"LEAVE NONE TO TELL THE STORY"

Genocide in Rwanda

written by Alison Des Forges

based on research by

Alison Des Forges	Eric Gillet
Timothy Longman	Catherine Choquet
Michele Wagner	Trish Huddleston
Kirsti Lattu	Jemera Rone

Human Rights Watch
New York · Washington · London · Brussels

International Federation of Human Rights
Paris

ISBN: 1-56432-171-1
Library of Congress Catalog Card Number: 99-61313
Cover photograph © Gilles Peress
Cover design by Rafael Jiménez
Cartoons and cover from *Kangura* reprinted *Rwanda, Les médias du génocide,*
courtesy of Jean-Pierre Chrétien, Jean-François Dupaquier, Marcel Kabanda and
Joseph Ngarambe.

Addresses for Human Rights Watch
350 Fifth Avenue, 34th Floor, New York, NY 10118-3299
Tel: (212) 290-4700, Fax: (212) 736-1300, E-mail: hrwnyc@hrw.org

1522 K Street, N.W., #910, Washington, DC 20005-1202
Tel: (202) 371-6592, Fax: (202) 371-0124, E-mail: hrwdc@hrw.org

33 Islington High Street, N1 9LH London, UK
Tel: (171) 713-1995, Fax: (171) 713-1800, E-mail: hrwatchuk@gn.apc.org

15 Rue Van Campenhout, 1000 Brussels, Belgium
Tel: (2) 732-2009, Fax: (2) 732-0471, E-mail:hrwatcheu@skynet.be

Web Site Address: http://www.hrw.org

Listserv address: To subscribe to the list, send an e-mail message to
majordomo@igc.apc.org with "subscribe hrw-news" in the body of the message
(leave the subject line blank).

Human Rights Watch is dedicated to
protecting the human rights of people around the world.

We stand with victims and activists to prevent
discrimination, to uphold political freedom, to protect people from inhumane
conduct in wartime, and to bring offenders to justice.

We investigate and expose
human rights violations and hold abusers accountable.

We challenge governments and those who hold power to end abusive practices
and respect international human rights law.

We enlist the public and the international
community to support the cause of human rights for all.

HUMAN RIGHTS WATCH

Human Rights Watch conducts regular, systematic investigations of human rights abuses in some seventy countries around the world. Our reputation for timely, reliable disclosures has made us an essential source of information for those concerned with human rights. We address the human rights practices of governments of all political stripes, of all geopolitical alignments, and of all ethnic and religious persuasions. Human Rights Watch defends freedom of thought and expression, due process and equal protection of the law, and a vigorous civil society; we document and denounce murders, disappearances, torture, arbitrary imprisonment, discrimination, and other abuses of internationally recognized human rights. Our goal is to hold governments accountable if they transgress the rights of their people.

Human Rights Watch began in 1978 with the founding of its Europe and Central Asia division (then known as Helsinki Watch). Today, it also includes divisions covering Africa, the Americas, Asia, and the Middle East. In addition, it includes three thematic divisions on arms, children's rights, and women's rights. It maintains offices in New York, Washington, Los Angeles, London, Brussels, Moscow, Dushanbe, Rio de Janeiro, and Hong Kong. Human Rights Watch is an independent, nongovernmental organization, supported by contributions from private individuals and foundations worldwide. It accepts no government funds, directly or indirectly.

The staff includes Kenneth Roth, executive director; Michele Alexander, development director; Reed Brody, advocacy director; Carroll Bogert, communications director;Cynthia Brown,program director; Barbara Guglielmo, finance and administration director; Jeri Laber special advisor; Lotte Leicht, Brussels office director; Patrick Minges, publications director; Susan Osnos, associate director; Jemera Rone, counsel; Wilder Tayler, general counsel; and Joanna Weschler, United Nations representative. Jonathan Fanton is the chair of the board. Robert L. Bernstein is the founding chair.

The regional directors of Human Rights Watch are Peter Takirambudde, Africa; José Miguel Vivanco, Americas; Sidney Jones, Asia; Holly Cartner, Europe and Central Asia; and Hanny Megally, Middle East and North Africa. The thematic division directors are Joost R. Hiltermann, arms; Lois Whitman, children's; and Regan Ralph, women's.

The members of the board of directors are Jonathan Fanton, chair; Lisa Anderson, Robert L. Bernstein, William Carmichael, Dorothy Cullman, Gina Despres, Irene Diamond, Adrian W. DeWind, Fiona Druckenmiller, Edith Everett, James C. Goodale, Vartan Gregorian, Alice H. Henkin, Stephen L. Kass, Marina Pinto Kaufman, Bruce Klatsky, Alexander MacGregor, Josh Mailman, Samuel K. Murumba, Andrew Nathan, Jane Olson, Peter Osnos, Kathleen Peratis, Bruce Rabb, Sigrid Rausing, Anita Roddick, Orville Schell, Sid Sheinberg, Gary G. Sick, Malcolm Smith, Domna Stanton, and Maya Wiley. Robert L. Bernstein is the founding chair of Human Rights Watch.

CONTENTS

Rwandan terms

Akazu
President Habyarimana's entourage, particularly persons linked to his wife.

Inkotanyi
Members of the RPF, a term that recalls the important armies of nineteenth century Rwanda.

Inyenzi
Literally, cockroaches, a scornful term for members of the RPF implying ties with assailants who came by night in the 1960s.

Umuganda
Obligatory labor for the public good, a practice existing in some areas before the arrival of Europeans but generally thought of as having been imposed by the colonial administration.

Kubohoza
To "free" someone against his or her will, to force people to change political parties or more loosely to injure or pillage for political ends.

Nyumbakumi
A person responsible for the residents of a unit of ten households.

Ibyitso
"Accomplices" of the RPF (singular icyitso).

Interahamwe
Militia attached to the MRND party.

Impuzamugambi Militia attached to the CDR party.

Glossary

MRND National Republican Movement for Development and Democracy. Formerly the single party in Rwanda, centered on Juvénal Habyarimana, its founder; strongest in the northwest.

MDR Democratic Republican Movement, rooted in the Parmehutu, the party which led the revolution of 1959 and unseated the Tutsi aristocracy; strongest in the center of the country.

CDR Coalition for the Defense of the Republic, a stridently anti-Tutsi political party that sometimes worked together with the MRND and perhaps served as a way for that more mainstream party to enunciate radical ideas.

RPF Rwandan (also Rwandese) Patriotic Front, an armed movement, initially composed largely of Rwandans who had lived in exile for a generation.

RTLM The radio station, Radio Télévision Libre des Mille Collines, jointly owned by many members of the akazu and others close to Habyarimana, that became the voice of the genocide.

PSD Social Democratic party, most popular in southern Rwanda.

PL Liberal Party, largely based in urban areas and supported by commercial or professional groups, said to be closest to the RPF.

UNAMIR The United Nations Assistance Mission in Rwanda, a peacekeeping force established under the terms of the Arusha Accords

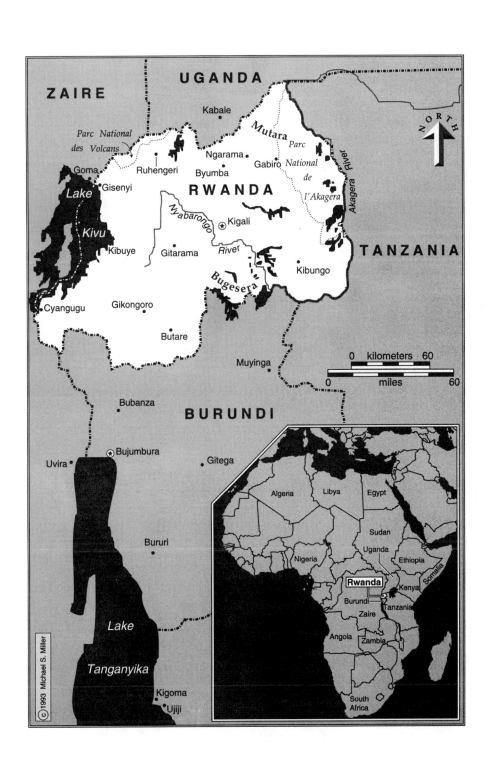

ZAIRE

UGANDA

Kabale

Parc National
des Volcans

Mutara

Goma

Lake

Gisenyi

Ruhengeri

Byumba

Ngarama

Gabiro

Parc
National
de
l'Akagera

Akagera River

Kivu

RWANDA

Kibuye

Nyabarongo

Kigali

Gitarama

River

Kibungo

TANZANIA

Cyangugu

Gikongoro

Bugesera

Butare

Muyinga

0   kilometers   60

0   miles   60

Bubanza

BURUNDI

Uvira

Bujumbura

Gitega

NORTH

Bururi

Algeria   Libya   Egypt

Sudan

Nigeria   Uganda   Ethiopia

Rwanda

Somalia

Burundi   Kenya

Zaire   Tanzania

Lake

Angola   Zambia

Tanganyika

Kigoma

Ujiji

South
Africa

INTRODUCTION

"When I came out, there were no birds," said one survivor who had hidden throughout the genocide. "There was sunshine and the stench of death."

The sweetly sickening odor of decomposing bodies hung over many parts of Rwanda in July 1994: on Nyanza ridge, overlooking the capital, Kigali, where skulls and bones, torn clothing, and scraps of paper were scattered among the bushes; at Nyamata, where bodies lay twisted and heaped on benches and the floor of a church; at Nyarubuye in eastern Rwanda, where the cadaver of a little girl, otherwise intact, had been flattened by passing vehicles to the thinness of cardboard in front of the church steps; on the shores of idyllic Lake Kivu in western Rwanda, where pieces of human bodies had been thrown down the steep hillside; and at Nyakizu in southern Rwanda, where the sun bleached fragments of bone in the sand of the schoolyard and, on a nearby hill, a small red sweater held together the ribcage of a decapitated child.

In the thirteen weeks after April 6, 1994, at least half a million people perished in the Rwandan genocide, perhaps as many as three quarters of the Tutsi population. At the same time, thousands of Hutu were slain because they opposed the killing campaign and the forces directing it.

The killers struck with a speed and devastation that suggested an aberrant force of nature, "a people gone mad," said some observers. "Another cycle of tribal violence," said others. The nation of some seven million people encompassed three ethnic groups. The Twa, were so few as to play no political role, leaving only Hutu and Tutsi to face each other without intermediaries. The Hutu, vastly superior in number, remembered past years of oppressive Tutsi rule, and many of them not only resented but feared the minority. The government, run by Hutu, was at war with the Rwandan Patriotic Front (RPF), rebels who were predominantly Tutsi. In addition, Rwanda was one of the poorest nations in the world and growing poorer, with too little land for its many people and falling prices for its products on the world market. Food production had diminished because of drought and the disruptions of war: it was estimated that 800,000 people would need food aid to survive in 1994.

But this genocide was not an uncontrollable outburst of rage by a people consumed by "ancient tribal hatreds." Nor was it the preordained result of the impersonal forces of poverty and over-population.

This genocide resulted from the deliberate choice of a modern elite to foster hatred and fear to keep itself in power. This small, privileged group first set the majority against the minority to counter a growing political opposition within Rwanda. Then, faced with RPF success on the battlefield and at the negotiating

1

table, these few powerholders transformed the strategy of ethnic division into genocide. They believed that the extermination campaign would restore the solidarity of the Hutu under their leadership and help them win the war, or at least improve their chances of negotiating a favorable peace.They seized control of the state and used its machinery and its authority to carry out the slaughter.

Like the organizers, the killers who executed the genocide were not demons nor automatons responding to ineluctable forces. They were people who chose to do evil. Tens of thousands, swayed by fear, hatred, or hope of profit, made the choice quickly and easily. They were the first to kill, rape, rob and destroy. They attacked Tutsi frequently and until the very end, without doubt or remorse. Many made their victims suffer horribly and enjoyed doing so.

Hundreds of thousands of others chose to participate in the genocide reluctantly, some only under duress or in fear of their own lives. Unlike the zealots who never questioned their original choice, these people had to decide repeatedly whether or not to participate, each time weighing the kind of action planned, the identity of the proposed victim, the rewards of participating and the likely costs of not participating. Because attacks were incited or ordered by supposedly legitimate authorities, those with misgivings found it easier to commit crimes and to believe or pretend to believe they had done no wrong.

Policymakers in France, Belgium, and the United States and at the United Nations all knew of the preparations for massive slaughter and failed to take the steps needed to prevent it. Aware from the start that Tutsi were being targeted for elimination, the leading foreign actors refused to acknowledge the genocide. To have stopped the leaders and the zealots would have required military force; in the early stages, a relatively small force. Not only did international leaders reject this course, but they also declined for weeks to use their political and moral authority to challenge the legitimacy of the genocidal government. They refused to declare that a government guilty of exterminating its citizens would never receive international assistance. They did nothing to silence the radio that broadcast calls for slaughter. Such simple measures would have sapped the strength of the authorities bent on mass murder and encouraged Rwandan opposition to the extermination campaign.

When international leaders did finally voice disapproval, the genocidal authorities listened well enough to change their tactics although not their ultimate goal. Far from cause for satisfaction, this small success only underscores the tragedy: if timid protests produced this result in late April, what might have been the result in mid-April had all the world cried "Never again."

This study, summarized in the introduction, describes in detail how the killing campaign was executed, linking oral testimony with extensive written documentation. It draws upon interviews with those who were marked for extinction but managed to survive, those who killed or directed killings, those who saved or sought to save others, and those who watched and tried not to see. It presents minutes of local meetings where operations against Tutsi were planned and correspondence in which administrators congratulated their subordinates for successfully destroying "the enemy." It analyzes the layers of language and the silences that made up the deceptive discourse of genocide, broadcast on the radio and delivered at public meetings. It places the genocide in the immediate political context, showing how local and national political rivalries among Hutu influenced the course of the campaign to eliminate Tutsi. It traces changes in the tactics and organization of the campaign as well as its collapse as the RPF defeated the genocidal government.

Drawing on many sources, including previously unpublished testimony and documents from diplomats and United Nations staff, the study shows how international actors failed to avert or stop the genocide. It ties the expansion of the killing campaign to early international inertia and it shows that international protests against the slaughter, when they finally came, were discussed even at local meetings on the distant hills of Rwanda. Thus the study establishes that the international community, so anxious to absent itself from the scene, was in fact present at the genocide.

The Genocide
The Strategy of Ethnic Division

President Juvenal Habyarimana, nearing the end of two decades in power, was losing popularity among Rwandans when the RPF attacked from Uganda on October 1, 1990. At first Habyarimana did not see the rebels as a serious threat, although they stated their intention to remove him as well as to make possible the return of the hundreds of thousands of Rwandan refugees who had lived in exile for a generation. The president and his close colleagues decided, however, to exaggerate the RPF threat as a way to pull dissident Hutu back to his side and they began portraying Tutsi inside Rwanda as RPF collaborators. For three and a half years, this elite worked to redefine the population of Rwanda into "Rwandans," meaning those who backed the president, and the "ibyitso" or "accomplices of the enemy," meaning the Tutsi minority and Hutu opposed to him.

In the campaign to create hatred and fear of the Tutsi, the Habyarimana circle played upon memories of past domination by the minority and on the legacy of the revolution that overthrew their rule and drove many into exile in 1959. Singling out most Tutsi was easy: the law required that all Rwandans be registered according to ethnic group. Residents of the countryside, where most Rwandans lived, generally knew who was Tutsi even without such documentation. In addition, many Tutsi were recognizable from their physical appearance.

But shattering bonds between Hutu and Tutsi was not easy. For centuries they had shared a single language, a common history, the same ideas and cultural practices. They lived next to one another, attended the same schools and churches, worked in the same offices, and drank in the same bars. A considerable number of Rwandans were of mixed parentage, the offspring of Hutu-Tutsi marriages. In addition, to make ethnic identity the predominant issue, Habyarimana and his supporters had to erase—or at least reduce—distinctions within the ranks of the Hutu themselves, especially those between people of the northwest and of other regions, those between adherents of different political factions, and those between the rich and the poor.

From the start, those in power were prepared use physical attacks as well as verbal abuse to achieve their ends. They directed massacres of hundreds of Tutsi in mid-October 1990 and in five other episodes before the 1994 genocide. In some incidents, Habyarimana's supporters killed Hutu opponents—their principal political challengers—as well as Tutsi, their declared ideological target.

Habyarimana was obliged to end his party's monopoly of power in 1991 and rival parties sprouted quickly to contend for popular support. Several of them created youth wings ready to fight to defend partisan interests. By early 1992, Habyarimana had begun providing military training to the youth of his party, who were thus transformed into the militia known as the *Interahamwe* (Those Who Stand Together or Those Who Attack Together). Massacres of Tutsi and other crimes by the Interahamwe went unpunished, as did some attacks by other groups, thus fostering a sense that violence for political ends was "normal."

Preparations for Slaughter

Through attacks, virulent propaganda, and persistent political manoeuvering, Habyarimana and his group signficantly widened divisions between Hutu and Tutsi by the end of 1992. During 1993 a dramatic military advance by the RPF and a peace settlement favorable to them—which also stipulated that officials, including the president, could be prosecuted for past abuses—confronted Habyarimana and his supporters with the imminent loss of power. These same events heightened concerns among a broader group of Hutu, including some not previously identified with Habyarimana. Increasingly anxious about RPF ambitions, this growing group was attracted by the new radio Radio Télévision Libre des Mille Collines (RTLM) and by a movement called Hutu Power, which cut across party lines and embodied the ethnic solidarity that Habyarimana had championed for three years. In late October, Tutsi soldiers in neighboring Burundi seized and murdered the Hutu president, freely and fairly elected only months before. In massacres touched off by the assassination, tens of thousands of Burundians died, both Hutu and Tutsi. The crime, energetically exploited by RTLM, confirmed the fears of many Rwandan Hutu that Tutsi would not share power and swelled the numbers supporting Hutu Power.

Meanwhile the Habyarimana circle was preparing the organization and logistics to attack the minority. During 1993, some loyalists from Habyarimana's party expanded the recruitment and training of the Interahamwe. But others, perhaps concerned that the militia were too tainted by partisan rivalries, proposed a "civilian self-defense force" which was to recruit young men through administrative rather than party channels. The recruits were to be trained by former soldiers or communal police who would direct them in attacking the "enemy" in their communities. In early 1993, Col. Théoneste Bagosora sketched out elements of the program in his appointment book, the intellectual Ferdinand Nahimana advocated such a force in a letter to friends and colleagues, and administrators began preparing lists of former soldiers who could command its ranks.

Soldiers and political leaders distributed firearms to militia and other supporters of Habyarimana in 1993 and early 1994, but Bagosora and others concluded that firearms were too costly to distribute to all participants in the "civilian self-defense" program. They advocated arming most of the young men with such weapons as machetes. Businessmen close to Habyarimana imported large numbers of machetes, enough to arm every third adult Hutu male.

Aware of these preparations, the RPF anticipated further conflict. They too recruited more supporters and troops and, in violation of the peace accords, increased the number of their soldiers and firearms in Kigali. They understood the risk that renewed combat would pose to Tutsi, particularly those who had come out publically in support of the RPF in the preceding months, and warned foreign observers to this effect.

The Attack

By late March 1994, Hutu Power leaders were determined to slaughter massive numbers of Tutsi and Hutu opposed to Habyarimana, both to rid themselves of these "accomplices" and to shatter the peace agreement. They had soldiers and militia ready to attack the targeted victims in the capital and in such outlying areas as Cyangugu in the southwest, Gisenyi in the northwest and Murambi in the northeast. But elsewhere they had not completed the arrangements. In the center of the country, they had successfully disseminated the doctrine of Hutu Power, but they were unsure how many ordinary people would transform that ideology into action. In other areas, particularly in the south, they had not won large numbers of supporters to the idea, far less organized them to implement it.

On April 6, the plane carrying President Habyarimana was shot down, a crime for which the responsibility has never been established. A small group of his close associates—who may or may not have been involved in killing him—decided to execute the planned extermination. The Presidential Guard and other troops commanded by Colonel Bagosora, backed by militia, murdered Hutu government officials and leaders of the political opposition, creating a vacuum in which Bagosora and his supporters could take control. Soldiers and militia also began systematically slaughtering Tutsi. Within hours, military officers and administrators far from the capital dispatched soldiers and militia to kill Tutsi and Hutu political leaders in their local areas. After months of warnings, rumors and prior attacks, the violence struck panic among Rwandans and foreigners alike. The rapidity of the first killings gave the impression of large numbers of assailants, but in fact their impact resulted more from ruthlessness and organization than from great numbers.

Recruiting for Genocide

The genocide was not a killing machine that rolled inexorably forward but rather a campaign to which participants were recruited over time by the use of threat and incentives. The early organizers included military and administrative officials as well as politicians, businessmen, and others with no official posts. In order to carry through the genocide, they had to capture the state, which meant not just installing persons of their choice at the head of the government, but securing the collaboration of other officials throughout the system.

Bagosora and his circle sought first to obtain the backing, or at least the acquiescence, of the majority of military commanders. They began negotiating for this support even as troops under their command slaughtered civilians in the streets. Bagosora's first proposal, to take power in his own right, was rejected by a number of influential officers as well as by the ranking representative of the United Nations in Rwanda. But his next move, to install a regime of extremists masquerading as a legitimate government, was accepted by the soldiers, the U.N. representative, and the international community. The day after Habyarimana's death, the RPF renewed combat with the government forces, a response to the continuing attacks by the Rwandan army on civilians and on RPF headquarters. With the resumption of the war and the ensuing pressure for solidarity, officers opposed to Bagosora found it increasingly difficult to challenge his actions.

As the new leaders were consolidating control over military commanders, they profited enormously from the first demonstration of international timidity. U.N. troops, in Rwanda under the terms of the peace accords, tried for a few hours to keep the peace, then withdrew to their posts—as ordered by superiors in New York—leaving the local population at the mercy of assailants. Officers opposed to Bagosora realized that a continuing foreign presence was essential to restricting the killing campaign and appealed to representatives of France, Belgium and the U.S. not to desert Rwanda. But, suspecting the kind of horrors to come, the foreigners had already packed their bags. An experienced and well-equipped force of French, Belgian, and Italian troops rushed in to evacuate the foreigners, and then departed. U.S. Marines dispatched to the area stopped in neighboring Burundi once it was clear that U.S.citizens would be evacuated without their help. The first impression of international indifference to the fate of Rwandans was confirmed soon after, when the Belgians began arranging for the withdrawal of their troops from the U.N. peacekeeping force. Ten of these soldiers, a contingent different from those of the evacuation expedition, had been slain and, as the organizers of the violence had anticipated, the Belgian government did not want to risk any further casualties.

Against the backdrop of Rwandan military acquiescence and foreign flight, Bagosora and his circle moved to recruit administrators and political leaders for the killing campaign. They expected and received support from politicians, prefects and burgomasters associated with Habyarimana's party, but to expand the killing campaign more broadly they needed the collaboration also of administrators and local leaders from the other parties, those that were predominant in central and southern Rwanda. Adherents of these parties, stunned by the murder of their Hutu colleagues in the first days, were ready to oppose soldiers and militia whom they believed to be fighting to restore exclusive control to Habyarimana's party. The new authorities hurried to dispel these concerns in a meeting of prefects on April 11 and through radio appeals for Hutu unity broadcast by the minister of defense and influential politicians on April 12. They stressed that partisan interests must be put aside in the battle against the common enemy, the Tutsi.

By April 15, it was clear that the U.N. Security Council would not order the peacekeepers to try to stop the violence and might even withdraw them completely. By this date, the organizers of the genocide had also expanded their ranks considerably and were strong enough to remove opponents and impose compliance with the killing campaign. On April 16 and 17, they replaced the military chief of the staff and the prefects best known for opposing the killings. One prefect was later imprisoned and executed and the other was murdered with his family. Three burgomasters and a number of other officials who sought to stop the killings were also slain, either by mid-April or shortly after. The leaders of the genocide held meetings in the center and south of the country to push hesitant local administrators into collaboration. At the same time, they sent assailants from areas where slaughter was well under way into those central and southern communes where people had refused to kill and they used the radio to ridicule and threaten administrators and local political leaders who had been preaching calm.

The Structure

By April 20, two weeks after the plane crash, the organizers of the genocide had substantial, although not yet complete, control of the highly centralized state. The administration continued to function remarkably well despite the disruptions in communication and transport caused by the war. Orders from the prime minister were handed down to the prefect, who passed them on to the burgomasters, who called local meetings throughout the communes where they read the instructions to the population. The same language echoed from north to south and from east to west, calling for "self-defense" against "accomplices." Slaughter was known as "work" and machetes and firearms were described as "tools." Reports on the situation at the local level and minutes of meetings held by people out on the hills were handed back up through the administrative channels.

By appropriating the well-established hierarchies of the military, administrative and political systems, leaders of the genocide were able to exterminate Tutsi with astonishing speed and thoroughness. Soldiers, National Police (*gendarmes*), former soldiers, and communal police played a larger part in the slaughter than is generally realized. In addition to leading the first killings in the capital and in other urban centers, soldiers and National Police directed all the major massacres throughout the country. Although usually few in number at sites of massive killing, their tactical knowledge and their use of the weapons of war, including grenades, machine guns, and even mortars, contributed significantly to the death tolls in these massacres. It was only after the military had launched attacks with devastating effect on masses of unarmed Tutsi that civilian assailants, armed with such weapons as machetes, hammers, and clubs, finished the slaughter. In addition, the military encouraged and, when faced with reluctance to act, compelled both ordinary citizens and local administrators to participate in attacks, even travelling the back roads and stopping at small marketplaces to deliver the message.

The administrators were charged with driving Tutsi from their homes and gathering them at places of slaughter, with assembling the masses of assailants, providing transportation and "tools" for the "work," arranging for the disposal of the corpses, and directing the division of looted property and confiscated land. They transformed administrative practices, benign in themselves, such as obligatory labor for the common good (*umuganda*) or the use of security patrols, into mechanisms for executing the genocide.

The political leaders provided the militia for attacks, dispatching them around the country as needed. They prodded reluctant administrators and military officers to greater activity, sometimes using party supporters to harass or threaten those who hesitated to participate. Political leaders also incited Hutu to kill in more direct language than that used by officials who often spoke in ambiguous and allusive terms.

Even as leaders of the genocide were exploiting existing hierarchies, they also created a fourth channel dedicated to implementing the "civilian self-defense" program. The system was formalized only late in May, but such key elements as the recruitment of participants by administrators and the reliance on former soldiers to command them were in use during the massacres of early April. With headquarters in Bagosora's own office, the "civilian self-defense" hierarchy was staffed largely by retired officers-cum-politicians, much like Bagosora himself.

Through these hierarchies, organizers carried out a killing campaign, a perversion of previous campaigns that called on citizens and officials alike to contribute extra efforts for some public good. The urgency and importance of the objective was deemed to justify departing from usual bureaucratic practice. Zeal for killing took on more significance than formal rank: subordinates could prevail over their superiors, in both civilian and military spheres, if they showed greater commitment to the genocide. This flexibility encouraged ambition and initiative among those willing to trade human lives for personal advantage. Actors could also bypass the usual limits set by law or administrative practice, with politicians or soldiers speaking for government officials, militia approving candidates for administrative position, and medical assistants calling in military strikes.

These practices, which promoted rapid and effective execution of the killing campaign, now complicate the task of assessing responsibility for crimes. All who seek accountability for the genocide must take care to ensure that officials of lesser rank but greater power not escape blame for crimes that are wrongly imputed to their superiors alone.

Strategies of Slaughter
In the first days of killing in Kigali, assailants sought out and murdered targeted individuals and also went systematically from house to house in certain neighborhoods, killing Tutsi and Hutu opposed to Habyarimana. Administrative officials, like the prefect of the city of Kigali, ordered local people to establish barriers to catch Tutsi trying to flee and to organize search patrols to discover those trying to hide.

By the middle of the first week of the genocide, organizers began implementing a different strategy: driving Tutsi out of their homes to government offices, churches, schools or other public sites, where they would subsequently be massacred in large-scale operations.

Towards the end of April, authorities declared a campaign of "pacification," which meant not an end to killing, but greater control over killing. Sensitive to criticism from abroad—muted though it was—authorities ended most large-scale massacres. They also sought to rein in assailants who were abusing their license to kill, such as by slaying Hutu with whom they had disputes or who were allowing Tutsi to escape injury in return for money, sexual favors or other considerations. They ordered militia and other citizens to bring suspects to officials for investigation and then murder instead of simply killing them where they found them. Authorities used "pacification" also as a tactic to lure Tutsi out of hiding to be killed.

By mid-May, the authorities ordered the final phase, that of tracking down the last surviving Tutsi. They sought to exterminate both those who had hidden successfully and those who had been spared thus far—like women and children—or protected by their status in the community, like priests and medical workers. As the RPF advanced through the country, assailants also hurried to eliminate any survivors who might be able to testify about the slaughter.

Throughout the genocide, Tutsi women were often raped, tortured and mutilated before they were murdered.

Popular Participation

The density of the administrative and political hierarchies, characteristic of Rwanda for many years, gave genocidal leaders rapid and easy access to the population, but did not guarantee mass participation in the slaughter. As authorities played on popular fears and greed, some people picked up their machetes and came readily. Others came more slowly and some refused to come, even at the risk of their lives.

Both on the radio and through public meetings, authorities worked to make the long-decried threat of RPF infiltration concrete and immediate. Throughout the country they disseminated detailed false information, such as reports that Tutsi had hidden firearms in the bushes behind the Kibungo cathedral, or that they had prepared maps showing fields to be taken from Hutu in Butare, or that they had killed local administrative officials in Nyakizu. Authorities counted on such news to convince Hutu that their Tutsi neighbors were dangerous agents of the RPF who had to be eliminated. Community leaders and even clergy assured Hutu that they were justified in attacking Tutsi as a measure of "self-defense."

Authorities offered tangible incentives to participants. They delivered food, drink, and other intoxicants, parts of military uniforms and small payments in cash to hungry, jobless young men. They encouraged cultivators to pillage farm animals, crops, and such building materials as doors, windows and roofs. Even more important in this land-hungry society, they promised cultivators the fields left vacant by Tutsi victims. To entrepreneurs and members of the local elite, they granted houses, vehicles, control of a small business, or such rare goods as television sets or computers.

Many poor young men responded readily to the promise of rewards. Of the nearly 60 percent of Rwandans under the age of twenty, tens of thousands had little hope of obtaining the land needed to establish their own households or the jobs necessary to provide for a family. Such young men, including many displaced by the war and living in camps near the capital provided many of the early recruits to the Interahamwe, trained in the months before and in the days immediately after the genocide began. Refugees from Burundi, in flight from the Tutsi-dominated army of Burundi, had also received military training in their camps and readily attacked Rwandan Tutsi after April 6.

In some regions, particularly those where Habyarimana's supporters were strongest, authorities needed to do little more than give the signal for Hutu to begin attacking Tutsi. In other areas, such as central and southern Rwanda, where Tutsi were numerous and well integrated and where Habyarimana's party had little standing, many Hutu initially refused to attack Tutsi and joined with them in fighting off assailants. Only when military and civilian authorities resorted to public criticism and harassment, fines, destruction of property, injury, and threat of death did these Hutu give up their open opposition to the genocide.

In some places, authorities apparently deliberately drew hesitant Hutu into increasingly more violent behavior, first encouraging them to pillage, then to destroy homes, then to kill the occupants of the homes. Soldiers and police sometimes threatened to punish Hutu who wanted only to pillage and not to harm Tutsi. Authorities first incited attacks on the most obvious targets—men who had acknowledged or could be easily supposed to have ties with the RPF—and only later insisted on the slaughter of women, children, the elderly, and others generally regarded as apolitical.

Just as communities were readier to kill some Tutsi than others, so individual Hutu would agree to attack one person and not another or, in an extension of the same logic, would attack one person and save another. Hutu who protected Tutsi ordinarily helped those to whom they were linked by the ties of family, friendship, or obligation for past assistance, but sometimes they also saved the lives of strangers. Even such persons as Colonel Bagosora and leading figures of the interim government saved the lives of Tutsi close to them, testimony to the extent to which ties between Hutu and Tutsi survived even the most persistent efforts to eradicate them. In some cases, former officials now seek credit for saving the lives of a few favored Tutsi, as if having done so reduced their responsibility for directing or permitting the slaying of so many others.

The Masquerade of Legitimacy

Many Rwandans say that they killed because authorities told them to kill. Such statements reflect less a national predisposition to obey orders, as is sometimes said, than a recognition that the "moral authority" of the state swayed them to commit crimes that would otherwise have been unthinkable.

Itself the chief actor in a masquerade of legitimacy, the interim government gave its officials and citizens the cover of "legitimate" orders to hide from themselves and others the evil they were doing. Administrators broke the genocide down into a series of discrete tasks which they executed without consideration of the ultimate objective of the work. Cultivators turned out for the long-standing practice of communal labor although they knew that they were to cut down people as well as the brush in which they found them. Priests announced public meetings without consideration of the message to be delivered there. Businessmen contributed money to the "self-defense" fund established by the government as they had contributed to similar collections in the past, even though the money was to buy "refreshments" for the militia and fuel to transport them to their places of "work."

As part of the"pacification" effort in late April, authorities ordered churches, schools, hospitals, and shops to resume their functions, ignoring the absence of Tutsi who used to participate in these various activities. They presumed to create a veneer of "normalcy" in a world where untold numbers of people were violating the laws, religious teachings, and cultural norms that they had always lived by.

Survival Tactics

Many Tutsi and those Hutu associated with them fought to save their lives. We know of their heroic resistance, usually armed only with sticks and stones, at such places as the hills of Bisesero, the swamps of Bugesera, and the church at Cyahinda, but we have no way of knowing about the countless small encounters where targeted people struggled to defend themselves and their families in their homes, on dusty paths, and in the fields of sorghum.

Some tens of thousands fled to neighboring countries and others hid within Rwanda, in the ceilings of houses, in holes in the ground, in the forest, in the swamps. Some bought their lives once, others paid repeatedly for their safety over a period of weeks, either with money or with sexual services.

Many Tutsi who are alive survived because of the action of Hutu, whether a single act of courage from a stranger or the delivery of food and protection over many weeks by friends or family members.

The End of Hutu Power

When organizers of the genocide gained control of the state, they suppressed dissent but did not extinguish it. In May and June, when the interim government was weakened by military losses and by the first signs of international disapproval, Hutu in one community after another began refusing to undertake further searches or to participate in guarding barriers. As the majority of participants withdrew, they left execution of the genocide in the hands of smaller, more zealous groups of assailants, who continued to hunt and kill in hopes of profit or because they were committed to exterminating the last Tutsi.

With the campaign against Tutsi no longer a strong bond, Hutu of different areas and parties once more began to fight against each other. Some revived old battles. Others competed in new rivalries over power or over goods and property taken from Tutsi. Interahamwe and other young men who had been authorized to terrorize Tutsi began robbing, raping, and killing Hutu as the number of Tutsi declined.

Hutu used the discourse of the genocide in conflicts with other Hutu: they accused each other of being Tutsi, of having hidden Tutsi, or of supporting the RPF. Just as some charged enemies with too great lenience towards Tutsi at this time, so others would charge their opponents with violence against Tutsi once the genocide was ended.

The Rwandan Patriotic Front

In defeating the interim government and its army, the RPF ended the genocide. At the same time, its troops committed grave violations of international humanitarian law by attacking and killing unarmed civilians. Unlike the genocidal authorities who undertook a complex campaign involving all the machinery of the state and aiming to involve all Hutu citizens, the RPF ran a straightforward military campaign where civilians generally provided only information or support services.

The RPF permitted its soldiers to kill persons whom they took to be Interahamwe or other supposed participants in the genocide. They killed some in the course of their military advance, but they executed most in the days and weeks after combat had finished. They selected the victims from among civilians grouped in camps, sometimes relying on accusations by survivors, sometimes on their own interrogations. They executed some persons apparently because they were linked with parties opposed to the RPF or showed potential for becoming political leaders rather than because they were thought guilty of involvement in the genocide.

In a number of places, such as in the communes of Ntyazo, Mukingi and Runda, RPF soldiers massacred unarmed civilians, many of them women and children, who had assembled for a meeting on their orders. The people were told to come to receive food or to be given instructions or to gather before being transported to another site. The RPF soldiers also massacred several hundred people in the Byumba stadium in mid-April.

In a series of raids in Kigali in early April, RPF soldiers killed dozens of political and military leaders, many of them past government employees or persons close to Habyarimana's political party. They killed family members, including women and children, in a number of these cases.

The RPF was commonly acknowledged by military experts to be a highly disciplined force, with clear lines of command and adequate communication. Although it may have become less disciplined during the months of the genocide due to the incorporation of new recruits, RPF commanding officers like General Paul Kagame maintained the authority necessary to ensure compliance with their orders. The crimes committed by RPF soldiers were so systematic and widespread and took place over so long a period of time that commanding officers must have been aware of them. Even if they did not specifically order these practices, in most cases they did not halt them and punish those responsible.

In early November 1994, the RPF reported that it had arrested twenty-five soldiers for capital crimes, eight of them accused of killing civilians between June and August 1994 and by the end of the year military prosecutors had supposedly completed investigations in some twenty such cases. One major, one corporal and four soldiers indicted for these crimes were tried and convicted in 1997 and 1998. The major was sentenced to life in prison and the others to imprisonment for terms ranging from two to five years.

After some early but limited reports of killings by the RPF, the first substantial charges against RPF forces were made by Robert Gersony, a consultant to the U.N. High Commissioner for Refugees. After interviewing hundreds of Rwandans inside and outside the country in July and August 1994, he concluded that the RPF had engaged in widespread and systematic slaughter of unarmed civilians. In September 1994, the U.N., in agreement with the U.S. and perhaps others, agreed to suppress the report but demanded that the RPF halt the killings. The number of killings declined markedly after September in the face of this international pressure.

Numbers

Establishing a reliable toll of those killed in the genocide and its aftermath is important to counter denials, exaggerations, and lies. The necessary data have not been gathered but speculation about death tolls continues anyway, usually informed more by emotion than by fact. In July 1998, the Rwandan government announced plans for a census of genocide survivors.

Even the size of the Tutsi population in Rwanda on April 6, 1994 is debated. Demographer William Seltzer, who has studied the data, estimates the number as 657,000, a figure extrapolated from 1991 census data. Some critics assert that the number of Tutsi was underreported in that census and in the prior census of 1978 because the Habyarimana government wanted to minimize the importance of Tutsi in the population. Although frequently said, no documentation has been presented to support this allegation. The 1991 data show Tutsi as forming 8.4 percent of the total population. This figure seems to accord with extrapolations from the generally accepted census data of 1952, taking into account the population loss due to death and flight during the 1960s and the birth rate, which was lower for Tutsi than for Hutu.

Whether or not census data were purposely altered to reduce the number of Tutsi, the figures underestimated the Tutsi population because an undetermined number of Tutsi arranged to register as Hutu in order to avoid discrimination and harassment. Although many Rwandans know of such cases, there is at present no basis for estimating how many persons they represented.

Deliberate misrepresentation of ethnicity complicates assessing how many of the victims were actually Tutsi. At a reburial ceremony for a family slain during the genocide, the only two survivors, both priests, talked separately with our researchers. One maintained that his family was Tutsi but claimed to be Hutu while the other declared that the family was really Hutu, but was said to be Tutsi by neighbors who coveted their wealth. In addition to such cases of questionable identity, there are Hutu who were killed because they looked like Tutsi.

A U.N. expert evaluating population loss in Rwanda estimated that 800,000 Rwandans had died between April and July 1994, but this figure included those who had died from causes other than the genocide. Seltzer estimated the number of persons killed in the genocide as at least one half million. Professor Gérard Prunier estimated that 130,000 Tutsi were alive in July, but his figures did not include those in Zaire or Tanzania, perhaps another 20,000. If this number of 150,000 survivors is subtracted from an estimated population of 657,000 Tutsi, this leaves 507,000 Tutsi killed, close to Seltzer's minimum assessment, and representing the annihilation of about 77 percent of the population registered as Tutsi. Using other data from Butare prefecture, our researchers computed an estimated loss of 75 percent of the Tutsi population in that prefecture. Based on these preliminary data, we would conclude that at least half a million persons were killed in the genocide, a loss that represented about three quarters of the Tutsi population of Rwanda.

Estimates of persons killed at any one site vary widely, often by a factor of ten or more, perhaps because most have been made by untrained observers. At the parish of Rukara, for example, estimates ranged from 500 to 5,000. In 1995, a Rwandan government commission set the death toll at the Murambi Technical School in Gikongoro at some 20,000, a figure which some have since raised to 70,000, although the bodies exhumed there at the time of the 1996 commemoration of the genocide numbered in the range of 5,000. As many as 50,000 have been said to have perished at Bisesero, but a recent list of persons killed at that site totaled just over 5100 names. Similarly, some claim that 35,000 were slain in the Nyamata church, which appears to have a capacity of some 3,000.

Establishing the number of persons killed in the genocide will not help much in assessing the number of people involved in their execution. The circumstances of the crimes varied enormously: there were professional soldiers armed with machine guns or grenade-launchers firing into crowds, each of whom may have killed dozens, if not hundreds, of people, and there were groups of assailants armed with clubs or sharpened pieces of bamboo who jointly killed a single person. There can be no simple formula to assess how many killers murdered one victim or how many victims were slain by one killer.

The first estimate of numbers slain by the RPF was made by Gersony in his 1994 report. He concluded that the RPF killed between 25,000 and 45,000 persons in the months of April to August 1994. Seth Sendashonga, former minister of the interior and early member of the RPF, estimated that the RPF killed some 60,000 people between April 1994 and August 1995, with more than half killed in the first four months of that period. It seems likely, although not certain, that these estimates include persons killed in the course of combat, both civilians and militia.

Although our research indicates considerable killing of civilians by RPF forces during this period, including massacres and executions, we have too little data to confirm or revise these estimates. In any case, they appear more likely to be accurate than claims that the RPF killed hundreds of thousands of people from April to August 1994.

International Responsibility
The Rwandans who organized and executed the genocide must bear full responsibility for it. But genocide anywhere implicates everyone. To the extent that governments and peoples elsewhere failed to prevent and halt this killing

campaign, they all share in the shame of the crime. In addition, the U.N. staff as well as the three foreign governments principally involved in Rwanda bear added responsibility: the U.N. staff for having failed to provide adequate information and guidance to members of the Security Council; Belgium, for having withdrawn its troops precipitately and for having championed total withdrawal of the U.N. force; the U.S. for having put saving money ahead of saving lives and for slowing the sending of a relief force; and France, for having continued its support of a government engaged in genocide. In contrast to the inaction of the major actors, some non-permanent members of the Security Council with no traditional ties with Rwanda undertook to push for a U.N. force to protect Tutsi from extermination. But all members of the Security Council brought discredit on the U.N. by permitting the representative of a genocidal government to continue sitting in the Security Council, a council supposedly committed to peace.

Tolerating Discrimination and Violence

From 1990 on, influential donors of international aid pressed Habyarimana for political and economic reforms. But, generally satisfied with the stability of his government, they overlooked the systematic discrimination against Tutsi which violated the very principles that they were urging him to respect. They discussed but did not insist on eliminating identity cards that showed ethnic affiliation, cards that served as death warrants for many Tutsi in 1994.

When the Rwandan government began massacring Tutsi in 1990, crimes that were solidly documented by local and international human rights groups and by a special rapporteur for the U.N. Commission on Human Rights, some donors protested. At one point, the Belgian government went so far as to recall its ambassador briefly. But none openly challenged Rwandan explanations that the killings were spontaneous and uncontrollable and none used its influence to see that the guilty were brought to justice.

In addition, the lack of international response to the 1993 massacres in Burundi permitted Rwandan extremists to expect that they too could slaughter people in large numbers without consequence.

Economies and Peacekeeping

In September 1993, U.N. staff and member states wanted a successful peacekeeping operation to offset the failure in Somalia. They believed that Rwanda promised such success because both parties to the conflict had requested the U.N. presence and because the agreement between them, hammered out in a year of negotiation, seemed to have resolved all major issues.

Faced with escalating costs for peacekeeping operations, the U.N. staff and members wanted not just success, but success at low cost. Demands for economy, loudly voiced by the U.S. and others, led to the establishment of a force only one third the size of that originally recommended and with a mandate that was also scaled down from that specified by the peace accords. Peacekeeping staff had proposed a small human rights division, which might have tracked growing hostility against Tutsi, but no money was available for this service and the idea was dropped.

Belgium, too, wanted to save money. Although it felt concerned enough about Rwanda to contribute troops to the force, it felt too poor to contribute the full battalion of 800 requested and agreed to send only half that number. Troops from other countries that were less well trained and less well armed filled the remaining places, producing a force that was weaker than it would have been with a full Belgian batallion.

As preparations for further conflict grew in February 1994, the Belgians were sufficiently worried by the deteriorating situation to ask for a stronger mandate, but they were rebuffed by the U.S. and the United Kingdom, which refused to support any measure that might add to the cost of the operation.

The concern for economy prevailed even after massive slaughter had taken place. When a second peacekeeping operation was being mounted in May and June, U.N. member states were slow to contribute equipment needed for the troops. The U.S. government was rightly ridiculed for requiring seven weeks to negotiate the lease for armored personnel carriers, but other members did not do much better. The U.K., for example, provided only fifty trucks.

Warnings, Information and the U.N. Staff

A January 11, 1994 telegram from General Roméo Dallaire, commander of the U.N. peacekeeping force, to his superiors was only one, if now the most famous, warning of massive slaughter being prepared in Rwanda. From November 1993 to April 1994, there were dozens of other signals, including an early December letter to Dallaire from high-ranking military officers warning of planned massacres; a press release by a bishop declaring that guns were being distributed to civilians; reports by intelligence agents of secret meetings to coordinate attacks on Tutsi, opponents of Hutu Power and U.N. peacekeepers; and public incitations to murder in the press and on the radio. Foreign observers did not track every indicator, but representatives of Belgium, France, and the U.S. were well-informed about most of them. In January, an analyst of U.S. Central Intelligence Agency knew enough to predict that as many as half a million persons might die in case of renewed conflict and, in February, Belgian authorities already feared a genocide. France, the power most closely linked to Habyarimana, presumably knew at least as much as the other two.

In the early months of 1994, Dallaire repeatedly requested a stronger mandate, more troops and more materiel. The secretariat staff, perhaps anxious to avoid displeasing such major powers as the U.S., failed to convey to the council the gravity of warnings of crisis and the urgency of Dallaire's requests. The paucity of information meant little to the U.S. and France, which were well-informed in any case, but it led other council members with no sources of information in Rwanda to misjudge the gravity of the crisis. Instead of strengthening the mandate and sending reinforcements, the Security Council made only small changes in the rate of troop deployment, measures too limited to affect the development of the situation.

When the violence began, the secretary-general's special representative, Roger Booh-Booh minimized both the extent and the organized nature of the slayings. Meanwhile Dallaire was fairly shouting the need for immediate and decisive action. Given the two points of view, the staff generally presented the more reassuring assessment to council members.

By late April, representatives of the Czech Republic, Spain, New Zealand and Argentina sought information beyond that provided by the secretariat and became convinced that the slaughter was a genocide that must be stopped. They pushed the Security Council to support a new peacekeeping operation with a stronger mandate to protect civilians. Had these non-permanent members been fully informed earlier—such as on January 11—they might have found their voices in time to have called for firm measures to avert the violence.

Obfuscation and Misunderstanding

From the first hours after the killings began, U.S., Belgian, and French policymakers knew that Tutsi were being slain because they were Tutsi. Dallaire delivered that same information in a telegram to U.N. headquarters on April 8. Early accounts by journalists on the spot also depicted systematic, widespread killings on an ethnic basis. The simultaneous selective slaughter of Hutu opposed to Hutu Power complicated the situation but did not change the genocidal nature of attacks on Tutsi and, in any case, killings of Hutu diminished markedly after the first days. Given the pattern of killings, given previous massacres of Tutsi, given the propaganda demanding their extermination, given the known political positions of the persons heading the interim government, informed observers must have seen that they were facing a genocide.

They knew, but they did not say. The U.S. may have been the only government to caution its officials in writing to avoid the word "genocide," but diplomats and politicians of other countries as well as staff of the U.N. also shunned the term. Some may have done so as part of their effort at neutrality, but others surely avoided the word because of the moral and legal imperatives attached to it.

Instead of denouncing the evil and explaining to the public what had to be done to end it, national and international leaders stressed the "confusing" nature of the situation, the "chaos" and the "anarchy." After a first resolution that spoke fairly clearly about the conflict, the Security Council issued statements for several weeks that left both the nature of the violence and the identity of its perpetrators unclear. Secretary-General Bhoutros Bhoutros-Ghali spoke of the genocide as if it were a natural disaster and depicted Rwandans as a people "fallen into calamitous circumstances."

Some policymakers could not get byeond the old cliches, like one official of the U.S. National Security Council who described the genocide as "tribal killings," an explanation echoed by President Bill Clinton in June 1998 when he talked of "tribal resentments" as the source of troubles in Rwanda. In a similar vein, an adviser to French President François Mitterrand suggested that brutal slaughter was a usual practice among Africans and could not be easily eradicated. Other diplomats, more up to date, promoted the idea of a "failed state," ignoring all indications that the Rwandan state was all too successful in doing what its leaders intended. They seemed unable to dissociate Rwanda from Somalia, although the two cases had few points of comparison beyond their common location on the African continent. Most journalists simply exploited the horror and made no effort to go beyond the easy explanations. A leading columnist for the *New York Times* even managed on April 15, 1994 to put the new and the old cliches in the same sentence, referring to a "failed state" and to a "centuries-old history of tribal warfare."

Genocide and War

From the start, the genocide was intertwined with the war and the war complicated efforts to halt the extermination campaign. The organizers used the slaughter of Tutsi to draw the RPF into renewed combat. Later, in the face of RPF advances, they demanded a cease-fire as a prerequisite for ending the genocide. The RPF resumed the war in part to stop the massacres and insisted on an end to the genocide as a condition for a cease-fire. An early initiative by the RPF to halt the genocide failed at least in part because combat had resumed. RPF representatives proposed a joint operation against the killers with Rwandan army troops not involved in the slaughter and with U.N. peacekeepers, but even Rwandan soldiers previously opposed to Habyarimana would not switch sides during a war and U.N. troops could not move because there was no longer a peace to keep. At about this time, France and Belgium, and perhaps the United States, briefly discussed using troops of the evacuation force to halt the killings, but they dropped the idea. The RPF, suspicious of French intentions, warned that it would attack soldiers who stayed longer than was necessary to evacuate foreigners and Rwandan government soldiers, who had already proved that they would kill Belgian troops, were presumed ready to kill more. Whether these risks provided the real reason or merely a pretext for their rapid departure, the French and Belgian troops boarded their planes and flew away. According to Dallaire, the evacuation force left him and the peacekeepers "on the tarmac, with the bullets flying and the bodies piling up" around them.

Foreign policymakers treated the genocide as a tragic byproduct of the war rather than as an evil to be attacked directly. Accustomed to dealing with wars, not with genocides, diplomats addressed the familiar part of the problem in the usual way, by promoting a dialogue between the belligerents and seeking a cease-fire. To increase the chance of success, they sought to maintain a posture of neutrality between the parties, which meant not condemning the genocide. This was true for the staff of the U.N. as well. Dallaire was instructed to concentrate on getting a cease-fire even though he believed that objective was unattainable and clearly secondary to ending the killings. But diplomatic hopes of halting the genocide by ending the war could not produce results so long as the organizers of the slaughter saw the genocide as a way of winning the war.

Some policymakers, particularly in France and in Belgium, were wedded to the notion that an ethnic majority was necessessarily the same as a democratic majority. They could not bring themselves to condemn the genocide because they feared increasing the likelihood of an RPF victory and the subsequent establishment of a government dominated by the minority.

Military Action and Inaction

Of approximately 7,000 Rwandan army forces in the vicinity of the capital on the day that the slaughter was launched, some 1,500 to 2,000 elite troops—the Presidential Guard plus soldiers of the paracommando and reconnaissance units—backed by some 2,000 militia carried out most of the killings of civilians. When the RPF renewed hostilities with the Rwandan army late that day, their 1,000 or so soldiers drew some of the Rwandan troops away from attacks on civilians, but not enough to halt the slaughter. Three days later, when the RPF proposed assembling a force with Rwandan army soldiers opposed to the attacks and U.N. peacekeepers, they believed 900 soldiers would suffice to end the killing of civilians. The commander of the Belgian contingent of the peacekeepers concluded that the U.N. troops together with the evacuation troops present from April 9 to

April 15 would have been strong enough to halt the violence. Dallaire too agreed that a joint force could have stopped the killers and he was ready to lead the peacekeeping soldiers themselves into action, if he received additional troops and materiel.

The number of troops needed to restore order grew as participants from more areas were drawn into the killing campaign, but, according to Dallaire and other military experts, 5,000 experienced soldiers could have ended the genocide even in the later weeks.

Because the operation of the genocide was highly centralized, stopping the killing in Kigali would have quickly quelled violence elsewhere in the country. Any serious challenge from foreign troops would have signaled that the interim government was illegitimate in the eyes of the international community and unlikely to receive the support it would need to survive, far less prosper. This would have discouraged Rwandans from joining the killing campaign and might even have stimulated some opponents of the genocide to come together to oppose it.

But instead of using the peacekeeping troops to stop the genocide, the U.N. sought primarily to protect its soldiers from harm. Dallaire was ordered to make avoiding risk to soldiers the priority, not saving the lives of Rwandans. To do so, he regrouped his troops, leaving exposed the Rwandans who had sought shelter in certain outposts under U.N. protection. In the most dramatic case—for which responsibility may belong to commanding officers in Belgium as much as to Dallaire—nearly one hundred Belgian peacekeepers abandoned some two thousand unarmed civilians, leaving them defenseless against attacks by militia and military. As the Belgians went out one gate, the assailants came in the other. More than a thousand Rwandans died there or in flight, trying to reach another U.N. post.

The next day and for several days after that, the Security Council debated the complete withdrawal of the peacekeeping operation, a decision which would have abandoned some 30,000 unarmed civilians then in U.N. posts, just as the others had been deserted the day before. The Belgians promoted this idea aggressively outside the council while the U.S. led the forces in its favor at the council table. A member of the secretariat even suggested that protection of civilians might not be an appropriate activity for a peacekeeping operation. But Nigeria, other council members, and finally the secretary-general insisted that the lives of "innocent civilians of Rwanda" must be taken into account. They delayed the decision long enough for U.S. policymakers and others to reconsider their position.

On April 21, the Security Council withdrew most of the U.N. troops and left only a few hundred peacekeepers to protect civilians already directly under the U.N. flag. Eight days later, after refugees began pouring out of Rwanda in numbers massive enough to threaten stability in the entire region, the secretary-general and Security Council acknowledged that the war and the genocide could be addressed separately and that they should try to halt the killings.

When the U.N. began discussing sending a new force with a stronger mandate to protect Tutsi civilians, the RPF categorically opposed the move, fearing that such a force might intervene in the war and rob them of a victory that they now were confident of achieving. In an April 29 press release, they declared that a new military force would serve no purpose because "the genocide is almost completed" and most Tutsi were already dead or had fled. At the time some 100,000 Tutsi were alive and awaiting rescue. The RPF certainly knew of the 60,000 in Kigali, Kabgayi and Cyangugu and of untold thousands of others clustered at Bisesero or in Bugesera and scattered throughout Butare, where large scale killing had begun only nine days before. RPF opposition to a new U.N. force complicated and slowed the effort to mount a rescue operation for Tutsi civilians. RPF troops had proved their effectiveness and peacekeeping staff and member states preferred not to risk direct combat with them. Whether the RPF would in fact have fired on a U.N.force seems unlikely: it would later make similar threats against the French but in the end reached an accomodation with them.

Discussion about the size, mandate, and strategy for a new peacekeeping force continued until May 17, in part because of U.S. rigidity in applying its new standards for approval of peacekeeping operations, in part because of hesitations sparked by RPF opposition to any intervention. Manoeuvering by nations supplying troops and those supplying equipment consumed another two months, so that the second peacekeeping force landed only after the RPF had defeated the genocidal government. The slowness and ineptness of national and international bureaucracies in mounting the operation was not unusual, nor was the attempt by participating nations to get the most or give the least possible. What was extraordinary was that such behavior continued to be acceptable in the context of genocide, by then openly acknowledged by national and international leaders.

In early April some French authorities considered using the soldiers of their evacuation force to back the Rwandan army against the RPF but decided not to do so. In mid-June they undertook Operation Turquoise purportedly to save lives but also to preserve "territory and legitimacy" for the interim government. French soldiers went to rescue Tutsi in southwestern Rwanda, to the general acclaim of press and public. Others who went to the northwest, ready to impede the RPF advance and to protect the interim government, were hailed by RTLM but drew little foreign notice. Some French soldiers were slow to act to save Tutsi, as at Bisesero, apparently because they accepted the official Rwandan explanation that the Tutsi were RPF infiltrators. In the humanitarian zone which they established,

French troops took some measures against the militia but they permitted genocidal officials to continue exercising their functions. Even after conceding a RPF victory, the French took no action against the genocidal authorities, permitting—and apparently in some cases assisting—them to flee the country.

Some 2,500 well-equipped elite French forces saved 15,000 to 17,000 lives. The barely 500 U.N. peacekeepers, poorly equipped and minimally supplied, protected about twice that number during the course of the genocide.

Tolerating Genocide

During the first weeks, when firm opposition to the genocide would have saved hundreds of thousands of lives, international leaders refused even simple actions which would have required no military force and no expense. Complicit in the refusal to speak the word "genocide," they failed to denounce the evil, either jointly—which would have been most effective—or even singly, in outraged voices. Condemning evil, warning of its consequences, and naming the authorities apparently responsible for it would have made clear to Rwandans that these leaders were branded outlaws by the world community. Representatives of various governments and branches of the U.N. were in touch with Rwandan authorities and may have criticized the genocide, but they did so discreetly. Anthony Lake, national security adviser to the president, did issue a single appeal to Rwandans leading the genocide, calling on them by name to stop the killings. This innovative step, excellent in itself, was not followed by the others needed to give it real force.

In 1994, as for the preceding several years, Rwanda depended heavily on foreign financial support. Donor nations and the World Bank had withheld aid or threatened to do so to pressure the Rwandan government at several critical moments, including when it balked at signing the peace accords. All Rwandans in positions of responsibility understood the importance of foreign financial support: even burgomasters and communal councils were responsible for raising funds for local development projects by direct appeals to foreign governments. Any public condemnation of the genocide by the combined donors and the World Bank, particularly if accompanied by an explicit warning that they would never fund a genocidal government, would have shown Rwandans that the interim government was unlikely to succeed and made them less likely to implement its orders.

Radio RTLM, which had incited to genocide before April 6, communicated the orders for implementing the killings after that date. It instructed people to erect barriers and carry out searches; it named persons to be targeted and pointed out areas which should be attacked. Even the more restrained national radio, Radio Rwanda, broadcast directives important to the execution of the genocide. So important was this means of communication that officials admonished citizens to keep listening to the radio for instructions from the interim government. Broadcasts from these stations could have been interrupted without military action on the ground. The U.S., and perhaps other nations, considered jamming the radio broadcasts, but in the end rejected the measure.

After more than two weeks of massacres, most governments refused to admit Rwandan representatives sent to try to justify the genocide. Egypt and France, however, did receive them. The French action had great importance—because France was the strongest past supporter of the Rwandan government, because the delegation was received at the highest levels, and because one of the Rwandans was the effective head of the most virulently anti-Tutsi party in the country and clearly identified with the genocide. Two weeks later, when a Rwandan army officer came to Paris to request aid, a high-ranking official told him that France had just sent some communications equipment to Rwanda and that further aid could be forthcoming if Rwanda managed to end bad publicity about the slaughter.

Members of the Security Council gave more importance to maintaining diplomatic procedures than to condemning perpetrators of genocide. Rather than demand that the Rwandan representative resign from the council, they continued collaborating with him, thus treating his government as an honorable member of the world community. They did not insist that he absent himself from discussions about Rwanda or even that he observe the usual custom of abstaining from such discussions. They thus afforded him the chance to know and communicate to his government all proposals for U.N. action in Rwanda.

The Security Council also received the delegation meant to repair the Rwandan image abroad and heard it out with the customary courtesy. Faced with representatives just arrived from the capital of a genocidal government, most members of the council failed to denounce the slaughter clearly and forcefully. On an occasion of great symbolic importance, they once more put decorum before the obligation to speak as the conscience of the international community.

Although many genocidal killings were done with machetes, clubs, or other such weapons, military and militia used firearms to begin major massacres, to execute some persons, and to threaten opponents of the genocide into compliance. Rwandan soldiers also needed ammunition for the war against the RPF. Imposing an embargo on arms to Rwanda would have been another effective, cost-free way of indicating international condemnation of the interim government, but this measure, first raised in the Security Council at the end of April, was implemented only on May 17.

During the genocide, the frequently ignored nonpermanent members of the Security Council in the end showed the strongest committment to action. Nigeria made an effort in the first week to have the U.N. force strengthened and reminded others to think not just about the foreigners, relatively little at risk, but also about the Rwandans who were targeted by the violence. Later, the Czech Republic, Spain, Argentina, and New Zealand demanded that a second and stronger force be sent to Rwanda. As the Czech representative declared at one point, "Rwanda is not a priority for the Czech government, but as a human being I cannot sit here and do nothing."

Rwandans Listened

When foreign governments, the pope, and the secretary-general began to find their voices, Rwandans listened. The major business and financial leaders feared loss of international funds and high-ranking military officers feared interruption of the supply of arms and ammunition. Leading intellectuals debated strategies to counter international criticism and diplomats were sent on mission to persuade the world of a series of lies: that the killings were less serious than depicted abroad, that they were a spontaneous outburst of rage by a grief-stricken people, that they were justified by the need of "self-defense," and that—in any case—they had been halted.

After France insisted that Rwanda avoid further international criticism, Radio RTLM immediately broadcast the news that the French were ready with further aid, but on condition that there be "no more cadavers visible on the roads" and that people "no longer kill...while others stand around and laugh." After the U.S. communicated its disapproval, Rwandan authorities cared enough to send orders down to the hills that killings should be brought under control and removed out of sight. At a communal council meeting in remote Bwakira commune in the western prefecture of Kibuye, the burgomaster warned local leaders that satellites passing over head could track continued violence and that such displays would make re-establishment of good relations with the U.S. impossible.

International censure, timid and tardy though it was, prompted Rwandan authorities to restrict and hide killings. If instead of delaying and temporising, international leaders had immediately and unambiguously called the genocide by its awful name, they would have shattered the masquerade of legitimacy created by the interim government and forced Rwandans to confront the evil they were doing. Once Rwandans were faced with the consequences for themselves as individuals and for their nation of being declared international outlaws, they would have made choices in a different context. Perhaps those completely committed to exterminating Tutsi would have continued that course. But they had been few at the start and they would have found it more difficult to recruit others—or to retain their loyalty—once it was clear that the interim government could not succeed in the international arena.

For international condemnation to achieve maximum effect would have required complete and public support by all major international actors in Rwanda. These policymakers sadly lacked the breadth of vision to see that genocide in Rwanda was detrimental to the interests of their own nations and the world community as well as to the people of Rwanda. They placed lesser diverse interests of their governments before the need to avert or end a genocide and so violated the pledge of "Never again" made nearly fifty years before.

The Future

Even as the international community resolves not to repeat the culpable passivity of 1994, it risks yet another kind of inertia: that of not acting until confronted by a catastrophe similar in kind and scale to that of the genocide. Circumstances have changed. Although some of the insurgents currently attacking the Rwandan government may intend to continue exterminating Tutsi, they lack the means to execute campaigns of the extraordinary scale and speed of the 1994 genocide. Rather they carry out limited but ongoing slaughter that deadens public concern simply by its very repetitiveness. Meanwhile the Rwandan government, eschewing any genocidal ideology, has nonetheless engaged in massive slaughter of civilians whom it counts as supporters of the enemy, both in Rwanda and in the Democratic Republic of Congo.

It is increasingly difficult to assess the nature and extent of violence and to identify leaders responsible for it. Faced with possible punishment for massacring large numbers of civilians, government officials have restricted access to troubled regions, interfered with efforts to gather testimony, destroyed evidence, and misrepresented events. Their opponents, the insurgent leaders, often remain in the shadows, with their programs and even their names unknown. Although their alleged crimes are generally more widely publicized, it is difficult to find the information needed to assess the truth of the charges against them.

International leaders, chasing the ever-moving goal of stability, ignore crimes against humanity and tolerate obstruction of efforts to reveal the full horror of ongoing abuses in the region. By failing to demand accountability for current crimes, they undermine the credibility of justice being meted out for the genocide and by tolerating impunity for present slaughter, they help perpetuate insecurity. As long as they decline to take a principled, public and effective stand against the killings of civilians, they offer neither model nor encouragement to forces—whether in government or in the insurgency—who themselves might oppose such violence. By accepting the "normality" of slaughter for political reasons, they may be contributing to the conditions that will produce the very repetition of genocide they have vowed to prevent.

The Research Project

Human Rights Watch and the International Federation of Human Rights Leagues (FIDH) each documented human rights abuses in Rwanda before, during and since the genocide. The two organizations joined with the International Center for Human Rights and Democratic Development and the Interafrican Union of Human and Peoples' Rights to sponsor an international commission that reported in 1993 on massacres of Tutsi and other human rights violations by the Rwandan government and on abuses by the RPF. In addition, the Arms Division of Human Rights Watch documented the arms trade and military preparations of both the Rwandan government and the RPF in 1993 and later arms deliveries to former Rwandan army soldiers and militia in camps in Zaire.

When the April 1994 slaughter was launched, Human Rights Watch and FIDH fought together with other human rights and humanitarian organizations to oblige policymakers, the press and the public to recognize the genocidal nature of the killings and to honor moral and legal obligations to intervene to halt the genocide.

Since 1994 staff and lawyers associated with both organizations have initiated and helped Rwandans initiate legal actions in the U.S. and in Belgium against persons accused of genocide. They have served as expert witnesses and supplied documentary evidence to prosecutors in legal proceedings related to the genocide in the U.S., Canada, Belgium and Switzerland and at the International Tribunal. They have provided testimony and documentation also to the Belgian Senate, the French National Assembly and the U.S. Congress in their inquiries into the genocide.

In early 1995, the two organizations began documenting the genocide, attempting to analyze the killing campaign from the level of the local security committee to the that of the U.N. Security Council. Researchers carried out hundreds of interviews and located, organized, and translated administrative records from communes and prefectures. They also amassed extensive materials from judicial cases and from various diplomatic sources.

The study presents both an overview of the genocide throughout the country and a closer examination of its course in southern Rwanda, where people opposed the killing campaign longer than elsewhere in the country and where the role of the authorities in directing the genocide is particularly clear.

The researchers comprised an international team of historians, political scientists, and lawyers with extensive experience in the region. All acknowledge with deep respect and appreciation the contributions of hundreds of Rwandans to this work, most of whom are not named for their own protection.

Alison Des Forges directed the research for this project, assisted by Eric Gillet. Des Forges wrote this study with the collaboration of Gillet for the chapter on justice and of Timothy Longman and Michele Wagner for the chapters on Nyakizu. In addition to these persons, the research team included Lynn Welchman, Kirsti Lattu, Trish Hiddleston, Catherine Choquet, and Christine Deslaurier. Deslaurier and Anne Boley prepared the maps. Janet Fleischman supplied critical advice, logistical assistance and encouragement and Jemera Rone helped establish the field project in Butare. Georgette Uwase, Alphonse Nkunzimana, Medard Ndawumungu, Daniel Kanyandekwe, and Aimable Twagirimana provided skilled assistance with translation from Kinyarwanda into French and English.

Michael McClintock and Peter Takirambudde edited the English version of the report and Eric Gillet, Catherine Choquet, Valerie Pons-Mello and Emmanuelle Robineau-Duverger edited the French version. Mariam Abou-Zahab translated the report from English to French. Juliet Wilson, Roger Des Forges, Peter Bouckaert, Patrick Minges and Sybil Liebhafsky assisted with the production of the English version of the report. Kim Mazyk, Marcus Watson and Maria-Theresia Schütte helped with classifying documents. Gilles Peress graciously contributed his photograph for the cover.

The research team gratefully acknowledges the assistance and cooperation of officials from the Rwandan Ministry of Justice and from the prefectural and communal administrations in Butare, Gikongoro, Gitarama and Kibuye.

The team thanks Alter-Ciné, Jean-Pierre Chrétien, Alain Destexhte, André Guichaoua, Lindsey Hilsum, Chris McGreal, Catharine Newbury, David Newbury, Gasana Ndoba, Gérard Prunier, Filip Reyntjens, William Seltzer, Astri Suhrke, and Claudine Vidal for assistance with documentation and in interpreting evidence.

The research team gratefully acknowledges the funding which made this study possible. Novib-Netherlands, Oxfam, and the Harry Frank Guggenheim Foundation supported the work of Human Rights Watch in this project and FIDH was funded by the Comité Catholique Contre la Faim pour le développement; Développement et paix (Canada); Broederlink Delen; Oxfam (Canada); Trocaire; Swiss Cooperation and Danida.

The public interest demands that crimes as grave as those committed in Rwanda be known and that those responsible for them be identified. We understand the limitations of even the most careful investigative techniques and recognize that despite our best efforts this work may contain errors. We stress that this work does not and is not meant to establish "judicial truth" as to the guilt or innocence of any person, which is the responsibility of legally established national and international tribunals. Indeed, we publish the results of our research in part to encourage public support for the efforts of judicial authorities responsible for finding and judging those guilty of genocide.

All who have invested their energy and resources in this study hope that it will contribute to a deeper analysis of events and to a more honest and complete delineation of responsibility both inside and outside Rwanda.

Language, Spelling and Names

Kinyarwanda is generally pronounced as written, with the accent on the second to last syllable of the word. The singular or plural of nouns is indicated by the prefix: an accomplice is icyitso, two or more accomplices are ibyitso. Most Kinyarwanda terms in this study are written with the prefix, but in conformity with general practice, the nouns Tutsi, Hutu and Twa are used without the prefix and in the same form in the singular and the plural.

Kinyarwanda has been written only since the beginning of the century. Although there is an official orthography, it is not always followed. In citations, Kinyarwanda terms are reproduced here as they were found in the original sources. The term for burgomaster, for example, may be found as burugumestri or burugumesteri.

Most Rwandans have names particular to themselves and do not share a common family name. When two people have the same name, this is usually a coincidence rather than an indication that they are related.

HISTORY

Rwandans take history seriously. Hutu who killed Tutsi did so for many reasons, but beneath the individual motivations lay a common fear rooted in firmly held but mistaken ideas of the Rwandan past. Organizers of the genocide, who had themselves grown up with these distortions of history, skillfully exploited misconceptions about who the Tutsi were, where they had come from, and what they had done in the past. From these elements, they fueled the fear and hatred that made genocide imaginable. Abroad, the policy-makers who decided what to do—or not do—about the genocide and the journalists who reported on it often worked from ideas that were wrong and out-dated. To understand how some Rwandans could carry out a genocide and how the rest of the world could turn away from it, we must begin with history.

The Meaning of "Hutu," "Tutsi," and "Twa"

Forerunners of the people who are now known as Hutu and Tutsi settled the region over a period of two thousand years. Originally organized in small groups based on lineage or on loyalty to an outstanding leader, they joined in building the complex state of Rwanda. They developed a single and highly sophisticated language, Kinyarwanda, crafted a common set of religious and philosophical beliefs, and created a culture which valued song, dance, poetry, and rhetoric. They celebrated the same heroes: even during the genocide, the killers and their intended victims sang of some of the same leaders from the Rwandan past.[1]

In early times, as now, most people in the region were cultivators who also raised small stock and occasionally a few cattle. A far smaller number of people scorned cultivation and depended on large herds of cattle for their livelihood. Cultivators and pastoralists lived interspersed in most areas, although the cool, wet highlands of the north had few pastoralists and the drier, hotter east had more. With fertile soil and regular rainfall, the region was productive and population grew to a point where Rwanda was in 1994 the most densely populated nation on the African continent.

When Rwanda emerged as a major state in the eighteenth century, its rulers measured their power in the number of their subjects and counted their wealth in the number of their cattle. The two were usually related. Giving or temporarily granting cattle was a way of winning supporters; a large number of supporters

---

[1]Jean-Pierre Chrétien, Jean-François Dupaquier, Marcel Kabanda, Joseph Ngarambe, *Rwanda, Les média du génocide* (Paris: Editions Karthala, 1995), p. 358.

helped to win cattle, both in conflicts with other members of the elite and in adventures abroad. But not all cattle-owners held state positions. The pastoralists known as Bagogwe, clustered in the northwest, and those called Bahima, located in the northeast, sought to avoid state power rather than to share in it. Conversely, not all members of the elite were born rich in cattle, although those lacking such wealth ordinarily acquired it along with power. Cultivators skilled in making war and able to mobilize large groups of followers rose to importance through the military system, particularly under the late nineteenth century ruler Rwabugiri, who brought Rwanda to the height of its power. In its drive to expand, Rwanda attacked neighboring peoples regardless of whether they were pastoralists or cultivators and regardless of whether they were organized in lineages or in states.[2]

Rwandan institutions were shaped by both pastoralists and cultivators. Although the power of the ruler derived from control over the military and over cattle, his authority was buttressed also by rituals firmly rooted in agricultural practices.[3] By the end of the nineteenth century, the ruler governed the central regions closely through multiple hierarchies of competing officials who administered men, cattle, pasturage, and agricultural land. He exercised a looser kind of suzerainty over other areas, particularly on the periphery, which were dominated by powerful lineage groups, some of them pastoralists, some cultivators. In addition, he tolerated the existence of several small states within the boundaries of Rwanda, usually because their rulers were thought to control rainfall, crop pests, or some other aspect of agricultural productivity important for Rwanda as a whole. The late President Habyarimana and his circle counted themselves as the proud contemporary representatives of Bushiru, the largest such state within Rwanda at the beginning of the colonial era.

As the Rwandan state grew in strength and sophistication, the governing elite became more clearly defined and its members, like powerful people in most societies, began to think of themselves as superior to ordinary people. The word "Tutsi," which apparently first described the status of an individual—a person rich in cattle—became the term that referred to the elite group as a whole and the word "Hutu"—meaning originally a subordinate or follower of a more powerful person—came to refer to the mass of the ordinary people. The identification of

---

[2]Alison L. Des Forges, "When a Foreign Country Rebels: The Ideology and Practice of War in Eighteenth and Nineteenth Century Rwanda," Symposium on Warfare and Society in Africa, Yale University, 1990.

[3]M. D'Hertefelt and A. Coupez, *La Royauté Sacrée de l'Ancien Rwanda* (Tervuren: Musée Royale de l'Afrique Centrale, 1964).

Tutsi pastoralists as power-holders and of Hutu cultivators as subjects was becoming general when Europeans first arrived in Rwanda at the turn of the century, but it was not yet completely fixed throughout the country. Rulers of small states embedded in the larger nation, important lineage heads and some power-holders within the central state hierarchy exercised authority even though they were people who would today be called "Hutu."

Most people married within the occupational group in which they had been raised. This practice created a shared gene pool within each group, which meant that over generations pastoralists came to look more like other pastoralists—tall, thin and narrow-featured—and cultivators like other cultivators—shorter, stronger, and with broader features. Within each group there were also sub-groups, the result of some distant common ancestry or of more recent patterns of marriage. Thus among pastoralists, some whose ancestors had arrived centuries ago were distinctly shorter, plumper, and redder-skinned than the taller and blacker-skinned descendants of nineteenth-century immigrants. Cultivators, who were relatively sedentary and chose mates from areas close to home, often exhibited traits characteristic of their places of origin: those from the south, for example, were generally shorter and slighter than those from the north central region.

Although it was not usual, Hutu and Tutsi sometimes intermarried. The practice declined in the late nineteenth and early twentieth centuries as the gap widened between Tutsi elite and Hutu commoners, but rose again after Tutsi lost power in the 1959 revolution. With the increase in mixed marriages in recent decades, it has become more difficult to know a person's group affiliation simply by looking at him or her. Some people look both "Hutu" and "Tutsi" at the same time. In addition, some people who exhibit the traits characteristic of one group might in fact belong to the other because children of mixed marriages took the category of their fathers, but might actually look like their mothers.[4] During the genocide some persons who were legally Hutu were killed as Tutsi because they looked Tutsi. According to one witness, Hutu relatives of Col. Tharcisse Renzaho, the prefect of the city of Kigali, were killed at a barrier after having been mistaken for Tutsi.[5]

The Twa, a people clearly differentiated from Hutu and Tutsi, formed the smallest component of the Rwandan population, approximately 1 percent of the

---

[4]If the child were born out of wedlock, he or she would take the classification of the mother.

[5]Human Rights Watch/FIDH interview, Kigali, June 30, 1995.

total before the genocide. Originally forest dwellers who lived by hunting and gathering, Twa had in recent decades moved closer to Hutu and Tutsi, working as potters, laborers, or servants. Physically distinguishable by such features as their smaller size, Twa also used to speak a distinctive form of Kinyarwanda. While the boundary between Hutu and Tutsi was flexible and permeable before the colonial era, that separating the Twa from both groups was far more rigid. Hutu and Tutsi shunned marriage with Twa and used to refuse even to share food or drink with them. During the genocide, some Twa were killed and others became killers. Because Twa are so few in number and because data concerning them are so limited, this study does not examine their role.

Colonial Changes in the Political System

The Germans, who established a colonial administration at the turn of the century, and the Belgians who replaced them after the First World War, ended the occasional open warfare that had taken place within Rwanda and between Rwanda and its neighbors. Both Germans and Belgians sought to rule Rwanda with the least cost and the most profit. Making use of the impressive indigenous state was the obvious way to do so, but the colonialists found its complexities troublesome. The multiple hierarchies which had allowed the ruler to maximize his control by playing off rival officials now permitted both ruler and his subordinates to evade control by the colonialists. The dense administration within central Rwanda—with the least important representatives of the ruler sometimes governing only a few hundred people—required a relatively high proportion of local goods and labor for its support. The colonialists preferred to have these resources at their own disposal, to cover their expenses and to pay the costs of building an infrastructure to link Rwanda to the world economy. At the same time, the Belgians saw the autonomous enclaves, where central control was light, as anomalies potentially disruptive of good order.

In the 1920s, the Belgians began to alter the Rwandan state in the name of administative efficiency. Always professing an intention to keep the essential elements of the system intact, they eliminated the competing hierarchies and regrouped the units of administration into "chiefdoms" and "sub-chiefdoms" of uniform size. They used force to install state officials in the autonomous enclaves, destroying the power of the heads of lineages and of local small states. They fixed and made uniform the goods and services that local officials could demand, thus—they thought—reducing the burdens on the population.

Rwandan officials were not helpless pawns but rather real players in the game of administrative reform. Politically astute, they understood how to evade the intent of European orders even while apparently conforming to them. Chiefs and sub-chiefs seemed to accept the reduction in numbers of officials, but in fact kept on using unofficial representatives out on the hills who continued living off the local people. As a result, the density of administration and consequent customary burdens on the people diminished little, if at all, in the central part of the country, while in the north and southwest, they actually increased because of the installation of resident officials. At the same time, the chiefs and sub-chiefs—and later other administrative agents—enforced a series of wholly new demands imposed by the colonialists as part of their effort to integrate Rwanda into the world economy. They often found ways to turn these new requirements, such as building roads or planting cash crops, to their personal profit.

The elite profited not just from direct European backing but also from the indirect and unintended consequences of the administrative changes. Under the old system of multiple officials, power-holders ordinarily limited demands on subordinates, knowing that those who felt unreasonably exploited could seek protection from rivals or could move elsewhere, even clearing new land in the forest, if need be, to escape exactions. In the 1920s and 1930s, the Belgians made it far harder for the weak to escape repressive officials; not only did they eliminate the multiple hierarchies but they also restricted changes in residence from one region to another and they prohibited new settlement in the forests. The one avenue of escape still possible was migration abroad and thousands took that route beginning in the 1920s. But those who preferred not to leave Rwanda had little choice but to submit to increased exploitation of officials now freed from the constraints that once limited their demands.

European administrators generally overlooked the abuses of those officials who got the taxes collected, the roads built, and the coffee planted. They established European-style courts which they expected would protect the ordinary people, but they usually did not. The judges saw themselves as defenders of the elite, not the masses.

At the same time that the Belgians enabled the officials to demand more from the people, they decreed that Tutsi alone should be officials. They systematically removed Hutu[6] from positions of power and they excluded them from higher education, which was meant mostly as preparation for careers in the administration. Thus they imposed a Tutsi monopoly of public life not just for the 1920s and 1930s, but for the next generation as well. The only Hutu to escape relegation to the laboring masses were those few permitted to study in religious seminaries.

---

[6]They also removed women who had exercised authority.

The Transformation of "Hutu" and "Tutsi"

By assuring a Tutsi monopoly of power, the Belgians set the stage for future conflict in Rwanda. Such was not their intent. They were not implementing a "divide and rule" strategy so much as they were just putting into effect the racist convictions common to most early twentieth century Europeans. They believed Tutsi, Hutu, and Twa were three distinct, long-existent and internally coherent blocks of people, the local representatives of three major population groups, the Ethiopid, Bantu and Pygmoid. Unclear whether these were races, tribes, or language groups, the Europeans were nonetheless certain that the Tutsi were superior to the Hutu and the Hutu superior to the Twa—just as they knew themselves to be superior to all three. Because Europeans thought that the Tutsi looked more like themselves than did other Rwandans, they found it reasonable to suppose them closer to Europeans in the evolutionary hierarchy and hence closer to them in ability. Believing the Tutsi to be more capable, they found it logical for the Tutsi to rule Hutu and Twa just as it was reasonable for Europeans to rule Africans. Unaware of the "Hutu" contribution to building Rwanda, the Europeans saw only that the ruler of this impressive state and many of his immediate entourage were Tutsi, which led them to assume that the complex institutions had been created exclusively by Tutsi.

Not surprisingly, Tutsi welcomed these ideas about their superiority, which coincided with their own beliefs. In the early years of colonial rule, Rwandan poets and historians, particularly those from the milieu of the court, resisted providing Europeans with information about the Rwandan past. But as they became aware of European favoritism for the Tutsi in the late 1920s and early 1930s, they saw the advantage in providing information that would reinforce this predisposition. They supplied data to the European clergy and academics who produced the first written histories of Rwanda. The collaboration resulted in a sophisticated and convincing but inaccurate history that simultaneously served Tutsi interests and validated European assumptions. According to these accounts, the Twa hunters and gatherers were the first and indigenous residents of the area. The somewhat more advanced Hutu cultivators then arrived to clear the forest and displace the Twa. Next, the capable, if ruthless, Tutsi descended from the north and used their superior political and military abilities to conquer the far more numerous but less intelligent Hutu. This mythical history drew on and made concrete the "Hamitic hypothesis," the then-fashionable theory that a superior, "Caucasoid" race from northeastern Africa was responsible for all signs of true civilization in "Black" Africa. This distorted version of the past told more about the intellectual atmosphere of Europe in the 1920s than about the early history of Rwanda. Packaged in Europe, it was returned to Rwanda where it was disseminated through the schools and seminaries. So great was Rwandan respect for European education that this faulty history was accepted by the Hutu, who stood to suffer from it, as well as by the Tutsi who helped to create it and were bound to profit from it. People of both groups learned to think of the Tutsi as the winners and the Hutu as the losers in every great contest in Rwandan history.

The polished product of early Rwando-European collaboration stood unchallenged until the 1960s when a new generation of scholars, foreign and Rwandan, began questioning some of its basic assumptions.[7] They persuaded other scholars to accept a new version of Rwandan history that demonstrated a more balanced participation of Hutu and Tutsi in creating the state, but they had less success in disseminating their ideas outside university circles. Even in the 1990s, many Rwandans and foreigners continued to accept the erroneous history formulated in the 1920s and 1930s.

Once the Belgians had decided to limit administrative posts and higher education to the Tutsi, they were faced with the challenge of deciding exactly who was Tutsi. Physical characteristics identified some, but not for all. Because group affiliation was supposedly inherited, genealogy provided the best guide to a person's status, but tracing genealogies was time-consuming and could also be inaccurate, given that individuals could change category as their fortunes rose or fell. The Belgians decided that the most efficient procedure was simply to register everyone, noting their group affiliation in writing, once and for all. All Rwandans born subsequently would also be registered as Tutsi, Hutu, or Twa at the time of their birth. The system was put into effect in the 1930s, with each Rwandan asked to declare his group identity.[8] Some 15 percent of the population declared themselves Tutsi, approximately 84 percent said they were Hutu, and the remaining 1 percent said they were Twa. This information was entered into records at the local government office and indicated on identity cards which adult Rwandans were then obliged to carry. The establishment of written registration did not completely end changes in group affiliation. In this early period Hutu who

---

[7]Among the new Rwandan historians were Emmanuel Ntezimana, distinguished also for his courage as a human rights activist, and Ferdinand Nahimana, now indicted by the International Criminal Tribunal for Rwanda for his role in fomenting hatred of the Tutsi through broadcasts of Radio Télévision Libre des Mille Collines.

[8]It is often said that all Rwandans who owned ten or more cattle were classed as Tutsi, but this is not correct. Tax regulations in the 1930s did indeed distinguish between owners of ten or more cattle and those who had fewer, but the procedure for population registration took no account of ownership of cattle.

discovered the advantages of being Tutsi sometimes managed to become Tutsi even after the records had been established, just as others more recently have found ways to erase their Tutsi origins. But with official population registration, changing groups became more difficult.

The very recording of the ethnic groups in written form enhanced their importance and changed their character. No longer flexible and amorphous, the categories became so rigid and permanent that some contemporary Europeans began referring to them as "castes." The ruling elite, most influenced by European ideas and the immediate beneficiaries of sharper demarcation from other Rwandans, increasingly stressed their separateness and their presumed superiority. Meanwhile Hutu, officially excluded from power, began to experience the solidarity of the oppressed.

The Hutu Revolution

Belgium continued its support for the Tutsi until the 1950s. Then, faced with the end of colonial rule and with pressure from the United Nations, which supervised the administration of Rwanda under the trusteeship system, the colonial administrators began to increase possibilities for Hutu to participate in public life. They named several Hutu to responsible positions in the administration, they began to admit more Hutu into secondary schools, and they conducted limited elections for advisory government councils. Hardly revolutionary, the changes were enough to frighten the Tutsi, yet not enough to satisfy the Hutu. With independence approaching, conservative Tutsi hoped to oust the Belgians before majority rule was installed. Radical Hutu, on the contrary, hoped to gain control of the political system before the colonialists withdrew.

The ruler who had been in power since 1931, Mutara Rudahigwa, had served to reassure all parties and to keep the situation calm. But he died unexpectedly in 1959[9] and was succeeded by a young half-brother, Kigeri Ndahindurwa, who appeared to be heavily influenced by the most conservative Tutsi group. Moderate parties that sought to organize across the Hutu-Tutsi divide lost ground as the Parmehutu (Parti du mouvement de l'émancipation des Bahutu), identified exclusively with Hutu, and the Union Nationale Rwandaise (UNAR), a royalist Tutsi party, gained in strength. In November 1959, several Tutsi assaulted a Hutu

---

[9]Mutara collapsed and died just after seeing a Belgian doctor in Bujumbura, the capital of neighboring Burundi. Conservative Tutsi accused the Belgians of having poisoned him, a charge which some Rwandans still believe, although no proof has been advanced to support it.

sub-chief. As the news of the incident spread, Hutu groups attacked Tutsi officials and the Tutsi responded with more violence. Several hundred people were killed before the Belgian administration restored order. The Belgians then replaced about half the Tutsi local authorities by Hutu. With the help of many of these local administrators, the Parmehutu easily won the first elections in 1960 and 1961. In September 1961, some 80 percent of Rwandans voted to end the monarchy, thus confirming the proclamation of a republic the previous January 1961 by the Parmehutu-led government. These events became known as the "Hutu Revolution."

In later years, and particularly during the genocide, Hutu politicians waved the flag of the revolution, knowing they would get an overwhelming response from their audiences. In fact the revolution was neither so heroic nor so dramatic as it was later presented. In their struggle for power, the Hutu were "helped" considerably by the Belgians, both politically and militarily. At the start, Hutu attacked power-holders and those related to them, leaving their ordinary Tutsi neighbors in peace. They usually sought to drive Tutsi away rather than to destroy them. The assailants cleared the north most completely, the area where Tutsi officials had been installed three decades before by the colonial administration. Many displaced Tutsi resettled elsewhere in Rwanda, particularly in the sparsely populated region known as Bugesera, but another 10,000 took the road to exile.

In 1961 some of these refugees began to attack Rwanda, an effort they would repeat ten times over the next six years. After these incursions, Hutu officials led reprisal attacks on Tutsi still within the country, accusing them of having aided the invaders—the same kind of charges often repeated at the time of the genocide.[10] Only one of these attacks, that of late December 1963, posed a real threat to the new republic. But Hutu leaders used them all to bolster the sense of Hutu solidarity, to solidify their own control and to eradicate the last vestiges of respect for Tutsi authority. From these attacks they crafted the myth of the Hutu revolution as a long and courageous struggle against ruthless forces of repression. For them, the battle had been legitimate as well as brave: the Hutu, as the "great majority," the "rubanda nyamwinshi," had the right to rule over the minority. In their eyes, the ethnic majority was necessarily the same as the democratic majority.

At this time, Hutu politicians also established the link between "patriotism" and profit. In attacking the supposed enemies of the nation and the revolution, the Hutu stood to gain, both in the short term from goods pillaged and in the long term from lands appropriated from Tutsi who were driven away. Given the political and

---

[10]René Lemarchand, *Rwanda and Burundi* (New York: Praeger, 1970), pp. 222-26.

material gains from anti-Tutsi violence, officials and others had strong incentives to widen the circle of people targeted from the narrow group of former power-holders to all Tutsi. By 1967 when both the incursions and the attacks on Tutsi within Rwanda ended, Tutsi were at risk of attack for the simple fact of being Tutsi. During these years, some 20,000 Tutsi were killed and more than 300,000 were forced to flee abroad.[11]

The new republican government continued labeling all Rwandans as Hutu, Tutsi, or Twa, but the identity cards which had once served to guarantee privilege to Tutsi now served as a means to discriminate against them, both in employment and in education. Just as the new leaders maintained population registration, so they perpetuated the distorted concepts that had underlain the practice. Hutu used the ideas once prized by the Tutsi—ideas about Tutsi distinctiveness, foreign origins, and complete control over the Hutu—to justify the violence of the revolution and the discriminatory measures of the years after.

Following the revolution, the percentage of Tutsi in the Rwandan population declined sharply, partly because many had been massacred or fled, partly because some found ways to redefine themselves as Hutu. Said to represent 17.5 percent of the population in 1952, Tutsi were counted as only 8.4 percent of the total in 1991.[12]

Habyarimana in Control

Over a period of several years, the Parmehutu leaders, who were based in the south, eliminated Hutu rivals as well as the once powerful Tutsi and created what was in effect a single party state. By the end of the first decade of the republic, however, they were increasingly challenged by Hutu from the north who saw that all rhetoric about Hutu solidarity notwithstanding, the southerners were monopolizing the benefits of power. In the face of this growing split between Hutu of the north and Hutu of the south, "Public Safety Committees" and other groups began a campaign of intimidation and assaults on Tutsi in early 1973. Some attributed the attacks to southerners who hoped to minimize differences with northerners by reminding them of the common enemy; others laid them to northerners who hoped to create sufficient disorder to legitimate a coup d'état by the army, an institution dominated by northerners. Regardless of which group had

---

[11]Gérard Prunier, *The Rwanda Crisis, History of a Genocide* (New York: Columbia University Press, 1995), p.62.

[12]See discussion in the Introduction.

initiated the campaign, the tactic was clear: seek to resolve differences among Hutu at the expense of the Tutsi.

In July 1973, General Juvénal Habyarimana, the most senior officer in the army, took power, promising to restore order and national unity. He established the second republic in what was at the time a bloodless coup, although some fifty of the most prominent leaders of the first republic subsequently were executed or died in prison.

The Single-Party State

Two years after the coup, in 1975, Habyarimana made Rwanda officially a single-party state under the National Revolutionary Movement for Development (Mouvement Révolutionnaire National pour le Développement, MRND).[13] All Rwandans of whatever age were automatically members of the party. Over the years, Habyarimana constructed a cohesive monolith, with himself as president of the republic and president of the party and, at each level below him, the relevant government official simultaneously heading the corresponding level of the party.

At this time, Rwanda was divided into ten prefectures,[14] each of which included sub-prefectures, administrative units without much political importance. Below them were the communes, the essential building blocks of the administration. Numbering 145 in 1991, the communes ranged in population from less than 30,000 for the smallest to over 100,000 for the largest, with most counting between 40,000 and 50,000 residents. The head of the commune, the burgomaster, of course ranked below the prefect or sub-prefect, but he exercised more immediate and pervasive power over the ordinary people than did his superiors. In a style that harked back to the pre-colonial and the colonial era, the burgomaster held court one or more times a week, receiving the ordinary people who brought him their grievances or who came to give thanks for help received. He determined the use of land that belonged to the commune or was temporarily under its control. He mediated conflicts over property, settled family disputes, found places in secondary school, dispensed political advice, and even judged a substantial number of cases that in principle should have been taken to court. In accord with the communal

---

[13]The party changed its organization somewhat in April, 1991 and adopted the name of National Republican Movement for Democracy and Development but kept using the same initials.

[14]An eleventh prefecture was added in 1992 when the city of Kigali was established as an independent unit and a twelfth, Mutara, was formed in the northeast in August 1996.

council, he hired and fired the employees of the commune, including the communal policemen who were at his command, and he also intervened in personnel decisions of local schools, health centers, and development projects, although sometimes the presence of expatriates on project staffs limited his influence in this domain. The ultimate authority at the local level, he was clearly and directly the president's man out on the hills. Although nominally responsible to the minister of the interior, the burgomasters were named by Habyarimana and removed by him. All were known to him and some were very close to him personally.

The communes were divided into sectors, each of which had a population of some 5,000 people. The sectors were represented by elected councilors who together formed the communal council that supposedly advised the burgomaster, but more often simply implemented his decisions. The sector was in turn composed of cells, each of which grouped together approximately 1,000 people. The cell had an elected committee of five persons, headed by a *responsable* (cell head), who were charged more with executing orders from above than with representing the views from below. That small part of the population employed in urban salaried jobs participated in the party at their place of work, where the work unit was also a party cell.

This intensive administration had two objectives: control and mobilization. The control was implemented not just by the high ratio of officials to ordinary people but also by regulations governing population registration and movement. The Habyarimana government continued the use of identity cards and also required people moving from one location to another to register with the local authorities. Each commune submitted monthly, quarterly, and yearly reports of births, deaths, and movement into and out of the commune. The burgomaster kept agents of the secret service informed of any suspicious persons seen in his district. In his first months in office, Habyarimana ordered important government employees with master's degrees or higher to take military training, apparently with the intention of providing one more channel for instilling habits of obedience to orders.

The mobilization of the population aimed at first towards building the economic infrastructure and improving conditions for agriculture. Exploiting the practice of unpaid, communal labor imposed by the colonial administration, the MRND required the population to do *umuganda*, work for the public good, such as repairing roads, digging anti-erosion ditches, or clearing the brush. Umuganda was supervised by the *nyumbakumi*, a neighborhood leader in charge of a group of ten households, who had the power to fine those who failed to appear for the communal work sessions.

Once the MRND was firmly established, mobilization took on an added aspect: glorifying the party and its head. In addition to the work days, people were obliged to participate in weekly sessions of *animation*, propaganda meetings leavened with poetry, music, and dance created to honor Habyarimana and the MRND. Propaganda teams of singers and dancers vied for honors in regular competitions, often dressed in fine costumes bought by contributions from the party faithful. Rwandans often proclaimed their loyalty to Habyarimana, wore his image on portrait pins, and posted his picture in their houses or places of business.

The Army, the Church and the Akazu

As head of the army, Habyarimana had the allegiance of some 7,000 troops of the Rwandan Armed Forces (Forces Armées Rwandaises, FAR), about 1,200 of whom were part of the National Police (Gendarmerie). He was loyally supported especially by the elite units, made up largely of men from his home region: the Presidential Guard, estimated at between 1,000 and 1,300 troops, the paracommandos and the reconnaissance troops. He occasionally had to counter plots by other officers, however, including that attributed to Col. Alexis Kanyarengwe in 1980. Kanyarengwe, who had served as minister of interior, was forced to flee the country.

Habyarimana also enjoyed active support from the heads of the parastatal corporations that controlled public services like gas, water and electricity, or bus transport, and those that oversaw the production and marketing of cash crops. He knew he could count on the intellectual elite, including professors at the national university and heads of hospitals. To keep their posts, they would avoid criticizing him even if some declined to join in glorifying him. He could call on the heads of private enterprises to contribute materially and politically to his cause, knowing they needed his approval for the state concessions that made their businesses profitable.

He benefited enormously from the support of the hierarchy of the Catholic Church, which counted 62 percent of Rwandans among its adherents. The church, initially a pillar of support for the Tutsi elite, switched sides even before the colonial administration did and helped make the Hutu revolution. Although the majority of clergy, religious brothers, and sisters were Tutsi—some 70 percent according to one knowledgeable estimate—seven of the nine bishops in place at the start of the genocide were Hutu.[15] The archbishop of Kigali, Mgr. Vincent Nsengiyumva, was an ardent supporter of the president, known for wearing

---

[15]Guy Theunis, "Le Role de l'Eglise Catholique dans les Evénements Récents," in André Guichaoua, ed., *Les Crises Politiques au Burundi et au Rwanda* (Lille: Université des Sciences et Technologies de Lille, second edition, 1995), p. 293.

Habyarimana's portrait pin on his cassock while saying mass. He served as a member of the central committee of the MRND for many years and resigned only when church authorities insisted that he end his openly political role in 1985.

The various Protestant churches, representing 18 percent of the population, had no unified position towards Habyarimana, but the Anglican hierarchy and the Baptist church generally supported him. The president of the Presbyterian Church was a member of the prefectural committee of the MRND in Kibuye.

Both Catholic and Protestant clergy cooperated with officials by passing on state announcements from the pulpit and by serving on councils, particularly those that reviewed development projects at the prefectural or communal level.

One more link strengthened the connections from top to bottom of this highly structured system: the network of personal relations. Members of the elite who left home for positions in the capital or at the university maintained close ties to their communes of origin, where they had parents or other relatives. They visited home often and were the messengers of choice if some special order needed to be transmitted from the top to local officials. This practice existed long before Habyarimana took power—in December 1963, for example, ministers had gone home to organize the killings of Tutsi out on the hills, but he exploited it to maximum advantage, as did those who took over from him during the genocide.

The *akazu,* or "little house," was a special circle within the larger network of personal connections that worked to support Habyarimana. It was composed mostly of the people of Habyarimana's home region, with Madame Habyarimana and her relatives playing a major role. Some exercised authority openly, such as Protais Zigiranyirazo, who was once prefect of Ruhengeri, or Seraphin Rwabukumba, who headed a powerful enterprise, La Centrale, while others operated behind the scenes, such as Colonel Elie Sagatwa, who was Habyarimana's private secretary. When necessary, this group drew on military officers, like Col. Théoneste Bagosora, Major Leonard Nkundiye, and Captain Pascal Simbikangwa, to ensure their continued hold on power.[16] Christophe Mfizi, once close to Habyarimana and head of the national information service, denounced the activities of this group, which he called the "Zero Network." In an August 15, 1992 public letter to the president resigning his membership in the MRND, he declared that the intimates surrounding

---

[16]Professor Filip Reyntjens and Senator Willy Kuypers identified members of the akazu at a press conference reported in *La Libre Belgique*, October 3, 1992.

Habyarimana had taken control of the state and were milking it for private benefit.[17]

Prosperity, Short-Lived and Superficial

At the head of what was taken to be an honest and energetic administration, Habyarimana attracted substantial foreign assistance in the 1970s and 1980s. With such help, the government constructed an impressive infrastructure, particularly of roads and telephone and electric service. For the first decade, the economy did better than others in the same region, with a net increase in gross national product in relation to population, an achievement all the more remarkable given that Rwanda also had one of the highest rates of population growth on the continent.[18] Donor nations applauded these accomplishments, regarding Rwanda as one of the few promising "models" in Africa. The expatriate experts who implemented the assistance projects in the country took great satisfaction not just in the results obtained but also in the personal ties that they developed with Rwandan counterparts.[19]

Some Rwandans were indeed getting rich: those who worked for the state directly, those employed by its offshoots, parastatal enterprises, and those who ran economic development projects controlled by state officials. State employees and the military also used access to preferential treatment to build profitable private businesses. But the prosperity was both fragile and superficial. The mass of the people stayed poor and faced the prospect of getting only poorer. More than 90 percent lived from cultivation and while the population grew, the amount of land did not. The land available to ordinary cultivators actually diminished in some regions as local officials appropriated fields for development projects and as members of the urban elite bought out the poor, establishing themselves as absentee landlords. According to a government study done in 1991, the richest 16 percent of landowners held 43 percent of the land, while the poorest households tried to eke out a living on holdings that ranged from one quarter to three-quarters of a hectare,

---

[17]Christophe Mfizi, "Le réseau zéro," Kigali: August 15, 1992; Filip Reyntjens, *L'Afrique des Grands Lacs en Crise* (Paris: Editions Karthala, 1994), pp. 189-190.

[18]Reyntjens, *L'Afrique des Grands Lacs*, p. 35.

[19]On May 13, 1998, former French Minister of Cooperation Robert Galley told the French National Assembly inquiry on Rwanda that, for many, Rwanda was the model of transition from the colonial period to democracy. See Peter Uvin, *Aiding Violence, The Development Enterprise in Rwanda* (West Hartford, Kumarian Press, 1998).

or less than an acre of land.[20] In the most densely populated regions, some young people could not marry because they could not find land and, according to custom, a man without land could not take a wife. This situation was so critical in Ngoma commune, Butare prefecture, that large numbers of young people were cohabiting and having children without marrying, a practice that broke dramatically with past standards of behavior. Of the births registered in Ngoma, Butare prefecture, in January 1994, nearly 50 percent of the children had been born out of wedlock.[21]

At the end of the 1980s, coffee, which accounted for 75 percent of Rwanda's foreign exchange, dropped sharply in price on the international market. Suddenly Rwanda found itself among the many debtor nations required to accept strict fiscal measures imposed by the World Bank and the donor nations. The urban elite saw its comfort threatened, but the rural poor suffered even more. A drought beginning in 1989 reduced harvests in the south and left substantial numbers of people short of food. Habyarimana at first refused to acknowledge the gravity of the food shortage, an attitude that exemplified the readiness of the urban elite to ignore suffering out on the hills.[22]

The imbalance in wealth and power was a question not just of the usual urban-rural disparities but also of increasingly evident discrimination against Tutsi and against Hutu from areas other than the "blessed region," that is, the northwest. Habyarimana had established a system of quotas, supposedly to assure equitable distribution of resources and opportunities to all Rwandans. In fact, officials used the system to restrict the access of Tutsi to employment and higher education, and increasingly to discriminate against Hutu from regions other than the north. By the

---

[20]James K. Gasana, "La Guerre, La Paix et La Démocratie au Rwanda," in Guichaoua, *Les Crises Politiques,* pp. 214-15.

[21]Raporo y'abaturage, ukwezi kwa Mutarama, annex to letter of Joseph Kanyabashi, Burgumestri wa Komini y'Umujyi ya Ngoma to Bwana Responsable wa Service Statistique, no. 99/04.05/1 16 February 1994. [N.B. Provenance of unpublished documents is noted in parentheses after the first mention of each, except where the document was delivered on condition that its source not be revealed. This document was found by our research team at the Butare prefecture.]

[22]For economic development in Rwanda, see Catharine Newbury, "Recent Debates over Governance and Rural Development," in G. Hayden and M. Bratton, eds., *Governance and Politics in Africa* (Boulder: Lynne Riemer, 1992) and F. Bezy, *Rwanda. Bilan socio-économique d'un régime, 1962-1989* (Louvain-la-Neuve: Institut d'étude des pays en développement, Etudes et Documents, 1990).

mid-1980s, Habyarimana's home prefecture of Gisenyi, one of ten in the country at the time, had provided the office holders for one-third of the most important jobs in government as well as virtually all the leaders of the army and security service. Gisenyi and the adjacent prefecture of Ruhengeri enjoyed a similarly disproportionate share of national resources, whether measured in terms of funds for development or places available for higher education.[23]

Threats to the MRND Monolith
Opposition within Rwanda
Confronted by the dramatic economic decline and the evidence of increasing corruption and favoritism on the part of Habyarimana and his inner circle, political leaders, intellectuals, and journalists began demanding reforms. These critics within Rwanda echoed demands for greater democracy being heard elsewhere in Africa and in other parts of the world. They were in turn backed by donor nations that now saw political reform as necessary for economic progress. In July 1990, Habyarimana agreed to discuss change and announced that a national commission would be formed to examine the question. Two months later, a group of thirty-three intellectuals and leaders of the awakening civil society declared that in their view the issue needed no further examination: Rwanda should return to a multi-party system. In that same month of September, four journalists were brought to trial for having published reports of government corruption. They were led by Abbé André Sibomana, editor of *Kinyamateka*, the oldest and most influential newspaper in the country. In denouncing abuses of power, Sibomana broke with the position of the archbishop and others in the hierarchy, who continued to give Habyarimana apparently unquestioning support.[24] After presenting considerable evidence to substantiate their charges, the four were acquitted in a decision that seemed both to confirm the accuracy of the reports and to herald a new era of freedom for the press. The next week, Habyarimana named the members of the commission to examine political reform. Just as these changes were promising greater participation in the political system, the RPF attacked Rwanda.

---

[23]Reyntjens, *L'Afrique des Grands Lacs,* pp. 33-34.

[24]Sibomana would continue to publicize corruption and human rights violations in the months to come, at considerable risk to himself. He would also serve as the chief inspiration for an extraordinary pastoral letter issued by the Kabgayi presbyterium on December 1, 1991, "Convertissons-nous pour vivre ensemble dans la paix" which criticized the closeness of the church to the political establishment.

The RPF Attack

By the late 1980s, the Rwandan community in exile had swelled to approximately 600,000 people,[25] most of whom lived in the countries surrounding Rwanda. Except in Tanzania, where the government had encouraged their integration into the local population, the refugees existed precariously, with few rights or guarantees. In Uganda, thousands of refugees had been expelled to Rwanda in 1982, only to be pushed back again across the border shortly after. In 1986 Rwandan authorities had declared that the country was too overpopulated to permit the return of the refugees, a statement that helped spark renewed activity in the refugee community. At a meeting in Washington D.C. in 1988 Rwandans affirmed their right to return home, by force if necessary. In 1989 the Rwandan government created a commission to deal with the refugee problem. It met jointly with Ugandan authorities three times, the last in July 1990, and appeared to be making some progress in clearing the way for the refugees to return.

The RPF, however, decided to go home on its own terms, proclaiming its goals to be not just the return of the refugees, but also the ouster of Habyarimana and the establishment of a more democratic government. Its leaders, part of a generation that had grown up in Uganda, were well prepared to launch this effort. Many of them had learned to make war in the forces of the National Resistance Army, where they had helped Yoweri Museveni win control of the Ugandan state. Among them was Paul Kagame, once deputy head of military intelligence for the NRA, who took command of the Rwandan Patriotic Army (RPA),[26] the fighting force of the RPF, in the early days of the war. His forces consisted of some seven thousand soldiers, about half of whom were Rwandan refugees who had deserted from the Ugandan army, bringing along their arms and other equipment.[27]

---

[25]André Guichaoua, "Vers Deux Générations de Réfugiés Rwandais?" in Guichaoua, *Les Crises Politiques*, p. 343.

[26]Although the fighting force of the RPF is properly known as the Rwandan Patriotic Army, we use the term RPF for both the army and the political organization before July 17, 1994 in order to avoid confusion with the current Rwandan army which is also known as the RPA.

[27]Human Rights Watch Arms Project, "Arming Rwanda, The Arms Trade and Human Rights Abuses in the Rwandan War," *A Human Rights Watch Short Report,* vol. 6, issue 1, January 1994, p. 8.

The Government Response to the Attack

Rumors that the RPF was about to attack had circulated in both Uganda and Rwanda since mid-September 1990. The Rwandan commander at the frontier, aware of these reports, wired headquarters to ask for reinforcements. He got none, leading him and others to speculate that Habyarimana wanted the invasion. On October 1, 1990, the RPF crossed the border, easily overpowered the small detachment there, and headed for the capital.[28]

The attack offered Habyarimana the opportunity to rebuild his eroding base of power by rallying Rwandans against the enemy. In response to the news, the great majority of people, Tutsi and Hutu opponents of the regime included, came to the support of the government. But Habyarimana understood that the attack posed a risk as well as an opportunity: it might embolden the opposition within the country and even lead to its alliance with the enemy. Rather than rely on a spontaneous coalescing of support from all sides, Habyarimana decided to pursue a more forceful strategy, to sacrifice the Tutsi in hopes of uniting all Hutu behind him.

On October 4, the RPF had advanced a considerable distance into Rwanda but was still forty-five miles from Kigali. That night, however, heavy firing shook the capital for several hours. In the morning the government announced that the city had been attacked by RPF infiltrators who had been driven back by the Rwandan army. Under the pretext of assuring security, the government began making massive arrests in Kigali and elsewhere in the country, eventually imprisoning some 13,000 people. The detainees would be held without charge, thousands of them for months, in deplorable conditions. Many were tortured and dozens died. The last of them were finally liberated in April 1991.[29]

Many Rwandans and apparently all foreign observers believed the government account of the battle and the infiltration. In fact, the attack had been faked. Habyarimana staged the event to have credible grounds for accusing Tutsi of supporting the enemy. He disclaimed any such intention, declaring on October 5 that there was no question of considering "our brothers and sisters of whatever ethnic group" responsible for what had had happened.[30] But certainly he knew and

---

[28]Human Rights Watch/FIDH interview, Kigali, January, 1993.

[29]Human Rights Watch/FIDH interview, Brussels, October 19, 1997; Africa Watch, "Rwanda: Talking Peace and Waging War, Human Rights Since the October 1990 Invasion," *A Human Rights Watch Short Report,* vol. 4, issue no. 3, February 27, 1992, pp. 7-11.

[30]Reyntjens, *L'Afrique des Grands Lacs,* p. 94, note 10.

approved of the plan as well as of the arrests that resulted from it. The minister of justice spoke more openly. In the first use in the 1990s of the term that was to become so famous, he declared that the Tutsi were *ibyitso*, "accomplices" of the invaders. He continued that "to prepare an attack of that scale required trusted people [on the inside]. Rwandans of the same ethnic group offered that possibility better than did others."[31]

In accusing the Tutsi, the authorities reverted to the tactics of the 1960s, but in a departure from the earlier practice, they included Hutu as well among the "accomplices." Unwilling to wait for the scapegoating of the Tutsi to produce solidarity among the Hutu, they sought to hasten the effect by imprisoning Hutu opponents, hoping to silence and perhaps even eliminate some while at the same time intimidating others into rallying to the president.

The faked attack served another purpose: to ensure help from friendly foreign nations. When asked the reason for all the firing on the night of October 4, one Rwandan army officer is reported to have replied, "It was fireworks to welcome our friends, the French," who did, in fact, arrive that night.[32] Pretending that even the capital was at risk, Habyarimana was able to enlist immediate support from Belgium and Zaire as well as from France. The Belgian forces stayed only a month and the Zairian soldiers were sent home for indiscipline, but the French soldiers remained to become a solid support for the Rwandan army and the Habyarimana regime.

With the help of foreign troops, Rwandan soldiers drove the RPF back towards the Ugandan border. As they advanced through the region called Mutara, the Rwandan forces killed between 500 and 1,000 civilians. The unarmed victims were Bahima, a people usually identified with Tutsi, and they were accused of having aided the RPF.[33]

The government instituted a series of security measures, including requiring citizens to participate in patrols at night and to man barriers to monitor traffic on

---

[31]Ibid., p. 94.

[32]Human Rights Watch interview, Kigali, November 8, 1991.

[33]Africa Watch (later Human Rights Watch/Africa), International Federation of Human Rights Leagues, Interafrican Union for Human and Peoples' Rights, and the International Center for Human Rights and Democratic Development, "Report of the International Commission of Investigation on Human Rights Violations in Rwanda since October 1, 1990," March 1993, p. 34. Hereafter cited as "Report of the International Commission."

roads and paths. The neighborhood official, the nyumbakumi, was responsible for enforcing these measures and for keeping track of any strangers who entered his part of the commune. Except in communes adjacent to battle zones, these measures did not last long, but they did help convince people that there was a real danger of enemy infiltrators.

Consolidating the Opposition

The imprisonments of October reinforced the image of the Habyarimana government as a repressive regime and instead of driving Tutsi and Hutu opposition apart, strengthened bonds between them. In a January 1991 letter, prefects urged Habyarimana "to vigorously destroy the manoeuvers of the enemy, both...the INYENZI[34] terrorists and those of the opposition that has developed inside the country." They advised him to "fight openly against what could be called the 'Kanyarengwe effect' which poses a serious threat to the necessary solidarity of the BAHUTU."[35] Colonel Kanyarengwe, the important officer who had fled Rwanda in 1980 after accusations that he was plotting against Habyarimana, had joined the RPF and was serving as its president. Because he was a Hutu—and from northern Rwanda besides—his participation in the RPF exemplified the dreaded union of dissatisfied Hutu and the RPF.

Knowing of RPF pressure on the regime, its opponents were encouraged to demand more rapid change. The Rwandan human rights movement was stimulated by the massive arrests at the start of the war. The first of the groups, the Rwandan Association for the Defense of Human Rights (Association Rwandaise pour la Défense des Droits de l'Homme, ARDHO) had been established the night before the RPF attack and faced its first challenge in dealing with the arrests. Two others were founded directly in reaction to the imprisonments: the Rwandan Association for the Defense of Human Rights and Public Liberties (Association Rwandaise pour la Défense des Droits de la Personne et des Libertés Publiques, ADL) developed from a network of those who tried to bring relief to the prisoners and their families and Kanyarwanda was established by former prisoners once they

---

[34]*Inyenzi*, literally cockroaches, was a term used to describe Tutsi who invaded Rwanda in the 1960s. It was revived in 1990 to refer to members of the RPF.

[35]Jean Marie Vianney Mugemana, Ministre de l'Intérieur et du Développement Communal to Monsieur le Président de la République Rwandaise, no. 035/04.09.01/16, January 31, 1991 (Butare prefecture).

were liberated.[36] These organizations quickly began insisting on reforms necessary to permit full enjoyment of civil and political rights. Donor nations, too, urged Habyarimana to open up the political system, hoping this would speed an end to the war.

In announcing the national commission on reform in July 1990, Habyarimana had anticipated a two-year period of study before it would submit its report. But only eleven months later, in June 1991, he was obliged to accept the constitutional amendment that made multiple political parties legal. Even before the amendment was adopted, opponents began to organize the Democratic Republican Movement (Mouvement Démocratique Républicain, MDR), which would constitute the chief threat to the MRND. Within months another fifteen parties had been formed, the most important of which were the Social Democratic Party (Parti Social Démocrate, PSD), Liberal Party (Parti Libéral, PL) and the Democratic Christian Party (Parti Démocrate Chrétien, PDC).

With the organization of parties, the opposition had structures to mobilize protest against the establishment. Their first goal was to force Habyarimana to accept a coalition government which would give them a chance to share in power. He resisted their demands for some months but after the opposition parties mounted massive street demonstrations early in 1992, he was obliged to begin talks with them. As these negotiations were going on, a group of Hutu announced the establishment of a new party, the Coalition for the Defense of the Republic (Coalition pour la Défense de la République, CDR). They asserted that "no party, no institution, no person had been able to defend the interests of the majority [i.e., the Hutu] publicly and consistently," and so they must take their fate in their own

---

[36]Two other human rights organizations were later established: the Association of Volunteers for Peace (Association pour les Voluntaires de la Paix, AVP) and the Christian Human Rights League (Ligue Chrétienne pour la Défense des Droits de l'Homme, LICHREDHOR, later renamed League for the Promotion and Defense of Human Rights in Rwanda, Ligue Pour la Promotion et la Défense des Droits de l'Homme au Rwanda, LIPREDHOR). In July 1992, the five groups formed the Coalition of Leagues and Associations for the Defense of Human Rights (Collectif des Ligues et Associations de Défense des Droits de l'Homme, CLADHO). Kanyarwanda withdrew some months later but often acted informally with CLADHO even after having dissolved its official link with the committee.

hands.[37] The CDR openly criticized the MRND and even Habyarimana personally for conceding too much to the opposition parties and to the RPF. Despite this criticism, the CDR collaborated frequently with the MRND, leading some observers to conclude that this bitterly anti-Tutsi party existed only to state positions favored by the MRND but too radical for them to support openly.

Habyarimana agreed to incorporate the major opposition parties in a coalition government, which took office in April 1992. In it, Habyarimana continued as president of the republic and the MRND was able to retain nine of the nineteen cabinet posts, including the key ministries of defense and interior. But the largest of the new parties of opposition, the MDR, obtained the post of prime minister as well as two other ministeries. In addition, the PL and the PSD each had three seats and the PDC had one. The new CDR, representing only a small number of adherents, was not included.

Once at the cabinet table, the opposition parties next aimed to divorce the MRND from the state, the natural consequence of introducing a multi-party system. At their insistence, the minister of interior directed administrative officials to show neutrality in the exercise of their functions instead of being cheerleaders for the MRND.[38] Once able to count on buildings, vehicles, office equipment, and supplies that belonged to the state, the MRND would henceforth have to provide its own resources. The divorce was faster and more complete in regions where the opposition parties had established a solid base, less so in the northwest where the continued preeminence of the MRND made it futile to protest its privileges. Wherever possible, the MRND naturally delayed yielding its advantage. Radio Rwanda, for example, continued for some time to play MRND songs, supposedly because it had no other tapes in its music collection.

To make their participation in power real and convincing—and hence to draw more adherents to their flags—the opposition parties had to end the MRND monopoly over government posts. They had to deliver to their members the jobs

---

[37]Reyntjens, *L'Afrique des Grands Lacs,* p. 127. Reyntjens indicates that Shyirambere Jean Barahinyura was the primary force behind this party, which appears surprising since he was not long before a member of the central committee of the RPF. Barahinyura was, however, only one of several important politicians who changed position dramatically toward the Hutu-Tutsi problem. Both Colonel Kanyarengwe and Pasteur Bizimungu, now president of Rwanda, were known previously for hostility to the Tutsi.

[38]Ministeri y'Ubutegetsi bw'Igihugu n'Amajyambere ya Komini to Bwana Perefe, Bwana Su-perefe, Bwana Burugumesitiri, no. 585/04.09.01, Kigali, August 5, 1992 (Gikongoro prefecture).

usually associated with controlling the state and they had to be in a position to ensure that the policies they favored would be executed. They quickly put their own people behind the desks in the ministries they headed, but determining appointments in Kigali was not enough. They needed to control at least some of the local administration whose support was usually essential to winning elections. Within a few months of joining the government, the MDR, the PL and the PDC each had gotten one post of prefect. It was even more important for them to have the support of burgomasters, who could do much to sway election results within their communes. This took longer and it was only in February 1993 that the MRND agreed to changing burgomasters in about one third of the communes.

One of the first domains where the opposition ended exclusive MRND control was access to education. In 1991, only 8 percent of Rwandan children were able to study at secondary school.[39] Through the Ministry of Primary and Secondary Education, the MRND had regulated access to government-supported high schools, supposedly assigning places according to quotas for ethnic and regional groups. The quotas were both inaccurately computed and unfairly applied, favoring children from the northwest or those whose families could pay in money or other benefits for access to education. With the April 1992 government, Agathe Uwilingiyimana took office as minister of primary and secondary education.[40] A representative of the MDR, she promptly abolished the quota system and decreed that access to higher education would be decided on merit alone. Almost immediately after, she was assaulted by armed men who forced their way into her house and beat her. Thousands of students and mothers turned out to march in support of her new policy.[41]

Kubohoza, "To Help Liberate"

In the early months after the parties were established, their supporters saw the new organizations as the hope of the future—for themselves personally as well as for the nation. In a brash and exuberant rush to publicize their cause and to recruit new members, party activists sporting caps and shirts with the party colors held demonstrations and meetings in small commercial centers out on the hills as well

---

[39]Martial Laurent, "Panorama Succinct des Economies de la Région des Grands Lacs Africains," in Guichaoua, *Les Crises Politiques,* p. 424

[40]Named prime minister in July 1993, the first woman to hold this office in Rwanda, she was killed by Rwandan army soldiers on April 7, 1994.

[41]Reyntjens, *L'Afrique des Grands Lacs,* pp. 115-16.

as in the capital. Local leaders flew the party flag on poles outside their homes or businesses, proud to be identified as the key persons for mobilizing adherents in that area. Party leaders organized groups of singers or dancers to enliven meetings with musical versions of party propaganda, mirroring the "animation" that had once been the exclusive domain of the MRND.

MRND officials naturally feared the development of opposition parties. The prefect of Butare, for example, wrote his subordinates in early 1992 to warn that parties posed a risk to the "unity of the popular masses." Like many others at the time, he cast the danger in terms of defeat by the enemy, not in terms of the loss to some rival political party within the country. He insisted that if Hutu opponents continued contesting MRND control, the Tutsi would take power.[42] MRND leaders at the national level were concerned enough about the threat from other contenders to direct local authorities, still all nominally MRND supporters at that time, to do a poll of political loyalties within some of their districts. In Bwakira commune, sector leaders reported that in some places Habyarimana and the MRND would be chosen by only 50 percent of the voters.[43]

The MRND authorities did their best to slow the organizing efforts of rivals by using security regulations to hinder their travel and public meetings. They looked the other way when MRND members disrupted demonstrations of the opposition and stole or destroyed their party insignia. In some places they tolerated or even encouraged MRND supporters to assault members of the opposition or to burn and pillage their houses. Seeing the power of the state used for partisan ends, adherents of opposition parties also adopted force as a means of winning the political struggle. Taking political recruits by force or by threat became known as *kubohoza* or "to help liberate," an ironic use which suggests that the captive might have been "freed" against his or her will. Originally undertood to mean liberating from the MRND monolith, the term later was used to refer to aggressive action against any political opponent.

The parties organized youth wings which increasingly engaged in violence against rivals. The MDR youth wing, the *Inkuba* or "Thunder," led in harassing MRND supporters, sometimes with the help of the *Abakombozi*, "The Liberators" of the PSD. Confronted with this opposition, the MRND moved to a new level of

---

[42]Justin Temahagali, Préfet de Butare, to Monsieur le Ministre de l'Intérieur et du Développement Communal, January 3, 1992, enclosing the minutes of a meeting he had held with all the burgomasters and sub-prefects (Butare prefecture).

[43]Documents identified by sector, but otherwise unlabeled, listing seven questions about local political opinions and the results for each sector (Bwakira commune).

intimidation by transforming its youth group, the *Interahamwe*, into a real militia. Besides being more numerous and better organized than the youth of other parties, the Interahamwe received military training from regular soldiers beginning in 1992. They were sometimes backed by the CDR youth group, the *Impuzamugambi,* "Those With a Single Purpose." During 1992 and 1993, politically motivated attacks by Interahamwe and other groups took some 200 lives and injured scores of people in different communities.[44]

If the target to be "liberated" was sufficiently important, the process could involve rewards as well as threats. In the commune of Nshili, Gikongoro prefecture, for example, an ambitious young teacher named Paul Kadogi decided to join the MDR in part because he was having difficulties with the burgomaster, an MRND stalwart who had held the post for some thirty years. Because Kadogi, described by MRND higher authorities as a "very virulent" propagandist for the MDR, was attracting considerable support among teachers and others in the commune, the MRND dispatched a "mission" in June 1991 to win Kadogi back. The senior member was secretary-general of the Ministry of the Interior and a native of the region. He was assisted by a burgomaster from an adjacent commune who was also a member of the prefectural committee of the MRND and by the sub-prefect of the region. The MRND emisssaries combined what they called "muscular persuasion" with the promise to name Kadogi himself burgomaster if he agreed to rejoin the MRND "with all the people who had followed him into the MDR." On August 12, 1991 the prefect of Gikongoro "took great pleasure" in writing the minister of the interior to announce that the "recovery" of Kadogi and his numerous followers had been completed. The prefect had just returned from the ceremony installing Kadogi as burgomaster of Nshili where he had "forcefully and enthusiastically" invited all the MDR members in the crowd to follow his example of rejoining the MRND. In his report on the mission, the sub-prefect stressed the effectiveness of visits by important officials from the capital who were native to the region in rallying people to the MRND. The prefect, in his report, assured the minister of the interior that: "We remain vigilant and ready to dismantle in the

---

[44]Africa Watch, "Beyond the Rhetoric: Continuing Human Rights Abuses in Rwanda," *A Human Rights Watch Short Report,* vol. 5, no. 7, June 1993, pp. 6-10. See also, Ligue Indépendante pour la Défense des Droits de l'Homme (LIDEL), *Rwanda: Le Non-Dit sur la Violation des Droits de l'Homme,* Kigali, January 1993. This group, apparently a tool of the Habyarimana government, published data on abuses by other political parties against members of the MRND.

same way any effort or campaign that might be launched here...by other parties developing at the expense of the MRND."[45]

The MDR adherents did not count themselves defeated although it apparently took them some months to recover from Kadogi's defection. By November 1992, they were ready to use kubohoza and went so far as to attack and take hostage National Policemen. A month later, the police shot and killed a member of the MRD youth group in the same region. This provoked MDR activists in several communes to threaten the sub-prefect and the prefect whom they accused of using the police to destroy their party. The prefect, Laurent Bucyibaruta, protested his complete neutrality and his readiness to permit demonstrations by other political parties, provided their organizers were willing to "take the consequences if another part of the population decides to react against these demonstrations."[46]

In this case, the prefect and sub-prefect avoided assault, but other MRND authorities, higher as well as lower in rank, were attacked, particularly in 1992 and early 1993. Several burgomasters were driven from their communes and forced to resign. The minister of youth was assaulted while driving through a commune hostile to him. The home of the minister of labor was attacked in the prefecture of Kibungo.[47]

The illegitimate use of public powers for private or partisan benefit discredited not just the office-holders, but also the institutions themselves in the eyes of the population. In communes where the burgomaster was accused of governing badly, people refused to pay taxes, the situation in a considerable number of communes by mid-1992. In those places where the land-hungry cultivators had been obliged by the state to cede fields to development projects that brought no visible improvement to their lives, they took back the land by force. In communes where umuganda obligatory work was bringing no benefit to the ordinary people, they began refusing to turn out for the day of labor.

---

[45]Gérard Terebura, Sous-préfet, Rapport de Mission effectuée samedi 29/6/1991 auprès de certains adherents du MDR dans la commune Nshili, 2/7/1991; Joseph Habiyambere, Préfet, to Monsieur le Ministre de l'Intérieur et du Développement Communal, no. 1111/04.09.01, August 12, 1991 (Gikongoro prefecture).

[46]Laurent Bucyibaruta, Préfet, to Monsieur le Ministre de l'Intérieur et du Développement Communal, no. CN 132/04.17.02, December 14, 1992 (Gikongoro prefecture).

[47]LIDEL, *Rwanda, Le Non-dit*, p. 93.

Impunity and Insecurity

When people engaged in kubohoza, they sometimes covered their faces with chalk, wore banana leaves, attacked at the signal of a whistle, marched to a drum and manned barriers along the roads to catch their prey. During the genocide, some assailants did the same things. More important by far than these surface resemblances was the continuation of an attitude spread by kubohoza, an attitude that accepted violence as "normal" in the pursuit of political ends. Just as MRND officials frequently tolerated or encouraged violence by MRND members, so did officials of other parties condone or incite the use of force by their supporters. When authorities halted or punished violence, it was often because the perpetrators belonged to political parties to which they themselves were opposed. The National Police and soldiers sometimes refused to assist civilian officials who were attempting to maintain order and sometimes they even launched politically motivated attacks themselves against opponents of the MRND or CDR.[48] The judiciary did no better than the executive branch in upholding a state of law. The courts, underfunded and understaffed, rarely functioned as they should have.[49]

During 1992 and 1993, apparently random attacks by unindentified assailants increased dramatically: grenades thrown into houses, bombs placed in buses or at markets, and mines laid along roads. The Rwandan army general staff issued a press release identifying RPF infiltrators and their "accomplices" as responsible for this violence, an assessment generally accepted by supporters of Habyarimana.[50] Those opposed to Habyarimana attributed the attacks to his agents, who, they charged, were operating a death squad which they called by Mfizi's name of the "Zero Network." The International Commission of Investigation On Human Rights Violations in Rwanda, a group sponsored by four international human rights organizations that examined the situation in Rwanda in early 1993, concluded that the Zero Network was linked to the highest circles of power in Kigali and was

---

[48]Jean-Baptise Habyalimana, Préfet, to Alison Des Forges, Butare, February 8, 1993.

[49]For an examination of the problems with the judiciary, see François-Xavier Nsanzuwera, *La Magistrature Rwandaise dans l'Etau du Pouvoir Executif* (Kigali: Editeur CLADHO, 1993).

[50]Assemblée Nationale, Mission d'information commune, *Enquête sur la tragédie rwandaise (1990-1994)*, Tome I, Rapport, pp. 94, 113.

responsible for many of the attacks.[51] Whether executed by agents of Habyarimana or by others, the random violence, like the targeted violence of kubohoza, showed Rwandans that the government either could not or would not protect its citizens.[52]

In the absence of an impartial, effective enforcement of the laws, those who attacked with political motives multiplied their abuses. Common criminals profited too from the laxity of law enforcement to increase assaults and robberies. Firearms had suddenly become easy to get, partly as a result of the war-time increase in the circulation of guns, partly as the result of distribution of weapons by officials. Grenades could be bought at the market for less than U.S.$2.[53] The availability of guns and grenades made the work of criminals easier, more certain to be profitable, and more likely to prove fatal for the victims. In some communities, National Police and soldiers raped, pillaged, or even murdered the civilians they were supposed to be protecting.[54] Unable to count on protection from the state, law-abiding Rwandans who feared attack because of their politics or their wealth also invested in guns, some of which were registered as required by law, others of which were kept hidden until the genocide.[55]

The Military Defines "The Enemy"

After the initial RPF attack in October 1990, the Rwandan government forces, assisted particularly by the French, repulsed the invaders, killing many of them. The RPF regrouped and, in a surprise attack, took the important northwestern town

---

[51]"Report of the International Commission," p. 43.

[52]Africa Watch, "Beyond the Rhetoric," pp. 12-14.

[53]Ibid., p.14.

[54]Ibid., p. 8; "Report of the International Commission," pp. 32-33.

[55]See, for example, James Gasana, Ministre de la Défense, to J.B. Hakizamungu, Sous-préfet, no. 0913/06.1.9, March 11, 1993; Jean-Baptiste Habyalimana, Préfet, to Messieurs les Bourgmestres (tous), no. 138/04.09.01 April 16, 1993 and Joseph Kanyabashi, Bourgmestre de la Commune Urbaine de Ngoma, to Monsieur le Préfet, no. 308/04.09.01, April 30, 1993 (Butare prefecture).

of Ruhengeri in January 1991, but held it for only one day.[56] Reduced to only about 3,000 soldiers, the RPF retreated into a series of guerrilla incursions which were met with ripostes from the Rwandan army.[57] The combat was punctuated by occasional efforts at cease-fires and negotiations, but it was only after the MDR, the PL, and the PSD joined the government in April 1992 that they were able to oblige Habyarimana to enter into serious negotiations with the RPF. At the same time, the RPF launched an important offensive in the northeast, apparently to assure a strong position at the start of peace talks. They drove Rwandan army troops back from several communes in Byumba prefecture along with some 350,000 civilians who thus began years of misery as displaced persons. The RPF and the Rwandan government signed a cease-fire at Arusha, Tanzania in July 1992 and in August 1992 they signed the first of a series of agreements that would be known as the Arusha Accords. The Organisation of African Unity (OAU) facilitated the negotiations and agreed to provide a small observer force to monitor the cease-fire.

By the time serious talks with the RPF began in 1992, the Rwandan army had grown to some 30,000 soldiers. An important number of them opposed the negotiations, not just because they did not want to give up the fight, but also because they dreaded demobilization. The thousands of troops who had been recruited since the start of the war had become accustomed to the advantages of the military life. The MRND and the CDR fed their fears by spreading rumors that soldiers would be thrown out onto a disintegrating economy without hope of finding work. The prime minister, Dismas Nsengiyaremye of the MDR, attempted to reassure the troops by talking of using demobilized soldiers in economic development projects, such as draining marshes to obtain new land for cultivation. This proposal incensed the soldiers further; it was just such menial labor that they thought they had left behind in their new military careers.

In May and June, 1992, soldiers mutinied in the northern towns of Gisenyi, Ruhengeri, and Byumba killing scores of civilians and pillaging or destroying hundreds of thousands of dollars worth of property. Soldiers rebelled again briefly

---

[56]In the brief day or so when the RPF controlled Ruhengeri, they freed prisoners from the local jail, including Col. Théoneste Lizinde, an important officer imprisoned by Habyarimana at the time of the 1980 coup attempt. He retreated with the RPF and joined their forces, another example of the feared "Kanyarengwe effect."

[57]Col. Déogratias Nsabimana to Liste A, Comdt Sect OPS (Tous), No. 1437/G2.2.4, Kigali, September 21, 1992 (International Commission).

in October at the Kanombe military base near the capital.[58] Responding to pressure from the military as well as from civilian hard-liners, Habyarimana disavowed the Arusha Accords in a speech in Ruhengeri on November 15. Making clear that he did not intend to implement the agreement that he had signed three months before, Habyarimana called the Accords "a scrap of paper."

In principle prohibited by law from membership in political parties, soldiers and police nonetheless did not hesitate to demonstrate their political leanings. Habyarimana himself was only the most obvious case, serving until 1992 as general and commander-in-chief of the Armed Forces while also being president of the MRND. Particularly those soldiers who shared a northern origin with Habyarimana, of whom there were many, put loyalty to the president above all else. Some officers of the army general staff promoted fear and hatred of Tutsi and of Hutu opposed to Habyarimana both among the troops and among the civilian population. In early December 1991, the high command of the Rwandan army issued two press releases that proclaimed in a pro forma way their support for democratization and neutrality towards all political parties. But the military leaders then went on to condemn Rwandans who "knowingly or unknowingly, aided the enemy under the cover of political party activities." They declared that newpapers critical of the president were subsidized by the RPF. They blamed RPF infiltrators and their "acolytes" for the increase in crime and acts of random violence and they concluded one press release by asking the secret police to "neutralize all collaborators identified with the enemy."[59] Col. Léonidas Rusatira, then secretary-general of the Ministry of Defense, apparently opposed the broadcast of these releases, but he was overruled by Habyarimana himself who decided to make them public.[60] The minister of the interior circulated the first of these press releases, directing that burgomasters make its contents widely known. The prefect of Kibuye, passing on the order, told burgomasters to "use it [the press release] to its full value in meetings to raise the consciousness of the population about the ideals

---

[58]"Report of the International Commission," p. 33; Reyntjens, *L'Afrique des Grands Lacs,* p. 118.

[59]Africa Watch, "Rwanda: Talking Peace and Waging War," pp. 20-21.

[60]Reyntjens, *L'Afrique des Grands Lacs,* p. 185.

of peace and unity."[61] The release must certainly have had the opposite effect, itself fueling the "ethnic and regional tensions" that it accused opponents of fostering.

On September 21, 1992, Colonel Déogratias Nsabimana, chief of staff, sent a top secret memorandum to his commanders identifying and defining "the enemy."[62] The memorandum was part of a report from a commission of ten officers established the previous December to examine how to defeat the enemy "in the military, media and political domains." Among the measures recommended by the commission was the removal of some high-ranking officers who held these posts by virtue of their connections to members of the akazu, particularly Madame Habyarimana, rather than by virtue of their military abilities. Habyarimana had accepted their recommendations in June 1992 and had obliged a number of officers to retire, among them Colonels Serubuga and Rwagafilita.[63] The memorandum remained restricted to a small circle of high-ranking officers until Nsabimana ordered its dissemination in September, several weeks after the signing of the first of the Arusha Accords. Rwandan military authorities at this time feared a new RPF offensive was being prepared and Nsabimana hoped the memorandum would "lead our men to be more vigilant and to not count on political negotiations alone." He ordered:

> You will distribute this document widely, insisting especially on the sections relating to the definition of the enemy, identification of the enemy, as well as the groups within which the enemy is recruited. You will inform me of the impact made by the contents of this document on the men under your orders.

The report divided the enemy into two categories, the principal enemy and partisans of the enemy. The principal enemy was:

> the Tutsi inside or outside the country, extremist and nostalgic for power, who have NEVER recognized and will NEVER recognize the realities of the 1959 social revolution and who wish to reconquer power by all means necessary, including arms.

---

[61]Gaspard Ruhumuliza, Préfet de Kibuye, to Monsieur le Bourgmestre (Tous), December 12, 1991.

[62]Col. Déogratias Nsabimana to Liste A, September 21, 1992.

[63]Human Rights Watch/FIDH interview, by telephone, August 29, 1996.

The partisans of the enemy were defined as anyone who supported the principal enemy. Like the December 1991 press releases, the document made the necessary nod towards democratic openness:

> Political opponents who want power or the peaceful and democratic change of the current political regime of Rwanda are NOT to be confused with the ENI [enemy] or with partisans of the ENI.

Again like the earlier communiques—and sometimes in the same language—the fourteen page document then went on to condemn Tutsi and those Hutu who opposed Habyarimana and his party. Nowhere did it caution against confusing the RPF as a political group with Tutsi as an ethnic group. In several places, it used "Tutsi" as equivalent to enemy. As one of the advantages of the enemy, it listed "A single political will and a single political ideology, which is Tutsi hegemony."

The document deplored the loss of Hutu solidarity, which it blamed on enemy machinations rather than on understandable resentment of the corruption and repression of the Habyarimana regime. It listed the establishment of multiple political parties as an advantage for the enemy and warned that infiltrators had convinced these parties to support the RPF. Repeating the accusation of the December 1991 press release that the enemy was sharpening conflict between individuals and regions, the memorandum asserted that opponents were "turning public opinion from the ethnic problem to the socio-economic problem between the rich and the poor." It stated that the enemy and its partisans were recruited primarily among:

- Tutsi refugees
- the NRA (Ugandan army)
- Tutsi inside the country
- Hutu dissatisifed with the regime in power
- Unemployed people inside and outside the country
- Foreigners married to Tutsi wives
- the Nilo-Hamitic people of the region
- criminals in flight [from the law]

The document warned that the enemy had infiltrated the government and had corrupted various officials by offering them advantageous business deals, which was easy for them to do because the enemy predominated in business circles. It identified a number of "enemies" by name, including Evariste Sissi and Antoine Sebera.[64]

Many of the themes of this document sent to the soldiers on September 21 are echoed in a CDR tract issued the next day. In its "Notice No. 5," the CDR warned of the dangers from enemies inside Rwanda, who were supposedly aiding the RPF. It asserted that these enemies had highly placed friends in the government, who were permitting them to work against the interests of the great majority, the rubanda nyamwinshi. Among the enemies named are the same Evariste Sissi and Antoine Sebera who were cited in the military document. The CDR finished by demanding action:

> The CDR party calls upon the government and the president to deal with this problem. If it does not, the great mass [rubanda nyamwinshi] cannot stand by and do nothing. An enemy is an enemy. Anyone who cooperates with the enemy is a traitor to Rwanda.[65]

The similarities in the statements of CDR radicals and of high military authorities foreshadowed their later cooperation which made the genocide possible.

---

[64]Col. Déogratias Nsabimana to Liste A, September 21, 1992.

[65]Itangazo no. 05 ry'ishyaka CDR, 22 September 1992 (International Commission).

PROPAGANDA AND PRACTICE

Rwandans—Tutsi as well as Hutu—were frightened by the RPF attack. Tutsi recalled the reprisal killings at the time of invasions by refugee groups in the 1960s and feared they would be targeted again. Hutu remembered the slaughter of tens of thousands of Hutu by Tutsi in neighboring Burundi in 1972, 1988, and in 1991 and dreaded killings on a similar scale by the RPF. Authorities at the highest level knew that the RPF had been reduced by losses during the first months to a number less than half that of the Rwandan army and that their own army was backed by several hundred highly trained and well-armed French troops. Well aware of the fears of their own subordinates and of ordinary citizens, they could have put the danger in perspective and calmed the population.[1] Instead Habyarimana and his advisers exaggerated the risk in hopes of increasing support for themselves. As one Rwandan put it, "With the invasion, the politicians began to beat the drum." The drum was both a usual signal of attack and the instrument used to keep all the dancers moving to the same rhythm.

Propagandists echoed and magnified the hatred and suspicion sown by Habyarimana and officials around him. Under the cover of the newly-established freedom of the press, they blared forth messages disseminated more discreetly by officials, such as many of the conclusions about the "enemy" presented in the military memorandum of September 21, 1992.

Propagandists developed the same themes over and over, both before and during the genocide. While some of the similarities in their messages may result simply from sharing the same cultural milieu, other similarities in technique suggest deliberate coordination among propagandists and between them and government officials. In a mimeographed document entitled "Note Relative à la Propagande d'Expansion et de Recrutement," found in Butare prefecture, one propagandist tells others how to sway the public most effectively. Obviously someone who had studied at university level, the author of the note presents a detailed analysis of a book called *Psychologie de la publicité et de la propagande*, by Roger Mucchielli, published in Paris in 1970.

---

[1]Joseph Habiyambere, Préfet de Gikongoro, to Monsieur le Président de la République Rwandaise, no. 794/04.17.02, May 29, 1991; no. 831/04.17.02, June 5, 1991; no. 842/04.17.02, June 7, 1991; Paul Kadogi, Bourgmestre de la Commune Nshili, to Monsieur le Préfet de Gikongoro, no. 661/04.17.02, September 6, 1991; Préfet de Gikongoro to Monsieur le Col. Elie Sagatwa, November 21, 1991; Col. Athanase Gasake to Liste A Comdt Secteurs OPS (Tous), May 21, 1993 (Gikongoro prefecture).

The author of the note claims to convey lessons learned from the book and drawn from Lenin and Goebbels. He advocates using lies, exaggeration, ridicule, and innuendo to attack the opponent, in both his public and his private life. He suggests that moral considerations are irrelevant, except when they happen to offer another weapon against the other side. He adds that it is important not to underestimate the strength of the adversary nor to overestimate the intelligence of the general public targeted by the campaign. Propagandists must aim both to win over the uncommitted and to cause divisions among supporters of the other point of view. They must persuade the public that the adversary stands for war, death, slavery, repression, injustice, and sadistic cruelty.

In addition to these suggestions, the propagandist proposes two techniques that were to become often used in Rwanda. The first is to "create" events to lend credence to propaganda. He remarks that this tactic is not honest, but that it works well, provided the deception is not discovered. The "attack" on Kigali on October 4-5, 1990 was such a "created" event, as were others—the reported discovery of hidden arms, the passage of a stranger with a mysterious bag, the discovery of radio communications equipment—that were exploited later, especially during the genocide.

The propagandist calls his second proposal "Accusation in a mirror," meaning his colleagues should impute to enemies exactly what they and their own party are planning to do. He explains, "In this way, the party which is using terror will accuse the enemy of using terror." With such a tactic, propagandists can persuade listeners and "honest people" that they are being attacked and are justified in taking whatever measures are necessary "for legitimate [self-] defense."[2] This tactic worked extremely well, both in specific cases such as the Bugesera massacre of March 1992 described below and in the broader campaign to convince Hutu that Tutsi planned to exterminate them. There is no proof that officials and propagandists who "created" events and made "accusations in a mirror" were familiar with this particular document, but they regularly used the techniques that it described.

The Media

One of the most virulent voice of hate, the newspaper *Kangura*, began spewing forth attacks on the RPF and on Tutsi immediately after the October 1990 invasion. It was joined soon after by other newspapers and journals that received support

---

[2]Anonymous, "Note Relative à la Propagande d'Expansion et de Recrutement," mimeographed, undated (Butare prefecture).

from officials and businessmen linked to the regime. According to authors of an intensive study of the media of genocide, at least eleven of the forty-two new journals founded in 1991 were linked to the akazu.[3] The newspapers were published and sold in the capital, but urban workers who often went home for weekends carried copies of the better-known newspapers out to the hills. Some 66 percent of Rwandans are literate and those who knew how to read were accustomed to reading for others. In many cases, the written word was underscored by cartoons, most of which were so graphic that they could not be misinterpreted.

The radio was to become even more effective in delivering the message of hate directly and simultaneously to a wide audience. Before the war, Rwanda had only one radio station, the national Radio Rwanda, but listening to the radio was a popular distraction among ordinary people and elite alike. In 1991, some 29 percent of all households had a radio.[4] The number of radio sets was presumably much higher by the start of the genocide. In some areas, the government distributed radios free to local authorities before the genocide and they may have done so after the killing began as well.[5] One foreign religious sister who traveled from Kibuye to Butare during the height of the genocide reported that she had seen new radios at every one of the dozens of barriers where she had been stopped en route.[6] People without radios listened to broadcasts in the local bar or got information from neighbors.

Until 1992, Radio Rwanda was very much the voice of the government and of the president himself. It announced prefectural or national meetings, nominations to and removals from government posts, and the results of admissions examinations to secondary schools.[7] Before the daily news programs, Radio Rwanda broadcast

---

[3]Chrétien et al., *Rwanda, Les médias*, p. 45.

[4]In urban areas, the figure was far higher, 58.7 percent, while in rural areas 27.3 percent of the households owned radios. *Recensement général de la population et de l'habitat au 15 août 1991* (Kigali: Service National de Recensement, July 1993), p. 31.

[5]Human Rights Watch/FIDH interview, Brussels, February 15, 1997; Chrétien et al., *Rwanda, Les médias*, pp. 57, 74.

[6]Human Rights Watch/FIDH interview, Brussels, February 6, 1996.

[7]Clément Kayishema, former Prefect of Kibuye, and Sylvain Nsabimana, former Prefect of Butare, are among the officials who say that they learned of their appointments from radio announcements. Human Rights Watch interview, Kibuye, July, 1992; Human

excerpts of Habyarimana's political speeches. This national radio sometimes broadcast false information, particularly about the progress of the war, but most people did not have access to independent sources of information to verify its claims.

In March 1992, Radio Rwanda warned that Hutu leaders in Bugesera were going to be murdered by Tutsi, false information meant to spur the Hutu massacres of Tutsi. Following the establishment of the coalition government in April 1992, the MDR, PL, and PSD insisted on a new direction for Radio Rwanda. Ferdinand Nahimana, a stalwart supporter of the MRND, was removed from his post at the Rwandan Office of Information (ORINFOR), where he had supervised Radio Rwanda. Several months later, Jean-Marie Vianney Higiro, a member of one of the parties opposed to Habyarimana, was named director to steer the radio towards a more nonpartisan stance. By December 1993, Radio Rwanda had agreed to include the RPF among political parties participating in its broadcasts, although the decision had not been implemented by the time the genocide began.[8]

Soon after the start of the war, the RPF established its own station, Radio Muhabura, but its signal did not reach throughout the country. At first, many Rwandans were afraid to listen to it, but its audience grew steadily during 1992 and 1993. Although it glorified the RPF, it did so in a nationalist rather than an ethnic context, consistent with the general RPF emphasis on minimizing differences between Hutu and Tutsi.[9]

With the new direction at Radio Rwanda and the voice of the RPF increasingly strong, Hutu hard-liners decided to create their own station. They began planning their radio in 1992, incorporated it as Radio Télévision Libre des Mille Collines (RTLM) in April 1993, and began broadcasting in August 1993.

Of the fifty original founders, forty were from the three prefectures of northern Rwanda, all but seven of those from Gisenyi and Ruhengeri, the region identified with Habyarimana. One of the chief financiers of the project was Félicien Kabuga, a wealthy businessman whose daughter was married to a son of President Habyarimana. Another contributor was Alphonse Ntilivamunda, a son-in-law of President Habyarimana, and an important official at the Ministry of Public Works.

Rights Watch/FIDH interview, by telephone, Nairobi, March 25, 1996.

[8]Jean-Marie Vianney Higiro, "Distorsions et Omissions dans l'ouvrage *Rwanda, Les médias du génocide,*" *Dialogue,* no. 190, avril-mai 1996, p. 166.

[9]See chapter on the RPF below.

Two ministers were among the founders, Augustin Ngirabatware, the minister of planning, and son-in-law of Kabuga, and André Ntagerura, the minister of telecommunications. Simon Bikindi, an employee of the Ministry of Youth who was also an extremely popular musician best known for his virulently anti-Tutsi songs, was part of the group, as was Pasteur Musabe, general director of the Banque Continentale Africaine. Augustin Ruzindana, governor of the National Bank of Rwanda, joined later. The MRND was represented among the founders by Joseph Nzirorera, subsequently its executive secretary, and later by Mathieu Ngirumpatse, who served as president of the MRND after President Habyarimana left that post. In addition, Georges Rutaganda, vice-president of the MRND militia, the Interahamwe, was among the founders. The CDR was represented by Jean-Bosco Barayagwiza, its chief ideologue, and by Stanislas Simbizi. Subsequently the minister of defense, the officer who would become chief of staff of the Rwandan army, and a protestant bishop would buy shares in the station.[10]

Although nominally private and opposed to Radio Rwanda, RTLM in fact was linked in a number of ways with the national radio, with other state agencies and with the MRND. RTLM was allowed to broadcast on the same frequencies as the national radio between 8am and 11am, when Radio Rwanda was not transmitting, an arrangement that encouraged listeners to see the two as linked, if not as identical. The new station also drew personnel from Radio Rwanda, including Nahimana, who played a leading role at RTLM after having been dismissed from ORINFOR, and announcer Noel Hitimana. Its editor-in-chief, Gaspard Gahigi, and announcer Kantano Habimana had previously worked for *Umurwanashyaka*, party organ of the MRND. Gahigi had also been employed by Radio Rwanda and was a member of the central committee of the MRND.[11] The ostensibly private station used equipment belonging to various government ministries and perhaps some equipment taken from Radio Rwanda. It had access to an emergency source of electric power which some said was a free-standing generator, but others said was linked to the emergency electrical system of the presidential residence, across the street from its studio.[12]

---

[10]François-Xavier Nsanzuwera, Manuscript on the RTLM.

[11]Higiro, "Distorsions et Omissions," p. 161.

[12]Ibid., p. 164; Chrétien et al., *Rwanda, Les médias,* p. 70.

According to Rwandans who listened to RTLM, the station won an audience rapidly because of its lively music and informal style. Higiro, the director of Radio Rwanda, analysed its initial success this way:

These broadcasts were like a conversation among Rwandans who knew each other well and were relaxing over some banana beer or a bottle of Primus [the local beer] in a bar. It was a conversation without a moderator and without any requirements as to the truth of what was said. The people who were there recounted what they had seen or heard during the day. The exchanges covered everything: rumors circulating on the hills, news from the national radio, conflicts among local political bosses...It was all in fun. Some people left the bar, others came in, the conversation went on or stopped if it got too late, and the next day it took up again after work.[13]

Introducing the concept of interactive broadcasting to Rwanda, RTLM invited listeners to call in to express their opinions. People called to ask for a song to be broadcast or to pass on some piece of news or gossip. The announcers broadcast this information without ever checking on it. RTLM departed from the more staid and formal tone of Radio Rwanda. The announcer Kantano Habimana was known for his wit, which was appreciated even by some Tutsi who were the objects of his barbs. Another, Valerie Bemeriki, was remarkable for the speed and passion of her delivery, which increased when she had violence to report.

Rwandans learned from experience that RTLM regularly attributed to others the actions its own supporters had taken or would be taking. Without ever having heard of "accusations in a mirror," they became accustomed to listening to RTLM accusations of its rivals to find out what the MRND and CDR would be doing.

RTLM took up many of the same themes, sometimes in the same words, that were being popularized in the written press. Hassan Ngeze, the editor of *Kangura*, welcomed the arrival of the new ally in the "fight to defend the republic."[14] Before long, RTLM, with its greater drawing power, was displacing *Kangura* and other journals as the voice of extremism. Once the genocide began, Radio Rwanda was pulled into the orbit of RTLM. Its director Higiro fled the country, himself targeted for death by RTLM broadcasts, and was replaced by Jean-Baptiste Bamwanga, a journalist fired from Radio Rwanda in 1992 for his role in inciting the massacre of

---

[13]Higiro, "Distorsions et Omissions," p. 171.

[14]Chrétien et al., *Rwanda, Les médias,* p. 68.

Tutsi in Bugesera. RTLM announcer Kantano Habimana celebrated the transformation of Radio Rwanda from a "rival" to a "sister."[15] During the genocide, when communications and travel became difficult, the radio became for most people the sole source of news as well as the sole authority for interpreting its meaning. At that time, RTLM and Radio Rwanda collaborated to deliver a single message about the need to extirpate the "enemy."

Validating the Message

Propagandists naturally wove references to political authorities past and present into their materials as often as possible. Grégoire Kayibanda, the father of the revolution and first president of the republic, as well as Habyarimana, appeared often in pictures and through use of their quotations. In addition, the propagandists acknowledged the great respect Rwandans have for formal learning by occasionally asserting that their information came from "intellectuals" or "professors at the national university." A large number of university faculty were from Habyarimana's home region—because they had been the ones to profit from university education and study abroad—and ranked among his sincere supporters. Others teaching at the university or at government-sponsored schools (the vast majority in the country), as well as the staff of research institutes, knew that advancement and perhaps continued employment could depend on backing the government position. Both those within Rwanda and those studying abroad wrote letters and made public statements that reported facts wrongly or misinterpreted data to support the official line (see below).[16]

Two academics left the university to devote themselves to supporting Habyarimana through propaganda and active political organizing. One was Nahimana, a historian from the northwestern prefecture of Ruhengeri, who had benefited from the opportunity to study in Paris. He gave up teaching to take charge of government propaganda at ORINFOR. After being forced from this position, Nahimana was supposed to become the Rwandan ambassador in Bonn, but the German government refused to accept him. He tried to go back to the university, but his colleagues there also protested against his return. Appointed then to direct RTLM, he regained the opportunity to shape public opinion, this time through the most effective propaganda medium in Rwanda.

---

[15]Ibid., p. 79; Higiro, "Distorsions et Omissions," p. 178.

[16]Chrétien et al., *Rwanda, Les médias,* p. 97.

The other professor-turned-propagandist was Léon Mugesera, who had done advanced university studies in Canada. After teaching briefly at the National University of Rwanda, he moved on to positions with the Ministry of Information, the national headquarters of the MRND, and the Ministry for the Family and the Promotion of Women. The author of two propaganda pamphlets in 1991, he is even better known for a speech that is analyzed below.

In addition to calling on political and intellectual leaders to support their ideas, propagandists used religion and the church to validate their teachings. *Umurava Magazine* declared "It is God who has given Habyarimana the power to direct the country, it is He who will show him the path to follow."[17] Most propagandists did not go so far, but they did frequently couch their ideas in religious language or refer to passages from the Bible. Cartoons sometimes portrayed Habyarimana as a saint or a priest, and one depicted God cursing the leaders of the political opposition. Following killings of Hutu in Burundi in 1991, *Kangura* featured the Christ child with Mary and Joseph on the cover of the January issue. Mary asks the Christ child to save the Hutu of Burundi. He replies that he will tell them to love each other. Joseph comments, "No, instead tell the Hutu of the world to unite."[18] In a country where 90 percent of the people called themselves Christian and 62 percent were Catholic, these references to religion helped make the teachings of fear and hate more acceptable.

The Message

The propagandists built upon the lessons Rwandans had learned in school. It was hardly necessary even to repeat the basic assumption that Hutu and Tutsi were different peoples by nature, representatives of the larger and equally distinct "Bantu" and "Nilotic" ("Nilo-Hamitic," "Hamitic," or "Ethiopid") groups. In some passages, propagandists equated the Hutu-Tutsi difference with the fundamental difference between male and female.[19] Those who married across group lines produced "hybrids" for children and people from one group who tried to pass for members of another were said to be like "beings with two heads."[20] The radicals rejected the idea that Rwandans were a single people, charging that this concept

---

[17]Ibid., p. 46.

[18]Ibid., pp. 371-74, 256.

[19]Ibid., pp. 96-97.

[20]Ibid., pp. 102, 108.

Document: Cover of *Kangura*, December 1993: A photograph of Grégoire Kayibanda, leader of the Hutu Revolution and first president of Rwanda, accompanied by a machete, a cynical comment about Tutsi being the race of God, and a question about what arms can be used to defeat the Inyenzi once and for all.

SPECIAL

BATUTSI
BWOKO BW'IMANA !

NI IZIHE NTWARO TUZAKORESHA KUGIRA NGO DUTSINDE INYENZI BURUNDU ??

Document: Cartoon from *Echo des 1000 collines*, July 1991, with a figure representing a Tutsi killing Hutu and a caption warning that Tutsi are going to exterminate the Hutu.

Les pogromes justifiés par l'autodéfense : "Fuyez, un Tutsi va exterminer les Hutu"
(Echo des 1000 collines, juillet 1991, n°3, p.10)

was a Tutsi trick to divide and weaken the Hutu by destroying their sense of ethnic identity. As *Kangura* assured the Hutu, "You are an important ethnic group of the Bantu...The nation is artificial but the ethnic group is natural."[21] The propagandists stressed that Tutsi were foreign to the area and had stolen Rwanda from its rightful inhabitants. The ruthless conquerors had ground the Hutu under their heel in a "repressive and bloody regime...epitomized by [the queen-mother Kanjogera who] to get up from her seat leaned on two swords planted between the shoulders of two Hutu children!"[22] But when the great mass—rubanda nyamwinshi—had become conscious of its own strength and had come together, it had been able to overthrow the "feudal" oppressors in the great revolution of 1959.[23]

"Tutsi Unity"

To these assumptions, propagandists added the myth of Tutsi unity, a clannishness held to have facilitated their conquests in the past and to enable them to continue exercising undue influence in the present. In the September 21, 1992 memorandum mentioned above, the military officers listed singleness of purpose as an advantage of the enemy. The propagandists linked Tutsi living inside Rwanda today both with those who had exploited Hutu in the past and with the RPF. Thus the circle was complete and the links among Tutsi of different times and places were said to be solid and unbreakable. In March 1993, *Kangura* published an article entitled "A cockroach cannot give birth to a butterfly." After 1990, opponents of the RPF called its troops Inyenzi, cockroaches, while the RPF itself used the term *Inkotanyi*, a name taken from a nineteenth-century military formation. The article said:

We began by saying that a cockroach cannot give birth to a butterfly. It is true. A cockroach gives birth to another cockroach...The history of Rwanda shows us clearly that a Tutsi stays always exactly the same, that he has never changed. The malice, the evil are just as we knew them in the history of our country. We are not wrong in saying that a cockroach gives birth to another cockroach. Who could tell the difference between the Inyenzi who attacked in October 1990 and those of the 1960s. They are all linked...their evilness is

---

[21]Ibid., pp.111, 109.

[22]Ibid., p. 110.

[23]Ibid., p. 118.

the same. The unspeakable crimes of the Inyenzi of today...recall those of their
elders: killing, pillaging, raping girls and women, etc.[24]

Like the soldiers who wrote the September 21, 1992 memorandum,
propagandists often used the terms Tutsi and RPF together or interchangeably. One
example of the association of Tutsi and RPF is the cover of the December 1993
issue of *Kangura*. Below the ironic title "Tutsi, Race of God" are shown a machete
and the question, "What weapons can we use to defeat the Inyenzi once and for
all?" And to complete the association, the final question asks "What if someone
brought back the Hutu Revolution of 1959 to finish off these Tutsi cockroaches?"[25]
During the genocide, officials would occasionally declare that not all Tutsi were
"accomplices" of the RPF, but such statements were too few and too late to destroy
the widespread and carefully constructed identification between them.

"Infiltration"
The propagandists asserted that the Tutsi, as Ethiopids or Nilotics, had no right
to inhabit Central Africa and that they had deviously infiltrated all aspects of
Rwandan state and society. Many Tutsi were found in the Liberal Party but some
had made their way into other parties as well. *Kangura*, among others, insisted that
this "infiltration" must stop and that Tutsi should not join parties that belonged to
the Hutu majority. The propagandists said the Tutsi had infiltrated the
economy,—at one point *Kangura* claimed that 70 percent of the rich in Rwanda
were Tutsi—monopolized credit at the banks, and won a disproportionate share of
the highly coveted import and export licenses. In a clear effort to divert the
resentment otherwise directed towards Hutu from Habyarimana's region,
propagandists argued that it was Tutsi, not other Hutu, who occupied the jobs
which southern Hutu wanted and failed to get. They also accused the Tutsi of
having taken a disproportionate share of places in secondary school and university
and, because of their educational advantages, of having dominated the professions
and government. They claimed that even the church had been infiltrated by Tutsi.
On all these points, the propagandists were delivering to the public the same

[24]Ibid., p.156.

[25]Ibid., pp. 114, 119, 128, 257.

message sent by the Rwandan general staff to its troops in the memorandum defining the enemy.[26]

If Tutsi men failed to penetrate some aspect of national life, said the propagandists, they sent in their women to seduce the Hutu who controlled that domain. According to *Kangura*, "The inkotanyi will not hesitate to transform their sisters, wives and mothers into pistols" to conquer Rwanda.[27] The propagandists, like the authors of the military memorandum, agreed that Tutsi wives and mistresses manipulated foreign men for the Tutsi cause. They agreed, too, that male and female Tutsi had infiltrated international organizations, including both official agencies, like the U.N., and nongovernmental organizations, like human rights groups.[28]

To support the argument that Tutsi had slipped "like snakes" into places unnoticed, propagandists asserted that many people who claimed to be Hutu were in fact Tutsi who had changed their identity papers. In a wildly exaggerated estimate, *Kangura* charged that 85 percent of Tutsi had changed their ethnic identification. It warned:

> The other calamity...is the detestable habit that many Tutsi have adopted of...changing their ethnic group...which allows them to pass unnoticed and to take places normally reserved for Hutu in the administration and the schools. If this disease is not treated immediately, it will destroy all the Hutu.[29]

"Real" Hutu were cautioned to be on the lookout for such people, recognizable usually by their too great tolerance for Tutsi and their lack of commitment to Hutu solidarity. To demonstrate how the pretense might be discovered, the journal *Ibyikigihe* published an examination of the background of Faustin Twagiramungu in its December 1993 issue. Twagiramungu, then the head of the MDR, was

---

[26]Ibid., pp. 92, 159-60.

[27]Ibid., p. 161. For propaganda against Tutsi women, see Human Rights Watch/Africa, Human Rights Watch Women's Rights Project, and the Fédération Internationale des Ligues des Droits de l'Homme, *Shattered Lives, Sexual Violence during the Rwandan Genocide and Its Aftermath* (New York: Human Rights Watch, 1996).

[28]Ibid., p. 269-73, 318. In March 1997, a message on the internet asserted that a Rwandan woman wrote the reports of Human Rights Watch/Africa.

[29]Ibid., pp. 103, 159.

accused of being Tutsi, a wolf disguised in sheep's clothing. To document its charges, the newspaper published excerpts from local government records going back to 1948.[30]

Effective in discussions of economic, social, and political life, this notion of "infiltration" was even more powerful when transferred to the domain of actual warfare. Echoing the position adopted by the government in October 1990, the propagandists fulminated that "It is because of this Tutsi infiltration into society that the country has no more secrets and they have been able to invade it with no trouble at all." The Tutsi as "accomplice" was said to be everywhere. *Kangura* estimated in 1991 that 85 percent of all Tutsi were "accomplices" who never put down their arms, "who were working night and day...."[31] The propagandists sometimes added specifics to these general charges. In one of two pamphlets he produced, the professor-turned-propagandist Léon Mugesera justified imprisoning thousands of persons "suspected of plotting with the enemy":

> ...because they were found with stocks of weapons, supplies of ammunition, radios for communicating with the enemy, or compromising documents, such as descriptions of the authorities and plans for attack.[32]

Officials and propagandists would use the same excuses—"created" events—to cover arrests and attacks on Tutsi and their Hutu allies for the next three years and throughout the genocide.

"Restoring the Old Regime"

From the first days of the war, officials and propagandists alike warned that the RPF had come to re-establish their total Tutsi control over the Hutu. One Rwandan army officer stationed near the Ugandan frontier in October 1990 reported that his superiors ordered him to spread the word among the civilian

---

[30]Ibid., p. 101.

[31]Ibid., p. 149.

[32]Association des Femmes Parlementaires pour la Défense des Droits de la Mère et de l'Enfant en collaboration avec Dr. Mugesera Léon, "Respect des Droits de la Personne par le Rwanda," Kigali, April 1991, p. 3 (Obtained from Comité Pour le Respect des Droits de l'Homme et de la Democratie au Rwanda).

population that the RPF had attacked to restore the monarchy.[33] In defining the "enemy," the military high command focused on those Tutsi "who refused to accept the revolution and wanted to reconquer power by any means." Civilian administrators in Butare, acting in the same vein, organized demonstrators in November 1990 to protest against any attempt to recreate the old regime. The demonstrators were sent out into the streets with signs like:

"Let slavery, servitude and discord be finished forever!"
"We condemn the exploitation and servitude of the people!"
"Long live the republic! Down with the monarchy!"
"No more feudalism! No more Kalinga!" [the drum that symbolized the power of the ruler][34]

Propagandists insisted that an RPF victory would mean a return to all the evils of "feudalism," with Hutu whipped and forced to work without pay for Tutsi masters. The singer Simon Bikindi stressed that danger in one of his most famous songs, "Bene Sebahinzi," "The Descendants of Sebahinzi," a proper name which means the "Father of the Cultivators." In a refrain that was repeated endlessly on RTLM, Bikindi sang about the importance and benefits of the 1959 revolution, "a heritage that should be carefully maintained...and transmitted to posterity": He went on:

...the servitude, the whip, the lash, the forced work that exhausted the people, that has disappeared forever. You, the great majority [rubanda nyamwinshi], pay attention and, descendants of Sebahinzi, remember this evil that should be driven as far away as possible, so that it never returns to Rwanda.[35]

Bikindi sang that the revolution should be preserved "especially by we who have benefited from it," a reminder that should the Tutsi win, they would not just reverse all the political changes of the revolution but also reclaim all the property

---

[33]Alison Des Forges, "The Ideology of Genocide," *Issue, A Journal of Opinion*, vol. XXIII, no. 2, 1995.

[34]Anonymous, Amwe Mu Magambo Yanditse Ku Byapa Abamilitante n'Abamilita Bitwaje Mu Rugendo Rwo Gushyigikira Ingabo Z'u Rwanda n'Umugaba Wazo W'Ikirenga, Mu Mujyi wa Butare Kuwa 3 Ugushyingo 1990 (Butare prefecture).

[35]Chrétien et al., *Rwanda, Les médias*, pp. 347, 353.

that had once been theirs, leaving many Hutu destitute. This argument carried great weight with cultivators who were working lands received after the expulsion of the Tutsi and who feared above all being reduced to landless laborers.

"Genocide of the Hutu"

The propagandists went further. They insisted that not just the freedom and prosperity of Hutu were at risk but their very lives. They warned that the Tutsi minority could not hope to reestablish their control over the majority without killing large numbers of Hutu. By December 1990, *Kangura* had begun charging that the Tutsi had prepared a war that "would leave no survivors." Another pamphlet produced by Mugesera declared in February 1991 that the RPF planned "to restore the dictatorship of the extremists of the Tutsi minority," by "a genocide, the extermination of the Hutu majority."[36] As the conflict progressed, the warnings became increasingly explicit and hysterical. By mid-1993, propagandists were asserting, "We know that they have attacked us with the intention of massacring and exterminating 4.5 million Hutu and especially those who have gone to school...."[37] Particularly after April 6, 1994, propagandists and media circulated the story that Tutsi had prepared pits to serve as mass graves for the Hutu. RPF troops had indeed dug trenches to protect their positions, which may have given some support to these rumors. Hard-liners even claimed that Tutsi had prepared holes in the dirt floors of their houses to accommodate Hutu corpses. That custom—not to mention concerns of health and odor—made such burial unthinkable did not discourage speculation that they intended to dispose of the bodies in this way.[38]

---

[36]Association des Femmes Parlementaires pour la Défense des Droits de la Mère et de l'Enfant en collaboration avec Dr. Mugesera Léon, "Toute la Vérité sur la Guerre d'Octobre 1990 au Rwanda," Kigali, February 1991, p. 5. An English version of the pamphlet, published in March 1991 under the title "The Whole Truth on the October 1990 War Imposed upon Rwanda by the Aggressors from Uganda Armed Forces" differs slightly in wording from the original French (International Commission).

[37]Chrétien et al., *Rwanda, Les médias,* pp.159-60, 180, 186, 290-91, 293, 323. In making this argument, propagandists often recalled the slaughter in Burundi of tens of thousands of Hutu, particularly "intellectuals," by the Tutsi-dominated military in 1972.

[38]Solidarité Internationale pour les Réfugiés Rwandais, *Le Non-Dit sur les Massacres au Rwanda,* vol. 2, January 1995, p. 11 and vol. 3, July 1995, pp.124-37; Chrétien et al., *Rwanda, Les médias,* p.266.

In warning that the Tutsi were planning a genocide against the Hutu, several publications appear to have have followed closely the propaganda tactic of "accusation in a mirror." Some attributed to Tutsi the words that Hutu themselves would eventually use in inciting the slaughter of Tutsi. In September 1991, *La Médaille Nyiramacibiri* stated that the Tutsi wanted to "clean up Rwanda...by throwing Hutu in the Nyabarongo [River]", a phrase that would become notorious when Mugesera applied it to Tutsi a year later. *Kangura* reported that RPF soldiers captured by the government forces said that they "had come to clean the county of the filth of Hutu."[39] During the genocide, Hutu would often talk of cleansing their communities of the filth of the Tutsi. In April 1992, the newspaper *Jyambere* charged opposition parties with distributing arms to their youth wings, revealing by its "accusations in a mirrror" exactly what the Habyarimana forces were then doing.[40]

The Regional Context

Echoing the military memorandum which had identified the "Nilo-Hamitic people of the region," in general, and Tutsi in Uganda, Zaire, and Burundi, in particular, as sources of support for the "enemy," propagandists stressed the regional aspect of the RPF attack. The RPF had launched its operation from Uganda with the support, though unacknowledged, of the Ugandan authorities. Some of the most important leaders of the RPF had served in the Ugandan army under the command of Ugandan President Yoweri Museveni, who supposedly was related through a grandmother to the Bahima. The Bahima are pastoralists, a small number of whom lived in northeastern Rwanda, and are generally grouped with Tutsi. In neighboring Burundi, Tutsi dominated the army and economy, although they briefly lost control of political power after the election of a Hutu president and his party in June 1993. Tutsi were also powerful in adjacent regions of Zaire. From these disparate pieces of information, propagandists like those at *Kangura* concluded that:

There is indeed a diabolical plan prepared by the Tutsi and related groups and targeting the systematic extermination of the Bantu population as well as the extension of a Nilotic empire from Ethiopia...and Douala to the sources of the Nile and from...Gabon to Lesotho going through the vast basins of the Kongo,

---

[39]Chrétien et al., *Rwanda, Les médias,* pp. 160, 176.

[40]Ibid., p. 255.

the Rift Valley of Tanzania...down to the Cape and the Drakensberg Mountains....What are the Bantu peoples waiting for to protect themselves against the genocide that has been so carefully and consciously orchestrated by the Hamites thirsty for blood and for barbarian conquests and whose leaders dispute the golden medal of cruelty with the Roman emperor Nero....[41]

In his pamphlet, Mugesera weighed in with the same idea, asserting that the Tutsi intended to:

"Establish in the Bantu region of the great lakes (Rwanda, Burundi, Zaire, Tanzania, Uganda) a vast kingdom for the Hima-Tutsi, an ethnic group that considers itself superior, on the model of the Aryan race, and which uses Hitler's Swastika as its emblem."[42]

Mugesera's linking the plot for a Tutsi empire to the Nazis was picked up by *Kangura* several months later. In its September 1991 issue, it repeats the charge that neo-Nazi Tutsi, nostalgic for power, dream of "colonial expansion," and adds to this the accusation that they are cannibals besides.[43] Mugesera and *Kangura* appear to have been implementing the tactic of "accusation in a mirror" by connecting the Tutsi with the Nazis. It may have been Habyarimana and his intimates instead who were the admirers of Hitler. Copies of films about Hitler and Naziism were apparently found in Habyarimana's residence after the family fled in early April 1994.[44]

The propagandists buttressed their argument about the plan to create a grand Tutsi empire by referring to an apparently apocryphal letter, dated 1962, about a Tutsi program to "re-colonize" the region starting from the Kivu region of Zaire. They also talked of a plan supposedly formulated by a Tutsi politician named Arthémon Simbananiye in Burundi for killing off the Hutu population over a period of decades. This purported plan, frequently discussed by Hutu in Burundi,

[41]Ibid., p. 169.

[42]Associations des Femmes Parlementaires, "Toute la Vérité sur la Guerre d'Octobre 1990 au Rwanda," p. 5.

[43]Chrétien et al., *Rwanda, Les médias*, p. 178.

[44]Ibid., photo facing p. 257.

seemed credible in a country where Tutsi had in fact slaughtered tens of thousands of Hutu.[45]

"The Hutu as Innocent Victim"

Underlying much of this propaganda is the image of the Hutu as the innocent victim—victim of the original aggression by Tutsi conquerors some centuries ago, of the "infiltration" of the state and society, and of the 1990 invasion. After April 6, 1994, President Habyarimana himself would become the ultimate symbol of Hutu as innocent victim.

When the government was criticized for killing Tutsi in the years before the genocide, officials and propagandists alike tried to demonstrate that the Tutsi had slaughtered more than the Hutu. In September 1991, the pro-Habyarimana publication *La Medaille Nyiramacibiri* discounted reports that Hutu officials had been responsible for killing Tutsi and offered instead to give readers lists of the Hutu killed by Tutsi so "then you will know who are the real criminals."[46]

In 1992 and 1993, Habyarimana came under increasingly severe attack for human rights abuses, including the slaughter of some 2,000 Tutsi. In February 1993 the RPF violated a cease-fire and killed hundreds of civilians in their military advance and several dozen others by summary executions. Hoping to divert attention from the criticism against Habyarimana, propagandists and officials like the Rwandan ambassador to the U.S. launched exaggerated accusations against the RPF. Depicting the Hutu as the true victims, they asserted that the RPF had killed 40,200 civilians.[47] In a letter to the pope and various heads of state, a group of people identifying themselves as "intellectuals of the city of Butare," and using the Butare campus of the National University as their return address, accused the RPF of genocide. They went so far as to indicate how many of the 40,200 victims had come from each of the communes affected by the latest RPF attack. Even had the number of estimated victims not raised suspicions, such spurious detail would have caused doubts, given that the letter was dated only eleven days after the attack. A group of seventeen Rwandans studying in the United States sent out a similar letter

---

[45]Ibid., pp. 163, 167.

[46]Ibid., p. 177.

[47]Africa Watch, "Beyond the Rhetoric," p. 23.

to American political leaders and organizations on February 24.[48] In a speech on March 23, 1993, President Habyarimana did not go so far, but claimed merely that the RPF had slaughtered several tens of thousands of civilians.[49]

"The Tutsi Cause Their Own Misfortune"

According to the propagandists, the suffering of the Hutu was real and grievous, but the misery of the Tutsi was a sham or, if real, had been their own fault. Those Tutsi apparently killed by official direction had in fact committed suicide, they said, or had left the country to go join the RPF. Those who had been driven from homes that had then been burned and pillaged had actually destroyed their own property to give Hutu a bad name or to cover their departure for the ranks of the RPF. In a speech to military commanders on March 13, 1993, President Habyarimana suggested that it was possible that the RPF itself had "organized and aggravated" the massacres of the Tutsi that had taken place at the end of January 1993 (see below) in order to give themselves a pretext for violating the cease-fire.[50] And, once again relying on the easy identification of all Tutsi with the RPF, propagandists said Tutsi deserved whatever ill befell them because it was they who had launched the war in the first place.

"Hutu Solidarity"

Propagandists and officials constantly reminded Hutu that they had one important advantage in facing this ruthless and insidious enemy: they were rubanda nyamwinshi, the great majority. *Kangura* encouraged them, "Your unity, your mutual understanding, your solidarity are the certain weapons of your victory." But this advantage could be thrown away. As *Kangura* warned, "you understand that when the majority people is divided, [then] the minority becomes the majority..."[51] Hutu must not be divided by regionalism or by conflicting party loyalties. Any who trusted in the Tutsi rather than in their fellow Hutu would suffer the consequences.

---

[48]Letter with four pages of signatures, a total of 104 names, to the pope and other international dignitaries, Butare, February 19, 1993; Letter from the Cercle Rwandais de Reflexion to Africa Watch, February 24, 1993.

[49]Africa Watch, "Beyond the Rhetoric," p. 23.

[50]Chrétien et al., *Rwanda, Les médias,* pp. 63, 155, 177, 337; Africa Watch, "Beyond the Rhetoric," p.16; "Report of the International Commission," p. 25.

[51]Chrétien et al., *Rwanda, Les médias,* pp. 154, 220.

Should the Tutsi win, they would pay no attention to place of origin or political party membership—they would oppress all Hutu in the same way.

The propagandists, like the authors of the military memorandum, railed against any Hutu who would dare to break ranks: such traitors could not possibly act from worthy motives but must have succumbed to money or women offered by the Tutsi. The need to maintain Hutu purity and to avoid contamination from the Tutsi was taught in a notorious set of "Ten Commandments." It specified that any Hutu who married or consorted with Tutsi women were traitors, as were any who engaged in business with Tutsi. It demanded that all strategic posts in politics or administration be reserved for Hutu and that the armed forces be exclusively Hutu.[52] The virulence of the attacks against Hutu who opposed Habyarimana showed how much the president and his supporters dreaded the "Kanyarengwe effect." Discrediting those already in the opposition was not enough; they had to make it unthinkable for others to join them.

The popular singer Simon Bikindi spread this message in a song entitled "I Hate Hutu." In one version, he particularly targets the Hutu of Butare:

Let us start in the region of Butare where they like feudalism [the reign of the Tutsi], who would blame me for that? I hate them and I don't apologize for that. I hate them and I don't apologize for that. Lucky for us that they are few in number...Those who have ears, let them hear![53]

Once propagandists had established the supposedly overwhelming threat to Hutu—to their lives and to their very existence as a people, as well as to their freedom and material well-being—it was an easy step to arguing their right—indeed their duty—to defend themselves, their country, and the revolution. The best-known expression of this idea before the genocide came in a speech delivered on November 22, 1992 by Léon Mugesera.

The Mugesera Speech: "Do Not Let Yourselves Be Invaded"
Party meetings offered propagandists an essential opportunity to spread the doctrine. In emotion-filled gatherings, where music, dancing performances and beer warmed the audience, propagandists could send their message directly into the

---

[52]Ibid., pp. 141-42.

[53]Recording of RTLM broadcasts, October 17-31, 1993 (tape provided by Radio Rwanda).

hearts of their listeners. Speakers caught up in the excitement of playing to a responsive crowd often delivered the message of the moment in a more dramatic and intense form than what might be printed in a newspaper or broadcast over the radio. They could also use the opportunity to test what ideas could be made acceptable to the party faithful. Few such speeches are available for analysis, but one has been preserved in its entirety, probably because its ideas and style of expression were so extreme and called forth a vigorous response from the opposition.

The setting was an MRND meeting at Kabaya, not far from Habyarimana's home, in the northwestern prefecture of Gisenyi. The speaker, Mugesera, was then vice-president of the MRND for the prefecture as well as an official of the Ministry for the Family and the Promotion of Feminine Affairs. The date was November 22, 1992, one week after a well-publicized speech by President Habyarimana in the adjacent prefecture of Ruhengeri in which he had disavowed the Arusha Accords. Habyarimana had also talked about elections that would someday be held in Rwanda, promising that the MRND militia, the Interahamwe, would serve as a striking force to ensure his victory.

In a speech that weaves together the major themes of pro-Habyarimana propaganda, Mugesera stresses above all the danger of being invaded. In opening his remarks, he tells the audience: "At whatever cost, you will leave here with these words...do not let yourselves be invaded." And after having returned to the phrase about not being invaded another ten times in the half hour speech, he concludes, "I know you are men...who do not let themselves be invaded, who refuse to be scorned."

The invasion to which he refers is two-pronged: of course, that of the RPF, and, in addition, that of the political parties opposed to Habyarimana. In the most frequently cited passages, Mugesera attacks the "Inyenzi"—he insists that they must be called Inyenzi, never the more respectful Inkotanyi—but he assails with equal force those political parties which he labels "accomplices" of the RPF. He condemns the MDR, the PL, and the PSD as "traitors" for talking with the RPF and for demoralizing and causing mutinies in the Rwandan army by raising the question of its eventual demobilization. He accuses them of having given away the prefecture of Byumba because they favored a cease-fire and negotiations after the RPF had taken part of that region. He insists that ministers of opposition parties who pretend to represent Rwanda in the peace negotiations do not in fact speak for the nation. "They are Inyenzi talking to [other] Inyenzi." Taking his cue from Habyarimana's rejection of the Arusha Accords the previous week, he asserts that "we will never accept these things."

Mugesera shows concern also for the way the MDR, PL, and PSD are destroying Hutu unity. He berates them for having "invaded" the MRND in various ways: by bringing their party flags and regalia into the northwestern prefectures, by "tak[ing] our men," by challenging MRND leadership in Nshili commune (see above), and by replacing MRND functionaries with their own supporters in ministeries under their control. Saying that the MRND is "at war" with members of these parties, he warns that these opponents are armed and have "begun to kill." He demands that they clear out of the region because "we cannot accept that such people shoot us down while pretending to live among us."

Saying that the enemy's objective is extermination, Mugesera exhorts his audience to "rise up...really rise up" in self-defense. He cites the Bible several times and declares that the MRND has a new version of the Biblical adage to turn the other cheek: "If you are struck once on one cheek, you should strike back twice..." He says that the law provides the death penalty for both politicians inside the country and "Inyenzi" who have betrayed the national interest. If the judicial system is not going to act to execute this punishment, then the people have the right to do so themselves and "to exterminate this scum." In referring to the "Inyenzi," he says that it was a mistake that some of them were allowed to get away in 1959. He recounts a conversation in which he warned a member of the PL, "I am telling you that your home is in Ethiopia, that we are going to send you back there quickly, by the Nyabarongo [River]." For the audience, "member of the PL" could not have meant anything other than Tutsi, and the mention of transportation by the Nyabarongo had to be understood as killing the people in question and dumping the bodies in the river, a usual practice in past massacres of Tutsi. [The Nyabarongo feeds into the rivers of the Nile watershed and hence is supposed to permit passage to Ethiopia.] Mugesera directs the faithful to keep careful track of all the people who come into their neighborhoods and to "crush" any accomplice so that "he will not be able to get away."

Speaking before Rwandans, who ordinarily value sophisticated, allusive rhetoric, Mugesera chose unusually blunt words to convey his message. Using a coarse term not often heard in a public address, he talks of members of other parties coming to MRND territory to defecate. He depicts the opponent as dying, in the agony of death, knocked down, and under ground. He calls them "vermin" that must be "liquidated." And at the end, he gives a final warning, "Know that the person whose throat you do not cut now will be the one who will cut yours."[54]

Mugesera's speech was tape-recorded. Excerpts were broadcast on the national radio and copies of the cassette were circulated among people in Kigali and other towns. One newspaper published the text. Many persons, and not all of them opposed to the MRND, expressed outrage at this bald summons to slaughter. Jean Rumiya, a professor at the university and former colleague of Mugesera, wrote him an open letter to criticize this "true call to murder." He remarked that Mugesera, someone who had done much textual analysis in his work, certainly understood exactly what he was doing with his use of coarse language and terms like "cutting throats." He pointed out that whether by coincidence or by design, Mugesera had used the same kind of language heard at the time of recent Tutsi massacres in the northwest. As a former member of the central committee of the MRND, he regretted that a speech so full of ethnic hatred and political intolerance could be presented at a MRND meeting and particularly without eliciting a protest from the audience. He had believed, he wrote, that "the time of ritual murders for political ends was finished."[55]

The minister of justice, a member of the PL, issued a warrant for Mugesera's arrest for inciting to violence. Mugesera dropped from view. According to some witnesses, he sought refuge at a military camp for a few weeks before pro-Habyarimana soldiers helped him escape from the country in early 1993. He returned to Canada where he had once studied at Laval University. On July 11, 1996, the Canadian arbiter Pierre Turmel, ajudicator in an administrative proceeding brought by the Ministry of Citizenship and Immigration, found that Mugesera had incited to genocide by his November 1992 speech and ordered him expelled from Canada on a number of charges.[56]

---

[54]Léon Mugesera, "Discours Prononcé par Léon Mugesera lors d'un Meeting du M.R.N.D. Tenu à Kabaya le 22 novembre 1992." The version of the speech quoted here was the French text submitted by the Canadian government in legal proceedings against Mugesera in September 1995.

[55]Jean Rumiya, Lettre ouverte à M. Mugesera Léon, Butare, December 9, 1992 (International Commission).

[56]La Commission de l'Immigration et du statut de réfugié, Section d'Arbitrage, *Décision dans la Cause entre Léon Mugesera et Le Ministre de la Citoyenneté et de l'Immigration,* Dossier no. QML-95-00171, Montréal, 11 juillet 1996. Mugesera appealed the decision, but the appeal was rejected in November 1998.

Practicing Slaughter

To execute a campaign against Tutsi effectively took practice. Before the grim background of war, economic distress, violent political competition, insecurity and impunity, and to the accompaniment of virulent propaganda, radicals staged the practice for the catastrophe to come. The rehearsals took place in more than a dozen communities, the most important being the commune of Kibilira in October 1990, March 1992, December 1992, and January 1993; in several communes in northwestern Rwanda, including Mukingo, Kinigi, Gaseke, Giciye, Karago, and Mutura in January and February 1991; in the region known as Bugesera, commune Kanzenze, in March 1992; in several communes of Kibuye in August 1992; and again in the northwest in December 1992 and January 1993.[57] These attacks slaughtered some 2,000 Tutsi and dozens of Hutu and established patterns for the genocide of 1994.

Choosing the Target

The organizers launched the attacks where they could be sure of success, in regions most identified with Habyarimana and his supporters. Of the seventeen incidents of serious violence in the years 1990-1993, fourteen took place in the northwest quadrant of the country and the fifteenth took place in Bugesera, where considerable numbers of Hutu from the northwest had settled relatively recently.

Authorities tolerated and incited small-scale, sporadic killings of Tutsi throughout this period, but they also initiated five more important attacks, each time in reaction to challenges that threatened Habyarimana's control. They sought to use ethnic violence to transform the threats into opportunities to strengthen their position. The first two challenges were military, the October 1, 1990 invasion and the lightning strike by the RPF at Ruhengeri on January 22, 1991. Massacres of Tutsi began ten days after the first, almost immediately after the second. By organizing reprisals against the Tutsi, the regime got rid of some "enemies" and fostered solidarity among Hutu who actually or vicariously joined in the killing. At

---

[57]Information for this section is drawn from two reports published by Africa Watch, "Talking Peace and Waging War" and "Beyond the Rhetoric," and from the "Report of the International Commission," which treat these massacres in detail. See also Human Rights Watch, *Slaughter Among Neighbors; The Political Origins of Communal Violence* (New Haven: Human Rights Watch and Yale University Press, 1995), pp. 13-32; Eric Gillet and Andre Jadoul, "Rapport de Deux Missions Effectuées par Eric Gillet et André Jadoul, avocats au barreau de Bruxelles, au Rwanda du 9 au 17 janvier et du 2 au 5 février 1992," Bruxelles, mai 1992; and the 1992 and 1993 reports of the Rwandan human rights group ADL.

the same time, it was able to claim to have located the reason for the setback—"infiltrators"—and to have dealt with it successfully.

The other three challenges were political. The first was the unexpectedly strong demand by the new parties of opposition for a place in the government. They were able to turn out tens of thousands of demonstrators in January 1992 and kept up pressure on Habyarimana throughout discussions during the following month. The next was the first protocol of the Arusha Accords, which Habyarimana signed under heavy domestic and international pressure in August 1992. The last was the January 1993 signature of a further protocol of the Accords concerning the transitional government that was to govern in the interim between the signature of the peace treaty and elections. In these three instances, Habyarimana and his supporters used massacres of Tutsi to create the appearance of massive opposition to concessions to other political parties and to the RPF.

The first three of these rehearsals for slaughter targeted only Tutsi. But during the August 1992 attack and the violence at the end of 1992 and in early 1993, assailants killed both Tutsi and Hutu members of parties opposed to Habyarimana, presaging the catastrophe of 1994.

Feeding the Fear

Before these attacks, authorities used lies, exaggeration, and rumors about the local situation to make the general propaganda against Tutsi more immediate and frightening. They staged incidents or reported events which had not in fact occurred to "prove" that Tutsi inside Rwanda were "accomplices" of the RPF. This accusation, repeated constantly and by officials and community leaders alike, was itself a recurring "created" event, meant to bring the threat inside and to make the danger real.

In Kibirira in October 1990, some officials told people that Tutsi planned to exterminate the Hutu and had killed two Hutu in their region. Others told the local population that Tutsi had killed two important military men from the region, Colonel Serubuga and Colonel Uwihoreye. Still others spread the rumor that Tutsi had attacked children at local schools.

To incite Hutu to kill the Bagogwe, generally seen as a subgroup of the Tutsi, in the communes of northwestern Rwanda in early 1991, authorities blamed them for having helped the RPF stage its surprise attack on Ruhengeri on January 23, 1991. To increase fear further, the military followed the successful precedent of the October 1990 "attack" on Kigali and staged a fake assault on the important Bigogwe military camp in the region. This worked so well that in one commune the burgomaster had trouble persuading the Hutu not to flee—their immediate reaction—but instead to stay and attack their Bagogwe neighbors.

In Bugesera, where large numbers of recent Hutu migrants from the northwest had settled adjacent to groups of Tutsi resident there since the revolution, local authorities whipped up Hutu sentiment against Tutsi by publicizing the departure of young Tutsi who crosssed the nearby Burundi border to join the RPF. In late February and early March 1992, Hassan Ngeze, editor of *Kangura*, visited Bugesera several times to spread tracts and rumors about the danger of "Inyenzi" infiltration and attacks. Following a local meeting of the PL on March 1, such a tract was distributed in the community accusing the PL leader of being a rebel and an assassin and closing with words reminiscent of Mugesera's speech a few months before: *they must not escape us*! On March 3, Radio Rwanda five times broadcast the "news" that a "human rights group" in Nairobi had issued a press release warning that Tutsi were going to kill Hutu, particularly Hutu political leaders, in Bugesera. Some Hutu took this to be the truth and the next night began slaughtering Tutsi.

In communes in northwestern Rwanda in December 1992 and January 1993, officials warned that killers were lurking in the nearby Gishwati forest and they organized the population to "clear the brush." "The brush" referred to Tutsi who were thought to provide cover to the RPF, allowing them to infiltrate without being noticed because they looked like resident Tutsi. Also in this region officials cautioned that strangers had been sighted, including a "man with a red bag," a shadowy figure who had also supposedly put in an appearance in Kibirira at one time. They also asserted that a young Tutsi who had left—to join the RPF, they said—had returned carrying a suspicious-looking bag.

Directing the Attacks

Local officials at the level of cell, sector, and commune directed the early massacres. In several places, such as the communes of Gaseke and Giciye, they told the people that participating in the attacks was their umuganda or communal work obligation. Other community leaders, such as teachers, health workers, the staff of developments projects, and party heads also helped turn out killers.

In Bugesera in March 1992, authorities used the Interahamwe to slaughter Tutsi for the first time. Drawing on experience gained in the violence of kubohoza, the militia knew how to take the lead, making it possible for government officials to play a less public part in the slaughter. At the end of 1992 and in early 1993, they again supported Hutu attacking Tutsi in the northwest, confirming their usefulness in ethnic violence.

Officials determined the end as well as the start of the slaughter. In Kibirira, for example, authorities needed only to send two policemen to blow their whistles and announce the end to the killing. The police did not need to fire a single shot to restore order. In January 1993 two burgomasters halted the attacks against Tutsi during the visit of an international commission investigating human rights violations, saying the slaughter would resume when the group left. Indeed, the killings began within hours of its departure.

Officials often directed assailants first to pillage property, guaranteeing them immediate profit as they accustomed themsleves to attacking their neighbors. In communities where people showed no enthusiasm for even this level of violence, the attacks went no further. But where officials were able to generate enough fear and greed, assailants moved to the next stage of destroying houses and then to killing the inhabitants of the houses.

Just as the attacks could increase in intensity, so they could increase in area, with attacks in one sector or commune sparking similar crimes in the adjacent regions.

Once massacres began in an area, authorities held victims hostage by refusing them the permits needed to leave for other regions or by physically barring their escape routes with barriers. Tutsi attempting to pass the barriers were usually identified by their identity cards and then slain. Those who decided not to flee were killed in their homes.

Civilian authorities played the major role in directing attacks, but they occasionally called on the military for support. In northwestern Rwanda in early 1991, soldiers rounded up Bagogwe to be slain and helped civilians when they encountered resistance from their intended victims. In Bugesera in March 1992, soldiers in civilian dress joined groups of killers while others in uniform disarmed Tutsi and kept them cornered until the killing teams could arrive.

In the northwest and in Bugesera, civilian and military authorities occasionally rounded up groups of several dozen people to be massacred all at one time at a site such as a communal office. But for the most part, they did not attack large groups who gathered spontaneously at such sites—particularly at churches. Instead they cut their access to food and water to force them to return home. They were not yet ready to launch the large-scale attacks that became usual during the 1994 genocide.

Lying about the Violence

When confronted with reports of killings, the authorities often simply denied that the slaughter had taken place. This strategy worked best in cases where the killings had taken place in an inaccessible location. Because the Bagogwe, for example, lived far from the capital and in an area where access was controlled by the military, the authorities were able to continue pretending there had been no slaughter until outside investigators insisted on visiting the region and revea.cu the lie.[58]

When the massacre was too widely known to be plausibly denied, authorities had ready a range of excuses, most of which asserted that the victims had brought the slaughter on themselves—by boasting of imminent RPF victory, by threatening Hutu, or by having planned to attack Hutu. They ordinarily concluded by equating Tutsi with the RPF and declaring that Tutsi were being killed because they had launched an unjustified war against Rwanda in the first place.

Well aware of how easily foreigners accepted explanations of "ancient, tribal hatreds," the authorities repeatedly underlined the "tribal" nature of the killings when called to account by the international community. They insisted that they had been simply unable to control the outburst of spontaneous, popular rage. Then, turning the explanation into a plea for additional foreign support, they would express regrets that the government was so poor that it could not provide officials with the needed resources to keep order in such difficult circumstances.

Impunity

No one, neither official nor ordinary citizen, was ever convicted of any crime in connection with these massacres. Some suspected assailants were arrested after the Kibilira massacre, but were released several weeks later. The prefect of the adjacent prefecture warned in early 1991 that the killings might begin again because those apparently guilty at Kibilira had been liberated and "were boasting of 'brave deeds' that had gone unpunished."[59] The government removed several officials from their posts in areas where attacks had occurred, particularly after foreign criticism of the killings and after the installation of the coalition government when officials opposed to Habyarimana could influence appointment of personnel. But, more discreetly, national authorities also removed local officials who had protected Tutsi or tried to prevent the spread of violence against them.

International Response to the Massacres

In pursuing ethnic violence as a way to keep political power, Habyarimana and his supporters stayed alert to any international reaction to the killings. Even before the war, Rwanda needed foreign financial assistance to keep the government

---

[58]"Report of the International Commission," p.17.

[59]Gaspard Ruhumuliza, Préfet de Kibuye, to Monsieur le Ministre de la Défense Nationale, no. 017/04.18, February 11, 1991 (Kibuye prefecture).

running. With military expenditures, the war-time damage to the economy and the burden of feeding hundreds of thousands of displaced persons, it had become even more dependent on donor nations, both for direct aid and for support through such multilateral institutions as the World Bank and the European Union. Leaders of whatever political persuasion—even radicals of the CDR—understood the importance of maintaining some level of international respectability.

Foreigners—diplomats, aid experts, clergy, technocrats resident in the country—also wanted to maintain the positive image of this clean, well-organized, hard-working little country. Even as evidence of human rights abuses mounted, many were reluctant to admit wrongdoing by the government. In July 1991, consultants from outside the system and thus unaffected by this enthusiasm for the Habyarimana regime found representatives of the major donors in Kigali unwilling to admit that ethnic conflict posed serious risks. When they advised donors to insist on the removal of ethnic classification on identity cards as a condition for continued aid, none of them took the advice.[60]

Donors hoped to correct what they viewed as inadequacies in the regime by fostering the growth of a "civil society," including Rwandan human rights groups. Activitists like Monique Mujyawamariya of ADL, Alphonse-Marie Nkubito of ARDHO, Bernadette Kanzayire of AVP, and Fidele Kanyabugoyi of Kanyarwanda pressured the government for reforms and also kept diplomats in Kigali well-informed of violations. On the occasion of particularly egregious abuses, such as the Bugesera massacre, they actually took diplomats to witness the events. When confronted by such evidence, the diplomats ordinarily intervened with the Rwandan government, discreetly in less important cases, more formally by a joint visit to the authorities in cases like that of Bugesera. These occasional protests sometimes resolved short-term problems but failed to affect Habyarimana's overall policy. Donor nations regarded human rights abuses generally as the result of the war and they chose to work on ending the war rather than on addressing the violations as such. Many would adopt the same position at the time of the genocide. Habyarimana understood the foreign reluctance to intervene and when questioned about massacres, he was always ready with suitable expressions of regret and promises to avoid such mishaps in the future. The foreign donors easily swallowed this reassurance.

---

[60]A team of consultants gave this advice in July 1991 to a group that included ambassadors and others from the embassies of the U.S., France, Canada, Germany, and Belgium. The French at one point recommended that Rwandans remove ethnic categories from identity papers but failed to exert the necessary pressure to have this done.

The International Commission of Inquiry into Human Rights Abuse in Rwanda

Rwandan activists expected more from the donors who always spoke so highly about the importance of human rights. To focus foreign attention on the seriousness of the problem, the activists in the coalition CLADHO pressed international human rights organizations to mount a joint commission to examine the human rights situation in Rwanda. Four agreed to do so: Human Rights Watch (New York), the International Federation of Human Rights Leagues (Paris), the International Center for Human Rights and Democratic Development (Montreal) and the Interafrican Union of Human and Peoples' Rights (Ouagadougou).

During an inquiry in Rwanda in January 1993, the International Commission amassed substantial data to show that "President Habyarimana and his immediate entourage bear heavy responsibility for these massacres [from October 1990 through January 1993] and other abuses against Tutsi and members of the political opposition."[61]

The commission also presented evidence of abuses by the RPF, but given that the RPF then controlled a population of only 3,000 people, this part of the report attracted relatively little attention.

The commission report, published on March 8, 1993, put Rwandan human rights abuses squarely before the international community. It was widely distributed among donor nations and was even handed out by the U.N. Department of Humanitarian Affairs to representatives meeting to discuss assistance to Rwanda.[62] International donors accepted its conclusions and expressed concern, but took no effective action to insist that the guilty be brought to justice or that such abuses not be repeated in the future. French President François Mitterrand directed that an official protest be made and explanations demanded from the Rwandan government, but French authorities made no public criticism of the massacres documented in the report.[63] Belgium reacted most strongly by recalling its

---

[61]"Report of the International Commission," p.51.

[62]Howard Adelman and Astri Suhrke, *Early Warning and Conflict Management,* Joint Evaluation of Emergency Assistance to Rwanda, March 1996, p. 32. This is the second volume of a larger study of the international response to the Rwandan crisis, now commonly called "the Danish report." Funded by a consortium of the donor nations, it provoked a critical response from France, which withdrew its sponsorship of the report.

[63]Assemblée Nationale, Mission d'information commune, *Enquête sur la tragédie rwandaise (1990-1994)*, Tome III, Auditions, Volume 1, pp. 322, 330.

ambassador for consultations but in the end made no significant changes in its aid program. The U.S. redirected part of its financial aid from official channels to nongovernmental organizations operating in Rwanda so that the Rwandan government could not profit from it, and Canada also cut back on its aid. But both donors weakened the impact of their decisions by linking them to Rwandan fiscal mismanagement or shortage of their own funds as much as to human rights abuses.

The report of the International Commission was presented to the United Nations Human Rights Commission, but it declined to discuss the matter in open session, reportedly because it had too many other African nations already on its docket. The United Nations Special Rapporteur on Summary, Arbitrary and Extrajudicial Executions undertook a mission to Rwanda in April 1993 and produced a report in August 1993 that largely confirmed the report of the International Commission. Referring to the possibility, raised by the International Commission, that the massacres of the Tutsi might constitute genocide, the special rapporteur concluded that in his judgment the killings were genocide according to the terms of the 1948 Convention for the Suppression and Punishment of Genocide.

To forestall any further damage to his image, Habyarimana responded to the charges of the International Commission in a formal statement, signed jointly with Prime Minister Dismas Nsengiyaremye on April 7, 1993. In it, the Rwandan government "recognizes and regrets the human rights violations committed in our country." But continuing to deny that officials had taken the initiative in any of these abuses, the government declared only that it had failed to assure the security of citizens who were attacked. It did, however, promise to undertake a series of human rights reforms that closely followed the recommendations of the commission. Habyarimana at the same time launched efforts to discredit the commission, calling into existence four fake human rights organizations that published a scurrilous pamphlet attacking commission members and sponsored a European speaking tour for two representatives to refute the report. The attempt to discredit the commission was too clumsy to succeed, but Habyarimana had secured the continuing favor of donors in any case by his April 7 profession of good intentions.

In the months after the publication of the report, there were no more massacres of Tutsi and the international community hoped that the ethnic violence would not be repeated. But its willingness to accept excuses for lesser massacres and its continuing acceptance of impunity for killers in official positions contributed to the very result they wished to avoid, more slaughter and this time catastrophic in scale and unambiguously genocidal in nature.

In the episodes of violence from 1990 to 1994, Habyarimana's supporters perfected some of the tactics they would use during the genocide: how to choose the best sites to launch attacks, how to develop the violence—both in intensity and in extent—from small beginnings, how to mobilize people through fear, particularly fear aroused by "created" events, how to use barriers and bureaucratic regulations to keep a target group restricted to one place, and how to build cooperation between civilian, military, and militia leaders to produce the most effective attacks. Perhaps equally important, they had learned that this kind of slaughter would be tolerated by the international community.

downside of presence

CHOOSING WAR

The Rwandan government and the RPF signed a cease-fire in July 1992 and the first protocol of the Arusha Accords the next month, but progress to peace was one step forward and two steps back. On August 17, 1992, the day after the protocol was signed, Habyarimana declared on the radio that he would not permit negotiators to "lead our country into an adventure it would not like."[1] Three days later, MRND and CDR supporters killed dozens of Tutsi and members of parties opposed to Habyarimana in the Kibuye massacre described above. During these weeks, the president was apparently conducting private negotiations with the RPF through a Jesuit priest, seeking to obtain assurance of a amnesty for himself in return for his resignation. As it was becoming clear that these talks would lead nowhere, Habyarimana and his supporters learned that more than a million dollars worth of arms had been seized in Orlando, Florida. They supposed that these arms, apparently en route to Kampala, were meant to resupply the RPF and they anticipated an RPF attack at the end of September or beginning of October.[2] It may have been these events which prompted the Rwandan army high command to disseminate on September 21 its memorandum defining the enemy, which had been sitting in a drawer for a number of months. In mid-October, the MRND ministers indicated that the government was divided over peace negotiations and three days later, the CDR took to the streets to protest the talks. At the end of October, nonetheless, the Rwandan government and the RPF signed the second part of the Arusha Accords. Two weeks later, Habyarimana disavowed the agreements in his "scrap of paper" declaration, and a week after that MRND propagandist Mugesera invited his fellow party members to engage in mayhem against Tutsi and Hutu opposed to the MRND.[3]

At the end of December 1992, the MRND (with Habyarimana as party president), the CDR, and several allied smaller parties issued a vigorous rejection of the Accords, calling it "a plan for treason" which "[we] must prepare to defeat."[4]

---

[1]Prunier, *The Rwanda Crisis*, p.161.

[2]Human Rights Watch/FIDH interview, by telephone, Lausanne, August 29, 1996.

[3]Reyntjens, *L'Afrique des Grands Lacs,* pp. 204-05; Prunier, *The Rwanda Crisis*, pp. 162-63, 171.

[4]Antoine Jouan, "Rwanda 1990-1994: de la transition politique au génocide," Fondation Médecins sans Frontières, December 1995, pp. 34-35.

Two weeks later, the Rwandan government agreed to another part of the Accords, the one which decided political arrangements for the transitional period before elections. But not quite two weeks after that, the secretary-general of the MRND, Mathieu Ngirumpatse, again denounced the Accords, a position echoed several days later by Habyarimana himself who said that certain provisions must be renegotiated.[5] The MRND and CDR mobilized their followers in the streets to protest the agreement and launched the January 1993 massacre, described above, to disrupt the whole peace process.

He Who Wishes for Peace Prepares for War
Arms
Even as peace talks lurched uncertainly forward, the Rwandan army prepared for further war. After having obtained U.S.$6 million worth of arms from Egypt the previous March, the Ministry of Defense took delivery of a further U.S.$5.9 million worth of arms and ammunition from South Africa on October 19, 1992. The March purchase included some 450 Kalashnikov rifles, a standard infantry assault weapon and the one then used by most Rwandan soldiers, and the October purchase included 20,000 R-4 rifles. At the time of the March purchase, the Rwandan army also bought two thousand rocket-propelled grenades, which require a significant amount of instruction to use effectively, but no hand grenades; in October they purchased 20,000 hand grenades, which could be used by persons with relatively little training.[6]

The October purchase of small arms seems remarkably large, given that the armed forces then numbered some 30,000 men and was not being expanded. Any recruitment then being carried out was just to replace deserters.[7] Although there were perhaps a thousand or so deserters per year, they did not all leave with their guns, and arming their replacements did not require 20,000 new weapons.[8]

---

[5]Jouan, "Rwanda 1990-1994," p. 35; Reyntjens, *L'Afrique des Grands Lacs*, p. 205.

[6]Human Rights Watch Arms Project, "Arming Rwanda," p. 22.

[7]Human Rights Watch/FIDH interview, by telephone, Lausanne, August 29, 1996.

[8]Estimates based on correspondence between the prefect and burgomasters of Gikongoro concerning the identification of deserters throughout 1992 and 1993, particularly Laurent Bucyibaruta, Préfet, to Bourgmestre (Tous), no. 169/04.09.01/1, August 9, 1993 (Gikongoro prefecture).

Some of the newly purchased weapons may have been intended for resale to other governments but thousands of them were distributed to members of the armed forces, making possible the recycling of their weapons to communal police and ordinary citizens.[9]

Not quite two weeks after the first part of the peace accords was signed, burgomasters were ordered to prepare lists of materials needed by their local police, usually a force of ten or so policemen and ordinarily armed lightly, if at all. Several burgomasters submitted unremarkable requests for raincoats and handcuffs, but others, perhaps alerted to the possibilities by some unofficial communication, presented very different lists. The burgomaster of Nyamagabe reported that his police needed three Kalashnikov rifles and one BREN machine gun with amunition. The burgomaster of Nshili—who had been successfully brought back to the MRND by the kubohoza described above—asked for twelve automatic weapons and six other arms as well as 1,000 bullets of one kind and fifty of another. The burgomaster of Mudasomwa, one of the first communes to launch genocidal killing in April 1994, requested eight automatic weapons and two pistols.[10]

At this time, the training and arming of communal police was supervised by Col. Alphonse Ntezeliyayo, who was seconded from the Ministry of Defense to the Ministry of the Interior. Colonel Ntezeliyayo, originally from the southern prefecture of Butare, was apparently not well-regarded by his colleagues from the north, who taxed him with being too accommodating to Tutsi and Hutu dissidents, a position he would change during the genocide.[11]

Presumably at Ntezeliyayo's direction, authorities began in January 1993 to distribute new weapons to some communes considerably in excess of the number of policemen who were slated to use them. The commune of Ngoma, in the prefecture of Butare, added eight new Kalashnikovs to its supply of twenty-six rifles and at the same time received 960 bullets. Six months later, it received an

---

[9]In March 1993, a jeep loaded with weapons destined for Palipehutu insurgents in Burundi was involved in an accident in Kigali. The weapons had been sold or otherwise delivered by soldiers at the Kanombe military camp.

[10]Laurent Bucyibaruta, Préfet de Gikongoro, to Monsieur le Ministre de l'Intérieur et du Développement Communal, no. 039/04.15, le 22/9/1992 (Gikongoro prefecture).

[11]See the chapters below on Butare prefecture.

additional 144 bullets, although it had used only fifteen.[12] At the time, the commune had eighteen policemen, an unusually large force because it served the needs of the important town of Butare, but not one that would have required thirty-four rifles. Given the severe financial problems of the government and the cost of firearms, it is unlikely that a surplus of sixteen rifles was simply stored in Ngoma without some plans for their use.[13]

Lists

The distribution of arms to the communes, presumably for the communal police but apparently for others as well, indicates that some highly placed military officers anticipated fighting an "enemy" dispersed in the population, not just concentrated on a war front. In the months that the arms were being distributed, both civilian and military authorities were gathering information on the "enemy" and where to find him.

In September and October 1992, prefects relayed secret orders to the burgomasters to compile lists of people who were known to have left the country surreptitiously. The lists, for "the purpose of security" were to include complete identification and were to be provided urgently. The prefects told the burgomasters to remove the registration cards of these people from the usual file and to put them aside until further instructions.[14] Burgomasters were providing lists of "persons who joined the ranks of the inkotanyi" at least through August 1993.[15] In his November 1992 speech, Mugesera several times attacked families that permitted their children to go join the RPF, insisting that these people should leave Rwanda while they still could, because "the time has come for us also to defend ourselves."

[12]Joseph Kanyabashi, Bourgmestre, to Monsieur le Préfet, Butare, no. 68/04.17, January 31, 1993; no. 257/04.17, April 13, 1993; and no. 904/04.17.01, November 24, 1993 (Butare prefecture).

[13]Ibid.

[14]Laurent Bucyibaruta, Préfet, to Monsieur le Bourgmestre, no. Ls 23/04.17.02, September 2, 1992; Laurent Bucyibaruta, to Monsieur le Bourgmestre, Nyamagabe, Mudasoma, Karama, Kinyamakara, Rwamiko, Kivu, Karambo, Musange, Muko, Musebeya, No. LS 047/04.17.02, October 2, 1992 (Gikongoro prefecture).

[15]Francois Xavier Njenyeli, Bourgmestre, Commune Gituza, to Préfet, Byumba, no. 247/04.17.02, August 2, 1993, Dossier Planification Genocide (RPF Human Rights Commission, Kigali).

Mugesera asked the crowd, "Why do we not arrest these parents who have sent their children away and why do we not exterminate them?" A moment later, he continued,

> I would like to tell you that we are now asking for those people to be put on a list and for them to be brought to court so that they can be judged before us. If they [the judges] refuse...we should do it ourselves by exterminating this scum.[16]

In late September or early October 1992, the army general staff directed all units and military camps to provide lists of all people said to be "accomplices" of the RPF. When the order came to light in February 1993, Prime Minister Dismas Nsengiyaremye, protested against this "witch hunt" and demanded that any lists so compiled be turned over immediately to the Ministry of Justice for appropriate action.[17] His initiative was apparently ignored by the military.

Several weeks later, the chief of staff, Colonel Nsabimana—the same man who had signed the September 21 letter circulating the definition of the enemy—was injured in an automobile accident. After he was taken to the hospital, a document was found in his car entitled cynically "Memo for the Protection of Human Rights" (Aide-Mémoire pour la protection des droits de la personne). It included a "list of persons to contact" (Personnes á contacter), 331 persons thought to be supporters of the RPF. The notes for some persons gave a brief description of the charges against them as well as their names and locations. Some were accused of having allowed their children to go abroad to join the RPF, others of having held suspicious meetings of Tutsi in their houses or of having stockpiled arms for the RPF. Several were named because they had been detained as "accomplices" in the October 1990 arrests.[18] In the prefecture of Butare, and presumably in other prefectures as well, lists had been kept of all local people arrested in 1990. Some of the lists had been brought up to date with more current information about the

---

[16]Léon Mugesera, "Discours Prononcé par Léon Mugesera lors d'un Meeting du M.R.N.D. Tenu à Kabaya le 22 novembre 1992."

[17]Dr. Dismas Nsengiyaremye, Premier Ministre, to Monsieur le Ministre de la Défense, no. 071/42.3.5, February 2, 1993 (ARDHO).

[18]Guichaoua, *Les Crises Politiques,* pp. 662-67. Note that the document is incorrectly dated to March 1994; it should be March 1993.

persons named.[19] All these lists offered a ready source of information for any who wanted to attack Tutsi and Hutu opponents of Habyarimana.

As the existence of some of these lists became publically known, people from all sides found it increasingly easy to believe rumors of other lists and adversaries frequently traded accusations about such compilations. During the genocide, assailants often justified killing Tutsi by claiming that they had found lists of Hutu marked for execution on the person or property of their intended victims. Many such accusations were false, although some RPF supporters did apparently make lists of likely backers or opponents as part of the data about local communities that they supplied to the RPF.[20]

The Militia and "Self-Defense"

Beginning in March 1992 the Interahamwe had proved their effectiveness in attacking Tutsi and Hutu who supported the MDR, the PSD, or the PL. Foreseeing the role they could play against such "enemies" in case of renewed combat, Habyarimana and his supporters stepped up the recruitment and training of the militia. Hoping to keep the effort secret, they sent the recruits to training camps distant from the capital. One was at Gabiro, near a hotel in the Akagera game park, and another was in the northwestern Gishwati forest, adjacent to the Hotel Mont Muhe, which belonged to Habyarimana and his circle. The recruits at Gishwati lived in tents in the forest and were visited on the weekends by important MRND officials and businessmen who came up from Kigali to cheer them on. According to a witness present on one such occasion in January 1993, the hotel staff killed and roasted a cow to honor the visitors and the trainees. The tired and sweaty recruits came out of the forest fifteen or so at a time to enjoy the barbecue and plentiful beer. After several groups had eaten, they gathered the remaining food and drink and transported it into the forest in a pickup truck for their fellow trainees. When the festivities were finished, the dignitaries spent the night at the Mont Muhe Hotel or at hotels in the nearby town of Gisenyi.[21]

---

[19]Justin Temahagali, Préfet, to Bwana Burugumesitiri wa Komini, no. 090/04/01, April 5. 1991 (Butare prefecture).

[20]Col. Théoneste Lizinde to Abahuza-Bikorwa Ba FPR mu Rwanda (Bose), March 22, 1994, includes a questionnaire about political, social and economic conditions to be filled out by RPF agents in the various communes (Kibuye prefecture).

[21]Human Rights Watch/FIDH interview, Kigali, June 23, 1995.

The militia, however, were limited by their close identification with the MRND. They would not seek to recruit—or would not in any case be able to recruit successfully—young men committed to other parties. Because of the bitterness of past kubohoza struggles, members of other parties regarded them with suspicion and sought to discover and expose their training programs, particularly any that used Rwandan army soldiers. The need for secrecy required complicated and sometimes costly logistical arrangements to get recruits to the remote training sites.

A government program of civilian self-defense offered a simpler, cheaper, and perhaps equally effective way of mobilizing civilians for eventual action against the "enemy." Immediately after the RPF invasion, the government had instituted such a program, similar to one established by authorities to counter guerrilla attacks in the 1960s.[22] It required citizens to man blockades on roads and to carry out patrols at night. But the effort lapsed throughout most of the country soon after the RPF was driven back at the end of October 1990. In late December 1990, a group of university faculty including Vice-Rector Jean-Berchmans Nshimyumuremyi and Professor Runyinya-Barabwiriza proposed that the minister of defense establish a "self-defense" program for all adult men. Citing the adage, "He who wishes for peace prepares for war," the group advocated a population in arms as a way to "assure security" inside the country if the army were occupied in defending the frontiers. It suggested that men be trained locally, within the comune, under the command of soldiers, and that they should particularly learn to fight with "traditional weapons," because they were cheaper than firearms.[23]

The idea was not implemented at the time but in September 1991, as the RPF multiplied its incursions across the Ugandan border, Colonel Nsabimana, then the local commander, proposed training and arming one person from each unit of ten households. The persons to be armed would be chosen by the communal council, would be ideally between twenty-five and forty years old, married, patriotic, and of high moral character. They would be locally trained and would continue to live at home, going into action under the orders of National Policemen, or, if they were not available, of soldiers from local military units. The program was to be

---

[22]Lemarchand, *Rwanda and Burundi,* p. 223.

[23]Jean-Berchmans Nshimyumuremyi, Vice Rector of the U.N.R., Butare Campus, to the Minister of National Defense, P2-18/813/90, December 26, 1990 (Butare prefecture).

implemented first in three communes near the Ugandan frontier and then extended to the rest of the country as money became available to pay for the arms.[24]

During 1992, small groups of local residents carried out patrols and engaged in skirmishes near the border, usually in the company of one or two soldiers. Often one or two of the civilians were armed with guns while others carried such weapons as machetes, spears or bows, and arrows. According to the local people, they fought more fiercely than the professional soldiers, but some in the top ranks of the army opposed the program, claiming that many civilians fled at the first sign of danger, leaving their guns behind for the RPF to pick up.[25]

The AMASASU and Colonel Bagosora

The high-ranking officers associated with the akazu were among those who continued to favor civilian self-defense. Col. Laurent Serubuga, for example, lent his prestige to Léon Mugesera, sitting on the platform while the MRND propagandist called repeatedly for the people to rise up and defend themselves.

The congruence of interest between hard-line soldiers and anti-Tutsi militants reappeared in January 1993 just after the third of the Arusha protocols was signed. On January 20, a group of soldiers calling themselves AMASASU sent an aggressive open letter to Habyarimana.[26] They explained that their name meant The Alliance of Soldiers Provoked by the Age-old Deceitful Acts of the Unarists (Alliance des Militaires Agacés par les Séculaires Actes Sournois des Unaristes); Unarists referred to the Tutsi royalist party from the years of the revolution. The real meaning of the cumbersome name lay not in the component words but in the acronym: *amasasu* means bullets in Kinyarwanda. "Commandant Mike Tango," writing for the Supreme Council of the AMASASU, appears to have shared ideas with Mugesera, including the increasingly familiar phrase, "He who wishes for peace prepares for war." Both warn that supporters of the RPF had better clear out of the country before it is too late. Both threaten to deliver their own form of "justice" to the "accomplices" if the competent authorities fail to act against them. Commandant Mike goes even further. He declares that the RPF is preparing a

---

[24]Col. Déogratias Nsabimana to Monsieur le Ministre de la Défense Nationale, no. 181/G5.3.0, September 29, 1991 (International Commission).

[25]Human Rights Watch/FIDH interview, Rebero, January 19, 1993; Human Rights Watch/FIDH interview, by telephone, Lausanne, August 29, 1996.

[26]Commandant Tango Mike to Monsieur le Président de la République Rwandaise, January 20, 1993 (International Commission).

major attack and he asks Habyarimina, if that happens, "how do you expect to stop us from delivering an exemplary lesson to traitors inside the country? After all, we have already identified the most virulent of them and will strike them like lightning."

Repeating Mugesera's call for self-defense, Commandant Mike advocates establishing in each commune at least one battalion of "robust young men," who will receive a minimum of military training on the spot. "They will stay [at home] on the hills, but will be ready to form a popular army" to support the regular army. The Ministries of Youth, Defense and the Interior will take charge of training and commanding this "popular army."

Commandant Mike was a pseudonym, of course, but it seems likely that he is either Col. Théoneste Bagosora or someone working closely with him. Bagorosa was born in 1941 in the commune of Giciye, next to Habyarimana's home commune, and had devoted his life to the Rwandan army. He describes himself as the son of a "Christian and relatively well-off" family, with a father who was a teacher. He took military courses in Belgium and France and commanded the important military camp of Kanombe in Kigali until 1992. When the recently-installed coalition government made changes in the army high command in June 1992, forcing the retirement of Colonel Serubuga, Col. Pierre-Celestin Rwagafilita, and others, Habyarimana sought to have Bagosora named chief of staff. Ministers of opposing political parties refused this arrangement, seeing Bagasora as no improvement over the other hard-liners. In a compromise, Colonel Nsabimana, thought to be more moderate, was named to head the general staff and Bagosora was installed as head of the administration at the Ministry of Defense, where he was well placed to keep an eye on Minister of Defense James Gasana, who was seen as unsympathetic to hard-line positions. According to some observers, Habyarimana actually distrusted Bagosora, who had been trying for years to escape from Habyarimana's shadow. The two presented much the same political profile, with Bagosora somewhat more militantly anti-Tutsi, and they drew on the same constituencies. Bagosora, who was ambitious, was said to believe that he, too, was qualified to run Rwanda and hoped for the chance to do so. Bagosora reportedly enjoyed the support of Habyarimana's wife and her brothers and of his own younger brother, Pasteur Musabe who directed a large commercial bank, and was described by one insider as the most important civilian in the akazu.[27]

---

[27]Human Rights Watch/FIDH interview, August 30, 1996; Prunier, *The Rwanda Crisis,* p. 167.

In an essay entitled "L'assassinat du Président Habyarimana ou l'ultime opération du Tutsi pour sa reconquête du pouvoir par la force au Rwanda," Bagosora makes clear that he held firmly to the radical ideas of the CDR, as propagated by RTLM and such newspapers as *Kangura*. He has no hesitation in stating repeatedly that the struggle, one that is age-old (*séculaire*), is between the "Hutu people" and the Tutsi, not between political groups.[28] For this reason, the negotiations at Arusha should have been between Hutu and Tutsi rather than between political parties and any future discussions should be held between two ethnically defined sides. The same theme is sounded in *Kangura*, which in February 1993 published a call for discussions between the head of the CDR and Kigeli V Ndahindurwa, the exiled former king of Rwanda, instead of wasting further time with negotiations at Arusha where the real actors were not present.[29] For Bagosora, the Hutu are the legitimate possessors of the region, where they lived "harmoniously" with the Twa since the ninth century. The Tutsi "never had a country of their own to allow them to become a people"; they are and will remain "naturalised nilotic immigrants" who have arrogantly tried to impose their supremacy over the rightful local inhabitants.[30] Repeating all the usual clichés about the supposed nature of these peoples, Bagosora describes the Tutsi as "masters of deceit," "dictatorial, cruel, bloody," "arrogant, clever and sneaky," while he speaks of the Hutu as "modest, open, loyal, independent and impulsive."[31]

Like Commandant Mike, the authors of the September 21 memorandum defining the enemy, and many of the anti-Tutsi propagandists, Bagosora is insistent that the RPF is simply a continuation of the old UNAR, determined to restore "feudal-royalist servitude." Like them, he stresses the RPF reliance on support from Uganda and its president Museveni, whose supposedly Hima origins he points out. Like *Kangura*, he refers to the "Simbananiye plan" that Tutsi had purportedly

---

[28]Colonel BEMS Bagosora Théoneste, "L'assassinat du Président Habyarimana ou l'ultime opération du Tutsi pour sa reconquête du pouvoir par la force au Rwanda," Yaoundé, October 30, 1995, p. 7. See also Jean-Marie Aboganena, "Bagosora S'Explique," *Africa International*, no. 296, July-August 1996, p. 18.

[29]Chrétien et al., *Rwanda, Les médias*, p. 136.

[30]Bagosora, "L'assassinat," pp. 12-13.

[31]Ibid., pp. 12, 14, 18; see also Communiqué de Presse du Parti CDR, February 25, 1993 (Provided by Comité pour le respect des droits de l'homme et la démocratie au Rwanda, CRDDR).

created to eliminate Hutu in Burundi, and he attributes to the RPF the assassination of Hutu political leaders of varying political views in Rwanda.[32]

Like the propagandists of Hutu solidarity, Bagosora refers to Kayibanda, the leader of the 1959 revolution, whose supposed words he uses to validate his argument that the Tutsi have brought suffering on themselves. He asserts that in attacking the Rwandan government, the Tutsi have knowingly and "coldly decided to expose their brothers to reprisals." In a reference that is inaccurate both in its date (March 11, 1963 instead of 1964) and in its content, Bagosora quotes Kayibanda as warning that further Tutsi attacks from outside the country would mean "the total and precipitate end of the Tutsi race."[33]

The essay, intended as a public justification for his position, shows how Bagosora fit into the ideological context of anti-Tutsi extremism. A second document, not intended for publication, shows how he intended to implement this ideology. When Bagosora fled Kigali in 1994, he left behind in his house a small black appointment book. On the cover is "Agenda 1993, Banque de Kigali," and inside is written Bagosora's name and telephone number.[34]

Beginning on the page for February 1 is a series of notes sketching out a plan for civilian self-defense. As with previous proposals, recruits are to live at home and to be trained locally. Bagosora writes, "The communal police should be up to training its militia," indicating by his use of the word "militia" the link he is making between the community-based self-defense units and those organized by the party. If they are not available, military reservists, meaning former soldiers, would give the instruction. The recruits are to be married men "who have something to defend" and, in a later passage, "reliable persons" chosen among those displaced by the war. Elsewhere he adds that each cell and each sector are to elect the men to be armed. In one entry, Bagosora indicates that three times as many men are to be trained as there are arms available; in another he notes that sixty men should be trained for each commune. They are to be organized by sector

[32]Chrétien et al., *Rwanda. Les médias*, p. 237.

[33]Ibid., p. 16. The printed text of Kayibanda's speech does not include these words. République Rwandaise, Commission Spéciale sur les problèmes des émigrés rwandais, *Le Rwanda et le problème de ses refugiés* (Kigali: 1990), pp. 95-6.

[34]Human Rights Watch/FIDH researchers examined and copied the original of this document, held by an RPF representative. An expert in handwriting analysis found the writing in the appointment book to be consistent with a sample of Bagosora's handwriting.

Document: Page from Bagosora's appointment book, month of February 1993, sketching elements of the "civilian self-defense" program.

---

februari / february / februar — donderdag jeudi / thursday / donnerstag

4

— Le minimum d'armes par secteur

— Un système de coordination entre eux avec les militaires —

— le Conseiller Communal les policiers communaux —

— Former le triple d'hommes par rapport aux armes

— Organisation des ... communaires

Kibombe
Ngalinya
Nkingo
Nkuli
Nyakinama
Nyarutovu

---

vendredi vrijdag / viernes friday / venerdì freitag — février / febrero / febbraio

5

— Principes :

— plans

— Le Calendrier —

— Communes menacées mais encore habitées ?
— Communes déjà occupées partiellement —
— Les communes occupées — en force

— Qui armer ? — Les mariés ou qui ont quelque chose à défendre

— Organisation locale formation... encadrement —

— contrat avec la commune.

— Éviter les contradictions partisanes — leur désinformation
... de l'information

Document: Page from Bagosora's appointment book, month of February 1993, sketching elements of the "civilian self-defense" program.

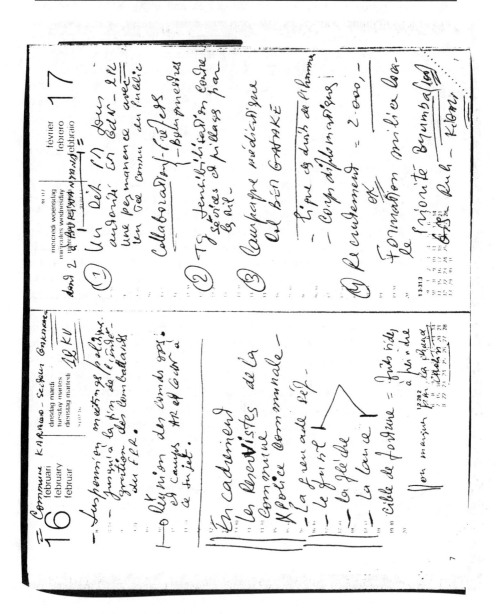

with coordination between military authorities and the local administration, including communal councilors, and local police.

Bagosora identifies the city of Kigali and the prefectures of Byumba, Ruhengeri, and Gisenyi as the areas where the self-defense program should be launched first. He projects the need for 2,000 weapons, 300 for Kigali, 700 for the prefecture of Byumba, 600 for Ruhengeri, and 400 for Gisenyi,[35] and seems to indicate that the first 2,000 recruits should be trained by soldiers, perhaps to get the program started in the right way. An entry later in the month of February speaks of ordering 2,000 Kalashnikovs "to bring to 5,000 the number for the communes." On this page, he scribbles a proposal that three to five weapons be distributed for each cell. On another page, he jots the note "hand grenades" next to a list of the names of six communes. Aware of the possible conflicts that might arise out of arming a part of the population, Bagosora remarked on the importance of "avoiding partisan considerations during the distribution."

Not just a planner, Bagosora was evidently also involved in implementing the details of the self-defense program. He is concerned with obtaining vehicles and with finding appropriate storage places for the weapons. He even sketches out the main headings of a training program that would teach the use of the hand grenade, the rifle, bows and arrows, and spears. He proposes making targets out of empty tins with bulls eyes painted on or marked with chalk. One task to which he refers often is that of "organizing information," that is, propaganda. On one page, he notes "censorship of the radio" and "listen to all radio broadcasts." On another, he writes about radio broadcasts by heads of the political parties. Elsewhere he proposes the contents of a radio program which, he writes, should include songs by Bikindi, the singer well-known for his anti-Tutsi lyrics. He proposes entrusting a more general propaganda campaign, aimed at human rights organizations and the diplomatic corps, to Col. Gasake, a respected older soldier who had recently returned from years of diplomatic service abroad. Bagosora also jotted down remarks about the need to ban meetings of political parties and the possibility of amnesty for war crimes.

In a first effort to launch the self-defense program in northwestern Rwanda, Bagosora ordered about 500 firearms distributed in the communes of Mutura, Giciye, Karago, Rubavu, and Rwerere at the end of January or the beginning of

---

[35]There appears to be a mistake in arithmetic here because five Gisenyi communes are listed, Karago, Mutura, Rwere (an error for Rwerere), Rubavu, and Kanama, each with the number 100 next to it, which would make 500 for the prefecture and a total of 2,100 weapons needed.

February 1993. In doing so, he overrode the specific orders of the minister of defense. According to a document obtained at the time by Human Rights Watch, 193 firearms were delivered in the commune of Mutura to primary school teachers, government employees, communal councilors, army reservists, and shopkeepers, just the same kinds of people who would be found using guns during the genocide.[36] On March 1, 1993, the burgomaster of the commune Gituza wrote to the prefect of Byumba, acknowledging delivery of forty-four firearms and thanking him in the name of the population for his efforts to provide for their security and self-defense.[37]

Defense Minister Gasana, who had been away at the Arusha negotiations, returned to Kigali and learned of the distribution. He ordered the 500 firearms collected, but not all of them were returned to the authorities.[38] Bagosora and other hard-liners tried to discredit Gasana within the MRND.[39] Perhaps anticipating the success of this attempt, Bagosora noted in his datebook in early March that Gasana would be replaced as minister by Felicien Ngango, a lawyer who was an important member of the PSD. The information was wrong and Gasana continued to serve until July 1993. With Gasana still in place and political conditions not yet ripe, Bagosora temporarily shelved his plans for distributing guns to civilians.

Locating Potential Leaders

On the page for February 21 of his appointment book, Bagosora had noted the need for "identification of reservists."[40] A store of relevant information already existed, assembled by administrative authorities who tracked the location of former soldiers for a variety of reasons from mid-1992 on. By March 1993, the continued gathering of such information became more discreet, linked to political loyalties.

---

[36]Africa Watch, "Beyond the Rhetoric," p. 14.

[37]Francois Xavier Njenyeli, Burgomestre, Commune Gituza, to Préfet, Byumba, March 1, 1993, Dossier Planification Genocide (RPF Human Rights Commission, Kigali).

[38]Human Rights Watch/FIDH interview, Washington, D.C., September 10, 1996.

[39]Human Rights Watch/FIDH interview, August 30, 1996.

[40]Correspondence between the prefect and burgomasters of Gikongoro concerning the identification of deserters throughout 1992 and 1993, particularly Laurent Bucyibaruta, Préfet, to Monsieur le Bourgmestre (Tous), no. 169/04.09.01/1, August 9, 1993 (Gikongoro prefecture); Human Rights Watch/FIDH interview, Kigali, July 13, 1996.

At this time, the prefect of Kigali city asked two burgomasters who were MRND supporters to provide lists of former soldiers who were living in the capital, but he did not address the same request to the third, who was a member of the PSD. When that burgomaster asked why he had not been told to gather this information, he was informed that the order had come from the party, not from the administration.[41]

As the problems of insecurity grew throughout 1993, local officials enlisted increasingly active citizen participation in security committees that included judicial, police or military personnel, administrators, heads of local political parties, clergy, and other community leaders. In a number of communes, the security committees established patrols of citizens or of watchmen paid by citizens to supplement the inadequate efforts of local police.[42] Although the involvement of ordinary citizens in police functions may have brought short-term improvements in security in some places, it created a precedent that would be exploited for the opposite purpose during the genocide.

The February 1993 Attack

On February 8, 1993, the RPF violated the July 1992 cease-fire and launched a massive attack all along the northern front and rapidly drove back the government troops. The civilian population also fled south, joining hundreds of thousands of persons displaced earlier in the conflict to make a total of some one million displaced, about one seventh of the total population. The RPF, critical of international inaction, claimed that they had to attack to halt the late January massacres of Tutsi and others.[43] In fact, the slaughter of Tutsi had stopped more than a week before the RPF moved, suggesting that the real motive for the attack had been to force progress on the negotiations that Habyarimana had sought to stall by killing Tutsi.

The RPF initiative was a great success in military terms, but far less so in political terms. The MDR, PSD, and PL, cooperating more or less successfully with the RPF since May 1992, felt betrayed by the sudden resumption of combat. Some of their members began to question if the RPF really wanted a negotiated peace, or

---

[41]Human Rights Watch/FIDH interview, Kigali, July 14, 1996.

[42]Minutes of the meetings of these committees can be found in communal or prefectural archives in the prefectures of Butare, Gikongoro, and Kibuye. See, for example, Damien Biniga, Sous-Préfet, to Monsieur le Bourgmestre, Rwamiko, no. 494/04.17.02, August 13, 1993 (Gikongoro prefecture).

[43]Human Rights Watch/FIDH interview, Washington, D.C., September 10, 1996.

if it was determined to win an outright victory and impose its own control, replacing one repressive regime with another. Rwandan and international human rights organizations published credible charges that the RPF had assassinated at least eight Rwandan government officials and their families, had executed some fifty persons thought to be supporters of the MRND, and had killed at least two hundred other civilians in the course of its advance.[44] News of these abuses contributed to disillusionment about RPF methods and goals among Rwandans and foreigners alike.

Faced with this growing discontent, the RPF was also militarily over-extended on a very wide front and so badly placed to risk open combat with French troops that had been brought in to reinforce the Rwandan army. The RPF agreed to a new cease-fire and pulled back to its original positions, leaving a sizable buffer zone between its lines and those of the government army.

After the RPF attack, more voices clamored for a civilian self-defense program. In a radio address four days after the RPF attack, Habyarimana advocated a self-defense force armed with traditional weapons rather than with guns.[45] He repeated this idea in a speech to sector commanders of the Rwandan army on March 13, when he called for the population to "organize to defend itself."[46] Political activist Ferdinand Nahimana wrote others of the political and intellectual elite, urging that young people, especially those displaced by the RPF advance, be trained as part of a "civil defense operation." Like the academics who had advocated self-defense in 1990, he stressed the usefulness of this popular force in "safeguarding peace inside the country," implying that it would act against civilians rather than against the RPF. He proposed that the force should be provided with "arms and other light materials that could be used directly in the defense of the population."[47] In February, *Kangura* wrote:

> We must remark to the Inyenzi that if they do not change their attitude and if they persevere in their arrogance, the majority people will establish a force

---

[44]Africa Watch, "Beyond the Rhetoric," pp. 23-24.

[45]Pasteur Bizimungu to Africa Watch, February 13, 1993.

[46]General Juvénal Habyarimana, "Exposé Introductif du Général-Major Habyarimana Juvénal à la Réunion des Commandants de Secteurs du 13 mars 1993."

[47]Ferdinand Nahimana, "Le Rwanda: Problèmes Actuels, Solutions," February 21, 1993, included in a letter of Nahimana to Chers amis, March 28, 1994 (confidential source).

composed of young Hutu. This force will be charged with breaking the resistance of the Tutsi young people [literally, children]. We should stop fooling around.[48]

In a press release dated February 25, 1993, the CDR warned that the RPF were planning a genocide of Hutu throughout the country in their pursuit of a Hima-Tutsi empire. It demanded that the government provide the people with the means necessary to defend themselves.[49]

Splitting the Opposition
Even before the February 8 attack, some hard-liners sensed a new possibility of attracting members of rival parties—particularly the MDR—back to the side of the MRND. In the January 20 AMASASU letter, for example, Commandant Mike is conciliatory towards Prime Minister Dismas Nsengiyaremye of the MDR, a position far different from that taken by Mugesera, who had equated him with the devil in his speech three months before. Foreign advisers also saw the benefit of an MDR-MRND alliance. In a letter dated January 20, Alain De Brouwer, political counselor of the Christian Democratic International, (Internationale Démocrate Chrétienne, IDC) advised Mathieu Ngirumpatse, secretary-general of the MRND, to explore a "permanent and open MRND-MDR collaboration." He suggested calling a "national conference" to form an alliance that would allow these parties to seize the initiative from the RPF, both at the next round of peace talks and beyond.[50] The IDC, a conservative, European-based coalition of Christian Democratic political parties, firmly supported the MRND. At the end of February, the French minister of cooperation, Marcel Debarge, added his voice and urged creating a "common front" against the RPF.[51]
Habyarimana needed no lessons in how to play the game. In early March he called a "national conference"—in fact a small-scale meeting—that attracted

---

[48]Chrétien et al., *Rwanda, Les médias*, p. 136.

[49] Communiqué de Presse du Parti CDR, February 25, 1993.

[50]Alain De Brouwer, Conseiller Politique, Internationale Démocratique Chrétienne, to Mathieu Ngirumpatse, January 20, 1993 (CRDDR). For an analysis of the role of conservative Christians in Rwanda, see Léon Saur, *Influences Parallèlles: L'Internationale Démocrate Chrétienne au Rwanda* (Brussels: Editions Luc Pire, 1998).

[51]Prunier, *The Rwanda Crisis,* pp. 178.

members of the MDR, PSD, and PL, as well as a number of less important parties. This first effort led nowhere. The MDR, PSD, and PL had just finished papering over their differences with the RPF, and their leaders disavowed those party members who "had neither the mandate nor the power" to carry on discussions with Habyarimana.[52] But this was only Habyarimana's opening shot in what would eventually be a successful campaign to win back disaffected Hutu. Those who attended his first meeting included Donat Murego of the MDR and Stanislas Mbonampeka of the PL, both already hostile to the elected presidents of their respective parties and both major actors in leading segments of their parties into an alliance with Habyarimana by the end of the year.

As Habyarimana sought new ties with the MDR and other parties, he was attacked by the CDR which exploded in anger at the terms of the new cease-fire with the RPF. In a press release issued March 9, the CDR called acceptance of the cease-fire "an act of high treason" and said that by signing it, Habyarimana showed that he no longer cared about the interests of the nation.[53]

Just how crucial alliances with other parties would be to Habyarimana's future was made clear at the end of March 1993 when a form of limited election was held to replace burgomasters removed for unsatisfactory performance or who had fled or resigned their posts as a result of kubohoza. In each commune, the councilors, members of cell committees, heads of development projects, clergy, and heads of local political parties were permitted to vote, a group that amounted to some fifty people in most communes. The MRND won only sixteen of the forty posts contested, all those available in the northern prefectures of Gisenyi and Ruhengeri with the rest scattered elsewhere in the east and southwest. In contrast, the MDR took eighteen posts, including all those in the central prefecture of Gitarama, the stronghold in the 1960s of the Parmehutu party, of which the MDR was the direct descendant. The PSD and the PL divided the rest of the posts, all of them in the south.The results represented only a rough approximation of political strength—and in somewhat less than a third of the communes in the country.[54] But,

---

[52]Ibid., pp. 178-79.

[53]Ibid., p. 182.

[54]In a second election of the same kind in September 1993, the MRND won all eight places being contested, but once again, these were all in the north. Reyntjens, *L'Afrique des Grands Lacs,* p. 227. Our statistics for the earlier elections differ slightly from those given by Reyntjens, p. 226, and are based on a tally provided by Rwandan government sources at the time.

the MRND had also lost burgomasters—and others—who had switched parties in communes where no elections were held. Habyarimana and his party would have to win back followers or build solid alliances with other parties if they were to hope to dominate political life. Habyarimana would clearly be strongest if he were to win back support from adherents of the MDR, PSD, and PL and at the same time attract backing from those who had joined the CDR.

At the same time as Habyarimana was working to put together a new coalition, a promising and well-connected young politician named Emmanuel Gapyisi was also exploring a realignment of political forces across party lines in a new group called the Peace and Democracy Forum (*Forum Paix et Démocratie*). A leader of the MDR from Gikongoro prefecture, Gapyisi hoped to bring together all those who were equally opposed to the RPF and to Habyarimana, regardless of party affiliation. He attracted a number of restless politicians, among them several who had been engaged in discussions with Habyarimana in March, including Murego of the MDR and Mbonampeka of the PL. Just as Gapyisi's movement was beginning to gather steam, he was assassinated on May 18, 1993 by a very efficient hit-squad. With his death, the Forum movement collapsed, leaving the field open to the original actors. Habyarimana used the assassination to try to discredit his political adversaries and accused the RPF and some MDR leaders of the killing. They in turn charged Habyarimana with the crime, an allegation substantiated by an investigation but never brought to court.[55]

Gapyisi's assassination focused attention on the increased insecurity and the continuing impunity for both political and common crime. After Gapyisi's killing, attempts were made to slay PL leader Stanislas Mbonampeka, CDR leader Dr. Céléstin Higiro, and Defense Minister Gasana. Soldiers in Kigali were killing civilians at the rate of four or five a day and did not hesitate even to strangle a man at noon in front of the Kigali post office, then walk off leaving his corpse behind. Abuses by soldiers reached such a level that Habyarimana himself found it necessary to criticize military misconduct in a speech to sector commandants on March 13, 1993. Random violence continued as well, with bombs exploding at markets and other public places in Butare, Gisenyi, and Kigali. Tutsi in some rural communes were so afraid of night-time attacks that they regularly slept outdoors

---

[55]Guichaoua, *Les Crises Politiques,* p. 629; Prunier, *The Rwanda Crisis,* pp. 182-85.

instead of at home.[56] A number of local administrators cited the growing insecurity as a reason for requesting permission to own a gun or to obtain a gun from the Ministry of Defense.[57]

Efforts at compiling lists of enemies continued during these months. Col. Nsabimana told a family member that a list of some 500 people to be killed existed in April 1993.[58] In a secret memorandum to all commanders, Col. Athanase Gasake, temporarily replacing Nsabimana as chief of staff, distributed the names of families whose sons had purportedly left to join the RPF. He reported that the Collège APACOPE in Kigali was a hotbed of RPF activity and noted that its students could not be bothered now because the government was on the point of signing a peace agreement with the RPF, but that the appropriate services had identified them and recorded their names. He also warned of infiltrators who were operating as household help, clerks, watchmen, tailors, prostitutes, traders, and especially taxi drivers. In an exaggerated way, the memorandum stressed the possibility of imminent attack from Uganda, Tanzania, Burundi, Zaire, or all four at once and urged the officers to communicate the need for constant vigilance to all their soldiers.[59]

Against this background of unpunished abuses and preparations for further violence, the prime minister wrote to Habyarimana, accusing him of wanting to cause troubles inside Rwanda and to start the war again in order to get a settlement that would protect his own power:

---

[56]Africa Watch, "Beyond the Rhetoric," pp. 7-14; Joseph Matata, Permanent Secretary of ARDHO to Alison Des Forges, May 12, 1993; Human Rights Watch/FIDH interview, by telephone, Lausanne, August 29, 1996.

[57]James Gasana, Ministre de la Défense, to Monsieur le Préfet (Tous), no. 0655/06.1., February 23, 1993; Ministre de la Défense to Monsieur le Ministre de l'Intérieur et du Développement Communal, no. 0895/06.1.0, March 10, 1993; Laurent Bucyibaruta, Préfet to Monsieur le Bourgmestre, no. 483/04.06, May 19, 1993; Jean Baptiste Hakizamungu, Sous-préfet, to Monsieur le Ministre de la Défense, February 12, 1993; James Gasana, Ministre de la Défense, to Monsieur Hakizamungu Jean Baptiste, no. 913/06.1.9, March 11, 1993 (Butare and Gikongoro prefectures).

[58]Marie-France Cros, "Jean Birara: 'Belges et Français auraient pu arrêter les tueries.'" *La Libre Belgique*, May 24, 1994.

[59]Col. Athanase Gasake Chef EM AR(ai) to Liste A, Comdt Sect OPS (Tous), May 21, 1993 (CRDDR).

Terrorist groups are now preparing attacks on various politicians and disturbances throughout the country to try to start the war again. In other words, you feel you must find a subterfuge that would enable you to avoid signing the peace agreement, to bring about the resignation of the present government—so as to put in place a bellicose government devoted to you—to begin the hostilities again in an effort to push the RPF troops back to their former positions...and to demand the renegotiation of certain terms of the protocols that have been signed already.[60]

The violence feared by Nsengiyaremye was not launched immediately, perhaps because Habyarimana had not yet pulled enough dissidents back to his side. In mid-July, Habyarimana and his supporters moved nearer that goal when the MDR, the chief threat to the MRND, split apart. The immediate issue was replacing Nsengiyaremye, whose mandate as prime minister had ended, but this question covered a larger struggle for control of the party—complicated by personal ambitions—and a division over the issue of how far to trust the RPF. As the prospects for peace grew, politicians looked forward to the distributions of posts that would take place when a transitional government was formed and they sought to position themselves as advantageously as possible. The president of the MDR, Faustin Twagiramungu, who stood for continued cooperation with the RPF, named Agathe Uwilingiyimana, minister of primary and secondary education, as the party's choice for prime minister. Dissident leaders like Donat Murego and Frodouald Karamira, suspicious of the RPF since its February attack, challenged Twagiramungu's control at a national congress. They designated Jean Kambanda, a lesser known politician from Butare, as the party choice for prime minister.[61] They went so far as to expel both Twagiramungu and his nominee Uwilingiyimana from the party. Twagiramungu ignored the dissidents' effort to expel him and continued to regard himself as the president of the party, while the dissidents, greater in numbers by far than Twagiramungu's supporters, claimed that they were in fact the MDR.

Habyarimana accepted Twagiramungu's nomination of Uwilingyimana and rejected the protests of the dissidents, seeing this as a way to widen the gap

---

[60]Dismas Nsengiyaremye, Premier Ministre, to Monsieur le Président de la République Rwandaise, no. 528/02.0, June 6, crossed out and replaced by July 6, 1993 (ARDHO).

[61]Disappointed at this time, Kambanda would later serve as prime minister of the interim government.

between the two parts of the MDR. On July 18, 1993, the new government was established with Uwilingiyimana as prime minister, the first woman to serve in this capacity, and the struggle over which part of the MDR was the *real* MDR was moved to the courts. On July 19, James Gasana, who was supposed to continue in his post as minister of defense, fled to Europe, to be followed not long after by the former prime minister, Dismas Nsengiyaremye. Both said their lives were threatened. They no doubt had in mind recent assassinations, attempted assassinations, massacres and random violence when they decided it was too dangerous to stay in Rwanda, but perhaps they also knew more than most others about the risk of future violence.

French Support for Habyarimana

From the outset of the war with the RPF, Rwanda had been firmly backed by France. Able to rely on this steady support from a major international actor, Habyarimana was in a strong position to confront threats from the RPF, reproaches from other foreign powers, and opposition from dissidents within Rwanda. Fluent in French, apparently a devout Catholic, Habyarimana impressed French president François Mitterrand and others with his assimilation of French values. In the French system, where the president exercised enormous control over African policy, Mitterrand's bond with Habyarimana counted for a great deal. The French ambassador in Kigali, Georges Martres, also was close to Habyarimana, whose home he visited frequently. Habyarimana found his support so precious that he wrote Mitterrand in January 1993 asking that Martres not be retired for reasons of age, as French regulations required, but rather allowed to continue his service in Kigali. Mitterrand, to his regret, could prolong his term only until April 1993. High-ranking military officers, both those in the field and those in Paris, were strongly committed to helping their Rwandan colleagues fight a force that some of them labeled the "Khmers Noirs," a reference to the Khmer Rouge terrorists in Cambodia. The French Foreign Ministry officials were less enthusiastic about the Rwandan president; but they could do little to change policy so long as he enjoyed the firm support of Mitterrand and the military.[62]

The readiness to back Habyarimana rested on broader bases than personal connections. Mitterrand, like many French policy-makers, believed that France must continue to have strong links with African allies if it were to have any stature on the international scene. By definition, such allies were French-speaking. Among them, Rwanda had a special status because it was not a former French colony, but

---

[62]Jouan, "Rwanda 1990-1994," p. 23.

an ally that had been won away from Belgium, its old colonial master. Backing Rwanda offered the chance not just to outdo Belgium but also to humiliate the Anglo-Saxon forces thought to be behind the largely English-speaking RPF. According to former French minister Bernard Debré, Mitterrand believed that the U.S. had "hegemonic aims" in the region.[63] François Leotard, former minister of defense, agreed with this assessment. He told members of the French assembly,

> The President of the Republic was the person who in his comments seemed to define best the balance of power between the Anglo-Saxons and the French in this part of the world, and to do so with the greatest precision and sense of strategy and history.[64]

This reasoning, so redolent of nineteenth-century colonial passions, seems in fact to have motivated much of French policy about Rwanda. The French dreaded an upset in Rwanda, which they had come to regard as part of their backyard, *le pré carré*. If Habyarimana were to lose, it would be the first time that a regime loyal to France had been removed without prior French approval. Powerholders dependent upon French support elsewhere on the continent were watching the outcome carefully and might judge the usefulness of a continuing French alliance according to the result.[65] Gérard Prunier, an analyst well-informed about the French Defense Ministry, has suggested that Habyarimana may have helped France with some illegitimate business in the past, perhaps passing on arms shipments to embargoed countries, and thus made the French feel more obligated to support him.[66]

In addition to these general considerations, French policymakers also supported Rwanda in order to have a firm base for dealing with potential crises in Zaire. In January 1993, a report by the Treasury concluded that "with the risks of

---

[63]Assemblée Nationale, Mission d'information commune, *Enquête*, Tome III, Auditions, Volume 1, p. 413.

[64]Ibid., p. 112.

[65]Hubert Vedrine, minister of foreign affairs, expressed such a concern. Ibid., p. 212.

[66]Prunier, *The Rwanda Crisis*, pp. 102-6, 147-49, 163-64, 278-79; Reyntjens, *L'Afrique des Grands Lacs*, pp. 178-79.

Zaire disintegrating, Rwanda remains an interesting pole of political and economic influence in the region."[67]

Habyarimana and his supporters appreciated French backing and welcomed French troops warmly. In the December 1990 issue where *Kangura* presented the "Ten Commandments of the Hutu," it printed a picture of Mitterrand on the back cover with the comment, "It is in hard times that you know your real friends." When the CDR demonstrated against peace negotiations in October 1992, they acknowledged French support by chanting "Thank you, President Mitterrand" and "Thank you, French people."[68]

Besides steady political and moral backing, France gave Rwanda more immediately practical help, a contingent of soldiers in October 1990 and reinforcements in later times of crisis. Although French authorities generally asserted that only some 600 soldiers were in Rwanda, they in fact maintained as many as 1,100 there at one time.[69] The troops included two groups, one called the Noroît detachment, supposedly there to protect French citizens, and the other, a military assistance mission to "train" Rwandan soldiers. The "protection of French citizens" was only a cover—the French numbered only a few hundred and were not threatened—but the training was real. As the Rwandan army expanded from fewer than 10,000 to more than 30,000 soldiers, the French played an important role in training both the combatants and soldiers who would in turn serve as instructors for others. Some of these French-trained soldiers passed on their knowledge to the party militia Interahamwe and Impuzamugambi.[70]

French soldiers sometimes delivered their "training" in a surprisingly direct manner. On February 3, 1992, the Rwandan Ministry of Foreign Affairs wrote to the French embassy in Kigali to ask approval for naming Lieutenant Colonel

---

[67]Jouan, "Rwanda, 1990-1994," p. 24.

[68]Prunier, *The Rwanda Crisis*, p. 163.

[69]Ibid., p. 164, n. 9.

[70]Several foreign diplomats based in Kigali, who had seen French soldiers at a militia training site at Gabiro, in the game park in eastern Rwanda, even asserted that the French themselves had trained militia. Prunier, usually well-informed about French military matters, has said that the French may well have trained militia without distinguishing them from regular recruits, who were receiving training so summary that it differed little from that given to the irregulars. Adelman and Suhrke, *Early Warning,* p. 87, n. 50; Human Rights Watch/FIDH interview, Washington, December 9, 1995.

Chollet, head of the French military assistance mission, adviser to Habyarimana. In this capacity, Chollet would advise on "organization of the defense and on the operations of the military," duties which would require him to "work in close collaboration" with officers even at the local level. The arrangement would have effectively placed responsibility for military operations in French hands. The letter was leaked to the press and the proposal seemed to have been aborted. But, in April 1992, Lt. Col. Jean-Jacques Maurin was named adjoint to the French military attache in Kigali and filled just the role proposed for Chollet. He advised the Rwandan chief of staff in such tasks as drawing up daily battle plans, accompanied him around the country, and participated in daily meetings of the general staff.[71] In addition, French soldiers on the ground were assisting in combat, in interrogating military prisoners, and in enforcing control measures on the civilian population.[72] A former French army chief of staff later denied that French troops joined in fighting, but admitted that, given the small size of the country, French troops were "close to combat."[73] The former Rwandan minister of defense, James Gasana, stated that Rwandan military could use heavy weapons given by France only after having received French permission to use them.[74] According to one French "instructor," French trainers positioned the heavy artillery to bombard the RPF and then stood back to let Rwandan soldiers push the button to fire the weapon. French soldiers played such a key role in defending Ruhengeri in January 1991 that a

---

[71]Guichaoua, *Les Crises Politiques*, pp. 712-13; Assemblée Nationale, Mission d'information commune, *Enquête*, Tome I, Rapport, pp. 151-52.

[72]Testimony of Eric Gillet, reported in *L'événement du Jeudi*, June 25-July 2, 1992; Assemblée Nationale, Mission d'information commune, *Enquête*, Tome I, Rapport, pp. 158-68.

[73]Testimony of Amiral Lanxade, Mission d'Information, May 6, 1998; Assemblée Nationale, Mission d'information commune, *Enquête*, Tome III, Auditions, Volume 1, p. 241.

[74]Assemblée Nationale, Mission d'information commune, *Enquête*, Tome III, Auditions, Volume 2, p. 47.

French commander asked the Rwandan government to award medals to some of the troops.[75]

France officially supported peace efforts and was one of the sponsors of the Arusha Accords which stipulated the withdrawal of all foreign troops, except those involved in bilateral military cooperation arrangements. According to Gasana, however, who participated in some of the Arusha negotiations, the French were far less intent on a negotiated solution than were the U.S. and Belgium. Their support for Habyarimana and the MRND was such that they gave the impression that they actually favored a military solution to the conflict.[76] On August 26, 1992, three weeks after the first part of the Accords was signed, Ambassador Martres formally agreed with the Rwandan government to expand the limited French military training program to the whole Rwandan army, making it possible to increase the number of "instructors" while removing combat troops. On January 18, 1993, Mitterrand addressed the delicate problem of continued military assistance in a letter to Habyarimana. Remarking that he would not want France to be reproached with having undermined the Arusha Accords, he continued, "I wish to confirm that on the question of the presence of the Noroît detachment [the combat troops], France will act in accord with [the wishes of] the Rwandan authorities."[77]

In February 1993 French authorities once more proved their support by sending more than 500 troops to "indirectly command" and assist the Rwandan forces in halting the RPF advance.[78] They also stepped up delivery of arms and ammunition, sending up to twenty tons of arms a day, enough to cut into the stocks

---

[75]Human Rights Watch Arms Project, "Arming Rwanda," p. 24; Reyntjens, *L'Afrique des Grands Lacs,* pp. 176-77; Prunier, *The Rwanda Crisis*, pp. 149, 177; Adelman and Suhrke, *Early Warning*, pp. 22-23 and notes; Stephen Smith, "France-Rwanda: Lévirat Colonial et Abandon Dans la Région des Grands Lacs," in Guichaoua, *Les Crises Politiques*, p.450; Guichaoua, on pages 720-21, reprints the important account of French military activity by Hervé Gattegno, published in *Le Monde*, September 22, 1994.

[76]Assemblée Nationale, Mission d'information commune, *Enquête*, Tome III, Auditions, Volume 2, p. 53.

[77]Guichaoua, *Les Crises Politiques,* p. 714; Reyntjens, *L'Afrique des Grands Lacs,* p. 205; Prunier, *The Rwanda Crisis*, p.173.

[78]Assemblée Nationale, Mission d'information commune, *Enquête*, Tome I, Rapport, pp. 157, 159.

of the French army itself.[79] After a visit to Rwanda to assess the situation, then Minister of Cooperation Marcel Debarge reported to Mitterrand that the "indirect military support" provided by France was not enough and that a "real intervention force" (une veritable force d'interposition) was necessary to enforce the Arusha Accords. Unwilling to have France supply such a force, Mitterrand then ordered his subordinates to get the U.N. more involved.[80] French diplomats worked so hard to get a U.N. peacekeeping force to replace its soldiers in aiding their ally that, according to one member of the Security Council, the effort became "a standing joke."[81]

From the beginning of the war in 1990, French authorities understood the risk of genocide. Colonel Rwagafilita, Habyarimana's close associate, told the general who directed French military cooperation in Rwanda that the Tutsi "are very few in number, we will liquidate them."[82] Many of the French who dealt with Habyarimana believed that he wanted to keep the extremists in check and could do so only with their continued political and military support. They were well aware of the massacres and other human rights violations carried out by his government and they pressed him—but only discretely—to end such practices. Reluctant to weaken their loyal client in any way, they sought to minimize any criticism of him. Thus Ambassador Martres dismissed reports of massacres as "just rumors"[83] and a supporter within the French Foreign Ministry wrote soon after the International Commission published its report that the Habyarimana regime was "rather respectful of human rights and on the whole concerned about good administration." In a shocking echo of extremist Hutu propaganda, this author explained that the RPF, and not Habyarimana, should be blamed for the massacres of the Tutsi, because their agents (provocateurs) had infiltrated and caused the Bugesera

---

[79]Smith, "France-Rwanda," p. 450.

[80]Assemblée Nationale, Mission d'information commune, Enquête, Tome III, Auditions, Volume 2, p.14.

[81]Adelman and Suhrke, Early Warning, p. 27.

[82]Assemblée Nationale, Mission d'information commune, Enquête, Tome I, Rapport, p. 276.

[83]Smith, "France-Rwanda," p. 451; Assemblée Nationale, Mission d'information commune, Enquête, Tome III, Auditions, Volume 1, p. 122.

massacre as well as the slaughter of the Bagogwe in 1991.[84] As part of an effort to shore up Habyarimana and discredit further the RPF, the French secret service (Direction Générale des Services Extérieurs, DSGE) planted news stories about supposed Ugandan support for the guerrilla movement. On February 21, 1993, the reputable *Le Monde* published an account of a RPF massacre of hundreds of civilians that had in fact never taken place.[85]

When the French National Assembly held an inquiry on Rwanda in 1998, French political leaders, bureaucrats, and military officers all declared that their policy was intended to encourage political reform and respect for human rights within Rwanda as well as to avoid a military victory by the RPF. On the basis of the unstinting support received from Mitterrand on down, Habyarimana and his circle concluded that the French valued the second objective more than the first. Thus convinced, they dared to continue the campaign against the Tutsi that would finally reach the point of genocide.

The Costs of War

Fragile at the start, the Rwandan economy had crumbled under the burden of the costs of war. In 1990 war-related expenses accounted for 15 percent of the budget, but by 1993, they consumed some 70 percent of the operating expenses of the state.[86] In 1993, agricultural production, the mainstay of the economy, declined 15 percent, partly because hundreds of thousands of displaced persons were no longer able to work their fields, partly because of poor weather conditions. Foreign assistance increased nearly 100 percent from 1989 to 1993, when it amounted to U.S.$334 million, to which was added some U.S.$130 million in direct emergency aid in 1993. The additional support notwithstanding, living conditions worsened dramatically, as per capita income that stood at U.S.$320 in 1989 (nineteenth poorest in the world) fell to U.S.$200 in 1993.[87]

Under the provisions of the structural adjustment program, government expenses were supposedly carefully regulated, both in amount and in intended use. To evade these regulations and escape supervision by foreigners, Rwandan officials

---

[84]Jouan, "Rwanda 1990-1994," p. 31.

[85]Prunier, *The Rwanda Crisis*, p. 176 and note.

[86]Mission d'information commune, *Enquête*, Tome III, Auditions, Volume 1, p. 165.

[87]Laurent, "Panorama Succinct," pp. 423-27.

diverted resources intended for civilian purposes to use by military or militia, such as buying military trucks with money allocated for civilian vehicles. Authorities at the Ministry of Health permitted Interahamwe to requisition vehicles from the ministry and to collect gas coupons each week for their fuel. Military officers imported luxury goods that escaped the high tax ordinarily imposed on such imports and sold them in special shops for profits that were used for the war effort. Authorities at the National Bank, under the direction of Habyarimana's brother-in-law, Séraphin Rwabukumba, reportedly hid deductions of foreign exchange used for arms purchases in a category of "errors and omissions." In addition, authorities apparently siphoned off funds from the government employees pension fund and other sources to fund military expenditures.[88]

Despite these various efforts, the Rwandan government was close to bankrupt by mid-1993 and desperately needed foreign assistance to keep operating.

Although the nation suffered enormously from the costs of war, Habyarimana personally seems to have profited from the conflict. According to one banker, the president earned commissions on arms sales and deposited the money in European bank accounts held by several of his associates and their children.[89]

The Arusha Accords

In July 1993, after a year of negotiations, agreement, disavowal, and then renewed negotiations, Habyarimana was still looking for ways to avoid signing the final peace treaty. He was finding it increasingly difficult to delay because even France was pushing him to accept the Accords. Habyarimana's most ardent supporters in the French military may have flinched little at the successful RPF thrust in February. But others, particularly those at the Foreign Ministry who had believed for some time that Habyarimana could not win the war, used the RPF military success to support their argument for a negotiated settlement. At the same time, a change of ambassador in Kigali in April 1993 removed one of

---

[88]Human Rights Watch/FIDH interview, Pierre Galand, by telephone, Brussels, March 27, 1997, based on his work and that of Professor Michel Chossudovsky; Frédéric Moser, "Rwanda: Comment le Nord a Financé le Génocide, *Télé Moustique*, No. 9/3708, February 19, 1997; Jean-François Pollet, "Rwanda: les fonds internationaux ont financé le génocide," *Demain le Monde,* no. 12/13, mars-avril 1997; Tribunal de Première Instance de Bruxelles, Compte-rendu de la Commission rogatoire internationale exécutée au Rwanda du 5 juin au 24 juin 1995, dossier 57/95 (confidential source).

[89]Tribunal de Première Instance de Bruxelles, Compte-rendu...du 5 juin au 24 juin 1995.

Habyarimana's strong supporters and in Paris the installation of Edouard Balladur as prime minister brought to power someone who cared less for African adventures than did his predecessor.

By late July, the donor nations—including France—had lost patience and used the ultimate threat. In combination with the World Bank, they informed Habyarimana that international funds for his government would be halted if he did not sign the treaty by August 9. With no other source of funds available, Habyarimana was obliged to sign along with the other parties, on August 4, 1993.[90]

The international actors celebrated this hard-won success, particularly important as the first peace negotiated with the assistance of the Organization of African Unity (OAU). Tanzania had served as the chief facilitator. France, Belgium, the U.S., Germany, Burundi, Senegal, Uganda, and Zaire had been represented throughout and the U.N. had sent observers for the final sessions. The international community so present in forging the treaty promised also to help implement it by providing a U.N. peacekeeping force.

The Accords appeared to have dealt with all the major issues in a detailed series of agreements that covered the establishment of the rule of law, the transitional institutions to govern until elections could be held, the repatriation of refugees, the resettlement of displaced persons, and the integration of the two opposing armies. They laid out a clear schedule for implementation of the Accords. In the broad-based transitional government, power was to be shared among three forces: Habyarimana and his group, the RPF, and the block of MDR, PSD, and PL, with the addition of the Democratic Christian Party (PDC). Habyarimana would remain as president, but would lose most of his power to a Council of Ministers, and in that body the MRND was to have only five of nineteen places, instead of the nine held previously. The RPF also was to hold five seats, but received in addition the newly-created post of vice prime minister. The MDR, PL, PSD, and PDC were to have nine ministries plus the post of prime minister, which remained in the hands of the MDR. The parties that composed the broad-based transitional government were also to dominate the transitional legislative assembly with a small number of additional seats allocated, one each for less important parties.[91]

In the integrated army, the Rwandan government was to provide 60 percent of the troops, but would have to share command posts fifty-fifty down to the level of

---

[90]Human Rights Watch/Africa interview, Brussels, February 12, 1994.

[91]Reyntjens, *L'Afrique des Grands Lacs*, gives a clear and complete analysis of the Accords, pp. 248-256. See also Adelman and Suhrke, *Early Warning*, pp. 24-27.

battalion with the RPF. The new army was to count no more than 19,000 soldiers and 6,000 national police, so both forces, the Rwandan army with more than 30,000 soldiers and national police and the RPF with some 20,000 troops, would have to demobilize at least half their military personnel.[92]

The carefully calibrated three-part division of power in the government made it unlikely that any one group could dominate and thus be able to disrupt the movement toward elections and real peace. But the hope of progress depended on each of the groups remaining coherent and able to act as a counterweight to the others. As the negotiators all knew, that was a doubtful premise given the division of the MDR just three weeks before the signature of the treaty. The Accords actually named Faustin Twagiramungu, head of the smaller of the two MDR factions, as the prime minister to take office when the broad-based transitional government was installed. This designation, approved by Habyarimana, permitted the signature of the Accords, but did not resolve the dispute within the MDR. The division in its ranks and the possibility that similar splits could take place—or could be caused—in other parties offered opponents of the settlement the chance to upset the whole peace process.

Opposition to the Accords
Even as the crowds were celebrating peace in the streets of Kigali, the radicals were hardening their opposition to the terms of the Accords. Two days after the treaty was signed, Belgian military intelligence reported much dissatisfaction among both soldiers and civilians, warning that "a wave of demonstrations, clashes and even assassination attempts" might begin within the next few days.[93] Many soldiers were angry that Habyarimana had yielded to foreign pressure when the army had not been decisively defeated. Despite their rapid retreat before the RPF the previous February, some continued to believe that the Rwandan army could win if the battle were begun again. Soldiers disavowed the accords for personal as well as for political reasons. With the planned demobilization, many would lose the chance to live relatively well—from exactions if not from salary. This was particularly true for senior officers, many of them of Habyarimana's age-group, who would be among the first demobilized because of their age. Colonel Bagosora,

---

[92]United Nations, *The United Nations and Rwanda, 1993-1996* (New York: United Nations Department of Public Information, 1996), p. 224.

[93]Sénat [Belge], *Rapport du Groupe Ad Hoc Rwanda à la Commission des Affaires Etrangères*," [Hereafter Sénat, *Rapport du Group AdHoc*] January 7, 1997, p. 22.

although already retired, spoke for those whose careers would be ended by the Accords. He was completely opposed to the agreement and scorned those Hutu who had signed it as "House Hutu and opportunists."[94] Presumably he included Habyarimana among this group.

Like the soldiers, some burgomasters and prefects feared losing their positions when the Accords were implemented. Administrators were to be subject to review within three months of the installation of the broad-based transitional government and those found to be incompetent or involved in prior human rights abuses were to be removed. Having seen a similar review process remove about one quarter of the burgomasters in February 1993, many administrators had no desire to expose themselves to the same fate.[95]

The CDR, opposed to the Accords from the start, had no place in the transitional institutions and continued to attack the agreement. Although CDR leader Jean-Bosco Barayagwiza held an important post in the foreign affairs ministry that had participated in negotiating the treaty, he visited the Belgian Ministry of Foreign Affairs two weeks after its signing to "explain the reasons why the Arusha Accords are unacceptable and why their implementation will bring even more bloodshed."[96] Radicals found their fears of Tutsi domination confirmed by the terms of the Accords, but even moderate Hutu, first disillusioned by the February 1993 attack, experienced growing concern that the RPF had gotten more than its fair share of power and might not want to continue cooperating with other parties.

In the months following the signing of the Accords, hard-liners pushed ahead with activities that appear linked to the "self-defense" program. In entries in his appointment book early in the year, Bagosora several times stressed the importance of controlling the flow of information to the public. In August the radio station RTLM began broadcasting, drawing listeners primarily with its popular music, building an audience for the time several months later when it would begin blasting forth propaganda and directives.

---

[94]Aboganena, "Bagosora S'Explique," p.18-19.

[95]Article 46, Protocol of Agreement on Power Sharing, Part I, signed October 30, 1992.

[96]Sénat, *Rapport du Group AdHoc*, p. 58.

Buying Machetes

If the war were to resume and a self-defense force were to be put into action, its recruits would need arms. According to an entry in the appointment book, Bagosora had foreseen being able to provide firearms for only one third of the recruits. The others were to operate with traditional weapons: spears, bows and arrows, and machetes. Spears and bows and arrows were not easily available on the world market, but machetes were another matter. Requests for import licenses from January 1993 through March 1994 show that 581,000 kilograms of machetes were imported into Rwanda as part of a larger quantity of 3,385,000 kilograms of metal goods including also hammers, picks, and sickles. Assuming the average weight of a machete to be one kilogram, this quantity would equal some 581,000 machetes or one for every third adult Hutu male in Rwanda. This was about double the number of machetes imported in previous years. These importations were remarkable not just for the extraordinary quantity but also for the identity of the importers. The most significant was Félicien Kabuga, a businessman from Byumba and friend of Habyarimana, to whom he was connected through the marriage of their children. Kabuga had built his wealth through the export of coffee and the import of a variety of goods, chiefly used clothing, food, and household goods. During this period, Kabuga ventured into large-scale importation of metal goods, including machetes, for which he received seven licenses for a total value of 95 million Rwandan francs, or about U.S.$525,000. One cargo of 987 cartons of machetes, weighing some 25,662 kilograms, was shipped to him from the Kenyan port of Mombasa on October 26, arriving in Kigali in early November.[97]

The only local manufacturer of machetes was Rwandex Chillington, a joint venture between Plantation & General Investments, based in the United Kingdom, and Rwandex, a coffee processing company. According to *La Lettre du Continent,* a Chillington employee said that in February 1994, the company had sold more machetes than it had during the entire preceeding year. The news account reported that Chillington officials found this so alarming that they had notified representatives of the United Nations peacekeeping force.[98] Sebastian Hobhouse, Executive Director of Plantation & General Investments, categorically denied this information, saying there was no increase in sales whatsoever during the first three

---

[97]Human Rights Watch/FIDH interview, Pierre Galand, March 27, 1997; Elisabeth Levy, "Un protégé de Berne a importé 25 tonnes de machettes au Rwanda," *Le Nouveau Quotidien,* January 16, 1997. Levy provided the copy of the receipt published here.

[98]*La Lettre du Continent,* no. 213, June 26, 1994.

months of 1994.[99] But, according to the production manager, quoted in the *Sunday Times*, the Chillington factory sold "an unusually high number" of the 16,000 machetes produced between August and December 1993 to two Rwandex employees, Eugene Mbarushimana and François Burasa.[100] Mbarushimana was secretary-general of the Interahamwe and a son-in-law of Kabuga. Burasa, a retired member of the armed forces, was the older brother of CDR leader Barayagwiza. Researchers from Human Rights Watch and FIDH questioned both the local manager, Joe Hazel, and Hobhouse about machete production and sales as well as about general operating procedures of the plant during these months. Hazel found Hobhouse's information that the company supplied only 5 percent of the local machete market (a figure that Hobhouse subsequently raised to 8 percent) to be far too low, but he refused to provide his own assessment without consulting London. Hazel declared that there had been no foreign manager of the plant for about six months before his arrival in March 1994 and that the plant had been managed by Rwandan staff with only occasional visits by foreign staff based outside Rwanda. Hobhouse, on the other hand, asserted that there had been no gap in resident foreign supervision.[101] These contradictions suggest that further investigation might produce useful information on the production and distribution of machetes in the months before the genocide.

Recruiting Supporters

In late 1993 and early 1994, hard-liners stepped up the recruitment and training of militia. As the training became increasingly public knowledge, Minister of Finance Marc Rugenera raised a question about it in the Council of Ministers. The minister of defense at the time, Augustin Bizimana, admitted that the training was going on, but said it was only to prepare the young men to be guards for the national parks and forests. In a document dated June 1996, Col. Bagosora and

---

[99]Human Rights Watch/FIDH interview, Sebastian Hobhouse, London, October 4, 1996.

[100]Jason Burke et al, "British Firm Sold Machetes to Hutu Killers," *Sunday Times* (London), November 24, 1996.

[101]Human Rights Watch/FIDH interview, Sebastian Hobhouse; Human Rights Watch/FIDH interview, Joe Hazel, by telephone, Kigali, April 26, 1996. Letter from Sebastian Hobhouse to Human Rights Watch, May 9, 1996.

Document: Receipt for the transport of 25,662 kilograms of machetes to be delivered to Félicien Kabuga, Kigali, October 26, 1993.

_____

S.T.I.R. - KENYA
TRANSPORTERS: S.T.I.R.S.A.

Lettre de Transport No. 0766 '93
Letter of Transport

CL. FOR TPT DEPT. (KIGALI)

Nature du véhicule-CAMION et REMORQUE / Type of Vehicle & Trailer: CAMION ET REMORQUE
Marque / Make: BENZ
Chargements / Loaded at: MOMBASA
Déchargements / Offloaded at: KIGALI
Plaque / Reg. No.: AB 8442 - LA 0392

Propriétaire / Owner: STIR (KABUGA FELICIEN)
Chauffeur / Driver: RABWARA GERALD

COLIT DATE	Marques et numéros des colis / Marks & Number of Packages	Nombre et nature des colis No. & Type of Package	Nature de la marchandise / Nature of Goods	Poids/Gross/KG Gross Wt./cnm.	Destination Consignee	Payable Payable at	COADHED
C34 no:0551 of 8.9.93	AS PER T.B. IMPLIC 010/88814-LC CDI 33380	987 CARTONS	MATCHETS	25662 kgs	from: STIR MOMBASA BRANCH-225/93-part-order of COMMER. BK OF RWANDA NOTIFY:KABUGA FELICIEN - BP 741, KIGALI R. RWN/4		
C34 no:1532 of 29.9.95	AS PER T.B.	2 FLTS	STEARIC ACID	1060 kgs	from:RELIANCE CLEARING AGENCY LTD NOTIFY: SACIRWA BP 44, KIGALI		
C34 no: 0526 of 1.10.93	--do--	1 FLT	PREVENTOL	130 kgs	Notify:RAMCO BP 555, KIGALI		
C34 no:1541 of 29.9.95	--do--	6 PLTS	ONYA VIOLET LABEL CRAIE	7308 kgs	--do--		

QUICONQUE FAIT LA COMMANDE DES SERVICES DE TRANSPORT DE LA SOCIETE ADHERE PAR LE FAIT MEME AUX CONDITIONS GENERALES DE TRANSPORT REPRISES AU VERSO DE LA PRESENTE.

FAIT A:
DATE: Oct 26 1993.'vcs

contents not checked

Déchargement terminé le

WHOEVER UTILISES THE TRANSPORT SERVICES OF THE COMPANY, ACCEPTS IPSO FACTO THE GENERAL TRANSPORT CONDITIONS ON THE BACK OF THIS DOCUMENT.

GOODS TRANSPORTED AT OWNERS RISK

S T I R
MOMBASA BRANCH

eleven others accused of genocide gave the same explanation.[102] When the burgomaster of Butamwa commune asked questions about militia training at a cassiterite pit in his commune in early 1994, the military trainers told him that the trainees were preparing for work with private security companies and that the training program had been authorized by Minister of Defense Bizimana.[103]

The radical military group AMASASU had proposed in their January 1993 letter that the Ministry of Youth join with the Ministries of Interior and Defense to mount the civilian self-defense program. The minister of youth at the time was Callixte Nzabonimana, an MRND member, who has been accused of participating in the genocide in his home commune. In mid-October, the Ministry of Youth notified burgomasters that it would henceforth provide the salary for youth leaders at the commune level. Such posts had existed in the past but had been eliminated in many communes because of lack of funds. The financial situation of the national government had not improved in the meantime, but the minister of youth had decided nonetheless that the services of professional youth leaders were important enough to justify subsidizing their salaries.[104] The subsidy allowed at least one of the communes, Nyakizu, to hire a youth organizer who was said to be an anti-Tutsi extremist and who may have assisted in the militia training programs that were carried out in Nyakizu in the months before the genocide. Youth organizers apparently continued to work throughout the genocide in Kibuye, when most other public services were not functioning.

Recruitment by the RPF

Not convinced that the Accords would be implemented, the RPF continued to enlist young people to be soldiers and trained them in the part of northern Rwanda under their control. At the same time, it intensified preparations for the political struggle. Since the start of the war, a small number of supporters had worked for the RPF within Rwanda, largely collecting money for the guerrilla effort. In late July or early August 1993, the RPF brought increasing numbers of young people

---

[102]African Rights, *Rwanda, Death, Despair and Defiance* (London: 1995), pp. 55-56; Théoneste Bagosora et al., "Le Conseil de Sécurité de l'ONU Induit en Erreur sur le Prétendu 'Génocide Tutsi' au Rwanda," June 1996, p. 13.

[103]Human Rights Watch/FIDH interview, Brussels, January 25, 1997.

[104]J.M. Vianney Habineza, Bourgmestre, Commune Maraba, to Monsieur l'Encadreur Préfectoral de la Jeunesse et des Associations, Butare, no. 472/04.09.01/10, December 21, 1993 (Butare prefecture).

to their zone to train them as political agents to broaden this network within the country. They prepared them with two or three weeks of theoretical and Marxist lectures on philosophy, history, and economics and then sent them home to gather information on local conditions and to organize sympathizers for the movement. According to witnesses who participated in or observed this program, only one day or one half day was spent on training in arms and most trainees were allowed to fire only one bullet. An apparently authentic notebook kept by a trainee and later captured by the Rwandan army substantiates this information. Of forty-seven pages of notes, only one and a half record information on guns, information apparently delivered in one two-hour session.[105]

RPF supporters organized several hundred cells during 1993, each including between six and twelve members. Leaders apparently insisted that each group include Hutu as well as Tutsi because they feared groups of Tutsi alone would be too easily isolated and attacked. If adherents could not attract Hutu participants, then the group was not to be formally constituted as a cell. Unarmed and virtually untrained in combat skills, these young agents hardly constituted a military threat. Even in the political domain, they did not yet threaten the Habyarimana regime. Some bolder supporters publically declared their affiliation with the RPF after the peace treaty was signed, but most still kept their preference hidden. Although the majority operated quietly, particularly outside of Kigali, the elite of Habyarimana supporters, military and civilian, knew they had arrived. Here, they said, were the "infiltrators" they had been talking about for so long.[106]

The United Nations Peacekeepers

The U.N. Security Council was still smarting under the failure of its peacekeeping efforts in Somalia when the request for a Rwandan force was presented. Members of the council were reassured by the detailed nature of the Accords and they were impressed that a joint delegation representing both sides had come to ask for a peacekeeping force. As one diplomat remarked, they thought

---

[105]Notebook provided by Solidaire-Rwanda, a nongovernmental organization close to the former Rwandan government.

[106]Human Rights Watch/FIDH interview, by telephone, March 22, 1996; Human Rights Watch/FIDH interview, Kigali, February 14, 1997; Commandement des Forces Armées Rwandaises en Exil, "Contribution des FAR à la Recherche de la Verité sur le Drame Rwandais," Décembre, 1995, pp. 39, 42-43.

"Rwanda would be a winner."[107] Had they consulted the diplomats who had extracted the signature from the reluctant Habyarimana, they might have had a more realistic assessment of the chances of future success. Partly because they counted on an easy success, partly because they were not disposed to invest much in resolving the situation in Rwanda anyway, the Security Council failed to devote the resources necessary to ensure that the hard-won Accords were actually implemented.

From the start, Rwandans and some knowledgeable foreign observers recognized the precariousness of the Accords. The longer the delay before the installation of the broad-based government, the greater the likelihood that the entire structure would collapse into renewed war. The Accords called for a U.N. peacekeeping force to arrive thirty-seven days after the signing of the agreement. As experienced diplomats certainly knew, it would be impossible to keep to such a schedule. It took three weeks beyond the thirty-seven days for the Security Council even to pass the resolution creating the force. Despite the warning by the U.N. secretary-general that delay would "seriously jeopardize" the agreement, it was another two months before substantial numbers of peacekeepers were in the country. As critical observers later commented, the Rwandan operation lacked a powerful patron among council members to force the normally slow pace of the U.N. bureaucracy. Only France had the interest to play that role, but its effectiveness was undercut by its close identification with the Habyarimana government.[108]

Resources and Mandate

Not only was the U.N. slow, it was also stingy. The United States, which was assessed 31 percent of U.N. peacekeeping costs, had suffered from the enormous 370 percent increase in peacekeeping expenses from 1992 to 1993 and was in the process of reviewing its policy on such operations. In the meantime, it was determined to keep the costs of the Rwandan operation as low as possible, which meant limiting the size of the force. One U.N. military expert had recommended that UNAMIR include a minimum of 8,000 soldiers. General Romeo Dallaire, named as commander, had asked for 4,500. The U.S. initially proposed 500. When

---

[107]Adelman and Suhrke, *Early Warning,* p. 35.

[108]Ibid., p. 36.

the Security Council finally acted on October 5, 1993, it established the U.N. Assistance Mission in Rwanda (UNAMIR) at a level of 2,548 troops.[109]

The UNAMIR budget was formally approved on April 4, 1994, two days before the beginning of the genocide. The delay in funding, in addition to other administrative problems, resulted in the force not receiving essential equipment and supplies, including armored personnel carriers and ammunition. When the killing began in April, UNAMIR lacked reserves of such basic commodities as food and medicine as well as military supplies.[110]

Constrained by the relatively small size of the force as well as by a determination not to repeat the mistakes made in Somalia, the diplomats produced a mandate for UNAMIR that was far short of what would have been needed to guarantee implementation of the Accords. In a spirit of retrenchment, they weakened several important provisions of the Accords. Where the Arusha agreement had asked for a force to "guarantee overall security" in Rwanda, the Security Council provided instead a force to "contribute to" security, and not throughout the country, but only in the city of Kigali. At Arusha, the parties had agreed that the U.N. peacekeepers would "assist in tracking of arms caches and neutralization of armed gangs throughout the country" and would "assist in the recovery of all weapons distributed to, or illegally acquired by, the civilians." But, in New York, diplomats conscious of the difficulties caused by disarmament efforts in Somalia completely eliminated these provisions. In the Accords, the peacekeepers were to have been charged with providing security for civilians. This part of the mandate was first changed to a responsibility for monitoring security through "verification and control" of the police, but in the end it was limited to the charge to "investigate and report on incidents regarding the activities" of the police.[111]

Paragraph 17

Rules of Engagement translate the general policy directives—the mandate—of the Security Council into regulations that govern the conduct of the soldiers. Soon after General Dallaire and his staff arrived in Rwanda, they drew up these rules for

---

[109]Ibid., pp.35-6.

[110]Human Rights Watch/FIDH interview, Plainsboro, New Jersey, June 14, 1996; Adelman and Suhrke, *Early Warning*, p. 36.

[111]Compare articles B1, B3 and B4 of the Arusha Accords with articles 3a and 3h of Security Council Resolution 872 of October 5, 1993.

UNAMIR. Like other such operations, UNAMIR was to use weapons "normally for self-defense only." The use of force for deterrence or retaliation was forbidden and self-defense, which was legitimate, was defined to mean "resistance to attempts by forceful means to prevent the Force from discharging its duties under the mandate of UNAMIR." The overriding rule was to be the use of minimum force. In accord with these directions, the force was lightly armed.

Dallaire specified that the maintenance of law and order was normally the job of Rwandan police, assisted, if necessary, by the U.N. police unit, UNCIVPOL. He added that it was "a very real possibility" that UNAMIR soldiers might be required to assist UNCIVPOL and local authorities in maintaining law and order.

In paragraph 17, Dallaire spelled out in extraordinarily strong and clear language the responsibility of the force if confronted with crimes against humanity. It reads:

> There may also be ethnically or politically motivated criminal acts committed during this mandate which will morally and legally require UNAMIR to use all available means to halt them. Examples are executions, attacks on displaced persons or refugees, ethnic riots, attacks on demobilized soldiers, etc. During such occasions UNAMIR military personnel will follow the ROD[112] outlined in this directive, in support of UNCIVPOL and local authorities or *in their absence, UNAMIR will take the necessary action to prevent any crime against humanity.*[113]

The first paragraph of the document indicates that these Rules of Engagement "are drafted by the Force, but are approved by the U.N. and may only be changed wth U.N. authority."[114] This document was a second version that included changes proposed in Kigali by Belgians and others involved in UNAMIR. Although the document was marked "interim," it was accepted by U.N. headquarters in New

---

[112]This is apparently a typographical error for ROE or Rules of Engagement.

[113]Force Commander, "Operational Directive No. 02, Rules of Engagement (Interim), File No. 4003.1, 19 November 1993, U.N. Restricted, p.7 (emphasis added).

[114]Force Commander, "Operational Directive No. 02," p. 1.

York and was not amended by it. It was circulated to the member states that provided troops to UNAMIR and was in effect at the time of the genocide.[115]

The Assassination of Melchior Ndadaye and Violence in Burundi

Had the situation in the region remained stable, there would have been at least some hope for actual implementation of the Accords. But it did not. On October 21, 1993, Tutsi army officers assassinated Melchior Ndadaye, the president of Burundi, setting off massive killings of both Hutu and Tutsi. This nation just to the south of Rwanda has a similar population of Hutu, Tutsi, and Twa, but had experienced a different political history, in part because Tutsi retained power after independence in 1962. Hutu had tried to win control several times, only to be put down by the Tutsi-dominated army, most savagely in 1972 when some 100,000 Hutu were slaughtered. In 1988, Hutu attacks on Tutsi had provoked excessive and unjustified military repression in parts of northern Burundi near the Rwandan frontier and tens of thousands of Hutu refugees fled into Rwanda. Under international and domestic pressure, the Burundi government then had initiated a series of reforms that culminated in a free and fair election in June 1993. The victor, Ndadaye, was the first Hutu to hold this office and his election was hailed as a great victory by Hutu in Rwanda as well as in Burundi. A moderate, he named a Tutsi prime minister[116] from the opposing party and approved a politically and ethnically balanced cabinet. Ndadaye moved to establish his party's control over the administration, but left the Tutsi-dominated army largely untouched. Hutu in Rwanda, where he had once been a political refugee, followed his progress with interest and pride. Those Rwandans who most feared the RPF were reassured by Ndadaye's election because, they believed, it would eliminate the possibility that a Tutsi-dominated Burundi government might permit the RPF to invade Rwanda from the south.

---

[115]Sénat, *Rapport du Groupe Ad Hoc*, p. 81. At a meeting in Washington on December 9, 1998, U.N. Assistant Secretary-General Alvaro De Soto asserted that UNAMIR troops used a different and shorter version of the rules of engagement which did not include paragraph 17. A senior UNAMIR commander, however, confirmed that troops were operating under the rules cited here, including paragraph 17. Human Rights Watch/FIDH interview, by telephone, Brussels, December 14, 1998.

[116]The prime minister was a capable economist, Sylvie Kinigi, the first woman to serve in that capacity in this part of Africa. The nomination of Agathe Uwilingiymana as Rwandan prime minister the next month created the remarkable situation of two women serving as heads of governments in adjoining central African nations.

Four months after the election, soldiers murdered Ndadaye and leading members of his government during an attempted coup. Although forced by apparently unanimous international pressure to return to the barracks and restore power to a civilian government, the soldiers had nonetheless taken the first step to a gradual reassertion of Tutsi control over the administrative system. In the days after the murder, Hutu retaliated, killing thousands of Tutsi, often at the incitement of local administrative officials. Under the guise of restoring order, the Tutsi army took savage reprisals, even in communities where there had been little or no violence against Tutsi.

The murder of Ndadaye and the ensuing killings worsened the situation in Rwanda immediately and dramatically. Moderates who had hoped that a peaceful transition in Burundi would show that Hutu and Tutsi could share power found it increasingly difficult to remain optimistic about the peaceful integration of the RPF into the government. Tutsi saw their fears of slaughter by Hutu justified once more and concluded that Tutsi control of the state was the only way to protect themselves. The CDR and MRND hard liners saw the assassination as irrefutable proof that Tutsi were bent on dominating the entire region and would use force, if necessary, to achieve that goal.

For the anti-Tutsi propagandists, the assassination of the Burundian president offered just the kind of tragedy most helpful to their cause. It gave RTLM the chance to establish itself as the most virulent voice in the campaign against Tutsi. Eager to whip up revulsion against the assassins, its announcer Habimana Kantano came on the air for the evening news declaring:

> Burundi first. That's where our eyes are looking now. Even when the dog-eaters are few in number, they discredit the whole family. That proverb was used by the [Burundian] minister of labor, Mr. Nyangoma, meaning that those Tutsi thugs of Burundi have killed democracy by torturing to death the elected president, Ndadaye. Those dog-eaters have now started mutilating the body. We have learned that the corpse of Ndadaye was secretly buried to hide the mutilations that those beasts have wrought on his body.[117]

The press, too, circulated accounts that Ndadaye had been tortured and, some said, castrated before death. Even the national television, not ordinarily much involved in such propaganda, displayed a bloated and mutilated body for hours,

---

[117]Recording of RTLM broadcasts, October 17-31, 1993 (tape provided by Radio Rwanda).

wrongly claiming it was Ndadaye's corpse. All the reports of torture and mutilation were false.[118]

Rwandans in the southern prefectures of Butare and Gikongoro were more directly touched by the killings in Burundi than people who lived further from the border. Some 300,000 refugees streamed into southern Rwanda in the weeks after the Ndadaye assassination.[119] They joined several tens of thousands of Burundians who had sought refuge in Rwanda following earlier episodes of violence. By the very misery of their existence in refugee camps, as much as by the tales of horror they related, these refugees showed Rwandan Hutu the damage that could be done by a Tutsi-run army.

Since at least the end of December 1991, several hundred Hutu guerrillas from Burundi had been living and training in refugee camps in Gikongoro.[120] With the arrival of the new flood of refugees, the training increased to such a level that a representative of the U.N. High Commissioner for Refugees wrote to the Rwandan authorities, reminding them that such activities violated international agreements on refugees. In late November, Prime Minister Uwilingiyimana visited the largest camps to insist that the training stop.[121] Camp directors and local authorities ignored her orders. The training even expanded to include recruits from Rwandan militia. By January, many diplomats in Kigali had heard reports of the training

---

[118]Human Rights Watch, the International Federation of Human Rights Leagues, SOS-Torture, and the Human Rights League of the Great Lakes organized an international commission of inquiry similar to that which had documented abuses in Rwanda. The commission arranged for an autopsy by a forensic physician who found that Ndadaye had been killed by several blows of a sharp instrument, probably a bayonet. The body had not been mutilated and showed no signs of torture. See Commission Internationale d'Enquete sur les Violations des Droits de l'Homme au Burundi depuis le 21 octobre 1993, *Rapport Final,* New York and Paris, July, 1994, Annexe B.

[119]Butare prefecture received the largest number, with 276,626 refugees in mid-November. Jean-Baptiste Habyalimana, Préfet, to Monsieur le Ministre de l'Intérieur et du Développement Communal, no. 1389/04.09.01/1, November 14, 1993 (Butare prefecture).

[120]Préfet, Gikongoro, to Monsieur le Ministre de l'Intérieur et du Développement Communal, December 19, 1991; Bourgmestre, Nshili, to Monsieur le Préfet, February 11, 1992; Laurent Bucyibaruta, Préfet, to Monsieur le Ministre de l'Intérieur et du Développement Communal, February 19, 1992 (Gikongoro prefecture).

[121]Telegram, S/Préfet, Busoro, to Mininter, no. 375/04.09.01/14, December 3, 1993 (Butare prefecture).

from representatives of international humanitarian agencies working in the camps.[122]

The murder of Ndadaye had great impact on the Rwandan situation in one further way: it showed once again that the international community was willing to tolerate slaughter in the pursuit of political ends. Once the Burundian army had bowed to international pressure and apparently returned control of the government to civilians, donor nations did nothing to insist that the guilty be brought to trial, neither those army officers responsible for the assassinations of the political leaders and the killing of other Hutu civilians, nor the Hutu administrators and ordinary people who had slaughtered Tutsi. Those most implicated in the killings continued to exercise power as they had before.[123]

In the days after the murder of Ndadaye, Hutu attacked Tutsi in many parts of Rwanda. They killed some forty in Cyangugu, twenty each in Butare and Ruhengeri, seventeen in Gisenyi, thirteen in Kigali and drove many others from their homes. Assailants tried to assassinate Alphonse-Marie Nkubito, a high-ranking judicial official and human rights activist who had frequently defended Tutsi, although himself a Hutu.[124]

Hutu Power

The movement known as Hutu Power (pronounced Pawa in Kinyarwanda), the coalition that would make the genocide possible, was built upon the corpse of Ndadaye. The doubts about RPF intentions, sown by the February 1993 attack and fed by the extent of RPF gains at Arusha, ripened following the assassination in Burundi. As one political leader commented during the genocide, "...Who didn't have his eyes opened by what happened in Burundi...[where they] elected President Ndadaye, who really wanted Hutu and Tutsi to live together, but you know what they did [to him]...."[125]

---

[122]Human Rights Watch/FIDH interview, by telephone, Washington, October 26, 1996.

[123] Commission Internationale d'Enquete, *Rapport Final.*

[124]CLADHO to Madame le Premier Ministre, October 29, 1993 and CLADHO, Memorandum Adressé à la Minuar et aux Missions Diplomatiques en Rapport avec les Tueries en Cours dans le Pays, December 8, 1993.

[125]Chrétien et al., *Rwanda, Les médias,* p. 294.

First announced at a meeting in Gitarama, Hutu Power drew widespread support at a rally in Kigali on October 23, 1993 where adherents met to deplore Ndadaye's assassination and to draw lessons from it. Present were members of the part of the MDR now resolved to reject cooperation with the FPR, members of the MRND and CDR, and even some Hutu members of the PL, increasingly sceptical of their party's link with the RPF. The second vice-president of the MDR, Froduald Karamira, took to the podium to declare that the RPF, including specifically its leader General Kagame, were among the plotters who had killed Ndadaye. Asserting that Kagame was depriving the people of Burundi of democracy, Karamira went on to say he would do the same thing in Rwanda because "he lied to us in Arusha when they were signing for peace and democracy..." Karamira called for all Hutu in Rwanda to stand up and take "appropriate action" which, he said, does not mean "uttering words just to 'heat heads,'" but rather unifying into one effective Hutu mass. Sounding very much like the MRND propagandist Mugesera one year before, Karamira reviled Twagiramungu, the MDR president who had been named to serve as prime minister in the transitional government, Agathe Uwilingiyimana, prime minister at the time, and Anastase Gasana, one of the chief negotiators for the Accords, calling them Inyenzi or "puppets of the Tutsi."

He continued, "We are not simply 'heating heads' by saying we have plans 'to work'...."[126] and then he told the crowd that they must help authorities "to look for what is within us. The enemy among us here. We cannot sit down and think that what happened in Burundi will not happen here, since the enemy is among us." Karamira insisted that Hutu who work against Hutu solidarity are also part of the enemy. "We have clarified what we must avoid. Avoid fighting another Hutu. We have been attacked, so let us not attack ourselves. Let us avoid the invasion of the enemy who may steal our government." In a conclusion that evoked wild enthusiasm from the crowd, Karamira shouted:

Hutu Power! MRND Power! CDR Power! MDR Power! Interahamwe Power! JDR Power! All Hutu are One Power!

---

[126]"To work" in this context means "to kill Tutsi," a usage developed in the 1959 revolution.

After each shout, the crowd roared its response, "*Power! Power! Power!*"[127]

The split in the Liberal Party, signaled by the attendance of some of its leading members at this rally, was formalized several weeks later. After months of effort, Habyarimana had achieved his objective of splitting two of the parties that opposed him. The politicians immediately responsible for the rifts were hardly naive pawns in the game. They made their choices knowingly, based as much on calculations of personal interest as on their supposedly more principled opposition to the RPF. Some members of the MDR would try to repair the rift in their ranks in December, but without success.[128] Rivalries among leaders troubled the PSD, too, but members would desert its ranks for the Power movement only after the genocide began.

With the consolidation of Hutu Power, party allegiances faded before the imperative of ethnic solidarity: political life was reorganized around the two opposing poles of Hutu and Tutsi. Hutu Power was the coalition that Habyarimana needed, but it was not yet his for sure. In his speech, Karamira had criticized the president, reiterating the CDR stand of the previous March that Habyarimana had conceded too much to the RPF. To take leadership of the Power movement, Habyarimana would have to carry through to its logical conclusion the position he had advocated since 1990. He would have to stand up to the RPF and rid the country of their "accomplices."

Hutu Power was to be implemented by the "popular army of strong young men" as sketched out by the AMASASU and by Bagosora the previous January. This army of self-defense was to supplement rather than to replace the party militia. Just a week after the Hutu Power rally, a commission of the Rwandan armed forces met to plan its organization. Perhaps aware of Bagosora's early caution that party considerations should be avoided in the distribution of guns, they decided that firearms should be distributed "within the framework of legal work" and that trainees who received them should be recruited so as "to avoid suspicions among the different layers of population and among political parties." They called for clear

---

[127]Recording of RTLM broadcasts, October 17-31, 1993 (tape provided by Radio Rwanda).

[128]The parts of the MDR and the PL associated with Hutu Power will be referred to as MDR-Power and PL-Power.

definition of administrative and technical responsibilities for what was now called "popular self-defense" or "civilian self-defense."[129]

At the end of March 1994, army officers—presumably members of the same commission—met again at the operations center to plan "defense of neighborhoods [and] the tracking down and neutralisation of infiltrators." In a letter to the minister of defense reporting on the meeting, Chief of Staff Colonel Nsabimana again echoed the ideas of Bagosora and the AMASASU. He specified that soldiers living outside their camps as well as former soldiers would command the recruits and, because the supply of firearms was limited, he proposed that the civilian population in communes outside Kigali should be instructed in the use of machetes, spears, swords, and bows and arrows.[130]

Rwandan military authorities writing later asserted that the new self-defense mechanisms were not yet in place when the catastrophe began. It appears that the system might indeed not have been *fully* in place by April 7, but what was already there served the intended purpose most effectively.

---

[129] Commandement des Forces Armées Rwandaises en Exil, "Contribution des FAR," Décembre, 1995, Chapitre V, L'Auto-Défense Populaire.

[130]Ibid.; Guichaoua, *Les Crises Politiques*, p. 514.

WARNINGS

The U.N. had to move first to implement the Arusha Accords: its peacekeeping force had to be in place in Kigali so that representatives of the RPF could also take up residence in the capital and begin to function as part of the broad-based transitional government. At the end of December 1993 UNAMIR had finally deployed nearly 1,300 peacekeepers in Rwanda, some 400 of them Belgian soldiers assigned to the capital.[1] UNAMIR was then able to escort the RPF civilian leaders, accompanied by some 600 of their soldiers, into Kigali. The RPF contingent was quartered at the national parliament building, the Conseil National de Développement (CND), an imposing structure set on a hillside a short distance from downtown Kigali. The choice seemed reasonable: there was no other space large enough and secure enough to house the troops. But it underlined how much the old regime had lost to the newcomers.

With UNAMIR in place, the next move fell to the Rwandans. Whether still hoping to win new ground through political maneuvering or whether simply to gain time for more preparations for war, Habyarimana—with the help of members of the Hutu Power block of the PL and MDR—launched a series of challenges to the interpretation of the Accords. He sought to assure ministerial posts for representatives of the PL Power and MDR Power wings and to get a seat in the transitional assembly for the CDR. He was most anxious to be able to count on one-third plus one of the total votes in the transitional assembly, the amount needed to block decisions of major importance—such as impeachment proceedings that could strip him of his power and leave him vulnerable to prosecution for past crimes.[2] The RPF refused all such initiatives. As one weary observer remarked, the struggle during these months was like negotiating the Accords all over again. The installation of the new government, originally set for January, was postponed to February and then postponed again to March 25, and then again to March 28, and then again to early April.

As the weeks passed, preparations for renewed conflict increased. The warnings of catastrophe multiplied, some public, like assassinations and riots, some discreet, like confidential letters and coded telegrams, some in the passionate pleas

---

[1] United Nations, *The United Nations and Rwanda*, p. 28.

[2] Cmdr. HQ Sector [Col. Luc Marchal, Commander of the Belgian contingent, UNAMIR] to COPS, no. 1554, January 15, 1994 (confidential source); Filip Reyntjens, *Rwanda, Trois Jours Qui Ont Fait Basculer l'Histoire* (Brussels: Institut Africain, 1995), pp. 17-18.

of desperate Rwandans, some in the restrained language of the professional soldier. A Catholic bishop and his clergy in Gisenyi, human rights activists in Kigali, New York, Brussels, Montreal, Ouagadougou, an intelligence analyst in Washington, a military officer in Kigali—all with the same message: act now or many will die.

In Kigali, diplomatic representatives followed events carefully. Belgium, the U.S., France, and Germany all had good sources of information within the Rwandan community and frequently consulted with each other, even though there was little formal interchange among their military intelligence services.[3] Like other U.N. peacekeeping operations, UNAMIR itself had no provision for gathering information about political and military developments. Belgian troops within UNAMIR, however, set up their own small intelligence operation and also gathered information informally from Belgian troops who were present as part of a military assistance project unrelated to the peacekeepers. Occasionally UNAMIR passed on confidential information to some of the diplomats, in one case only to find they already knew about it.[4] Diplomats rarely shared what they knew with the peacekeepers. Dallaire later commented on this in the Canadian press:

> "A lot of the world powers were all there with their embassies and their military attachés," Dallaire said. "And you can't tell me those bastards didn't have a lot of information. They would never pass that information on to me, ever."[5]

Obviously no one observer, whether in Kigali, in a capital abroad or at U.N. headquarters, followed all the ominous signs during the months before the genocide. But, as the compilation below makes clear, the warnings of catastrophe were many and convincing; although international decision makers did not know everything, they knew enough to have understood that disaster lay ahead.

---

[3]Sénat de Belgique, Commission d'enquête parlementaire concernant les événements du Rwanda, *Rapport*, 6 Décembre 1997, pp. 334-5 [Hereafter cited as Commission d'enquête, *Rapport*]. Note that this report reprints the report of the Groupe Ad Hoc of the Belgian Senate.

[4]Human Rights Watch/FIDH interview, by telephone, October 25, 1997.

[5]Allan Thompson, "Nightmare of the Generals in 1994," *The Sunday Star*, October 5, 1997.

Chronology
November 1993

Lt. Marc Nees, an intelligence officer with the Belgian paratroopers, among the first UNAMIR troops to arrive in Rwanda, reported that a meeting chaired by Habyarimana on November 5 at the Hotel Rebero decided "to distribute grenades, machetes and other weapons to the Interahamwe and to CDR young people. The objective is to kill Tutsi and other Rwandans who are in the cities and who do not support them [i.e., the Interahamwe and CDR]. The distribution of the weapons has already begun."[6] These measures may have been linked to the military meeting on "self-defense" held at the end of October.

November 17-18: Unidentified assailants killed some forty persons, including local authorities, in a highly organized attack in the northern communes of Nkumba, Kidaho, Cyeru, and Nyamugali. One attack was in the immediate vicinity of a U.N. military observer post. UNAMIR investigated the killings, but never published any results. This was the first case to suggest that UNAMIR could not in fact assure the security of civilians nor even bring assailants to justice.[7]

November 23: The human rights group, Association des Volontaires de la Paix, issued a statement describing attacks on civilians throughout the country, many by members of the MRND and the CDR. Among other measures, they recommended closer supervision of Burundian refugee camps to ensure that the international prohibition of military activity in the camps was respected.[8]

November 23: The CDR issued a press release calling for the resignation or dismissal of the president and prime minister if they failed to act following the killings of November 17-18. If they do nothing, the CDR said, it would consider

---

[6]Walter de Bock and Gert Van Langendonck, "Legerstaf wist alles over nakende genocide Rwanda," *De Morgen*, November 4, 1995, p. 1.

[7]Sénat, *Rapport du Groupe Ad Hoc,* pp. 69, 74; Commandement des Forces Armées Rwandaises en Exil, "Contribution des FAR," p. 24; Human Rights Watch/FIDH interview with diplomat present in Kigali at the time, by telephone, Washington, January 13, 1997.

[8]"Declaration de l'Association des Volontaires de la Paix sur la Sécurité au Rwanda depuis la Signature des Accords d'Arusha," November 23, 1993 (AVP).

them "accomplices" of the RPF. The CDR asked the "majority population" to be ready to "neutralize by all means its enemies and their accomplices."[9]

November 26: The Belgian ambassador in Kigali reported to his ministry of foreign affairs that RTLM had called for the assassination of Prime Minister Uwilingiyimana and of Prime Minister-designate Twagiramungu.[10]

A Belgian Red Cross truck was deliberately targeted by government soldiers and blown up by a mine.[11]

November 29-30: Unidentified assailants killed more than a dozen persons in the northwestern commune of Mutura.[12]

December 1993

Early December: Six buses full of Interahamwe trainees stopped to refuel at a military camp en route home from a training session at Gabiro. The officer in charge, unsure if he was authorized to provide fuel to the Interahamwe, radioed an inquiry to Kigali. He was later reprimanded for having asked his question over the nation-wide military communications network and having thus revealed official support for the Interahamwe. He then changed his story to say the trainees were park guards.[13]

Early December: UNAMIR received reports of suspicious movements by armed militia. It noted that RTLM was broadcasting relentless and increasingly inflammatory propaganda urging Hutu to stand up to Tutsi. U.N. representatives

---

[9]Communiqué du CDR, signed by Martin Bucyana, Kigali, November 23, 1993 (RPF Human Rights Committee, Kigali).

[10]Sénat, *Rapport du Groupe Ad Hoc*, p. 70.

[11]Ibid., p. 29.

[12]Commandement des Forces Armées Rwandaises en Exil, "Contribution des FAR," p. 22; Human Rights Watch/FIDH interview with diplomat present in Kigali at the time, by telephone, Washington, January 13, 1997.

[13]Human Rights Watch/FIDH interviews, January 26, 1996, Brussels, August 13, 1998; Adelman and Suhrke, *Early Warning*, p. 87, n. 50.

asked diplomatic missions in Kigali to become more actively involved in expediting the installation of the transitional government.[14]

December 1: The Rwandan human rights organization ARDHO published a report of recent attacks on Tutsi, warning that the assailants "declare that this population is an accomplice of the Inkotanyi because it is mostly Tutsi and its extermination would be a good thing."[15]

December 2: Assailants armed with machine guns fired on a UNAMIR patrol in northern Rwanda.[16]

December 3: Senior officers of the Rwandan Armed Forces wrote to General Dallaire, drawing his attention to recent killings of civilians at Kirambo, Mutura, and Ngenda and informing him that "More massacres of the same kind are being prepared and are supposed to spread throughout the country, beginning with the regions that have a great concentration of Tutsi....This strategy aims to convince public opinion that these are ethnic troubles and thus to incite the RPF to violate the cease-fire, as it did in February 1993, which will then give a pretext for the general resumption of hostilities."

The officers specified also that opposition politicians would be assassinated, including the Prime Minister-designate Twagiramungu and Félicien Gatabazi, head of the PSD. They remarked that Habyarimana himself initiated this "Machiavellian plan" with the support of a handful of military officers from his home region. They identified themselves as having been part of this circle until recently when a sense of the national interest "inspired us with revulsion against these filthy tactics."[17]

December 3: The Belgian ambassador in Kigali informed his foreign ministry that the Presidential Guard was training young men in three camps for "raids"on Kigali.[18]

---

[14]Anonymous, "Rwanda, Chronology," Document by U.N. staff member not otherwise identified (confidential source).

[15]Sénat, *Rapport du Groupe Ad Hoc*, p. 70.

[16]Ibid., p. 37.

[17]Anonymous to Monsieur le Commandant de la Mission des Nations unies pour l'assistance au Rwanda, December 3, 1993 (confidential source). The letter is reprinted in Guichaoua, *Les Crises Politiques,* p. 654, where General Rusatira is listed among the signers. Rusatira, however, denies having signed the letter.

[18]Sénat, *Rapport du Groupe Ad Hoc*, p. 65.

December 8: The human rights coalition CLADHO addressed a memorandum about killings throughout the country to UNAMIR and the diplomatic missions in Kigali. They asked that the militia be disarmed.[19]

December 17: A coalition of nongovernmental organizations working for development issued a press release asking the army to discipline its troops and calling for disarming and dismantling the militia.[20]

December 24: According to its mandate, UNAMIR was charged with contributing to the security of Kigali, which was to be free of weapons. On this date, the procedures for establishing the weapons-free zone went into effect. UNAMIR, in cooperation with the National Police, was to enforce the ban on weapons.[21]

December 27: Belgian intelligence reported on a meeting of military commanding officers held from 11 am to 3 pm December 22 in the office of Chief of Staff Nsabimana, promoted several months before to the rank of general. A number of officers were ordered to supply light arms, ammunition, spare parts, and uniforms to Hutu extremists. The report said, "The Interahamwe are armed to the teeth and on alert. Many of them have been trained at the military camp in Bugesera. Each of them has ammunition, grenades, mines and knives. They have been trained to use guns that are stockpiled with their respective chiefs. They are all just waiting for the right moment to act."[22]

December 28: The bishop and clergy of the diocese of Nyundo, in northwestern Rwanda, issued a press release in which they noted the distribution of weapons in their parishes and asked the authorities "to explain clearly to the public the use [intended] for these weapons that have been handed out recently."[23]

---

[19] CLADHO, Memorandum Adressé à la Minuar et aux Missions Diplomatiques en Rapport avec les Tueries en Cours dans le Pays, December 8, 1993.

[20] Consultative Council of Organizations Supporting Grass-roots Initiatives (Conseil de Concertation des Organisations d'Appui aux Initiatives de Base, CCOAIB), Communiqué de Presse, December 17, 1993.

[21] Sénat, *Rapport du Groupe Ad Hoc*, p. 83.

[22] Walter de Bock, "Belgische 'Wijkagenten' zagen voorbereiding genocide," *De Morgen*, November 4, 1995, p. 5.

[23] Msgr. Wenceslas Kalibushi and priests of Kibuye and Gisenyi, Communiqué de Presse, December 28, 1993 (ADL).

The Kigali prosecutor asked the help of UNAMIR in arresting Setiba, head of a militia group that had been receiving training by the Presidential Guard in the Gishwati forest. UNCIVPOL, the police attached to UNAMIR, undertook the mission but returned empty-handed because a detachment of Rwandan soldiers was camped in the vicinity of Setiba's house and appeared ready to protect him.[24]

With the installation of the RPF in the capital at the end of December, young people began taking political training courses in their Kigali headquarters. Others were recruited to go to RPF areas in the north for military training.[25]

January 1994

January 1-2: According to a report submitted by Belgian intelligence, Rwandan army units surrounded the CND building where the RPF were quartered and checked to be sure the building was within range of their weapons at those locations. They then withdrew to their own barracks.[26]

January 3: Belgian UNAMIR troops under the command of Colonel Luc Marchal seized hidden stocks of arms, ammunition, and explosives. But later they returned the weapons to the Rwandan army, which was said to have been their owner.[27]

January 4: The Belgian ambassador in Kigali reminded his ministry of foreign affairs about the distribution of weapons by supporters of the president. At a meeting the same day, Belgian officers had discussed the locations of stocks of arms and of training camps. This information was reported to General Dallaire.[28]

January 5: A crowd of CDR supporters attacked the Tanzanian ambassador whom they regarded as too favorable to peace negotiations.[29]

---

[24]Human Rights Watch/FIDH interview, by telephone, Brussels, January 26, 1997.

[25]Human Rights Watch/FIDH interviews, Butare, July 2, 1995; Kigali, July 13, 1996.

[26] Walter de Bock, "Belgische 'Wijkagenten' zagen voorbereiding genocide," *De Morgen,* November 4, 1995, p. 5.

[27]Document 6, Belgian Military Intelligence, January 8, 1994 (confidential source).

[28]Sénat, *Rapport du Groupe Ad Hoc*, pp. 61, 65.

[29]Adelman and Suhrke, *Early Warning*, p. 38.

January 6: In a cable to the U.N. in New York, Dallaire reported that UNAMIR had no proof of who committed killings in northern Rwanda in November, but "the manner in which they were conducted, in their execution, in their coordination, in their cover-up, and in their political motives, leads us to firmly believe that the perpetrators of these evil deeds were well-organized, well-informed, well-motivated and prepared to conduct premeditated murder. We have no reason to believe that such occurrences could not and will not be repeated again in any part of this country where arms are prolific and ethnic tensions are prevalent."[30]

January 6: The Security Council reviewed the situation, as was stipulated in the resolution establishing UNAMIR, to ensure that progress had been made toward implementing the Accords. It decided to deploy troops designated for phase II of the operation, even though the broad-based transitional government which was supposed to have been installed prior to the deployment had not been sworn in. General Dallaire requested the additional troops because he feared that violence might spread from Burundi to southern Rwanda and he wanted to post troops there. The Security Council stressed that continued support for UNAMIR depended on full and prompt implementation of the Accords.[31]

January 8: During a violent demonstration by Interahamwe—involving also the sub-prefect of Kigali and soldiers of the Presidential Guard in civilian clothes—the National Police did nothing to intervene. In a meeting afterwards, U.N. officers remarked that the events of the morning make "us think how few possibilities we have to deal with this kind of action." They acknowledged that UNAMIR might have to intervene more actively "to compensate for the lack of effectiveness of the National Police," even if doing so worsened relations with the population, which was already shouting anti-Belgian slogans that morning.[32]

January 8: Belgian intelligence reported on a January 7 meeting at MRND headquarters that reportedly brought together MRND president Mathieu

---

[30]General Dallaire to U.N., New York, Code Cable MIR 39, January 6, 1994 (confidential source).

[31]Anonymous, "Chronology-Rwanda," Draft document by U.N. staff member not otherwise identified, March 16, 1994 (confidential source).

[32]Service de Police Judiciaire auprès de la Justice Militaire, En cause de Dewez Joseph and Marchal Luc, Annexe A/5 au PV no. 1210 du 6/11/95; Major Hock to Maison Militaire du Roi Ministre de la Défense Nationale and others, February 2, 1994 (confidential source).

Ngirumpatse, Minister of Defense Augustin Bizimana, Army Chief of Staff Nsabimana, National Police commander Gen. Augustin Ndindiliyimana, and the president of the Interahamwe, Robert Kajuga, as well as agents of the secret police (SCR). In response to the UNAMIR arms raid five days before and to avoid further losses, they decided that weapons would be stored at the homes of army officers loyal to the MRND and that their owners would come get them when necessary.

The leaders decided also to remove all hidden arms to new locations and to order Interahamwe to fight, with stones if necessary, to defend the weapons from UNAMIR.

In addition, the leaders resolved to disrupt relations between Rwandan police and the UNAMIR officers who were working with them and to create trouble between the Rwandan population in general and UNAMIR, particularly its Belgian contingent.[33]

January 8: The association Professional Women United (Pro-Femmes Twese Hamwe), the human rights coalition CLADHO, and the council representing nongovernmental organizations working for development, CCOAIB, issued a declaration appealing to Rwandan and international leaders to implement the Arusha Accords rapidly. They deplored the insecurity in the country, including massacres and grenade attacks, the terror caused by the army and the militia, and the risk of resumed war. They called on politicians and the media to cease their incitation to hatred and "condemned unreservedly" the distribution of weapons to civilians by those who seek "to provoke a civil war that would be devastating for the country."[34]

January 9: General Ndindiliyimana explained to Belgian UNAMIR officers that the National Police had not intervened in the demonstration the day before in order to avoid confrontations "that would inevitably lead to losses, especially when the population had many grenades."[35]

January 9: RTLM broadcast that UNAMIR was opposed to the Interahamwe and Impuzamugambi and in favor of the RPF and parties allied to it. Such propaganda had begun sometime before in the written press and had stressed the

---

[33]Document 6, Belgian Military Intelligence, January 8, 1994.

[34]Pro-Femmes Twese Hamwe, CLADHO, CCOAIB, "Declaration des Collectifs Relative au Retard de la Mise sur Pied des Institutions de Transition Definies dans l'Accord de Paix d'Arusha," January 8, 1994 (CLADHO).

[35]Service de Police Judiciaire auprès de la Justice Militaire, En cause de Dewez Joseph and Marchal Luc, Annexe A/5 au PV no. 1210 du 6/11/95.

supposed success of Tutsi women in seducing UNAMIR soldiers, including the commander himself.[36]

January 10: A five hour meeting took place between leaders of the CDR and of the Palipehutu, an exiled guerrilla group from Burundi active in the Burundian refugee camps.[37]

January 10: Belgian UNAMIR officers met with an informant named Jean-Pierre, an Interahamwe commander, who offered to show the location of a weapons cache in return for protection for himself and his family. He said the Rwandan Armed Forces provided these weapons, as well as training, to the militia. He asserted that he could move the weapons wherever UNAMIR would like them put and that he could get back part of the guns already distributed. He also informed the officers that UNAMIR had been infiltrated with informers and that he was aware of everything that went on inside the U.N. forces. He revealed that the January 8 demonstration had been meant to provoke a confrontation with the Belgian UNAMIR soldiers, but that since no conflict had developed, he had never given the order to open fire.

January 11: Interahamwe and CDR supporters demonstrated again, with the participation of Ministers Pauline Nyiramasuhuko and Callixte Nzabonimana and authorities of Kigali prefecture.[38]

January 11: In a coded cable to Gen. Maurice Baril at the Department of Peacekeeping Operations in New York, General Dallaire passed on information received the previous day from Jean-Pierre. He reported that, according to the informant, the Interahamwe had trained 1,700 men, 300 of them since UNAMIR had arrived, in three-week sessions at Rwandan army camps. The training had focused on "discipline, weapons, explosives, close combat and tactics." Jean-Pierre stated that he had believed that the Interahamwe were to defend Kigali against the RPF. But since the arrival of UNAMIR [late November and early December], his superiors had ordered him to make lists of all Tutsi in Kigali, which persuaded him that the Interahamwe were to be used for a different purpose. Dallaire wrote:

---

[36]Document 7, Belgian Military Intelligence, January 9, 1994 (confidential source).

[37]Document 8, Belgian Military Intelligence, January 10, 1994 (confidential source).

[38]Human Rights Watch/FIDH interview, Brussels, August 13, 1998; Augustin Ndindiliyimana, "Témoignage à la Commission Spéciale Rwanda," Brussels, April 21, 1994, (*sic*) p. 20.

"Informant states he disagrees with anti-Tutsi extermination. He supports opposition to RPF, but cannot support killing of innocent persons." The informant estimated that the men he had trained, who were scattered in groups of forty throughout Kigali, could kill up to 1,000 Tutsi in twenty minutes. He had distributed 110 guns and had a stockpile of another 135 which he was willing to show to UNAMIR.

The informant confirmed that the January 8 demonstration, which he had commanded, had been meant in part to create conditions for killing Belgian UNAMIR soldiers, in the expectation that this would cause Belgium to withdraw its troops from Rwanda. He also confirmed that forty-eight Rwandan paracommando soldiers and some National Policemen in civilian dress had participated in the demonstrations for which the Rwandan army and the Interahamwe had provided radio communication.

In the chain of command, Jean-Pierre reported directly to the chief of staff of the Rwandan army and to the president of the MRND. Speaking of Habyarimana, he stated that "the president does not have full control over all elements of his old party/faction." He also warned, "...hostilities may commence again *if political deadlock ends*."[39]

Dallaire had some reservations about the "suddenness of the change of heart" of the informant and said the possibility of a trap was not excluded. Two days later he sent a UNAMIR officer to verify the information about hidden arms and found it to be accurate.

Dallaire informed New York that he planned to seize the arms within thirty-six hours. He concluded by saying, "Where there's a will, there's a way. Let's do it." Dallaire also asked for protection for the informant, who wanted to be assured of a U.N. guarantee before providing further information.[40]

January 11: The French military attaché, Colonel Cussac, and the Kenyan ambassador came separately to ask UNAMIR officers about evacuation plans for foreigners in the event of a serious crisis. They may have been reacting to the

---

[39]Emphasis added. As is shown above, Habyarimana and his circle often used massacres and other violence to disrupt a political process which was working.

[40]Outgoing Code Cable from Dallaire\UNAMIR\Kigali to Baril\DPKO\UNations New York, January 11, 1994.

demonstration on January 8 and to the latest failure to install the transitional government.[41]

January 12: Dallaire received a response from Iqbal Riza, writing over the signature of Kofi Annan, head of peacekeeping operations, stating that the UNAMIR mandate did not permit the planned operation against the arms caches. Riza directed Dallaire to discuss Jean-Pierre's information with Habyarimana and to inform the ambassadors of Belgium, France, and the U.S. He stated further that the U.N. could not offer protection to Jean-Pierre.[42]

January 12: The Secretary-General's Special Representative Jacques-Roger Booh-Booh, the diplomat reponsible for political matters for the U.N. in Rwanda, joined Dallaire in meeting with representatives of the Belgian, French, and U.S. embassies. In a fax to New York the next day, Booh-Booh and Dallaire reported that these diplomats "expressed serious concern about the alleged activities and indicated that they would consult with their capitals for instructions and would act accordingly." Shortly after talking with the diplomats, Dallaire and Booh-Booh met President Habyarimana and warned him that the Security Council would be informed immediately if any threat of violence were carried out. According to the fax, Habyarimana "appeared alarmed by the tone of our démarche. He denied knowledge of alleged activities of the militia and promised to investigate." The U.N. team went on to meet with the president and secretary-general of the MRND, who suggested that any problems—apparently such as those at the demonstration of January 8—came from "infiltrators and bandits" who hid behind MRND party insignia. Booh-Booh and Dallaire concluded:

> The initial feedback that we have received indicates that both the president and officials of his political party were bewildered by the specificity of the information at our disposal. The president of MRND seemed unnerved and is reported to have subsequently ordered an accelerated distribution of weapons.[43]

---

[41]Service de Police Judiciaire auprès de la Justice Militaire, En cause de Dewez Joseph and Marchal Luc, Annexe A/6 au PV no. 1210 du 6/11/95 (confidential source).

[42]Philip Gourevitch, "The Genocide Fax," *The New Yorker,* May 11, 1998, pp. 43-46.

[43]Fax from Jacques-Roger Booh-Booh and General Dallaire to DPKO, U.N., January 13, 1994 (confidential source).

Adding that the extent of UNAMIR knowledge of their plans might force Habyarimana and the MRND to "decide on alternative ways of jeopardizing the Peace Process," the force commander and special representative of the secretary-general said they would continue to coordinate their strategies with the ambassadors of Belgium, France, and the U.S.[44]

January 13: The Belgian ambassador in Kigali reported to his ministry of foreign affairs that UNAMIR would have problems acting against the Interahamwe because its mandate was limited strictly to peacekeeping. Any investigation would have to be done together with the National Police, but since many of them were apparently involved with the militia, such an effort would be futile. For this reason, Boutros-Ghali decided instead to do a rapid démarche to Habyarimana and to push him to act within forty-eight hours. The ambassador remarked that any action by Habyarimana was unlikely.[45]

January 13: Belgian UNAMIR officers discussed Jean-Pierre's information with the Belgian ambassador and later saw Jean-Pierre himself, who was still ready to share information and to indicate the location of the arms caches. The informant urged prompt action, saying that the weapons might be moved before Tuesday of the following week. A Senegalese officer of UNAMIR visited several of the arms caches with him, including one at the headquarters of the MRND. One of the Belgian officers concluded after meeting with the informant, "The situation seems more and more ripe and with the information in our possession, it seems really unfortunate to not be able to intervene. New York has not changed its position."[46]

January 13: CLADHO again appealed to the international community and Rwandan leaders to implement the peace accords and once more condemned the violent broadcasts of RTLM, the distribution of arms, the military training for militia, as well as numerous exactions of the Rwandan army.[47]

---

[44]Ibid; "Answers to Questions Submitted to Major-General Dallaire by the Judge-Advocate General of the Military Court," pp. 7-8 (confidential source).

[45]Sénat, *Rapport du Groupe Ad Hoc,* p. 85.

[46]Service de Police Judiciaire auprès de la Justice Militaire, En cause de Dewez Joseph and Marchal Luc, Annexe A/6 au PV no. 1210 du 6/11/95.

[47]CLADHO, "Memorandum Relatif au Retard de la Mise en Place des Institutions de la Transition Elargie Adressé aux Hommes Politiques Rwandais," January 13, 1994 (AVP).

January 14: Acting in the name of Dallaire, Colonel Marchal, who headed the Kigali sector of UNAMIR, asked the Belgian Ambassador Johan Swinnen to give asylum to Jean-Pierre and his family. After long discussion, the request was refused for fear of compromising Belgian neutrality within the UNAMIR force.[48]

January 14: The Belgian and U.S. ambassadors and the French chargé d'affaires visited Habyarimana to urge implementations of the Arusha Accords. The secretary-general had asked these diplomatic representatives to stress the urgency of acting on the information from the January 11 telegram, but they said nothing specific about it, apparently because the French opposed doing so.[49]

January 14: The secretary-general prohibited the operation to confiscate arms (apparently confirming the decision of his subordinates) because he feared an escalation that would force UNAMIR into a peacemaking rather than a peacekeeping role. According to the Belgian ambassador in Kigali, Boutros-Ghali was:

> concerned about the serious political repercussions that such an action would cause and therefore before beginning such an operation, there must be serious reflection....That is why New York insists on inquiries and measures from Habyarimana's side.[50]

If Habyarimana did not act, Booh-Booh was to report this to the secretary-general who was to report to the Security Council which would make all this public and take appropriate measures.[51]

---

[48]Col. Luc Marchal, "Considérations relatives aux conditions dans lesquelles j'ai exercé ma fonction de Commandant du Secteur Kigali au sein de la MINUAR (Mission des Nations Unies d'Assistance au Rwanda) du 04 décembre 1993 au 19 avril 1994" (confidential source).

[49]Sénat, *Rapport du Groupe Ad Hoc*, p. 41; United Nations, *The United Nations and Rwanda*, p. 32. According to the report of the French National Assembly, the three diplomats made a demarche to Habyarimana "in the same sense"—but not identical to—that of the U.N. representatives. Assemblée Nationale, Mission d'information commune, *Enquête*, Tome I, Rapport, p. 203.

[50]Sénat, *Rapport du Groupe Ad Hoc*, p. 86.

[51]Ibid, p. 86.

January 14: In Belgium, the military intelligence service briefed military commanders on fears that the Interahamwe might attack the peacekeepers, particularly those who were Belgian. They reported "Indeed, there are increasingly well substantiated indications of secret links and/or support to Interahamwe by high ranking officers of the Rwandan army or National Police."[52]

January 15: Colonel Marchal, who originally thought that Rwanda would prove to be "a textbook case" of peacekeeping, had become so concerned about the prospects of "grave troubles" that he asked his commanding officers in Belgium what role he should play in case of evacuation of foreigners. Would he keep his blue beret as a UNAMIR officer or would he act as a member of the Belgian military? He also urgently requested heavier arms than had thus far been provided to the force, foreseeing the need for such weapons if the airport had to be defended to assure a foreign evacuation.[53]

January 15: In a long message to his ministry of foreign affairs, the Belgian ambassador in Kigali reported that UNAMIR would have to act soon because otherwise the arms were going to be distributed to Interahamwe and other civilians. The ambassador expressed the opinion that UNAMIR regulations permitted Dallaire to seize the arms, but, he said, the commander was unwilling to act without explicit approval from New York.[54]

January 16: Four thousand to five thousand MRND supporters, many from outside the city, met at the Nyamirambo stadium in Kigali. The meeting looked like a general mobilization, but it was calm, with no indication of why it had been called. In one of the speeches, Justin Mugenzi, leader of the Hutu Power faction of the Liberal Party, played on ethnic divisions. Two days later, UNAMIR officers learned that arms were distributed at this meeting.[55]

---

[52]Ibid., p. 41.

[53]Comdr. HQ Sector to COPS, Nb Cir. 1554, January 15, 1994 (confidential source).

[54]Sénat, *Rapport du Groupe Ad Hoc*, p. 86.

[55] Marchal, "Considerations relatives," p. 14; Annexe A/7 au PV no. 1210 du 6/11/95 du Service de Police Judiciaire auprès de la Justice Militaire.

January 17: Booh-Booh told assembled African diplomats that "We have proof of the existence of training camps for many recruits." He added that weapons of different calibres had been distributed widely to the population.[56]

January 18: Because none of the countries contacted (Belgium, France, U.S.) was willing to offer him asylum, Jean-Pierre ended his contacts with UNAMIR but he continued speaking informally with a Belgian officer for several more weeks.[57]

January 19: In a letter to MRND ministers, Prime Minister Uwilingiyimana accused the minister of defense of refusing to implement the order of the council of ministers to collect arms that had been illegally distributed to the population.[58]

January 20: Assassins tried to kill Justin Mugenzi, president of the Liberal Party and head of its Hutu Power faction.[59]

January 20: The Belgian ambassador to the U.N. reported to his ministry of foreign affairs that he had met Iqbal Riza, the assistant to Kofi Annan, to voice Belgian concerns over the situation in Rwanda and over the safety of its troops. Riza explained that the U.N. had chosen a diplomatic approach to try first to make Habyarimana take responsibility and, if that did not work, they would inform the Security Council. Riza also said that Habyarimana's behavior should be evaluated in two areas: first, disarming the population and dismantling the stocks of weapons and second, forming the transitional government. He admitted that first reports from Kigali were not encouraging since the militias were apparently continuing to distribute arms to the population.[60]

January 21-22: A French DC-8 landed secretly at night with a load of arms including ninety boxes of sixty mm mortars originally made in Belgium but coming from France. UNAMIR discovered the shipment, which violated the terms

---

[56]Walter de Bock and Gert Van Langendonck, "Falende VN-bureaukratie werd blauwhelmen fataal," *De Morgen,* November 7, 1995.

[57]Commission d'enquête, *Rapport,* p. 253.

[58]Sénat, *Rapport du Groupe Ad Hoc,* p. 62.

[59]Anonymous, "Rwanda, Chronology."

[60]Sénat, *Rapport du Groupe Ad Hoc,* pp. 44, 87.

of the Arusha Accords, and put the arms under joint UNAMIR-Rwandan army guard.[61]

January 22: Dallaire again appealed to New York for a broader interpretation of the mandate.[62]

January 22: Belgian intelligence reported that RTLM was planning to install a new broadcast tower of 1,000 watts on Mont Muhe, in Habyarimana's home region, and that it had been assigned two new frequencies for broadcasting. It later began broadcasting from the new tower.[63]

January 24: Booh-Booh complained to the press that "weapons are distributed from arms caches around Kigali and even inside town."[64]

January 24: Interahamwe were arrested for bombing a house in Kigali and other Interahamwe rioted in the streets.[65] In a separate incident, assailants shot at Belgian peacekeepers guarding Booh-Booh's residence.[66]

January 25: The Belgian ambassador in Kigali informed his ministry of foreign affairs that Dallaire had appealed to New York for new instructions concerning the UNAMIR mandate, indicating that the force must either be allowed to enforce the ban on arms in Kigali more strictly or UNAMIR must be withdrawn completely.[67] He also reported a meeting with Donat Murego, secretary of the MDR, an intellectual of considerable standing who had become increasingly identified with Hutu Power. Murego warned that the Interahamwe were going to launch a civil war in which they would exploit hostility against the Belgians. He

---

[61]Ibid; Sénat, *Rapport du Groupe Ad Hoc*, p. 133; Filip Reyntjens, *Rwanda, Trois Jours*, p. 19.

[62]Anonymous, "Rwanda, Chronology."

[63]Document 12, Belgian Military Intelligence, January 22, 1994 (confidential source); Human Rights Watch/FIDH interview, Brussels, August 13, 1998.

[64]Adelman and Suhrke, *Early Warning,* p. 38.

[65]Anonymous, "Rwanda, Chronology."

[66]Sénat, *Rapport du Groupe Ad Hoc*, p. 38.

[67]Sénat, *Rapport du Groupe Ad Hoc*, p. 87.

blamed Habyarimana, the businessman Kabuga, MRND president Ngirumpatse and propagandist Nahimana for fostering this anger against the Belgians.[68]

January 26 and 27: Two grenades exploded at the CND building where the RPF were quartered.[69] In another incident, assailants fired on Belgian peacekeepers who were on patrol.[70]

January 26: MRND leaders, including Joseph Nzirorera, Edouard Karemera, Jean Habyarimana, and Robert Kajuga, president of the Interahamwe, reportedly met to discuss ways to create conflict beween Interahamwe and Belgian soldiers of UNAMIR. The militia were ordered to never obey orders from Belgian soldiers, to call Interahamwe from surrounding areas whenever confronted by Belgians, and to get as many local people as possible to witness the confrontation. The final order was to try to create "a collective psychosis" among UNAMIR troops by using all possible deceptions.[71]

January 27: RTLM broadcast a call for Hutu to defend themselves to the last man. After a long diatribe against UNAMIR, the radio station called on the population to "take responsibility" for what was happening because otherwise the Belgian soldiers would give Rwanda to the Tutsi.[72]

January 30: Colonel Marchal reported to his superiors that UNAMIR found it impossible to act effectively and that the troops of other nations in the force were of poor quality. After 924 mobil patrols, 320 foot patrols, and establishing 306 checkpoints, UNAMIR had collected only nine weapons.[73]

January 30-31: A Belgian soldier threw stones and broke windows at the home of Jean-Bosco Barayagwiza, the CDR leader, and supposedly threatened him. RTLM and Radio Rwanda both broadcast the news that Belgian soldiers had tried to kill Barayagwiza. The incident focused attention on the inappropriate behavior

---

[68]Ibid., p. 45.

[69]Anonymous, "Rwanda, Chronology."

[70]Sénat, *Rapport du Groupe Ad Hoc,* p. 38.

[71]Document 15, Belgian Military Intelligence, January 29, 1994 (confidential source).

[72]Document 14, Belgian Military Intelligence, January 27, 1994 (confidential source).

[73]Sénat, *Rapport du Groupe Ad Hoc,* p. 88.

of some Belgian soldiers who clearly showed their disdain for pro-Habyarimana forces.[74] In another incident, an assailant threw a grenade at UNAMIR headquarters.[75] The same day, RTLM broadcast that "the time has come to take aim at Belgian targets."[76]

Late January: According to a confidential source, a U.S. government intelligence analyst estimated the potential loss of life should there be renewed conflict in Rwanda. He reportedly described three possibilities, the worst of which would result in the loss of one half million lives. A colleague of the analyst told a Human Rights Watch researcher that this person's work was usually highly regarded but that his superiors did not take this assessment seriously.[77]

Late January: The Human Rights Watch Arms Project published a report documenting the flow of arms into Rwanda. After detailing the distributions of arms to civilians, it concluded:

> It is impossible to exaggerate the danger of providing automatic rifles to civilians, particularly in regions where residents, either encouraged or instructed by authorities, have slaughtered their neighbors. In light of the widespread and horrific abuses committed by Hutu civilian crowds and party militia armed primarily with machetes and spears, it is frightening to ponder the potential for abuses by large numbers of ill-trained civilians equipped with assault rifles.[78]

February 1994

February 2: In a thirteen-page memorandum on the Interahamwe to various Belgian authorities, including Lieutenant General Mertens at the Maison Militaire du Roi and the Chef du Cabinet of the Ministry of Defense, Belgian military intelligence summarized much of what was known about the militia. It described their plan to attack Belgian UNAMIR troops in order to get Belgium to withdraw

---

[74]Document 16, Belgian Military Intelligence, February 1, 1994 (confidential source).

[75]Sénat, *Rapport du Groupe Ad Hoc,* p. 38.

[76]Ibid., p. 46.

[77]Human Rights Watch interview, Washington, December 8, 1995.

[78]Human Rights Watch Arms Project, "Arming Rwanda," p. 27.

its soldiers from Rwanda, their targeting of Tutsi and members of parties opposed to Habyarimana, and their training and arming by the Rwandan army. The memo remarked that close links were reported between the Interahamwe and some Rwandan soldiers, particularly some in the Presidential Guard and the National Police. Noting that both Habyarimana and the president of the MRND denied the military activities of the Interahamwe, an intelligence officer concluded that the denials changed nothing and that there were strong indications that authorities close to the president of the republic and to the party were involved.[79]

February 2: Booh-Booh cabled New York that Habyarimana had done nothing to investigate or act on the security issue.[80]

February 3: Dallaire cabled New York:

> We can expect more frequent and more violent demonstrations, more grenade and armed attacks on ethnic and political groups, more assassinations and quite possibly outright attacks on UNAMIR installations...Each day of delay in authorizing deterrent arms recovery operation will result in an ever deteriorating security situation and may if the arms continue to be distributed result in an inability of UNAMIR to carry out its mandate in all aspects."[81]

In response, U.N. headquarters increased somewhat Dallaire's authority to make decisions on his own. It permitted him to assist Rwandan authorities in recovering weapons, but continued to insist that the mandate did not permit UNAMIR to conduct such operations alone.[82]

February 3: The Belgian ambassador in Kigali reported to his ministry of foreign affairs that UNAMIR was powerless and that it was urgent to halt the distribution of arms and to eliminate the stocks already built up.[83] The same day,

---

[79]Major Hock, Service Générale du Renseignement et de la Sécurité, to Maison Militaire du Roi, Ministre de la Défense Nationale, and others, February 2, 1994.

[80]Fax from Booh-Booh to DPKO, New York, February 2, 1994 (confidential source).

[81]General Dallaire to U.N., New York, Code Cable MIR 267, February 3, 1994 (confidential source).

[82]Anonymous, "Rwanda, Chronology."

[83]Sénat, *Rapport du Groupe Ad Hoc*, p. 88.

in Belgium, officers of the general staff informed the Ministry of Foreign Affairs that in their opinion the grenade attacks that caused insecurity in Kigali were the result of "an organized plan."[84]

February 6: Marchal and Dallaire suspended weapons searches at UNAMIR checkpoints following a number of incidents with Rwandan soldiers, the most recent with Chief of Staff Nsabimana himself. Marchal feared "a deliberate intention to create incidents with soldiers of the Belgian detachment."[85]

February 8: Marchal asked Dallaire to take action against the "continuous propaganda" of RTLM.[86]

February 11: Belgian Foreign Minister Willy Claes warned Boutros-Ghali that Rwandan leaders themselves "admit that a prolongation of the current political deadlock could result in an irreversible explosion of violence." He welcomed Boutros-Ghali's instructions to Booh-Booh to push harder for the installation of the transitional government and added,

> It seems to me, however, that this higher profile of the United Nations on the political level should be accompanied by a firmer stance on the part of UNAMIR with respect to security. I am aware of the complexity of the situation, and of the constraints imposed on you under Security Council resolution 872. Nevertheless, unless the negative developments we are witnessing are halted, UNAMIR might find itself unable to continue effectively its basic mission of playing a major supporting role in the implementation of the Arusha Peace Agreement.[87]

February 14: The Belgian ambassador at the U.N. reported that the reaction of the secretariat to the foreign minister's February 11 letter was "rather perplexed" because they had already authorised Dallaire to help local authorities collect arms

---

[84]Ibid., p. 71.

[85]Ibid., pp. 47, 89.

[86]Colonel L. Marchal to Force Commander, Nr CO/008, February 8, 1994 (confidential source).

[87]United Nations, *The United Nations and Rwanda*, p. 244, where the letter is dated 14 March 1994. The Sénat, *Rapport du Groupe Ad Hoc* publishes extracts in French, p. 89, and dates the letter to February 11. This date is confirmed in the *Rapport* of the Commission d'enquête, p. 242, n. 1.

and dismantle weapons stocks. Dallaire had not come back to the issue of a more active role for UNAMIR although the week before he had said he would make some concrete proposals.[88]

February 14: The first February issue of *Kangura* published a cartoon on its cover depicting the prime minister and the minister of finance as rats. Both were Hutu opposed to Habyarimana. A man is about to strike them with a wooden club studded with nails, a weapon that was often used in the genocide. The assailant refers to himself as "No Pity," recalling one of the Ten Commandments of the Bahutu which directs Hutu to have no pity on the Tutsi.

February 15: Dallaire and Booh-Booh again insist on the importance of recovering illegal weapons and ask for clarification of the mandate.[89]

February 15: Belgian military intelligence reported that the Rwandan army chief of staff had put all troops on alert, canceled leaves, ordered a check of stocks of ammunition and other war materials, and asked for recruitment of more soldiers.[90]

February 17: Senior officers of the National Police met with Habyarimana to express fears that war might resume. Habyarimana responded, "If the RPF begins the war, we have plans to deal with their accomplices." When they asked for details, Habyarimana suggested that Minister of Defense Augustin Bizimana brief them. Bizimana declined and sent them to the Army Chief of Staff Nsabimana. He too refused to explain the plan.[91]

February 17: In response to information from the secretary-general delivered on February 10 and February 16, the Security Council "expressed concern" over delays in establishing the transitional government and over the deterioration in the security situation. It discreetly reminded the parties to "respect the weapons-free zone" and warned that UNAMIR would be supported only if they rapidly

---

[88]Commission d'enquête, *Rapport*, pp. 380-81.

[89]Anonymous, "Rwanda, Chronology."

[90]Document 17, Belgian Military Intelligence, February 17, 1994 (confidential source).

[91]Human Rights Watch/FIDH interviews, Brussels, May 26, 1997, August 13, 1998.

implemented the Arusha Accords. In a blunter release issued in Kigali, UNAMIR called for an end to militia training and "massive arms distributions."[92]

Mid-February: The Rwandan minister of defense requested landing authorization for three planes carrying arms. UNAMIR refused.[93]

February 20: Assassins tried to kill Prime Minister-designate Twagiramungu and did kill one of his bodyguards.[94] In another incident, a crowd stoned Belgian peacekeepers and they had to fire 63 shots in the air in order to free themselves.[95]

February 20: Army Chief of Staff Nsabimana showed a relative, repected banker Jean Birara, a list of 1,500 persons to be eliminated in Kigali.[96]

Late February: Major Stanislas Kinyoni reportedly summoned the heads of National Police brigades in Kigali and told them to prepare lists of persons suspected of ties with the RPF. Some of the National Police officers refused and the effort was dropped.[97]

February 21: Assassins killed the minister of public works and head of the PSD party, Félicien Gatabazi. This murder, like that attempted the day before on Twagiramungu, had been predicted by high-ranking military officers in their December 3 letter to Dallaire, mentioned above. Investigations by UNCIVPOL reportedly revealed participation by several persons close to Habyarimana, including Captain Pascal Simbikangwa, long identified with secret service tortures, and Alphonse Ntilivamunda, son-in-law of Habyarimana.[98] When U.N. police later

---

[92]United Nations, *The United Nations and Rwanda,* pp. 32-33, 243; Prunier, *The Rwanda Crisis, p. 205.*

[93]Human Rights Watch interview, General Romeo Dallaire, by telephone, Kigali, February 25, 1994.

[94]Anonymous, "Chronology-Rwanda."

[95]Sénat, *Rapport du Groupe Ad Hoc*, p. 38.

[96]Marie-France Cros, "Jean Birara: 'The Belgians and French Could Have Stopped the Killing,'" *La Libre Belgique,* Foreign Broadcast Information Service (FBIS), Central Africa, May 25, 1994.

[97]Anonymous, "La Milice Interahamwe."

[98]Reyntjens, *Rwanda, Trois Jours*, p. 61.

helped arrest a suspect, RTLM reviled them. Several persons, including Simbikangwa, threatened the Kigali prosecutor who had ordered the arrest.[99]

February 22: Martin Bucyana, president of the CDR, was killed by a mob in Butare in retaliation for the killing of Gatabazi. In another incident, a UNAMIR convoy escorting the RPF was attacked with grenades; one RPF soldier was killed and a U.N. military observer was wounded. High-ranking RPF leaders were supposed to have been part of the convoy but at the last minute changed their plans.[100]

February 23: UNAMIR peacekeepers sent to rescue a judge exchanged fire with attackers.[101]

February 22-26: Interahamwe killed some seventy people and destroyed property in Kigali. Belgian officers described the situation as "explosive," but UNAMIR, limited by its mandate, could do little to stop the violence.[102]

February 24: Boutros-Ghali called Habyarimana to insist that the Accords must be implemented and to warn that the international community would not take responsibility if the situation exploded.[103]

February 25: The Belgian Ministry of Foreign Affairs wrote the Belgian ambassador at the U.N. about the need to strengthen the UNAMIR mandate. Among its points were the following:

- "[A] new bloodbath" could result from the political murders and unrest. (Point 1.)

- Under the present mandate, UNAMIR cannot carry out "a strong maintenance of public order." (Point 4.)

---

[99]Human Rights Watch/FIDH interview by telephone, Brussels, January 26, 1997.

[100]Sénat, *Rapport du Groupe Ad Hoc,* p. 38; Anonymous, "Chronology-Rwanda."

[101]Sénat, *Rapport du Groupe Ad Hoc,* pp. 48-49.

[102]Tribunal de Première Instance de Bruxelles, Deposition de Témoin, dossier 57/95, September 18, 1995 (confidential source); Ibid., p. 38.

[103]United Nations, *The United Nations and Rwanda,* p. 34. According to another source, the call may have been made several days later, following growing Belgian pressure. Human Rights Watch/FIDH interview, by telephone, October 25, 1997.

- *"In case the situation were indeed to deteriorate and the UNAMIR orders mentioned above remain in force, public opinion would never tolerate having Belgian peacekeepers remain passive witnesses to genocide and having the U.N. do nothing."* (Point 5.) [Emphasis added.]

- "UNAMIR should play a more active role and raise its profile to reinforce the credibility of the international community." (Point 6.)

- "The question is whether this is possible without a new mandate from the Security Council. If strengthening UNAMIR requires a new mandate (a new Security Council resolution), there would be problems given the current policy of the United States. At this point, an extension of the operation (peacekeepers, funding) appears excluded for them." (Point 7.)

- "It will be extremely important to see how the action can be reinforced under the present mandate (including Austrian peacekeepers? More decision-making powers for Dallaire? Temporary deployment of peacekeepers from other operations in the region?) and how to effectively increase diplomatic and political pressure." (Point 8.)

The memorandum closed by stressing that the Belgians themselves had made no decisions, but that they wanted these points taken into consideration (presumably at the U.N.) before new steps were taken.[104]

In response, the Belgian ambassador at the U.N. replied that he had discussed the matter with the secretariat and with principal members of the Security Council. (From minutes of a meeting between the Ministries of Foreign Affairs and Defense on March 3, it is clear that "secretariat" in fact means the secretary-general himself.[105]) The discussions yielded the following conclusions:

1. that it is unlikely that either the number of troops or the mandate of UNAMIR would be enlarged; that the United States and Great Britain oppose

[104]The Senate *Rapport du Groupe Ad Hoc* publishes points 1 and 5 as part of a telex dated February 25, 1994 (p. 77) and points 4 and 6-9 as part of a telex dated February 24, 1994 (p.90). The report of the Commission d'enquête (p. 393) shows them to have been part of the same document, dated February 25.

[105]Sénat, *Rapport du Groupe Ad Hoc*, p. 91.

this both for financial reasons and because the operation was undertaken under chapter 6;

2. that it is also unlikely that the ROE [Rules of Engagement] would be modified;

3. that Austrian troops could be called on only when troops were rotated and then only after Austria had formally requested this;

4. that General Dallaire could help Rwandan authorities plan and carry out the elimination of weapons stocks and could do this in a visible way;

5. that two companies of the Ghanaian battalion will be transferred from the demilitarized zone [in northern Rwanda] to Kigali.[106]

February 25: Robert Kajuga presided over a meeeting of Interahamwe leaders that recommended greater vigilance against Tutsi in the city of Kigali and asked that lists of Tutsi be drawn up. The leaders decided on a system of communication using telephones, whistles, runners, and public criers. They ordered militia members to be ready to act at any moment using traditional weapons and, for the more experienced—former soldiers and trained militia members—using firearms. In directions presaging collaboration between political parties during the genocide, leaders told the Interahamwe to be ready to come to the aid of members of the militias of the CDR and the MDR. Interahamwe were advised to have nothing to do with thugs who stole, raped, or otherwise harassed people in the name of Interahamwe.[107]

February 25: The human rights group AVP issued a declaration enumerating victims of recent violence in Kigali, condemning calls for the extermination of the Tutsi heard on RTLM, and urging UNAMIR to establish security in the city.[108]

---

[106]Sénat, *Rapport du Groupe Ad Hoc*, p. 77.

[107]Document 18, Belgian Military Intelligence, [February 27, 1994?] (confidential source).

[108]AVP, "Declaration de l'Association des Volontaires de la Paix sur l'Assassinat des Hommes Politiques Rwandais et les Massacres des Populations Civiles par les Milices CDR et Interahamwe," February 25, 1994.

February 25: Habyarimana warned Booh-Booh that his life was in danger.[109]

February 27: Dallaire again sought approval from New York for a plan to confiscate weapons. He also requested reinforcement by a company of 150 soldiers. On this date or shortly after, he expressed fears about a civil war. The peacekeeping office reminded him that the Rules of Engagement permitted the use of weapons only for self-defense and told him to concentrate on getting the new transitional government installed.[110]

February 27: Belgian intelligence reported on continuing arms deals for the Rwandan army. The arms, bought from Unita in Angola, supposedly were delivered through the Zairean military base at Kamina. From there they were sent to Goma and then across the border into Gisenyi, in northwestern Rwanda.[111]

February 25-28: The clearly anti-Tutsi character of continuing violence drove Tutsi to seek shelter in religious centers and with U.N. employees. On February 28, the U.N. opened two centers, one near Amahoro stadium and another at the Magerwa storehouse, for Tutsi who were seeking protection.[112]

February 28: A shell struck between the CND building where the RPF was quartered and the UNAMIR headquarters.[113]

Late February: The second issue of *Kangura* for February talked of "The Final Attack" that the RPF was supposedly preparing to make on Kigali. Saying that they knew where Inyenzi were hiding, the journalists mentioned that many were in the part of the city called Biryogo. They ask that "all who are concerned by this problem" be on the alert because "We will not perish little by little."[114]

---

[109]Anonymous, "Rwanda, Chronology;" Human Rights Watch/FIDH interview, by telephone, October 25, 1997.

[110]Anonymous, "Rwanda, Chronology."

[111]Document 19, Belgian Military Intelligence, February 27, 1994 (confidential source).

[112]Sénat, *Rapport du Group Ad Hoc*, pp. 71-72.

[113]Ibid., p. 39.

[114]*Kangura*, no. 57, février 1994, p. 4.

March 1994

March 1: According to the Belgian ambassador in Kigali, RTLM was broadcasting "inflammatory statements calling for the hatred—indeed for the extermination" of the Tutsi.[115]

March 2: An MRND informant told Belgian intelligence that the MRND had a plan to exterminate all the Tutsi in Kigali if the RPF should dare to resume the war. The informant said this was possible because now "all Hutu speak the same language and are behind a Hutu leader, that is, President Habyarimana." Regional divisions are now ended and the morale of the army is higher than ever. The informant concluded that "if things go badly, the Hutu will massacre them without pity."[116]

March 3: UNAMIR Major Podevijn reported to Dallaire about the distribution of weapons to militia in Gikondo, a section of Kigali.[117]

March 6: A jeep involved in an automobile accident near the RPF headquarters at the CND was found to be fully loaded with ammunition and grenades. Assumed by many to have been destined for the RPF, the weapons had actually been sold by Rwandan soldiers to Burundian insurgents.[118]

March 10: UNAMIR discovered the manifest of a shipment of heavy weapons for the Rwandan army.[119]

March 10: Belgian intelligence again reported new arms and new recruits for the Rwandan army and improvement in its morale.[120]

March 10: Belgian intelligence reported that the MRND executive committee was angry that Habyarimana had gone off for discussions with President Museveni of Uganda without consulting them. The president of the party, Mathieu

---

[115]Sénat, *Rapport du Group Ad Hoc*, p. 78.

[116]Document 20, Belgian Military Intelligence, March 2, 1994 (confidential source).

[117]Sénat, *Rapport du Groupe Ad Hoc*, p.63.

[118]Reyntjens, *Rwanda, Trois Jours*, p. 19; Human Rights Watch/FIDH interview, Brussels, July 29, 1998.

[119]Anonymous, "Rwanda, Chronology."

[120]Document 21, Belgian Military Intelligence, March 10, 1994 (confidential source).

Ngirumpatse, said this constituted "a serious political error." Habyarimana had to explain his actions to the party leaders.[121]

March 13: Dallaire again requested reinforcements of 150 soldiers.[122]

Mid-March: Dallaire once more sought authorization to seize arms caches, again without success.[123]

Mid-March: After visiting Rwanda, Belgian Minister of Defense Léo Delcroix reported that Kigali, supposedly a weapons-free zone, was full of arms. He proposed that the mandate, soon to be renewed, be amended to provide "more freedom of movement," and "more persuasive action." [124]

March 14: Marchal asked his Belgian superiors to respond promptly to his January 15 request for more ammunition. Five days later he remarked that the likelihood of serious conflict was "hardly a fantasy."[125]

March 15: The sponsors of the International Commission on Human Rights Abuse in Rwanda (Human Rights Watch, the International Federation of Human Rights Leagues, the International Center for Human Rights and Democratic Development, and the Interafrican Union of Human Rights) were joined by Amnesty International in a declaration deploring the growing violence in Rwanda, the distribution of arms, the delays in implementing the Arusha Accords and the efforts of the MRND to obtain a promise of amnesty for those involved in previous human rights abuses.[126]

---

[121]Ibid.

[122]Adelman and Suhrke, *Early Warning,* p. 88, n. 60.

[123]Walter de Bock and Gert Van Langendonck, "Falende VN-bureaukratie werd blauwhelmen fataal," *De Morgen,* November 7, 1995, p. 6.

[124]Sénat, *Rapport du Groupe Ad Hoc,* p. 91.

[125]Comdr. HQ Sector to COPs, Nb Ctr: 2600, March 14, 1994 and Luc Marchal to Monsieur l'Ambassadeur, March 20, 1994 (confidential source).

[126]Amnesty International, Human Rights Watch, Interafrican Union of Human Rights, International Center for Human Rights and Democratic Development, International Federation of Human Rights Leagues, "Declaration of Five International Human Rights Organizations Concerning the Delays in the Implementation of the Peace Agreements in Rwanda," March 15, 1994.

March 15: The Belgian ambassador in Kigali reported that UNAMIR had blocked the delivery of loads of arms for the Rwandan army from the Mil-Tec Corporation of the United Kingdom and the Société Dyl-Invest of France.[127]

March 17: A repected source in the National Police (probably Chief of Staff Ndindiliyimana) told Belgian officers that the UNAMIR mandate should be strengthened so that it could take the initiative and act more firmly. According to him, the National Police was unable alone to carry out the role assigned to it by the Arusha Accords.[128]

March 22: Georges Ruggiu, a Belgian announcer on RTLM radio, warned that the Belgians wanted to impose a RPF government of bandits and killers on Rwanda and that the Belgian ambassador had been plotting a coup. He told the Belgians to wake up and go home because, if not, they would face a "fight without pity," "a hatred without mercy."[129]

Third week of March: The officer in charge of intelligence for the Rwandan army told a group including some Belgian military advisers that "if Arusha were implemented, they were ready to liquidate the Tutsi." (*Si Arusha était exécuté, ils étaient prets a liquider les Tutsis.*)[130]

March 26: Dallaire told New York that he needed contingency plans in case an "extreme scenario takes place."[131]

March 28: Ferdinand Nahimana sent around to members of the elite his call for "self-defense" originally circulated in February 1993 and asked for suggestions for a "final solution" to the current problems. In the document, he calls for national unity, condemns "the Tutsi league" with its plan for a "Hima empire" and insists that the elite not remain "unconcerned" but rather work with local administrators to rouse the population to the danger of war.[132]

---

[127]Sénat, *Rapport du Groupe Ad Hoc,* p. 133.

[128]Sénat, *Rapport du Groupe Ad Hoc*, p. 91.

[129]Ibid., p. 49.

[130]Commission d'enquête, *Rapport, p. 334.*

[131]Human Rights Watch/FIDH interview, by telephone, October 25, 1997.

[132]Nahimana, "Le Rwanda: Problèmes Actuels, Solutions."

March 30: CLADHO issued a declaration detailing attacks by soldiers, including the Presidential Guard, and Interahamwe. It again demanded that the soldiers be disciplined and the militia be disarmed.[133]

March 31: Assailants killed Alphonse Ingabire (known as Katumba), operational head of the CDR. Militia of the CDR killed a member of the PSD and wounded three others.

March 31: In the last days of March, RTLM broadcast increasingly bitter attacks on UNAMIR, including Dallaire, the Belgians, and some Rwandan political leaders.

March 31: With the UNAMIR mandate about to expire, leaders of Rwandan human rights associations and other nongovernmental organizations issued a plea to the Security Council "to maintain and reinforce" UNAMIR because its withdrawal "would be interpreted as abandoning the civilian population to the worst of calamities."[134]

April 1994

April 2: RTLM announced that military officers had met with the prime minister to plan a coup against Habyarimana.[135]

April 2: Army Chief of Staff Nsabimana told Colonel Marchal that the Rwandan military expected an offensive soon by the RPF.[136]

April 3: RTLM broadcast a prediction that the RPF would do "a little something" with its bullets and grenades on April 3 to April 5 and again from April 7 to 8. This may have been an "accusation in a mirror"—like that advocated by the disciple of the propaganda expert Mucchielli—with Hutu hard-liners accusing Tutsi of preparing to do just what they themselves were planning.[137] The prediction increased fears in an already tense situation. Some people who felt at risk sent their

---

[133]CLADHO, "Declaration sur les Violations Systematiques et Flagrantes des Droits de l'Homme en Cours dans le Pays Depuis Les Tentatives de Mise en Place des Institutions de Transition," March 30, 1994 (CLADHO).

[134]Société Civile, c/o Centre Iwacu, "Déclaration de la Société Civile au Rwanda dans sa réunion du 31 mars 1994."

[135]Human Rights Watch/FIDH interview, Brussels, August 4, 1998.

[136]Human Rights Watch/FIDH interview, by telephone, Brussels, July 24, 1998.

[137]RTLM, April 3, 1994, recorded by Faustin Kagame (provided by Article 19).

children away from Kigali while others took refuge in places thought to be safe havens.

April 3: The German ambassador, speaking for the European Union, expressed concern about increasing insecurity, proliferation of weapons and the "unacceptable role of some media." He suggested that continued support depended on implementing the Accords.[138]

April 4: At a party to celebrate the national day of Senegal, Bagosora told people that "the only plausible solution for Rwanda would be the elimination of the Tutsi." Among those present at the time were Dallaire, Booh-Booh, Marchal, and Shariyah Khan, adviser to Booh-Booh. Bagosora reportedly told Marchal that if the RPF attacked successfully, the Rwandan forces had plans for guerrilla warfare against them.[139]

The U.N. Response to the Warning

The preparations for violence took place in full view of a U.N. peacekeeping force. The commander of that force reported evidence of the worsening situation to his superiors who directed him to observe the narrowest possible interpretation of his mandate. He was in effect to do nothing but keep on talking with the authorities while they kept on preparing for slaughter.

The secretary-general and his subordinates ordered this apparently aberrant interpretation of peacekeeping in an effort to keep within the constraints set by the Security Council. They knew that council members did not regard Rwanda as a priority and were reluctant to invest any more troops or funds in keeping the peace there. Stopping the preparations for slaughter required firm action, which itself might lead to an escalation of violence and the need for more troops and funds. Staff feared that requests for more resources might provoke the council simply to end the mission, thus marking another in a series of failures for the U.N. and its peacekeeping office.[140]

When Dallaire sent his January 11 telegram, he understood his mandate to permit seizing illegal arms: he stated that he was undertaking the operation rather than requested authorisation for it. But his initiative drew an immediate and

[138]Prunier, *The Rwanda Crisis,* p. 209.

[139]Sénat, *Rapport du Groupe Ad Hoc,* p. 79; Human Rights Watch/FIDH interview, by telephone, Brussels, July 24, 1998.

[140]See the statement of Kofi Annan, then Undersecretary-general for Peacekeeping. Assemblée Nationale, Mission d'information commune, *Enquête*, Tome I, Rapport, p. 204.

supposedly unanimous negative response from the secretariat staff. Recalling that an attempt to confiscate arms had sparked violence and subsequent failure for the U.N. operation in Somalia, they ordered Dallaire not to act. Hiding behind legalities, they insisted that UNAMIR had no authority to create an arms-free zone, only to enforce one created by other parties.[141]

Dallaire sent five more messages about the need for action, on January 22, February 3, February 15, February 27 and March 13.[142] In the last two, sent after the violence set off by Gatabazi's assassination on February 21, Dallaire requested more troops as well as for a broader interpretation of the mandate.

Dallaire's demands for action and grim predictions caused friction with his superiors, including the U.N. senior military adviser, Gen. Maurice Baril. Dallaire later protested that he never considered himself "a cowboy," that is, someone ready to leap to action without forethought, but Baril—a former classmate—and others saw him that way. Baril felt he had to keep Dallaire "on a leash" and other secretariat staff believed he was right to do so.[143] Authorities in New York, apparently including the secretary-general, preferred Booh Booh's reports to those of Dallaire. A diplomat from Cameroon, Booh Booh reportedly thought highly of Habyarimana and presented optimistic assessments of his intentions. Following the late February killings of Tutsi, for example, Booh-Booh reported that there was no proof that the attacks had been ethnically motivated.[144]

With the UNAMIR troops limited to a passive role, Dallaire's predictions proved accurate. Unable to seize arms, to prevent the bloodshed of late February, or even to interrupt the broadcasts of RTLM, the force lost credibility rapidly.

Having prohibited Dallaire from acting militarily, the secretary-general sought to move Habyarimana through talk—his own, that of his special representative, and that of other foreign diplomats—combined with threats to take the matter to the

---

[141]Sénat, *Rapport du Groupe Ad Hoc*, pp. 89-91; United Nations, *The United Nations and Rwanda*, p. 32.

[142]One request was for permission to raid Habyarimana's home commune where military had reportedly stored heavy weapons removed from the capital to evade monitoring by UNAMIR. It was denied "because of the political implications." Thompson, "Nightmare of the Generals in 1994."

[143]Jess Sallot and Paul Knox, "Rwanda a Watershed for Baril," *Globe and Mail*, September 25, 1997.

[144]Code Cable MIR 409, 24 February 1994 (confidential source).

Security Council if Habyarimana remained intransigent. On January 13, Boutros-Ghali set a goal of getting Habyarimana to halt the preparations for violence within forty-eight hours, but he then waited until February 10 to take the matter to the Security Council, despite indications much earlier that the Rwandan president did not intend to cooperate. The mild statement issued by the council on February 17 "expressing concern" over the situation only reinforced the impression of U.N. timidity—or perhaps indifference—in face of the preparations for slaughter.

Even though discussions seemed to be leading nowhere, Boutros-Ghali refused to push the Security Council to strengthen the mandate because he believed it was futile to propose a change that the U.S. was sure to oppose. Through early March, he also refused Dallaire's request for new troops, although he did permit the transfer of 200 Ghanaian peacekeepers from the demilitarized zone in the north to Kigali, changing the location but not the number of soldiers.

When the omens of disaster were multiplying, Boutros-Ghali kept on with the usual practices of the U.N. bureaucracy, doing his best to avoid any open conflict with the powerful members of the Security Council. Accused later of having failed to bring like the January 11 telegram to the attention of the Security Council, Boutros-Ghali and some of his staff asserted that they laid the matter—if not the document itself—before the Security Council the next day. This is not true.[145] Although one staff member drew attention to the importance of the telegram by placing it in a black folder, the usual signal that this was a matter for urgent attention, the cable was not delivered to the council members nor were its contents communicated in summarized form, as was often the case for such messages. The subsequent treatment of the document suggests that someone regarded it as potentially damaging. When researchers consulted files from this period, they found the January 11 cable present but not in the appropriate order. Attached to it was the explanation that it had been at one point missing from the folder and was later put back into it. Some months after the genocide, a representative of a nongovernmental organization delivered a copy of the telegram to one high-

---

[145]United Nations, *The United Nations and Rwanda*, p. 32; Human Rights Watch/FIDH interviews with a council member and others, in New York and by telephone, March 8, 1995, February 19, 1996, December 23, 1997. Iqbal Riza, then Assistant Secretary-General for Peacekeeping Operations, admitted in a British Broadcasting Company telecast on December 7, 1998 that the secretariat had not given the telegram the importance it deserved. He had confirmed in an earlier Canadian Broadcasting Company telecast that the telegram had never been presented to the Security Council.

ranking U.N. official who had stated that there was no such telegram and that rumors of its existence were propaganda by Rwandan extremists.[146]

In a confidential assessment of the Rwandan crisis, one U.N. staff member concluded that the peacekeeping office had failed to respond to Dallaire's calls for support and that it was "too conservative in meeting the challenge...[H]ad we used our imagination we could have prevented the crisis by advising the [Security] Council of the increased tensions and rearmament activities that were going on."

Such readiness to admit error is welcome from staff, but the ultimate responsibility naturally rests with the secretary-general. His decision not to inform the council fully about the situation limited the possible courses of action open to council members. Even if discussion of the risks of massive slaughter—and of genocide—had not altered the policies of such members as the U.S., the U.K., and France, it might have prompted action by members who ultimately behaved responsibly after April 6. Had these members, the representatives of the Czech Republic, Argentina, Nigeria, New Zealand, and Spain been apprised of the preparations, they might have countered the inertia of others. And had the general public been alerted to the genocidal plans, some citizens and nongovernmental organizations would have had the chance to use the information to press their governments to take the issue seriously.

Responses of the French, U.S., and Belgian Governments

As the foreign governments most involved with Rwanda, France, the U.S., and Belgium followed the deteriorating situation and cooperated with the U.N. and with each other in trying to speed implementation of the Arusha Accords. Despite the clear signs of imminent violence, both France and the U.S. failed to respond with any new initiatives and continued to operate within the same constraints that had shaped their policy towards Rwanda for some time. Belgium, spurred by the added responsibility of having troops on the ground, sought a greater international commitment to prevent the disaster, but failed to invest the energy needed to make the other powers respond.

With close ties to Habyarimana and other high-ranking Rwandan officials and with an undercover intelligence operation in place, France certainly knew about the preparations for killing Tutsi and opponents of Hutu Power. French diplomats and military officers discussed the risk of genocide beginning in 1990 and, according

---

[146]Human Rights Watch interviews, Washington, December 8, 1995; by telephone, April 26, 1998. According to one source, there were two cables, one coded and one not, one dealing with more political matters, the other with more military issues.

to former Ambassador Martres, the 1994 genocide could have been foreseen in October 1993.[147] Bound by its old loyalties, however, France continued to support the Rwandan government diplomatically, in discussions in the Security Council, for example, and militarily, with the delivery of arms. After the January 11 telegram, Boutros-Ghali had looked to France, Belgium, and the U.S. to support his efforts to get Habyarimana to halt the preparations for violence. According to Belgian diplomatic correspondence, it was France that prevented the three from addressing the issue when they met with the Rwandan president. Along with the others, France refused to give shelter to the informant.

In the U.S., senior officials may not have listened to the prediction of potential widespread carnage from within their own ranks, but, according to Anthony Lake, then national security adviser to the president, they were aware of Belgian efforts to alert them to such a risk. On one occasion, civilian and military authorities discussed the possibility of sending more troops to Rwanda, but they decided that the number was already too large if the soldiers were there only to observe and that if the proposed reinforcements were sent, the force would still be too small to stop a conflict.[148] The U.S. was ready to use diplomatic pressure to improve the situation in Rwanda—and sent Associate Secretary of State for African Affairs Prudence Bushnell to Rwanda for that purpose—but it was not ready to spend more money. U.S. officials refused to support broadening the mandate or any other measure that would substantially increase the expense of UNAMIR.

Belgium tried hardest to respond to the warnings of imminent slaughter. Its representative at the U.N. pushed the secretary-general and members of the peacekeeping staff to permit Dallaire greater freedom of action and to demand faster progress from Habyarimana. Although Foreign Minister Claes conceded on February 11 that broadening the mandate was out of the question, he changed his mind after the killings of late February and actively campaigned for a stronger mandate. One Foreign Ministry official acknowledged the risk of genocide in late February—even using that term—and argued that "If conditions deteriorate, the U.N. and Belgium could not really allow themselves to withdraw from Rwanda."[149]

---

[147]Assemblée Nationale, Mission d'information commune, *Enquête*, Tome I, Rapport, pp. 226, 281, Tome II, Annexes pp. 133-4.

[148]Human Rights Watch/FIDH interviews, by telephone, Washington, May 4, 1998 and Washington, July 16, 1998; Commission d'enquête, *Rapport,* pp. 244, 336.

[149]Commission d'enquête, *Rapport,* p. 393.

The first Belgian effort to strengthen the mandate failed when the U.S., along with the U.K., refused to consider the proposal and even suggested they would favor a complete withdrawal should the difficulties continue. In mid-March, after the visit of Minister of Defense Léo Delcroix to Rwanda, the Belgians again raised the issue. In discussions with representatives of France and the U.S. on March 22, Belgium proposed that the mandate, about to expire, should be renewed for only a brief period and should be strengthened. France refused to support a stronger mandate, but all agreed that the new term of the mandate should be brief, in order to exert greater pressure on the parties for concrete progress. Delcroix still maintained the importance of a more flexible mandate and on March 29 even threatened to end Belgian participation in UNAMIR if no revision were made.[150] Although Belgian authorities invested far less energy in trying to change the mandate than they would several weeks later when attempting to end UNAMIR completely, they still did more than other international actors to try to interrupt the movement towards catastrophe.

A Solemn Appeal
On March 28, at the end of the seventh month since the signing of the Accords, Habyarimana and his supporters failed to appear for yet another of the ceremonies scheduled for swearing in members of the broad-based transitional government. The issue this time was whether the CDR should have a seat in the assembly. The RPF and other parties had refused, insisting that the Accords provided for representation of only those parties that subscribed to the Accords, which, at the start, the CDR vociferously did not. But recently the CDR had changed its position and finally subscribed to a code of ethics for political parties, an essential precondition for participation in the assembly. Habyarimana was determined to have the CDR seated because it could provide him with the final vote necessary to block any effort to impeach him.

The same day, the special representative of the secretary-general, the apostolic nuncio, the ambassadors of Belgium, France, Germany, the U.S., Zaire, Uganda, Burundi, and the representative of the Tanzanian facilitator joined in "a solemn appeal" to all parties to resolve their differences and implement the Accords. They expressed the opinion that all political parties in existence at the time the Accords were signed should be represented in the Assembly, that is, that the CDR should have a place. This was in line with the thinking of many diplomats since the

---

[150]Commission d'enquête, *Rapport,* p. 281.

beginning—that it was wiser to include the extremists than to attempt to shut them out of power.

With this concession from the international community in hand, Habyarimana set off for Dar es Salaam a few days later to meet with heads of neighboring states. It was expected that this meeting of his peers would exact from him a final commitment to install the new government. Col. Elie Sagatwa, responsible for the security of the president, met twice with Colonel Marchal to plan for the installation ceremonies, which also contributed to the impression that Habyarimana really meant to permit the new government to take power.[151] The international actors also knew, as the French ambassador reported to Paris on March 28, that "the cash-drawer was empty."[152] Since the donor nations refused to provide more money until the broad-based government was installed, they may all have counted on near-bankruptcy forcing cooperation, as had been the case with the signing of the Accords the previous August.

Renewing the Mandate

Although some of the signs at the very end of March seemed promising, they did not outweigh the grim indications of trouble ahead. Called upon to assess the situation in his formal report on UNAMIR at the end of its mandate, the secretary-general on March 30 detailed the warnings of the previous months: the distribution of arms, the training of militia, the assassinations, the violent demonstrations, and the laying of mines. Boutros-Ghali could have used this opportunity to insist on strengthening the mandate and sending reinforcements to the peacekeepers, but he did not. To have done so would have involved confronting the reluctance of the Security Council—and specifically the U.S.—to devote the resources needed to improve the situation. It would also have required negotiating with other member states over the numbers of troops to be provided and the duties with which they would be charged.

The secretary-general was ready, however, to risk confrontation over the length of the mandate. The major international actors in Rwanda, as well as the department of peacekeeping, had agreed that the new mandate must be for a brief term of two or three months in order to keep the greatest possible pressure on the parties to implement the Accords. In a surprise move, Boutros-Ghali recommended an extension of six months. Such a time span would have restricted leverage over

---

[151]Human Rights Watch/FIDH interview, by telephone, Brussels, May 4, 1998.

[152]Jouan, "Rwanda, 1990-1994" p. 43.

Habyarimana and opened the way to further delays and continued preparations for violence. After strong reaction from the council members, the term was finally settled at four months.

In analyzing the deteriorating security in Kigali, the secretary-general had noted that "most incidents can be attributed to armed banditry."[153] This explanation was astonishingly like that made by leaders of the MRND on January 12 when Dallaire and Booh-Booh reproached them for violence in the capital. Only secondarily did Boutros-Ghali remark that "ethnic and politically motivated crimes" also had increased. Having stressed that common crime was the problem in Kigali, Boutros-Ghali was in a good position to propose a small increase in the ranks of UNCIVPOL as the solution. At a time when the UNAMIR commander was requesting 150 experienced troops to deal with the threat of ethnic and political violence and his second was calling for heavy weaponry to defend the airport, the secretary-general asked the Security Council for forty-five policemen. He assured council members that "the cost implications of this proposed personnel increase will be minimal."[154] It was the cheaper solution—or so it seemed.

---

[153]United Nations, *The United Nations and Rwanda,* p. 249.

[154]Ibid., p. 250.

APRIL 1994: "THE MONTH THAT WOULD NOT END"

By early April, the increasingly vicious incitements to hatred and violence, the frequent predictions of imminent catastrophe, the recurring delays in implementing the Accords, the widespread awareness of training and arming of militia, and the threat that UNAMIR and other foreign actors might end or reduce their role in Rwanda had all caused great anxiety, particularly among people in the capital. Both the Hutu Power group and the RPF understood the likelihood of violence and were moving their forces into position.

Hutu Power advocates were far from done implementing their "self-defense" program, but they did already have some 2,000 militia in place in Kigali. In addition, there were some 7,000 regular troops in Kigali and its environs, although not all of them were combat troops.[1] Many feared renewed battle, but those committed to Habyarimana were buoyed by the new solidarity of Hutu Power and felt a renewed sense of purpose. On April 3, a RTLM commentator declared that the people were ready to serve as a "fourth column" against the "enemy." He said:

> The people, there is the real shield, it is the true army that is strong...the armed forces [i.e., the regular Rwandan army] fight, but the people, they say: we protect your rear, we are your shield. The day when the people rise up and want no more of you, when they hate you all together and from the bottom of their hearts, when you make them sick to their stomachs, I...I wonder then where you will escape to. Where will you go?[2]

The RPF had strengthened its position by secretly bringing arms and several hundred troops into Kigali to supplement the 600 soldiers permitted by the Arusha Accords. The movement had also grown politically, both in Kigali and throughout Rwanda. With a RPF role in government assured by the peace agreement, supporters previously reluctant to declare their loyalties now acknowledged that they were RPF members. Political organizers who had gone to the RPF zone for training programs returned home eager to recruit new members. By early April, the RPF had some 600 cells throughout the country, 147 of them in Kigali. With each group counting between six and twelve members, this made a total of between

---

[1] Human Rights Watch/FIDH interviews, by telephone, Montreal, May 22, 1996; by telephone, Antwerp, April 15, 1997; Brussels, October 20, 1997.

[2] RTLM, April 3, 1994, recorded by Faustin Kagame (provided by Article 19).

3,600 and 7,200 persons who had openly or privately declared their support for the RPF. The greatest number, some 700 to 1,400, were in the capital.[3]

Well-aware of the training and arming of the Interahamwe, the RPF had begun exploring the organization of a joint militia with the MDR and the PSD to counter possible attacks. The MDR rejected the plan but the PSD was still considering it in early April. Few RPF members had firearms.[4] Those who did had apparently not received them from the movement but had bought them on their own initiative. During the genocide, Hutu Power supporters talked incessantly about "infiltrators" and their stocks of arms. Although the RPF soldiers brought into Kigali in contravention of the terms of the peace agreement could be called "infiltrators," unarmed and untrained Tutsi citizens—even if they happened to back the RPF—could not be described by that term. When these Tutsi residents were attacked after April 6, virtually all resisted with sticks, stones, machetes or spears, not with Kalashnikovs or grenades.[5] The vast majority who survived owed their lives to their own strength, good fortune or the assistance of Hutu, not to previous military training.

The Attack on Habyarimana's Plane

The genocide of the Tutsi, the murders of Hutu opposed to Habyarimana, and the renewed war between the Rwandan goverment and the RPF were all touched off by the killing of President Habyarimana. This extremely significant attack remains largely uninvestigated and its authors unidentified.

Habyarimana died on Wednesday evening, April 6, 1994, when the plane bringing him home from Dar es Salaam was shot down. He had been attending a meeting of heads of state where he had supposedly finally consented to put in place the broad-based transitional government. The president of Burundi, Cyprien Ntaryamira, who had also attended the meeting, had decided to fly home in

---

[3]Human Rights Watch/FIDH interviews with a former UNAMIR officer, Plainsboro, New Jersey, June 13, 1996; by telephone, Nairobi, March 22, 1996; Kigali, February 14,1997.

[4]Human Rights Watch/FIDH interviews, by telephone, Nairobi, March 22, 1996; Kigali, February 14,1997.

[5]Among the cases of Tutsi with firearms are Antoine Sebera in Kigali, two persons at Ndora commune and others with guns and grenades at Sake commune. Article 19, *Broadcasting Genocide, Censorship, Propaganda & State-Sponsored Violence in Rwanda 1990-1994*, October 1996, p. 125; African Rights, *Rwanda, Death,Despair*, pp. 1056-7.

Habyarimana's plane rather than in his own. He too died in the crash as did General Nsabimana, chief of staff of the Rwandan army, and several others. As the plane was coming in for a landing, it was hit by ground to air missiles shot from a location near the Kigali airport. The Rwandan army later stated that it had recovered two launchers from the missiles. The registration numbers on the launchers identified them as SA 16s, sophisticated weapons that require a certain level of training to be used sucessfully.[6]

The RPF, politicians opposed to Habyarimana, and the circle of his own supporters all might have wanted the Rwandan president dead and could have found the means to bring down his plane.

The RPF might have launched the missiles either because they believed that Habyarimana would never permit the Accords to be implemented or, conversely, because they thought he was about to do so and they preferred a clear military victory to sharing power as part of a coalition. In support of allegations of RPF responsibility for the crime, former French Minister of Cooperation Bernard Debré, asserted that records of RPF communications prove that their soldiers were ordered to begin advancing towards Kigali on the morning of April 6.[7] Some Rwandans present in the region north of the capital at the time also assert that RPF troops began their march south before they could have known of Habyarimana's death.[8]

Hutu moderates, either alone or with the RPF, could have assassinated the president. The small group who had supposedly discussed the possibility of a coup with Prime Minister Uwlingiyimana a few days before might have believed that killing Habyarimana offered the only hope of preempting the violence that was planned.[9]

Some in Habyarimana's own circle might have wanted to eliminate him to avoid the installation of a new government that would diminish their power. The CDR and even MRND leaders had criticized Habyarimana for talking with Museveni in early March and some feared that he would return from Dar es Salaam ready to implement the Accords. Enoch Ruhigira, Habyarimana's chief of staff,

---

[6]Reyntjens, *Rwanda, Trois Jours*, pp. 44-45; Stephen Smith, "6 avril 1994: deux missiles abattent l'avion du président Habyarimana," *Libération*, April 6-7, 1996.

[7]Assemblée Nationale, Mission d'information commune, *Enquête*, Tome III, Auditions, Volume I, p. 415.

[8]Human Rights Watch/FIDH interview, by telephone, Atlanta, September 2, 1996.

[9]Reyntjens, *Rwanda, Trois Jours*, pp.34-35.

says that the president had, in fact, made such a decision and had told him to bring an announcement to that effect to the airport when he came to welcome him home.[10] The expectation that the new government was about to be installed would have increased pressure on Hutu Power advocates to launch the violence immediately, whether fully prepared or not. Once the new authorities were in place, the RPF would take over the Ministry of the Interior and Communal Development and the MRND would lose control of the administrative structure so helpful in mobilizing the population. Some of the Hutu Power group, including Bagosora himself, would lose their posts and would have no more authority to give orders.[11]

There are indications that Bagosora and other soldiers may have expected something to happen at the time of Habyarimana's return. According to one witness, Bagosora left Kigali for vacation on March 30 or 31 but then suddenly returned on April 4. Several witnesses assert that soldiers of the Presidential Guard had put up barricades and were patrolling the neighborhood inhabited by ministers and other MRND leaders, either before or within minutes after the plane was shot down.[12] Sporadic gunfire began almost immediately after the crash in the vicinity of the Kanombe camp that housed the Presidential Guard. Soon after, soldiers from the paracommando battalion, one of those most closely linked to the hard-liners, began killing the people who lived on Masaka hill, the site from which the missiles had been launched. These soldiers of one of the best trained units in the Rwandan army apparently continued the sweep against the Masaka civilians for thirty-six hours after the renewal of combat with the RPF, when they could presumably have been better used against the military foe. Since the local people clearly had not been the ones to shoot the missiles, the soldiers could not have been seeking revenge and may have been trying to eliminate witnesses to the crime.[13]

---

[10]Ibid., p. 23.

[11]Aboganena, "Bagosora S'Explique," p. 19.

[12]Tribunal de Première Instance de Bruxelles, Compte-Rendu de la Commission rogatoire internationale exécutée au Rwanda du 5 juin au 24 juin 1995, Dossier no. 57/95, pp. 2, 22; République Rwandaise, Parquet de la République de Kigali, PV no. 143. This and depositions cited hereafter from this source are all from dossiers labeled CRIM/ KK/KGL 95, CRIM/KK-DA/KGL/95 or an abbreviated form of these designations (confidential source).

[13]Reyntjens, Rwanda, Trois jours, pp. 25, 27.

Habyarimana's supporters accused the Belgians of involvement in the assassination, but never presented any proof. Others have suggested that the French—probably a nucleus of powerful individuals rather than the government as such—assisted in assassinating a leader who was no longer useful to them. According to some European intelligence sources, the missile launchers bore numbers that identified them as weapons that France captured from Iraq during the Gulf War. One French soldier confirmed this information and another reported attempts to buy such missiles from a private arms dealer and from a French company authorized to export them.[14] The French government denies these allegations. A source in the United States intelligence service thought it unlikely that France had captured the missiles in Iraq but that it could well have obtained them elsewhere.[15] Former minister Debré claimed that the U.S. was the source of the missiles, having provided them to Uganda which then gave them to the RPF.[16] Uganda did in fact have some of the missiles, as did other governments in the region like Tanzania and the Sudan. Mercenaries could also easily have purchased the weapons and put themselves and the missiles at the service of anyone ready to pay their fee.

Other unexplained elements suggest a link to French actors. The plane, a gift of the French government, was operated by a crew of three French citizens, supposedly employed by a private company. French officials recognized that the crewmembers had died in the service of their country, but undertook no public investigation into the downing of the plane. Nor did French authorities draw attention to the murders of two French policemen, apparently communications experts, and the wife of one of them, who were found in a house near the airport and killed by the RPF on April 8.[17] In another unexplained case, François de Grossouvre, a confidant and adviser to President Mitterrand on African affairs, committed suicide on April 7 at the presidency in Paris. De Grossouvre had been linked to Habyarimana and to Captain Paul Barril, a former French policeman who

---

[14]Reyntjens, *Rwanda, Trois jours*, p. 45; Patrick de Saint-Exupéry, "France-Rwanda: Dangereuses Liaisons," *Le Figaro*, March 31, 1998.

[15]Human Rights Watch/FIDH interview, by telephone, Washington, September 7, 1996.

[16]Assemblée Nationale, Mission d'information commune, *Enquête*, Tome III, Auditions, Volume I, p. 416.

[17]Smith, "6 avril 1994."

had been employed to provide security for Habyarimana. Barril, who was in Rwanda on April 7, continued in the service of Madame Habyarimana, notably in trying to persuade the press that the RPF was responsible for downing the plane.[18]

Responsibility for killing Habyarimana is a serious issue, but it is a different issue from responsibility for the genocide. We know little about who assassinated Habyarimana. We know more about who used the assassination as the pretext to begin a slaughter that had been planned for months. Hutu Power leaders expected that killing Tutsi would draw the RPF back into combat and give them a new chance for victory or at least for negotiations that might allow them to win back some of the concessions made at Arusha.

The Presidential Guard began the slaughter of Tutsi and other civilians shortly after Habyarimana's death. Sixteen hours later the RPF came out of their headquarters to engage the Rwandan soldiers and the war had begun again.

Taking Control
Bagosora In Command
With the death of Habyarimana, Colonel Bagosora took charge. The minister of defense, Augustin Bizimana, and two members of the general staff, Col. Aloys Ntiwiragabo and Col. Gratien Kabiligi, were abroad and the chief of staff had died with Habyarimana. When sixteen high ranking officers got together to decide on a course of action just after the crash, Bagosora ran the meeting. Although only a retired officer, he took precedence over senior officers in active service, he says, because he was the ranking official present from the Ministry of Defense and the meeting was "to discuss questions of a politico-military nature."[19] Bagosora prevailed in taking the chair, but he lacked strong support in the group. Some senior officers closest to him, such as the commander of the Presidential Guard, the commander of the paracommandos, and some of the territorial commanders, were absent.

Bagosora proposed naming Col. Augustin Bizimungu, then commander at Ruhengeri and an officer whom he could trust, as the new chief of staff. The group rejected Bizimungu, who was junior in rank and experience to a number of other officers. Col. Léonidas Rusatira, present at the meeting, was the senior ranking

---

[18]Reyntjens, *Rwanda, Trois Jours*, pp. 30-31; Prunier, *The Rwanda Crisis*, pp. 217-19.

[19]Commandement des Forces Armées Rwandaises en Exil, "Contribution des FAR," p. 91; Bagosora, "L'assassinat," p. 9.

army officer and a northerner, but Bagosora saw him as a rival. Some time before, Bagosora and his supporters had succeeded in relegating Rusatira to the command of the Ecole Supérieure Militaire, a school where he had no combat troops under his orders. Rusatira's name was proposed, but, perhaps anxious to avoid a conflict during this time of crisis, the officers passed over him and chose Col. Marcel Gatsinzi as interim chief of staff.[20] At that time, Gatsinzi was commanding the southern sector in Butare. Originally from Kigali, he was not a member of the inner circle of powerful officers from the northwest and would be unlikely to be able to mobilize a following strong enough to challenge Bagosora and his group.[21]

Bagosora pushed hard for the military to take control of the government, but on this matter, too, he was rebuffed. General Dallaire, who was at the meeting, declared that any military take-over would result in the immediate withdrawal of UNAMIR. He urged the officers to make contact instead with Prime Minister Uwilingiyimana to arrange for a legitimate continuation of civilian authority. Bagosora adamantly refused the suggestion, which Dallaire made several times.[22] Bagosora, like other Hutu Power advocates, distrusted Dallaire, whom he believed favorable to the RPF. Under pressure from the other officers, Bagosora did agree to consult the special representative of the secretary-general. Booh-Booh also insisted that some form of civilian authority was necessary and Bagosora finally accepted that advice. Like Dallaire, Booh-Booh pressed for contacts with the prime minister and again Bagosora refused, saying that "the military would not accept her" and that "her own government and the Rwandan people had rejected her."[23] Bagosora had only contempt for Mme. Uwilingiyimana who had, he later asserted, "morally and materially demobilized" the Rwandan army when it was fighting for its life against the RPF.[24] Acting on Booh-Booh's recommendation that the MRND

---

[20]République Rwandaise, Parquet de la République, PV no. 0259, no. 253, no. 143; Police Judiciaire près le Parquet du Procureur du Roi de Bruxelles, No. 41.312, dossier 57/95; Commandement des Forces Armées Rwandaises en Exil, "Contribution des FAR," p. 91.

[21]Reyntjens, Rwanda, Trois Jours, p. 53.

[22]Human Rights Watch/FIDH interview, Plainsboro, N.J., June 14, 1996; Commission d'enquête, Rappport, pp. 420-21.

[23]Reyntjens, Rwanda, Trois Jours, p. 54.

[24]Bagosora, "L'assassinat," p. 9.

provide a candidate to replace Habyarimana as president, Bagosora contacted the party leaders to ask them to nominate someone to the post.

At the meeting with the military commanders, Dallaire asked them to keep the militia under control and to recall to barracks the Presidential Guard, which was already out on the streets. Bagosora assured Dallaire of "all necessary cooperation required by the situation" and asked in return that UNAMIR keep close watch over the RPF headquarters at the CND. Dallaire saw the importance of having the peacekeepers visible throughout the city and he arranged for them to do joint patrols with the National Police.[25]

"The Prime Minister Isn't Working Anymore..."

As discussions went on for an orderly transition, soldiers and National Police were active throughout the city preparing just the opposite. Since Gatsinzi had not yet come from Butare, Bagosora was the effective military commander and apparently directed these operations in a series of private telephone conversations carried on during the meeting. He also had at his disposal a direct and private radio link with the Presidential Guard.[26]

Rwandan soldiers blocked Belgian UNAMIR troops at the airport twenty minutes after the plane crashed. Within an hour, soldiers of the Presidential Guard and the reconnaissance battalion were blockading the home of the prime minister. Two hours later soldiers from the Presidential Guard began evacuating MRND politicians and their families from the neighborhood of Kimihurura to a military camp. They ordered leading politicans from other parties to remain in their homes in the same neighborhood. The Ministry of Defense had recently transferred responsibility for the security of MRND leaders from the National Police to a unit of the regular army, an arrangement which facilitated their evacuation on April 6.

Lt. Col. Innocent Bavugamenshi feared violence as soon as he heard that MRND politicians had been moved to the military camp and other leaders left behind. As head of the National Police unit responsible for other political leaders, he sent reinforcements to the home of the prime minister and tried in vain to get others from UNAMIR and from National Police headquarters. His commander, General Ndindiliyimana, could not be found, either at home or at headquarters. At

---

[25]Reyntjens reprints the minutes of the meeting in *Rwanda, Trois Jours,* pp. 125-6.

[26]General Roméo Dallaire, "Answers to Questions Submitted to Major-General Dallaire By the Judge-Advocate General of the Military Court" (confidential source); République Rwandaise, Parquet de la République de Kigali, PV no.0142, 148 ; Reyntjens, *Rwanda, Trois Jours,"* p. 57.

about midnight, Bavugamenshi was informed of the first killing of a government official, the administrative head of the Ministry of Foreign Affairs.[27]

Between 1 and 2 a.m., Interahamwe were out on the streets patrolling. By 2:30 a.m., the military had blanketed the middle of the city so thoroughly with barriers that UNAMIR soldiers ordered to the home of the prime minister needed three hours to cover a distance usually traversed in fifteen minutes.[28]

Mme. Uwilingiyimana had been alterted to the danger she faced half an hour after the crash and she called for more protection from military headquarters. The additional police sent by Bavugamenshi never reached her home. At 1 a.m., Booh-Booh had informed her that the military rejected her authority, but she refused to flee. She arranged for UNAMIR soldiers to escort her to the radio station in the morning so that she could speak to the nation and show that the civilian authority was in control and committed to the Arusha Accords. This was exactly what those in command intended to prevent. When one officer called headquarters to ask about gunfire he had heard at about 5 a.m., Lt. Col. Cyprien Kayumba, the officer on duty, supposedly told him "That's us. We want to keep the prime minister from going to the radio."[29] Shortly after that, a UNAMIR officer told Rwandan soldiers at the radio station that the prime minister would be arriving shortly to make a broadcast. The Rwandans replied, "The prime minister isn't working anymore..."[30] Other Rwandan soldiers told a different group of peacekeepers that only orders from the minister of defense, whose authority was then being exercised by Bagosora, could permit the prime minister to address the nation on the radio.[31]

When UNAMIR soldiers arrived in four jeeps at the prime minister's home on the quiet, tree-lined street soon after 5:30 a.m., Rwandan soldiers opened fire on

[27]République Rwandaise, Parquet de la République de Kigali, PV no. 143.

[28]République Rwandaise, Parquet de la République de Kigali, PV no. 0033, no. 0034, no. 143, and no. 0146; [Belgium] Auditorat militaire près le Conseil de guerre, Declaration Pro Justitia, January 3, 1995 (confidential source); Lt. Col. J. Dewez, Kibat [Kigali Battalion], "Chronique, 06 avr-19avr 1994," September 1995, pp.7, 9, 12, 13-14,16, 18.

[29]République Rwandaise, Parquet de la République de Kigali, PV no. 0148.

[30]Reyntjens, *Rwanda, Trois Jours*, p. 67; République Rwandaise, Parquet de la République, de Kigali, PV no. 143.

[31]Dewez, "Chronique," p. 13.

them and immediately disabled two of the four jeeps. The peacekeepers, unable to withdraw, and Mme. Uwilingiyimana waited in vain for reinforcements. Just before 8:30, she and her husband tried first to scale the wall to get to the residence of an American diplomat next door. When that proved impossible, they fled in the other direction to the adjacent home of a U.N. employee.

Rwandan soldiers took the fifteen UNAMIR peacekeepers prisoner and, at about 9 a.m., delivered them to the Kigali military camp, only a few hundred meters from the prime minister's residence. There the five Ghanaian peacekeepers in the group were led away to safety and the ten Belgians were left at the hands of a furious crowd of soldiers, including a number who had been wounded in the war. The Rwandan soldiers had been prepared to hate the Belgian troops by months of RTLM broadcasts and believed the rumor—spread by their officers and later broadcast by RTLM—that the Belgians had helped the RPF shoot down Habyarimana's plane. They set upon the Belgian peacekeepers and battered most of them to death. The surviving Belgians took refuge in a small building near the entrance to the camp. They killed a Rwandan soldier and got hold of his weapon. Using that, they fought off the attackers for several more hours.[32]

At 10 o'clock that morning, about one hundred officers of the Rwandan armed forces assembled under the leadership of Bagosora to discuss a transitional government. The meeting took place at the Ecole Supérieure Militaire, just adjacent to the camp where the UNAMIR soldiers were being held. Bagosora once again proposed that the military take control of the government, but was once again rebuffed by his fellow officers who argued that soldiers had no place in politics. They did agree, however, to create a "crisis committee" to assist civilian politicians in forming a government. At about 10:30, the camp commander came to inform Bagosora and General Ndindiliyimana that Belgian soldiers were under attack at the camp, but they did nothing, not even shortly after when the sound of gunfire from the camp interrupted the meeting briefly.[33]

Just before 11 a.m., Dallaire drove to the meeting, passing by the entrance to the military camp where he saw that several UNAMIR soldiers lay on the ground. He wanted to enter the camp, but was prevented from doing so by his Rwandan

---

[32]Ibid., pp.11-14; Dallaire, "Answers to Questions;" Alexandre Goffin, *10 Commandos Vont Mourir* (Editions Luc Pire, n.p. n.d.), pp. 63-65, 73-77; Reyntjens, *Rwanda, Trois Jours,* pp. 67-69.

[33] République Rwandaise, Parquet de la République de Kigali, PV. no. 0370, no. 0146, no. 0034, no. 0201, and no. 0112; [Belgium] Auditorat militaire près le Conseil de guerre Declaration Pro Justitia, January 3, 1995.

military escort. At the meeting, he did not raise the question of the UNAMIR soldiers at the camp until the session ended at about noon. Dallaire then asked Ndindiliyimana to intervene to rescue them. Ndindiliyimana reportedly told him that Bagosora would take care of the problem.Throughout the day, Dallaire tried repeatedly to obtain permission to enter the camp, but Bagosora, who was clearly in charge, refused to allow him to do so. Dallaire believed that his troops and resources were too limited to fight his way into the camp to rescue the peacekeepers.[34]

As the leaders of the Rwandan armed forces debated the future government in the presence of the commander of the U.N. peacekeepers, soldiers continued their search for the current prime minister in the neighborhood just across the road from the meeting place. Capt. Gaspard Hategekimana of the Presidential Guard, apparently in charge of finding the prime minister, kept checking at various barricades, insisting that Mme. Uwilingiyimana could not have escaped the blockade that had been in place since the night before. Shortly before noon, soldiers discovered Mme Uwilingiyimana in her hiding place. Other soldiers in the area heard the applause and shouts of joy and knew that she had been captured. She came out quickly and without struggle, apparently because she wanted to protect her children who were hiding in the same area. She tried to persuade the soldiers to take her to the military camp. A small group, including some from southern Rwanda, were willing to do so. Others refused and wanted to execute her immediately. Captain Hategekimana reportedly arrived and gave the order to kill her on the spot. A lieutenant of the National Police, who was in training to become a judicial officer, shot the prime minister, blowing away the left half of her face. Witnesses who came to the house soon after found her nearly naked body on the terrace and carried it into the house. Another witness who passed an hour or so later found that her dressing gown had been thrown up over her upper body and that a beer bottle had been shoved into her vagina.[35] Her husband and two other men were

---

[34]Dallaire, "Answers to Questions."

[35]Opponents had often called the prime minister a whore and accused her of sexual relations with other political leaders. The first woman to hold such high office in Rwanda, she was said to have been raped in an attack by political adversaries two years before.

also slain, but her five children escaped and were eventually brought to safety by Capt. Mbaye Daigne, a Senegalese officer of the U.N. contingent.[36]

Officers leaving their meeting just after noon learned that the prime minister had been killed. At that time, Bagosora went to the military camp next door. Shortly after, Rwandan soldiers renewed the attack on the last Belgians, overcame their resistance, and killed them in the early afternoon.[37]

Early that same morning, soldiers and police had executed the two candidates for the presidency of the transitional assembly, Félicien Ngango of the PSD, and Landoald Ndasingwa of the PL, one of whom would have replaced Habyarimana according to the Arusha Accords. They had also murdered Joseph Kavaruganda, the president of the Constitutional Court, who would have been needed to swear in new authorities. RTLM had targeted Ndasingwa since December and, in February, the radio station had remarked of Kavaruganda that "we should rid ourselves of [him], one of the biggest accomplices of the RPF."[38] Rwandan soldiers and National Police had attacked the other heads of opposition political parties, either killing them or forcing them to hide or flee. They had worked from lists that allowed them to locate their victims efficiently.[39]

By mid-day April 7, the Presidential Guard, with the help of soldiers of other elite battalions and some National Policemen, had eliminated those leaders who could have legitimately governed. Bagosora, who was giving the orders to these soldiers, had failed in his effort to get himself installed officially as head of a new government, but he still had the chance to influence—if not to dictate—the choice of persons who would form a new government. At the same time, Rwandan

---

[36]République Rwandaise, Parquet de la République de Kigali, PV. no. 0370, no. 0146, no. 0034, no. 0201, and no. 0112; [Belgium] Auditorat militaire près le Conseil de guerre, Declaration Pro Justitia, January 3, 1995; Guichaoua, *Les Crises Politiques*, p. 709.

[37]République Rwandaise, Parquet de la République de Kigali, PV. no. 0370, no. 0146, no. 0034, no. 0201, and no. 0112.

[38]Communiqué de Mme. Annunciata Kavaruganda; Declaration of Louise Mushikiwabo, Appendix of Declarations and Statutory Materials in Support of Plaintiffs' Motion for Default Judgment, United States District Court, Southern District of New York, No.94 Civ. 3627 (JSM), Louise Mushikiwabo, et al., against Jean Bosco Barayagwiza.

[39]Dewez, "Chronique," pp. 7, 9,16; Human Rights Watch interview, Kigali, October 29, 1994; Human Rights Watch interview, by telephone, Nairobi, May 5, 1994; Dallaire, "Answers to Questions."

soldiers had killed ten Belgian peacekeepers, the first step in the plan revealed in the January 11 cable for getting rid of an effective UNAMIR force. The afternoon of April 7, both Bagosora and Ndindiliyimana told Dallaire that the killings at Camp Kigali showed that it might be best for Belgian troops to leave Rwanda.[40] While the leadership of the Rwandan armed forces and of UNAMIR sat in the meeting room at the military school, just outside the decisive blows had been struck against both Rwandan and foreign forces that could have assured a peaceful transition and that could perhaps have averted a genocide.

Ambiguities and Double Language

In the afternoon of April 7, Bagosora carried on the pretense of restoring order by issuing a press release in the name of the Rwandan army about efforts "to stabilize the situation in the country rapidly." Knowing that it was the Presidential Guard and other elite units that were engaged in slaughter throughout the city, he "invited" the armed forces to "restore order in the country." Fully aware that the prime minister and other leading officials had been slain, he urged creating the "conditions necessary for authorities to work in good order." He asked the "government in power" to do its job knowing that there was no such government. He called for speedy implementation of the Arusha Accords although preventing this had been his stated objective for months. And he asked the population to resist all efforts to increase hatred and all kinds of violence even as he was presumably counting on just such hatred and violence to achieve his objective.[41]

Many military officers understood that Bagosora and his supporters were saying one thing and doing another. One officer observed, "The official orders were to restore order. But it was clear that, in fact, other orders were also being given."[42] A high-ranking officer declared in a sworn statement that there were "operations carried out by soldiers, including those of the PG [Presidential Guard] which implemented a preestablished plan that was known to a hidden network."[43] When a senior officer ordered Col. Muberuka, who commanded the zone of Kigali, to have the Presidential Guard halt their attacks, he replied that he had tried to do

---

[40]Dallaire, "Answers to Questions."

[41]Reyntjens, *Rwanda, Trois Jours*, pp. 132-33.

[42]Human Rights Watch/FIDH interview, January 26, 1996.

[43]République Rwandaise, Parquet de la République de Kigali, PV no.0142.

so but that the immediate commander of the unit asserted that all his troops were already in camp.[44]

Not everyone playing a double game was part of the "hidden network." In the first day or two, other officers, unsure who would finally dominate and what the program would be, temporized and tried to please superiors—and foreigners—who had different objectives. Commanding officers made commitments that their subordinates failed to honor, leaving open the question of whether it was the superior officer or the subordinate who was obeying instructions from the hidden network. Throughout the first days, for example, Ndindiliyimana repeatedly professed willingness to collaborate with UNAMIR, but many of his men delayed or refused participation in joint patrols, sometimes asserting they had received no orders to do so. In one case, National Policemen even backed a hostile crowd attacking UNAMIR soldiers. In another, Ndindiliyimana reportedly sent National Police to protect endangered people at the Ecole Technique Officielle (ETO), a technical school in Kigali, but the troops joined the assailants rather than stopping them. Elsewhere in Kigali, National Police officers at a barrier confronted each other over the question of whether armed militia should be allowed to pass without being disarmed. Each was obeying a different set of instructions.[45]

Not even the new chief of staff was safe from the double game. Bagosora had called Colonel Gatsinzi in Butare at 2 a.m. to inform him of his nomination and to insist that he come to Kigali before dawn. Gatsinzi refused to travel at night, given the uncertainty of the situation. When he did arrive in the capital the next day, his vehicle was fired on as it approached the city and one of his escort was wounded. The newly named interim president, Dr. Théodore Sindikubwabo, was also traveling with Gatsinzi. It is unclear whether one or both were targeted and by whom, but the attack may have represented one more effort to prevent the installation of a civilian government or of a military chief of staff not chosen by Bagosora himself.[46]

With Gatsinzi at least nominally in command of the armed forces, he, Rusatira, and Ndindiliyimana sought to wrest control from Bagosora. When the crisis

---

[44]Ibid.

[45]République Rwandaise, Parquet de la République de Kigali, PV no. 0004; Human Rights Watch/FIDH interviews, Plainsboro, N.J., June 14, 1996; January 26, 1996; Brussels, August 3, 1998; Dewez, "Chronique," pp. 11-12,19; Goffin, 10 Commandos, p. 100.

[46]Reyntjens, Rwanda, Trois Jours, p. 83.

committee met on the evening of April 7, they refused to allow him to run the meeting. He insulted the others, particularly Rusatira and boycotted the rest of the meeting. The others made some plans for bringing the Presidential Guard under control and for setting up a government based on the Arusha Accords.[47]

To outvote Bagosora was much simpler than it would have been to outfight him. The Presidential Guard, with the best trained and best armed soldiers in the Rwandan armed forces, stood outside the normal command structure and had been under the orders of Col. Elie Sagatwa, Habyarimana's private secretary who had died in the plane crash. Bagosora reportedly took control of this unit after Sagatwa's death and also had the loyalty of the commanders of the reconnaissance and paracommando battalions, the other two strongest units in the Rwandan army. The Presidential Guard numbered between 1,300 and 1,500 men, having been strengthened soon after the Arusha Accords by the transfer of two companies from the paracommandos.[48] The majority of these troops were posted in Kigali. With some 800 men of the paracommando and reconnaissance battalions, this made a total of some 2,000 elite troops that Bagosora could count on. In contrast, Rusatira, head of a school instead of a fighting unit, had about 100 soldiers at his command, his personal bodyguard and the staff and students of his school. Gatsinzi headed a battalion, but it was located in Butare. Ndindiliyimana commanded thousands of National Police, but, with the resumption of the war, some of the force was integrated into the regular army command, thus limiting his freedom of action. He had perhaps 1,000 men in Kigali and its vicinity but his troops lacked both the battle experience and the heavy weaponry of combat soldiers.[49] In addition, they had surrendered many of their best weapons, R 4 rifles, to UNAMIR in mid-March as part of the process of creating a weapons-free zone for Kigali, while the Presidential Guard had not given over any of theirs. Before dawn on April 7, the reconnaisance battalion recalled to Kigali the armored personnel carriers that they

---

[47]République Rwandaise, Parquet de la République de Kigali, PV no. 0259, 0142; Police Judiciaire près le Parquet du Procureur du Roi de Bruxelles, No. 41.312, dossier 57/95 (confidential source).

[48]Human Rights Watch/FIDH interview, Brussels, May 26, 1997.

[49]Human Rights Watch/FIDH interviews, by telephone, Antwerp, April 15, 1997 and Brussels, October 20, 1997; Police Judiciaire près le Parquet du Procureur du Roi de Bruxelles, No. 41.312, dossier 57/95.

had sent to Rambura, in the north, to evade UNAMIR control.[50] Bagosora's clear superiority in arms and troop strength was no doubt one reason the other officers preferred to challenge him at the committee table rather than on the battlefield.

Resumption of the war late in the afternoon of April 7 complicated the struggle for dominance within the Rwandan government forces. RPF leader Tito Rutaremara had warned Ndindiliyimana and Bagosora that the RPF would attack if the slaughter of civilians did not stop. When the killings continued, RPF troops came out of their CND headquarters and engaged the Presidential Guard.[51] With the RPF in the field, those opposed to Bagosora had the possibility of cooperating with them to restore order and they explored this possibility through the good offices of Dallaire. General Kagame was receptive and even sent Seth Sendashonga with an offer to create a joint force composed of 300 soldiers each from the RPF, the Rwandan army units opposed to Bagosora, and UNAMIR to bring an end to the massacres.[52] During the weekend of April 9 to 10, Radio Muhabura, the voice of the RPF, encouraged Rwandan government soldiers to dissociate themselves from their fellows who were slaughtering civilians. They even publicized the names of officers who, they said, were threatened because they had refused to participate in such killings.[53]

The senior officers opposed to Bagosora either could not bring themselves to join forces with the long-standing enemy or did not believe that they could lead a substantial number of soldiers into such an arrangement. They looked instead to the international community for support. Dallaire would have liked to help what he saw as a "new army," but he was blocked by the narrow interpretation of the mandate as well as by a shortage of troops and equipment. Ndindiliyimana explored the possibility of foreign support with the Belgian ambassador Johan Swinnen on the evening of April 7 and Rusatira had contacts with Swinnen, with representatives of the U.S., and with a French general in Paris. But diplomats in

---

[50]République Rwandaise, Parquet de la République de Kigali, PV. no. 0034, no.143, no. 0370; Police Judiciaire près le Parquet du Procureur du Roi de Bruxelles, No. 41.312, dossier 57/95.

[51]Reyntjens, *Rwanda, Trois Jours*, pp. 82-83.

[52]Human Rights Watch/FIDH interviews, Plainsboro, N.J., June 14, 1996; by telephone, Nairobi, March 7, 1998.

[53]Radio Muhabura, April 11, 1994, BBC Summary of World Broadcasts, AL/1970 A/5, April 13, 1994.

Kigali, as well as their ministries back home, were all focused on evacuating citizens of their own countries. No one had resources to offer to dissenters who hoped to oust Bagosora and stop the slaughter of Rwandans.[54]

The Interim Government

Early on the morning of April 8, Bagosora assembled party leaders to fashion a civilian government, all of them, not surprisingly, from the Hutu Power end of the political spectrum. The MRND was represented by its president Mathieu Ngirumpatse, Edouard Karemera, and Joseph Nzirorera, an intimate of the Akazu; MDR by its Power leaders, Froduald Karamira, the Hutu Power orator of October 1993, and Donat Murego, one of those originally courted by Habyarimana in March 1993; and PL by its Power advocates, Justin Mugenzi and Agnes Ntamabyaliro. It had been difficult to locate representatives of the PSD because its entire national committee had been killed or was in hiding, so two members of the political committee, François Ndungutse and Hyacinthe Nsengiyumva Rafiki were pressed into service. In attendance for the PDC were Jean-Marie Vianney Sibomana, Célestin Kabanda, and Gaspard Ruhumuliza, another who had been attracted by Habyarimana a year before.[55]

On the recommendation of MRND leaders, the group decided to install Dr. Théodore Sindikubwabo, an aging pediatrician and politician from Butare as president. Described by another public official as "someone with no personality," Sindikubwabo was a lonely figure, who was often found reading in his office. He had barely held on to his seat in the parliament at the time of the last election and played the figure-head role of president of that body with suitable docility.[56] Claiming that the Arusha Accords had not yet taken effect, the politicians made Sindikubwabo president of Rwanda under the terms of the 1991 constitution.

For prime minister the politicians settled on Jean Kambanda, a far younger and more vigorous man, but one with relatively little standing or experience at the national level. An economist and banker, he had unsuccessfully challenged Agathe

[54]Human Rights Watch/FIDH interviews, Plainsboro, N.J., June 14, 1996; by telephone, Brussels, April 27, 1997 and July 22, 1998; Reyntjens, *Rwanda, Trois Jours*, p. 84.

[55]Reyntjens, *Rwanda, Trois Jours*, pp. 86-87 and note.

[56]Human Rights Watch/FIDH interviews, Plainsboro, N.J., June 14, 1996; by telephone, Kigali, November 8, 1996; Tribunal de Première Instance de Bruxelles, Deposition de Témoin, September 18, 1995 Dossier 57/95.

Uwilingiyimana for the post of prime minister in August 1993. On April 7, Kambanda had fled to a nearby military camp where Karamira and Bagosora found him the next day and offered him the post. He reportedly accepted unwillingly and was driven away in a military vehicle.[57]

Sindikubwabo and Kambanda supported different parties—the MRND and MDR-Power—but both were from Butare. In addition, the minister of family and feminine affairs, Pauline Nyiramasuhuko, who had held the same post in the previous government, was from Butare, as was a newcomer to politics, Dr. Straton Nsabumukunzi, who was named minister of agriculture. The minister of interior, a hold-over from the previous cabinet, happened to be abroad at the time and refused to return to Rwanda.[58] Until a replacement was named at the end of May, the administrative head of the ministry acted in his place. He was Callixte Kalimanzira, also from Butare. Never before had Butare been so well represented in the most important positions of power. In inviting so many southerners to join them, Hutu Power advocates hoped both to increase their legitimacy generally and to augment the effectiveness of their control in the south. The arrangement corresponded exactly to what Bagosora had specified in his diary in early 1993 when he had written "War for the Bakiga, Politics for the Banyanduga." "Bakiga" meant people of the north and "Banyanduga" meant people of the central and southern part of the country.[59]

Bagosora presented the interim government to the crisis committee and other high-ranking military officers soon after its formation on April 8. As they looked over the proposed new authorities, the military officers saw quickly that Bagosora "had chosen these men himself and that this was not at all what the meeting the night before had decided."[60] But the same officers who for two days had resisted Hutu Power in the military incarnation of a Bagosora now accepted it in the

---

[57]Human Rights Watch/FIDH interview, Brussels, May 26, 1997; Notes of Chris McGreal, interview with Jean Kambanda, Bukavu, August, 1994.

[58]Faustin Munyazesa had been minister of interior since 1991, during the period of smaller-scale massacres of Tutsi and preparation for the genocide. He remained in Dar es Salaam after the April 6 meeting that he had attended with Habyarimana. When he heard of the plane crash, he exclaimed, "Forget Rwanda! It is finished! It is finished! It is finished!" Human Rights Watch/FIDH interview, by telephone, Kigali, December 19, 1997.

[59]Bagosora, "Agenda, 1993," entry for February 15.

[60]République Rwandaise, Parquet de la République de Kigali, PV. no. 0142.

political form of a self-proclaimed government. With the RPF pushing ahead vigorously, they felt pressure to shun politics and devote themselves completely to the work of being soldiers. Perhaps they also felt that they had taken their opposition as far as they could given the relative troop strength of the two sides and the absence of encouragement from foreign powers. Having accepted a proposed government that fell far short of the balanced group that some had expected, the crisis committee adjourned, never to meet again.[61]

The interim government presented itself as a legitimate continuation of the previous one, formed, like it, under the terms of an agreement between the parties signed on April 16, 1992. The party representatives summoned by Bagosora to set up the government even drew up a protocol to make their arrangements look proper.[62] But anyone aware of the divisions within the parties and acquainted with the positions of their representatives could see through the pretense: the interim government may have adhered to the letter of the 1992 arrangement, but it completely violated the spirit, representing as it did a single point of view. In announcing its goals, the interim government carried on the deception. The interim president Sindikubwabo declared that the new government would rapidly re-establish security and would continue negotiations with the RPF in order to install the broad-based government within six weeks. The actions of the new authorities would reveal what the words did not. Security would be limited to Hutu who supported their position and serious negotiations would not take place. The third of the stated goals, to cope with the problem of famine was genuine, a response to the increasingly serious shortage of food in the country.[63]

The interim government took office on April 9 and fled from the capital on April 12, just after the first RPF troops from northern Rwanda arrived in Kigali to reinforce those previously quartered in the city. It operated for a number of weeks at Murambi, near the capital of the prefecture of Gitarama, before fleeing further west and then north to Gisenyi and leaving Rwanda in mid-July.

---

[61]Human Rights Watch/FIDH interview, Plainsboro, N.J.; June 14, 1996; Reyntjens, *Rwanda, Trois Jours*, pp. 90-91.

[62]Reyntjens, *Rwanda, Trois Jours*, pp. 134-6.

[63]Ijambo Perezida w'Inama y'Igihugu Iharanira Amajyambere Dr. Sindikubwabo Théodore Ageza ku Banyarwanda Kwa 8 Mata 1994, enclosed in Fawusitini Munyazeza, Minisitiri w'Ubutegetsi bw'Igihugu n'Amajyambere ya Komini, [actually signed by C. Kalimanzira] to Bwana Perefe wa Prefegitura (Bose), April 21, 1994 (Butare prefecture).

Launching the Campaign
The Initiators

By April 6, hundreds of thousands of Rwandans counted themselves part of Hutu Power, but those who launched the genocide and slaughter of Hutu adversaries were few in number. The initiators appear to have included military officers like Bagosora and the commanders of the three elite units, Major Protais Mpiranya of the Presidential Guard, Major Francois-Xavier Nzuwonemye of the reconnaissance battalion, and Major Aloys Ntabakuze of the paracommando battalion, as well as Lt. Col. Léonard Nkundiye, formerly head of the Presidential Guards, Captain Gaspard Hategekimana, who oversaw the execution of the prime minister, and Major Bernard Ntuyahaga, who apparently directed killings in the central residential area of Kigali and celebrated them afterwards in noisy parties at his home.[64] Given the number of attacks that took place almost immediately in the northwestern prefecture of Gisenyi, Col. Anatole Nsengiyumva, the local commander, seems to have been among the first implementers of the killing plan.[65] Col. Tharcisse Renzaho, a military man who was prefect of Kigali, quickly marshalled his administrative subordinates to organize the patrols and barriers needed to capture and kill Tutsi. He also maintained links with the militia who accorded him immediate obedience when he went around the city.[66]

Some militia were out in the streets before dawn April 7 and others, identifiable as MRND and CDR members through their distinctive caps, were digging up buried weapons at daybreak.[67]

The president and vice-president of the Interahamwe, Robert Kajuga and George Rutaganda, as well as the heads of the MRND and the CDR, Mathieu Ngirumpatse and Jean-Bosco Barayagwiza, may have called them out. Ngirumpatse and other politicians, such as Froduald Karamira, Joseph Nzirorera, Edouard Karemera, Justin Mugenzi, and Donat Murego, put together the interim government at the request of Bagosora and hence were responsible for the

---

[64]Tribunal de Première Instance de Bruxelles, Compte-Rendu de la Commission rogatoire internationale exécutée au Rwanda du 1er au 13 mai 1995, dossier no. 57/95.

[65]République Rwandaise, Parquet de la République de Kigali, PV. no. 0133.

[66]Human Rights Watch/FIDH interview, New York, May 15, 1996.

[67]Tribunal de Première Instance de Bruxelles, Deposition de Témoin, September 18, 1995 Dossier 57/95.

composition of this group that put the state at the service of genocide. They also mobilized their followers, directly and by radio, to join in the killings.

Some members of the akazu appear to have played significant, but less public, roles. Witnesses present during the first two days after the plane crash claim that Mme. Habyarimana was involved in political decisions, including the naming of Gatsinzi to the post of chief of staff of the army, an assertion which she has denied. The witnesses also declared that she and others followed events closely and that "...all the family that was there, including the religious sisters, rejoiced when they announced the death of one or another opponent. It was the Presidential Guards who announced that and they boasted about these murders."[68] Madame Habyarimana was evacuated from Rwanda on April 9 by the French government. She may have continued to influence decisions from Paris, but it is unlikely that she was involved in detailed management of political affairs at that distance.

The activities of others close to the Habyarimana family should be investigated for possible links to killings. Michel Bagaragaza, the director of the Rwandan tea marketing office OCIR-Thé and linked to Mme. Habyarimana, was at home on April 6 and 7 near the parish of Rambura, supposedly to prepare for a family wedding. Rambura was the site of some of the first killings outside Kigali. Three priests at the parish were slain at dawn, followed soon after by three Belgian volunteers who worked at a school run by persons linked to the akazu, including Bagosora.[69] During the days of large-scale slaughter, Colonel Rwagafilita, a member of the akazu, was frequently seen at the military camp in Kibungo. Soon after militia and military had massacred some 1,000 people at the St. Joseph Center at the bishopric, a witness found Rwagafilita at the camp drinking beer with Cyasa Habimana, the local head of the Interahamwe who had led the attack, and the camp commander, Col. Anselme Nkuliyekubona.[70]

The first killers, like the first leaders, represented only a small part of the number who would finally be drawn into participation. In Kigali, where the

---

[68]Auditorat Militaire, Bruxelles, PV no. 1013, Dossier no. 02 02545 N94 C8 (confidential source). Two sisters of Habyarimana were members of a religious congregation.

[69]Commission d'enquête, *Rapport,* pp. 461-62.

[70]Human Rights Watch/FIDH interview, Kibungo, January 30, 1995; Commission pour le Mémorial du Génocide et des Massacres au Rwanda, "Rapport Préliminaire d'Identification des Sites du Génocide et des Massacres d'avril-juillet 1994 au Rwanda," February 1996, pp. 113-5.

violence was most concentrated, they included more than a thousand Presidential Guards along with several hundred troops from other elite battalions or from the National Police. The militia provided another 2,000.[71] Outside the capital, assailants killed Tutsi at sites that were widely dispersed, but relatively few in number, perhaps some two dozen in the first day or two. The killers who responded to the initial call to slaughter probably numbered no more than 6,000 to 7,000 throughout the country.

For the first few days, it was not clear how many more of the hundreds of thousands who had been influenced by the ideas of Hutu Power were prepared to kill, rape, maim, burn, or pillage in its name. But by the middle of the following week, the initiators were assured of the support they needed to attempt the wholesale elimination of the Tutsi.

Sharpening the Focus on Tutsi

By Monday, April 11, an estimated 20,000 Rwandans had been slain, the vast majority of them Tutsi.[72] But because some of the first victims had been highly visible Hutu and because assailants continued to target Hutu adversaries of the MRND and the CDR, many Hutu also feared for their lives. They saw the killings as broader than a genocide and as constituting also an extreme form of kubohoza with victims chosen on partisan, regional or economic grounds. Both in Kigali and elsewhere, Hutu cooperated with Tutsi in fighting off militia attacks or they fled together to places of refuge. Often Hutu made such decisions not just because of their political beliefs but also because of ties of family or friendship with Tutsi.[73]

Bagosora and his supporters set out to reorient the violence on more specifically ethnic grounds, both to break the bonds between Hutu and Tutsi and to win over Hutu from outside the MRND and the CDR who feared that the new authorities had seized power for the exclusive benefit of these parties. They first distanced themselves from the "serious troubles" that had resulted in the murders of Hutu political leaders, like Prime Minister Uwilingiyimana, and blamed these

---

[71]Human Rights Watch/FIDH interview, Bruxelles, May 26, 1997.

[72]Terry Leonard, "New Fighting is Reported in Rwanda as Foreigners Flee," Associated Press, April 11, 1994.

[73]Human Rights Watch interviews, by telephone, Kigali, April 7, 8, 10, 1994; Dr. Clément Kayishema, Préfet, "Rapport sur la Sécurité dans la Précture Kibuye," April 10, 1994, p. 3 (Kibuye prefecture).

crimes on unruly troops acting without orders.[74] Then on April 11 and 12, political and governmental leaders began working more actively to build an anti-Tutsi alliance that cut across party and regional lines.

On Monday, April 11, the new authorities summoned the prefects to Kigali, but only five attended the meeting. Four posts were vacant—one because the Ruhengeri prefect had just been killed by the RPF—and two other prefects did not attend. The meeting was brief and seemingly inconclusive. The interim prime minister had hardly come to terms with his new power, the minister of interior was absent and represented by a subordinate, and the success of the new authorities was hardly assured. Still the session permitted national leaders to track the progress of the slaughter and to evaluate the willingess of the administrators to be drawn into further action. After making their reports, the prefects were sent home without clear orders or any additional resources to end the violence. In this highly centralized political system where superiors regulated even minor details of policy implementation, the absence of a message was itself a message: attacks were to continue.

The next day, both political and governmental leaders began mobilizing popular support for genocide. By inciting the people against Tutsi, they clarified the indirect message delivered the previous day to the administrators. Speaking on Radio Rwanda early on the morning of April 12, MDR-Power leader Frodauld Karamira told his listeners that the war was "everyone's responsibility," an idea that would be repeated frequently in the next few weeks. He called on people to "not fight among themselves" but rather to "assist the armed forces to finish their work."[75] This was a directive to the MDR-Power supporters to forget their differences with the MRND and the CDR and to collaborate with them in tracking Tutsi. Without this collaboration, advocated by Karamira since his "Hutu Power" speech the previous October, the genocide would have remained limited to strongholds of the MRND and the CDR.

An hour later, Radio Rwanda broadcast a press release from the Ministry of Defense. It denied "lies" about divisions in the armed forces and among Hutu generally and insisted that:

---

[74]Ijambo Perezida w'Inama y'Igihugu Iharanira Amajyambere Dr. Sindikubwabo Théodore Ageza ku Banyarwanda Kwa Mata 1994 (April 8, 1994).

[75]Radio Rwanda, "Radio Rwanda broadcasts appeal by official of the pro-army faction of the MDR," April 12, 1994, SWB, AL/1970 A/2, April 13, 1994.

Soldiers, gendarmes [National Police], and all Rwandans have decided to fight their common enemy in unison and all have identified him. The enemy is still the same. He is the one who has always been trying to return the monarch who was overthrown....the Ministry of Defence asks Rwandans, soldiers and gendarmes the following: citizens are asked to act together, carry out patrols and fight the enemy.[76]

One witness recalled: "They talked only about uniting together, saying we had to fight the enemy. They said that parties and kubohoza were no longer important."[77] In the streets of Kigali, people were singing a little song that told it all:

Umwanzi wacu n'umwe	Our enemy is one
turamuzi	We know him
n'umututsi[78]	It is the Tutsi.

The RPF sought to counter this effort to redefine the violence on ethnic grounds. On Radio Muhabura, Kagame denounced the use of ethnic strife as a pretext and declared that it was clear "that these acts of murder are political."[79] Much as Radio Muhabura had played upon divisions between moderate and Hutu Power soldiers, so, too, it stressed the partisan and regional nature of attacks on civilians.[80]

RTLM in turn sought to discredit the image of Hutu-Tutsi cohesion within the RPF by broadcasting a false report that Kagame, the Tutsi general, and

---

[76]Radio Rwanda, "Defence Ministry communique urges Rwandans to ignore 'the lies' of RPF radio,"April 12, 1994, SWB, AL/1970 A/5, April 13, 1994.

[77]Human Rights Watch/FIDH interview, Mukingi, July 10, 1996.

[78]Human Rights Watch/FIDH interview, Kigali, February 14, 1997.

[79]"RPF Leader Kagame Says His Forces Will Act Against the Presidential Guard," April 9, 1994, SWB, AL/1968 A/4, April 11, 1994.

[80] Radio Muhabura, "RPF radio reports killings by presidential guards and pro-Habyarimana militia,"April 11, 1994, SWB, AL/1970 A/5, April 13, 1994.

Kanyarengwe, the Hutu president of the RPF, had killed each other in a power struggle.[81]

As RTLM and Radio Rwanda increasingly defined the Tutsi as the target, officials moved to prevent their escape from the country. On April 13, an officer of the army general staff telephoned the official in charge of immigration at the Butare prefecture and ordered him to grant no more authorisations for travel to adjacent countries. That night, Tutsi attempting to cross the river to Burundi were slaughtered at Nyakizu. Authorities in Gisenyi also refused permission to Tutsi to cross into Zaire.[82] As Mugesera had declared in November 1992, and many others had echoed since, authorities had made a serious mistake in permitting Tutsi to flee after the 1959 revolution. That mistake, they said, must not be repeated.

Military Opposition: The April 12 Statement

After having permitted Bagosora to install the interim government, the senior officers opposed to him briefly suspended open political action. Whether motivated by hope, fear, or opportunism—or simply absorbed in combat with the RPF—they made no public protest as the bodies mounted on the streets of Kigali. But, on April 12, Rusatira, who had presented himself to foreign diplomats as the liaison of the new government three days before, decided that he must seek to halt the slaughter.[83] That day he escorted dozens of persons whom he had been sheltering in his own Kigali home to Gitarama. En route Rusatira saw many cadavers, including those of two National Policemen shot because they were Tutsi or because they had been trying to defend civilians. At Gitarama he sought out political leaders and tried in vain to persuade them to halt the killings. When Rusatira returned to Kigali, he enlisted nine other officers to sign a statement that he drafted. Without the approval of the interim government, they had the declaration broadcast on the radio, calling for an "end to this tragedy." They proposed a truce to facilitate talks with the RPF to "promptly restore order in the country and install the broad-based

---

[81] Agence France Press, "RPF official tells AFP that reports of death of RPF leader are a 'rumour,'" April 11, 1994 SWB, AL/1970 A/5, April 13, 1994.

[82] Des prêtres du diocèse de Nyundo, "Des Rescapés du Diocèse de Nyundo Témoignent," p. 59 and Soeur Patricia Massart, "A Butare, Au Jour Le Jour," p. 78, *Dialogue*, no.177, August-September, 1994. For Nyakizu, see chapter nine.

[83] Human Rights Watch/FIDH interview, by telephone, July 22, 1998.

transitional government, in order to avoid continuing to spill innocent blood for no reason at all."[84]

This effort came too late. The initiators of genocide had chosen their strategy and were prepared to stand behind it. Bagosora and his supporters were outraged by the officers' initiative and regarded it as proof that the signers were traitors. Rusatira was informed that a squad of the Presidential Guard was to assassinate him that night and went into hiding. Soon after, Minister of Primary and Secondary Education André Rwamakuba and MDR-Power leader Shingiro Mbonuyumutwa reportedly denounced the officers who had signed the statement during a public meeting at Kibilira, in Gisenyi prefecture. Whether to respond to the senior officers or to external pressure, the interim government named a delegation to talk with the RPF, but the discussions went nowhere.[85]

Strategies of Slaughter
Priority Targets

From the start, in Kigali and out on the hills, leaders directed two kinds of killing: that of specific individuals and that of Tutsi as a group.[86] The organizers aimed first to eliminate any authorities who could stand in the way of their taking power. They kept track of their deaths and, according to one military witness, "passed on the news of each assassination like a trophy."[87] They were angered at the escape of a few intended victims, like Prime Minister-designate Faustin Twagiramungu, and pursued them relentlessly. The organizers also sought to kill other individuals who had criticized the Habyarimana regime and who could be expected to criticize the interim government: leaders of the MDR, PL, PSD, and PDC who rejected Hutu Power, members of the judiciary, human rights activists, clergy, journalists, and other leaders of civil society. Most of the targeted political authorities were Hutu, as were many of the leaders of civil society. In addition, the

---

[84]Colonels Rusatira, Gatsinzi, Muberuka, Ntiwiragabo, Kanyamanza, Murasampongo, Hakizimana and Lieutenant Colonels Rwabalinda, Rwamanywa, and Kanyandekwe, "Communiqué du Commandement des Forces Armées Rwandaises," Kigali, April 12, 1994. Ndindiliyimana was said to have supported the statement but did not sign.

[85]Human Rights Watch/FIDH interview, by telephone, Brussels, April 27, 1997.

[86] Jean-Pierre Godding, "Refugié d'un Rwanda à Feu et à Sang," Dialogue, no. 177, August-September 1994, p. 39.

[87]République Rwandaise, Parquet de la République de Kigali, PV. no. 0370.

organizers marked particular Tutsi as priority targets, either because of their wealth and influence or because of their real or presumed support for the RPF.

As early as daybreak on April 7, the organizers had already distributed lists of the names of these specially targeted persons, both Hutu and Tutsi, to squads of killers. At 7:30 that morning, one Rwandan soldier on the outskirts of the city heard gunfire near his house. When he went out to see what was happening, he observed a typical scene:

> ...I saw nine soldiers of the paracommando battalion and of the GP and a civilian who was apparently guiding them. He held a list of names in his hand. It was a list of people to be killed. They went to another neighbor and threw grenades and shot open the door of the house. They killed the people inside. They left on foot. My household worker, whom I sent to follow them, told me later that they had shot at a series of houses (four families).[88]

Radio RTLM involved the general public in hunting down named individuals, directed killers where to find them and then announced their murders. One person who was targeted recalls that he and others at risk listened to RTLM because it "indicated the victims and we wanted to know if we were on the list of people selected to be hunted."[89] On April 8, announcer Valérie Bemerki told listeners that RPF hiding at the home of Tutsi businessman Antoine Sebera had been attacked and "now they are being grilled right there...now they are burning."[90] In fact, Sebera's home had not yet been attacked but the report set it up as a target and it was besieged and burned soon after. Several days later, Noël Hitimana announced that the home of Joseph Kahabaye in Kivugiza was a RPF bastion, with many agents hidden in the ceiling. Militia attacked the area within hours and killed Kabahaye. Charles Kalinjabo, too, was murdered after having been denounced on RTLM.[91] On April 10, Bemerki read a list of thirteen "responsables du FPR," important agents of the RPF, their addresses, places of work, and where they spent

---

[88]République Rwandaise, Parquet de la République de Kigali, PV. no. 0146.

[89]Tribunal de Première Instance de Bruxelles, Deposition de Témoin, September 18, 1995 Dossier 57/95.

[90]Article 19, *Broadcasting Genocide*, p. 125. Sebera had been one of the Tutsi named in the above-mentioned September 1992 military memorandum defining the enemy.

[91]Ibid., p. 127.

their leisure time. The information had supposedly come from a document found in the possession of a RPF agent. Asserting that these people were preparing to kill Hutu, Bemerki urged all people who wanted security to "rise up" against these "spies":

> ...you have heard their names, with their sectors and their cells, so we find that these people are really plotting with the Inyenzi-Inkotanyi in order to kill...Rwandans.[92]

She invited listeners who would like to look for these persons to call her for more information.

Targeted individuals who escaped were tracked by authorities to the other side of Kigali, to other communes, or even to the island of Idjwi in Zaire.[93] Tutsi who fled to the large displaced persons camps at Kabgayi in central Rwanda were followed by people from their home regions who appeared, list in hand, to search for them among the crowds. In one well-known case, a group of Tutsi assembled in this way at Kabgayi were stripped naked and forced on a bus that took them to Ngorerero in Gisenyi, where they were killed.[94]

Even when assailants were preparing to massacre large numbers of Tutsi at places of refuge, they often had in mind specific persons whom they wanted to be sure to kill. A survivor of the massacre at Mugonero hospital in Kibuye reported that he heard such a list read over a loudspeaker before the attack began.[95] Another survivor declared that once the killing was finished,

> They sent people in among the bodies to verify who was dead. They said, "Here is the treasurer and his wife and daughter, but where is the younger child?" Or, "Here is Josue's father, his wife and mother, but where is he?" And then, in the days after, they tried to hunt you down if they thought you were

---

[92]RTLM broadcast, April 10, 1994, recorded by Faustin Kagame (provided by Article 19).

[93]African Rights, *Rwanda, Death, Despair*, p. 439.

[94]Human Rights Watch/FIDH interview, Butare, March 7, 1996; Commission pour le Mémorial du Génocide et des Massacres au Rwanda, "Rapport Préliminaire," p. 67; African Rights, *Rwanda, Death, Despair*, p.439.

[95]Human Rights Watch/FIDH interview, Kigali, September 12, 1995.

still alive. They would shout out, "Hey Josue, we see you now" to make you jump and try to run so that they could see you move and get you more easily.[96]

Thorough Elimination: "Begin on One Side..."

As squads sought out the most wanted victims on the morning of April 7, Bagosora was reportedly overheard directing the commanders of the elite military units, "*Muhere aruhande*," "Begin on one side...," ordering a systematic sweep of Tutsi and opponents of Hutu Power from one side of the city through to the other.[97]

A witness in the section known as Remera related the progress of the killers in her neighborhood in telephone conversations every half hour of the first night of the genocide. She told a Human Rights Watch researcher in the United States how a group of soldiers were shooting people in houses on the street below her home. Then she recounted how they were moving up her street, from one house to the next. With the sound of gunfire in the background, she described how three neighbors from the house next door were being executed at the corner of the street. When the soldiers banged on her own door, she hung up the phone. She fled, hid for several days, and was finally evacuated to safety.[98]

Both RTLM and Radio Rwanda identified areas of Kigali to be attacked, like Gikondo or the buildings of the law faculty of the university. RTLM announcer Hitimana congratulated those who had searched out Tutsi:

> ...the population is very vigilant, except in certain sectors...where people are still downcast; otherwise, everywhere else, they have sacked all the houses, the rooms, the kitchens, everywhere! They have even torn out all the doors and windows in all the uninhabited houses, [and] in general they find inkotanyi hidden inside. They have searched everywhere!...If they [the inkotanyi] get

---

[96]Human Rights Watch/FIDH interview, Kigali, September 12, 1995.

[97]Reyntjens, *Rwanda, Trois Jours*, p. 58.

[98]Human Rights Watch/Africa, eight interviews, by telephone, Kigali, April 7, 1994. Many relatives and friends of Rwandans in Europe and North America received similar calls. The Belgian peacekeepers' log of these days gives some sense of the horror. See Dewez, "Chronique."

hungry, they'll all come out before you arrive. That is why you must act very fast! Force them to come out! Find them at whatever cost.[99]

Georges Ruggiu, the Belgian announcer who worked for RTLM, enthusiastically joined in inciting violence. He alerted listeners that:

around the hill Mbunabutuso [sic, Mburabuturo], in the woods...suspect movements of people have been observed...People of Rugonga [sic, Rugunga], of Kanongo [sic, Kanogo], by the gas station, pay attention, go to check out that woods, go ensure security and that the inyenzi have not gotten in there.[100]

By mid-day April 7, assailants were killing and pillaging Tutsi in the northwest, in the town of Gisenyi, and at Byangabo, Busogo, Busasamana, Mudende, Muramba, Kivumu, and Rambura; south of Kigali, at Ruhuha and Sake; northeast of Kigali at Murambi; in Gikongoro at Muko and in the far southwestern town of Cyangugu. Later that night and the next day, the killers began their "work," as they called it, in other regions in the east and west.

Massacres

At first assailants generally operated in small bands and killed their victims where they found them, in their homes, on the streets, at the barriers. But, as early as the evening of April 7, larger groups seized the opportunity for more intensive slaughter as frightened Tutsi—and some Hutu—fled to churches, schools, hospitals, and government offices that had offered refuge in the past. In the northwestern prefecture of Gisenyi, militia killed some fifty people at the Nyundo seminary, forty-three at the church of Busogo, and some 150 at the parish of Busasamana. A large crowd including Burundian students and wounded soldiers took on the task of massacring hundreds of people at the campus of the Seventh Day Adventist University at Mudende to the east of Gisenyi town.[101] In Kigali,

---

[99]Police Judiciaire près le Parquet du Procureur du Roi de Bruxelles, PV no. 30339, Dossier 36/95.

[100]Ibid.

[101]G. Leonard, "Le Carnage à Busogo," pp. 31-33; Godding, "Refugié d'un Rwanda à Feu et à Sang," p. 40; and Des prêtres du diocèse de Nyundo, "Des Rescapés," pp. 60-61, 64-65, Dialogue, no. 177, August-September 1994; Agence France Presse, "Massacres de Rwandais dans une mission franciscaine au nord du pays," Bulletin Quotidien

soldiers and militia killed dozens at a church in Nyamirambo on April 8 and others at the mosque at Nyamirambo several days later. On the morning of April 9, some sixty Interahamwe led by Jean Ntawutagiripfa, known as "Congolais," and accompanied by four National Policemen, forced their way into the church at Gikondo, an industrial section of Kigali. They killed more than a hundred people that day, mostly with machetes and clubs.[102]

RTLM encouraged these attacks on April 8 when announcer Hitimana broadcast advice which he described as especially credible because it came from "a Doctor [whom] I really trust." The "Doctor" said that seeing people gathering in churches was "not good at all," especially when the RPF had put them there along with grenades and other arms. RTLM followed up this general counsel with specific warnings about the church and the mosque in Nyamirambo that spurred almost immediate attacks on these places of worship.[103]

Even when news of the massacres began to spread, some Tutsi still sought sanctuary in public places because the choice seemed no worse and perhaps better than staying at home or attempting to flee much further away. Some did, in fact, survive at the gathering places, either as the fortunate few who escaped at the time of a massacre or because their place of refuge was not attacked. In the two most remarkable cases, some 24,300 Tutsi in the camps at Kabgayi, a large church complex in the central province of Gitarama, were rescued by the arrival of the RPF and another 10,000 at Nyarushishi, in Cyangugu, were protected by National Police under Colonel Bavugamenshi until the arrival of French troops under Operation Turquoise. Tutsi at Rukara in eastern Rwanda were saved when the gunfire from advancing RPF troops frightened away assailants who were besieging the church.[104]

Beginning in the week of April 11, government officials exploited the Tutsi impulse to seek refuge and promised them protection if they would assemble in designated sites. Those who declined the offer were often forced to go there anyway. This effort was so general throughout the country that it must have

---

d'Afrique, no. 14189, 11/04/94, p. 39.

[102]U.S. Committee for Refugees, "Genocide in Rwanda: Documentation of Two Massacres during April 1994," pp. 4-9.

[103]Article 19, *Broadcasting Genocide, Censorship, Propaganda & State-Sponsored Violence in Rwanda, 1990-1994* (October 1996), pp. 130-131.

[104]U.S. Committee for Refugees, "Genocide in Rwanda," p. 16.

reflected orders from above. As Rwandans remarked, "it was like sweeping dry banana leaves into a pile to burn them more easily." The prefects of Kibuye and Cyangugu directed Tutsi to assemble in the local stadiums. In Kivumu commune, Kibuye prefecture, the burgomaster reportedly drove a white pick-up truck around to gather Tutsi who were straggling along the road. He was anxious to get them to Nyange church, where they would later be massacred by a bulldozer that flattened both the church and the people inside. In some cases, authorities did not order the massacre immediately after people assembled, apparently because they were waiting to gather either the maximum number of people or the forces necessary to attack them. In the meantime, they restricted supplies of food and water to the displaced persons, or prohibited them completely, so weakening the population in readiness for the attack. Often several National Policemen or communal policemen "guarded" the displaced persons. This "protection" reassured the Tutsi and encouraged them to remain quietly at the site. If any did try to leave, the "guards" were there to stop them.[105]

From April 11 to the first of May, killers carried out the most devastating massacres of the genocide, in some cases slaying hundreds or even thousands of people in one or two days. This kind of slaughter took place near the ETO school in the city of Kigali; at Ntarama and Nyamata in Kigali prefecture; at Kiziguro in Byumba; at Musambira, Mugina, and Byimana in Gitarama; at Nyarubuye church, Rukara church, Rukira commune, and the St. Joseph center in Kibungo; at the church and stadium in Kibuye town, Mubuga church, Birambo and Mugonero church and hospital in Kibuye prefecture; at Shangi, Nyamasheke, and Mibirizi churches in Cyangugu; at Kibeho, Cyanika, and Kaduha churches in Gikongoro; at Cyahinda, Kansi and Nyumba churches, Butare hospital and the university in Butare; and at Nyundo Cathedral in Gisenyi.

When Hutu who had feared attack because of their political convictions heard that "Tutsi alone were for killing," most left their places of refuge to return home. But other Hutu, particularly those who had taken refuge with Tutsi family members, remained in the churches, schools, and hospitals. Killers generally tried to restrict slaughter to the Tutsi and directed others to leave before the attack. Often

---

[105]Human Rights Watch/FIDH interviews, Kigali, July 11, 1996; Kivumu, July 9, 1996. In some cases, the guards did in fact protect people at these sites. See chapter 8.

soldiers, National Policemen, or militia verified identity papers to ensure that only those classed as Hutu left.[106]

Hutu with Tutsi relatives faced wrenching decisions about whether or not to desert their loved ones in order to save their own lives. At Mugonero church in Kibuye, two Hutu sisters, each married to a Tutsi husband, faced such a choice. One decided to die with her husband. The other chose to leave because she hoped to save the lives of her eleven children. The children, classed as Tutsi because their father was Tutsi, would not ordinarily have had the right to live, but assailants had said that they could be allowed to depart safely if she agreed to go with them. When she stepped out of the door of the church, she saw eight of the eleven children struck down before her eyes. The youngest, a child of three years old, begged for his life after seeing his brothers and sisters slain. "Please don't kill me," he said. "I'll never be Tutsi again." He was killed.[107] If assailants tried as much as possible to kill only Tutsi, so they tried, too, to kill all Tutsi. Survivors and other witnesses from many parts of Rwanda speak of the killers approaching the destruction of the crowds at a church, hospital, or hilltop as a piece of work to be kept at until finished. One compared killers to government workers putting in a day at the office; another likened them to farmers spending a day at labor. In case after case, killers quit at day's end, to go home and feast on food and drink they had pillaged or been given, ready to come back the next morning, rested and fit for "work." At Mugonero hospital, after hours of slaughter, assailants tossed tear gas cannisters in among the bodies. They wanted to make any survivors cough so they could locate them and finish them off.[108] If killers were too tired to complete the "work" on any given day, they assured the Tutsi that they would come back. And, generally, they did.

Impeding Flight: Barriers and Patrols

Organizers tranformed practices once instituted to promote security into mechanisms for genocide and the killing of political adversaries. Even before the October 1990 invasion, guards maintained barriers on roads and paths where they examined the papers and belongings of passersby. More recently the administration

---

[106]Human Rights Watch/FIDH interviews, Kigali, August 29, 30, 1994; Butare, October 2, 1994; Kibungo, January 30, 1995; Nyarubuye, March 5, 1995; Kigali, July 7, 1995; Kigali, July 11, 1996; U.S. Committee for Refugees, "Genocide in Rwanda," p.6.

[107]Human Rights Watch/FIDH interview, Kigali, September 13, 1995.

[108]Human Rights Watch/FIDH interview, Kigali, September 12, 1995.

had established patrols to check rising crime and political attacks within neighborhoods in town or out on the hills. Soldiers or National Police manned important barriers on main roads, but it was communal police and citizens themselves who were responsible for the others and who made up the neighborhood patrols. In Butare town, workers at the university and other persons with salaried employment hired *zamu* or nightwatchmen to do this work in their stead. Security committees at the various levels from sector to prefecture oversaw the implementation of these measures within their areas of jurisdiction.

At the start, authorities instructed Rwandans to stay at home. The curfew allowed authorities and local political leaders to put in place the barriers and patrols necessary to control the population, multiplying them in communities where they were already functioning and reestablishing them in places where they were no longer in operation. Tutsi as well as Hutu cooperated with these measures at the start, hoping they would ensure their security. The hope was disappointed. RTLM, which had at first encouraged Tutsi to join Hutu at the barriers and on the patrols, subsequently began advising listeners to look carefully at coworkers and examine their motives for participation. Incited by such messages from the radio and from local leaders, Hutu in some communities turned on Tutsi at the barriers or on patrols and killed them.[109]

By restricting movement, the barriers made it less likely that people at risk would dare to flee and they also offered a means of catching those who did try to escape. Their keepers scrutinized papers, particularly that line under the photograph that gave the ethnic affiliation of the bearer, to ensure that no changes had been made or false data entered. They examined facial characteristics and configuration of the body to "expose" Tutsi who were trying to pass as Hutu. In some cases, they wrongly assumed that Hutu were Tutsi because they looked Tutsi. They checked passersby for other supposed signs of links with the RPF, marks on their shoulders made by the rubbing of a gunstrap or traces on their ankles resulting from the chafing of boots, or even scars or other marks that could be labeled tattoos indicating loyalty to the RPF.[110]

Barriers were often set up in front of local bars or in nearby commercial centers. Local businessmen or other well-to-do people sponsored barriers, which

---

[109]Human Rights Watch/FIDH interview, by telephone, Brussels, January 26, 1997.

[110]Tribunal de Première Instance de Bruxelles, Deposition de Témoin, September 18, 1995 Dossier 57/95; Fergal Keane, *Season of Blood, A Rwandan Journey* (London: Viking, 1995), p. 168.

meant supplying the guards with food, drink, and sometimes marijuana as well.[111] As in the past, soldiers and National Police manned barriers on the main roads while communal police, militia, and other civilians guarded others. Even at the barriers maintained by civilians, at least one of the guards would often carry a firearm and others might have grenades as well as machetes.

The guards, drunk or sober, had the power of life and death over those who sought to pass and sometimes over persons captured and brought to them by patrols in the area. In considering the case, they might evaluate if the person looked Tutsi or was known personally to any of them as being Tutsi or a RPF supporter. They might also weigh how much the person could pay to save his or her life and, if a woman, how desirable she would be either as an object for rape or for longer-term sexual service. Then the guards as a group, or the leader among them, decided whether the person was to be killed on the spot, raped, kept for service or future execution, or perhaps released. Barriers sometimes served as temporary places of detention.

Some barriers were manned by opponents of the genocide who participated under threat of death to themselves or their families if they were to refuse. Survivors remembers these barriers as "good" ones where Tutsi would not be killed and where the guards might warn of more dangerous barricades further down the same road.[112]

Patrols searched for Tutsi in and out of their houses, in the fields, in the bush, in the swamps, wherever they might be hiding. Often they invaded the homes of Hutu as well under the pretext of verifying reports about hidden arms or a stranger who was residing there. They checked the space between ceiling and roof, under the beds, in the cupboards, in the latrines. In the search, they often helped themselves to whatever goods attracted them. In addition to the patrols that did regularly scheduled tours of the neighborhood, there were others organized in response to reports from informers who had noticed suspicious indications, such as unfamiliar clothes hung out to dry in a backyard or unusual kinds or quantities of food being purchased.[113]

---

[111]Human Rights Watch/FIDH interview, Maraba, June 14, 1995; Chrétien et al, *Rwanda, Les médias*, p. 266.

[112]Human Rights Watch/FIDH interviews, Butare July 12, July 13, 1996.

[113]Human Rights Watch/FIDH interview, Maraba, June 14, 1995; Butare, October 21, 1995.

Rape and Sexual Servitude

During the genocide, tens of thousands of women and girls were raped, including one who was only two years old.[114] The assailants raped as part of their attempt to exterminate Tutsi, some of them incited by propaganda about Tutsi women disseminated in the period just before the genocide. The women had been depicted as devious and completely devoted to the interests of their fathers and brothers. Generally esteemed as beautiful, Tutsi women were also said to scorn Hutu men whom they found unworthy of their attention. Many assailants insulted women for their supposed arrogance while they were raping them. If assailants decided to spare the lives of the women, they regarded them as prizes they had won for themselves or to be distributed to subordinates who had performed well in killing Tutsi. Some kept these women for weeks or months in sexual servitude. In the commune of Taba, women and girls were raped at the communal office, with the knowledge of the burgomaster.[115] At the Kabgayi nursing school, soldiers ordered the directress to give them the young women students as *umusanzu*, a contribution to the war effort. The directress, a Hutu, Dorothée Mukandanga, refused and was killed.[116]

Assailants sometimes mutilated women in the course of a rape or before killing them. They cut off breasts, punctured the vagina with spears, arrows, or pointed sticks, or cut off or disfigured body parts that looked particularly "Tutsi," such as long fingers or thin noses. They also humiliated the women. One witness from Musambira commune was taken with some 200 other women after a massacre. They were all forced to bury their husbands and then to walk "naked like a group of cattle" some ten miles to Kabgayi. When the group passed roadblocks, militia there shouted that the women should be killed. As they marched, the women were obliged to sing the songs of the militia. When the group stopped at nightfall, some of the women were raped repeatedly.[117]

---

[114]Human Rights Watch/FIDH, *Shattered Lives,* p.24.

[115]Fondation Hirondelle, "L'ancien maire de Taba aurait encouragé au viol de femmes Tutsies," October 23, 1997.

[116]Boniface Musoni, "Holocauste Noir," *Dialogue,* no. 177, August-September 1994, p. 88.

[117]Human Rights Watch/FIDH, *Shattered Lives,* pp. 54, 62-64.

Crimes of Extraordinary Brutality

Some killers tortured victims, both male and female, physically or psychologically, before finally killing them or leaving them to die. An elderly Tutsi woman in Kibirira commune had her legs cut off and was left to bleed to death. A Hutu man in Cyangugu, known to oppose the MRND-CDR, was killed by having parts of his body cut off, beginning with his extremities. A Tutsi baby was thrown alive into a latrine in Nyamirambo, Kigali, to die of suffocation or hunger. Survivors bear scars of wounds that testify better than words to the brutality with which they were attacked. Assailants tortured Tutsi by demanding that they kill their own children and tormented Hutu married to Tutsi partners by insisting that they kill their spouses. Victims generally regarded being shot as the least painful way to die and, if given the choice and possessing the means, they willingly paid to die that way.

Assailants often stripped victims naked before killing them, both to acquire their clothes without stains or tears and to humiliate them. In many places, killers refused to permit the burial of victims and insisted that their bodies be left to rot where they had fallen. Persons who attempted to give a decent burial to Tutsi were sometimes accused by others of being "accomplices" of the enemy.[118] The Hutu widow of a Tutsi man killed at Mugonero in Kibuye expressed her distress at the violation of Rwandan custom, which is to treat the dead with dignity. Speaking of Pastor Elizaphan Ntakirutimana of the Adventist church, she stated:

> What gives me grief is that after the pastor had all these people killed, he didn't even see to burying them, including his fellow pastors. They lay outside for two weeks, eaten by dogs and crows.[119]

Strategies of Survival
Resistance

Tutsi fought for their lives at Bisesero, Karongi, and Nyamagumba in Kibuye; at Nyakizu, Nyamure, and Runyinya in Butare; at Bicumbi and Kanzenze and in the swamps of Bugesera in Kigali; at Gashihe in Gisenyi; at Gisuma and Cyangugu stadium in Cyangugu; at Kibeho and Kaduha churches in Gikongoro; at the Muhazi

---

[118]Human Rights Watch/FIDH interview, Brussels, February 26, 1997.

[119]Human Rights Watch/FIDH interviews, Kigali, September 9, 1995.

and Rukira communal offices in Kibungo.[120] The names of these and other major sites of resistance are known, but unrecorded are the thousands of places where Tutsi struggled hand to hand with their aggressors, in their homes, on the paths and in the fields. Each place of struggle has its own story of heroism, but most share common elements: Tutsi (in the early days, in some places, mixed groups of Tutsi and Hutu) repelled the initial attack; the aggressors obtained reinforcements in people and material, usually from soldiers or National Police; the aggressors attacked repeatedly until they overcame the resistance. Some Tutsi survived, hidden among the bodies or elsewhere, or by fleeing.

At some sites, the besieged people formulated strategies for fighting or for fleeing. At Rubona in Butare and at Bisesero at Kibuye, resisters used a tactic called "merging," or *kwiunga*.[121] This involved lying down and waiting until assailants had moved in among the intended victims, then rising up to face them in close combat. This tactic decreased the likelihood that assailants would shoot because they would fear being caught in fire from their own side. The two sites where the tactic was used are far apart and probably had no communication between them during the genocide. Perhaps the RPF had taught this way of fighting during training sessions for its adherents or had disseminated it in some other way. At Bisesero, where the numbers of resisters were large and the struggle long, the Tutsi put into place a command structure. Leaders directed the combat and even beat those who refused to advance under attack.[122] In Nyakizu, most Tutsi were besieged for only a few days under attack, but they too worked out a division of tasks in the combat. When they decided to flee, they arranged the departure of groups at different times and in different directions to increase their chances for escape.

---

[120]Human Rights Watch interviews, seven by telephone, Kigali, between April 6 and May 28, 1994; Human Rights Watch/FIDH interviews, Kigali, September 9, 12, 13, 1995; Commission pour le Mémorial du Génocide et des Massacres au Rwanda, "Rapport Préliminaire," pp. 92, 136, 142, 148-58, 173-76, 186-8, 241; Missionnaires d'Afrique, Guy Theunis and Jef Vleugels, fax no. 12, May 9, 1994.

[121]Human Rights Watch/FIDH interview, Rusatira, March 23, 1996; African Rights, *Resisting Genocide, April-June 1994,* Witness, No. 8, p. 16.

[122]African Rights, *Resisting Genocide*, p. 17.

The best known case of resistance was that of Bisesero, a mountainous ridge in Kibuye where Tutsi stood off militia and military from April 8 until July 1. In explaining why Tutsi had fled to Bisesero, one survivor related:

> We fled to the hill because it was high and we could see the attackers coming....It had lots of woods on it and so many hiding places. The attackers would come to kill during the day and at night they would go off to eat and drink.[123]

Others recalled that Bisesero had been an important site for defense at the time of the 1959 revolution, a consideration which determined the choice of site for people in other prefectures as well. According to some witnesses, Radio Muhubura encouraged Tutsi to assemble at Bisesero.

During the genocide people living in the town of Kibuye became used to the sound of the vehicles rolling by en route to Bisesero with their loads of assailants. Obed Ruzindana, a local businessman and prefectural head of the CDR, is accused of having led attacks on the hilltop along with a councilor, Mika Muhimana. One survivor declares that Dr. Gerard Ntakirutimana, son of Pastor Elizaphan Ntakirutimana, who headed the Adventist church, came to the hill often, "wearing white pants and a white and red sweater and carrying a R4 rifle." The witness thought that Dr. Ntakirutimana would help him because their fathers had exchanged cattle, a sign of a close and enduring bond. He says, "So I fled to Ntakirutimana for protection, but instead he shot at me." The burgomaster, Charles Sikubwabo, a former soldier, helped organize the repeated assaults on the hill. From time to time, Alfred Musema, head of a nearby tea factory, came to observe.[124]

The local militia, gathered from three surrounding communes, was not enough to overcome resistance on the hill, so the organizers called in reinforcements from a considerable distance. A militia leader well-known in Cyangugu, John Yusufu Munyakazi, brought his men from that prefecture and both militia and soldiers came from Gisenyi. In late April, the resisters, using spears and machetes, killed a lieutenant of the Presidential Guard and four National Policemen. There followed a respite of two weeks. Then on May 13, soldiers, backed by eight busloads of

---

[123]Human Rights Watch/FIDH interview, Kigali, September 12, 1995.

[124]Human Rights Watch/FIDH interviews, Kigali, September 9, 1995; July 11, 1996.

Une rumeur a circulé qu'une attaque venant de MURUNDA allait tuer le Bourgmestre et sa famille, alors une contre attaque de ± 5.000 personnes s'est organisé pour défendre le Bourgmestre; cette défense provenait des hautes altitudes. Je me suis rendu sur les lieux en empruntant l'itinéraire Kibuye-Kabona-Crête Zaïre-Nil. La réalité est que l'attaque de MURUNDA n'était pas préparée, mais nous avons trouvé un document du M.D.R.-RUTSIRO qui soulignait qu'ils sont pour le M.D.R. Parmehutu Pawa; et parmi les signataires c'est là où il y a eu deux mortalités (KAYUMBA vers le 29/05/1994 et MBWIRABUMVA le 31/05/1994). Ce qu'on ne peut pas oublier c'est que la mort de KAYUMBA provient des supçons qu'il avait des communications avec le FPR et que les auteurs de la mort seraient des Interahamwe. Alors il y a eu la peur des représailles des deux côtés. Lors de mon passage le 1/6/1994, j'ai calmé la population qui voulait la défense (via les conseillers des secteurs) mais la parti qu'on disait qui voulait attaquer je n'ai pas pu la contacter. Le Bourgmestre a regagné sa commune le 1/6/1994, situation semble être calme mais c'est à suivre de près.

4o Les rumeurs me parviennent qu'il y aura une attaque du FPR sur KIBUYE par une jonction de Nyanza (Nyabisindu)- Karongi-Ile Idjwi. Actuellement il y a une infiltration FPR parmi la population en déplacement.

Honneur vous demander un renfort militaire pour aider la population à surveiller les hautes altitudes de Karongi et les plantations théicoles de Gisovu. Les fusils et munitions pour la protection civile sont urgents pour Kibuye. Rappel que KARONGI possède Station FM et Poste de Transformation Electrogaz et Usine à Thé Gisovu et aussi coin stratégique militaire.
Sommes entrait d'organiser des camps des déplacés hors la ville de Kibuye et des grands centres.

Très haute considération.

Fait à Kibuye, le 2/6/1994.

Le Préfet de Préfecture KIBUYE
Dr KAYISHEMA Clément.-

Document: (Kibuye prefecture) Letter from Minister of the Interior requesting military support for the population in executing sweeps at Bisesero which has become "a sanctuary for the RPF."

Monsieur le Lieutenant-Colonel
Anatole NSENGIYUMVA,
Commandant du Secteur
Opérationnel de Gisenyi
GISENYI

Objet: Opération de ratissage
à Kibuye

Monsieur le Commandant de Secteur,

J'ai l'honneur de vous informer que lors du Conseil des Ministres de ce vendredi 17 juin 1994, le Gouvernement a décidé de demander au Commandement du Secteur Opérationnel de Gisenyi d'appuyer le Groupement de la Gendarmerie à Kibuye pour mener, avec l'appui de la population, l'opération de ratissage dans le secteur Bisesero de la Commune Gishyita, qui est devenu un sanctuaire du FPR.

Le Gouvernement demande que cette opération soit définitivement terminée au plus tard le 20 juin 1994.

En l'absence du Ministre de la Défense qui est en mission à l'étranger, le Ministre de l'Intérieur et du Développement Communal a été mandaté pour vous communiquer cette décision et en assurer le suivi.

Le Préfet de la Préfecture Kibuye ainsi que le Commandant de Groupement Kibuye à qui je réserve la copie de la présente, sont priés de prendre les dispositions qui s'imposent pour faciliter la réalisation cette opération dans les délais vous impartis.

Le Ministre de l'Intérieur et
du Développement Communal
Edouard KAREMERA

Copie pour information:
- S.E. Monsieur le Premier
  Ministre
  KIGALI
- Monsieur le Ministre de la Défense
  KIGALI
/- Monsieur le Préfet de la
  Préfecture de Kibuye
  KIBUYE
- Monsieur le Commandant de Groupement
  KIBUYE

militia, charged the hill. They killed thousands of Tutsi. According to a survivor whose wife and mother were killed there, the assailants "speared women through the vagina to their heads, saying 'May you give birth to a child.'"[125]

During the weeks on the hilltop, the Tutsi first consumed supplies they had brought with them and then foraged for food and stole from the fields of farmers. The attackers were divided into two teams, those who assaulted the hill during the day and those "who went around at night trying to find where people were hiding by smelling or seeing their cooking fires."[126]

The prefect, Dr. Clément Kayishema informed his superior on May 5 about the continued existence of "a little spot of insecurity in the Bisesero zone,"[127] and wired them on June 2 to request "military reinforcements to help the population monitor the [areas of] high altitude." Perhaps to ensure a prompt and positive response, Kayishema reminded his superior that this region included a radio transmitter, an installation of Electrogaz, and the tea factory. He also reported that there were RPF infiltrators among incoming refugees and that an RPF attack was rumored to be coming from Nyanza to the east and from Idjwi island in Lake Kivu.[128]

The prefect got the response he wanted some two weeks later when the council of ministers instructed the military commander at Gisenyi to send troops to join the National Police at Kibuye "to lead a search operation, with the help of the population, in sector Bisesero...which has become a sanctuary of the RPF." The interim government insisted that the operation be "finished definitively" by June 20 at the latest, perhaps because they anticipated the arrival of French troops of Operation Turquoise at about that time.[129] The attack took place, killing and maiming many of the ragged and starving survivors who clung to life on top of the hills. A foreign witness present in Kibuye town heard the militia and troops coming

---

[125]Ibid.

[126]Human Rights Watch/FIDH interview, Kigali, September 12, 1995.

[127]Dr. Clément Kayishema, Préfet, to Monsieur le Ministre de l'Intérieur et du Développement Communal, no. 0286/04.09.01, May 5, 1994 (Kibuye prefecture).

[128]Dr. Clément Kayishema, Préfet, telegram to Ministre MININTER, no. 003/04.09.01, June 2, 1994 (Kibuye prefecture).

[129]Edouard Karemera, Ministre de l'Intérieur et du Développement Communal to Monsieur le Lt. Col. Anatole Nsengiyumva, Commandant du Secteur Opérationnel de Gisenyi, no classification number, June 18, 1994 (Kibuye prefecture).

home shouting their *ibyivugo*, a formalized boast that dates to the precolonial period, declaiming the numbers they had slain and the details of how they had killed them.

A survivor estimated that of the thousands of Tutsi hidden in the woods on top of the Bisesero hills, fewer than 1,500 survived.[130]

Flight, Hiding, and Buying Safety

Many of the Tutsi alive today fled in search of safety, some many times over. A young man from Bisesero first fled south with a group heading for Burundi, but they were caught in the Nyungwe forest by the Presidential Guard. They escaped and made their way back to Bisesero. He tried again, heading southeast, planning to circle through the northern part of Gikongoro to reach the RPF zone. Forced to retreat again to Bisesero, he started out a third time to the northeast, through Birambo but once more was driven back to the hilltop. As he remarks, "All this was in April, the month that would not end."[131] Some fled from one place to another, like a group that escaped from the massacre at Kibeho and went to Muganza and from there to Cyahinda and from there to Agatobwe to Nkomero and finally across the border to Burundi. Tracked by assailants from their places of origin, harassed by new attackers along the way, those in flight traveled at night, frequently backtracking and following circuitous routes. One witness needed six days to traverse a distance that he could normally walk in two hours.

Many hid in every imaginable kind of space: latrines, ceilings, unused wells, in trees, in empty buildings in the city and in fields of sorghum or sugar cane. Some profited from a momentary distraction or temporary weakening of will on the part of a captor. One woman at the crowded Kabgayi camp who was selected for killing by militia begged the chance to suckle her infant one last time. While she was doing so, her captor got bored and looked away and she disappeared into the crowd. A teenaged girl was lined up with others waiting to be killed at the edge of a grave. When the killers began to dispute the division of the spoils taken from the victims, she sped off into the night. Some bought their lives once with a watch or a small sum of money; others made payments to soldiers or militia every day or every week throughout the genocide. Some negotiated a temporary reprieve through wit and promises, staying alive day by day.

---

[130]Human Rights Watch/FIDH interview, Kigali, September 9,1995.

[131]Ibid.

Resisters in places like Bisesero or the Bugesera swamps seem to have been largely self-sufficient, but others who survived through flight, hiding, or buying their safety usually needed help from Hutu. Some of those who opened their doors, showed a path, or delivered food acted from principle, responding to a sense of common humanity with the victim, even if a stranger. Some acted from family feeling, friendship, or sense of obligation for past services rendered. Others sold their help, but, in doing so, they, too, saved lives.

Authorities and political leaders defined aiding Tutsi as helping the "enemy." In many places, they specifically ordered Hutu not to assist Tutsi and threatened them with death or other punishment if they did so. Hutu who disobeyed such orders and were caught often had to pay fines. In some cases, the protectors, like those whom they were trying to protect, were raped, beaten, or killed. These cases were widely known in local communities and often led other Hutu to refuse or end their assistance to Tutsi.[132] When an elderly Tutsi in Bisesero appealed to an old Hutu friend to hide his grandsons, the old friend responded, "I would like to, but I can't. The orders are that I must not."[133]

---

[132]Human Rights Watch/FIDH, interviews, Butare, May 29, 1995, Kigali, July 18, 1995; Brussels, December 18, 1995; Human Rights Watch/FIDH, *Shattered Lives*, pp. 66-67.

[133]Human Rights Watch/FIDH interviews, Kigali, July 12, 1995.

THE ORGANIZATION

In the past, the Rwandan government had often mobilized the population for campaigns of various kinds, such as to end illiteracy, to vaccinate children, or to improve the status of women. It had executed these efforts through the existing administrative and political hierarchies, requiring agents to go beyond their usual duties for a limited period of time for some national goal of major importance. The organizers of the genocide similarly exploited the structures that already existed—administrative, political, and military—and called upon personnel to execute a campaign to kill Tutsi and Hutu presumed to oppose Hutu Power. Through these three channels, the organizers were able to reach all Rwandans and to incite or force most Hutu into acquiescing in or participating in the slaughter.

The organization that ran the campaign was flexible: primacy depended more on commitment to the killing than on formal position in the hierarchy. Thus within the administrative system, sub-prefects could eclipse prefects, as they did in Gikongoro and Gitarama, and in the military domain, lieutenants could ignore colonels, as happened in Butare. This flexibility encouraged initiative and ambition among those willing to purchase advancement at the cost of human lives. To preserve appearances, an inferior might obtain the approval of his superior for decisions he made, but those receiving the orders knew who really had the power.[1]

Similarly, actors bypassed the usual legal and bureaucratic limits on their activities. Military men, retired or in active service, took charge in the civilian domain, as did Col. Simba when he took the chair of prefectural meetings away from the prefect of Gikongoro, and civilians, even those with no legal authority, obtained military support for their attacks on Tutsi. Administrators gave orders to militia groups and Interahamwe leaders intervened in the administrative realm, as when their national committee ruled on the acceptability of the candidate to replace the prefect of Butare. Party leaders like Karemera of the MRND and Murego of the MDR-Power participated in meetings of the council of ministers while others like Ngirumpatse of the MRND represented the interim government abroad in its efforts to legitimate the genocide.[2] The prime minister and the Ministry of the Interior directed prefects to involve local politicians in the efforts to assure "security." They

---

[1]Details of the cases mentioned in this chapter are found in chapters on Gikongoro and Butare.

[2]Karemera was subsequently named minister of the interior and community development and Barayagwiza became secretary of the assembly created just before the interim government left the country.

did and they made sure their subordinates did the same.[3] Like officials of the administration, important party leaders were protected by military guards and, like them, they toured the hills bringing the message of the government to the people.

Individuals from other sectors—the akazu, the church, the business community, the university, schools and hospitals—backed the efforts of the officials.

The Military

Soldiers and National Police, whether on active duty or retired, killed civilians and they gave permission, set the example, and commanded others to kill. Although fewer in number than civilian killers, the military played a decisive role by initiating and directing the slaughter. In the first hours in Kigali, soldiers of the Presidential Guard and the paracommando and reconnaisance battalions, along with some National Policemen, carried out the carnage in one neighborhood after another. Soldiers, National Police and the communal police also launched the slaughter and organized all large-scale massacres elsewhere in the country.

Witnesses in Kigali and other towns have identified as killers certain soldiers and National Policemen whom they knew before the genocide. But elsewhere, witnesses found it difficult to identify the persons or even the units responsible for given crimes because soldiers and National Police wore the same uniforms and only sometimes wore the berets of different colors which indicated the service to which they belonged. Witnesses often say that soldiers from the Presidential Guard attacked them, but troops from other army units or from the National Police may actually have committed some of these crimes.[4]

Regardless of the responsibility of individuals or units, the widespread and systematic participation of military personnel throughout the entire period of genocide indicates that the most powerful authorities at the national level ordered or approved their role in the slaughter. Bagosora, as shown above, has been identified by other officers as the leader who launched the genocide. General Bizimungu, named chief of staff with Bagosora's support, and Minister of Defense

---

[3]Ministiri w'Ubutegetsi bw'Igihugu n'Amajyambere ya Komini [actually signed by C. Kalimanzira] to Bwana Perefe wa Perefegitura (Bose), April 21, 1994 and Yohani Kambanda, Ministiri w'Intebe, to Bwana Perefe wa Perefegitura (Bose) April 27, 1994 (Butare prefecture).

[4]In interviews by Human Rights Watch/FIDH, researchers found "Presidential Guard" used as a generic term for military personnel who killed Tutsi and "Interahamwe" used as a generalized description for civilian bands of killers.

Augustin Bizimana at the least collaborated actively with Bagosora, while officers in charge of the elite units, Majors Protais Mpiranya, François-Xavier Nzuwonemeye, and Aloys Ntabakuze, as well as others like Colonel Tharcisse Renzaho, Lieutenant Colonels Léonard Nkundiye and Anatole Nsengiyumva, Captain Gaspard Hategekimana, and Major Bernard Ntuyahaga carried out the killings of Tutsi and Hutu civilians.

On April 10, Colonel Gatsinzi, then temporarily chief of staff, and the Ministry of Defense each ordered subordinates to halt the killings of civilians, using force if necessary. The Ministry of Defense sent a second, weaker command on April 28 "to cooperate with local authorities to halt pillage and assassinations." But neither the general staff nor the Ministry of Defense enforced the orders, leaving subordinates to conclude that the directives had no importance. In fact, as some officers had observed from the start, the authorities countermanded the official orders by another message, passed discreetly to like-minded officers who executed the informal order to kill rather than the official directive to stop the killings.[5]

The military also led militia and ordinary civilians in slaughter, giving orders to citizens directly and through civilian administrators. At the national level, civilian and military authorities directed the population to obey these orders, insisting that civilians must "work with," "assist," or "support" the army.[6] According to a foreign witness, soldiers taught hesitant young people to kill on the streets of Kigali. When the young people balked at striking Tutsi, soldiers stoned the victims until the novices were ready to attack.[7] In the prefecture of Gitarama, soldiers said to be Presidential Guards drove around in a black Pajero jeep, killing and inciting others to kill in the communes of Musambira and Mukingi. Others launched the killing of Tutsi at a market in the commune of Mugina. In Kivu and Kinyamakara communes in Gikongoro, soldiers or National Police directed crowds gathered at market and people found along the roads to attack Tutsi. Soldiers led killing in Cyangugu starting on April 7.[8]

---

[5]Commandement des Forces Armées Rwandaises en Exil, "Contribution des FAR," pp. 96-103 and Appendix IV (Annex D); Human Rights Watch/FIDH interview, January 26, 1996.

[6]Chrétien et al, *Rwanda, Les médias*, p. 299.

[7]Fergal Keane, *Season of Blood*, pp. 134-35.

[8]Human Rights Watch/FIDH interviews, Butare, August 18 and 19, 1995; Kigali, August 21, 1995; Mukingi, July 10, 1996. See below for more detail.

Document: (Ntyazo commune) Request for police support in attacking Tutsi who have turned out to be "stronger than expected."

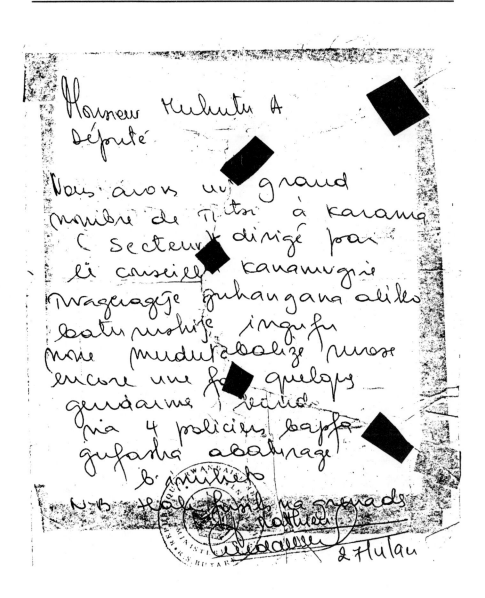

Document: (Butare prefecture) Order from Minister of the Interior to prefects, directing them to make the population aware of the need to continue "tracking the enemy wherever he is or wherever he might have hidden his arms..."

REPUBULIKA Y'URWANDA
MINISTERI Y'UBUTEGETSI
BW'IGIHUGU N'AMAJYAMBERE
    YA KOMINI.
  B.P. 446 KIGALI

KIGALI, kuwa 21 Mata 1994

Bwana Perefe wa Perefegitura (bose)

Bwana Perefe,

    Nshingiye ku miterere y'ibihe by'imidugararo Igihugu cyacu kirimo, nkwandikiye ngusaba kwita kuri ibi bikurikira kugirango umutekano ugaruke vuba muri Perefegitura uyobora :

1. Kwihutira gukoresha Inama y'Umutekano ya Perefegitura yaguriwemo n'Abayobozi b'Amashyaka kugirango itate ingamba zo kugarura umutekano mu Gihugu;

2. Gukangurira abaturage gukomeza gutahura umwanzi aho yihishe n'indiri z'intwaro ze badahohotera inzirakarengane;

3. Kwihanangiriza abantu bose kudahohotera ubuzima n'umutekano w'abandi kubera amashyari, inzangano no gushaka kwihimura;

4. Guhagurukiriza Abayobozi b'inzego z'ubutegetsi zose, ari ba Burugumesitiri, Abajyanama n'abagize Komite za selire kugarura no kubumbatira umutekano w'Abaturage n'uw'ibintu byabo;

5. Gufatanya n'inzego z'amadini kugarura amahoro mu mitima y'Abatura-Rwanda kugirango barusheho kwihanganirana no kubabarirana;

6. Kwigira hamwe n'abo bireba uburyo amaduka yokongera agafungura, amasoko akarema n'imyuga y'ingeri zose igakorwa kugirango abantu babone uko bahahirana;

7. Kworohereza abacuruzi ba buri karere, cyane cyane abacuruza imyaka kwihutira kugeza ku bantu ibiribwa;

8. Guhamagarira abakozi kwihutira gusubira ku mirimo yabo aho bishoboka.

    Ngusabye guhita ushyira mu bikorwa ibikubiye muri aya mabwiriza.

          Minisitiri w'Ubutegetsi
          bw'Igihugu n'Amajyambere
             ya Komini.
          MUNYAZEZA Fawusitini

Bimenyeshejwe :

– Bwana Minisitiri w'Intebe
    KIGALI.

Document: (Bwakira commune) Minutes of meeting setting rules for conduct at the barrier near the Trafipro shop.

Inama yateranye kuwa kabiri taliki ya 17/%/1994 iyoborwa na NSENGIMANA Apollinaire .Yitabiriwe nabantu benshi bageze kuri 25 bashinzwe kujya bakorera kuriyo barrière.

Ibyari k'umurongo w'ibyigwa ı 1Kureba uko barrière yarushaho gukora neza.

        2.Kureba uko iriya barrière (abayishinzwe)batavunisha abandi.

        3. Ibibazo rusange.

Ku kibazo cya mbere,abari mu nama basabwe ko barushaho kuba maso abagenzi ntibakazabashukishe amafaranga kuko byatuma umwanzi ahita.Ikindi kandi kuri barrière hagombwa gusuzuma ibi bikurikira:

- Guusuzuma Iranga muntu

-Gusaka imizigo n'amamodoka

-Umugenzi agomba kubazwa iyp ajya(Umusozi,Segiteri,Serire)ndetse akabazwa n'abantuazi kuri uwo murenge agiyeho.Iyo atabimenye aba abeshya bityo agafatwa agashyikirizwa ubutegetsi.

Ku ngingo ya kabiri;Kubera ko bamwe bavunisha abandi kandi agasanga abariho bakora mukajagari,ugasanga umuntu yasinze ,agasagarira abagenzi, hakabura uwafata ibyemezo cyangwa gukemura impaka kubibazo bibonetse.Kugira ngo ibyo bitazongera kubaho,abari mu nama bemeje ko hagomba gukorwa amakipi kandi ikagira umuyobozi.Bityo ikibaye cyose kuri barrière akaba ariwe wabisobanura.Kandi akaba ashinzwe imigendekere myiza y'irondo.Buri kipe igomba kugira umunsi wayo wo gukora..

Mubibazo rusange ,abari mu nama bifuje ko Komini yabafasha ikabaha intwaro cyangwa bitashoboka hakaboneka umupolisi umwe.

Ikindi basabye inkunga y'abaturage kuko gusaka abantu bitaharirwa barrière gusa kuko abantu bose batanyura kuri za barrière.Ni ukuvuga ko no mugiturage cyangwa muri za kabare zose bagombye kujya babaza imbyangombwa buri muntu wese utazwi.

Nyuma yibyo bitekerezo byose hakurikiyeho kubaka amakipe .Mukuyubaka ari abakozi ari abatarabakozi bifuje ko bavangwa bakajya bakorera hamwe hamwe nta vangura.

AMAKIPE YAKOZWE KURI UBU BURYOı

.../...

Document: (Ndora commune) Letter claiming the Hutu identity of the undersigned family and asking the burgomaster to confirm this identity and so end attacks that have killed family members and destroyed their property.

GAKWAYA Antoine
Perefegitura BUTARE.

Butare, kuwa 25/05/1994

Impamvu: Gusaba ko ikibazo
cy'umuryango w'ABACYABA
cyarobanuka.

Bwana Burupumeritiri wa
komini NDORA.

À traiter par ....
ate entrées: 0 2 JUIN 1994
N° Classement: 17.37/04.04.13

Bwana Burupumeritiri;

Nyuma y'ibyago byagwiririye
umuryango wacu mu gihe cy'imvururu, bitewe n'ishyari
n'irrangano bamwe mu baturage bari basanewe badufitiye,
ibintu byacu bigasahurwa amazu agasenywa, ndetse na bamu
mu bawandimwe bacu bakiwa npo hato hatazagira usigara
akazababaza maze bakitwaza kutwitirira ubwoko bw'Abatutsi,
ndetse n'abashoboye kuba bariho bagacumbikishirizwa n'umu
na wabo w'ingabo y'igihugu, abo baturage bakaba bakiba-
kunikiranye mu bukungiro;

Tubardikiye twifuza kardi
tubasaba ko ikibazo cyacu cyare cyare icy'ubwoko abaturage
bitwaje mwagisobanurira abaturage kuko ubwoko bwacu turi
kardi twenera Turi Abahutu. Aha mukaba mwakwifashisha
abategetsi babababanjirije mu kuyobora komini NDORA, muke-
reye mu gihe cya Ntawamuvulira Alas, mubare Bwana
Kamasei Joseph wayoboye komini NDORA igihe kiriri, n'abandi
bakunikiranye. Ndetse no muri Segikeri dutuyemo kuva ku
mukorerye wa mbere Munyakazi Joseph, Nkundwarabake
Casmir wamurimbuye n'uriho ubu.

Ikindi gishobora gutuma musobanu-
kirwa ni uko igisukuru cyacu kiri muri komini Gishamvu, bere
wacu bose bo muri iyo komini bakaba bahari nta kibazo.
Abakuze muri bo cyare cyare nk'umusaza BINYENZI wo
muri Segikeri MUSUMBANO alaba yabisobanura.

Turangije tubasaba gusuzunara
ubushishozi iki kibazo cyacu kuko kituremereye cyane. Mugire
amahoro.

Bimenyeshejwe:
* Bwana Perefe wa Perefegitura BUTARE
* Bwana Supeefe wa Supeefegitura
       GISAGARA
* Bwana Prokireri wa Repubulika
          BUTARE

Abahagarariye umuryango:
1. GAKWAYA Antoine
2. MUZAMUZI Fidèle
3. Madamu USABA Léonille

Soldiers and National Police distributed arms and ammunition to civilians discreetly before April 6 and openly after that date.[9] They also provided reinforcements in men and materiel to civilians who found it impossible to overcome resistance from Tutsi. A medical assistant who was trying to kill Tutsi in the commune of Ntyazo at the end of April asked for military support:

Mr. Muhutu A.
Deputy

We have a large number of Tutsi at Karama (sector headed by the councilor Kanamugire). We have tried to fight them, but they have turned out to be stronger than we expected. So we ask for your help once again; send us a few National Police and four other [communal?] police to help the population that is fighting with bows.

P.S. We have guns and grenades.

Mathieu
27/4/94[10]

Military personnel also ensured the spread of the genocide by refusing assistance to authorities, including the prefect of Gitarama and burgomasters in Gitarama, Gikongoro, and Butare who tried to stop killing and other acts of destruction.[11]

In addition, soldiers and National Police used force or the threat of force against Hutu who tried to resist the slaughter. At the request of administrators, like the burgomaster of Nyakizu, they intimidated citizens into joining in attacks. Even more extraordinary, they directed or permitted militia to exert the same kind of pressure on administrators if they dissented from the campaign of genocide.

---

[9]Augustin Ndindiliyimana, Témoignage à la Commission Spéciale Rwanda, Le Sénat Belge, April 21, 1994, p. 14.

[10]Mathieu [Ndahimana, Medical Assistant in Ntyazo] to A[dalbert] Muhutu, Deputy, April 27, 1994 (CLADHO).

[11]Fidèle Uwizeye, "Aperçu Analytique sur les Evénements d'Avril 1994 en Préfecture de Gitarama, Rwanda," August 18, 1994 (confidential source).

Soldiers who had been wounded in war formed a particularly brutal category of military killers. Some joined in beating Belgian UNAMIR peacekeepers to death, others attacked Tutsi at the Adventist university at Mudende, and still others killed and harassed Tutsi in the town of Butare, at Kabgayi, and near the hospital at Cyakabili.[12]

Politicians and Militia

Political leaders at every level championed the genocide, launching themselves into the killing campaign as a way to increase their own importance and to displace rivals. They were uninhibited by any of the formal responsibilities that sometimes constrained administrators and led them to disguise their intentions in indirect language. Invited by authorities to participate fully in official meetings from the national to the local level, they took the floor to demand ruthless action against Tutsi and those who helped them.[13]

Politicians used their personal authority and channels of communication within their parties to direct attacks on Tutsi. In Taba commune, Gitarama prefecture, the local MRND leader Silas Kubwimana distributed arms and launched killings.[14] In Butare prefecture, National Assembly Deputy Muhutu arranged military support for civilian killers, Deputy Bernadette Mukarurangwa ordered barriers put up, and Deputy Laurent Baravuga reportedly patrolled with his own band of killers.[15] In some cases, politicians organized "security" measures in accord with the local administrators. In other cases, where administrators showed no commitment to the

---

[12]Des Prêtres du diocèse de Nyundo, "Des Rescapés du Diocèse," p. 61.

[13]Fawusitini Munyazeza, [signed by Callixte Kalimanzira] Minisitiri w'Ubutegetsi bw'Igihugu n'Amajyambere ya Komini to Bwana Perefe (all), April 21, 1994, no identifying number (Butare prefecture).

[14]Kubwimana's role is described by many witnesses in the trial of Jean-Paul Akayesu, burgomaster of Taba, before the International Criminal Tribunal for Rwanda. See the testimony of the witness identified as DZZ, as reported by Ubutabera, No. 28, November 24, 1997, found at http://persoweb.francenet.fr/-intermed.

[15]Human Rights Watch/FIDH interviews, Butare, December 19 and 29, 1995 and January 2, 1996; "Inama y'Abaturage ba Komini Ndora yo kuwa 7 kamena 1994," in Célestin Rwankubito, Burugumesitiri wa Komini Ndora, no. 132/04.04/2, June 16, 1994; Dominiko Ntawukuriryayo, S/prefe wa S.prefegitura Gisagara to Bwana Prefe, no. 083/04.09.01/4, April 15, 1994 and no. 008/04.17.02, June 8, 1994 (Butare prefecture).

genocide, political leaders effectively took over the extermination campaign in their communities.

Politicians claimed to speak for the people in demanding the extermination of the Tutsi when in fact they often incited them to make that demand.[16] In person and on the radio, Shingiro Mbonyumutwa of MRD-Power, son of the president of the first Rwandan Republic, used his considerable prestige to whip up fear and hatred of the Tutsi. In a use of the now-familiar "accusation in a mirror," he told Radio Rwanda listeners that Tutsi intended to carry out a genocide of the Hutu:

> They are going to exterminate, exterminate, exterminate, exterminate [ugutsembatsemba-tsembatsemba]...They are going to exterminate you until they are the only ones left in this country, so that the power which their fathers kept for four hundred years, they can keep for a thousand years![17]

The Militia

Political organizations provided the civilian striking force of the genocide, the militia. Before April 6, the militia—in the sense of those who had at least some training and experience fighting as a unit—numbered some two thousand in Kigali, with a smaller number outside the capital in communes where the MRND and the CDR were strong. Once the genocide began and militia members began reaping the rewards of violence, their numbers swelled rapidly to between twenty and thirty thousand for the country as a whole.[18]

The Interahamwe was an unincorporated organization supposedly independent of the MRND, but heavily influenced by it. The militia was directed by a national committee that included Jerry Robert Kajuga, president (himself the son of a Tutsi father and Hutu mother), Phénéas Ruhumuriza, first vice-president, George Rutaganda, second vice president, Eugene Mbarushimana, secretary-general, Dieudonné Niyitegeka, treasurer and, as councilors, Bernard Maniragaba, Joseph Serugendo, Ephrem Nkezabera, Jean-Marie Vianney Mudahinyuka, and Alphonse Kanimba. The Interahamwe had committees at the prefectural level, but it is unclear how important a role they played in the genocide. The best trained groups,

---

[16]Commission pour le Mémorial du Génocide et des Massacres, "Rapport Préliminaire," pp. 132, 155, 190, 192, 195-6.

[17]Chrétien et al., *Rwanda, Les médias*, p. 300.

[18]Human Rights Watch/FIDH interview, Brussels, May 26, 1997.

those in Kigali, operated under the command of local leaders like "Congolais" in the region of Gikondo and Kigingi and Jean-de-Dieu in Nyamirambo.[19] The Impuzamugambi had no leaders apart from those of the CDR, the best known of whom was Barayagwiza.

Once the genocide began, there was virtually no distinction between Impuzamugambi and Interahamwe in the field, although members of each might still wear the distinctive garb or colors belonging to their parties. Some men participated in both groups, attacking when and where action seemed most profitable. As early as February, the Interahamwe were directed to cooperate also with Inkuba, the MDR-Power militia, but in the first days of the genocide, many MDR members—including those identified with MDR-Power—fought against the Interahamwe and Impuzamugambi. After Karamira's April 12 message on the radio and similar directives by other party leaders, however, MDR youth groups began cooperating with the Interahamwe in attacking Tutsi. In Butare, the young supporters of the PSD also eventually participated in attacks with the Interahamwe, exchanging one party hat for another and putting into effect the order that it was time to forget party loyalties for the larger good of the killing campaign.[20]

From the start of the genocide, political leaders put the militia at the disposition of military. In a statement prepared for judicial proceedings, General Dallaire declared:

> ...[W]henever we attempted to establish communications with the Interahamwe leadership for cease-fire and humanitarian operations, our most sure and effective conduit to them was Colonel Bagosora. I believe, based on my experiences with the cross-line refugee exchanges in particular, that the militia and the control thereof seemed to be responsive to direction received from Col. Bagosora.[21]

As Interahamwe head Kajuga explained to a reporter,

---

[19]Anonymous, "La Milice Interahamwe"; Human Rights Watch/FIDH interview, by telephone, Brussels, September 23, 1996.

[20]République Rwandaise, Parquet de la République de Kigali, PV. no. 0053; Radio Rwanda, "Radio Rwanda broadcasts appeal by official of the pro-army faction of the MDR," April 12, 1994, SWB, AL/1970 A/2, April 13, 1994.

[21]Dallaire, "Answers to Questions," p. 39.

The government authorises us. We go in behind the army. We watch them and learn....We have to defend our country. The government authorises us to defend ourselves by taking up clubs, machetes and whatever guns we could find.[22]

In his radio address on April 12, Karamira used the same phrase, remarking that the militia "go in behind the army." At major massacres, such as the attack on Gikondo church on April 9, witnesses report that militia were clearly following the orders of the soldiers on the spot.[23]

In an account written later, CDR leader Barayagwiza recounts how the militia became real paramilitary forces once the "interethnic massacres" began. He admits that they attacked Tutsi civilians:

The targets were no longer the youth of other political parties [as in the days of kubohoza] but the soldiers of the RPF, especially infiltrators in the ranks of civilians, as well as the civilian accomplices of the enemy.[24]

Militia also carried out the commands of civilian administrators. Witnesses report that prefect Renzaho gave orders to the Interahamwe during their attack in late April at the Centre d'Etudes des Langues Africaines (CELA) in Kigali and that Odette Nyirabagenzi, a communal councilor in Kigali, sent militia to seize Tutsi to be killed at the Sainte Famille church and the adjacent St. Paul's center. In another case, a witness relates that he was attacked by Interahamwe at the direction of Rose Karushara, also a communal councilor in Kigali, who urged the assailants to kill him.[25]

In response to needs identified by the authorities or party heads, the militia leaders displaced their men from one area to another. These temporary transfers of

---

[22]Lindsey Hilsum, "Hutu Warlord Defends Child Killing," *Observer* (London), July 3, 1994.

[23]"Radio Rwanda broadcasts appeal"; U. S.Committee for Refugees, "Genocide in Rwanda," pp. 4-9.

[24]Jean-Bosco Barayagwiza, *Rwanda, Le Sang Hutu Est-il Rouge?* (Yaoundé: 1995), p. 246.

[25]African Rights, *Rwanda, Death, Despair*, pp. 645, 704; Human Rights Watch/FIDH interview, Gitarama, July 12, 1995.

assailants demonstrate the extent to which the genocide was centrally directed. Leaders dispatched militia from Kigali to Butare town and others from Nyabisindu were ordered to Gatagara in Butare prefecture. They sent militia from other locations to participate in massacres at Kaduha church in Gikongoro, at Rutonde commune in Kibungo, and at Ntongwe commune in Gitarama. They transported militia from Gisenyi to Kibuye, where they lodged at the Golfe Eden Rock Hotel and assisted the military and the local population in attacking the large groups of Tutsi at Karongi and Bisesero. They ordered militia from several places to help attack Mugonero hospital in Kibuye. A survivor of that massacre identified the party affiliation of the assailants from their distinctive garb, the blue and yellow print boubou of the Interahamwe and the black, yellow, and red neck kerchiefs and hats of the Impuzamugambi. He could tell, too, that they came from several regions. As was common in such large-scale attacks, assailants wore leaves from the plants found in their home regions to distinguish themselves from the victims. The witness saw assailants wearing leaves from tea plants, probably from Gisovu, others with leaves from coffee plants, presumably from Gishyita and Mubuga, and those of a third group with leaves from banana plants, apparently from Cyangugu.[26] In mid-June when national authorities began to fear increased RPF pressure on the capital, Interahamwe leaders broadcast orders over RTLM recalling their men to Kigali.[27]

National leaders used militia, as they did the military, to destroy Hutu opposition to the genocide. They sent groups across communal and prefectural boundaries to intimidate reluctant Hutu into attacking Tutsi.

Although generally responsive to directives from civilian and military authorities, leaders of the militia represented a force with its own base of power—particularly as the number of their members grew—and they dealt with authorities at the highest level. On occasion they met with ministers, prefects, and the chief of staff of the army.[28] Like the leaders of political parties, they often claimed to speak for the people in demanding the most extreme measures against Tutsi. In early May, militia attacked a convoy of civilians leaving the Hotel Mille Collines although it had received a safe conduct from General Bizimungu. In a

---

[26]Human Rights Watch/FIDH interviews, Kigali, September 12, 1995; July 11, 1996; Butare, October 12, 1995.

[27]Ntaribi Kamanzi, *Rwanda, Du Génocide à la Defaite* (Kigali, Editions Rebero, n.d.), p. 146.

[28]UNAMIR, Notes, Radio Rwanda, 20:00 hrs, April 24, 1994.

similar case in mid-May, U.N. officers negotiated for three hours to obtain the authorization of military and civilian authorities to evacuate a group of orphans. Then some young militia members in tee shirts and jeans stood up and imposed conditions that made the operation impossible. The officials said nothing and the effort failed.[29] In such cases the greater radicalism of the militia may have been contrary to the stated position of officials but in conformity with their real, hidden intentions. If militia acted without military approval and soldiers wished to stop them, they generally had little difficulty doing so. When General Bizimungu disapproved of an Interahamwe attack on the Hotel Mille Collines on June 17, for example, he quickly expelled them although he had only his personal guard at hand to enforce his order.[30]

The Administration

The military and the militia brought essential skills and and firearms to the slaughter, but they were too few to kill Tutsi on a massive scale in a short span of time. Executing an extermination campaign rapidly required the mobilization of hundreds of thousands of ordinary people, tens of thousands to actually slaughter and the others to spy, search, guard, burn, and pillage. In some situations, crowds were needed immediately and for only a few days to participate in a massacre; in others, a reliable supply of long-term "workers" was required to do patrols, man the barriers and track survivors. Bagosora, the AMASASU, the CDR, and Kangura had foreseen that turning out large numbers of civilians was the only way to attack an "enemy" dispersed in the population. As Karamira had said in his radio speech of April 12, this "war" had to become everyone's responsibility.

The interim government directed the administration to carry out this mobilization. Some ministers already known for their determined support of Hutu Power, such as Minister of Family and the Promotion of Women Pauline Nyiramasuhuko, Minister of Commerce Justin Mugenzi, Minister of Information Eliézer Niyitegeka, Minister of Youth Callixte Nzabonimana, and Minister of Primary and Secondary Education Dr. André Rwamakuba were apparently the most insistent about executing the genocide.[31] Judging from the way Interim

---

[29]"Ce sont les miliciens qui commandent', selon Bernard Kouchner," BQA, no. 14217, 20/05/94, p. 18.

[30]Human Rights Watch/FIDH interview, Brussels, November 8, 1998.

[31]Fidèle Uwizeye, "Apercu Analytique"; Human Rights Watch/FIDH interviews, by telephone, Brussels, April 27, 1997; Brussels, October 19 and 20, 1997.

President Sindikubwabo and interim Prime Minister Kambanda were assigned their roles in the government, they probably lacked the stature to influence major decisions, but they nonetheless shared responsiblity for implementing them.[32]

Passing the Word

On April 19, Interim President Sindikubwabo identified his government as "a government of saviors" that would come directly to the people "to tell you what it expects of you."[33] Ministers and other high-ranking government representatives did indeed go out to the countryside, exhorting and insisting on the need to support the genocide, promising rewards to supporters and threatening sanctions against dissenters.[34] The practice of going out to the hills had been used to mobilize people for projects of public good, but it also harked back to the 1960s when ministers used tours of rural areas to set off the killing of Tutsi.[35]

In the continuing absence of the minister of interior and communal development, the administrative head of the ministry, Callixte Kalimanzira, was responsible for implementing the government policy. He counted on a bureaucracy that was known for executing orders promptly and fully. When he directed subordinates to "alert the population to the necessity of continuing to track the enemy wherever he is to be found and wherever he hid his arms," most of them did so. To make clear that directives about "security" came from the highest authorities and must be obeyed, Kalimanzira ordered that speeches by the president and the

---

[32]Jean Kambanda confessed and pleaded guilty to genocide at the International Criminal Tribunal for Rwanda. On September 4, 1998, he was sentenced to life in prison.

[33]"Discours du Président Thodore Sindikubwabo prononcé le 19 avril 1996 à la Préfecture de Butare" (Recorded by Radio Rwanda, transcription and translation, confidential source). The term "saviors," *abatabazi*, described heroes of the Rwandan past who sacrificed their lives to protect the nation from foreign attack.

[34]Callixte Kalimanzira, Umuyobozi mu biro bya Ministere y'Ubutegetsi bw'Igihugu n'Amajyambere ya komini, to Bwana Prefe wa Prefgitura ya Butare, May 24, 1994 (Butare prefecture); Dr. Clément Kayishema, Préfet, to numerous recipients, no. 0282, April 30, 1994 (Kibuye prefecture).

[35]Lemarchand, *Rwanda and Burundi*, p. 223.

prime minister be disseminated widely. This would serve, he said, to make citizens "more determined to assure their own security and to warn all troublemakers."[36]

When Kalimanzira directed that meetings about security be held, prefects passed the order to burgomasters, who scheduled meetings and alerted councilors and cell heads. The burgomaster of Bwakira, for example, wrote to subordinates on April 19, ordering them to inform all residents of a series of scheduled meetings. He told them to use whistles and drums to summon the population "so that no one will be absent."[37] Prefects and sub-prefects expected and received reports of these meetings, many of which were recorded in minutes that were carefully taken and neatly transcribed.[38]

Administrators were responsible for informing their superiors about all important developments within their jurisdictions. In correspondence, in telephone conversations, and in meetings they regularly reported on the "state of security."

In orders passed down the administrative hierarchy as in the reports passed back up, crucial elements were sometimes left unstated, or were expressed in vague or ambiguous language.[39] Superiors told their subordinates to seek out the "enemy" in their midst, but did not specify what was to be done with him when found. Subordinates reported on the capture of "accomplices" but neglected to mention what measures had been taken against them. No one asked for further clarification because everyone understood.

As was usual in Rwanda, authorities at the national level dealt even with matters of detail. The widespread use of banana leaves or other foliage to distinguish attackers from intended victims throughout the country suggests a

---

[36]Fawusitini Munyazeza, [signed by Callixte Kalimanzira] Minisitiri w'Ubutegetsi bw'Igihugu n'Amajyambere ya Komini to Bwana Perefe (all), April 21, 1994, two letters, no identifying numbers (Butare prefecture).

[37]Tharcisse Kabasha, Bourgmestre wa Komini Bwakira, to Madame, Bwana Conseiller wa Segiteri (Bose), Bwana Responsable wa Cellule (Bose), no. 0.293/04.09.01/4, April 19, 1994 (Bwakira commune).

[38]For one example, see Dominiko Ntawukuriryayo, S/prefe wa S/prefegitura Gisagara to Bwana Burugumesitiri wa Komini (Bose), no. 088/04.09.01/16, May 14, 1994 (Butare prefecture).

[39]The International Criminal Tribunal for Rwanda in the Matter of the Trial of Jean-Paul Akayesu, case no. ICTR-96-4-T, draft transcripts (hereafter ICTR-96-4-T), Testimony of Jean-Paul Akayesu, March 12, 1998.

decision made in Kigali, as does the frequent reliance on whistles as a means of communication among assailants.

Mobilizing the Population

Prefects transmitted orders and supervised results, but it was burgomasters and their subordinates who really mobilized the people. Using their authority to summon citizens for communal projects, as they were used to doing for umuganda, burgomasters delivered assailants to the massacre sites, where military personnel or former soldiers then usually took charge of the operation. Just as burgomasters had organized barriers and patrols before the genocide so now they enforced regular and routine participation in such activities directed against the Tutsi. They sent councilors and their subordinates from house to house to sign up all adult males, informing them when they were to work. Or they drew up lists and posted the schedules at the places where public notices were usually affixed.

Burgomasters were responsible for ensuring the continuity of the genocidal work over a period of weeks, a task that many found difficult. "Intellectuals" were needed at barriers to read documents presented by passersby, but many disliked the duty and tried to evade it. Some councilors tired of making the rounds to check on the functioning of barriers. Burgomasters threatened sanctions against laggards and removed councilors who failed in their responsibilities.[40] The administrators also had to resolve squabbles among participants and sometimes resorted to having them draw up written agreements, such as that produced by workers assigned to the checkpoint near the Trafipro shop in the commune Bwakira. All the participants agreed to "be more vigilant" and to refuse bribes. They were reminded to check identity cards and baggage carefully and to interrogate all passersby. They were cautioned against drunkenness and disagreements. "To avoid such disorders, the meeting resolved to create teams, with a leader for each team. The leader will be accountable... for whatever happens at his checkpoint. He will be responsible for the success of the patrol. Every team will have its own patrol day." And because "it is not easy to check everyone, since some travellers dodge checkpoints," the group asked the whole population to stop and interrogate any unfamiliar person, wherever encountered.[41]

---

[40]These problems are described in documents from Bwakira commune, Kibuye, and from many communes in Butare prefecture, including Ngoma, Nyakizu, and Mbazi.

[41]Bwakira commune, "Inyandikomvugo y'Inama y'Abashingzwe Gucunga Barriere yo kuri Trafipro, May 17, 1994" (Bwakira commune).

Burgomasters, as well as those above and below them in the hierarchy, worked with local councils in implementing the genocide. In some cases, the elected communal council assisted them, but more often a committee or council[42] devoted specifically to security played this role. Security committees had existed before April 6 at the level of the prefecture and commune and, in some places, in sectors and cells as well. At the prefectural and communal levels, they had included government employees, military or police officers, and other locally important people such as clergy. At the lower levels, they were comprised mostly of community leaders. After the genocide began, administrators set up security committees for jurisdictions where they had not previously existed and gave new importance to committees that had existed before in name only. The officials regularly invited party leaders to meetings, as was being done at the national level and as they had been directed to do by Kalimanzira.[43]

In some communes, the security committee did little but approve decisions made privately by the burgomaster and his immediate circle, but in others they helped determine the daily details of the genocide, such as whose house would be searched and where and by whom barriers would be maintained. As the following document from Ntyazo commune shows, the committee sometimes determined the fate of Tutsi who had been caught.

Monsieur Gatwa Abias
"Barrier chief at Bugina"

Concerning the three girls of Gapfizi, I ask you to find two or three men to take them very early tomorrow morning to the sector councilor [illegible] where the measures will be carried out regarding them as was decided at the last meeting of the communal security committee that was held on May 13, 1994.

Ndahimana Mathieu
Assistant Médical

---

[42]Both terms were used.

[43]Fawusitini Munyazeza [signed by Callixte Kalimanzira], Minisitiri w'Ubutegetsi bw'Igihugu n'Amajyambere ya Komini to Bwana Perefe (all), April 21, 1994.

P.S. [illegible] asks permission to miss the patrol because he is very tired.[44]

Burgomasters occasionally called in soldiers or National Policemen, particularly if there were many Tutsi to kill. More usually they relied on local resources: the population, militia, and the communal police. In the course of the preceding months, many communal police had received new firearms or additional supplies of ammunition so they were well-equipped to serve as the local force for slaughter. They often guarded the sites where Tutsi had gathered until groups of assailants were organized for the attack and they then helped direct the massacre. Others led search parties to capture and kill Tutsi in their homes or in the bush.[45] Although most communal police followed orders to participate in the extermination, some did refuse. Others were killed themselves, either because they were Tutsi or because they tried to save the lives of Tutsi.

Burgomasters used the same forces to oblige dissident citizens to join in the genocide. They directed or permitted communal police, militia, or simply other citizens to burn down houses and to threaten the lives of those who refused to join in the violence.[46]

They also offered powerful incentives to draw the hesitant into killing. They or others solicited by them provided cash payments, food, drink and, in some cases, marijuana to assailants. They encouraged the looting of Tutsi property, even to the point of having the pillage supervised by communal police. In many areas, authorities led the people from one stage of crime to the next as they directed them from pillaging property to burning homes to killing the owners of the homes. In several places, police reprimanded those people who wanted only to pillage and not to kill. Assailants at Nyundo reminded each other "Kill first and pillage later."[47]

One of the most important resources for the burgomaster in enlisting participants was his authority to control the distribution of land, a much desired and

---

[44]Mathieu Ndahimana, Medical Assistant to Abias Gatwa, Barrier chief, Bugina (CLADHO).

[45]ICTR-96-4-T, Testimony of Jean-Paul Akayesu, March 12, 1998.

[46] Jacques Broekx, "Les Evénéments d'Avril 1994 à Rusumo," *Dialogue*, no. 177, August-September, 1994, p. 100; Buchizya Mseteka, "We Were Trained to Kill Tutsis," Reuter, May 20, 1994; Tina Susman, "Quiet Parish Paradise Destroyed by Massacre," Associated Press, May 31, 1994.

[47]Les Prêtres du diocèse de Nyundo, "Des Rescapés du Diocèse," p. 65.

scarce source of wealth for the largely agricultural population. Hutu who had attacked Tutsi in the 1960s had acquired the fields of their victims. A generation later, people again hoped to get more land by killing or driving Tutsi away. As Pasteur Kumubuga commented in a meeting in Bwakira commune "Those who killed say that the properties of the victims belong to them."[48] At a later meeting, another participant commented that people were cultivating lands taken from victims "to reward themselves for the work they had done."[49] As usual, "work" meant "killings."

Enforcing Regulations

The burgomaster did more than just recruit and organize participants in attacks and patrols. As head of the local administration, he became the arbiter of life and death through the implementation of administrative regulations. Because population registration was done at the commune, the burgomaster was the ultimate authority in cases of contested ethnic classification. In the commune of Bwakira, the burgomaster responded to an appeal from a woman named Mujawashema who said people accused her children of being Tutsi and wanted to kill them. The burgomaster carried the research back three generations to the status of Nsengiyumva, grandfather of the children's father. From a file completed on April 16, 1948, the burgomaster learned that the greatgrandfather of the children was Hutu. He concluded, "Therefore, no one must harm those children."[50]

In the commune of Ndora, members of a family accused of being Tutsi wrote to the burgomaster:

> After the misfortunes that have struck our family in the course of the recent troubles, misfortunes caused by the jealousy and the hatred spread by certain residents of the commune against us and which resulted in the pillage

---

[48]Bwakira commune, "Inyandiko-mvugo y'inama ya Komini yateranye kuwa 5.5.94" (Bwakira commune). "Inyandiko-mvugo" (sometimes with variant spellings) means minutes of a meeting. After the first citation, subsequent citations will be "Inyandiko-mvugo" and the date.

[49]Bwakira commune, "Inyandiko-mvugo y'inama ya Komini yateranye kuwa 20.5.94" in Tharcisse Kabasha, Bourgmestre wa Komini Bwakira to Bwana S/Prefe, no. 0329/04.04/2, May 31, 1994 (Bwakira commune).

[50]Tharcisse Kabasha, Bourgmestre wa Komini Bwakira to Bwana Conseiller wa Segiteli Shyembe, no. 0.359/04.03/3, June 21, 1994 (Kibuye prefecture).

of our goods, in the destruction of our houses, and even in the massacre of several of our family under the pretext that they could try to make them [i.e., the wrongdoers] pay for what they had done, and to this end, they have accused us of belonging to the ethnic group of the Batutsi, to the point that those [among us] who are safe owe this to their having a son in the national army; and even so, these residents are still pursuing them in the place where they have sought refuge.

We are writing to ask your help especially concerning the question of our ethnic affiliation, which is the pretext put forward by the residents of the commune, that it be clarified and explained to them because the ethnic group in which we believe and with which we identify is that of the Bahutu.[51]

They concluded by giving the names of four past and present officials in Ndora commune and others in Gishamvu, where the family had originally lived, who could verify their Hutu identity.

Persons who hoped to pass for Hutu often "lost" their identity cards and then requested temporary papers from the councilor or a new card from the burgomaster, hoping the administrator would be persuaded to falsify the document. In testimony at the International Tribunal about his powers during the genocide, one former burgomaster declared, "In the countryside, the mere fact of giving an attestation to a person sufficed to save him."[52] Tutsi who succeeded in obtaining such papers in their home communes sometimes found themselves caught by less obliging officials as they tried to flee through other communes. In another manoeuvre, Hutu mothers of children fathered by Tutsi sometimes tried to protect their children by claiming they were illegitimate and seeking to have them registered on their cards—as Hutu—rather than on the cards of the fathers. The burgomaster of Huye commune, reluctant to deal with these issues, passed such a case to the local judicial official, who passed it back to him with a bare explanation of the law that gave no real guidance on how to deal with the problem.[53]

---

[51]Antoine Gakwaya, Fidele Muzamuzi, and Madame Leonille Usaba to Bwana Burugumesitiri wa Komini Ndora, May 25, 1994 (Butare prefecture).

[52]ICTR-96-4-T, Testimony of Witness R, January 28, 1997, p. 83.

[53]Jonathan Ruremesha, Bourgmestre wa Komini Huye to Bwana Procureur wa Repubulika, no. 154/04.05/2, May 18, 1994; Mathias Bushishi, Prokireri wa Republika, to Bwana Burugumesitiri wa Komini Huye, no. C/0520/D11/A/Proc., May 24, 1994 (Butare prefecture).

In several cases, the burgomaster himself or members of his family were accused of hiding a Tutsi identity behind an officially Hutu exterior. One of them, the burgomaster of Mabanza, appealed to the Kibuye prefect, Kayishema, to defend him. He wrote:

> Regarding my personal problem—[accusations] that my wife is a Tutsi, that I am supposedly an accomplice of the enemy, that I protect Tutsi and Hutu with Tutsi wives—these rumors are spread by my political opponents who want to replace me. My wife is a Hutu of the Bagiga, a large Hutu family who live at Rubengera, commune Mabanza.
>
> The accusations that my mother-in-law is Tutsi are groundless as well. And if she were, children take the ethnic identity of their father, not their mother. Those who say that my mother-in-law is Tutsi are wrong: she is from sector Ruragwe, commune Gitesi, from the Barenga family, a well-known Hutu family, as the burgomaster of Gitesi explained in his letter no. D 249/04/05/3 of June 6, 1994, addressed to the councilor of sector Ruragwe and of which you have a copy.[54]

Administrative officials recorded changes in the population extremely carefully before the genocide, noting births, deaths, and movement into and out of the commune on a monthly as well as a quarterly basis. With this data, officials knew how many Tutsi, whether male or female, adult or child, lived in each administrative unit, information useful in any attempt to eliminate them. Prefect Kayishema was so concerned about the accuracy of this data that he took time in early May to review census data submitted by burgomasters for the last quarter of 1993. He found errors in at least two of the reports, that of Mabanza, which recorded the increase in female Tutsi as fifty-two instead of fifty-three, and that of Rwamatamu where an error of seven was made in accounting for the male Tutsi population and an error of six was made in recording that of female Tutsi.[55]

---

[54]Ignace Bagilishema, Bourgmestre de la Commune Mabanza to Monsieur le Préfet, no. 0.365/04.09.01/4, June 21, 1994.

[55]Dr. Clément Kayishema, Prefe, to Bwana Burugumesitiri wa Komini Rwamatamu, no 0290/04.05/1, May 5, 1994 and to Bwana Burugumesitiri wa Komini Mabanza, no. 0291/04.05/1, May 11, 1994; Dr.Clément Kayishema, Préfet, to Monsieur le Bourgmestre de la Commune Gitesi, no. 0292/04.05/l. Among documents found by researchers from Human Rights Watch and FIDH, there was no indication of error in statistics for the Hutu populations (Kibuye prefecture).

Even before April 1994, Rwandans were supposed to be registered in the communes of residence if these differed from their communes of birth. Nyumbakumi, cell heads, and councilors all were involved in making sure that no strangers lived unnoticed in a commune. With the start of the genocide and the renewal of combat, tens of thousands of people fled the capital, some heading directly south, others returning to their communes of origin, wherever they might be. Authorities and radio announcers warned from the start that the Tutsi among these displaced persons were often "infiltrators" in disguise and stressed the need to keep close track of them. Officials usually directed the displaced to a common gathering place and sought to discourage their taking shelter with private families, where it would be harder to keep track of them. But recognising that some went to stay with friends or family, burgomasters passed instructions down to councilors, cell heads, and nyumbakumi that such people must be registered immediately.[56] Administrative officials also insisted that clergy or persons responsible for sheltering the displaced provide as much data as possible about those whom they were lodging. Administrators generally declared that such data was needed to assure adequate food supplies, but the information also allowed them to know how many Tutsi were still alive and where they were staying. Often a gathering place was attacked soon after officials had collected data on the displaced persons sheltered there.[57]

Authorities also revived an earlier requirement that persons wishing to travel outside their communes receive written authorisation to leave (*feuilles de route*). Burgomasters controlled the distribution of these documents which could permit Tutsi to try to flee for their lives. During periods of curfew, burgomasters also decided who must obey the regulations to remain at home. Officials insisted that Tutsi remain in their houses while granting passes to assailants who could then move freely around the commune to attack them.

Burgomasters and other officials sought to keep accurate records on the dead and missing. In Bwakira, for example, the burgomaster ordered subordinates to prepare such lists on April 29. Five days later councilors submitted lists, by sector, of household heads who had died, the number of people in the household killed,

---

[56]"Réunion de Conseil de Sécurité Elargi du 11 Avril 1994," Dr. Clément Kayishema, Préfet, Dirigeant, Janvier Tulikumwe, Rapporteur (Kibuye prefecture); Dominiko Ntawukuriryayo, S/Prefe wa S/Prefegitura Gisagara to Bwana Burugumesitiri wa Komini Ndora, no. 085/04.09.01/4, April 15, 1994 (Butare prefecture).

[57]Telegram from Minitranso to Préfet (tous), no. 016/94, May 4,1994 (Butare prefecture).

and the number from the household who had fled.[58] In Butare, at Kabgayi and elsewhere, some Tutsi were sent back to their home communes to be killed, in part to enable local officials to verify that they were actually dead. Burgomasters kept track not just of overall numbers of dead, but also of the elimination of those persons named as priority targets for their communes. They seem to have borne final responsibility for ensuring that such persons had in fact been slain. Where there was any doubt that a person in question had in fact been killed, authorities would insist on seeing the body to confirm the death. In some cases, burgomasters tracked down escapees from their communes into adjacent areas, including those who had just sought temporary refuge in their jurisdiction before being driven away.

Burgomasters were also charged with disposing of the bodies. Sometimes they left the bodies unburied for days or weeks, a practice which contributed to the "normality" of violent death, but after a while public health considerations dictated disposal of the remains. Authorities summoned people for umuganda which consisted of stuffing bodies down latrines, tossing them in pits, throwing them into rivers or lakes, or digging mass graves in which to bury them. In Kibuye, workers used a bulldozer to push bodies into a pit behind the little church on a peninsula jutting into the lake. In Kigali, Gikongoro, Butare, and elsewhere, authorities also called upon drivers of bulldozers to assist in disposing of the bodies. In Kigali, prisoners went through the streets every three days to gather up the bodies, a service that prisoners performed in Butare as well. One witness related his shock in the early days of killing when he came across a group of prisoners, dressed in their pink prison shirts and shorts, tossing cadavers into a truck. They were appropriating all valuables from the bodies, stripping glasses and watches from them, plunging their hands into pockets to be sure they had extracted all they could from the dead, and then squabbling among themselves over the division of the spoils.[59]

Support Services: Ideas and Money

Behind the intertwined triple hierarchy of military, administrative, and political authorities stood another set of important, but unofficial and less visible actors. A

[58]Bwakira commune, "Inyandiko-Mvugo y'Inama ya Komini Bwakira Yateranye Kuwa 29/4/94" in Tharcisse Kabasha, Bourgmestre wa Komini Bwakira to Bwana S/Prefe wa S/Prefegitura Birambo, No. 0. 316/04.04/2, May 18, 1994 (Bwakira commune).

[59]Human Rights Watch/FIDH examination of the grave site, Kibuye church, February 1995; Human Rights Watch/FIDH interview, Butare, May 25, 1995.

number of them, left over from the akazu, came together under the leadership of Félicien Kabuga, the wealthy businessman who had helped organize RTLM and who had ordered the thousands of machetes imported in 1993 and early 1994. In early April, many of the group retired to the luxury of the Hotel Meridien or other comfortable lodgings in the pleasant, lakeshore town of Gisenyi. From there they gave advice to the interim government on finance, foreign relations, food supply, and even military strategy.

On April 24 and 25, Kabuga brought together a group of local elite and important persons displaced from Kigali to discuss how to support the army "and the young people," i.e., militia. The meeting established a "Provisional Committee," including Kabuga, Abijah Kwilingira, and Stanislas Harelimana to present their ideas to the government. In an April 26 "Message to the Government," the group urged the interim government to improve its image abroad, an objective that it had just decided to address by sending delegations abroad to try to justify the genocide. Several days later, the Rwandan ambassador in Bruxelles released a statement detailing the "pacification" efforts of the interim government and supposed massacres by the RPF of 20,000 civilians.[60] The memo by Kabuga and his group also urged immediate action against the Rwandan ambassador in Paris, Jean Marie Vianney Ndagijimana, who had denounced the interim government on French radio. Four days later, the interim government removed Ambassador Ndagijimana. The committee asked the interim government to accuse Uganda and Belgium formally of aiding the RPF. Two weeks later, the Rwandan representative to the U.N. filed a complaint of aggression against Uganda with the U.N. secretary-general and requested an urgent meeting of the Security Council to examine the charges.[61]

Kabuga and his group also demanded that all young people receive military training. Repeating the language used by the military commission writing about self-defense at the end of March, they urged that "large quantities of traditional weapons" be found for the recruits since there would not be enough firearms for all of them. Several weeks later, Minister of Interior Edouard Karemera ordered

---

[60]François Ngarukinyintwali, Situation Actuelle au Rwanda sur le Plan de la Securité, April 30, 1994 (Butare prefecture).

[61]Félicien Kabuga, Prezida, Abijah Kwilingira, Visi Prezida, Stanislas Harelimana, Umunyamabanga, Komite y'agateganyo, Ubutumwa Bugenewe Guverinoma, April 25, 1994 (Butare prefecture).

prefects to have people arm themselves with such weapons and soon after, several communes established training camps to teach young people how to use them.[62]

Kabuga and his associates announced a fund to support the "youth" and contributed the first monies for the account. The committee called on the government to publicize this idea rapidly so that others could contribute.[63] Within ten days, the project had been relayed to Washington and probably other foreign capitals as well. The Rwandan ambassador in Washington wrote Rwandan citizens resident in the U.S. and asked them to send contributions to an account he had established at Riggs National Bank.[64] Within the country, prefects directed their subordinates, businessmen, and the heads of government departments to collect contributions for such a fund from the people under their authority. The contributions solicited by Kabuga from his immediate circle, 25 million Rwandan francs, about U.S.$140,000, was divided among the prefectures and the Ministry of the Interior to allow each to establish its own account. Dr. Jean-Berchmans Nshimyumuremyi, the vice-rector of the National University of Rwanda, pressed faculty and staff of the university to contribute and within five days had more than 6 million Rwandan francs, about U.S.$34,000 available for deposit in the local fund. The money was transferred from the university "Caisse d'Epargne," the savings plan of university employees, suggesting that the vice-rector had taken some or all of it from this account. If so, he would have followed the model of the national government which apparently diverted money from the pension fund for state employees to pay the expenses of war.[65]

---

[62]Edouard Karemera, Ministre de l'Intérieur et du Développement Communal, to Monsieur le Préfet (Tous) May 25, 1994; [Dominiko Ntawukuriryayo, S/prefe]to Bwana Burugumesitiri wa Komini (Bose), no. 009/04.09.01, June 16, 1994 (Butare prefecture).

[63]Félicien Kabuga, Prezida, Abijah Kwilingira Visi Prezida, Stanislas Harelimana, Umunyamabanga, Komite y'agateganyo, Ubutumwa Bugenewe Guverinoma, April 25, 1994; Félicien Kabuga, Perezida, Komite y'Agateganyo y'Ikigega Ndengera-Gihugu (F.D.N.) to Nyakubahwa Bwana Ministiri w'Intebe, May 20, 1994 (Butare prefecture).

[64]Human Rights Watch/Africa, press release, May 11, 1994. After being notified by Human Rights Watch of the existence of this account, the U.S. government insisted that it be closed.

[65]Jean-Berchmans Nshimyumuremyi, Le Vice-Recteur de l'U.N.R. [Université Nationale du Rwanda] to Monsieur le Préfet de la Préfecture de Butare, P2-18/226/94, May 25, 1994 (Butare prefecture).

The previous government had also solicited contributions to help pay the costs of war, but this fund was different because it was destined "to help civilians fight the enemy," as wrote the prefect of Kibuye.[66] The Ministry of Interior instructed that the money was to be used to pay the expenses of the militia, including their "refreshments," meaning certainly the beer and, in some cases, drugs used to intoxicate the killers before an attack. The funds were meant also to buy traditional weapons and communications equipment and to pay the costs of transporting the militia (gasoline and the maintenance of vehicles) to the sites of their "operations."[67] The need for "refreshments" was so important that the prefect of Kibuye requested a police escort for a boat bringing beer from the BRALIRWA brewery in Gisenyi to remedy "the scarcity of drinks" in his prefecture.[68] Before money became available through the fund, administrators were forced to find resources themselves to pay the costs of keeping militia active. The prefect of Kibuye emptied the MRND youth fund to pay transportation costs and the burgomaster of Taba used funds of the commune to buy food and beer for militia.[69]

In addition to responding rapidly to the solicitation of money for the civil defense fund, university staff in Butare shared ideas with both Kabuga's group and the interim government. In an April 18 press release, the "intellectuals of Butare" laid out a justification for the genocide that would be exploited by delegations sent abroad the following week. They blamed the RPF for having refused a cease-fire and for having thus obliged Rwandan troops to remain at the front instead of going to save Tutsi. At a meeting arranged by Vice-rector Nshimyumuremyi in mid-May, interim Prime Minister Kambanda thanked the intellectuals of the university for the ideas and other support they had provided in the past. In the discussion that followed, speakers repeated some of the ideas enunciated by Kabuga on April 26:

---

[66]Dr. Clément Kayishema, Préfet, to Bwana Burugumesitiri (bose), no. 0.330/04.01.01, June 9, 1994 (Kibuye prefecture).

[67]Undated document, Instruction Ministerielle Aux Préfets de Préfecture Relative à l'Utilisation du Fonds Destiné au Ministère de l'Interieur et du développement Communal dans le Cadre de l'Auto-défense Civile (Kibuye prefecture).

[68]Dr. Clément Kayishema, Préfet, to Monsieur le Commandant de Place, Gendarmerie, no. 0283/04/.09.01/6, May 4, 1994 (Kibuye prefecture).

[69][Dr. Clément Kayishema] "Rapport de Conseil de Sécurité Elargi du 11 avril 1994" (Kibuye prefecture); ICTR-96-4-T, Testimony of Witness K, January 10, 1997, pp. 74-75.

the importance of a rapid media response to RPF charges against the government, the usefulness of accusing Uganda and Belgium of supporting the RPF, and the need for civilians to help the army fight the war. These same ideas had appeared in a press release on May 10 by the Groupe de Rwandais Défenseurs des intérêts de la Nation and would be discussed at a later meeting of this group and another at the university, Le Cercle des Republicains Universitaires de Butare.[70]

The Clergy

Within the first twenty-four hours after the plane crash, it was clear that Tutsi clergy would be killed like any other Tutsi and, a day after that, it was evident that the churches would be desecrated by slaughter carried out at the very altar. Still, four days later, the Catholic bishops promised their "support to the new government." They asked all Rwandans to "respond favorably to calls" from the new authorities and to help them realize the goals they had set, including the return of peace and security. The bishops balanced the statement with a denunciation of troublemakers and a request to the armed forces to protect everyone, regardless of ethnic group, party or region.[71] The statement was issued from the Vatican, where the first synod of African bishops was beginning. The Rwandan bishops had been scheduled to attend, but did not leave Rwanda because of the onset of violence.

As the slaughter continued, the bishops reportedly felt the need to temper their early support of the government with criticism but were not allowed to broadcast such a firm statement.[72] On April 17, the bishops spoke again, but only to call for an end to bloodshed for which they held both the RPF and the government responsible. It was only a month later that four Catholic bishops, the Anglican archbishop and other Protestant clergy took a stronger position, urging an end to the war, massacres and assassinations. They "condemned all scandalous acts" and,

---

[70]Anonymous, Handwritten Notebook recording prefectural security council meetings, entry for 5/14/94. (Butare prefecture.) Hereafter cited as Notebook 1; Le Groupe de Rwandais Défenseurs des Intérêts de la Nation, "Document no. 5: Complicité des Eléments Belges de la Mission des Nations Unies pour l'Assistance au Rwanda (MINUAR) avec Le Front Patriotique Rwandais," May 10, 1994 (Butare prefecture); Chrétien et al., *Rwanda, Les médias*, p. 303.

[71]Agence France Press, "Les évêques du Rwanda promettent leur soutien au nouveau gouvernement," BQA, No. 14190, 12/04/94, p.29.

[72]Human Rights Watch/FIDH interview, by telephone, Brussels, April 27, 1997.

without explicitly denouncing the genocide, asked all Christians to refuse to kill.[73] With the hierarchy slow to take a clear stand against the genocide, many local clergy, both Catholic and Protestant, gave tacit approval to the slaughter by participating in security committee meetings.

By not issuing a prompt, firm condemnation of the killing campaign, church authorities left the way clear for officials, politicians, and propagandists to assert that the slaughter actually met with God's favor. Sindikubwabo finished a speech by assuring his listeners that God would help them in confronting the "enemy."[74] RTLM announcer Bemeriki maintained that the Virgin Mary, said to appear from time to time at Kibeho church, had declared that "we will have the victory." In the same vein, the announcer Habimana said of the Tutsi, "Even God himself has dropped them."[75]

Far from condemning the attempt to exterminate the Tutsi, Archbishop Augustin Nshamihigo and Bishop Jonathan Ruhumuliza of the Anglican Church acted as spokemen for the genocidal government at a press conference in Nairobi. Like many who tried to explain away the slaughter, they placed the blame for the genocide on the RPF because it had attacked Rwanda. Foreign journalists were so disgusted at this presentation that they left the conference.[76]

Some clergy who might have been able to save lives refused to even try to do so. On April 15 Abbé Pierre Ngoga, who had fled the Kibeho church after soldiers and local people had begun massacring thousands of Tutsi there, called the Bishop of Gikongoro. Abbé Ngoga asked him to rescue the Tutsi who had survived and faced renewed attack. The bishop reportedly refused to help, saying that he had no soldiers to accompany him to Kibeho and that the Tutsi had been attacked because they had arms with them.[77]

---

[73]Missionnaires d'Afrique, Guy Theunis and Jef Vleugels, fax no. 10, April 25, 1994 and no.15 and annex, May 26, 1994.

[74]"Ijambo Perezida wa Repubulika yongeye kugeza ku Baturarwanda kuwa 14 Mata 1994," in Fawusitini Muyazeza, Minisitiri w'Ubutegetsi bw'Igihutu n'Amajyambere ya Komini to Bwana Perefe wa Perefegitura (Bose), April 21, 1994 (Butare prefecture).

[75]Chrétien et al, *Rwanda, Les médias*, pp. 329, 326.

[76]African Rights, *Rwanda, Death, Despair*, pp. 900-902.

[77]République Rwandaise, Parquet de la République de Kigali, PV. no. 0117.

Some clergy, Rwandan and foreign, turned away Tutsi who sought their protection, whether from fear, from misjudgment of the consequences of their action, or from desire to see them killed.[78] In other cases, the clergy protected most who sought refuge with them, but nonetheless sacrificed others. At the large Catholic church center at Kabgayi, some 30,000 refugees gathered under the protection of the Archbishop of Kigali, two bishops, and many clergy. Of that number, about 25,000 were Tutsi, 1,500 of whom would be extracted in small groups from the camps and killed during the course of the genocide. In some cases, burgomasters or militia leaders arrived to collect individuals from their communes to take them home to be killed. In other cases, militia, soldiers, and National Police passed through the crowds and chose persons to execute because they looked like members of the elite. They also took women to rape and sometimes to kill afterwards. Shortly before the arrival of the RPF, four soldiers and five militia members presented the archbishop with a list of names of clergy and lay people whom they were seeking because they had links with the "enemy." The archbishop stood aside and allowed the squad to search the rooms. The killers departed several hours later with sixteen persons, seven religious brothers, four priests, one religious sister, and four lay persons. The nun, Sister Benigna, an older Hutu who was known throughout the region for her work with single mothers and orphans, was apparently battered to death with a hammer. Her body was found in the woods next to the church center.[79]

A small number of clergy and other religious persons have been accused of having incited genocide, delivered victims to the killers or even of having killed themselves. Pastor Elizaphan Ntakirutimana has been indicted before the International Criminal Tribunal for Rwanda in connection with the massacre at Mugonero and Abbé Wenceslas Munyeshyaka of the Sainte Famille Church in Kigali has been charged in France with torture. Two Rwandan priests have been found guilty of genocide and condemned to death by a Rwandan court.

Despite the silence of many clergy, some did defend Tutsi, even at the risk of their own lives. Bishop Frédéric Rubwejanga went to the local military camp to ask protection for Tutsi attacked at the St. Joseph center in Kibungo, as described

[78]Soeur Gertrude Consolata Mukangango to Bwana Burugumesitiri wa Komini Huye, May 5, 1994 (Butare prefecture); Gabriel Maindron, "Rwanda, L'Horreur," *Dialogue,* no. 177, August-September, 1994, p. 49; African Rights, *Rwanda, Death, Despair,* p. 923.

[79]Human Rights Watch/Africa interview, Kabgayi, August 29, 1994; Missionnaires d'Afrique, Guy Theunis and Jef Vleugels, fax no. 16, June 2, 1994.

below. Mgr. Thaddée Ntihinyurwa of Cyangugu preached against the killing of civilians on April 10 and went to Nyamasheke when he learned that Tutsi in the church were under attack. When he returned to the town of Cyangugu the next day, he tried to evacuate Tutsi religious brothers but was unable to protect them from militia who stopped the cars on the road. The three brothers were killed before his eyes.[80]

One of the most courageous examples of opposition to the genocide was that of Felicitas Niyitegeka of the religious congregation of the Auxiliaires de l'Apostolat. A Hutu, she had given shelter to many Tutsi in Gisenyi since the start of the genocide and had helped them across the border to Zaire. Her brother, Col. Alphonse Nzungize, who commanded the nearby Bigogwe military camp, heard that she was threatened with death for her work and asked her to give it up. She refused. On April 21 she was taken to a cemetery for execution with forty-three persons, including other religious sisters and Tutsi who had sought refuge with them. Once there, militia members who feared retaliation from her brother offered her the chance to leave. She refused to abandon the others. They repeated the offer after they had slain thirty people. She still refused and was shot and thrown naked with the others into the common grave. When her brother heard the news, he went to find her body and had it dressed and properly buried.[81]

The Radio: Voice of the Campaign

Throughout the genocide, Radio Rwanda and RTLM continued to broadcast both incitations to slaughter and the directions on how to carry it out. Authorities knew that they could reach a far wider audience through the radio than through popular meetings and so told people that they should listen to the radio to know what was expected of them. The burgomaster of Bwakira commune, for example, reminded people that they "have to follow all orders transmitted in meetings or on

---

[80]Missionnaires d'Afrique, Guy Theunis and Jef Vleugels, fax no. 10, April 25, 1994.

[81]Nzungize himself had saved several hundred Tutsi in the first days of slaughter in a case described in chapter seven. République Rwandaise, Parquet de la République de Kigali, PV. no. 0117; Missionnaires d'Afrique, Guy Theunis and Jef Vleugels, fax no. 17, June 9, 1994.

the radio."[82] Radio Rwanda also alerted listeners that heads of political parties would use the airwaves to "send messages to their members concerning how they should behave during these times when all of us should be alert and protect the sovereignty of our country."[83] Repeatedly authorities used the radio to caution against "infiltrators" who were said to be coming to kill Hutu and to ask the population to be vigilant in watching out for them.[84]

On April 12, the same day when Karamira and the Ministry of Defense used the radio to make clear that Tutsi were the target of killing, Prefect Renzaho used Radio Rwanda to give detailed instructions about where to look for them:

> ...we ask that people do patrols [*amarondo*], as they are used to doing, in their neighborhoods. They must close ranks, remember how to use their usual tools [i.e., weapons] and defend themselves...I would also ask that each neighborhood try to organize itself to do communal work [*umuganda*] to clear the brush, to search houses, beginning with those that are abandoned, to search the marshes of the area to be sure that no *inyenzi* have slipped in to hide themselves there...so they should cut this brush, search the drains and ditches...put up barriers and guard them, chosing reliable people to do this, who have what they need...so that nothing can escape them.[85]

Authorities used the radio to recall retired soldiers to active duty and to summon the personnel needed for special tasks, such as the drivers of bulldozers

---

[82]Bwakira commune, "Inyandiko-mvugo y'inama ya Komini yateranye kuwa 24.5.94" in Tharcisse Kabasha, Bourgmestre wa Komini Bwakira to Bwana Suprefe wa Suprefegitura, Birambo, no. 0.340/04.04/2, June 6, 1994 (Bwakira commune); Article 19, *Broadcasting Genocide*, p. 139.

[83]Radio Rwanda, "Radio Rwanda broadcasts appeal by official of the pro-army faction of the MDR," April 12, 1994, SWB, AL/1970 A/2, April 13, 1994.

[84]Valerie Bemeriki, RTLM, April 8 and 13, 1994 recorded by Faustin Kagame (Provided by Article 19).

[85]Chrétien et al, *Rwanda, Les média*, p. 298.

who were urgently called to Kigali prefecture, presumably to help in digging trenches to dispose of bodies.[86]

Throughout the genocide, RTLM continued its informal, spontaneous style, with announcers recounting what they had seen on their walks around Kigali. The radio made the war immediate for people distant from the front: listeners could hear the explosions of mortars being shot at RTLM. So lively was the wit of the announcers that even wounded RPF soldiers listened to RTLM from their hospital beds. The station carried not just the rhetoric of politicians but also the voice of the ordinary people who took time off from their work on the barriers to say hello to their families back home. The consistency of the message, delivered by the man in the street as well as by ministers and political leaders, increased its impact on listeners. They were convinced by hearing one of the "abaturage," the masses, declare that a person who could not present the right identity card at a barrier should "maybe lose his head there."[87]

The announcers replayed all the now familiar messages of hate: the inherent differences between Hutu and Tutsi, the numerical superiority of the Hutu—the *rubanda nyamwinshi*, the majority people—the cleverness of the Tutsi in infiltration, their cruelty, their cohesiveness, their intention to restore past repression, the risk they posed to the gains of the 1959 revolution, and, above all, their plan to exterminate the Hutu. Such messages concluded with calls to action, like the following by Kantano Habimana: "Fight them with the weapons that you have at hand, you have arrows, you have spears...go after those *inkotanyi*, blood flows in their veins as it does in yours...." One RTLM announcer promised that a "shining day" would dawn when there would be not a single Inyenzi left in the country and the word could be forgotten.[88]

The radio castigated those who failed to participate enthusiastically in the hunt. One listener remembers RTLM saying:

[86]Police Judiciaire près le Parquet du Procureur du Roi de Bruxelles, PV no. 30339, Dossier 36/95; Missionnaires d'Afrique, Guy Theunis and Jef Vleugels, fax no. 5, April 8, 1994.

[87]Sezibera Saverini, RTLM broadcast, May 15-May 30, 1994 (tape provided by Radio Rwanda).

[88]Chrétien et al., *Rwanda, Les médias*, pp. 193, 304.

All who try to protect themselves by sympathizing with both sides, they are traitors. It is they who tell a lot to the Inyenzi-Inkotanyi. It is they whom we call accomplices [ibyitso]. They will pay for what they have done.[89]

Disseminating the message that "there is no place for moderates," RTLM heaped scorn on those who refused to participate:

The inhabitants of certain sectors don't dare search! They say that the houses are occupied and that their owners are shut up inside them; they don't dare search even in the banana groves![90]

They warned that those who refused to search could expect sanctions and they cautioned that those who deserted the barriers could expect severe punishment, just as did soldiers who deserted the battlefront.[91]

RTLM occasionally went beyond government policy. While officials and political leaders were directing militia to follow the lead of the army and not get ahead of the professionals, RTLM exhorted the people of Rubungo commune to attack on their own. It urged them:

Courage! Don't wait for the armed forces to intervene. Act fast and don't allow these enemies to continue their advance! If you wait for the authorities, that's your problem. They are not the ones who are going to look out for your houses during the night! You must defend yourselves.[92]

RTLM announcer Kantano Habimana even dared criticize the interim government for its decision to withdraw to Gitarama. He asked when these authorities would return to Kigali to support the population and the soldiers and he hoped, "that they aren't spending their time, sitting inside, receiving their friends...." Instead they

---

[89]Tatien Musabyimana, "R.T.L.M.," *Traits d'Union RWANDA,* July 15, 1994, p. 5.

[90]Police Judiciaire près le Parquet du Procureur du Roi de Bruxelles, PV no. 30339, Dossier 36/95.

[91]Ibid; RTLM, 15-30 May 1994 (tape provided by Radio Rwanda).

[92]Police Judiciaire près le Parquet du Procureur du Roi de Bruxelles, PV no. 30339, Dossier 36/95.

should "go out on the hills...to support the people, to teach them how to dodge the *inkotanyi*, how to cut them off, how to kill them with spears...."[93]

Deception, Pretext, and Pretense

Authorities, military, administrative, and political, engaged in deception with three objectives in mind: they wanted to confuse foreigners in order to avoid criticism and perhaps even to win support; they wanted to mislead Tutsi to make it easier to kill them; and they wanted to manipulate Hutu into participating energetically in the genocidal program. Sometimes a given strategem served more than one purpose and misled two or even all three target audiences at once. The whole effort of deception was remarkably coherent, with diplomats abroad proclaiming the same lies as those told at home and with officials and politicians using the same pretenses in widely separated communities at the same time.

Just as the organizers used genocide to wage war, so they used the war to cover the genocide. Whether speaking in foreign capitals or at sector meetings out on the Rwandan hills, representatives of the interim government always began with a reminder that the RPF had invaded Rwanda in 1990 and from that deduced that the RPF was responsible for all subsequent developments, including the massive killing of Tutsi by Hutu. Without hesitation, they blamed the assassination of Habyarimana on the RPF, making it an illustration of the larger theme of Tutsi aggression and ruthlessness.

In early April, Sindikubwabo described the violence as a spontaneous outburst of rage sparked by "sorrow and aggressive feelings of frustration" after the assassination.[94] Kambanda explained that Habyarimana was "not an ordinary man, not a man like any other," and asserted that his killing created "a certain frustration among people, a certain vague anger that made it impossible for people to keep control after the death of the head of state."[95] The excuse of "spontaneous anger" echoed the attempts at justification during the Habyarimana period when authorities attributed killings of Tutsi to uncontrollable popular wrath.

The pretext of popular anger was meant not just to confuse foreigners about the organized and systematic nature of the violence, but also to encourage Rwandans to feel justified in participating in it. According to witnesses, many

---

[93]Chrétien et al, *Rwanda, Les médias*, p. 305.

[94]Ijambo Perezida wa Repubulika...kuwa 14 Mata 1994.

[95]Chrétien et al., *Rwanda, Les médias*, p. 301.

assailants declared during attacks that Tutsi deserved to die because the Inyenzi had killed the president. After the militia leader, Cyasa Habimana, led the slaughter of some 1,000 persons at the Saint Joseph center in Kibungo, the bishop confronted him to ask why he had killed. The militia leader pointed to the portrait pin of Habyarimana that he wore on his chest and said, "They killed him."[96] In the days just after the plane crash, many Rwandans in the MDR stronghold of Gitarama prefecture began wearing such portrait pins, which had not been seen in the region since the end of the MRND monopoly of power in 1991. The widespread appearance of the pins demonstrated the success of the campaign to make a martyr of the president.[97]

In another reprise from the Habyarimana years, authorities occasionally tried to shift the blame for violence from the guilty to someone else, even to the victims themselves. In the first days of the genocide, military authorities claimed that it was not soldiers of the Rwandan army but others wearing their uniforms who were slaughtering political leaders. When they could not sustain this pretense, they assigned guilt to a few unruly elements who were said to have disobeyed orders. Later, RTLM announcer Bemeriki asserted that Interahamwe attacks on the Hotel des Mille Collines and the Sainte Famille church were carried out by "people disguised as Interahamwe." Soon after she claimed that Tutsi were responsible for burning their own houses as a way to trap and kill Hutu.[98]

Also familiar from the Habyarimana years was the claim that authorities were doing everything posssible to restore order. In speeches on April 13 and 14, Sindikubwabo even went so far as to assert that the "troubles and killings" had ended with the installation of his government. He later retreated to a position of claiming only that the government was there "to prevent the worst" and would work to see "that these troubles, murders, and thefts are ended in Rwanda once and for all." When Kambanda took office on April 9, he promised that the government "will do everything possible to restore peace as soon as possible, let us say within about two weeks." Whether coincidence or indication of prior planning, it was

---

[96]Human Rights Watch/FIDH interview, Kibungo, January 30, 1995.

[97]Human Rights Watch/FIDH interview, Brussels, May 17, 1997.

[98]"'Armed forces' acting COS says RPF attacks 'contained,' appeals for peace talks," Radio Rwanda, April 10, 1994, SWB, AL/1969 A/1, April 12, 1994; Chrétien et al, *Rwanda, Les médias*, p. 337.

fifteen days later that authorities began real efforts to make killing more circumspect.[99]

The "spontaneous anger" excuse became less plausible as the days passed and the killings continued, so authorities replaced it with the pretext of slaughter as "self-defense." On April 15, the foreign ministry directed Rwandan diplomats to inform the world that "the civilian population which rose as a single man...has greatly contributed to the security of persons and property as well as to exposing the FPR combatants who had infiltrated different parts of the city."[100] On his tour abroad to explain the genocide, Mathieu Ngirumpatse would proclaim, "The population is trying to defend itself."[101]

Authorities and propagandists insisted that the war was present throughout the country, even if it were not apparent, and the enemy was everywhere, even if he were not obvious.[102] Beginning on April 8, Bemeriki had cautioned that "*Inkotanyi* are now dispersing...spreading out amongst the inhabitants."[103] Hitimana warned that "they are taking off for the hills...They know how to hide and reappear!"[104] In another broadcast, RTLM declared that Inkotanyi were arriving "dressed as civilians and unarmed," leading listeners to believe that all who looked like the "enemy," i.e., Tutsi, should be considered RPF soldiers.[105] As Bemerki exhorted on April 13,

---

[99]Ijambo Perezida wa Repubulika...kuwa 14 Mata 1994; Ijambo Perezida wa Repubulika yagejeje ku Baturarwanda kuwa 13 Mata 1994, in Fawusitini Muyazeza, Minisitiri w'Ubutegetsi bw'Igihugu n'Amajyambere ya Komini to Bwana Perefe wa Perefegitura (Bose), April 21, 1994 (Butare prefecture). "New prime minister addresses parliament, says talks with RPF will continue," Radio Rwanda, April 9, 1994, SWB, AL/1968 A/2.

[100]Guichaoua, *Les crises politiques,* p.680.

[101]Thadee Nsengiyaremye, "Bombardments Blast Apart Rwandan Rebel Ceasefire," United Press International, April 27, 1994.

[102]UNAMIR, Notes, Radio Rwanda broadcast, 10:00 hrs, April 26, 1994.

[103]Article 19, *Broadcasting Genocide,* p.121.

[104]Ibid., p. 121.

[105]Ibid., p.115.

People have to look at who is next to them, look to see if they are not plotting against them. Because those plotters are the worst. The people must rise up, so that the plotters will be exposed, it is not hard to see if someone is plotting against you...[106]

On April 17, MDR leader Karamira informed Radio Rwanda listeners that the RPF soldier "is not a soldier in any obvious way..." He added that many "are not in uniform and are hidden among the people..."[107] In mid-April, the radio intensified this campaign by reporting that not only individual Tutsi but also organized RPF brigades were operating throughout the country and were responsible for alleged attacks, such as on the burgomaster of Runda.[108]

The "enemy" who was everywhere was extraordinarily cruel, according to the propagandists. Announcers on RTLM frequently reminded listeners of the dozens killed at Kirambo the previous November and insisted that the RPF had committed that massacre. Bemeriki charged the RPF with cannibalism, saying they killed people by dissecting them and cutting out their hearts, livers, and stomachs.[109] On the air and in public meetings, officials and political leaders also contributed to this sense of a people besieged by a heartless enemy. In an April 15 broadcast, the minister of defense charged the RPF with "extreme cruelty," saying that it had massacred 20,000 people and had burned people with gasoline at Nyamirambo in Kigali.[110]

To make the need for "self-defense" seem more pressing, RTLM and Radio Rwanda announcers broadcast false news reports of Belgian or other European

---

[106]Valérie Bemerki, RTLM, April 13, 1994, recorded by Faustin Kagame (Article 19).

[107]Chrétien et al., *Rwanda, Les médias*, p. 302.

[108]Solidarité Internationale pour les Refugiés Rwandais, "Le Non-dit sur les Massacres," p.12. The first reference to Cyahinda rather than Runda on this page is apparently an error.

[109]Chrétien et al., *Rwanda, Les médias*, p. 162. The interim foreign minister made the same charge before the U.N. Security Council. [See below.]

[110]Chrétien et al, *Rwanda,Les médias*, p. 299.

assistance to the RPF or of invasions being planned or actually under way by troops from Uganda or Burundi.[111]

Like the "spontaneous anger" justification, this effort at legitimating violence through "self-defense" was meant both to quiet foreign critics and to incite Hutu to kill more. When the propagandist who disseminated his summary of the work of Mucchielli wrote about "accusations in a mirror," he recommended that adversaries be accused of terrorism because "honest people" will take action if they believe they are legitimately defending themselves.[112] Officials and propagandists alike encouraged Hutu to feel righteous anger at the Tutsi and to give "them the punishment they deserve."[113]

Local authorities invoked several kinds of "proof" to convince Hutu that Tutsi were planning to attack them and hence should be killed first. Both the practice of presenting such "evidence" and the kinds of "evidence" presented were remarkably uniform throughout the country, indicating the central direction to the deception. They also echoed the strategems of the Habyarimana years. In some cases, the "proof" was a local replay of the nationally-broadcast scenario of Hutu being attacked. In Huye commune near Butare, Tutsi were said to have attacked a soldier. In the town of Butare itself, Tutsi were said to be preparing to kill Hutu. In Kibuye, the rumor circulated that the RPF would launch a helicopter strike to free Tutsi in the stadium.[114]

A still more widely used "proof" of Tutsi guilt was the supposed possession of arms. At the western most reaches of Rwanda, the first Tutsi killed in Kibuye town was accused of having grenades stored in his toilet and Pastor Ezekiel Semugeshi was accused of having arms and Inkotanyi at his home in Mugonero.

---

[111]UNAMIR, Notes, Radio Rwanda, 20 hrs, 22. [04.94]; 13:00 hrs, 24.[04.94]; 10:00 hrs, 26[04.94]20:00 hrs, 05 [05.94];19:00 hrs, 11.05.1995 [sic, 1994] (confidential source); RTLM, 12:00 hrs, 13 [.04.94]; 17 hrs, 22 [.04.94] 15 hrs, 26 [.04.94].

[112]See chapter two.

[113]Kantano Habimana, RTLM, April 13, 1994, recorded by Faustin Kagame (provided by Article 19).

[114]République Rwandaise, Parquet de la République de Kigali, PV. no. 0053 and P.V. no. 0117; Fondation Hirondelle, "Des Rumeurs à l'Origine des Massacres de Kibuye, Selon un Témoin," June 23, 1998. Bagosora supposedly alleged that Rwandan soldiers who killed the ten Belgian peacekeepers had only been protecting themselves after the Belgians had attacked their military camp, Reyntjens, *Rwanda, Trois Jours*, p. 77.

In Kibungo, all the way to the east, soldiers showed the bishop four guns supposedly found in a hedge next to the church to justify their slaughter of the Tutsi who had sought shelter there. In the north, at the parish church of Gisenyi, Abbé Ntagara was accused by RTLM of having "replaced the communion hosts with ammunition." And in the south, Tutsi were accused of having arms at Kibeho church.[115]

Authorities also discredited Tutsi by reporting that they possessed suspicious documents, ordinarily lists of Hutu to be killed, but alternatively records of RPF meetings or of dues collected for the RPF, maps with houses marked for attack, letters supposedly from RPF members, or diagrams showing how land was to be redistributed in the community once all the Hutu were eliminated. Just as some authorities displayed arms supposedly found in searches, so others produced actual pieces of paper to add credibility to the charges. The prefect of Kibuye kept examples of such suspicious papers to show to foreign visitors in an effort to legitimate the killing that had taken place in his prefecture.[116] Militia at a barrier in Kigali asserted that a newspaper containing a letter from RPF president Alexis Kanyarengwe was proof that the person in whose house it had been found was in communication with the RPF.[117] Echoing the speech by Léon Mugesera in November 1992, as well as many subsequent similar statements, some local authorities charged families with having sent their children to join the RPF. They also leveled other accusations that had been heard in prior years: that the Tutsi were holding secret meetings, that they had radio equipment for contacting the RPF, and that they had traveled abroad recently. Some said the very flight of Tutsi to churches and other places of refuge showed that they planned some terrible crime and wished to be clear of the scene before the plot was put into operation.

In some instances, Tutsi did have arms or were assisting the RPF, and authorities did have real evidence of their actions. But the cases were few and instead of dealing with them responsibly, officials exaggerated their importance and used them to cast suspicion upon all Tutsi.

---

[115]Human Rights Watch/FIDH interviews, Kibungo, January 30, 1995; Kigali, June 30 and September 12, 1995, July 11, 1996; Butare, October 26, 1995; Neuchatel (Switzerland), December 16, 1995; by telephone, Brussels, April 27, 1997; Chrétien et al., *Rwanda, Les médias*, p. 328.

[116]Human Rights Watch/FIDH interview, Buffalo, N.Y., September 21, 1997.

[117]Human Rights Watch/FIDH interview, Kigali, September 12, 1995.

Officials and political leaders used some of the same "proofs" as pretexts for attacking Hutu opposed to them, but more often they charged them with hiding Tutsi. They also accused them of having changed their identity from Tutsi to Hutu.

The "intellectuals" of Butare discussed the need for "uniformity and harmony" of language at two meetings that they held during the genocide.[118] In official statements made at meetings, in correspondence among administrators and politicians, and in radio broadcasts, this "uniformity and harmony" prevailed and in the vocabulary used even long after the fact by participants, it still prevails. Some ordinary words carry a special meaning, like "to work," which appears frequently and almost casually, meaning to kill Tutsi and their Hutu supporters. The word refers back to the 1959 revolution and its violence against Tutsi, a link indicated in phrases that advocate "finishing the work of the revolution." "Work" requires "tools," that is, firearms, machetes, clubs, spears. In a report on security meetings that he conducted, one sub-prefect declares that he made people understand what they needed to do for their own welfare. In parentheses he adds, "to work."[119]

Always using the war to cover the genocide, authorities refer to massacres as "battles" and to the genocide as "interethnic fighting." The enemy was the Tutsi. Such was the message of the street song, but it was rarely stated openly. Instead Tutsi were described as "accomplices," "infiltrators," "Inyenzi," "Inkotanyi" and "the minority." The Hutu were called "the great mass" (the rubanda nyamwinshi) or "the majority people" and "the innocent," meaning the innocent victims of the Tutsi aggressors. Officials also spoke of "the Rwandans," when they clearly meant only Hutu, thus reinforcing the belief that Tutsi were alien. The interim government repeatedly announced that it intended to ensure security, peace, and the protection of property, but they meant those benefits only for the Hutu, not for all Rwandans.

Authorities issued statements carrying a double message, knowing that Rwandans would be able to decipher their real meaning. In an April 14 speech that is a model of ambiguity, Sindikubwabo began by preaching the need for "peace in the hearts of our citizens so that they will be tolerant of each other and pardon each other." He directed them to "keep calm, to forget all feelings of anger, hatred or vengeance." But then he insisted that people must collaborate with the government

---

[118] Dr. Eugène Rwamucyo for Le Cercle des Républicains Universitaires de Butare and Groupe des Défenseurs des Intérêts de la Nation, "Table Ronde Politique à Butare," June 22, 1994 (Butare prefecture).

[119] Chrétien et al., *Rwanda, Les médias*, pp. 304-5.

in "denouncing any person who still has the evil intention of making us return to the situations of the past," a phrase that could refer only to Tutsi. He returned to the more benign mode to counsel good behavior so that no one would be unjustly injured. Then, immediately after, he switched to the attack again: "On the other hand, point out [enemies] and alert the army and security authorities, do patrols...."[120] In a similarly ambiguous statement on April 15, the minister of defense urged listeners to work with the army to put the enemy "to flight and exterminate [kumulimbura] him wherever he is" but also stated that "we cannot permit the people to begin killing each other."[121] A week later, Kalimanzira of the Ministry of Interior ordered prefects to "Make people aware of the need to continue to hunt the enemy wherever he is...[but] without doing harm to the innocent."[122]

The deceptions in language were echoed and intensified by the deceptions in action, such as the pretense of providing police protection to sites where Tutsi had taken refuge. On a number of occasions, authorities or political leaders used promises to lure Tutsi into situations where they could be attacked: in Musebeya, it was the assurance of transport home; in Muko, it was the guarantee of a ride to the Kaduha church; and at Mugonero, it was the promise of protection by U.S. forces who were said to have arrived in the area. A councilor in the Kicukiro commune, Kigali, offered to hide Tutsi, then reportedly put them in a truck and delivered them to militia. Busloads of displaced persons were transported by order of the prefect of Cyangugu from the stadium to a camp at Nyarushishi. En route, one bus took another route and all the persons on it were killed.[123]

In other cases, those who had escaped death by flight and hiding were summoned to return home, by drum, voice or loudspeaker. The authorities assured them that the killing was finished. When they came out, they were set upon and slain. In a variant of that deception, survivors were told that the killing was over at the end of an attack, only to see the killers reappear later to finish off those who

---

[120]"Ijambo Perezida wa Repubulika...kuwa 14 Mata 1994."

[121]Chrétien et al., *Rwanda, Les médias,* p. 299; Commandement des Forces Armées Rwandaises en Exil, "Contribution des FAR," p. 96.

[122]Ministiri w'Ubutegetsi bw'Igihugu n'Amajyambere ya Komini [actually signed by C, Kalimanzira] to Bwana Perefe wa Perefegitura (Bose), April 21, 1994.

[123]Human Rights Watch/FIDH interviews, Kigali, August 29, 1994, September 12, 1995; Anonymous, "Les Massacres au Stade de Cyangugu," *Dialogue,* no. 177, Août-Septembre, 1994, p. 95. See chapter on Gikongoro.

were still alive.[124] After the previously mentioned massacre at the Kibungo bishopric, the leaders of the attack assured the bishop that the survivors would be permitted to live. The militia had even delivered survivors of other attacks to the Saint Joseph center to receive medical care. At the Kibungo military camp three days later, the bishop raised the issue and was again told by Colonel Nkuliyekubona, the camp commander, Colonel Rwagafilita of the akazu, and the local militia leader Cyasa Habimana that the survivors would not be harmed. He returned directly to the bishopric several kilometers away and found that, in his brief absence, the survivors had been loaded into a truck and taken to a large mass grave near the hospital. There the survivors—more than half of them children—were slain and buried or buried alive. The bishop returned to the camp to confront the three leaders. The two colonels seemed to indicate that it was the militia leader who was responsible, but they made no move to arrest him or otherwise hold him accountable for the massacre.[125]

Deception was central to the genocide. Without being persuaded that the war was in every community, no matter how far from the line of battle, and without believing that all Tutsi—whether strangers on the road or neighbors known for a lifetime—were enemies, some people would have found it harder to transform their Hutu Power beliefs into deadly action.

Popular Participation

When the national authorities ordered the extermination of Tutsi, tens of thousands of Hutu responded quickly, ruthlessly and persistently. They killed without scruple and sometimes with pleasure. They jogged through the streets of Kigali chanting, "Let's exterminate them all." They marched through the streets of Butare town shouting "Power, Power." They returned from raids in Kibuye singing that the only enemy was the Tutsi. They boasted about their murders to each other and to the people whom they intended to kill next.

---

[124]Human Rights Watch/FIDH interviews, Butare, October 24, November 9, November 30 1995, March 26, 1996; Kigali, September 9, 1995; Des Prêtres du diocèse de Nyundo, "Des Rescapés du diocèse," p. 63; African Rights, *Rwanda, Death, Despair,* pp. 433, 436, 439, 458, 494, 516, 541, 615, 624.

[125]Human Rights Watch/FIDH interviews, Kibungo, January 30, 1995.

Many of these zealous killers were poor, drawn from a population 86 percent of whom lived in poverty, the highest percentage in the world.[126] They included many young men who had hung out on the streets of Kigali or smaller commercial centers, with little prospect of obtaining either the land or the jobs needed to marry and raise families. They included too thousands of the displaced who focused their fear and anger on the RPF and defined that group to include all Tutsi. As Bagosora and Nahimana had anticipated, young men from the camps were easily enlisted in the "self-defense" effort. Convinced partisans of the MRND or the CDR, particularly those from the northwest who had grown up hearing accounts of Tutsi oppression and who had little contact with Tutsi in their daily lives, constituted another important pool of assailants.

Many refugees from Burundi, who transferred their anger from their Tutsi-dominated government at home to the Tutsi of Rwanda, also rushed to join the killing campaign. They had been trained at some camps by Rwandan soldiers and militia since late 1993 and were prepared to strike. Refugees from Gisali camp in Ntongwe commune launched attacks on Tutsi in the vicinity, while others killed at Gashora commune in Kigali, at Mugina in Gitarama, at Nshili in Gikongoro, and at Nyakizu, Muyaga, Mugusa, and Butare town in Butare.[127]

Some Rwandans, previously scorned in their communities, seized on the genocide as an opportunity to gain stature as well as wealth. Using their physical strength, their fighting skills, or their knowledge of weapons, men generally regarded as thugs organized bands to serve as ready-made militia to exterminate Tutsi. Women and children sometimes joined in pillaging or destroying property. Less often they too injured or killed Tutsi. As one UNAMIR officer remarked, "I had seen war before, but I had never seen a woman carrying a baby on her back kill another woman with a baby on her back."[128]

Not all killers were poor and living in misery. The authorities who directed the genocide constituted a substantial part of the Rwandan elite, vastly richer and better established than the masses—whether participants or victims.

---

[126]Uvin, *Aiding Violence*, p. 117. These data refer to the total population, including Tutsi, but figures pertaining exclusively to Hutu would presumably be nearly the same.

[127]Human Rights Watch/FIDH interview, Brussels, February 26, 1997; Commission pour le Mémorial du Génocide et des Massacres, "Rapport Préliminaire," pp. 8, 28, 178.

[128]Human Rights Watch/FIDH interview, Plainsboro, NJ, June 13, 1996.

Nor were all the poor killers. Some refused to attack Tutsi, even when offered the prospect of pillage or the chance to acquire land that might provide security for their families. The people of Butare, arguably the poorest and most over-populated prefecture, were the last to join the killing campaign. Those who initially rejected violence wanted only to get on with their own lives. They hoped mostly for an end to war and the seemingly interminable political squabbles of the elite.

Some who refused at the start became convinced to act when all authorities seemed to speak with one voice, when the leaders of their parties joined with administrators to demand their participation and when the military stood behind, ready to intimidate those who hesitated. At this point, the hesitant accepted the deceptions of the supposedly legitimate officials and hid behind them to commit crimes unthinkable in ordinary circumstances.

Unlike the zealous assailants, the reluctant set limits to their participation: they might massacre strangers in churches or at barriers, knowing only that they were Tutsi, and refuse to attack neighbors, knowing that they were Tutsi but knowing also that they were not enemies. They might agree to pillage a Tutsi envied for his wealth and refuse to burn the house of a poor widow; they might join in killing a young man who loudly proclaimed his loyalty to the RPF but refuse to slay an infant. Some became more hardened with experience and learned how to slaughter even those whom they had once refused to harm; others went the other way, apparently swept up by fear or greed in the first days of slaughter, they were later repelled by the efforts to exterminate even the vulnerable.

Tens of thousands of Hutu refused to join the killing campaign and saved Tutsi lives. Hundreds of thousands more disapproved of the genocide but did nothing to oppose it or to help its victims. They did not answer the call of the local cell leader but neither did they respond to the cries of Tutsi in distress. As one witness reported, "We closed the door and tried not to hear."[129]

---

[129]Human Rights Watch/FIDH interview, Musebeya, June 7, 1995.

EXTENDING THE GENOCIDE

In the first days of the genocide, its leaders rapidly rallied support among military, militia, and administrators who supported the MRND and the CDR. The next week, with the announcement on April 12 that Tutsi were the only enemy, they attracted increasing numbers of officials from MDR-Power and other parties to the killing campaign. But by mid-April, they still had not won the support of some influential military officers and administrators. The prefects of Butare and Gitarama and many of the burgomasters under their direction as well as isolated administrators elsewhere, like the burgomasters of Giti in Byumba and of Musebeya in Gikongoro, continued traveling through their regions to deter attacks, facing down crowds of assailants, and arresting the aggressors. In those areas, there were relatively few Tutsi killed before the interim government decided to extend the genocide.[1]

The leaders of the killing campaign had to invest considerable political and military resources to end opposition to the genocide and they did so, belying their assertion that they were trying to halt the slaughter. They killed or removed some of the dissenting soldiers and officials and intimidated others into compliance. They left other opponents of the slaughter in place, but destroyed their effectiveness—by bypassing them, by sapping their political control, or by withholding or withdrawing the military or police support they needed.

As they extended the slaughter, national leaders also sought to tighten control over it by formalizing the system of "civilian self-defense." They hoped to improve their image abroad by making the killing more discreet as well as to curb dissension among Hutu as they finished the "work" of eliminating Tutsi. As the number of Tutsi diminished, Hutu attacked each other over questions of property and power, often using the same accusations and deceptions against each other that they had been using against Tutsi. In the end, the leaders of the genocide failed in their goal of creating Hutu solidarity, which they had been ready to purchase at the cost of so many Tutsi lives.

The rapid advance of the RPF spurred some authorities to more frenetic killing but also showed others, officials and ordinarily people alike, the futility of trying to fight the war through the genocide. With the final victory of the RPF, the interim

---

[1] Human Rights Watch/FIDH interview, Kigali, July 11, 1996; Commission pour le Mémorial, "Rapport Préliminaire, pp. 136, 195, 239; Broekx, "Les Evénéments d'avril 1994 à Rusumo," p. 99. See chapters below for cases from Gikongoro and Butare.

government fled to Zaire, leaving behind a people divided by fear and hatred as never before in their history.

Removing Dissenters

Ten days after the start of the genocide, leaders of the killing campaign had to contend with continuing opposition within Rwanda but faced no challenge from abroad to their policy. The evacuation of foreigners, begun a week before, had been concluded and the troops sent for that purpose had also left Rwanda without intervening in the slaughter. The Belgians had withdrawn their soldiers from the peacekeeping force and, at the end of its April 15 meeting, the Security Council was leaning towards a total recall of UNAMIR, although no decision had been made. The Rwandan ambassador to the U.N., a member of the Security Council at the time, no doubt promptly communicated the tenor of the debate to the interim government.[2]

The next morning, on April 16, the ministers—presumably assisted, as usual, by political leaders—felt sufficiently confident to move against opponents of the genocide. In the military domain, they removed Gatsinzi as chief of staff of the armed forces and named instead Col. Augustin Bizimungu, whom Bagosora had first proposed on April 6. They promoted Bizimungu to general and did the same with Gatsinzi and Rusatira, perhaps hoping in this way to win their support.[3]

The Ministry of Defense also recalled to active duty certain officers who had been obliged to retire sometime before, including Bagosora himself and Colonels Rwagafilita, Serubuga, and Gasake, all supporters of Bagosora. Gatsinzi signed the recall shortly before his removal and then tried to cancel it after learning that he could invalidate the order on a technicality. His radio announcement voiding the recall was apparently ignored.[4]

In the civilian sphere, the government on April 17 removed Prefect Jean-Baptiste Habyalimana of Butare who had been successfully opposing the killings. The radio had prepared public opinion for Habyalimana's removal by announcing earlier in the week that he had not attended the April 11 meeting of prefects, an unusual item to broadcast as part of the news and one which implied negligence on

---

[2]See chapter fifteen for these decisions.

[3]UNAMIR, Notes, Radio Rwanda, 20:00, April 16, 1994; Human Rights Watch/FIDH interviews, by telephone, Brussels, April 27, 1997 and July 22, 1998.

[4]République Rwandaise, Ministère de la Justice, Parquet de la République, P.V. no. 0142.

his part. Unlike Gatsinzi who lost his post but escaped with his life, the prefect of Butare was arrested and later summarily executed by soldiers or National Police. His family was slaughtered after his execution. Prefect Godefroid Ruzindana was also fired. He had tried to prevent slaughter in his prefecture of Kibungo, but had done so less successfully than Habyalimana, perhaps because important leaders like Colonel Rwagafilita had struck swiftly and ruthlessly after April 6. Ruzindana and his family were massacred while trying to flee.[5]

In naming candidates to replace these prefects and to fill vacant posts in the three northern prefectures, the government chose men whom they expected would support the genocidal program. François Karera, previously a sub-prefect, who was named to head the prefecture of Kigali, had no hesitation later in justifying the massacres to a *New York Times* reporter by saying that Tutsi were "originally bad." Another new prefect was Elie Nyirimbibi, the first member of the CDR ever to be given such a post.[6]

The interim government anounced Gatsinzi's removal on April 16 and the administrative changes on Sunday evening, the 17th. The dismissal of Habyalimana, the outstanding opponent of slaughter, was announced just after a presidential address to the nation about "pacification."

After having replaced Prefect Habyalimana, the interim government in May and June dismissed several dozen other administrators—prefects, sub-prefects, and burgomasters—and they permitted or encouraged local authorities to replace councilors and cell heads during these same months. By substituting apparently committed supporters of the genocide for those who did not back the program, they also warned others about the loss of post—and possibly life—that might result from continued opposition to the new power-holders.

At the same time the authorities showed their willingness to pay for collaboration, scarce though public funds were. At the end of April the interim government agreed to begin paying salaries to cell heads, local officials who had not previously been remunerated by the state and whose cooperation was important to the success of the killing campaign. In July, as the interim government was preparing to decamp to Zaire, the prefect of Kibuye sought to arrange for payments

---

[5]Human Rights Watch interview, Kigali, by telephone, April 29, 1994; Human Rights Watch/FIDH interview, Buffalo, January 12, 1997. For Habyalimana, see chapters 11 and 12. Note that the prefect spelled his name with the letter "l," while the president used "r." In kinyarwanda, the sounds are nearly interchangable.

[6]Jane Perlez, "Under the Bougainvillea, A Litany of Past Wrongs," *New York Times*, August 15, 1994; UNAMIR, Notes, Radio Rwanda, 20:00 April 17, 1994.

to communal youth organizers, who had apparently been actively supporting the genocidal program in the preceding months.[7]

Continued Conflicts Among the Military

With the beginning of the genocide, even Tutsi in the armed forces were accused of being ibyitso. Virtually no Tutsi had risen to command positions in the army, but a small number had become officers in the National Police. They, as well as Tutsi in the ranks, were targeted by fellow military and by militia. At barriers on the outskirts of Kigali, National Police were disarmed and killed by soldiers and militia because they were Tutsi—or thought to be Tutsi.[8] Maj. François Kambanda, initially saved by Ndindiliyimana, was later killed by militia at Nyanza. Lieutenant Mpakaniye was shot on the parade ground in the military camp at Cyangugu, reportedly by Lt. Samuel Imanishimwe. Adjutant Karwanira was killed by a corporal from Gisenyi in the cafeteria of the National Police camp. The murderer then fled to the camp of the Presidential Guard, where soldiers at first protected him but eventually allowed the National Police to arrest him.[9]

Some military men, especially those from the south, had wives or other relatives who were Tutsi and they feared for the lives of these family members. Military men were supposedly not allowed to marry Tutsi women, but in fact some did so. Once the genocide began, National Policemen at Kacyiru camp in Kigali and soldiers at the Bigogwe camp in Gisenyi had to protect their Tutsi wives from local assailants. Soldiers and National Policemen moved Tutsi relatives and friends to military camps or National Police brigades in hopes they would be safe there.[10] As the slaughter continued, many learned that relatives and friends had in fact been killed—not just those who were Tutsi, but also others who were mistaken for Tutsi or had tried to help Tutsi. Lieutenant Colonel Nzungize, commander of the

---

[7]Anonymous, Notebook 1, entry for 14/05/94; Felix Bahati, Encadreur Préfectoral de la Jeunesse et des Associations to Monsieur le Préfet de Préfecture, no. 33/21.01/06, July 11, 1994 (Kibuye prefecture).

[8]Human Rights Watch/FIDH interviews, Brussels, October 19 and 20, 1997, and by telephone, April 27, 1997.

[9]Anonymous, "La Milice Interahamwe, La Main à Tuer des Genocidaires"; Human Rights Watch/FIDH interview, Brussels, May 16, 1997.

[10]Human Rights Watch/FIDH interview, Brussels, May 16, 1997; Commandement des Forces Armées Rwandaises en Exil, "Contribution des FAR," p. 98.

Bigogwe camp, had a grandson—Hutu like himself—slain in Gikongoro because he looked Tutsi. He also lost a sister, Felicitas Niyitegeka, who was killed, as described above, because she was rescuing Tutsi.[11]

Some soldiers and National Policemen showed their opposition to the genocide by trying to save lives. On April 7, Lieutenant Colonel Nzungize cooperated with Belgian soldiers, still present as part of a military assistance program, to bring to safety some 350 to 400 people. Other officers whose names are not known saved lives in the early days, including National Police lieutenants at Busogo and Nyamirambo, an army lieutenant at Nyundo, and an army major who protected people at the Institut Africain et Mauricien des Statistiques et d'Economie Appliquée outside Kigali. National Police Majors Jean-Baptiste Jabo at Kibuye and Cyriaque Habyarabatuma at Butare sought to prevent slaughter in areas under their jurisdiction. Lieutenant Colonel Bavugamenshi later protected thousands of Tutsi at a displaced persons camp in Cyangugu, as mentioned above. Major Jean-Baptiste Nsanzimfura was one of the gendarmes who protected Tutsi at churches and the Hotel Mille Collines in Kigali; he also rescued Tutsi who had hidden for weeks at the churches of Ruli and Rwankuba.[12]

Bagosora and his supporters tried to suppress dissent against himself and the program of slaughter. Lieutenant Colonel Bavugamenshi was attacked with a grenade and Major Augustin Cyiza was arrested and returned to Kigali in handcuffs when he tried to escort his family to safety elsewhere. Like Rusatira, they went into hiding for a week or more in the early days of the genocide. Major Habyarabatuma of the National Police in Butare was warned that Capt. Ildephonse Nizeyimana of the local military camp, was planning to kill him. As Bagosora's power increased, his supporters occasionally openly disobeyed and even insulted their superiors who

---

[11]République Rwandaise, Parquet de la République de Kigali, PV. no. 0117.

[12]Human Rights Watch interviews, by telephone, Kigali, April 29 and May 3, 1994; Human Rights Watch/FIDH interviews, Kigali, July 11, 1996; Arusha, February 17, 1997; Brussels, November 8, 1998; République Rwandaise, Parquet de la République de Kigali, PV. no. 0034; Leonard, "Le Carnage à Busogo," pp. 33, 35; Des Prêtres du diocèse de Nyundo, "Des Rescapés du diocèse," p. 61; Commission d'Enquête CLADHO-KANYARWANDA, Rapport de l'Enquête sur les Violations Massives des Droits de l'Homme Commises au Rwanda à partir du 06 avril 1994, pp. 331, 333.

were known to be opposed to the new authorities.[13] When Rusatira summoned Major Mpiranya, head of the Presidential Guard, in early April, he refused to come. Ndindiliyimana had an armored personnel carrier under his authority appropriated by a junior officer of the reconnaissance battalion. He protested to the chief of staff, but was unable to get the vehicle restored to his command.[14]

Throughout this period, the interim government frequently transferred troops, both units and individual officers, supposedly in response to the demands of the war. In some cases, these changes served to prevent the development of resistance to the new authorities and to advance the genocide. With thousands of combat troops at its disposal, the general staff transferred National Police under Majors Jean-Baptiste Jabo and Habyarabatuma to the battlefront, removing them from posts where they could have protected Tutsi from attack. In Gikongoro, the National Police commander, Maj. Christophe Bizimungu, who tried to restrain a subordinate who favored attacks against Tutsi, was replaced by an officer who made no effort to stop the killings.[15]

Although their position was clearly out of favor, some high-ranking officers persisted in trying to get an end to attacks on civilians. On April 16, Rusatira sought out interim Prime Minister Kambanda and Minister of Defense Bizimana at Murambi, in Gitarama prefecture, to tell them that the departure of the government from Kigali had spurred further violence, both in the capital and in Gitarama. He urged them to stop the killings.[16] Six days later, on April 22, Rusatira came back again, this time accompanied by Ndindiliyimana, to try to convince officials of the interim government and political party leaders that the genocide was destroying the morale of the troops and could discredit Rwanda with foreign

---

[13]Human Rights Watch/FIDH interviews, January 26, 1996, Brussels, by telephone, April 27, 1997; République Rwandaise, Parquet de la République, P.V. no. 0143; Article 19, *Broadcasting Genocide,* p. 124. Ndindiliyimana found an excuse to leave Rwanda in early June, supposedly to try to arrange the purchase of arms, and he never returned.

[14]Human Rights Watch/FIDH interviews, Brussels, June 21, 1997; by telephone, Brussels, April 27, 1997, September 3, 1997, and July 22, 1998.

[15]Human Rights Watch/FIDH interviews, New York, Plainsboro, N.J., June 13, 1996 and Brussels, June 21, 1997; by telephone, Brussels, April 27, 1997.

[16]Human Rights Watch/FIDH interviews, by telephone, Brussels, April 27, 1997 and July 22, 1998.

governments whose support was essential. In a meeting that reportedly included Kambanda and political leaders like Murego, Mugenzi, Karemera, and Shingiro, the officers argued that the slaughter was "a prelude to defeat." The politicians refused to heed their warnings. They insisted that the killings were "self-defense" and must continue. They reportedly declared that if soldiers refused to collaborate in the killing campaign, they had another way to carry it out.[17]

In mid-April, General Ndindiliyimana and Colonels Gatsinzi and Rusatira summoned Gaspard Gahigi of RTLM and Jean-François Nsengiyumva of Radio Rwanda to the military school in Kigali. The officers supposedly told them that the radios must stop calling for violence against Tutsi and discrediting military officers opposed to the genocide. Announcer George Ruggiu had questioned Rusatira's intentions in making frequent contacts with General Dallaire and another RTLM announcer incited militia to attack Ndindiliyimana by reporting that he was transporting RPF soldiers in his vehicle—for which the license plate number was given—when he was trying to help Tutsi escape. Major Habyarabatuma was also threatened on RTLM.[18]

Either the message was not clearly enough delivered or the propagandists of hate knew they were supported by other more powerful soldiers. Instead of tempering their calls for violence against Tutsi, the radios at about this time began broadcasting spurious reports that RPF brigades were threatening civilians in different parts of the country.[19] Nor did they soften their stance on dissident military. Throughout the rest of the war RTLM continued to issue general warnings about military opposed to the interim government who were responsible, they said, for each loss by the government forces to the RPF.[20]

---

[17]Human Rights Watch/FIDH interview, by telephone, Brussels, April 27, 1997; Human Rights Watch/FIDH interview, by telephone, January 26, 1997; Human Rights Watch/FIDH interviews, Brussels, October 19 and 20, 1997, June 22, 1998.

[18]Human Rights Watch/FIDH interviews, January 26, 1996; Brussels, October 19 and 20, 1997; Brussels, by telephone, April 27, 1997.

[19]Human Rights Watch/FIDH interviews, Brussels, October 19 and 20, 1997 and by telephone, July 22, 1998; Commandement des Forces Armées Rwandaises en Exil, "Contribution des FAR," p.98.

[20]Chrétien et al., *Rwanda, Les médias*, pp. 266-67.

On April 29, the general staff of the army wrote to the minister of defense complaining that the National Police, which had been used in combat in Mutara and Kibungo, had been responsible for the defeats by the RPF in those regions. Officers of the National Police learned of the letter and suspected that some army officers intended to simply dissolve their force. Although no such step was taken, the incident contributed to hostile feelings between officers of the two services. RTLM exacerbated the ill-feeling by making derogatory comments about the National Police, who were thought too tolerant of Tutsi and southerners.[21]

Destroying Opposition in Gitarama

Among the opponents of genocide left in place after April 16 were the prefect, Fidele Uwizeye, and most of the burgomasters of Gitarama prefecture. The government may have retained these men because they feared alienating their party, the MDR, which was the predominant political organization in Gitarama, or because they expected to be able to oblige them to change their position. Over a period of several weeks officials, political leaders, the military, the militia, and the media worked together to force such a change.

As elsewhere in Rwanda, the MDR in Gitarama was divided between moderates and advocates of Hutu Power. In the first days of the genocide, not just the moderates, but even some of the MDR Power politicians refused to join the killing, believing that the MRND and the CDR had launched the violence simply to capture power for themselves.

When the people of Gitarama refused to attack Tutsi, MRND and CDR militia raided across the prefectural boundary, striking first and most vigorously from the city of Kigali and its periphery. Setiba, the Interahamwe leader whom UNAMIR police had been afraid to arrest and disarm the previous December, now put his weapons to good use. Supported by a few soldiers, he led his militia in attacks against the communes of Runda and Taba. The prefect complained about the raids to officials, including presumably Kalimanzira, who was acting for the minister of the interior, and to MRND leaders, but without result. Militia from communes of Kibuye, Gisenyi, and Ruhengeri prefectures also began crossing boundaries to raid and burn in Gitarama. These incursions were intended both to kill Tutsi and to force hitherto inactive Hutu to join in the attacks.[22]

---

[21]Human Rights Watch/FIDH interviews, Brussels, May 26, October 19 and 20, 1997; Anonymous, "La Milice Interahamwe."

[22]Fidèle Uwizeye, "Aperçu Analytique."

Uwizeye organized his burgomasters to defend the prefecture. Under the direction of local officials, Hutu and Tutsi fought together to drive off the assailants and killed a number of them. In communes further from prefectural boundaries, like Nyamabuye, where attacks from outside the prefecture were less of a problem, burgomasters successfully opposed the efforts of local troublemakers to begin the killing campaign. Uwizeye and several of his burgomasters also prohibited establishing barriers, although RTLM was encouraging people to do so. Some burgomasters, like the one of Nyamabuye, discouraged people from even listening to RTLM.[23]

When the interim government moved its headquarters to a training school in Murambi on April 12, it brought the political, military, and administrative leaders of the genocide into the heart of Gitarama prefecture, just a few miles from the prefectural offices. In later testimony before the International Criminal Tribunal for Rwanda (ICTR), the man who had been burgomaster of Nyamabuye was asked if it would have been possible to prevent killings in his commune if the national government had not relocated to Gitarama. He responded:

Yes, it is possible if other people—if other forces did not come from outside to come back—to fight against what the burgomaster was doing in his commune. I believe that if the government had not come into Gitarama prefecture with many soldiers and Interahamwe, it would have been possible.[24]

Elsewhere in his testimony, the former burgomaster remarked:

The Presidential Guard and the Interahamwe who were present in Gitarama were moving within the country, talking to the population, teaching the ideology of killing, of massacres. They incited the population to hate the local authority by saying that those who did not kill the Tutsi were accomplices of the Inkotanyi.[25]

---

[23]ICTR-96-4-T, Testimony of Witness R, January 28, 1997, pp. 37, 40, and January 30, 1997, p. 34; Witness K, January 14, 1997, p. 9; Jean-Paul Akayesu, March 12 and 13, 1998, unpaginated.

[24]ICTR-96-4-T, Testimony of Witness R, January 29, 1997, p. 18.

[25]ICTR-96-4-T, Testimony of Witness R, January 28, 1997, p. 45.

The same day that the government moved to Gitarama, MDR-Power leader Karamira had exhorted MDR supporters to collaborate with the MRND and the CDR in fighting the common enemy. The MRND minister of youth and cooperatives, Callixte Nzabonimana, himself from Gitarama, brought the message home even more dramatically. He freed men arrested by the burgomaster of Rutobwe for having slaughtered Tutsi cattle and publicly slapped the burgomaster for refusing to join the killing campaign. Nzabonimana also addressed a large public meeting near the church of Kivumu, where "he asked the local population why they had not done their 'work'" and suggested that the Tutsi cattle were just waiting to be eaten.[26]

Hundreds of militia—perhaps somewhat more than a thousand—followed the interim government from Kigali to Gitarama, where they took up residence in schools in Runda and Taba. Now inside the prefecture, they were better placed to reinforce directives from the national leaders. They forced the burgomasters of Kayenzi, Mugina, Musambira, and Taba to flee their communes briefly. One of the Interahamwe shot at the burgomaster of Taba and killed the communal policeman who was accompanying him. Later, another man stabbed a communal policeman in Taba and then joined the Interahamwe for protection. The burgomaster of Nyamabuye also recalled having been threatened by the Interahamwe.[27] At a session of the International Tribunal he declared:

> I received messages saying that if I continued to protect people I would be killed. They also asked soldiers to shoot at me. They did in fact shoot at me but I was not struck by a bullet. They prevented me from driving about in the commune, and if I did, they would stop me at the roadblock....[28]

Prefect Uwizeye pleaded for reinforcements from the National Police, but was told that all were occupied at the front. The burgomaster of Nyamabuye later remarked that even had National Police been available, most of those stationed in Gitarama supported the slaughter and would not have tried to restore order. Uwizeye found few persons of stature ready to support his struggle to halt the

---

[26]Kamanzi, *Rwanda, Du Génocide à la Defaite*, p. 110; African Rights, *Rwanda, Death, Despair*, p. 361.

[27]Uwizeye, "Aperçu Analytique;" ICTR-96-4-T, Testimony of Akayesu, March 12 and 13, 1998.

[28]ICTR-96-4-T, Testimony of Witness R, January 28, 1997, p. 64.

genocide. One was Abbé André Sibomana, the highly respected editor of the widely-read journal *Kinyamateka* who managed to flee to Gitarama from Kigali, where militia had been looking for him. Sibomana met with the prefect and encouraged his opposition to the killing.[29]

Early on Monday, April 18, the morning after Butare Prefect Habyalimana's replacement had been announced, Prefect Uwizeye called together the burgomasters and local party leaders and clergy to discuss the growing political and military pressure for genocide. When the interim prime minister heard of the planned meeting, he ordered the session moved from the prefectural center to Murambi. Uwizeye and his subordinates arrived there to find a group that reportedly included interim Prime Minister Kambanda, interim ministers Callixte Nzabonimana, André Rwamakuba, Dr. Straton Nsabumukunzi, Eliézer Niyitegeka, Jean de Dieu Habineza, and Justin Mugenzi as well as MDR-Power leaders Murego and Shingiro and MRND leader Edouard Karemera.[30]

The Gitarama prefect and his burgomasters asked the national authorities to begin restoring order by stopping the distribution of arms and by terminating incitements to slaughter by RTLM. They also asked members of the Presidential Guard to help end the violence. The interim prime minister failed to address the problem directly and replied instead with a cliché-ridden speech about national unity and the need to support the new government. When the prefect asked once more for concrete measures to help himself and his subordinates, the interim prime minister stepped aside to allow Hutu Power political leaders to deliver a more explicit response. They railed at the Gitarama officials for failing to support the militia who were protecting Rwanda against the enemy. According to the burgomaster of Nyamabuye, one of the MRND ministers denounced their opposition to genocide by saying:

> that he knew very well that some of the commune leaders in Gitarama were Inkotanyi accomplices, and furthermore if these people continued to work in this manner, that there will be very serious consequences for them.[31]

---

[29]Uwizeye, "Aperçu Analytique;" ICTR-96-4-T, Testimony of Witness R, January 29, 1997, p. 42; Human Rights Watch/FIDH interview, Brussels, by telephone, April 27, 1997.

[30]ICTR-96-4-T, Testimony of Witness R, January 28, 1997, pp. 67-69; Testimony of Akayezu, March 12 and 13, 1998; Uwizeye, "Aperçu Analytique."

[31]ICTR-96-4-T, Testimony of Witness R, January 28, 1997, p. 76.

Two of the burgomasters who attended the meeting subsequently told the International Tribunal that official authorities never directed them specifically to kill Tutsi. Rather they offered no assistance in putting down violence by militia and soldiers and they indicated that continuing to resist violence would have many costs and no rewards. Pressed on the question of whether they were given any directions about exterminating Tutsi, the burgomaster of Nyamabuye replied, "When you are threatened and somebody tells you that you are an Inkotanyi accomplice, it is the same as saying go on and do that."[32] He related that the meeting ended inconclusively and that the participants, all frightened, returned home without discussing the session. Asked by one of the judges if such behavior after a meeting were normal, the burgomaster replied, "We were in an abnormal situation."[33]

The Gitarama officials understood the message and some responded to it promptly. According to the prosecutor and many witnesses at the International Tribunal, Jean-Paul Akayesu, the burgomaster of Taba, was one of those who changed from a protector to a killer of Tutsi immediately after the meeting of April 18.[34] At about the same time that the interim government and national political leaders were applying pressure from above, Akayesu also had to contend with a challenge from newly-strengthened Interahamwe inside the commune. Silas Kubwimana, an honorary vice-president of the Interahamwe at the national level and a political rival of Akayesu, had left the commune some months before when Akayesu was powerful. Now he returned with the backing of the national Interahamwe leadership and with guns, grenades, and military uniforms to distribute to his followers. A former communal policeman testified at the International Tribunal that there were nine communal policemen armed with seven firearms in Taba at this time to face the far more numerous and well-armed militia.[35] Akayesu maintains that Kubwimana effectively took over running the commune, directing killings, harassing opponents, and even appropriating a vehicle

---

[32]ICTR-96-4-T, Testimony of Witness R, January 30, 1997, p. 20.

[33]ICTR-96-4-T, Testimony of Witness R, January 28, 1997, p. 95.

[34]See the testimony of witnesses K, C, H and JJ, among many others.

[35]As mentioned above, one of the police was killed and another wounded by Interahamwe. "Les miliciens n'auraient pas menacé Akayesu, selon un ex-policier," Fondation Hirondelle, News du 19 novembre 1997. Accounts of the proceedings of the tribunal are posted on the internet by Fondation Hirondelle and Ubutabera.

from the burgomaster. While not disputing that the Interahamwe leader played a role, the prosecutor and many witnesses conclude that Akayesu was not the frightened tool of Kubwimana, but his active partner.

According to Akayesu, he was also threatened by charges, made by RTLM and others, that he himself was Tutsi. The radio talked about his height and light, brown skin and warned listeners that he intended to "exterminate the Interahamwe." In addition, the burgomaster had to deal with large numbers of displaced persons, including many originally from Byumba, who were pushed south by the fighting in and around Kigali. Embittered by their long months of misery, they swelled the numbers of persons ready to kill Tutsi. Akayesu told the International Tribunal of one case where he had supposedly attempted to save a Tutsi woman from a crowd of displaced persons. The sub-prefect of Byumba who was with the crowd told him it was no use even to try to defend her. As if to prove his colleague's good intentions, Akayesu reported that the sub-prefect had bought her a soda even if he did not save her from the assailants who presumably finally killed her.[36]

In other communes as well, RTLM hammered home the risks of continued dissent while militia multiplied their attacks. RTLM encouraged militia to strike in the commune of Mukingi, broadcasting: "All the enemies have gone to hide at Mukingi."[37] The burgomaster who had at first saved Tutsi by transporting them to the church center at Kabgayi lost heart under such attacks, particularly after he tried to get help from the National Police and was refused. In addition, a person of national importance mobilized killers inside the commune, playing a role much like that of Kubwimana in Taba. Lt. Col. Aloys Simba, a well known military and political figure, organized young men from the Byimana commercial center to attack the Tutsi who had taken shelter in the schools and communal office of Mukingi. He distributed large quantities of beer as a reward. Under these pressures, the burgomaster reportedly gave up trying to quell the attacks.[38]

Before April 18, Justin Nyandwi, burgomaster of Musambira, also opposed Hutu Power and the violence it espoused. On a trip into the city of Kigali, he encountered Rose Karushara, councilor of Kimisigara and a supporter of the killing campaign. She reportedly directed her Interahamwe to attack him and the three communal police who accompanied him, but they were saved by the intervention

---

[36]ICTR-96-4-T, Testimony of Akayesu, March 12 and 13, 1998.

[37]Human Rights Watch/FIDH interview, Mukingi, July 10, 1996.

[38]Ibid.; Uwizeye, "Aperçu Analytique."

of Major Nyamuhimba of the National Police. On April 14, RTLM increased the pressure on Nyandwi by naming him as an opponent of the massacres. On April 20, a group of Interahamwe came in a pickup truck to attack him at home, but he escaped death and temporarily fled the commune. A survivor from his commune described him as a good man who was finally overwhelmed by the forces against him. Although he gave up his opposition to the genocide, he still failed to satisfy the interim government, which replaced him with MRND leader Abdelrahman Iyakaremye, who was committed to carrying out the genocide promptly and thoroughly.[39]

The burgomaster of Nyamabuye, although subjected to the same pressures as the others, says that he continued to protect Tutsi, by taking them to safety at Kabgayi, by dissuading local people from attacking the camps where they had sought refuge, and by providing them with needed documents. Instead of carrying out these activities openly as he had before April 18, however, he worked at night to avoid being seen by Presidential Guards. He continued going around the commune out in the countryside, but he avoided the town where soldiers were more likely to be found and, he said, "I tried to not go where the Interahamwe were."[40] He was supported by some—although not all—of the communal police and with their backing he could rescue people from barriers provided the guards were not soldiers and were not armed. But if he encountered soldiers or armed militia, neither his authority nor the guns of the local police were enough to obtain the release of the persons being held. Instead, he told the court,

> ...we had recourse to all the means. Sometimes we would give them money to buy beer, or we would tell them that we are going to take these people to the highest authority. We used all other means like that.[41]

The burgomaster of Mugina commune, Callixte Ndagijimana persisted in trying to protect Tutsi even at the cost of his own life. After the April 18 meeting, the six National Police who had been assigned to help him in the commune were recalled. For two days more he kept on opposing the killings and organizing

---

[39] Human Rights Watch/FIDH interviews, Gitarama, July 12, 1995; African Rights, *Rwanda, Death, Despair*, p. 624.

[40]ICTR-96-4-T, Testimony of Witness R, January 28, 1997, p. 84.

[41]Ibid., pp. 85-86. See also p. 87.

transport for Tutsi to Kabgayi. On April 20, the same day that the burgomaster of neighboring Musambira was attacked, Interahamwe from Kigali invaded Mugina and murdered Ndagijimana. With the chief resister against the genocide removed, a local judge came to the market the next day to get the killing started. The soldiers accompanying him fired their guns in the air and then told the crowd, "We want you to destroy Tutsi houses and kill Tutsi."[42] In the next days, local people, who had earlier refused to kill, began to join the slaughter. Led by Burundian refugees from a nearby camp, they massacred an estimated 5,000 to 7,000 people in their homes and in the parish church. The prefect managed to save 176 wounded survivors whom he had brought to the church center at Kabgayi.[43]

The prefect meanwhile sought to limit the violence by such measures as suspending the prefectural security committee, a step he took because he believed some members would use the committee to increase the slaughter. But he could not count on support from the National Police, not trusting them even to provide the guard for his own family. Instead he called on communal police from Nyamabuye for that duty. Nor did his own subordinates back his efforts to prevent the slaughter. In his estimation, five of six sub-prefects actively encouraged the killing. When confronted by determined killers like one lieutenant who reportedly slaughtered thirty-one people in the commune of Nyakabanda, the prefect could do little but complain to higher authorities. Finally convinced of the futility of continued opposition, Uwizeye fled west to Kibuye at the end of May. The interim government removed him from office and named Major Jean-Damascene Ukurukiyezu prefect of Gitarama.[44]

The combined pressure by political and military authorities, militia, and the radio succeeded in destroying open opposition to the interim government and its genocidal program in Gitarama. But the killing campaign failed to exterminate all the Tutsi of the region, in part because Hutu officials and ordinary people continued to aid Tutsi, even if only furtively, and in part because the rapid assemblage of thousands of Tutsi at Kabgayi created an agglomeration protected by its sheer size. From the start many Tutsi had fled spontaneously to the extensive

---

[42]Human Rights Watch/FIDH interview, Kigali, July 15, 1995.

[43]Human Rights Watch/FIDH interview, Kigali, July 15, 1995; Uwizeye, "Aperçu Analytique;" Commission pour le Mémorial du Génocide et des Massacres, "Rapport Préliminaire," p. 86.

[44]Uwizeye, "Aperçu Analytique;" ICTR-96-4-T, Testimony of Witness R, January 29, 1997, p. 42.

grounds of the Catholic diocese at Kabgayi. Governmental authorities also encouraged and helped Tutsi to assemble there, some of them believing that people at risk were safer at Kabgayi than in their home communes, others because they understood that gathering Tutsi together was part of the genocidal plan. Military and militia never launched an open assault on the extensive camps, but were preparing to do so when the RPF took Kabgayi in early June.[45]

The extension of the genocide in Gitarama was part of a larger campaign to spread the slaughter throughout the country. After having delivered the message to Prefect Uwizeye and his burgomasters, the interim authorities moved south to ensure that the killing campaign would be implemented in Butare and Gikongoro. Everywhere they went, their "pacification" visits sparked or increased the slaughter.

"The Population Is Trying to Defend Itself"

As political leaders extended the genocide by force into the center and south of the country, they also moved to tighten control over the whole killing campaign by establishing a formal structure for the "civilian self-defense" force. Proposed by AMASASU, sketched in Bagosora's appointment book, discussed by a committee of the Rwandan army on October 30, 1993 and again on March 30, 1994, the force had not been completely organized by early April. The basic plan of mobilizing civilians by administrative division and putting them under the command of retired soldiers or other military men had nonetheless been put quickly into effect, particularly during the early weeks of large-scale massacres. It was no doubt this force—which RTLM called "the real shield, the true army"[46]—that politicians had been referring to when they told dissident military leaders that they had another way to execute the genocide if the regular soldiers refused to participate.[47]

The force was vigorous but needed greater discipline and organization. Having delivered a license to kill the "enemy," authorities found that some civilian executioners were deciding for themselves—on partisan or personal grounds—who was the "enemy." In some cases, the killers ignored the message that "there is one

---

[45]Human Rights Watch interview, Kabgayi, August 29, 1994.

[46]RTLM, April 3, 1994, recorded by Faustin Kagame (provided by Article 19).

[47]Human Rights Watch/FIDH interviews, by telephone, Brussels, April 27 and May 4, 1997; Human Rights Watch/FIDH interview, by telephone, Arusha, January 26, 1997; Commandement des Forces Armées Rwandaises en Exil, "Contribution des FAR," p. 98.

enemy and he is the Tutsi" and slaughtered other Hutu. On April 21, Kalimanzira of the Ministry of Interior directed prefects to ensure that people not kill others for reasons of "jealousy, hostility, or spirit of vengeance."[48] National leaders worried not just that some Hutu were being killed, but also that some Tutsi were escaping death as local authorities and ordinary executioners yielded to entreaty or bribe. On RTLM Kantano Habimana railed against those who would allow Tutsi to buy back their lives, saying "If you are an inyenzi, well, then, you are an inyenzi; let them kill you, there is no way that you can buy yourself out of it."[49]

In communes where militia were already operating, the "civilian self-defense" program offered a way to expand them, to make them more legitimate, and, at the same time, to subject them to tighter control. As militia leaders told the press, their groups provided the elite striking force (fer de lance) of "civilian self-defense." They had been carrying out the same duties that were now assigned to the "civilian self-defense" groups: to assist regular troops in protecting the population and public property, to "obtain information on the enemy presence" in their communities, and to "denounce infiltrators and accomplices of the enemy."[50] The training of the militia became the model for the "self-defense" groups, a brief program carried out by retired soldiers or others with military training. Once trained, "self-defense" recruits joined the militia at the barriers and on patrol. They sometimes went into actual combat together, as they did at Nyanza under Lieutenant Colonel Simba. Officials and administrators, Bagosora among them, recognized that militia and self-defense groups were essentially the same when they used one term for the other.[51] In the order concerning the "self-defense fund" mentioned above, the minister of the interior specified "refreshments for the

---

[48]Fawusitini Munyazeza, Minisitiri w'Ubutegetsi bw'Igihugu n'Amajyambere ya Komini [actually signed by Callixte Kalimanzira] to Bwana Perefe wa Perefegitura (bose), April 21, 1994.

[49]Chrétien et al., Rwanda, Les médias, p. 193.

[50]Prime Minister Jean Kambanda to Monsieur le Préfet (Tous), "Directive du Premier Ministre aux Prefets pour l'Organisation de l'Auto-Défense Civile," no. 024/02.3, May 25, 1994 (Butare prefecture).

[51]Bagosora, "Agenda, 1993," entry for February 1.

militia" and expenses for their transport to operations as legitimate uses for the money.[52]

Within a week of the plane crash and nearly two weeks before the formal announcement of "civilian self-defense," soldiers were teaching military skills to young men on the streets of Kigali.[53] Soon after, authorities began recruiting new forces throughout the rest of the country. On April 21, for example, the army commander for Butare-Gikongoro asked local burgomasters to furnish recruits for the program.[54]

The authorities announced the new program on Radio Rwanda on April 26, explaining that it was necessary because "the war was being fought all over the country," but it was another month before the interim prime minister revealed the formal organizational plan. The structure was almost a parody of the Rwandan penchant for administrative complexity. It included supervisory committees at the national, prefectural, and communal and sectoral levels to facilitate collaboration between administrative, military, and political party authorities. In urban communes, the organization was carried down to the level of the cell. The duties of the committee members at each level echoed the division of tasks at the army general staff: a member in charge of personnel (G1 of the army), another in charge of intelligence and communication (G2), another responsible for operations (G3), and a fourth in charge of logistics and finance (G4). At the national level, the committee included eight designated members, chaired by the minister of the interior and including also the minister of defense and the army commander in chief. The officer in charge of operations was supposed to be a major and the one in charge of logistics and finance was required to have at least a bachelor's degree in economics or accounting. An "experienced" person was to be responsible for intelligence. At the prefectoral, communal, and sectoral level, elected councils were to oversee the corresponding supervisory committee. At the prefectoral level, retired soldiers, political party leaders, and the local military commander were also to monitor the work. Communal policemen and former soldiers were to train both the young recruits and the population in general about how to dig trenches, how to

---

[52]Human Rights Watch/FIDH interview, Brussels, by telephone, July 22, 1998; "Les miliciens hutus affirment assurer la 'défense civile,'" BQA, no. 14213, 16/05/94, p. 30.

[53]"Les résistants hutus chassent le rebelle 'infiltré' à Kigali," BQA, no. 14192, 14/04/94, p. 29.

[54]Lt.-Col. Tharcisse Muvunyi, Comd. Place BUT-GIK to Monsieur le Bourgmestre, no. 0085/MSC.1.1, April 21, 1994 (Butare prefecture).

gather intelligence, and how to obtain necessary supplies. Although the program had been publically announced, participants were to keep the details of its operation as secret as possible.[55]

In creating this system, the interim government added a fourth chain of command to the military, political, and administrative hierarchies that had henceforth executed the genocide. The new channel was to allow for more direct, efficient control over civilian assailants. The officers named to staff the program were a remarkably homogenous group, very like each other and very like Bagosora in age, background and, apparently, in political ideas. More likely to follow Bagosora's lead than the broader group of officers who had refused to allow him to take power on April 7 and 8, they were the ideal candidates to direct a paramilitary force that would implement his orders without question. The direction of the "civilian self defense" program was lodged in Bagosora's office at the Ministry of Defense.[56]

The commander at the national level was Colonel Gasake, who had temporarily replaced Nsabimana as chief of staff the year before. In 1993, Bagosora had already noted the possibility of using Gasake to head a propaganda campaign. The two men were apparently personal friends as well as colleagues. Among the regional commanders were Lieutenant Colonel Simba for Butare and Gikongoro, Colonel Rwagafilita for Kibungo, Maj. Protais Bivambagara for Kigali, Maj. Jean-Damascene Ukurukiyezu for Gitarama, and Lt.-Col. Bonaventure Ntibitura for Ruhengeri. Col. Laurent Serubuga was reportedly named to the post for Gisenyi but refused it. Several of the group, like Simba and Rwagafilita, had already been involved in genocidal killings before their appointment. They were all retired officers and they were ordered to designate other soldiers no longer in active service as their seconds in command.[57]

Three of these officers, Ukuruliyezu, Ntibitura, and Simba, had been deputies in parliament, all of them representing the MRND. A fourth, Rwagafilita, was due

[55]Kambanda, "Directive du Premier Ministre aux Prefets pour l'Organisation de l'Auto-Défense Civile;" Edouard Karemera, Le Ministre de l'Intérieur et du Développement Communal, to Monsieur le Préfet (Tous), May 25, 1994 (Butare prefecture).

[56]Human Rights Watch/FIDH interviews, by telephone, Brussels, May 4, 1997; Brussels, October 19 and 20, 1997.

[57]Ibid; Augustin Bizimana, Ministre de la Défense to Lt. Col. e.r. Aloys Simba, no. 51/06.1.9/01, May 15, 1994 (Butare prefecture); Bagosora, "Agenda, 1993," entry under February 20.

to take his seat as deputy for the MRND as soon as the transitional government was installed. Both Serubuga and Rwagafilita were part of the akazu.[58]

Of these officers, at least one shared Bagosora's contempt for soldiers opposed to the genocide. In May, Simba sought to discredit Rusatira, who had been posted to Gikongoro, and incited militia to attack the general and his staff, whom he labeled Inkotanyi. Although none of Simba's supporters dared openly assault the officers, Rusatira was unable to stop the accusations.[59]

In a lengthy order on May 25, the minister of interior directed administrators to assist the "civilian self-defense" effort by recruiting staff, such as retired soldiers, preparing inventories of firearms available, helping people to obtain traditional weapons, locating appropriate means of communication within and between groups, monitoring the work of barriers and patrols, and—as usual—keeping the population ready to "defend" itself whenever necessary. One task not listed but already current practice was supervising the distribution of the firearms being made available under the program.[60]

The new program offered an opportunity to force changes in the attitudes of administrators who opposed the genocide or to remove them altogether. The minister of interior ordered the prefects to identify local authorities "who could potentially hinder the execution of the strategy of self defense" and he warned against the danger of "infiltration by elements working for the enemy cause."[61] When the interim authorities removed the prefect of Gitarama in late May, they replaced him with the local "civilian self-defense" councilor, Major Ukurukiyezu, a further indication of how the new structure could be used to shape the administrative system already in place.

Because the organizers of the "civilian self defense" program made no distinction between the civilian Tutsi population and RPF soldiers, they expected recruits to go to battle against the advancing RPF troops as well as to assist in the genocide of the Tutsi. The young men were badly trained and most of them were armed only with bows and arrows, spears and machetes. The authorities exhorted them to take the Vietnamese as an example of what a courageous people could do,

[58]Human Rights Watch/FIDH interviews, by telephone, Brussels , May 4, 1997.

[59]Human Rights Watch/FIDH interviews, Brussels, December 18, 1995; by telephone, Brussels, May 4, 1997.

[60]Karemera to Monsieur le Préfet (Tous), May 25, 1994.

[61]Ibid.

even without modern weapons. In combat against the RPF in Nyanza, Mugusa, and Muyaga in early June, the "civilian self-defense" forces suffered heavy casualties.[62]

Tightening Control

The change in structure represented by "civilian self defense" was paralleled by a change in tactics, a shift from the open and often large-scale killing that had characterized the first weeks of the genocide to a less public, smaller-scale approach to eliminating Tutsi. Instead of attacking sizable concentrations of Tutsi, such as those at churches in Kigali, assailants came in squads, night after night, to take away small numbers to be executed elsewhere. In May and June, authorities transported some groups of Tutsi to less accessible sites. They sent people from the Cyangugu stadium, for example, to the remote Nyarushishi camp and moved other groups back to their home communes, presumably with the intention of slaughtering them with less attention. The cut off in massive slaughter was neither immediate nor total: massacres, begun later in Butare, were continuing even as the new policy was being broadcast and horrible, if less frequent, attacks were launched elsewhere in May and June. But, in general, the worst massacres had finished by the end of April.

The new policy of more disciplined killing was called "pacification," borrowing the term the interim government was already using to disguise its efforts to increase killing in the south and center of the country. "Pacification" meaning "more killing" merged into "pacification" meaning "more discreet killing." It enlarged to a national scale the small deceptions that were already taking place in communities where killers had announced an end to the slaughter in order to lure victims from hiding or in order to give them a false sense of reassurance before launching a new attack.

The authorities began "pacification" after they had exterminated a substantial part—perhaps half—of the Tutsi population of Rwanda and after they had begun to hear faint sounds of indignation from the international community.

Restoring to Rwanda "Its Good Name"

From the early days of the genocide, the interim government demonstrated its concern with international opinion. Interim President Sindikubwabo talked about the need for Rwanda to restore "its good name, so that friendly countries will trust

---

[62]Human Rights Watch/FIDH interview, Brussels, February 26, 1997.

us once again."[63] Near bankruptcy, the interim government depended on foreign funds to function; at war with the RPF and engaged in a genocide in which firearms were used, it needed foreign deliveries of arms and ammunition; burdened with hundreds of thousands of displaced persons, it required international humanitarian assistance to keep people alive. Not just national authorities and the urban-dwelling intellectuals but even most ordinary people knew the importance of foreign assistance which had brought the benefits of development projects to their own or adjacent communes.

The interim government was increasingly discredited as human rights and humanitarian organizations stressed the genocidal nature of the killings. On April 19, Human Rights Watch called the slaughter genocide and demanded that the U.N. and its member states meet their legal obligation to intervene. Respected and articulate human rights activists who had fled Rwanda, like Monique Mujyawamariya and Alphonse-Marie Nkubito, arrived in Europe and North America where their accounts were attracting the attention of officials and journalists. On April 22 Anthony Lake, National Security Adviser to U.S. President Bill Clinton, received Mujyawamariya and a representative of Human Rights Watch, who described the extent of the genocide and the importance of the military in its execution. Later that day Lake issued a statement from the White House, calling on Bagosora, Bizimungu, and other military officers by name to halt the killings. The statement was the first by a major international actor to publicly assign responsibility for the ongoing killing to specific individuals, but it stopped short of calling the slaughter genocide.

That same day—although too early to have been in reaction to the Lake statement—the chief of staff, General Bizimungu, called for "the people to stop fighting each other and forget about ethnic differences. They have to stand side by side and help the government forces fight the enemy, the RPF." Radio RTLM broadcast Bizimungu's statement as well as another in a similar vein by Ndindiliyimana.[64]

Also on April 22, the interim government announced the departure abroad of delegations "to explain the government position on the Rwandan crisis."[65] Minister

---

[63]"Ijambo Perezida wa Repubulika...kuwa 14 Mata 1994."

[64]UNAMIR, Notes, RTLM, 17:00 hrs, April 22, 1994; Commandement des Forces Armées Rwandaises en Exil, "Contribution des FAR," p. 104.

[65]UNAMIR, Notes, RTLM, 17:00 hrs, April 22, 1994.

of Commerce Justin Mugenzi and MRND president Mathieu Ngirumpatse went to Kenya and other African states. Foreign Minister Jérôme Bicamumpaka and CDR head Jean-Bosco Barayagwiza traveled to Europe and the U.N. where they sought to convince officials and the press that the Hutu had risen up in justifiable rage after the death of their president. "Inter-ethnic fighting" had followed in which, according to Bicamumpaka, "the Tutsi and Hutus have massacred each other to an equal extent."[66] The Rwandan spokesmen did their best to minimize the number of fatalities. Bicamumpaka described the estimates recently given by the International Committee of the Red Cross (ICRC) of 100,000 dead as "grossly exaggerated" and suggested that 10,000 might be more accurate. He concluded that no one could know because "There are no witnesses to give evidence." He asserted that, in any case, "There is no more killing."[67] The Rwandan ambassador in Brussels did his part by sending around an open letter explaining how Kambanda and other national authorities had undertaken "pacification actions" throughout Rwanda.[68]

Meanwhile, in a Nairobi press conference, Mugenzi and Ngirumpatse told the press that the government was simply overwhelmed because all of its soldiers were occupied at the front. When journalists protested that they had seen soldiers killing civilians in Kigali, Ngirumpatse said that some soldiers were on leave and that all armies had some ill-disciplined elements. Taking up the argument presented by the "intellectuals of Butare" on April 18, he asserted that a cease-fire would end the killing of Tutsi civilians. He commented, "The best way of stopping those mass killings is to stop the shooting from the RPF and tell people: 'You are secure and have no reason to hunt down people from the RPF.'"[69]

On April 27, Bicamumpaka and Barayagwiza met with French President Mitterrand, Minister of Foreign Affairs Alain Juppé, and other highly placed

---

[66]BBC, SWB, AL/1989, May 5, 1994.

[67]BBC, SWB, AL/1989, May 5, 1994.

[68]François Ngarukiyintwali, Ambassadeur, to Cher Compatriot, Brussels, May 5, 1994.

[69]Thadee Nsengiyaremye, "Bombardments Blast Apart Rwandan Rebel Ceasefire," UPI, April 27, 1994.

officials. They apparently heard from these usually understanding supporters that the killings were undermining Rwandan standing in the international community.[70]

On April 30, the U.N. Security Council issued a sterner warning by reminding Rwandan leaders that they would bear personal responsibility for violations of international law. Without using the word genocide, the statement spoke in the language of the genocide convention about the attempt to destroy an ethnic group. In addition the council called on all nations to provide no further arms or military aid to the parties to the conflict and declared itself in principle ready to impose an embargo on arms deliveries to Rwanda. The interim government attributed this initiative to the Belgians and Radio Rwanda reported it as their work. The U.S. also took a strong stand in favor of an embargo, as the interim government knew.[71]

The next day, the U.S. reinforced the Security Council message through a telephone call by Deputy Assistant Secretary of State for African Affairs, Prudence Bushnell, to the chief of staff. She had asked to speak to Bagosora, but, as always happened, he declined to come to the phone so Bushnell delivered the message to Bizimungu instead. She reiterated Lake's message that the United States authorities at the highest levels would hold these officers responsible if they failed to stop the massacres. Bizimungu replied in a flip manner, "How nice of them to think of me," but he was concerned enough to write to the Ministry of Defense the next day saying that it was "urgent...to stop the massacres everywhere in the country."[72]

On May 3, the pope issued a strong condemnation of the genocidal slaughter and the next day Secretary-General Boutros Ghali stated that there was "a real genocide" in Rwanda.[73]

Rwandan authorities judged the international outcry in the light of the Security Council decision to withdraw most of the peacekeepers made just days before. With this in mind, they found the protests important enough to stop the major massacres, but not important enough to stop all killing and prevent its recurrence.

---

[70]Prunier, *The Rwanda Crisis,* p. 277; Alain Girma, French Embassy, Washington, D.C. to Holly Burkhalter, Human Rights Watch, April 28, 1994.

[71]United Nations, Statement by the President of the Security Council, S/PRST/1994/21, 30 April 1994.

[72]Human Rights Watch/FIDH interview, by telephone, Nairobi, September 16, 1996; Commandement des Forces Armées Rwandaises en Exil, "Contribution des FAR," pp. 69, 98, 104.

[73]United Nations, *The United Nations and Rwanda,* p. 51.

"Violence....Should Stop"

On April 24, administrative, military and militia leaders met to discuss measures to make the slaughter more circumspect. Prefect Renzaho, General Bizimungu for the army, and Col. Laurent Rutayisire for the National Police and the heads of the militia agreed that the bands of killers would end slaughter at the barriers and on the roads; they would instead take "suspects" to the appropriate authorities to have their cases investigated and decided. The militia would continue to search out "infiltrated RPF elements," but would do so in a more orderly fashion than previously through "crisis committees," a name echoing that of the military committee established at Bagosora's direction on April 7. The authorities asked all who were armed "to rationalize the use of these weapons." They also directed militia to allow staff and vehicles of the ICRC to pass without hindrance. There had been several incidents in which militia had taken wounded persons from their ambulances and executed them. The international protest that greeted such incidents illustrated just the kind of censure that Rwandan authorities wanted to avoid.[74]

The president of the Interahamwe, Robert Kajuga, went on the radio twice to instruct his men in the new approach. Two days later, Kajuga and his vice president, George Rutaganda, delivered a signed statement to the ICRC, expressing the laudable but vague desire to "see the massacres end as soon as possible," and, in any case, committing the militia to observing the new policy.[75] Prefect Renzaho reinforced the orders to militia and others by a long radio message on April 27, condemning the murder of innocent people and pillaging.[76]

On April 27 also, the interim prime minister declared that "violence, pillage, and other acts of cruelty should stop." He directed that barriers should be established by local authorities in conjunction with military officers and that guards and members of patrols "should avoid committing acts of violence against the innocent." He clarified the new approach by stating that the population should

---

[74]UNAMIR, Notes, Radio Rwanda, 20:00 hrs, April 24, 1994; International Committee of the Red Cross, Communication to the press No 94/16, 14 April 1994.

[75]Human Rights Watch interviews, by telphone, Kigali, April 29, 1994; UNAMIR, Notes, Radio Rwanda, 20:00 hrs, April 24, 1994; C. Ls., "Kigali s'est vidée des trois quarts de sa population," *Le Monde*, April 28, 1994; Broekx, "Les Événéments d'Avril 1994," p. 102.

[76]Otto Mayer, "Trois Mois d'Enfer au Jour le Jour," *Dialogue*, no. 177, August-September 1994, p. 25.

continue seeking out the enemy but should deliver him to the authorities, rather than dealing with him on the spot. If necessary, the people could call the armed forces for help in doing so. To show that this was not really a message to leave Tutsi in peace, he repeated the usual directive that the authorities, civilian and military, should be ready to help the population "defend itself when it is attacked." He reminded prefects of the means at their disposal to implement the more discreet elimination of the Tutsi: they and their subordinates were to enforce rigorously the requirement that people traveling between communes and between prefectures must have written authorisations from the appropriate authorities.[77]

To show the population that the period of large-scale murder and pillage had ended, the interim prime minister ordered the prefects to restore "normality" to daily life "as soon as security is restored in your prefecture[s]." They were to make sure that offices were functioning, that markets were held, and that factories were back on schedule. Farmers should return to their fields.[78]

As part of the "pacification," the interim prime minister announced that the enemy was the RPF and advised people to avoid ethnic, regional, or partisan divisions which would weaken resistance against them.[79] Even RTLM announcer Gaspard Gahigi adopted this position for a brief time, explaining in a broadcast that "nobody should be killed because of his ethnic group" and that Tutsi, "even those with an aquiline nose," who love their country should not be attacked.[80] This effort to depict the slaughter as politically rather than ethnically motivated coincided with the change from large-scale massacres—where a whole group was slaughtered on what could only be ethnic grounds—to more selective executions of smaller groups and individuals, for whom there could be a pretense of establishing that they were actually linked with the RPF.

"No More Cadavers...On the Road"
Prefects received the "pacification" message from the interim prime minister and passed it on to their subordinates who called the population to meetings to hear

---

[77]Yohani Kambanda, Ministiri w'Intebe, to Bwana Perefe, no. 007/02.3.9/94, April 27, 1994 (Butare prefecture).

[78]Ibid.

[79]Ibid.

[80]Gaspard Gahigi on RTLM, Selections from RTLM, May 15-May 30, 1994 (tape provided by Radio Rwanda).

about the new policy. At the same time that administrators explained "pacification," they announced the official establishment of barriers and patrols as part of the "civilian self-defense" effort. Many of the barriers and patrols already functioning had been set up by militia or local political leaders on their own initiative. Now burgomasters ordered all men to participate in these "self-defense" measures, making government authority rather than informal community pressure the force that assured participation. The radio repeated the same message, ensuring that even those who had not come to the meetings would know what they were expected to do. Measures which had been used to catch and kill Tutsi became part of the program of "self-defense" and known killers were named to direct the "pacification" effort. In Taba and adjacent communes, Silas Kubwimana, the honorary vice-president of the Interahamwe and leader of the genocide in Taba, for example, was assigned responsibility for "pacification."[81]

Given the double message of "pacification," some militia felt free to continue killing. Georges Rutaganda, vice-president of the Interahamwe, himself led an attack on the Cyahafi neighborhood of Kigali just four days after the militia leaders called for an end to open violence.[82] Militia continued to kill at some barriers outside Kigali and they attacked the cathedral at Nyundo on May 1, where they slaughtered 218 survivors of previous assaults. The same day they killed more than thirty orphans and Rwandan Red Cross workers in Butare and several days later they attacked Marie Merci School at Kibeho where they massacred some ninety students.[83]

RTLM announcers showed their understanding of "pacification" by declaring a general "clean-up" of Tutsi left in Kigali. They asked listeners to finish killing all the Tutsi in the capital by May 5, the date when Habyarimana's funeral was supposed to take place.[84]

On May 3, soldiers of the paracommando battalion ignored a safe-conduct signed by Chief of Staff Bizimungu and halted a convoy of Tutsi and others en route from the Hotel Mille Collines to the airport for evacuation. UNAMIR

---

[81]ICTR-96-4-T, Testimony of Akayesu, March 13, 1998.

[82]ICTR, Testimony of witness AA, as reported in Ubutabera, no. 22 (1e partie), October 13, 1997.

[83] Broekx, "Les Evénéments d'Avril 1994," p. 102. For details on the Butare incident, see chapter 12.

[84]Human Rights Watch interview, Kigali, by telephone, April 29, 1994.

peacekeepers escorting the convoy stood aside and permitted the paracommandos to force the persons under their protection out of two of the four trucks. The soldiers had begun beating the civilians when militia, apparently alerted by RTLM, arrived and joined in the attack. One of the militia fired, attempting to kill Kigali prosecutor Francois-Xavier Nsanzuwera who was among the evacuees, but instead he wounded a soldier. In the ensuing confusion, a lieutenant of the paracommandos ordered people back into the trucks. Prefect Renzaho and Rutaganda then intervened and directed the convoy to return to the Hotel Mille Collines.[85]

On May 9, the Interahamwe leaders reaffirmed the earlier directives to their members and declared support for the "pacification" visits of authorities throughout the country. They repeated that the neutrality of the Red Cross must be respected and added that the same kind of treatment should be accorded to UNAMIR and other U.N. personnel. This may have been both a response to the May 3 attack on the convoy and also a warning concerning the expected visit of U.N. High Commissioner for Human Rights José Ayala Lasso, which was scheduled for the next week.[86]

Rwandans directly in touch with international opinion may have felt more pressure to end the slaughter—or at least to appear to have ended it—than others in the interim government. Bizimungu and others responsible for fighting the RPF, for example, took seriously the threat of an arms embargo and understood that continued killing of Tutsi might well result in such a measure. In addition to the radio message of April 22 and his May 1 letter about stopping the massacres, Bizimungu reacted to the killing of the orphans in Butare—and the international censure of the incident—by directing his subordinates in that town "to do everything [necessary] to stop these barbarities."[87] After having approved the evacuation of Tutsi and others from the Hotel Mille Collines, he reportedly intervened twice more to protect the highly visible hostages whose safety was closely monitored by foreigners.

---

[85]Human Rights Watch/FIDH interviews, by telephone, Brussels, January 25 and May 4, 1997; Broekx, "Les Evénéments d'Avril 1994," p. 102. Guichaoua, *Les crises politiques,* p. 708; Commandement des Forces Armées Rwandaises en Exil, "Contribution des FAR," p. 98.

[86]UNAMIR, Notes, Radio Rwanda, 19:00 hrs, May 9, 1994 and RTLM, 17h 30, May 9, 1994; Human Rights Watch/Africa, Press Release, May 11, 1994.

[87]Commandement des Forces Armées Rwandaises en Exil, "Contribution des FAR," p. 98.

It was not just the fear of international censure but also the hope of concrete support that pushed Rwandan authorities to change their way of killing. Ten days after the Rwandan apologists of genocide were well received by French officials, the interim government sent Lt.-Col. Ephrem Rwabalinda to French military cooperation headquarters in Paris with a list of the arms, ammunition, and equipment most needed by the Rwandan army. Rwabalinda was told that French assistance would depend on improving the Rwandan image abroad.[88]

The day Rwabalinda finished his four day mission, Kantano Habimana of RTLM began a series of announcements calling for violence to end. On May 13, he berated those who kept on killing, saying "the president of the Interahamwe, the prime minister, the president of the republic, everyone, each of them says, 'Please, the killings are finished, those who are dead are dead.'"[89] Two days later, he explained the need for controlling the killings. "Since we have begun to restrain ourselves, the international community will certainly not fail to notice and will say, 'Those Hutu are really disciplined, we should understand them and help them, hum!'" Three days later, he was more explicit still, announcing cheerfully that France had promised to begin aiding Rwanda again, "with considerable aid, with promises to increase it. Only, for this good news to continue coming, they ask that there be no more cadavers visible on the roads and also that no one kill another person while others stand around and laugh, instead of delivering the person to the authorities."[90]

"Pacification" as Deception
A remarkable series of minutes from meetings of the security committee in the commune of Bwakira, in the hills of western Rwanda, show how quickly and efficiently the administration transmitted orders from the center to the communes, how the concerns of the military influenced policy—or at least were used to justify that policy—and how well the double meaning of "pacification" was disseminated at local level.

---

[88]Lt. Col. BEM Ephrem Rwabalinda, "Rapport de Visite Fait Auprès de la Maison Militaire de Cooperation à Paris," enclosed in Lt. Col. BEM Ephrem Rwabalinda to Ministère de la Défense and Chef EM AR, undated. See chapter 16 for details.

[89]Chrétien et al, *Rwanda, Les médias*, p. 201. It is unclear whether his mentioning the president of the Interahamwe before the two leaders of the government reflected his own unconscious ranking or a deliberate choice meant to impress his listeners.

[90]Ibid., pp. 316-17.

On April 29, the burgomaster described the major issue of the day for the committee: all the ammunition used against the RPF is imported; the governments that provided that ammunition "are reluctant to arm us while we are killing one another"; and the interim government has expressed its "wish for the war [i.e., killing Tutsi] to end so that we can straighten out our relations with the international community." So, the burgomaster concluded, "People should obey government orders and stop carrying their weapons around with them. This is serious business, not a joke."[91] The next week, the burgomaster explained that the Belgian government wanted to impose an embargo on Rwanda. To avoid this happening, he recommended that people go back to work, as the government asked, and stop thinking that every Tutsi was Inkotanyi. At the meeting of May 20, the burgomaster relayed the demands of the U.S., apparently those specified in Bizimungu's May 1 conversation with Bushnell. They were:

The Rwandan Government must end all killings before it will be recognized by the international community. It must arrest and bring to trial all soldiers and youth [i.e., militia] who committed crimes. It must release all detainees [i.e., Tutsi still held hostage in the Hotel Mille Collines and elsewhere] and let them seek refuge in countries of their choice.[92]

At a meeting four days later, the burgomaster repeated the message and added,

You must enforce security. Some people imagine that what happens on their hills is not known because they do not know that there are satellites in the sky which take pictures. Killings must stop for good. The councilors must transmit these orders in meetings with the population.[93]

Local authorities elsewhere delivered the same "pacification" messages, complete with cautions about the likelihood of satellite surveillance, to the people in their jurisdictions.

---

[91]Bwakira commune, "Inyandiko-mvugo...kuwa 29/4/94."

[92]Bwakira commune, "Inyandiko-mvugo...kuwa 20/5/94."

[93]Bwakira commune, "Inyandiko-mvugo...kuwa 24.5.94."

The burgomaster of Bwakira followed up his announcements of "pacification" by drafting a model of a reprimand for councilors to use in writing to persons who continued to assault others.

But, in Bwakira, as elsewhere in Rwanda, "pacification" was not what it seemed. On May 5, immediately after telling people to stop killing, the burgomaster related that an RPF soldier had been caught in sector Nyabiranga of the neighboring commune of Gitesi. He was searched and found to be carrying an unidentified white power. When he was forced to eat it, he died immediately. This supposed incident replicated the features of the scare tactics used since October 1990: a soldier is purportedly found in the vicinity—near enough to be threatening but not so near as to permit easy verification of the story—in possession of the means to kill people and apparently on a mission to do so. The burgomaster in the next breath said that people must do patrols conscientiously at night to catch such infiltrators.[94]

At the council meeting of May 24, one member dared to raise the difference between rhetoric and reality. Remarking that most of the Tutsi had already been killed or driven from the commune, he declared:

> It is a shame that only people of the same ethnic group are left. Authorities do not deal with problems consistently. Some say one thing, but act differently. It is not the ordinary people who kill, but the authorities who fail to carry out the laws that they know well.[95]

Others pointed out that violence continued because the authorities did nothing to enforce orders against the killing. One citizen commented that at Shyembe, "people kill any Tutsi they see, despite the fact that in the last meeting held there, people were elected to a security committee." Another person responded that the security committee must enforce the law. He remarked that the violence against Tutsi in 1959 ended only after some people had been arrested and put in jail.[96]

As directed by their superiors, administrators disseminated the message of "pacification" and called on Tutsi to come out of hiding. In some communities, they used a sound-truck to deliver the news up and down the streets of the town.

---

[94]Bwakira commune, "Inyandiko-mvugo...kuwa 5.5.94."

[95]Bwakira commune, "Inyandiko-mvugo...kuwa 24.5.94."

[96]Bwakira commune, "Inyandiko-mvugo...kuwa 24.5.94."

Out on the hills, they beat a drum to attract attention to the message that killings had ended. Those Hutu who were hiding Tutsi carried the word to them.

Some Tutsi understood the deception. Pastor Kumubuga who was in touch with the Tutsi hidden around Bwakira told others at the committee meeting, "The people say that the advice to leave the bushes will lead to their death....they say that it is a political game."[97] Tens of thousands understood that and stayed hidden. But others, perhaps thousands of others, still had faith in the integrity of their authorities. They came out and were slain. The policy of "pacification," meant to tighten control over the killing and to impress the foreigners, also in the end served the additional purpose of enticing more Tutsi to their deaths.

"Justice" During the Genocide

The interim prime minister's message of April 27 spoke about reopening courts that had been closed and using the judicial system to punish killings and deter further violence. But by that time, "justice," like "security," was meant only for the Hutu.

That had not been the case in the first days of the genocide when officials opposed to the slaughter had actually tried to use the judicial system to protect Tutsi. They arrested assailants and pillagers and began preparing cases against them. But as soon as the national leaders of genocide exerted their influence in the communes, the burgomasters released the detainees. The liberation of persons who had been seen burning and pillaging property and killing Tutsi signaled the community that the local authority had decided to tolerate, if not to support, violence against Tutsi.

Few prosecutors heeded the interim prime minister's call to resume work at the end of April. Where they did and began investigating cases, the nature of the charges varied from murder to the theft of mud-guards from a bicycle. The cases had a common element: the victim was Hutu.

No longer the beneficiary of official judicial protection, Tutsi became the accused in an unofficial parody of justice. In communal offices, at barriers, or in bars, they were "tried" on charges of being the "enemy." Since the start of the genocide, some Tutsi had been brought to the burgomaster in a continuation of the earlier practice of handing over any suspected criminal to the local authorities. With the "pacification" campaign, the number delivered apparently increased, with Tutsi being brought to the burgomaster, the councilor, a security committee, or to the head of a barrier or a patrol. There they would be interrogated about the

---

[97]Bwakira commune, "Inyandiko-mvugo...kuwa 20/5/94."

pretexts that supposedly proved their guilt, such as possessing arms or lists of people to kill. If the accused were women, they might be distributed to male militia members for sexual service instead of being killed.[98]

Spurious as the process was, it formed a logical sequel to the denunciations against individuals. By carrying it through, the authorities added credibility to the whole deception and may have convinced some doubters that the person charged had actually worked for the RPF. Most of those captured were slain after perfunctory questioning. In some cases, the Tutsi were released, but just as condemnations usually had nothing to do with guilt having been established, so the reprieves rarely had to do with innocence having been proved. They resulted rather from bribes, personal connections, or some inexplicable stroke of good fortune.

Many killers treated the directive to take Tutsi to the authorities as just one more pretense. In mock compliance, the killers in Gisenyi labeled the cemetery, a usual place of execution, "the commune." Elsewhere assailants announced that they were taking the Tutsi "to the burgomaster" when they led them into a banana grove or off into the bush to be killed.[99]

Mid-May Slaughter: Women and Children as Victims

Through the last days of April, the RPF made dramatic advances. They took Byumba in the northeast on April 21, Rwamagana in the east on April 27, and Rusumo in the southeast on April 29-30. In a major blow to the Rwandan army, they swung west and in mid-May cut the main road linking Kigali to Gitarama. At this time, authorities ordered a new wave of killings. Militia and military launched new large-scale attacks on Tutsi at Bisesero and a raid was planned on the Hotel Mille Collines, although it was never carried out. RTLM, too, returned to frankly genocidal calls for slaughter. Kantano Habimana insisted:

> Let 100,000 young men be rapidly recruited, so that they all rise up and then we will kill the Inkotanyi, we will exterminate them all the more easily since...the proof that we will exterminate them is that they are a single ethnic

---

[98]Human Rights Watch/FIDH, *Shattered Lives,* p. 59.

[99]Commission pour le Mémorial du Génocide et des Massacres, "Rapport Préliminaire," p. 63; Des prêtres du Diocèse de Nyundo, "Des rescapés du diocèse," p. 64.

group. So look at a person and see his height and how he looks, just look at his pretty little nose and then break it.[100]

In many communities, women and children who had survived the first weeks of the genocide were slain in mid-May.[101] In the past Rwandans had not usually killed women in conflicts and at the beginning of the genocide assailants often spared them. When militia had wanted to kill women during an attack in Kigali in late April, for example, Renzaho had intervened to stop it.[102] Killers in Gikongoro told a woman that she was safe because "Sex has no ethnic group."[103] The number of attacks against women, all at about the same time, indicates that a decision to kill women had been made at the national level and was being implemented in local communities. Women who had been living on their own as well as those who had been kept alive to serve the sexual demands of their captors were slaughtered. In the note quoted above, the head of the barrier is directed to deliver "the three girls of Gapfizi" early the next morning so that the measures which the security council has decided can be carried out. This document, almost certainly the death warrant for the three young women, dates to mid-May.[104]

Some killers urged eliminating Tutsi women because, they said, they would produce only Tutsi children, regardless of the ethnic group of their husbands. This argument, which reversed the usual custom of assigning children to the group of their fathers, paved the way to demanding death also for Tutsi wives of Hutu husbands. Many were killed at this time, some by their own husbands. In some communities, however, local authorities worked to keep these women alive, particularly if their husbands were men of some importance. Depriving a man of the productive and reproductive capacities of his wife harmed his interests and a man injured in this way might demand punishment for the murderers or some other form of satisfaction. Because these cases involved the interests of a Hutu as much as the life of a Tutsi, a husband thus injured could expect support at least from his immediate kin and friends. Burgomasters and communal security committees spent

[100]Chrétien et al, *Rwanda, Les médias*, p. 193.

[101]Human Rights Watch/FIDH, *Shattered Lives,* p. 41.

[102]African Rights, *Rwanda, Death, Despair,* p.645.

[103]Human Rights Watch/FIDH interview, Maraba, June 14, 1995.

[104]See chapter six.

a substantial amount of time trying to balance the interests of the husbands, generally acknowledged as valid, against the demands for action by hard-liners within the community. Often the support of authorities was not enough and husbands had to pay assailants to leave their wives unharmed; others fought, sometimes successfully, to save their wives.

Infants and young children who had survived or been saved in the first weeks were also slain in mid-May. Killers sought to justify their slaughter by repeating a phrase about Kagame or Rwigema, the RPF commander who had led the 1990 invasion, having once been a baby too. This explanation, voiced uniformly throughout the country, carried the idea of "self-defense" to its logically absurd and genocidal end. Hutu who tried to buy the lives of children or save them in other ways had little success and sometimes had to pay fines for having protected them.

"Opening a Breach to the Enemy": Conflicts Among Hutu
In the later part of May and in June, administrators found ordinary people were deserting the barriers and refusing to do the patrols. With the great majority of Tutsi dead, gone, or in hiding, people wanted to return to that "normality" preached by the authorities themselves. In permitting or directing the slaughter of the weak, the elderly, women, and infants, who posed no threat to anyone, authorities discredited the justification that killing was an act of self-defense. Prefects pressed burgomasters who pressed councilors who pressed the citizens to carry out their assigned duties, but with shrinking success.

As the more stable and established citizens withdrew, the militia and young men from the "civilian self-defense" program increasingly dominated the barriers and the patrols. They sometimes were armed with guns or grenades and had received enough training in military skills to intimidate others. With far fewer Tutsi to be caught, they spent more time harassing, robbing, and killing Hutu passersby. The minister of interior asked that those at the barriers and on patrols "use better judgment and not confuse the guilty with the innocent."[105] Several days later, the prefect of Kibuye reported to him that young people at a barrier tried to help themselves to the beer and tobacco from passing trucks that belonged to an important government official. The prefect had intervened to protect the goods, but, he commented, the incident showed "that there are people who still do not

---

[105]Edouard Karemera, "Ijambo rya Ministri w'Ubutegetsi bw'Igihugu n'Amajyambere ya Komini," May 31, 1994 (Butare prefecture).

understand the role of the barriers."[106] Burgomasters and members of the councils of several communes expressed their anger at the abusive young men who controlled the roads and paths of their communities. One critic remarked later, "It is a good thing that the RPF arrived when it did. The thugs were beginning to take over."[107]

Political Struggles

With the genocide, the accepted criteria for success in the political and administrative domains had been supplanted by new measures of worth: hostility to Tutsi and efficiency in getting them killed. This led to struggles for power as people in each community nurtured new enmities and built new alliances to deal with the changes in standards and leaders. People from one sector attacked those in the adjacent sector and residents of one commune raided those of another.

The disputes sometimes involved cattle or land or revenge for previous killings, but questions of political party loyalty often underlay the other considerations. Burgomasters, party leaders, and other locally important persons generally had the services of armed guards, sometimes communal policemen or, if they could be obtained, National Police or soldiers. They sent these guards to intimidate or assault other officials or party leaders. A number of these cases resulted in deaths, such as a conflict between authorities of Gishyita and Gisovu that ended with seven persons dead, two of them National Policemen. In early June, the burgomaster of Rutsiro feared an attack by people from the adjacent commune of Murunda because of "unexplained mortality among certain people of the MDR in the region of Murunda."[108]

National authorities intended "pacification" to limit conflict among Hutu, but some local authorities used the policy as a pretext for harassing their political adversaries. Just as some burgomasters had once charged opponents with refusing to participate in killings of Tutsi, so some now accused adversaries of continuing such attacks.

---

[106]Dr. Clément Kayishema, Préfet, to Ministre MININTER KIGALI, no. 003/04.09.01, June 2, 1994 (Kibuye prefecture).

[107]Human Rights Watch/FIDH interview, Butare, August 19, 1995.

[108]Kayishema to Ministre MININTER, June 2, 1994.

Disputes Over Property

Many Hutu fought over the property left by Tutsi. At the start of the genocide, authorities froze Tutsi bank accounts, presumably intending to appropriate these funds for the national government. In at least one commune, that of Gisovu, the burgomaster supposedly got there first and embezzled 726,000 Rwandan francs (some U.S.$4,800) from "missing clients." Minister of Information Eliézer Niyitegeka, who was from the region, used this allegation and other charges to demand that the burgomaster be replaced by a candidate he favored. To cap a number of allegations of corruption and mismanagement, Niyitegeka added what he apparently supposed would be the ultimate charge, that the burgomaster lacked enthusiasm for "civilian self-defense."[109] In Bwakira commune, thieves who were caught trying to rob a bank protested that they were just separating money belonging to Tutsi from money belonging to Hutu.[110]

Most people fought not over money but over land, cattle, or crops. Some disputed the boundaries of fields they had been allocated and others tried to harvest crops that had been assigned to someone else. In Gisovu, the burgomaster and the councilor fought so bitterly over pillaged cattle that "the matter created an open hatred" between them.[111] Communal councilors in Bwakira had to deal with assailants who wanted the cattle of Tutsi eaten immediately—to the enjoyment of many—rather than kept alive—for the profit of a few.[112] Looters fought over the distribution of the goods taken from development projects, schools, and hospitals as well as over Tutsi belongings.

Authorities directed burgomasters to deal with the disposition of Tutsi goods and land promptly to avoid trouble. As early as mid-April in some places, burgomasters ordered their subordinates to prepare inventories of the property of Tutsi who had been killed or driven away. One reason for the lists of people killed, initiated also at this time, was to identify which households were completely eliminated, meaning that their property was available for redistribution, and which had some survivors, meaning the land would be available only after further killing. Rural burgomasters were most preoccupied with distributing fields for cultivation;

---

[109] Eliézer Niyitegeka to Monsieur le Ministre de l'Intérieur et du Développement Communal, no classification number, no date [received July 8, 1994] (Kibuye prefecture).

[110]Bwakira commune, "Inyandiko-mvugo...kuwa 5.5.94."

[111]Kayishema to Ministre MININTER, June 2, 1994.

[112]Bwakira commune, "Inyandiko-mvugo...kuwa 20/5/94."

authorities in the towns like Butare also allocated houses and even market stalls during the months of May and June.

Communal councils spent more time discussing property than any other issue except "security" measures themselves. Most communities divided the property into three categories, so similar from one commune to the next as to indicate they were determined at the national level. Pillaged goods belonged to the one who took them, except for particularly valuable items that were supposed to go to the authorities to be sold; land reverted to the commune, as was customary, for short-term rental or permanent allocation; and crops already standing were to be protected and harvested by individuals for their own benefit or by the authorities for the public good. In some cases, authorities directed that grain of the dead Tutsi be brewed into beer to reward the militia or to be sold to help pay the costs of war.[113]

In documents where recipients of vacated lands are identified, it appears that one or a small number of persons sometimes benefited more than others in the community. In some cases, the rewards may have corresponded to the extent of participation in the genocide. The prompt parceling out of the victims' land demonstrated the solid advantage to be gained by joining in attacks and no doubt tempted some to kill who would not otherwise have been done so.

"Where Will It End?"

Soldiers and National Police, both those posted in a region and those who had returned home after deserting the battlefront, exacerbated conflicts by pillaging and commiting exactions against the local population. Administrators or politicians, emboldened by having soldiers or police as armed guards, also committed abuses against people in their jursidictions.

The number of firearms and grenades available meant that conflicts often had serious consequences. From the first days of the genocide, officials opposed to the killings had tried without success to locate and, if possible, confiscate the weapons that had already been distributed in preparation for the killing. Beginning in late April, those who approved the genocide also saw the need to control the use of firearms. The minister of interior insisted that the "tools" which have been "put at the disposition of people" were to be "used only for the purpose for which they have received them and not for anything else."[114]

---

[113]Bwakira commune, "Inyandiko-mvugo...kuwa 5/5/94."

[114]Karemera, "Ijambo rya Ministri."

In various communes, council members deplored the vandalism and banditry of armed young men. In Bwakira, council member Dr. Kamanzi raised the issue of "young men who possess grenades and guns while we do not have any. We do not even know where those guns came from. I wish they could be taken away from them."[115] The burgomaster was ready to disarm some, but not all who had such weapons. He declared:

> Each person's particular conduct must be taken into consideration, however, since some of those people have good behavior and own grenades only to protect themselves in case they are assaulted.[116]

In late May, the minister of the interior ordered burgomasters to prepare inventories of all the firearms in their communes, suggesting that they might be confiscated and redistributed. The order occasioned a flood of letters from persons who had firearms and wanted to obtain official authorisation for them, as the law required. When authorities distributed thousands of firearms beginning in mid-May, many competed to obtain a weapon.

As the scramble to obtain firearms demonstrated, many Hutu felt more rather than less afraid after the majority of Tutsi—the supposed enemy—had been eliminated. The RPF was, of course, increasingly a threat, but, in addition, Hutu feared other Hutu.

After some weeks of slaughter, people were beginning to understand that a system dedicated to the destruction of Tutsi provided no security for Hutu either. One witness described the astonishment and indignation of his Hutu neighbors when one of their number was seized by a soldier. "We defended him, saying he is Hutu. You are supposed to be killing Tutsi, so why take him? If you start taking Hutu, where will it end?"[117]

RPF Victory
In late May, the RPF took both the airport and the major military camp at Kanombe in Kigali and, on May 27, the militia leaders and many of their followers fled although Rwandan army troops continued to hold on to part of the capital. On

---

[115]Bwakira commune, "Inyandiko-mvugo...kuwa 20/5/94."

[116]Bwakira commune, "Inyandiko-mvugo...kuwa 29/4/94."

[117]Human Rights Watch/FIDH interview, Butare, October 26, 1995.

May 29, they took Nyabisindu and on June 2, Kabgayi, only a few miles from Gitarama. The Rwandan army counterattacked, backed by militia and "civilian self-defense" forces, but the RPF routed them and rolled on to take Gitarama on June 13. Leaders of the interim government fled west to Kibuye and then north to Gisenyi. There they created a new national assembly in a last vain effort to establish legitimacy.

As the RPF advanced into each region, authorities managed to galvanize killers to hunt for the last remaining Tutsi. They launched these final attacks in June and early July, on dates that varied according to the moment of the RPF arrival nearby. In early June, assailants had surrounded at least one of the three large camps of Tutsi at Kabgayi, but were overwhelmed by a rapid RPF advance before they could carry out the planned attack. In late June, militia and military tried to complete the annihilation at Bisesero, as is described above. Others poised to launch a major attack on the some ten thousand Tutsi at Nyarushishi camp in Cyangugu failed to move because of the presence of National Police under Lieutenant Colonel Bavugamenshi.

In June Bemerki pushed killers to complete the elimination of Tutsi, "their total extermination, putting them all to death, their total extinction."[118] On July 2 Kantano Habimana exultantly invited his listeners to join him in a song of celebration.

> Let's rejoice, friends! The *Inkotanyi* have been exterminated! Let's rejoice, friend. God can never be unjust!...these criminals...these suicide commandos...without doubt they will have been exterminated...Let us go on. Let us tighten our belts and exterminate them...so that our children and our grandchildren and the children of our grandchildren never again hear of what is called *Inkotanyi*.[119]

Two days later the RPF took Kigali and two weeks after that the authorities responsible for the genocide fled Rwanda.

---

[118]Chrétien et al, *Rwanda, Les médias,* p. 338.

[119]Ibid., pp. 205-06.

GIKONGORO PREFECTURE

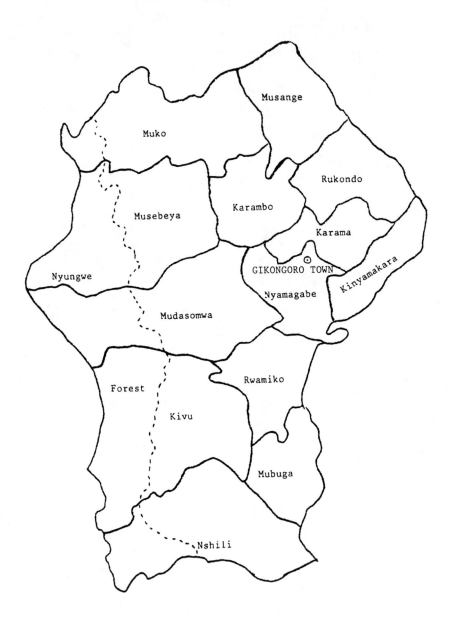

GIKONGORO

Some of the earliest attacks as well as some of the worst massacres of the genocide took place in Gikongoro. MRND supporters launched the violence at three points and from there spread it into adjacent areas, much as they expanded disorder outward from Kigali and its vicinity into the prefecture of Gitarama. In some communes, like Musebeya, Kivu and Kinyamakara, administrators opposed the genocide and initially drew strength from the people in their communes who refused to kill. But as prefectural authorities failed to act against the violence and national authorities pressured for more and faster slaughter, they lost power to local rivals who saw the killing campaign as an opportunity to establish or reestablish their power. The dissenters judged continuing opposition futile and dangerous and either withdrew into passivity or themselves took up the role of killers.

Background

The government created the prefecture of Gikongoro shortly after independence, largely to weaken the Tutsi influence that continued strong around the former royal capital of Nyanza. It attached the southern and western outskirts of the Nyanza region to a highlands area further west inhabited largely by Hutu. Like Hutu of northern Rwanda, these "hill people" were sometimes called *Bakiga* and like them, they resented Tutsi control that had been imposed during the colonial period.[1] Thus cobbled together, Gikongoro lacked the cohesiveness enjoyed by other prefectures as a result of geography or history. It was also one of the least favored prefectures. Its only real town, also called Gikongoro, had a population of fewer than 10,000 in 1994. It was not much more than a motley collection of shops, offices, and a bank stretched out on either side of the one paved road that passed through the region. Perched high on one hill overlooking the road was the recently built prefectural office. On another more distant hill sat the newly established Catholic bishopric of Gikongoro. The town had no more history or coherence than the prefecture it served.

Secondary schools were few and local people lacked the opportunity for higher studies needed to obtain important government posts. With few people in power, Gikongoro had little chance to win the foreign-supported projects that could have improved opportunities for its residents. The most promising of the political leaders from Gikongoro, Emmanuel Gapyisi, had been assassinated in 1993 and a second,

---

[1]René Lemarchand, *Rwanda and Burundi* (New York: Praeger, 1970), p. 224.

303

the minister and PSD head Frederic Nzamurambaho, was killed at the start of the genocide.

As elsewhere in Rwanda, most people in Gikongoro eked out a living from the soil. The one bright spot in the beautiful but bleak landscape of wind-swept hills were tea plantations where some farmers were able to earn small amounts from this cash crop. But control of the local tea factories at Kitabi and at Mata as well as of OCIR-Thé, the national tea marketing office that ran them, remained in the hands of people from the favored regions of northwestern Rwanda, linked by loyalty and kinship to the Habyarimana family.[2] The stagnation brought on by the war aggravated the poverty of the region. In addition, as multiple parties began to flourish, some people began refusing to pay their taxes as part of the rejection of the MRND and authorities seen to be related to it. The income of the communes fell off by some 20 percent in 1993 and communal authorities were obliged to lay off employees.[3] Fighting to counter the decline, the prefect encouraged communes to exploit to the fullest the few foreign-aided projects in their areas, but even some of them were beginning to suffer cutbacks from foreign funders. Several years of poor growing conditions cut food production. At the end of 1993, the prefect estimated that 64 percent of the population faced food shortages and that 48 percent were in real danger of famine during 1994.[4]

During the 1960s and again in 1973, Gikongoro was the scene of serious violence against Tutsi, but there had been no major attacks on them right after the October 1990 attack by the RPF. Janvier Afrika, who confessed to helping organize slaughter of Tutsi in northwestern Rwanda in 1991 and in Bugesera in 1992, told the International Commisson investigating human rights abuse that Gikongoro was supposed to be the next place for him to cause trouble. But after a falling out with

---

[2]Michel Bagaragaza, head of OCIR-Thé, was from Habyarimana's home region. In March of 1992 the tea marketing office delivered one million dollars worth of tea and mortgaged future crops as part of a six million dollar arms deal with the Egyptian government. Human Rights Watch Arms Project, "Arming Rwanda," pp. 18-19.

[3]Laurent Bucyibaruta, Préfet, telegram to Monsieur le Sous-Préfet (tous), February 1, 1993 (Gikongoro prefecture).

[4]Laurent Bucyibaruta, Préfet, to Mininter, fax no. 244/04.09.01/4, December 13, 1993 (Gikongoro prefecture).

others of the akazu, he was imprisoned and never put the plans into effect.[5] Following the death of Burundian President Ndadaye and the arrival of thousands of refugees from Burundi in late 1993, Hutu in several parts of Gikongoro attacked Tutsi. In the commune of Nshili, assailants burned the homes of Tutsi and drove them across the prefectural border into Butare.[6]

From the start of the war, some local authorities depicted Gikongoro as virtually besieged by the RPF. There was no real basis for such concern, but authorities feared that a dense stretch of rain forest that covered the western 20 percent of the prefecture could serve as a natural route for RPF infiltration from Burundi into the heart of Rwanda. Local people, however, seemed little touched by the war before 1994, except for those who became soldiers to escape the lack of opportunities in the region.[7]

Once multiple political parties were permitted, prefectural authorities—then all representatives of the MRND—fought hard to hinder the growth of the new parties.[8] They had little success, however, and during 1992 and 1993, the MRND was losing support steadily, primarily to the MDR, but also to the PSD and the PL.

Throughout 1993, prefectural and local authorities participated in the measures described above that later facilitated the genocide: the efforts to locate former soldiers, to identify families of young people said to have left the country, and to increase the arsenal of communal police.[9] During the months preceding the genocide, the commanders of the National Police in Gikongoro and in Butare

---

[5]Field notes, the International Commission on Human Rights Abuse in Rwanda, January 19, 1993.

[6]Joachim Hategekimana, Sous-Préfet, to Préfet, Gikongoro, no. 114/04.17.02, February 8, 1993; Laurent Bucyibaruta, Préfet, to Commandant de Groupement Gendarmerie, Butare, no. 161//04.17.02, February 12, 1993; Augustin Gashugi, Bourgmestre, to Préfet, Gikongoro, no. 573/04.17.02, November 29, 1993; Laurent Bucyibaruta, Préfet, to Monsieur le Responsable du CLADHO, no. 116/04.09.01, December 30, 1993 (Gikongoro prefecture).

[7]Human Rights Watch/FIDH interviews, Butare, August 18, 1995; Kigali, July 16, 1995.

[8]See the case of Nshili commune described in chapter one.

[9]Laurent Bucyibaruta, Préfet, to S/Préfet Munini, Bourgmestre Nyamagabe, telegram no. 94/004/04.06, January 20, 1994 (Gikongoro prefecture).

posted small detachments in several locations around the prefecture. One group had been sent to Musebeya after some protests over non-payment of salary at a local development project in August 1993; they had been kept there, although the dispute was long since settled. Another group had been dispatched to Nshili following conflicts between MDR and MRND supporters, but once more that problem had been resolved and yet the police were still there in April 1994. Another detachment was located at the tea factory at Mata in commune Rwamiko and another under the orders of the sub-prefect at Munini. According to one account, National Police were posted to the sub-prefecture of Kaduha for no apparent reason several days before the plane was shot down.[10]

Despite the presence of National Police, attacks on persons and property increased in 1993, whether from political or simply criminal motives, with such incidents as the burning of communal reforestation projects, attacks by grenades, and the attempted assassination of a former burgomaster and his wife.[11] The number of firearms also increased in the region. In late 1993, the burgomaster of Nshili reported that some persons in his commune had a stock of seventy grenades, one of which he was able to buy for the equivalent of three dollars U.S.[12] The burgomaster of Musebeya, who belonged to the PSD, was attacked in his home as was the burgomaster of Kivu, who was a member of the MDR. Aware that their enemies from the MRND and the CDR had access to firearms, they asked the prefect for guns of their own. [13]

---

[10]Laurent Bucyibaruta, Préfet, to Monsieur le Bourgmestre, Musebeya, no. 28/04/17/02, April 1, 1994; Prosecutor Celse Semigabo to Commander of Brigade, Groupement Gikongoro, No. D/776/D.11/A/PRORE, September 2, 1993 (Gikongoro prefecture); Human Rights Watch/FIDH interview, Butare, October 19, 1995; African Rights, *Rwanda, Death, Despair*, p. 317.

[11]Celse Semigabo, Procureur de la République, to Monsieur le Commandant de la Brigade, Gikongoro no. D/776/D.11/A PRORE, September 2, 1993; Laurent Bucyibaruta, Préfet, to Monsieur le S/Préfet (tous), Monsieur le Procureur, Monsieur le Bourgmestre de la Commune (tous), no. 227/04.17.02, November 18, 1993 (Gikongoro prefecture).

[12]Laurent Bucyibaruta, Préfet, to Bourgmestre, Nshili, No. 200/04.17.02, October 14, 1993 (Gikongoro prefecture).

[13] Laurent Bucyibaruta, Préfet, to Muhitira Juvénal, Bourgmestre, Kivu, no. 243/04.06, December 7, 1993 (Gikongoro prefecture).

Bypassing the Prefect

Hutu attacked Tutsi in several parts of Gikongoro beginning on April 7. The prefect, a MRND loyalist, was one of the first officials to come out in support of the interim government on national radio but he seems to have been less important in the early onset of violence and in its later expansion than some of his subordinates, such as Damien Biniga, and some party leaders who were not part of the administration at all, such as retired Lt. Col. Aloys Simba.

The prefect, Laurent Bucyibaruta, was originally from Gikongoro and had devoted himself to the service of party and state through the decades when the two were identical. An administrator, subsequently a deputy in the parliament, and then again an administrator, he came home to Gikongoro in 1992 after several years as prefect of Kibungo in eastern Rwanda. A man who took his responsibilities seriously, he had been openly loyal to the MRND until the new regulations of the multiparty era required that administrative authorities treat all parties equally. He then dutifully professed objectivity and rarely showed his preference publicly. His MDR opponents taxed him with favoritism from time to time. Occasionally a partisan phrase escaped him, such as when he indicated that demonstrators of other parties should be prepared to take the consequences if MRND members reacted negatively to their demonstrations.[14] But to judge from his correspondence generally as well as from evaluations by observers from other parties, he appears to have executed his duties responsibly, frequently cautioning subordinates against being influenced by party loyalties. In a hotly contested election in Musebeya commune in June 1993, for example, he gave the victory to the PSD candidate over that of the MRND and defended his decision when challenged by superiors. That same month, he directed the burgomaster of Rwamiko to look into the case of a man whose identity card had been changed from "Umuhutu" to "Umututsi" over his protests. Bucyibaruta refused the above-mentioned requests of the PSD and MDR burgomasters for their own guns and he also ordered all his subordinates to divest themselves of any weapons that they might have appropriated from the communal police. If they needed protection, he told them, they were to rely on the communal police as guards; they must not keep police weapons in their own possession. When notified that the burgomaster of Nshili had bought a grenade, he

---

[14]Laurent Bucyibaruta, Préfet, to Monsieur le Ministre de l'Intérieur et du Développement Communal, no. CN 132/04.17.02, December 14, 1992 (Gikongoro prefecture).

directed him to hand it over promptly to the National Police because the communes had no right to have this kind of arms.[15]

Sub-Prefect Damien Biniga

One of Bucyibaruta's immediate subordinates was the sub-prefect Damien Biniga, who was in charge of communes in the southern part of Gikongoro, adjacent to the border with Burundi. Described by others in the administration as "brutal" and "hard-core MRND," Biniga had served as deputy in the parliament and as a member of the prefectural committee of the MRND. Once a sub-prefect in Ruhengeri, he maintained ties with military from that region. According to a witness who was himself an official in Gikongoro at the time, Biniga came to the prefecture to organize the Interahamwe. Supporters of the MDR clashed with Biniga and in September 1992 organized a demonstration against him, hoping to get him removed. At one point, the people of Kivu commune—presumably adherents of the MDR—were so angry at his favoring the MRND that they barred the road to prevent him from passing through their commune.[16]

Biniga was active also at the national level of the MRND. Trading upon his status as party loyalist, he bypassed the prefect to communicate with President Habyarimana himself or with other high-ranking officials in Kigali.[17] Bucyibaruta disapproved of his subordinate's open favoritism of the MRND and tried unsuccessfully to interrupt his direct links with Kigali.[18]

---

[15]Laurent Bucyibaruta, Prefe, to Bwana Ministri w'Ubutegetsi bw'Igihugu n'Amajyambere ya Komini, no. 647/04/09.01, July 8, 1993; Laurent Bucyibaruta, Préfet, to Monsieur le Bourgmestre, Musebeya, no. 0961/04.09.01/9, October 21, 1993; Laurent Bucyibaruta, Préfet, to Monsieur le Bourgmestre, Rwamiko, no. 528/04.07, June 9, 1993; Laurent Bucyibaruta, Préfet, to Bourgmestre, Nshili, No. 200/04.17.02, October 14, 1993 (Gikongoro prefecture).

[16]Human Rights Watch/FIDH interviews, Butare, August 20, October 12, October 19, 1995; Sous-Préfet, Munini, to Préfet, Gikongoro, telegram 130950 B, October 13, 1992; Sous-Préfet, Munini to Préfet, Gikongoro, telegram 130830 B, November 13, 1992; Sous-Préfet, Munini, to Monsieur le Ministre de l'Intérieur et du Développement Communal, telegram 201330B, November 21, 1992 (Gikongoro prefecture).

[17]Sous-Préfet Munini to Présidence de la République, telegram, 200900B, November 21, 1993 (Gikongoro prefecture).

[18]Laurent Bucyibaruta, Préfet, to Monsieur le Sous/Préfet, Munini, no. 452/04/01/01, May 10, 1993 (Gikongoro prefecture).

Once the genocide began, Bucyibaruta supposedly encouraged Tutsi to assemble at the Murambi technical school, site of one of the worst massacres in the prefecture, and he visited students at the Kibeho school just before they were attacked and slaughtered.[19] But Biniga seems to have been the more dynamic figure, seen inciting to killings in many parts of the prefecture as well as in Butare. Given Biniga's close links with Habyarimana's circle, they may have chosen to deal with him directly rather than with the prefect.

Lieutenant Colonel Simba

One administrative official commented that throughout this period, "military figures were deciding government strategies and actions" increasingly and that civilian administrators were losing power proportionately.[20] One of the soldiers who exercised this power in Gikongoro was retired Lieutenant Colonel Simba. A native of Gifurwe sector of Musebeya commune, Gikongoro, Simba had followed the military path to success. He was of the same generation as Habyarimana and had been one of the small circle of officers who had helped install him as president in 1973. Retired from active duty, Simba had made a second career in the MRND, serving as deputy in the parliament. Although based in Kigali, he became president of the MRND for the prefecture of Gikongoro and occasionally returned home to steer local activities. In January 1993, for example, he directed a rally against the Arusha Accords in the town of Gikongoro just when MRND and CDR leaders were launching violence elsewhere in the country to stall the peace process.[21]

Simba drew his power from his old military contacts and links with the president rather than from a local base. He had apparently been away too long and had done too little for his home commune to be considered a favorite son. So alienated was he from Musebeya that its burgomaster initially refused to support his candidacy for parliament in 1988 and then did so only because of pressure from Kigali. Because the burgomaster had opposed him, Simba had joined forces with some locally dissatisfied MRND members, including teacher Jean-Chrysostome Ndizihiwe, to use kubohoza tactics to oust him. After the burgomaster was forced to resign, a limited form of communal election was held to replace him in June

[19]African Rights, *Rwanda, Death, Despair*, p.300.

[20]Human Rights Watch/FIDH interview, Butare, August 20, 1995.

[21]Préfet Gikongoro to Mininter, fax no. 006/04.09.01, January 20, 1993 (Gikongoro prefecture).

1993. Simba arrived to use his influence—some say his money as well—to ensure that his protégé Ndizihiwe was chosen. He was accompanied by Daniel Mbangura, minister of higher education, also a member of MRND and at the time the only minister from Gikongoro.[22] Ndizihiwe was narrowly defeated—one more sign of the general ebbing of MRND influence throughout the country—and Simba was humiliated. When the results were announced, the youth wings of the parties that had opposed Ndizihiwe, the Abakombozi of the PSD and the Inkuba of the MDR, joined together in singing "Simba has failed."[23] As mentioned above, Prefect Bucyibaruta played a correct role in this contest, apparently putting the requirements of administrative neutrality above any preference for the MRND.

Soon after Habyarimana's death, Simba came home to Musebeya, in a Mercedes-Benz belonging to the MRND, to spread the message that the enemy was the Tutsi. According to one resident of Musebeya, Simba went around "...dressed as a colonel, with his stars, his uniform, his escort, saying 'The situation is dangerous. Even I have been recalled to military service to help hunt Tutsi.'"[24] Simba at first stayed with his sister in the sector Gifurwe, but the location was distant from the center of the commune and had no easy means of communication. After a few days, he moved his headquarters to the buildings of the Crête-Zaire-Nil (CZN) project, a foreign-funded development project that was closely linked to the MRND and the akazu. There, at a place called Gatare, Simba found adequate quarters for his guard, which grew from a modest six soldiers to an impressive eighteen. There he presumably also had the use of the CNZ short-wave radio for communication. During his time in Musebeya, he had access to a supply of fuel, which he sold to favored traders who needed the gasoline to carry on commerce. His control over this scarce commodity gave him one more lever of power in the community.[25]

---

[22]Apparently comfortable in such company, Mbangura would continue as minister of higher education in the interim government until he was named counsellor to the interim president, Sindikubwabo.

[23]Laurent Bucyibaruta, Préfet, to Mininter, fax no. 006/04.09.01, January 20, 1993; Human Rights Watch/FIDH interview, Kigali, July 16, 1995.

[24]Human Rights Watch/FIDH interviews, Kigali, July 16, 1995 and Musebeya, August 28, 1995.

[25]Human Rights Watch/FIDH interview, Musebeya, August 28, 1995.

While Biniga apparently became one of the most active civilian leaders of genocide in Gikongoro, he remained in principle subordinate to the prefect. Simba, as a high-ranking military officer, had no such restrictions. Not long after his arrival, he was "co-chairing" prefectural security council meetings with Bucyibaruta.[26] His control was later formalized by his appointment as "counsellor for civil defense."[27]

According to a number of well-placed witnesses, another military figure important in directing the genocide was Captain Sebuhura, a National Police officer from northern Rwanda. He was nominally subordinate to Major Christophe Bizimungu, commander of the Gikongoro post of the National Police, who was from the southwestern province of Cyangugu. But Sebuhura seems to have eclipsed his superior much as Biniga did Bucyibaruta. Because there was no army post in Gikongoro, the National Police were the only important force in the prefecture, essential to either spread or suppress the genocide. One witness then part of the civilian administration reported that at first "Major Bizimungu was not officially replaced, but he had no voice....[I]t was his assistant Sebuhura who had the real power. It was he who organized things, sending teams of National Police right and left."[28] As Bizimungu attempted to control his subordinate, the hostility between the two officers extended into the ranks and the National Policemen in the Gikongoro camp lined up behind one of the two, ready to fight each other in late April or early May. The general staff sent an officer to calm the situation and finally resolved the conflict definitively by removing Bizimungu. His replacement, Captain Gerace Harelimana, shared Sebuhura's views and worked well with him.[29]

First Attacks

The attacks in Gikongoro began at three different centers on April 7 and April 8. Two operations were launched in the south, one in Rwamiko commune, an area under Biniga's direct supervision, the other in neighboring Mudasomwa commune.

---

[26]Human Rights Watch/FIDH interviews, Gikongoro, June 19, 1996 and Butare, July 19, 1996.

[27]Laurent Bucyibaruta, Préfet, to Monsieur le Bourgmestre (tous), no. 183/04.09.01/1, May 18, 1994 (Gikongoro prefecture).

[28]Human Rights Watch/FIDH interview, Gikongoro, June 19, 1996.

[29]Human Rights Watch/FIDH interviews, Brussels, June 21, 1997; by telephone, Brussels, April 27, 1997.

In both communes, tea factories dominated local economic and political life. The directors of the factories were from the north, a man named Denis Kamodoka at the Kitabi factory in Mudasomwa and another named Ndabarinzi at Mata in Rwamiko. Their employees, many of them supporters of the MRND or the CDR, led the first attacks with the help of local administrators.[30]

Just as assailants were burning the first houses in Mudasomwa and Rwamiko on April 7, other attackers were preparing to kill Tutsi in Muko, a commune tucked away in the mountainous northwestern corner of Gikongoro. Muko was remote from the prefectural center, but in the early days of the genocide, the telephone still functioned and connected communal authorities with others elsewhere in the region and even in Kigali. Muko was also far from Biniga's area of administrative responsibility, but it was his commune of origin and, according to several witnesses, Biniga maintained close ties with the Muko burgomaster, Albert Kayihura, who had been in power there for years. As one witness from the area stated, "Biniga came often to monitor developments in Muko."[31]

At about 4 p.m. on April 7, Abbé Kumunyange, priest at the parish of Mushubi went the short distance from his church to the commercial center of Muko to check on the atmosphere there. In passing by the communal office, he found Burgomaster Kayihura meeting with the brigadier, head of the communal police, and with the chauffeur for the commune. At the center, all was quiet.

When he returned to the parish, he found a small group of Tutsi had arrived to seek shelter: Michel Gacenderi, the accountant for the commune, his wife and five children; Jean-Baptiste Kaberuka, the head of the health center, and his family; and Emmanuel Bayingana, the clerk of the local court, and his family. Because these men had had problems before with the burgomaster, they feared attack. Two hours later, Burgomaster Kayihura arrived and tried to persuade them to return to their homes. But when the abbé insisted that they be allowed to stay, Kayihura agreed and sent two communal police to guard the parish, as the priest requested.

At about 10 p.m. a crowd of some one hundred people attacked and pillaged the home of the assistant burgomaster, a Hutu, on the pretext that his wife was Tutsi. They continued up the hill to the parish, yelling and screaming. The brigadier of the communal police, armed with a rifle, led the way along with the communal chauffeur, Mucakari, and his brother. The cook of the parish, Manasé, joined them as well. Among the assailants were several boys, aged between twelve and fifteen.

---

[30]Human Rights Watch/FIDH interview, Kigali, June 4, 1996.

[31]Human Rights Watch/FIDH interview, Kigali, June 4, 1996.

The attackers forced their way into the parish house, a single-story building constructed around a garden. They broke down the door to the priest's room with a large stone. They beat him, looted his room, and then went on to the others. A witness recalls, "Then they broke the door to the other rooms. I heard blows. There were no cries."[32] The assailants killed Gacenderi, Bayingana, and Kaberuka and the wives of the first two. The wife of Kaberuka bought her life for about U.S.$800, but was later killed at the home of her husband's family. Assailants struck Leo, one of the small children, with a machete. He died from the wound the next morning. The other children were not harmed. The attackers also pillaged the large stock of food stored at the parish for distribution to the poor. They used the vehicle of the commune to carry off the goods and they finally left the parish at 4:30 a.m.[33]

The next morning, when the abbé called the prefect for help, Bucyibaruta ordered the burgomaster not to harm the priest. The burgomaster locked the priest into an annex to his house and then sent him to the town of Gikongoro the day after.

Moving the Violence Outward

Within a day or two, local leaders elsewhere in Gikongoro launched attacks on their own, following the nearby model, and assailants from the original centers carried the attacks over into areas which had previously been quiet. In Musebeya, for example, the first attacks came from Muko, the commune to the north, and a few days later, also from Mudasomwa to the south. Assailants from Rwamiko raided into neighboring Mubuga and Kivu, while those from Karambo carried the violence into Musange. Attackers crossed prefectural lines as well, with some from Mwendo in Kibuye attacking into the northern part of Gikongoro and others from Gikongoro exporting the violence to Butare.[34]

National Police, former soldiers, and communal police played an essential role in extending the violence, foreshadowing the even more important part they would play in later large-scale massacres. Assailants who burned and pillaged Tutsi houses in Kivu commune declared that they had been authorized to do so by a

---

[32]Human Rights Watch/FIDH interview, Gikongoro, May 23, 1995.

[33]Ibid.

[34]Human Rights Watch/FIDH interviews, Musebeya, June 1 and June 8, 1995; Maraba, June 14, 1995.

passing National Police patrol, apparently including guards of Sub-Prefect Biniga.[35] In Kinyamakara, two National Policemen, who described themselves as responsible for security, went through the area telling people along the road to attack the 2,000 Tutsi of the commune. They did it discreetly, speaking to small clusters of people here and there, rather than gathering a public meeting. They told Hutu that if they failed to burn the houses of Tutsi, the police would be back to burn all the houses in the region since, as strangers, they would have no way to distinguish the homes of Hutu from the homes of Tutsi.[36] When attackers could not defeat the population—Hutu and Tutsi—of a hill in Karambo commune who were defending a Tutsi woman from attack, they retreated only to come back the next day with National Police to back their assault.[37]

In these first days of burning, pillaging, and killing, there was some confusion about who was being targeted. Because it was known almost immediately that government leaders who were Hutu and members of the MDR, PSD, and PL had been slain in Kigali, people elsewhere at first believed that local supporters of these parties were to be attacked also. In Musebeya, for example, Hutu supporters of the PSD or the MDR, particularly those who were thought to be rich, were harassed and threatened by backers of the MRND and CDR. Reacting to the intimidation as if it were a continuation of kubohoza tactics, several wealthy traders moved to protect themselves by resigning from the PSD or MDR and buying off their attackers with money for beer. One Hutu known to oppose the MRND and CDR felt so intimidated that he fled to the Bushigishigi health center for protection.[38] In many places Hutu fled together with Tutsi or joined with them in fighting off the attackers who began burning houses on April 11.[39]

The Radio Targets Tutsi

After the first two or three days of violence, attackers in Gikongoro followed national directives and targeted only Tutsi. Hutu who had sought safety elsewhere

---

[35]Human Rights Watch/FIDH interview, Butare, October 19, 1995.

[36]Human Rights Watch/FIDH interview, Butare, August 19, 1995.

[37]Human Rights Watch/FIDH interview, Maraba, June 14, 1995.

[38]Human Rights Watch/FIDH interview, Musebeya, June 23, 1995.

[39]Human Rights Watch/FIDH interviews, Musebeya, June 1 and June 8, 1995; Maraba, June 14, 1995.

were reassured enough to return home. At the church of Muganza, for example, the Hutu who had taken refuge together with Tutsi on April 11 left the following day.[40] The focus on eliminating Tutsi resulted from the new solidarity among Hutu and sealed that solidarity. When Biniga learned of the death of Prime Minister Uwilingiyimana, he supposedly bought drinks for everyone in a bar to celebrate the end of hostility between the MRND and the MDR. He reportedly said, "Everything is equalized," meaning that now both parties had lost their leaders and on the basis of their mutual loss could join together in defeating the Tutsi enemy.[41]

Witnesses remember that it was the radio that disseminated the message. As one commented:

> We found out from RTLM that it was the inkotanyi that were supposed to be killed. This was on April 9, the day they named a new government in Kigali. The government called for calm and stated there was one common enemy—the inkotanyi-inyenzi.[42]

Another witness declared, "After April 10, the orders to kill were coming from above, and the radio was transmitting them." He added that the radio station itself went beyond the official pronouncements in "...pushing people to see this as ethnic." He continued, "People were listening to RTLM which was telling them, 'You people, ordinary people, the Tutsi killed your president. Save yourselves. Kill them before they kill you too.'"[43] On April 17, the telephone link with other parts of Rwanda was broken and the people of Gikongoro depended even more on the radio for information. At most barriers, there was a radio where the guards stayed tuned to RTLM during their long hours of keeping watch. And when patrols went out to kill, they went off singing the songs heard on RTLM, such as those of the popular Simon Bikindi.[44]

---

[40]Human Rights Watch/FIDH interview, Butare, October 19, 1995.

[41]Ibid.

[42]Human Rights Watch/FIDH interview, Musebeya, June 23, 1995.

[43]Human Rights Watch/FIDH interviews, Kigali, July 16, 1995; Musebeya, June 7 and August 28, 1995.

[44]Human Rights Watch/FIDH interviews, Musebeya, June 7, 1995; Kigali, July 16, 1995.

The importance of RTLM was underscored by a group of men from Nyarwungo sector, Musebeya, who stated that from the time of the plane crash, they started listening to the radio. Those who had no radios visited neighbors who had them so that they could know what might be coming next. The genocide, they said, was a concept they understood from the radio, not having known before what it meant.[45]

Musebeya

As at the national level, so at the local level, relatively few authorities were committed to a killing campaign at the start. One dissenter was Higiro, the burgomaster of Musebeya. This mountainous commune, remote from the prefectural center and bordered on the west by the Nyungwe forest was home to just under 40,000 people in April 1994, only 300 to 400 of them Tutsi. Only one percent of the population, the Tutsi were so few and so well-integrated with Hutu through marriage, friendship, and clientage arrangements—some of them spanning up to five generations—that Musebeya looked unlikely to be a center of virulent anti-Tutsi sentiment. In addition, Higiro was a member of the PSD and hence seen as sympathetic to the RPF and probably to Tutsi in general.

Higiro had defeated Simba's candidate, Ndizihiwe, to become burgomaster less than a year before and was engaged in an ongoing struggle for power with this MRND leader. He had supported several teachers in their efforts to oust Ndizihiwe as director of their school. Ndizihiwe was then implicated in a grenade attack which killed one of these teachers. He had been removed from the directorship of the school and was facing judicial charges when the genocide began. When teachers at the school were asked to elect a new director, Higiro played a role in defeating Ndizihiwe's candidate, providing yet one more reason for enmity between the two men. Higiro's house was attacked in January 1993 and, believing that Ndizihwe was armed, the burgomaster sought unsuccessfully to obtain a gun for his own protection.[46]

The PSD and hence Higiro had local support partly because the minister of agriculture, who was a PSD leader, had taken the side of local people in a dispute over the use of land by the CZN project. Supposedly intended to increase agricultural production for local residents, the foreign-funded project had been turned to other ends by powerful actors, including high-ranking soldiers linked to

[45]Human Rights Watch/FIDH interview, Musebeya, June 7, 1995.

[46]Human Rights Watch/FIDH interview, Kigali, July 16, 1995.

Habyarimana. In a region where fertile land was scarce, CZN had been allowed to displace cultivators from plots they had farmed and improved for years. In addition, the project had transformed lightly wooded areas on the edge of the forest into pasturage for the cattle of the wealthy rather than into arable plots for the hungry. Foreign funding for CZN evaporated during 1993. In August, the CZN in Musebeya was unable to pay some of its workers, who then went on strike. At this point a detachment of National Police were sent to Gatare, to the CZN headquarters, where they still were in April 1994. The director of the CZN in Musebeya was Celestin Mutabaruka, who was president of the Union social des démocrates chrétiens (UNISODEC) political party, a small offshoot of the MRND.[47] Because Mutabaruka's party was linked to the MRND and because many of the people who profited from the project were, part of the akazu, the local people extended their anger against the CZN to the MRND.[48]

It was because conflict between the MRND and the PSD in Musebeya was still so bitter that some Hutu also feared attack and fled on April 7 while others renounced the PSD or MDR for a safer haven within the MRND in the days just after the violence began.

The Burgomaster Opposes the Genocide

When Higiro learned of Habyarimana's death on the morning of April 7, his first reaction was to seek direction and help from above. He began calling his party leaders and other important people in Kigali. No one answered. Those party leaders and other powerful people who might have provided guidance and helped organize opposition to the genocide were all dead or in flight. Higiro recalls, "I was lost."[49] When several important members deserted the local PSD for the MRND, Higiro saw his support from below shrink as well.[50] Increasingly isolated, he could rely on an important source of help in trying to keep order: Major Cyriaque

---

[47] Mutabaruka was also a fervent member of the Pentecostal church. According to several observers in the commune, he denied benefits of participation in the project to anyone who was unwilling to join his party and his church.

[48] Ironically, some staff at the project had once been Tutsi so that in the eyes of poor local people, their exploitation had originally been seen as a Tutsi-MRND-akazu-military plot. Human Rights Watch/FIDH interview, Butare, August 18, 1994.

[49] Human Rights Watch/FIDH interview, Kigali, July 16, 1995.

[50] Human Rights Watch/FIDH interview, Musebeya, June 23, 1995.

Habyarabatuma, a native of Musebeya, who was commander of the National Police of Butare prefecture. Based in the town of Butare, an hour and a half away by road, Habyarabatuma came home to Musebeya right after the plane crash to insist that anyone who killed others would himself be killed. In the first few days, Higiro used this threat to intimidate potential assailants. The burgomaster also had support from the four communal police, who were commanded by a brigadier who was himself Tutsi.[51]

Beginning on April 8 and 9, assailants crossed into Musebeya from Muko to attack Tutsi in Nyarwungo and Rugano, the two sectors closest to Muko and the two with the highest concentration of Tutsi population. The Musebeya people, Tutsi and Hutu, resisted the attacks. Beginning on April 8, the burgomaster went around the commune, trying to persuade people to stay at home as the government had requested over the radio.[52] He also called together the councilors to get information on what was happpening in the various sectors. Later in the day, he closed down the usual Friday market because he feared the crowd might get out of hand. On April 9 he held a meeting in the sector Nyarwungo, to urge people to continue resisting attacks from Muko.[53] In testimony about the period, one survivor who had been hidden by a Hutu family commented spontaneously about Higiro:

> There was the burgomaster whose name was Higiro Viateur. When people were killing others, he prevented them from killing, saying: "don't kill." He held meetings in the sectors to prevent attacks. I know this because the people who were hiding me told me so.[54]

Meanwhile active supporters of the MRND challenged Higiro's authority and his message. A group of "intellectuals"—that is, people with higher education and salaried employment—who gathered frequently at a bar owned by a teacher named Etienne Mugema urged others to take revenge against the "accomplices" who were responsible for Habyarimana's death. These troublemakers, reportedly led by

---

[51]Human Rights Watch/FIDH interviews, Musebeya, June 23, 1995; Musebeya, May 5, 1995 and January 26, 1996.

[52]Human Rights Watch/FIDH interview, Musebeya, June 7, 1995.

[53]Human Rights Watch/FIDH interviews, Musebeya, May 5,1995 and June 7, 1995; Butare, June 14, 1995.

[54]Human Rights Watch/FIDH interview, Maraba, June 14, 1995.

Ndizihiwe, turned Higiro's request for people to stay at home against him, saying that he wanted to keep people in their houses so that the Inkotanyi could come and kill them there. Ndizihiwe denies this charge, saying that he stayed at home during these days, a contention supported by his wife.[55]

During the weekend of April 9 and 10, as RTLM pushed people to see the Tutsi as the prime enemy, the raiders from both the north and the south attacked Musebeya and convinced a few residents of the commune to cooperate with them, first by pointing out the homes of Tutsi, then by joining in the attacks.[56] By Monday morning April 11, some thirty Tutsi families had been attacked. Seeing a steady increase in the extent and intensity of the attacks, Higiro called for help from the prefect, Bucyibaruta, who sent four National Policemen from the detachment in Gikongoro town.

Higiro put the police to use almost immediately. A Hutu who was protecting Tutsi was attacked and he sent a child to get help from the burgomaster. Higiro went to the place immediately with three of the National Policemen who dispersed the large crowd simply by firing in the air. As the threatened Hutu recalls:

> Before the burgomaster and the police left, they spread the word that we should bring everyone who was in hiding to them. "I'll protect them at the commune," the burgomaster said. So I looked for those who had hidden in the[fields of] sorghum and in the bush. I brought them to my house. Then, at night, I took them to the commune. We arrived there very early in the morning. Even though this was dangerous, I wanted to do it. I wanted to do it for my friends, my neighbors. I didn't want them to have problems.[57]

These Tutsi stayed a day or two at the commune, fed by Hutu neighbors and friends and guarded by the communal and National Police. Then they decided to leave for Butare where several of them had a relative, a brother of the Marist congregation. After a telephone conversation with the brother, they asked Higiro's help in leaving. He arranged for the health center ambulance to transport as many as possible of the group and he also took care to get the needed fuel. He sent them

---

[55]Human Rights Watch/FIDH interviews, Kigali, July 16, 1995; Musebeya, June 23 and August 28, 1995; Butare, May 17 and June 14, 1995.

[56]Human Rights Watch/FIDH interviews, Musebeya, June 1 and June 8, 1995; Maraba, June 14, 1995.

[57]Human Rights Watch/FIDH interview, Musebeya, June 8, 1995.

off with an assistant burgomaster and two National Policemen whom he paid for the service. When the group arrived in the town of Gikongoro, half an hour away from the final destination of Butare, the authorities there refused to allow them to go any further. The Tutsi were taken to the bishopric in Gikongoro town. Soon after they were transported to a still unfinished government technical school set high on a hill at a place called Murambi just northwest of town. There all except one of the Musebeya people were slaughtered with thousands of other Tutsi. The survivor, an eight-year-old child, lay hidden under the body of his father. The child was found by local people, who took him in and cared for him for two years. In 1996, he was reunited with an uncle, one of the few surviving adults in the family.[58]

Simba Takes the Lead

Once Simba arrived, he took charge of the genocide in Musebeya as well as in the wider area.[59] Relying on his obvious wealth and power, his association with the slain president, his status as colonel, his position as head of the MRND in Gikongoro, Simba effectively countermanded Higiro's directives about keeping order. He congratulated assailants, pushing them to do more. In the company of his local supporters, Simba supposedly did the rounds of the bars "buying beer for people, saying 'Organize—you!' and then going on to the next center to do the same." Everywhere Simba went, he incited Hutu to "work" and he reportedly distributed money to young men in payment for their assaults on Tutsi. When people objected that the burgomaster had told them not to do such things, Simba supposedly replied, "Whom do you trust? Now the situation is different from what it was."[60] Indeed it was very different from nine months before when Higiro had been able to defeat Simba's candidate for the post of burgomaster. Now the

---

[58]Human Rights Watch/FIDH interviews Kigali, May 18, 1995, June 4, 1996. At the time of the 1996 commemoration ceremonies for the genocide, victims from mass graves at Murambi were exhumed and laid out in the classrooms before being reburied. Daniele Lacourse, a Canadian film producer, visited the school, where sixty-six classrooms were filled with between forty and sixty bodies each, totalling between some 2,600 and 4,000 victims exhumed. Current Rwandan government sources speak of 50,000 slain at Murambi, a toll difficult to reconcile with the number of bodies exhumed, even assuming that there are graves yet to be opened and that not all victims were buried.

[59]Human Rights Watch/FIDH interview, Kigali, July 16, 1995.

[60]Human Rights Watch/FIDH interview, Musebeya, May 5, 1995. For Simba's similar efforts at Byimana in Gitarama, before he came to Gikongoro, see chapter seven.

genocide had begun, proclaimed by national leaders via the radio. As the local leader of that campaign, Simba had grown stronger and Higiro, deprived of protection from above and unsure of support from below, was weakened.

With Simba's leadership, new recruits joined the original small group of organizers, including former soldiers, staff of the CZN and other assistance projects, teachers, councilors, and local party leaders, including some from MDR-Power as well as MRND and parties related to it. Simba's son and a soldier who was a nephew of Ndizihiwe reportedly helped their relatives lead the campaign.[61] In the first days, those advocating attacks on the Tutsi had worked furtively at night, but as they grew in number, they became bolder.[62]

Before April 6, the MRND, the MDR and the PSD had youth wings—some even used the same names as the names used for the militia elsewhere in Rwanda—but they served primarily as singers and dancers for party propaganda sessions. Witnesses agree that they had not been armed or trained to kill, a conclusion that seems reasonable given the continuing conflict between the burgomaster and his MRND rival. It would have been difficult for the MRND or the CDR to have given military training to young people without having attracted the attention of Higiro, who would have had every reason to publicize and oppose such preparations.

In the absence of militia ready to strike, leaders at first gathered assailants informally, often recruiting them from bars in the evenings. After attackers returned from early raids gloating over the goods they had pillaged, others decided to participate as well. As one witness remarked, "They said to themselves, 'I am poor and young. My friends have gone out and brought back things and here I am with nothing. I'll go too.'"[63] Older people who wanted to recapture the glory and profit of the 1959 revolution remembered having killed and pillaged then without punishment and decided to do it again. MDR-Power leader Samuel Rutasi was reportedly involved in killings in 1963 as well as in 1994. One witness whose families suffered from both these attacks found it understandable that Rutasi would

[61]Human Rights Watch/FIDH interviews, Musebeya, May 5, 1995, August 28, 1995; Kigali, June 4, 1996.

[62]Human Rights Watch/FIDH interviews, Butare, June 14, 1995; Kigali, May 16 and May 18, 1995.

[63]Human Rights Watch/FIDH interview, Kigali, July 16, 1995.

attack again since he had not been punished the first time. He commented, "This is an example of what happens when there is no justice."[64]

Sometimes the attackers donned banana leaves, particularly if they were going to raid outside the commune, where they might not be immediately recognized as part of the strike force. Those led by traders or other well-to-do leaders were transported out to the site of the attack and back in vehicles. The others set off on foot, following a leader who usually had a whistle which he blew to attract other participants as the group went along. The chief organizer was entitled to certain benefits, such as possession of any cattle taken in the raid. As the attackers followed the path, they would often sing, both to build up courage and to draw others into joining them. The groups agreed more or less upon "territories" to attack so that they avoided conflict with each other.[65]

While greed motivated some, fear induced many others to attack or to refuse help to Tutsi. People were afraid of the RPF who, the radio said, were killing Hutu with great cruelty.[66] But many Hutu were more immediately afraid of fellow Hutu, including local authorities and political leaders.

At the start, some Hutu opened their homes to Tutsi; but as the violence grew, more and more simply closed the door. A group of women from Nyarwungo sector recalled the genocide as a time when "Everyone was for himself." They explained:

Life was paralyzed. Children didn't go to school. Cultivators didn't go to the fields. The churches and markets stopped. All due to fear....We asked ourselves if night would come to be followed by a day that we would wake to see....We knew it was the time to hide, just hide and not look so they wouldn't kill you.[67]

A witness from another sector spoke in the same vein: "People wanted to stay at home so as not to see anything awful. But, of course, you heard things anyway."[68]

---

[64]Human Rights Watch/FIDH interview, Kigali, May 18, 1995.

[65]Human Rights Watch/FIDH interview, Kigali, July 16, 1995.

[66]Chrétien, et al., *Rwanda, Les médias*, pp. 162, 178, 189.

[67]Human Rights Watch/FIDH interviews, Musebeya, June 7, 1995.

[68]Human Rights Watch/FIDH interview, Musebeya, June 7, 1995.

Another resident traced the role of fear in transforming Musebeya from a place where Tutsi were protected to a place where most Tutsi were slain.

On the first day, those who went out were people from the MRND, the CDR, and former soldiers. But on the following days, others joined...those who refused to participate were called "accomplices" (ibyitso) and the others threatened them:

"Come with us and join us or we will kill you." Pushed to go out with their neighbors, they were pushed again once they were out with them. For example, the group would capture someone and then say, "Now kill her to show that you are really with us!"[69]

The Barriers

With the burgomaster opposed to executing the genocide, local leaders of the CDR and MDR-Power put up the first barriers, followed soon after by Celestin Mutabaruka, the director of CZN project, who reportedly established a total of three roadblocks in the vicinity of the project headquarters at Gatare. Those who maintained the barriers counted on robbing their victims, but they also enjoyed regular support from the patrons who had established the roadblocks. Thus Mutabaruka was said to have distributed 20,000 francs to the men at the three CZN barriers and to have provided them regularly with beer and meat.[70] Government employees "financed"—that is, supplied the beer for—the guards at the barrier at Gatovu, an important intersection with the road that went to Kaduha.[71]

After national authorities insisted that everyone must participate in the work of barriers and patrols as part of the "self-defense" effort, the burgomaster and councilors also put up barriers and ensured that they were carefully guarded particularly towards the end of April, when the flow of displaced persons from the

---

[69]Human Rights Watch/FIDH interview, Kigali, July 16, 1995.

[70]Human Rights Watch/FIDH interview, Gikongoro, June 19, 1996. Twenty thousand Rwandan francs amounted to about U.S.$100; in the context of Rwandan poverty, this represented a considerable sum of money.

[71]Human Rights Watch/FIDH interview, Musebeya, August 28, 1995; Maraba, June 14, 1995.

east increased.[72] Ordinarily at least one former soldier was posted at each of the most important barriers, those at Gasenyi, at Gatovu, at Kwitaba, and at the CZN project.[73] In describing how the officially-sanctioned barriers functioned, one resident of Musebeya stated:

All men worked at the barriers. This was required. It was organized by the councilor of the sector who compiled a list of those who would work. He would go to the families and write down the name of the head of the family and all those boys over eight years old. The councilors and the cell leaders verified who went and who did not....The cell leader did much of the listing of who lived in his cell. It was not random choosing. There was hierarchy and politics involved in the choice of who would work....Also the councilor and the cell leader had to find the place to put up the barrier. Then they had to find the people...and inform them which day they had to go to work.[74]

She then went on to make a distinction between guarding a barrier and actually taking lives: "Going to work at the barrier was obligatory. But killing was by choice. Authorities required people to work at the barrier, but not to kill."[75] Those barriers where guards were disposed to kill easily were known and identified by witnesses as more dangerous than others. A witness recounted that the one at Gatovu was particularly difficult to pass and that a number of people fleeing from killings at Kaduha and Mushubi, some of them already wounded, were slain by machete there. "At the barrier, you showed your identity card and they killed you if you were Tutsi." Another witness stated that a Hutu relative of his was killed at a barrier because his identity card included the notation "I." which was taken by the guards to stand for Inkotanyi and the person was killed.[76]

[72]Human Rights Watch/FIDH interview, Musebeya, August 28, 1995; interview, Butare, June 14, 1995.

[73]Human Rights Watch/FIDH interview, Musebeya, August 28, 1995.

[74]Human Rights Watch/FIDH interview, Musebeya, June 7, 1995.

[75]Human Rights Watch/FIDH interview, Musebeya, June 7, 1995.

[76]Human Rights Watch/FIDH interviews, Musebeya, June 7, 1995; Maraba, June 14, 1995.

"We Must Exterminate Them All!"

Many survivors have testified about the dogged tracking of Tutsi throughout the genocide. A woman of Musebeya related the narrative of her weeks of hiding as if in a trance, the twisting of her long hands and the goose-flesh on her arms the only visible signs of emotion. First attacked on April 9, she was not safe until early July when French troops arrived in Musebeya.

The witness had been born in Karambo commune. A widow with three daughters, she had married a widower with four sons who lived in Musebeya. The family lived in the sector of Rugano, near the border of Karambo on the east and Muko on the north. She learned of the killings in Mushubi parish, Muko, on April 7 and, she says, "The next day, Friday the 8th, I stayed at home. I was waiting to be killed." The attackers reached her home the morning after, April 9, at 10 a.m. As the family ran away, the attackers pillaged everything in the house. Her husband fled with his sons toward Kaduha parish but he was killed on the way "because he ran more slowly than the boys." She fled to a neighbor but was found the next morning. The attackers permitted her to return home because she was a woman and had only daughters with her. Three hours later they came again, demanding money. When she said she had none, they said they would kill her, but they left her under the guard of one of their group while they went after other Tutsi. The guard permitted her and her daughters to escape. She declared:

> I fled, following a small river. The attackers saw us and said, "Ah! Catch that little animal who is fleeing!" As we ran, I knew that we were being pursued. We went toward the bush. I saw a man and asked him, "Are they nearby?" He told me, "They are looking for you in the banana grove. Other people say you have passed there." This man who helped me was named Faustin.[77]
>
> I crossed into Karambo commune where I spent the night at Faustin's house and hid there the next day, all day. Faustin had a brother in the National Police, who is now in Zaire. The leader of the attack told Faustin's brother, "We must find the Inkotanyi who have gone back to their home communes." Faustin hid us, telling his brother that there was nobody there.
>
> On Monday, April 11, a group of about forty people from Musebeya attacked the hill where I was hiding in Karambo. The whole hill from Karambo went to resist the attack at the Rurongora River. The Karambo people asked those coming from Musebeya, "What are you looking for?" The

---

[77]"Faustin" is a pseudonym.

Musebeya people replied, "We are looking for this woman." The Karambo people asked, "Why are you seeking her, did she do something bad?" The Musebeya people said, "Because we killed the others and to complete our work, we must kill her too." Then they began to fight, with the Karambo people saying, "You'll take her after you die in this attack!"

The Musebeya attackers fought for some time and then said, "You are strong. We will go and get the National Police and come back with them tomorrow!" Among the National Policemen was Faustin's brother. Faustin told us, "I've got to move you away from here to save you." He brought us to a small forest. We rested there, hiding. We saw people passing through, coming from pillaging....I told the children, "Do not scream!" They stayed quiet. Later Faustin brought food for the children to the forest. He had to return home fast because he did not want anyone to notice.

While we were hiding in the forest, we saw old women who could not flee together with their grandchildren. They were being killed on the Musebeya side of the river. The old women were wearing *pagnes* [lengths of cloth] and the attackers took them off and killed them all with machetes. I left the forest and went on to sector Rusekera [back in Musebeya.] When I got there, I met some friendly families who took one of my children, and another family took another, and I was left with only the youngest child. I left my children with these families in order to hide. But still attackers were coming to look for us.

Most people in this sector did not participate in the genocide. In fact, when the attackers came, the people chased them away. This occurred every day I was there and I stayed there for some time. The family that hid us sometimes told us that we could go out and stretch ourselves and get some exercise. When I went out occasionally, I could see what was happening on the nearby hills because this was during the day. I could see—and they told me—that attackers were still searching on the nearby hills. People came to the house to give the news that even Tutsi girls who were married to Hutu men were being killed.

The attackers in Musebeya wore banana leaves, especially around their heads like a kind of crown, and carried spears, but the people in Karambo wore banana leaf belts and other leaves tied around their shoulders and chests. They carried wooden clubs studded with nails. I saw National Police who shot at the houses that were made of durable material, because the walls were not so easily broken as walls of mud and packed earth. I saw the houses doused with gasoline to make them burn more easily.

The attackers made lots of noise and blew on whistles. And they shouted, "We must exterminate them all." Even if people were hiding, the attackers could find them in the night and then they blew on whistles to call the rest of the group to come. Sometimes they seemed intoxicated on marijuana.[78] Women came behind the attackers to pillage. They also did a kind of security detail to see who was hiding. For example, they would keep track of who was in a house by the kind of laundry that was put out to dry.

During that time there were also barriers. They stopped everyone at the barriers to see if they were from my family and if they were, they would be killed. Those who were fleeing at night accidentally ran into barriers. When I was leaving the forest, I passed at Gasenyi and saw a fire. The fire showed that there was a barrier. If there had been no fire, I would have walked into the barrier.

In the final week, the family who was hiding me met the burgomaster[79] and he said, "Get out of here! You are hiding Inkotanyi. But on Monday, I'll be coming!"

Fortunately, on Saturday the French came and they took us away to Gikongoro. The family that had hidden me did not go with us to Gikongoro. When the attackers saw the vehicle leaving, they said to that family, "You said you never had any Inyenzi at your place, but now we see that they are leaving in a vehicle for Gikongoro!"[80]

"No Words for Solving the Problem"

Like the burgomaster of Musebeya, some other authorities apparently reacted initially by trying to stop the violence. The burgomaster of Kinyamakara imprisoned those whom he caught pillaging and burning in the first few days.[81] In Kivu commune, the burgomaster set off with communal police, the Judicial Police Inspector and other judicial authorities to halt the burning and theft that began on April 11. They frightened the criminals by shooting in the air and then arrested

---

[78]Marijuana is grown in Musebeya. Habyarimana's government supposedly made efforts to control the illegal trade in the drug, but some of those in power may have actually been involved in the business themselves.

[79]By this time, Ndizihiwe had replaced Higiro. [See below.]

[80]Human Rights Watch/FIDH interview, Maraba, June 14, 1995.

[81]Human Rights Watch/FIDH interview, Butare, August 19, 1995.

three.[82] On April 8, the sub-prefect of Kaduha also began arresting assailants and by April 20 had imprisoned eighty-five persons accused of attacking Tutsi.[83]

Having given at least a semblance of an appropriate response, these administrators looked to the prefect, Bucyibaruta, for guidance and support. The prefect, however, had decided to support the interim government and had dutifully answered the summons to a meeting with his fellows and national authorities in Kigali on April 11. When Bucyibaruta returned to Gikongoro, he gathered together his sub-prefects and burgomasters to review the security situation. According to an administrator who attended, the burgomasters of Gikongoro, like those of Gitarama, received no support in trying to quell the violence. He declared:

> In that meeting, there were no words for solving the problem. They were lost. Some said, "exterminate." Others were afraid. This is why it turned into a catastrophe. They were saying, "We have to stop this," but those who were making decisions did not know what to do.[84]

Another official present at the meeting made a similar assessment:

> There were never any directives. In the meetings of the burgomasters, we were never told what to do. Each burgomaster would just report what was happening in his commune, how many people were killed, where there was violence. And then the meetings would close. We would just make reports, but we were never given any guidance. The burgomasters were just left on their own. [85]

The absence of support for efforts to protect Tutsi was a powerful, though unstated, message. Administrators did not need to be told "kill Tutsi" to understand that this was the approved policy. Bucyibaruta does not seem to have been an enthusiastic supporter of the genocide, but, a loyal bureaucrat, he failed to oppose his superiors and left those who were opposed to the killing without a model and without

---

[82]Human Rights Watch/FIDH interview, Butare, October 19, 1995.

[83]Human Rights Watch/FIDH interview, Butare, October 12, 1995; Kaduha, June 12, 1996.

[84]Human Rights Watch/FIDH interview, Butare, October 12, 1995.

[85]Human Rights Watch/FIDH interview, Gikongoro, June 19, 1996.

protection, making it unlikely that any of them would take risks to stop the slaughter.

Attacking Dissenters

Although the burgomaster of Musebeya had received no encouragement or direction from the April 12 meeting with the prefect, he was still willing to try to halt the killings. In the early afternoon of the next day, April 13, a crowd attacked Tutsi in sector Rugano. En route home, they passed not far from the communal office, screaming and blowing their whistles. Higiro, backed by the Judicial Police Inspector and four National Policemen, went out to confront the assailants. They numbered about 150 people, mostly from Mudasomwa but strengthened by some from Musebeya. Under the command of a former soldier, they were armed with machetes, swords, bows and arrows, and spears. Higiro's police went after the leader and beat him badly. His followers carried him home to Mudosomwa where he died almost immediately. After the struggle, Higiro went back to the office and telephoned the sub-prefect and the prefect, who supposedly listened to his report and "said nothing."[86]

Organizers of the genocide within Musebeya found Higiro was hindering their efforts and they sought to get rid of him. Borrowing a tactic often used in kubohoza to oust unpopular local officials, they wrote to higher authorities, including the president and the minister of defense, complaining about Higiro and asking for his removal. The first letter, dated April 14, the day after Higiro had confronted the killers, declared that the burgomaster had helped Tutsi flee to Butare, referring to the group whom he had helped get as far as Gikongoro several days before. It said that these Tutsi intended to go to Burundi to join up with the RPF so that they could return later to attack Rwanda. Between April 18 and April 24, the group sent other letters, at least one reportedly signed by Celestin Mutabaruka of the CZN project, to the National Police at Gikongoro. They asked for help in getting rid of Higiro whom they accused of being paid by the RPF.[87]

Higiro had often been called an "accomplice" privately in the months before, but it was only during the genocide that opponents dared bring the charge openly against him. One day the councilor Innocent Ngiruwonsanga, a protégé of Ndizihiwe, and others caused a commotion in the market by blowing whistles and shouting that they had seen Inkotanyi at Higiro's house. A crowd gathered and

---

[86]Human Rights Watch/FIDH interviews, Musebeya, August 28, 1995.

[87]Ibid.

went to surround Higiro's house. He called the four National Police from the communal office to come defend him and then permitted his house to be searched. The crowd found nothing. After this incident, his wife begged Higiro to flee Musebeya that night but he refused to do so.[88]

On another occasion, Higiro tried to take some Tutsi past the CZN barrier run by the head of the CDR. He was detained by aggressive guards who demanded to know who were these Inkotanyi. He was able to continue on his way only after long discussion.[89]

In the commune of Kinyamakara, the burgomaster Charles Munyaneza—though a member of the MRND—tried to quell violence against the Tutsi during the early part of April. The son of a Tutsi mother, he was known for his good relations with Tutsi. But, as in Musebeya, local political leaders were ready to act if the burgomaster refused to support the slaughter. After National Policemen passing through the commune had given the signal to start killing Tutsi, a sector leader for MDR-Power reportedly brought together about one hundred assailants who burned and pillaged first in his own sector of Kiyaga, then in other sectors.[90] An official who observed the spread of violence remarked,

> Before this time, there had been killings in Mudasomwa and no one had reacted. There had been killings at Nyamagabe and no one had reacted. Killings were going on in Kivu and Nshili. So it is not surprising that it also started in Kinyamakara....[When it began] the councilors had no power to stop the attacks because they had no guns. They continued to have power only if they cooperated with the attacks. [T]he burgomaster was the only one who could oppose the attacks because he had guns at his disposal.[91]

When the burgomaster did try to stop the killing, he was labeled an "accomplice" of the enemy. A crowd attacked his house where he had hidden Tutsi who had fled from slaughter in the neighboring commune of Nyamagabe. In the assault,

---

[88]Ibid.

[89]Human Rights Watch/FIDH interview, Musebeya, August 28, 1995.

[90]Human Rights Watch/FIDH interview, Butare, August 19, 1995.

[91]Ibid.

Munyaneza and those with him managed to fight off the assailants, killing five in the process.[92]

National Authorities Spur the Slaughter

Just as the interim government and its political and military collaborators decided to extend the genocide to Gitarama and Butare, so they decided to intensify and accelerate it in Gikongoro. To implement this decision, Interim President Sindikubwabo came to Gikongoro in person on April 18 or 19, just before his visit to Butare. He met with the prefect and a few others, certainly including the commander of the National Police in Gikongoro and his second in command. The message he delivered was not broadcast, but everyone could surmise what he had said because his speech in neighboring Butare was transmitted on the national radio. Everyone understood. Dissenters, particularly among local authorities, found themselves increasingly threatened. A burgomaster expressed the isolation and futility that he felt:

> The burgomaster, who is the immediate head of security for the commune, has to report to the sub-prefect and to the police commander. The burgomaster has to submit to the system. The sub-prefect, who was my direct superior, and to whom I reported, did nothing. The police commander of Gikongoro, who is in charge of security, did nothing. Ultimately, the system to which I submitted did nothing to help me.[93]

With the unmistakable signs that those bent on genocide were in control, those who had opposed the killing withdrew into passivity or themselves took on the active role of genocidal leaders.[94]

Kivu: Evading Responsibility

The burgomaster of Kivu, Juvénal Muhitira, reportedly tried to avert a tragedy at the church of Muganza, located in his commune. He chose to do so in a way which offered the least risk to himself, even though it was also the least likely to guarantee protection to Tutsi who had sought refuge in the church.

---

[92]Ibid.

[93]Human Rights Watch/FIDH interview, Butare, October 19, 1995.

[94]Human Rights Watch/FIDH interview, Butare, March 5, 1996.

He began correctly enough by posting four communal policemen at the church where hundreds of Tutsi, many of them women and children, had gathered.[95] Around 10 a.m. on April 12, a crowd of 300 to 400 armed people moved towards the church, some of them from the sectors of Kivu commune near Mudasomwa, others from neighboring Rwamiko commune. When the burgomaster confronted the attackers they demanded that the Tutsi, as the "chief enemy" be chased from the commune.[96] The burgomaster used his authority to calm the crowd and then went to summon the Sub-Prefect Biniga. The sub-prefect came back, talked some with the leaders of the assailants, and told them to disperse for the moment until he had time to talk with the prefect. Biniga did not return or communicate further with the burgomaster until three weeks later when he came back, "singing victory," and boasting about the slaughter of the Tutsi and the MRND victory.[97]

With no word from Biniga and the crisis unresolved, Muhitira decided to take the issue to the prefect. By this time, the commune no longer had a working telephone. Instead of sending a messenger to the prefecture, as was usual, he set off in the communal vehicle, knowing it was in poor repair. He spent the entire day going to and from the prefecture, with no result because the prefect was dealing with another crisis and unable to see him. When he returned home, he learned that the church had been attacked in his absence and that one of the assailants had been killed.[98]

When Muhitira went to the church the next morning, he found that many more Tutsi had streamed in from the communes of Rwamiko, Mubuga, and Nshili as well as from Kivu. He estimated the crowd as numbering 16,000, with no food and, for most, no shelter. The Tutsi themselves supposedly asked him to appeal once more to the prefect both for protection and for food. Rather than send a written appeal, Muhitira set out once more for Gikongoro the next morning, Friday, April 15. He was finally able to see the prefect in the afternoon and was sent on to Major Bizimungu who commanded the police brigade. Presented with the request for National Police, the major responded that since so many of his men had been transferred to the front to fight the RPF, he had none to send to protect the church.

---

[95]Human Rights Watch/FIDH interview, Butare, October 19, 1995.

[96]Ibid. A witness says Muhitira joined in the April 12 attack. African Rights, *Rwanda, Death, Despair*, p. 333.

[97]Ibid.

[98]Ibid.

But he told Muhitira to go ask for help from the police post at Nshili, in the commune next to Kivu, and he gave him a note to the officer in charge there.[99]

Muhitira returned to Kivu that evening, April 15, to learn that the assailants had again attacked the church. They were people from Kivu commune, sectors of Shaba, Cyanyirankora and Kivu, led by former soldiers or National Policemen. The assailants had been driven back by the Tutsi and had then gone to the communal office, where they had overpowered the communal policemen and stolen some guns and ammunition. The attackers returned to attack the church once more. This time they killed twenty-four Tutsi and lost one or more of their own number. According to Muhitira,

> The attackers fought until the bullets were all used. Then they fled....And they left behind a threat for me. "They've got guns," I told myself. I couldn't sleep at my house. I slept outdoors with two policemen. My family left the house also.[100]

The same kinds of political realignments that had weakened the burgomaster of Musebeya were also taking place in Kivu. Muhitira was a member of the MDR which together with the PSD had displaced the MRND as the leading party in the commune. With the new focus on the ethnic issue, with the increasingly angry accusation that the PSD was a party of the Inkotanyi, and with the slaughter of their leaders in Kigali, PSD members felt threatened and quit the party. They rejoined the MRND, leaving Muhitira and his MDR supporters now in the minority. Muhitira had been hearing threats against himself for several days, but he took them more seriously after the assailants captured the communal guns and ammunition.

Muhitira left at daybreak April 16 for the police post at Nshili. To avoid being seen by the assailants, he took a less traveled road through the forest instead of the usual road that passed by the church. At Nshili, the lieutenant in command had gone to Gikongoro and none of his subordinates could help Muhitira. He states:

---

[99]Ibid.

[100]Human Rights Watch/FIDH interview with Juvenal Muhitira, Butare.

There were already twenty-four dead and now there was no help [to be had]. This overwhelmed me. I had planned to get the National Police and then conduct a meeting in the commune. But now I had no National Police.[101]

During the night of April 15 to 16, the vast majority of people at Muganza church fled. They had heard of a horrible massacre the previous day at Kibeho church and anticipated the same fate for themselves if they did not act. When the assailants arrived at the church on the morning of April 16—no doubt at about the same time when the burgomaster was deliberately taking the other road away from the church—they slaughtered those who were left, those too old, weak, or injured to have fled with the others. Fewer people were killed at Muganza than at other churches, probably hundreds rather than thousands of people, but the relatively low death toll was due to Tutsi having taken the initiative of fleeing, not to officials having succeeded in protecting them.[102]

At about 10 in the morning of April 16, Muhitira returned to discover the slaughter at the church and once more took the road to Gikongoro to tell the prefect what had happened. The prefect said he was "sorry." At this point, Muhitira tried to resign, apparently out of concern for his own safety as much as from revulsion against the genocide. In addition to the threats on his life, he had been attacked at a barrier in Rwamiko, where the windshield of his vehicle was broken. The prefect persuaded him to stay on. Muhitira says, "He told me to follow the orders of the military," meaning the National Police.[103] Muhitira then went to the National Police headquarters, where he saw the second in command, presumably Captain Sebuhura, who had with him the lieutenant from the Nshili camp. They promised to assure his security and gave him a National Police guard. Muhitira and the guard returned to the commune, where the National Policemen organized the burial of the bodies.

Eliminating the Tutsi at Musebeya

On April 18, a crowd of some 300 assailants massed outside the Musebeya office, where there were then forty-seven Tutsi taking shelter. The attackers were

---

[101]Ibid.

[102]Ibid.

[103]These are his words, but, as the context makes clear, he is referring to the head of the National Police group in Gikongoro, not to a military headquarters as such. There was no army post in Gikongoro.

mostly local people, armed with spears, machetes, and clubs, but included also some former soldiers armed with grenades.[104]

The burgomaster Higiro reasoned with the crowd until late in the afternoon. Although he had police to back him up, he did not order them to shoot. In the opinion of one witness, even had Higiro done so, his order would have been ignored.[105] At the end of the afternoon, Higiro convinced the assailants to go away and come back the next day. That night he arranged to transport the Tutsi to the parish at Kaduha, near the center of the sub-prefecture. Tutsi from Musebeya and other communes had taken refuge at Kaduha in prior times of trouble and some, anticipating that they would again have security there, had fled to the Kaduha church spontaneously as early as April 9. The commune had no vehicle large enough to transport the Tutsi, so they took up a collection for the money needed to rent a truck. The next morning at 4 a.m., Higiro, along with some policemen, escorted the Tutsi to Kaduha and installed them in one of the classrooms at the parish school with the help of the sub-prefect Joachim Hategekimana and other officials. He then returned to Musebeya.[106] As with the earlier attempt to send Tutsi to safety in Butare, the transport to Kaduha in the end only postponed the slaughter. Higiro may well have anticipated or even known that such would be the result; taking them to Kaduha removed them from the commune but may not have completely ended his responsibility for their fate.

Also on April 18, some seventy Tutsi were taken from the small church at Gatare and were slain on the grounds of the nearby CZN project. The Tutsi had been promised transportation to some safe place, perhaps to Kibuye or to Kaduha. Both Higiro and CZN director Mutabaruka have been accused of having encouraged the Tutsi to leave under the guard of National Policemen. They were taken off in four vehicles, a Mitsubishi that belonged to the sub-prefecture, a minibus belonging to the CNZ project, a Land Rover belonging to the project

---

[104]Human Rights Watch/FIDH interviews, Musebeya, May 5, 1995 and June 8, 1995; Kigali, July 16, 1995.

[105]Human Rights Watch/FIDH interviews, Musebeya, June 8, 1995.

[106]Human Rights Watch/FIDH interviews, Musebeya, May 5, 1995, June 7, 1995, June 8, 1995; Maraba, June 14, 1995; African Rights, *Rwanda, Death, Despair*, pp. 316, 320.

director, and a double-cabin pickup truck belonging to Simba's son Robert.[107] Sergeant Sothere, in command of the National Policemen in Musebeya, came with six of his men in a blood-soaked vehicle to report the deaths at the communal office. He told the brigadier of the communal police to inform the burgomaster that the people from Gatare were dead. A witness reports, "They didn't explain anything. They just told the brigadier, 'Tell the burgomaster that the people from Gatare are dead.'"[108]

The lure of safety at Kaduha was used to get Tutsi to embark willingly on a journey to death in the neighboring commune of Muko as well. The burgomaster loaded the Tutsi men who had been camped at the communal office for about ten days into vehicles, promising to deliver them to the church at the sub-prefectural center. They were all massacred en route. Those who had stayed at the communal office, women and children, were killed some time after.[109]

Massacre at Kaduha

The church at Kaduha sits high on a hill, with a primary school just above and a hospital down to the left. At the time the Human Rights Watch/FIDH team visited the site in February 1995, authorities had recently exhumed hundreds of bodies after rains had washed away the soil from three shallow mass graves near the church. Between 500 and 1,000 bodies lay on two biers, each about ninety feet long. There were other mass graves near the school and twelve more across the road from the church and school. At the time of the visit, classes had recently resumed at the school. Clothing and bones were still strewn about the site. Some school children played next to scattered rib-bones of other small children. The church buildings showed signs of forcible entry and desperate struggle. The kitchen area had been blown apart, probably by a grenade. Some of the doors had been pried open. Bloody finger streaks were on the walls, as were marks of machetes. Windows and walls were pocked with bullet holes.

---

[107]Human Rights Watch/FIDH interviews, Kigali, May 18 and June 4, 1995; Musebeya, June 8, 1995, August 28, 1995. Human Rights Watch/FIDH interview, Gikongoro, June 19, 1996.

[108]Ibid. The National Police posted at Gatare and at Kaduha were reportedly part of a single detachment and rotated men between the two places.

[109]Human Rights Watch/FIDH interviews, Gikongoro, May 23, 1995; June 19, 1996.

Soon after the news arrived of Habyarimana's death, "intellectuals" began spreading the rumor that Tutsi were preparing to kill Hutu. Sub-prefect Joachim Hategekimana called for National Police from Gikongoro on April 7. Three policemen were sent but instead of protecting Tutsi they arrested four that same evening, supposedly for having violated the curfew. They detained them, including two employees of the Projet de Développement Agricole de Gikongoro, for several days and beat them badly before releasing them.[110]

The sub-prefect brought together his administrative subordinates early in the crisis and, like the prefect, directed them just to ensure that information was reported up the chain of command, from the heads of cells to the councilors to the burgomasters to the sub-prefect. According to an administrative official, they "were to follow [each incident], reacting after something happened but not in advance."[111]

The sub-prefect arrested assailants beginning on April 8, when he went to investigate the killings at Mushubi church in Muko.[112] When he came across a group besieging a Tutsi house, he and the police with him gave chase and shot and killed one of the assailants. A week later, on April 15, he and some policemen disarmed a large crowd of people at the Masizi market who were massing to attack Tutsi who had sought refuge at the Musange communal office. According to a witness, the police fired in the air and the crowd dispersed, leaving behind enough spears, machetes, clubs, and other weapons to "nearly fill a room."[113]

But Hategekimana declined to take responsibility for protecting Tutsi at his own office. One witness who arrived at the sub-prefecture at about 6 p.m. on April 9 with a group from Muko explains, "We went there because it was the seat of government power for the region and we thought we would get protection there."[114] The hope may have been all the greater because Kaduha was the home region of the prefect himself and people trusted that he would not allow massacres in his own backyard. The sub-prefect collected the machetes and spears which the Tutsi had

---

[110]Human Rights Watch/FIDH interviews, Butare, August 20, 1995, March 5, 1996, and April 15, 1996; African Rights, *Rwanda, Death, Despair,* p.317.

[111]Human Rights Watch/FIDH interview, Butare, October 12, 1995.

[112]Human Rights Watch/FIDH interview, Kaduha, June 12, 1996.

[113]Human Rights Watch/FIDH interviews, Butare, August 20, 1995, March 5, 1996, and April 15, 1996.

[114]Human Rights Watch/FIDH interview, Kaduha, June 12, 1996.

brought with them and directed them to Kaduha church, saying there was no refuge to be had at his office. At this time, the churches had not yet become slaughterhouses and the Tutsi willingly took shelter there.[115]

As the attacks expanded from one hill to the next and from one commune to another, Tutsi found it impossible to stay in their homes and increasingly difficult to hide with Hutu neighbors. Assailants in Muko, for example, were threatening to make Hutu protectors kill any Tutsi whom they had sheltered.[116] First hundreds, then thousands of people from Musebeya, Muko, Karambo, and Musange communes gathered at Kaduha parish center, in the church itself, in the adjoining schools, in the health center and in all the spaces in between. Tutsi from more distant regions, like parts of Muko, came first. Tutsi in the immediate vicinity of the church moved there only about April 14, when they were threatened with attacks by Hutu from the hills.[117] Many Tutsi had come on their own, but some had come with the help of local officials, like those transported from Musebeya.[118] In Muko, and perhaps elsewhere, the burgomaster had at first refused to help Tutsi flee to Kaduha, but later changed his position and began encouraging them to go there.[119] Some survivors believe that authorities decided at a meeting at the sub-prefecture to attract Tutsi to Kaduha for one enormous massacre rather than to continue killing them in smaller numbers throughout the area. Such a decision would have been consistent with the pattern of killings elsewhere in the country.

Hategekimana installed five National Policemen to protect Tutsi at the church center. For the first week or so, the situation was calm, with Tutsi even going home when necessary to replenish their food supply. According to one witness,

> During all of this time, Hutu and Tutsi in the community remained close together. Hutu neighbors brought food and brought the livestock that their

---

[115]Human Rights Watch/FIDH interviews, Kaduha, February 28, 1995; June 12, 1996.

[116]African Rights, *Rwanda, Death, Despair,* p. 326.

[117]Human Rights Watch/FIDH interview, Kaduha, June 12, 1996.

[118]Human Rights Watch/FIDH interview, Muko, June 5, 1996.

[119]Ibid.

Tutsi neighbors had left behind. Some people went home themselves to get things they had left.[120]

The witness indicates that the situation changed dramatically on April 17, just after the adoption of the more aggressive policy at the national level and the arrival of a new National Police officer, Sergeant-Major Ntamwemezi. She continues,

> But, beginning the 17th, they began to prevent people…from bringing food and the Tutsi could no longer leave the church freely. They were stopped by people who put up barricades. If you decided to go out, if you decided to go home and get some food, they could kill you. Some people who went out were killed.[121]

On April 18, the newly arrived police sergeant-major together with the sub-prefect reportedly forced Tutsi to leave the hospital and go to the church area. A German nun, Sister Melgitta Kösser, who ran the health center was allowed to keep only Tutsi patients who appeared seriously ill.[122]

On April 19, the sub-prefect stopped arresting people for attacking Tutsi. On April 20, an administrative official observed that "all around there were groups who were organizing to come to Kaduha and exterminate the camp [i.e., the Tutsi camped at the church]." He stopped to speak to young people whom he did not recognize in the neighboring commune of Musange. They claimed to be from the area. He reports the exchange:

> I saw that these young people were strangers and wearing military uniforms. But I could not really question this. I could not interfere with the military, but I suspected that they had been sent secretly. I saw that they were not from our region. I sensed that the situation had changed. I asked the head of the National Police, who was from Ruhengeri, but he said, "Don't worry."[123]

---

[120]Human Rights Watch/FIDH interviews, Kaduha, June 12, 1996.

[121]Ibid.

[122]African Rights, *Rwanda, Death, Despair,* p. 320.

[123]Human Rights Watch/FIDH interview, Butare, October 12, 1995.

According to one witness, the sub-prefect himself searched Kaduha church for weapons the same day.[124]

Just before noon on April 20, the crowd raided livestock and other property of the people at the church. The Tutsi turned back the assailants with no loss of life. The National Police guarding the church were said to have persuaded the raiders to give up, perhaps because they realized the force was too small to overcome the Tutsi. Some witnesses say that the National Police advised the attackers to "go search for others and then return."[125]

That day, the parish priest, a Burundian named Father Robert Nyandwi, sought out a Tutsi teacher at the parish elementary school who was hiding at her home. The teacher lived near a bar that was known to be a gathering place for the CDR. The priest told her that the attack would be launched from there. He reportedly insisted, "I'll take you to the CND," an ironic reference to the Conseil National de Développement, the national parliament building which was serving as RPF headquarters in Kigali. The teacher relates:

> He grabbed me by the arm and...dragged me out into the street and we started to go on foot to the church. But when we got to the path, I saw there was a huge crowd of people wearing banana leaves and carrying machetes. I broke free from him and ran. I went to hide in the home of a friend. He [Father Nyandwi] wanted to turn me over to the crowd that was preparing to attack the church.[126]

The final attack began before dawn on April 21 when assailants threw grenades into the house where a number of Tutsi men had sought refuge, including those first arrested and beaten on April 7. When morning broke, a crowd of thousands from Musebeya, Muko and other communes attacked, supported by National Police, soldiers in civilian dress, and former soldiers. After several hours of shooting and throwing grenades, the assailants paused temporarily while awaiting new supplies of ammunition. During that period, they continued killing by machete, spear, club, and other weapons. A witness who was in hiding nearby recounts,

---

[124]Human Rights Watch/FIDH interview, Kaduha, February 28, 1995.

[125]Ibid.

[126]Human Rights Watch/FIDH interview, Kaduha, June 12, 1996.

I could hear gunfire and the explosion of grenades and the cries of people being killed. The attackers fired their guns and threw grenades into the crowd and then groups of killers with traditional weapons came in and killed those who were still alive. This began early in the morning on the 21st and it continued all day Thursday and all day Friday. On Friday, they mostly searched for people who were hiding.[127]

Another witness, present in the church, said that the grenade explosion served as a signal for the attack. He states:

The National Police who were supposed to protect us were lodged in the agricultural school. When we awoke and found we were surrounded, we tried to defend ourselves. We were more than they and so we were able to force them back by throwing rocks. But the National Police came to reinforce them....They began to organize the crowd. They fired their guns and threw grenades.[128]

This witness fled in a large group—he estimates it as about 1,000—at about 11 a.m., heading to the southeast. Another group also broke out of the encirclement and fled to the northeast. Each group encountered military and civilian assailants waiting along the roads for them. A new radio antenna had been installed in Kaduha shortly before and it may have made it easier for the police to inform their troops about the movements of the refugees. When the military encountered the fleeing Tutsi, they ordered them to sit down and then began firing on them and throwing grenades into their midst.[129]

The same day, assailants in Kaduha killed Oscar Gasana, the assistant prosecutor, his Tutsi wife and several of their children. Gasana was a moderate Hutu who had refused to cooperate in anti-Tutsi measures before the genocide began. He was one of those who could have mobilized resistance to the genocide

---

[127]Ibid.

[128]Human Rights Watch/FIDH interview, Kaduha, June 12, 1996.

[129]Ibid.

in Kaduha. The bodies of Gasana and his wife were left naked on the street for some days, a mute reminder of the consequences of resisting.[130]

Simba was in Kaduha the day before the major attack in the company of militia leaders and, according to one witness, he arrived with a detachment of military from Gikongoro to launch the first attack with firearms on the church.[131] National Police officers, led by Sergeant-Major Ntamwemezi, former soldiers and local soldiers in active service directed the attacks at Kaduha. A witness remarked on the role played by local soldiers and National Police who had returned home the week before from active duty elsewhere. He declared, "At the church I saw only National Police in uniform. These other soldiers and National Police....were camouflaged in civilian clothing, but they still had guns. I saw them myself."[132] Military also led the ambushes of groups in flight and directed the search for and execution of individual survivors. Militia, including groups brought from outside the region, such as the group sighted in Musange on April 20, backed up the professional military. Secondary school students from the north, temporarily housed at Kaduha, and staff of the health center also joined in the slaughter. One witness relates that the sergeant-major gave a prize of 30,000 Rwandan francs (about U.S.$170) to a student who had been the best killer and that Father Nyandwi rewarded him with a "radio cassette."[133] Here, as elsewhere, "intellectuals," like teachers, school inspectors, and traders with access to vehicles, provided important support with logistics and organization.[134]

---

[130]Human Rights Watch/FIDH interview, Kaduha, June 12, 1996; African Rights, *Rwanda, Death, Despair,* p. 323.

[131]From the context, it is clear that the witness is referring to the first day of the attack, which was actually April 21. Human Rights Watch/FIDH interviews, Kaduha, February 28, 1995, June 12, 1996.

[132]Human Rights Watch/FIDH interviews, Kaduha, June 12, 1996; Kigali, June 4, 1996; African Rights, *Rwanda, Death, Despair,* p. 317. The International Commission that investigated the 1993 violence in Burundi noted the unusually high number of soldiers home on leave at the time of killings in their communities. Commission Internationale d'enquête sur les violations des droits de l'homme au Burundi depuis le 21 octobre 1993, "Rapport Final," July 5, 1994, p. 33.

[133]African Rights, *Rwanda, Death, Despair,* pp. 322-23.

[134]Human Rights Watch/FIDH interview, Kaduha, June 12, 1996; African Rights, *Rwanda, Death, Despair,* pp. 321-22.

The great mass of assailants was made up of ordinary people from the surrounding communes, particularly Musebeya and Muko, as well as from Kaduha itself. One witness estimates that some 400 people came from Musebeya to kill and pillage. Many of them were transported to the first attack by vehicle, but in subsequent days they went on foot. The same persons who apparently organized the extermination of Tutsi in their home commune gathered together the assailants to kill at Kaduha. The day after the first attack, the organizers could be recognized by the new clothes that they were wearing, pillaged from the vicitims. According to one witness, they included communal councilors, party leaders like the local head of the CDR, and other "intellectuals" and traders. A witness from Musebeya states:

> This group had motorcycles, and they went around from sector to sector to organize people to go to Kaduha. The people would come back at night, every night, and meet at Bar Mugema. They would buy drinks for everyone who helped them. Other people were told that if they joined in, they could get drinks bought for them as well. They said, "You can get free beer. Come with us tomorrow and then you can join us at the bar." Every evening there was a meeting there at the bar to expand their group.[135]

Two witnesses place the sub-prefect Hategekimana at the church during the attack while other testimonies do not mention his presence.[136] He asserts that he was at home at the time. He states that he heard the grenade explosions from his house:

> It was in the night, at about 3 o'clock. I was not there. I stayed home, thinking, "This is the end of me." The shooting went on until 2 p.m....When it stopped, a neighbor who was a methodist pastor came to my house and told me, "They have attacked the camp." I told him, "Go home." There were barriers all over the place. At 5 p.m., I did not hear any more shots. I started talking to the neighbors. At 6 p.m., I went and I saw the carnage. I saw that the National Police had participated also. I asked what they had hoped to accomplish...[but]they did not have to explain [to me].

---

[135]Human Rights Watch/FIDH interview, Gikongoro, June 19, 1996.

[136]Human Rights Watch/FIDH interview, Kaduha, February 28, 1995.

I asked myself, "Where will I go?" But there were barriers everywhere. Where could I go with my children. And do what?[137]

Hategekimana knew the attack on Kaduha was being prepared, but did nothing to stop it, apparently because he was afraid of the military. When it was over, he reported the massacre to the prefect.[138] Right after the massacre, "higher authorities" released the eighty-five persons whom Hategekimana had arrested at Kaduha during the previous two weeks and drove off in their car without further explanation. Hategekimana made no further arrests.[139]

One woman who survived the slaughter saw the National Police come back to the church on April 23 to organize burying the dead. They set about killing the survivors whom they found there. They hit the witness with a hammer and threw her into a pit. She managed to scramble out, but they caught her and threw her in again. She escaped once more and ran into the bush, where she hid for nine days. Then she was able to creep back to the residence of the nuns where she took shelter until the French arrived.[140]

The slaughter in Kaduha reinforced the message delivered by Sindikubwabo a few days before. Civilian officials understood and "took orders from the military" as the prefect had told the burgomaster of Kivu to do. In Kinyamakara, the burgomaster who at first tried responsibly to suppress the violence apparently became a leader of the slaughter after April 20. He released from the Kinyamakara jail Hutu who had been detained for their attacks on Tutsi and he supposedly mobilized the Hutu of his commune for attacks across the prefectural border into the hitherto peaceful commune of Ruhashya in Butare. "The violence came especially from the military authorities and no one could stop them," was the assessment of one official.[141]

Higiro, the burgomaster, gave up public resistance in Musebeya after the Kaduha massacre. Although well aware of the steady erosion of his support within the commune, Higiro had had no sign of official disapproval from his superiors

[137]Human Rights Watch/FIDH interview, Butare.

[138]Human Rights Watch/FIDH interview, Butare, July 19, 1996.

[139]Human Rights Watch/FIDH interview, Butare, October 12, 1995.

[140]Human Rights Watch/FIDH interview, Kaduha, February 28, 1995.

[141]Human Rights Watch/FIDH interview, Butare, August 19, 1995.

before Sindikubwabo's visit. But, after that, when he went to Gikongoro town to attend a meeting mentioned to him by the burgomaster of Muko, he found that he was excluded from certain administrative gatherings. The sub-prefect for political and administrative affairs, Celestin Mushenguzi reportedly confronted him in the hall of the prefecture and asked why he had come when he had not been invited. Shut out by the hard-liners, Higiro went home. He states:

> I went home in fear. At any time, they could set up a barrier for me and it would be finished. I had no means of escape. They kept me like a mouse inside a house. I was running around looking for hole in order to escape.[142]

Major Habyarabatuma had also been sent from his post in Butare to the front shortly before, leaving Higiro without a powerful military protector. The burgomaster reports that he hid with friendly families, not daring to stay in his own home. When he felt the need to show up at the communal office, he sent someone ahead to scout out the situation before going himself.[143]

Tightening Control

By the end of April, assailants had slain Tutsi in one attack after another in churches, schools, health centers, and communal offices. According to one administrative official, by this time "just about all the camps had been exterminated."[144] In smaller incidents out on the hills, assailants had killed large numbers of Tutsi either in the initial attacks or as they fled the sites of massacres. As one witness remarked, "Those Tutsi not killed the first day were pursued everywhere until they were finally slaughtered."[145]

"Pacification" in Gikongoro

On April 26th, Prefect Bucyibaruta assembled the sub-prefects and the burgomasters to carry out orders from Kalimanzira of the Ministry of the Interior to tighten control over the killing campaign. Three days later, he issued a long and complex message to the population, summarizing the meeting. He insisted that

[142]Human Rights Watch/FIDH interview, Musebeya.

[143]Human Rights Watch/FIDH interview, Musebeya.

[144]Human Rights Watch/FIDH interview, Butare, March 5, 1995.

[145]Human Rights Watch/FIDH interview, Butare, August 19, 1995.

reckless killing must be halted and remarked with concern, "The troubles are beginning to take on other dimensions [by which he apparently means other than killing Tutsi]: we see that people are being attacked for their property or are betrayed and killed out of hatred." Later in the text, he elaborated on the different conflicts that were turning people against one another: quarrels over pillaged goods, disputes over land, harvests or other property left by Tutsi, and the desire to settle old scores, all of which caused divisions that could facilitate the advance of the enemy.

The prefect also explained that the disorder in Rwanda had caused foreigners to stop aiding the country. He warned, "As long as we are unable to rapidly stop these troubles, the enemy will profit from this and the international aid that was destined for our country may be delivered to the enemy instead of to us." He bemoaned the damage and losses to schools, hospitals, and other public facilities in the course of the attacks and the paralysis of international and domestic trade that had resulted from the massive disorder. In great detail he depicted the consequences of the violence on the lives of all in the prefecture: the loss of educational opportunity for children, the difficulty of getting medical care, even the impossibility of getting prescriptions filled with pharmacies closed. He cautioned that involving children in violence now could result in harm to their parents in the future and he called for repentance and returning to God in shunning all evil acts.

After this grim preamble, the prefect announced a series of measures that would replace the looser conglomerate of killers with a more tightly controlled force through the self-defense program. He indicated that burgomasters had been directed to recruit people from each sector who would be given arms and proper training on how to use them. He called for the security committees to meet at the sectoral level to establish barriers and patrols to "discover the enemy who often infiltrates using different disguises." He then prohibited "massacres, pillage, and other acts of violence of whatever kind" because the enemy could use such acts to blacken the reputation of Rwanda in the international community, causing the loss of much needed aid. He also directed the security committees to "publicly disavow" those who attacked others and he ordered officials to use force, if necessary, to eliminate groups of assailants. He insisted that people taken at barriers or during patrols be turned over to authorities instead of being dealt with by their captors. He also declared that any military materials, such as grenades, guns, uniforms and so on, must be turned in to the authorities before the next week. Persons found with such materials in their possession after that time would be considered "killer[s] or troublemaker[s]...who will be prosecuted according to the law without mercy."

To avoid further conflict over property, the prefect ordered that land and other goods left by Tutsi would be administered by the communal authorities, who should begin to inventory such property immediately.

Bucyibaruta directed burgomasters to read his message to meetings of the population in their communes, for which he prepared a schedule. He delegated a prefectural official to be present at each meeting along with the burgomaster. Bucyibaruta informed the burgomasters that they were free to add their own ideas if they found something missing in his words, but they were to do so only after having read his message. Perhaps the presence of the prefectural officials was meant to ensure that this order be obeyed.[146]

Bucyibaruta himself took the liberty of adding to the message transmitted to him by the Ministry of the Interior. His text stretches to seven pages, while the original directive is less than a page long. Rather than merely mouthing the usual appeals for order, he crafted what appears to be a real and well-argued plea for ending the violence, stressing, of course, its unfortunate consequences for the population in general rather than the loss of lives among the Tutsi.[147]

The "pacification" meetings took place and the message was delivered, but the killing did not stop. Indeed, in many cases, the message simply presaged new slaughter as Tutsi were lured out of hiding. In the commune of Kinyamakara, the burgomaster held the meeting to announce the reestablishment of order, as directed, on April 29. Taking the directive to be genuine, an official brought his young brother-in-law to the meeting. He had been protecting the Tutsi at his house, which had been attacked twice. Anti-Tutsi leaders like the MDR-Power sector leader who had launched the first attacks in the commune (see above) and the head of the MRND youth wing wanted to attack both the official and his Tutsi relative immediately. A witness declared:

> At the meeting, some asked, "Is it time to stop the killing while there are still Tutsi alive?" They had no shame asking that, even in public. It was the time

---

[146]Laurent Bucyibaruta, Prefe, to Bwana Suprefe, Kaduha, Karaba, Munini; Bwana Umuyobozi w'imirimo uri mu kanama k'umutekano, Bwana Burugumestri wa komini (bose), no. 125/04.17.02, April 27, 1994 (Gikongoro prefecture).

[147]Laurent Bucyibaruta, Ubutumwa bwa Prefe wa Prefegitura ya Gikongoro Bwo Kugarura Umutekano Kuri Prefegitura, April 29, 1994 (Gikongoro prefecture).

to kill. They did not even see that it was a human being that they were busy killing.[148]

In this case, the burgomaster protected the threatened persons, announcing that anyone who killed them would himself be pursued. But, after the meeting and its declaration of renewed security, says one witness, "authorities continued to meet with the leaders of the band to plan and direct searches for the [other] remaining Tutsi."[149] In many cases, Tutsi who emerged after the proclamation of the "peace" were immediately killed. The regularity with which the slaughter followed the statement of reassurance makes clear that the promise of safety was not a sincere guarantee which authorities were simply unable to enforce but rather a deliberate tactic to carry forward the genocide.

"Civilian Self-Defense" in Gikongoro
As is clear from the prefect's message of April 29, burgomasters had already been charged at this time with recruiting young men for the self-defense units, which were to be organized by sector. But it was only on May 18 that the prefect notified burgomasters of Col. Simba's appointment as "Civil Defense Counsellor" for the prefectures of Gikongoro and Butare, an arrangement which replicated the formal military structure with its commander responsible for both prefectures.

Sometimes people who had played little or no role in the genocide joined the self-defense program, but often it was the very same persons who led the killings at the start who later directed the self-defense recruitment.[150] In Musebeya, the group who gathered regularly at Mugema's bar are said to have organized the self-defense group, which took the name "The Nyungwe Battalion." Those who were intended to do the fighting, however, were younger men who were trained by former soldiers and communal police as well as by Interahamwe militia who arrived from outside the region.[151] Simba was in charge of distributing the guns which were then handed out, usually by the burgomasters in each commune.[152]

---

[148]Human Rights Watch/FIDH interview, Butare, August 19, 1995.

[149]Ibid.

[150]Ibid.

[151]Human Rights Watch/FIDH interview, Gikongoro, June 19, 1996.

[152]Human Rights Watch/FIDH interview, Butare, August 19, 1995.

Simba eventually led some of these units, such as those from the communes of Kinyamakara, Rukondo, and Karama in attacking RPF troops near the town of Nyabisindu in Butare prefecture. The attack occurred at night and cost many, perhaps hundreds of lives, among the self-defense units. Poorly trained and inexperienced in handling their weapons, they were no match for the battle-hardened RPF troops. After this one experience, the self-defense units from Gikongoro apparently did not go to combat again.

The stated objectives of self-defense included not just fighting against the RPF but also "obtaining information about the actions or presence of the enemy in the commune, the cell or the neighborhood" and "denouncing infiltrators and accomplices of the enemy."[153] As the self-defense units were trained, they began to replace the less skilled and less structured groups on the barriers and in the patrols. According to one official, there were two kinds of barriers: "barriers against the war and barriers against an ethnic group, and these [i.e., the latter] were far away from the war."[154]

Authorities put increasing importance on catching Tutsi at the barriers in May and June when many tried to flee, hidden in the tens of thousands of displaced persons who streamed into Gikongoro from the north and east, often en route for Cyangugu and eventually Zaire. They hoped that the self-defense units, commanded by people with military training, could be kept focused on eliminating the remaining Tutsi instead of drifting off into attacks for profit or for reasons of private vendetta against other Hutu. The importance of tightening control over the violence was underlined in mid-May when a group of Hutu killed Charles Nyilidandi, the Hutu burgomaster of Mubuga commune, apparently when he was trying to stop them from pillaging the property of a local development project.[155]

With the self-defense units being set up, ordinary citizens were in part relieved of the burden of killing and were supposed to return to "normality." In accord with orders from the Ministry of the Interior, the prefect and his subordinates had

---

[153]Kambanda, "Directive du Premier Ministre aux Préfets pour l'Organisation de l'Auto-Défense Civile."

[154]Human Rights Watch/FIDH interview, Butare, October 12, 1995.

[155]Laurent Bucyibaruta, Préfet, to Monsieur Hategekimana Jean, Conseiller, Nyarushishi, no. 1365/04.01.01, May 17, 1994; Laurent Bucyibaruta, Préfet, to Monsieur le Ministre de l'Intérieur et du Développement Communal, No. 136/04.17.02, May 18, 1994 (Gikongoro prefecture); Human Rights Watch/FIDH interview, Kigali, July 16, 1994.

directed everyone to return to work on May 2.[156] In early May they pressed hard to have schools reopened, which was done several weeks later. But beneath the veneer of normality, the killing continued. The massacres were finished, but individuals remained to be tracked down. In a new burst of activity in mid-May assailants intensified their searches, combing the bush and the fields of sorghum for survivors. At this time, they slaughtered many Tutsi women, including wives of Hutu, spared in most communities until then.[157] Hutu husbands in Musebeya, for example, had been able to buy the safety of their Tutsi wives, to defend them by force, or to hide them successfully until May 16. On that date, many of these women were killed.[158]

Removing the Burgomaster of Musebeya

Under attack by local rivals, outweighed by the power of Simba, and unsupported by his superiors, Higiro had little authority to command the attention of local residents.[159] His power slipped further when the four National Policemen who had been supporting him were recalled to the prefecture. His opponents then came around threatening him, "singing outside my office, that they were in control, that I was an Inyenzi accomplice. When I went to have a drink, they would announce as I went by in the bar, 'There goes the Inyenzi.'"[160] Higiro's growing alienation from many local people came to a head over his failure to stop a group of pillagers who attacked the sector of Bushigishigi to raid cattle from wealthy Hutu. Higiro claimed he had not intervened because he had feared an ambush, but other accused him of having been in league with the pillagers.[161]

Higiro was removed as burgomaster following a meeting of prefects with higher members of the government at Gitarama on May 28, 1994. The sub-prefect of Kaduha, Hategekimana, informed Higiro of the decision immediately, but it was

---

[156]Laurent Bucyibaruta, Préfet, to Monsieur le chef de service (tous) et Monsieur le Bourgmestre (tous), no. 127/04.01.01., May 2, 1994 (Gikongoro prefecture).

[157]Human Rights Watch/FIDH interview, Maraba, June 14, 1995.

[158]Human Rights Watch/FIDH interview, Musebeya, April 11, 1995.

[159]Human Rights Watch/FIDH interview, Musebeya, May 5, 1995.

[160]Human Rights Watch/FIDH interview, Musebeya, August 28, 1995.

[161]Ibid.

not announced until June 17. According to an official, Higiro was removed because "he was not dynamic, was leaning towards the RPF and was running a business in pillaged materials."[162] A Tutsi survivor from Musebeya had another assessment:

> People said, "Give us a burgomaster who thinks as we do." So they overthrew Higiro and they put in Ndizihiwe who was the chief of the attackers and the barriers. The family who was hiding me met Ndizihiwe Jean-Chrysostome at the market. Ndizihiwe was there saying, "Who favors Inkotanyi?" When he saw them, he confronted the family who was hiding me. He confronted them and intimidated them, saying, "It is thanks to Higiro that you are hiding Inkotanyi. You are doing this because he favors you. I will kill you all!"[163]

The sub-prefect Hategekimana arranged a semblance of consultation with the population and installed Ndizihiwe as burgomaster.[164] The decision only confirmed officially the suffocation of opposition to the genocide that had happened over a period of weeks.

Symbolic of the change was the reaction of the new burgomaster to a call for help from a wealthy Hutu trader with a Tutsi wife. His home was attacked six times during the genocide. The first time, when assailants sought to kill Tutsi whom he had been sheltering, he had called for and received help from Higiro who had come with National Policemen to drive away the assailants. When assailants had returned on four subsequent occasions demanding his wife, the Hutu had bought them off or fought them off with the help of neighbors. When a crowd approximately one hundred strong appeared on July 2, anxious to kill one of the few Tutsi left in the community, the Hutu hurried to the commune for help. This time, the burgomaster was Ndizihiwe and there were no more National Police in Musebeya resisting the genocide. Ndizihiwe refused to help. When the husband returned home, he found his wife and her mother had been captured by the crowd. Fortunately, his neighbors had followed the attackers and persuaded them to relinquish the women.[165]

---

[162]Human Rights Watch/FIDH interview, Butare, August 18, 1995.

[163]Human Rights Watch/FIDH interview, Maraba, June 14, 1995.

[164]Human Rights Watch/FIDH interviews, Butare, May 17, 1995; Musebeya, August 28, 1995.

[165]Human Rights Watch/FIDH interviews, Musebeya, June 1 and June 8, 1995.

By early July, there were no more authorities to provide protection to Tutsi in Gikongoro. The prefect, able to craft a convincing appeal for an end to violence, never tried to back his words with action. The sub-prefect, who had found that the military owed him no explanation, had shut his door on preparations for a massacre. Muhitira of Kivu had given up public opposition and was "following the orders of the military" and Munyaneza of Kinyamakara was organizing attacks into the prefecture of Butare. Higiro of Musebeya, who had stood up to crowds of assailants on several occasions, had lapsed into inaction and had finally been replaced by Ndizihiwe.

The only ones left to protect the Tutsi were ordinary people, without authority but with a sense of common humanity.

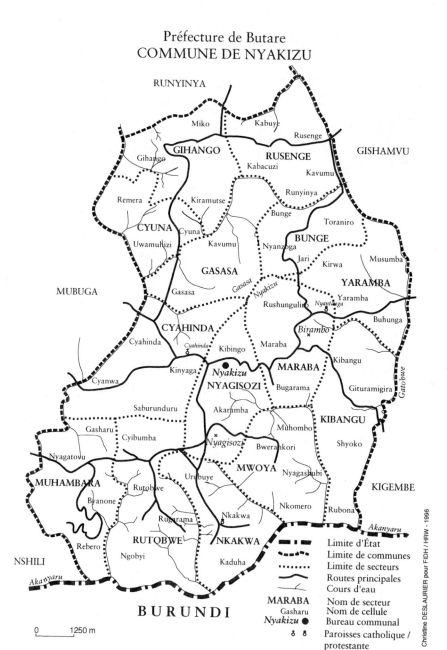

Préfecture de Butare
COMMUNE DE NYAKIZU

RUNYINYA

Miko   Kabuye
        Rusenge   GISHAMVU
GIHANGO   RUSENGE
Gihango   Kabacuzi
                           Kavumu
Remera   Kiramutse   Runyinya
                Bunge
CYUNA   Cyuna   Toraniro
Uwamulizi   Kavumu   Nyanzoga   BUNGE
                                        Musumba
GASASA   Jari   Kirwa
                                          YARAMBA
MUBUGA   Gasasa   Gasasa   Nyakizu   Yaramba
                    Rushunguliro Nyantanga   Buhunga
CYAHINDA   Birambo
Cyahinda   Cyahinda   Kibingo   Maraba
                                      Kibangu
Cyanwa   Kinyaga   Nyakizu   MARABA
                NYAGISOZI   Bugarama   Gituramigira
        Saburunduru   Akaramba   KIBANGU
Gasharu   Cyibumba   Muhombo   Shyoko
Nyagatovu   Nyagisozi   Bwerankori
                          MWOYA   Nyagashubi   KIGEMBE
MUHAMBARA   Rutobwe   Urubuye
Byanone   Nkomero   Rubona
              Rugarama   Nkakwa   Akanyaru
        Rebero
NSHILI   RUTOBWE   NKAKWA
        Ngobyi   Kaduha   Limite d'État
Akanyaru   Limite de communes
                            Limite de secteurs
                            Routes principales
0   1250 m   Cours d'eau
                  MARABA   Nom de secteur
                  Gasharu   Nom de cellule
B U R U N D I   Nyakizu ● Bureau communal
                  ♂ ♀   Paroisses catholique /
                            protestante

Christine DESLAURIER pour FIDH / HRW - 1996

NYAKIZU:
THE MASSACRES

In the early days of the genocide, Tutsi saw the prefecture of Butare in southern Rwanda as the ultimate haven. For nearly two weeks, it held out the hope of safety, largely because the prefect, backed by the local police commander, insisted on protecting Tutsi. Following his model and covered by his authority, most of his subordinates offered protection too. The burgomaster of Nyakizu was one who did not: he launched the first killing campaign in Butare directly in opposition to the prefect's efforts to keep order. Already experienced in using force to build his political base, he imitated leaders at the national level in exploiting ethnic bonds to tighten his hold on power. With the assistance of supporters loyal to him personally and to MDR-Power, he murdered opponents of the genocide and intimidated other dissenters into silence. He led National Police, soldiers, and the people of Nyakizu and adjacent communes in massacring Tutsi at the Cyahinda church, on hilltops where they had taken refuge, and along the paths as they tried to flee.

Butare: The Prefect and the Prefecture

Hutu from the northern part of Rwanda sometimes used to say there are no Hutu in Butare, meaning that the Hutu population there was so fully integrated with the Tutsi that it had lost any distinctively Hutu characteristics. With a population more than 17 percent Tutsi, Butare was the prefecture with the highest concentration of Tutsi and it was reputedly the part of Rwanda where Hutu and Tutsi had intermarried most often. The old royal capital of Nyanza, in the northwestern corner of the prefecture, had been renamed Nyabisindu to purge it of its association with the past, but it remained nonetheless a historical symbol unifying Hutu and Tutsi of the region. The town of Butare, long second only to Kigali in size and importance, had been eclipsed in the 1980s by the northwestern town of Ruhengeri, but it remained very much the focus of interest and activity for Butare prefecture. It was above all a university town, home to the National University of Rwanda which was established after independence, and to a number of other institutions of higher education, including the Groupe Scolaire, the first high school in Rwanda. As intellectual center of the nation and focus of a region where Hutu and Tutsi long lived together, Butare had a reputation for tolerance and moderation. In the Habyarimana years, a branch of the university had been opened in Ruhengeri and an important number of northerners had been awarded posts in faculty and administration on the Butare campus. With its predominance challenged by the Ruhengeri campus and the character of its faculty changed, the

Butare campus was no longer the model of moderation it had once been, but the ideal of respect for the individual once associated with it continued to figure in the image of the prefecture as a whole.

The prefect, Jean-Baptiste Habyalimana, was the exemplar of the openness and rationality for which Butare was known. The only Tutsi prefect in the country, he was also the only member of the relatively small Liberal Party to direct a prefecture. He was exceptional, too, in having been able to pursue higher studies abroad and he had received a PhD in engineering from an American university. A slender, bespectacled figure, he looked very much like the intellectual that he was. While he was in the U.S., several friends had counseled him to claim political asylum rather than return to Rwanda where Tutsi suffered such discrimination. But he had great faith in his fellow Rwandans and a strong sense of the need to bring home the skills that he had acquired abroad. He returned in 1990 to teach at the university and was almost immediately swept up in the October arrests. Later released, he returned to teaching, which he reluctantly gave up in July 1992 when he agreed to accept the post of prefect. Soon after, he told a Human Rights Watch researcher that the nomination proved the correctness of his decision to return home: now he had the opportunity to play a leading role in enhancing democracy and respect for human rights.[1]

Nyakizu Commune

In many respects, Nyakizu was much like other communes in Butare, desperately poor and densely populated. It was located in the southwestern corner of the prefecture, on the border with Burundi. According to the March 1994 figures, the population was 61,366 with a density of 451 persons per square kilometer, far more than the land could productively support within the constraints of the technology available.[2] Because farmers were forced to keep their fields in almost constant cultivation, the fertility of the soil was declining. In the western part of the commune, where the hills were higher and the slopes sharper, erosion was a serious problem. More people lived in the eastern part of the commune where the hills were lower and broader, both easier to cultivate and less eroded. In addition to food staples like beans or sorghum, some farmers raised a small amount

---

[1]Human Rights Watch/Africa interview with Jean-Baptiste Habyalimana, Butare, July 11, 1992.

[2]Commune Nyakizu, Raporo y'ibarura ry'abaturage ukwezi kwa gashyantare 1994 (Nyakizu commune).

of coffee to sell for cash to buy such necessities as soap or, if they were wealthy enough, to pay the costs of sending children to school.

The commune itself was the main source of salaried work, with some sixty employees, followed by the Catholic and Baptist churches with their associated schools and health centers. A small number of traders, profiting largely from commerce across the frontier to Burundi, rose far enough above the usual level of poverty to own vehicles and solid homes.[3] Although those with paid employment earned usually less than a hundred dollars a month, the approximate salary of the burgomaster, they lived a far more comfortable life than did ordinary farmers.[4] In addition, they often had cash available to acquire land when their poorer neighbors were in need and forced to sell or rent their fields. The salaried elite thus built up larger holdings of land which the land-poor or landless then cultivated in order to earn a living. The elite were also able to pay for at least some of their children to leave the commune to attend secondary school, making it far more likely that they would have well-paying jobs in the future.

More than 18 percent of the population of Nyakizu was Tutsi in early 1994, just above the percentage for the prefecture as whole and considerably above the national level, which official statistics placed at some 8 percent.[5] Extremists would argue that the large number of Tutsi in the commune increased the likelihood of RPF infiltration and even of actual attack across the nearby border from Burundi. The RPF's Radio Muhabura also reportedly talked of strong RPF support in the commune which added weight to these charges.

Burgomaster Ntaganzwa: Victory Through Kubohoza

Like the prefect of Butare, the burgomaster of Nyakizu, Ladislas Ntaganzwa, was relatively new to politics. Trained as a medical assistant, he was working at the Cyahinda health center in Nyakizu, his home commune, when multiple political parties were authorized in 1991. He was strong and athletic, proud of the karate that

---

[3]Five entrepreneurs operated small carpentry workshops that provided salaried jobs to a total of about one hundred workers. Human Rights Watch/FIDH interview, Butare, August 19, 1995.

[4]Prefecture de Butare, Liste du Personnel Communal au 30 juin 1993, Commune Nyakizu.

[5]Commune Nyakizu, Raporo y'ibarura ry'abaturage ukwezi kwa gashyantare 1994. Calculation based on a total population of 61,366, including 5,527 Tutsi men and 5,786 Tutsi women.

he had mastered at secondary school. Respected for his competence in medicine and generally liked by people of the commune, he had become head of the local branch of the MDR. He organized a vigorous youth wing, the Jeunesse Démocrate Républiciane (JDR), and with its help used kubohoza to destroy the MRND. A communal councilor related:

> In kubohoza, what they were doing was forcing people out of the MRND and into MDR. To give you examples of people who were treated this way, there was Ndekezi Thadée who was a victim of kubohoza. He was beaten, but afterward, he agreed to join the other party....And there was Mutagano Innocent who did not agree to change parties and was injured.[6]

Another person who lived through the experience described it this way:

> The MDR came to knock on the door. You had to come out. "Go to your room and bring out your MRND card." And then they could beat you or force their way into your house. You would bring your card, and...there were these poles on which they placed the card after stabbing a hole in it. They did the same thing to your MRND hat, impaled it and displayed it on a pole. The card represented the person who was the target of kubohoza. After being the target of kubohoza, the person was now visibly MDR.

> They also beat up people, although they did not do this to women. But they beat up respected older men, including my father. They brought you with the group and herded you to a public place like the market, as if you were a goat. They herded you with the others who were also being targeted by kubohoza, the people who were called *abahoza*. The JDR chanted and sang, "We've done well! Our party has won!" They did this openly during the day. They passed from house to house, gathering the group of people to be targeted. They herded everyone together, with the JDR singing and they beat those who resisted.[7]

The enforcers of kubohoza even made written reports of their campaigns, in which they noted the names and places of residence of the persons "liberated"

---

[6]Human Rights Watch/FIDH interview, Cyahinda church, Nyakizu, June 26, 1995.

[7]Human Rights Watch/FIDH interview, Maraba, Nyakizu, May 3, 1995.

along with remarks about whether cards or hats were taken at the time of the "visit." They extorted payments from the victims in order to guarantee that the party president, Ntaganzwa, look favorably on the requests for admission to the MDR. Should Ntaganzwa not accept the requests, the unfortunates would continue to be harassed until their next opportunity to "apply" for admission.[8]

By the middle of 1992, Ntaganzwa was feeling strong enough to turn kubohoza against the burgomaster himself, Jean-Baptiste Gasana, a member of the MRND. According to people in the commune, supporters of Ntaganzwa came to Gasana's home with trucks full of machetes and other weapons, suggesting that they would be used against him. Some informants claim that he was beaten. Gasana fled his home and then left the commune with his family.[9]

The PSD had helped Ntaganzwa and the MDR break the power of the MRND. In November 1992, after Gasana left, the PSD leader and Assistant Burgomaster Jean-Marie Gasingwa was named interim burgomaster, sparking a new political struggle in the commune. Ntaganzwa now tackled Gasingwa, who was only twenty-four years old and recently named as assistant burgomaster. The contest in Nyakizu had reverberations at the national level. With Ntaganzwa's forceful tactics, the MDR stood a chance of taking Nyakizu, thus establishing a first foothold in a region where the MDR had never before been strong. Athanase Sebucocyero, an important official in the ministry of transportation, was from Nyakizu and, according to witnesses in the commune, served as Ntaganzwa's chief supporter in the national level of MDR. At the same time, the PSD was in the process of establishing itself as the leading party in the prefecture and it was anxious to support Gasingwa who might be able to resist the MDR and to keep Nyakizu within the PSD camp.

During the time when the MDR was fighting to establish its predominance, crime was increasing in Nyakizu, as elsewhere in Rwanda. Local authorities repeatedly expressed concern over the mounting number of robberies, arsons, and violent attacks on persons, including five murders in the course of 1992. Often the line between common crime and politically motivated attacks was blurred. Political activists engaged in kubohoza might rob as well as beat political opponents while

---

[8]Human Rights Watch/FIDH interview, Butare, October 19, 1995.

[9]Human Rights Watch/FIDH interviews, Cyahinda church, June 26, 1996; Butare, October 9, 1995; Nyakizu, August 28, 1995.

criminals might cover their wrongdoing by claiming to be acting for political ends.[10]

In behavior that presaged the comportment of many authorities during the genocide, officials did little to halt this violence. The local judicial official declared he was unable to carry out his responsibilities. The interim burgomaster asked to be relieved of his functions. Other officials avoided going to work if they believed a conflict was in the offing.[11]

As partisan struggles grew, authorities ordered an election for burgomaster with a limited number of voters, as was done in other communes at the time. On March 23, 1993, Ntaganzwa ran as a candidate for burgomaster against Gasingwa of the PSD and Etienne Muragizi of the PL. Ntaganzwa and Gasingwa each received seventeen votes, while Muragizi received two.[12] The several dozen electors, apparently fearing reprisals if Ntaganzwa were not chosen, at first asked authorities simply to designate the new burgomaster. When officials insisted that another election be held, members of the MDR threatened that if the PSD candidate won, the party would be forced to "leave the commune."[13] A second poll was taken in May and Ntaganzwa was unanimously elected. According to one of the participants in the election, "We elected MDR to save our lives. I needed to save my life and my family. I was afraid....The threat was real."[14]

---

[10]Nyakizu commune, minutes from security meeting November 17, 1992.

[11]Nyakizu commune, minutes from security meeting November 17, 1992; telegram no. 757/04/09.01, S/Préfet, Busoro to Préfet, Butare, November 19, 1992; telegram no. 763/04.09.01, S/préfet, Busoro to Préfet, Butare, November 20, 1993; telegram no. 733/04.09.01 from the S/préfet, Busoro to Préfet, Butare, November 11, 1992 (Butare prefecture).

[12]Jean-Baptiste Habyalimana, Préfet, to Monsieur le Ministre de l'Intérieur et du Développement Communal, undated (Butare prefecture).

[13]Telegram from S/Préfet, Busoro, to Préfet, Butare, November 20, 1993.

[14]Human Rights Watch/FIDH interview, Butare, August 19, 1995.

Consolidating Control

Once elected, Ntaganzwa used his authority as burgomaster to consolidate his own power and that of his party.[15] First he removed opponents—personal and political—from the communal payroll. When he took office, the financial situation of Nyakizu was desperate. The debt of some U.S.$30,000 that had burdened the commune in 1990 and 1991 had nearly doubled to more than U.S.$50,000 by the end of 1992. Ordered by his superiors to cut costs, Ntaganzwa began by eliminating the posts of employees who were long-serving and apparently competent but who had not given him their unqualified support. This effort brought Ntaganzwa immediately into conflict with the prefect, who sought to ensure that fiscal considerations not be used to cover a form of administrative kubohoza. The powers of the prefect to intervene were limited, however, so long as Ntaganzwa had the support of the communal council for the decisions. After extensive correspondence, Ntaganzwa emerged the victor on most of these questions.[16]

But Ntaganzwa could not bring the entire administrative system into line right away. Gasingwa, for example, his chief rival and the PSD candidate for burgomaster, could not be simply removed from his post as assistant burgomaster because he was named by the Ministry of Interior. As long as Gasingwa was in place, other communal employees and councilors also retained their membership in the PSD or its ally, the PL.

The burgomaster continued to rely on the young people who had helped bring him to power. To increase their effectiveness, he organized them by sector, each of which had its "youth president." In November 1993, on the same day when the commune dismissed several employees for lack of funds, Ntaganzwa rehired a "youth organizer" whose job had been ended in 1989. The national government, though facing a severe shortage of funds, was to pay part of the youth organizer's salary in Nyakizu and in other communes. The hard-strapped local and national authorities found money for these posts just as preparations for the genocide were intensifying. Some months before, Bagosora had noted in his appointment book

---

[15]Runyinya Barabwiliza, President of the MRND in Butare prefecture, to Madame le Premier Ministre, October 5, 1993 (Butare prefecture).

[16]Among other examples are: letters of Symphrose Mukankusi to Bwana Prefe, Nyakizu, July 8 and 9, 1993; Approbation no. 924 du 15/07/1993 du Prefet du Proces verbal de la Réunion des Conseillers de la Commune Nyakizu, du 30/06/1993 et envoyé au Prefet au 30/07/1993 (Butare prefecture).

that young people formed an important pool of recruits for the "self-defense" program.[17]

Ntaganzwa also developed links with many intellectual, religious, and business leaders in Nyakizu. One of the most influential of this circle was François Bazaramba, a Hutu refugee from the 1972 massacres in Burundi who was the youth director of the Baptist church at Maraba. The Baptists, important first in Burundi, established themselves in Rwanda in the 1950s and were usually identified far more with Hutu than with Tutsi interests. In addition to helping to direct one of the two Baptist churches in Nyakizu, Bazaramba was connected through marriage with other persons in the Baptist system. A man of some means, he ran a prosperous bar along with his other activities. Among others in the group were Geoffrey Dusabe, the school inspector who had considerable influence because he supervised teachers throughout the commune and distributed their salaries; Sampson Marembo, from the sector of Rutobwe; Festus Nyamukara, director of the primary school at Nyantanga; and Celestin Batakanwa, the director of the Center of Integrated Rural Artisanal Education (CERAI), a vocational secondary school at Muhambara.

Those communal councilors who were MDR and loyal to Ntaganzwa also formed part of his circle, but those whose party ties or views on Tutsi differed from those of Ntaganzwa were informally and unofficially replaced by men from Ntaganzwa's own network.[18] As one observer commented,

In sectors where the councilor was not MDR, he would be eclipsed by one of two other persons, either the representative of MDR or the JDR representative. In Rutobwe, for example, the councilor had been MRND before. Under pressure he had switched to MDR. But he had a wife who was Tutsi, so no one listened to him. The representative of the MDR was Sampson Marembo. He replaced the councilor at the end of April 1994. Even before that, he was the

---

[17]Ladislas Ntaganzwa, Bourgmestre, to Monsieur l'Encadreur Préfectoral de la Jeunesse et des Associations, Butare, no. 7941/04.01.02, received December 10, 1993 (Butare prefecture). Shortly before the genocide, a youth organizer, identified by title but not by name, was included on a list of anti-Tutsi "extremists" that circulated at Nyakizu. Another was accused of involvement in the genocide in Kivu commune. The Kibuye prefect urged that the organizers be paid in July 1994, a time when most government salaries were not being paid. The role of youth organizers in the genocide should be investigated further.

[18]Human Rights Watch/FIDH interview, Butare, October 19, 1995.

"real" head of the sector. In Rutobwe sector, the JDR members were called to meetings but the councilor was not.[19]

Faced with Ntaganzwa's official authority as burgomaster, his informal network of support, and the ever-present threat of violence by the JDR, the vast majority of the population came to accept Ntaganzwa's control. Asked to define the basis of his power, people said repeatedly and simply: fear.

Hutu Power
When Ntaganzwa became burgomaster, the MDR was still a single party, but several months later it divided into MDR and MDR-Power. Forced to chose his camp, Ntaganzwa opted for MDR-Power and thus acquired a new weapon to forge support, the ideology of ethnic loyalty. Like Hutu Power politicians at the national level, Ntaganzwa saw that he and his party could benefit from identification with the Hutu cause.

By the time the MDR divided, Ntaganzwa was strong enough to prevent any challenge by supporters of the other branch. He was even able to block a visit from the prime minister—a leader of the MDR—to the commune in late 1993, so denying her the opportunity to contest him on his own territory.[20] Most of the MDR-Power leaders at the national level, such as Donat Murego or Froduald Karamira, were from other regions of Rwanda, but the future interim Prime Minister Kambanda was from Gishamvu, the commune adjacent to Nyakizu. He appears to have had a special relationship with Ntaganzwa and came to see and reward him during the genocide. (See below.)

With the arrival of Hutu Power, kubohoza was used to enforce not just political loyalty but also ethnic solidarity. A politically active businessman declared, "When Hutu Power was installed here, everything changed. Anyone who was Tutsi or who did not speak the language of Hutu Power was the enemy."[21] By early 1994, MDR-Power claimed to be the only channel for Hutu to oppose the RPF, Ntaganzwa was its unquestioned local leader, and force was the "normal" way of separating supporters from the "enemy."

---

[19]Human Rights Watch/FIDH interview, Butare, October 19, 1995.

[20]Telegram no. 310/04.9.01, S/Préfet, Busoro to Madame le Premier Ministre, c/o MININTER, undated (Butare prefecture).

[21]Human Rights Watch/FIDH interview, Nyakizu, October 20, 1995.

The Border and the Burundians

Rwandans who lived near the frontier traded easily across the border at a number of points where there were no government agents and they crossed the river between the countries easily and often. Many had friends or relations in Burundi whom they trusted to keep them informed of events there. Their own observations and information from their contacts in Burundi made them think there was no danger of RPF attack from Burundi.[22] But, as in Gikongoro, civilian and military authorities further removed from the frontier saw the situation from a larger perspective and many of them supposed that the RPF could suddenly mount an attack from the south just as they had once launched an invasion from the north. Although they took no concrete measures to defend the frontier, they talked enough about the possible danger to plant fear among community leaders in Nyakizu.[23]

On April 23, 1993, the communal council first took note of a recent warning from the Ministry of Interior about the possibility the RPF could be transporting arms in fake funeral possessions, then it went on to look at the specific threat to Nyakizu. The minutes from that meeting read:

> As Nyakizu commune is located on the frontier, it is possible for the Inkotanyi to infiltrate easily here. The chair asked the councilors to give their opinions and proposed solutions for preventing the Inkotanyi from infiltrating and bringing in arms. Each participant spoke and everyone recognized that it is not easy to stop the Inkotanyi because they may have valid identity cards delivered by Rwandan authorities. They suggested restoring the old system of laissez-passer. Since it seems difficult to do this surveillance and since the councilors themselves cannot do it, they asked the representatives of the parties to get their supporters to help the councilors keep track of who was entering the commune by patrolling at night. The interim burgomaster agreed to put the decision into effect immediately.[24]

---

[22]Human Rights Watch/FIDH interviews, Nyagisozi, Nyakizu, January 5, 1996; interview, Nyakizu, January 5, 1995.

[23]Human Rights Watch/FIDH interview, Brussels, December 14, 1995.

[24]J.M.V. Gasingwa, Inyandiko-Mvugo y'Inama ya Komini yo Kuwa 23/4/1993, enclosed in J.M.V. Gasingwa, Burgmestri a.i. wa Komini Nyakizu, to Bwana Prefe wa Prefegitura, no. 54/04.01.02, April 26, 1993 (Butare prefecture).

Turning to the political parties to help organize patrols was an important precedent for the genocide, establishing that security was as much the concern of the party and the individual citizen as of the government. The reliance on citizens to deal with problems of insecurity in Nyakizu paralleled efforts in other communes to recruit citizens for patrols to counter growing crime.[25]

After the assassination of President Ndadaye, approximately 15,000 primarily Hutu Burundians flooded into Nyakizu, a number that equaled one quarter of the total population of the commune. Some 13,000 of these refugees were installed in a large camp at Uwimfizi in Nyagisozi sector, not far from the communal office and Cyahinda church, while the rest found shelter with Rwandan families in the commune.[26]

Having been driven from their homes by the largely Tutsi army in Burundi, many of the refugees feared and hated Tutsi and encouraged similar feelings among the Hutu of Nyakizu. As the refugees began arriving, some Tutsi in the commune were frightened by rumors that Hutu would attack them. A Tutsi woman from Nyagisozi explains, "When the Burundians arrived here in Nyakizu, some Tutsi families fled to the church. They sensed even then that something was wrong." Assured by the burgomaster that they were not in danger, they returned to their homes.[27] During the month of November, unidentified assailants destroyed several bars owned by Tutsi in Rusenge sector, people from Yaramba sector accused others of supporting Inkotanyi, and people from Maraba speculated that some from their sector had gone to Burundi to join the RPF and wondered "what kind of welcome people would give them the day that they came back." The councilor from Maraba commented that "all conflict between two individuals has begun to have an ethnic coloration."[28]

---

[25]As discussed above for Rwamiko, Gikongoro prefecture, and below, for Ngoma, Butare prefecture.

[26]Jean Baptiste Habyalimana, Préfet, to Monsieur le Ministre de l'Intérieur et du Développement Communale, "Rapport sur la situation des réfugiés Burundais," November 14, 1993 (Butare prefecture).

[27]Human Rights Watch/FIDH interview, Nyakizu, August 28, 1995; Inama ya Komini yo kuwa 12/11/1993, enclosed in Ladislas Ntaganzwa, Burugumesitiri wa Komini Nyakizu to Bwana Prefe wa Perefegitura, no. 498/04.01.02, November 23, 1993 (Butare prefecture).

[28] Inama ya Komini yo kuwa 12/11/1993.

According to regulations, the refugees were not supposed to cultivate or engage in trade, but many were soon participating in local economic life, making use of contacts established when they were still in Burundi. Many sent their children to the local school and formed drinking friendships with local people.[29] More important for the history of the genocide, the Burundians also became part of the political life of the commune. François Bazaramba, the Baptist youth director, was named chief of the camp, an official post that allowed him to serve as liaison between the refugees and the government and other outside agencies. With his church connections and his own origin as a refugee from Burundi, he was well suited for the job. As one of Ntaganzwa's closest associates, he drew the refugees into the group supporting the burgomaster.[30] The communal administrator—the equivalent of a burgomaster—of the Burundi commune of Kabarore was among the refugees. He was reportedly lodged at a house belonging to another one of Ntaganzwa's inner circle.[31] One witness described the changes that followed the arrival of the refugees:

> It became more tense when the Burundians came. They wanted to continue the killing that they had started over in Burundi. [A]fter the arrival of the Burundians, there was only one party here [MDR-Power]....The Burundians were favored. They were given the right to speak in meetings. They even had their own "burgomaster of the Burundians," who fled together with the Rwandans to Zaire.[32]

Burundian refugees had engaged in military training at camps elsewhere in Rwanda for some time and those newly arrived in Nyakizu soon began similar activities. In November, 1993 the office of U.N. High Commissioner for Refugees in Kigali protested this training which violated international convention and U.N.

---

[29]Human Rights Watch/FIDH interview, Butare, August 19, 1995.

[30]Telegram from Prefect to MINITRASO, no.150.3/04.09.01/4, December 14, 1993 (Butare prefecture).

[31]Human Rights Watch/FIDH interviews, Butare, October 21, 1995; Nyakizu, August 28, 1995.

[32]Human Rights Watch/FIDH interview, Nyakizu, August 28, 1995.

regulations and asked the Rwandan authorities to halt it.[33] Ntaganzwa did not intervene although he must have known that some fifty refugees were being trained not far from the communal office.[34] According to one witness, Ntaganzwa had been selling arms to militants even while they were in Burundi. He had acquired the weapons from Rwandan authorities, claiming he needed them to defend the frontier and then had sold them at a profit to Burundians.

A leading Hutu businessman and former parliamentary deputy, Ange Nshimiryayo, wrote to warn the prime minister about the growing probems in Nyakizu.[35] At the end of November 1993, Prime Minister Uwilingiyimana visited the commune to try to ease tensions between Hutu and Tutsi and, specifically, to warn the refugees that they must halt their military training.[36]

Training and Arms

Witnesses from Nyakizu state that some young men from the commune began their own military training sessions as early as September or October 1993, with local military reservists as instructors.[37] Most of the Rwandans trained appear to have been from the JDR, but young men from other parties also were included, so long as they were Hutu.[38] Several witnesses report having seen young men picked

---

[33]United Nations High Commissioner for Refugees to the Minister of Foreign Affairs and Cooperation, Kigali, November 18, 1993 (International commission).

[34]Human Rights Watch/FIDH interview, Butare, October 19, 1995.

[35]Ladislas Ntaganzwa, Burgumesitiri wa komini Nyakizu to Bwana Perefe wa Prefegitura wa Butare, no. 143/04.09.01/4, June 27, 1994 (Butare prefecture).

[36]Telegram no. 375/04.09.01/14, S/Préfet, Busoro to MININTER, December 3, 1993 (Butare prefecture).

[37] In 1990 there were four reservists in the commune. By 1994, the number was certainly higher. Burgomaster Jean Baptiste Gasana to the Commandant de Place, Butare-Gikongoro, January 19, 1990.

[38]Human Rights Watch/FIDH interview, Nyantanga, Nyakizu, June 20, 1995.

up in the communal truck from throughout Nyakizu and taken to a training site. Another reported that young men were taken out of the commune for training.[39]

Once the Burundians arrived, Rwandan militia trained together with them, sometimes under the supervision of Bazaramba.[40] Another who reported that the "intellectuals" had learned how to shoot from the Burundians added:

> Before the genocide, there was military training going on here. It was former soldiers who trained people. I never saw them directly, but they did training at night and exercises. At four in the morning, they would run and do exercises. They didn't sing [as soldiers in training in Rwanda commonly do], but you could hear their feet....Burundians helped in the military training, including these 4 a.m. exercises.[41]

Nyakizu received three new "commando rifles" in an official distribution in January 1994 and apparently other arms were delivered through informal channels as well.[42] Once the genocide began several dozen men, former soldiers and members of Ntaganzwa's circle, brought out firearms and grenades. Ntaganzwa and his supporters stockpiled traditional arms as well as firearms and distributed them when the killing began. Assailants obtained spears from the neighboring commune of Gishamvu where they were made by specialists, but they made their own cruder weapons, such as nail-studded clubs.[43]

In February, 1994, the popular PSD leader Gatabazi was assassinated in Kigali and the CDR president Bucyana was lynched in retaliation the day after, near Butare. As people on all sides became more frightened, Ntaganzwa launched a new

---

[39]Human Rights Watch/FIDH interviews, Cyahinda church, June 26, 1995; Cyahinda church, July 7, 1995; Maraba, Nyakizu, June 20 and August 16, 1995; Gasasa, Nyakizu, August 9, 1995.

[40]Human Rights Watch/FIDH interview, Cyahinda church, June 26, 1995.

[41]Human Rights Watch/FIDH interview, Nyakizu, August 28, 1995.

[42]Human Rights Watch/FIDH interview, Nyakizu, August 28, 1995; telegram no 56/04.06, Préfet, Butare to Bourgmestres, Muyira, Ntyazo, Muganza, Muyaga, Kibayi, Kigembe, Nyakizu, Nyabisindu, Ngoma, January 20, 1994 (Butare prefecture).

[43]Human Rights Watch/FIDH interviews, Gasasa, August 9, 1995; Butare, June 12, 1995; Maraba, August 16, 1995.

campaign of kubohoza in which political and ethnic loyalties were now completely intertwined. One witness declared:

Many people were imprisoned in February 1994. It was a time of great kubohoza. They were saying "Inkotanyi are attacking." They traumatized a lot of people looking for accomplices of the Inkotanyi. They had many meetings, particularly in February.[44]

One older man reported:

Kubohoza was very strong here. I myself was a victim. My wife was Tutsi, and in February 1994, they brought me to my knees and made me give money [for party membership dues]. I was PL, but they made me give 2,000 francs [about U.S.$10] and become MDR-Power. They also put me in prison, beat me, and threatened my wife.[45]

Beginning in February 1994, the communal administration insisted that the security patrols begun the previous April be done more regularly. As one witness remembers:

There had been organization before and people guarding and such, but in February there was a whole new level of organization. Before there had been patrols, but in February...they were each night. The councilor or cell leader was involved in organizing them....People who were not in the burgomaster's party and also the Tutsi were obliged to join the patrols, but they did not work at the barriers.[46]

In addition, during this period, a contingent of gendarmes was sent from Butare to help maintain order in the commune.

---

[44]Human Rights Watch/FIDH interview, Nkakwa, Nyakizu, August 15, 1995.

[45]Ibid.

[46]Human Rights Watch/FIDH interview, Nkakwa, August 15, 1995.

In March 1994, a newly arrived group of Hutu refugees got into a dispute with the political leader and businessman Ange Nshimiryayo and on March 23 tried to shoot him.[47]

As these signals of danger to Tutsi and moderates multiplied, an unidentified person circulated a handwritten list of "Extremists in the Commune of Nyakizu," naming "the burgomaster and his group at the head," many Burundian refugees, the youth organizer, several policemen, teachers, and the inspector of schools, Geoffrey Dusabe, "and his friends." The list was sent to the prefect who wrote to ask Ntaganzwa about it. The burgomaster replied by denying that there were any problems in Nyakizu except for sickness and hunger.[48]

Shortly before the genocide began, leaders of MDR-Power from Nyakizu met several times with their counterparts from communes in Gikongoro. During this period, Ntaganzwa himself was reportedly seeing the sub-prefect Biniga.[49] The burgomaster went to Kigali for a meeting on March 31 or April 1, just after the March 30 meeting on civilian self-defense at the army headquarters (see above). According to one witness, neither his wife nor his driver knew—or would admit to knowing—exactly where he had gone or for what purpose.[50]

Beginning the Genocide

The use of violence against political opponents, the identification of all Tutsi with the RPF, the ideology of Hutu power, growth of insecurity, the pressure from the Burundian refugees, the training of the militia, and the demand for loyalty to the burgomaster all worked together to prepare for genocide in Nyakizu. As elsewhere, the catalyst would be the killing of Habyarimana, but as one informant asserted, "If the president had not died, still something would have happened."[51]

As in other parts of Rwanda, most residents of Nyakizu heard about the death of President Habyarimana from the radio. That same afternoon, witnesses saw

---

[47]Human Rights Watch/FIDH interview, Nyakizu, January 5, 1996.

[48]Ladislas Ntaganzwa, Burugumesitiri wa Komini Nyakizu, to Bwana Perefe wa Perefigutura wa Butare, no. 68/04.09.01/4, March 7, 1994, and attached Liste des Extrêmists en commune Nyakizu (Butare prefecture).

[49]Human Rights Watch/FIDH interview, Gasasa, August 9, 1995.

[50]Human Rights Watch interview, Nyakizu, August 28, 1995.

[51]Human Rights Watch/FIDH interview, Nyakizu, August 19, 1995.

smoke from the first houses burning far away in the Gikongoro commune of Rwamiko and, soon after, people fleeing from Gikongoro began arriving in Nyakizu.[52] At first, people were unsure what was happening. The restrictions on movement and the cancelling of the Friday market meant they could not gather news from others as they usually did. But as people began arriving from Gikongoro, Hutu as well as Tutsi were afraid and some fled their homes.[53] A Hutu informant from the northern-most sector of Gihango recalled:

> The first people who fled Gikongoro arrived in our sector on Thursday and...said that the Interahamwe had attacked them. Their houses were being burned in Gikongoro all the time from Thursday through Saturday. When we saw the people whom we knew, I thought to myself: this is the war....I fled with my family on Tuesday of the next week, after I saw houses burning nearby. I was really afraid....I fled with Gikongoro people toward Rusenge...where I got information about the war: it was a war for killing Tutsi. At the beginning, I didn't know who was attacking whom. It was just houses burning. Gikongoro people said that...it was first of all for killing Tutsi and...so we returned home.[54]

In Rutobwe sector, removed by the entire length of the commune from Gihango, people also learned on Tuesday, April 12, that it was Tutsi who were being targeted. The prosperous trader Charles Rwahama gathered the information from Tutsi at the church of Cyahinda and brought the news to Rutobwe. As one witness recalls:

> We saw smoke, but we didn't know who in particular was in danger. But Charles Rwahama came to tell us that it was Tutsi especially who were seeking refuge in the parish. He decided to go to Burundi...He went together with his younger brother who was a student. He left his family behind. He didn't know

---

[52]Human Rights Watch/FIDH interview, Gasasa, August 9, 1995.

[53]Human Rights Watch/FIDH interviews, Cyahinda church, November 8, 1994 and Butare, October 19, 1995.

[54]Human Rights Watch/FIDH interview, Butare, October 9, 1995.

anything about the seriousness of the situation, or he would have taken them....And when he came back, his family was dead.[55]

A survivor from Bunge described how hostility grew against the Tutsi:

When we heard that the president was dead, we also heard that Kigali was having problems. And here, when you spoke to Hutu, you got no response. Except they said threateningly, "Things are going to happen." Hutu stopped speaking to us completely when they saw people coming here from Gikongoro. We knew that now it would be our turn. We knew we would have to seek refuge. Then one week after the president's death, houses began burning here.[56]

Gathering the Tutsi, Mobilizing the Hutu
As was so often the case during the genocide, public reassurances masked the secret organization of the killings. A Hutu witness who lived near the communal office reported:

We saw the burgomaster at the center and asked what we could do so that it [the violence] would not happen here. "It is the Interahamwe of Damien Biniga who are doing it," that's what the burgomaster said. "The Tutsi here don't have to worry because there are no Interahamwe here. We are all MDR and PSD." After reassuring us, he held another meeting with his inner circle at the communal office to tell them what was really going to happen. I saw him summoning them to this meeting by name. I was not invited because he did not trust me.[57]

Ntaganzwa used his inner circle of party and personal supporters to carry out the genocide, backing up the cooperative members of the official hierarchy and supplanting those opposed to the slaughter. He sent them first to organize patrols in each sector and particularly to monitor the area to the west and north where people were arriving from Gikongoro. Some were hoping to flee to Burundi, but

---

[55]Human Rights Watch/FIDH interview, Butare, October 19, 1995.

[56]Human Rights Watch/FIDH interview, Nyantanga, June 20, 1995.

[57]Human Rights Watch/FIDH interview, Cyahinda church, November 8, 1994.

others expected to find safety at Nyakizu. The burgomastcr insisted that the Tutsi go to Cyahinda church rather than seeking shelter with families. Ntaganzwa's supporters, JDR and MDR leaders, communal councilors, cell leaders, and police, both communal and national, all helped direct the new arrivals to the church. According to one witness from Gikongoro:

> I was in Mubuga....The assailants from Gikongoro were behind us together with the sub-prefect of Munini [Biniga]. In front of us was Nyakizu, and the burgomaster of Nyakizu was at the border...reassuring us: "If you come to my commune, you'll be safe." He was together with the community leaders and with some ordinary people. They did patrols in the night to reassure the people that Nyakizu was safe.[58]

According to a Nyakizu resident:

> As thc Gikongoro people came fleeing in this direction, they were saying: "There are cadavers!" But the burgomaster said "That is not going to happen here. I am protecting you."[59]

Another elderly survivor recalled:

> The burgomaster welcomed people who were being pursued, saying, "Go to Cyahinda." And the intellectuals and other authorities assisted people to come to Cyahinda. That is how I came with my family to Cyahinda.[60]

Ntaganzwa directed a communal employee to organize the Tutsi at the church by their sector of origin and to appoint a leader for each group, thus reinforcing the impression that he did intend to take responsibility for their welfare.[61]

In addition to controlling the flow of people, the patrols were supposed to prevent troublemakers from Gikongoro from raiding Nyakizu or, alternatively, to

---

[58]Human Rights Watch/FIDH interview, Cyahinda church, July 7, 1995.

[59]Human Rights Watch/FIDH interview, Cyahinda church, June 26, 1995.

[60]Human Rights Watch/FIDH interview, Cyahinda church, July 7, 1995.

[61]Human Rights Watch/FIDH interview, Butare, August 19, 1995.

prevent infiltration by the RPF who might hide among the crowds. Initially Tutsi took part in the patrols.[62] As a Tutsi from Yaramba recounts:

> I participated in the patrols from April 7 through April 11. They said, "The president is dead and Inyenzi are going to invade." We all did turns during the nights....If we encountered a person whom we did not know, we put the person somewhere, and in the morning we called the chief of the hill [*chef de colline*] who would ask, "Who are you?" to see if the person was Inyenzi or not.[63]

One patrol in the Cyahinda sector captured a man who had come to pillage. They turned him over to the burgomaster, who put him in the communal lockup but then freed him the next day. After this incident, the burgomaster directed people, "Keep your eyes open. Stay together. Do not let anyone be alone."[64] Tutsi then began to realize that the patrols were not so much for general security as to keep track of their movements and they stopped participating in them.

Even while the authorities were taking measures supposed to promote security, Ntaganzwa's men were promoting fear of the Tutsi. A witness from Rutobwe linked the anti-Tutsi propaganda directly to Ntaganzwa's meetings with his circle:

> At these meetings, every sector was represented by one or more people, friends of the burgomaster, who kept his secrets. They were the *abanyamabanga*.[65] From Rutobwe, the person was Celestin Batakanwa of the CERAI. Those people trusted by the burgomaster came out of the meetings and they spoke to others. They went to the leaders of the party, saying: "Be careful, those Tutsi are going to kill us. There are RPF all over. They have hidden arms."
>
> In this way, by spreading these rumors, they made a large part of the population afraid of the RPF. I remember once I was speaking with one of my

---

[62]Human Rights Watch/FIDH interview, Cyahinda church, November 8, 1994.

[63]Human Rights Watch/FIDH interview, Maraba, Nyakizu, October 20, 1995.

[64]Human Rights Watch/FIDH interviews, Butare, August 19, 1995; Nyantanga, June 20, 1995.

[65]Literally, "people of the secret," the term once referred to ritualists and advisers who surrounded a ruler.

students, and I told him: "You're crazy to say that all Tutsi are armed RPF." Even though he said these things, I really didn't believe that he was serious. "Did you ever *see* an RPF soldier?" I asked him. But he was serious. They cultivated fear.[66]

The message reached even ordinary people on the outskirts of the commune. One said that he had heard rumors "that the Inkotanyi would take power. It was said that the Tutsi had to be killed, or they would kill the Hutu."[67] Many people prepared for the worst. One Hutu married to a Tutsi woman said they had discussed the situation and decided simply to remain in their home and to die together.[68]

The First Killings

On April 13, RTLM warned that Inyenzi were hiding themselves among crowds of people fleeing into the prefectures of Gitarama and Butare. The shrill Valérie Bemeriki broadcast: "I have told you repeatedly...that the Inkotanyi say that they will make their breakthrough especially in the prefecture of Butare and that they will find an opening there and we are not unaware that they have 'accomplices' everywhere there...."[69] That night assailants killed the first Tutsi, quietly, along the banks of the Akanyaru River, in the sector of Nkakwa.

A Tutsi survivor who lived in a house from which he could see across the river into Burundi, reports having seen groups of armed Hutu patrolling along the banks of the river on the Burundi side for several days. On April 13, they stopped a group of Tutsi, apparently from Gikongoro, who had forded the river and they brought them back across to Rwanda, where armed civilians were waiting. The Rwandans and Burundians together used machetes and other traditional weapons to kill the Tutsi, then threw their bodies into the river. Because both the burgomaster and the ordinary people of Nyakizu had frequent contacts with people on the other side of the frontier, this kind of cooperation was easily arranged. One witness who lived

---

[66]Human Rights Watch/FIDH interview, Butare, October 21, 1995.

[67]Human Rights Watch/FIDH interview, Nyagisozi, January 5, 1996.

[68]Human Rights Watch/FIDH interview, Nyakizu, October 20, 1995.

[69]RTLM, April 13, 1994, recorded by Faustin Kagame (provided by Article 19).

near the river stated, "Rwandans promised Burundians cows if they would help. I heard neighbors say this and, after the massacres, the cows were given."[70]

Also on April 13, in the sector of Maraba in the center of the commune, a young Tutsi night watchman saw the local patrol pass through a cluster of shops and houses and begin to mount the hill towards the bar owned by François Bazaramba. Sector president of MDR-Power, head of the Burundian refugee camp and supporter of Ntaganzwa, Bazaramba reportedly had organized the local patrol and was in the group that night along with a former communal policeman and a former councilor. The watchman saw the patrol intersect a group of twenty-one people who were hurrying through the night, including the elderly, women and children. Presumably they were coming from Gikongoro and headed for the border. The patrol forced them to go up the hill and to sit down next to Bazaramba's bar. The watchman followed a short distance behind, afraid of being seen in the bright moonlight. He saw them kill four men, apparently the strongest of the group, bludgeoning them with hammers and clubs. Then the former councilor intervened to stop the killing, saying that the patrol should take the people to the authorities in the morning. The patrol stopped, threw the bodies of the four they had killed into a latrine and in the morning took the others to the communal office.[71]

Thursday morning, the school inspector Geoffrey Dusabe led a public meeting in the market square at Birambo in Yaramba sector, apparently to rally people to participate in patrols. Among the other party activists who attended was a young man named Kabano, the head of the JDR for the sector. A Tutsi teacher from Yaramba who was present at the market found the atmosphere so hostile by midday that he decided to leave. Later in the afternoon he heard that Tutsi were fleeing on a nearby hill and he and his brother went to ask them for information. On their way home, they were intercepted by a patrol of some twenty young men led by Kabano. The patrol forced them to sit down and began interrogating them about why they were not participating in efforts to ensure the security of the commune. The teacher said he had to return home for something to eat and to get his arms before beginning. They were allowed to leave, but that night their house was surrounded, apparently by the same patrol. In the morning, the women of the household succeeded in leaving, with the family cattle, and the teacher slipped out to hide in a banana grove. From there, he saw the patrol loot the house and then drag out his father, who had been unable to flee with the others because he was sick. The JDR

---

[70]Human Rights Watch/FIDH interviews, Nyagisozi, January 5, 1996.

[71]Human Rights Watch/FIDH interview, Maraba, Nyakizu, August 16, 1995.

assailants piled dried banana leaves around him and set him on fire. When the teacher left his hiding place that night to flee Nyakizu, his father still had not died. The women of the family were killed later in the commune of Kigembe where they had sought shelter.[72]

While Dusabe was conducting the meeting for the eastern part of the commune at Birambo, the burgomaster was mobilizing the rest of Nyakizu through a meeting at Cyahinda. He warned that people must carry out the patrols just as he had directed. He also ordered local people to stay away from the church, thus beginning the isolation of the Tutsi that would end in their elimination, a pattern found also at Kibeho, Kaduha and elsewhere.[73]

Shortly after the meetings to mobilize the population, Ntaganzwa directed his subordinates to collect all the weapons held by the Tutsi at the church, a measure just like that taken at other massacre sites. But a university intern working temporarily at the commune refused the order, apparently with the support of the assistant burgomaster Gasingwa. The student states:

On Thursday, April 14, at around 3:00 or 4:00 in the afternoon, the burgomaster told us to go take from the Tutsi anything they might use to defend themselves, such as spears, arms, any kind of weapon. They had these arms for protection, because they had come with their cows and their houses had been burned. Now, the burgomaster instructed us to confiscate these arms. We refused. We said that these people had come with their herds and they were afraid. They wanted to protect themselves. To take away their arms would be too difficult....We said, let the people guard their herds, because right now they are really upset.[74]

Ntaganzwa was angered at this insubordination but did not force the issue. Instead he met with his inner circle at the communal office and then left to continue his work elsewhere in the commune.[75]

---

[72]Human Rights Watch/FIDH interviews, Maraba, Nyakizu, May 3 and October 20, 1995.

[73]Human Rights Watch/FIDH interview, Butare, August 19, 1995. For Kibeho and Kaduha, see chapter 8.

[74]Human Rights Watch/FIDH interview, Butare, August 19, 1995.

[75]Ibid.

Nkakwa

Despite efforts to direct all those in flight to Cyahinda, large numbers continued to head for the frontier. On Thursday, there were so many that they formed a line stretching from Nyarubuye to the hill of Kwishorezo, just overlooking the river, a distance of more than three kilometers. Three barriers had been set up in Nkakwa, the sector at the border, but the guards had not halted the flood of people, supposedly because they were overwhelmed by the number. The apparent reluctance of the sector councilor, Albert Nzimbirinda, to participate in the killing (see below) may help explain this failure. Once in sight of the river, the Tutsi hesitated before attempting the crossing, intimidated by armed patrols on one side or the other. Hundreds gathered in an open area at a small commercial district on top of one of the hills bordering the river.[76]

According to several witnesses, Ntaganzwa arrived at Nkakwa at about 6 p.m. in a red pickup truck. He was apparently accompanied by two or three teachers and the head of the communal police. Using a hand-held loudspeaker, Ntaganzwa supposedly exhorted people to protect the commune by keeping the rebels—meaning the Tutsi—from fleeing to Burundi. He declared that the men intended only to take their wives and children to safety and then to return to attack Rwanda. Since Nkakwa was close to Burundi, the people there would be particularly vulnerable to attack.[77] After speaking at Nkakwa, the burgomaster went on to another border sector, Rutobwe, where he is said to have delivered the same message.[78]

Approximately an hour after Ntaganzwa's departure, the killers, under the direction of two leaders from the JDR and another from MDR-Power, attacked the Tutsi using machetes and other traditional weapons. One witness reports, "Rutobwe did not have many Tutsi, so people came from there to help at Nkakwa."[79] Some

---

[76]Human Rights Watch/FIDH interviews, Nkakwa, August 10 and August 15, 1995.

[77]Human Rights Watch/FIDH interview, Nyagisozi, January 5, 1996.

[78]Ibid; Human Rights Watch/FIDH interviews, Butare, October 19, 1995; Nyagisozi, January 5, 1996.

[79]Human Rights Watch/FIDH interview, Nyagisozi, January 5, 1996.

Burundians also crossed the river to assist. Witnesses from Nkakwa say Ntaganzwa returned twice during the night to supervise the killing.[80]

As dawn approached, Ntaganzwa was busy going around the commune collecting carefully chosen supporters, those who were "sure," to finish the "work" at Nkakwa. One witness reports:

> Those who participated [in the] killing at Nkakwa....had been chosen by the burgomaster and his friends. The people selected for this—the burgomaster knew what he was doing. He had sorted people out and had chosen those who were active in the MDR. These people meant to kill, and they also pillaged.[81]

To ensure that local Tutsi residents not take flight, Ntaganzwa used the loudspeaker to make an announcement as he went by in the vehicle:

> Stay at home. There is no problem. We're taking care of the people who attack us. I believe that this message was directed particularly at Tutsi who were in their homes—which was nearly all of them. They didn't know that people were being massacred at Nkakwa all throughout the night. We didn't hear anything. The killing was just by machete.[82]

At first light, Ntaganzwa returned to the border accompanied by several vehicles full of assailants whom he had picked up in various parts of the commune. A witness returning from his work as a nightwatchman that night says he heard the burgomaster give orders as he dropped off the killers, "Get to work. Leave no one alive."[83] The leaders brought by Ntaganzwa organized the local assailants into groups and used drums and whistles to communicate with each other and to frighten the victims. After killing most of the Tutsi on top of the hill known as Mu Gisoro, they pushed the others back towards the river. Burundian killers waited on the opposite bank determined not to let the Tutsi cross. They shouted that the Tutsi must not be allowed to enter Burundi and become official refugees and obtain protection. Caught between the two groups of killers, hundreds of Tutsi were

---

[80]Human Rights Watch/FIDH interviews, Nkakwa, August 15, 1996.

[81]Ibid.

[82]Human Rights Watch/FIDH interview, Butare, October 19, 1995.

[83]Human Rights Watch/FIDH interview, Nkakwa, August 15, 1995.

slaughtered. Very few escaped, scattering to hide in the bush. Of these survivors, many were caught later that day or in the following days by patrols. Ntaganzwa sent National Police to the border later on Friday to help with searches and witnesses report that they then heard gunfire from that direction.[84] The bodies of those killed near the river were simply thrown in the water. The others would be buried in a number of mass graves on the hills Kwishorezo and Mu Gisoro.[85]

After finishing at the river's edge, the killers set out to hunt down local Tutsi in their homes, both in Nkakwa and in Rutobwe. One witness awoke to hear others in his household giving the alarm because a neighbor's house had just been attacked. He remembers them saying, "Over at Rwamgampuhwe's house, they have just set fire. He was at home! He has been killed with his children!"[86] A Baptist pastor and the director of the Baptist school are said to have participated in these killings.[87] According to one Tutsi farmer from Nkakwa:

The killing had gone on all night. They came to attack my home at 4 a.m. It was a group of five neighbors. I saw them coming. My wife and children had gone to hide with Hutu families, and I stayed at the house to guard the cows. When I saw them coming, I went to hide behind a latrine. They broke down the doors of the house and took everything inside. They took all of the animals—four cows, two pigs, seven chickens. They began to burn the house, so I fled into the bush. My wife and children were found and killed. And my mother. They were all killed by the people of Nkakwa.[88]

As this testimony and many others make clear, some Hutu tried to protect their Tutsi neighbors, particularly those to whom they were bound by the ties of marriage, clientage, or long-standing friendships. Other Hutu opposed the killings

---

[84]Ibid; Human Rights Watch/FIDH interviews, Nkakwa, August 10, 1995; Nyagisozi, January 5, 1996; Nyakizu, August 19, 1995.

[85]Field notes, Human Rights Watch and FIDH researchers, August 10 and 15, 1995.

[86]Human Rights Watch/FIDH interview, Butare, October 19, 1995.

[87]Human Rights Watch/FIDH interviews, Nkakwa, August 15, 1995; Butare, October 21, 1995.

[88]Human Rights Watch/FIDH interview, Nyagisozi, January 5, 1996.

on the grounds of principle. Such seems to have been the case with the communal councilor, Albert Nzimbirinda, who apparently refused to kill and even tried to stop others from killing, an effort which led to his removal several weeks later.[89] Perhaps anticipating that Nzimbirinda would refuse to participate, Ntaganzwa had made sure that JDR and MDR-Power leaders were on the spot to replace him in directing the slaughter.

The killers pillaged the goods of their victims, whether Tutsi in flight or local residents. One witness recounts seeing "people returning from Nkakwa with bags of beans, clothing, mats." As the news spread that "the family of so and so has fled and they have left behind their belongings," other people not involved in the killings went off to loot, some of them apparently unaware that a massacre had taken place. During the morning many people returned from Nkakwa and "everyone brought back something on his head." The witness continued:

One man came by with cushions for a couch. He had six of them. He wanted to sell them in order to buy beer. "Where did you get this?" I asked. "At Charles' [Rwahama][90] place!" he told me.

The National Police took the beer and the beer-crates from the stock at Charles' place. They took everything until it was empty....Ordinary people had nothing to fear. They were encouraged by the example of the National Police. People were returning with things which they had found free. There was no punishment. It was like a festival. And they were selling these things for next to nothing. For example, a radio normally costing 20,000 francs now cost 2,000 francs. As usual, they bought beer with the money.[91]

After men pillaged larger, heavier, and more valuable items, women helped themselves to what was left.

---

[89]Ibid; Ladislas Ntaganzwa, Umwobozi w'inama, and Geoffrey Dusabe, Umwanditsi w'inama, Inyandiko mvugo y'inama ya Komite y'Umutekano yateranye tariki ya 18/5/1994 (Nyakizu Commune). Hereafter cited as Nyakizu commune, "Inyandiko mvugo...18/5/1994."

[90]Rwahama was the prosperous trader who went to Burundi on April 12, leaving behind his family. [See above.]

[91]Human Rights Watch/FIDH interview, Butare, October 19,1995.

Cyahinda

The Catholic church at Cyahinda, a weathered fifty-year-old brick building, sat atop a hill within view of the communal office. A major social center for the commune, it offered a place not just for religious services, but also for meetings of women's associations, youth groups, scouts, and various other organizations throughout the week. To the left of the long church building were large, flat grounds and to the right, the land fell off steeply. In addition to its religious programs, the church ran a primary school, a vocational high school and a health center at Cyahinda. A large complex of school buildings extended behind the church, enclosing several sizable courtyards. Just down from the church complex, on the road to the communal office, there was a commercial and residential center where many of the employees of the church lived. The main intellectual center of the commune, Cyahinda was viewed as a "Tutsi community," in part because the priest and several other church employees were Tutsi.

When a researcher from Human Rights Watch first visited the church in November 1994, the main doors, marked by bullet holes, stood open. A burn mark on the inside wall just above the door showed that at least one grenade had been thrown in through that entrance. Bullets shot into the church had left holes on several walls and had broken some of the stained glass windows. There were blood stains on the floors and walls. Bleached bits of human bone were mixed with the dirt on the ground around the church. Just next to the church was the grave of the priest. Three mass graves lay behind and below the church and a long line of graves ran next to the church on the right side. Behind the church, on the left side, was a long row of latrines that had been stuffed full of bodies.

The Tutsi who arrived at Cyahinda beginning on April 8 hoped to find sanctuary there as many had in previous such disasters, a hope that Ntaganzwa encouraged. Others who had planned instead to escape to Burundi were alarmed by news of the massacre at Nkakwa and Rutobwe and so they too sought shelter at the church. With violence behind them and violence ahead of them, they had little choice.

On Friday morning, April 15, assailants leaving the killing at Nkakwa and Rutobwe began attacking Tutsi elsewhere in Nyakizu while fresh recruits joined in the "work" as well. They killed some Tutsi that morning and drove many others from their homes, which they then burned so that they could not return.[92] Even those Tutsi who had not yet been attacked had good reason to fear and many fled to the church. As one witness states, "When we heard gunfire [at Nkakwa], we

---

[92]Human Rights Watch/FIDH interview, Nyakizu, May 24, 1995.

knew we could not escape south to Burundi, so we went to take refuge at Cyahinda."[93]

The burgomaster went to see Tutsi who remained at home and told them to go to the church.[94] According to one elderly Tutsi from Cyahinda sector:

> The burgomaster arrived at my home together with communal police, the National Police, and militia. They instructed me to go to the church. The burgomaster reassured people that even though they could see people fleeing from other places, there would be no violence in his commune.[95]

The witness did not really believe this promise. He states, "I saw guns and machine guns. I thought it was for killing, but the burgomaster said that it was for protecting us. We had doubts, but we were not sure." He felt he had no choice but to go. Within twenty minutes, this man and his family gathered a few belongings and hurried to Cyahinda. When he arrived at the church, he turned and saw his own home burning on the hill behind him.[96]

The local Tutsi who arrived on Friday found the church, the buildings of the school, and the yards surrounding them overflowing with people and their animals and other possessions. One survivor estimated that Tutsi from six communes were there. "The church was full" she said. "It was really full."[97]

As the gangs of assailants went about burning and pillaging, an employee of the commune and sector head of MRND raised the alarm, saying the commune was being attacked from Gikongoro. Once he had gotten a crowd together and excited at the Maraba health center, Ntaganzwa arrived to take over, announcing that it was Tutsi who were the real threat to security. He reportedly asked why nothing had yet been done in his commune, when the killing was already finished elsewhere. According to several informants, Tutsi in the vicinity were taken and killed on the

---

[93]Human Rights Watch/FIDH interview, Nyakizu, August 28, 1995.

[94]Human Rights Watch/FIDH interview, Gasasa, August 9, 1995.

[95]Human Rights Watch/FIDH interview, Cyahinda church, June 26, 1995.

[96]Ibid.

[97]Human Rights Watch/FIDH interview, Cyahinda church, July 7, 1995.

spot as soon as Ntaganzwa had finished speaking. Other Tutsi in Maraba fled when they heard of the killings.[98]

The "Battle"

On Friday, April 15 assailants launched a preliminary attack against the Tutsi at Cyahinda at about 10 a.m., just as the killing at Nkakwa was winding down. A witness who was hiding in the bush at Nkakwa that morning states, "I heard people saying that they should go over to Cyahinda, where there were many Tutsi, and help in the killing there."[99] Some of the attackers were armed with guns and fired into the crowd around the church. The Tutsi scattered and started throwing stones to defend themselves. They had the advantage of a superior location and drove back the assailants, who were trying to fight their way uphill. After about an hour, the attackers drew back, some of them carrying off the animals or goods they had plundered. Others began searching for individuals and small groups hiding around the edges of the church complex, while Tutsi tried to find safety in the church itself or in its adjacent buildings. Some of the Tutsi gathered the injured and moved them to a protected area where they could receive care. Profiting from a lull in the shooting, others fled the church to take refuge at nearby Nyakizu hill or headed out of the commune altogether. At the same time, other Tutsi arrived, believing the church still offered the best hope of sanctuary. The parish priest, Abbé Charles Ncogoza, advised the people at the church to defend themselves as best they could.[100]

At about 2 p.m., the burgomaster arrived in the communal pickup truck, accompanied by National Policemen, communal policemen, and a former soldier named Kambanda.[101] Witnesses report that some of the "intellectuals" who joined

---

[98]Human Rights Watch/FIDH interviews, Maraba, Nyakizu, August 16, 1995; Nyantanga, June 20, 1995.

[99]Human Rights Watch/FIDH interview, Nyagisozi, January 5, 1996.

[100]Human Rights Watch/FIDH interviews, Cyahinda church, November 8, 1994; Nyantanga, June 20, 1995; Nyakizu, August 28 and October 20, 1995 and January 5, 1996.

[101] A policeman named Gashagaza, identified by several witnesses, may have been among the National Police since he was apparently not a communal policeman at the time. Our witnesses estimate the number of National Police participating in the attack between four and sixteen. Apparently thirty were stationed in the commune at the time, at least ten of them at the camp for Burundian refugees. An account published by African Rights gives

Ntaganzwa were armed, including Geoffrey Dusabe, François Bazaramba, a university student, and the director of a vocational high school.[102] They were backed by approximately two hundred Burundian refugees, some of whom were also armed, by the MDR-Power activists and by one to two thousand others.

Several witnesses, including one from Gikongoro, stated that Damien Biniga, sub-prefect of Munini, participated in the attack along with his Interahamwe. They said that some of the attackers from Gikongoro wore banana leaves across their chests or tied in clumps on their arms so that assailants could be easily distinguished from victims. They also used the greeting "*Power*" and they saluted each other, "Turatsembatsemba abatutsi" or "We will exterminate the Tutsi."[103]

Using a loudspeaker to address the crowd, the burgomaster demanded that they put down their weapons. Some did so. One of the National Policemen began threatening those who refused. The burgomaster then insisted that the people from Gikongoro leave the church, perhaps wanting to divide the crowd so that it would be easier to attack.[104]

He said, "Everyone [from Gikongoro] must leave, or you will see what happens." And he counted to three, "One, two, three." And just after that, they began to fire. It was chaos. Everyone ran. Many people fled from the church, but many others of us stayed there and hid. I hid behind some houses of the convent. There were some *militaires* [National Policemen] who found me

---

the number of National Police at the attack as between eight and eleven. African Rights, *Rwanda, Death, Despair,* p.340.

[102]This person was mentioned by title, not by name. It could have been either Celestin Batakanwa, director of the Muhambara CERAI or Joel Setabaro, director of the Nyakizu CERAI.

[103]Human Rights Watch/FIDH interviews, Cyahinda church November 8, 1994 and July 7, 1995; Butare, August 19 1995; Gasasa, August 9. 1995. African Rights, *Rwanda, Death, Despair,* p. 340.

[104]African Rights, *Rwanda, Death, Despair,* p. 339.

there. One of them wanted to kill me, but the others said to leave me alone. They knew my husband [a Hutu] and said that he was a good man.[105]

Since early on April 15, Burundian refugees—particularly women and children—had left their camp and headed towards the border. Men capable of fighting stayed in Nyakizu, probably about one thousand of them, and many of them killed ferociously. One witness, who identified the Burundians by hearing them shout in Kirundi, declared:

The Burundians were killing anyone they saw. At the church, the shooting continued. People were scattering, coming out of the church. And the Burundians were hunting them down.[106]

When the afternoon attack began, the Tutsi took a stand on the large soccer field behind the church and school. There, near the summit of the hill and protected by school buildings on either side, they again hurled rocks to defend themselves. In July 1995, a survivor from Gikongoro walked over the site with Human Rights Watch and FIDH researchers, recalling the massacre:

When the attack started, we scattered, running down to the soccer field to fight....Most of my family died on the soccer field. Three children died here. My wife died here....I myself got shot. This was on the 15th of April. We were destroyed together. I lay down with my dead family as the killers attacked....The attackers included military men and civilians, one person in uniform with lots of civilians. Since they did not have many bullets, they shot only the strong people and attacked the weak ones with machetes. And I was shot in the leg. I couldn't run, so I lay down among the cadavers. The attackers whom I saw were not drunk. They wore banana leaves. The ones in Gikongoro

---

[105]The term "*militaire*" means literally a military person, member of the armed forces. Rwandans often use the term and its Kinyarwanda equivalent *umusirikare* to mean any person in uniform, particularly if carrying a gun. Because National Policemen wore the same uniform as regular soldiers (except for distinctive berets), witnesses cannot ordinarily distinguish National Police from soldiers on the basis of appearance alone. Here we specify National Policemen because we do not know of any soldiers at the church on April 15. Human Rights Watch/FIDH interview, Butare, August 19, 1995.

[106]Human Rights Watch/FIDH interview, Butare, August 19, 1995.

had also worn banana leaves. And they wore chalk on their faces so that you couldn't recognize them. They wore that both in Gikongoro and here.

When the first line of civilians with traditional arms was failing, they moved back and the second line of attackers which had been behind them came forward. They had guns and they shot, which caused us on the soccer field to scatter. Then, the first attackers came forward again and they chased us, moving onto the field with machetes to attack us.[107]

During the afternoon a large group of Tutsi fled from the parish. One of the group recalls:

We left with many women and children. I carried children, and my wives carried children. We left everything else behind, including the pigs. We left in a big line—so that nobody else could get in between us. At that time, the attackers had turned their attention in another direction. They were engaged in shooting and didn't pursue us. They had not yet formed a human enclosure around the church. On the path to Gasasa, we did not encounter attackers. We could see that elsewhere people living around there were watching and even assisting in the attack. The neighbors who did see us were afraid to attack us, because we had strong men in the line, and they knew that one of the National Policemen had already been killed. Local people avoided us, except for saying "Kagame has deceived you."[108]

During the attack, the Tutsi managed to kill two National Policemen. As the police moved forward firing across the field, some Tutsi came out of buildings behind them and ran to overpower them. They killed one policeman by machete, but apparently shot the second with the gun taken from the first.[109] The national radio would later report the incident, saying that National Police who were trying

---

[107]Human Rights Watch/FIDH interview, Cyahinda church, July 7, 1995.

[108]Ibid.

[109]Ibid; Human Rights Watch/FIDH interviews, Butare, October 19, 1995 and February 5, 1996.

to reach the church to protect the Tutsi had been attacked by salvos of bullets from automatic weapons.[110]

In another incident that afternoon, a Tutsi charged the burgomaster with a machete in an attempt to kill him. According to one survivor:

> Just after he [the burgomaster] spoke, one man ran up to try to kill him. He said, "I am going to die, but I will save a lot of people." He was stopped, of course, but this frightened the burgomaster, so he left right after that. He took his family to safety in Butare and went to get more military men.[111]

Another informant who saw the event confirms this version. She reports that the assailant, who was her uncle, was stopped before he even reached the burgomaster and that the burgomaster was not injured in the attack.[112]

Ntaganzwa and his supporters made full use of these incidents to heighten fear of the Tutsi exactly as the disciple of the propaganda expert Mucchielli had directed. The burgomaster traveled throughout the commune with his head bandaged warning the population that RPF soldiers were in the church, hiding in the midst of the Tutsi civilians. He insisted that everyone must help defend the commune. A Hutu witness from Rutobwe recounts:

> The burgomaster went around doing propaganda meetings, during which he said that the people of Cyahinda had thrown a grenade at him and that he had escaped by a miracle. There were witnesses who said that it was only a stone, but the burgomaster said that it was a grenade. He got in his pickup truck with his head bandaged and went around telling the population: "They tried to kill me!" People saw that his head was bandaged and they believed. I believed it myself when I saw his bandage. Only later did I find out that he had taken advantage of the stone to arouse anger in the commune: a stone had become a grenade. And the truth? Well, people saw the bandage and believed it was the truth.[113]

---

[110] Solidarité Internationale pour les Refugiés Rwandais, *Le Non-Dit sur les Massacres,* vol.2, p. 12.

[111] Human Rights Watch/FIDH interview, Nyakizu, January 5, 1996.

[112] Human Rights Watch/FIDH interview, Butare, March 13, 1996.

[113] Human Rights Watch/FIDH interview, Butare, October 19, 1995.

Eager to multiply pretexts for the massacre, Ntaganzwa and his circle also claimed to have found a list of names of people who had given money to the RPF, a claim just like that heard in so many other places in Rwanda. The witness who reported this remarked:

> I did not know if this was true, but it generated a lot of anger among the people. And who could verify these claims? Those who knew the truth were afraid, and people were not supposed to be going out.[114]

Improving Participation

Although many Tutsi had been killed or wounded, they had successfully withstood the attacks on Friday. By that evening, Ntaganzwa saw the need to reinforce the attackers, especially because the Burundians who had played such an important part in the assault declared that they would not continue their "work" the next day unless they could be assured of more support from the Rwandans. The burgomaster apparently called for reinforcements from Butare and from communes in Gikongoro. He also decided to take measures to improve participation among the people of his own commune.[115]

Large numbers of people had turned out to pillage, which was not surprising given the overwhelming poverty and actual hunger in Nyakizu. Even if the person targeted were just as poor as the pillager, the criminal still went home richer than he had begun. And if the target was in fact more prosperous—in the case of some traders and members of the elite, considerably more prosperous—the pillagers were indeed happy to share in such a "festival." At Cyahinda, some of the assailants also pillaged the schools and health center, disappearing down the paths laden with mattresses from the dormitories, computers from the offices, and microscopes from the health center.[116]

If many wanted to steal, fewer were ready to destroy or to kill. Out on the hills, a JDR leader had to insist that assailants burn and destroy houses instead of just pillaging and moving on to the next target. The National Police reportedly had to

---

[114]Ibid.

[115]Human Rights Watch/FIDH interview, Cyahinda church, November 8, 1994.

[116]Human Rights Watch/FIDH interviews, Cyahinda church, November 8, 1994; Nyakizu, October 20, 1995; Butare, October 19, 1995; Ladislas Ntaganzwa, Bourgmestre, to Monsieur l'Administrateur communal (Kabarore) et Monsieur le Bourgmestre (Nshili, Mubuga, Kigembe, Gishamvu), no. 102/04.02.01/7, May 10, 1994 (Butare prefecture).

press people to attack persons because they were too focused simply on looting and leaving.[117] One woman fleeing with her children to Cyahinda thought they would be killed when they stumbled on a group of assailants on a back path through the sorghum fields. But, as she reported, "They were busy killing cattle and cutting them up. They were too busy with that to bother with us. So we were able to get to Cyahinda."[118]

To turn pillagers into killers and resisters into participants, Ntaganzwa decided to eliminate several moderate Hutu leaders who were providing a model and a cover for others who would not kill. The most important was Jean-Marie Vianney Gasingwa, the PSD leader in the commune and Ntaganzwa's rival for political control since more than a year before. As assistant burgomaster, Gasingwa spoke with authority as well as reason. He asked people, "Why kill? What will it get you? Why do it?"[119] He had refused to disarm the Tutsi the day before the massacre, thus encouraging a similar refusal from a university student who worked as an intern at the communal office, and perhaps from others.[120] The student recalls that after the Friday massacre, Gasingwa and several other moderates had decided to spend the night at the communal office:

We were at the commune, and the burgomaster sent a message calling us to Nyagisozi: Come to my place for a drink. They went, but I didn't go because I was guarding my home....On their return, they had walked about 100 meters, and [they were killed] ... [by] a group of Burundians accompanied by friends of the burgomaster. [The killers] were armed with machetes....Saturday morning, I was at my place and I got the news that my friends had been murdered. "And you are also in danger," I was told by the person who brought me the news. I decided to flee.[121]

Three other communal employees, Jean-Damascene Nkurikiyeyezu, the cashier, Jean-Marie-Vianney Ntawukuliyayo, the accountant, and Cansius Kalisa,

---

[117]Human Rights Watch/FIDH interview, Butare, October 19, 1995.

[118]Human Rights Watch/FIDH interview, Nyakizu, August 19, 1995.

[119]Human Rights Watch/FIDH interview, Cyahinda church, November 8, 1994.

[120]Human Rights Watch/FIDH interview, Butare, August 19, 1995.

[121]Ibid.

the agronomist were killed with Gasingwa. A fifth government employee, the director of the Centre de Formation de la Population, was slain later while passing the communal office on his motorcycle, which was then appropriated by National Policemen.[122]

The national radio reported these murders, but in one of the cynical deceptions common during the genocide, it said the moderates had been slain by Tutsi from Cyahinda church. Thus those committed to the genocide not only rid themselves of dissidents but used their deaths to heighten fear and hatred of the "enemy."[123]

According to a witness from the commune, "Killing these officials was very important in shaping popular thinking (*sensibilisation*)."[124] Several other persons corroborated this judgment, one of them saying, "When the party leaders got killed, that scared the lesser PSD people."[125] As in so many other places in Rwanda, people who had begun just by fearing the RPF now had reason to fear their own officials and political leaders. Because Ntaganzwa had already demonstrated his ruthlessness before April 6, people could easily believe that he would use force against any who opposed the genocide.

Beginning the next morning, April 16, the National Police added their direct pressure to the threat implied in the Friday night murders. One witness declared:

> The National Police appropriated the pickup trucks at the commercial center and beginning on Saturday, they took everybody along the road. "Let's go fight the RPF!" As if there were RPF in each Tutsi family and in the buildings at the church and the CERAI. They believed that there were lots of soldiers at the church. But, in fact, there were no soldiers of the RPF at the parish. There were ordinary people. Cyahinda was full of children, women, and men, not soldiers.[126]

---

[122]Ibid.; Human Rights Watch/FIDH interview, Cyahinda church, November 8, 1994.

[123]Human Rights Watch/FIDH interview, Butare, October 19, 1995.

[124]Ibid.

[125]Human Rights Watch/FIDH interview, Gasasa, August 9, 1995.

[126]Human Rights Watch/FIDH interview, Butare, October 19,1995.

During the night, most Tutsi had stayed put at Cyahinda, in part for lack of any clear idea where else to go, in part because guards were present to keep them from leaving. Some witnesses report that on Saturday morning fresh troops arrived from Butare, probably more National Policemen. Ntaganzwa and his assistants organized local assailants more tightly than before in groups of about fifty men. In some cases, the leaders presented themselves with their groups already assembled, in others, the burgomaster named the heads. Most of the groups included one or two policemen, former soldiers or others with guns, to strengthen a force otherwise armed with traditional weapons.

A survivor of the massacre recounts what happened in a brief time of quiet just after dawn:

> People began to assemble in groups, looking for members of their families. It was just after daybreak....I went up to some buildings in the church complex to look for my three children. I was in a kitchen there, just behind the door, when the firing started again. This was around seven or eight in the morning. If I had not been behind the door, I would have been killed. The bullets hit the door, and people came falling into the room shot dead.[127]

Groups of attackers came rushing up the hill from several directions at once, trying to surround the Tutsi and to push them into a smaller space where they could be more easily slaughtered.

The killing went on all day, but still the Tutsi were so many that the assailants could not get to the church building. The killers went home in the late afternoon, establishing a schedule that they would follow for the next few days. As one witness reported, "They came exactly at 7 a.m. each morning, just like government employees. They worked until 5 p.m. and then came back the next morning at 7 again." In the evening, they went home singing Hutu Power songs to feast on the cattle they had pillaged.[128]

On Saturday evening, a large group of Tutsi arrived from Kivu commune in Gikongoro, driving their cattle before them. Many may have been survivors of the killings at Muganza church who had fled from there Friday night. They were such a large crowd that people along the way were apparently intimidated by them and let them pass. Tutsi at the church were at first suspicious, afraid that some

---

[127]Human Rights Watch/FIDH interview, Nyakizu, January 16, 1996.

[128]Human Rights Watch/FIDH interview, Cyahinda church, November 8, 1994.

Interahamwe might have infiltrated the group, and tried to drive them away. But then the Cyahinda crowd accepted the others, who thus swelled the mass to confront the assailants the next morning.[129]

Promises of Help, Threats of Reprisals

On Sunday, April 17, the killing started again in the morning, but stopped for a time in the early afternoon with the arrival of Prefect Habyalimana, Major Habyarabatuma, and other officials. Habyalimana and Habyarabatuma were struggling to keep control in the prefecture in the face of multiple challenges to their authority, of which the killing at Nyakizu was the most serious. In the face of the growing hopelessness of the situation, the prefect sought to reassure the Tutsi. According to a woman who was at the church:

> He came and spoke to the crowd. He announced that he would bring troops to defend the Tutsi and that he would bring food....The killing died down for a little while just after his visit. But very soon after, it started again.[130]

That evening, as the prefect was returning to Butare, the national radio announced that he had been removed from his post. He was never able to keep his promise to help the people at Cyahinda.

Sunday afternoon, Ntaganzwa and his supporters continued their intimidation of those who were not participating in the killing. They wanted to ensure that no new leaders stepped forward to replace Gasingwa and the others killed for opposing the genocide. The burgomaster, the director of the vocational high school, four National Policemen and about thirty others from the neighborhood called on a teacher who had considerable standing, both because of his education and because he came from a large family. They searched his house, looking for Tutsi. Although they found none, they warned the teacher, "If you do not come with the others [to kill], you are an accomplice of the Inkotanyi." He was so frightened by the threat that he did not dare go out to the road after the incident. He reports, "I said to myself, 'If they see me, they can send someone to kill me.'"[131]

---

[129]Human Rights Watch/FIDH interview, Nyakizu, January 16, 1996.

[130]Ibid.

[131]Human Rights Watch/FIDH interview, Butare, October 19, 1995.

The same day that this visit took place at the southern most limit of Rwanda, Froduald Karamira, Vice-President of MDR-Power, approved such searches in a statement on Radio Rwanda. He said:

> The people...are now systematically searching all homes, looking for any person hidden there, any person who has not done patrols with others, who has not been seen with others, because such a person is suspected of hiding guns, since there are armed people who are not in military uniform who have hidden among the people....[132]

Whether or not Ntaganzwa and his group heard this particular statement before visiting the teacher, they were in fact carrying out the policy of the national leaders like Karamira whose words they virtually echoed in threatening the teacher.

Other dissidents, too, would have heard Karamira's speech or similar pronouncements and they would have understood the meaning of Habyalimana's removal. They would have understood that Ntaganzwa's killings and threats had the backing of those above him both in the administrative hierarchy and in the party system. With no likelihood of support from higher authority outside the commune and with the local leaders of the opposition dead, those who might have opposed the genocide in Nyakizu gave up. Some fled, like the student intern. Those who stayed formed a disapproving, but silent block who went into hiding, refused to participate or participated as little as possible. Many continued to take risks privately to protect Tutsi with whom they had ties, but they did not dare oppose the genocide publicly.[133]

On Monday morning, police, national and communal, former soldiers and armed civilians joined in launching a more vigorous attack on the parish. By this time, the civilian attackers had grown to such numbers that they could completely enclose the complex to cut off any escape. Witnesses watching from a distance described it as a "fence of people," with various groups assigned to guard each area. These witnesses say that they could see sub-prefect Biniga organizing these groups to form the cordon of killers.[134] The armed attackers moved methodically

---

[132]Chrétien et al, *Rwanda, Les médias,* p. 302.

[133]Ibid.; Human Rights Watch/FIDH interviews, Cyahinda church, November 8, 1994; Butare, August 19 and October 9, 1995; Gasasa. August 9, 1995.

[134]Human Rights Watch/FIDH interview, Gasasa, August 9, 1995.

from one building or enclosure to the next. A survivor of the massacre described a courtyard in the church complex this way:

> Here it was completely full of people, and they shot into this dense crowd with machine guns. A lot of people died here. There are no bullet holes on the walls, because the crowd was so dense that the bullets went into their bodies. Even if the bullets passed through one person's body, they went into the body of another person.[135]

The assailants with guns then forced their way into the church through the main doors and the doors on the right side. Others, armed with machetes, clubs, and spears, followed closely behind.

The violence was so extraordinary in scale and ruthessness that a witness, hiding in her home and watching from the window, rubbed her eyes in disbelief and asked the person with her, "Do you see what I see?"[136]

That day a second important outsider came to offer help at Nyakizu, but to the killers rather than to their intended victims. Interim President Sindikubwabo stopped briefly at the communal office in the course of his tour to mobilize the people of southern Rwanda. His audience was small because most of the people of the commune, including the burgomaster, were busy attacking the church. A witness who was among the 200 or so persons who heard him speak reported that he said:

> People of Nyakizu, this is the first time you have had a visit from the president of Rwanda. I have come to encourage you and to thank you for what you have done so far. I am going back now to get some people to help you with this work and to see about a reward for you.[137]

Another witness saw the visit as a turning point. He recalls:

> In the evening, the information about this visit spread in the sectors. On the radio they said that the president had passed at Nyakizu and had told people,

---

[135]Human Rights Watch/FIDH interview, Cyahinda church, June 26, 1995.

[136]Human Rights Watch/FIDH interview, Cyahinda church, November 8, 1994.

[137]Ibid.

"We have to do as in 1959!" In Kinyarwanda, "Mukore nko 1959!" This referred to the revolution....The president just passed through. He gave permission. The participants said to themselves, "We are following the true path. We have been blessed by the president. The others are Inkotanyi."[138]

According to another informant, Sindikubwabo told people, "Even if you have to demolish the church to get rid of the Tutsi, do it. I will take responsibility."[139]

Unlike the prefect, Sindikubwabo was in a position to keep his promise. The next day twelve soldiers arrived in army jeeps, under the command of a young lieutenant, most likely Lt. Ildephonse Hategekimana from the Ngoma camp in Butare. The soldiers brought some heavy weapons which they used to fire a few rounds at the church from the communal office across the valley. They joined the other assailants in slaughtering those left at Cyahinda. They pursued people throughout the church, into the vestry, the sacristy, and onto the altar, leaving walls splattered with blood and brains. After nearly two years and countless washings, the stains remained as a testimony to the massacre. By Tuesday night, April 19, the killing at Cyahinda was complete, and the church and surrounding buildings and grounds were strewn with corpses.

That weekend in mid-April, the church at Cyahinda, some 1,050 square meters in area, probably sheltered between 3,000 and 3,500 people. The schools and outbuildings in the complex may have held 4,000 to 5,000 more. It is more difficult to judge the number who might have been on the grounds. The land falls away rapidly on the right side of the church, so it is unlikely that more than a few hundred people would have been there, but in front, behind and to the left of the church, there was space for several thousand to gather.

The total Tutsi population of Nyakizu just before the genocide was about 11,300,[140] of whom perhaps 7,000 to 8,000 went to Cyahinda. There were also thousands of Tutsi from outside Nyakizu who took shelter in the church complex. On April 15, prefectural authorities estimated that 20,000 people were at Cyahinda, many of whom would have been women, children, and the elderly.[141] Adolescent

---

[138]Human Rights Watch/FIDH interview, Butare, October 19, 1995.

[139]Human Rights Watch/FIDH interview, Nyakizu, January 16, 1996.

[140]Commune Nyakizu, Raporo y'ibarura ry'abaturage ukwezi kwa gashyantare 1994.

[141]Anonymous, Notebook 1, entry for April 15, 1994.

or adult males actively defending the church probably numbered fewer than 4,000 to 5,000.

The maximum number of persons with firearms in Nyakizu in early April was apparently between sixty and seventy, including some thirty National Police, twelve regular soldiers, five or six communal policemen, and another two dozen civilians—former soldiers, Hutu power leaders, and militia—who had been given guns and grenades. At the height of the attack on Cyahinda, when the soldiers were present, there many have been as many as thirty assailants armed with guns. In terms of other attackers, one witness estimated that "half the commune" or as many as 10,000 assailants participated. A report filed in March 1994 records a population in Nyakizu of some 24,700 Hutu males, about half of whom would have been under the age of fifteen or sixteen.[142] Of the some 12,350 adult Hutu males, perhaps 10 to 15 percent would have been too old or unable to participate in the attack for some other physical reason. This leaves a group of potential adult male assailants of some 10,000, some of whom refused to participate and others of whom were occupied elsewhere in the commune at the time. It is possible that some women or adolescents, say between the ages of thirteen to fifteen, also participated, but no witness has ever indicated sizable numbers of either group among those who besieged the church. In addition, there were assailants from neighboring communes, probably at least several hundred, and an equal or larger number of Burundian refugees. The attackers were not strong enough to storm the church for the first three days, even with the help of a certain number of guns. Once they entered the building, they needed two days to finish the killing. This suggests that there were fewer assailants than victims, perhaps between 6,000 and 8,000.

Just after the massacre, clergy in Butare who knew the church well estimated that 5,500 Tutsi died in the Cyahinda massacre.[143] The number may have been considerably higher, perhaps between 10,000 and 15,000, men and women, old people and young, all condemned for the simple fact of being Tutsi. Apparently the last to die from the attack on the church was a schoolgirl who was thrown alive in a deep hole, probably filled with cadavers. Other children came to give her water to drink. When the burgomaster learned of this, he ordered the hole covered.[144]

---

[142]Commune Nyakizu, Raporo y'ibarura ry'abaturage ukwezi kwa gashyantare 1994.

[143]Alison Des Forges to Ambassador Karel Kovanda, Representative of the Czech Republic at the United Nations, May 15, 1994.

[144]Human Rights Watch/FIDH interview, Cyahinda church, November 8, 1994.

The Hilltops

The hill from which Nyakizu commune draws its name rises steep-sloped in the center of the commune. More than 2,000 meters high, it provides a clear view of surrounding sectors. Sparsely populated, much of it is planted in trees that provided some protection to those in hiding. Some people came directly to Nyakizu hill, assuming it would afford more safety than other locations. One woman recounted:

> We were fleeing and arrived at Nyakizu and...decided to hide near the forest. There was a Hutu living nearby who agreed to hide us. He invited me to go inside, but I was afraid. I had the three-year-old on my back. I went to hide outside in the sorghum. The child began crying, and the attackers heard the cries. They came. I tried to put the child on my back, but I was shaking so badly that I could not tie the knot in the cloth.[145] I started to run. Behind me, the attackers were chasing me. The child fell. The attackers hit the child on the head with a stick, and the child died.
>
> I kept running. Ahead, I encountered another attacker. I gave him 9,000 francs [about U.S.$50] to save me....He had banana leaves on his hips and along his neck and shoulders. He had a machete. He was like a madman. He grabbed me by my clothing at the neck and dragged me. I made signs that I had money, and he let me go. By this time it was night, and I decided to return to Nyakizu hill.[146]

Others who were on their way to Cyahinda stopped at Nyakizu when they saw that the church was under attack while still others who were first at the church fled to the hill during the days of the siege.

As was often the case elsewhere, the first attack at Nyakizu hill was a preliminary skirmish. On Saturday, April 16, a group of people, mostly from the eastern sectors of the commune, attacked armed with traditional weapons. A former soldier and employee of Bazaramba at the Baptist Church led the charge. The night before Bazaramba had reportedly given guns to him and a nightwatchman at his bar. As at Cyahinda, the Tutsi at Nyakizu defended themselves by throwing stones,

---

[145] Women in Rwanda usually carry small children on their backs in slings made of pieces of cloth.

[146] Human Rights Watch/FIDH interview, Nyantanga, June 20, 1995.

benefiting from their position higher on the hill. According to one participant, there was no plan to the defense except "not to be killed like sheep" and all, men and women, children and the elderly, joined in. The Tutsi fended off the attack without fatalities, but some felt that their position was too vulnerable and they fled to the church even as some people were leaving Cyahinda for the hill.[147]

On Sunday, a larger crowd of assailants attacked the hill, armed with four guns. Witnesses report that Bazaramba himself led the charge. According to a survivor, "The attackers were numerous enough to fill the whole market place....They were stronger than we were, because they had guns."[148] Another witness remarked, "They killed like people go to the fields, going home when they get tired,"[149] leaving the remainder of the work to be finished the next day.

On Monday, April 18, the people at Nyakizu hill could see that Cyahinda was encircled. Hearing the gunfire and the explosions of the grenades, they knew that the "work" there would soon be completed and that the crowds of killers would be able to focus on Nyakizu. Several groups of Tutsi who managed to break out of the encirclement and to make their way to the hilltop confirmed that the massacre at Cyahinda would soon be over. Many Tutsi decided to flee Nyakizu hill before Tuesday morning.

Some trekked on to another peak of the Nyakizu ridge known as Gasasa. There they found Tutsi from the sector Gasasa who had fled to the hill together on April 15 after a meeting with their cell leader and councilor. Other Tutsi had come from Cyahinda, swelling the group to many thousands. On April 18, they had discussed the grim choices they faced but did not reach a common decision on what to do. The next day, most left, in three groups heading in different directions. A fourth group, those who would have trouble fleeing, stayed at Gasasa. The one point that all accepted was that those who fled should leave their cattle behind on the hilltop. They hoped that this rich booty would distract the killers and give them more time to escape.[150]

The killers attacked at Gasasa on April 20 and 21, after the assault on Nyakizu hill. A survivor described what he saw:

---

[147]Human Rights Watch/FIDH, interviews Maraba, Nyakizu, August 16, 1995.

[148]Ibid.

[149]Ibid.

[150]Human Rights Watch/FIDH interviews, Gasasa, July 20 and August 9, 1995.

The attackers came from all the sectors of Nyakizu and with them were Burundians. The first attackers came from...Cyahinda. The others came from the left side. They surrounded the hill, taunting us, watching us. They formed a circle around the hill, then they sat down. They were not in a line exactly, but in groups that formed a kind of circle around the hill....There were different groups of attackers who were off burning houses, and there were others who were sitting surrounding the hill.

Then a person blew a whistle, and they all came together and they began climbing the hill toward us. I saw them climbing. I saw them coming and I heard three guns behind me. There were also shots coming from the right side. And I saw the burgomaster's truck in front, but the burgomaster was behind us, up on top of the hill with a hand-held loudspeaker.[151]

When the attack began, the burgomaster immediately recognized the risk that the attackers might focus more on securing their share of the loot than on the killing. From his commanding position on top of the hill, he announced over his loudspeaker that the attackers should leave the cows alone, that they would be compensated later for not touching them at the time.[152] One man who survived came a short distance down the hill and hid behind a tree. He recounted:

My wife and my children were killed by machetes here on this hill. You know, they didn't kill the children who were younger than two years old, and down the hill...a woman was killed. I saw her child trying to nurse at her breast and the killers said, "Don't worry, we'll give you something to drink!"

They finished killing by 2 p.m. and then they shouted out that those who were hiding should show themselves. By 4 p.m. I was still here hiding, and I saw the red truck with the burgomaster and some councilors inside. They [got out and] looked to see if any of the people were still alive by kicking the bodies. They shouted, "I see the body of so-and-so," as they went examining the bodies. And they shouted, "Have you seen the body of the Gasasa counselor?" "No." "You've done nothing unless we find this body! Find him!" They also wanted the body of the leader of Kinyaga cellule, which is in Cyahinda sector, but he

---

[151]Human Rights Watch/FIDH interview, Gasasa, July 20, 1995.

[152]Ibid.

was killed at Nshili. The burgomaster wanted to see the bodies of the local authorities.[153]

When Human Rights Watch and FIDH researchers visited Gasasa in July 1995, they followed the path that wound in a spiral around the hill. Alongside it were a number of mass graves. They passed through fields of coffee plants, where bones, clothes and household goods were scattered. They examined a skull, half covered with earth, its mouth open in a perpetual scream. They stopped to investigate a child's red sweater and found the little rib cage intact inside it. Past the last destroyed house, on the flat hilltop, there was only tall grass littered with the remains of the people who had sought safety there: a broken rosary, a school notebook with an agriculture lesson in fine penmanship, women's underwear, wooden vessels for holding milk. There were large mass graves on top of the hill but they did not contain all the bones. Scattered about were ribs, vertebrae, shoulder blades.

Flight

On April 19, the people from Gasasa hill set off in three groups, one towards the west, through Nshili to Burundi, another to the east towards Gishamvu and then to Burundi, and a third to the northeast to Muyogoro in Butare. Those who fled from Nyakizu hill also took different paths, some heading northeast for the hill Bitare, on the border of Nyakizu and Gishamvu, others striking out more directly east to the main paved highway that led south to Burundi, others heading west to Nshili, hoping to pass through that commune to get to Burundi. All were attacked, no matter which way they headed. One person in the group to leave Nyakizu hill for Nshli reported:

After we arrived in Nyarure [in Kamana sector, Mubuga commune], we were attacked by the local people who killed many among us. A military man from Gisororo named Senkindi—I knew him, because my father had land and a wife at Gisororo, so I knew people there—told everybody to sit down. Then they attacked. They shot and killed the three strong men who had been protecting the group and then the civilians attacked the group with machetes. I was already injured and I fell. I was with three children. They cut off the head of one of the children. My sister-in-law was killed with her whole family. One of the children fell down and dead bodies fell on top of the child. The child

---

[153]Ibid.

survived underneath the dead bodies. The burgomaster and a soldier led the attackers.[154]

Of four groups that left in one night along the same route to the southwest, the one that left last had the most survivors because by the time they arrived the attackers had run out of ammunition and were too tired to kill as thoroughly. A survivor who made the trek in the last group relates:

We arrived at Gisenyi [Gisororo sector, Nshili commune]. The burgomaster and the soldiers attacked until there were no more bullets. So the burgomaster said, "Leave them. They'll be killed by FRODEBU." When we got to Burundi, we encountered FRODEBU [members] who killed some of the people. But the Burundi government sent its soldiers to welcome refugees.[155]

Another large group that headed to the east found the same kinds of civilian and military killers, wearing the same leaves used by assailants elsewhere, and motivated by the same goal. According to an elderly Tutsi man who was part of this group:

We left with about 1,600 all grouped together in a line. At Agatobwe, they shot at us, at our line. We fled out on the highway. There was no other way to escape, because on the small paths people with traditional arms were waiting for us. But on the open road, we were in a better position to defend ourselves. We had machetes and small sticks.[156]

At 6 a.m., we met soldiers....They asked us, "Why are you fleeing?" They ordered us: "Go back and sit down at Nkomero" [the commercial center near the border]. We saw people coming wearing leaves and carrying machetes. The soldiers disarmed those who tried to escape, while the local people threw rocks at them and hit them with machetes. The local people were approaching from one side, and the soldiers were approaching from the other. Then the soldiers started shooting. People hid in sorghum fields and others swam the

---

[154]Human Rights Watch/FIDH interview, Cyahinda church, July 7, 1995.

[155]Ibid. FRODEBU is the largely Hutu political party of Burundi.

[156]Human Rights Watch/FIDH interview, Gasasa, August 9, 1995.

river to Burundi. Many of the large group stayed together and were killed together. It was not easy for them to scatter and flee, because the attackers would follow after them and cut them down with machetes.

The attackers wore leaves. The women wore the leaves on their hips. The men wore them crossed like an "X" across the chest, in the style of *intore*. They had chalk around the eyes, as if for *kubandwa*, and they shouted "*tuzabatsembatsemba!*" [We have come to exterminate!][157]

Ntaganzwa, Bazaramba, Dusabe and others chased those who fled to Bitare, on the Gishamvu border. A woman from Nyakizu declared:

At Bitare, the attackers included neighbors [from Nyakizu], some government people, including former soldiers and communal police and our burgomaster. I saw that the attackers had vehicles. There was an attack by the burgomaster of Nyakizu, Ntaganzwa Ladislas, who said "Come ahead, but you will not get away."[158]

By April 22 the killers had finished at the church and on the hilltops, having done their best to execute the threat shouted by one killer during an attack, "You are snakes. Your god does not exist. We will exterminate you."[159]

---

[157]Ibid. The ntore were the elite in the military system that existed before the arrival of the Europeans. Kubandwa is a religion widely practiced in the central lakes region since the sixteenth century. In its rituals, participants sometimes put kaolin, or chalk, on their faces.

[158]Human Rights Watch/FIDH interviews, Maraba, Nyakizu, August 16, 1995; Butare, May 24, 1995.

[159]Human Rights Watch/FIDH interview, Nyantanga, June 20, 1995.

NYAKIZU:
THE ADMINISTRATION OF GENOCIDE

During the ten days of massacres, the burgomaster Ntaganzwa and his men worked methodically, directing incoming Tutsi to Cyahinda while cutting the escape route to Burundi, enticing or coercing local Tutsi to gather in the church before slaughtering them, day after day, from 7 am to 5 pm. With that "work" completed, they moved on to destroy those clustered on the hilltops, all the while using patrols and barriers to intercept those who tried to escape. Ntaganzwa's network functioned efficiently, collaborating with or eclipsing members of the regular administration depending on the extent of their acceptance of the genocide. He received important support from the outside: the National Police and later regular soldiers provided essential tactical knowledge and firepower; the interim president and the interim prime minister offered praise and encouragement; assailants from adjacent regions, some of them directed by their local officials, supplemented the attackers from Nyakizu itself and intercepted Tutsi who tried to leave Nyakizu; and national party leaders gave advice and directives over the radio and perhaps by other means as well.

Ntaganzwa used support from inside and outside Nyakizu to push into action many who doubted the need to kill. In the end, local leaders of the genocide mobilized a significant part of the total Hutu population to violate all the usual moral and legal rules. People who had never before taken a life learned to kill. Men who had coveted Tutsi women from a distance now raped them or forced them into cohabitation. Entire families who had lived in desperate poverty helped themselves to furniture and cooking pots, mattresses and clothes, windows and doors belonging to their neighbors. Those who rarely ate meat came home to feasts of looted cattle and goats.

At the very start of the genocide, Ntaganzwa violated the orders of his administrative superior, the prefect, who hoped to resist the killing. But as the interim government made clear by Habyalimana's removal, it was the prefect and not the burgomaster who was out of step with the program set by the new authorities. Just as the higher authorities removed the prefect, so Ntaganzwa purged dissenters from the communal council. By mid-May, authorities in Nyakizu were speaking with one voice and they were treating the elimination of the Tutsi as one more national goal to be met. They nearly succeeded.

Restoring "Normal" Life

At the end of April, Ntaganzwa began the "normalization" ordered from above: the wholesale disruption of life in which all were called to kill was to give

Kilangu Le 11/6/1994

Uyu munsaje Halindintwari
Muvene Nsahulwera

Impunzi yavuye i Bugesera
yaragijeje Igihe Cyogufata
Indangamuntu Akaba
Asabwe kyishutira NAI
Gushaka Ikemezo gisimbue
na Indangamuntu

Konseye Wasegiteri
Kilangu Muzungu Leopold

[official stamp: CONSEIL ... SECTEUR NYAKIZU ... BP 639 BUTARE]

Document: (Nyakizu commune) Form for permission to leave the commune with Hutu ethnic group (*umuhutu*) already printed on it.

/K.P./
REPUBLIQUE RWANDAISE

Nyakizu, le..19/06/1994

N°..

Préfecture de Butare
Commune de Nyakizu

B.P.8ᵗ⁹ BUTARE

Objet:

URUHUSHYA RW'INZIRA

Jyewe NTAGANZWA Ladislas,Burugumestiri wa Komini NYAKIZU,Prefegitura ya BUTARE,ntange uruhushya rw'inzira rwa ....
.BUCUMI..........mwene .MBOZE...............na .NGENZUKABONYA. ucumbitse Segiteri Mulindoro.Komini ya NYAKIZU,Prefegitura ya BUTARE rwo kujya i Mubumbano,ubwoko bwe ni umuhutu.

Impamvu..Guba mu i Burundi..........................
....

Uruhushya ruzamara iminsi .3..

Burugumesitiri wa Komini NYAKIZU
NTAGANZWA Ladislas

way to a more tightly administered campaign of extermination. In early May, the burgomaster ordered markets reopened, so signaling that people were once more to rely on production rather than pillage for their needs.[1] Not long after, some schools resumed sessions and officials made great efforts to get parents to send their children to classes. At the instruction of national authorities, the burgomaster ordered everyone who had firearms to register them. Local residents responded promptly, requesting the needed authorisation to keep their weapons. One person specified he needed the kalashnikov "for his own protection and that of the population," while another indicated that he wanted to keep his pistol for use during patrols.[2]

The communal administration functioned, although some services could not be restored due to the death or flight of personnel (including the four Hutu ordered killed by the burgomaster). The burgomaster, councilors, and cell leaders all held meetings with the population to discuss security, each time stressing that they were transmitting orders from the national government. They ordinarily opened these meetings with the same ritualized explanations of the war, beginning with its origins.

The burgomaster was able to call on both National Police and communal police to keep order, but he used them in a very restrictive way. He directed them to arrest Hutu who harassed, pillaged, or killed other Hutu but did not order them to arrest Hutu who killed Tutsi. Rather he had them detain Hutu who protected Tutsi. The local judicial police inspector prepared cases against persons suggested by the burgomaster, particularly his political enemies. He seems to have investigated only one murder during this period, that of a Hutu, and he did not, apparently, investigate any of the killings of Tutsi. The administration continued the effort to keep track of the population, more difficult but even more important during the genocide. As groups of displaced persons arrived from the north in May and June fleeing the RPF advance, councilors prepared lists of the heads of household, the number of dependents for each, and their communes of origin. The burgomaster and his subordinates provided the documents necessary to travel

---

[1]Ladislas Ntaganzwa, Burugumesitiri wa Komini Nyakizu, to Bwana Superefe wa superefegitura ya Busoro, no. 101/04.05/1, May 10, 1994 (Nyakizu commune, second copy in Butare prefecture).

[2]François Bazaramba to Bwana Burugumesitiri, May 20, 1994; Nzeyimana Vénuste to Bwana Burugumesitiri, June 25, 1994; Ladislas Ntaganzwa, Burugumesitiri wa Komini Nyakizu, to Bwana Nzeyimana Vénuste, no. 145/04.09.01/4, June 27, 1994 (Nyakizu commune).

outside the commune and issued attestations of identity for people from Nyakizu and elsewhere who had lost their identity cards. The forms prepared for such use included the information that the bearer was Hutu; Tutsi apparently were not expected to apply for the papers necessary for their safe passage outside the commune.[3]

The burgomaster reported to his superiors about the progress of the genocide, but in a discreet way. He informed them of the names of Tutsi captured and when and where they were taken. He did not usually describe their fate, although he sometimes suggested it. In one letter, for example, Ntaganzwa wrote:

> We arrived there very early in the morning. We arrested the whole group and took them to the commune, but the man named Mpakaniye was very difficult to get under control because he was armed with a spear.

Without further details, the burgomaster concluded by saying, "The population is working to help the authorities safeguard security."[4]

In another letter, the burgomaster reported the arrest on May 17 of some "Inkotanyi" found with grenades in their possession and of two other young men, strangers to Nyakizu, caught walking through the commune at night on May 19. He said nothing about the disposition of their cases except through implication, closing with the reminder that the RPF intends to take Nyakizu by force.[5]

The Language of War

The massacres at the church and on the hilltops had been conducted like military operations: the large numbers of assailants, the participation of former soldiers, communal police, National Police, and later regular soldiers, the heavy weaponry and grenades, the use of military strategy, all this suggested combat. All

---

[3]Ladislas Ntaganzwa, Burugumestiri wa Komini Nyakizu, and Geoffrey Dusabe, Umwanditsi, "Inyandiko mvugo y'inama yo kuwa 2/6/1994," enclosed in Ladislas Ntaganzwa, Burugumestiri wa Komini Nyakizu, to Bwana Perefe wa perefegitura ya Butare, no. 129/04/09/01/4, June 13, 1994 (Nyakizu commune). Hereafter cited as Nyakizu commune, "Inyandiko mvugo...2/6/1994."

[4]Ladislas Ntaganzwa to Bwana Superefe wa superefegitura ya Busoro, May 10, 1994.

[5]Ladislas Ntaganzwa, Burugumesitri wa Komini Nyakizu, to Bwana Su-Prefe wa Su-Prefegitura, Busoro, No. 109/04.09.01/4, May 20, 1994 (Butare prefecture).

that was missing was a real armed enemy. Playing upon these military trappings and mimicking the language of the national leadership, Ntaganzwa spoke of "the war that raged at Cyahinda" and of the "battle" in which the "refugees"—meaning the Tutsi—had attacked Nyakizu along with the RPF. Ntaganzwa, like officials elsewhere and like authorities in prior years, tried to justify the killings by claiming that Tutsi had hidden arms for the RPF or were in possession of military plans, maps, or lists of Hutu to be killed. When Ntaganzwa and his supporters talked of carrying out a "search for arms," they meant hunting down Tutsi.

Many understood how ridiculous it was to pretend that war had come to Nyakizu. As one citizen remarked, "Where was the war? Who was here but ordinary people? It was just the language: all Tutsi, even those still inside the wombs of mothers, were Inkotanyi." But few dared voice such opinions at the time because, as the same witness explained, "The Tutsi was Inyenzi and any one who did not talk that way was also Inyenzi."[6]

Occasionally the authorities themselves slipped and revealed the falseness of the pretense. In his famous speech at Butare, discussed below, Sindikubwabo describes the prefecture as a place as yet untouched by war. In a letter at the end of May, Ntaganzwa writes of preparing measures to be implemented "if the Inkotanyi should attack Nyakizu."[7] Indeed, the whole effort at returning life to "normal" belied the claim that the region was under attack.

Like national leaders, Ntaganzwa sought to heighten the fear of attack in order to solidify his personal control. Repeatedly he stressed the need to "be always on guard."[8] He found the demands of war-time security a useful cover for murdering rival Hutu as well as for massacring Tutsi, as is shown below. Others too adopted the same language and used the accusation of "helping the enemy" to discredit teachers who failed to show up for work, slackards who did their jobs poorly and criminals who robbed their neighbors.[9]

---

[6]Human Rights Watch/FIDH interview, Nyakizu, October 20, 1995.

[7]Reports of meetings held in the sectors enclosed in Ladislas Ntaganzwa, Burugumesitiri wa Komini Nyakizu, to Bwana Su-Prefe wa Su-Prefgitura Busoro, no. 120/04.09.01/4, May 31, 1994 (Butare prefecture).

[8]Ladislas Ntaganzwa to Bwana Su-Prefe, May 10, 1994.

[9]Geoffrey Dusabe, Umugenzuzi w'Akarere k'Amashuri, to Barimu, Barezi, no. 08.03/08/113 [114?], June 8, 1994 (Butare prefecture).

Ntaganzwa used the pretext of imminent attack also to justify asking his administrative superiors for ever more weapons, which he wanted to arm his supporters and perhaps also to continue the trade which he had apparently established to Burundi. Carrying on the use of "to work" as a code word for killing, Ntaganzwa in one document referred to guns as "tools," adding in parenthesis "weapons" to be sure his meaning was clear.[10] On May 31, Ntaganzwa prepared an order for ammunition for five different kinds of weapons, totaling 7,600 bullets, suggesting that the commune was well-supplied with arms.[11] But soon after he complained to the interim prime minister that Nyakizu had only two guns to protect itself; the patently false declaration was meant to spur delivery of more firearms.[12] When Robert Kajuga, president of the Interahamwe, arrived in the town of Butare, Ntaganzwa wrote him about "defending the sovereignty of our country." After thanking the militia head for his "spirit of patriotism," Ntaganzwa asked him also to provide weapons as quickly as possible to counter an attack from the Inyenzi.[13]

Cleaning Up

On April 28, several days after the last of the massacres, the burgomaster summoned the communal councilors, the heads of cells and political party leaders to the communal office "to examine the situation after the battle of Cyahinda."[14] He began by reviewing the history of the war—that is, the responsibility of the RPF for having launched the war and hence for all the misery that followed from it. He talked at some length also about the "refugees" who had been in the church—where they had come from and why they had collaborated with the

---

[10]Ladislas Ntaganzwa, Burugumesitiri wa komini Nyakizu, to Bwana Superefe [June 4, 1994] (Nyakizu commune).

[11]Ladislas Ntaganzwa, Burugumesitri wa Komini Nyakizu, "Amasasu Akenewe Muli Komini Nyakizu, May 31, 1994" (Nyakizu commune).

[12]Ladislas Ntaganzwa, Bourgmestre de la Commune Nyakizu to Monsieur le premier ministre [no date, no number] (Nyakizu commune).

[13]Ladislas Ntaganzwa, Burugumesitiri wa komini Nyakizu, to Bwana Kajuga, no. 124/04.09.01/4, June 3,1994 (Nyakizu commune).

[14]Ladislas Ntaganzwa to Bwana Superefe, May 10, 1994.

(78)

Busoro, le 3/6/94

11h.

Monsieur le Bourgmestre,

Nari nzi ko kugeza num masaa fine (10h) uyu munsi bari bube bampaye Amabwiriza yo kuguhumaho ngo wohereze bamwe muri rwa rubyiruko, ariko kugeza kuri iyi saha ntacyo baramunyesha (ESO ou Camp Ngoma). Ndacyategereje rero, namwe mugomba guhora mwiteguye, aussitôt que mbonye amabwiriza nzabita nkoherereza intumwa.

Ni ngufnmera ko mungambi wo gutsinda iyi ntambara kandi abatunape bahyzi bshwa guhora bari maso, ntibarambirwe kuko tutazi izaraupirira. Komite zisli-zwe guhumikiraniza koti ibyi iyi ntambara num ngefo zose (sefiti, kii aditse na selire) zikore akazi kayo ko guhora bifisha abatunape ibyo kwirengera, kandi bajagajage muri selire hose hanbe aho umwanzi ari bamurumbue, bamuhashye.

Nompeye kugushim va ko Ko—i NYAKIZU ikonuje kunyereka ko yahapunkije gutsinda umubunzi. Nimumva aho umwanzi ari, abatunape bose bahapunkire icypnimwe banuhashye atarakwira muri ko—i yose.

Amahoro.

SINBALIKURE Asriel.

Document: (Nyakizu commune) Burgomaster reports personnel changes occasioned by "troubles caused by the RPF that resulted in the death of several people, including communal employees."

/K.F./

REPUBLIQUE RWANDAISE

Nyakizu, le 19/5/1994

N° 116/04.02.01

Préfecture de Butare
Commune de Nyakizu
B.P.639 BUTARE

A traiter par ....
Date entrée : 0 1 MAI 1994
N° Classement : 1724/04.04/2

Objet: Isimburwa rya Konseye
wa Segiteri GASASA.

Bwana Perefe wa Perefegitura
BUTARE.

Bwana Perefe,

Imvururu zashojwe na F.P.R. muri Komini NYAKIZU zahitanye abantu benshi harimo n'abakozi bamwe ba Komini. Konseye wa Segiteri GASASA bwana Laurent RUHIGANGOGA kugeza ubu ntituramenya aho aherereye.

Kubera ikibazo cyihutirwa cy'iyi ntambara turimo twabaye tumusimbuje umwe mu ba Responsable MUKWIYE Tharcisse.

Uwo MUKWIYE yahiswemo hakoreshejwe itora hagati ye n'abandi ba Selire bari aho;nkuko Komite ya Segiteri yari yanditse ibisaba tariki ya 14/5/1994.

Burugumesitiri wa Komini NYAKIZU
NTAGANZWA Ladislas

Bimenyeshejwe:

-Bwana Su-Prefe wa Su-Prefegitura
BUSORO.

Inkotanyi to attack Nyakizu.[15] After this review, everyone agreed—or so Ntaganzwa told his superior—that they must follow the orders of the government in order to win the war.

Everyone may, in fact, have accepted this general principle and one of the national directives that Ntaganzwa announced seems to have caused no discussion: the implementation of the "self-defense" program. He informed them that all the communes of Butare and Gikongoro were to select ten "sure and patriotic" young men from each sector to learn the basics of "individual tactics" and how to handle firearms and grenades. The program formalized the arrangements used during the massacres, with local police and former soldiers commanding and training the civilians. The military commander of the zone would supervise the program.[16]

Explaining the second order—to carry on patrols and searches for the "enemy" and his materiel—Ntaganzwa insisted that the "the enemy is still here, the war goes on," "patrols must be done," and "we must look in the bush to see if the enemy is hiding there." But some community leaders hesitantly opposed this program. One speaker remarked that "people are wondering whom we are looking for? Tutsi?" He or another of the same leanings objected that the National Police had once prohibited barricades while another speaker interjected that people who had begun doing rounds on their own now had stopped doing them. A councilor complained that he could not be everywhere at once, presumably meaning to supervise barriers and patrols, and another speaker reported that it was too difficult to give everyone the papers necessary to get by the barriers. The councilor from Maraba sector, apparently seeking to set himself apart from the others, wanted it known that he had always told the population to do patrols. He suggested that "those who are more intelligent can make those who are less intelligent understand" the need for this work. In the end, Ntaganzwa and his supporters prevailed on this issue. The meeting decided: "Inyenzi: search tomorrow starting at 7 a.m.; discover all the possible hiding places."[17]

The third order from above—"to avoid conflicts among ourselves"—provoked as much discussion as the second. One of Ntaganzwa's firm supporters, Festus Nyamukaza, reminded the meeting that it was important to know "the truth" about

---

[15]Ibid.

[16]Lt.-Col. Tharcisse Muvunyi, Comd. Place But-Gik, to Monsieur le Bourgmestre de la Commune Nyakizu, no. 0070/Msc.1.1, April 21, 1994 (Nyakizu commune).

[17]Document entitled "Security: 28/04/1994," notes taken during the meeting at the bureau communal on that date, Nyakizu (Nyakizu commune).

the war "to avoid dividing our forces." As the discussion about searches had showed, not everyone saw "the truth" as Nyamukaza did. But, beyond the larger division over the need to pursue Tutsi lay a host of lesser conflicts over the disposition of the property of the victims. Some people had appropriated the fields of "those who fled" or had destroyed crops, including coffee, that could have been left to ripen for harvest. To avoid further conflict, the council adopted rules apparently suggested from above: the land left by Tutsi would belong to the state, to be divided at some future time; the standing crops were to belong to the commune and were to be protected by the people of the sector in which they were located; and other goods, including cattle and other animals, could be taken as loot, except for exceptionally valuable items which were to be delivered to the authorities for public sale. In addition, someone suggested adopting the rule that "no one could pillage unless the National Police were there." One of the group asserted that pillaging without adequate supervision produced greed among certain people. He added: "The person who takes something himself [that is, without official authorisation] is a thief." The burgomaster and some others were especially distressed at the pillage of goods from the health center and secondary school, property which belonged to the community rather than to the Tutsi. They demanded that goods taken from such places be returned immediately and warned that authorities would search houses for property that was not returned. They also stated that many items had been transported to other communes or across the border to Burundi. The burgomaster undertook to write his fellow administrators to ask their aid in recovering the stolen property.[18]

Once the questions of property had been discussed, there was one further pressing issue: disposing of the cadavers. Some bodies had been dumped into the long row of latrines near the church and others, those of persons killed near the frontier, had been tossed into the river. But thousands remained unburied. They smelled and they constituted a threat to public health. Several days after the massacres ended, the burgomaster started to organize burials. One survivor from Cyahinda who watched from the bushes near Nyakizu hill, reported:

On April 24, I was hiding in a small forest nearby. I could see from there that the burgomaster was making people bury cadavers. They had a Daihatsu truck

[18]Ibid.; Ladislas Ntaganzwa to Bwana Superefe, May 10, 1994.

and four pickup trucks and they gathered up the cadavers and they dug lines of holes.[19]

At the meeting on April 28, the community leaders decided that "since the refugees who stayed at Cyahinda had left behind a lot of filth"—that is, their cadavers—people would be called to do umuganda to clean up the church.[20] When people failed to respond to the call, National Police went around in a pickup truck that belonged to the Red Cross, taking men by force to bury the bodies just as they had taken some by force to do the killing. Men hid to avoid being obliged to do the work. The umuganda continued for six days. The authorities then halted the increasingly unpopular work although many bodies still remained to be buried.[21]

"Clear the Remaining Brush"
In early May, the Tutsi left alive in Nyakizu included young children—usually those under two years of age were spared—and some women, either wives of Hutu or women who had been forced into temporary cohabitation with Hutu. In addition, there were a few important Tutsi men who had not been found, such as the priest of Cyahinda, Father Charles Ncogoza, who had escaped from the church during the siege. While Ntaganzwa and his agents were directing ordinary people to resume their usual occupations, they established a new and more specialized committee to supervise the genocide of the Tutsi who remained. On May 9, Ntaganzwa called a meeting of the head of the National Police detachment, councilors, heads of cells, leaders of the political parties, and members of the Technical Commission, a group of businessmen and other community leaders that usually advised on economic development. On cue from Ntaganzwa, the meeting recommended that security councils be established for the commune and for the sectors of Nyakizu. The move foreshadowed a directive to come from the national level two weeks later with the formal establishment of the "civilian self-defense" program.[22] The declared

---

[19]Human Rights Watch/FIDH interview, Cyahinda church, June 26, 1995.

[20]Ladislas Ntaganzwa to Bwana Superefe, May 10, 1994.

[21]Human Rights Watch/FIDH interviews, Cyahinda church, November 8, 1994; Butare, October 21, 1995.

[22]Assiel Simbalikure, S/Prefe wa S/Prefegitura Busoro, to Bwana Burugmestre wa Komini Nyakizu, no. 62/04.09.01/4, June 1, 1994; Assiel Simbalikure, S/Préfet de S/préfecture Busoro, to Monsieur le Bourgmestre de la Commune Gishamvu-Kigembe-

purposes of the councils were to keep "track of the development of the war and to propose ways to win it" and to resolve conflicts over property taken from the victims. But for Ntaganzwa there was an unspoken objective as well: to replace the existing communal council by a group more committed to him and to the genocide. At a later meeting, one resident asked why security councils had been set up. Ntaganzwa's supporter Francois Bazaramba answered that the new councils "were truly necessary to serve as intermediary between the population and the authorities," implying that existing organizations were insufficient for this purpose.[23]

The community leaders elected Ntaganzwa's firmest supporters to the nine seats on the communal security council, including Celestin Batakanwa, Francois Bazaramba, Festus Nyamukaza, and Geoffrey Dusabe. The election recognized the role that these leaders had played since the start of the genocide as part of Ntaganzwa's inner circle. According to one witness, Batakanwa took charge of installing the security councils within the sectors. Following this meeting, Ntaganzwa and his aides reorganized the barriers and patrols, which had been neglected since the end of the massacres. The former soldier Celestin Rucyahana reportedly directed the patrols and did so in such a satisfactory fashion that he was later named to the post of communal policeman.[24]

As part of the "pacification" effort decreed by the national authorities, prefectural officials on May 20 scheduled a series of meetings to inform the population about the new approach.[25] The meeting for Nyakizu was scheduled for the next afternoon at the Viro marketplace. The morning of the next day, the priest who had escaped death at Cyahinda church was discovered. According to a witness:

Nyakizu-Runyinya, no 74/04.04/1, June 7, 1994 (Butare prefecture).

[23]Etienne Munyakazi, Konseye, "Inyandikonvugo y'inama y'umutekano muri segiteri Maraba yo kuwa 26/6/1994," June 27, 1994 (Nyakizu commune). Hereafter cited as "Inyandikonvugo...26/6/1994."

[24]Ladislas Ntaganzwa, Burugumesitiri wa Komini Nyakizu, to Bwana Su-Perefe wa Su-Prefegitura ya Busoro, no. 115/04.09.01/4, May 30, 1994 (Butare prefecture); interview, Butare, October 21, 1995.

[25]Anonymous, Notebook 1, entry for May 20, 1994.

Document: (Nyakizu commune) The burgomaster reports to the sub-prefect the capture and killing of Inyenzi who had first confessed that some thirty other inflitrators had penetrated the region.

/K.P./

REPUBLIQUE RWANDAISE

Nyakizu, le...31/5/1994............

N° 130/04.09.01/4 ....

A traiter par ....

Date entrée : 0 1 JUIN 1994

N° Classement : 1727/04.09.01

Préfecture de Butare
Commune de Nyakizu
B.P.639 BUTARE

Objet: **Umutekano**

Bwana Su-Prefe wa Su-Prefgitura
BUSORO.

Bwana Su-Prefe,

Impunzi ziva i Bugesera muri Komini Ngenda zimaze kuba nyinshi kuburyo harimo abo dukeka ko atari abyabyn.
Ubusanzwe hazaga abantu kavukire ka Nshiri tukabareka bakajya muri Nshiri,abandi ari kavukire ka Nyakizu tukabareka bakajya muri Segiteri bakomokamo mu miryango yabo.

Ubu rero tumaze kubona n'abakavukire ka Ngenda.Hari kandi n'impapuro ngo bandikirwa n'abakonseye baho baturuka (=muri Ngenda tudashira amakenga).

Hari inyenzi zafatiwe muri Segiteri KIBANGU,ngo imbere yo kwicwa yababwiyeko hari n'izindi mirongo itatu zigomba kuba zaraje.Ubu nafashe icyemezo cyo gushakisha hose muri Segiteri zose za Komini NYAKIZU kugirango umugambi wazo tuwuburizemo.

Ndasaba ko mwakongera mukababaza niba batakwihutisha kuduha twadutwaro.

Mboneyeho n'umwanya wo kuboherereza raporo y'amanama yakorewe mu masegiteri mu mpera z'iki cyumweru.

Burugumesitiri wa Komini NYAKIZU
NTAGANZWA Ladislas

Bimenyeshejwe:
√-Bwana Perefe wa Perefegitura
BUTARE
-Bana Komanda de Place
BUTARE-GIKONGORO.

Document: (Nyakizu commune) Report of the discovery and killing of the priest of Cyahinda church.

REPUBLIQUE RWANDAISE

Préfecture de Butare
Commune de Nyakizu
B.P.639 BUTARE

Objet: **Umutekano**

Nyakizu, le 26/5/1994

N° 112/04.09.01/4

Bwana Su-Prefe wa Su-Prefgitura
BUSORO.

Bwana Su-Prefe ,

Tariki ya 21/5/1994 i Cyahinda haramutse umutekano muke bitewe n'uko abaturage bari bavumbuye uwitwa Karori NCOGOZA wari Padiri Mukuru wa Paruwasi Cyahinda wari warihishe kwa Alexis wari usanzwe ukora aho mu gipadiri.

Naje kuhagera mu masaa yine,bamaze kumwica bafashe abari bamucumbikiye harimo na Konseyewa Segiteri Cyahinda bakekaga ko bari babiziranyeho kubera urupapuro bafashe rwari rwandikiwe uwo Padiri ruvugako K seye yahinduwe.

Nyuma baje gusaka abaturage ba Konseye bavumbura n'abandi bari bahishwe kwa Sherebuka.

Ubu abo bari bahishe Padiri bose narabarekuye basubira iwabo kuko abaturage bari hamaze gushira uburakari.

Burugumsitiri wa Komini NYAKIZU
NTAGANZWA Ladislas

-Bimenyeshejwe:

-Bwana Prefe wa Prefegitura
BUTARE .

-Bwana Komanda de Plase
BUTARE-GIKONGORO

-Bwana Komanda wa Jandarumori
BUTARE.

The priest had been hidden at the home of one of the workers at the church. Other people realized that someone was at his home when the worker went to buy beer and bread. They saw this and they asked, "How is it that such a poor man is buying bread like that?" And people began talking among themselves. The talk went all the way to the sergeant [of the National Police, presumably Sgt. Corneille Ndindayino] who organized a search of the worker's house. They found the priest. It was at Cyanwa. They brought the priest to the church, and they showed him the destruction. They said it was all his fault, because he had invited the Inkotanyi to the church. He was an accomplice. Then he was killed by one of the National Police and he was buried there. This was several weeks after the massacre. It made a lot of people angry.[26]

That the priest was found and murdered on the day important officials were expected to visit the commune may be coincidental, but it seems more likely that his hiding place had been known for some time and that it was the anticipated visit that precipitated his killing. Given that popular opinion seems to have opposed his murder, the burgomaster may have acted on that day in order to benefit from the support of the visitors, if there were a negative reaction, and to have a recent accomplishment to present for their praise.

In addition to relating the news of the priest's death to his visitors that day, the burgomaster also submitted a written report to the sub-prefect several days later. He wrote:

On the morning of May 21, there was trouble at Cyahinda caused by the discovery of Charles Ncogoza, who was the priest of Cyahinda parish and who had fled and hidden at the home of Alexis, who ordinarily worked at the parish.

When I arrived at 10 a.m., they had killed him and had arrested the people who had protected him, including the councilor of Cyahinda sector, who was suspected of complicity with those who had hidden him because they found a note addressed to the priest that talked about the councilor being replaced.

Soon after they searched the houses of all the councilor's neighbors and they found other people who had been hidden at the home of Sherebuka.

---

[26]Human Rights Watch/FIDH interview, Butare, October 21, 1995.

I released all those who had hidden the priest because I thought popular anger against them had cooled down.[27]

As the testimony of the witness suggests, the popular anger may in fact have been directed more at those who killed the priest than at those who protected him.

In the afternoon of May 21, Lieutenant Colonel Simba, head of the self-defense program of Butare and Gikongoro, Lt. Col. Tharcisse Muvunyi, commander of the military district of Butare and Gikongoro, and at least one other high-ranking prefectural official arrived to show the importance that the authorities attached to altering the execution of the genocide. Witnesses in the commune mention the presence of the person "who would become the prefect," Col. Alphonse Nteziryayo, then "assisting" the prefect of Butare but later to replace him. Another witness, who traveled to Nyakizu with the group, states that the prefect at the time, Sylvain Nsabimana, was among the delegation and does not mention Nteziryayo.[28] Like similar "pacification" visits by persons of importance to other locations, this one touched off a new round of killings. Only a few days before RTLM had reinforced the message that "pacification" did not mean an end to pursuing Tutsi. Kantano Habimana had declared the need to continue a war that would "exterminate the Tutsi from the globe...make them disappear once and for all...."[29]

Colonel Simba also recommended identifying all who had failed to participate in the killing thus far and searching their houses for evidence of support for the RPF.[30] According to a woman survivor from the sector of Nyagisozi:

Simba came in May to do the final cleanup. At that time, there were still many people hiding. For example, a family might have been hiding their cousins or their nieces. Now it was time for the final order. Those who had been hidden, now it was time to kill them all. There were single women who had been forced to cohabit with Hutu men and they were still alive. So there was a meeting in the marketplace. Lots of people were there. After that, there were

---

[27]Ladislas Ntaganzwa, Burugumesitiri wa Komini Nyakizu, to Bwana Su-Prefe wa Su-Prefegitura, Busoro, no. 112/04.09.01/4, May 26, 1994 (Butare prefecture).

[28]Human Rights Watch/FIDH interview, by telephone, Nairobi, April 3, 1996.

[29]Chrétien et al, *Rwanda, Les médias*, p.205.

[30]Human Rights Watch/FIDH interview, Butare, October 21, 1995.

eight children who had been hidden by their grandmother—all eight little grandchildren were killed. And the girls married by force, who had accepted in order to have a hiding place, they were killed that night.[31]

Another witness confirms this information:

> After the Cyahinda massacre, the next propaganda meeting took place at Viro market when Lt. Col. Muvunyi Tharcisse and Col. Simba Aloyis, and the person who later became the prefect came here from Butare. The situation had calmed down, but this meeting stirred everything up again. Their message was *"contre guerrilla."*
>
> One thing they said that I remember well was "Clear the remaining brush," in Kinyarwanda "Mukureho ibihuru byasigaye." Following these orders, they [the assailants] sought out Tutsi who were still hidden in families. Etienne Muragize, who had hidden eleven children at his house, was caught at this time....Etienne tried to pay off those who had come to search his house. He offered them 2,000 francs at first, then he added 3,000 more (about U.S.$27). He added a goat. But the eleven children were killed anyway.[32]

After the visit, authorities directed a new hunt for Tutsi. They also launched a new round of searches against Hutu who had refused to kill, accusing them of harboring accomplices or of stocking arms or of having documents, such as incriminating lists, in their houses. Often Hutu whose homes were searched had to pay a sum of money, such as 1,000 francs, to get the crowd to leave.[33]

Speaking With One Voice

During their visit to Nyakizu, Simba and the other prefectural dignitaries strengthened Ntaganzwa by publicly expressing great appreciation for what he had done against the Inkotanyi. This approval encouraged him in efforts he had begun three days before to eliminate any possible opposition to himself and to the

---

[31]Human Rights Watch/FIDH interview, Nyakizu, August 28, 1995.

[32]Human Rights Watch/FIDH interview, Butare, October 21, 1995. See chapter two for the use of the phrase "Clear the brush" during killings of Tutsi at the end of 1992 and in early 1993.

[33]Human Rights Watch/FIDH interviews, Cyahinda church, November 8, 1994; Butare, October 21, 1995.

genocide from the communal council. The recently-created security committee was his tool and the demands of war-time security his pretext. He began the May 18 meeting of the security committee by asserting that some members of the communal council had failed to pass on his orders or had wrongly reported the content of council meetings. This created the risk of what his loyal supporter Bertin Bagaragaza described as "a conflict of authority."[34] Unless the authorities spoke with one voice, the people would be confused and would not know whom to follow.

Then, one after another of Ntaganzwa's followers spoke up to accuse the communal councilors: Etienne Ntampuhwe, sector Mwoya, of living outside his sector and not knowing what was happening there; Albert Ndimbilinda, sector Nkakwa, of being too old for this work; Etienne Rugwizangoga, of having hidden accomplices, of having stopped patrols in some sectors, and of having pillaged goods; Innocent Mutaganda, sector Cyahinda, of having tried to set Hutu against each other; Laurent Ruhigangoga, of having fled the country; Emmanuel Ntakirutimana, of having hidden accomplices; Joseph Semigabo, sector Rusenge, of being very old; Daniel Niyirora, sector Yaramba, of having hidden six accomplices.

Adopting the language favored by Ntaganzwa, his men competed in heaping scorn on the communal councilors. Athanase Lindiro asked how anyone could work with those councilors who hid accomplices. Geoffrey Dusabe insisted that these councilors be removed before they "betrayed us and allowed the enemy to come in and attack us." Continuing the pretense that Tutsi were the aggressors, Festus Nyamukaza denounced a councilor "whose sector was attacked a whole week long in his absence and the people defended themselves, and when it was all over, when he came back, he did not utter a single word of encouragement [for what they had done.]" The minutes of the meeting commented that Nyamukaza was known for recommendations that were "full of good sense" which presumably enhanced the value of his proposal "to remove these people as quickly as possible, tomorrow if possible, because the more we delay, the more the enemy will profit from the situation." He was much applauded for his recommendation.[35]

---

[34]Ladislas Ntaganzwa, Umwobozi w'inama, and Geoffrey Dusabe, Umwanditsi w'inama, "Inyandiko mvugo y'inama ya Komite y'Umutekano yateranye tariki ya 18/5/1994" (Nyakizu commune). Hereafter cited as Nyakizu commune, "Inyandiko mvugo...18/5/1994."

[35]Ibid.

Document: (Nyakizu commune) Letter informing sub-prefect of the creation of a security committee "to follow the progress of the war." All named are teachers or government employees.

REPUBLIQUE RWANDAISE

Nyakizu, le 30/5/1994

N° 115/04.09.01/4

A traiter par _____

Date entrée : 0 1 JUIN 1994
N° Classement : 1728 04.09.01

Préfecture de Butare
Commune de Nyakizu

B.1.679 BUTARE

Bwana Su-Prefe wa Su-Prefegitura ya
BUSORO.

Objet:

Umutekano

Bwana Su-Prefe,

Mu rwego rwo kubambatira umutekano no gukurikira
nira hafi intambara. Tariki ya 9/5/1994 hakozwe inama ku biro bya
Komini NYAKIZU,ibuza ABAKONBEYIDUPUGUKE muri Komini,Abahagarariye
amashyaka muri Komini na Segiteri,n'uhagarariye abajandarume muri Komin
Bwana NDINDAYINO Corneille.

Abari mu nama bunguranye ibitekerezo cyane cyane
kubyrekeye intambara turwana n'umwanzi,basanga dushobora kuyitsinda
turamutse twirinze amacakubiri,gusahura,n'ibindi byose bishobora gutuma
abantu batumvikana.

Kubirebana n'imilima yeze yasinzwe n'abahunze,
hashyizweho Komisiyo muri buri Segiteri,iyo Komisiyo ikaba arinayo
inagenda ikemura ibibazo byose birebana n'iyi ntambara.

Abari mu nama basanze ari ngombwa ko hashyirwah
urwego rwa Komini rushinzwe gukurikiranira hafi uburyo bwose bw'iyi
ntambara n'uburyo twayitsinda.Abari mu nama bakiriye icyo gitekerezo
bahita banatora abantu icyenndari bagize Komisiyo. ikubuxarixxya

Dore abatowe:

1. NYAMUKAZA Festus(Ancien Burugumesitiri)
2. BAZARAMBA François(Umuyobozi w'Urubyiruko muri UEBR)
3. BAGARAHAZA Bertin (Umwarimu muri CERAI NYAKIZU)
4. BATAKANWA Célestin(Directeur wa CERAI MUHAMBARA)
5. KAYINAMURA Eugène (Umwarimu)
6. LINDIRO Athanase (Directeur wa Ecole Primaire)
7. DUSABE Geoffrey(Inspecteur Scolaire)
8. MIKANGARA André(Inspecteur de Police I.P.J.)
9. NKURIZA Evariste(Umwarimu)

Inyandiko mvugo y'inama izabereka neza
uburyo inama yagenze.

Burugumesitiri wa Komini NYAKIZU
NTAGANZWA Ladislas

Dec '95
83

Bimenyeshejwe:

-Bwana Prefe wa Prefegitura
BUTARE.

-Bwana Komanda w'Ingabo z'Igihugu
Akarere ka BUTARE-GIKONGORO.

REPÙBLIQUE RWANDAISE

Nyakizu, le.....................

N°..............................

Préfecture de Butare
Commune de Nyakizu

Objet:
GIHANGO:

      Lindiro yavuze ko hamaze gukorwa amanama atatu ku buryo abaturage basobanukiwe neza iby'intambara.

      Twakoze fouille tuvumbura inkotanyi 5 zikomoka muri komini Ngoma
Hari kandi n'abandi baducitse bitwa:Nkundizera na Munyankindi ubu bara-shakishwa.

RUSENGE:

      Lindiro yavuze ko hakiri urugomo kuri za bariyeri zimwe na zimwe bambura abantu bakanabahohotera . Hakwiye umupolisi wo gufasha abaturage gucyaha abnyarugomo.
Lindiro yanavuze ko abaturage b'ako karere bishimiye ko Burugumesitiri n'abajandarume babasura buri gihe (kenshi).

CYUNA:

      Nkuriza Evariste yavuze ko nyuma y'inama yo kuwa 28/5/1994 Burugumesitiri yakoresh umutekano umeze neza.Abari baronnye imyaka bafunzwemo babiri,ubu abandi baratinye.
Hakozwe amanama muri buri serire ku buryo ubu abaturage bifashe neza.Nkuriza kandi yana-menyesheje abari mu nama ko hari mumntu uherutse kugwa Mumu Cyuna ubu anketi iri kwa II Amarondo arakorwa neza.

GASASA:

      Nkuriza yavuzeko abaturage baho bameze neza uretse kwikanga i Nyakizu ko haba hari inyenzi mu ishyamba. Ati hakwiye imbunda hafi yaryo.

IBINDI.

1.Bariyeri zose zigomba kujya ahemejwe n'ubutegetsi.
2.Bariyeni yegereye Komini ikwiye umupolisi.
3.Gusaka imbunda no kuzishakisha.

      a)Ahakwiye gushakishwa intwaro
  - Aho Sezikeye yari atuye
  - Aho Gashugi Emmanuel yari atuye
  - Aho Gashugi Seresitini yari atuye
  - AHO Rwahama Karoli yari atuye
  - Aho Kabanda Yozefu yari atuye.

      b)Abakwiye gusakwa:

-Nshimiryayo Anga
-Rugwizangoga Etinna
-Hareramana J Baptiste.

4.Umusozi wa Nyakizu ukwiye gucungwa cyane.

      B. GUSOZA.

After having agreed to remove eight of fourteen communal councilors, the security committee immediately named "competent replacements who could work well with the intelligent people in their sectors," people "whose bravery was appreciated by the people and on whom they could count in this bad period of war." The replacements were Bertin Gategero, Ngendamabago, Francois Ndagije, Misigaro, Mukama, Callixte Sahoguteta, and Tharcisse Mukwiye.[36] With this action, Ntaganzwa completed his takeover of communal government, with a security committee composed of his staunchest supporters and a communal council purged of all opposition.

The councilors removed by Ntaganzwa belonged to the PSD and the MRND while those he appointed were all of the MDR. Those ousted from office protested to the prefect that Ntaganzwa had acted simply to favor his own party. They also rallied support among fellow party members in Butare town and Ntaganzwa was officially reproved for having acted without appropriate authorization from his superiors.[37]

The affair eventually reached even the interim Prime Minister Kambanda, one of Ntaganzwa's patrons in MDR-Power. In writing to him, Ntaganzwa turned the charge of partisanship back on his critics, once again using the cover of war-time needs. He wrote: "Thus you see that while some are sweating blood to make war, others are instead hung up with the affairs of their parties."[38] He condemned the councilors who had been removed, saying it was their fault that the patrols and barriers were not being implemented satisfactorily. For example, he said, the Gihango councilor obstructed orders so much that the people of his sector had had to tie him up in order "to get him to work, but it was wasted effort; the patrols still were not done." Any delay in replacing the slackards would "leave us open to the enemy, since the patrols, the barriers and the meetings take place only at their [i.e.,

---

[36]Ibid.

[37]Assiel Simbalikure, S/Perefe wa S/Perefegitura Busoro, to Bwana Burugumestre, May 26, 1994 and no. 62/04.09.01/4, June 1, 1994; Albert Nzimbirinda, Etienne Ntampuhwe, Etienne Rugwizangoga, Innocent Mutaganda, Daniel Niyirora, Emmanuel Ntakirutimana and Joseph Semigabo, Councilors, to Nyakubahwa perefe wa perefegitura Butare, June 27, 1994 (Butare prefecture).

[38]Ladislas Ntaganzwa to Monsieur le premier Ministre, [no date].

the councilors'] direction."[39] Ntaganzwa assured his superiors that the replacements "all distinguished themselves as great leaders in the war that took place at Cyahinda" and were the ones "who directed the attacks when Cyahinda was liberated" (for which he uses the kinyarwanda word "kubohoza").[40]

Other sources confirm that some of the councilors, like Albert Nzimbirinda and Innocent Mutaganda seem to have actually opposed the genocide. Natganzwa's accusations, however, should not be taken as proof of resistance to the slaughter. He might have falsely charged persons opposed to him personally with opposition to the genocide just to discredit them and to justify removing them from the council. If his assessment were accurate, then an important part of the political leadership of Nyakizu in fact disapproved of the killing of Tutsi, although they showed that disapproval with varying amounts of courage and persistence.[41]

Ntaganzwa sought to ensure that the ordinary people also speak with the same voice as the authorities. He called a series of meetings to inform the population about the changes in communal councilors, which, he reported to his superiors, were greeted with popular satisfaction everywhere. Following the usual model, Ntaganzwa began the meeting in Mwoya sector on May 29 by explaining "the origins of this war, dating back to the events of 1959." He went on to insist that the Hutu could win "if they stayed united, if they put their forces together and avoided anything that could divide them." Perhaps inspired by Ntaganzwa's rhetoric, a local resident asked that an umuganda be called to cut the brush where the Inyenzi might hide and everyone present agreed to participate. In Cyahinda sector the same day, Ntaganzwa was helped by Ambroise Serubibi in explaining the history of the war. Serubibi then publicly blamed the members of his own family for hindering the genocide. He said, "It is really unfortunate and sad to see that you hide Inyenzi."

---

[39]Ladislas Ntaganzwa, Burugumesitiri wa Komini Nyakizu, to Bwana Perefe wa Perefegitura ya Butare, no. 118/04.02.01, May 30, 1994 (Butare prefecture).

[40]Ladislas Ntaganzwa to Bwana Perefe wa Perefegitura ya Butare, May 30, 1994; Ladislas Ntaganzwa to Monsieur le premier Ministre [no date].

[41]Ladislas Ntaganzwa to Bwana Perefe wa Perefegitura ya Butare, May 30, 1994; Ladislas Ntaganzwa to Monsieur le premier Ministre [no date]; Ladislas Ntaganzwa to Bwana Su-Perefe, May 26, 1994; Human Rights Watch/FIDH interview, Nkakwa, August 15, 1995.

In his report, the burgomaster remarked that the blame was well placed because "many people were found hidden in this family."[42]

At the direction of the burgomaster, communal councilors and their subordinates held frequent meetings to "galvanise public awareness" during May and June.[43] In sector Rutobwe, for example, the councilor Celestin Batakanwa said that he "held many meetings to explain the whole war situation to the people, so that now they were no longer afraid and were ready to fight."[44] The meetings were public occasions for reaffirming commitment to the genocide and for accusing others of insufficient zeal. Francois Bazaramba reported that at a sector meeting in Maraba, he had raised "a little problem at Birambo" where some Hutu workers had protected Tutsi. The Tutsi "had left," but "there was still a climate of suspicion" surrounding those workers. One of those suspected, a man named Gideon who was not native to Nyakizu, had taken the floor "to accept his error and to ask pardon." The apology was not accepted and Gideon was chased from the commune, an appropriate action said Festus Nyamukaza because Gideon was "a bad type, very sneaky." Approving this, "the meeting decided that such people should not trouble public security and instead should go back to their home communes." Nyamukaza also raised the problem of Hutu men who had Tutsi wives, saying that they too "created a climate of mistrust in the heart of the population." There is no indication of immediate action to deal with this "mistrust," but the discussion indicated that such men might expect to be attacked in the future.[45]

Approval from Above

In pushing so hard to increase his own power, Ntaganzwa sometimes drew reproaches from above, but for his vigorous pursuit of the genocide, he received only praise. Soon after the security committee removed the communal councilors, Interim Prime Minister Kambanda came to Nyakizu, armed and in military

---

[42]Report enclosed in Ladislas Ntaganzwa to Bwana Su-Prefe wa Su-Prefegitura, May 31, 1994.

[43]Callixte Sahoguteta, Konseye at Yaramba, "Rapporo," June 20, 1994; Etienne Munyakazi, Conseiller at Maraba, "Raporo y'inama rusange yateranye kuwa 28/6/94" (hereafter cited as Munyakazi, "Raporo...28/6/94."); Nyakizu commune, "Inyandiko mvugo...2/6/1994."

[44]Nyakizu commune, "Inyandiko mvugo...2/6/1994."

[45]Ibid.

uniform. He was said to have delivered 200,000 francs (about U.S.$1000) to Ntaganzwa to help with local expenses. The money allowed Ntaganzwa to solve the problem of the cadavers left unburied from the April massacres: the burgomaster used 8,000 francs (U.S.$40) to buy beer to pay workers to finish the job.[46] But the political capital represented by Kambanda's visit was even more important than the money. According to one witness, "People here saw it as a gesture of encouragement." [47]

Throughout the genocide, Assiel Simbalikure, the sub-prefect of Busoro, who was Ntaganzwa's immediate superior, also strongly backed his activity against the Inyenzi. On May 26, he wrote:

> I thank you with all my heart for your determination in protecting and assuring the security of Nyakizu commune...with the help of the population as is shown in your letters no. 106/04/09.01/4 of May 17, 1994 and no. 109/04.09.01/4 of May 20, 1994.
>
> I encourage you to keep on in the same way and each time that the enemy, that is, the Inyenzi-Inkotanyi, shows his head, capture him so that he can be punished.[48]

On June 1, Simbalikure wrote to thank the burgomaster for the "good ideas" he had presented to the people of the commune in a series of meetings about the war and for "the careful attention" that he had shown "to finding the enemy Inyenzi-Inkotanyi."[49]

In another letter, also dated June 1, the sub-prefect sent Ntaganzwa and his fellow burgomasters instructions about the self-defense program, including:

---

[46]Human Rights Watch/FIDH interviews, Cyahinda church, November 8, 1994; Nyakizu, October 20, 1995.

[47]Human Rights Watch/FIDH interview, Butare, October 21, 1995.

[48]Assiel Simbalikure, S/Prefe wa S/Prefegitura Busoro, to Bwana Burugmestre wa Komini Nyakizu, no. 60/04.09.01, May 26, 1994 (Butare prefecture).

[49]Assiel Simbalikure, S/Prefe wa S/Prefegitura Busoro, to Bwana Burugmestre wa Komini Nyakizu, no. 63/04.09.01/4, June 1, 1994 (Butare prefecture).

Search everywhere in the commune for the enemy because he is clever and can sneak in like a snake. The people of the commune should do this [i.e., search] in every cell every day and the barriers should be well guarded.

He concluded:

I thank you again for the courage that you always show in these difficult times. Do not tire; the enemy is always the same and he is not yet disarmed.[50]

Two days later, Simbalikure again insisted that "the enemy must be sought everywhere and must be flushed out and neutralized once and for all." And again he thanked Ntaganzwa for having shown him "that the people of Nyakizu have decided to defeat the enemy."[51] Two days after that, he closed a letter wishing the bourgmaster "peace and even greater zeal."[52]

The Security Committee

Just like innumerable other councils and committees that filled Rwanda's recent administrative past, the security committee met regularly, discussed at length, and recorded its activities in minutes of the meeting. The procedure of the administration was normal; its objective was not. Like the more innocuous committees established earlier in other regions to assure public security, it purported to be protecting the population, but it did so by trying to eliminate that part of the population identified as Tutsi and friends of Tutsi. After mid-May, it carried out its responsibilities largely through the young men trained in the "civilian self-defense" program. According to the minutes of the May 18 meeting, these young men were to protect the sectors from which they came and to train other young men at the level of the cells. [53]

---

[50]Assiel Simbalikure, S/Prefe wa S/Prefegitura Busoro, to Bwana Burugmestre wa Komini Gishamvu, Kigembe, Nyakizu, Runyinya, no. 64/04.09.01/4, June 1, 1994 (Butare prefecture).

[51]Assiel Simbalikure, S/prefet, to Monsieur le Bourgmestre, handwritten, no number, June 3, 1994 (Nyakizu commune).

[52]Assiel Simbalikure, S/Prefe wa S/Prefegitura Busoro, to Bwana Burugmestre wa Komini Nyakizu, no. 66/04.09.01/4, June 5, 1994 (Butare prefecture).

[53]Nyakizu commune, "Inyandiko mvugo...18/5/1994."

In good administrative practice, the council ordinarily began by reviewing action taken since the last meeting. Thus on June 2, Lindiro of Gihango sector reported:

> We searched and we discovered five Inkotanyi originally from Ngoma commune. There were others named Nkundizera and Munyankindi who escaped whom we are still looking for.[54]

At the same meeting Batakanwa of Rutobwe sector reported an unsuccessful search for an Inkotanyi named Jean Nzirabatinyi who was not found at Rugwiganzoga's house, where he had been said to be hiding.

The participants ennumerated meetings held—apparently always with satisfactory results—and reported on the functioning of barriers and patrols. They identified troublemakers, such as Pascal Burindwi, who was obstructing patrols in the sector of Yaramba. They examined causes of concern, such as the continued sighting of lights in the forest of Nyakizu hill, which might indicate that the enemy still lurked among the trees despite the massacre of the Tutsi there. They assigned tasks, directing that the "self-defense" recruits should take over barriers and patrols. They specified that men with the most education should be assigned to the barriers during the day when passersby were most numerous because they were most able to scrutinize identity papers for any irregularities. They stated needs: flashlights for night searches, but especially more weapons. And they designated the next targets: on May 18, this was the whole sector of Cyahinda; on June 2, it was certain deserted homes—presumably of Tutsi who had been killed or fled—and the homes of Hutu known to oppose the genocide.[55] Ntaganza set the stage early in the June 2 meeting by announcing that an informant had recently revealed that many arms were hidden in the commune. Using the usual pretext to cover looking for Tutsi, he insisted that people must "search with the greatest care in all places where arms might be hidden." The council took its cue. Under the heading "Miscellany," the minutes record:

1). All barriers should be put at places designated by authorities.
2). The barrier next to the communal office needs a policeman.
3). Carry out searches, looking everywhere for arms.

---

[54]Nyakizu commune, "Inyandiko mvugo...2/6/1994."

[55]Ibid.; Nyakizu commune, "Inyandiko mvugo...18/5/1994."

a. Places where we must search for arms:
  - Where Sezikeye used to live
  - Where Gashugi Emmanuel used to live
  - Where Gashugi Celestin used to live
  - Where Charles Rwahama used to live
  - Where Joseph Kabanda used to live

b. People whose homes must be searched
  - Nshimiryayo Ange
  - Rugwizangoga Etienne
  - Harerimana Jean Baptiste

4). Nyakizu hill must be carefully guarded.[56]

The Burgomaster: More Feared than Trusted

Even after having secured his control of the communal council, Ntaganzwa continued using the cover of security concerns to attack his personal enemies. One of the persons targeted by the Security Committee, Rugwizangoga, was a councilor who had been removed on May 18. Ntaganzwa was particularly anxious to destroy him because he opposed the genocide and because he continued to have standing in the community. The burgomaster had harassed Rugwizangoga for some time and immediately after the June 2 council meeting he had him beaten badly and thrown in the communal lockup.[57]

Another whose house was targeted by the Security Committee was Nshimiryayo, a prosperous businessman, older than Ntaganzwa and a former deputy in the assembly. Linked to the moderate MDR leader Twagiramungu, he had posed a challenge to Ntaganzwa even before the genocide. On April 15, Nshimiryayo had been warned that his house was about to be attacked and he fled with his family to Cyahinda just before the massacre there began. They survived and later escaped from the commune, his wife and children going in one direction while Nshimiryayo went in another and took shelter in the adjacent commune of Mubuga. In official correspondence throughout May and June, and presumably in informal contacts with people of the commune, Ntaganzwa fired one accusation after another against Nshimiryayo: that he was trying to cause conflicts among Hutu and thus allow the enemy to infiltrate; that he had a Tutsi wife who behaved

---

[56]Ibid.

[57]Assiel Simbalikure, Suprefe wa Suprefegitura Busoro, to Bwana Burgmestri wa Komini Nyakizu, handwritten, June 3, 1994 (Nyakizu commune).

like a real Inyenzi; that his son was a recruit to the RPF; that his son was in Burundi preparing an attack on Nyakizu, planning to kill the local authorities; that he was among the Inkotanyi who tried to conquer Nyakizu on April 15; that a booklet containing the statutes of the RPF had been found stuck in the fence around his house (a later version was that the booklet was found on Nshimiryayo himself); that he had gone to Mulindi (the RPF base) to meet General Kagame; that he had prepared a grenade attack against Ntaganzwa.[58]

Just after the June 2 meeting, Ntaganzwa arrested Nshimiryayo but he feared him too much to kill him or even to keep him in prison in Nyakizu, so he sent him to the prefectural capital of Butare and asked the prosecutor to deal with him. The prosecutor found no grounds for arrest and passed the case to the prefect as an administrative affair. In the meantime Nshimiryayo was able to enlist the help of two sub-prefects, one of whom was a relative by marriage, the other of whom was from Nyakizu, and he was released from jail. In the meantime, assailants had pillaged and destroyed the several buildings of his prosperous residence.[59]

Ntaganzwa's attempt to destroy Nshimiryayo led the burgomaster into conflict with authorities in neighboring Mubuga, where Nshimiryayo had fled for protection. He traded accusations with the burgomaster of Mubuga and even arrested him in mid-May, accusing him of having come to Nyakizu to kill him. It was in fact the burgomaster of Mubuga who was then murdered, killed by a crowd in his own commune, whether with the involvement of Ntaganzwa is not known.[60] Disputes between people from Nyakizu and people from Mubuga continued into the weeks after.

---

[58]Ladislas Ntaganzwa letters to Bwana Suprefe, no. 103/04.09.01, May 10, 1994; to Bwana Su-prefe, no. 119/04.09.01.04, June 1, 1994; to Bwana Suprefe, [June 4, 1994] (Nyakizu commune); to Bwana Suprefe, no. 125/04.09.01/4, June 6, 1994; to Bwana Perefe, no. 128/04.09.01/4, June 8, 1994; to Bwana Prefet, June 13, 1994; to Bwana Su-Prefe, no. 134/04/09.01/4, June 15, 1996; to Bwana Perefe, no. 143/04.09.01/4, June 27, 1994; to Monsieur le Premier Ministre [no date] (Nyakizu commune). (All others from Butare prefecture.)

[59]Ladislas Ntaganzwa to Bwana Su-Prefe, June 15, 1994; Silvani Nsabimana, Perefe wa Perefegitura ya Butare, to Bwana Burugumestri wa Komini ya Nyakizu, no. 289/04.05/3, June 18, 1994 (Butare prefecture); and Ladislas Ntaganzwa to Bwana Perefe, June 27, 1994.

[60]Ladislas Ntaganzwa, Burugumesitiri wa Komini Nyakizu, to Bwana Su-Prefe, no. 106/04.09.01/4, May 18, 1994 (Butare prefecture).

When the prefect learned of the Nshimiryayo case, the difficulties between the communes, and perhaps also the beating of Rugwizangoga, which had been brought to the attention of the sub-prefect, he reproached Ntaganzwa for having gone too far. He ordered Ntaganzwa to moderate his behavior several times, once instructing him:

> Avoid everything that could encourage quarrels, disputes, and hatreds in the commune; we understand that there are many false accusations, lies, and unexplained murders and that many residents have more fear than trust for their authorities, to such an extent that some have preferred leaving their commune.[61]

From the context, it is clear that the "unexplained murders" referred only to Hutu victims, not to Tutsi. Ntaganzwa made his reply in the same terms. With apparently no sense of the outrageousness of his words, he wrote the prefect that his political enemies had defamed him "by spreading unfounded rumors that there had been many killings in Nyakizu."[62]

Allies into Enemies

Ntaganzwa exercised increasingly harsh control over Nyakizu during May and June. The communal councilors who had been removed in May wrote the prefect in June asking for protection for themselves and their families against the burgomaster.[63] The assistant burgomaster, Augustin Namahungu, who had been involved in a dispute with the burgomaster some time before, was attacked by "bandits" who completely destroyed his house, taking even its doors. He was left with nothing but the clothes on his back and by early June was forced to beg help from the burgomaster to get reestablished in his own home.[64]

---

[61]Silvani Nsabimana to Bwana Burugumestri, June 18, 1994.

[62] Ladislas Ntaganzwa to Bwana Perefe, June 27, 1994.

[63]Albert Nzimbirinda, Etienne Ntampuhwe, Etienne Rugwizangoga, Innocent Mutaganda, Daniel Niyirora, Emmanuel Ntakirutimana and Joseph Semigabo, Councilors, to Nyakubahwa perefe wa perefegitura Butare, June 27, 1994.

[64]Augustin Namahungu to Monsieur le Prefet de la Prefecture Butare, April 1, 1994; Augustin Namahungu to Bwana Burgmestri wa Komini Nyakizu, June 7, 1994 (Nyakizu commune).

Even those Hutu who had loyally supported Ntaganzwa suffered if they seemed to hinder his drive to increase his wealth and power. One such person, who had helped Ntaganzwa against political rivals during the months before the genocide, complained to the burgomaster that he was so harassed that he was afraid to report for work:

> Since you know what I did during the time of multipartyism and how I have behaved in this war...what advice would you give me since I have had to give up working in order not to be killed by those who are after me, especially now that a tract is going around saying that we are Inyenzi and that we are against the Government of National Salvation [guvernoma y'abatabazi] when you know how much I like that government and am working for it!

After reminding the burgomaster of his previous services, he asks plaintively, "And now have I really become an Inyenzi?"[65]

One of the "unexplained murders" referred to by the prefect was that of François Nzaramba, once Ntaganzwa's loyal supporter. The burgomaster accused Nzaramba of having allied with the Mubuga burgomaster against him. Soon after Nzaramba was found dead and local people were convinced that Ntaganzwa had had him killed.[66]

"A Thirst for Possessions"

In many cases, Ntaganzwa fell out with former supporters, including the head of the JDR, over the division of the spoils, whether from Tutsi who had been killed, from public property that had been pillaged, or from loot taken at the barriers. According to one witness, "Ntaganzwa had a thirst for possessions."[67] In addition to automobiles, he claimed other major items that had been stolen, including computers, medicines and medical equipment, solar panels, and sewing machines. He demanded that ordinary people who had taken such items hand them over and he even beat those who did not comply promptly. Many of these items he funneled south of the border to his colleague, head of the adjacent commune in Burundi,

---

[65]Anonymous to Ntaganzwa Ladislas, Bourgmestre wa Komini Nyakizu, June 10, 1994 (Nyakizu commune).

[66]Human Rights Watch/FIDH interview, Butare, October 9,1995.

[67]Human Rights Watch/FIDH interview, Nyakizu, August 28, 1995.

even as he wrote him—at the request of the communal council—asking his help in getting such stolen goods returned.[68]

As in his drive for power, so too in his search for possessions, Ntaganzwa was ready to murder even Hutu who shared his commitment to the genocide. In the most dramatic case of this kind, Ntaganzwa was apparently responsible for killing three Interahamwe from Mubuga commune in order to get their Suzuki jeep. In recounting the incident, the burgomaster described coming upon the three stopped by barrier guards:

> We realized that these people were Inkotanyi because they were carrying maps of the city of Kigali (neighborhoods of Kicukiro and Kacyiru) on which were written the names of people like Colonel Bagosora. They also had two grenades. These people also had other pieces of paper, including one with the numbers of firearms and a list which summarized donations given to the Inyenzi.[69]

As with similar correspondence about Tutsi who had been killed, the letter said nothing more about the fate of those taken, but closed simply with the request for more arms.

Perhaps to forestall any questions, Ntaganzwa himself raised the incident at the next security committee meeting. He began with the usual reminder that ever since the time "when the war was raging at Cyahinda," the Inkotanyi had made clear their intention of capturing Nyakizu. He then pointed out that the three taken at the barrier had all been Hutu and he assured the council "that it would be fatal to continue the mistake of thinking that it was Tutsi [alone] who were the Inkotanyi." It is remarkable that Ntaganzwa felt sufficiently secure to risk killing people who were well-known as Interahamwe.[70] It is even more remarkable that he covered his crime by the brazen lie that they were Inkotanyi, which he "proved" by the same supposed proof that he used against Tutsi: the presence in their possession of arms,

---

[68]Ibid.; Human Rights Watch/FIDH interview, Butare, October 21, 1995; Ladislas Ntaganzwa, Bourgmestre de la Commune Nyakizu to Monsieur l'Administrateur communal, Kabarore, no. 102/04.02.01/7, May 10, 1994 (Butare prefecture).

[69]Lasislas Ntaganzwa, Burugumesitiri wa Komini Nyakizu, to Bwana Su-Prefe wa Su-prefegitura, May 18, 1994.

[70]Human Rights Watch/FIDH interviews, Nyakizu, August 28, 1995; Butare, October 19, 1995.

lists, and material for attacks. It is also worth noting that Bagosora was the figure whom Ntaganzwa cited to exemplify the national leaders who were supposedly going to be killed.

In a number of subsequent incidents, passing Hutu were stopped at barriers in Nyakizu and were arrested, supposedly because their papers were not in order or for some other reason. The letters reporting these incidents do not indicate whether they were simply robbed and then released or whether they suffered some worse fate. In reporting one case, Ntaganzwa again argued that it was justifiable to arrest Hutu on charges of being Inkotanyi. He wrote that people coming to Nyakizu without appropriate documents should expect to be detained and should not "count on their Hutuness" as a protection.[71]

With the greed of the burgomaster as model, others in the commune raided fellow Hutu to get goods originally pillaged from Tutsi. Joseph Musayidire and his group, for example, attacked Daniel Munyambibi to steal four sewing machines, saying that they had been looted from Tutsi. Ntaganzwa seems to have been particularly annoyed over this case because Musayidire, a communal policeman whom he had fired a few months before, claimed to be confiscating the goods in the name of the authorities. Ntaganzwa had the gang arrested and put in the communal jail.[72]

Like the burgomaster, the young people at the barriers "attacked anyone if he looked like he had money." The young people took identity cards from those whom they assaulted, tore them up and then killed the victims.[73] Older members of the community complained that young men who had been trained in the use of arms were "so undisciplined that they have become completely ungovernable." Even when not working at the barriers or on patrol, they hung about on the roads, playing cards and looking for someone to victimize. At a meeting of the security committee in early June, participants complained that at Nyagisozi these men "profit from the situation to create disorder, above all by stopping passersby and taking from them whatever they have on them." At the same meeting, one participant said a communal policeman had to be put at the barriers in Rusenge to

---

[71]Ladislas Ntaganzwa, Burugumesitiri wa Komini Nyakizu, to Bwana Su-Prefe wa Su-Prefegitura, Busoro, no. 110/04/09.01/4, May 26, 1994; see also his no. 114/04.09/01/4 of the same date (Butare prefecture).

[72]Ladislas Ntaganzwa, Burugumesitiri wa Komini Nyakizu, to Bwana Su-Prefe wa Su-Prefegitura Busoro, no. 113/04.09.01/4, May 26, 1994 (Butare Prefecture).

[73]Human Rights Watch/FIDH interview, Butare, October 19, 1995.

stop the misbehavior of the guards.[74] The young men also pillaged crops in the fields left by the Tutsi and sometimes vandalized crops that were not yet ripe.

While the young engaged in theft and pillage, their elders were busy appropriating fields left by the Tutsi or cutting the trees in their afforestation plots. Men apparently seized the property of Hutu widows of Tutsi husbands. People from sectors where there had been few Tutsi raided crops in areas where there had been more and tried to take over vacant land, efforts which caused conflicts between the different sectors.[75]

The "Enemy" Arrives at Nyakizu

In late May and early June, people from communes to the north and the northeast began to stream through Nyakizu. Some were Hutu fleeing the advance of RPF troops. Others were the last of the Tutsi fleeing the genocide. Ntaganzwa wrote the sub-prefect that he feared that infiltrators, carrying suspect identity papers, were hidden among the displaced persons. He reported that an Inyenzi captured and killed in Kibangu sector supposedly revealed before he died that thirty others had infiltrated the region. Ntaganzwa resolved to "hunt them down in all the sectors of Nyakizu commune to abort their plans," for which he of course needed an immediate delivery of more weapons.[76] The prefectural security committee had decided to assemble all the displaced persons in the commune of Gishamvu and so, the sub-prefect said, Ntaganzwa had the right to bar them from his commune. He advised Ntaganzwa: "Search among the local residents, search throughout the commune, ferret out the enemy, show him that the commune of Nyakizu is inviolable."[77] The burgomaster then organized a new wave of killings, targeting Tutsi among the displaced persons.

---

[74]Geoffrey Dusabe, Umugenzuzi w'Akarere k'Amashuri, to Barimu, Barezi, June 8, 1994; Munyakazi, "Raporo...28/6/94"; Nyakizu commune, "Inyandiko mvugo...2/6/1994."

[75]Report included in Ladislas Ntaganzwa to Bwana Su-Prefe wa Su-Prefegitura, May 31, 1994; Munyakazi, "Raporo...28/6/94."

[76]Ladislas Ntaganzwa to Bwana Su-Prefe wa Su-Prefegitura, May 31, 1994.

[77]Assiel Simbalikure to Bwana Burugmestre wa Komini Nyakizu, no. 63/04.09.01/4, June 1, 1994.

In early June Ntaganzwa heard that Burundian soldiers were moving into position to invade Rwanda and passed on the rumor to his superiors.[78] This news turned out to be false—there is no indication that the largely Tutsi army of Burundi ever planned to attack—but the push of the RPF towards Butare and Gitarama was real. As the RPF troops marched nearer, the local administration stepped up the preparations for self-defense. The sub-prefect of Busoro ordered that the communal police and the young men trained in the "civilian self-defense" program teach the population how to dig trenches and how to encircle the enemy. He directed that they should increase their vigilance and search for Inyenzi every day throughout the commune. In contrast to the position taken by the government later, the sub-prefect insisted that the people should not flee. Instead they were to hide in trenches until the shooting stopped and then "rise up all together to attack the enemy, flatten him and kill him."[79]

As the "enemy" that had been so long the focus of Ntaganzwa's efforts came ever closer to Nyakizu, the burgomaster seemed to pay less attention to them than to local political challengers. During the month of June, he lost favor with his superiors and the people of the commune turned away from him, two developments that were certainly related. The men whom Ntaganzwa had tried to destroy, Nshimiryayo, Rugwizanzoga, and others, called important outsiders to their defense. The prefect criticized Ntaganzwa harshly, both in meetings and through correspondence, and then disciplined him by ordering him to hand over two of the vehicles that were part of his booty, including the one taken from the three Interahamwe from Mubuga.[80]

In addition, Ntaganzwa continued to have disputes with authorities in the adjacent commune of Mubuga and in the prefecture of Gikongoro, where the sub-prefect Biniga had become hostile to him. Ill-feeling between the authorities was

---

[78]Telegram from S/Préfet Busoro to Minter Kigali, June 2, 1994 (Butare prefecture).

[79]Assiel Simbalikure to Bwana Burugumesitiri wa Komini Gishamvu-Kigembe-Nyakizu-Runyinya, no. 64/04.09.01/4, June 1, 1994.

[80]Assiel Simbalikure, S/Prefe wa S/Prefegitura Busoro to Bwana Burgmestri wa Komini Nyakizu, no. 80/04.04/1, June 28, 1994 (Butare prefecture).

mirrored by squabbles between people of the two communes.[81] These divisions among Hutu who otherwise agreed on the genocide were just the kind of splits that national authorities had feared and tried to avoid.

Ntaganzwa tried to defend himself by appealing to Robert Kajuga, the president of the Interahamwe, with whom he solicited an interview so that he could "explain clearly what is happening here and explain some things that you seem not to understand very well."[82] Ntaganzwa also wrote a long appeal to the interim prime minister and even organized a meeting on June 18 in Butare town of people originally from Nyakizu, presumably to discuss security concerns, but probably also to deal with his own political problems.[83]

As the people of Nyakizu became aware that Ntaganzwa no longer enjoyed unqualified support from his superiors, they felt freer to question his authority. Those long disgusted by the genocide as well as others more narrowly concerned with attacks on local Hutu leaders joined in a "mass rising" against him. As one witness put it, "People rose up saying, he is killing everyone, even the priest."[84]

The realization that the RPF were advancing and that the massive slaughter of Tutsi had done nothing to guarantee security also contributed to popular rejection of Ntaganzwa. From the Hutu fleeing through the commune, people heard that the RPF troops were rolling forward, news that contradicted the optimistic official bulletins being broadcast over the radio. At the same time, they heard that the RPF were killing many civilians, information that reinforced the fears created by radio reports.[85] In mid-June, soldiers of the Burundian army fired on Hutu on their side of the border, causing a number of them to flee briefly to Nyakizu. Not of great

---

[81]Ladislas Ntaganzwa, Burugumesitiri wa Komini Nyakizu, to Bwana Konseye Usimbura Burugumesitiri wa Komini Mubuga, no. 117/04.02.01, May 30, 1994; Ladislas Ntaganzwa, Burugumesitiri wa Komini Nyakizu, to Bwana Su-Prefe wa Su-Prefegitura Busoro, no. 139/04.05/1, June 16, 1994 Ladislas Ntaganzwa, Bourgmestre de la Commune Nyakizu to Monsieur le Premier Ministre, [no date] (Nyakizu commune).

[82]Ladislas Ntaganzwa to Bwana Kajuga, president des interahamwe au Rwanda, June 3, 1994.

[83]Ladislas Ntaganzwa, Burugumesitiri wa Komini Nyakizu, to Bwana..., no. 132/04.09.01/4, June 14, 1994 (Butare prefecture).

[84]Human Rights Watch/FIDH interview, Nyakizu, August 28, 1995.

[85]Nyakizu commune, "Inyandiko mvugo...2/6/1994."

significance in itself, this incident also added to the insecurity felt by many in the commune.[86]

Ntaganzwa and his supporters sought to counter the growing fear and discouragement among the people—and their own loss of control—by multiplying meetings and increasing exhortations about the importance of security measures. But people stopped coming to meetings and they no longer showed up to do patrols or man the barriers. By the time of its last meeting on July 3, the security committee was finding it impossible to get men to do this work and was forced to offer to pay men to do it.[87]

At that meeting, the burgomaster announced that the RPF had taken the town of Butare. He declared that the council must make a common decision on what to do next, whether to stand and fight or to flee. Sergeant Corneille, head of the National Police whose men had "defended" Nyakizu so well against the unarmed Tutsi civilians announced that if the Inkotanyi came in large numbers, then there would be no choice but to flee. In mid-May, when the "enemy" was mostly women and children left from the first massacres, the councilor Festus Nyamukaza had declared that "it is lack of firmness that can lead us to defeat."[88] In early July, faced with a real enemy, he showed considerably less resolve. He declared: "If the soldiers were not able to handle the situation at the front, we cannot deceive ourselves or the people by saying that we can do it when we are not even armed. The people cannot succeed where the soldiers have failed."[89]

---

[86]Ladislas Ntaganzwa, Burugumesitiri wa Komini Nyakizu, to Bwana Su-Prefe wa Su-Prefegitura, Busoro, no. 135/04.09.01/4, June 15, 1994 (Nyakizu commune, second copy in Butare prefecture).

[87]Munyakazi, "Raporo...28/6/1994;" Geoffrey Dusabe, Umwanditsi, "Inyandiko mvugo du Conseil Communal de Securité du 3/07/1994" (Nyakizu commune). Hereafter cited as "Inyandiko mvugo...3/07/1994."

[88]Nyakizu commune, "Inyandiko mvugo...18/5/1994."

[89]"Inyandiko mvugo...3/07/1994."

With the "enemy" finally in sight, Ntaganzwa and his followers fled westward through Gikongoro and then on to Zaire. They left behind more than 20,000 Tutsi slain by their "work."[90]

---

[90]According to the current burgomaster of Nyakizu, 21,015 persons had been exhumed from mass graves and reburied in Nyakizu commune by October 1995. Among the victims were most of the 11,213 Tutsi recorded as living there when the genocide began. In addition, many Tutsi from other communes trying to escape to Burundi were slain in Nyakizu, as were a certain number of Hutu, killed by Ntaganzwa and his men or by arriving RPF soldiers.

BUTARE:
"LET THEM STAND ASIDE FOR US AND LET US WORK"

For Tutsi, Butare was the last hope both as a refuge in itself and as a way station en route to Burundi. For leaders of the genocide, it was a troublesome obstacle to completing the national campaign to exterminate the Tutsi. To achieve that goal required eliminating the some 140,000 Tutsi residents of Butare and the tens of thousands of others who had sought refuge there.[1] It also necessitated extirpating the very idea that Hutu and Tutsi could live peaceably together.

In trying to resist this catastrophe, Prefect Jean-Baptiste Habyalimana was at first able to count on the local commander of the National Police and on his own subordinates, with the exception of the burgomaster of Nyakizu. But otherwise, the prefect was opposed by powerful forces committed to genocide: military officers, the militia, intellectuals, and Burundian refugees. In addition, assailants from both the west and the northeast invaded Butare, attacking Tutsi who had fled from Gikongoro, Kigali, and Gitarama as well as those resident within the prefecture.

The Setting

The town of Butare, the prefectural center, was located in Ngoma commune, which had a population of about 26,600 people. About one quarter of them were Tutsi, a percentage far higher than the national average and higher also than the 17 percent Tutsi population of the capital.[2] A sleepy little town, Butare stretched out along a ridge on either side of the main highway that ran south to the border with Burundi. The central district could be traversed on foot in fifteen or twenty minutes, but several of its neighborhoods jutted out from the main axis along other ridges, separated from one another by largely uninhabited valleys. To travel from

---

[1]According to the 1991 census, Butare had a Tutsi population of just over 128,000, the largest by far of any prefecture. Françoise Imbs, François Bart, and Annie Bart, "Le Rwanda: les données socio-géographiques," *Hérodote, 72-73.* Janvier-juin 1994, p. 265. Extrapolations based on population growth yield an estimate of 140,000 Tutsi in 1994, a figure confirmed by a second set of extrapolations from 1994 population reports from three-quarters of the communes.

[2]In addition to there being both a prefecture and a town of Butare, there was both a commune of Ngoma and a sector Ngoma of that commune. Of the 26,650 residents of Ngoma commune, 6,947 were registered as Tutsi at the end of February 1994. Joseph Kanyabashi, Bourgmestre, to Monsieur le Préfet, no. 153/04.05/1, March 14, 1994 (Butare prefecture).

432

BUTARE PREFECTURE

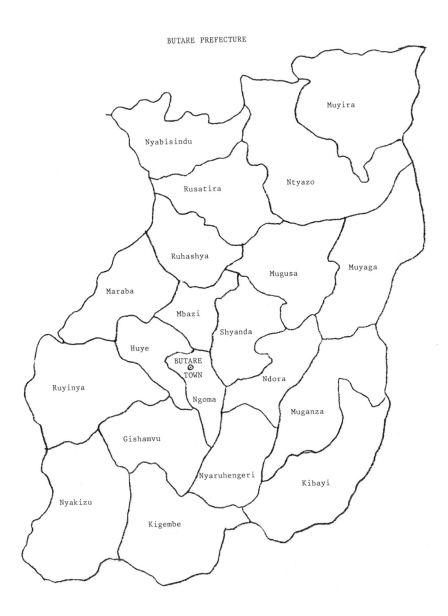

the far point of one sector to that of another could take more than an hour walking by road, but local people cut that time by using foot paths through the valleys.

As befit its status as the intellectual center of the country, the town of Butare was heralded to the north by a handsome new historical museum, which both by its architecture and its contents paid tribute to the old monarchy so disavowed by the new Hutu republics. At the northern entry to town, on either side of the main road, although not visible from it, lay a school for social workers and Catholic and Protestant theological institutes and seminaries. Just beyond the commercial district and off to the left of the main road stood the cathedral, the extensive complex of the Groupe Scolaire secondary school, and a training school for veterinarians. Leaving town to the south, the wooded campuses of the university to the left of the road and of a scientific research institute to the right completed the impressive concentration of institutions devoted to the life of the mind. A large university hospital, a short distance from the main road, abutted the research institute and a smaller hospital was located just beyond the Groupe Scolaire.

Buye, the neighborhood at the northern entry of the town, encompassed the tree-lined avenues of slightly decrepit colonial-era houses and newer residences of university professors, doctors, government employees, and military officers. The sector of Ngoma, originally built by the colonial administration to house its Rwandan employees, lay a respectable distance from the Buye residences, down a dusty and largely uninhabited road, past the airfield. The orderly rows of modest, look-alike brick houses had been expanded in recent years by larger and more varied structures, but Ngoma still looked like a working class neighborhood. At the entry of Ngoma stood a military camp, housing only some fifty soldiers, the rest of its troops having been sent to the front. Back on the main road, a row of shops bracketed by the two oldest and best-known hotels in town, the Ibis and the Faucon, formed the commercial center, which spilled over onto adjacent streets.

Down one of those streets stood an open-air market and beyond it a school for training junior military officers, the Ecole des Sous-Officiers (ESO). The school housed some one hundred soldiers and served as the headquarters for the military command of Butare and Gikongoro prefectures. Its senior officers lived in Buye, not at the camp. Tumba and the two sectors known as the Cyarwas (Cyarwa-Cyimana and Cyarwa-Sumo) lay beyond the university and included some substantial residences of university or medical professionals, as well as more modest homes. The headquarters of the National Police, located in Tumba, commanded some 300 gendarmes, the majority based in the town of Butare and with a second important group at Nyabisindu in the northern part of the prefecture. A week or ten days after the start of the genocide, some 120 of the National

Policemen were transferred north to the battlefront.[3] The semi-rural sectors of Matyazo in the north of the commune and Nkubi and Sahera in the south represented the transition from the town to countryside beyond. The main street of town was paved as were short sections of intersecting roads, but other roads were dirt or gravel.

The Military

The military camps in Butare were troubled by the same regional and political divisions that existed elsewhere in the armed forces. Gen. Marcel Gatsinzi, the local commander of all forces in Butare and Gikongoro, was from Kigali and Lt. Col. Tharcisse Muvunyi, who replaced him when he was briefly named chief of staff on April 6, was from Byumba. Neither was associated with the Hutu Power advocates from the northwest. Capt. Ildephonse Nizeyimana of the junior officers' school was from the northwest and was reportedly a relative of Bagosora. Nominally subordinate to the other two, he could and did ignore their orders or act counter to them. Symbolic of the power relationships among the officers was the number of their guards. General Gatsinzi had six men while Nizeyimana, only a captain, had twelve, all of them from his home region of Ruhengeri. Acknowledged leader of the hard-line military group in Butare, Nizeyimana was celebrated in local songs for his virulent hatred of Tutsi. The chief of Ngoma camp, Lt. Ildephonse Hategekimana, stood with Nizeyimana although he was not himself from the northwest. A subordinate officer recently posted to Ngoma, Lt. (jg) Niyonteze, backed up Hategekimana.[4]

Among the National Police, the commander Cyriaque Habyarabatuma had been counted as a fair-minded moderate since 1990 when he had helped Tutsi and members of the political opposition arrested by President Habyarimana. Nizeyimana could not tolerate Habyarabatuma and in the days just after the start of the genocide Habyarabatuma believed that Nizeyimana was preparing to kill him. Habyarabatuma's second in command, Maj. Alfred Rusigariye, originally

---

[3]Human Rights Watch/FIDH interviews, Kigali, November 21, 1995; January 26, 1996; Butare, February 5, 1996.

[4]Human Rights Watch/FIDH interviews, Kigali, November 21, 1995; Brussels, September 24, 1994, December 12, 1995; January 26, 1996; March 4, 1996; Butare, February 5, 1996; by telephone, February 4, 1998.

from Gisenyi, supported the genocidal line of Nizeyimana and Hategekimana rather than the policy of his superior.[5]

Following the February 1994 troubles, the general staff transferred to Butare several soldiers and police who supported the Hutu Power position. Once combat resumed, Kigali headquarters on occasion rotated fresh troops from Butare to the front and sent men who had been in combat to Butare. The soldiers who had been fighting the RPF, and particularly those who had been wounded in battle—were reportedly more ruthless against Tutsi than others.[6]

Before the genocide, a small group of Presidential Guards protected the home in Buye of Dr. Séraphin Bararengana, a physician who was President Habyarimana's brother. Once Sindikubwabo was named interim president, a contingent of Presidential Guards established a small post outside his house which was situated just at the entry of Tumba, a short distance from the National Police headquarters. Outside the usual hierarchy, the Presidential Guards were commanded directly from Kigali, but they often frequented the ESO, where they had links with Nizeyimana and other Hutu Power advocates.[7]

The Intellectuals

Prefect Habyalimana had been a professor at the university and knew that the intellectual community was split between those for and those against Hutu Power. As early as 1990, some professors had provided the intellectual justifications for what would become Hutu Power and had reportedly even participated in drafting the "Ten Commandments of the Bahutu." Since that time, they had supplied propaganda declarations to influence the international community to favor Habyarimana. (See above.) The vice-rector of the university, Jean-Berchmans Nshimyumuremyi, led this group and overshadowed the rector, who was reportedly far more moderate. Increasingly alienated from colleagues who were Tutsi or tolerant of Tutsi, these hard-liners encouraged similar sentiments among students. In 1993 students who backed President Habyarimana insisted on creating a new

---

[5]Human Rights Watch/FIDH interviews, Kigali, November 21, 1995; January 26, 1996; Butare, December 19, 1995; February 5, 1996; Brussels, October 19 and 20, 1997.

[6]Human Rights Watch/FIDH interviews, Kigali, November 21, 1995; January 26, 1996; Butare, February 5, 1996; Butare, March 26, 1996; by telephone, Rome, February 4, 1998.

[7]Human Rights Watch/FIDH interviews, Kigali, November 21, 1995; January 26, 1996; Butare, February 5, 1996.

student organization, the Rwandan Student League (Ligue des Etudiants du Rwanda, LIDER) to rival the established General Association of Rwandan National University Students (Association Generale des Etudiants de l'Université Nationale du Rwanda, AGEUNR). In that year, too, Habyarimana's supporters demonstrated outside the university and threatened to close it down. They were led by the wife of the university rector, Pauline Nyiramasuhuko, minister of family and women's affairs and their son, Shalom Anselme Ntahobari, a one-time student who had dropped out of the university and who would become the most important local militia leader in Butare town after April 6.[8]

The Militia and Political Parties

In the period just before the genocide, there was little indication of the problems to be posed by the militia after April 6. The MRND, the CDR, and the MDR had too few adherents to have built up significant groups of trained men in the town or in most of the communes of Butare. As discussed above, militia had begun training in Nyakizu in September and October 1993, and, according to witness testimony, young men from the commune of Maraba had been secretly taught military skills beginning at about the same time. At least three recruits had left Maraba for about a month, transported in the vehicle of the commune to some unknown destination for further training.[9] Another member of the Interahamwe, active in Butare during the genocide, reported that he had been trained in Kigali.[10] Militia from outside Butare had reportedly arrived after April 6 and lodged quietly in a local motel until April 19 when they moved to other quarters, on orders from the military. Although the presence of this group was not generally noticed, people had remarked that armed strangers, either militia or disguised Presidential Guards, were quartered at the Rwandan Match Company (Société Rwandaise des Allumettes, SORWAL). Questioned about this at a public meeting in the early days

---

[8]Human Rights Watch/FIDH interviews, January 26, 1996; Butare, January 13, 1996; Kigali, January 19, 1996; "Inyandiko-Mvugo y'Inama ya Perefegitura Ishinzwe Umutekano yo kuwa 24 gicurasi 1993" (Butare prefecture).

[9]Human Rights Watch/FIDH interview, Nyangazi, Maraba, June 28, 1995.

[10]Human Rights Watch/FIDH, Butare, December 18, 1995.

of the genocide, Prefect Habyalimana wrongly declared that there were no unknown armed persons at the match factory.[11]

While organized anti-Tutsi militia were not widely seen in Butare before early April, young supporters of PSD, the party which dominated politics in town and in a number of communes, caused trouble in February 1994. Enraged by the assassination the previous day of Felicien Gatabazi, the popular PSD leader, a crowd of young men caught and lynched Martin Bucyana, the national head of the CDR who was popularly held responsible for the crime. When members of the PSD were arrested and charged with Bucyana's murder, party leaders organized a demonstration demanding that they be released and used quieter forms of pressure as well to slow the investigation. In the days after Bucyana's murder, PSD members threatened proponents of Hutu Power generally and northerners in particular. The CDR leaders at Tumba, Deputy Laurent Baravuga and Simeon Remera, believed it necessary to take shelter temporarily at the police brigade. At this time, when Tutsi were being killed in Kigali, advocates of Hutu Power made their own threats against Tutsi and friends of Tutsi. At the university, some Tutsi and opponents of the MRND felt so threatened that they moved from their campus dormitories into town.[12]

The Burundians

Several hundred Burundians lived in town, including some university students, teachers, and other professionals who had been refugees for some years, and unemployed young men who had found their way into town from refugee camps or directly from Burundi. Many of the more than 100,000 refugees in the camps headed back to Burundi after April 6, but some 65,000 were still in Butare prefecture in May, including hundreds who had undergone military training in the camps. Well aware of the attitudes and experience of these young refugees, the

---

[11]Alphonse Higaniro, director of SORWAL, was the son-in-law of President Habyarimana's personal physican, who supposedly helped Prefect Habyalimana get a scholarship to study abroad. The prefect was said to have counted Higaniro and his wife as friends. Habyalimana might have been misled about the presence of armed men at SORWAL or he might have known but decided not to admit they were there. Human Rights Watch/FIDH interview, Butare, July 6, 1995.

[12]Human Rights Watch/FIDH interviews, Butare, December 29, 1995; January 2, 3, and 13, 1996; Kigali, January 19, 1996.

prefect from the start insisted that the refugees be provided with adequate food in order to minimize the risk of their turning to violence.[13]

Early Violence

On the two days after the plane was shot down, Butare people stayed at home as directed by the Ministry of Defense over the radio. Satisfied with the relative calm, the prefect ordered public services resumed and markets opened on April 9. Soldiers from the Ngoma camp, however, notified at midnight April 6 of Habyarimana's death, had already begun killing Tutsi on April 7. A few went out from Ngoma camp and brought back young men tied up in the back of their pickup truck, beating them on the way. The next day soldiers from the camp, including some recently arrived northerners, picked up twelve young men from Matyazo. When notified of the detentions, Major Habyarabatuma secured the release of one or more of the men, but at least one of the others, Jean-Bosco Rugomboka was tortured by being burned with an iron and then killed by stabbing. One rumor that was circulated to justify his murder was that he had been caught in the process of "planning to kill Hutu." Because Rugomboka had been a PSD supporter and because PSD members had repeatedly challenged northerners and Hutu Power supporters after the deaths of Gatabazi and Bucyana, some Hutu took the rumor so seriously that they left Ngoma temporarily for Nyakizu and other places outside of town. Another rumor, apparently lent credence by being repeated by Joseph Kanyabashi, burgomaster of Ngoma, at a public meeting five days later, was that Rugomboka had been found in possession of a RPF tee shirt. On Monday, April 11, Ngoma soldiers arrested eight young men and women who had just returned home to Butare on foot from Kigali. They tortured them as they had Rugomboka, killed them and dumped their bodies near the road leading out of town to the Burundi border, perhaps as a warning to any who were considering fleeing the country.[14]

The military used not just threats, arrests and violence but also political action to pull the young Hutu of Ngoma to their side. Between April 7 and 21, groups of young men, many of them supporters of the PSD, reportedly spent a few days

---

[13]Gemmo Lodesani, Directeur du PAM Burundi, to Monsieur Ignace, May 11, 1994 (Butare prefecture).

[14]Human Rights Watch/FIDH interviews, Neuchatel, December 16, 1995; Butare, March 26, 1996; by telephone, Rome, February 4, 1998; République Rwandaise, Parquet de la République, PV no. 0117.

being indoctrinated at the ESO. They returned to the streets of Ngoma far more hostile towards Tutsi and more supportive of Hutu Power.[15]

Not many Butare residents knew of the first killings by the soldiers, but many saw the smoke of houses set aflame in neighboring Gikongoro on April 7 and 8. On April 9, Butare people received the first displaced persons from Gikongoro into the western communes of Runyinya, Maraba, and Nyakizu. Major Habyarabatuma sent National Police to the border of Gikongoro to protect the displaced persons and to try to keep out their assailants. Burgomasters of Runyinya and Maraba organized Hutu and Tutsi to defend their communities from invasion by the assailants. Displaced persons began arriving also in northeastern Butare, coming from adjacent communes in Kigali and Gitarama. National Police were sent to the commune of Ntyazo to protect against attacks from those prefectures.[16]

Preoccupied by evidence of disturbances in neighboring regions, the prefect and others witnessed the passage on April 9 of convoys of foreigners fleeing south to Burundi. They recognized that their hasty departure reduced the chances of any foreign intervention to halt the slaughter. Two of a small U.N. contingent present in Butare during the first week of April appeared at the funeral of the young Tutsi Rugomboka on Sunday, April 10. They inquired about the circumstances of the murder, but they did nothing, neither then nor in the ten days remaining before they left town.[17]

Trying to Keep Control

The prefect called burgomasters and sub-prefects to report on the situation at an urgent meeting of the prefectural security council on Sunday morning, April 10. The sub-prefect of Nyabisindu began by reporting rumors that Presidential Guards had arrived in town and that soldiers were going around checking on the names of owners of various houses. Some forty-five children had been sent to take refuge in the church or elsewhere. Some people had received threats over the telephone and gunfire had been heard in the middle of the night. The burgomaster of Nyabisindu commune added that his house had been attacked during the night and that many people had chosen to spend the night outside, fearing murder if they slept at home.

---

[15]Human Rights Watch/FIDH interview, by telephone, Rome, February 4, 1998.

[16]Human Rights Watch/FIDH interview, January 26, 1996; Maraba, May 16, 1995; Anonymous, Notebook 1, entries for April 9, April 10, and April 13, 1994.

[17]République Rwandaise, Parquet de la République de Kigali, PV. no. 0117.

The burgomaster of Nyaruhengeri reported threats against religious sisters who ran a clinic and the burgomaster of Muyira stated that soldiers and civilians armed with traditional weapons had come into his commune from Kigali prefecture and killed one person and pillaged goods. The burgomaster of Runyinya declared that military and civilian authorities in Gikongoro were doing nothing to combat violence in that prefecture and that more than a thousand displaced persons had fled into his commune.[18]

After listening to the lengthening list of problems, the prefect stressed that "Responsibility belongs to the burgomasters." Recognizing that crises elsewhere could spill over into their areas, he directed them to keep order by combating rumors and providing the necessary supplies to the fast-growing groups of displaced persons. He announced that he would go to Nyabisindu to deal himself with the problem of military men[19] who were challenging the civilian authorities. Lieutenant Colonel Muvunyi apparently supported the prefect by urging the authorities to fight anything that could set one ethnic group against the other. He urged that troublemakers be identified and held responsible should anything happen. Speaking from a different point of view, the commander of Ngoma camp, insisted that all those who spread rumors to discredit the army be identified, presumably a reference to the report about military misbehavior in Nyabisindu.[20]

The prefect, no doubt well aware of problems with soldiers and police in Butare town as well as in Nyabisindu, reacted promptly the next day when he heard that a group of soldiers from the ESO had entered Ngoma church to look for ibyitso, "accomplices" of the RPF. He called the parish priest and insisted that he never again acquiesce in such a search unless it were authorized by a proper warrant.[21]

On April 11, Habyalimana refused the summons to a meeting of all prefects with the new government in Kigali. Some say that he had been warned of a plot to assassinate him en route, but he might also have been simply trying to decide how

---

[18]Anonymous, Notebook 1, entry for April 10, 1994.

[19]Literally, *militaires*, but almost certainly National Police rather than regular soldiers.

[20]Anonymous, Notebook 1, entry for April 10, 1994.

[21]République Rwandaise, Parquet de la République de Kigali, PV. no. 0117.

far to obey the interim government.[22] The next day, April 12, when the Defense Ministry announcement and Karamira's speech on the radio showed that the interim government was bent on genocide, Habyalimana again refused an order of national authorities. The general staff directed the Butare prefecture to deliver no more authorizations to Rwandans to leave the country. Several hours later, the prefect, backed by the prefectural security council, directed the local head of the immigration service to give the necessary papers to Rwandans trying to flee with foreign religious sisters. The next day, the sisters were stopped by a soldier who appeared to be on drugs at a barrier just south of Butare town. He refused to allow the Rwandans to pass and took them away to police headquarters. One of the sisters appealed to passing U.N. soldiers for help, but they said they could do nothing. She next appealed to a high-ranking military officer, probably Lieutenant Colonel Muvunyi, who arranged for one of his officers to escort the Rwandans beyond the barrier.[23]

The order prohibiting travel authorizations was one of the last direct telephone communications received by authorities in Butare from the national government. On the night of April 12, long-distance telephone service was cut leaving Habyalimana and others in outlying prefectures isolated. They would continue to receive information delivered over the radio and to communicate with other officials through brief messages transmitted by telegram. But no longer could they engage in substantive dialogues with distant authorities nor could they quickly and easily exchange information or verify official claims with like-minded colleagues in the capital.

At the security meeting on Wednesday morning, April 13, Habyalimana discussed the disintegrating situation. He acknowledged that military officers in Gikongoro were encouraging the troubles, that civilian authorities in Nyabisindu—by which he meant the sub-prefect—were not telling people the truth, and that the ordinary people were beginning to participate in the disorder. He stressed again that the people had no right to make their own laws, that they had no excuse for threatening others, and that they could not set up patrols and barriers that were not officially authorized. Although he directed that government services reopen and that the curfew be lifted to reassure people and to restore some sense of normality to life, he also prepared for a continuing crisis by requisitioning

---

[22]Human Rights Watch/FIDH interview, Butare, July 6, 1995.

[23]Massart, "A Butare, au jour le jour," p. 78.

vehicles and fuel, along with stocks of food to provide for the rapidly increasing flow of displaced persons.[24]

Prefect Habyalimana ordered his subordinates to hold meetings throughout the prefecture to try to calm people and prevent disorder. At one such meeting at the stadium on April 14, he tried to reassure the residents of Ngoma. A university professor, Jean-Marie Vianney Maniraho, stood to ask why there were so many soldiers out of their camp and present in town and a farmer from an outlying area asked in a quavering voice why people were burning houses in nearby Maraba commune. The prefect responded that citizens would be protected as guaranteed by law. Repeating his advice to the priest of Ngoma church, he stressed that citizens should not permit searches of their homes or arrest by any person who did not produce the appropriate warrant.[25] Burgomaster Kanyabashi and Major Habyarabatuma delivered similar guarantees of protection to more than 500 displaced persons from Gikongoro who were gathered at a health clinic in Matyazo. In the commune of Ndora, the burgomaster told Tutsi that there was no threat and that they should return to their homes at night instead of sleeping out of doors.[26]

The reassurances rang hollow as people began arriving in Butare, bearing news of disasters elsewhere, worst of all the massacre of thousands at Kibeho church just across the Gikongoro border on the night of April 14. Early reports by those who had fled the carnage, including the parish priest Abbe Pierre Ngoga, were confirmed by the staff of Doctors Without Borders (Medecins sans Frontiers, MSF) who were turned back a few hundred yards short of the church on the morning of April 15. En route to treat the wounded and carrying a general letter of authorisation signed by Lieutenant Colonel Muvunyi, they were stopped and forced to leave by drunk militia and communal policemen who told them that Muvunyi's authorisation meant nothing to them. As they turned their cars and drove away,

---

[24]Anonymous, Notebook 1, entry for April 13, 1994.

[25]Human Rights Watch/FIDH interviews, Butare, July 6 and October 26, 1995.

[26]République Rwandaise, Parquet de la République de Kigali, PV no. 0117; P. Célestin Rwankubito, Bourgmestre wa Komini Ndora, to Bwana Perefe wa Perefegitura, no. 097/04.09.01/7, April 20, 1994 (Butare prefecture).

they heard heavy gunfire and many screams. They returned to their base in Butare town and informed the authorities.[27]

At a meeting of the prefectural security council on April 15, the prefect reported on the Kibeho massacre and then summed up the situation in various parts of the prefecture. Most serious was the problem at Nyakizu, where some 20,000 people were massed at the church complex and where many Tutsi homes had been burned down. Assailants, some of them armed with guns and grenades, were crossing into Butare at various points along the border with Gikongoro. The numbers of displaced persons in other communes adjacent to Gikongoro continued to mount and some 1,000 people were gathered at the Burundi frontier, stopped by border guards and soldiers from crossing the river. A policeman in Maraba was shooting at innocent people and an assistant burgomaster had been caught in the act of pillaging with the population. In several communes, including Nyakizu, Maraba, and Runyinya, assailants—both local and from outside the prefecture—had killed Tutsi. Despite all this bad news, there had been no major catastrophes as of the morning of April 15 and most of the troubles had been imported into the prefecture from the outside. Officials had organized patrols and barriers, with Hutu and Tutsi working on them together, just as they were standing together against incursions from outside.[28]

The prefect and security council imposed a total curfew in communes where there had been violence. The next day, April 16, they sent teams of officials to these areas to try to restore calm.[29]

Responding to Attacks from Gikongoro

While other officials tried to restore order after the fact, the prefect himself tried to address the cause of the problem by meeting with the Gikongoro prefect. At the end of the session, the two prefects issued a communique that seems to have represented a compromise between Habyalimana, who rejected the new authorities and Bucyibaruta, the MRND loyalist, who did not want to challenge them. They did not recite the virtually obligatory historical preamble that blamed the RPF for the crisis, but neither did they acknowledge the official role in the attacks. Instead

---

[27]ICTR-96-4-T, Testimony of Dr. Rony Zachariah, January 16, 1997; Human Rights Watch/FIDH interview, Butare, March 26, 1996.

[28]Anonymous, Notebook 1, entry for April 15, 1994.

[29]Ibid.

they attributed the extent of the disturbances to the famine that had disrupted the local economy. They named the communes in Gikongoro where people had been killed, thus making clear exactly which officials were meant by their otherwise general appeal to "prefectural authorities at all levels" to halt the violence. In an effort to end the attacks against Butare, they forbade any travel outside the sector, except for reasons of work, and any gathering of people into groups.

The prefects broke with the official myth that the Tutsi were the aggressors and the Hutu the victims trying only to defend themselves. They ordered local officials to establish barriers and patrols against "troublemakers and wrongdoers." By using these simple words instead of the code terms for Tutsi—"infiltrators," "accomplices," "enemy," "Inyenzi," and "Inkotanyi"—the prefects showed that they wanted action against the real criminals, not against those targeted by the government. Other authorities had been instructing the population to listen to the radio and follow its orders, but the two prefects urged people to avoid being misled by rumors and to "listen with a very critical ear" to everything said on all radios. They asked the authorities to prosecute those who spread false information and they asked people to report to the authorities anyone who possessed unauthorized firearms. They urged the army, the public prosecutors and local officials all to make full use of the law to prevent and punish any and all acts of violence. And, in a final indication of how alone they felt in confronting the catastrophe, they entreated the government to restore long-distance telephone service.[30]

In their communique, the prefects failed to mention the one obvious cause of the violence. When summarizing the statement for the prefectural security council the next morning, Habyalimana added the element omitted in the published statement: "extremists."[31]

Dealing with the Displaced

On April 15, assailants attacked the estimated 20,000 displaced persons at Cyahinda church in Nyakizu and on the 16th, they continued killing throughout the

---

[30]Bwana Lawurenti Bucyibaruta, Perefe wa Perefegitura ya Gikongoro and BwanaYohani Batisita Habyalimana, Prefe wa Perefegitura ya Butare, Itangazo Lisoza Inama y'UmutekanoYahuje Abategetsi Ba Perefegitura ya Butare Na Gikongoro, April 16, 1994 (Butare prefecture).

[31]Anonymous, Notebook 1, entry for April 17, 1994. Anonymous, Notebook 2, entry for April 17, 1994 (Butare prefecture). This second notebook, with notes of prefectural security council meetings recorded in a handwriting different from that of the first, will be cited as Notebook 2.

day. This tragedy brought to the prefecture the large-scale slaughter experienced elsewhere in Rwanda and underscored the risk that such massacres might be staged wherever significant numbers of Tutsi gathered. The radio insisted over and over that "infiltrators" were hidden among the displaced and that they were planning to attack the Hutu as they moved into their communes.[32]

On April 16 and 17, prefectural authorities began sending displaced persons to centers some distance from Butare town, attempting also to disarm them whenever possible, even though they were carrying only traditional weapons. In a number of communes, including Ruhashya, Mbazi, and Nyaruhengeri, burgomasters at this time or soon after refused to allow the displaced to congregate at the communal offices, apparently on orders from their superiors. They directed them instead to other locations, such as a stadium or church. Some of those refused refuge at the Ruhashya communal offices went to the Institute of Agricultural Sciences of Rwanda (Institut des Sciences Agronomiques du Rwanda, ISAR) at Rubona.[33]

On April 16, Burgomaster Kanyabashi and Lieutenant Hategekimana directed the more than 1,500 displaced persons at the Matyazo health center to move to Karama church in Runyinya or to Simbi church in Maraba. Abbé Jerome Masinzo of Ngoma church and Catholic lay leader Laurien Ntezimana insisted that the displaced not be moved until the security of the locations had been checked. Ntezimana went first to Runyinya and found the area already burning. The next day, Lieutenant Hategekimana insisted that Abbé Masinzo escort the displaced to Simbi. When the Abbé and Ntezimana set out with the group, they found Simbi also besieged. Only when they brought the displaced back to Ngoma and presented the lieutenant with a fait accompli did he agree to leave them at Matyazo.[34] That same day, authorities sent nearly 500 people who arrived in Sahera sector of Ngoma south to Nyumba church in the commune of Gishamvu and directed others at the Nyakibanda seminary to move to Nyumba also. No one checked the security

---

[32]Valerie Bemeriki, RTLM, April 8 and 13, 1994 recorded by Faustin Kagame (provided by Article 19).

[33]African Rights, *Witness to Genocide*, issue 7, September 1997, pp. 17, 45. For Nyaruhengeri, see below.

[34]Human Rights Watch/FIDH interviews, Butare, March 26, 1996; Brussels, January 19 and 29, 1998; by telephone, Rome, February 4, 1998.

of these locations. The displaced were apparently transferred to both places, the sites of massacres soon after.[35]

Habyalimana feared that the 3,000 people waiting to cross the boundary into Burundi would be massacred if they did not move away from the frontier. At the time, Radio Rwanda was inciting people of the region to attack them. On the 8 p.m. news on April 16, it had declared that the gathering of displaced persons near the frontier was meant to open a new front in the war. It concluded "The government is appealing to the population to remain vigilant and help restore order and peace."[36] When soldiers moved the displaced back to a small commercial center called Nkomero, a prefectural delegation, apparently including Habyalimana, went to preach calm and to promise them aid.[37]

The military authorities presumably made the decisions about regrouping the displaced persons at certain sites, about disarming them, and about moving them back from the frontier. But Habyalimana himself and other civilian and church leaders—some of them Tutsi like Habyalimana—persuaded the displaced to cooperate in these measures.[38] Perhaps they had no choice. Or perhaps they hoped to undercut the government strategy of presenting the agglomerations as a threat to local Hutu. By having Tutsi surrender their weapons and move away from sensitive locations, like the town and the frontier, Habyarimana and others may have hoped to demonstrate that the Tutsi had no intention of taking the offensive.

Prefect Habyalimana Removed

After meeting with the Gikongoro prefect on Saturday, Habyalimana spent the weekend dealing with one crisis after another. The violence had spread from its first major center along the western frontier in the communes of Maraba, Runyinya and Nyakizu, to adjacent communes further to the east and south in Huye, Gishamvu, Kigembe, Muganza, and Nyaruhengeri. Another center of violence that had been established in the northeast by raids from Kigali and Gitarama was expanding south and west through the commune of Muyira. The attacks were no longer the work of outsiders alone: people from Butare were taking up their machetes to join killers from Gikongoro and the other prefectures.

---

[35]Anonymous, Notebook 1, entries for April 16 and April 17, 1994.

[36]UNAMIR, Notes, Radio Rwanda, 20:00, April 16, 1994.

[37]Anonymous, Notebook 1, entry for April 17, 1994.

[38]Ibid.

Attackers from Maraba commune had begun burning the sector of Sovu in Huye commune, driving women and children to the Sovu health center and Rugango church. The men of Huye—still Hutu and Tutsi together—were attempting to fend off the attackers.[39]

Assailants had driven some 1,000 persons, many from Nyakizu or Gikongoro, to seek refuge at the Kigembe communal office. In Nyaruhengeri, people were being conscripted by officials and political leaders to go attack Nyumba church in neighboring Gishamvu where, it was falsely alleged, a soldier had been killed. Others were being sent to attack Tutsi at Gisagara in Ndora commune and at Mugombwa in Muganza. They were told to take banana leaves with them. Some returned hurt and required medical attention while others who came back without injury were then dispatched to other sites.[40]

In the northeast of the prefecture, displaced persons continued to arrive in the commune of Muyira fleeing soldiers and other assailants from Kigali and Gitarama. Their attackers, too, had worn banana leaves and had covered their faces with chalk and ashes.[41]

In the early afternoon of April 17, other soldiers were driving the roads of Maraba and Runyinya in a red pickup truck, giving armed men who stood along the road the thumbs up sign. The attackers, who also wore banana leaves around their necks, shouted back with approval, "Power!" The church and adjacent buildings at Simbi in Maraba commune were full of displaced persons. A double row of armed assailants had encircled the buildings and were just waiting for the agreed-upon hour of 7 p.m. to begin the slaughter. A dense network of road blocks was in place to catch any Tutsi who tried to flee. One of the barriers was manned by a proud twelve-year-old, under the watchful eyes of adults nearby. He told a passerby that he had been present at the planning meeting where the hour of attack had been set. Asked why the Tutsi should be killed, he replied with assurance, "Because they are evil."

According to a witness, Jean-Marie Vianney Habineza, the burgomaster of Maraba, was present at the church, wearing a pistol and accompanied by armed

---

[39]République Rwandaise, Parquet de la République de Kigali, PV. no. 0117; Human Rights Watch/FIDH interviews, Butare, March 26, 1996; Brussels, by telephone, January 19, 1998.

[40]Human Rights Watch/FIDH, Brussels, May 17, 1997; Anonymous, Notebook 1, entry for April 17, 1994.

[41]African Rights, *Rwanda, Death, Despair*, p. 355.

communal policemen that Sunday afternoon. When soldiers arrived to deliver an additional group of displaced persons from Ngoma commune, the burgomaster refused to accept them and complained that he had already told the Ngoma burgomaster Kanyabashi that morning to send him no more Tutsi. The displaced persons walked back to Ngoma to the sounds of whistles and the shouts of "Power!" from groups of children and young people along the way.[42]

Kanyabashi was supposedly astonished to learn that Simbi was besieged and promised to alert Lieutenant Colonel Muvunyi. Informed of the pending attack, the Bishop of Butare also promised to call Muvunyi. A message was left too for Major Habyarabatuma, who was not at police headquarters. The National Policeman who took the message stated that Habyarabatuma was angry at the death of two of his men at Cyahinda and would not intervene again "if it was just to have his policemen killed by Tutsi."[43]

Someone seeking to avert the disaster at Simbi also called Habyalimana, but was told by his wife that he was still at Nyakizu. By that time, Habyalimana could hardly have helped in any case. As the 8 p.m. news on Radio Rwanda announced, he was no longer prefect.[44]

That night a rotation of the troops took place. Captain Nizeyimana reportedly sent away those soldiers who showed no enthusiasm for killing Tutsi civilians. This may also have been the time when about half the Butare contingent of the National Police was sent to the battlefront. It was not replaced in Butare.[45]

Hutu Power Gains in Butare

With the increasing raids from outside the prefecture, the multiplication of attacks within, and the incitement to violence by the military, Habyalimana and those associated with him were clearly losing ground to the forces of genocide. Other administrators and political leaders, motivated by fear or opportunism, then followed the lead of the Nyakizu burgomaster and began inciting people in their areas to genocide. Many were anxious to profit from or at least not to be excluded by the forces shaping the radically and rapidly changing political situation. François Ndungutse, a native of Shyanda commune and one of the few leaders left

---

[42]République Rwandaise, Parquet de la République de Kigali, PV. no. 0117.

[43]Ibid.

[44]Ibid; UNAMIR, Notes, Radio Rwanda, 20:00, April 17, 1994.

[45]Human Rights Watch/FIDH interview, Neuchatel, December 16, 1995.

at national level in the PSD, reportedly helped push the PSD towards the side of Hutu Power. The one important party to have resisted the efforts to divide it in 1993, the PSD had lost most of its national leaders during the first days of the killings in Kigali and Ndungutse apparently hoped to strengthen it by cooperating more closely with the MRND. Observers in town noticed that the young men of PSD were drinking and strolling the streets with soldiers and before long, those who had worn the hats of the PSD were seen sporting the caps of MRND or even the CDR. One remarked:

> The PSD was strong in Butare, but after April 6, there was no more PSD. There was only two ethnic groups, Tutsi and Hutu: Tutsi to be killed and Hutu to be killed if they didn't want to kill.[46]

Adherents of the MRND hoped to reassert their hold over at least some parts of Butare prefecture while supporters of MDR, particularly MDR-Power, saw the opportunity to establish a base as Ntaganzwa had done in Nyakizu. These supporters of Hutu Power, including even those of the CDR, moved quickly to exploit the new cooperative spirit that they found among members of the PSD.[47]

Massacre at Simbi

Burgomaster Habineza of Maraba was one official who changed abruptly from an opponent to a supporter of killings. At first, he had led Hutu and Tutsi from his commune to the border to fight off incursions from neighboring Gikongoro. When assailants penetrated to the vicinity of the church where Tutsi had taken shelter, he went to the nearby playing field of the school to frighten them off by firing his pistol.[48]

The raiders from Gikongoro, wearing banana leaves and carrying machetes, hoes, and clubs, were backed by men with firearms, either former soldiers or National Police. Some assailants wore a kind of cannister on their backs from which they sprayed gasoline on houses before setting them alight. Vehicles followed behind carrying fuel to refill the cannisters as needed. The assailants'

---

[46]Human Rights Watch/FIDH interview, Butare, August 20, 1995.

[47]Human Rights Watch/FIDH interview, by telephone, Rome, February 4, 1998.

[48]Human Rights Watch/FIDH interviews, Simbi, Maraba, May 3 and 16, 1995; Kizi, Maraba, May 13 and June 23, 1995.

access to fuel and vehicles, already under state controls, was further proof of official sponsorship of the attacks.[49]

When Habineza was unable to halt the attacks, backed as they were by officials of the neighboring prefecture, he asked support from the prefecture. The prefectural security council on April 15 sent several National Policemen along with the public prosecutor Mathias Bushishi and a sub-prefect named Evariste Bicamumpaka to Maraba. From the point of view of the prefect, the delegation was meant to reinforce Habineza's efforts to keep order; and they did actually arrest an assistant burgomaster who was accused of encouraging the attacks. According to observers in the commune, however, the burgomaster stopped opposing the genocide soon after this visit. Some believe that one of the visitors took the burgomaster aside and persuaded him to give in to the violence.

Whatever changed the mind of the burgomaster, his decision was soon clear. He unexpectedly insisted that the Tutsi leave the church and move to a camp where they would be more exposed to attack. After the parish priests protested, he did allow them to remain in the church but he took away one group, largely of girls and young women. He was supposedly transporting them to a safer location, but they were never heard from again.[50] At about that same time, Habineza tolerated, if he did not actually encourage, the murder of the local judicial inspector, a man with whom he had often had conflicts in the past. When a group of young men armed with spears and machetes raided the home of the judicial inspector, he fled to the nearby home of the burgomaster. Habineza refused to let him in. As the judicial inspector turned away, he was struck in the back with a machete. Reportedly, the head of the communal police took him to the brigade to finish him off.[51]

Many in the commune followed the lead of the burgomaster. As one witness remarked,

---

[49]Human Rights Watch/FIDH interview, Nyangazi, Maraba, June 28, 1995. From the description of several witnesses, these cannisters sound like the devices used to spray insecticide on plants at tea plantations in Rwanda. If so, they had probably been delivered by staff from the Mata and Kitabi tea plantations in Gikongoro. (See above.) The use of such devices has also been recorded in Nshili commune in Gikongoro. See Africans Rights, *Rwanda, Death, Despair*, p. 1016.

[50]Human Rights Watch/FIDH interviews, Simbi, Maraba, May 3 and 16, 1995; Anonymous, Notebook 1, entry for April 15, 1994.

[51]Human Rights Watch/FIDH interview, Simbi, Maraba, May 16, 1995.

In the first days, the refugees [i.e., the Tutsi] would walk out and around the area, go out of the church to buy sorghum beer and so on. But, after April 15, no one would serve them beer. This was just one sign that things were changing.[52]

The first group of National Police to come to Maraba had worked to keep order, but after April 17 another team came with the opposite goal. They arrived in Nyangazi sector of Maraba in a pickup truck and found a group of people pillaging the homes of Tutsi. Seeing that the assailants hesitated to kill, "the police encouraged them." The witness declared:

Right over there the National Police killed Hategeka because he was pillaging the house of Gasarabwe and they ordered him to kill, not to just pillage. Hategeka was armed with a grenade and a machete [but he was not killing]. After the police had killed Hategeka, the people killed some of those who were fleeing, a man called Kabera and a woman called Mukakaremera and her seven children. The National Police went on towards Ruhashya.[53]

Maraba assailants borrowed methods and equipment from the Gikongoro attackers: they too used the portable spray devices to make it easier to burn houses quickly. A driver who worked for the commune reportedly used one of the commune pickup trucks to supply the arson squads with fuel.[54]

Hundreds of assailants, some local, some from Gikongoro, attacked the Simbi church and health center at about 9 a.m. on April 18. They wore banana leaves and had chalk on their faces and they made a lot of noise with drums and shouting. One priest, who was Tutsi, had escaped the night before and the other, who was Hutu, was in the church baptizing people in anticipation of their imminent deaths when one of the attackers threw a grenade into the building. The killers slaughtered all day and into the night, then stopped to feast on the cattle that they had looted. They returned to resume the slaughter on April 19 and 20. According to one survivor

---

[52]Human Rights Watch/FIDH interview, Simbi, Maraba, May 16, 1995.

[53]Human Rights Watch/FIDH interview, Nyangazi, Maraba, June 28, 1995.

[54]Ibid.

from Maraba, some of the killers were "like madmen," but many others had been forced by the authorities to kill.[55]

Eight soldiers, who had arrived in a red pickup truck, directed the massacre with the help of communal policemen. On the first day, a second group of uniformed men also arrived, driving in a van, apparently to ensure that the others did not need help. The soldiers in the van distributed grenades to assailants as it drove around the area. The burgomaster, armed and present before the attack, was not reported seen during the slaughter itself.

Most of the 3,000 to 5,000 persons in the church and outbuildings at the time of the attack were slain. The few who escaped were caught in the dense web of barricades that covered roads and paths "at every ten paces."[56] During the attack, three Hutu nuns were killed, apparently because they opposed the pillage of the health center.

Burgomaster Habineza rewarded with one kilogram of rice each person who helped bury the victims in shallow graves around the church. The rice had been stored by church authorities for distribution to the hungry.[57]

Habineza reportedly participated in the pillage of the health center and subsequently confiscated valuable goods from ordinary people who had looted them from Tutsi homes. He almost immediately organized local meetings to divide up the fields of those who had been killed.[58]

Massacre at Kansi

In the commune of Nyaruhengeri also, local leaders decided that April 18 was the time to begin large-scale killing. Until that day, Hutu and Tutsi had worked together at road blocks and on patrols. Near the church of Kansi, Tutsi teachers had at first been afraid to take their places at the barrier and did so only after Hutu had promised that they would not harm them. Thousands of people had sought shelter in the church and adjacent buildings after the burgomaster, Charles Kabeza, had refused to let displaced persons come to the communal offices. Saying he had been

---

[55]Human Rights Watch/FIDH interview, Kizi, Maraba, June 23, 1995.

[56]République Rwandaise, Parquet de la République de Kigali, PV. no. 0117.

[57]Human Rights Watch/FIDH interviews, Simbi, Maraba, May 3, May 5 and May 16, 1995.

[58]Human Rights Watch/FIDH interviews, Simbi, Maraba, May 3, May 5 and May 16, 1995; Nyangazi, Maraba, June 28, 1995.

ordered not to allow them to gather at the offices, he had put a barrier in place to keep them at a distance. The parish priests had sought without success to get the Red Cross to provide food for the displaced, who were also lacking water.[59]

In the afternoon of April 18, retired soldiers or military men in civilian dress came to goad Hutu into attacking Tutsi at the barrier near the church. At first the Hutu hesitated, but then they began to throw stones at the Tutsi, who threw stones back. That night, armed men attacked the church complex and killed some Tutsi. The next morning workers warned the priests, who had spent the night in the rafters of the church, that a major attack would come that night. The priests, who had not been able to get even food for the displaced despaired of getting any protection for them. They advised the crowd to flee, but leaders of the group asked "Flee to where?" Many were already weakened by lack of food and water. Unable to save the thousands of people, one of the priests gave them absolution and left. As he passed behind the church, he was caught by an assailant who put his machete to the priest's neck and warned him to stay clear of the killing that was going to take place.[60]

That afternoon assailants killed the director of the school outside the convent of the Bernadine sisters. Shortly after, former soldiers and communal councilors led thousands of armed men in attacking the church and school buildings, beginning with grenades and finishing with machetes. In a few hours of intense slaughter, they killed between 10,000 and 10,500 persons. During the attack leaders used plastic whistles to direct the activities of the killers. Among the killers were Burundian refugees who had been housed at the Nyange camp not far from the church.[61]

The next day, one of the priests found ten or fifteen survivors outside the main door of the church. As he stood talking with them, he heard assailants blowing their whistles in the same rhythm that they had used the day before. From the woods behind him, a crowd surged forward and killed the survivors before his eyes. When the priest later entered the classrooms, the killers once more came after him and

---

[59]Human Rights Watch/FIDH interviews, Buffalo, N.Y., April 23, 1997; Brussels, May 17, 1997.

[60]Human Rights Watch/FIDH interview, Brussels, May 17, 1997.

[61]Human Rights Watch/FIDH interviews, Buffalo, N.Y., April 23, 1997; Brussels, May 17, 1997.

killed babies who had survived the massacre of the day before. When he asked them why they were murdering infants, they replied, "They are the enemy."[62]

For the next six days, local people were too occupied with searching for survivors and plundering to help dispose of the bodies. Dogs came to eat some of them. After the six days, the burgomaster sent men to help with the burial. The church paid for the labor.

Pillagers made off with everything portable from the church and school buildings, even items for which they had no possible use. When the burgomaster appealed for the return of some of the goods, people did bring them back. Some who regretted having killed asked the clergy, "Will God punish us?"[63]

The Hutu at the barrier who had promised the Tutsi teachers that they would not harm them kept their promise. Burundian refugees killed them instead.[64]

On April 18, the same day as the massacres at Simbi and Kansi, administrative officials and political leaders launched the slaughter of between 2,000 and 3,000 people who had taken refuge at the communal offices in the commune of Kigembe, just south of Nyaruhengeri.[65] On the same day, assailants spread out over the hills of the commune Huye, burning and killing in all sectors except Mpare.[66] And in the northeast, assailants from outside the prefecture and others from the commune of Muyira drove Tutsi, including those displaced from further north, from Muyira into Ntyazo, just to the south.[67]

Welcoming the New Prefect

Although many had already moved to violence on or before the 18th, the first day when people became generally aware of Habyalimana's dismissal, the commune of Ngoma and others forming a protective shield to its north—Mbazi, Ruhashya, Mugusa, Shyanda, and Ndora—were largely, if not completely, quiet.

---

[62]Human Rights Watch/FIDH interview, Brussels, May 17, 1997.

[63]Ibid.

[64]Human Rights Watch/FIDH interviews, Buffalo, N.Y., April 23, 1997; Brussels, May 17, 1997.

[65]Human Rights Watch/FIDH interview, Kigali, July 14, 1996.

[66]Human Rights Watch/FIDH interview, Butare, March 26, 1996.

[67]African Rights, *Rwanda, Death, Despair,* p. 355.

In many places Hutu and Tutsi were still patrolling or guarding barriers together. In Mbazi, the burgomaster Antoine Sibomana had coordinated an effective defense of Hutu and Tutsi against attacks from the adjacent commune of Maraba, in one instance killing several of the assailants. He had arrested commune residents, including his own brother, who had attacked Tutsi.[68] In the northeastern commune of Ntyazo, Hutu, and Tutsi came together for an effective defense that would last for ten days.[69] Several burgomasters still hoped the armed forces would help them to keep the peace. The burgomaster of Runyinya, who had provided both protection and food to people who had fled from Gikongoro, appealed to Major Habyarabatuma for additional help from the National Police. In a letter to the local military commander, the burgomaster of Ndora described how he had been able to intervene successfully to stop an attack against a man who was accused of hiding "unknown persons" in his house and asked the commander to send a patrol from time to time "to quiet the troublemakers."[70]

In accord with orders from the prefect, many burgomasters and other officials held meetings about security between April 14 and 18. They organized patrols and guard duty on the barriers and they also addressed the fears felt by people, whether Hutu or Tutsi. One witness from the commune of Ngoma recalls such a meeting where Kanyabashi urged the people of Cyarwa to avoid violence and to fight together against attacks from Huye and Gikongoro, while others recall a similar session that he led in Rango to encourage resistance against attacks from Gishamvu.[71] In a foreshadowing of events to come, Hutu Power advocates took over several of the meetings and used the occasions to frighten Hutu. At the meeting at Kabutare in Butare town, for example, Hutu pressed Tutsi to explain

---

[68]Human Rights Watch/FIDH interviews, Butare, October 29, 1994; August 19, 20, and December 13, 1995; Brussels, December 18, 1995, February 2, 1996; African Rights, *Witness to Genocide,* issue 7, September 1997, pp. 7-8.

[69]Anonymous, Notebook 2, entry entitled "Ntyazo."

[70] Human Rights Watch/FIDH interviews, Butare, August 19 and 24, 1995; January 26, 1996; P. Celestin Rwankubito, Bourgmestre de la commune Ndora, to Monsieur le Commandant de Place, no. 093/04.09.01/7, April 18, 1994 (Butare prefecture) African Rights, *Witness to Genocide,* issue 7, September 1997, pp. 7-9; African Rights, *Rwanda, Death, Despair,* pp. 345, 348.

[71]Human Rights Watch/FIDH interviews, Butare, October 29, 1995; January 2 and January 27, 1996.

why they had sent their children away if they were not intending to cause trouble in the community. In a sector meeting in Tumba, also in Butare, a well-known local doctor, Sosthène Munyemana, reported wrongly that the RPF had attacked people in Kigembe and had caused fifteen people to flee to his home in Butare. Witnesses in the community declared that his speech and the angry reaction to it sparked dissension among Hutu and Tutsi who had previously worked well together to avoid violence.[72]

To hold together the dwindling island of peace in the swell of genocidal violence would have required great political skill and force of character. The man named by the interim government as prefect, Sylvain Nsabimana, was not known for these characteristics but rather for his cordial good nature and readiness to have a good time. The decision-makers had wanted to appoint someone from the PSD since the party was dominant in Butare and its young adherents were showing greater openness to Hutu Power. They hoped that a prefect from the PSD would be able to bring local people into line with government policy.

PSD leaders François Ndungutse and Etienne Bashamiki welcomed the idea and set about recruiting Nsabimana, an agronomist who headed the PSD in the commune of Mbazi, but had little experience with politics at the national level. At first Nsabimana refused the post, citing his lack of experience, but then he was swayed by the argument that it might go to the MRND if he did not take it. He and others in the PSD feared that a prefect from the MRND might harass the party (and perhaps Nsabimana himself) over PSD involvement in the February murder of CDR head Bucyana, a case that was still being investigated. Nsabimana maintains that he still had not actually accepted the offer when the interim government announced the appointment on the radio. Three days later he heard on the radio that the interim president was coming to install him in the post. Forced to decide whether to accept or not, he went that morning to buy a suit and then to be installed as prefect. He thus assumed a position of major responsibility in a government which had already made clear its genocidal program.[73]

---

[72]Human Rights Watch/FIDH interview, October 24, 26 and 29, 1995; African Rights, *Witness to Genocide,* issue 2, February 1996, pp. 6-11.

[73]Transcript of interview of Sylvain Nsabimana by unidentified interviewer, October 1, 1994 (provided by Sylvain Nsabimana; hereafter "Interview of Sylvain Nsabimana, October 1, 1994").

Months later, Nsabimana learned that his appointment had been examined and approved by the executive committee of the Interahamwe, an indication of the power exerted at that time by the militia within the circles of government.[74]

The formalities of installation took place on the morning of April 19 in the Salle Polyvalente, a large auditorium on the main street of Butare, built to house meetings of the MRND in the closing days of the single-party era. The assemblage included a host of dignitaries of the interim government: Prime Minister Kambanda, Minister of Trade and Industry Justin Mugenzi, Minister of Family and Womens' Affairs Pauline Nyiramasuhuko, Minister of Information Eliezer Niyitegeka, and Minister of Justice Agnes Ntamabyaliro. The interim president attended but, according to witnesses, came in late. Minister of Agriculture Straton Nsabumukunzi may have been there as well. Their presence underscored the importance of the occasion and placed it firmly within the context of the program to extend the genocide which they had already begun executing the day before at the meeting with local officials in Gitarama. A number of high-ranking military officers were in the audience, as were most local burgomasters and councilors. The heads of various prefectural administrative departments, many of them Tutsi, were there as well.[75]

Callixte Kalimanzira, still temporarily in charge of the Ministry of the Interior, served as master of ceremonies for a program which included speeches by the president, the prime minister, the ministers Mugenzi and Niyitegeka, the newly appointed prefect, and the burgomaster of Ngoma. Contrary to usual practice and to emphasize the humiliation of the outgoing prefect, Habyalimana was not given the opportunity to speak. Once he was officially dismissed, Habyalimana was in effect told to leave and he did so. This further humiliation shocked some of those who had been his subordinates and roused their fears of a similar fate.[76]

The interim prime minister apparently spoke first. Declaring that the current conflict was the "final war" that had to be carried to its ultimate conclusion, he

---

[74]Two of the committee, Dieudonné Niyitegeka and Ephrem Nkezabera, reportedly later stated that the committee had known little about Nsabimana when it approved his nomination and implied that they had been disappointed in his performance on the job. Human Rights Watch/FIDH interview, by telephone, Nairobi, April 3, 1996.

[75]Human Rights Watch/FIDH interviews, Butare, August 19, 1995; January 26, 1996.

[76]Human Rights Watch/FIDH interviews, Butare, August 19,1995; Brussels, November 2, 1995.

insisted that the government would no longer tolerate those who sympathised with the enemy and helped him by sapping the morale of the Rwandan army. He mentioned burgomasters who had supposedly gone for training with the RPF and asked that their colleagues warn them that the government was determined to win the war.[77]

Kanyabashi, the most senior burgomaster, both by length of service and because of the importance of his commune, responded to Kambanda's speech.[78] The Ngoma burgomaster presumably understood the threat implicit in the prime minister's accusation about RPF training. Some months before, a group of PSD party members had gone to the RPF zone, supposedly for a friendly football match, but the rumor was that they had gone for military training with the RPF. Burgomasters who supported the PSD, as did Kanyabashi, would most likely have realized that their loyalty was in question simply because of their party affiliation, a reason to declare support for the government even if they did not feel obligated by party solidarity to endorse the new appointee. In Kanyabashi's case, the pressure may well have been greater because he was known to have a Tutsi wife and because he had already been criticized so frequently for his friendships with Tutsi.[79] The man described by some colleagues as "supple" and by others as "an opportunist" took the safe course of supporting a government that was carrying out a genocide. According to the transcript of the speech recorded and subsequently played over Radio Rwanda, he declared:

> We promise you once more, as we have not stopped showing, that we support your government and that we will continue to do everything that is in our power to permit it to realise its objectives.

After professing support also for the army, he continued:

---

[77]Discours du Premier Ministre Jean Kambanda, transcript of a recording broadcast by Radio Rwanda, April 21, 1994 (provided by Jean-Pierre Chrétien).

[78]It has been generally supposed that Kanyabashi took the floor after both the president and the prime minister had spoken, but this may not have been the case. In his salutation Kanyabashi addresses only the prime minister, which makes it seem unlikely that the president had already delivered his remarks. Given that the president's speech was so much more incendiary than that of the prime minister, the question of whether Kanyabashi was responding to both or to only one has considerable importance.

[79]Human Rights Watch/FIDH interview, by telephone, Antwerp, March 8, 1997.

We will do everything in our power to keep our country from falling into the hands of the "inyangarwanda" (those who hate Rwanda), we will do everything in our power to make every citizen understand that national sovereignty is his concern. In addition, we will maintain security wherever this can be done while also trying to restore it wherever it is absent.

Perhaps revealing his discomfiture at having pronounced this endorsement, he remarked that it was "difficult to find the right words," and then concluded that the people of Butare would put into action whatever was possible to protect the security of the prefecture.[80]

Interim President Sindikubwabo presented a seemingly casual series of remarks, directed primarily at the new prefect, whom he addressed with the affectionate term "sha." He reviewed briefly the visits he had made the day before to Maraba, Nyakizu, and Nyumba church in Gishamvu, using the chance to reinforce the myth that the "refugees" gathered in these locations were armed with "very sophisticated weapons," including rifles and grenades. Because of this, he said, they had badly frightened the local populations. Quoting the minister Mugenzi, he stressed that the "refugees," the Tutsi, were being well fed and cared for in the churches while "the great majority," the Hutu, received no such care as they wandered about in the pouring rain.

He chastised authorities in Gikongoro and Butare for requesting help from National Police who were needed for "other obligations." Sindikubwabo recounted that he had asked in one commune if there were no more men there, meaning men who could deal with "security" problems themselves, only to be told that there were few left because most others were preoccupied with enriching themselves. This passage echoed the directives, like those heard at Nyundo, Nyakizu, and Maraba, that killing Tutsi was more important than pillaging them.

Stressing that each burgomaster was responsible for protecting his commune, Sindikubwabo told them, "Act like adults and protect our prefecture." He insisted that officials could not hide behind excuses, such as not being in the office when there was work to be done. They could not just watch while others did the work.

In the harshest passages of the speech, he remarked that people of Butare were well known for their know-it-all attitude, for their approach of "it's not my business." He declared,

---

[80]Discours du Bourgmestre Joseph Kanyabashi, transcript of a recording broadcast by Radio Rwanda, April 21, 1994 (provided by Jean-Pierre Chrétien).

What this means is that "the actors who only watch," the "those who feel it's not their business," should be exposed. Let them step aside for us and let us "work" and let them look from outside our circle. He who says "that's not my business and I'm even afraid," let him step aside for us. Those who are responsible of getting rid of such a person, let them do it fast. Other good "workers who want to work" for their country are there.

Referring back to the prime minister's mention of officials who had gone to the RPF for training, Sindikubwabo asked anyone acquainted with such people to get rid of them. He predicted that the interim government would win the war once it had eliminated those who felt the war was not their business.

Sindikubwabo excused himself for speaking in "an almost authoritarian voice," but said he had to do so to make his audience understand the gravity of his message. Because the country was at war, "these are not ordinary words." The interim president said that he had delivered only a part of his message "because the way is still long." Before continuing the message, Sindikubwabo said, he "would first observe the conduct of each person. I am speaking especially of the authorities." The implication was that the rest of his message—with dismissals of other officials—would follow if local authorities failed to join the killing campaign. He concluded by insisting,

> ...I want you to learn to understand us and to interpret our remarks as they are intended. You should understand the reason that pushes us to talk this way, analyze every word so that you understand why it was delivered in such a way and not in another. It is because we are living through extraordinary times. Jokes, laughing, taking things lightly, indifference, all must for the time being give way to "work."[81]

Two of the ministers most known for their virulently anti-Tutsi views, Mugenzi and Niyitegeka, also spoke. Their remarks clearly were less important than those of Sindikubwabo, not only because they were lower in status than he, but also because they were not native to the region. Even so, their incitements to

---

[81]As in so many official pronouncements throughout the genocide, "work" here means to kill Tutsi as it did in the 1959 revolution. Discours du Président Théodore Sindikubwabo prononcé le 19 avril à la Préfecture de Butare.

action multiplied the pressures on the listeners.[82] When the formal addresses were finished, Jonathas Ruremesha, burgomaster of Huye, asked what he should say to the people of his commune who wanted "to begin conflicts." As in the meeting in Gitarama the day before, the highest authorities stood back and allowed Mugenzi to respond for the government. He stated unequivocally, "If the population gets angry, it should be allowed to do what it wants." Ruremesha reportedly decided at that point that he would make no further attempts to halt violence.[83]

After being sent from the auditorium that morning, Jean-Baptiste Habyalimana crossed the road to the prefectural offices. The main building, a long, decrepit one-story structure, faced a large expanse of beaten earth. The prefect's office was at the far end, to the left. To the right stood the small and dark jail that housed prisoners arrested by the National Police. A witness at the prefecture on the morning of April 19 observed some 500 displaced persons gathered in front of the prefecture. As he watched, soldiers loaded men from the crowd into three trucks which departed full and returned empty about twenty minutes later. In an hour's time, the trucks made three roundtrips to an unknown destination. The women and children stayed at the prefecture. The witness, a foreigner who needed some assistance from the administration, sought out the prefect who was seated at the desk in his office. When he stated his business, Habyalimana said that he could not help because he was no longer prefect. As he was leaving, the visitor thanked Habyalimana for being one of the three men who had tried to keep the peace in Butare. Habyalimana asked, "Which three?" When the visitor mentioned Habyalimana, Major Habyarabatuma, and Kanyabashi, the former prefect exclaimed with anger and disgust, "Kanyabashi!" The visitor asked what Habyalimana would do next. He answered, "I used to be a professor. I will probably go back to teaching." As he said this, he turned his face away so that his tears would not be seen.[84]

Disappointed though Habyalimana might have been in Kanyabashi's performance, the burgomaster of Ngoma was, according to one witness, still trying to prevent the killing in the late afternoon of April 19. He told a crowded meeting

---

[82]Sylvain Nsabimana, "The Truth About the Massacres in Butare," undated manuscript (provided by Sylvain Nsabimana).

[83]Arrondissement de Bruxelles, Tribunal de Première Instance, Deposition de Témoin, November 30, 1995, Dossier 57/95.

[84]Human Rights Watch/FIDH interview, Neuchatel, December 16, 1995.

at the Ngoma sector office that the slaughter must not happen, but he apparently could offer no concrete advice on how to avoid it.[85]

The day after his installation in office, the new prefect met with his predecessor to go over financial records and other paperwork related to the change in administration. Nsabimana agreed to allow Habyalimana to keep the two National Policemen who were supposed to protect him and to permit him and his family to remain in the official residence of the prefect, a modest house near the airport. After this meeting, Habyalimana went into hiding, stalked by Pauline Nyiramasuhuko and her collaborators.[86]

Nsabimana spent some time after Habyalimana's departure searching through documents in the prefect's office and in a storeroom adjacent to the auditorium, looking for proof that his predecessor had actually supported the RPF as he had been told was the case. He found nothing. Similarly, he had been assured that the security service had files on burgomasters and others who had gone to RPF headquarters in Mulindi for military training, but none was ever produced to confirm the assertion.[87]

On the day Habyalimana left his post, Major Habyarabatuma came home in the late morning after having directed security patrols in various sectors. He found a telegram from the army general staff that had been delivered at about 9 a.m. ordering him to report to the battlefield in Kigali at 2 p.m. that same day. Deprived of about half the police under his command a few days before, he had experienced growing difficulty in getting compliance with his orders and had had to discipline some subordinates, even imprisoning a lieutenant, junior grade, who had participated in the Cyahinda massacre. Still he had remained an important presence in discouraging violence. His departure, like the replacement of Habyalimana, marked the defeat of forces opposed to the genocide. He left the National Police in Butare under the command of Major Rusigariye, who was known to support the slaughter.[88]

---

[85]Human Rights Watch/FIDH interview, Butare, March 26, 1996.

[86]Human Rights Watch/FIDH interview, Nairobi, by telephone, March 25, 1996.

[87]Human Rights Watch/FIDH interview, Nairobi, by telephone, April 3, 1996.

[88]Human Rights Watch/FIDH interviews, Kigali, November 21, 1995; January 26, 1996; Butare, February 5, 1996.

South of Butare

By April 19, some 12,000 Rwandans had sought safety in Burundi. Many others wanted to leave, but just as the need for escape was becoming more pressing, so flight across the border was becoming more difficult. One man in Butare was able to convince a soldier to escort his wife to safety in return for 10,000 Rwandan francs (about U.S.$55), but few had that kind of resources or connections.[89]

Foreign aid workers witnessed the violence directed against residents of the area south of town and people trying to flee across the frontier. On the morning of April 19, several staff members of MSF drove the thirty-five miles south from Butare through the communes of Gishamvu and Kigembe to the Burundi frontier to pick up some medical supplies. They had to pass through twenty to twenty-five road blocks, most of them made out of rocks and limbs of trees. The most important, such as the one just outside Butare and another near the frontier, were manned by soldiers, some of them armed with machine guns and grenades. Others were guarded by civilians with machetes and one or two men with firearms. At several places, the MSF staff noticed men wearing bright yellow wool scarves, as had Interahamwe both at the Kibeho church massacre and in the town of Butare. Guards were interested in checking the identity papers only of Africans in the group. At one barrier, they examined the cargo in the pickup truck asking "Are you carrying Tutsi?"[90]

When the cars reached one of the road blocks in Gishamvu, the staff began seeing dead bodies alongside the barriers and scattered among the houses. Dr. Rony Zachariah saw people being pulled violently out of their houses and handed over to groups of two, three, or four people who were armed with machetes. Often the victims were made to sit down before being struck. He recalled the entire landscape being "spotted with corpses" virtually all the way to the border. In some of the piles, there were between sixty and eighty corpses.

As the MSF convoy approached the border, Zachariah saw a group of ten militia armed with machetes chasing sixty to eighty people who were running on the road "like cattle in a stampede." Zachariah recalled:

In front of us there was a man who looked very elderly to me because he had white hair. He could not run so fast and he stumbled. The militia [member]

---

[89]Human Rights Watch/FIDH interview, Butare, October 26, 1995.

[90]ICTR-96-4-T, Testimony of Dr. Rony Zachariah.

took his machete and he hit him with the machete on the side of the neck, right there before our eyes, directly in front of our car. We could see the blood that was gushing out....It was done in such a professional manner that he was cut, there was blood gushing out and the old man just fell down in the middle of the tarmac. The militia [member] started chasing the group of people along with the others. It was very close to the car, so I had to swerve the car in such a way that I would not drive over him. I tried to get past this group of people—and the people were trying to get into the car. They were crying for help, "Take us in!" But we had raised the window glass and the doors were locked. We could not take anybody in. We crossed [passed] them and we reached the border. But at the border there was another group of militia that was waiting. All these civilians, sixty to eighty of them were pursued and hacked to death. There were six, perhaps ten, that managed to cross the bridge between Rwanda and Burundi with their wounds.[91]

A representative of Action Internationale Contre la Faim (AICF) who had come from Bujumbura to meet a convoy from Butare wrote a description of a similar scene that he witnessed at the same crossing point several days later. At one moment, everything was quiet at the border, where the two barriers marking each side were separated by two hundred yards of paved road. Suddenly a crowd surged over the top of a nearby hill, some twenty Tutsi being chased by many others, and rushed towards the frontier.

The witness described the total unreality of the scene; he had trouble believing that he was really seeing the blows fall and hearing the cries and moans:

My position made the situation even more hallucinatory; alone, I stood deliberately in the middle of the carnage. I was so naive as to believe that my presence might restrain the violence of the assailants, so I stayed in the middle of the slaughter. But they paid no attention at all to me, completely cut off by their own rage. When one scene of violence began several yards of away, I went there, just to be there, to make my presence troubling, but at the same time, another was happening on the right and I wanted to go there too, then another and still another, always the same thing, a man trying to flee and the others catching him and hitting him, a man on the ground not even trying to protect himself, immobilized by the blows, resigned, and other men crushing his flesh with blows of clubs and machetes, spears, bows, and arrows.

---

[91]Ibid.

The assailants did not finish off a victim, but injured each just enough to immobilize him before going after another. The witness continued:

> Not everyone was armed with weapons, but everyone was armed with hate, ready to trip up a Tutsi who was passing, to slap in passing the miserable person who was running, out of breath, out of strength, who, exhausted fell flat on the macadam. Scarcely was he down when the blows fell with twice the force. Children...made a game of it all, following their older brothers in running after the Tutsi, throwing stones at them, and laughing at each Tutsi who was caught.

> A Zairian who was also trying to cross the border stood next to his car, watching the scenes of horror. As broad as he was tall, massive and solid, the forty-year-old man was built to inspire respect. This man watched what was happening before his eyes and sobbed silently.

When the awaited convoy arrived, the aid worker went to get in his own car to lead them across the border. As he did so, two women with babies on their backs, ignored by the crowd, murmured a plea to be taken in one of the cars. The aid worker feared that doing so would attract the attention of the crowd to the cars and the Tutsi inside whom they were hoping to get across the border. He recalled that "I would have preferred dying on the spot to saying no to these women and condemning them to death, but that is what I had to do."[92]

The Meeting of April 20

After having delivered his message to the administrators and politicians on April 19, Interim President Sindikubwabo carried the word to the population by visits to the Cyamukaza and Muzenga sectors of his home commune of Ndora, where he reportedly demanded violence against Tutsi even more bluntly than at the Butare meeting. He also delivered instructions to the people of other communes, such as Shyanda, and to the sub-prefectural center at Gisagara, where he apparently helped prepare assailants for the massacre that began the next day at Kabuye.[93]

---

[92]Jean-Fabrice Pietri, Untitled manuscript.

[93]Human Rights Watch/FIDH interviews, Butare, October 27, 1995; Brussels, September 24, 1994 and March 4, 1996; UNAMIR, Notes, Radio Rwanda, 21:00, April 21, and 20:00, April 22, 1994; Human Rights Watch/FIDH, *Shattered Lives*, p. 51.

On some of these visits, he was joined by Callixte Kalimanzira, who would appear in the region with growing frequency to prod and supervise the prefect and his subordinates into efficiently implementing the genocide. As a long-standing member of the MRND, Kalimanzira had little hope of being named prefect in a prefecture so hostile to his party, but he expected and was expected by others to run the prefecture through Nsabimana, given the new prefect's lack of experience with the territorial administration. Sindikubwabo and Kalimanzira together allegedly put great pressure on those burgomasters who still hesitated to kill, such as Théophile Shyirambere of Shyanda, stressing that if they failed to perform satisfactorily and were removed their lives might be in danger.[94]

While the national authorities were reinforcing the message, the new prefect began the work of implementing it. He subsequently claimed that he did not go to his office between April 20 and 26 and that there was no one in charge during those days. He described the first week after he took office as "total disorder."[95] But the day after his installation he chaired a well-attended meeting of the prefectural security committee. Notes taken by a participant reflect a carefully planned agenda and a well-structured discussion. The participants agreed that "infiltrators" accounted for the mounting violence. Proceeding from the government doctrine that local Tutsi residents were in fact armed RPF agents, the participants agreed that such persons must be arrested and brought to the authorities; that military operations would be executed to "disarm those who are armed"; that search operations should be carried out whenever solid information indicated the need; and that administrative meetings should be held the next day with subordinate officials and other local leaders "who could contribute to restoring security." They singled out several places as needing special attention, including the Burundi border and Nyakizu, with its "problems of armed people," no doubt meaning the last resisters on top of Nyakizu hill. The participants also considered what to do at Maraba and concluded "The burgomaster should work there first; he should identify everyone from his commune who is at Gihindamuyaga," a monastery where Tutsi had taken refuge.

Reflecting the wish to deal only with those who were their own responsibility, the participants stressed that "refugees" should go back home "to be helped" in their places of origin. Gikongoro people, in particular, should be the responsibility

---

[94]Human Rights Watch/FIDH interviews, Brussels, September 24, 1994 and March 4, 1996.

[95]"Interview of Sylvain Nsabimana, October 1, 1994."

of Gikongoro authorities. Recognizing that all those without identity papers were likely to be killed, the participants declared that care should be taken to ensure that the "innocent not become victims as well," no doubt meaning those Hutu who had fled their homes without the necessary documents.

Apparently planning ahead for the hunt that would follow the first massacres, the participants talked of eliminating hiding places, such as empty houses, and of directing all residents to cut the brush around their houses.

The participants dealt with some administrative arrangements to facilitate the "restoration of security," such as exchanging information with Gikongoro authorities, and allocating fuel, which was in short supply.

Jean-Marie Vianney Gisagara, the burgomaster of Nyabisindu, known for his vigorous resistance against attackers from Gikongoro, was apparently the only one to openly dissent from the program. He described the grief among the people in his commune over the removal of the previous prefect and over the deaths of their relatives. He reported that they were discussing creating a territorial base to resist the genocide.[96] Other participants did not challenge the unspoken genocidal program and made no suggestions for dealing with the violence. One assessed the tenor of the meeting by saying, "At that time, there was no way to stop the killing."[97]

On the last line of the entry for this meeting, the notetaker wrote "Ndora - Rusatira -," and then instead of continuing the list of names of communes, he struck it out and wrote simply, "All on Friday except Mbazi." There were attacks in most of the previously untouched communes on Friday, April 22, except for Mbazi, which was targeted the following Monday, April 25.

After the attacks from Gikongoro, after killers had mobilized in half the communes of Butare, after the prefect and the police commander who fought for order had been removed, and after the leading officials of the national government had come to deliver incendiary speeches, the security meeting of April 20 destroyed the last hope of most burgomasters opposed to the genocide. Bourgomasters like Ruremesha of Huye, Hategekimana of Runyinya, and Sibomana of Mbazi seem to have left the meeting ready to accept if not to encourage the genocide in their communes. Faced with pressure from above,

---

[96]Anonymous, Notebook 1, entry for April 20, 1994. Gisagara is apparently the person referred to as "the bourgmestre of Gisagara" by African Rights in *Rwanda, Death, Despair,* pp. 1043-44.

[97]Human Rights Watch/FIDH interview, by telephone, Nairobi, April 3, 1996.

burgomasters also had to confront grass-roots political leaders determined to carry forward the genocide. A witness on the spot recalls hearing the former soldier and militia leader Emmanuel Rekeraho remark that "it could turn out badly for the burgomaster of Mbazi, who, according to him, was trying to hold back the revolution."[98] Tutsi were attacked at the communal office in Huye even while the prefectural security meeting was going on and a messenger brought the news to the burgomaster there. The burgomaster, Ruremesha, who the day before had asked the assembled ministers what to do if conflict threatened, set off for his office but took along no soldiers or National Police. He had apparently decided that there was no point in asking for their help.[99]

Some burgomasters passed the new message of violence to their subordinates and the people of their commune by public meetings. Elie Ndambayaje of Muganza commune reportedly openly incited people to kill at such meetings. Others were more circumspect. On April 21, at the stadium in his commune of Mbazi, Sibomana delivered a speech described by one witness as "very complex." Some say he cited proverbs to convey his meaning, the most important being *Iyo inzoka yizilitse ku gisabo ugomba kikimena ukabona uko uyica.* Literally the sentence means "In killing a snake curled around a gourd, you break the gourd if you must to kill him," in other words, you do what you must to eliminate a danger.[100] Sibomana admits having used the proverb, but protests that it was on another occasion and that the speech has been misconstrued.[101]

Officials also made the new program clear by releasing from jail those who had been arrested for attacking Tutsi. Immediately following the meeting at Mbazi, Sibomana and the public prosecutor for Butare, Mathias Bushishi, released the

---

[98]Dr. Alexandre Rucyahana, untitled typescript.

[99]République Rwandaise, Parquet de la République de Kigali, PV. no. 0117.

[100]Rwandans attach great importance to large gourds, used in the past to hold milk and to churn it into butter. Breaking such a vessel was a serious mistake that could bring unfortunate consequences. In the terms of this proverb, killing a snake is so important as to excuse even the fault of breaking a gourd. In *Witness to Genocide*, issue 7, African Rights quotes this proverb three times on pages 10 and 16. The first citation, correct in kinyarwanda, is wrongly translated.

[101]African Rights, *Witness to Genocide,* issue 7, p, 86. Human Rights Watch/FIDH interview, Butare, August 19, 1995.

persons whom Sibomana had arrested for having attacked Tutsi.[102] In Nyabisindu, where Gisagara, the burgomaster opposing the genocide, had arrested the former soldier Abel Basabose and others for attacking Tutsi homes, National Policemen insisted on their release and restitution to them of the weapons taken at the time of arrest. As in similar cases in Gikongoro and Gitarama, the release of those who had openly killed Tutsi and destroyed their property demonstrated that Tutsi no longer enjoyed the protection of the law.[103]

In a number of sectors, councilors held smaller meetings on the night of April 20 from which they excluded Tutsi and during which they planned attacks for the following days. In Tumba, for example, the councilor told participants that lists had been found proving that Tutsi were planning to kill Hutu and that they must attack first to protect themselves. In Cyarwa a Tutsi who tried to attend a security meeting was insulted and spat at. In Kabutare, participants were told that the RPF was attacking in a neighboring sector and that the people needed to organize patrols immediately to combat the enemy. At the university, the vice-rector told students that if they heard shooting, it was soldiers "fighting infiltrators here in Butare." He told them that they must take measures to protect themselves.[104] He also summoned faculty to a similar meeting for the next morning, but by then the slaughter was too widespread for any more talk.[105]

---

[102]Human Rights Watch/FIDH interview, Butare, August 19 and 20, December 13, 1995; Brussels, December 18, 1995.

[103]Human Rights Watch/FIDH interview, Buffalo, by telephone, October 29, 1997; African Rights presents what may be two different versions of the same incident. See *Rwanda, Death, Despair*, pp. 358, 1044. For Gikongoro, see above.

[104]Human Rights Watch/FIDH interviews, Neuchatel, December 16, 1995; Butare, October 26, 1995; République Rwandaise, Ministère de la Justice, Parquet de la République, PV no. 0156.

[105]Dr. Jean-Berchmans Nshimyumuremyi, Vice-Recteur, to Membres du personnel enseignant et scientifique, du personnel académique associé supérieur et du personnel administratif et technique des catégories de conception et de coordination, Butare, April 21, 1994, P2-18/210/94 (Butare prefecture).

BUTARE:
"THIS IS AN EXTERMINATION"

As in Kigali, where troops and militia launched the genocide while army officers and politicians were talking of "restoring order," so in Butare soldiers launched the period of most extensive slaughter while the April 20 security meeting was taking place. At 11 a.m., just as the session was beginning at the auditorium in town, a detachment of soldiers commanded by Lt. (jg) Pierre Bizimana, acting under the orders of Capt. Nizeyimana, invaded the modest home of Rosalie Gicanda, a short distance up the main street in the northern part of town. Gicanda was the widow of Mutara Rudahigwa, the ruler of Rwanda who had died in 1959 just before the revolution that overthrew aristocratic Tutsi rule. About eighty years old, she lived a quiet life as a devout Catholic, sharing her home with her bed-ridden mother and several women and girls who cared for them both. Because she eschewed any involvement in politics and behaved with discreet dignity, even the most anti-Tutsi politicians had left her largely undisturbed throughout the thirty years of Hutu rule. When the killing began, she trusted that Prefect Habyalimana would look out for her. As his power waned, she began to receive threatening telephone calls. According to testimony, she called on Burgomaster Kanyabashi for protection, but he replied that he could do nothing for her. The soldiers passed through the wooded enclosure that protected the house from the main street and entered the little house with its air of faded respectability. They seized the former queen and six others, leaving her bed-ridden mother and one girl to care for her. The soldiers passed by the ESO and then took Gicanda and the others to a place behind the national museum where they shot them. One teenaged girl, left for dead, survived to recount the murders. The soldiers returned to pillage Gicanda's home in the afternoon and, two days later, they killed her mother. At the request of a priest, Kanyabashi sent prisoners to recover Gicanda's body and bury it in the yard next to her house.[1]

The news that this gracious lady and others from her household had been taken away by soldiers in the back of a pickup truck spread rapidly and alarmed Tutsi and

---

[1]Human Rights Watch/FIDH interview, October 20, 1995; Police Judiciaire près le Parquet du Procureur du Roi de l'arrondissement de Bruxelles, P.V. no. 37221, Dossier 37/95 (confidential source); Musoni, "Holocauste Noir," pp. 83-4. A Rwandan military court found Bizimana and Private lst Class Aloys Mazimpaka guilty of genocide and killing Gicanda and her family. Chambre Specialisée du Conseil de Guerre de Butare, case no. LMD 187, LP 0001-PS 97, Judgment pronounced July 27, 1998. Bizimana was sentenced to death, Mazimpaka to life in prison.

470

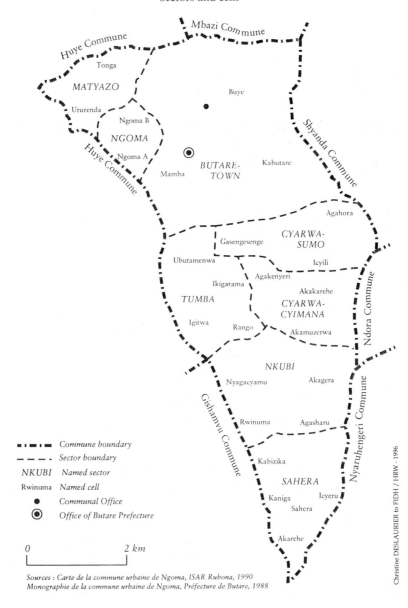

Butare Prefecture
URBAN COMMUNE OF NGOMA
Sectors and cells

Mbazi Commune

Huye Commune

Tonga

MATYAZO

Buye

Ururenda

Ngoma B

NGOMA

Shyanda Commune

Huye Commune

Ngoma A

BUTARE-
TOWN

Kabutare

Mamba

Agahora

Gasengesenge

CYARWA-
SUMO

Ubutamenwa

Icyili

Agakenyeri

Ikigarama

Akakarehe

TUMBA

CYARWA-
CYIMANA

Igitwa

Rango

Akamuzerwa

Ndora Commune

NKUBI

Nyagacyamu

Akagera

Gishamvu Commune

Rwinuma

Agasharu

Nyaruhengeri Commune

Kabizika

SAHERA

Kaniga

Icyeru

Sahera

Akarehe

▪▪◾■ ▬   Commune boundary
‑ ‑ ‑ ‑   Sector boundary
NKUBI   Named sector
Rwinuma Named cell
●   Communal Office
◉   Office of Butare Prefecture

0   2 km

Sources : Carte de la commune urbaine de Ngoma, ISAR Rubona, 1990
Monographie de la commune urbaine de Ngoma, Préfecture de Butare, 1988

Christine DESLAURIER to FIDH / HRW · 1996

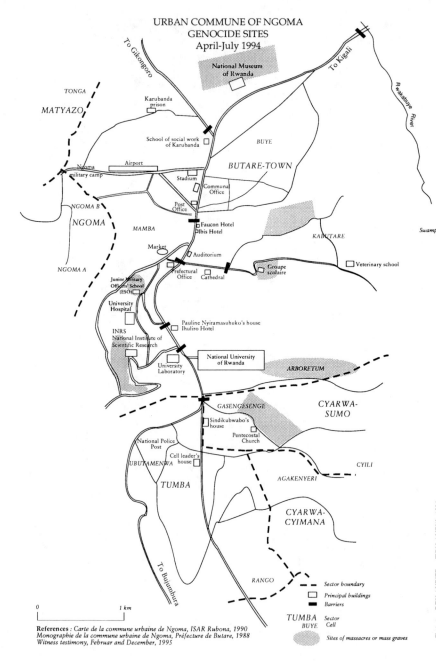

URBAN COMMUNE OF NGOMA
GENOCIDE SITES
April-July 1994

To Gikongoro

National Museum
of Rwanda

To Kigali

Rwakabuye River

TONGA

MATYAZO

Karubanda
prison

BUYE

School of social work
of Karubanda

BUTARE-TOWN

Ngoma
military camp

Airport

Stadium

Communal
Office

NGOMA B

Post
Office

NGOMA

MAMBA

Faucon Hotel
Ibis Hotel

KABUTARE

Swamps

Market

Auditorium

NGOMA A

Junior Military
Officers' School
(ESO)

Prefectural
Office

Cathedral

Groupe
scolaire

Veterinary school

University
Hospital

INRS
National Institute of
Scientific Research

Pauline Nyiramasuhuko's house
Ihuliro Hotel

University
Laboratory

National University
of Rwanda

ARBORETUM

CYARWA-
SUMO

GASENGESENGE

Sindikubwabo's
house

Pentecostal
Church

National Police
Post

Cell leader's
house

UBUTAMENWA

CYILI

AGAKENYERI

TUMBA

CYARWA-
CYIMANA

To Bujumbura

RANGO

Sector boundary

Principal buildings

Barriers

TUMBA   Sector
BUYE   Cell

Sites of massacres or mass graves

0   1 km

References : Carte de la commune urbaine de Ngoma, ISAR Rubona, 1990
Monographie de la commune urbaine de Ngoma, Préfecture de Butare, 1988
Witness testimony, Februar and December, 1995

Christine DESLAURIER to FIDH / HRW - 1996

all others who opposed the genocide. They concluded that if soldiers dared to seize even this revered person, then no one was safe. On the afternoon of April 20, physics professor Pierre-Claver Karenzi called colleagues to suggest trying to find a safe place for women and children, but knowing of the massacres elsewhere, others hesitated to bring Tutsi together into too large a group.[2]

Shortly after Gicanda was taken, soldiers at a barrier just south of the auditorium killed four young men whom they hauled out of a vehicle bearing license plates from Burundi.[3] After killing them, one of the soldiers checked the identity card of a priest who was stopped at the roadblock. He demanded, "Give me a cigarette, I've just killed four Tutsi." Then he allowed the priest to continue on his way. At about that time, witnesses who lived in the Kabutare area just adjacent to this barrier saw five men brought by pickup truck to an area next to the psychiatric center. They were shot and left there. Soon after a truck returned with eight more who were killed in the same way. Later that afternoon, a witness saw sixteen young men tied up in a pickup at the barrier. One was being beaten by a soldier. Suddenly a number of soldiers set upon the others in the back of the truck, yelling that they were "Inyenzi," insulting and beating them. The truck then took them up the road into the ESO.[4]

Barriers in Butare, as elsewhere in Rwanda, often became the sites of murders. On April 22, witnesses passing the barrier in front of the Hotel Faucon saw soldiers from the ESO beating fifteen children who had fled from Gikongoro. When they returned shortly after, eight or nine of the children lay dead.[5] The Presidential Guard kept a barrier across one of the main roads entering Cyarwa and allowed virtually no one to pass there. They diverted pedestrians and vehicles to another road to the east where there was also a barrier in front of the bar known as Chez Ngoga. Alphonse Ngoga, former burgomaster of Kigembe, worked as an employee of the prefecture and was a stalwart supporter of the MRND. His son, Micomyiza, known as Mico, was a university student who organized a crowd of young toughs, many of them from Burundi, to guard this barrier. They were reportedly

---

[2]Human Rights Watch/FIDH interview, July 6, 1995.

[3]MSF staff had witnessed a man clubbed to death at this barrier three days before. ICTR-96-4-T, Testimony of Dr. Rony Zachariah.

[4]Human Rights Watch/FIDH interviews, Butare, October 24, 26, and 29, 1995; République Rwandaise, Parquet de la République, P.V. no. 0117.

[5]ICTR-96-4-T, Testimony of Dr. Rony Zachariah.

responsible for killing many people, including the university student Gilbert Ntazane[6]

Systematic Slaughter in Town
Killing the Targeted Individuals

As in Kigali, soldiers—particularly Presidential Guards, members of Nizeyimana's bodyguard, and troops from Ngoma camp—along with National Police began the slaughter by targeting people from the intellectual and political elite of Butare. They went directly to the homes of those selected ahead of time for slaughter, sometimes relying on local guides or asking directions from neighbors. Militia backed up the members of the regular armed forces. In addition to the dozens of Interahamwe who had apparently been discreetly brought in during the previous ten days, one hundred or so Presidential Guards and militia arrived in Butare on April 20. A C-130 transport plane landed at Butare airport between 4 and 5 p.m., perhaps the first time such a large craft had used the small landing strip. Struck by the arrival of such an unusual plane and by the appearance of unknown soldiers and militia in town that evening, many people assumed that the strangers had been flown into Butare. In fact, they had arrived by bus while the plane, flown by Belgian pilots, had come from Nairobi to evacuate a group of European nuns and U.N. military observers. In addition to militia from outside Butare, local killers reportedly led by Shalom Ntahobari, also began the most damaging of their attacks on April 20.

Although soldiers and militia killed some people in their homes, they took many to be executed at one or another of the main killing grounds, like that behind the museum or in the arboretum of the university or near the psychiatric center and the Groupe Scolaire. Beginning late in the day of April 20 and continuing for the next three days, residents of Butare town reported hearing frequent bursts of gunfire, particularly from these execution grounds.[7]

The soldiers began the slaughter in the pleasant neighborhood of Buye, striking leading Tutsi like Professor Karenzi. Presidential Guards from the group that protected Habyarimana's brother, Dr. Bararengana, came for Karenzi at about 2 p.m. on April 21 and took him to the barrier manned by soldiers of the ESO in

---

[6]Human Rights Watch/FIDH interview, Neuchatel, December 16, 1995; Butare, December 29, 1995 and January 13 and February 5, 1996.

[7]Human Rights Watch/FIDH interview, Butare, December 18, 1995; Jef Vleugels and Guy Theunis, Société des Missionnaires d'Afrique, fax no. 10, April 25, 1994.

front of the Hotel Faucon. There he was lined up with a number of other people, including another professor who was accused of having falsified his identity card. According to a witness, a militia member from out of town then killed two men, two women, and five children under the eyes of Prefect Nsabimana and Vice-Rector Nshimyumuremyi who stood a short distance down the street, in front of the Hotel Ibis. One of the other men bolted and ran for his life and Professor Karenzi was shot and killed immediately afterwards. Soldiers returned shortly after to the Karenzi home and murdered the professor's wife. The children and young people of the household were hidden in the ceiling and escaped, although all except one would later be killed too (see below).[8]

When killing began in Cyarwa, witnesses immediately recognized that it was being done systematically. One man first heard shots behind his house at about 1 p.m., then others from a house next door. He stated:

> The soldiers who came had very clear objectives: Ndakaza was a supporter of the PL, a Tutsi, who lived in the house behind mine; Sinzi Tharcissse, who was at the national university; Simpunga who worked at the Butare Economat and who was a member of the PSD; and Gregoire Hategekimana, an administrator from the university, who was a member of the MDR. The soldiers went down the street behind me and then up my street and stopped at these particular houses.[9]

Another witness to the same events not only heard the perpetrators, but saw them clearly from his enclosure. He declared:

> The trouble began in Cyarwa on the afternoon of the 21st. We heard gunfire first from the direction of Rango. People coming from the market said that soldiers had shot a man named Venuste and then had gone to his home and had killed everyone there. The soldiers then proceeded down the line, killing as they went. I could hear the sound of gunfire, moving in a line around my house, since the street behind follows a wide arc that circles back towards my house.

---

[8]République du Rwanda, Parquet de la République, P.V. 0054 and no. 0117.

[9]Human Rights Watch/FIDH interview, Kigali, November 30, 1995.

A few of those killed were officially Hutu on their identity cards, but someone had done research and had learned that they had previously been Tutsi. Someone had gone to the home communes of those who were suspected to check on whether they were really Hutu or Tutsi.

I saw the deputy [Laurent] Baravuga leading three or four soldiers who were carrying South African rifles [probably R-4 rifles]. He had a list. He knew the area well and could direct them. The soldiers were Presidential Guards and they were followed by a large crowd of people. After the soldiers had finished and moved on, the crowd would move in and loot the house. I saw people streaming by carrying refrigerators, radios, anything. Nearly everyone from Cyarwa joined the crowd and they were happy to steal.[10]

During the first days of attacks, a crowd of militia and others in Cyarwa found that not all Tutsi were to be considered targets. They forced their way into a large building where several women friends of interim President Sindikubwabo had taken refuge with their families. The assailants were rounding up the Tutsi and preparing to kill them when Presidential Guards from Sindikubwabo's house hurried to the scene and ordered them to leave. The assailants did not want to give up their intended victims, but the Presidential Guards threatened them with grenades and made them withdraw.[11]

In addition to political and intellectual leaders, the military targeted the rich. In the heart of Butare, soldiers invaded the home of a prosperous businessman on April 20 and extorted some 300,000 Rwandan francs (about U.S.$1,700) as the price of his own life and that of his family. Two days later, a young soldier named Claude[12] came back with three Interahamwe, reportedly from the group headed by Shalom. They took five young adults and a twelve-year-old boy with them and

---

[10]Human Rights Watch/FIDH interview, Butare, December 19, 1995.

[11]Human Rights Watch/FIDH interviews, Butare, December 19 and 29, 1995, January 2, 1996.

[12]A young man named Claude, usually identified as a soldier, was involved also in violence against the children of Prof. Karenzi and in temporarily abducting Alphonsine Kabengera in Tumba. A militia member named Claude Murekezi is also accused of participating in killing in Butare, but it is unclear if this is the same person. See Pie-Joseph Ngilimana, "Vision Synoptique des Massacres à Butare à partir du 7 avril 1994," August 19,1994.

walked the short distance to the killing field at the Groupe Scolaire where they murdered them.[13] In Tumba six National Policemen led a crowd in attacking the home of a Swiss entrepreneur who had a Tutsi wife. The ordinary people were armed with machetes, spears, and even a bow and arrow—wielded by a young man wearing a baseball cap with the visor behind, in the fashion of foreign young people. The National Policemen fired a couple of warning shots and forced their way in. After having robbed the family of several hundred thousand Rwandan francs, they called in the civilians, who looted the house. Some of the crowd stole valuable items, but others seemed almost embarassed at what they were doing and took items of little or no value, like a cooking pot full of potatoes or a child's toy. To one observer, they seemed to be participating because they had no choice. They left without injuring anyone.[14]

Soldiers killed important Hutu who were thought to oppose the genocide, just as other troops had killed Hutu officials of the national government in Kigali. According to witnesses, Nizeyimana and soldiers of his guard murdered his neighbor, Deputy Prosecutor Matabaro. Soldiers also slew the professor Jean-Marie Vianney Maniraho, who had criticized the heavy military presence in town at a public security meeting, and his family. In Cyarwa, soldiers burned down the home of a Hutu woman related to a national leader of the MDR who opposed Hutu Power. Several days later, she was killed at a barrier, reportedly on the order of Deputy Baravuga. Soldiers and militia killed the sub-prefect Zéphanie Nyilinkwaya and fourteen others of his family during the night of April 21. A Hutu member of the PSD, Nyilinkwaya was seen as a potential leader of resistance to the slaughter of Tutsi. A MSF doctor came by Nyilinkwaya's house early on the morning of April 22 and found the corpses of the family scattered over the drive in front of the house. Among them was a child three months old, shot in the back of the head, lying at his mother's breast, which had also been blown open by a bullet. The doctor found two survivors, a girl about seventeen years old, who had been shot by a bullet that had passed through both breasts, and a fourteen-year-old boy. When he prepared to take them to the hospital, two soldiers came at the run to stop him.

---

[13]Human Rights Watch/FIDH interviews, Butare, October 26, 28, and 29, 1995.

[14]Human Rights Watch/FIDH interview, Neuchatel, December 16, 1995.

It was only by insistent negotiating that the doctor won the right to take the wounded for treatment.[15]

Killing by Neighborhood

While most soldiers concentrated on the elite targets, others, together with National Police supervised the militia that swept through neighborhoods eliminating Tutsi. A frail resident of the working-class neighborhood of Ngoma, in her mid-eighties, observed the genocide with horror. She had seen the killing of Tutsi since the 1950s but, she said, this slaughter was different because "it killed babies on the back, children who were beginning to walk, pregnant women, old people." She declared:

> The militia always came escorted by soldiers, two or three of them. The soldiers did not kill, they just accompanied the militia and watched them kill. They came many times over many days: attack, leave, attack, leave. They came during the night, attacking one family, then leaving. Then they came the next night and attacked another family. Maybe three families in this place in one night. Then, tomorrow, five families over there.

> During the day, there were rumors about who would be attacked that night. They had meetings in town to plan. Sometimes, they said, "Tonight we will attack a family with this number of people in the household, this number of children." Those listening tried to guess which family was being talked about. Children especially would move about, listening, and come to give warnings. Children and household workers moved between houses, between houses and the meetings, between houses and the bush. Sometimes they would get paid for going to listen. But there were other children, too, who spied on those who were giving warning.

> While some were in meetings others were out on the streets, moving around, poking around, trying to find the people who were hiding inside houses. Those who did the spying included women, prostitutes, and girls who did not have husbands.

---

[15]Human Rights Watch/FIDH interviews, Butare, October 25, 1995 and January 13, 1996; Brussels, December 12, 1995; ICTR-96-4-T, Testimony of Dr. Rony Zachariah.

The old lady lived in a well-built house at the corner of two streets. One street runs along the ridge on which most of Ngoma sits; the other cuts across the first and descends steeply into the valley which separates Ngoma from the rest of the town of Butare. Starting on the night of April 21, she saw the crowds surging down the street, some of them dressed in banana leaves, and always with their military escort:

> I hid and saw it from the window, from behind the curtain, cowering there in the corner. I saw them driving the groups of people ahead of them, shouting and shoving them with sticks and wooden clubs. Behind them came the soldiers with their guns, but they did not shoot. I saw a pregnant woman get hit in the stomach and fall back. I heard her cries. They took them down to the valley and killed them with nail-studded clubs, with hoes and machetes. I heard no shots, only the cries of horror and pain from the valley.

The elderly woman, herself a Hutu, became a target when informers told the militia that she was hiding her Tutsi grandchildren. Knowing that sheltering Tutsi put her own life at risk, the elderly woman also took in one teenaged girl who was not part of her family but who had fled to her home in the middle of the night. While the witness was peeking out from behind her curtain, she saw the girl run, bent over, into the enclosure that surrounded the house. She opened the door and the girl threw herself inside and collapsed unconscious on the floor. When the girl revived, she recounted how the rest of her family had been slain or fled to an unknown destination. The old woman allowed her to stay with the young people of her family. They hid in the bush during the night and came in furtively during the day to get something to eat.

The militia who came three times to search this home included people from the neighborhood and those from the adjacent sector of Matyazo. The two groups, which joined together outside her front door, were supervised by two soldiers. Most came on foot, but they also had a couple of vehicles to transport whatever they were able to pillage from this house or others they intended to attack that night.

At the time of the second search, Shalom Ntahobari led the group. He particularly wanted to find the girl whose midnight arrival had been noticed by local informers. He knew her older sisters well and had often dined and spent the evening at the girl's home.[16] Shalom and his followers forced their way into the house and demanded to know where the girl and the others were hiding. He had a

---

[16] Human Rights Watch/FIDH interview, October 20, 1995.

machete stuck in his belt. When the old woman said there was no one there, he grabbed her by her two ears and twisted them to try to make her talk. She said nothing. They searched the house thoroughly, but found no one. Two days later, they returned, again ready to kill. Once more they had to leave empty-handed and angry. Soon after, someone came to rescue the old woman and her charges. As they drove away, she saw the crowd arriving for another search.

The witness remarked that many who invaded her house were strangers, but, she added, "Even the ones I knew, I couldn't recognize them. They had transformed themselves into animals. They were like lions."[17] Another witness in Ngoma remembered what he saw outside his window:

> I saw people out on the street, carrying clubs, axes, and machetes. They were all wearing MRND or CDR hats. Those without hats wore banana leaves around their necks or over their shoulders. They wore portrait pins of President Habyarimana on their chests. Even the youngest also tried to carry a weapon or a stick and were wearing the portrait pin. Even the young members of the PSD were wearing the hats of the CDR and the MRND and the portrait pin. We could not understand how that was possible because the PSD was opposed to the MRND and the CDR.[18]

After the first attacks on April 20, assailants moved on to other neighborhoods in the following days. In Cyarwa, soldiers and militia herded the crowd of Tutsi down the street in the middle of the day and beat them to death at a bridge, at a place known as Gateme. In one part of Tumba, the physician Munyemana reportedly organized the patrols and supervised the arrest and detention of Tutsi who were locked in the sector office, to which he had a key. In another part of the sector, the cell leader and employees of the university laboratory guided National Police to the homes of Tutsi. In both Cyarwa and Tumba, Hutu and Tutsi had collaborated until April 20 in protecting their sectors from outsiders, so some Tutsi joined the patrols organized on April 21, believing they were still part of the defense, not the enemy. They were killed by their fellow patrol members.[19] In the

---

[17]Human Rights Watch/FIDH interviews, May 29 and July 5, 1995.

[18]République Rwandaise, Parquet de la République, P.V. no. 117.

[19]Human Rights Watch/FIDH interviews, Butare, October 27 and December 29, 1995.

sector of Sahera, assailants attacked the home of Aristarque Rwigimba, who was able to hold them off with the help of a stout door and a bow and arrow. But the assailants returned the next day with a communal policeman, who shot two of the resisters, making it possible for the assailants to kill nine others in the house.[20]

At Kabutare, teachers and staff members from the Groupe Scolaire secondary school lived in a tight-knit community just down the road from the school buildings. Of the sixty-five or seventy families in one neighborhood, five were Tutsi or mixed Tutsi-Hutu households. Soldiers, reportedly guided by the cell leader, Faustin Twagirayezu, arrived one morning and went directly to the houses where Tutsi lived. They were followed by a gang of street kids who tagged along after the soldiers to watch the violence. According to one of the community who was present that morning,

> We stood in front of our houses, unable to do anything at all. We waited, knowing what had happened elsewhere, waiting our turn to have it happen here, waiting with our arms folded.[21]

The soldiers took several Tutsi men, one Tutsi woman, and a Hutu and headed down towards the psychiatric center. According to one witness, they chose people at random from the onlookers and tried to get them to beat the Tutsi to death, but those selected refused to do the job.[22] The soldiers locked the captives in the local canteen, saying they were too hungry to kill at the moment. They went away, telling local people to guard them. In the opinion of one onlooker, that measure was not necessary because they would not have tried to flee anyway. Later that day, the soldiers returned with civilians from outside the community. They beat the captives to death. A witness who heard the soldiers coming a second time called his children to come in the house, not wanting them to see what would happen. He went outside himself, pretending to read a notice that was posted on a tree. He saw the soldiers go into the house of a neighbor named Joseph and then went back inside his own home and closed the door. All those taken away were killed and

---

[20]Human Rights Watch/FIDH interview, Brussels, November 6, 1995.

[21]Human Rights Watch/FIDH interview, October 26, 1995.

[22]This detail was not mentioned by other witnesses and may have been an effort to portray local people in a favorable light.

their families were killed three or four days later. The witness added, "That finished our neighborhood and they never came back."[23]

Once the killing campaign was launched, soldiers and militia acted as though they had license to kill anyone who looked Tutsi. On April 23, a Zairean couple, Mr. Kisasa Lukasa and his wife, were traveling through Butare and stopped at the market. While Mr. Lukasa went to make some purchases, his wife stayed in the car. Militia or soldiers passing by the vehicle noticed her and asked for her identity papers. When she could not produce them immediately, they killed her on the spot.[24]

Slaughter at the University and the Hospital

While some soldiers and militia were targeting neighborhoods in town, others began killing at the university. Classes were in recess for the Easter vacation, but some students had stayed in residence to prepare for examinations and others fled to the university once killing began elsewhere because they hoped to be safe there. Beginning on April 8, soldiers had restricted movement to or from the campus and authorities had prepared a list of students in residence, supposedly to facilitate their passing the soldiers' barrier. Students, already polarized by previous events such as the February killings, formed into two groups, that of Hutu Power and that of Tutsi and those willing to support them. The Hutu Power students, known as the LIDER group from the name of their student association, began playing the music of anti-Tutsi singer Bikindi and staying up at night to see what the others were doing. The Tutsi students and others of their group also organized into four teams of guards who took turns keeping watch at night. They moved to rooms other than those where they usually slept and the LIDER students tried to keep track of where they were.

At mid-day April 21, soldiers killed a student at the campus barrier and another either at the barrier or in town. That evening, they came to round up Tutsi students as they entered the cafeteria, checking them off on a list as they were taken. A few Tutsi students saw the roundup beginning and managed to flee along with Hutu friends. The soldiers took those captured either to the arboretum adjacent to the campus or across the road to a woods on the grounds of the national research institute. LIDER students then took up the search for those students not yet found

[23]Human Rights Watch/FIDH interview, October 26, 1995.

[24]Préfet Cyangugu to Préfet Butare, telegram no. 94/040, 8:15, May 2, 1994 (Butare prefecture).

by the soldiers. As they discovered Tutsi who had hidden in the rooms, under the beds, or elsewhere, they took them out to deliver to the soldiers. One student was found at about 3 a.m. by a group of fellow students who kicked and beat her before taking her and another student across the road to the soldiers in the woods. As the student recalled,

> The soldiers there said that these were the last students they would take. They said not to bring any more to them, because they were finished for the day. The two soldiers took us and pushed us into the woods. They cocked their guns and I thought it was all over. But then they spoke to us. They asked us if we would have anywhere to hide if they let us go. I said I had an aunt in Cyarwa and Aimable had a cousin in town. And so the soldiers told us to run. They fired their guns into the air so that the students would think that we had been killed and they left.

> Aimable and I went further into the woods. It was full of cadavers. There were bodies everywhere, many, many of them. There was nowhere else we could go, so we had to stay there until it got light, there among the bodies.[25]

The next morning, the two students sought refuge at the nearby university hospital, which was still quiet. One of the two was eventually killed, but the second survived.

According to the vice-rector, some 650 students were at the university on April 20 with more arriving all the time. On May 31, there were 212 students on campus, 190 of them Rwandan, the rest from Burundi. Some students had fled, but the great majority had been killed. In a later exhumation of a mass grave near the university, some 600 bodies were found. Most of these victims were students—a significant part of the national intellectual elite in training at the university.[26]

During the night of April 22, after students had come to seek shelter at the hospital, soldiers of the ESO and the Presidential Guard came and killed some forty Tutsi patients. One remarked to MSF staff who worked there, "The hospital stinks with Tutsi and we must clean it up." The next morning, the soldiers continued

---

[25]Human Rights Watch/FIDH interview, Kigali, January 19, 1996.

[26]Anonymous, Notebook 1, entry for April 20, 1994; Le Vice-Recteur, "Effectif des Déplacés de Guerre Logés au Campus Universitaire de Butare," May 31, 1994 (Butare prefecture).

removing patients from the wards and even from the operating rooms. They also took away hospital personnel because their names were on the list of those to be killed. One of the nurses taken and beaten to death behind the hospital was a Hutu who had been caring for wounded FAR soldiers. She was seven months pregnant with a baby fathered by a Tutsi. Over a two day period, the soldiers killed between 140 and 170 people at the hospital. After meeting authorities at the prefectural offices on April 23 to protest the killings, the head of the MSF mission, Dr. Zachariah, returned to the hospital. He later recalled:

> I looked around me with my team and people were just being taken out in groups of threes, fives, going behind the hospital. We could hear the screams. I told my team, "We are getting out of here! There is nothing more to do."[27]

Like the university students, others had sought refuge at the hospital in late April, some of them occupying tents in the courtyard that had once housed refugees from Burundi, others hidden in the wards, closets or kitchen of the conglomerate of rambling buildings. In the days following the first killings at the hospital, soldiers returned repeatedly to search out those in hiding. One evening they took a law student named Épiphanie who was pretending to be one of the hospital staff. By this time, authorities had proclaimed an end to the killings (see below) and had said that anyone who was threatened should call for help, so Épiphanie screamed repeatedly. But no one came to her rescue and the soldiers took her away to the woods below the hospital. There they raped and beat her. A military doctor named Rwanyonga heard of the attack and went to find her in the woods. He brought her back and put her in the intensive care ward for treatment. At about 11:30 p.m., four soldiers returned and took her away and killed her.[28]

Some of the Tutsi who had taken refuge at the hospital were from the commune of Huye. Soon after the soldiers killed the patients and medical staff, militia from that commune came, with an escort of soldiers, to collect the men and boys from Huye. The militia forced them to set out for Huye and reportedly killed them, either en route home or shortly after arriving there. According to testimony, the burgomaster of Ngoma helped pressure the Huye people to leave and allegedly

---

[27]ICTR-96-4-T, Testimony of Dr. Rony Zachariah.

[28]Human Rights Watch/FIDH interviews, Butare, November 9, 1995; Kigali, January 19, 1996. According to one witness, the soldiers also took Hutu women students to rape when they had finished killing Tutsi. Human Rights Watch/FIDH interview, January 3, 1996.

also returned several times in the next two weeks, twice in the company of soldiers, to see that other Tutsi be put out of the hospital. Some of those expelled were reportedly killed at a barrier just a short distance down the road from the hospital.[29]

Dr. Alphonse Karemera, dean of the medical school, produced an attempted justification for "cleaning up" the hospital in an official plan dated April 24—while the slaughter was still going on. Entitled "Socio-hygenic and Humanitarian Action for Victims and Persons Displaced by the War: A Proposal of the Faculty of Medicine concerning the functioning of the UH [University Hospital] in this period of provoked catastrophe," it was forwarded by Vice-Rector Nshimyumuremyi with his approval to the prefect. The plan called for removing refugees, displaced persons, and those not critically ill from the hospital and the tents on the hospital grounds. Those persons who, in the words of the vice-rector, "clutter up the UH without good reason" were to be handed over to humanitarian organizations and the administration. In the proposal, Dr. Karemera complained of the "suffocating lack of support personnel." Without remarking on the reason for this sudden loss of staff, he merely asked for authorization to begin recruitment for provisional replacements. He also insisted on immediate action to remedy the critical hygenic and sanitary situation in the region, that is, to remove the bodies which could become a hazard to health. Noting that the post of medical supervisor was empty for the moment, he offered the help of the faculty of medicine in supervising this work. It was apparently Dr. Eugène Rwamucyo, a member of the medical staff known for his virulent anti-Tutsi attitude (see below) who undertook this task.[30]

On May 2, Prefect Nsabimana informed the vice-rector that the prefectural security council agreed with the proposed plan. He noted that the administration was looking for ways to take care of the remaining refugees and displaced persons still at the hospital.[31] That same day, the director of the hospital told those who had

---

[29]Human Rights Watch/FIDH interviews, Butare, November 9, 1995; Kigali, January 19, 1996; interview, May 21, 1996; ICTR-96-I, The Prosecution of the Tribunal against Joseph Kanyabashi, Indictment.

[30]Dr. Alphonse Karemera, "Action Socio-Sanitaire et Humantaire (sic) en Faveur des Victimes et Deplacés de Guerre: Une Proposition de la Faculté de Médecine Concernant le Fonctionnement de l'HU en Cette Période de Catastrophe Provoquée," enclosed in Dr. Jean Berchmans Nshimyumuremyi, Vice-Recteur de l'UNR, to Monsieur le Préfet de la Préfecture de Butare, P2-18/211/94, April 25, 1994 (Butare prefecture).

[31]Sylvain Nsabimana, Préfet, to Monsieur le Vice-Recteur, no. 274/04.09.01, May 2, 1994 (Butare prefecture).

sought shelter at the hospital to go to the prefecture; he even provided transportation to take some there. One witness who was present remembers being told that they were to go to the prefecture to get the documents necessary to go home. According to another witness:

> Then they said that everyone who was at the hospital had to go to the prefecture. The burgomasters wanted them to go back to their homes and the burgomasters were going to come fetch their people and take them back to their hills.[32]

One of the two university students who had been captured and then allowed to escape was among those sent to the prefecture. She reported:

> At the prefecture, the Interahamwe were waiting. They had been told that we were coming and there were Interahamwe from each of the communes waiting to take their own people to kill. Our students were there too. When we arrived, we were surrounded by Interahamwe, they encircled us. A soldier tapped me on the shoulder and asked if I was a student from the university. I said that I was. He asked if I was alone, and I said that no, I was with another student. He asked us to follow him. He took us to the brigade. There was a crowd of people there, and they beat us. After they were done, they told us to leave. We went outside, and when we went out, another soldier tapped me on the shoulder. He asked if I knew him and I said no. And he asked if I knew what this was, and he handed me my identity card. He said that he was the soldier who was supposed to have killed me but let me go....He said that he would help me and so he escorted me to Cyarwa. I really do not know why.[33]

Not all those from the hospital were taken back to their communes at this time. Some joined the group of Tutsi already at the prefecture and remained there for another two weeks.

---

[32]Human Rights Watch/FIDH interview, Butare, November 9, 1995.

[33]Human Rights Watch/FIDH interview, Kigali, January 19, 1996.

Collective Slaughter
Butare Town

In Butare prefecture, as elsewhere, the largest numbers of Tutsi were killed in the shortest time in massacres at churches, public buildings, and other gathering places. In the town of Butare, however, the worst massacres took hundreds rather than thousands of lives because officials had not permitted massive assemblages of Tutsi within town limits.

In the first two weeks of April, several hundred Tutsi had assembled in the broad space before the prefectural offices. On April 19, as described above, soldiers removed the men from that group and apparently took them to be executed. Those left behind, mostly women and children, formed the nucleus of a group whose presence would trouble authorities until the end of June. They were shifted from place to place and dozens of them were seized at night, but they were never openly attacked in town.

Authorities had transferred six to seven hundred children from an orphanage in Kigali to the Groupe Scholaire and also had allowed several hundred other displaced persons from Kigali to take shelter in the school buildings and courtyard. On April 21, soldiers and Interahamwe, some of whom were wearing the distinctive green and yellow patterned tunic of the militia, came to the Groupe Scolaire as the orphans and displaced persons were eating their noon meal. They called them out to the courtyard, separated them into two groups on the basis of their identity cards, and began killing the Tutsi, mostly with machetes and clubs. Local residents, reportedly under the direction of the cell head Faustin Twagirayezu and including especially Burundians, also joined in the slaughter. According to one witness, several women, both Rwandan and Burundian, killed other women and children.[34]

Some people from Kigali and elsewhere, at least several hundred of them, had dispersed quietly throughout the town with family or friends. Small numbers of them, like locally resident Tutsi, sought protection clandestinely in convents and other church facilities. Larger groups took refuge openly at the Ngoma church and the Rwandan Episcopal Church (Eglise Episcopale Rwandaise).

Ngoma Commune: Matyazo and Kabakobwa Massacres

Not permitted to congregate in massive numbers inside town, the displaced did assemble in the thousands at Matyazo and Kabakobwa, two sites just outside of town but within Ngoma commune. Authorities had first tried to send displaced

---

[34]Human Rights Watch/FIDH interview, October 29, 1995.

persons gathered at Matyazo to churches at Karama and Simbi, as mentioned above, but when this failed, Burgomaster Kanyabashi had installed them at the Matyazo health center and had arranged for police to be posted there as guards. As with such groups elsewhere, the displaced at first had freedom of movement, to go out and buy food, for example. After April 19, those inside were no longer permitted to leave. On April 21, soldiers touched off the attack on the health center by firing grenades into the enclosure and then shooting some of the people inside. Militia and local people followed up with machetes and clubs, killing most of the two to three thousand persons who had sought refuge there. A witness on a hill facing Matyazo could hear clearly the sounds of the massacre. He remembered:

> I heard all the noise from Matyazo, the explosions of grenades, preceded by the shouts of the young who yelled "Power," the blasts on the whistles and the beating of the drums. It went on until 5 a.m.[35]

Children and infants who survived the Matyazo massacre were left alone among the bodies for three days. Then some women came to take the little girls home, probably to raise them as servants. On April 25, the councilor of the sector, Athanase Nshimiyimana, and the communal policeman, Marc Polepole, drove a truckload of injured children to the hospital at the Groupe Scolaire. When they attempted to transport a second group of sixty-two injured children, the soldiers at Ngoma camp said it was forbidden to transport Inyenzi and refused to allow them past their barrier. They left the children, who ranged in age from a few months to four years old at Ngoma parish, not far from the barrier, where some four hundred other people had already taken refuge. The priests at Ngoma tried to get the Red Cross to come to take the children to the hospital, but they also replied that it was no use because the children would just be killed en route. A nurse, Domitilla Mukabaziga, who was among those who had taken shelter at the church, cared for the wounded children despite the lack of supplies and equipment. Mukabaziga was the sister-in-law of Burgomaster Kanyabashi and called him repeatedly during these days to ask him to rescue her, her children and her nephew. He reportedly answered that there was nothing that he could do for them.[36]

---

[35]République Rwandaise, Parquet de la République, P.V. no. 117.

[36] République Rwandaise, Parquet de la République, P.V. no. 0117; Human Rights Watch/FIDH interview, March 26, 1996.

The second major massacre of Ngoma commune was launched the same day as that at Matyazo, but at the opposite end of the commune. Matyazo lies at the northern most point of Ngoma while Kabakobwa, a gently sloping site where three valleys merge, lies between the two southernmost sectors, Nkubi and Sahera. Many Tutsi from Gikongoro and such Butare communes as Huye, Gishamvu, and Ngoma, some with their few heads of cattle, camped in the open space there while deciding whether or not to continue their flight some ten miles further to the Burundi border. From Kabakobwa, they could have gone directly south, following the Migina River, or they could have taken one of the two roads paralleling the river that led to the frontier. As the slaughter intensified, more Tutsi came to Kabakobwa, some of them told by authorities or advised by Hutu neighbors to go there. A mile or so north of Kabakobwa was the Rango market, one of the two markets functioning to serve Butare town and the immediate region. Thursday, April 21, was a market day. Some men in civilian dress arrived at the market in late morning by bicycle and began checking identity cards among the crowds trading there. The story quickly circulated that the men were soldiers, even that they were Presidential Guards. Either these men or others in uniform shot a Tutsi named Venuste at the market. Many people then fled from the market to Kabakobwa, swelling the number of persons there. According to some estimates, there may have been as many as 10,000 Tutsi at the site.[37]

That afternoon local people attacked the Tutsi, apparently with some support from the communal police, including at least one former soldier. At first the Tutsi repelled the attack. Some Tutsi, numbering perhaps 500, decided to flee Rwanda and headed southeast for the frontier in Kibayi commune. Most were killed before they could cross the river that forms the boundary between Rwanda and Burundi. The next morning, April 22, the communal police arrived in a Ngoma commune pickup truck and took away several Tutsi selected from the crowd. They returned later that day with soldiers and National Police who used rocket-propelled grenade launchers and machine guns to slaughter the Tutsi. That night, on the hills of Nyaruhengeri, on the other side of the valley, some local people celebrated the massacre with feasting, singing, and dancing.[38]

---

[37]Human Rights Watch/FIDH interviews, Neuchatel, December 16, 1995; Butare, August 20 and October 25, 1995.

[38]Ibid.; Human Rights Watch/FIDH interviews, Butare, December 19 and 29, 1995; Brussels, November 6, 1995; African Rights, *Rwanda, Death, Despair*, pp. 351-52.

Elsewhere in the Prefecture: The Devastating Third Week of April

In the week between April 18 and April 25 authorities accelerated and intensified the large-scale slaughter that was begun at Cyahinda on April 15. They had been slower than authorities elsewhere to launch the most devastating phase of the genocide. Now it was as if they had to hurry to catch up in order to meet the goals set by the extermination campaign. At any number of sites, particularly in the southern half of the prefecture, they massacred thousands of people, and at each of several places, they killed ten thousand or more at one time. They executed these massacres at churches such as Simbi, Kansi, Karama, Nyumba, Mugombwa, and Rugango; at health centers such as that at Sovu; on Mont Bisi and, continuing these killings, at the Senior Seminary at Nyakibanda; at the communal offices of Huye, Kigembe, Kibayi, Maraba, Muyaga, and Muyira; at the Mbazi commune stadium and at the Mugusa commune playing field; at the agricultural research stations at Rubona and Songa; at the market of Nkomero and the artisanal school at Nyaruteja; and at gathering places at Bitare in Gishamvu, Kabuye in Ndora, Nyamure in Ntyazo, and in the communes of Muganza and Kibayi. At the end, the churches were marked by the traces of grenade explosions, the benches overturned, the bodies strewn inside and outside the sanctuaries; the health centers were burned, with the remains of people and their possessions scattered about; and the communal offices looked like slaughter-houses.

Apparently more displaced persons were gathered at the church of Karama than at any other site in Butare. According to one count made the day before the massacre, some 75,405 people were present.[39] In a 1996 study of massacre sites, a commission set up by the Rwandan government established a lower but still remarkable number of 50,000 present at the center of Runyinya commune, the location also of the church. This study suggests that 40,000 persons died and that some 8,000 survivors fled to Burundi.[40] Others have estimated that as many as 43,000 died at Karama, while sources in the Catholic church, including a priest from a parish in the region, have proposed between 20,000 and 30,000 as the death toll. Investigators from the U.N. Human Rights Field Operation's Special Investigations Unit estimated that about 17,000 people were slaughtered there,

---

[39]African Rights, *Rwanda, Death, Despair*, p. 345.

[40]Commission pour le Mémorial du Génocide et des Massacres au Rwanda, "Rapport Préliminaire," p. 14.

basing that figure on the distribution of food rations shortly before the massacre.[41] Whatever the toll for Karama or any other single site, it is likely that more than 100,000 persons were slain in the large-scale massacres in Butare prefecture.

The Betrayal of "Pacification"

The slaughter in Butare prefecture, launched most intensively two weeks after the genocide began in Kigali and elsewhere, was still at its worst when national authorities were already proclaiming "pacification" on the weekend of April 23 to 24. Even as the massacres continued without relief at places like Kabuye and were yet to begin at others like the agricultural research stations at Songa and Rubona, authorities in Butare were repeating the new national line about "pacification." Here, as elsewhere, the promised end to killings served only to deceive both Rwandans and the international community.

Authorities drove through Butare town and its environs beginning on April 23, making announcements over a sound system or through a hand-held megaphone. They declared that the killing was finished, that people should put away their weapons and bury the dead, and that those in hiding should come out. In addition to this message, cited by witnesses from several different parts of town, some others remember hearing a specific call to women and girls, inviting them to return to their homes in safety. Others remember being told that the markets were open and that the hospitals were ready to receive the wounded. In addition, several witnesses remember a message reporting protests from the international community about the killings. In order to avoid such criticism, the announcement said, signs of the killing must be hidden from journalists flying over in helicopters and from surveillance satellites passing overhead. Most witnesses state that the message was delivered by communal authorities, if not by the burgomaster himself.[42] Prefect Nsabimana asserts that he also drove around, either delivering a similar message or calling people to meetings where he delivered such a message. He declares that this was his own initiative, not ordered by anyone. Yet the coincidence in timing and the similarity of the message with that delivered elsewhere in the country show

---

[41]Human Rights Watch/FIDH interviews, Brussels, May 17, 1997; by telephone, January 19, 1998; U.N. High Commissioner for Human Rights, Human Rights Field Operation in Rwanda, Special Investigations Unit, SIU Final Report on the Genocide Investigation, Kigali, April 12, 1995, p. 19; African Rights, *Rwanda, Death, Despair*, p. 345.

[42]Human Rights Watch/FIDH interviews, Butare, October 20, 24, 25, and 26, 1995; Neuchatel, December 16, 1995.

that the announcement of "pacification" was part of the campaign ordered at the national level.[43]

At a meeting at the Butare stadium on April 26, the prefect and other authorities declared an end to the killings and announced at the same time that all residents would be obliged to participate in a system of patrols and barriers.[44] Dr. Emmanuel Kazima attended the meeting and then returned home to find that the seven Tutsi whom he had been hiding had been taken away by soldiers. During the "pacification" meeting, the group, including a child two-and-a-half years old, were killed in a woods 200 yards from the house.[45] Many others in Butare, as elsewhere in the country, were slain in the days when the message of pacification was being disseminated: they had come out of hiding believing in the official guarantees of safety. One man who was a councilor at the time and who lost family members in the genocide remarked of the "pacification," "It was a strategy to get the Tutsi to come out from where they were hiding to be able to continue with the killings."[46] Prefect Nsabimana admits that Tutsi who emerged after hearing the message were slain, particularly at the barriers. As a result, he says, he decided not to promise safety again.[47]

Nsabimana carried out other pacification meetings on April 27, including one held jointly with Kanyabashi on the football field next to the Ngoma church. At the church were nearly 500 people who had escaped from the massacre at the Matyazo health center a few days before or who had been forced to flee when their homes had been attacked. The great majority were children whose parents had been killed or who had fled, leaving them behind. From inside the church, the priests and the displaced listened with growing hope to the prefect and the burgomaster as they delivered the pacification message. The church had been raided on April 22 by the councilor Said Hussein and others bent on looting. At the time, Said had remarked

---

[43]Human Rights Watch/FIDH interview, Nairobi, by telephone, March 25, 1996; "Interview of Sylvain Nsabimana, October 1, 1994."

[44]Human Rights Watch/FIDH interviews, Butare, December 18, 1995.

[45]Jane Perlez, "Rwandan Doctor's Journey Through Horror and Death," *New York Times*, August 8, 1994.

[46]Human Rights Watch/FIDH interview, Butare, November 9, 1995.

[47]Human Rights Watch/FIDH interviews, Butare, October 20, 24, 25, and 26, 1995; Neuchatel, December 16, 1995; Nairobi, by telephone, March 25, 1996.

on how many displaced had taken shelter there. Initially afraid that the pillage would be followed by slaughter, the people in the church began to breathe more freely after hearing the official announcement of the end to violence.[48]

The Massacres of April 30

The people at Ngoma church had only two days to enjoy the promise of safety. At 10 p.m. on April 29, militia and local crowds attacked the church buildings. One of the people inside reached the bell tower and sounded the bell for thirty-five minutes, alerting the entire region to the attack that was violating the promised peace. One of the priests called the Ngoma military camp, less than a mile distant. The soldier who answered inquired what kind of weapons the assailants carried and then told the priest, "Don't worry. They won't hurt you." Hardly reassured, the priest called the public prosecutor, Mathias Bushishi, a man from Ruhengeri who was thought to have influence with the local leaders of the genocide. Bushishi agreed to call the camp commander. Two hours later eight soldiers appeared, led by a lieutenant (jg) named Niyonteze. The officer directed his ire at the priests for sheltering such a large number of people in the vicinity of a military camp and showed no interest in arresting their attackers. He counted the number of displaced persons at the church and then he left. The assailants, kept at bay by a hail of stones from the roof, also left for the night.[49]

The next morning, at about 10 a.m., twenty-two soldiers returned under the command of Lt. Ildephonse Hategekimana, head of the Ngoma camp. After telling the displaced people that they would be not be killed but would be taken to prison, he called in the civilians to do the killing. A witness who was hidden heard the children crying and the women begging. He heard the "dull blows, followed by small cries," which he supposed were the sounds of children being clubbed to death. Then, after an hour, silence. There had been 476 people in the church, 302 of them children. Some victims were taken off to be killed in the nearby woods, a number of the women raped first. According to witnesses, the communal

---

[48]Human Rights Watch/FIDH interview, March 26, 1996; République Rwandaise, Parquet de la République, P.V. no. 0117.

[49]Human Rights Watch/FIDH interview, March 26, 1996; République Rwandaise, Parquet de la République, P.V. no. 0117.

policeman Marc Polepole particularly sought out the sister-in-law of the burgomaster and her children and delivered them to killers outside the church.[50]

It rained in the late morning, but when the rain ended in the early afternoon, killers came to finish off the wounded children who were still alive, lying on the grass. As they were clubbing them to death, a vehicle belonging to the Ministry of Health appeared and several officials got out. The killers chatted with them while continuing to club the children on the ground. After the officials left, the killers pillaged the remaining rice stocks of the church as payment for their "work."[51]

Some soldiers had searched especially for the parish priest, Abbé Jerome Masinzo, and reportedly intended to torture him before killing him, but two others helped him to hide just before the attack. One returned later and demanded 500,000 Rwandan francs (U.S.$2,800) to keep the secret of the priest's location. Without any such sum available, Abbé Masinzo appealed to other church contacts who managed to obtain 50,000 Rwandan francs from Burgomaster Kanyabashi. This was the first of a number of payments delivered to soldiers as the price of the priest's life. The burgomaster agreed to help Abbé Masinzo although he was said to have refused to save members of his own family who were killed in the Ngoma massacre. On several subsequent occasions, he reportedly refused aide to other relatives, including to two little girls, one aged seven, the other aged eight. He supposedly believed that help to relatives would be more quickly discovered than aid to others and would expose him to immediate reprisals.[52]

Apparently just after having launched the operation at Ngoma church, Lieutenant Hategekimana led another large group of soldiers, professional people from Buye, and others in searching the convent of a Rwandan religious order, the Benebikira. They brought a warrant signed by Lieutenant Colonel Muvunyi. Hategekimana ordered his soldiers and the professional people to round up everyone inside the extensive complex. Meanwhile a larger crowd of civilians stayed outside, moving around the wall of the compound, shouting and yelling.

---

[50]République Rwandaise, Parquet de la République, P.V. no. 0115 and no. 0117; Human Rights Watch/FIDH interview, March 26, 1996.

[51]Human Rights Watch/FIDH interview, March 26, 1996; République Rwandaise, Parquet de la République, P.V. no. 0117.

[52]Ibid; Human Rights Watch/FIDH interviews, by telephone, Brussels, January 19 and 29, 1998; and by telephone, Rome, February 4, 1998; République Rwandaise, Parquet de la République, P.V. no. 0115.

Among the Tutsi particularly sought by the soldiers were the children and young people from the household of Professor Karenzi, who ranged in age from a seven-year-old girl to a young woman of twenty-two. After Karenzi and his wife had been killed on April 21, the young people had hidden at first in a deserted house and then had been stopped by soldiers as they tried to move to another hiding place. After looking at their identity cards, the soldiers remarked "You are Inyenzi, Tutsi" and threatened to kill them. Several soldiers were unwilling to kill, complaining that they had already killed so many people that day. One claimed to have killed eight women, another to have killed thirteen girls. A Presidential Guard appeared and insisted that the young people be taken to the police brigade. At a barrier, soldiers instructed them to sit down and pray because they were about to die. In the end, the soldiers decided to be satisfied with money and, perhaps, with raping one or more of the girls. The soldiers accused one of the girls of having rebuffed the advances of soldiers before the genocide had begun. Finally the soldiers delivered them to the convent, where they had asked to go and where they remained until April 30.

When the search party located "the Inkotanyi from Karenzi's house" at the convent on April 30, they loaded them and others into the back of a pickup truck. The soldiers climbed in to stand on top of the children. In all, they took away twenty-five people, five of them men, the others women and children. The youngest was a little girl named Aimée, who was five years old. Just as soldiers had said that the people at Ngoma church would be taken to prison and not to be killed, so the assailants said that this group was being taken to the prefectural offices for protection. When the soldiers returned later in the afternoon to loot some beer that they had noticed during the search, the sisters asked what had happened to the young people. One answered, "That's not our job. We left that to the Interahamwe."[53]

An hour or so after the convent of the Benebekira was invaded, ten soldiers and thirty militia and other civilians demanded entry to the Junior Seminary at Karubanda, a short distance away. When asked why they had come, one of the group answered, "Even the clergy and the nuns have been found hiding arms for the RPF, so they can't be trusted...watch out if you hate our country...."[54] The search party checked the identity papers of those present and found two Tutsi employees, who were handed over to the militia. The Interahamwe took them to a

---

[53]Human Rights Watch/FIDH interviews, Butare, March 15 and 21, 1995.

[54]Musoni, "Holocauste Noir," p. 85.

nearby woods and beat them to death, then climbed on their bus to go home. At about 5 p.m., the soldiers returned to loot the seminary. They took a couple of the young women who were there caring for orphans as *umusanzu*, a "contribution" to the army. They raped them. Shortly after other soldiers came for the same purpose.[55]

Beginning on April 20, increasing numbers of soldiers wounded in war were transported to Butare to be treated in the hospital and to convalesce in the buildings of the Groupe Scolaire. On May 1, some of these soldiers slaughtered twenty-one children and thirteen Red Cross workers whom they believed to be Tutsi. They selected them from among the survivors of the April 21 massacre and those who had taken shelter at the Groupe Scolaire since that date. The brutal killing, reported in the foreign press, drew sharp international criticism and, probably as a consequence, a reprimand from the general staff.[56]

Surviving
Seeking Help
Hutu sometimes helped Tutsi spontaneously in an act decided and carried out in a minute or two of time. Donatilla Mukamusoni warned Tutsi in Mbazi of an impending attack and told them that wearing banana leaves would protect them, a warning for which she paid with her life. Students intervened to negotiate the release of fellow students who were being taken away by soldiers. A young Hutu woman lent her identity card to a Tutsi so that she could pass barriers on her attempted flight from death.[57]

But sometimes both those who needed protection and those who extended it were faced with dilemmas resolved only after agonizing discussion. A woman who had given birth while hidden in the home of a Hutu knew that the cries of her newborn would attract searchers who could kill her protectors as well as herself and her baby. She and her host debated many possibilities, including strangling the baby. In the end, they took the risk of trying to bribe soldiers and succeeded in

---

[55]Ibid. See above for a similar case at Kabgayi.

[56]Human Rights Watch/FIDH interviews, Butare, October 24 and 29, 1995; Contribution des FAR, pp. 97-98.

[57]Human Rights Watch/FIDH interviews, Butare, November 9, 1995 and Brussels, December 18, 1995.

finding a couple willing to smuggle the mother and child out of the community, the baby hidden among the grenades and ammunition in the military vehicle.[58]

In the southern part of Ngoma commune, a man of some standing in the community at first took in many relatives from his wife's Tutsi family as well as his Tutsi godson and his family. The godson related the events of that night:

> When I arrived at his place, I found many people hiding there. Many. By 6 p.m., it was clear that we couldn't all stay. Other people had seen too many of us going into his house. Without actually saying it, he let the others know that they had to leave his place. Without weeping or any other show of emotion, they did it. Only one boy showed his fear. He was trembling when he left. Among these people was his own son-in-law, the husband of one of his daughters. She spent the night weeping. As people left, he whispered in my ear: stay here. So I, my wife and our children stayed at his place that night. Nobody slept. Myself, I just sat on a chair, just sitting there, just sitting. My godfather's daughter was weeping because her father had sent her husband away. Then in the middle of the night, we heard shouting. Terrifying cries. I have never been afraid like I was at that moment. I was trembling in my chair, all through the night.[59]

In the morning, the witness left too, hoping thus to increase the chance that his wife and children would be left unmolested. In the end, he survived and they did not.

Resisting

In virtually all the sites where numbers of Tutsi gathered together, they did their best to protect themselves and their families. Those places where the agglomerations were largest, such as some of the churches, the agricultural research stations at Songa and Rubona, and Kabuye, the resisters held out the longest. Many Tutsi from Gikongoro and others who had survived the massacres at Kibeho and Cyahinda fled to the hill Bitare in Gishamvu, a place where Tutsi had successfully resisted Hutu attackers in the early 1960s. The first arrived on Friday April 15, but hundreds of others headed towards the hill on each of the next four days. Many traveled through the fields, trying to avoid groups of assailants who were lying in wait along the roads and paths. Even so, many of the weak stragglers were picked

---

[58]Human Rights Watch/FIDH interview, Brussels, December 18, 1995.

[59]Human Rights Watch/FIDH interview, Butare, May 25, 1995.

off by killers. The Tutsi who reached Bitare were not yet safe. Groups of Hutu
came to attack them so, as one witness reports, "The people at Bitare organized to
defend themselves. They gathered on the hill top and threw stones....during this
time, the men didn't sleep. They went to the river to protect the others from the
assailants."[60] Unable to overcome Tutsi resistance on their own, the attackers went
to get reinforcements from the military. They also obtained grenades and rifles for
themselves. On Tuesday, April 19, new Tutsi arrivals at Bitare talked of the
increased pace of attacks, saying "This isn't just a war. This is an extermination."[61]
The people decided then to try to escape over the Burundi border. They set out
together at dawn on the morning of April 20. When they reached the frontier,
soldiers met them with gunfire. Many died on the road or trying to flee into
adjacent fields, but several hundred made it across the border to safety.[62]

Of all the communes, the three most northern, Nyabisindu, Muyira, and
Ntyazo seem to have offered the most concerted resistance to the genocide. Perhaps
this reflected the history of the area, the heart of the old kingdom, where bonds
between Tutsi and Hutu were multiple, long-standing, and strong, disposing the
Hutu to defend Tutsi more vigorously. Remote from the major military posts,
resisters in the region also had more time to organize their efforts before substantial
military force was brought against them. Ntyazo and Muyira included low-lying
relatively sparsely populated regions fronting the border with Burundi, where a
river and swamps offered good terrain for hiding. Of the twenty burgomasters of
Butare prefecture, two refused to join in the genocide, both of them from this
cluster of northern communes. In taking this stand, they perhaps drew strength
from the depth of local revulsion against the genocide while at the same time
contributing to strengthening that sentiment.

Gisagara, the burgomaster of Nyabisindu, was a Hutu member of the PSD, but
unlike many others of his party who were being drawn into the Hutu Power
alliance, he rejected any such collaboration. From the start, he had vigorously
fought attackers of Tutsi and had jailed the former soldier Basabose and others who
participated in these attacks. He had sought to enlist the support of his superior and
fellow party member, Prefect Nsabimana, and others at the April 20 security

---

[60]Human Rights Watch/FIDH interview, Nyakizu, May 24, 1995.

[61]Ibid.

[62]Human Rights Watch/FIDH interviews, Nyakizu, May 24, June 20 and August
16, 1995.

Document: (Butare prefecture) Telegram informing the Interior Ministry that the Nyabisindu burgomaster is trying to organize resistance to the genocide. The National Police have been sent to find him.

2/4/94

MESSAGE

DTG: 241600 B

DE: S/PREFET NYABISINDU
POUR: MININTER
INFO: PREFET BUTARE

94/015 (-)

TEXTE: REMONTEL DU 22/04/1994 VOUS INFORME QUE BOURGMESTRE COMMUNE
NYABISINDU Mr GISAGARA J.M.V AVEC TOUS LES POLICIERS COMMUNAUX
CORROMPUS A QUITTE LA VILLE POUR SE RETIRER DANS LE SECTEUR
GAHANDA OU IL A ORGANISE AVEC UNE POPULATION QU'IL A CORROMPU UNE
ATTAQUE CONTRE UNE POPULATION QUI N'EPOUSSE PAS SES IDEAUX ET DE
LA POUR ATTEINDRE LA VILLE DE NYANZA(-) GENDARMERIE S'ETRE RENDU
SUR LES LIEUX OU ELLE A ETE CONTRE CETTE POPULATION MAIS LE
BOURGMESTRE ET SES POLICIERS N'ONT PAS PU ETRE RETROUVES (-)
RECHERCHES CONTINUENT(-) ME SUIS RENDU AU BUREAU COMMUNALE
NYABISINDU CE 23/04/1994 ET AI TROUVE LE BUREAU VIDE cÀd SANS
POLICIERS AUCUN(-) AI CAPTE UNE INFORMATION COMME QUOI AVANT DE
QUITTER LA VILLE,IL A CHERCHE LA CAISSIERE ET COMPABLE
ET ONT PASSE QUELQUE TEMPS AU BUREAU CERTENEMENT POUR PRENDRE
DE L'ARGENT(-)EN FAIT IL S'EST DECIDE A FAIRE LE " MAQUIS"
VOUS APPRENDS EGALEMENT QU'HIER 23/04/1994 Mr NYAGASAMA NARCISSE
BOURGMESTRE DE LA COMMUNE NTYAZO A ETE SURPRIS ET TUE PAR POPULA-
TION PANDANT QU'IL TENTAIT DE TRAVERSER L'AKANYARU AVEC D'AUTRES
GENS ET DES VACHES POUR LE BURUNDI (-)
TRES HAUTE CONSIDERATION   ==/==

IM: 25 15 RT N.CLAUDE
04 35 D. " "

Par relais de station
BUFORO

meeting. But he found no help in Butare and when he returned to Nyabisindu, he saw the military release Basabose, as described above. Gisagara and his supporters in the communal police then fled the town of Nyabisindu just as National Police and soldiers brought from Butare were moving into all sectors of the commune. They retreated to the home of one of the communal policemen in Gahanda sector where they may have hoped to rally people against the genocidal assailants. The sub-prefect, Kayitana, reported angrily to his superior that they had raided the communal safe before leaving and asserted that they intended to go underground to fight against the authorities. The military failed to find Gisagara on its first sweep of the area, but eventually they did locate and kill him.[63] With the elimination of the burgomaster and the beginning of military attacks, people from Nyabisindu fled southeast to an agricultural station at Songa in Rusatira commune. On April 29, the burgomaster of Rusatira expressed satisfaction that Tutsi had been "chased away" from Songa but asked for more help in getting rid of those from Nyabisindu who remained in the sector of Nyagisenyi.[64]

On April 23, the burgomaster of Ntyazo commune, Narcisse Nyagasaza, decided to flee rather than execute the genocide. He attempted to lead a group of people from his commune across the border to Burundi. They too were caught and killed. With no replacement named for either burgomaster until late June, Sub-Prefect Kayitana took over carrying out the genocide in their communes. He reportedly directed the slaughter of thousands at and near the Nyabisindu stadium.[65]

Despite the flight and death of the burgomaster, the people of Ntyazo continued to resist. The councilor of Ruyenzi protected Tutsi who had arrived from

---

[63]S/Prefet Nyabisindu to Mininter, telegram 94/015, April 25, 15:35 (Butare prefecture). Gisagara's family was also slaughtered by the military, in Kaguri according to our sources, in Cyahinda according to African Rights. Human Rights Watch/FIDH interview, Buffalo, by telephone, October 29, 1997; African Rights, *Rwanda, Death, Despair*, p. 1044.

[64]Vincent Rukelibuga, Burugumesitiri wa Rusatira, to Bwana Perefe wa Perefegitura, April 29, 1994 (Butare prefecture).

[65]S/Prefet Nyabisindu to Mininter, telegram 94/015, April 25, 15:35 (Butare prefecture); Human Rights Watch/FIDH interview, Buffalo, by telephone, October 29, 1995; Commission pour le Mémorial du Génocide et des Massacres au Rwanda, "Rapport Préliminaire," p. 18; African Rights, *Rwanda, Death, Despair*, p. 358. Gaetan Kayitana was posted to the Nyabisindu sub-prefecture in 1993 after having reportedly been involved in massacres of Tutsi and Bagogwe in northwestern Rwanda.

the north, expressing to them his despair that "Habyarimana's blood was wiping out Rwanda."[66] When he thought they faced too much of a risk in his area, he escorted them to the agricultural research station at Songa, presumably believing they would be safer there. After attacks at Songa drove some Tutsi back to Ntyazo, local Tutsi from Kimvuzo, Gatonde, and Munyinya joined them in Karama sector to try to ward off the attackers. Among the Tutsi, who numbered about 1,500, three had firearms, either because they were (or had been) soldiers or because they had a brother who was a soldier and who had provided a gun. In addition, a National Police first sergeant named Elisée Twagirayezu, who was "hidden among the population"—meaning perhaps that he was Hutu—was helping them and had even tried to shoot one of the communal policemen. At one point, the Tutsi reportedly killed two military men and burned a vehicle of the National Police. In some areas, Tutsi solidified Hutu support by paying them. In Gisasa sector, one hundred Tutsi paid fifty Hutu a cow—which they presumably slaughtered and ate—and 24,000 Rwandan francs (about U.S.$140) to help defend them.[67]

Mathieu Ndahimana, a medical assistant from Nyamure sector, led attacks against the Tutsi but found their resistance unexpectedly strong. On April 27, he asked Deputy Adalbert Muhutu, a former burgomaster and MRND member of parliament from Muyira, to send several National Policemen and four other police to help, a request that he had had to make before. (See above.) National Police under the command of Sergeant Major Philippe Hategekimana targeted the hill Nyamure in Nyamure sector and a site in Karama sector at the same time, slaughtering thousands of people.[68] Along with the military attack, authorities worked successfully to convince Hutu that they had a greater interest in assisting

---

[66]African Rights, *Rwanda, Death, Despair*, p. 1042.

[67]Anonymous, Notebook 2, entry entitled "Ntyazo;" Commission pour le Mémorial du Génocide et des Massacres au Rwanda, "Rapport Préliminaire," pp. 21-22; African Rights, *Rwanda, Death, Despair*, pp.355, 1042.

[68]Hategekimana's attack has been dated to April 24. If this is correct, it may have been executed in response to Nahimana's first request or it may have been initiated independent of Nahimana's request of April 27, which is firmly dated by the document itself. Mathieu [Ndahimana] to Monsieur Muhutu A, Député, April 27, 1994 (see chapter six); Commission pour le Mémorial du Génocide et des Massacres au Rwanda, "Rapport Préliminaire," pp. 21-22.

the authorities than in continuing their loyalty to Tutsi friends and relations. When most Hutu deserted the Tutsi, the assailants completed their genocidal "work."[69]

In the commune of Muyira, authorities had been obliged to bring in militia from neighboring areas to get the genocide started and the aggressors encountered stiff resistance. A corporal, Alexis Musoni, led Tutsi and Hutu in fighting off the National Policemen in sector Mututu, costing the attackers eighteen men. But, here, as in Ntyazo, a combination of military and political action weakened the resistance and made it possible to slaughter most of the Tutsi.[70]

Genocidal Operations
The "Muscular Assistance" of the Military

Throughout the period of the slaughter, government officials claimed that the number of soldiers and National Police available for duty away from combat areas was so limited that they could not halt the genocide. It is true that the number of troops in Butare prefecture was small. There were 150 or so soldiers posted in the town of Butare and about one hundred or so National Police available in the prefecture, most of them also headquartered in the town, although a sizable group was posted in the town of Nyabisindu in the northwest and smaller numbers were sent to other locations as needed. The Presidential Guard unit, probably numbering some fifty soldiers, was also based in Butare, making a total of approximately 300 soldiers and National Police in the prefecture. But to conclude, as did the authorities, that the forces in Butare were too few to stop the genocide was not only wrong but deliberately misleading: had the soldiers and National Police been used to save Tutsi, they would have sufficed to keep order. Instead they were used to provide what the burgomaster of Rusatira called approvingly the "muscular assistance"[71] necessary for the genocide.

The commanding officer for the Butare-Gikongoro operational zone during the worst of the killing was Lieutenant Colonel Muvunyi, acting as a temporary

---

[69]Commission pour le Mémorial du Génocide et des Massacres au Rwanda, "Rapport Préliminaire," pp. 21-22; African Rights, *Rwanda, Death, Despair,* pp.355.

[70]Commission pour le Mémorial du Génocide et des Massacres au Rwanda, "Rapport Préliminaire," pp. 20-21.

[71]Vincent Rukelibuga, Burugumesitiri wa Rusatira, to Bwana Perefe wa Perefegitura, April 29, 1994 (Butare prefecture).

replacement for General Gatsinzi.[72] He had charge of the soldiers at Ngoma camp and the ESO but he did not command the local unit of the Presidential Guard, which remained under the orders of an officer of the general staff. There is no doubt that Muvunyi officially exercised senior military authority in Butare during this period: he appeared publicly in that role and he signed documents in that capacity, like the search warrant mentioned above. But military and civilian witnesses present in Butare at the time agree that it was not Muvunyi but rather his subordinates Captain Nizeyimana and Lieutenant Hategekimana who agressively pushed the genocide, while accusing Muvunyi of being Tutsi himself and threatening him with death for his efforts to help Tutsi. At the end of May, he was put on leave for two weeks, reportedly on the initiative of two ministers from Butare who charged him with hindering the execution of the genocide (see below).[73] When questioned by other officers and civilian administrators about why soldiers were slaughtering Tutsi, Muvunyi claimed that he could not control the soldiers at the Ngoma camp who had been sent south after having fought the RPF and who were determined to kill Tutsi. At one point, he tried to excuse his troops—and hence himself—by asserting that the soldiers who killed actually came from some other unit, not from his troops. But according to a junior officer at Ngoma camp, it was not soldiers from elsewhere who were responsible. He declared that "the soldiers of Butare needed no reinforcement for the 'cleansing' of the town, except for the Interahamwe who were staying at the Ibis [hotel] who gave the ordinary people a hand from time to time."[74]

At the start of the massacres, the Ngoma camp, the ESO, and the National Police divided responsibility for the area around the town of Butare, with leadership in the hands of Nizeyimana and Hategekimana. According to one witness, Nizeyimana played more of a role in the first days, then ceded to Hategekimana. Another suggests that the officers and men of the Ngoma camp led the campaign from the start. Whatever the exact relations between the two, the division of territory was clear. Hategekimana and his troops were to kill Tutsi in Ngoma and Matyazo and other sectors abutting these parts of Ngoma commune,

---

[72]Once Gatsinzi was finished with his brief period as chief of staff, he was assigned to negotiating with the RPF and other duties that did not involve direct command of troops.

[73]Human Rights Watch/FIDH interview, Brussels, by telephone, January 29, 1998; République Rwandaise, Parquet de la République, P.V. no. 253.

[74]République Rwandaise, Parquet de la République, P.V. no. 0117.

an order that the lieutenant passed on to Corporal Nkurunziza.[75] A soldier of the camp showed the limits of his "work" to a National Policeman by pointing to the hills of the sector Matyazo and explaining, "They're all Inyenzi over there and we've been ordered to burn it down."[76] Hategekimana also provided the soldiers for most of the major massacre sites in the southern part of the prefecture, including Karama. According to witnesses, he led the assault on Ngoma church and on the convent of the Benebikira. His subordinate, Lieutenant (jg) Niyonteze, helped the burgomaster of Nyakizu get the soldiers he needed to finish the massacre at Cyahinda, an operation that Hategekimana himself may have commanded at the site. Another soldier under Hategekimana's command, Sergeant-Major Vénuste Gatwaza, reportedly launched the massacre at Mutunda stadium in Mbazi commune and three sergeants directed the attack at the agricultural station at Rubona.[77]

Nizeyimana and the soldiers of ESO killed in the central part of Butare town, including in the residential section of Buye where Nizeyimana himself supervised the murder of the Deputy Prosecutor Matabaro. The captain reportedly also ordered the murder of Rosalie Gicanda and his men carried out the raids on the hospital and the university. Soldiers had orders to take identity cards from those whom they killed. According to one witness, Nizeyimana regularly received these cards from his men as they reported on the progress of the killings. They often appeared at his house shortly after a volley of gunfire was heard and handed the cards to the captain with the report, "Mission accomplished." In the captain's absence, his wife received the cards. Corporal Ndayizeye, one of Nizeyimana's bodyguards, reportedly frequently implemented his orders for murder.[78]

The National Police, under Major Rusigariye, were responsible for the genocide in sectors south of the town center: Tumba, the Cyarwas, Nkubi, and Sahera. National Police from both Butare and from the Nyabisindu outpost also

---

[75]Human Rights Watch/FIDH interviews, Butare, July 6, 1995 and March 26, 1996.

[76]République Rwandaise, Parquet de la République, P.V. no. 0117.

[77]Human Rights Watch/FIDH interviews, Butare, October 27, 1995; Brussels, December 12, 1995; Human Rights Watch/FIDH, written communication from Nairobi, August 7, 1996. Witnesses identified Gatwaza as from the commune of Huye.

[78]Human Rights Watch/FIDH interview, Brussels, December 12, 1995; République Rwandaise, Parquet de la République, P.V. no. 189 and no. 260.

directed major attacks in the northern part of the prefecture, in Nyabisindu and Rusatira communes, at the Songa and Rubona agricultural research stations, and in the commune of Ntyazo.[79]

It is harder to assess responsibility for the Presidential Guards. Some crimes are well documented, such as the attack on Prof. Karenzi and his family or the murders carried out at their barrier, including that of the respected elderly businessman Camille Mbonyubwabo and his son. Residents of Tumba and Cyarwa, near the interim president's home, also talk with certainty about attacks by Presidential Guards whom they recognized from having seen them in the neighborhood. But, in other cases, particularly those that happened some distance from town, witnesses who accuse the Presidential Guards often cannot provide details to support their charges. Given the relatively small number of Guards in Butare and the obligation for some of them to be on duty at Sindikubwabo's house, it seems unlikely that they could have committed all of the attacks attributed to them. Witnesses who suffered at the hands of soldiers of the ESO or of the Ngoma camp may have assumed that their attackers were Presidential Guards because this unit was best known for its genocidal activities.

In town during the first week, the military did much of the killing themselves. Where they needed the support of larger numbers, they sometimes summoned civilians directly and told them what to do. On April 20, for example, soldiers told the head of Kabutare cell that local residents must immediately begin doing patrols, using as a pretext the falsehood that the RPF had attacked a mile or two away. In Cyarwa on April 22, five or six National Policemen gathered the men of the sector at the bar Chez Ngoga. They divided the civilians into groups and ordered them to "search the entire area for arms and for people who were hiding."[80] In Sahera, the soldiers passed through in several vehicles to insist that the people begin "working."[81] In Tumba, one soldier was assisted by two civilians when he came to abduct a Tutsi woman on Friday, April 22. Though they repeatedly threatened to kill her, they seemed to need authorisation from a superior, perhaps because she was married to a European. The three men drove her from place to place in Butare, stopping at the ESO, in the commercial section known as the Arab quarter, and at

---

[79]Major Habyarabatuma returned from the battlefront in June but was then on medical leave.

[80]Human Rights Watch/FIDH interviews, Butare, December 19 and 29, 1995, January 2, 1996.

[81]République Rwandaise, Parquet de la République, P.V. no.0113

the police brigade behind the prefecture building. At each stop, the soldier went searching and then returned saying, "He is not there." Because the group could not locate the officer who could authorize the killing, they returned the woman to her home. One of the civilians apologized to the woman for his part in the abduction, saying he had been "requisitioned" for the work.[82]

The military men were too few to direct daily operations out on the hills. There they moved through communities in pickup trucks or other vehicles, stopping briefly to spread lies and to whip up fear and hatred before moving on to the next location. It was National Police who incited to genocide in the outlying communes of Mugusa and Muyaga. On April 20, the area was still quiet but a visitor from Butare found the people concerned about the passage of a couple of National Policemen. He reported:

> They said that the National Police had come to the markets and caused problems. They tried to fill people with fear. The National Police told them that if they didn't kill Tutsi, the Tutsi would kill them. I tried to explain to them that they shouldn't believe the arguments of the police. They were ready to listen to me, but they asked, "If we are forced to kill, what should we do?" And I didn't know how to answer them.[83]

In the commune of Shyanda on April 22, as the burgomaster and councilors were holding a meeting in one place to persuade people to remain calm, soldiers were passing over the next hill ordering others to burn, pillage, and kill. The military also monitored how rapidly and thoroughly the violence was being carried out. Several returned to Shyanda a few days later to threaten men at a barrier for not having killed enough Tutsi. The civilians responded to the intimidation by seizing several Tutsi for execution.[84] In Kibayi, soldiers and militia went to the MSF center at the Saga camp for Burundian refugees. They separated the Tutsi staff from the Hutu and then handed machetes and guns to the Hutu, directing them

---

[82]Human Rights Watch/FIDH interview, Neuchatel, December 16, 1995.

[83]Human Rights Watch/FIDH interview, December 19, 1995.

[84]Human Rights Watch/FIDH interview, Butare, October 29 and November 9, 1995.

to kill their Tutsi colleagues. Those who refused were killed themselves. Thirty to forty persons were slain.[85]

Once the daily campaign of small assaults, burning, and pillage had driven the Tutsi into churches and other public places, the military launched the large-scale massacres. As in Gikongoro where it looks as though violence was planned to radiate out from three initial centers of violence, so in Butare the attacks spread in an apparently deliberate fashion from the west to east with a secondary thrust coming down from the northeast. The first major massacres (Cyahinda, Kansi, Simbi, Karama, Kabuye, frontier areas) were launched in the south, to be followed several days later by those further north (Mbazi, the two agricultural research stations, Nyamure at Ntyazo, Muyaga communal office). Given the limitations on the numbers of troops at their command, authorities made it a priority to massacre Tutsi who might have a chance of reaching and crossing the frontier. The radio often broadcast warnings about the risk of a southern front being opened, with either RPF or Burundian troops crossing the border to link up with Tutsi gathered in the southern communes. Although there appears to have been no evidence of any such activity, the propagandists used such fears to motivate soldiers and civilians alike. In any one area, attacks were often clustered, following each other in quick succession: Nyumba, Gisagara, and Muganza; the Sovu health center and the Huye communal office; Rugango church, the encampment at Gihindamuyaga, and Mbazi stadium; the Songa and Rubona agricultural research stations, and Nyamure in Ntyazo; the neighborhoods in town, the university, the hospital; Ngoma church, the Benebikira convent, and the Karubanda seminary. This pattern suggests careful planning to make the optimum use of the limited number of troops available.

Former soldiers and communal policemen, although not part of the regular forces, followed the orders of any regular soldiers or National Police who were present at massacre sites. In addition to contributing their own firepower, they served as a link between the regular forces and the civilians, transmitting orders and organizing the untrained masses in conformity with military practice. If regular soldiers or National Police were unavailable, former soldiers led the attacks as did Emmanuel Rekeraho in Maraba and Huye, Kamanayo in Huye, Christophe Kabanza, and a former corporal named Kimonyo, the bodyguard and chauffeur for

---

[85]ICTR-96-4-T, Testimony of Dr. Rony Zachariah.

Pauline Nyiramasuhuko.[86] At Kabuye hill, Ndora, it was a former National Police officer, Félicitée Semakuba, who helped direct the assault. Although pregnant, she "threw grenades as if she were sowing beans."[87]

Soldiers occasionally used their power to save instead of to kill, most often protecting individuals with whom they were linked before the genocide began. Lieutenant Colonel Muvunyi reportedly facilitated the escape or assured the safety of Tutsi and Hutu opposed to the genocide on several occasions. Even Captain Nizeyimana kept some Tutsi in his own house.[88] Sergeant-major Gatwaza, accused of leading the attack at Mbazi stadium, supposedly protected a Tutsi woman from that commune.[89] According to a list registering persons under the protection of soldiers at one of the Butare camps in mid-May, two of the fourteen were Tutsi.[90]

Several wives of military officers arranged transportation and hiding places for Tutsi and in one case provided a FAR military uniform to a young Tutsi woman who was able to flee across the border with this disguise.[91]

Assistance, sometimes freely given on the basis of ties of family or friendship or from simple humanity, was sold by soldiers and police on other occasions. While many Tutsi paid for their lives once or twice, others, like the family of a wealthy entrepreneur in Butare town or the priest of the Ngoma church, paid regular protection money to soldiers throughout the genocide.[92] An elderly Tutsi

---

[86]Human Rights Watch/FIDH interviews, Brussels, December 18, 1995, February 2, 1996; Anonymous, Notebook 1, entry for April 20, 1994; African Rights, *Rwanda, Not So Innocent* (London: August, 1995), p. 159.

[87]African Rights, *Rwanda, Not So Innocent*, p. 36.

[88]Human Rights Watch/FIDH interviews, Butare, July 6, 1995; Brussels, December 18, 1995; Nsabimana, "The Truth About the Massacres in Butare;" République Rwandaise, Parquet de la République, P.V. no. 260.

[89]African Rights, *Witness to Genocide,* issue no. 7, September, 1997, p. 74.

[90]Untitled list giving names, identity card numbers, places of origin, ethnic group, name and rank of protector (lieutenant to corporal), and date of arrival in camp (Butare prefecture).

[91]Human Rights Watch/FIDH interview, Brussels, March 4, 1996.

[92]Human Rights Watch/FIDH interviews, Kizi, Maraba, May 13, 1995; Butare, October 29, 1995.

man at Sovu gave a cow, probably more valuable to him than money, to a communal policeman who, he thought, would protect him. In the end, the payment did not save him from attack.[93]

The Militia and the Match Factory

Many of the militia active in the first days of slaughter had come from outside of Butare. According to local people, some had come in the weeks and months before the genocide and either just resided at SORWAL, the match factory, or were hired to work there. Others who arrived as the killing began made the factory their local headquarters, at least until late May when Interahamwe President Robert Kajuga arrived to set up his base at the Hotel Ibis.[94]

Northern supporters of Hutu Power perhaps felt safer and more at home at the match factory than elsewhere in Butare. A little removed from the heart of town, protected by its own guards, the factory offered privacy as well as security. The enterprise was a joint venture between the Rwandan government and foreign investors. Like many parastatal corporations, it was run by hand-picked associates of President Habyarimana. Mathieu Ngirumpatse, secretary-general of the MRND, sat on its board as representative of the Rwandan government. Among other board members was at least one French citizen. Its director, Alphonse Higaniro, was a former government minister and part of the inner circle of President Habyarimana both on his own account and through his marriage to the daughter of the president's physician, who was killed with Habyarimana in the April 6 plane crash. In Butare, Higaniro developed a close relationship with Captain Nizeyimana, who was ready to bend the rules to oblige him. Some time before April 6, Nizeyimana assigned soldiers to guard Higaniro at his request, an irregular arrangement that was not approved by Nizeyimana's superiors.[95]

Operating as an adjunct to the regular military forces, the militia must have had at least one liaison with the military officers who directed their operations. It appears that Martin Dusabe, a northerner and technical director of SORWAL, was such a link. According to a witness who lived in the neighborhood, Dusabe received visits from Captain Nizeyimana once or twice every day during the

---

[93]African Rights, *Rwanda, Not so Innocent,* p. 180.

[94]Human Rights Watch/FIDH interviews, Brussels, December 12, 1995; January 26 and March 4, 1996; by telephone, Nairobi, April 3, 1996.

[95]Human Rights Watch/FIDH interview, Brussels, December 15, 1995; République Rwandaise, Parquet de la République, P.V. no. 0142.

genocide. In this time of crisis, such regular visits could hardly have been for social purposes, nor did the two men have any ordinary business to transact. The match factory was not operating during this period.[96]

Other SORWAL employees or former employees, like Jacques Habimana and Edward Niyitegeka (also known as Nyagashi), may have passed on orders from Dusabe. Habimana directed attacks in the neighborhood of Ngoma and both helped lead the massacre at the Ngoma church. Nyitegeka's brother, Gatera, also participated in that attack.[97]

In addition, Dusabe and the chief financial and administrative officer of SORWAL, Jean-Baptiste Sebalinda, played important roles in the "civilian self-defense" program, as detailed below.

Higaniro himself left Butare on April 7 to participate in the funeral of his father-in-law in Kigali. He then withdrew to Gisenyi with other important backers of the interim government. He returned once to Butare, at the end of April or beginning of May, supposedly to get the match factory running again and then left once more for the northwest.[98] But from a letter that he wrote to his subordinate in Butare, it appears that he was directing his employees' involvement in the genocide even at a distance. He wrote: "For security in Butare, you must continue and finish the 'clean-up.'" Higaniro later admitted writing this letter, but explained that it was an order to clean up an oil spill in the parking lot of the factory and had nothing to do with eliminating Tutsi from Butare.[99]

Captain Nizeyimana seems to have been the link between Higaniro and Professor Vincent Ntezimana, a northerner who was a professor of physics at the university. Professor Ntezimana has acknowledged a close relationship with Captain Nizeyimana, whose house he visited virtually daily, he said, during the genocide. Professor Ntezimana and Higaniro were also acquainted and had jointly founded an association to promote the "cultural, apolitical" interests of their common home region. The professor denied any close link with Higaniro, yet when Higaniro was under pressure to leave quickly for Kigali on April 7, he took the time to let the professor know of his departure. Professor Ntezimana was sometimes transported around Butare in military vehicles and when he wished to

---

[96]Human Rights Watch/FIDH interview, Brussels, March 4, 1996.

[97]République Rwandaise, Parquet de la République, P.V. no. 0117.

[98]Human Rights Watch/FIDH interview, Brussels, December 15, 1995.

[99][Alphonse Higaniro] to SORWAL employee, date illegible (confidential source).

travel to the northwest, Captain Nizeyimana arranged for him to do so in a vehicle of SORWAL.[100]

The links among the three are shown also in their relationships to a young man named Innocent Nkuyubwatsi, a northerner from Ruhengeri. Once a soldier studying at ESO, he had left the army, supposedly because of some injury. Captain Nizeyimana then obtained a job for him at SORWAL and had lodged him and his sister in his own house. When the captain found his household getting too crowded, he asked Professor Ntezimana to take in Nkuyubwatsi. Professor Ntezimana agreed to do so and Nkuyubwatsi stayed with him during the genocide. Nkuyubwatsi, who often wore a military uniform, could come and go freely even when others had to observe a curfew. The professor watched Nkuyubwatsi murder a young Tutsi woman who also had been living in his house and then removed the body from his back yard and dumped it on the road by his house. Nkuyubwatsi apparently also joined in beating a young man to death at a barrier, an incident at which Professor Ntezimana was also present. Knowing Nkuyubwatsi to be a murderer, the professor continued to provide him with lodging.[101]

In addition to the militia linked to SORWAL, a second group operated under the orders of Shalom (Chalôme) Ntahobari, son of the minister, Pauline Nyiramasuhuko and the university rector, Maurice Ntahobari. A failed student turned killer, Shalom became a big man in Butare once the slaughter began. He swaggered around town with grenades hanging from his belt, often armed with a gun which he once aimed in insolent jest at a local burgomaster. One witness asserted that even military officers saluted Shalom. He controlled his own barrier in front of the family house near the university campus where he bullied his militia subordinates as well as passersby. One witness who had known Shalom as a fellow student witnessed him killing a man in order to rob him of his cattle. This was only one of numerous murders Shalom was said to have committed.[102] In addition to his activities in town, Shalom recruited and organized militia in Mbazi, a commune

---

[100]Human Rights Watch/FIDH interview, Brussels, March 4, 1996; Police Judiciaire près le Parquet du Procureur du Roi de Bruxelles, Section: Criminelle, Dossier: 37/95, P.V. nos. 182, 31.884, 32.765, and 33.088.

[101]Police Judiciaire près le Parquet du Procureur du Roi de Bruxelles, Section: Criminelle, Dossier: 37/95, P.V. nos. 55, 149, 31.876, 31.883, 32.996, and 34.250.

[102]Human Rights Watch/FIDH interviews, Butare, August 18, August 20, and October 20, 1995.

just outside of town that was home to his father's family. There he frequently told people, "If we don't kill them, they will kill us."[103]

Although Shalom and his group sometimes operated together with the military, he appears to have enjoyed considerable autonomy and status, probably because of his mother's influence. He collaborated with Nyiramasuhuko both in the general goals of the genocide and in the more specific effort to increase the power of the MRND at the expense of the MDR and the PSD. She in turn supported his murders, to the extent of accompanying him when he went to abduct those to be executed. (See below.)[104]

In addition to the militia associated with SORWAL and the local group recruited by Shalom, a third and even more prestigious cluster of killers arrived in early May with Robert Kajuga, the national president of the Interahamwe. They installed themselves at the Hotel Ibis, where they spent a great deal of time drinking with soldiers. Like local militia members, these militia members from Kigali wore portrait pins of Habyarimana, pieces of clothing imprinted with the image of the late president, or the green and yellow print tunics long associated with the Interahamwe. But they displayed also the assurance that came from being associated with the most important national leaders of the militia as they looted widely in town among Hutu as well as Tutsi.[105] Several young Tutsi women who were part of Kajuga's entourage moved freely about town and the market, their safety guaranteed by their protector. Kajuga also provided protection to some Tutsi of Butare, alerting their Hutu hosts whenever Shalom's militia was planning an attack on them.[106] The national president was sufficiently sure of his own power to ignore a request to come to the prefect's office to discuss the behavior of his followers. The prefect complained later that in contrast to professional soldiers with

---

[103]Human Rights Watch/FIDH interviews, Brussels, December 18, 1995 and February 2, 1996.

[104]Human Rights Watch/FIDH interviews, Butare, October 28 and 29, 1995; Brussels, December 12, 1995.

[105]Human Rights Watch/FIDH interviews, Butare, July 6, 1995; August 18, 20, and December 13, 1995.

[106]Human Rights Watch/FIDH interviews, Butare, October 20, 1995 and Nairobi, by telephone, April 3, 1996.

whom issues could be discussed, the Interahamwe were impossible to reason with: they wanted only to kill.[107]

The number of militia members grew enormously once the genocide began in Butare, both because previously organized groups recruited numbers of people into their ranks and because other groups formed around local leaders and called themselves Interahamwe. Kajuga's militia members particularly encouraged the street kids who spent their nights huddled in an improvised shelter across from the Ibis to follow their lead. They rewarded them with a share of the loot acquired in raids on Tutsi.[108]

Civilian Action

Administrators and political leaders ensured that the Tutsi would be available for easy attack by encouraging or ordering them to go to various sites, some of which were already occupied by Tutsi who had gathered on their own initiative. Prefectural authorities ordered Tutsi from Sahera to move to Nyumba and sent others from Nyakibanda to Nyumba. The sub-prefect of Gisagara, Dominique Ntawukuriryayo, insisted that displaced persons leave the market at Gisagara to join others at Kabuye and summoned Tutsi who lived in the area to come there as well. The sub-prefect of Busoro, Assiel Simbalikure, apparently supervised moving the displaced from the Burundi frontier back to the market at Nkomero. The burgomaster of Nyaruhengeri sent people to the church at Kansi. The communal authorities in Runyinya called on Tutsi to go to Karama. The burgomaster of Butare sought to move people from Matyazo to Karama and Simbi. According to witnesses, the burgomaster of Mbazi sent people to the commune stadium and also turned back crowds of people who wanted to leave the Rubona agricultural research station to go into Butare. Councilors and other local officials reportedly escorted the displaced to the agricultural research station at Songa and told people in Sahera to go to Kabakobwa.[109] Beginning on April 16, soldiers, with civilian

---

[107]"Interview of Sylvain Nsabimana, October 1, 1994;" Interview of Mr. Nsabimana Sylvain, September 18, 1994. (Transcripts provided by Sylvain Nsabimana.)

[108]Human Rights Watch/FIDH interviews, Butare, July 8 and December 13, 1995.

[109]Human Rights Watch/FIDH interviews, Butare, October 25, 1995, March 26, 1996; Brussels, November 6, 1995 and May 17, 1997; Anonymous, Notebook 1, entry for April 17, 1994); African Rights, *Rwanda, Death, Despair,* pp. 348, 355 African Rights, *Witness to Genocide,* issue no. 7, pp. 7, 17 and 20, but see apparently contradictory testimony on p. 8; pp. 44-45.

helpers, began forcing Tutsi to gather on the grounds of an artisanal school (Center of Integrated Rural Artisanal Education, CERAI) in Kigembe commune, often looting them of their belongings in the process. One woman who had fled to Kigembe recalled:

> The authorities made promises about our security. We believed their assurances because we thought we were in the hands of the state and not of the popular crowds who had attacked us in Nyakizu.[110]

After permitting the displaced to come and go freely for two or three days, burgomasters at communes like Nyaruhengeri, Mbazi, and Ngoma reportedly restricted them to the sites where they had gathered. If Hutu had assembled with Tutsi at these places, officials or militia leaders told the Hutu to go home shortly before the place was to be attacked. In the first day or two, some authorities provided food, as did the burgomaster at Kigembe to the Tutsi at the Nyaruteja CERAI, and others allowed church workers to deliver food, as they did at Sovu and Matyazo. But soon after authorities refused to deliver more provisions and discouraged or prohibited others from supplying food and water to the Tutsi. Such deprivation weakened the displaced persons both psychologically and physically.[111]

Administrative officials from the prefect down to the cell leader, assisted by local political figures, fed the hatred and panic already generated by propaganda. They permitted people to believe and, in many cases, actively encouraged them to believe that Tutsi posed a threat to the safety of Hutu and thus should be attacked. Whether in public meetings, such as that where the sub-prefect of Gisagara accused Tutsi of stocking firearms in churches, or in more spontaneous road-side exhortations, like those attributed to Minister Nyiramasuhuko, Prefect Nsabimana, and Burgomaster Kanyabashi officials gave license to attack Tutsi.[112] Burgomasters, including Habineza of Maraba, Ntaganzwa of Nyakizu, and Déogratias Hategekimana of Runyinya were reportedly present immediately before

---

[110]Human Rights Watch/FIDH interview, Butare, June 12, 1995.

[111]Human Rights Watch/FIDH interviews, Butare, June 12, 1995; Brussels, May 17, 1997; by telephone, January 19 and 29, 1998; African Rights, *Witness to Genocide*, issue 7, September 1997, pp. 18-20.

[112]Human Rights Watch/FIDH interviews, Brussels, December 18, 1995, May 17, 1997; République Rwandaise, Parquet de la République, P.V. no. 0290.

or during massacres and thus lent their authority to the killings.[113] If most burgomasters absented themselves during the actual attack, virtually all seem to have permitted or directed their subordinates, including communal police, councilors, and cell heads to join in the slaughter.[114]

In Ngoma, for example, many witnesses accuse the communal police of participating in massacres such as those at Kabakobwa, Matyazo health center, and the Ngoma church as well as in smaller attacks on local residences. The log book for the communal vehicle with registration number A 8979 appears to confirm that testimony, recording an extraordinary amount of activity by the police during the last ten days of April. The truck was driven only thirty-five and thirty-one kilometers per day for the two days of use registered in the week before April 7. Once the slaughter was launched in town, however, the vehicle was used to transport the communal police 266 kilometers on the bloody weekend of April 22 to 24 and another 510 kilometers in the six days after.[115]

Burgomasters and the prefectural staff provided logistical and financial support for the killing campaign. In addition to supplying communal vehicles, they requisitioned private vehicles to transport assailants and they provided the fuel both to run the vehicles and to burn Tutsi houses. They delivered the trucks and the bulldozer that made mass burials easier. Administrators and politicians paid for the "work" of assailants and, later, for the efforts of those who buried the bodies. According to one witness, authorities paid militia, the elite of the civilian assailants, 2,000 Rwandan francs (about U.S.$10) a day, while the burgomaster of Maraba gave rice and the minister Nyiramasuhuko offered beer to the ordinary people.[116]

---

[113]République Rwandaise, Parquet de la République, P.V. no. 0117; African Rights, *Rwanda, Death, Despair*, pp. 346-48.

[114]Human Rights Watch/FIDH interviews, Nyangazi, Maraba, June 28, 1995; Brussels, May 17, 1997; République Rwandaise, Parquet de la République, P.V. no. 0115; African Rights, *Witness to Genocide,* issue 7, pp. 29-30. For Nyakizu, see chapters nine and ten.

[115]Carnet de Route et de Controle de Circulation, plaque d'immatriculation no. A8979 (final digits nearly illegible) (Butare prefecture).

[116]Human Rights Watch/FIDH interviews, Simbi, Maraba, May 3, May 5 and May 16, 1995; Nairobi, by telephone, April 3, 1996; May 21, 1997; Musoni, "Holocauste Noir," p. 84.

Document: (Ngoma commune) Log of use of communal vehicle reflecting sudden increase after April 20 for transport of communal police.

Date	Compteur départ	Nom du chauffeur	MISSION EXACTE ET NOMS DES PERSONNES A BORD AUTORISEES	Jour ou Heures Départ	Fin de mission	Retour	Compteur au retour	Kms parcourus	Nom et signature Chef de Service	Consommations Carburants	Lubrifiants	H.mot-H.Frein	Observation
29/3/94	21610	KASTANZI	Circulac: Ville & Nyab	14h00			21646						
30/3/94	21646	"	Patrouille Ngoma	9h00									
			à Nyabisi	15h35									
31/3/94		"	Ngoma (Béatitudes)	9h05									
1/4/94		"	Visite des Sœurs										
			Ngoma CTK-CBay	8h15									
	21686	"	Ngoma CTK-CBay	7h30		11h00	9.017						
	21817	"	Ngoma (Ng.7)	9h30									
		"	(Ngoma-Nyanza)	14h45									
31-4-94	21979	Nsanzabahiz	Dépl Comm.t des Policiers dans tous les Secteurs										
			de la Commune Ngoma										
21-4-94	22072	Nsanzabahiz	Dépl.Comm.t des policiers dans tous les Secteurs	9h00 16h00	14h30	22077							
			de la Commune Ngoma										
22-4-94		Nsanzabahiz	"	9h00									
23-4-94		Nsanzabahiz	"										
24-4-94	22343	Nsanzabahiz	Déplacement dans tous les Secteurs avec le										
30-4-94	Mêmes déplacements	Nsanzabahiz	Policiers	9h00									
2-5-94	22853	Nsanzabahiz	venons la comptabilité										
3-5-94	22925	Nsanzabahiz	conduire les Policiers dans tous les secteurs	9h00			22925						

Local leaders, some relying on their political networks, others drawing power from militia and other less formal armed bands, helped organize the genocide in most communes. Some supplemented the efforts of administrators who were already working zealously at eliminating Tutsi; others displaced authorities who were less ready to kill or, by challenging their authority, pushed them to more extreme positions. Such pressures from local leaders who were committed to the killing campaign complemented the pressures that came from above, from national political and administrative leaders.

In Mbazi, Maraba, and Huye Emmanuel Rekeraho built upon his skills as a former soldier, his status as a local head of the MDR, and his position as aide to Colonel Simba in the "civilian self-defense" program to become a significant force who impressed administrators and frightened resident foreigners. Arbiter of life and death, he decided at one point that Tutsi sheltered at the Sovu convent could stay alive, a decision that he apparently changed some time later. In Mbazi, Jean-Baptiste Kagabo made use of his status as former burgomaster and as prefectural vice-president of the CDR to organize support for the genocide. Along with his sons and other local strongmen, he represented a serious challenge to the authority of Burgomaster Sibomana.[117] Bonaventure Nkundabakura, communal head of MDR-Power and his ally Bernard Mutabaruka, local head of the CDR, appear to have spearheaded the killing of Tutsi in Kigembe, displacing the burgomaster Symphorien Karekezi from leadership of the killing campaign. Jacques Habimana, a one-time SORWAL employee and self-described journalist, exploited his connections with militia to attack Tutsi as well as to build a personal base of power that got him installed as councilor of Ngoma sector, an unexpected success for someone from outside the community. In Tumba sector, Sosthene Munyemana allegedly used his considerable prestige as a physician to incite killing and acquired new power through his control over the neighborhood lock-up where Tutsi were confined before being sent off for execution. In the adjacent sector of Cyarwa, the CDR leader Simeon Remera rallied old and new adherents to his party to attack Tutsi. Innocent Bakundukize, a casual laborer previously without status in Cyarwa, acquired a firearm from a brother who was a soldier. He used the weapon to exert

---

[117]Alexandre Rucyahana, undated typescript.

authority over others and to insist that the community get rid of its Tutsi residents.[118]

In ten catastrophic days from April 20 to April 30, the military, administrative, and political leaders of Butare brought the prefecture into full compliance with the national program of genocide.

---

[118]Ibid; Human Rights Watch/FIDH interviews, Nyangazi, Maraba, June 28, 1995, Butare, October 25, 1995; African Rights, *Rwanda, Not so Innocent,* pp. 158-84; African Rights, *Witness to Genocide,* issue 2, February 1996. For more on Mbazi and Kigembe, see below.

BUTARE:
"WORKERS WHO WANT TO WORK FOR THEIR COUNTRY"

In two weeks of massacres, genocidal authorities annihilated more than half the Tutsi in Butare. Then they allowed violence to dwindle for a period of between ten days and three weeks at the end of April and into the first part of May, with the dates and length of the period varying somewhat from one community to the next. At this time, administrators pushed forward the organization of "civilian self-defense," meant to shift responsibility for "security" from military into civilian hands, official and unofficial.

Just as the week before Interim President Sindikubwabo had come to urge killings in Butare, so on April 27 he returned to tell the prefectural security committee that it was time to bring the slaughter under tighter control. The press release issued after that meeting and a more general message issued by the prefect the same day indicated that in Butare, as elsewhere, "pacification" meant greater circumspection in killing Tutsi: no one should be attacked unless "there is proof that he is a real supporter of the Inkotanyi" and such persons must be brought to the communal authorities.[1] At the same time, "pacification" represented an effort to halt the violence among Hutu, particularly that conducted on the pretext of association with the Inkotanyi. The messages from the authorities also demanded an end to the pillage of state property, to "criminal behavior," and to the unauthorized use of arms.[2]

The local speeches and national radio messages alike made clear that "pacification" was the prelude to "civilian self-defense." As the Ministry of Defense announced on Radio Rwanda, "security has been restored except in combat zones," meaning that the large-scale killing of Tutsi had been effective, but "the people must be vigilant because the Inyenzi are ready to infiltrate."[3] With the people being "vigilant" and increasingly tightly organized to exercise this vigilance, military forces would be left freer to confront the RPF. The burgomaster

---

[1]Sylvain Nsabimana, Prefe wa Prefegitura ya Butare, "Ubutumwa Bugamije Kugarura Umutekano mu Makomini ya Prefegitura ya Butare," April 27, 1994 (Butare prefecture).

[2]Ibid.; Sylvain Nsabimana, Prefe wa Prefegitura ya Butare, "Itangazo Kuri Radio Rwanda," (April 27, 1994) (Butare prefecture).

[3]UNAMIR, Notes, Radio Rwanda, 19:00, May 11, 1994. Similar messages were heard on RTLM, 17:00, April 22, 1994 and on Radio Rwanda, 20:00 May 5, 1994.

515

of Muganza on May 5 protested the recall of a National Police detachment from his commune, complaining that he could not complete the "pacification of the population" without its support. But the prefectural security council the next day reaffirmed that administrators were no longer to call on the armed forces, but rather to rely on such local resources as communal police "in cases of insecurity."[4]

"Civilian Self-Defense" in Butare
Leadership and Finance

The highly bureaucratic plan for "self-defense," incorporating civilian and military elements into an autonomous hierarchy, was sent to prefects on May 25 (see above), but the command structure in Butare was already being assembled in late April or early May. Colonel Simba was the local commander, an arrangement regularized by a mid-May letter of appointment. Acknowledging the important role to be played by former soldiers whom Simba would choose as his subordinates, the letter for the first time specified that such participants would be paid by the Ministry of Defense, unlike the great mass who would be unpaid volunteers.[5]

While Simba oversaw the military training of the recruits, Lt. Col. Alphonse Nteziryayo was in charge of coordination with the civilian authorities. A native of Kibayi commune, Nteziryayo had for some time been seconded from the army to the Ministry of Interior. In the opinion of some colleagues, northern officers had shunted Nteziryayo into this out-of-the-way position out of personal rivalry or because they suspected him of not sharing their ideas. At the Ministry of Interior, where he had charge of programs for the communal police, he presumably worked closely with Kalimanzira, then head of administration and a fellow native of Butare. Apparently it was Kalimanzira who arranged for Nteziryayo to come to Butare.[6]

---

[4]Chrysologue Bimenyimana, Bourgmestre de la Commune Muganza, to Monsieur le Commandant de Groupement Gendarme, no. 070/04.09.01/1, May 5, 1994; [Dominiko Ntawukuriryayo, S/Prefe wa S/Prefegitura Gisagara] to Bwana Burgumestri, no. 006/04.01.02, May 14, 1994 (Butare prefecture).

[5]Augustin Bizimana, Ministre de la Défense, to Lt. Col. e.r. Simba Aloys, no. 51/06.1.9/01 May 15, 1994 (Butare prefecture).

[6]Human Rights Watch/FIDH interviews, Butare, August 20, 1995; Kigali, November 21, 1995; Brussels, by telephone, January 25, 1997; Augustin Bizimana, Ministre de la Défense au Lt. Colonel e.r. Simba Aloys, no. 51/06.1.9/01, May 15, 1994 (Butare prefecture); "Interview of Sylvain Nsabimana, October 1, 1994"; Nsabimana, "The Truth

Nteziryayo took up residence at the Hotel Ibis shortly before Kajuga arrived with his Interahamwe. With the two of them lodged there, the Ibis became the informal local headquarters for the genocide campaign. According to one witness, the lieutenant colonel used militia members—dressed in ill-assorted combinations of civilian and military dress—instead of regular soldiers as his personal bodyguard. Nteziryayo reportedly eliminated Tutsi in his own immediate surroundings as well as organizing genocide throughout the prefecture. According to testimony, he and his men abducted three girls who worked at the hotel, two of whom were killed. The third was saved by a Protestant evangelical soldier who opposed the killings. Nteziryayo's group also reportedly bludgeoned to death three young men who had hidden at the Hotel Faucon and they were said to have killed Thomas Nyandwi, a Hutu, whom they accused of being an icyitso because he had taken in a Tutsi orphan.[7]

In promoting "civilian self-defense," Nteziryayo got his greatest support from the administrator, Kalimanzira, and from politician Pauline Nyiramasuhuko, who worked closely together throughout the prefecture. Kalimanzira and Nyiramasuhuko shared a loyalty to the MRND and years of experience in national politics. Another powerful politician who supported "civilian self-defense" was Felix Semwaga, a prosperous local merchant. Semwaga was treasurer of the MDR-Power for the prefecture, a member of the national governing body of the party, and a prefectural representative on the board of the national Chamber of Commerce. Throughout the genocide, he enjoyed the protection of two or three soldiers from camp Ngoma, a privilege that he may have negotiated directly with Lieutenant Hategekimana but which some attributed to his connection with the interim prime minister, also a MDR-Power politician from Butare. Party rivalries caused tensions between Semwaga and MRND supporters Kalimanzira and Nyiramasuhuko, but, at least in the early days, they minimized their differences in the larger interests of Hutu Power. Jean-Baptiste Ruzindaza, president of the Court of First Instance, agreed to help run the civilian part of the training program.[8]

Representatives of the political, intellectual, and commercial elite of the prefecture helped formalize the structure of "civilian self-defense." Neither

---

about the Massacres in Butare."

[7]Human Rights Watch/FIDH interviews, Butare, December 13, 1995; Nairobi, by telephone, March 25 and April 3, 1996.

[8]Human Rights Watch/FIDH interviews, Butare, August 18, 1995; Nairobi, by telephone, March 26 and April 3, 1996.

Kalimanzira nor Nyiramasuhuko appeared on the list of those preparing the organization and financing of the "Youth Meetings"—not surprising given that their importance was national rather than prefectural—but Semwaga figured among those listed on the organizing committee. This group included three representatives each from the MDR, the PSD, and the MRND block (two MRND, one CDR). Among them were a teacher, a medical assistant, an important businessman, a former soldier, and at least two prefectural employees. Semwaga and two teachers, one from the Groupe Scolaire and another the head of the Buye Centre de Formation made up a more restricted three person committee that supervised "civilian self-defense." The fund-raising committee included such notables as the rector and vice-rector of the university, the director of the university library, who was a former member of President Habyarimana's staff, two university professors, one other teacher, two doctors, two important businessmen and one burgomaster. Two members of this committee were employed at SORWAL. People identified by witnesses as organizers or participants in the killings that preceded the formal establishment of "civilian self-defense," including Emmanuel Rekeraho, Faustin Niyonzima, Simeon Remera, Céléstin Halindintwali, and Martin Dusabe, served on one committee or the other.[9]

Kalimanzira and Nyiramasuhuko reportedly insisted on generous contributions from the urban and intellectual elite of Butare to finance the "self-defense" effort. In response to their urging and in conformity with instructions from the national level, the prefect established a special fund for "civilian self-defense," as distinct from prior accounts for national and local security. The vice-rector contributed a check from the university employees savings association for six and a half million Rwandan francs (U.S.$36,000), as mentioned above. By late June, the "civilian self-defense" account amounted to about twelve million Rwandan francs, four million of which was added by the authorities after the public prosecutor confiscated and sold the property of a Tutsi trader whose nickname was Nouveau Riche. The rest was contributed mostly by local businessmen.[10] The committee with authority over the account included: Sub-prefect Faustin Rutayisire, Vice-Rector Nshimyumuremyi, Venant Gakwaya, an important businessman and

---

[9]"Amanama y'Urubyiruko" (undated document) (Butare prefecture).

[10]Dr. Jean-Berchmans Nshimyumuremyi, Vice-Recteur, to Monsieur le Préfet, P2-12/226/94, May 25, 1994; Sylvain Nsabimana, Préfet, to Monsieur le Vice-Recteur, Butare [no date, no number]; Dr. Jean-Berchmans Nshimyumuremyi, Vice-Recteur, to Monsieur le Préfet, P2-18/236/94, June 15, 1994 and attached payment order, no. 1955802 (Butare prefecture).

Document: (Butare prefecture) The prefect directs the bank manager to open a "Civil Defense" account and lists those who will have control over the account.

REPUBLIQUE RWANDAISE
PREFECTURE DE BUTARE

Butare, le 15 JUIN 1994
N° 84 /04.13

Monsieur le Gérant de la B.K.

Agence de BUTARE

Objet : Demande
        d'ouverture
        d'un compte.

Monsieur le Gérant,

                Le conseil de sécurité préfectorale
de Butare a décidé d'ouvrir un compte dans votre Banque,
dénommée "Préfecture Butare - Défense Civile". Les mandataires
sont : - Monsieur RUTAYISIRE Faustin, Sous-Préfet de Préfecture
       - Monsieur NSHIMYUMUREMYI J.Berchimans, Vice-Recteur UNR
       - Monsieur SEBALINDA, Chef administratif et financier
                            à la SORWAL
       - Monsieur GAKWAYA Venant, Secrétaire de la Chambre de
         alias SOCODE Commerce à Butare.
Ils agiront conjointement trois à trois pour toute opération
de retrait.

                Je vous demanderais donc de
faciliter l'ouverture de ce compte dans votre Banque.

                Dans l'attente d'une réponse
favorable, veuillez croire, en ma franche collaboration.

                                LE PREFET DE PREFECTURE BUTARE
                                NSABIMANA Sylvain

Document: (Ngoma commune) The "civilian self-defense" committee sends the burgomaster the names of five persons chosen to learn to shoot firearms.

Butare kuwa 27 Nyakanga 1994.

Bureau du Comité
T. Auto-Défense Civile
Suféchine Butare.

Kuri Bwana Burgomestri wa Komini
J. Umujyi wa Ngoma.

Impamvu: Kuvigisha abaturage
kurwanaho.

Bwana Burgomestri;

Nkwikije ibaruwa no 205/04.09.01 yo kuwa 20/06/1994 muri nitikije abakenewa ba za Segiteri zo muri Komini J. umujyi wa Ngoma mulasaba kuboherereza abakandida bo ku kwigisha mu buryo bwo kuriwanaho k'abaturage, tukoherereje abantu batanu batuye muri Segiteri Mubumbano, Komini Gishamvu, kugirango nabo bigishwe, bazunganire abarinda barijyeri iri ku iteme ryo Mukura ku muhanda Butare - Akanyaru Haut.

Abo ni aba: 1) Gintirikububa Pascal   4) Rugelinganya.
          2) Twagirumukiza J. Samascu 5) Karunganura.
          3) Nzayirana Theophile.

Abo bukanozu tuvabirijyejengwe na Conseiller wa Segiteri Mubumbano Bwana Bumeya Zephilii mu abaruwa yakoherereje uyu munsi.
Murakoze.

Pour le Bureau du Comité   Rugumintwali J.
T. Auto Défense Civile   Secretaire

secretary of the Butare Chamber of Commerce, and Jean-Baptiste Sebalinda, the administrative and financial head of SORWAL.[11] As the above-mentioned directive from the Ministry of the Interior ordered, the funds were to be spent for such items as weapons, supplies, and "refreshments" for the militia.

Training and Weapons

In Butare, as elsewhere in Rwanda, the "vigilant" masses were to be headed by young men trained to "lead the population so that it will be able to prevent the infiltration of the enemy [*Eni*]."[12] On April 21, just two days after Sindikubwabo's speech, Lieutenant Colonel Muvunyi wrote burgomasters explaining the program and ordering them to choose ten "reliable and patriotic" young men from each sector to be trained in the use of firearms and grenades. He emphasized the distinction between this program and regular army service, for which he had asked burgomasters to recruit men two days before. This second group of recruits, trained locally and living at home, were to be used against the "enemy" in the immediate region.

The authorities had no difficulty recruiting men for the self-defense training. According to one participant, people fought for the opportunity to participate.[13] Some no doubt were motivated by real fear and desire to protect their homes from the threat so dramatically depicted by the government. The inhabitants of Butamenwa cell seemed convinced of the need for such defense when they wrote to ask the prefect for guns. They explained that their request followed from:

...the government recommendations that require all people to assist the national army in safeguarding territorial integrity, in pursuing the Inyenzi wherever they may be, from wherever they come, whether they are among us or whether they come from the outside....[14]

---

[11]Sylvain Nsabimana, Préfet, to Monsieur le Gérant de la B.K., Agence de Butare, no. 884/—/04.13, June 15, 1994 (Butare prefecture).

[12]Augustin Bizimana, Ministre de la Défense au Lt. Col. e.r. Simba Aloys, no. 51/06.1.9/01, May 15, 1994 (Butare prefecture).

[13]Ibid.

[14]The inhabitants of the Butamenwa cell, Tumba sector, Ngoma commune to the Prefect, May 5, 1994 (Butare prefecture).

Many others hurried to the training because they wanted to have firearms and to know how to use them for personal or political ends as well as for fighting the "enemy." Although teaching men how to shoot was a primary goal of the program, some were also instructed in how to use spears and bows and arrows. Soon after the call for recruits went out, hundreds of men began training on the football fields and in stadiums and open spaces near government offices in the town of Butare and throughout the prefecture. In some places, one cycle of training immediately followed another. One group of trainees in town comprised about 400 men. In the end, several thousand men were trained.[15]

Local groups requested assurances that their members be allowed to participate. On April 25, Professor Vincent Ntezimana, a friend of Captain Nizeyimana, host to militia member Nkuyubwatsi, and president of the faculty association, and Professor J. Népomuscène Rutayisire, president of the security committee of Buye, asked the local commander to arrange for university faculty to learn how to shoot, and when appropriate, to provide them with arms.[16] Subsequently, the director of the Rubona agricultural research station requested that places in the self-defense training program be reserved for his staff and offered four former soldiers to be put at the disposition of the program. Students resident on the Butare campus asked to be trained to help keep "infiltrators" off the university grounds.[17]

Young men who had completed the training program took on responsibility for conducting patrols and manning the barricades. One set of five men sent to be trained from Gishamvu commune, for example, was scheduled to begin guarding the barrier at the bridge over the Mukura River as soon as they had finished their training. Those who successfully completed the training were sometimes rewarded

[15]Human Rights Watch/FIDH interview, Butare, November 1, 1995.

[16]Vincent Ntezimana and J. Népomuscène Rutayisire to Monsieur le Commandant de place de la Zone Butare-Gikongoro, April 25, 1994 (Butare prefecture).

[17]Venant Rutunga, Directeur du Centre Régional, ISAR, Station Rubona, to Monsieur le Préfet and Monsieur le Bourgmestre (undated, but received before May 26, 1994) and Anaclet Nkulikiyumukiza, Président, Pour le comité des étudiants déplacés de guerre logés à l' UNR-CUB to Monsieur le Commandant de Place, May 31, 1994 (Butare prefecture).

with a shirt or trousers from a military uniform which they wore with pride to show they ranked above ordinary citizens.[18]

At the start, few of those trained had access to firearms or grenades, which were even more highly prized than uniforms because they carried real and not just symbolic power. By mid-May, however, enough firearms had arrived in the prefecture to permit a distribution of weapons to communes thought most at risk of an actual RPF attack. On May 15, Colonel Gasake handed over fifty Kalachnikovs to Prefect Nsabimana for "civil defense" in the commune of Muyira and Colonel Simba distributed guns in various other places in the prefecture. Towards the end of May, a South African airplane delivered a large number of firearms to the Butare airport. A witness who observed the arrival of the firearms reported:

> The cases were unloaded in front of the prefecture. The Rwandans stroked them and admired them, so beautiful did they find them. All the militia members had new arms at the barriers the next day....[19]

Burgomasters in Butare for a meeting one day were issued sixty firearms at the prefecture. The sub-prefect of Nyabisindu collected weapons for the communes in his district where there were no burgomasters at the time. Burgomaster Kanyabashi, who at one point had sixty-eight firearms in his communal arsenal, handed them out to councilors of the sectors on May 28, requiring each to sign a receipt noting the registration number of the weapon. Communes in the north, like Muyira, or along the frontier, and urban agglomerations, like Butare and Nyabisindu, received the firearms first.[20] Less favored communes sought to hasten acquisition of

---

[18]J. Damascene Ruganintwali, Secrétaire, Bureau du Comité d'Auto-Défense Civile, to Bwana Burgmestri, June 20, 1994 (Butare prefecture); Human Rights Watch/FIDH interviews, Butare, December 29, 1995, January 2, 1996.

[19]Patrick de Saint-Exupery, "France-Rwanda: des mensonges d'Etat," *Le Figaro,* April 2, 1998.

[20]Bordereau de Livraison No. 002/D.C./94, signed by Colonel Gasake and Sylvain Nsabimana, May 15, 1994; Series of documents labeled "Inyandiko-mvugo yo guhererekanya imbunda," (Record of receipt of weapon), signed by Burgomaster Joseph Kanyabashi and councilors of Butare-ville, Cyarwa-Cyimana, Cyarwa-Sumo, Matyazo, Ngoma, Nkubi, Sahera, Tumba sectors of Ngoma commune, all May 28, 1994; "Verification Armament par Secteur," Commune Ngoma (undated but after May 28, 1994); Fidele

weapons by encouraging or requiring residents to contribute funds to the self-defense program so that it could buy more guns. In Ndora Commune, people were urged to drink less and give more to the "self-defense" effort while in Muyaga each family was required to contribute one hundred Rwandan francs to the program.[21]

Security Concerns Everyone

In meetings at every level of the hierarchy, administrators explained the new policy of more discreet killing. Having received the word from the interim president, the interim prime minister, and the prefect, sub-prefects transmitted the directives to burgomasters. One sub-prefect, Dominiko Ntawukuliryayo, even provided subordinates with a schedule of meetings to be held in the sectors for this purpose, complete with a list of those to be invited and the topics to be discussed. In a meeting with the burgomasters of his district, he ordered, "The people in the sectors should receive long explanations about how they should behave during these times...." stressing that "the enemy has not laid down his arms" and reminding them that they "must not lower their guard, that they should, on the contrary, reinforce their vigilance." At this, the burgomaster of Kibayi, Pierre Canisius Kajyambere reminded his colleagues to pay attention to the fields of sorghum and the bush because the "enemy" was more likely to pass that way to avoid the barriers.[22]

Burgomasters carried the word down to the population. Déogratias Hategekimana, burgomaster of Runyinya, for example, chaired the required meetings at which he ordered that everyone "must be ready at all times to fight the Inkotanyi in case they dare to appear." Each person should be "vigilant," and ready to grab his weapon. With this premise clear, he developed the same "principal ideas" that were being disseminated in Butare town and elsewhere in the prefecture: that public violence must end, that suspect persons must be delivered

---

Nzamwita, Bourgmestre wa Komine Muyaga, to Bwana S/Prefe wa S/prefegitura Gisagara, no. 1-/04/09/01/1994, May 27, 1994; Muyaga commune, "Imyanzuro y'Inama ya Komini Muyaga Yaguye yo kuwa 18/5/1994" (Butare prefecture).

[21]Burugumesitiri wa Komini Ndora, Célestin Rwankubito, "Inama y'Abaturage Ba Komini Ndora yo kuwa 7 kamena 1994;" Muyaga commune, "Imyanzuro y'Inama ya Komini Muyaga Yaguye yo kuwa 18/05/94" (Butare prefecture).

[22]Dominiko Ntawukuriryayo, Sous-Prefét, to Monsieur le Préfet de la Préfecture, no. 005/04.09.01/18, May 10, 1994; Proces-Verbal de la Réunion des Bourgmestres des Communes de la Sous-Prefecture Gisagara, tenue le 3 mai 1994 (Butare prefecture).

REPUBULIKA Y'U RWANDA
PREFEGITURA YA BUTARE

UBUTUMWA BUGAMIJE KUGARURA
UMUTEKANO MU MAKOMINI YA
PREFEGITURA YA BUTARE

                    Prefe wa Prefegitura ya Butare,
amaze kubona ko hari abantu bamwe bahohotera abandi, bakigabiza
ibyabo bitwaza ko ari ibyitso by'umwanzi wongeye kubura imirwano
muri iki gihe, arasaba abaturage bose ba Prefegitura ya Butare
ibi bikurikira :

   1) Buri wese agomba kubahiriza inshingano y'ibanze ya
      Guverinoma iriho ubu, yo kugarura amahoro n'umutekano mu
      gihugu. Ukora ibinyuranye n'iyi nshingano aba agaragaje ko
      ashyigikiye umwanzi.

   2) Buri wese agomba kwirinda rero kugira uwo ahohotera nta
      kigaragaza ko afatanyije n'inkotanyi.

   3) Abaturage bose bagomba kwirinda imvururu zose n'ubusahuzi,
      cyane cyane ubusahuzi mu mashuri, amavuriro n'ibindi bigo
      bya Leta.

   4) Ni ngombwa gushyiraho amarondo na za "barrières" bizwi,
      kandi bigenzurwa n'ubutegetsi bwa Selire, Segiteri na
      Komini muri Prefegitura yose, ku manywa kimwe na nijoro.

   5) Umuntu wese ukekwaho kuba afatanyije n'inkotanyi kimwe
      n'undi wese ufatiwe mu bikorwa by'ubusahuzi agomba guhita
      ashyikirizwa ubutegetsi bwa Komini.

                    Prefe wa Prefegitura ya Butare,
arongera kwibutsa akomeje abaturage b'iyo Prefegitura ko :

   - Mu gihe abantu basubiranamo ubwabo, bakanahugira mu bikorwa
     by'ubusahuzi, barushya Ingabo z'Igihugu zigomba kurwaña
     n'umwanzi no guhosha imvururu mu baturage;

   - Akaduruvayo kagomba guhagarara kugirango abaturage
     barusheho kongera guhumeka ituze, gushaka ikibabeshaho no
     kwitabira ibikorwa by'amajyambere.

                    BIKOREWE I BUTARE, KUWA 27/04/1994

                 PREFE WA PREFEGITURA YA BUTARE
                 NSABIMANA Sylvain

Document: (Ngoma commune) Document authorizing bearer to do patrols.

p.l 53a

REPUBLIKA Y'U RWANDA
PREFEGITURA YA BUTARE
KOMINI Y'UMUJYI YA NGOMA

No...

Icyemezo cyibakora amaronde
ICYEMEZO CYIBAKAZI .... /94 *na*
na mugi wa Butare

Jyewe KINYABASHI Joseph, Burgmestri wa Komini y'Umujyi
ya Ngoma, ndemeza ko uyu .... witwa ....
..............., ufite irangamuntu n° ....
Yihariwe gukora ironde muli quartier ya
na externe. - - - - Commune byayua.

Ahawe iyi cyemezo kugirango ashob re kuyerekana ....
ku kazi muri Komini y'Umujyi ya Ngoma. *bgoma kuwe.*
Bikorewe ; bgoma kuwe.

Bibonywe kandi byemewe   Bikorewe i Ngoma, kuwa ../../1994
na Komanda w'Ifasi   Burgmestri wa Komini y'Umujyi
BUTARE-GIKONGORO   ya Ngoma
                                        KINYABASHI Joseph

to the authorities, and that only authorized persons could bear arms, conduct searches, and guard barriers. As was ordered in Butare town, he directed that all bodies left out on the hills be buried immediately. And, as in town, he ordered that all strangers lodging in the commune be brought to authorities "so that they could make sure that there was no one collaborating with the enemy among them." In general, such persons were to be "sent back to their home communes so that their own authorities could examine their cases."[23]

Sub-prefects and burgomasters also passed on the other part of the "pacification" message: that the people, that is, the Hutu, must not "attack their brothers" and must "defend and maintain their unity at all costs."[24] The burgomaster of Runyinya, for example, warned that assailants must choose their targets carefully. He told the citizens of his commune "that it was forbidden to kill just anyone."[25]

Barriers and Patrols: Obligatory Participation

Authorities at various levels began the formal implementation of "civilian self-defense" by meeting with security committees, where they existed, or with less formal groups of councilors, political party heads, and locally important people. Together they determined the placement of barriers, the routes of patrols, and the schedules for participation.[26]

The burgomaster of Ngoma convoked such a meeting in Butare town on April 26 but then was called away for "other more urgent business" and handed the meeting over to Bernard Mutwewingabo and Jean-Bosco Nzitabakuze, both professors at the university. His readiness to leave arrangements for "self-defense"

---

[23]Déogratias Hategekimana, Burgmestri wa Komini Runyinya, to Bwana Perefe wa Perefegitura, no. 110/04.09.01/4, May 18, 1994 (Butare prefecture).

[24]Dominiko Ntawukuriryayo, Sous-Prefét, to Monsieur le Préfet de la Préfecture, no. 005/04.09.01/18, May 10, 1994; Proces-Verbal de la Réunion des Bourgmestres des Communes de la Sous-Prefecture Gisagara, tenue le 3 mai 1994 (Butare prefecture).

[25]He wrote *kwica uwo ariwe wese birabujijwe*. Had he meant to ban all killing, he would have been more likely to have said *kwica uwo birabujijwe* or *kwica ku muntu uwo ariwe wese birabujijwe*.

[26]Dominiko Ntawukuriryayo, Sous-Prefét, to Monsieur le Préfet de la Préfecture, no. 005/04.09.01/18, May 10, 1994; Proces-Verbal de la Réunion des Bourgmestres des Communes de la Sous-Prefecture Gisagara, tenue le 3 mai 1994 (Butare prefecture).

in the hands of local activists, who were known for their support of Hutu Power, recalls the interim prime minister's willingness to leave clarification of genocidal policies in the hands of political leaders at the meeting with authorities of Gitarama prefecture. The two professors explained the organization of a system of patrols and barriers set up in 1993 to deter crime in the neighborhoods of Kabutare and Buye and guided the other participants in setting up a similar system throughout the town.[27]

Some who participated later argued that the system simply continued the original effort against crime. Others depicted it as meant to detect the passage of unknown strangers, particularly RPF soldiers or agents. These objectives may have existed, but those who organized the system on April 26 clearly meant it primarily to catch any Tutsi hiding in the neighborhood. Leaders of the meeting remarked on the need to pay special attention to small woods or places with bushes as potential hiding places and they talked about asking the authorities to order a day of communal labor, umuganda, to cut the brush. They declared that even apparently "empty" houses must be searched because people might be hiding inside.

Participants at the meeting wanted to ensure that "innocent" people who happened to be staying in the neighborhood "not be mistaken for Inyenzi," an issue that was to be resolved by registering all such persons with those responsible for neighborhood security. Lists found in prefectural offices after the genocide recorded information about temporary residents, such as their names, places of origin, ages, and where they were lodged, evidence that the registration system was put in place. For Hutu, there was presumably no problem with being registered, but Tutsi faced a dilemma: if they registered, they exposed themselves to attack at the pleasure of the local security committee and if they did not, they risked immediate condemnation as Inyenzi if they were discovered.[28]

The organizers projected a need for some 300 men to fill all the posts and patrols twenty-four hours a day. They divided each cell of the sector into six or seven zones and they mapped out the routes to be taken by patrols within those zones. They prepared the schedules for work, complete with telephone numbers of those who had telephones at home.

---

[27]Ngoma commune, Butare town, "Inyandikomvugo y'inama yagizwe n'abatuye muli selire Butareville taliki ya 26/04/1994" (Butare prefecture); Human Rights Watch/FIDH interview, Brussels, December 14, 1995.

[28]Various lists of "Abacumbitsi," temporary residents (Butare prefecture).

At first it was arranged for the civilians to patrol the streets within each neighborhood with soldiers responsible for the main roads through town, but then the civilian elite prevailed upon the military to provide soldiers to accompany them within the neighborhoods as well. This presumably helped remedy the problem of too "few tools" that the organizers complained of, but the elite also asked that they be trained in the use of firearms as soon as possible. Although concerned to minimize any risk to which they might be exposed, some of the participants seemed to enjoy being soldiers in a popular army. One group described a "kind of general staff" that they had set up in their neighborhood and others insisted on the need for passwords so that strangers could not penetrate the system.[29]

It appears that many of the able-bodied adult men in Butare participated in the patrols and guarding the barriers. As one witness put it, "As for the barriers, there was nothing to discuss. They told you to do it and you had to do it."[30] Another witness from Cyarwa sector suggested that the youth were more involved than older men. He remarked:

The young men of each cell were organized into a group who were PAWA [Power]. They used the greeting "PAWA!" and you had to respond "PAWA" so they would know you were not an enemy. It was these groups who manned the barricades. When two PAWA patrols would meet, they would shout "PAWA!" to each other, so you would sometimes hear that.[31]

A few men, such as high-ranking clergy or government officials, were exempted by their status and a few others were able to refuse because they were protected by the powerful. Professor Ntezimana, for example, participated in patrols only twice and then refused to do more. He says he refused because he did not want to be involved in possible violence, but others present at the time say he refused because he was not given a firearm of his own. In any case, the organizers

---

[29]Ngoma commune, Butare town, "Inyandikomvugo y'inama yagizwe n'abatuye muli selire Butareville taliki ya 26/04/1994" (Butare prefecture); Human Rights Watch/FIDH interview, Brussels, December 14, 1995.

[30]Human Rights Watch/FIDH interview, Butare, November 1, 1995.

[31]Human Rights Watch/FIDH interviews, Butare, December 19 and 29, 1995.

probably tolerated his refusal because of his friendship with Captain Nizeyimana.[32]

One man, well-respected in his community, participated briefly in the patrols at the start and refused after that. He was regularly harrassed by others in the sector and his house was raided many times, supposedly to find Inkotanyi who were said to be hidden there. Many participated to avoid this kind of harassment and possible injury or death. Some who had Tutsi hidden in their homes had an additional motive to cooperate: they knew that refusal would arouse suspicions that would lead to a search of their houses, exposing the Tutsi to probable discovery and death. A university professor protecting Tutsi children from his wife's family took part in the barriers after his house had been attacked by soldiers and searched repeatedly by neighborhood teams. A doctor who had concealed his Tutsi neighbors in his backyard did the same. A priest, Abbé Denis Sekamana, manned the barrier in front of the African Catechism Institute (Institut Africain Catéchique, ICA) every day from April 28 to June 28. He had hidden seven Tutsi, two of them wounded, in his house.[33] Intellectual and moral leaders of the community who decided to participate under such circumstances no doubt increased the security of those whom they were protecting but did so at the price of contributing to the legitimacy of the genocidal system.[34]

Authorities outside of town generally settled for simpler and less bureaucratic arrangements for their patrols and barriers. But some, like the burgomaster of Runyinya, seem to have followed the model of the urban system. He too divided the cells into zones based on the number of available men, all of whom were to be properly registered for duty. Each team was to choose its own head who would receive written authorization from the burgomaster to direct the group. The burgomaster recommended also that residents contribute to the purchase of

---

[32]Human Rights Watch/FIDH interviews, Butare, July 6, December 19 and 29, 1995; Police Judiciaire près le Parquet du Procureur du Roi de Bruxelles, Section Criminelle, Dossier 37/95, P.V. unnumbered, April 27, 1995.

[33]At the time of our investigation Abbe Sekamana had not been formally charged with killing anyone, although he admitted to having seen soldiers attack a young man. Some accuse him of involvement in the death of Malik Karenzi, an allegation which we have not investigated. One witness, not questioned specifically about the priest, spontaneously offered the information that Sekamana protected people from harm at his barrier. Human Rights Watch/FIDH interview, Butare, October 29, 1995.

[34]Human Rights Watch/FIDH interviews, Butare, February 25, July 6, October 27, 1995; March 5, 1996.

Document: (Ndora commune) Order from sub-prefect to hold security meetings (including political party representatives), to establish patrols, and to keep track of any strangers.

/ R.A /

REPUBLIKA Y&U RWANDA
PREFEGITUKA YA BUTARE
S/PREFEGITURA GISAGARA.-

Gisagara, ku we 15 AVR. 1994
N° 065 /04.09.01/4

6

Bwana Burugumesitiri wa Komini
N D O R A.-

Bwana Burugumesitiri,

Nk'uko ahandi babikoze, ndagusaba ko :
wateranya vuba inama y'Umutekano irimo n'Abanyamashyaka
mukiga uko amarondo yajyaho vuba muri za nyumbakumi
n'uburyo yakora.

Icy'ingenzi ni ukumenya umuntu wese
winjiye muri izo ngo atahasanzwe.

S/PREFE WA S/PREFEGITURA GISAGARA
NTAWUKURIKIYIMANA Dominiko.

BIMENYESHEJWE:
Bwana Prefe wa Prefegitura
BUTARE.-

Document: (Ndora commune) Order to councilors to draw up lists of any strangers who have taken refuge in their sectors.

REPUBLIQUE RWANDAISE

Préfecture de Butare
Commune de Ndora

Ndora, le........18/04/1994.............

N°........095/04.09.01/7.....................

Objet: Umwirondoro w'abahungira ku
macuti yabo y'abanye—Ndora .

Bwana Conseiller wa Segiteri (Bose) .

Bwana Konseye ,

Nk'uko byemejwe mu nama y'umutekano
yabaye kuwa 17 Mata 1994 , ukimara kubona uru rwandiko , usabwe guhita ukora
umwirondoro w'abantu bose baba baraje bahungira ku baturage bo muri Segiteri
uyobora .

Uwo mwirondoro ugomba kugaragaza
izina , imyaka , igitsina , Selire , Segiteri Komini bakomokamo .

Birihutirwa !

Bourgmestre wa Komini NDORA
RWANKUBITO P. Célestin

BIMENYESHEJWE :

υ- Bwana Perefe wa Perefegitura
B U T A R E .

- Bwana Su-Perefe wa Su-Perefegitura
G I S A G A R A .

"communication equipment," "especially whistles," that could be used by the heads of the various "mobile alert squads."[35]

Security Committees

Security committees had existed at communal as well as prefectural level since 1990, but many were no longer functioning by 1994. In mid-April, Mugusa commune was one of the first to revive its security committee. Perhaps foreseeing the kinds of duties that would be involved, one person who had been part of the committee previously now asked how he could resign his position. In other communes, already existing committees started to work once more or new ones were set up, as in Nyakizu where the communal council appointed to it men who had led the first phase of the genocide and who supported the burgomaster. (See chapter ten.) By early May, Burgomaster Kanyabashi was directing the establishment of security committees at the sectoral level in Ngoma commune. Elsewhere in the prefecture, burgomasters and councilors set up sectoral committees during the third and last weeks of the month. Eventually, the more zealous administrators, like the sub-prefect of Gisagara, would urge the formation of such committees down to the level of the "sub-cell" or zone. He suggested calling the committees at communal level the "Etat-Major" or general staff of the commune, a phrase that was already in use in the town of Butare. As the phrase suggests, the security committees would in some places merge into the "civilian self-defense" committees specified for each administrative level in the plan issued by national authorities at the end of May.[36]

Some at least of the committees were elected by the local population but the bodies were not meant to be representative of public opinion so much as to provide administrative and political authorities with one more channel to implement the policies of the interim government. The committees had no power beyond

---

[35]Déogratias Hategekimana, Burgmestri wa Komini Runyinya, to Bwana Perefe wa Perefegitura, no. 110/04.09.01/4, May 18, 1994 (Butare prefecture).

[36][Dominiko Ntawukuriryayo, S/Prefe wa S/Prefegitura Gisagara] to Bwana Burgumestri, no. 006/04.01.02, May 14, 1994 and Dominiko Ntawukuriryayo, S/Prefe wa S/Prefegitura Gisagara, to Bwana Prefe wa Prefegitura, no. 007/04.09.01, May 28, 1994; Mugusa commune, "Inyandiko-mvugo y'inama z'umutekano za Komini Mugusa zateranye mu matariki ya 13 na 14 mata;" Joseph Kanyabashi, Burgmestri wa Komini y'Umujyi ya Ngoma, to Bwana Konseye wa Segiteri (Bose), no. 198/04.09.01, May 10, 1994 (Butare prefecture).

community opinion to enforce their decisions.[37] The meetings establishing the security committees and often the committees themselves incorporated leaders of the political parties (or, as Burgomaster Kanyabashi specified, of those parties now participating in the government) as well as other important people in the community. In Huye, for example, at meetings to set up the security committees, Rekeraho, representing MDR-Power and Joseph Muganga for the MRND spoke as well as the burgomaster. According to Burgomaster Ruremesha:

> Each [speaker] tried to make the people understand that anyone who does not follow the directives of the prime minister and of the prefect of the prefecture of Butare to the letter will have shown that he is an enemy and he will be prosecuted by the authorities after the security committee in the sector has examined his case.[38]

Anyone, for example, who did not do patrols was an enemy. The burgomaster recommended that committees should meet every Saturday with all the people of the sector to make them understand how they must support the "government of national salvation" (Abatabazi).[39]

Most security committees became active only after the period of massive slaughter had ended and did not plan or direct large-scale attacks. Instead they focused on tracking down the remaining Tutsi by gathering information, by searching houses, and by clearing the brush where they hid, as described below.

The committees were also meant to stop or at least reduce conflict among Hutu. The councilor of Cyarwa-Sumo explained that the committee was to help him investigate the "wrongdoings of troublemakers," among which he cited killing "innocent" people. He warned that anyone caught committing such abuses in the future would be severely punished.[40] In the adjacent sector of Cyarwa-Cyimana, the councilor and others went even further in condemning those who "liberate"

---

[37]Froduald Nsabimana, Umwanditsi, "Inyandiko Mvugo y'Inama Rusange ya Secteur Cyimana," May 15, 1994 (Butare prefecture).

[38]Jonathas Ruremesha, Bourgmestre wa Komini Huye, to Bwana Prefe, Huye, May 19, 1994 (Butare prefecture).

[39]Ibid.

[40]Nicodeme Hategikimana (sic), Conseiller, "Inama y'umutekano y'abaturage ba secteur Cyarwa-Sumo yateranye le 12 gicurasi 1994" (Butare prefecture).

Document: (Ngoma commune) Order to create security committees in each sector with the help of representatives of political parties that are participating in the government. Officers are to be elected for each committee, except for the president, who is to be the councilor.

REPUBLIKA Y'U RWANDA
PREFEGITURA YA BUTARE
KOMINI Y'UMUJYI YA NGOMA

Ngoma, kuwa 10/05/1994
N° 146 /04.09.01

Bwana Konseye wa Segiteri (BOSE)
KOMINI Y'UMUJYI YA NGOMA

Impamvu : Gushyiraho inzego
z'umutekano

Bwana Konseye,

Kubera ibibazo by'umutekano bigenda bifata indi ntera, nagirango mbasabe ko muri buri Segiteri hashyirwaho akanama ka Segiteri gashinzwe umutekano.

Kugirango uwo mutekano uzagere ku baturage bose, musabwe kwifashisha abahagarariye amashyaka agize Guvernoma, kandi muri buri Selire hagatoranywamo abagabo b'inyangamugayo batatu (3). Abo bose bazaba baturutse mu maselire yose bakazitoramo biro igizwe na Perezida, Visi-Perezida wa mbere, Visi-Perezida wa Kabili, umwanditsi n'umubitsi.

Icyitonderwa : Perezida w'ako kanama ntatorwa, agomba kuba ari Konseye, abandi nibo batorwa.
Segiteri Matyazo, Ngoma na Tumba ntibarebwa n'uru rwandiko kubera ko izo Komite zashyizweho mu minsi ishize.

Ndasaba abajyanama h'andi masegiteri asigaye kwihutira gushyiraho izo Komite bakamenyesha amazina y'abazigize.

Ikindi nsaba abajyanama, nuko haramutse hari abagize Komite za Selire babuze, mwabasimbuza abo bakurikiranaga mu majwi.

Birihutirwa.

Burgmestri wa Komini y'Umujyi
ya Ngoma
KANYABASHI Joseph

Bimenyeshejwe :
- Bwana Perefe wa Perefegitura
  BUTARE
- Bwana Komanda w'Ifasi
  BUTARE-GIKONGORO

(*kubohoza*) Hutu and their property, those who vandalize crops that are not yet ripe, and those who misbehave at the barriers. The councilor declared:

> It is becoming absolutely necessary to put a security committee in place that has the power to punish these terrorists; these abuses are beginning to go really beyond all bounds.[41]

Apparently oblivious to just how far beyond all bounds the abuses had already gone, he threatened that those guilty of such behavior risked their lives by continuing.[42]

Virtually all the committees helped execute the genocidal campaign as was intended. But in communities where the violence had begun to threaten Hutu also, some citizens may have understood that disregard for the lives of Tutsi led to disregard for the lives of Hutu and consequently tried to use the committees to halt all killings. Such appears to have been the case in Ngoma sector of Ngoma commune. Just as the presence of persons opposed to killing resulted in some barriers being "good" (see chapter five), similarly the presence of such people on security committees may have limited killings of Tutsi in some neighborhoods.

Most Tutsi residents of Ngoma sector had already been slain before the security committees were set up in May, but some survivors were hidden in a number of places, especially with members of the Muslim community. When Hutu residents of Ngoma came together to choose their security committee, they declared that they wanted an end to murder, rape and pillage. While some wanted to end such abuses against Hutu, others wanted also to protect the few remaining Tutsi.[43] The results of the election reflected these different wishes. Several locally powerful men who had been active in killing Tutsi, like Jacques Habimana and Edouard Niyitegeka, both associated with SORWAL and both involved in the

---

[41]Ngoma commune, Cyarwa-Cyimana sector, "Inyandiko Mvugo y'Inama y'Umutekano: Cyarwa Cyimana," May 13, 1994 (Butare prefecture).

[42]Froduald Nsabimana, Umwanditsi, "Inyandiko Mvugo y'Inama Rusange ya Secteur Cyimana," May 15, 1994 (Butare prefecture).

[43]République Rwandaise, Parquet de la République, P.V. No. 0304 and Ngoma commune, "Inyandiko Mvugo y'Inama Bourgmestre wa Commune y'Umujyi ya Ngoma Yagiranye na Commission y'Umutekano ya Secteur Ngoma"; Human Rights Watch/FIDH interview, Brussels, by telephone, January 19, 1998.

assault on Ngoma church, got themselves elected, but the community also chose Laurien Ntezimana, a Catholic lay leader known for protecting Tutsi.[44]

Ntezimana and Théophile Batware, a judicial police inspector, were only two of the nine committee members, but they were able to block numerous searches proposed by the others because the committee was supposed to act by consensus only. They reportedly exploited the new policy requiring "proof" of RPF connections before acting and were thus able to prevent the discovery and further killing of the Tutsi in their sector. Data on property left vacant by Tutsi owners suggests that, for whatever reason, a far lower percentage of Tutsi were killed in Ngoma sector than in other sectors of the commune (see below).[45]

The councilor of Ngoma sector, Said Munyankumburwa, had tried to defend Tutsi early in the genocide. He had been threatened and fled, but later returned to resume his post. He then became involved in pillaging with soldiers and eventually disputed the division of the loot with them. Soon after the committee was set up, a soldier named Gatwaza[46] abducted the councilor and another person from a meeting. Ntezimana telephoned Burgomaster Kanyabashi for help, but the soldiers summoned by the burgomaster arrived half an hour later, too late to save Said. With the backing of Gatwaza, Habimana of the security committee became the new councilor, an arrangement at least nominally approved by the burgomaster.[47]

Even with Habimana in charge of the sector, however, there was reportedly only one more killing in Ngoma through July. A young man known as Kivenge was murdered, supposedly by Habimana and Niyitegeka who wanted to pillage a house that he was occupying. Given that Kivenge was not in hiding at the time, he was presumably Hutu. Habimana and Niyitegeka both implicated soldiers, particularly a Corporal Uwamahoro, in the crime. Batware, acting as judicial police

---

[44]Human Rights Watch/FIDH interviews, Butare, February 9, 1995; Brussels, by telephone, January 19 and 29, 1998; République Rwandaise, Parquet de la République, P.V. no. 0117; Production Alter ciné, "Chronique d'un génocide annoncé."

[45]Human Rights Watch/FIDH interviews, Brussels, by telephone, January 29 and February 15, 1998; Rome, by telephone, February 4, 1998.

[46]Probably the same one who launched the slaughter at the Mbazi stadium. See above.

[47]République Rwandaise, Parquet de la République, P.V. No. 0304; Human Rights Watch/FIDH interviews, Butare, February 9, 1995; Brussels, by telephone, January 19 and 29, 1998; Production Alter ciné, "Chronique d'un génocide annoncé."

inspector, had Habimana and Niyitegeka arrested but they spent only one night in jail before soldiers forced their release. Kivenge's family was so outraged at this that they complained to the prosecutor that ordinarily someone who killed even a chicken would spend longer than one night in jail.[48] The murders of Said and Kivenge, like some of Ntaganzwa's murders in Nyakizu, showed that those who killed Tutsi with impunity might then go on to killing Hutu. Those who wanted the security committee to protect Tutsi as well as Hutu had perhaps come to that realization.

The Murders in May

While still talking of "pacification," some Butare authorities joined in the renewed attack on Tutsi called for by RTLM in the last days of April.[49] At its May 6 meeting, the prefectural security committee decided to put up more barriers for "pacification," or, as a parenthetical note made clear, to catch "persons who have disappeared without our knowledge." Like the Ngoma sector committee, they presented themselves as following the pacification directives to seize only proven members of the RPF, but their standards of proof were low. They identified five "members of the RPF who are still in town and who should be apprehended." They included Abbé Furaha, Modeste, Kayitakire, J.B. Habyalimana, and Professor Alexis. Abbé Justin Furaha was a priest at the parish of Save, the oldest parish in Rwanda, just north of Butare. Modeste was almost certainly the Abbé Modeste Mungwarareba, former head of Karubanda seminary, who was working in the reconciliation program with Laurien Ntezimana. J.B. Habyalimana was the former prefect; next to his name was the note "no one knows where he is." Kayitakire and Professor Alexis were not otherwise identified. Next to Abbé Furaha's name was the notation, 2,000,000 frw. (about U.S.$11,000). In a different hand was added the explanation that this was the reward to be delivered to those who provided information leading to his capture.[50]

---

[48]République Rwandaise, MINADEF, Gendarmerie Nationale, Brigade de Butare, Projustia [no number], P.V. d'Interrogatoire du Prévenu Niyitegeka Edouard, May 18, 1994 et Projustia no. 195, P.V. d'Interrogatoire du Prévenu Habimana Jacques; J. Chrysostome Ndakaza to Bwana Procureur wa Republika i Butare, June 3, 1994 (Butare prefecture).

[49]Human Rights Watch interview, Kigali, by telephone, April 29, 1994.

[50]If in fact meant to represent a reward, the sum may have been intended for the capture of any or all of the group listed. Two million francs seems too large an amount to have been intended for information about just one of those sought. The note in the different

Within three days, the first of the five, Abbé Furaha, had been caught and imprisoned, as had Abbé Ngoga of Kibeho. Ngoga was not on the Butare prefecture list, but he was the object of a reward posted in his home prefecture of Gikongoro, by sub-prefect Biniga and the head of the Mata tea plantation: Ngoga had been recognized and captured at Ngoma church. In accord with the new emphasis on following orderly procedures the prosecutor Mathias Bushishi questioned them and confirmed their detention.[51] Ten days later, on May 20, Abbé Ngoga and Abbé Mungwarareba were both attacked on RTLM by Valérie Bemeriki. In a diatribe against eighty-eight Tutsi who were ready "to commit the irreparable," that is, kill Hutu, she accused Abbé Ngoga of having fired on Hutu when Kibeho church was being attacked and she charged Abbé Mungwarareba with having hidden guns and ammunition in the sacristy of a church. She asserted that priests distributed guns to displaced persons who had taken refuge in churches. Thus armed, she claimed, the Tutsi would make sorties out of churches to liquidate Hutu and then retreat back into the churches, "daring to profane the dwelling of the Lord."[52]

Bemeriki's attack on the clergy suggests that national authorities had decided to eliminate those, like clergy, who had previously been protected by their status in the community just as they were now determined to eliminate women and children, earlier protected by their sex or age. Assailants killed three religious brothers in Butare on May 8, along with two women and perhaps others who had taken shelter with them. Three priests who had been confined in the Butare prison were sent home to Gikongoro to be killed on May 13. The parish priest of Cyahinda was slain on May 21 in Nyakizu. Rather than execute priests who were known to be in their custody, authorities released Abbé Ngoga and Abbé Furaha, along with Abbé Firmin Butera of Higiro parish, on May 31, 1994. They were set upon by assailants and killed just after leaving the prison.[53]

---

script may have been added some time after the rest of the entry was written.

[51]Musoni, "Holocauste noir," pp. 86-7.

[52]Chrétien, *Rwanda, les médias*, pp. 327-28.

[53]In a number of cases where authorities did not want to be blamed for murder, they released the persons in their charge to near immediate assault and death. République Rwandaise, Parquet de la République, P.V. no. 117; Guy Theunis, "Liste des prêtres, religieux, religieuses et laïcs consacrés tués au Rwanda," *Dialogue*, no. 177, August-September 1994, pp. 123, 125. Militia killed clergy and one nun at Kabgayi on May 24. (See

Document: (Butare prefecture) Notes of Security Council meeting, May 6, 1994 listing "RPF" in town who must be caught, including the former prefect.

Réunion Conseil Sécurité (6.5.94)

1- Situation générale de sécurité (couvre-feu : 18h à 6h)
2- Contacts avec Gouverneur Kayanza
3- Divers :
  - Radio S/T Usiagara
  - Enquêtes judiciaires, Nkubi
  - Maisons abandonnées
  - Titres de voyage vers l'Etranger
  - Sécurité Kanyam-Bas
  - Abanyeshuri bifuza gusubira iwabo
  - Autorisations de circuler
  - Cotisation pour nourrir les recrues
  - ~~Nyakunikunikunikunikunika~~
  - Barrages sur la route Butare - Abanyam

- - - - - - -

I - Barrages aishyirwaho
  - Tacification (personnes disparues à notre insu)
  - Abajewa babemora amuzu, gusaka (reconnaissance)
    Ls arrêter Mafene, Richard, Sekaganda momenta-
    nément
- Cas isolés d'assassinat :
    - Mbonyubwabo Camille et son fils Usarangwa Bon.
    - Abashikari benshi mu mugi (invalides + déserteurs)
      = peloton PM en vigilance =
    - Militaires travaillant de mèche avec les bandits civils
    - Aba FPR bakiri mu mugi bagomba gufatwa
      (- Abbé Fneaha : 2.000.000Frs) kufumunta vive...
      - Modeste
      - Kayitakire
      - Habyarimana J.B. → ngo ntibazi aho aba
      - Professeur - ... Alexis
  - Nyabisindu, Mujejende < Gebahunga
▶ Kivol avec violence no kwiba abayoze b'abandi (kuandi-
  kina ba Burugumestiri kuri iryo kibaro 33 Instituti
  datant des années 63/64 sur ibintu betimukanwa).
  Imyaka hafatwa icyemezo cyo kuyasarurira hamwe
  bakagira iryo bayagenera (Kgmbe ngo barata imigende.
  Gnid?).

a:

Abbé Mungwarareba was more fortunate. On April 20, he had hidden unnoticed in the sacristry of the cathedral, where he spent the next nine days, living from two packets of communion wafers and two buckets of water. When these supplies were exhausted, he had managed to attract the attention of nuns passing the window, and had them bring him food. On April 30, the nuns informed him that military authorities were insisting that the bishop say mass in the cathedral the next day to show that "life was continuing as normal." If a mass were to be said, the sacristry would be opened, so Abbé Mungwarareba moved first to the convent, then back to a nearby office where he sat for two days squeezed against a wall between two windows so that he could not be seen from the outside. He then moved to his own office, where he lay under a table, concealed from any passersby who might look in the window. On May 13, he heard a group searching the church compound and decided that he must leave. That night, he moved to a convent in another part of Butare, where he remained hidden until the arrival of French troops in early July.[54]

Jean-Baptiste Habyalimana evaded capture in the weeks after his removal from office, hiding, some said, with the bishop of Butare at one time, with his grandmother at Save at another. According to one witness, Pauline Nyiramasuhuko and Straton Nsabumukunzi were the most determined to catch the former prefect. A week or so after the prefectural security committee pushed for new efforts to locate Habyalimana, he was captured at his home reportedly by Jean-Baptiste Ruzindaza, the president of the Tribunal de Première Instance, and one of the local leaders of "civilian self-defense." Habyalimana was imprisoned in the small, dark lock-up next to the prefecture building where he had once had his office. Prefect Nsabimana apparently knew he was there, but did not intervene to save him. After a brief period, Habyalimana was sent to the headquarters of the national government in Gitarama, where he was executed. In late May and June, his residence looked unoccupied, with its grass uncut, but Habyalimana's wife and two daughters continued living there until near the end of June. At one point the prosecutor, Bushishi, took charge of the widow and her little girls, but at another time, it seems that the sub-prefect Faustin Rutayisire was responsible for her. She appealed to the prefect to help her return to Ndora, her commune of origin, but

---

chapter six.)

[54]Human Rights Watch/FIDH interview, Butare, April 12, 1995.

before she could leave, she and her daughters were killed by soldiers from the ESO.[55]

The fourth of the five named in the list, a man named Kayitakire, was apparently the businessman and former teacher Athanase Kayitakire. At first hidden by Gakwaya, the businessman involved in "civilian self-defense," Kayitakire was discovered in early May. Like the three priests mentioned above, he and his wife were imprisoned briefly and then released only to be murdered immediately after. Shalom and his militia are said to have killed them on the road near the cathedral. We have been unable to identify definitively Professor Alexis, but he may have been a teacher at the Groupe Scolaire.[56]

As at the summit of the prefecture, so too at the lower levels of sector and cell, officials and security committees intensified efforts to locate Tutsi in early and mid-May. In Matyazo, the councilor, soldiers, and local people raided the house of Froduald Gatabazi and found four Tutsi, all children of a man named Sugira, and two cattle also belonging to Sugira. A participant in the raid reported that the people took away the cattle, slaughtered, and ate them. He says nothing about what they did to the Tutsi.[57] On May 7 in the commune of Mbazi, cell head Savien Ntivuguruzwa and his committee decided to destroy the house of an elderly Hutu woman, Judith Mukandabalinze, because she was said to be hiding her Tutsi grandsons. Some seventy-five men carried out the order immediately, but the targeted Tutsi escaped.[58]

In the effort to carry the genocide to completion, authorities once again warned against helping Tutsi. On May 12, for example, the security committee for Cyarwa-Cyimana directed, "People who had hidden others should bring them out, so that we can all do patrols together as well as the other activities of every day." Then, showing that the order was not motivated by a simple desire to have everyone share

---

[55]Human Rights Watch/FIDH interview, Nairobi, by telephone, March 25, 1996.

[56]Human Rights Watch/FIDH interview, by telephone, February 4, 1998; Pie-Joseph Ngilimana, "Vision Synoptique des Massacres à Butare à partir du 7 avril 1994," typescript, August 19, 1994.

[57]Enias Semashinge Ntamushobora, to Bwana Conseiller wa Segiteri ya Matyazo, May 16, 1994 (Butare prefecture).

[58]République Rwandaise, Ministère de la Défense, Gendarmerie Nationale, Groupement Butare, Pro Justitia/Procès-Verbaux de Renseignement of Emmanuel Gakuru and Sikubwabo, May 17, 1994 (Butare prefecture).

in the same activities, they went on to warn, "Those who are caught while they are still in hiding will be considered as enemies."[59]

When the killing began in Butare town, Vincent Kageruka had tried to flee to Burundi but had been driven back to his Tumba neighborhood, where he had hidden in a hole from late April until May 14. One of those who found him that day seemed inclined to try to save him and two others were willing to exchange his life for money, but the news of his discovery spread rapidly, making any prospect of help—paid or otherwise—impossible. A large crowd came to his house, shouting "Power," "Power." Calling him the "king of Tumba," they congratulated themselves on having captured one of the few remaining educated Tutsi of the sector. Jailed with ten others, first in the sector under the control of Dr. Munyemana and later at the prefectural lock-up, Kageruka escaped on May 24 when the ten others were taken off to be killed.[60]

As in Nyakizu and elsewhere in the country, assailants multiplied attacks against Tutsi women beginning in mid-May. They tracked them down in places around Butare town like Buye, Tumba, and Matyazo and in communes as far afield as Ntyazo and Ndora. In some communes, burgomasters were still instructing assailants to leave in peace Tutsi women who were married to Hutu men. The burgomaster of Huye declared: "anyone who attacks these women does it as a deliberate provocation because the husband will certainly take vengeance."[61] Those with less formal liaisons with Hutu, including those taken for sexual service during the genocide, however, were no longer protected and many of those women were killed at this time. Some women avoided death by formalizing their relationships with Hutu men. At such a marriage ceremony, the Mbazi burgomaster reportedly made clear that becoming the wife of a Hutu male was the only possible avenue to safety for the Tutsi women before him. One woman who felt obliged to enter into such a marriage remembers him saying:

---

[59]Ngoma commune, Cyarwa-Cyimana sector, "Inyandiko mvugo y'Inama y'umutekano: Cyarwa Cyimana," May 13, 1994 (Butare prefecture).

[60]Human Rights Watch/FIDH interview, October 25, 1995.

[61]Jonathas Ruremesha, Bourgmestre wa Komini Huye, to Bwana Perefe, May 19, 1994 (Butare prefecture).

Now that you are married to Hutu, you have the right to live and to enjoy the country. However, you must always be aware that it is on account of your Hutu husbands that you are alive.[62]

As with women, so too with children. Only those children with an acknowledged Hutu protector might hope—even if only temporarily—for safety. On May 31, a person of Ndora commune asked Sub-prefect Ntawukuliryayo what should be done with children left by the people who had gone away, that is, Tutsi children. The sub-prefect answered that they should all be registered with the authorities. This measure, innocuous on its face, facilitated the elimination of these children whenever the authorities so chose.[63]

Protection
Given and Refused
In the early days of May the push to eliminate remaining Tutsi brought new attention to locations where the presence of Tutsi had been thus far tolerated. In the commune of Shyanda, the extensive Catholic church compound of Save had been attacked and pillaged in late April. Some of the sisters of the Benebikira congregation had left the convent and sought to hide among the local population. Prefect Nsabimana reportedly intervened to have the sisters recalled to the convent and to have them protected by local police. In the first days of May, either the sisters or Nsabimana himself felt the need for a greater protection. Sister Felicienne Uzarama prepared a list of 146 persons, some of them Tutsi, who were lodged in the Benebikira buildings. Included in the group were dozens of sisters who had fled from congregations throughout the region and more than a dozen lay workers and temporary residents. Reportedly with Nsabimana's support, the sisters obtained permission from Lieutenant Colonel Muvunyi for these persons to stay in the convent. With a military guard provided by Muvunyi, the sisters, lay workers, and temporary residents remained safe until July.[64]

---

[62]African Rights, *Witness to Genocide,* issue 7, September 1997, p. 57.

[63]Célestin Rwankubito, Burugumesitiri wa Komini Ndora, "Inyandiko-Mvugo y'Inama y'Abaturage B'Amasegiteri Gisagara, Mukande, Ndora na Cyamukuza yo kuwa 31 Gicurasi 1994" (Butare prefecture).

[64]List entitled "Benebikira Maison-Mère Save" with note of authorisation signed by Lieutenant Colonel Muvunyi, dated May 6, 1994 (Butare prefecture); Nsabimana, "The Truth About the Massacres in Butare."

de l'annonciation
B.P232 Butare

Sovu le 5/05/1994

Impamvu:kwitabaza ubutegetsi

Bwana Burugumesitiri wa
Komini Huye
BUTARE

A traiter par ....

Date entrée **09 MAI 1994**
N° Classement : **1650/04.09.01**

Bwana Burugumesitiri

Muri ibi byumweru bishize, hari abantu bagiye baza muri Monastère y'i Sovu ku buryo busanzwe ari abashyitsi bahumura iminsi akenshi iturenga icyumweru,abenshi bari muri za mission abandi baje kuruhuka cyangwa gusenga.

Aho intambara yuburiye igatera igihugu cyose,hari abandi bagiye baza ku buryo butunguranye,bakaba bose bigundiriza kuba hano kandi nta buryo na bukeya dufite bwo kubatunga dans l'illégalité. Nkaba maze iminsi narabasabye ko ubutegetsi bwa Komini bwaza bukabaha itegeko ryo gusubira iwabo,cyangwa ahandi bashaka kuba, kuko hano muri Monastère nta buryo na bukeya tugifite.

NDABASABA NKOMEJE BWANA Burugumesitiri ko mwadufasha ntibirenze taliki ya 6/05/1994 ibyo bitarangiye,kugitango imiri mo Monasiteri isanzwe ikora iyikomeze nta mitima ihaguze.

Tubaragije Imana mu musengesho.

Umukuru w'urugo
Soeur Gertrude Consolata
Mukangango

Copie pour information

Monsieur le Préfet de
Préfecture BUTARE

Monsieur le Commandant de
Place BUTARE

A similar situation at Sovu in Huye commune had a tragically different outcome, perhaps because local leaders—religious, administrative, or political—were less courageous, perhaps because assailants were more ruthless. The Benedictine sisters at the Sovu convent had been sheltering some sixty persons since mid-April. On April 17 and 18, women in the area had taken refuge in the Sovu health center, while men had stayed on the hills to fight off attackers. On April 20, when attacks led by Emmanuel Rekeraho became too strong, the men also retreated to the health center. The next day, Rekeraho and other MDR-Power activists led an assault on the health center which caused many Tutsi to flee to the convent itself. There, despite locked gates, they managed to force their way in. The mother superior, Sister Gertrude Consolata Mukangango, supposedly feared that the convent would be attacked if the Tutsi remained and got the help of communal police and six soldiers to force most of them to leave. Many of those expelled returned to the health center and were slain on April 22 and 23. Tutsi related to members of the congregation and some others had been permited to stay at the convent and constituted the group, largely women, children, and the elderly who were still there in early May.[65]

On May 5, Sister Gertrude wrote the burgomaster declaring that the convent had no way to keep "illegal visitors." She complained that she had asked the communal authorities to come several days before to order them out, either to go home or somewhere else. She continued:

I urgently ask your cooperation, Mr. Burgomaster, to see that these people are gone by May 6 at the latest, so that the convent can again take up its usual activities without anxiety.[66]

On May 6, after morning prayers, Sister Gertrude reportedly ordered all sisters who were protecting displaced persons in the convent to put them out immediately. She talked of the need to protect the convent and she warned that she would force the

---

[65]Survivors have accused Sister Julienne Kizito of having been present at the attack on April 23, but she may have fled with other sisters to Ngoma church, Butare between April 22 and 24. The question needs further research. African Rights, *Rwanda, Not so Innocent*, pp. 161-81; Human Rights Watch/FIDH interviews, Butare, March 26, 1996 and by telephone, Rome February 4, 1998; République Rwandaise, Parquet de la République, P.V. no. 0117.

[66]Soeur Gertrude Consolate Mukangango to Bwana Burugumesitiri wa Komini Huye, May 5, 1994 (Butare prefecture).

departure of any who did not go of their own accord. That afternoon she went to get the burgomaster, who came in his own vehicle with communal police. The police forced the displaced persons to leave the convent, reportedly stealing from them in the process. Of those expelled, many were killed, either immediately or en route to their homes. The burgomaster took away in his vehicle those who came from outside the immediate region. It is not known if they were killed in Huye or if they were sent to their home communes "so that their own authorities could examine their cases," as the administrators liked to say.[67]

Some time later, a Benedictine sister defended Sister Gertrude, saying she had tried without success to buy protection for the Tutsi who were being expelled. She stated that Sister Gertrude had been told by the burgomaster and "another important person" that the Tutsi must leave or that everyone—including Tutsi members of the congregation—might be killed.[68] The tone of the letter to the burgomaster, however, suggests that it was Sister Gertrude who took the initiative, although it is not impossible that she acted under pressure either from "another important person" or from local assailants, such as Rekeraho.

Sister Gertrude was only one of several religious to give up Tutsi to the killers. In addition to the clergy who permitted militia to take Tutsi from church complexes in Kigali and Kabgayi, a European brother in Butare allowed an armed group to take away the Rwandan brothers from his congregation on April 22. Rekeraho, who was leading the crowd, claimed that the brothers had been summoned to see a military officer. As the assailants led them away, the European brother expressed the hope that none would be killed. The assailants escorted the eight or nine brothers a short distance down a path. There they asked for their identity cards and separated the Hutu from the Tutsi.[69] According to a witness, Rekeraho accused the two Tutsi of being Inkotanyi and directed his armed followers, "Go on, get rid of that filth for me." And they did.[70]

---

[67] African Rights, *Rwanda, Not so Innocent*, p. 185.

[68] Ibid., p. 187-88.

[69] Church sources identify the two as Brothers Gaëtan Gatera and Antoine Rutagengwa, but a local witness referred to one of the two as Brother Innocent. Theunis, "Liste des prêtres," p. 131.

[70] Human Rights Watch/FIDH interview, Brussels, December 18, 1995.

Others, whether Rwandan or foreign, clergy or lay people, soldiers or civilians refused protection to Tutsi.[71] Some occasionally tried to mitigate the consequences of the refusal by finding another form of help for them. Those who yielded the Tutsi to murderers sometimes express regret for the decision but say it was necessary to save their own lives or those of others. These claims should not be rejected out of hand, but for some they served only to cover willing participation in the genocide.

Partial Protection: The Group at the Prefecture

From the start of violence elsewhere in the prefecture, some Tutsi had sought protection at prefectural offices in town. Many of the men in that group had been removed by soldiers on April 19, as mentioned above. The rest stayed and grew in number in the following days, particularly after Tutsi were forced out of the hospital in the first days of May. Some displaced Hutu or street children also moved in and out of the crowd, whenever they saw a chance to find food or protection close to the government building.

When Tutsi arrived from the hospital, Interahamwe from various communes were at the prefecture waiting to identify them and escort them back home. On several subsequent days, burgomasters like Ruremesha of Huye came to pick up residents of their communes, many of whom were killed when they returned home. But the effort to send the Tutsi home to be "taken care of" in their own communes was only partially successful. On the one hand, some Tutsi evaded capture when authorities arrived to look for them. On the other, some burgomasters began refusing to come to collect the Tutsi from their communes, asserting that they would be killed if brought home. Some may have been motivated by a desire to save lives, believing the Tutsi safer in front of the prefecture than out on the hills. Others had perhaps tired of the genocide campaign and simply did not want to bother with the additional work of collecting, killing, and burying these Tutsi who were already outside the limits of their territorial responsibility.[72]

During the days when the prefectural offices were open, the group was relatively safe. But at night and during week-ends, soldiers and militia arrived to take men to be killed and women to be raped and killed. In some cases, the crimes

---

[71]Beginning, of course, with the UNAMIR forces.

[72]Human Rights Watch/FIDH interviews, Butare, November 9, 1995; Kigali, January 19, 1996; Nairobi, by telephone, April 3, 1996; Nsabimana, "The Truth About the Massacres in Butare."

were committed behind the prefectural building and men from the group were called to bury the bodies the next day before the offices opened. In other cases, the Tutsi were taken away in a van or pickup truck, usually never to be seen again. One woman, taken to be killed, escaped death by agreeing to sexual servitude. She reported that the killings were carried out in the valley of Rwabayanga, behind the ESO. A number of witnesses have testified that Shalom led the operations to seize people at the prefecture and raped women taken from the crowd there. His mother, the minister Nyiramasuhuko, reportedly sometimes accompanied him and once stood watching as a woman who resisted being forced into the vehicle was killed on the spot.[73]

In early May, Kalimanzira and others on the prefectural security council decided that the group must be moved away from the prefecture to some place less visible. At about this same time authorities in Cyangugu began moving Tutsi from the stadium in town to a deserted refugee camp in the woods at Nyarushishi. Administrators in these two prefectures were probably implementing a policy determined at the national level, where authorities were becoming increasingly concerned to hide evidence of the genocide from foreigners whose visits were expected in the near future. (See chapter seven.) Butare authorities moved the Tutsi from the prefecture to a nearby complex of buildings belonging to the Episcopal church, where other Tutsi had already sought refuge. During the next ten days or two weeks, soldiers, some of them wounded in battle, and militia continued the same kind of abuses committed at the prefecture. They took women to rape and men to kill. They often clubbed the men to death in the nearby woods. According to testimony, Shalom himself came to seize men for killing on at least two occasions. On May 18 or 19, Monsignor Ndandari, the Episcopal authority in charge, insisted that the Tutsi return to the prefecture. He said that their presence would hinder plans to reopen the primary school at the compound, but he really wished simply to end the killings and other abuses on church premises.[74]

Kalimanzira and the others did not want the Tutsi back at the prefecture, so the prefect and his staff arranged to send them to Nyange, a deserted camp for Burundian refugees in the commune of Nyaruhengeri, a short distance outside of town. On May 30, the prefect requisitioned a bus from the National Population

---

[73]Human Rights Watch/FIDH interviews, May 21, 1997; Nairobi, by telephone, April 3, 1996; African Rights, *Rwanda, Not So Innocent,* pp. 94, 99-104.

[74]Human Rights Watch/FIDH interviews, May 21, 1997; Nairobi, by telephone, April 3, 1996.

Document: (Butare prefecture) In the name of the prefect, the sub-prefect authorizes persons named on the list to go to the Nyange camp in Nyaruhengeri commune. Guards at the barriers are asked to accept this attestation of the prefecture.

Uruhushya rwo kwinjira

Jyewe, NSABIMANA Sylvain, Préfet wa Prefegitura ya Butare, mpaye uburenga-nzira aba baturage bakulikira (reba liste yabo) kugirango bajyanwe muri komini Njaruhengeri, mu nkambi y'impungi. (i NYANGE)

Abari kuri za barrières bose, na Bourgmestre wa komini Njaruhengeri basabwe kubahiriza iki cyemezo cyi ubutegetsi bwa Prefegitura.

Prefe wa Prefegiture ya BUTARE - NSABIMANA Sylvain P.O. P.O. S/Préfet ACT Rutagishie faustin

Office for the purpose of "national defense." It is likely that this was one of the three vehicles that set out to take Tutsi to Nyange.[75] Witness testimony differs about the kind of vehicles, about whether all three reached Nyange and about how many people were left there.[76] But it is clear that once the Tutsi reached Nyange, they were attacked by either local militia or communal policemen, or both. A number of the Tutsi were killed, but according to several witnesses, local authorities then called a halt and refused to kill any more. They declared that the Tutsi should go home and be killed by the Hutu on their own hills.[77]

The Tutsi who escaped, some of them injured and many of them stripped of clothing and other possessions, headed back towards Butare. The prefect, perhaps aware that an attack had taken place, found them on the road the next morning. He arranged with the local councilor to house them temporarily at Rango. That night or the next day, the local people began threatening the Tutsi and they took off once more. Those who knew the region well went through the valleys and wooded areas to return to the prefecture, but others who were not from the area were caught by militia or soldiers on the roads and killed there.[78]

The prefect apparently then arranged a guard of National Police to protect the Tutsi, a measure which improved their security, although it did not assure it completely. A team of foreign journalists present in mid-June remarked that some people were still being seized from the group at the prefecture. Soldiers or National Police, presumably on orders from above, reacted to the presence of the foreigners by prohibiting further nighttime raids by militia.[79]

---

[75]S/Prefet Rutayisire, for the prefect, Proces-verbal de requisition, for vehicle from ONAPO, license number A8285, May 30, 1994 (Butare prefecture).

[76]Two witnesses declare that only one of the vehicles reached Nyange and that the others were stopped at the barrier of the Presidential Guard at Cyarwa and returned to the prefecture.

[77]Human Rights Watch/FIDH interviews, May 21, 1997, Nairobi, by telephone, April 3, 1996; African Rights, *Rwanda, Not So Innocent,* p. 100.

[78]Human Rights Watch/FIDH interviews, May 21, 1997, Nairobi, by telephone, April 3, 1996; Nsabimana, "The Truth About the Massacres in Butare."

[79]Nsabimana, "The Truth About the Massacres in Butare;" Fergal Keane, *Season of Blood* (London:Viking, 1995), p.175; African Rights, *Rwanda, Not So Innocent*, p. 104.

Seeking Intellectual Reinforcement: The Interim Prime Minister and the Professors

By mid-May, RPF forces had swung south through the eastern part of Rwanda, reached the southeastern frontier and were moving west towards the center of the country. They had taken the major military camp at Gako, in the region known as Bugesera, and were at the main highway that connected the capital to the southern part of Rwanda.[80] The interim government in Gitarama was at risk of being encircled or at least of being cut off from the southern prefectures. With the war against the RPF going so badly, Interim Prime Minister Jean Kambanda came to the university on May 14 seeking support and new ideas. Most of the faculty, as well as local officials, like the prefect, attended the session, which was organized by the vice-rector. The interim prime minister obviously felt the need to try to explain all the slaughter that had been taking place in the town and surrounding areas. Kambanda asserted that "there had been no massacres in Butare and Kibungo as the RPF claimed; the population had been attacked and had defended itself. There was a war."[81] His statement fit well with those being broadcast by RTLM at about the same time. Six days after the meeting, Valérie Bemeriki declared on the radio:

> So you have understood that the troubles in Butare are nothing but the wickedness of the Tutsi who have started it all to make it look like it was the Hutu and the GP [Presidential Guard] when instead it is the Tutsi who tried to exterminate the Hutu....[82]

Kambanda tried, apparently without much success, to justify the killing of former Prefect Habyarimana. He also did his best to minimize the losses to the RPF, declaring scornfully that "they have not taken any place; rather we have given it to them." And, conversely, he emphasized the achievements of his government, such as the appointment of new prefects and sub-prefects and the promise that cell heads would be paid by the government for duties that had previously been done without salary. Responding apparently to the pressure to make training in the use of arms and the firearms themselves available to all, the interim prime minister declared

---

[80]Kamanzi, *Rwanda, Du Génocide à la Defaite*, pp.145-46.

[81]Anonymous, Notebook 1, entry for May 14, 1994.

[82]Chrétien, *Rwanda, Les médias*, p. 194.

that such universal preparedness should be the goal rather than the earlier, more limited aims of civilian self-defense. He advocated training one hundred young men for each sector of Ngoma commune, instead of the ten previously proposed, but indicated that this idea would have to be worked out between heads of the political parties together with Colonels Gasake and Simba. Either he or others at the meeting spoke about buying some 200 firearms for men in the community, which would cost an estimated seven million Rwandan francs (about U.S.$39,000).[83] Some ten days later, the vice-rector deposited the above-mentioned six and a half million Rwandan francs, nearly the amount needed to buy the weapons.[84]

The interim prime minister called for the professors to work on a number of commissions: to develop ideas for the government on winning the war; to organize "civilian self-defense"; to deal with displaced persons and others in need; to obtain supplies from abroad; and to improve foreign relations, including preparing accusations against Uganda and Belgium for their alleged support of the RPF. Many professors agreed to participate and several of the commissions subsequently met for two or three sessions. But apparently none ever produced a report.[85]

Among the faculty who responded to the interim prime minister's address on May 14 was a physician, Eugène Rwamucyo, who spoke for four political parties: the MRND, the MDR, the PSD, and a small, relatively new party, the Party of Democratic Renewal (Parti du Renouveau Démocratique, PRD), recently organized by Professor Ntezimana. Rwamucyo, who had apparently taken charge of removing bodies throughout the town, also represented a group called the Cercle des Républicains. He called for stronger state action, for uniformity of language among authorities, and for doing away with the "myth of the icyitso." He did not specify what was to replace the "myth of icyitso," but certainly the doctrine of genocide as a form of self-defense was the idea that dominated the proceedings. He also echoed Sindikubwabo's April 19 speech by saying that "every person must

---

[83]Anonymous, Notebook 1, entry for May 14, 1994; Human Rights Watch/FIDH interview, Butare, July 5, 1996.

[84]Dr. Jean-Berchmans Nshimyumuremyi, Vice-Recteur, to Monsieur le Préfet, P2-12/226/94, May 25, 1994; Sylvain Nsabimana, Préfet, to Monsieur le Vice-Recteur, Butare [no date, no number]; Dr. Jean-Berchmans Nshimyumuremyi, Vice-Recteur, to Monsieur le Préfet, P2-18/236/94, June 15, 1994 and attached payment order, no. 1955802 (Butare prefecture).

[85]Human Rights Watch/FIDH interview, Butare, July 6, 1996.

understand that he must 'work' in order to win the war." After other speakers reinforced these ideas, Eugène Uwimana took the floor to urge careful controls against Inyenzi at the barriers and assistance to all those who wanted to buy guns "to defend themselves."[86]

Not all the faculty approved the position presented by Kambanda. Some demanded the right to see a list that university authorities had supposedly prepared of "enemies" remaining among faculty members. They were refused.

Students did not attend the meeting with Kambanda, but some hastened to express their complete support. The university and secondary school students of Muganza commune several days later distributed a statement echoing the sentiments expressed on May 15 by Kambanda and their professors. Perhaps prompted by Elie Ndayambaje, a former burgomaster turned university student, soon to be named burgomaster once more, the young people of the commune "condemned vigorously the diabolical intentions of the inyenzi inkotanyi to eliminate the popular democratic mass" in order to take power. Like their elders, they called for military training for all young people and for the rapid distribution of "effective methods of direct self-defense." They also condemned the RPF "lies" that the intellectuals of the region had been massacred and they denounced the RPF propaganda that was "intoxicating" public opinion abroad. They called for the population to "remain vigilant, to denounce and to fight any suspect element that could undermine public security."[87]

While some professors, teachers, and medical personnel participated in these activities only under pressure and to protect themselves or Tutsi hidden in their houses, others undertook a far more active role. Professors Nzitabakuze and Mutwewingabo, who led the meeting for organizing the patrols and barriers for Butare town, were reportedly also seen in the burgomaster's office in mid-May, looking like they had just finished a hunt in the bush. They were wearing dirty clothes and had whistles around their necks.[88] Nzitabakuze later led a search at the home of a departed European. He found a gun there and wrote to the military

---

[86]Anonymous, Notebook 1, entry for May 14, 1994. Police Judiciaire près le Parquet du Procureur du Roi de Bruxelles, Section Criminelle, PVs. no. 22.192 and no. 44.450.

[87]Anatole Havugimana, Emmanuel Mbarushimana, and Domina Ntakirutimana, Itangazo ry'Abanyeshuri b'i Muganza and its French translation, Declaration des Etudiants de la Commune Muganza, May 21, 1994 (Butare prefecture).

[88]République Rwandaise, Parquet de la République, P.V. no. 0115.

...e du Bourgmestre

г г

Butare le 1/5/94

Monsieur le Commandant de Place
de Butare

Objet : Demande de militaires pour
renforcer les rondes de civil
dans la cellule Buye

Monsieur le Commandant de Place

Par la présente, je vous demande
de bien vouloir nous envoyer au moins 20 militaires pour
renforcer les rondes nocturnes des civils organisés
dans la cellule Buye.
Les positions des barrières sont données ci-dessous :
Zone 1 : Responsable : Dr. J. Népo Nsengiyumva
  1. Extension Universitaire 2. Chez Dusabe Martin 3. Kiosque THERESE
X Zone 2 (a) Responsable : Dr. Nsengiyu Mr. Mutagoma Denys
  1. Hotel Ineza 2. Chez Biranda 3. Chez Kageruka (Enface de la gare)
  4. Chez le Préfet
Zone 3 : Responsable : Rutayisire J. Népo
  1. ICA 2. Avenue coopération 3. KATIMBA
  4. Ecole Française 5. Dépanneur 6. Pasi 7. Théologie
Zone 4 : Responsable : Karukeli Papicès
  1. Chez Seminega Pharcisse 2. Chez Joseph Hakizamungu
  3. Kiosque ITABA
Zone 5 : Responsable : J. Bosco Nzitabakuze
  1. Chez Abdallah 2. Chez Camille 3. Petit Séminaire Baptiste
  4. Chez a. Munyantore.
X Zone 6 (2) Responsable : Bernard Hutwerongabo
  1. Chez Prosper Munyankindi 2. Chez Faustin RUTAyisire
  3. Chez NDAHAGE
    Ces militaires seront répartis comme suit
Zone 1 : 2   Zone 2 : 2   Zone 3 : 4   Zone 4 : 4
Zone 5 : 4   Zone 6 : 4
    Pour plus d'informations, Veuilly nous contacter au 30682
        Franche collaboration
          Coordinateur des ronde dans la
          cellule Buye RUTAYisiro JN

Document: (Ngoma commune) Receipt identifying firearms delivered by the burgomaster to a communal councilor.

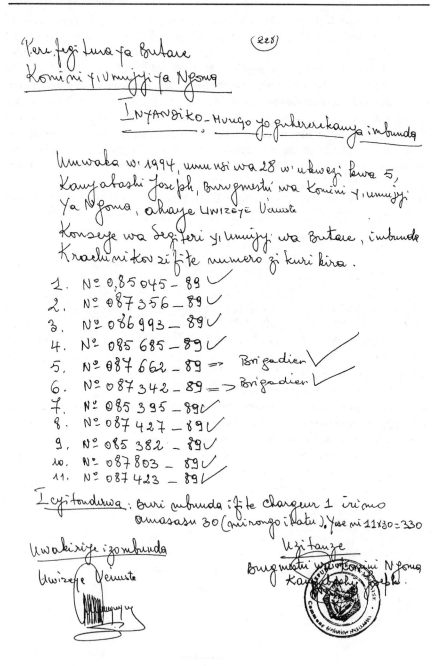

Repu. fegi tuna ya Butare

Komini yi umujyi ya Ngoma

(228)

INYANDIKO - Hungo yo gukererekanya imbunda

Umwaka w' 1994, umu nsi wa 28 w' ukwezi kwa 5, Kanyabashi Joseph, Burugmesti wa Komini yi umujyi ya Ngoma, ahaye UWIZEYE Venuste

Konseye wa Segiteri yi umujyi wa Butare, imbunda Kraleni mi kov zifite numero zi kuri kira.

1. N° 0,85 045 — 89
2. N° 087 356 — 89
3. N° 086 993 — 89
4. N° 085 685 — 89
5. N° 087 662 — 89 => Brigadier
6. N° 087 342 — 89 => Brigadier
7. N° 085 395 — 89
8. N° 087 427 — 89
9. N° 085 382 — 89
10. N° 087 803 — 89
11. N° 087 423 — 89

Icyitonderwa : Buri mbunda ifite Chargeur 1 irimo amasasu 30 (mirongo itatu). Yose ni 11x30 = 330

Uwakiriye izo mbunda

Uwizeye Venuste

Uzitanze

Burugmesti wa Komini Ngoma

Kanyabashi Joseph.

commander to ask permission to keep it for his patrol group in zone seven of Buye.[89] Faustin Ndayisaba, also a staff member at the university, similarly reported to the burgomaster that he had found three hunting rifles in a search at the Ibis Hotel. He reported that he had kept one of the weapons for "our barrier" and left the other two with the Interahamwe at the Ibis Hotel. He assured the burgomaster: "Nothing, nothing at all was damaged. Just to prove that, I was with Dr. Kageruka, soldiers and a crowd of people." Dr. Kageruka was Dr. Martin Kageruka, a member of the staff at the university hospital.[90] Dr. Kageruka himself allegedly led a search team that visited the Benebikira convent at the end of May. The other members were two university professors, a deputy prosecutor, a sub-prefect, and a merchant. Armed with their own weapon, the searchers had no soldiers with them, an indication that by this time the "civilian self-defense" program was operating as planned.[91]

Guhumbahumba: To Track Down the Last Tutsi

When the prefectural security council met to assess the situation on May 20, the senior administrators—most likely led by Kalimanzira—were far from satisfied. Despite the capture and killing of targeted individuals and the slaughter of previously protected people the zeal of ordinary citizens for guarding barriers and doing patrols had rapidly diminished. Burgomasters and other local authorities were not getting the work done. To make the situation more critical, the FAR were fleeing before the RPF and had abandoned the battlefield in Ntyazo in the northern part of the prefecture.

At the prefectural security meeting on that day, a senior administrator complained that "the burgomasters give the impression of being asleep" and the military commander expressed annoyance that many things were talked of but never implemented. "All decisions should be executed," he said. The meeting resolved to once more convoke a series of meetings with the people. According to the notes of the meeting:

---

[89]Prof. J. Bosco Nzitabakuze to M. Le Commandant de place, June 9, 1994 (Butare prefecture).

[90]Faustin Ndayisaba to Monsieur le Maire de la C.U. de Ngoma, June 9, 1994 (Butare prefecture).

[91]Human Rights Watch/FIDH interview, Butare, March 15, 1995.

Self-Defense: we should go to the cells to raise political consciousness; it ["civilian self-defense"] will be carried out if everyone knows what he is supposed to do.[92]

The participants decided to go first to the most exposed communes, those on the periphery of the prefecture. They set out a schedule of dates and hours for senior administrators and military officers to meet with the population in eight of the twenty communes. They were to impress upon the people the importance of doing patrols, guarding barriers, and searching everywhere for the "enemy." According to witnesses from Nyakizu, it was such a meeting that provoked a new round of killings in the commune, particularly of women and small children. (See chapter ten.) RTLM disseminated a new term for this final stage of the killing campaign: guhumbahumba, meaning to track down the last remaining Tutsi.

The sub-prefect of Gisagara was responsible for conducting meetings in the five communes of his district and reported on the successful completion of his assignment on May 28. He had informed people about:

1). security and aid to the armed forces in this war
2). raising their consciousness about their own welfare (to work)

The parenthetical explanation "to work" apparently meant that the subprefect had told his audiences that their welfare depended on killing Tutsi.

The sub-prefect found the population receptive, or so he said. He reported that they were ready to contribute (presumably money and food) to the soldiers and anxious to receive as quickly as possible the tools (ibikoresho, literally, the things to work with), meaning firearms, needed in their sectors. But clearly not everyone showed the same zeal, for Ntawukurkiryayo found it necessary to give severe and repeated warnings. Using the same phrases made current by Sindikubwabo in his April 19 speech, the sub-prefect declared that those whose attitude was "this doesn't concern me" (ntibindeba) must disappear from the communes. He insisted:

Anyone who does not help his fellow Rwandans to fight the RPF is also an enemy and must be treated as an Inkotanyi....Whoever hides and does not

---

[92]Anonymous, Notebook 1, entry for May 20, 1994.

show up to carry out the plans decided on by the administration is also an enemy.[93]

An additional order prohibited hiding *ibyitso* "when the people denounce them." This showed that "to fight the RPF" meant to attack local Tutsi in the area, not to combat RPF soldiers at the front.[94]

Burgomasters passed on to their subordinates the reprimands they had received at the May 20 meeting. The burgomaster of Mbazi wrote the councilor of Mwulire sector, for example, about the absence of guards at a barrier next to the main paved road:

> Several times in the course of our meetings together, I have reminded you about the question of keeping a reinforced guard on that barrier, but I see that it was wasted effort.
>
> So I am asking you to let me know if you have on your own arrived at the conclusion that the war is finished and security assured [or] if you have other forces that you can count on besides the citizens at the barriers and doing patrols.[95]

From the start, authorities had used clearing the brush both as a way to catch Tutsi hiding there and to remove the cover that might provide them protection in the future. In the days just after the systematic slaughter of April 21 to 25 in Butare town, residents of sectors like Ngoma and neighborhoods like Kabutare were summoned to days of umuganda to cut the brush. Less frequent for a short while, these operations were ordered again after the middle of May. The cell committee of Tonga, for example, decided on May 18 that all residents would get up early the next morning to go cut "bad branches" in the Gafurwe forest. They directed, "When this work is finished, the people will go to Nyabitare where they will cut all the bushes and they should search all the empty houses to see if there isn't someone

---

[93]Dominiko Ntawukuriryayo, S/Prefe wa S/Prefegitura Gisagara, to Bwana Prefe wa Prefegitura, no. 007/04.09.01, May 28, 1994 (Butare prefecture).

[94]Ibid.

[95]Antoine Sibomana, Burugumestri wa Komini Mbazi, to Bwana Konseye wa Segiteri Mwulire, no. 112/04.09.01, May 20, 1994 (Butare prefecture).

hidden in them."[96] The same day, the security committee for Muyaga commune directed the people "to destroy the brush that could serve as hiding places for the enemy."[97]

The prefectural security council decided on larger-scale brush cutting operations, probably at its May 20 meeting, and on May 24, Burgomaster Kanyabashi instructed the councilors to turn out the people at 7 a.m., May 27 for umuganda. They were to bring machetes and other cutting tools and to clear the brush along the Rwabayanga road and along the main road leading to the university.[98]

Searching the Fields, Forests and Valleys

A further RPF advance at the end of May spurred an apparent panic among high-level administrators. At a May 31 meeting, the prefectural security council decided that there would be a large-scale search on June 2 in Mugusa, Muyaga, and Rusatira. They directed searchers to bring a three day supply of food and warned them against looting along the way. One participant recorded the orders in his notebook:

> From tonight, increase the number of men; they should search everywhere in their own places; each one should take a weapon. Signal: how to recognize each other. Determine the departure line: cell heads.[99]

The sub-prefect Ntawukuriryayo hurried directly from the prefectural meeting to a communal meeting in Ndora to impress on participants the need to "search the houses of everyone who is suspected of collaborating with the enemy." After hearing his warning that the RPF might have already infiltrated the town of Nyabisindu, the participants at the meeting agreed that no market would be held the next day and that everyone must "search the sorghum fields and the forests and

---

[96]Banyangilike Etienne umwanditsi, "Inyandiko-mvugo y'inama yateranye le 18/5/94" (Butare prefecture).

[97]Muyaga commune, "Imyanzuro y'Inama ya Komini Muyaga yaguye yo kuwa 18/05/94" (Butare prefecture).

[98]Burgmestri wa Komini y'Umujyi ya Ngoma, Joseph Kanyabashi, to Bwana Konseye wa Segiteri, no. 200/04.09.01, May 24, 1994 (Butare prefecture).

[99]Anonymous, Notebook 1, entry for May 31, 1994.

Document: (Ngoma commune) Order to councilors to have population turn out in large numbers with their machetes to "cut the brush" on May 27 at 7 a.m.

REPUBLIKA Y'U RWANDA
PREFEGITURA YA BUTARE
KOMINI Y'UMUJYI YA NGOMA

Ngoma, kuwa 24/05/1994
N° 200 /04.09.01

A traiter par ....

Daie .... 26 MAI 1994
N° Classement: 2718/04.09.01/11

Bwana Konseye wa Segiteri
NGOMA
MATYAZO
CYARWA-SUMO — BUTARE-VILLE
KOMINI Y'UMUJYI YA NGOMA

Impamvu : Umuganda wo
kuwa 27/05/1994

Bwana Konseye,

Inama ya Perefegitura ishinzwe umutekane yafashe ibyemezo byo gutemesha ibihuru byose biri mu mujyi wa Butare no mu nkengero zawo. Ni muri urwo rwego twifuza ko kuwa gatanu tariki ya 27/05/1994 guhera saa moya hazakorwa umuganda aha hakurikira : Umuhanda wa Rwabayanga uva muri DGB ugana mu Rwabayanga, hazakorwa n'abaturage bahegereye cyane cyane abo mu cyarabu kab'i Ngoma.

Abaturage ba Tumba naba Cyarwa-Sumo bazakora umuganda wo gutema ibihuru ku muhanda wo kuri Université hagati ya Curphametra na Laboratoire.

Nsabye abajyanama kubimenyesha abaturage bakazaza ari benshi; ibikoresho bazitwaza ni imihoro, imipanga na za coupe-coupe.

Burgmestri wa Komini y'Umujyi
ya Ngoma
KANYABASHI Joseph

Bimenyeshejwe :

- Bwana Perefe wa Perefegitura
  BUTARE

wherever the enemy could be hidden." The day after the local search, Ndora people were to join the search ordered by prefectural authorities and were to assist the people of Mugusa commune in beating the bushes at Ngiryi, along the banks of a river that flowed down from the commune of Muyaga. They were told: "Everyone must go with the others, with his arms, and anyone who fails to go will be taken to be an icyitso."[100]

The burgomaster of Runyinya worried about the hiding places offered by the forests and caves in the high hills of his territory and by the extensive tea plantations in the valleys. Apparently the survivors of attacks on large agglomerations of Tutsi had retreated into these areas just as Tutsi had sought refuge on the hilltops of Bisesero in Kibuye. At almost the same moment when the prefect of Kibuye was requesting military help to eliminate the survivors at Bisesero, the Runyinya burgomaster was asking for ten firearms, presumably for the use of the fifty former soldiers who were at his disposition in Runyinya. To underscore the need for this help, the burgomaster wrote:

> Our worries are well founded, since last week the people discovered five unknown people in the forests of Rukara-Gikombe; three were taken but refused to reveal their identities; two succeeded in escaping into the forest and are still being sought. We could not bring those captured to the higher authorities because they refused to be brought to the communal office; those who caught them killed them on the spot.[101]

Authorities aimed to find not just Tutsi who were locally resident, but also those who had escaped killing in their home regions further north. These survivors were moving south and west into and through Butare prefecture with the masses of other displaced persons fleeing the RPF advances. After the sub-prefect of Gisagara aroused new zeal for tracking Tutsi by his late May security meetings, he asked the prefect to arrange for at least ten soldiers "to support the population and its [communal] police." He was anxious that "the enthusiasm that the people show

---

[100]Burugumesitiri wa Komini Ndora, Célestin Rwankubito, "Inyandiko-Mvugo y'Inama y'Abaturage B'Amasegiteri Gisagara, Mukande, Ndora na Cyamukuza yo kuwa 31 Gicurasi 1994" (Butare prefecture).

[101]Déogratias Hategekimana, Burgmestri wa Komini Runyinya, to Bwana Commandant de Place, no. 118/04.06, June 3, 1994 (Butare prefecture).

not be allowed to die" but rather be directed with the help of the soldiers towards "making sure that there are no enemies hidden in this crowd of refugees."[102]

Kalimanzira, as the most senior official of the territorial administration in the area, spurred this increasingly fanatical tone among his subordinates. Both he and the sub-prefect of Gisagara were dissatisfied with the lack of zeal shown by the burgomaster of Ndora: one or both of these higher ranking officials sometimes took over the burgomaster's meetings with the people of his commune. This was particularly easy for the sub-prefect because his offices were located in the commune of Ndora. Kalimanzira also managed to appear at a number of these local meetings, sometimes in the company of other dignitaries.

At a meeting in Ndora commune on June 7, Kalimanzira was flanked by several locally important people, including Bernadette Mukarurangwa, deputy of the national assembly. Kalimanzira gave the usual canned review of the orgins of the war and warned the people that the Inkotanyi had "elaborated a plan to eliminate all the Hutu everywhere in the country, from the level of the prefecture down to that of the cell." He declared, "The Inkotanyi send their spies (supporters of the RPF)...who tell them about what is going on." Trying to explain away the recent RPF advance into Ntyazo commune, he said that a mere handful of their soldiers had succeeded there because they had been helped by people whom they called "refugees," but who were really their spies hidden in the sorghum fields, "refugees who were carrying radio sets," meaning two-way radios for communicating with the RPF. To ensure the capture of such "spies," Kalimanzira insisted on a closer examination of all who passed through barriers, including interrogation about their origins and destination. He also demanded thorough searches of the whole commune to catch those who got around the barriers by going through valleys and swamps.

At this meeting, Kalimanzira warned even that "The Inkotanyi use small children (*abana bato*)," suggesting that they too were enemies to be killed.

On the issue of "civilian self-defense," Deputy Mukarurangwa wanted her opinion heard about the best way to recruit and train young people. On the recommendations of the authorities, the people at the meeting then resolved to arm themselves with traditional weapons and asked those who knew how to make bows and arrows to turn out enough so that they could be sold at market. As Kalimanzira had specifically directed, they also decided to form batallions of 600 young men

---

[102]Dominiko Ntawukuriryayo, S/Prefe wa S/Prefegitura Gisagara, to Bwana Prefe wa Prefegitura, no. 007/04.09.01, May 28, 1994 (Butare prefecture).

armed with such weapons to be commanded by one former soldier with a firearm.[103]

Searching Butare Town

The RPF advances also spurred renewed efforts to find Tutsi in Butare town. In the first days of June, militia and soldiers discovered Tutsi hidden in the convent of the Benebikira near the cathedral. They had tied up the men and apparently were preparing to kill them when Lieutenant Colonel Muvunyi arrived, having been summoned by the mother superior. He prevented the killings and sent the Tutsi to join those gathered in front of the prefecture, some of them just returned from Nyange.[104] On June 3, there was a raid at the Junior Seminary at Karubanda in which three women and two infants were taken and killed, without any effective effort by the priests to intervene. On June 5 and 6, there was a new "sweeping out" of the hospital, forcing out the last Tutsi who were hidden there.[105]

Also on June 5, the security committee of Cyarwa-Cyimana, "following the orders received from the government of salvation about the security of the Rwandan people," decided to raid the home of Margueritte Kaniwabo. They carried out the search the next day, together with the local people, and found four "traitors," two of them women, hidden in the ceiling of the house. According to those reporting the incident to the prefect,

All these people were being guarded by Eric Mujyambere, who had a firearm, and he had received that firearm from the communal authorities so that he, along with other inhabitants, could assure the security of the population. Those

---

[103]Célestin Rwankubito, Burugumesitiri wa Komini Ndora, "Inama y'Abaturage ba Komini Ndora yo kuwa 7 Kamena 1994" enclosed in Célestin Rwankubito, Burugumesitiri wa Komini Ndora, to Bwana Perefe wa Perefegitura, no. 132/04.04/2, June 16, 1994 (Butare prefecture).

[104]At least several of those sent to the prefecture were then transferred to Rango, where they remained until the arrival of the RPF, African Rights, *Rwanda, Not So Innocent*, p. 104.

[105]Human Rights Watch/FIDH interview, Brussels, December 12, 1995; République Rwandaise, Parquet de la République, P.V. no. 117; African Rights, *Rwanda, Not So Innocent*, p. 103.

carrying out the search had to defend themselves and the above-named ibyitso got into the fray and lost their lives.[106]

On June 7, a committee met to plan another drive to clear the brush in Butare town, where residents continued to report the presence of Inyenzi in wooded areas such as the arboretum next to the university.[107] The minutes of the meeting suggest how ordinary citizens acting in accord with the policy of "civilian self-defense" took on the tasks of officials in implementing the genocide. Bernard Mutwewingabo, the university professor and Faustin Twagirayezu, the secondary school teacher, active in organizing the system of patrols and barriers, seem to have led the meeting. Ayobangira and Elisée Mutereye, members of the finance committee for "civilian self-defense," participated as did Vénuste Uwizeye, councilor of Butare town,[108] representing the administration. Several agents of the forest or agricultural service attended, apparently to give technical advice on burning the brush. After listing the eight wooded areas in and around the town, the participants decided whether each was to be burned or cut down and who was to do the work. The minutes refer several times to the "head" (*umuyobozi*) of the commune, without ever using his title of burgomaster. He is noted always as the recipient, not the initiator of requests—or perhaps even orders—from the other participants. He is directed to arrange with the prefect for a day of umuganda to cut the brush in the Rwasave valley; he is asked to order the councilor of Tumba sector to have residents of that sector cut the brush near the hospital; and he is told to "make the councilor of Ngoma sector understand that he has to get the people in this sector to cut the brush." The group decided that the people of neighboring Shyanda commune would also have to be involved because they would need to cut a firebreak to protect their fields. One of the group, Jean Mubiligi, an agricultural

---

[106]Abahagarariye abaturage ba Cyarwa-Cyimana to Nyakubahwa Perefe wa Perefegitura ya Butare, June 6, 1994 (Butare prefecture).

[107]Nicodème Hategekimana, chair of the meeting, "Inama y'umutekano y'abaturage ba secteur Cyarwa-Sumo yateranye le 12 gicurasi 1994" (Butare prefecture).

[108]Identified in the minutes of the meeting as councilor, Uwizeye was only acting in that capacity at this time. He was named to the post some two weeks later after the previous councilor, Francois Semanzi, was killed. [See below.]

researcher and a person with no official authority, volunteered to go tell the burgomaster of Shyanda that he would have to arrange for this to be done.[109]

Fired with zeal to confront the "enemy" and strengthened by a sense of their own importance, such self-appointed leaders clearly expected to be heard by civilian and military officials. In a letter to the military commander of Butare, the "coordinator of patrols" J.N. Rutayisire asks him to send twenty soldiers to assist civilians with patrols and even informs him how they should be assigned to the various teams. When this message and a second, on a related subject, did not produce the expected prompt response, Rutayisire wrote to the burgomaster two days later informing him that the citizens of Buye "would like an immediate positive response" to their two letters. They ask Kanyabashi to "stand up firmly" for their requests in the prefectural security council and, if this is impossible, to arrange for them to meet directly with military authorities to explain the urgency of their security concerns.[110]

"Civilian self-defense" organized a substantial part of the population to hunt down Tutsi, either to kill them immediately or to hand them over to local authorities for execution. It also recruited and trained several thousand young men in the prefecture and provided them with firearms, making it possible for them to supply the firepower needed to support the "work" of the larger body of civilians. While many citizens appear to have participated with little zeal or under coercion, withdrawing as soon as possible, a small number willingly shouldered the burdens of leadership in the genocidal system. The materials available for this study make clearest the role played by intellectuals in the town, but other community leaders—businessmen, successful farmers, clergy, teachers—apparently played the same role out on the hills. Led into the killing campaign by local and national officials, they were the good "workers who want to work" for their country solicited by Sindikubwabo in his April 19 speech.

---

[109]Bernard Mutwewingabo, Rapporteri, "Inyandikomvugo y'inama ya komisiyo yashyinzwe kwiga uko ibihuru bigomba kuvanwaho mu mashyamba akikije umugi wa Butare" (Butare prefecture).

[110]J.N. Rutayisire, Coordinateur des rondes dans la cellule Buye, to Monsieur le Commandant de Place, May 1, 1994; J.N. Rutayisire to Monsieur le Bourgmestre de la Commune de Ngoma, May 3, 1994 (Butare prefecture).

BUTARE:
"NO ONE WILL BE SAFE FROM DISORDER"

On May 12, the burgomaster of Rusatira commented that "the enemy has been seriously beaten."[1] He meant that most local Tutsi had been slain and this assessment was accurate. But for the actual RPF, the situation was the opposite: it had begun its ultimate advance that would finally engulf the capital and defeat the genocidal authorities. The RPF success showed the hollowness of the claim that killing Tutsi would guarantee the safety of Hutu and made murderous fools or liars of the authorities who had promised it would.

Even had RPF progress been less dramatic, the decision by the interim government to push the genocide ever deeper into the community undermined its authority. People found it hard to believe that women, children, and the elderly and infirm posed the same threat as armed soldiers. Many of the women targeted after mid-May were wives or mothers of Hutu and many of the clergy, teachers, and medical personnel were highly esteemed by their Hutu neighbors. Hutu solidarity, at most a short-lived myth, crumbled as protectors of these newly specified targets clashed with others whose own personal or political interests were served by continuing the genocide.

The killing campaign created new opportunities for getting rich as Tutsi property became available for appropriation and it generated new possibilities for acquiring power as political alliances shifted. In struggles over these resources as in revivals of old conflicts, contenders used the same accusations against each other as they had used against Tutsi. The frequency and ease with which these charges were made discredited them and called into question their original use against Tutsi.

With the prospect that the interim government was headed for defeat and with the realization that anyone could be charged as an "accomplice," popular participation diminished. The activists carrying out the killing campaign at the end were, as at the start, a small number whose hatred and fear of Tutsi were intertwined with what they saw as their own opportunities for success.

These embittered killers sometimes turned on the communities and the authorities who had given them license to kill. The authorities found that the legitimacy which they had used at the start to cover the genocide had been

---

[1]Vincent Rukelibuga, Burugumestiri wa Komini Rusatira, to Bwana Perefe wa Perefegitura, May 12, 1994 (Butare prefecture).

consumed during the course of the killing campaign and that they no longer had the authority to control the assassins whom they had armed.

Hutu Against Hutu

As the Hutu of Butare fell into conflict on personal, political or regional grounds, they used the discourse of genocide against their opponents. In such struggles, having zealously implemented the genocide was no guarantee of safety and anyone, regardless of attitude toward Tutsi, could be accused of being icyitso.

Personal and Political Conflict

In quarrels between ordinary people, such as one that took place in mid-May in Butare town, one of the contenders could arrange for a soldier to kill the other, using the easy excuse that the intended victim was icyitso. In Rusatira, the burgomaster complained about certain residents of the commune who sought to use the troubled times to bring back the bad habits of vengeance and who confused personal enemies with the enemy of the country, the Inkotanyi.[2] In Vumbi, Runyinya commune, twenty-four Hutu were reportedly killed because they were accused of being Tutsi.[3] In Cyarwa-Cyimana sector of Ngoma commune, participants at a security committee meeting complained that "tall persons" were being attacked "even though they are Hutu."[4] The burgomaster of Ruhashya deplored unjustified attacks by Hutu against Hutu in his commune. He reported,

[The assailants] even attacked the man named Dominique Bigwiro, pillaged his goods, destroyed his house and in the confusion, he lost his life, on the unconfirmed pretext that he had hidden refugees in his house and in his banana plantation. His mother's house was also pillaged when she had nothing to do with the accusations against her son. Another person named Jean-Baptiste Rutegesha had his house pillaged in an abusive and vindictive way by these people for the sole reason that he was not able to find the money to pay off

---

[2]Ibid.

[3]Human Rights Watch/FIDH interview, Butare, August 20, 1995.

[4]Ngoma commune, Cyarwa-Cyimana sector, "Inyandiko mvugo y'Inama y'Umutekano," May 13, 1994 (Butare prefecture).

those who accused him of sheltering ibyitso and who went so far as to stick an ethnic label on him that was not even his own.[5]

With the enormous instability introduced by the genocide, political actors at all levels jostled for power for themselves and their parties. At the prefectural level, MRND stalwarts Nyiramasuhuko and Kalimanzira struggled against the growth of MDR-Power represented by men like Semwaga. This struggle intensified towards the end of the genocide when Shalom, as head of the MRND Interahamwe, prepared attacks against the sector Gatobotobo of Mbazi, where Semwaga and Prefect Nsabimana were protecting Tutsi. The MRND group called RTLM to their assistance and the radio station broadcast information about the continued presence of Tutsi in that sector. Semwaga also previously fought challenges from a CDR leader, the former burgomaster of Mbazi, Kabuga, who been one of the most zealous organizers of the genocide in that commune. According to local observers, Semwaga apparently was behind the abduction and murder of Kabuga and his associates like Masumbuko. Soldiers, including Sergeant Gatwaza, reportedly arrived one day in May to carry them off along with Emmanuel Sakindi, a councilor who was said to be Tutsi. The supposed Tutsi and the apparent killers of Tutsi were reportedly all killed by the same people at the same time, but for different reasons. Whether or not Sibomana, the burgomaster of Mbazi, participated in instigating the murder, as is sometimes charged, he benefited from the elimination of Kabuga, who had challenged his authority.[6]

At the national and prefectural level, Kalimanzira and Nyiramasuhuko lined up against PSD leaders like agriculture minister Straton Nsabumukunzi and Prefect Nsabimana. At the local level they opposed at least one PSD burgomaster, Vincent Rukelibuga of Rusatira, even though he had vigorously supported the genocide. Like politicians in Mbazi, Rukelibuga was troubled by a local CDR leader. In early May, Rukelibuga complained that supporters, "who had helped us to contain these troubles"—meaning who had helped kill Tutsi—had disappeared and could not be found anywhere. The disappearance of his supporters presaged his own removal

---

[5]Martin Rudakubana, Burugumestiri wa Komini Rushashya, to Bwana Perefe wa Perefegitura wa Butare, no. 910/04.09.01/4, June 3, 1994 (Butare prefecture).

[6]Human Rights Watch/FIDH interviews, Butare, August 18, 19, and 20, 1995; Nairobi, by telephone, March 26, 1997.

in late June, his record of killing Tutsi apparently not enough to protect him from partisan enmity.[7]

In the commune of Kigembe, partisan conflict surfaced at the end of April when Bonaventure Nkundabakura, the head of MDR-Power, was accused of having arranged the murder of the head of the other MDR faction. Nkundabakura then allied with his previous rival, the CDR leader Bernard Mutabaruka, to combat the PSD burgomaster, Symphorien Karekezi. In the struggle, which continued until the end of June, the MDR/CDR group accused the burgomaster of being Inkotanyi and subsequently charged that he was trying to avenge Tutsi relatives apparently killed by Nkundabakura. The burgomaster asked the prosecutor in Butare to order Nkundabakura to stop making such charges "because you know what that means these days."[8] More than once, supporters of the two sides resorted to violence and, at different times, both called in National Police to strengthen their positions.[9]

Dominique Ntawukuriryayo, sub-prefect of Gisagara, and Bernadette Mukarurangwa, deputy to the national assembly, seem to have shared a commitment to the killing campaign, but otherwise clashed. Mukarurangwa spread the word that Ntawukuriryayo was planning to flee and that he was hiding Tutsi; she used this as a pretext for ordering a local crowd to put up a barrier to stop him. The crowd forced him to return to his house, which they then searched, as they did that of the burgomaster of Ndora. Finding nothing at either place, they turned back on the instigator and demanded payment from her since they had not been able to pillage elsewhere.[10]

In divisions at the level of sector and cell, opponents used the same kinds of accusations against each other. The councilor of Nkubi, Augustin Kanyawabahizi, identified as a protector by some survivors, arrested five persons for their role in

---

[7]Vincent Rukelibuga, Burugumesitiri wa Rusatira, to Bwana Perefe, May 12, 1994; Callixte Kalimanzira, Umuyobozi mu biro bya Ministeri y'Ubutegetsi bw'Igihugu n'Amajyambere ya komini, to Bwana Prefc wa Prefegitura ya Butare, May 24, 1994 (Butare prefecture).

[8]Symphorien Karekezi, Burgumestre wa Komini Kigembe, to Bwana Prokireri, no. 094/04.09.01, May 3, 1994 (Butare prefecture).

[9]Ibid; Record of interrogation of J. Bosco Nsabimana, April 30, 1994; series of fourteen letters among various parties to the affair, May 1-June 29, 1994 (Butare prefecture).

[10]Dominiko Ntawukuriryayo, S/Prefe wa S/Prefegitura Gisagara, to Bwana Prefe wa Prefegitura, no. 008/04.17.02, June 8, 1994 (Butare prefecture).

"conflicts which broke out and cost the lives of some persons and destroyed much property" around April 26.[11] The victims apparently had been Tutsi. Fifty-six residents of the sector petitioned the prosecutor for the release of the detainees because "these persons are above reproach" in the community.[12] When they got no satisfaction and another person of the same group was arrested, 114 residents petitioned for their release, saying that they had violated no law and that their continued detention caused insecurity in the sector.[13] Receiving no support from the prosecutor, they sought other ways to discredit the councilor.[14] Kanyawabahizi, reportedly a protector of at least some Tutsi, reacted to the increasing pressure by appealing to Interahamwe president Kajuga. He asked him to provide the "materiel necessary for these difficult moments"—that is, firearms that would increase Kanyawabahizi's authority—and to send a representative to support him at a community meeting scheduled for two days later.[15] This strategy apparently failed and the residents of Nkubi wrote to the prefect on June 9 declaring that Kanyawabahizi was, in fact, a Tutsi who had changed his ethnic group in the 1960s and that "he had put in prison the people most opposed to the enemy." They asked for his removal and for the release of the detained persons.[16]

---

[11] If he, in fact, arrested them for killing Tutsi, it would be the only such arrest that we discovered for the period after the killing began on April 20. He may have had another reason for the arrest and merely used the accusation of murdering Tutsi as a pretext. Abaturage ba Segiteri ya Nkubi to Nyakubahwa Bwana Prokireri wa Republika, May 3, 1994 (Butare prefecture).

[12]Abaturage ba Segiteri ya Nkubi to Nyakubahwa Bwana Prokireri wa Republika, May 3, 1994.

[13]Abaturage ba Segiteri ya Nkubi to Nyakubahwa Bwana Prokireri wa Republika, May 29, 1994 (Butare prefecture).

[14]Mathias Bushishi, Prokireri wa Republika, to Bwana Burugumesitiri wa Komini y'Umujyi ya Ngoma, no. C/0523/RMP49.394/S6/PRORE (Butare prefecture).

[15]Agusitini Kanywabahizi, Konseye wa Segiteri ya Nkubi, to Bwana Robert Kajuga, Prezida w'Interahamwe mu rwego rw'igihugu, June 6, 1994 (Butare prefecture).

[16]Segiteru Nkubi to Bwana Prefe wa Butare, June 9, 1994 (Butare prefecture).

Document: (Butare prefecture) People of Nkubi, angry that their councilor Kanyawabahizi arrested residents for killing Tutsi, seek to discredit him by accusing him of being Tutsi himself.

___

Abaturage basegitelo
Nkubi

Nkubi le 9/6/1994

Imin : Ngoma
Perefegitire : Butare
Comine : Agashari

Bwana Perefe wa Butare?

Kuri Perefe wa Perefegitire ya Butare mwaramuthe?
Ikiduteye kukwandikira twagiramgo tukumenyeshe akababaro dufite.
Twebwe Abaturage basegitelo ya Nkubi dutelwa Nuwitwa Konseye wayo yitwa Kamwabahize Augusta? wigize Kihutu re Muw 1960 Ashaka ubutegetsi wemamukumwe yitwa uraye eduwari wihibye izina Kasero? Doreko Nawa Kasero yatepekaga? Ieyiduteye kukwandikira Nuko uwo Kamwabahize ibyo aduKorera Ntawumde muteoetsi ukoramKawe? yatamoiye ahotumu fatama ibyitso? atamoira kuducarmo ieyuho?
hurimo mamurarmuwe witwa mpakamiye? Bioatuma ararkara eyame Bitumu aducarmo ieyuho agakuramo abijyendzi muretwe Akaba fum oisha Kueitumoo Abasicoaye Enyuma Babome aho bimjiciira? Nome Bwana Perefe wa Butare twebwe abaturage tukabatugusabyeko wa kwikorera anKeto ukadutumoureza abamtu yatumoishije baremoamoa? Karmdi tuwaamukeka amababa? tuduzeko auibyitso akatumenya yaduse Nyera Niyompamu tutaishyizeho amazima ya Cu?
KAndi memu Jyayo muzaijye Nde mwitonze kuko Neba adatiteamba Boitse Ntabuze ibimtu byakomoma umukejye? Ntu
mulakoze? Mulakoze duteoereje ioisubizo?

Segitera Nkubi

Document: (Ngoma commune) Letter of councilor Kanyawabahizi asking for arms and political support from Kajuga, national head of the Interahamwe.

KOMINI Y'UMUJYI YA NGOMA   Nkubi, taliki ya 06/6/1994

SEGITERI YA NKUBI

B.P 35 BUTARE

8. 6. 1994

Kuli Bwana Robert KAJUGA

Prezida w'Interahamwe mu rwego

rw'igihugu -

        KIGALI

Impamvu: Gusaba inkunga

Bwana Prezida,

Nkimara kumenya ko muli hano i Butare muli iyi minsi, nihutiye kubiyambaza Bwana Prezida, kugirango niba bishoboka, mushobore kuba mwatwunganira ku byerekeye kubona udukoresho duhagije muli ibi bihe bikomeye byo kurwana inkundura turwana ku busugire bw'igihugu cyacu.

Na none ali ibishobotse Bwana Prezida, nabasabaga ko mwatwohererereza intumwa yanyu ikaza kutwungura ibitekerezo mu nama y'abaturage izabera hano ku Nkubi ejo bundi kuwa gatatu taliki ya o8/6/1994 i saa munani.

Mu gihe tugitegereje igisubizo cyanyu cyiza, tubaye tubashimiye Bwana Prezida.

B   Konseye wa Segiteri ya NKUBI

                       Agusitini KANYWABAHIZI

Bimenyeshejwe:

-Bwana Burgmestri wa KOMINI NGOMA

AAbagize Komite y'umutekano

  ya Segiteri ya Nkubi.

Regional Conflict

Behind the facade of unity against a common enemy, regional rivalries continued. Northerners doubted the loyalty of people from the south while southerners feared that the northerners would end by excluding them from power. On April 27, some 600 secondary school students from the Groupe Scolaire Byumba, most of them northerners, were installed in the buildings of the Butare veterinary school. Although supposedly restricted to the campus, small groups of them participated in attacks on Tutsi and pillaging in town. During the first days of May, the northern students killed two southerners—apparently Hutu—who were housed with them, one a student, one an adult. Later that month, the director of the veterinary school, himself a southerner, foresaw a war to the finish between people from the south—Butare—and those from further north, including people from Gitarama, now won over to Hutu Power. Semwaga, the MDR-Power leader, was from Gitarama and felt so threatened by the people of Butare that he requested a military guard.[17]

Northerners resident in Butare had been frightened by the outpouring of anger against them following the February assassination of Gatabazi. Some were so afraid in the first days of April that they took steps to leave for the north or at least to send their children back to their home region. The head of SORWAL, Alphonse Higaniro, went to Gisenyi in early April and returned to Butare only briefly to get the factory operating again in early May. The northerner, Captain Nizeyimana, and his ally Lieutenant Hategekimana were transferred from their posts at the ESO and the Ngoma camp in early May. This change may have increased the insecurity felt by northerners. On May 19, the head of SORWAL was so concerned about the safety of his personnel and property that he asked the military commander to increase the number of soldiers protecting the facility. Professor Ntezimana, the university professor who was often seen as representing the interests of northerners, left Butare on May 20 convinced the town was no longer safe. Certainly the northerners feared the RPF advance, but they also faced risks within Butare itself. On May 24, SORWAL was attacked by local armed intruders who arrived in a vehicle, exchanged fire with the SORWAL guards and then left. Two days later, the technical director, Martin Dusabe, wrote to the commander once more to

---

[17]Human Rights Watch/FIDH interviews, Butare, August 18 and October 26, 1995; Raporo y'Imikoreshereze Mibi y'Imbunda Itunzwe ya Mbarushimana Théophile, Directeur wa EAVK-Kabutare, May 25, 1994 (Butare prefecture).

urgently request additional soldiers to guard the factory.[18] SORWAL employee
Pierre Nsabimana, who had taken over a house from a dead or departed Tutsi in the
sector of Tumba, returned the property to the commune in early June because he
was afraid to live in that neighborhood.[19]

Within the south itself, there were local conflicts that pitted the people of some
Gikongoro communes against those of Butare, or of one Butare commune against
another, or of one sector or cell against another. These conflicts ordinarily centered
on pillage or control of land, but often were expressed in terms of eliminating the
"enemy." People from Maraba commune and from Gikongoro, particularly from
Kinyamakara commune, made sorties into Rusatira and Ruhashya "at times and
dates which they decided themselves,"[20] "killing innocent people and pillaging
houses,"[21] all under the pretext of eliminating Tutsi. For his efforts to prevent this
kind of "disorder and anarchy" in his commune, the burgomaster of Ruhashya was
labeled icyitso. He rejected this accusation and assured the prefect that he and the
people of his commune were quite capable of "harassing the enemy and their
ibyitso" on their own and that they would prefer that those troublemakers who
came claiming to help would just stay home.[22] The people of Cyarwa-Cyimana
recognized, too, the "serious conflicts" that resulted when people of one commune
or one sector pillaged in another. They decided that any "liberation" (kubohoza)

---

[18]Human Rights Watch/FIDH interview, Brussels, December 15, 1995; Martin
Dusabe, Directeur Technique, for Alphonse Higaniro Directeur Générale de la SORWAL,
to the Commandant de Place, Butare-Gikongoro, no. 271/02/0594, May 26, 1994 (Butare
prefecture).

[19]Pierre Nsabimana to Monsieur le Bourgmestre, June 10, 1994 (Butare
prefecture).

[20]Martin Rudabukana, Burugumestiri wa Komini Ruhashha (sic), to Bwana Perefe
wa Perefegitura, no. 910/04.09.01/4, June 3, 1994 (Butare prefecture).

[21]Rusatira commune, "Imyanzuro y'inama ya komini ishinzwe umutekano yo ku
wa 5/6/1994 yagenewe ingabo z'igihugu na perefe wa perefegitura Butare," in Vincent
Rukelibuga, Bourgmestre wa Rusatira to Bwana perefe wa perefegitura, June 5, 1994
(Butare prefecture).

[22]Martin Rudabukana, Burugumestiri wa Komini Ruhashha (sic), to Bwana Perefe
wa Perefegitura, no. 910/04.09.01/4, June 3, 1994.

operations in other sectors were prohibited, except by prior arrangement between the authorities of the sectors.[23]

In some communities, people understood the consequences of adding firearms to the already existing tensions. In Cyarwa-Cyimana, for example, the people of the sector pointed out the problems that could result if people were chosen to learn how to shoot on the basis of party affiliation.[24]

Property and Women

As a nation of farmers in a country short on land, Rwandans had been concerned about control over property for many years. Anti-Tutsi propagandists exploited the issue even before the genocide began by suggesting that the RPF intended to overthrow the 1959 social revolution and repossess the lands that Hutu had acquired after killing Tutsi or driving them out of their communities in the 1960s. The fears thus raised motivated some people to participate in the attacks on Tutsi, as did the hope of acquiring more property in the new round of violence. Authorities knew that once Tutsi were again forced from their homes and murdered, local people would immediately begin competing for their property and other goods and so they did.

On April 16, just a day after the first major massacre had begun in the prefecture, the prefectural security council dealt with the disposition of Tutsi possessions, decreeing that they should be sold at public auction. Several weeks later, the commune of Ngoma removed four truckloads of clothing from the Butare market, goods belonging to "disappeared businessmen," presumably to be sold to the highest bidder. The profits from this sale may have formed part of the some four million Rwandan francs (about U.S.$2,300) obtained through the sale of Tutsi property and then contributed to the "civilian self-defense" fund, as mentioned above.[25] These measures dealt with valuable goods but not with land, which was customarily not sold but subject to redistribution by the burgomaster if the property was deemed vacant. On April 25, the council established a commission to oversee

---

[23]Ngoma commune, Cyarwa-Cyimana sector, "Inyandiko mvugo y'Inama y'Umutekano," May 13, 1994.

[24]Froduald Nsabimana, Umwanditsi, "Inyandiko mvugo y'Inama Rusange ya Secteur Cyimana," May 15, 1994 (Butare prefecture).

[25] Receipt (Bon de Dépense) no. 154/94 to Harelimana Jean et Cie, May 28, 1994 (Butare prefecture).

an inventory of land, houses, and automobiles that had been "abandoned by their owners."[26]

At its May 6 meeting, the prefectural security council decided to renew instructions on property from 1963-64, when most Tutsi land and belongings had been forcibly appropriated. Although not further explained in the minutes of this meeting, the policy seems in practice to have been the same as that being implemented elsewhere in the country. Local authorities would appropriate the most valuable goods for eventual sale, but would concede other goods to looters; they would redistribute land; and they would leave standing crops to the disposition of the people of the cell or sector.[27] In Huye commune, and perhaps elsewhere, the people decided to use the crops to prepare beer to reward those who had done umuganda, that is, searches for Tutsi.[28]

Recognizing the possibility that property disputes could result in serious conflicts in the community, the burgomaster of Ngoma insisted that councilors produce prompt and careful inventories of available houses and land. He warned them, "The way in which you complete this work will show us how well you understand the commitment we expect from you."[29] The inventories, due by June 5 and submitted by or soon after that date, included also lists of the dozens of market stalls that had been held by Tutsi and that now were available for redistribution.

The decision to begin distributing property led to several dozen requests to the burgomaster and to the prefect for the grant of houses under the authority of each. One communal employee was directed to ensure that such requests be treated in the order received. Both in town and out on the hills, some did not wait for the

---

[26]Anonymous, Notebook 1, entries for April 16 and April 25, 1994.

[27]Anonymous, Notebook 2, entry for May 6, 1994.

[28]Dominiko Ntawukuriryayo, Sous-Prefét, to Monsieur le Préfet de la Préfecture, no. 005/04.09.01/18, May 10, 1994, enclosing Proces-Verbal de la Réunion des Bourgmestres des Communes de la Sous-Prefecture Gisagara, tenue le 3 mai 1994; Jonathas Ruremesha, Bourmestre wa Komini Huye, to Bwana Perefe, May 19, 1994.

[29]Joseph Kanyabashi, Burgmestri wa Komini y'Umujyi ya Ngoma, to Bajyanama ba Komini y'Umujyi ya Ngoma (Bose), no. 199/04.004/2, May 24, 1994 (Butare prefecture).

Document: (Ngoma commune) Receipt for payment to Jean Harelimana and Co. for transport of clothing taken from market stalls of "traders who have disappeared from Butare market."

REPUBLIQUE RWANDAISE

Préfecture de _Butare_

Commune de _Ngoma_

N° _154/94_

Art ...... S/Art ...... Litt.....

Frs = 4.800 =

Bon de Dépense

Payé à _HARELIMANA Jean et Cie_

La somme de (en toutes lettres) _Quatre mille huit cent francs_

Pour _avoir chargé et déchargé 4 tous ple ballots de vêtements des Commerçants disparus au marché de Butare_

Vu et approuvé
Le Bourgmestre
(Signature)

_le_ 26 05 19 94

Le Comptable
(Signature)

Pour acquit
(Signature ou
2 témoins)

L.C. n° .... du .... 19......

formalities but simply moved into empty homes and began cultivating fields that had belonged to Tutsi.[30]

The inventories of vacant property for five of the eight sectors of Ngoma commune suggest that the genocide varied in severity from one to the other. Survivors have confirmed this analysis, stressing primarily the importance of local leadership in determining the intensity and thoroughness of the attacks. From official data gathered in mid-June, it appears that the greatest proportion of Tutsi suffered in Cyarwa-Sumo and Sahera, where approximately 85 percent and 79 percent of Tutsi landholders were dead or driven away. In Cyarwa-Cyimana and Nkubi, some 62 percent and 58 percent of Tutsi proprietors were said to have vanished. In Ngoma sector, by far the lowest percentage of Tutsi, some 40 percent, were reported dead or fled.[31]

The mid-June inventories for some sectors also included names of persons who had already appropriated or been granted fields or parts of the fields of the departed. So great was the competition for land and the number of contenders to be rewarded that holdings were ordinarily granted to at least two and more often four or five recipients. In the cell Akamuzerwa of Cyarwa-Cyimana sector, the land of Laurenti Masabo was granted to nineteen landholders. In this cell and in the neighboring cell of Agakenyeli, a number of men each received two or three new parcels. The size or number of parcels acquired almost certainly reflected the political weight of the recipients and may also have been related to the zeal shown in slaughtering Tutsi or in driving them from their homes.[32]

At first, local authorities including Burgomaster Kanyabashi ordered the destruction of Tutsi homes, apparently as part of the effort to expose Tutsi to death or to drive them away. After the first massive slaughter had finished, however, authorities in Ngoma and perhaps elsewhere countermanded this directive and insisted that usable structures be left intact, either to serve as housing or for some

---

[30]The first letters making requests are dated May 6 in a series that continues throughout the month and into June; undated and unsigned instructions for Suzanne, not otherwise identified (Butare prefecture).

[31]Calculations were based on data from the December 1993 population report and mid-June property inventories of these sectors. (Butare prefecture).

[32]Ngoma commune, Cyarwa-Cyimana sector, Akamuzerwa cell, "Imbonerahamwe yabaguye numvururu zo 1994"; Ngoma commune, Cyarwa-Cyimana sector, Agakengeli cell, "Imbonerahamwe y'ibarura ry'ibintu byasizwe nabaguye mu mvururu zo muli 1994" (Butare prefecture).

public function, such as a school or an office for the cell. By June 10, national authorities had ordered a return to the earlier policy, at least for any houses that could not be promptly repaired and inhabited. They knew that foreign investigators would be arriving to examine charges of genocide and they wanted damaged houses destroyed "completely and immediately" before they arrived (see below).[33]

Despite official efforts to avoid controversy by early action, questions about property figured importantly on the agenda of most popular meetings in May and June. In late June, the burgomaster of Ngoma had to admit that "certain councilors hadn't handled the operation well." To clear up some misunderstandings, he asked a councilor to prepare a list of all who had received houses from the commune and to have the list countersigned by the local security committee.[34]

Authorities often discussed disputes over women at the same time as they considered problems of property. This was not just because issues of marriage and inheritance were often related but also because men were thought to have an interest in their wives or female relatives comparable to their interest in property. Thus Hutu men were generally recognized to have a right to protect their wives, even if they were Tutsi. Hutu men also intervened to defend their sisters, even if they were married to Tutsi husbands.

At the same May 6 meeting where the prefectural security council decided to implement the 1963-64 rules concerning property, prefectural authorities decided also to write to burgomasters about the need to stop "rapes with violence, seizing and sequestering wives of other men."[35] Referring presumably to sexual servitude involving Tutsi women with family ties in the Hutu community or Hutu widows of Tutsi husbands, the councilor of Cyarwa sector, Ngoma commune declared that the "unions of couples that are happening these days, without a proper marriage contract" was "a form of kidnapping which could cause much enmity, enmity that

---

[33]Human Rights Watch/FIDH interview, Brussels, November 6, 1995; République Rwandaise, Parquet de la République, P.V. no. 0290; Nicodeme Hategikimana (sic), Conseiller, "Inama y'umutekano y'abaturage ba secteur Cyarwa-Sumo yateranye le 12 gicurasi 1994;" Ngoma commune, Cyarwa-Cyimana sector, "Inama ya Comité de Sécurité yo kuli le 23.5.94"; Célestin Rwankubito, Burugumesitiri wa Komini Ndora, "Inyandiko-Mvugo y'Inama y'Abagize Komite Zatowe mu Masegiteri muri Komini Ndora yo kuwa 10 kamena 1994" (Butare prefecture).

[34]Jean Nepo Nzeyimana, Umwanditsi, "Inama yo kuwa 27/06/1994" (Butare prefecture).

[35]Anonymous, Notebook 2, entry for May 6, 1994.

Document: (Butare prefecture) Letter complaining of a woman who pretends to be Hutu and who claims to be protected by Interim President Sindikubwabo.

Butare,kuwa 20 /5 / 1994

Buana Préfet wa Prelegitima ya
B U T A R E

Buana Préfet,

U.ASETSIKAZI MUKAMKUSI Consolata
we.pragaweho kuba initco mu magambo ye,uvuga ngo Prezida
wa Republika SINDI UBWABO Théodore niwe umushyigikiye
mu buhungiro bwe. Uvuga ko umwene we w'umuhungu Prezida
wa Republika ndetse no kumwitwalira kugirango aba"
HUTU" batswice. Umaze gucumbika mu bigo tine ndetse
birerze. Wali warangiye kwicicha Jabo Innocent kugirango
-cebobore inzu ye mu Rwanza yali yaramucumbikiyemo.
Ugendana inyemezo by'ibihimbano atanawe na Kodini avukamo
cyangwa yashatseme by'ubuhutu kandi ali umututsi.
Bene wabo bali ibyitse bikonoye biawi kiawa n'izigacu aa.
Wojn'ibamnoumbikiye bakwiyo iki ? KANTARAMA dienne i Karama

KAMANAYO Jean de Dieu
B.P. 96 BUTARE

could lead far; it was a rape."[36] At a series of meetings with the people in Huye, the burgomaster found that the question of Tutsi wives of Hutu husbands was often raised. Participants in these meetings readily agreed to condemn anyone who attacked these women. With the increased killing of Tutsi women after mid-May, those determined to extend the genocide to all Tutsi women clashed increasingly frequently with Hutu men who wanted to protect their Tutsi wives.[37]

On the question of Hutu women married to Tutsi husbands, the burgomaster of Huye decreed that they should be allowed to keep their property if their husbands were gone or dead. Participants agreed with this decision also because they wished to protect the interests of women related to themselves and other Hutu in the community.[38]

Dissension Over the Genocide
Individual Protectors

Some Rwandans struggled tenaciously to protect certain individual Tutsi and in so doing clashed with those who aimed to eliminate all the Tutsi of a given area. The head of the rice factory in Mugusa commune, Augustin Nkusi, for example, used the soldiers assigned to protect the factory to assure the safety of his Tutsi relatives and others in the adjacent commune of Rusatira. The burgomaster, Rukelibuga, angrily denounced these soldiers whose presence meant that local people "responsible for security did not dare go on that hill." He demanded that these soldiers be removed "because they prevent the inhabitants and other people responsible for security from guaranteeing it and from working [*gukora*]." Once the soldiers were gone, he said, he wanted the local people to "be allowed to do the work that they were unable to do" while the soldiers were present.[39]

In Matyazo, a pastor of the pentacostal church had four soldiers threaten local people who had raided his house four times, each time apparently finding

---

[36]Froduald Nsabimana, Umwanditsi, "Inyandiko Mvugo y'Inama Rusange ya Secteur Cyimana," May 15, 1994.

[37]Human Rights Watch/FIDH interviews, Butare, December 19 and 29, 1995; African Rights, *Rwanda, Not So Innocent*, pp. 30-31.

[38]Jonathas Ruremesha, Bourmestre wa Komini Huye, to Bwana Perefe, May 19, 1994.

[39]Vincent Rukelibuga, Burugumesitiri wa Rusatira, to Bwana Perefe wa Perefegitura, April 29, 1994.

"unknown persons" hiding there. The pastor charged the search party with stealing and with threatening his Tutsi wife. The local people, intimidated by the soldiers, in turn asked the military commander to give them protection. Otherwise, they said, "we will stop doing patrols so that the pastor can hide all the people he wants without problem."[40] In another case, those troubled by a search charged that the searchers were under the influence of marijuana when they made their raids and they got soldiers at local roadblocks to harass one of the search party each time he passed.[41] When a group raided a home in a sector of Ngoma and killed Tutsi found there, the persons who had protected the Tutsi called in National Policemen who threatened to kill the search party. The aggrieved searchers asked the prefect for his support in their efforts "to prevent the enemy from living among us and installing his ibyitso here."[42]

When authorities who had led people to commit violence then undertook to protect certain Tutsi, those who had followed their lead under duress reacted with anger and resentment. In Muyira commune, assailants intending to attack a passing vehicle stopped short when they found Adalbert Muhutu, a member of the national assembly inside. One exclaimed, "It's you who tell us to kill people and then you help them to flee."[43]

Civilian and military authorities also sometimes engaged in disputes over the lives of individuals. The acting burgomaster for Ntyazo commune, for example, explained to the prefect that he was doing his best to obey orders from his superiors, but that he was blocked by Sergeant Elyse Twahirwa who was being paid to protect people known to "be in connivance with the enemy."[44] The burgomaster of Mugusa complained to the military commander about soldiers at

---

[40]Alexandre Nkulikiyimana and others to Bwana commandant de place, May 14, 1994 (Butare prefecture).

[41]Enias Semashinge Ntamushobora to Bwana Conseiller wa Segiteri ya Matyazo, May 16, 1994.

[42]Abahagarariye abaturage ba Cyarwa-Cyimana to Nyakubahwa Perefe wa Perefegitura ya Butare, June 6, 1994.

[43]African Rights, *Rwanda, Death, Despair*, p. 924.

[44]Nicodème Bizimana, Burugumestiri wa Komini Ntyazo, to Bwana Perefe wa Perefegitura Butare, April 30, 1994 (Butare prefecture). Bizimana was actually acting burgomaster at this time.

the barrier at the Hotel Faucon who had taken Camille Rwamanywa, accused of recruiting for the RPF, from him. He had supposed they intended to deliver him to the appropriate authorities, but the soldiers took a bribe from Rwamanywa and released him.[45]

Protection by the Community

Throughout the genocide, authorities had tried whenever possible to send Tutsi back to their home communes to be killed. In some cases, however, home communities offered a strong defense of local Tutsi. In Maraba, people protected an elderly woman out of gratitude for her husband's generosity in sharing his land with others.[46] When a group came from Tumba to kill a Tutsi woman in Cyarwa-Cyimana the neighbors joined to protect her. Her Hutu husband recounted, "They blocked the entrance to the enclosure and would not let the killers in."[47] In Tumba it was recognition for the acts of charity of a religious sister that prompted part of the community to defend others in her family. In the same sector, neighbors sought to protect a teacher, a father of five children, who was known to be a good and pious man. When a Burundian finally killed him, the people turned on him and killed him too, because "he had really carried it all too far."[48]

Local authorities sometimes confronted situations where part of the community rallied to protect a person whom the rest of the community wanted to kill. The burgomaster of Ndora, known for his continuing reluctance to kill, dealt with several such cases in May. In one, he directed that a woman be returned to her protectors because the people of the commune were divided over what to do with her. In another, a group accused Theodetta Mukangango, a medical assistant, of being named on a list of ibyitso supposedly found by students at a vocational school where the directress was also accused of supporting the RPF. According to the notes of a community meeting, "As soon as the people heard that, they let it be known that the communal committee would be attacked if anyone dared to touch Theodetta." As accusers and defenders of Theodetta were disputing the authenticity of the supposed proof, the subprefect arrived to warn that the people must support

---

[45]Andereya Kabayiza, Burugumestri wa Komini Mugusa, to Bwana Commandant de Place Butare-Gikongoro, no. 133/04.18, May 26, 1994 (Butare prefecture).

[46]Human Rights Watch/FIDH interview, Brussels, December 18, 1995.

[47]Human Rights Watch/FIDH interview, Butare, December 29, 1995.

[48]Human Rights Watch/FIDH interview, Neuchatel, December 16, 1995.

the government and combat the enemy. Asked about the case of Theodetta, he declared that everyone should search for her and the other women named in this case and that "the authorities would find a solution for her problem." He castigated the people of Ndora for being divided between sympathizers of the RPF and "others who wanted peace." He announced that "certain persons whom we took to be our brothers are hiding secrets from us."[49] When Theodetta was located several days later, the burgomaster subjected her to a charade of an interrogation about two trips that she had made the year before to Burundi, allegedly to contact the RPF, and about her supposed meetings with other women in the commune who were said to have supported the RPF. He then sent her to the prosecutor in Butare, apparently unwilling to decide her case in the face of strong community sentiment both for and against her.[50]

At the May 23 meeting of the security committee in the sector of Cyarwa-Cyimana, Ngoma commune, some participants complained about the ineffectiveness of their efforts to "punish" certain people in the community:

> Then another question was raised concerning the enemies of Rwanda who should be punished and those who should punish them who do not do it because of one or another member of the committee and yet all that is supposed to be planned in secrecy; also decisions made together are changed without there being another meeting to do it.[51]

Protection on Principle

In some communities, respected leaders opposed the entire killing campaign instead of just trying to protect persons close to themselves. Many such leaders were eliminated relatively early, either by being killed or by being forced to flee,

---

[49]Célestin Rwankubito, Burugumesitiri wa Komini Ndora, "Inyandiko-Mvugo y'Inama y'Abaturage B'Amasegiteri Gisagara, Mukande, Ndora na Cyamukuza yo kuwa 31 Gicurasi 1994."

[50]Célestin Rwankubito, Burugumesitiri wa Komini Ndora, Inyandiko-Mvugo y'Ibazwa rya Mukangango Theodetta Ukekwa Kuba Yari Mu Migambi Y'Umwanzi F.P.R. Inkotanyi, Utera U Rwanda and Raporo Y'Umugereka y'Inyandiko-Mvugo y'Ibazwa Iya Mukangango Theodetta, Ukekwa Kuba Yari Mu Migambi y'Umwanzi Utera U Rwanda, F.P.R. Inkotanyi (Butare prefecture).

[51]Ngoma Commune, Cyarwa-Cyimana sector, "Inama ya Comité de Sécurité yo kuli le 23.5.94."

but a few continued their opposition. A PSD member named Innocent Kabayiza, a teacher and dean at the Groupe Scolaire, seems to have been such a person in the Kabutare neighborhood of Butare town. He told a friend, "I detest this filthy business." Those who supported the genocide first accused him of being Tutsi. When this was not enough to garner wide support for his murder, they arranged to find incriminating "documents" in his home, just as was usually done with Tutsi. Defenders of Kabayiza apparently argued that the recently proclaimed "pacification" prohibited killing him, but his accusers countered by calling the military camp to ask permission to do so. The soldiers told them they should do what they thought right. The accusers beat Kabayiza to death.[52]

In Mbazi, the doctor Alexander Rucyahana began trying to halt attacks on Tutsi as soon as he returned to his home commune from Kigali in early April. Later, he hid two Tutsi women in his house, one of whom suffered complications while giving birth and had to be transported to the hospital, thus leading to public knowledge that she had been hidden at Rucyahana's house. From that time on, his house and the homes of his relatives were regularly searched for Tutsi. Several days after the massacre at nearby Rugango church, militia came to taunt Ruchyahana about being a "king" who had arrogated to himself the power to save Tutsi. They told him that a two-year-old Tutsi boy was still among the bodies at the church waiting to be saved. Rucyahana rescued the child, to much public criticism, and delivered him to the intensive care unit at the hospital.

Local leaders of the killing campaign decided to kill Rucyahana because of his opposition to the genocide. On May 10, they had their plans in place, even to the extent of having alerted potential customers to kinds of goods they would have for sale once they had finished pillaging his home. The pretext for the attack was that Rucyahana was himself a Tutsi who had changed his ethnic affiliation. Having heard of the plan, Rucyahana went to the authorities to ask that those planning the attack be arrested, but his opponents persuaded the National Police commander, Major Rusigariye, that Rucyahana was likely a Tutsi. The major reportedly threatened to kill Rucyahana himself if this were found to be true. In the meantime, he imprisoned Rucyahana, along with those accused of planning to attack him. A small circle including the prefect, the burgomaster Sibomana, the major, the vice-rector, and probably the militia leader Rekeraho, debated Rucyahana's fate the next day. Sibomana attested to Rucyahana's Hutu identity, although he reportedly said he was "almost a Tutsi" because of the efforts he had made to protect them.

---

[52]Human Rights Watch/FIDH interviews, Butare, August 20, October 26, December 19, and 29, 1995.

Another supported Rucyahana's Hutu identity, reporting that a 1973 inquiry had shown that Rucyahana's father was in fact Hutu. The major, unconvinced, wanted to have Rucyahana killed, but rather than do so in police custody, he released him along with those intending to kill him. A mobile unit of RTLM was on the spot, ready to publicize the case. Soldiers or National Police came to search for Rucyahana almost immediately, but he was able to flee Mbazi and escape from the country.[53]

Unruly Military

Soldiers and National Police, acting either on orders or as paid protectors, were drawn into some of the personal, political, and regional conflicts among civilian Hutu, raising the costs in lives lost and property damaged or stolen. They also committed their own abuses against Hutu as well as Tutsi, adding hostility between civilian and soldier to the other kinds of divisions in the prefecture. In addition to killing for pay, they took part in open pillage and in hidden theft, cooperating with civilian criminals and corrupting the children of the streets to assist in burglaries. They robbed each other of the booty looted from Tutsi. Soldiers, including a large number quartered at the Groupe Scolaire where they were convalescing from war injuries, raped Hutu women and girls in the immediate vicinity. Although some soldiers were arrested for their abuses, the prosecutions were apparently too few to have any effect on the behavior of others. When civilian authorities arrested civilians who had helped soldiers in crimes, the soldiers usually were able to obtain their release.[54]

Many people in Butare complained about military misconduct and asked why their people in government, including the interim president and prime minister, could not protect them from such abuses. Prefect Nsabimana and others demanded action from Lieutenant Colonel Muvunyi, who responded in early May by establishing more military police patrols to keep order. The abuses continued, however, and the prefect went to Gitarama to raise the matter with the interim prime minister. Kambanda replied that the problem was the same everywhere and

---

[53]Dr. Alexandre Rucyahana, untitled typescript. Human Rights Watch/FIDH interviews, Brussels, December 18, 1995; Brussels, by telephone, February 2, 1996.

[54]Among other examples: Sgt. Gd. Evariste Ugirase, Rapport à Charge pour le Cpl. Gatete, April 29, 1994; Sgt. Gd. Maximilien Habimana, Rapport à Charge du Mil. Cpl. Gd. Dukuzeyezu, May 3 1994; Cpl. Gd. Habinshuti to Cmd. Gpt. Butare, May 13, 1994 (Butare prefecture).

that military behavior was the responsibility of the minister of defense, not of the prime minister.[55]

Sometime in early May, Captain Nizeyimana was transferred to a military training program at Mata, Gikongoro. He was still often seen in Butare because his wife, also a military officer, continued to live there, but he no longer had an official post from which to command ESO soldiers. Lieutenant Hategekimana also was removed as head of Ngoma camp in May and replaced by Major Ntambabazi. Soon after, Captain Jean de Dieu Mugabo took over from Major Rusigariye as the interim head of the National Police.[56] These transfers may have resulted in part from protests about military misconduct.

Towards the end of May, Lieutenant Colonel Muvunyi was put on leave for two weeks, reportedly on the initiative of Pauline Nyiramasuhuko and Straton Nsabumukunzi. Nyiramasuhuko, who was often seen in military uniform, and Nsabumukunzi, who reportedly spent a great deal of time drinking with soldiers had good connections with the military. They are said to have labeled Muvunyi an icyitso and to have accused him of "sabotaging the development of political action in Butare."[57] Colonel François Munyengango, a native of Huye, replaced Muvunyi, supposedly because military authorities thought it wise to put a southerner in charge.[58]

The naming of new officers seems to have brought little change in the behavior of the soldiers. Their responsibility both for the genocide and for other abuses in Butare does not emerge clearly from data available at this time, perhaps because the tenure of each was so brief, perhaps because civilians had taken over much of the military role in hunting Tutsi.

Even civilians apparently zealous about the killing campaign and ordinarily on good terms with soldiers sometimes found the military abusive. On May 31, Dr. Munyemana tried in vain to save the life of a Hutu friend, an agronomist of the

---

[55]Human Rights Watch/FIDH interview, Nairobi, by telephone, April 3, 1996; Anonymous, Notebook 2, entry for May 6, 1994.

[56]Feuille de Route signed by Jean de Dieu Mugabo, Capt. Gd., Comd. Gpt. Butare (a.i.), May 24, 1994 (Kibuye prefecture).

[57]Human Rights Watch/FIDH interviews, Nairobi, by telephone, March 25 and April 3, 1996; Brussels, by telephone, January 29, 1998; République Rwandaise, Parquet de la République, P.V. no. 253.

[58]Human Rights Watch/FIDH interview, Brussels, December 12, 1995.

Rubona agricultural research station, who was seized by soldiers at the barrier at the Hotel Faucon. The soldiers, who suspected the agronomist was carrying a large sum of cash, took him to the arboretum next to the university and shot him.[59]

Some ten days later, in early June, Prefect Nsabimana declared an end to the road-blocks on the main roads leading out of Butare town, supposedly to eliminate some of the opportunities for soldiers and militia to kill and pillage. The commanding officer cooperated and the barriers came down, but Kalimanzira allegedly overruled them and, within a week, the barriers were back up again. At about this time, there was also a serious conflict between militia and military at barriers at the southern edge of town. This dispute may have been linked to the temporary suspension of the roadblocks. When they were resumed, the barriers of the militia and those of the military were some distance apart.[60]

As the FAR lost ground to the RPF, its troops became even more focused on personal profit. On May 24, some 600 soldiers engaged in pillage and rape as they fled the RPF at Ntyazo. One witness who saw the FAR flee from a later defeat recalls that they passed laden down with furniture and other loot. In at least two communes, Mugusa and Maraba, local people shot soldiers, in one case fatally, to punish them for abuses.[61]

Law and Order

As the numbers of Tutsi were reduced, the assailants deputed to kill them directed their violence increasingly against other Hutu. The young men who hung around the barriers, often drunk or under the influence of marijuana, plundered, raped, and even killed Hutu passersby. Sometimes they confiscated identity cards from victims so that they could claim that they were Tutsi. They paraded through the sectors with the firearms meant for use at the barriers, extorting what they

---

[59]Béatrice Musabeyezu to Monsieur le Commandant de Place, June 1, 1994 (Butare prefecture).

[60]Human Rights Watch/FIDH interviews, Butare, December 18, 1995; Nairobi, by telephone, April 3, 1996; Sylvain Nsabimana, "The Truth About the Massacres in Butare."

[61]Human Rights Watch/FIDH interviews, Butare, October 27 and November 9, 1995; Brussels, February 26, 1997; Anonymous, Notebook 1, entry for May 20, 1994; J.M.V. Habineza, Burgmestri wa Komini Maraba, to Bwana Commanda de Place Butare-Gikongoro, no. 122/04.09.01/4, June 13, 1994 (Butare prefecture).

wanted from unarmed neighbors.[62] On April 27, the interim prime minister and the prefect both called on representatives of the judicial system to help combat violence and disorder, meaning these abuses against Hutu. In this effort to reestablish law and order genocide was not counted as a violation.

Judicial Action

In Butare, the National Police, occupied for some weeks with the genocide, began once more making arrests and investigating crimes in mid-May. A representative of the Ministry of Justice scheduled a meeting on May 25 with the Butare prosecutor, the president of the court of first instance, and other judicial personnel to make sure that the system was beginning to function as ordered.[63] Administrative authorities urged fast and firm action by the police and courts. The burgomaster of Runyinya requested the immediate appointment of a judicial police inspector to help restore order in his commune and the burgomaster of Ngoma insisted that the murders of a group of displaced people—presumably Hutu passing through Matyazo be investigated immediately.[64]

Most of the crimes investigated in May and June involved some form of theft or pillage, including such minor affairs as a purse-snatching and the theft of the bicycle mud-guards mentioned above. In two cases, the accused were interrogated about having destroyed houses belonging to Hutu.[65]

Among the judicial records found in Butare prefecture, there was only one case of genocide suspects having been arrested by judicial authorities: the assailants

---

[62]Ngoma commune, Cyarwa-Cyimana sector, "Inama ya Comité de Sécurité yo kuli le 23.5.94;" Célestin Rwankubito, Burugumesitiri wa Komini Ndora, "Inyandiko-Mvugo y'Inama y'Abaturage B'Amasegiteri Gisagara, Mukande, Ndora na Cyamukuza yo kuwa 31 Gicurasi 1994" (Butare prefecture).

[63]Telegram, Minijust to Presindinstance et Prorep Butare, no. 034/94, May 24, 1994 (Butare prefecture).

[64]Déogratias Hategekimana, Burgmestri wa Komini Runyinya, to Bwana Perefe wa Perefegitura, no. 110/04.09.01/4, May 18, 1994; Joseph Kanyabashi, Burgmestri wa Komini y'Umujyi ya Ngoma, to Bwana Prokireli wa Republika, no. 203/04.09.01, June 10, 1994 (Butare prefecture).

[65]Among numerous examples: Pro Justitia, PV d'Interrogatoire de Bizimana Jean, May 14, 1994; PV d'Interrogatoire de Halindintwali Barthélémy, May 20, 1994; PV d'Interrogatoire du prévenu Ntegano Jonas, June 28, 1994; P.V. d'interrogatoire de Habimana, June 28, 1994 (Butare prefecture).

from Nkubi sector mentioned above. Their arrest seems to have stemmed as much from local power struggles as from any concern for justice.

That the objective of judicial activity was to restore greater security for the Hutu was made clear by the interrogation of a suspect in a case involving grenades. In Butare, as in Kibuye and elsewhere, authorities and established members of society were worried by the number of young men who possessed grenades and used them to terrorize others. On May 13, Sgt. C. Corneille Mudacumura questioned François Minani about his alleged use of grenades to steal a bicycle. He began by asking where Minani had obtained the grenades. Minani declared that he had received three of them from soldiers who were posted in Butare and that he still had two in his possession. When asked what he had done with the third, he stated that his friend Kamanzi had thrown it at the Inyenzi at Sovu. The interrogating officer then pursued questions about whether local authorities were aware that Minani had the remaining grenades and what assurances he could give that he would not misuse them. Sergeant Mudacumura showed no interest whatsoever in the use of the grenade at Sovu that almost certainly cost the lives of one or more Tutsi.[66]

Attempts at Community Control

Authorities hoped too that the "civilian self-defense" program might help establish control over the ill-disciplined assailants whom they themselves had turned loose on society in the first days of the genocide. But most of those who graduated from the program proved as ready to use violence for personal or partisan ends as those who had no such training. The commanders of "civilian self-defense" devoted their energies largely to recruitment and training and left supervision of those trained to local security committees.

Burgomasters, councilors, and security committee members sought to use regulations to reestablish control over the unruly. Burgomaster Kanyabashi railed against the misuse of guns and summoned a meeting for all who had been trained to shoot, except for a few who had to be left at the barriers to guard against the Inkotanyi. He planned to review the rules and regulations for the use of arms and for the functioning of barriers and patrols. Believing that clear identification of guards might help make them more responsible, he promised to prepare written authorization forms for those who were supposed to be working on the barriers. He

---

[66]République Rwandaise, Ministère de la Défense, Gendarmerie Nationale, Groupement Butare, BRG Butare, P.V. d'Interrogatoire du prévenu Minani François, May 13, 1994 (Butare prefecture).

had already put into use similar authorisations for those doing patrols. In Runyinya, too, the burgomaster hoped that the appropriate credentials might improve the orderliness of the patrols and barriers; he announced that the designated head of each group "would receive a written order from the burgomaster to direct the group."[67]

Following the lead of the Ngoma burgomaster, the security committee for Cyarwa-Cyimana tried to lay out its own set of rules. Firearms were to be kept by the heads of the cells and signed out by those who needed them. Those who took the weapons were to sign for them in a register and to account for any bullets used. Carrying a gun into a bar was strictly forbidden. The committee decided:

> As for the use of firearms, there are people who have learned how to use them but they must also respect the disciplinary rules that go with their use. That is why the security committee should present moral lectures (*causeries morales*) on the use of firearms. To do this, the security committee decided to have a meeting with those who have learned how to shoot to determine the rules which will govern the use of the weapons. The persons who are to use these arms as well as the cell heads who should keep them should sign these rules.[68]

Members of the security committee, not themselves trained to shoot, had no means to compel obedience from the young troublemakers. And, complicit as most were in the genocide, they had little grounds for appealing to them through "moral lectures."

At a meeting at the end of June, the burgomaster and a number of councilors, cell heads, and other local leaders in Ngoma again deplored the bad behavior of those at the barriers, those who attempted to search the houses of others while drunk, and those who threatened others with grenades. Implicitly recognizing that government officials had set loose these assailants, the burgomaster threatened to "withdraw their authority" from those who misused it but made no suggestions how this could be done. He remarked that problems like the proliferation and misuse of grenades happen in times of war and that higher authorities would have to find a

---

[67]Joseph Kanyabashi, Burgmestri wa Komini y'Umujyi ya Ngoma, to Bwana Konseye wa segiteri (Bose), no. 205/04.09.01, June 20, 1994; Déogratias Hategekimana, Burgmestri wa Komini Runyinya, to Bwana Perefe, no. 110/04.09.01/4, May 18, 1994 (Butare prefecture).

[68]Ngoma Commune, Cyarwa-Cyimana Sector, "Inama ya Comité y'Umutekano ya Cyarwa-Cyimana yateranye le 5-6-94," (Butare prefecture).

way to resolve them. The burgomaster directed his subordinates "to publically admonish the troublemakers; because if they are not admonished, no one will be safe from the disorder which will reign."[69]

International Contacts

As defeat neared, some authorities realized that the whole international community would come to know the scale and horror of the genocide. RTLM tried to counter worries that officials, soldiers, and political leaders would face international opprobrium and perhaps even actual trials for the crime of genocide. But many, including Kalimanzira, remained very concerned. In his years at the Ministry of the Interior, he had had frequent contacts with foreign diplomats and aid specialists and understood the consequences of implication in genocide, both for the government and for himself. He was one of those determined to shift the Tutsi grouped at the prefecture to another less visible location. When the visit of the Special Rapporteur for Rwanda of the U.N. Human Rights Commission was announced for early June, with other foreign delegations soon to follow, Kalimanzira gave orders to destroy all Tutsi houses that could not be easily repaired and inhabited. Burgomaster Kanyabashi, and presumably other burgomasters, passed on the directive to the people of their communes.[70]

While some engaged in trying to hide the signs of genocide, others sought to convince foreigners that they bore the Tutsi no ill will. When the Swiss humanitarian organization Terre des Hommes sought to evacuate 700 orphans—many of them Tutsi—in late May, its representative, Alexis Briquet, found officials at the Ministry of Defense quite willing to cooperate in drawing up the necessary agreement and others from the Ministry of Labor and Social Affairs ready to sign it.[71] According to former Prefect Nsabimana, Kalimanzira allegedly opposed the evacuation, saying that the children would grow up abroad and return

---

[69]Jean Nepo Nzeyimana, Umwanditsi, "Inama yo kuwa 27/06/1994."

[70]Célestin Rwankubito, Burugumesitiri wa Komini Ndora, "Inyandiko-Mvugo y'Inama y'Abagize Komite Zatowe mu Masegiteri muri Komini Ndora yo kuwa 10 kamena 1994;" Ngoma commune, Cyarwa-Cyimana and Cyarwa-Sumo sectors, "Inyandiko Mvugo y'Inama Cyarwa-Cyimana na Cyarwa-Sumo, June 27, 1994."

[71]Human Rights Watch/FIDH interview, by telephone, Lausanne, April 28, 1998; A. Briquet, Délégué, Terre des hommes, to M. Le Président et M. Le Premier Ministre, May 27, 1994, enclosing Protocole d'Accord (Butare prefecture); Nsabimana, "The Truth about the Massacres in Butare."

to attack Rwanda. If Kalimanzira expressed such
government, his view did not prevail over that ˎ
to improve relations with the international communɩ˷
  The Italian consul, Pierantonio Costa, was able to arnˎ
of a Swiss citizen, his Tutsi wife, and their children and to obtaɩɩ
prefectural civilian and military authorities that seventeen people, ɩɩˎ
children and young people, who had been living with the Sunier family wˎ˷
cared for by the Rwandan Red Cross and a religious order. Someone who deaˎ
with the case, presumably a prefectural official, wrote on a list giving the names
and ages of the seventeen, "these people are an international problem and should
be evacuated!" A subsequent document also remarked that this was "a litigious
case" and decided that the persons in question should be allowed to leave by the
Burundi border. In late June, a religious congregation, the Sisters of Sainte Marie
of Namur, obtained the agreement of the prefect of Butare to the departure of a
group of Hutu, Tutsi, and foreign sisters.[73]
  Prefect Nsabimana, anxious to impress foreigners favorably, cooperated with
foreign journalists as well as with those trying to evacuate people at risk.[74] He later
declared that he regarded foreign contacts as a resource for outmanoeuvering
Kalimanzira and, he asserted, for impeding the genocide. When the foreign staff
of MSF decided to leave after the April massacres at the hospital, Nsabimana
berated one of their Rwandan colleagues for not having stopped their departure.
The former prefect wrote:

Many, many people from Europe left the country, some through my office. I
asked them why they were going. Stay with us, I said, because I felt that if
there were foreigners around it would be very hard for them to keep killing.
If there were no foreigners it would be easy, I thought, for them to keep killing
because there would not be anybody to see it.

He continued:

---

[72]Nsabimana, "The Truth About the Massacres in Butare."

[73]P.A. Costa, Consul d'Italie, untitled document listing persons to be cared for by
the Red Cross and Brothers of Charity, May 11, 1994; hand-written document "Abana
baturutse muri Camp Kacyiru"; Sr. M. Jean Serafino to Autorités Préfectorales de Butare,
June 28, 1994 (Butare prefecture).

[74]Fergal Keane, *Season of Blood*, pp. 176-77, 178-82.

hen I told people not to go, it was because if people are going, leaving you, you have the feeling that you are living in a desert. When you have people around, when you are many, it is possible for people to try to think of ways of protecting themselves.[75]

If Nsabimana and some other officials saw the advantage in presenting a smiling face to foreigners, others sought to impress them with the strength and popular support of the government. When the Vatican representative Cardinal Roger Etchegaray arrived on June 24—after Nsabimana had been replaced by Nteziryayo—authorities in Butare ordered the local population to turn out for a demonstration meant to impress him. Reportedly organized by Dr. Munyemana, the demonstration was a parody of a military review, with crowds of men parading before the pope's representative in a "uniform" of banana leaves and woven grass, with their faces covered with chalk or charcoal.[76]

In Butare, as in Kigali the militia at first interfered with efforts by officials to seem conciliatory to foreign visitors, but eventually yielded to or were overruled by the authorities. Briquet was accosted by a group of militia while he was having a drink with the head of the local Boy Scouts, Réné Sibomana. One of the militia was a university professor who informed the others that Swiss from places like Lausanne or Geneva—as was Briquet—often had links with Belgians. The militia arrested Briquet and confined him to his hotel. They also beat and imprisoned Sibomana. After Briquet talked with Nsabimana, the prefect arranged for Sibomana's release.[77]

More seriously, militia attempted to interfere with the evacuation of orphans agreed to by national authorities. The first day that the children were sent to the border, there was no problem. But with a second convoy, the militia blocked the entrance to the Groupe Scolaire where the children were lodged. It took great effort by Colonel Munyengango to get them to move aside. The convoy was stopped at two barriers when it was leaving Butare. At the second one, militia climbed into the

---

[75]"Interview with Sylvain Nsabimana, October 1, 1994."

[76]Human Rights Watch/FIDH interview, Butare, January 2 and February 5, 1996; African Rights, *Witness to Genocide*, issue no. 2, February 1996, p. 11.

[77]Human Rights Watch/FIDH interviews, by telephone, Nairobi, March 26, 1996; Lausanne, April 28, 1998.

trucks and insisted that the children could not leave. At that moment, Nsabimana arrived and persuaded the militia to allow the convoy to proceed.[78]

Terre des Hommes established a center for orphans and other unaccompanied children in Butare at the Karubanda School. Several hundred more children were then delivered to them, including ten smuggled into the heart of town by a man from Cyarwa under cover of the excitement over the cardinal's visit.[79] A small number of Tutsi adults were also lodged there, some of them helping care for the children. Briquet asked for military protection for the school, but military patrols passed only from time to time. One day, when Briquet was absent, the militia seized a woman at the school and killed her. Briquet arranged to meet with Kajuga, president of the Interahamwe. Kajuga listened politely while Briquet explained the importance of guaranteeing security to humanitarian operations but promised nothing.[80]

The evacuation of a family group, a religious congregation, and of more than a thousand children demonstrates that when foreigners offered opportunities to save lives, there were some officials ready to exploit the possibility, whether for sincere humanitarian reasons or simply to enhance their standing with foreigners. The willingness of officials to evacuate the children like the concern for removing the traces of genocide before the arrival of foreign investigators suggests the extent to which authorities involved in the killing campaign remained concerned about the opinion of foreigners and open to pressure from them.

Permission to Leave

Apparently routine bureaucratic decisions sometimes spelled the difference between life and death for Tutsi. An official who granted permission to leave the commune or the prefecture offered the possibility of escape. In Butare, the prefect and his representatives held particular power because they could grant authorisation to cross the frontier with Burundi. Prefectural officials had been ordered in early April by the general staff to halt the departure of all persons from the country, but they later permitted certain individuals, as well as the groups mentioned above, to leave. A hand-written list records decisions of prefectural authorities concerning thirty-four persons who were apparently seeking authorization to flee the violence

---

[78] Ibid.

[79] Human Rights Watch/FIDH interview, Butare, January 2, 1996.

[80] Human Rights Watch/FIDH interview, by telephone, Lausanne, April 28, 1998.

of Rwanda. Of six "children" from the Kacyiru orphanage in Kigali, five were to be allowed to leave with the next convoy for the frontier, including two who were twenty-one years old. The sixth, a twenty-year-old, was said not to be an orphan and was to stay to work in the kitchen of the orphanage in Butare. Two children from Nyaruhengeri, a fourteen-year-old accompanied by a three-year-old, were to be given priority on the next convoy. A husband, wife, and mother-in-law who wanted to follow other relatives who had left the country were told that they must stay in Butare, as were the persons associated with the Sunier household. Hutu who were not local residents and who were refused permission to leave the prefecture were sent to a displaced persons camp at Mubumbano, in Gishamvu commune, while Tutsi—designated with an asterisk as well as a T next to their names—were sent to join other Tutsi at the prefecture. One person's affiliation was in question. Next to his name was "H? T?," as well as the notation "Mubumbano."[81]

Persons who were desperate did try to flee the prefecture and even the country without the necessary papers, but the likelihood of death was increased if they were captured and could not present even the fragile defense of having complied with regulations.

New Administrators, Dwindling Commitment to the Campaign

As the RPF took Kabgayi and moved towards Gitarama, the interim government called the "civilian self-defense" forces to back regular troops that were undertaking their one and only major counteroffensive of the war. The Ministry of the Interior directed the prefect of Butare to send the civilian forces to the northeast of the prefecture to try to halt the RPF advance.[82] The counteroffensive, launched June 6, failed, with considerable losses to the "civilian self-defense" forces. Several days later, the interim government fled from Gitarama, heading first west towards Kibuye, then northwest to Gisenyi. On June 13, the RPF took Gitarama.

On June 16, the French announced they would send troops for a "humanitarian intervention" in Rwanda. Immediately heartened by the prospect of French military support, the government saw new hope of protecting Butare and areas to the west from the RPF. The day after the French announcement, they made administrative

---

[81]Anonymous, handwritten list entitled "Abana baturutse muri camp Kacyiru" (Butare prefecture).

[82]Telegram, Mininter to Préfet Butare, no. 03 09 30 B, June 3, 1994 (Butare prefecture).

changes meant to give the Hutu of Butare new confidence to resist the RPF and new energy to complete the genocide. They removed Nsabimana as prefect, a decision he attributes to anger over his efforts to protect Tutsi, including by evacuating the orphans. But the national authorities were not so displeased as to want to sever all connection with Nsabimana: they offered him two other positions soon after his dismissal.[83] As his replacement, they named Lieutenant Colonel Nteziryayo of the "civilian self defense" program. They also removed the burgomaster of Ndora, Célestin Rwankubito, who never met Kalimanzira's expectations of zeal for the genocide. They replaced the burgomaster of Muganza with Elie Ndayambaje, a former burgomaster who had reportedly been more effective in organizing the genocide in the commune of Muganza than had the incumbent. The government named Matthieu Nahimana to the vacant post of burgomaster of Ntyazo, most likely to reward him for his efforts in eliminating Tutsi in that region. He was the local leader who had sent the above-mentioned messages calling for troops to reinforce local people confronting Tutsi resistance and asking for the delivery of "the three girls of Gapfizi." The government also removed Vincent Rukelibuga of Rusatira although he had shown zeal for killing Tutsi. Kalimanzira and Nyiramasuhuko had accused him of tolerating robbery of Hutu fleeing through his commune; this may have represented a serious effort to combat attacks by Hutu on Hutu or it may have simply been a pretext for getting rid of a political enemy.[84]

On the day that Nteziryayo took over as prefect, June 20, he ordered the displaced persons who had been outside the prefectural offices loaded on buses and sent to Rango, a short distance outside of town. Burgomaster Kanyabashi and one of the sub-prefects reportedly supervised the move. Although a first group went voluntarily, those who were left for a second dispatch of buses were more roughly handled and forced to go against their will. Many among them feared that they were being sent somewhere removed from the public eye in order to kill them without causing much stir. Once at Rango, the several hundred people—a mixture of Tutsi and Hutu—were kept in a guarded enclosure, where they were provided with food and water. Some witnesses report that militia watched the compound during the day and at night sneaked in to take out young Tutsi to be killed. The

---

[83]Telegram, Mininter to Lt. Col. Nteziryayo Alphonse, no. 94/060, June 20, 1994 (Butare prefecture); Nsabimana, "The Truth about the Massacres in Butare."

[84]Telegram, Mininter to Lt. Col. Nteziryayo Alphonse, no. 94/060, June 20, 1994; Lt. Colonel Ntezilyayo Alphonse to Monsieur le Gérant de la B.C.R., no. 293/04.13, June 27, 1994 (Butare prefecture).

militia also threatened that they would wipe out the entire group, but they were frightened away by the RPF before they could do that.

Soon after Nteziryayo became prefect, and presumably at his order, local authorities directed aggressive searches for the last remaining Tutsi, both in wooded areas around town and in outlying regions. The civilians went through the bushes, beating them, while accompanying soldiers fired in the air to frighten anyone who was hidden there. Some 300 Tutsi were found in the course of a search in Nyaruhengeri and Muganza communes, particularly around Mugombwa. The dirty, tattered, half-starved survivors of earlier massacres were made to sit together outside the building at Kibirizi on the day when the new prefect, resplendent in his uniform, arrived to meet the community leaders inside. During the meeting, two soldiers came in to report to the prefect about having found more Tutsi. The burgomaster reportedly was distressed about the presence of the group outside the door, apparently because he did not want the responsibility of killing the captives. He asked the prefect what was to be done with them. Nteziryayo was annoyed at the question and asked if the people of the commune wanted him to take care of them, implying that they should be willing to do the "work" themselves. No one spoke. Faced with the apparent unwillingness to kill any more, the prefect did not insist. The captives were sent off the next day, presumably headed for Butare. We do not know what happened to them after that.[85]

Throughout June, officials in Butare, as elsewhere, had growing difficulty getting people to do searches and patrols and to guard the barriers. In the sector of Cyarwa-Cyimana at the start of the month, the security committee resolved "to blame people who showed no enthusiasm for doing patrols and to invite the others to wake them up, by force if necessary."[86] By the end of the month, when the Nyakizu security council found it necessary to pay to attract participants, the Ngoma burgomaster was faced with people demanding payment in food for carrying out patrols.[87]

Intellectuals at the university who supported the interim government reacted to the growing dissension and sense of defeat by scheduling a new session of political discussion to reaffirm solidarity of purpose. Since the visit of the prime

---

[85]Human Rights Watch/FIDH interview, Brussels, May 17, 1997.

[86]Bernard Niyibizi, umwanditsi, "Inama ya Comite y'Umutekano ya Cyarwa-Cyimana yateranye Le 5-6-94" (Butare prefecture).

[87]Jean Nepo Nzeyimana, Umwanditsi, "Inama yo kuwa 27/06/1994."

minister in mid-May, the commissions established at that time to propose policy had made little progress. Dr. Eugène Rwamucyo, acting for Le Cercle des Républicains Universitaires de Butare and the Groupe des Défenseurs des Intérêts de la Nation, called for a round table discussion on June 23 to help authorities formulate a national plan for resistance and to understand the "uniformity and consistency necessary in political discourse about this war."[88]

The prefect meanwhile went out to the hills to try to inspire renewed support for the government program. According to a June 29 broadcast of RTLM, he went to the commune of Ndora to promise that the people would deliver "a deserved punishment to the RPF supporters."[89]

The Final Hunt in Butare

If a sense of the approaching end of the regime moved some to refuse or demand pay for further involvement in the genocide, it appears to have fired others with greater urgency and ruthlessness. A man who was caught twice, once in April and again in early July, compared the two assaults.

> [The first assailants] wore banana leaves and they carried weapons, machetes and others, but very few of them seemed convinced of what they were doing. They didn't seem all that dangerous to me. They seemed to be playing a kind of game. The people of July were very different. They made me really afraid. By July 2, they were savage, full of hatred.[90]

At the end of June, the militia in Butare town decided to eliminate some Tutsi whose presence had been known but tolerated for one reason or another. They killed François Semanzi, the councilor for Butare town, who had been hiding since April. Then Shalom himself directed an attack against the household of a wealthy businessman named Rangira. The family had been among the first targeted in April, when six persons had been taken and killed. After that, the family was not attacked, although they continued to live openly in central Butare. Military men who came, virtually daily, to extort money from the family, had afforded some

---

[88]Announcement of proposed meeting, signed Dr. Eugène Rwamucyo, Butare June 22, 1994 (Butare prefecture).

[89]UNAMIR, Notes, RTLM, 9: 00, June 29, 1994.

[90]Human Rights Watch/FIDH interview, Butare, May 25, 1995.

protection. In addition, one of the women in the family was married to a militia
member, which may have made other militia less ready to attack. But on June 27,
with the RPF only a few miles away, the militia broke down the kitchen door with
a sledgehammer just as the family was preparing for bed. One woman of the house
was able to flee, as were two young boys, and a sixteen-year-old hid in the ceiling
and was not found. But Shalom and his men captured Rangira, his wife, two
grandsons—one aged six, the other aged ten—and a teenaged girl who cared for
the children.[91] They put them in the back of a pickup truck, which Shalom drove.
The girl recalled:

> Then they took us to Cyarwa where they kill people. They told us to get out
> and they lined us up next to a mass grave. In it were other bodies, covered with
> sorghum leaves. They pulled the leaves aside when they were going to add
> other bodies. One of the Interahamwe asked the old man for his jacket. He was
> busy taking it from him and the others went to pick up the leaves.[92] I saw my
> chance and I took off. I just ran, not knowing where to go. I saw a ditch and
> jumped down inside it. The Interahamwe came looking for me with flashlights,
> but they didn't find me. They went back to the grave. I heard shots and then
> the truck drove away.[93]

The next morning, the girl made her way to the home of a family related to her
godmother. On the way, she pretended to be gathering firewood to allay any
suspicions from passersby. At that house, she was told that the councilor had
forbidden people to give shelter to Tutsi on pain of death, but she was allowed to
spend one night anyway. The next morning, the family directed her to the camp at
Rango, where the group from the prefecture had recently been installed. As she
approached the enclosure, she was set upon by Interahamwe who were lurking
nearby. They put her in a sack and beat her, saying that she was a messenger of the
Inkotanyi. They took her down to the road where Burgomaster Kanyabashi
happened to be driving by. He stopped and they explained that they had caught this
girl trying to sneak into the Rango camp and that she was probably a spy for the

---

[91]Human Rights Watch/FIDH interviews, Butare, October 26, 28, and 29, 1995.

[92]Killers were ordered to cover the bodies with leaves to conceal them from
observers in helicopters or airplanes overhead (see above).

[93]Human Rights Watch/FIDH interview, Butare, October 28, 1995.

Inkotanyi. Kanyabashi asked the girl, who had clearly been badly beaten, who she was and what had happened. She explained how she had been taken, along with others of Rangira's family. Kanyabashi asked if Rangira, whom he had known well, was dead. She replied that he had been killed a couple of days before. The girl later reported:

> Kanyabashi then told them to take me back to Rango. He said, "I'll think about it and I'll come back this afternoon at 2 p.m." He never came back. After two or three days, I knew that many people had fled, including Kanyabashi, because of the arrival of the Inkotanyi.[94]

Survivors

As the RPF neared Butare town, both the local authorities and the population fled south and west out of the prefecture. The roads were so clogged with the southward-moving flow that it was impossible to go north. By June 28, the sub-prefect of Nyabisindu and the burgomaster of Nyabisindu were in Gikongoro and the burgomasters of Muyira and Ntyazo had taken refuge in Butare town. That day, Kalimanzira reported that the RPF had moved into the commune of Mugusa and had taken the rice factory at Gikonko, which had been defended by FAR troops. In a desperate bid for help, Kalimanzira wired the ministries of interior and defense to get the French who had arrived in Cyangugu to come "protect these innocent people threatened by the Inkotanyi."[95]

By Wednesday, June 29, the RPF were close enough for the sounds of battle to be easily heard in town. Two days later, on July 1, a small French reconnaissance team entered Butare and the next day evacuated a number of persons by plane and helicopter. Knowing that substantial numbers of French troops were at Gikongoro, some thirty kilometers away, Hutu Power politicians and the FAR clung to the hope that they would come to their rescue. Prefect Nteziryayo told a journalist, "The French must come here to convince the RPF not to advance, pushing civilians in front of them."[96] In preparation for this much-desired arrival, flyers hailing Mitterrand and French soldiers lay ready for distribution in the

---

[94]Ibid.

[95]Directeur de Cabinet Mininter to Mininter-Minadef, no. 94/066, June 28, 1994; Directeur de Cabinet Mininter to Mininter, no. 94/065, June 28, 1994 (Butare prefecture).

[96]Lindsey Hilsum, "Rwandan rebels advance as French forces hang back," *Guardian*, July 2, 1994.

prefecture. They repeated the quotation, "It is in hard times that you know your true friends," that *Kangura* had published along with Mitterrand's photo and the Ten Commandments of the Bahutu in 1990. (See chapter three.)

On Friday and Saturday, the town emptied. One journalist described the scene on Saturday:

> The hills echoed with explosions. Trenches were manned by wide-eyed soldiers with bows and arrows, spears, and assault rifles. Tens of thousands of people—some on foot, balancing their weapons on their heads, some herding frightened livestock, others on bicycles so overloaded with personal possessions that they could barely ride them—filled the verges of the roads leading out of the city.[97]

Some left under duress. One university professor who saw no need to flee was warned by militia that he would be killed if he stayed. He boarded the last vehicle in a convoy of university staff heading west. The group was stopped at a barrier beyond Gikongoro while militia and soldiers examined their documents. The barrier guards had a list of persons to seize if they came through, including the professor, who was known to have protected a number of Tutsi children in his house. He was warned by someone who heard guards asking about him near the barrier. He retreated with the children and flagged down a passing French vehicle. The French could not understand why the professor, a Hutu, refused to go to the camp that housed tens of thousands of other Hutu, many militia among them, but they finally agreed to escort him and the children to Nyarushishi, where some ten thousand Tutsi were under their protection.[98]

A Tutsi woman, protected for ten weeks by her Hutu husband, fled with him and their children from their neighborhood of Cyarwa. At a barrier, the militia harassed her and tried to force her husband to take a gun to help defend the town. The family managed to get free and fled once more, this time down back roads towards Rango. As evening fell, the family clustered together with several other Tutsi wives and Hutu husbands. Nearby was a woman and Tutsi child, apparently eager for the protection of their company. The men stood guard all night. When the morning light broke, the woman had gone, leaving the child behind. Soldiers came by soon after and told them to move on to the west because the RPF would soon

---

[97]Robert Block, "Entire city flees the Rwandan rebels," *Independent*, July 4, 1994.

[98]Human Rights Watch/FIDH interviews, Butare, July 5 and 6, 1996.

arrive. Fearing the militia still at the barricades and patrolling the area, they stayed on the outskirts of Butare, hiding and moving from one hilltop to another for three or four days, until they were surrounded by an RPF patrol that told them how to get behind their lines. The witness relates:

> We applauded the RPF, but it was just to fool them. In reality, we did not trust them, even though many in our group were Tutsi. We had heard terrible things about what happened in the zones they controlled. After they passed, most of the group decided to go on towards Gikongoro, but I went back to Butare instead.[99]

On July 3, about one hundred French troops executed a rapid mission to Butare to "evacuate a number of people who needed help and who were in danger from both the militia and the RPF," as Col. Didier Thibaut, commander of the mission, put it.[100] They rescued some one hundred clergy and religious sisters, including Abbé Mungwarareba who ended his long weeks of hiding in various locations (see chapter thirteen) on July 3. Having heard that the French were at the bishopric, the sisters who had been sheltering him called them to come and get him. He was smuggled out of town with his head under a blanket. With the arrival of the French, Abbé Jerome Masinzo, a priest at Ngoma church, who had spent his life since April 30 in the ceiling next to the kitchen chimney and later in a cupboard in the church, was able to emerge also and to join the convoy out of town.

Outside Butare town other sisters and clergy tried to flee on their own. A priest from Kansi church set out to escort a Tutsi nun and three handicapped children across the Burundi border. At a barrier, militia and soldiers stopped their vehicle and insisted that everyone get out. They stripped the nun and put her and the children down in a ditch to kill them and made the others kneel and watch at the roadside. As they began sharpening a stick to use as a spear, the priest rushed forward to give the nun and children absolution. The assailants tried to stop him. In the struggle, they discovered his wallet with several hundred dollars in it. They took the money and told the priest to get back in his vehicle and to take the Tutsi

---

[99]Human Rights Watch/FIDH interview, Butare, January 2, 1996.

[100]Block, "Entire City flees the Rwandan Rebels."

with him. Others were less fortunate. Eight sisters from Sovu and two priests were caught on the road trying to head west a day or two later. They were killed.[101]

The French also evacuated some 600 orphans and unaccompanied children who had been gathered at the Karubanda school. Two of the group saved a teenager, recently graduated from secondary school, who had survived weeks of terror, loneliness, and privation. In late April, the girl, whom we will call Marthe, and her family had watched the spreading smoke and fire on hills facing their comfortable home in Buye and had heard the whistles of the assailants and the cries of their victims. On April 21, as the killing was beginning in town, Marthe and most of the family fled to a Muslim friend who owned an automobile repair business. Two of her sisters stayed at home, with a friend and the watchman for the property. On the morning of April 22, a woman with her arms badly cut by machetes and her baby dead on her back arrived to tell them to flee immediately. One of the girls wanted to pack a bag before leaving. The other, whom we will call Bernadette, tried to convince her that people in flight do not take baggage. While her sister was gathering some clothes, Bernadette heard the sound of a vehicle and peeked out from behind the curtain. She saw militia jumping the fence of the enclosure and soldiers in the truck outside. Shouting for her sister, Bernadette fled through the back fence and hid in a vacant house. There she heard the assailants beating the watchman, demanding to know where the family had gone. He refused to say. They found the girl and her friend in the house and tried to get information from them. The girl told them they had come too late for the others and that they would have to be satisfied with just her. The assailants pillaged the house and took the three away to be killed.

Bernadette rejoined the rest of her family and they stayed together for four days, hiding in a field, sheltered by banana plants. Their hiding place could be reached only through a hole in the back wall of the auto repair shop, itself hidden by a piece of scrap metal. The field was bordered on three sides by buildings and on the fourth by a fence. It was near enough the prison for the family to hear the prisoners, who had been burying the dead, exchanging shouts about who among the notable people of town had been most recently killed. On Tuesday, April 26, they heard a vehicle pass with a loudspeaker making the announcement, "The market is open. No one will kill you. Peace has been established."

Rather than emerge from hiding, the family decided to divide and to seek shelter at several places. Their protector escorted Marthe, dressed as a Muslim

---

[101]Human Rights Watch/FIDH interviews, Butare, March 26, 1996; Brussels, May 17, 1997; Theunis, "Liste des prêtres," p. 133.

woman, to an empty house where Europeans had lived and arranged with the watchman there to look after her. But when the local patrol group came to search the house, they beat the watchman and he revealed both that Marthe was hiding there and who had brought her. The patrol broke down the door, but by that time, Marthe had hidden behind a wardrobe and they did not find her. They went to question her protector and he denied having hidden anyone in that house. They returned, with soldiers this time, and searched again without success. Fearing that she would be found on the next attempt, Marthe fled that night to the home of her protector. He took her in once more and sent her to the field behind his house. There she passed her days in a hole. The household workers came every evening at about 7:30 p.m. and gave her some food. Then she would stretch and run around in the field. She explained:

> It was the only moment that I was really free. I didn't want to go to sleep because I wanted to enjoy those moments and sometimes I didn't go back in the hole until 5 a.m., without having slept at all. The workers were out and around town during the day and they told me that they heard everything about the girl who was hidden but whom no one had yet been able to find.[102]

The protector and his family had fled in early June and the household workers left on June 29 when the sounds of battle were heard in town. After three days without food, Marthe left the field. Having heard from the workers that the French might be coming, she went to the headquarters of a Franco-Rwandan exchange project, hoping she might find them there. But there was no one. She returned to the field. Believing her family to be dead and believing that she herself was going to die anyway, she decided that she might as well go and get herself killed. At 6 a.m. on Sunday July 3, she went to the barrier next to the gas station, at the start of the road to Gikongoro. She recalled:

> The first sergeant who was in charge of the barrier asked me, "Where are you coming from and where are you going?" I answered that I knew where I came from but that I didn't know where I was going. He said, "I'll kill her and that will show the Inkotanyi what we will do to them." He pushed me into a hole

---

[102]Human Rights Watch/FIDH interview, Butare, October 20, 1995.

after he had hit me and told the other soldiers at the barrier that no one should touch me. He said, "I'll take care of her myself."[103]

She stayed in the large hole near the barrier until about 11a.m., when another soldier came by and greeted her. She was too exhausted to do more than make a gesture of acknowledgement. This angered the soldier, who said, "You see how they are! I'm going to kill her." But as he took aim, one of the militia, who knew Marthe, intervened. A man named Clement, he was the son of Isaac Munyagesheke, an important distributor of beer and long-time MRND leader, who was also important in the "civilian self-defense" program. Clement told the soldier, "Why are you killing this girl instead of going to find the Inkotanyi and fighting them? You shouldn't kill this girl. There's no point in that." He pushed the soldier away and gave him 5,000 Rwandan francs (about U.S.$25) to leave.[104]

From the hole, Marthe could see and hear the many children playing in the yard at the Karubanda school, but thought that she would never be able to get there. Mortars were falling, including one that exploded in the nearby prison yard. Then French soldiers arrived. Marthe remembered:

> A jeep stopped not far from the hole where I was. I heard the French telling the Interahamwe, "In twenty minutes, you be out of town." I cried out because I could not stand up to get out of the hole. Then one of the French got me out.[105]

Marthe was put in one of the eight buses organized by the French to evacuate the children from Karubanda. As they drove south out of town, they passed the barrier in front of Nyiramasuhuko's house. The minister was there, at the barrier, in military uniform, with her son Shalom. At a second barrier further south, the French escort had to threaten the militia with their guns to be allowed to pass. The convoy was also protected overhead by a helicopter that followed it down to the border with Burundi. At the border, while Marthe was waiting to register her identity, she was looking at the children, some of them very small, a few months old, and some of them with their arms or legs badly cut or even missing altogether.

---

[103]Ibid.

[104]Ibid. Clement, the son of Munyagesheke, reportedly saved a Tutsi woman marked for death at the hospital by smuggling her away in the trunk of his car. Human Rights Watch/FIDH interview, Brussels, December 18, 1995.

[105]Human Rights Watch/FIDH interview, Butare, October 20, 1995.

Suddenly she saw her sister Bernadette step out of one of the vehicles. "We cried and we almost made a scene. It was unbelievable finding each other that way."[106]

As Colonel Thibaut had declared, the French had come also to evacuate those "who were in danger from...the RPF," including the former prefect Nsabimana. As they would do later with military and civilian authorities who fled into Zaire, they provided him safe passage to Burundi. The first night, Nsabimana stayed with the other evacuees in Bujumbura and showed great interest in hearing how they had survived. He was sought by Burundian soldiers but eluded them early the next morning when a car came from the Rwandan embassy in Bujumbura to collect him.[107]

As the French escorted their charges out of town to the south and west, the RPF arrived from the north. A few Tutsi emerged from hiding to applaud their arrival. One man had survived an unsuccessful effort to flee across the border to Burundi, had hidden for weeks in the bush, had been imprisoned and escaped when he was being transported to be killed, had again hidden in the woods, and had sneaked into Butare town at the end of June to lie hidden along the top of a wall, sheltered by a low-hanging avocado tree. He saw the RPF move in and came down from his perch to welcome them. Another emerged from a tiny, make-shift shelter of bricks where he had spent weeks of solitude and misery. Two parents and their two children who had passed their first weeks in an unused well and the last month and a half in a ceiling also came out to applaud their rescuers.

Authority and Responsibility

In the first days of the genocide in Butare, a Hutu of some standing but no official position tried to intervene when a militia gang was about to attack some Tutsi. They pushed him aside, asking why they should listen to him since he was neither prefect, nor burgomaster, nor councilor. By late June, even those who held such posts could no longer count on being obeyed or even respected. The prefect was insulted at a barrier by a university professor because he had protected the widow of an opponent of the genocide. The burgomaster of Ngoma received peremptory demands from other university professors who insisted he facilitate their requests for arms and military collaboration in doing their patrols. A councilor

---

[106]Ibid.

[107]Ibid.; Nsabimana, "The Truth about the Massacres in Butare"; Sylvain Nsabimana, "2e Edition du Rapport Africa Rights, pages 168-176, Le Point par Nsabimana Sylvain" (provided by Sylvain Nsabimana).

in Nyaruhengeri felt obliged to obey the rude order of a teenager armed with a grenade, explaining to a foreign observer that it was safer to obey "the authorities." Another councilor from Cyarwa-Cyimana remarked:

> Indeed there are people who say that authority no longer exists, for example, those who dared to tell the councilor, face to face, that they would make mincemeat of him with their machetes, when he is only preventing them from destroying his crops that are still growing—not even ripened yet—in the fields.[108]

In late May and June, other people contested the authority of their councilors with less violence but equal vehemence, demanding that they resign.

The erosion of authority was not the cause but rather the result of the genocide: by implementing the killing campaign, the administrators sacrificed their legitimacy and undermined their own authority. The "anarchy" and "chaos" which they deplored may have been real by the end of June but it did not exist in April and cannot be used to excuse the genocidal violence.

By the time of the removal of Prefect Habyalimana, he and his subordinates still presented a substantial obstacle to slaughter in many communes, although they had been overcome by extremists in the western and southwestern parts of the prefecture. After his removal and the recruitment of administrators as passive or active collaborators, the committed leaders of the campaign were able to annihilate the majority of the Tutsi in the prefecture in just ten days. The dramatic transformation of the situation in Butare demonstrates how important the administration was in first hindering and then in facilitating the genocide.

From written records and from the accounts of witnesses, it is clear that some administrators zealously executed their part in the genocide. But most seem to have collaborated reluctantly, from fear of losing their posts or their lives. While the first set took public leadership of the killing campaign, the second group stepped silently aside for activists from outside the administrative hierarchy: political leaders, intellectuals, or just local strong men suddenly become important through their ruthlessness and possession of firearms.

Regardless of personal conviction, the administrators undertook the bureaucratic implementation of the killing campaign. This did not entail taking up grenades or machetes and leading attacks, although a few lower level officials did

---

[108]Ngoma commune, Cyarwa-Cyimana sector, "Inyandiko mvugo y'Inama y'Umutekano," May 13, 1994.

so. Instead they participated by carrying on their usual functions of passing information down the chain of command, exhorting the population to action and organizing them for that purpose, and implementing the regulations connected with the campaign. They saw that recruits were selected and trained for "civilian self defense." They assigned communal police to "work" at massacre sites and on patrols. They recorded the distribution of firearms to subordinates and accounted for the numbers of bullets used. They logged in the miles driven by communal vehicles and the sums paid for the transport of the goods confiscated from Tutsi market vendors. They supervised the registration of nonresidents staying in the commune. They decided on the issuance of identity papers for persons who claimed to have lost theirs and they authorized—or did not authorize—permits to leave the commune or prefecture. By the regular and supposedly respectable exercise of their public functions, they condemned Tutsi to death for the mere fact of being Tutsi. Silent before the daily horror, they sought to hide behind the bureaucratic routine that divided the genocide into a series of discrete tasks, each ordinary in itself. But in the end, the semblance of administration as usual failed to disguise the ultimate objective of extermination.

In Butare, as elsewhere in Rwanda, people at all levels of responsibility saved some Tutsi even while carrying out the genocide. In some cases, the favored were relatives, friends, or at least acquaintances: like the women saved by Interim President Sindikubwabo, the priest ransomed by the burgomaster of Ngoma, the few who obtained false identity papers from the burgomasters of Huye and Shyanda, and the persons who hid under the beds of various councilors and communal employees.[109] In some rare cases, officials even assisted sizable numbers of persons to whom they were not personally linked, as the prefect did in helping to evacuate the orphans.

But some 105,000 Tutsi alive in Butare prefecture in early April 1994 had been slain by early July, in addition to tens of thousands of others who had fled there from other prefectures.[110] Military, civilian and political authorities must first take responsibility for slaughtering these vast numbers of Tutsi before they claim

---

[109]See above; also Jean de Dieu Kamanayo to Bwana Préfet wa Prefegitura wa Butare, June 20, 1994 (Butare prefecture); Human Rights Watch/FIDH interview, Brussels, December 18, 1995, March 4, 1996, and Neuchatel, December 16, 1995; African Rights, *Rwanda, Not So Innocent*, p. 167; African Rights, *Witness to Genocide,* issue 7, pp. 48-49.

[110]Estimate based on an original population of 140,000 and 35,000 survivors. See above and U.S. Committee for Refugees, *Life After Death: Suspicion and Reintegration in Post-Genocide Rwanda*, February 1998, p. 10.

credit for saving a few fortunate individuals from the genocide they themselves perpetrated.

IGNORING GENOCIDE

During the early weeks of slaughter international leaders did not use the word "genocide," as if avoiding the term could eliminate the obligation to confront the crime. The major international actors—policymakers in Belgium, the U.S., France, and the U.N.—all understood the gravity of the crisis within the first twenty-four hours even if they could not have predicted the massive toll that the slaughter would eventually take. They could have used national troops or UNAMIR or a combined force of both to confront the killers and immediately save lives. By disrupting the killing campaign at its central and most essential point, the foreign soldiers could have disabled it throughout the country. By serving as a counterweight to the elite forces under Bagosora, they could have encouraged dissenters to step forward as active opponents of the genocide.

Major international leaders were ready to collaborate on the common goal of evacuating their own citizens and expatriate employees, but they refused any joint intervention to save Rwandan lives. Instead they focused on issues of immediate importance for their own countries: Belgium on extricating its peacekeepers with a minimum of dishonor; the U.S. on avoiding committing resources to a crisis remote from U.S. concerns; and France on protecting its client and its zone of Francophone influence. Meanwhile most staff at the U.N. were fixed on averting another failure in peacekeeping operations, even at the cost of Rwandan lives.

Rather than undertake innovative and potentially costly ways to halt the slaughter, international leaders and the U.N. staff treated the extermination campaign as an unfortunate consequence of the war and devoted their energies to trying to obtain a cease-fire between the belligerents. They waited two weeks before taking action and then it was to reduce the number of peacekeepers in Rwanda.

Bagosora and his Hutu Power supporters exploited the two weeks of international inaction to argue that their program of genocide could in fact succeed without significant international reaction. They intimidated dissenters into silence and recruited growing forces to the killing campaign.

As political leaders in various national capitals and at the U.N. did nothing but talk, some of the peacekeepers took the initiative to save lives. Insignificant in terms of the numbers who needed to be saved, their effort to carry out their mission nonetheless protected thousands who would otherwise almost certainly have been killed.

595

UNAMIR

As the killers began their assaults, everyone in Rwanda—Rwandan and foreigner—looked to UNAMIR to see what it would do. The killers watched to see if it would threaten them; by and large, it did not. People at risk counted on it to protect them; for the vast majority of Rwandans, it did not do that either. Its success in protecting some Rwandans was commendable but also served to show how many more could have been rescued had the Security Council ordered that mission and provided the means to execute it.

"Defensive Survival Exercise"

The UNAMIR mandate permitted the peacekeepers to use force in self-defense, which was defined as including "resistance to attempts by forceful means to prevent the Force from discharging its duties under the mandate of UNAMIR." They were allowed to use their weapons "to defend themselves, other U.N. lives, or persons under their protection against direct attack" and, even more broadly, they were directed to use armed force "when other lives are in mortal danger."[1] In addition, the strong language of Paragraph 17 of the Rules of Engagement specified that the force was "morally and legally obligated" to "use all available means" to halt "ethnically or politically motivated criminal acts" and that it "will take the necessary action to prevent any crime against humanity."

Since January, however, headquarters in New York had insisted repeatedly on a narrow definition of what was permitted under the mandate and the Rules of Engagement. Consequently General Dallaire ordered troops over and over to negotiate and to avoid the use of armed force. Col. Luc Marchal, head of the Kigali command, had reinforced these orders with his men at the end of March, just before the start of the genocide, following two incidents in which UNAMIR soldiers had fired their weapons unjustifiably.[2] After April 6, officers on the spot believed that the rules must be revised before they could use force more freely in the changed circumstances. U.S. and Belgian authorities appear to have concluded the same and the Belgians at first asked New York for a broader interpretation of the rules. Headquarters said no change was necessary and that Dallaire had the authority to interpret the rules according to the needs of the situation. Iqbal Riza, the assistant secretary-general who directed the Rwandan operation, repeated in an interview

---

[1]Force Commander, "Operational Directive No. 02: Rules of Engagement" (Interim), File No. 4003.1, November 19, 1993 (confidential source), pp.1, 4, 6.

[2]Col. Luc Marchal, "Considérations relatives," p. 20.

later that Dallaire had broad authority to act. He asserted also that firing to prevent loss of life was within the "broad rules of engagement that apply to all peacekeeping operations." Even if doing so were not strictly within the mandate, "nobody would have blamed" peacekeepers had they opened fire to save lives.[3] But this was not the official position at the time, as is shown in Annan's remarks below. Officers in Rwanda understood that New York had confirmed the restrictive rules in place since January.[4] Some Belgian soldiers believed that there were virtually no circumstances in which they could legitimately fire their weapons—some attribute the capture of the ten peacekeepers who were later executed to that belief—and many Rwandan soldiers and militia believed that the UNAMIR soldiers would not fire, regardless of the provocation.[5] The policy on the use of firearms symbolized the more general and long-established reluctance of UNAMIR to take any deterrent action. As Dallaire had predicted in February, some Rwandans perceived this reluctance as weakness and were emboldened by it.

[handwritten margin note: what do the PK in the field see as their method?]

Even had Dallaire and his officers chosen to follow Paragraph 17 and use "all available means" against the violence, the means available to them were seriously limited. Administrative bungling and reluctance to spend money had left the force ill-prepared to deal with any crisis. It had food for less than two weeks, drinking water in some posts for only one or two days, and fuel for two to three days. It was critically short of ammunition and medical supplies. Its few armored personnel carriers, inherited from peacekeeping operations elsewhere, were in such poor condition that often only one or two were functioning at any given time. It had no ambulance.[6]

In addition to lacking supplies, UNAMIR was short on qualified, experienced troops, a problem which Dallaire had repeatedly asked his superiors to remedy. The

---

[3] F o u n d   o n   i n t e r n e t   a t http://www.pbs.org/wgbh/pages/frontline/shows/evil/interviews/riza.html;   Commission d'enquête, *Rapport*, p. 556.

[4]Commission d'enquête, *Rapport*, p. 450 and Annexe 5, pp. 24, 87.

[5]Commission d'enquête, *Rapport*, pp. 385-88, 452.

[6]Outgoing code cable from Booh-Booh UNAMIR to Annan/Goulding, April 8, 1994 (confidential source); Human Rights Watch/FIDH interview, by telephone, May 22, 1996; United Nations, *Comprehensive Report on Lessons Learned from United Nations Assistance Mission for Rwanda (UNAMIR), October 1993-April 1996* (Lessons Learned Unit, Department of Peacekeeping Operations, December 1996), p. 32.

mainstay of the force in Kigali was the 440 man Belgian contingent and some 200 Ghanaians recently brought down from the demilitarized zone in the north. The most numerous contingent in the capital, more than 900 soldiers from Bangladesh, were poorly trained and poorly equipped.[7] Once the shooting began, they could not be relied on to follow orders. On the afternoon of April 7, they refused even to open the gate of the stadium where they were quartered to admit a group of Belgian soldiers who were entrapped just outside by a crowd of Rwandan military and militia. The standoff between the Belgians and the hostile crowd went on for some two hours until the Belgians opened fire, ran to the stadium, and climbed over the fence.[8]

Within hours of the plane crash, Dallaire sent a message to New York saying, "Give me the means and I can do more." His superiors in the peacekeeping office, probably Gen. Maurice Baril, replied "that nobody in New York was interested in that." In a similarly futile telephone call on April 10, Dallaire again asked for 5,000 troops and a clear mandate to stop the killings.[9]

Despite the lack of support from New York, UNAMIR officers increased the number of peacekeepers on patrol around the city and the number assigned to protect political leaders. At first, the U.N. soldiers patrolled with National Policemen as they had in the past, but as the hours passed, fewer and fewer National Police showed up for these missions.[10] Some UNAMIR patrols went out unaccompanied. They encountered a growing number of threatening situations as did the peacekeepers guarding government leaders. After dawn, the rumor spread that Belgians had participated in shooting down Habyarimana's plane—misinformation later broadcast by RTLM—and Belgian officers ordered their men to use great caution and to restrict their movements to the "bare minimum."[11]

---

[7]United Nations, *The United Nations and Rwanda,* p. 35.

[8]Commission d'enquête, *Rapport,* Annexe 5, p. 28.

[9]Human Rights Watch/FIDH interview, by telephone, October 26, 1997. Assemblée Nationale, Mission d'information commune, *Enquête sur la tragédie rwandaise (1990-1994),* Tome I, Rapport, p.286.

[10]Commission d'enquête, *Rapport,* Annexe 5, p. 21.

[11]Ibid., p. 24.

When peacekeepers assigned to protect government leaders saw assailants arrive, usually in groups of twenty or thirty, they sometimes left almost immediately.[12] In other cases, they attempted to negotiate, as did three Belgian peacekeepers who were protecting the home of PSD leader Félicien Ngango early in the morning of April 7. Informed of the attack at Ngango's house, UNAMIR officers called for help from Bangladeshi peacekeepers, who had a functioning armored personnel carrier nearby, but got no response. A Belgian sergeant arrived with three soldiers and tried to persuade the assailants to allow the family to leave. They refused but were willing to let the Belgians depart alone. The peacekeepers left and not long after the Rwandan soldiers attacked the house and slaughtered the family.[13]

In a similar situation shortly after, the sector headquarters asked soldiers under the command of Lt. Luc Lemaire to save a Tutsi named Joseph Habimana "if possible." When a group of twenty police refused to allow the UNAMIR soldiers to take Habimana from his home, Lemaire himself went to negotiate. Unable to obtain satisfaction from the police on the spot, he and Habimana went to the local police headquarters, where he found the atmosphere hostile to Belgians and the angry subordinate officers barely controlled by their lieutenant. They insisted that Habimana had a gun and had shot at them. Judging this rescue to be not "possible," Lemaire returned Habimana to his home and went back to his post.[14]

In a cable the next day, Dallaire identified protecting government leaders as "the major task" for the force, one which must be undertaken even at the risk of the lives of UNAMIR soldiers. Protecting these persons was "the last means" of instituting the proposed new government and "saving the peace process." By the time Dallaire wired this message to New York, however, virtually all the major political leaders who needed protection were dead or in flight, in part because their UNAMIR guards had refused to take risks to protect them.[15]

As the force came under fire—sometimes deliberate, sometimes random—several times in the next day or two, UNAMIR moved into what Dallaire called "a defensive survival exercise" where protecting its own men became its

[12]Human Rights Watch interview, Kigali, October 30, 1994.

[13]Dewez, "Chronique," p. 16.

[14]Ibid., p. 17.

[15]Outgoing code cable from Booh-Booh UNAMIR to Annan/Goulding, April 8, 1994.

primary concern. Plans for UNAMIR had called for a rapid deployment group to be established, but it was not yet functional and there was no reserve available to rescue peacekeepers caught in a difficult situation. Particularly after the murder of the ten Belgian peacekeepers, Dallaire was ordered not to risk further losses or take actions that might lead to reprisals. He passed on the orders to his men, even though he disagreed with them. Dallaire later commented:

> An operation should begin with the objective and then consider how best to achieve it with minimal risk. Instead, our operations began with an evaluation of risk and if there was risk, the objective was forgotten. You can't begin by asking if there is a risk. If there is no risk, they could have sent Boy Scouts, not soldiers.[16]

Rwandans who suffered or saw others suffer while peacekeepers departed safe and sound from threatening situations did not know about the orders to avoid risk or the limitations on the mandate or the lack of supplies; they knew only that the soldiers to whom they looked for protection had disappeared.

The Mandate and Passive Witnesses to Genocide

As news of the crisis in Rwanda reached Europe, the Belgians reacted first with an effort to strengthen UNAMIR. When they had tried unsuccessfully to expand its mandate in late February, they had warned U.N. staff that "public opinion would never tolerate having Belgian peacekeepers remain passive witnesses to genocide." On April 7, Belgian Foreign Minister Willy Claes, who was in Bucharest, echoed those words. He wired Belgian diplomats that a military coup d'état or "widespread massacres"[17] might take place as a result of the killing of Habyarimana. He then commented, "If there should be many deaths, public opinion would not understand if UNAMIR remained passive, hiding behind the limitation of its mandate." He asked how authorities in New York, Washington and Paris would view the role of the peacekeepers in such a situation and suggested that

---

[16]Human Rights Watch/FIDH interview, Toronto, September 16, 1997.

[17]Commission d'enquête, *Rapport*, pp. 525, 530. The senior staff of the foreign affairs ministry, meeting in Claes' absence, also noted the possibility of "large massacres."

Document: Cartoon from *Kangura*, January 1994, showing UNAMIR soldiers helping Gen. Kagame of the RPF oppress the Hutu. The Belgian soldier asks: "Is this a Hutu or a Tutsi?" and Kagame answers, "It is a Hutu."

Les Belges alliés au FPR dans un racisme anti-hutu (*Kangura*, janvier 1994, n° 55, p. 12)
- Des Belges de la MINUAR : *Tu es hutu ou tutsi ?*
- Kagame (FPR) le pied sur un homme : *Ça c'est un Hutu.*
- Le "peuple majoritaire" cher à Kangura découvrant l'antiracisme : *Nous, nous sommes des Rwandais.*

Document: Cartoon from Kangura, February 1994, showing Tutsi women seducing UNAMIR soldiers. The caption says, "General Dallaire and his army have fallen into the trap of the seductresses."

Les femmes tutsi, responsables du ralliement des Blancs au FPR
(***Kangura***, n°56, février 1994 , n° 56, p. 15)
- *Le général Dallaire et son armée sont tombés dans le piège des femmes fatales.*

UNAMIR should be able to protect political leaders within the terms of its mandate and without sacrificing its neutrality.[18]

Not yet aware that Belgians had been killed in Rwanda, Claes also asked how the U.N. would view the possibility of the peacekeepers protecting or helping evacuate Belgians or other foreigners.[19] He treated this question as distinct from that of assistance to Rwandans but linked by the common issue of the limitations of the mandate.

In the absence of the secretary-general, who was in Europe, the Belgian ambassador to the U.N. raised these issues with Kofi Annan, the under secretary-general in charge of peacekeeping. Annan replied that UNAMIR would protect political leaders as much as it could, given the means at its disposal. As a result of contacts with UNAMIR, Annan and his subordinate Iqbal Riza knew at this time that government troops were already carrying out massacres of Tutsi in addition to murdering political leaders. Annan told the ambasador "that UNAMIR will do everything in its power to try to prevent or reduce the massacres."[20]

Concerning foreigners, Annan specified that Dallaire could order peacekeepers to help them, but only if this did not entail increased risk. He remarked that whatever was done must be governed by the Rules of Engagement and that the peacekeepers could not use armed force to save Belgians if they themselves were not threatened. At most, they could intervene by negotiation. Annan's reading of the rules seems unjustifiably restrictive, particularly as regards Paragraph 13 (b)(4) which permits peacekeepers to use armed force "when other lives are in danger." His interpretation did at least apply the same standard for foreigners as for Rwandans, rejecting armed intervention in both cases.

In response to the Belgian interest in seeing UNAMIR play a more active role, Annan replied that such a decision would require troop reinforcements as well as a change in the mandate. He stressed the time that would be required and the difficulty involved in moving from a Chapter VI to a Chapter VII operation,

---

[18]The Permanent Assistant Representative of Belgium to the U.N., Mr. Brouhns, says that he raised the issue of extending the mandate in order to protect Rwandans, but that instructions from Brussels did not. That may have been the case after April 8, but this document seems to establish that Claes was speaking of both Rwandans and Belgians on April 7. The response below from Annan confirms this interpretation. Commission d'enquête, *Rapport*, pp. 525-26.

[19]Commission d'enquête, *Rapport*, pp. 525-26.

[20]Commission d'enquête, *Rapport*, pp. 526-27.

particularly because UNAMIR was only nominally supported by the U.S., the U.K., and the Russian Federation. He added that the member states which had contributed the troops would also have to be consulted. He emphasized again the need for the same treatment for Rwandans and foreigners:

> Finally, it would be politically delicate to limit this broadening of the mandate to the protection of foreigners. It would of course have to be meant for the whole Rwandan population.[21]

In contrast to Annan's emphasis on the obstacles to prompt action, Riza would later assert that had the council wanted to act, the troops and tanks could have been airlifted in two days to Rwanda.[22]

By the evening of April 7, U.N. staff as well as the members of the Security Council knew that the Presidential Guard had killed Belgian peacekeepers, assassinated political leaders, and begun massacres of civilians.[23] In its first statement on the crisis, the council deplored the slaughter of government leaders and "many civilians" and strongly condemned "these horrific attacks and their perpetrators." The council then demanded that the "Rwandese security forces and military units and paramilitary units" halt the killings.[24] At this point, the council could have declared an emergency and moved to a Chapter VII mandate, but instead it delayed a decision until the secretary-general presented a written recommendation nearly two weeks later.

From the declaration, it is clear that council members knew that Rwandan government forces and militia were responsible for the slaughter, but it is not clear how many of them knew that many of the "civilians" were Tutsi and that that they were being targeted on an ethnic basis. Notes of the briefing that preceded the vote on the resolution make no mention of this information.

---

[21]Commission d'enquête, *Rapport*, p. 528.

[22] Found on internet at http://www.pbs.org/wgbh/pages/frontline/shows/evil/interviews/riza.html.

[23]Ibid., pp. 519, 526; Federal News Service, "State Department Regular Briefing," April 8, 1994, p. 2.

[24]Presidential Statement, Security Council, S/PRST/16, April 7, 1994, in United Nations, *The United Nations and Rwanda,* pp. 254-55.

Certainly the U.S., French, and Belgian delegates knew that ethnic slaughter had begun and anticipated extensive disorder. Both the Belgians and the U.S. began planning to evacuate their citizens by the evening of April 7 and the French were considering the move the next day.[25] General Christian Quesnot, then head of military affairs for the French presidency, recalled that "political as well as military leaders understood immediately that we were headed towards massacres on a scale far beyond any that had taken place before."[26] At a meeting on April 8, senior French military officers reportedly predicted that 100,000 Tutsi would die.[27]

Yet the U.S. decided on the evening of April 7 that the mandate could not be broadened from Chapter VI to Chapter VII and it began to suggest even that UNAMIR should be simply withdrawn. Several members of the Security Council—described as "permanent" and "western"—shared these points of view, probably meaning that at least the U.K. supported the U.S. position.[28] These "U.N. diplomats"—and presumably the U.N. staff who assisted them—insisted that UNAMIR must remain "neutral." To permit any apparent deviation from this position could result in military action against UNAMIR, a weak and lightly armed force unable to defend itself. Were UNAMIR attacked, member states might have to provide additional troops or funds to rescue it. They feared also creating a precedent (i.e., having another failure) that would have repercussions on other peacekeeping operations. They recalled the unfortunate consequences of a too assertive policy in Somalia, where the need for neutrality was ignored and failure ensued. Rather than intervene more actively to protect the population, all that the troops could do was to patrol and be visible in the city.[29] Both the U.S. and the U.K. had considered total withdrawal in February,[30] so it is not surprising to find

---

[25]Commission d'enquête, *Rapport*, pp. 519, 530; United Nations, Security Council, Notes on Informal Consultations, April 8,1994.

[26]Assemblée Nationale, Mission d'information commune, *Enquête sur la tragédie rwandaise (1990-1994)*, Tome III, Auditions, Volume I, p.344.

[27]Agnès Callamard, manuscript, "French Policy in Rwanda: A Diabolic Banality," p. 30.

[28]Commission d'enquête, *Rapport*, p. 532.

[29]Ibid., p. 531.

[30]See chapter five.

them adopting the same position again—except that in the meantime, massive ethnic slaughter had begun.

Although UNAMIR could not actively protect Rwandans, Assistant Secretary-General Riza suggested that it might be able to assist foreigners if its mandate were changed.[31] From this comment, it appears strong signals from certain "permanent" "western" members had caused the secretariat staff to consider applying the rules differently for foreigners and for Rwandans.

By April 8, as massacres of Tutsi increased, Belgium moved from seeking to use UNAMIR to protect both Rwandans and foreigners to proposing that the force help just foreigners. Claes once more used public opinion as a pretext for policy. The public which in February supposedly would not accept "passivity" in the face of a genocide and which the day before would not accept UNAMIR hiding behind the limitations of its mandate in the face of "many deaths," now was said to find it unacceptable for UNAMIR soldiers to "stay passive"[32] if there were more Belgian victims.

The secretary-general also foresaw using UNAMIR to assist foreigners, but he proposed helping an even more limited group, U.N. personnel exclusively. He wrote from Europe to ask the council to change the mandate and Rules of Engagement and to plan for recruiting an additional two or three battalions in order to make this assistance possible.

But that afternoon Annan in effect rescinded the request made by Boutros-Ghali and told Belgian, U.S., and French diplomats that sending two or three battalions under U.N. command would be too costly in time and money. It would be preferable for national governments to send troops for a "humanitarian" intervention, i.e., to evacuate foreigners. With the problems of troops to be resolved in this way, the question of mandate was no longer a problem. The U.S. in any case stated that there was "no need to change" the mandate "which was already quite broad enough (if interpreted flexibly)." The French had also indicated that the question of restrictions in the mandate could be resolved without difficulty.[33] They all preferred not to discuss a broader mandate, probably because they realized, as

[31]Commission d'enquête, *Rapport*, p. 532.

[32]Ibid., p. 535.

[33]Ibid, p. 533; United Nations, Security Council, Notes on Informal Consultations, April 8,1994.

had Annan, that any greater authority for UNAMIR would raise the issue of using that authority to protect Rwandans.

Under the plan for a "humanitarian" intervention by national governments, UNAMIR would cooperate in the evacuation of foreigners, including all U.N. staff. And, Annan proposed, UNAMIR itself should leave Rwanda with the evacuation force.[34]

That solution, proposed on April 8, certainly accorded with the thinking of certain "permanent" "western" members of the council, and would have kept UNAMIR soldiers from being "passive witnesses to genocide."

The Evacuation Force

If the U.S. and others made it impossible to use UNAMIR to influence events in Rwanda, various national governments could have employed their own troops. The possibility that they might do so was greatest for Belgium and France, the two countries most likely to launch an operation to evacuate foreigners from Rwanda. On April 8, the Belgian cabinet discussed the possibility of intervening with its own troops, if Rwandan authorities should request such an action. The Belgian ambassador believed it unlikely that the Rwandans would ask and the cabinet in the end found the idea inadvisable because it would constitute interference in an internal Rwandan conflict. A warning from Annan about the possible negative consequences on UNAMIR of any "military intervention" may have been meant to discourage such action. The Rwandan ambassador at the U.N. too hastened to react to rumors of "an imminent Belgian military intervention under the cover of pseudo-humanitarian reasons."[35] Through the good offices of the French ambassador of the U.N., he cautioned that the Presidential Guard controlled the airport and that the Belgians should not try even to evacuate their citizens. A French force, he said, would be welcome.[36]

In testimony before the Belgian Senate inquiry on Rwanda, Claes maintained that he sought support for such a military intervention, but that "Paris said a firm no and the Americans would not even think of it."[37] According to him, the French would support only a brief humanitarian intervention, an assertion that is confirmed

---

[34]Commission d'enquête, *Rapport*, p. 538.

[35]Ibid., p. 537.

[36]Ibid., p. 537.

[37]Ibid., p. 559.

by notes from Security Council consultations on April 8. But General Quesnot has a different recollection. At the French parliamentary inquiry on Rwanda, he remarked concerning stopping the massacres:

> There was a French effort anyway to try to do it: there were conversations with the Belgians and with the Italians. There were 300 American marines at Bujumbura. After a hope on the Italian side, it came to nothing. It was a political decision: France could not again intervene alone. What would they not have said? Stealing the victory from the RPF....[38]

Regardless of who should be credited with the idea and who blamed for its collapse, the plan was never realized. Instead Belgium and France cooperated—with some U.S. support at a distance—in a "humanitarian action" to evacuate foreigners, the idea proposed by Annan and favored by the U.S. and others on the Security Council.

The evacuation force comprised some 900 elite Belgian and French troops. They were backed up by an additional 300 U.S. marines at Bujumbura, less than half an hour away by plane, who were never called on to enter the country. Some eighty Italians arrived somewhat later than the others. Had these troops been combined with the 440 Belgian and the 200 Ghanaians UNAMIR soldiers available in Kigali, they would have made a force of nearly 2,000 capable soldiers. Had they needed reinforcements, there were another 600 Ghanaians north of Kigali in the demilitarized zone, 800 Belgian troops on standby in Nairobi, and hundreds of other U.S. marines just off the East African coast.[39]

Estimates of the number of Rwandan troops in Kigali on April 6 range up to some 7,000, but most military observers agree that of the total, only about 2,000 troops—the Presidential Guard and several hundred troops each from the paracommando and reconnaissance batallions—represented a serious force.[40] The

---

[38]Testimony of General Christian Quesnot, Mission d'Information, May 19, 1998, as reported on the Internet, http://www.paris.msf.org. The official version of this testimony (Assemblée Nationale, Mission d'information commune, *Enquête*, Tome III, Auditions, Volume I, p. 346) omits the first and last sentences quoted here. See following chapter for possible French plans to assist the Rwandan army.

[39]Commission d'enquête, *Rapport*, p. 558.

[40]Human Rights Watch/FIDH interviews, Brussels, May 26, October 19 and 20, 1997; by telephone, July 24, 1998.

likelihood that the Rwandan army would have attacked foreign troops—particularly if French soldiers were among them—was very small. A substantial number of the government soldiers were engaged in fighting the RPF. Others among them, recognizing that they were less well trained and armed than the foreign troops, would certainly have wished to avoid confronting them. In killing civilians, the military was backed by some 2,000 militia, but they had little formal military training and were armed at most with light firearms. They were hardly the equal of a professional fighting force. On the one occasion when UNAMIR soldiers opened fire on a mixed group of Rwandan military and militia—during the confrontation at the stadium described above—fifteen Rwandans were killed and the others fled immediately. They did not even stop to take the Belgian vehicles, some of which had been left with their motors running, and they caused no further trouble in the area for the next twenty-four hours.[41]

Having observed the situation and the relative strength of the forces on the ground, Dallaire believed that UNAMIR in combination with the evacuation force "could easily have stopped the massacres and showed the people at the barriers that it was dangerous to be there. They would have gone home."[42] Marchal agreed and stated afterwards that "the responsible attitude" would have been to combine the evacuation force with UNAMIR "to restore order in the country. There were enough troops to do it or at least to have tried."[43] General Quesnot was not in Rwanda at the time, but as a senior officer in the army most linked with the Rwandan forces, he presumably was well-placed to assess the force that would have been needed to end the massacres. He estimated that 2,000 to 2,500 "determined" soldiers would have sufficed to halt the slaughter.[44] The RPF, with more than three years experience fighting the Rwandan army and with the benefit of substantial local information, expected that 900 soldiers could stop the massacres.[45] An American colonel later estimated that 5,000 soldiers would have

---

[41]Commission d'enquête, *Rapport*, Annexe 5, p. 28; Goffin, *10 commandos vont mourir!*, pp. 94-104.

[42]Human Rights Watch/FIDH interview, Toronto, September 16, 1998.

[43]Marchal, "Considérations relatives," p. 15.

[44]Assemblée Nationale, Mission d'information commune, *Enquête*, Tome III, Auditions, Volume I, p. 346.

[45]Human Rights Watch/FIDH interview, by telephone, March 7, 1998.

been the maximum needed, but he was referring to the period after the killings had become widespread throughout the country.[46]

The RPF seemed unlikely to oppose foreign military intervention, if it were limited to ending the slaughter of civilians. On April 7 they had asked that UNAMIR troops begin protecting civilians and on April 8, they had urged that more UNAMIR troops be brought to Kigali.[47] They also asked Belgians to land their troops in the capital on April 10. Two days later they abruptly changed their position on the presence of the evacuation forces and warned the Belgians as well as the French to withdraw their troops within sixty hours or risk their being treated as hostile forces.[48] Had the Europeans insisted on staying to protect Tutsi—so long as they made no move to aid the Rwandan army—the RPF would not have been likely to engage them in combat.

In the days from April 8 to April 15, the very period when foreign governments were deciding on and executing the operation to rescue their citizens, Bagosora was in the process of establishing his power, winning support among military colleagues and installing a civilian government. It was the time when thousands of Rwandans were deciding how far they would oppose or collaborate with authorities whose program was genocide. During those days, soldiers and National Police opposed to the slaughter tried to work with UNAMIR and to hinder the attacks by the militia. Leading military officers opposed to Bagosora and his genocidal program made contact with Dallaire and with U.S., Belgian, and French diplomats or military figures to ask them to not "desert" Rwanda.[49]

During this week, large-scale massacres began claiming thousands of lives. If foreign troops, alone or in combination with UNAMIR forces, had stopped the killers in the capital, assailants throughout the country would have ceased their

---

[46]Colonel Scott R. Feil, "Preventing Genocide: How the Use of Force Might Have Succeeded in Rwanda," Prepublication Draft, December 1997.

[47]Belgium, Kabinet van de Eerste Minie, Betreft Ministeriele Vergadering over Rwanda, 8/4-15h00'-17h00' (confidential source); United Nations, Security Council, Notes on Informal Consultations on Rwanda, April 8,1994.

[48]Code Telex 198, ambabel (Belgian ambassador) nairobi to belext bru (Brussels), April 10, 1994; Code Telex 227 Ambabel Nairobi to Belext Bru, April 12, 1994 (confidential source).

[49]Human Rights Watch/FIDH interviews, Toronto, September 16, 1997; Brussels, June 22, 1998; by telephone, July 22 and 23, 1998.

attacks. In this highly centralized system, there was no alternative center of power to take over if the genocidal command structure had been dismantled in Kigali. An impressive show of foreign force would have demonstrated to all that the regime was not going to win foreign approval and would have swayed as yet uncommitted military officers and political leaders. With foreign troops as a potential counterweight to the elite troops engaged in slaughter, officers in charge of other units would have been in a stronger position to demand that Bagosora stop the carnage.

Assessing the role of foreigners who could have intervened and did not do so, Colonel Marchal wrote:

> When people rightly point the finger at certain individuals presumed responsible for the genocide, I wonder if after all there is not another category of those responsible by....omission.[50]

General Quesnot concurred, stating that.

> "...he would have wanted the international community to intervene at the start of the massacres because, from a technical point of view, they could have been stopped at that time since at the beginning, the abuses were the work of the militia and of the presidential guard which was behaving disgracefully. If the international community, not France alone, had not been so shortsighted...it could have stopped the massacres launched in Kigali."[51]

No Locals

Even after the U.N. and the Belgian and French governments had decided that troops under their control would not attempt to restore order in Rwanda, they still had the opportunity to save Rwandan lives in the process of evacuating foreigners. Taking Rwandans out of the country was a solution that could help only a tiny number of those at risk, but the presence of the evacuation force and the convoys they organized presented a chance to bring Rwandans to places of refuge within Kigali.

---

[50]Marchal, "Considérations relatives," p. 15.

[51]Assemblée Nationale, Mission d'information commune, *Enquête*, Tome III, Auditions, Volume I, p. 346.

When plans were first discussed for evacuating U.N. personnel, the rule was that no Rwandans, staff or not, could be taken along. Colonel Balis stated that he questioned Dallaire twice about the directive and was told, "Orders from New York: No Locals."[52] The rules were not always followed, even by the authorities in New York or by some U.N. agencies. In some cases, Dallaire was directed by headquarters to make an exception and rescue a particular Rwandan and he was deluged with similar demands from abroad as various governments sought to assure the safety of Rwandans whom they esteemed. In other cases, one or another peacekeeper was so overcome by the human tragedy of the genocide that he simply ignored the orders and did what he could to save lives.[53] When Lt. Luc Lemaire was ordered to evacuate only foreigners, he responded that the order was impossible to execute and that he and his men had already rescued Rwandans. On April 7, the Senegalese Captain Mbaye Diagne and a U.N. employee named Le Moal rescued the five children of Prime Minister Uwilingiyimana, who then left the country through the efforts of a French professor, André Guichaoua, who was in Kigali at the time.[54] Throughout the next weeks, Captain Mbaye became virtually a legend among Rwandans for his bravery and inventiveness in saving people and in deterring soldiers who sought to enter the Hotel Mille Collines at night to kill those whom he had saved during the day.[55]

UNAMIR did attempt at one point to evacuate a significant number of Rwandans by plane to Nairobi. But the government of Kenya, a long-time ally and supporter of the Rwandan government, refused entry to all those who did not have guarantees of safe conduct from other nations. Of course, none of the refugees had been able to obtain such documents before leaving Kigali. The plane was sequestered for a time in a cargo hanger, making it possible for two or three people to escape. But all the rest were returned to Kigali. This policy of the Kenyan

---

[52]Commission d'enquête, *Rapport*, p. 466.

[53]Human Rights Watch/FIDH interview, by telephone, May 22, 1996.

[54]Guichaoua, *Les Crises Politiques,* p. 696.

[55]Captain Mbaye was killed at the end of May by an RPF shell directed at a Rwandan army barrier where he happened to be stopped. See Guichaoua, *Les Crises Politiques,* p. 709.

government effectively ended efforts by UNAMIR to fly Rwandans at risk out of the country.[56]

The number of lives saved by UNAMIR soldiers was limited by the refusal of most to take risks. But some willing to take chances gave Rwandans an opportunity to escape. On April 11, for example, the Belgian peacekeeper Lieutenant DeCuyper was charged with escorting some fifty vehicles transporting some Rwandans as well as foreigners to the airport. After having passed through a barrier, Lieutenant DeCuyper noticed that Rwandan soldiers had halted the latter part of the convoy and were forcing the Rwandans to get out of their cars. He intervened and confronted a crowd that at first just threw stones and then began threatening him with grenades. He stood his ground and got all the Rwandans back in their vehicles and on their way. As he drove off, a sniper fired at him. He had to argue and bluff his way through several more such situations before delivering the convoy safely to the airport.[57] The reaction to this and similar incidents was an order from sector headquarters to take no more Rwandans in the convoys. The order was effectively countermanded the next day, however, when UNAMIR soldiers were told to include in airport covoys all Rwandans who wanted to go.[58]

A second constraint on the number of lives saved was simply the small number of soldiers and vehicles available to escort civilians—whether Rwandan or foreign— to the airport or to some other haven in Kigali. In the allocation of resources, foreigners got priority, even though they were far less at risk than Rwandans. Except for the Belgians who had been targeted over a long period by RTLM, most foreigners had not been even threatened, far less actually attacked.[59]

Although Annan had initially told the Belgians that UNAMIR "obviously had other priorities" than helping evacuate foreigners, this task did become their priority mission.[60] On April 10 and 11, UNAMIR was busy "escorting foreign

---

[56]Human Rights Watch interview, by telephone, April 27, 1994; Human Rights Watch/FIDH interview, by telephone, May 22, 1996.

[57]Dewez, "Chronique," p. 44-5.

[58]Ibid., pp. 45, 48.

[59]International Criminal Tribunal for Rwanda, The Prosecutor of the Tribunal against Georges Anderson Nderubumwe Rutaganda, case no. ICTR-96-3-I, Testimony of Luc Lemaire, September 30, 1997, p. 154.

[60]Commission d'enquête, *Rapport*, p. 528.

nationals leaving the country," according to a subsequent report to the Security Council.[61] The log of the Belgian battalion of UNAMIR makes clear that those soldiers believed evacuating foreigners was their most important objective at that time. On April 11, Lt. Col. J. Dewez ordered Lieutenant Lemaire to send part of his troops to Gitarama, some forty miles south of Kigali, to escort some Belgians back to the city. The lieutenant answered that to do so would "diminish the security of his post and reduce troops available to rescue refugees," meaning Tutsi and Hutu at risk because of their political beliefs. "The Gitarama mission has priority," Dewez replied.[62]

National governments also had to decide whether to evacuate Rwandans and, if so, whom to chose among the thousands who wished to go, including employees and friends but also others who had congregated on the grounds of embassies or ambassadorial residences. Some, like the U.S. government, did not want to take out any Rwandans and the ambassador simply told the several hundred people gathered at his residence that they would have to disperse because he was leaving. Others, like the Belgians and the Swiss, rescued hundreds of Tutsi and Hutu politicians, clergy, human rights activists, and other leaders of civil society. Many of those fortunate enough to be saved had persistent friends abroad who bombarded their own governments and the U.N. with demands that these people be rescued.[63] A few individuals, like the cook employed by one Belgian family, just happened to be present when the evacuation escort arrived and were taken along.[64]

The French were in a position to save Tutsi and others at risk with relatively little difficulty and yet they chose to save very few. French troops moved easily around the city, even when transporting Rwandans. Militia cheered them and gave them the thumbs up sign, while they greeted Belgian soldiers with a gesture of cutting their throats. In some cases, Belgian soldiers even removed insignia which

---

[61]"Confidential Summary of the Security Council Consultations on Rwanda, Monday 11 April 1994," signed by Kaz Kuroda (confidential source).

[62]Dewez, "Chronique," pp. 46, 31.

[63]Testimony before the Special Session of the U.N. Commission for Human Rights, Geneva, May 25, 1994; Commission d'enquête, *Rapport*, p. 539.

[64]Human Rights Watch interview, Buffalo, N.Y., December 22, 1994.

identified them as Belgians and passed themselves off as French.[65] In at least one case, French embassy personnel made no response to pleas for help from a Tutsi employee and in another they refused assistance to a Hutu prosecutor well-known for his opposition to Habyarimana. French soldiers on one occasion balked at escorting some Rwandan clergy to a safe haven but in the end gave in to pressure from UNAMIR soldiers and did so.[66] The French assisted the departure of some 400 Rwandans, virtually all of them closely linked to Habyarimana. They evacuated Madame Habyarimana and her family as well as a number of adult men apparently inexperienced in child care who were passed off as caregivers for children from an orphanage associated with Madame Habyarimana.[67]

In most cases, the evacuation troops, like the UNAMIR forces, did not intervene when they saw Tutsi being attacked. Nor did they make any systematic effort to escort Tutsi from their homes to places of greater safety. During the days when some 4,000 foreigners were evacuated—few of whom were actually at risk—some 20,000 Rwandans were slain.[68]

The foreign troops returned home to general applause for a job well done, even as television coverage showed them standing by while Rwandans were slain just next to them.

The Ecole Technique Officielle: "Do Not Abandon Us!"

In the end UNAMIR would make its greatest contribution to Rwandans at risk not by getting them out of Kigali but by affording some of them protection within the city. In the first days, this seemed unlikely to be the case. UNAMIR officers in charge of security and their superiors in New York feared that taking in Tutsi and others at risk would discredit the "neutrality" of the U.N., particularly since the

---

[65]Dewez, "Chronique," pp. 32, 44, 57; ICTR-96-3-I, Testimony of Luc Lemaire, September 30, 1997, p. 123.

[66]Vénuste Kayijamahe, "Lettre ouverte au Président de la République Française," *La Lettre de la FIDH*, nos. 548-49, July 28, 1994; Guichaoua, *Les Crises Politiques*, pp.706-7; ICTR-96-3-I, Testimony of Luc Lemaire, October 1, 1997, p. 6.

[67]Alain Frilet and Sylvie Coma, "Paris, terre d'asile de luxe pour dignitaires hutus," *Libération*, May 18, 1994, p. 5; Guichaoua, *Les Crises Politiques*, pp. 697-701.

[68]Estimate of the Deputy Head of the International Red Cross in Kigali. Terry Leonard, "New Fighting is Reported in Rwanda as Foreigners Flee," Associated Press, April 11, 1994.

interim government identified all Tutsi with enemies of the country. Some feared that the presence of displaced persons might lead to attacks, either from outside the U.N. compounds or from infiltrators who might enter, armed, among crowds of civilians.[69] In the first hours of the crisis, a U.N. officer directed a U.N. staff person to send away a "Very Important Person" who had sought refuge with him. The "Very Important Person," code for an important political leader, was Prime Minister Uwilingiyimana. She was not, in fact, forced to leave but was later discovered and captured in her hiding place.[70]

Dallaire was never ordered by headquarters to take in people at risk but he did so. He believed that both the mandate of contributing to the security of the city and the Rules of Engagement justified this decision.[71] As one person connected with UNAMIR commented, "If you wanted to do some good, you just had to do it and not ask New York."[72] It seems that Dallaire permitted rather than ordered his subordinates to grant refuge as well. A Belgian military commission investigating the performance of Belgian troops concluded later that the head of each local post in fact decided whether or not to admit Rwandans seeking refuge.[73]

Some who ended up under U.N. protection were rescued by peacekeepers, but most came to the posts on their own.[74] A trickle of Tutsi, frightened by rumors of impending violence, had been arriving even before April 6. With the beginning of the slaughter the next day, the trickle swelled rapidly. On April 7, for example, residents of the neighborhood of Gatenga fled to the Ecole Technique Officielle (Official Technical School, ETO), as Rwandan soldiers and militia swept through the area killing, raping, and robbing Tutsi and members of parties opposed to the MRND. The ninety UNAMIR troops posted at the ETO heard the gunfire and explosions of grenades all day long without attempting to intervene, but they did

---

[69]Human Rights Watch/FIDH interview, by telephone, May 22, 1996.

[70]Human Rights Watch/FIDH interview, by telephone, Antwerp, September 29, 1998.

[71]Human Rights Watch/FIDH interview, by telephone, May 22, 1996.

[72]Human Rights Watch/FIDH interview, by telephone, October 26, 1997.

[73]Commission d'enquête, Annexe 5, p. 29; ICTR-96-3-I, Testimony of Luc Lemaire, September 30, 1997, p. 96.

[74]Dewez, "Chronique," pp. 18, 31.

permit Tutsi to take refuge at the school. That night, Colonel Marchal ordered that all Rwandan displaced persons be out the gate of UNAMIR posts by 6 a.m. the next morning.[75] The order was not uniformly enforced any more than were other bans on assistance to Rwandans. When the Salesian Fathers, who ran the ETO, insisted that the people who had sought refuge with them be allowed to stay, Dewez agreed, saying that the Fathers had the right to determine who stayed on the property. The next morning at 5:17 a.m., shortly before the announced deadline, Lieutenant Lemaire asked his superior whether he should protect the displaced at the school or only the priests. Captain Choffay answered that he should protect everyone, in effect countermanding the order of the night before.[76]

On April 9, the Belgian command told its officers that all of UNAMIR might leave Rwanda since the cease-fire had collapsed and ordered troops to prepare to evacuate. That evening Lemaire had the foresight and concern to raise the difficult question of what would become of the displaced persons at the school when UNAMIR left. The log of the battalion, which records his question, does not record a similar query being made by other officers, although there were several who faced the same dilemma, nor does it record any answer.[77]

Lemaire discussed the problem first with the burgomaster of Kicukiro, one of the communes of the city of Kigali, who had taken refuge at the school and then presented it to the assembled Rwandans. He climbed up on a stool to address the crowd and explained that he might at any time be ordered to leave the school for another post. The crowd was panic-stricken and insisted that they would not be left behind, that the peacekeepers would have to take them along wherever they were going.[78]

By April 10, the number of displaced persons had grown to 2,000, at least 400 of them children, and many of them desperately needing food and medical care. Lemaire sought help in vain from Médicins sans Frontières, who could not get through to the post. Finally he got some sacks of rice from Colonel Rusatira who had come to the school looking for family members. Still with no answer to the question of what was to become of the Rwandans when the UNAMIR troops left,

---

[75]Ibid., p. 18.

[76]Ibid., pp. 25, 31.

[77]Ibid., pp. 28, 32.

[78]Human Rights Watch interview, Kigali, August 28, 1994; Human Rights Watch/FIDH interview, Kigali, July 14, 1996.

Lemaire asked Rusatira for help. Rusatira explained that he headed a military school, not an operational command, and had no soldiers available to defend the ETO. He reportedly passed the request for help to Ndindiliyimana, chief of staff of the National Police, but he could not or would not help.[79]

On April 11, at about 10:30 a.m., French soldiers came to evacuate the expatriates and—after strenuous objections—Rwandan clergy from the school. With the foreigners gone, the UNAMIR troops could be withdrawn as part of the regrouping ordered earlier to free soldiers "for the priority missions" of evacuating other expatriates. Aware that he would have to go, Lemaire preferred sooner rather than later, given "the more and more serious pressure from the armed bands" around the school. Remarking that the road just taken by the French troops with the evacuees was still open, he requested clearance to move his men out. Dewez checked with Marchal and then gave Lemaire and his troops authorization to leave. The log notes that the departure of the troops left 2,000 Rwandans unguarded and threatened by "armed bands." The senior Belgian officers knew this and knew as well what "the armed bands" were prepared to do as soon as UNAMIR left, but they made no attempt to provide for the Rwandans at ETO or in other similar situations elsewhere in the city.[80] Dallaire, who gave the initial order to regroup the troops dispersed throughout the city, supposedly knew nothing about the details of this case until informed sometime later by the RPF.[81]

Lemaire knew that some of the Tutsi had asked his men to shoot them rather than leave them to die at the hands of the militia. To avoid any difficulties at the time of departure, he gave the impression that his men were preparing to leave for a routine exercise and would be gone only briefly.[82]

The displaced persons at the ETO, who included human rights activists Fidele Kanyabugoyi and Jean-Paul Biramvu and their wives, had seen French troops arrive to escort the expatriates and the handful of chosen Rwandans to safety in the late morning. Shortly after 1 p.m., they saw the Belgian soldiers line up their jeeps,

---

[79]Dewez, "Chronique," p. 28. One witness relates that a lieutenant and several National Policemen came to the school, but that rather than protect the displaced they joined in the attack. Human Rights Watch interview, Kigali, October 29, 1994; Human Rights Watch/FIDH interview, Kigali, July 14, 1996.

[80]Dewez, "Chronique," p. 46.

[81]Human Rights Watch/FIDH interview, by telephone, May 22, 1996.

[82]ICTR-96-3-I, Testimony of Luc Lemaire, September 30, 1997, pp. 125-26.

preparing to move out, but they could not believe that they were being deserted before arrangements had been made for their protection. At the order to depart, the soldiers jumped into their jeeps and rapidly pulled out of the gate. Some of the Rwandans hurried to lie down in the road to block the departure, but they were too slow to stop the convoy. As some ran after the departing jeeps, shouting "Do not abandon us!" they were driven back by the UNAMIR soldiers firing over their heads. Lemaire had advised the displaced persons to try to leave in small groups under cover of night, but there was no question of that. As the Belgian troops left, the militia and Rwandan soldiers rushed through one gate and the displaced began fleeing out another.[83]

At 1:45 p.m. Lieutenant Lemaire moved out from the ETO with his ninety soldiers, including the battalion chaplain. He reported to his commanding officer by radio that he was leaving behind two vehicles that were no longer usable and one electric generator. He did not repeat that he was leaving behind 2,000 people.[84]

Lemaire's men were needed for various missions to protect and evacuate foreigners. At the Hotel Meridien, the sector headquarters, Dewez awaited his arrival to provide escort service for people from the Coopération Militaire Technique, the Belgian military assistance mission, an escort that was, in the end, provided by other troops.[85]

In his subsequent testimony at the international tribunal, Lemaire compared the situation at ETO to a large fire and says he was equipped only with a fire extinguisher when he needed a fire engine. He asserted that authorities in Belgium were aware that Tutsi at the ETO were dependent on protection by Belgian UNAMIR troops and that they could have permitted their rescue had they provided for a longer stay by the evacuation forces.[86] Lemaire recounted that he had tried to find a solution to the crisis himself. But, he said, escorting all the displaced persons elsewhere at one time would have required more men than the ninety available to him. If he had tried to move them in several smaller groups, the first group might have passed without difficulty but later groups would probably have been attacked

---

[83]Human Rights Watch interview, Kigali, November 3, 1994; Human Rights Watch/FIDH interview, Kigali, July 14, 1996.

[84]Dewez, "Chronique," pp. 25, 38, 44, 46.

[85]Ibid., p.44.

[86]ICTR-96-3-I, Testimony of Luc Lemaire, October 1, 1997, pp. 8, 29-31.

and he did not have enough ammunition to defend them.[87] Although some survivors from the school are understandably bitter about the desertion, at least one described Lemaire as a conscientious soldier who had no choice but to do what he did.[88] Lemaire maintains that he learned of the massacre that followed his departure only two years later.[89]

The Rwandans who escaped immediate slaughter on the school grounds tried to flee to the nearest major UNAMIR outpost, the Amahoro stadium. En route they encountered Rwandan soldiers who at first reassured them and said they would escort them to the stadium when a number of the group had congregated. But when a large group had gathered, soldiers and militia herded them up a hill to a ridge called Nyanza-Rebero. As they were being forced to move along by soldiers and armed civilians, a group of Ghanaian UNAMIR soldiers passed by but did not respond to their enreaties to stop. On the ridge, soldiers and militia ordered the people to sit down and they began firing and throwing grenades at them and attacking them with machetes. Most of the two thousand people were killed that afternoon, within hours of the departure of the peacekeepers.[90] When one of the survivors of the massacre took a Human Rights Watch researcher to Nyanza-Rebero in August 1994, the ridge was still littered with skulls, bones, clothing, and belongings of the people who had been slaughtered there. Most of the flesh had been eaten from the bones by dogs or other scavengers.

Belgian Policy
"Suspend the Activities of UNAMIR"
On April 8, the day after learning that the ten peacekeepers had been killed, the Belgian cabinet decided that Belgian participation in UNAMIR would end unless the mandate were broadened and the force were strengthened—with soldiers from a country other than Belgium. Hours earlier, the Belgian ambassador at the U.N. had informed Brussels that certain "permanent" members of the Security Council had decided against any such broadening of the mandate. So by the time members of the cabinet made this decision, they presumably knew that the U.S. and the U.K.,

---

[87]Ibid., pp. 197-99.

[88]Human Rights Watch/FIDH interview, Kigali, July 14, 1996.

[89]ICTR-96-3-I, Testimony of Luc Lemaire, September 30, 1997, p. 199.

[90]Human Rights Watch interview, Kigali, November 3, 1994; Human Rights Watch/FIDH interview, Kigali, July 14, 1996.

and apparently France as well, would block any broadening of the mandate. They submitted the request to Boutros-Ghali anyway but made no serious effort to win support for the proposal. On April 9, Belgian authorities knew that Nigeria still favored a broader mandate and intended to work for such a change in the week to come, but on April 10 they decided that the mandate was not likely to be strengthened and they made the decision to end Belgian participation in UNAMIR. They informed Boutros-Ghali on April 12 and delivered the message formally to the Security Council on April 13.[91]

When the decision was made on April 10, Belgians understood the nature and scale of the slaughter that was taking place. By the time of the official communication on April 13, the genocidal character of the killings was even more pronounced. Claes admits that Belgian authorities knew of the extent of the killing, a realization reflected in their communications with Washington and other governments.[92] He maintains that he no longer remembers exactly when he realized the slaughter was a genocide, but he is certain that he had not yet reached that conclusion when Belgium decided to pull out its soldiers.[93]

In the letter to the Security Council, Belgium referred to the "widespread massacres," but only as part of the "chaos" that jeopardized implementation of the Arusha Accords. Assuming that UNAMIR had and could have no role in halting the killings of civilians, the Belgians remarked that UNAMIR no longer had a reason for being, given that the peace process had collapsed. They cited the pointlessness of continued operations and the possibility of further loss among Belgian troops as reasons for the Belgian decision.[94]

Just as Belgian political leaders had in the past used public opinion as a reason for seeking broader involvement in Rwanda, so now they relied on it to try to justify their withdrawal. They referred to the "great emotion" caused in Belgium by the loss of the peacekeepers and to a public opinion "traumatized" by their deaths.[95] It appears that they consciously or unconsciously misread public opinion,

---

[91]Commission d'enquête, *Rapport*, pp. 519-20, 540, 556.

[92]Telex 181 to Washington, Objet: ONU/Rwanda, Avenir de l'Operation MINUAR, Position de la Belgique, April 12, 1994 (confidential source).

[93]Commission d'enquête, *Rapport*, pp. 560-61.

[94]United Nations, *The United Nations and Rwanda*, pp. 258-59.

[95]Commission d'enquête, *Rapport*, p. 534.

perhaps because they anticipated a reaction like that in the U.S. to the death of its peacemakers in Somalia. Belgian public opinion as measured by two polls showed no overwhelming demand for withdrawal. In one, 48 percent favored keeping Belgian troops in Rwanda and even sending more if needed and 40 percent believed that the stakes in Rwanda even justified further loss of Belgian lives. In another poll among Flemish-speakers, generally cautious about foreign involvement, 55 percent believed that peacekeepers should be assuring the security of Rwandans although 80 percent believed that the government should send no more Belgian soldiers for this task.[96]

Many Belgian soldiers wanted to stay in Rwanda to try to end the slaughter.[97] Marchal, who had been unsure of the best course of action before April 7, had no doubts about what should have been done after that date. Concerning the debate that developed over the withdrawal of Belgian troops, he later wrote:

> Under no circumstances could we leave the country. This was the point of view that I expressed to my superiors until the moment when the political decision was made to leave UNAMIR. Our political leaders should have known that in leaving UNAMIR, we would condemn thousands of men, women and children to certain death.[98]

Lemaire testified at the international tribunal, "If Belgium had been courageous enough to leave our men there, we would have been able to save people."[99]

"The Security of UNAMIR"

From the start, Belgium sought the withdrawal of all UNAMIR troops, not just its own. This manoeuvre, meant to disguise and lessen Belgian responsibility for deserting Rwanda, coincided with the U.S. policy to end UNAMIR in Rwanda and

---

[96]Ibid., p. 564; "Vlamingen Laten Ruanda Niet Vallen," *Het Volk*, April 19, 1994.

[97]Commission d'enquête, *Rapport*, p. 546.

[98]Marchal, "Considérations relatives," p. 15.

[99]ICTR-96-3-I, Testimony of Luc Lemaire, October 1, 1997, p. 29.

was probably encouraged by U.S. authorities with whom the Belgians were in close contact.[100]

In the interview where Claes announced the Belgian withdrawal to the secretary-general, he sought to persuade him that the entire UNAMIR force must be recalled and he thought that he had succeeded.[101] Boutros-Ghali in turn had an assistant call the force commander in Kigali to put considerable pressure on him to advocate withdrawal. Dallaire declares that the issue was for him "a matter of moral concern." He refused to recommend an end to the operation, a principled position taken also by the deputy force commander, Ghanaian Brigadier-General Henry Kwami Anyidoho. They instead requested delivery of large quantities of emergency supplies.[102] Belgian officers in Rwanda also notified Dallaire that additional Belgian troops on standby in Tanzania could cover the retreat of UNAMIR forces if he wished to lead them out.[103] Rejecting the Belgian judgment that a continued UNAMIR presence was futile, Dallaire remarked on how strange it was that the Belgians thought the field staff was unaware of the gravity of the situation. He noted, "they say we are too optimistic here."[104]

The Belgians launched a vigorous campaign to persuade Security Council members that its assessment was the correct one and that UNAMIR must be ended immediately. The effort devoted to this end far exceeded previous efforts to broaden the mandate. One Security Council member described an "extraordinary barrage" of attempted persuasion launched at passing members by a Belgian diplomat camped outside the door of the Security Council.[105] On April 15, Claes called the ambassador of New Zealand, then president of the Security Council, to

---

[100]Telegram /94/00661, New York - UNO - Deputy to Brussel, Objet: Rwanda. Entretien avec le Chargé d'affaires américain, April 12, 1994 (confidential source).

[101]United Nations, *The United Nations and Rwanda*, p. 40.

[102]Adelman and Suhrke, *Early Warning*, pp. 44, 91, n. 81.

[103]Human Rights Watch/FIDH interview, Plainsboro, New Jersey, June 14, 1996.

[104]Adelman and Suhrke, *Early Warning*, p. 91, n. 81.

[105]Human Rights Watch/FIDH interview, New York, May 15, 1996.

urge prompt action because of a "serious concern about the future safety of UNAMIR if any personnel remained in Rwanda beyond Sunday [April 17]."[106]

The Belgian foreign minister also insisted to his counterparts in Washington, London, and Paris that the U.N. must withdraw.[107] One U.S. State Department official remarked, "You can't overstate the impact on our policy process of the Belgians leaving."[108] That evaluation appears misleading with regard to the U.S., which was ready for total withdrawal at midnight on April 7 when the Belgians were still talking of extending the mandate. But the assessment was more accurate for other member states, particularly those with no past experience in the region.[109] Belgium had provided the best-trained and best-equipped troops for the force, which would be difficult to replace. And, as the former colonial power in the region, Belgium was assumed to be—and, in fact, claimed to be—the government best informed and most qualified to speak on Rwanda.

The "future safety" of its own troops and more broadly of all peacekeepers offered Belgium a most useful excuse for withdrawal from Rwanda. Still smarting from the failure in Somalia, policymakers both at the U.N. and in national governments talked more about the fate of the professional soldiers than about that of the defenseless civilians. Colonel Marchal recalls the bitter response of Booh-Booh's political counselor, when he was obliged to tell him of the Belgian decision to withdraw its troops. "Because Belgium has ten men dead, it does not give a damn about thousands of blacks who are going to be killed." Marchal obviously found the response appropriate. He remarks, "Everyone knew, even in Belgium, what was going to happen because the organization of the genocide had been in place for a long time. In such circumstances, it is very difficult to be the representative of your country."[110]

---

[106]Proceedings of the Security Council, Friday, 15 April 1994; Adelman and Suhrke, *Early Warning*, p. 90 n. 78.

[107]Adelman and Suhrke, *Early Warning*, p. 90, n. 78.

[108]Holly J. Burkhalter, "The Question of Genocide, The Clinton Administration and Rwanda," *World Policy Journal*, Vol. XI, No. 4, Winter 1994/95, p. 46; Alison Des Forges, "Face au Génocide, une réponse désastreuse des Etats-Unis et des Nations Unies," in Guichaoua, *Les Crises Politiques*, pp. 455-64.

[109]Human Rights Watch/FIDH interview, New York, May 15, 1996.

[110]Marchal, "Considérations relatives," p. 4.

After the loss of the ten Belgian soldiers, only two other peacekeepers were killed and several wounded, apparently none of them having been deliberately targeted. Once the Belgians had left, the interim government had no reason to drive away the others. The force would not interfere with the genocide and its presence lent the Rwandan authorities a semblance of international legitimacy. The RPF also had no objection to the presence of the peacekeepers and did not attack them.

U.S. Policy: "Another Somalia" and Other Misconceptions

One Washington official remembers the period when the decision about UNAMIR was made as a time of "total confusion." "We didn't know who was shooting at whom."[111] Yet officials in Washington certainly knew that the slaughter was organized, not spontaneous, and that Tutsi were the main targets. Even the press, poor as its coverage was overall, was reporting that. On April 11, the *New York Times* published a UNAMIR cable from Kigali reporting that thousands of civilians had sought refuge in U.N. buildings and camps because they were "terrified by the ruthless campaign of ethnic cleansing and terror." It said casualties were "quite heavy and primarily ethnic in nature."[112] *Libération* and *Le Monde* published solid testimony on April 11 and April 12 about squads "cleansing" neighborhoods systematically on the basis of lists. Groups like Human Rights Watch and Oxfam and clergy provided ample evidence to Washington officials to confirm that a genocide had begun. It was also apparent that the slaughter was extensive in area and in number of victims. The International Committee of the Red Cross had estimated some 20,000 dead by April 11, about half of them outside Kigali and remote from any battle zone.

The evidence of the first few days also accorded with all the warning signals of the previous weeks and months. Had the professional observers failed to grasp the meaning of the militia training, the distribution of guns, the message of RTLM, and the plans revealed in the January 11 telegram, surely they must have understood what was happening by late on April 7. In addition to all the precursors of violence, the pattern of the killings, like the excuses presented for them, were all familiar from the past.

---

[111]Thomas W. Lipman, "U.S. Troop Withdrawal Ends Frustrating Mission To Save Rwandan Lives," *Washington Post,* October 3, 1994.

[112]Paul Lewis, "U.N. Forces Shelter Thousands in Rwanda," *New York Times,* April 11, 1994.

If Washington officials described the killings as "chaos," it was in part because they saw Rwanda through the prism of Somalia. In this light, Rwanda was another "failed state," just one more of a series of political disasters on the continent. In such a case, they reasoned, any intervention would have to be large-scale and costly and would probably produce no measurable improvement anyway.[113]

Some high-level political and military officials, including at least one National Security Council staff member at the White House, believed that Rwanda was not just a "failed state," but one that had failed because of "tribalism."[114] Basically ill-informed about Africa, these officials thought in terms of the categories left over from years before. For them the Tutsi "tribe" were arrogant (if also tall and willowy) warriors who had come from the northeast to impose their control over the indigenous Hutu (short and stocky), thus beginning centuries of conflict. In this perspective, the hatred and violence was "age-old" and by implication could have no end. In stressing the permanent nature of strife in Rwanda, officials found still another reason for keeping away from the complex and difficult situation.

Some specialists at the State Department who had followed Rwanda for months certainly understood that a genocide had begun, even if they did not use that term. They accordingly argued for firm action. But those higher up in the department, those at the White House, and those in the military did not or would not hear them. Those at the top had little incentive to go beyond their misconceptions to understand the situation. Rwanda was small, poor, remote, and African—in their eyes, irrelevant to the "national interest" of the U.S. In addition, the officials heard no widespread outcry from the American people, a consideration of overwhelming importance for political leaders who at the time focused more on domestic than on international issues. At one meeting on Rwanda, President Clinton supposedly asked if the Congressional Black Caucus, the group of African-American members of Congress, had shown strong interest in the issue, and presumably heard that they had not. On another occasion, an ambitious, young staff person at the National Security Council asked what impact the Rwandan crisis would have on the elections in November 1994. In a third instance, when a Human

[113]Burkhalter, "The Question of Genocide," p.48.

[114]Human Rights Watch/FIDH interview, Washington, April 21, 1994.

"Tous les hommes regrettent la vie
lorsqu'elle leur échappe ".

Les vrais amis sont rares, l'adversité les fait
connaître.

VIVE FRANÇOIS MITTERAND

VIVE LA COOPERATION FRANCO - RWANDAISE

VIVE LES MILITAIRES FRANÇAIS AU RWANDA

O.S.

Rights Watch representative asked National Security Adviser Anthony Lake how to be more effective in influencing U.S. policy, he replied, "Make more noise."[115]

As the crisis developed, officials were just completing an evaluation of how to limit the U.S. role in peacekeeping operations. The policy that resulted, known as Presidential Decision Directive 25 (PDD25) was far from the ideas suggested by President Clinton during his campaign, when he favored international action for such purposes as protecting civilians in civil wars and providing humanitarian assistance to people at risk. Now his administration sought instead to reduce the number and cost of peacekeeping operations, which had grown significantly in recent years, and to avoid peacekeeping failures like that in Somalia. To qualify for U.S. support under the new policy, any peacekeeping operation had to contribute to U.S. interests and had to have firm sources of funding and troops as well as clearly defined goals and a fixed date of completion. PDD 25 as such was applied for the first time later in May when plans for a second UNAMIR force were under discussion, but the thinking behind it influenced the earlier decision on withdrawing the first UNAMIR force.[116]

U.N. Obfuscation: "A People Fallen into Calamitous Circumstances"

After the first statement by the Security Council on April 7 in which it identified "Rwandan military and paramilitary units" as responsible for the "horrific" attacks, the council, like the secretariat staff, fell into vague and confused statements that failed to come to terms with the real nature of the genocide.

Among council members, the U.S. and France shared information with each other, with Belgium, and, much of the time, with the U.K. Rwanda—by happenstance a council member in 1994—worked closely with France and with Djibouti and Oman, other nonpermanent members. Other members of the council seem to have taken their positions largely on the basis of data furnished them by the secretariat staff.

In preparing presentations on Rwanda, staff of the secretariat heard two quite different voices from the field, that of Booh-Booh and that of Dallaire. Some observers attributed the difference in their reporting to one being a diplomat and the other a soldier. Other observers suggested it had more to do with political loyalties. Booh-Booh, as a member of the elite of his home country of Cameroon,

---

[115]Human Rights Watch interview, Washington, April 22, 1994; Human Rights Watch/FIDH interviews, by telephone, April 9, 1998 and May 5, 1998.

[116]Burkhalter, "The Question of Genocide," p. 48.

was supposedly linked to the French, and thus was more sympathetic to the Habyarimana circle. Appointed by the secretary-general, who himself ordinarily benefited from strong French support, Booh-Booh enjoyed Boutros-Ghali's confidence more than did Dallaire.[117]

A cable addressed to New York headquarters on April 8 shows clearly the difference in how the two assessed the situation. Booh-Booh reports that the security situation is worsening, but attributes this to intensified fighting between the Presidential Guard and the RPF. He indicates that the rest of the country is "calm, although tense." The next paragraph states that "elements of the Presidential Guard" abducted "several" political figures, including the prime minister, and murdered "several" persons suspected to be RPF sympathisers. At paragraph nine, Booh-Booh says "I regret to confirm the death of ten (10) military personnel from the Belgian contingent who were seized and detained by elements of the Presidential Guard."

The second part of the cable is written all in upper case letters. As different in tone as in font from the first part, it emphatically transmits Dallaire's angry voice:

THE APPEARANCE OF A VERY WELL PLANNED, ORGANIZED, DELIBERATE AND CONDUCTED CAMPAIGN OF TERROR INITIATED PRINCIPALLY BY THE PRESIDENTIAL GUARD SINCE THE MORNING AFTER THE DEATH OF THE HEAD OF STATE HAS COMPLETELY REORIENTED THE SITUATION IN KIGALI. AGGRESSIVE ACTIONS HAVE BEEN TAKEN NOT ONLY AGAINST THE OPPOSITION LEADERSHIP BUT AGAINST THE RPF (BY FIRING AT THE CND), AGAINST PARTICULAR ETHNIC GROUPS (MASSACRE OF TUTSI IN REMERA), AGAINST THE GENERAL CIVILIAN POPULATION (BANDITRY) AND AGAINST UNAMIR (DIRECT AND INDIRECT FIRE ON U.N. INSTALLATIONS, VEHICLES, PERSONNEL AND AFFILIATED AGENCIES (I.E., UNDP) WHICH HAS RESULTED IN FATAL AND NON-FATAL CASUALTIES. THE PARTICULARLY BARBAROUS MURDER OF THE 10 CAPTURED BELGIAN SOLDIERS EMPHASIZES THIS SITUATION....[118]

---

[117]Human Rights Watch interview, New York, August 1994; Human Rights Watch/FIDH interview, New York, May 15, 1996.

[118]Outgoing code cable from Booh-Booh. Unamir to Annan/Goulding, 8 April 1994.

By speaking of "several" persons or residences attacked, Booh-Booh gives no sense whatsoever of a large-scale planned "campaign of terror" described by Dallaire. When Booh-Booh refers to the RPF engaging the Rwandan army in a "fierce exchange of fire," he neglects to mention the "aggressive actions" taken by the Rwandan army in firing at the CND where the RPF were quartered. Booh-Booh talks of "calm" outside Kigali, without remarking on what Dallaire called the "strong negative reactions" to Habyarimana's death in northwestern Rwanda.[119]

, After the start of the violence, U.N. staff briefed council members frequently on the situation, sometimes as often as twice daily. According to notes from these sessions as well as information from those present at the briefings, presentations after April 7 favored the Booh-Booh interpretation and gave no sense of the role of the Rwandan government in organizing the violence.[120] The slaughter was mentioned rarely and then depicted as "chaos with thousands of people killed," as Assistant Secretary-General Riza described it.[121] Four years later Riza acknowledged that early reports to New York from the field had been wrong and that "possibly we did not give all the details" of ethnic killings to council members. He declared, "I really can't tell you what happened then to prevent us from giving those details."[122]

The secretary-general, absent in Europe, did not participate in early discussions about the fate of UNAMIR and submitted his first formal report on the situation only on April 20. In it, he too avoided any clear description of the genocide that had been under way for two weeks. In comments much like those of Riza, he depicted the initial killings as the work of "unruly members of the presidential guard" that "spread quickly throughout the city." He related that "Authority collapsed, the provisional government disintegrated and some of its members were killed in the violence," a most misleading description of the purposeful slaughter of the prime minister and others in the government. He spoke of "violence in the

---

[119]Ibid.

[120] Human Rights Watch/FIDH interview, New York, May 15, 1996.

[121]"Confidential Summary of the Security Council Consultations on Rwanda, Monday 11 April 1994," signed by Kaz Kuroda; "Confidential Summary of the Security Council Consultations on Rwanda, Tuesday 12 April 1994."

[122] Found on internet at http://www.pbs.org/wgbh/pages/frontline/shows/evil/interviews/riza.html.

streets" and "mass killings" and "a people who have fallen into calamitous circumstances."[123]

In ignoring or misinterpreting the real nature of the slaughter, the secretary-general or members of his staff may have been just presenting material according to familiar formulae borrowed from other situations where violence against civilians had accompanied war. The vocabulary used by the secretary-general, however, seems to reflect the point of the view of the interim government, as reinforced no doubt by France.[124] According to Claes, it was the secretary-general who also decided to permit Rwanda to remain at the council table, a decision of great political significance that was supposedly dictated by legal considerations.[125]

Protecting "The Innocent Civilians of Rwanda"

For the two weeks from April 7 to April 21, the Security Council was mired in discussion about UNAMIR that seemed to lead nowhere and that rarely mentioned the fate of Rwandans. On April 13, the debate over broadening the mandate was revived briefly by Nigeria, which circulated a draft resolution on behalf of the Non-Aligned Members that expressed shock over the deaths of "thousands of innocent civilians" and called for increasing the troops and revising the mandate for the force. But this effort drew so little support that it was never even formally presented.[126] Otherwise the talk centered on how much of the force would be withdrawn and how fast the withdrawal would happen.

Throughout the debate, council members and staff focused on the war and how the presence of UNAMIR could assist in obtaining a cease-fire. There was no suggestion that UNAMIR was "morally and legally [obligated] to use all available means to halt" crimes against humanity, as paragraph 17 had provided, and there was even some reluctance for UNAMIR to play the far more passive role of simply protecting those who sought refuge from such crimes. The staff mentioned several

---

[123]Special Report of the Secretary-General on the United Nations Assistance Mission for Rwanda, S/1994/470, April 20, 1994.

[124]Human Rights Watch interview, New York, August 12, 1994; Human Rights Watch/FIDH interview, New York, May 15, 1996.

[125]Sénat de Belgique, Commission Spéciale Rwanda, Compte Rendu Analytique des Auditions, Audition de M.W. Claes, 18 avril 1997.

[126]Draft proposal, entitled "Rwanda," circulated by the Non-Aligned Members to others on the Security Council, undated.

times that UNAMIR was offering such protection as well as "carrying out some humanitarian functions ...[and] undertaking specific missions to take people to safety..." But in one discussion that touched on this role, Riza "raised the question of protecting civilian nationals [i.e., Rwandans] in the long term, and referred to the critical situation at the stadium and hospital. The protection of civilians would require more resources, and the council should consider whether PKOs [peacekeeping operations] should be assigned such tasks."[127] The Nigerian representative reacted to Riza's implication that protecting civilians was inappropriate for peacekeeping operations. He stressed "that the concern of the council should not be limited to the fate of U.N. personnel and foreigners but should also include the innocent civilians of Rwanda."[128]

Disregarding the evidence that UNAMIR was already protecting civilians, although in relatively limited numbers, the United Kingdom declared "there was no evidence, either now or in the foreseeable future, that UNAMIR would be in a position to protect civilians; the council should not lend itself to a 'tragic fiction' whereby it merely declared that something would be done." The representative of New Zealand also declared some reservations about the feasibility of protecting civilians. The next day, the representative of the United Kingdom again insisted that civilian protection be excluded from the mandate for a continued UNAMIR. "However painful it is to say," he remarked, "the council had no right to leave the thought lying around that two battalions of troops, or even less, could protect the civilian population of Rwanda."[129]

Immediately after the Belgians announced their withdrawal, the U.S. stated in the Security Council that UNAMIR had nothing more to do in Rwanda because there was no cease-fire to monitor. The next day it suggested withdrawing all but a small force, the day after that it talked about the need for an orderly evacuation, and on the next day, April 15, the U.S. announced it favored complete withdrawal. Several days before, the U.S. chargé and the Belgian ambassador had talked about what could be done with the persons who had sought protection under the U.N. flag if there were a complete withdrawal. They had concluded that the displaced should be put into a "safe environment," but without further indication of what that might

---

[127]Proceedings of the Security Council, Wednesday, April 13, 1994 (confidential source).

[128]Ibid.

[129]Proceedings of the Security Council, Informal Consultations, Thursday, April 14, 1994.

be. On April 16, a U.S. diplomat told the Belgian ambassador that it was "unacceptable" that concern for a "humanitarian drama" be used to justify keeping the peacekeeping force in Rwanda. If such arguments were to be used, it might make other peacekeeping operations "unworkable."[130]

Because Nigeria and other council members, as well as secretariat staff, were opposed to the total withdrawal advocated by the U.S., the council meeting of April 15 closed without a decision. Even without formal action, it was clear by the end of the first week of the genocide that the U.N. would not intervene to halt the slaughter. At best it would protect the thousands who had come under its care; and it might leave, relinquishing even them to the killers.

Reducing UNAMIR

By the morning of April 16, authorities of the interim government would have known about the firm position in favor of complete withdrawal taken by the U.S. During the course of that day, civilian and military leaders made the decision to extend the genocide, both in area and in intensity, a decision they began to implement the day after. By the middle of the next week, humanitarian agencies were estimating 100,000 people killed throughout Rwanda.

In Kigali, the regrouping of UNAMIR forces had been completed. Soon after the Belgians left, the Bangladeshi troops departed. Ghanaian troops that had been in the northern demilitarized zone had moved into the capital. UNAMIR soldiers had been moved to a smaller number of more centralized locations. As they closed some of their posts, the peacekeepers had on occasion thrust out the gates to their deaths some of the displaced persons who had taken refuge with them. UNAMIR continued to protect more than 15,000 persons, both Hutu and Tutsi, who had sought refuge at the Amahoro stadium. It also provided guards at other sites that were not U.N. posts, including the King Faisal Hospital where there were another 5,000-6,000 people. Dallaire established this protection in response to the overwhelming needs on the spot, not as a result of orders from New York.[131] The existence of these groups of protected persons shaped the final stages of the debate over UNAMIR, giving advocates of continued involvement an argument that in the end the diplomats could not ignore.

---

[130]Telegram /94/00661, New York - UNO - Deputy to Brussel, Objet: Rwanda. Entretien avec le Chargé d'affaires américain, April 12, 1994; Commission d'enquête, *Rapport*, p. 552.

[131]Human Rights Watch/FIDH interview, by telephone, May 22, 1996.

As the days of slaughter passed without a decision by the Security Council, international human rights and humanitarian groups called more and more loudly for action. On April 19, Human Rights Watch reported recent information from the field to the president of the Security Council and informed him that this slaughter "constitutes genocide." It urged the council to condemn by name the individuals in command of the forces executing the genocide and provided the council with the names and ranks of those in charge. It demanded also that UNAMIR forces be maintained at full strength in Rwanda.The International Federation of Human Rights Leagues addressed a similar letter to the secretary-general on April 21. With rumors circulating that the U.S. was insisting on the complete withdrawal of UNAMIR, representatives of Human Rights Watch and the Rwandan human rights organization ADL sought support for a continued U.N. presence from U.S. Ambassador Madeleine Albright. She favored keeping at least a small force in Rwanda and directed the delegation to the National Security Council, where the decision would be made. That day, apparently recognizing the growing pressure to protect at least those thousands already under the U.N. flag, the National Security Council staff reversed its earlier decision and backed keeping a small number of peacekeepers in Rwanda.

That was the decision taken by the U.N. Security Council, too, that same day, after it had rejected the more extreme measures proposed by the secretary-general, complete withdrawal—with the prospect of "very severe" loss of life—or a change to a Chapter VII mandate and increase in the troops needed to implement it.[132]

The resolution reveals the continuing reluctance to speak plainly about the genocide that had characterized the message of the secretary-general the day before. It speaks of "large-scale violence, which has resulted in the death of thousands of innocent civilians," "ensuing violence which has claimed the lives of the Prime Minister" and others, "ongoing violence...which endangers the lives and safety of the civilian population," and "mindless violence." But nowhere does it state that this violence was organized or by whom it was organized. Even the murders of the ten UNAMIR soldiers are "acts of violence" perpetrated simply by unnamed assailants. "[A]ll concerned" are condemned for the slaughter and asked to stop doing it.[133] Unable to muster even the necessary words—like genocide and crimes against humanity—the council was hardly ready to act to halt the slaughter.

---

[132]United Nations, *The United Nations and Rwanda*, p. 43.

[133]United Nations Security Council Resolution S/Res/912 (1994), 21 April 1994.

The council reduced the soldiers to a token force of 270 and set as its first priority securing a cease-fire, hardly the task for an army, whether small or large. Dallaire criticized this excessive emphasis on a goal that was unlikely to be met to the exclusion of doing something to stop the killings. Unwilling to halt the genocide, the council tried instead to alleviate the suffering by directing UNAMIR to assist in humanitarian relief operations "to the extent feasible." The council was not prepared to guarantee the safety even of those who sought refuge with UNAMIR and it ordered the force only "to monitor and report on developments...including the safety and security" of those who sought protection from them.[134]

Fortunately Dallaire and his subordinates stretched their limited orders in the weeks to come. They somehow never found the right time for a plane to land to evacuate the troops in excess of the allotted 270 and so they continued to function with about 540 soldiers.[135] They guarded or at least regularly visited sites where people had sought shelter and they facilitated the exchange of civilians from one side of the front to the other. In mid-April, Dallaire broadened the possibilities for intervention to protect Tutsi, although he continued to insist on the avoidance of risk. When RTLM warned that new attacks would be launched at the end of April, Dallaire posted peacekeepers at such places as the Sainte Famille Church and the Notre Dame school.[136] The peacekeepers sometimes failed to safeguard persons under their protection, such as those attacked in an evacuation convoy on May 3, and they failed to respond to some cries for help, such as one from priests who pleaded for protection for people who had sought shelter in their church in Nyamirambo.[137] Partial, sporadic help for a pitifully small number was all that UNAMIR could offer while international leaders, far from the horrors, awaited reports on "safety and security" in Rwanda.

---

[134]Ibid.

[135]Human Rights Watch/FIDH interview, by telephone, May 22, 1996.

[136]Aidan Hartley, "U.N. Guards Rwanda Hotel After Massacre Threat," Reuters, April 28, 1994; Agence France Presse, "La Minuar protège six mille autres réfugiés menacés à Kigali," April 30, 1994.

[137]Human Rights Watch/FIDH interview by telephone, Brussels, September 22, 1996.

An Exceptional Case: The Hotel Mille Collines

In the first month of the genocide, international authorities once spoke clearly to avert slaughter. They were heeded immediately.

Beginning on April 7, hundreds of people—most of them Tutsi or Hutu threatened by Hutu Power supporters—took shelter at the Mille Collines, a luxury hotel in central Kigali owned by Sabena airlines. Although set apart from city streets by its spacious, well-groomed grounds, this expensive hotel offered no defense against attack beyond its international connections. On April 15, Paul Rusesabagina, temporarily manager of the hotel, called for its protection in an interview with a Belgian newspaper, as did an official of Sabena, who spoke on Belgian television. Rwandan authorities responded by posting some National Police at the hotel. In later contacts with the press and others, by telephone calls and fax messages, occupants of the hotel made the Mille Collines a symbol of the fear and anguish suffered by the Tutsi and others during these weeks.[138]

On April 23, a young lieutenant of the Department of Military Intelligence, reportedly a nephew of Bagosora named Iyakamuremye, arrived at the hotel at around 6 a.m. and ordered Rusesabagina to turn out everyone who had sought shelter there. Told that he had half an hour to comply with the order, Rusesabagina went up to the roof and saw that the building was surrounded by military and militia. He and several of the occupants began telephoning influential persons abroad, appealing urgently for help. Their calls were presumably relayed by representatives of Sabena, who would have been eager both to save lives and to protect their costly investment. According to Rusesabagina, one of the foreign authorities called from the hotel was the Director General of the French Foreign Ministry. Before the half hour had elapsed, a colonel from the National Police arrived to end the siege and to oblige the lieutenant to leave.[139]

In a similar incident on May 13, a captain came to the hotel in the morning to warn that there would be an attack at 4 in the afternoon. On that day, the French Foreign Ministry "received a fax from the hotel saying that Rwandan government forces plan to massacre all the occupants of the hotel in the next few hours."[140] It directed its representative at the U.N. to inform the secretariat of the threat and

---

[138]Human Rights Watch/FIDH interview, Brussels, November 8, 1998.

[139]Ibid.

[140]Assemblée Nationale, Mission d'information commune, *Enquête*, Tome II, Annexes, p. 307.

presumably also brought pressure to bear directly on authorities in Kigali, as others may have done also. The attack never took place.

None of the people who took shelter at the hotel was killed during the genocide and none was killed at a small number of other sites under foreign protection, like the hospital in Kigali run by Doctors Without Borders and the International Committee of the Red Cross.[141] Perhaps these sanctuaries could not have been replicated so successfully elsewhere. But certainly it would have been right to try.

---

[141]Assemblée Nationale, Mission d'information commune, *Enquête*, Tome III, Auditions, Volume I, pp. 394, 397.

ACKNOWLEDGING GENOCIDE

The killers had counted on international inaction and they were right. It took three weeks of slaughter—well-publicized, brutal slaughter—for the international community to begin recognizing the genocide and three months to send the troops meant to stop it.

On April 29 Secretary-General Boutros-Ghali finally acknowledged that the killing of civilians was distinct from the war, although related to it, and that it had to be ended. The same day, nonpermanent members of the Security Council who had followed the lead of the dominant actors rejected their direction and began to insist on more responsible action. The process of creating a second UNAMIR force, set in motion at that time, delivered peacekeepers to Rwanda in late July. By that time, the RPF had defeated the interim government and driven it into exile.

International leaders had available means other than armed force to influence the interim government but did not use them. They could have eliminated the hate radio, an action which would have had great symbolic as well as practical effect, but they did not do so. Nor did major donors ever threaten publicly that all financial assistance in the future would be withheld from a government guilty of genocide. Such a warning would have raised immediate concern among the many Rwandans who knew how much local and national authorities depended on foreign support and might have caused them to reject the interim government. The leading international actors continued to conduct diplomacy as usual, dealing with the interim government as a valid party to the negotiations which they hoped to broker. Belgium and the U.S. at one time refused to receive representatives of the interim government, but the effect of this exclusion was lessened by the welcome they received in Paris and at the U.N. Fourteen members of the Security Council tolerated a representative of Rwanda at their daily meetings, putting the observance of procedural decorum before the need to denounce a genocidal government and the crime it was committing.

The Security Council discussed an arms embargo at the end of April but imposed it only in mid-May, after thousands more had been slaughtered. The U.N. Human Rights Commission decided in late May that genocide *might* have been committed and mandated an investigation, with the possibility of judicial action against its perpetrators.

The potential effect of these measures, timid and late to begin with, was weakened by continued French support of the interim government. Some French policymakers, led by Mitterrand, were determined to block an RPF victory, even if it meant continuing to collaborate with genocidal killers until they could locate better representatives of the "great majority." They launched Operation Turquoise as much to prevent an RPF conquest of the entire country as to save civilian lives. In the end, the French soldiers did rescue thousands of persons, but instead of arresting the perpetrators of genocide, they permitted—and in some cases apparently helped—them to escape.

Zaire and the Seychelles assisted the interim government in obtaining arms, and arms dealers in Israel, Albania, and the United Kingdom continued to do business with authorities engaged in genocide. In addition, Zaire blocked the flight of Tutsi trying to escape the killing campaign and Kenya returned some evacuees to an almost certain death in Kigali.

International leaders took a very long time to admit the appropriateness of the term "genocide" and even then never fulfilled the legal or moral obligation to stop it.

The End of April: Recognizing Genocide

In the last days of April, RTLM urged new attacks to finish "cleaning up" the city of Kigali before May 5, the day projected for Habyarimana's funeral. Dallaire, who took this call to slaughter seriously enough to deploy the guards mentioned above, also warned headquarters that the killers might be on the point of launching a new round of massacres. Dallaire or another "U.N. officer" in Kigali used the press to alert the public to the "catastrophic"situation and the continuation of massive killings. He stated that if UNAMIR received the necessary resources, it could halt killings by the militia in Kigali immediately. Then he warned, "Unless the international community acts, it may find it is unable to defend itself against accusations of doing nothing to stop genocide."[1] In the last week of April also, U.N. Undersecretary-General for Humanitarian Affairs Peter Hansen returned from a brief visit to Kigali, appalled by the extent of the horrors.

At the same time, U.N. officials reported outflows of hundreds of thousands of refugees, with the potential to upset the stability of adjacent countries. From April 28 to April 29, an estimated quarter of a million Rwandans fled to Tanzania. In Burundi, an attempted coup by paratroopers was averted, but served nonetheless to warn of the potential catastrophe if large-scale violence there were added to the slaughter in Rwanda.[2]

---

[1]Buchizya Mseteka, "U.N. Agencies Deal with Rwandan Catastrophe," Reuters, April 30, 1994.

[2]Buchizya Mseteka, "Heavy Shelling in Rwandan Capital," Reuters, April 25, 1994; Jonathan Clayton, "Uncertain Ceasefire Holds In Rwanda," Reuters, April 26, 1994.

Many criticized the decision to reduce UNAMIR as reports of the killings continued. The Organization of African Unity accused the U.N. of applying a double standard by cutting troops in Rwanda while strengthening involvement in the former Yugoslavia.[3] The president of Tanzania charged that the reduction of UNAMIR made it appear that "the tragedy was of no concern to the international community."[4] Human Rights Watch and FIDH stepped up their efforts to demand action from national governments and the U.N., as did a host of other humanitarian and human rights groups. On April 28, Oxfam issued a call for international action against the "genocidal slaughter," an appeal seconded on May 1 by the European coalition of nongovernmental organizations known as Eurostep, which also recognized the slaughter as "genocide." Oxfam organized a series of vigils that drew the attention of the secretary-general. The International Committee of the Red Cross said it had "rarely seen a human tragedy on the scale of the massacres."[5] All agreed that killers were slaughtering civilians away from the battlefront as part of a deliberate campaign against Tutsi and demanded that the U.N. protect them.

Statement by the Secretary-General

On April 29, the secretary-general finally acknowledged that the war and the civilian massacres constituted two different problems and that the mandate for UNAMIR established the week before dealt with the first, but not with the second. Although ready to assign responsibility for the massacres to "uncontrolled military" and "armed groups of civilians," he portrayed them as independent actors, motivated by "deep-rooted ethnic hatreds" and taking advantage of the breakdown of law and order. Thus he continued to obscure the government-directed nature of the genocide and lent his credibility to the deliberately inaccurate depiction of the slaughter being disseminated by some representatives of France and by the genocidal government itself. Citing estimates that 200,000 people had been killed in the previous three weeks and warning of the "implications for the stability of neighboring countries," he asked the council to consider "forceful action" to end the massacres. He suggested that rather than allocate the considerable resources required for a U.N. military operation, the council might chose to act through

---

[3]United Nations, *The United Nations and Rwanda*, pp. 269-70.

[4]Ibid., p. 273.

[5]Peter Smerdon, "Rebel Reinforcements Push on Kigali Despite Talks," Reuters, April 22, 1994; Oxfam, "Genocide in Rwanda: 28.4.94"; Le Collectif des ONG Européennes EUROSTEP, press release, May 1, 1994.

delegation to a member state. In this way, he opened the door to the later French military operation known as Operation Turquoise.[6]

Statement of the President of the Security Council

As the secretary-general was moving hesitantly towards dealing more effectively with the Rwandan crisis, the Security Council was forced by some of its nonpermanent members to confront the genocide for what it was. During the last week of April, the ambassador of the Czech Republic, Karel Kovanda, began to doubt the interpretation of the crisis as presented by the secretariat. Made aware of the genocidal nature of the slaughter through the press and information from Human Rights Watch and other groups, he called a Human Rights Watch representative on Saturday morning, April 30, to discuss the problem. He said, "You can understand that the issue of Rwanda is not a national priority for the Czech Republic, but as a human being, I cannot sit here and do nothing."[7] He had prepared a draft statement for the council that called the slaughter in Rwanda by its rightful name, genocide, and that warned the interim government of its responsibility for halting it. This attempt to lead the council to confront the genocide produced an acrimonious debate that lasted for eight hours. Rwanda profited from its seat on the council to delay proceedings and to attempt to weaken the statement. It was supported by its ally Djibouti, whose ambassador explained afterwards that some members of the council had not wanted to "sensationalize" the situation in Rwanda.[8] China, generally opposed to dealing with human rights issues in the Security Council, reportedly opposed the use of the term "genocide," as did Nigeria, a leader among the nonaligned members of the council. France continued its campaign to minimize the responsibility of the interim government for the slaughter. The delegate from United Kingdom, who initially derided the draft statement as "laughable" or words to that effect, opposed strong action by the council. As had been clear in the discussion of protection for displaced persons, his government wanted to keep commitments of the U.N. limited, apparently fearing the organization might collapse under the strain of trying anything more ambitious

---

[6]Boutros Boutros-Ghali to Colin Keating, President of the Security Council, April 29, 1994.

[7]Human Rights Watch/FIDH interview, by telephone, New York April 29, 1994.

[8]Evelyn Leopold, "UN Council Issues Statement, No Troops for Rwanda," Reuters, April 30, 1994.

than its usual role of diplomacy. The U.S. delegation supported a fairly strong statement but one without the word "genocide" in it.[9]

Colin Keating, the ambassador from New Zealand, was to finish his term as president of the council at midnight. As it drew near that time, Keating announced his firm intention to have a text decided before he left the chair. Because presidential statements must be adopted unanimously, the supporters of various positions would have to compromise. To ensure that they did so, Ambassador Keating threatened to use his prerogative to declare the meeting an open session, which would have made public the positions of the various delegations. Those most opposed to a strong statement did not want that and so were obliged to agree on a statement that included the wording of the genocide convention, although it did not use the word "genocide." The statement noted that most of the attacks on defenseless civilians had occurred in areas under the control of the interim government. It recalled that persons who instigated or participated in breaches of international humanitarian law were "individually responsible" and it directed the secretary general to suggest how to investigate reports of such violations.

The council could not be pushed to do much about the genocide at that time. It requested the secretary-general to consult with the OAU to find a way to restore order in Rwanda. In a more forceful vein, it asked states to end arms deliveries and military assistance to the interim government and said it was prepared to impose an arms embargo.[10]

Yet the council had finally been obliged to debate the Rwandan crisis in depth and to hear an interpretation of the Rwandan crisis far more damning of the interim government than that presented by the secretary-general. The nonpermanent members—particularly the Czech Republic, New Zealand, Spain, and Argentina—who at first had left leadership to the secretariat and to the dominant actors, took the initiative on April 30 to insist on measures to halt the genocide. They continued to inform themselves about the issue at a long briefing by a representative of Human Rights Watch organized by Kovanda two days later. In the weeks to come, they were among the most persistent members of the council in pushing for action in Rwanda. Had they been more accurately informed about

---

[9]Human Rights Watch/FIDH interview, by telephone, New York, May 15, 1996.

[10]United Nations Security Council, Presidential Statement, "Condemnation of all breaches of international humanitarian law and reiteration of demand for an immediate cease-fire and cessation of hostilities in Rwanda," S/PRST/1994/21, April 30, 1994.

the slaughter during the first week of April, they might have taken their responsible stand earlier and shamed other members and staff into joining them.

Diplomacy as Usual

Even as officials in foreign governments and the U.N. were beginning to acknowledge the organized nature and enormous scale of the killing in Rwanda, they continued to engage in diplomacy as usual. One U.S. State Department official remarked that the Rwandan crisis differed from others she had experienced because events happened much faster than analysts could interpret them. It is true that the genocide took its toll with astonishing rapidity. But in the Rwandan case, the problem was not just the speed of events but their extraordinary nature. Diplomats are accustomed to dealing with wars; they are not yet accustomed to dealing with genocides.

Although increasingly willing to admit that the slaughter of civilians was an issue apart from the combat, the U.S. and other governments remained stuck in the familiar track of trying to bring the belligerents together.[11] They sought to repeat their success at Arusha and, to this end, carried on contacts "with everyone imaginable," as one State Department official put it. In early May, the U.S. ambassador to Rwanda and the assistant secretary of state for human rights and humanitarian affairs traveled to the region to try to mobilize neighboring African governments to put pressure on the warring parties. The French sent their ambassador to various African governments to do the same.

Achieving a cease-fire remained an unlikely goal because the interim government demanded that the RPF put down its guns before it end the killings of Tutsi and the RPF refused to stop firing while the slaughter of civilians continued. Focusing on these diplomatic manoeuvers led the U.S. and others to continue treating the genocidal government as a valid interlocutor which supported its efforts to present itself as legitimate at home as well as abroad. The wish to ensure "neutrality" in order to mediate the conflict kept officials from the frank and forceful condemnation of the genocide that might have affected Rwandans, both those most implicated in the killing and the moderates who dissented from it. On April 22, at the urging of Human Rights Watch, National Security Adviser Anthony Lake issued a statement calling on General Bizimungu, Colonel Bagosora, Colonel Nkundiye, and Captain Simbikangwa to "do everything in their power to

---

[11]See, for example, Testimony of Assistant Secretary of State George E. Moose Before the House Subcommittee on Africa on the Crisis in Rwanda, May 4, 1994.

end the violcncc immediately."[12] This innovative step remained an exception. One State Department official who recognized the potential value of drawing attention to the alleged leaders of the genocide despaired of getting any further action from the U.S. government and suggested that nongovernmental organizations publish a full-page notice in the international press denouncing those responsible for the slaughter. President Clinton did make a one-minute radio address to Rwanda on April 30. But the message—that he hoped all Rwandans would recognize their common bonds of humanity—was so mild as to be worthless. In fact, it may have done more harm than good. Killers could take satisfaction that the U.S. president had no stronger words of reproach for them, while the victims could feel betrayed by the weakness of the remarks.

Human Rights Watch also asked both the State Department and the White House to mobilize the heads of all the major donor nations to make a joint statement, preferably in conjunction with the World Bank, vowing never to assist any government that had come to power through genocide. U.S. officials, and likely others, transmitted such warnings to General Bizimungu and other authorities privately, but they never delivered such a message publicly in a way that would have ensured its impact both on the genocidal authorities and on moderates who might have been encouraged to oppose them.[13]

Because it was well known that radio RTLM was inciting genocide, Human Rights Watch and others asked U.S. officials to jam the station. The State Department assigned a team of lawyers to examine the question, but they decided that an international agreement on broadcasting and the traditional American commitment to freedom of speech were more important than disrupting the voice of genocide. Efforts by FIDH and other organizations to obtain action on RTLM from European governments also produced no results.[14]

Throughout the first weeks of killing, international leaders refused to talk of "genocide," apparently because they feared the legal and moral obligations that would follow from recognizing the crime. The U.N. discouraged use of the term and apparently cautioned Dallaire not to use it, perhaps after the press statement mentioned above. Claes also corrected himself in public after he mentioned

---

[12]The White House, Statement by the Press Secretary, April 22, 1994.

[13]Human Rights Watch/FIDH interview, by telephone, September 16, 1996.

[14]Burkhalter, "The Question of Genocide," p.51.

"genocide," saying "We are not using that word, but that's what it is."[15] The U.S. State Department and National Security Council told staff to acknowledge only that "acts of genocide may have occurred."[16]

The pope actually used the word "genocide" in condemning the violence on April 27.[17] Boutros-Ghali followed suit a few days later and various national leaders, beginning with French Minister Alain Juppé and representatives to a meeting of the European Union, two weeks after that.[18] At the May 25 meeting of the United Nations Human Rights Commission, however, the delegates concluded only that genocide might have occurred and should be investigated (see below). The next day, the State Department declared that the question of whether genocide was taking place was "under very active consideration." Only after the directive to avoid using the term was revealed in the *New York Times* on June 10 and was ridiculed by critics did U.S. Secretary of State Warren Christopher agree that use of "genocide" was appropriate when talking of Rwanda.[19]

In one of the few routine diplomatic actions to show public disapproval of the interim government, the U.S., Belgium, and a number of other governments refused to receive its delegations sent abroad at the end of April. But the impact of this refusal was at least in part counterbalanced by their being received at the United Nations. There the undistinguished Foreign Minister Jérôme Bicamumpaka, supported and directed by CDR leader Jean-Bosco Barayagwiza, took the seat of the Rwandan delegation at the May 16 meeting of the Security Council. In a somewhat incoherent and unconvincing address, Bicamumpaka attempted to justify the genocide, recounting for the diplomats many of the lies and distortions ordinarily delivered over RTLM. In addition to the usual assertions about the hundreds of thousands of Hutu killed by the RPF "simply because they were Hutu,"

---

[15]Reuters, "Claes says U.N. Should Focus on Border Areas in Rwanda," May 17, 1994.

[16]Douglas Jehl, "Officials Told to Avoid Calling Rwanda Killings 'Genocide'," *New York Times*, June 10, 1994.

[17]Reuters, "Vatican Calls for Rwandan Peace Conference," April 27, 1994.

[18]United Nations, *The United Nations and Rwanda*, p. 51; Conseil Affaires générales - Interview du Ministre des Affaires étrangères Alain Juppé aux radios françaises.

[19]Michael R. Gordon, "U.S. Acting More Urgently To End Rwanda Slaughter," *New York Times*, June 16, 1994.

he introduced the novel allegation that RPF soldiers ate the hearts of their victims. He recounted that the radio in Rwanda was broadcasting messages of peace and that government leaders were crisscrossing the country to hold pacification meetings. He claimed in fact that the killing was finished, except in areas where fighting with the RPF continued.

The delegates of the fourteen other nations around the Security Council table then had a chance to comment. Given the rare opportunity to address directly a high-ranking official of a government that was even then carrying out genocide, representatives of Brazil, China, Djibouti, France, Oman, Pakistan, the Russian Federation, the United States, and Nigeria spoke only in the vaguest terms of humanitarian catastrophes, or at best said, "the killings must stop" without indicating who must stop them. Only the representatives of Argentina, the Czech Republic, New Zealand, Spain, and the United Kingdom addressed remarks of varying sharpness to the messenger who would shortly be returning to Rwanda. The delegate of Nigeria, who spoke last, called on the international community to support "the innocent civilians in Rwanda." But in this august setting, he and the representatives of eight other nations had missed an opportunity to do just that. They had failed to deliver a firm and unanimous denunciation of the genocide being executed by the government whose representatives sat at the table with them.[20]

Perhaps these Rwandan emissaries, or others who traveled to various African countries were subjected to frank criticism in private about the genocide, but, in public, diplomatic appearances were preserved. From what other Rwandans heard of these meetings abroad, they could surmise only that foreign governments and the U.N. as well had little knowledge of the genocide or did not think it merited serious comment.

The Organization of African Unity, which had promoted the Arusha negotiations and provided military observers before the U.N. became involved, proved no readier than the U.N. to call genocide by its rightful name. It opposed the reduction of UNAMIR, but referred to the slaughter as "carnage and bloodletting" and "massacres and wanton killings."[21] Fourteen heads of African states finally condemned "genocide" in early June, but at the OAU summit in mid-June, Interim President Sindikubwabo was seated as the representative from

---

[20]United Nations, Security Council, 3377th Meeting, Monday, 16 May, 1994, S/PV/3377.

[21]Adelman and Suhrke, *Early Warning*, p. 46.

Rwanda. That meeting, which described the killings as "crimes against humanity," provided the occasion for discussions that produced a cease-fire that was never executed.[22]

UNAMIR II

At the same meeting where Rwandan representatives tried to explain away the genocide, the Security Council finally voted to send a second UNAMIR force to Rwanda. Had the new force been mobilized quickly, it might have rendered real assistance to the "innocent civilians" spoken of by the Nigerian representative. But just as the council was slow in authorizing it, so the various national and international bureaucracies were slow in implementing it. The new force arrived too late to protect Tutsi from genocide.

The secretary-general had been asking member states to provide troops for Rwanda since early May. No nation outside the continent was likely to send soldiers to Rwanda and, in fact, it proved very difficult to muster the needed forces from other African countries. But by May 10, the supply of troops seemed well enough assured to proceed with crafting the mandate for the force. The U.S., in its first official application of PDD 25, wanted to go carefully through all the steps devised in Washington. Just when the process appeared finished and a resolution in sight for Friday, May 13, the U.S. delegation announced it had "no instructions" for the vote, forcing a postponement until May 16.[23]

In the resolution adopted on May 17,[24] the Security Council still eschewed the word "genocide" although once again using the words of the 1948 Genocide Convention. It mentioned again that such crimes were punishable under international law and, for the first time, drew attention to the role of the mass media in inciting violence. The mandate itself provided for contributing "to the security and protection of displaced persons, refugees and civilians at risk in Rwanda" and for providing security to humanitarian relief operations. It broadened the sphere of responsibility from the city of Kigali to Rwanda as a whole and it authorized "secure humanitarian areas," so recognizing and enlarging upon what UNAMIR had been doing in practice in Kigali since the start of the crisis. Although still

---

[22]Sibonginkosi Chigaro, "African States Pledge Troops to Rwanda," Reuters, June 3, 1994; Stephen Smith, "Le Sommet Africain Appelle Les Rwandais à un Cessez-le-feu, *Libération*, June 16, 1994.

[23]Human Rights Watch interview, New York, May 13, 1994.

[24]The vote took place after midnight, hence the resolution was dated May 17.

officially a Chapter VI mandate, this charge recognized that UNAMIR "may be required to take action in self-defense against persons or groups who threaten protected sites and populations," making it really a chapter "six and a half" operation. The difference in mandate from that of UNAMIR I was, in fact, very small, except in terms of the larger geographical area of responsibility. The real difference was in the size of force projected, some 5,500 troops, a number that Dallaire himself had said would be necessary to stop the genocide. The resolution also imposed an arms embargo against the government of Rwanda.[25]

At the time of the vote, the U.S. delegation required further information and field assessments before deploying the full force. Dallaire had proposed having UNAMIR II land in Kigali where its troops could most rapidly end the massacres, but the U.S. feared the force might then become caught in combat between the Rwandan army and the RPF. Instead it favored deploying the troops on the periphery of Rwanda where they could establish safe zones to protect civilians. One reason for caution was the strong position taken by the RPF against a second UNAMIR force (see below). Neither the U.N. nor the U.S. nor any other national actors wished to risk a confrontation between peacekeepers and a force that had appeared very effective in combat.

For the peacekeepers in Kigali, the wait for authorization of a new force had seemed interminable. They understood that action by the Security Council would not necessarily deliver prompt assistance to Rwanda and to UNAMIR I. Executive Director Abdul Kabiah tried to convey a sense of urgency that might spur the various national and international bureaucracies to faster action. He told the press:

> We need logistical support, armoured personnel carriers (APCs) and troops to stop the carnage. Everyone is appalled by the killing but the world must back up this kind of concern and act now.[26]

The lengthy exchanges about plans, troops, finances, logistics, and strategy between Washington and the U.N.—complete with mutual recriminations about unnecessary delays—finally produced the authorization for UNAMIR II on June 8, two months and a day after the first slaughter and more than five weeks after the secretary-general had announced the need for a new force. Because the African

---

[25]United Nations, Security Council Resolution, S/Res/ 918 (1994), 17 May 1994.

[26]Thaddee Nsengiyaremye, "U.N. Force in Rwanda Warns Delays Will Cost Lives," Reuters, May 18, 1994.

soldiers to be sent lacked essential equipment, the secretariat then engaged in further long exchanges to obtain the necessary provisions from better-equipped nations. In a process that was already well-established in other peacekeeping operations, the troop-supplying nations used this as an opportunity to squeeze the maximum amount from the wealthier nations, while the latter sought to keep their contributions to a minimum. The U.S. was much criticized for its outrageous delay of seven weeks in negotiating the conditions of delivery for fifty armored personnel carriers. It appeared that the problems had to do with adequate payment for transport and spare parts. But other wealthy nations also contributed little or contributed it slowly. The U.K., for example, came up with only fifty trucks.[27]

Such delays were not unusual in mustering U.N. operations. What was unusual was the context of the operation. In its June 8 resolution, the Security Council had finally used the word "genocide," not in its full brutality, but in the more tentative form "acts of genocide." Even though its members had acknowledged the crime for what it was, they could not get the additional troops to Rwanda in time to make any difference. In mid-June, Clinton was criticized by members of Congress and the press for tolerating the delays. He then directed U.S. officials to move faster to help get the new U.N. force to Rwanda.[28] But if this effort had results in Washington, it seems to have done little to cut through the red tape and to move the bureaucrats in New York. It was business as usual, as it had been diplomacy as usual, with no sense of the lives lost through delay. After the RPF had won the war and established a new government on July 19, there were still about the same number of UNAMIR soldiers in Rwanda as there had been at the time of the withdrawal in April.[29]

Human Rights Agencies

The genocide in Rwanda began just after José Ayala Lasso assumed the newly created post of the U.N. High Commissioner for Human Rights. The office had been established not only to give greater visibility to human rights but also to

---

[27]Burkhalter, "The Question of Genocide," pp. 50-51; Adelman and Suhrke, *Early Warning,* pp. 51-53.

[28]Michael R. Gordon, "U.S. Acting More Urgently to End Rwanda Slaughter," *New York Times,* June 16, 1994.

[29]United Nations, Security Council, Resolution 925 (1994), S/Res/925 (1994), June 8, 1994; United Nations, Letter of the Secretary-General to the President of the Security Council, S/1994/923, 3 August, 1994.

permit faster and more flexible reactions to crises than were possible with the somewhat cumbersome Human Rights Commission. At the request of various national governments and nongovernmental organizations, the high commissioner visited Rwanda in early May. There he pressed the interim government to allow the evacuation of Tutsi trapped at the Mille Collines and other sites in Kigali. Soon after the Rwandan authorities became more cooperative in permitting evacuations, perhaps as a consequence of his efforts and of their growing concern with their image abroad.[30] Lasso's report, issued on May 19, 1994 described the killings in Rwanda as "a human rights tragedy of unprecedented dimensions" and made clear that those in command of the killings must be held individually responsible for their violations of international law. But it was only in the context of urging "all players" to end the tragedy that he mentioned "genocide," asking for strict observance of international conventions, including that against genocide.[31]

Although the high commissioner showed early awareness of the crisis and courage in going to assess its extent personally, he failed to translate his concern into forceful action. Rather than suggest new strategies for coping with the catastrophe, he issued the expected calls to stop the violence and the usual warnings about the consequences of not stopping. He also proposed a special meeting of the Human Rights Commission and suggested that the commission consider appointing a special rapporteur with a supporting staff of human rights field officers. These measures, which were taken, were valuable, but only in the longer term.[32] After his initial visit and report, the high commissioner made no sustained, vigorous effort to keep the genocide before the international community and to insist on action in this crisis which, although just one of his responsibilities, was certainly the most urgent.

The U.N. Human Rights Commission, which had refused to discuss the case of Rwanda in open session in 1993, was called into emergency session on the initiative of Canada on May 25, 1994 to deal with the ongoing slaughter. After a day and a half of formal denunciations of the violence by professional diplomats, it heard an afternoon of less polished but more heart-rending testimony by

[30]José Ayala Lasso, "Urgent U.N. Measures Can Abate the Rwanda Killings," *International Herald Tribune*, May 24, 1994.

[31]Commission on Human Rights, "Report of the United Nations High Commissioner for Human Rights, Mr. José Ayala Lasso, on his mission to Rwanda, 11-12 May 1994," E/CN.4/-3/3, May 19, 1994.

[32]Ibid.

representatives of Rwandan and international nongovernmental organizations. Although a number of delegates, including those from France and the U.S. spoke of genocide or acts of genocide, the final resolution did not acknowledge that genocide had occurred. Rather it named a special rapporteur to investigate if genocide had in fact taken place.[33] At the meeting, diplomats and activists pressed for an international tribunal to bring to trial those accused of genocide.

The Human Rights Commission's special rapporteur on Rwanda, René Degni-Ségui, presented his first report on June 28. He concluded that genocide had been committed in Rwanda and should be punished by an international tribunal. He also condemned executions and assassinations of Hutu by the RPF.[34] On July 1 the Security Council created a Commission of Experts to evaluate the evidence of serious human rights violations including possible acts of genocide in Rwanda with the expectation that an international tribunal would be established to deal with them, as had been done recently in the case of former Yugoslavia.[35]

International denunciations and the associated threat of action by an international tribunal worried some of those responsible for the genocide. RTLM sought to dispel their concerns by claiming that the international disapproval resulted from RPF propaganda, such as that which had convinced U.S. senators to write to Clinton denouncing the killings as genocide.[36] Censure by foreigners would be fleeting said RTLM, having been provoked by "the action of the *Inkotanyi* girls who spread their legs in hotels...[to seduce the European] and recount to him the anguish of their brothers...in order to get the Rwandan government and the FAR [Rwandan army] condemned for genocide." The announcer continued,

> I would like...to remind the FAR that if we fight well and win, the Europeans will forget these stories of commissions; they will forget these stories of

[33]Economic and Social Council, Commission on Human Rights, Resolution E/CN, 4S-3/1, May 25, 1994.

[34]Economic and Social Council, Commission on Human Rights, "Report on the Situation of human rights in Rwanda submitted by Mr. R. Degni-Ségui, Special Rapporteur of the Commission on Human Rights, under paragraph 20 of Commission resolution E/CN, 4/S-3/1 of 25 May 1994."

[35]Security Council, Resolution 935 (1994), S/Res/935 (1994), July 1, 1994.

[36]Chrétien, et al., *Rwanda, Les médias*, p. 279.

embargoes; all these things that they are talking about, and even foreign aid will be re-established...

We cannot do anything else to shut up those people who try to discourage us by threatening to bring us before an international tribunal, or wherever...All who seek to demoralize us, we must fight them.[37]

RTLM responded quickly to news of the special rapporteur's report and the Security Council resolution. On July 2, Kantano Habimana declared that the international community had done nothing to punish slaughter in Burundi in 1972 or in 1993 and that the International Tribunal for Bosnia had not convicted anyone. Perhaps using the strategem of "accusing in a mirror," Kantano Habimana concluded, "So for Rwanda, they cannot say anything that will worry us...let us continue to do our work and to fight against the *Inyenzi-Inkotanyi* that began this combat and that has since already killed more than a million people."[38]

The apparent impact of international censure, even at this late date when so many had committed themselves to the killing campaign, suggests that similar denunciations, made earlier and more forcefully, could have swayed the decisions of those not yet active in the genocide.

Arms and Ammunition

The message of condemnation of the genocide, sent in a tardy and hesitant way, was counterbalanced throughout these months of horror by another message from international actors indicating acquiescence in the slaughter. A small number of persons, officially and unofficially—in such countries as France, the United Kingdom, Israel, Albania, South Africa, the Seychelles—supplied the weapons needed by the authorities who were executing the killing campaign. (For the case of France, see below.)

On April 10, in one of its first actions, the newly installed interim government made contact with the Mil-Tec corporation, arms dealers in the United Kingdom, to place an urgent order for U.S.$854,000 worth of arms and ammunition.[39] A week

---

[37]Ibid., p. 318.

[38]Chrétien, et al., *Rwanda, Les médias*, p. 319. For "accusation in a mirror," see above.

[39]Mil-Tec Corporation Ltd to Minister of Defense, Republic of Rwanda, December 7, 1994 (received from Massimo Alberizzi, correspondent for *Corriere della Sera*). Because Mil-Tec was incorporated in the Isle of Man, a territory with special status under British law,

later, it sent Lt. Col. Cyprien Kayumba on a two month mission to Kinshasha, Nairobi, Paris, Tunis, Cairo and Tripoli in search of arms.[40] Bagosora also went to the Seychelles and apparently to Malta and perhaps elsewhere to buy weapons.[41] Ndindiliyimana went to Europe in June with the charge to speed lagging deliveries.[42] Other emissaries may also have been sent to attempt to purchase firearms.[43]

Clearly the interim government placed great importance on ensuring a supply of weapons and ammunition. Clearly also it was ready even to change policy to avoid an interruption in the flow of arms. As official statements down to the level of the commune show, "pacification" was in part a response to the fear that the supply of arms would be disrupted. (See above.) On one level, continued deliveries were important to the legitimacy of the interim government, as an indicator that the international community was prepared to tolerate even if it did not approve of the genocide. On a practical level, the guns and bullets were needed to fight the RPF, a consideration which weighed especially heavily with the military officers in charge of combat. In addition, the firearms were needed in exterminating the Tutsi. Some foreign observers have minimized the importance of firearms in the genocide. Colonel Marchal, for example, stated that "the massacres were done by militias with machetes," an opinion voiced also by Kofi Annan.[44] Certainly most

---

it was not subject to the same regulations concerning the arms embargo as applied elsewhere in the U.K. Provision has since been made to ensure that such restrictions will apply there.

[40]Lt. Col. Kayumba Cyprien to Monsieur le Ministre de la Défense, December 26, 1994 (confidential source).

[41]United Nations, Letter dated 13 March 1996 from the Secretary-General to the President of the Security Council transmitting the final report of the International Commission of Inquiry, S/1996/195 in United Nations, *The United Nations and Rwanda,* pp. 679-81; United Nations, Letter dated January 22, 1998 from the Secretary-General addressed to the President of the Security Council, S/1998/63.

[42]Human Rights Watch/FIDH interview, Brussels, December 1, 1995.

[43]Lt. Col. Kayumba Cyprien to Monsieur le Ministre de la Défense, December 26, 1994.

[44]Jean de la Guérivière, "Un officier belge maintien ses déclarations sur l'attitude de la France lors du génocide rwandais," *Le Monde,* August 23, 1995; Assemblée Nationale, Mission d'information commune, *Enquête,* Tome II, Annexes, p. 331.

assailants killed Tutsi with machetes, hammers, clubs, and other such weapons. But, as the evidence above shows, soldiers and milita slew thousands of civilians with firearms and grenades. They used these weapons also to terrorize tens of thousands of others, paralyzing them before assailants who killed them by other means. At massacre sites, bullet shells litter the ground and holes in walls and ceilings testify to the use of the grenades. Witnesses from various regions agree that the attacks began with the use of firearms, including sometimes even heavy weaponry. They also agree that the guards at most important barriers had at least one firearm or several grenades which they used to execute Tutsi or to intimidate them to make it easier to kill them in other ways.

As is often the case with the profitable arms trade where a multiplicity of parties compete, official or unofficial actors from at least thirteen countries participated in the commercial transactions that kept Rwanda supplied with arms. In addition to the French authorities and private agents (discussed below), government officials in the Seychelles twice shipped arms to Rwanda. Bagosora himself went there to negotiate the delivery of some eighty tons of arms and ammunition at a cost of some U.S.$330,000. The government of Zaire provided an essential link in the supply line by permitting its airports at Kinshasha and Goma to be used for the delivery of arms that were then shipped on to Rwanda.[45]

Arms dealers in Israel, the United Kingdom, South Africa, and Albania had no scruples about selling weapons to authorities who were executing a genocide. Lieutenant Colonel Kayumba arranged for the delivery of five different shipments from the Mil-Tec Corporation, operated by two Kenyans, Anup Vidyarthi and Rakeesh Gupta, and under the directorship of two British subjects, John and Trevor Donnelly. Rwandan records show that Mil-Tec shipped U.S.$5.5 million worth of ammunition and grenades on April 18, April 25, May 5, May 9, and May 20. They obtained the first two shipments in Israel and the later ones from Albania. Shipping documents show that Mil-Tec used an aircraft registered in Nigeria but leased from a company in the Bahamas to make its deliveries.[46] In another case, a South African

---

[45]Human Rights Watch Arms Project, "Rwanda/Zaire: Rearming with Impunity," vol. 7, No.4, May 1995, pp. 9-12, 14; United Nations, *The United Nations and Rwanda,* pp. 679-81.

[46]Mil-Tec Corporation Ltd to Minister of Defense, Republic of Rwanda, December 7, 1994, and attached waybills and invoices; Lt. Col. Kayumba Cyprien to Ministre de la Défense, December 26, 1994; Christopher Elliott and Richard Norton-Taylor, "Arms sales to Rwanda questioned," *Guardian,* November 19, 1996.

plane reportedly delivered arms to Butare airport at the end of May, as mentioned above.

According to correspondence between Mil-Tec and the National Westminster Bank in the U.K., Mil-Tec deposited payments for arms sales to Rwanda in an account there. A U.N. commission investigating the traffic in weapons to Rwanda found that banks in Belgium (Banque Bruxelles Lambert), France (Banque National de Paris), Switzerland (Union Bancaire Privée, Geneva), Italy (Banca Nazionale de Lavoro), and in the U.S. (Federal Reserve Bank, Chase Manhattan Bank) also handled financial transactions involved in the purchase of weapons.[47]

Because the profitable trade in small arms is not subject to the same monitoring as the traffic in heavier weapons and involves so many actors, observers sometimes conclude that arms embargoes targeting such weapons can be nothing more than futile gestures. In the Rwandan case, once the Security Council had declared an arms embargo on May 17, arms dealers took the usual route of obtaining false declarations from friendly governments—in this case, Zaire—to hide continued traffic. Bagosora used this device in the Seychelles, presenting false documentation and claiming to be an officer in the army of Zaire. In another case, Zaire issued the necessary false documents for two arms dealers who intended to transfer arms stocked in Belgium to Goma for Rwandan use.[48]

Still the embargo did slow and hinder the delivery of weapons to the interim government. The government of Egypt, which had been negotiating an exchange of weapons for tea then stocked at Mombasa, ended discussions after the imposition of the embargo. The government of Libya, which had also promised arms, in the end delivered none, perhaps because of the embargo.[49] South African officials reportedly refused to violate the embargo but offered to help Bagosora

---

[47]Mrs. M. Franklin, Foreign Business Officer, National Westminster Bank, to Mil-Tec Corporation Limited, November 11, 1994; United Nations, *The United Nations and Rwanda,* p. 680; United Nations, Letter dated January 22, 1998 from the Secretary-General addressed to the President of the Security Council, S/1998/63; Lt. Col. Kayumba Cyprien to Ministre de la Défense, December 26, 1994.

[48]Human Rights Watch Arms Project, "Rwanda/Zaire: Rearming with Impunity," vol. 7, No.4, May 1995, p, 11; United Nations, Letter dated March 13, 1996 from the Secretary-General to the President of the Security Council transmitting the final report of the International Commission of Inquiry, S/1996/195.

[49]Human Rights Watch/FIDH interview, Brussels, August 1, 1997.

obtain arms by other means.[50] The government of the Seychelles asserts that it unknowingly violated the embargo because it believed the arms to be destined for Zaire and that it canceled a planned third shipment of arms when it learned this was not the case. In fact, Seychelles authorities may have known that the arms were meant for Rwanda even at the time of the first shipments. They may have refused to send the third shipment because the local press had embarrassed them by publicizing the deal.[51] In June, the British government issued an order prohibiting firms in the U.K. from selling arms from a third country to Rwanda as the Mil-Tec Corporation had been doing.[52] At about the same time, U.S. authorities may have blocked the transfer of funds from the Federal Reserve Bank that were intended to pay for the last shipment of the Mil-Tec Corporation.[53] In a case to be discussed below, the French company SOFREMAS, ready to do business for U.S.$8 million worth of arms on May 6 reportedly decided in the end not to do so because of the embargo.[54]

The arms embargo, first mentioned on April 30, was imposed only on May 17, after thousands more people had been slaughtered. After that time, governments acted to enforce compliance on individuals and corporations operating on their territory only slowly or not at all. Rwandan authorities feared a disruption in the flow of arms and the prospect of an embargo was one of the most important spurs to the policy of "pacification." Had the embargo been put in place earlier and enforced more rigorously, it might have pushed the interim government to end the slaughter instead of just changing the way it was carried out.

[50]Human Rights Watch Arms Project, "Rwanda/Zaire: Rearming with Impunity," p. 14.

[51]United Nations, *The United Nations and Rwanda,* pp. 679, 684.

[52]Elliott and Norton-Taylor, "Arms sales to Rwanda questioned."

[53]Lt. Col. Kayumba Cyprien to Monsieur le Ministre de la Défense, December 26, 1994 (confidential source).

[54]Bernard Duraud, "Rwanda: deux documents mettent la France en accusation," and Bruno Peuchamiel, "La réponse des sociétés mises en cause," *L'Humanité*, November 20, 1996.

"Vive La Cooperation Franco-Rwandaise"

Even as the number of victims of genocide mounted, some French officials pursued the goal of assuring the heirs of Habyarimana the predominant political role in Rwanda. In so doing they weakened the impact of weak and tardy efforts to halt the slaughter and strengthened the resolve of the genocidal government. The French had hoped to use the U.N. peacekeepers to protect the Rwandan government against the RPF, but this strategy collapsed with the renewal of combat and the withdrawal of UNAMIR into passivity. President Mitterrand and some of the military closest to him were not prepared to accept the prospect of a RPF victory. General Christian Quesnot, head of the president's own military staff, and General Jean-Pierre Huchon, who had been part of Mitterrand's military staff until he became head of the French military assistance program in mid-1993, apparently shared and shaped Mitterrand's analysis of the Rwandan situation.[55] Mitterrand, military officers with links to Rwanda, and many political leaders as well, had assimilated the doctrine of the rubanda nyamwinshi propagated by Hutu Power advocates. Like them, they unquestioningly equated the ethnic majority to the political majority. Whether they chose to speak of Hutu representing 80 percent of the Rwandan population or of Tutsi comprising 15 per cent of the total (the missing 5 percent was never mentioned), they never doubted that Hutu had the right to dominate political life. That the minority was supported by their Anglo-Saxon rivals only reinforced their loyalty to the Hutu.[56] With the resumption of combat, some high-ranking military officers held even more strongly to their belief that the RPF were "Black Khmers" and some privately challenged the Arusha Accords. One told a researcher, "Arusha is Munich," referring to the classic case of appeasement of the Nazis that preceded World War II.[57] Soldiers used terms like "Tutsiland" and "Hutu country" in private correspondence and even in official orders.[58] For policymakers and soldiers trapped in this ethnic analysis of the situation, Habyarimana had been the quintessential representative of the majority

---

[55]Assemblée Nationale, Mission d'information commune, *Enquête*, Tome III, Auditions, Volume I, pp. 127, 347. Callamard, "French Policy in Rwanda," p. 22.

[56]Assemblée Nationale, Mission d'information commune, *Enquête*, Tome III, Auditions, Volume I, pp. 208, 210, 341, 344; Chrétien et al., *Rwanda, Les médias*, p. 281.

[57]Callamard, "French Policy in Rwanda," pp. 16, 24.

[58]Assemblée Nationale, Mission d'information commune, *Enquête*, Tome II, Annexes, pp. 239, 279, 387.

people. With his death, they saw the circle of those identified with him as the only leaders likely to succeed in withstanding the RPF threat.

"Getting Your Hands Dirty"

The Rwandan politicians who formed the interim government on April 8 realized the importance of French support and kept French Ambassador Jean-Michel Marlaud well informed of their progress toward taking control. He found the new government acceptable even though it was composed exclusively of Hutu Power supporters and even though it had refused his suggestion to make Faustin Twagiramungu, designated prime minister by the Arusha Accords, head of the government instead of Kambanda.[59] The day after its installation, the interim government sent its foreign minister to ask Marlaud for French troops to "contain the situation."[60]

French soldiers were supposed to have left Rwanda in December 1993 under the terms of the Arusha Accords. Only twenty-four remained officially after this date, as part of a military training program for the army general staff, the National Police and other units. But according to Michel Roussin, then Minister of Cooperation, forty to seventy soldiers were actually in Rwanda in early April.[61] Within minutes after the plane was shot down, French soldiers were at the site of the crash, although UNAMIR soldiers were prevented by Rwandan troops from approaching it. The next morning, four French soldiers stood guard outside the Habyarimana's home while members of the Presidential Guard escorted visitors in and out.[62] Early on April 9, French soldiers secured the airport for the arriving evacuation force, working in close cooperation with Rwandan army troops, and

---

[59]Reyntjens, *Rwanda, Trois jours*, p. 89.

[60]Chris McGreal, Notes of interview with Jean Kambanda, Bukavu, August, 1994.

[61]Patrick de Saint-Exupéry, "France-Rwanda: des mensonges d'Etat, *Le Figaro,* April 2, 1998.

[62]Brussels, Détachement Judiciaire, Auditorat Militaire, P.V. no. 1013, June 22, 1994.

they served as intermediary between the Rwandan soldiers and the Belgian evacuation force, then regarded as hostile by the Rwandans.[63]

The deputy defense attaché at the French embassy, Lt. Col. Jean-Jacques Maurin, was in charge of the troops because the defense attaché was out of the country. Maurin, who had served as adviser to the general staff since 1992, was well-acquainted with Rwandan military leaders and presumably well-placed to influence them. According to Ambassador Marlaud, he and Maurin tried on the afternoon of April 7 to persuade Bagosora to "take control of the situation," ignoring the fact that he was already in control of the violence.[64] Otherwise there has been no account of the role played by these French advisers during the first days of the crisis, when the officers whom they had been training were ordering their troops to slaughter civilians. Nor has there been an explanation of the duties of the two French soldiers slain by the RPF, along with the wife of one of them, on April 8. They were supposedly found in possession of communications equipment. Some officers in Belgian military intelligence believed that the French had tapped the phone system in Kigali.[65]

For several days, the French considered meeting the request of the interim government for military assistance. According to a commission of the French National Assembly that investigated the Rwandan tragedy, the evacuation operation had a "strictly humanitarian purpose" but "could have developed into something other than a simple humanitarian operation."[66] They mention that the force came equipped with Milan missles and that a group of thirty-five men, at least one of them an intelligence expert, remained in Rwanda under Maurin's orders even after the embassy had been closed and all the foreigners and other French soldiers had been evacuated. The contingent left behind was ordered to gather information on the local situation, propose appropriate action, and guide air support

---

[63]Assemblée Nationale, Mission d'information commune, *Enquête,* Tome I, Rapport, pp. 257, 259.

[64]Assemblée Nationale, Mission d'information commune, *Enquête,* Tome III, Auditions, Volume I, p. 296.

[65]Stephen Smith, "6 avril 1994: deux missiles abattent l'avion du président Habyarimana;" Commission d'enquête, *Rapport,* p. 335-36.

[66]Assemblée Nationale, Mission d'information commune, *Enquête sur la tragédie rwandaise (1990-1994),* Tome I, Rapport, p. 262.

operations. As the commission notes, it is difficult to imagine for whom the air support might be destined if not the Rwandan army.[67]

The relative weakness of the government troops and the rapid advance of the RPF must have discouraged decision makers in Paris from attempting yet one more rescue of the Rwandan army. The French had also consulted with at least the U.S. and Belgium about some form of intervention, as mentioned above, and had found them unwilling to participate. According to official records, the last of the French troops was withdrawn on April 14.

Some soldiers long committed to supporting Rwandan colleagues regretted this decision. Col. Jean Balch, one of that group, commented:

...it would have taken very little (a few French military advisers) to reverse the situation. June 1992 and February 1993 [when French aid had halted the RPF] could perfectly well have been "replayed" in April 1994.[68]

Unwilling to provide military aid, the French provided discreet but vital political support to the interim government, at the U.N., in diplomatic exchanges with other governments, and through public statements.[69] They argued, as did the Kigali authorities, that the massacres were a virtually inevitable response to RPF military advances.[70] They often refused to acknowledge the role of Rwandan authorities in directing the genocide; as late as June 22, French military officers spoke of the need to help authorities reestablish control over the killers.[71] At other times, they admitted the responsibility of the interim government, but sought to minimize it by depicting the genocide as part of a particularly vicious "tribal war"

---

[67]Ibid., p. 264.

[68]Ibid, p. 263.

[69]Human Rights Watch/FIDH interview, New York, May 15, 1996.

[70]Assemblée Nationale, Mission d'information commune, *Enquête,* Tome III, Auditions, Volume I, p. 119.

[71]Assemblée Nationale, Mission d'information commune, *Enquête,* Tome II, Annexes, p. 387.

with abuses on both sides.[72] In an interview with representatives of Human Rights Watch and the International Federation of Human Rights Leagues, Mitterrand's chief adviser on Africa, Bruno Delaye, conceded that the "Hutu" had done terrible things, but he insisted that it was because they were fighting for their lives. It was regrettable, but that was the way Africans were.[73] On May 16, then Foreign Minister Alain Juppé became one of the first important statesmen to use the term "genocide" in referring to Rwanda, but in mid-June he wrote about "genocides," suggesting both sides were engaged in the crime.[74]

Using the pretext of keeping contact with all parties to the conflict, Juppé and Delaye welcomed to Paris the delegation of the interim foreign minister, Jérôme Bicamumpaka, and CDR head Jean-Bosco Barayagwiza. Although a French government spokesman described the visit as unofficial, the two were received at the French Presidency and at the Office of the Prime Minister. At the time, Human Rights Watch questioned a French representative in Washington about the meetings and was told that French officials had used the occasion to press for an end to the massacres.[75] In Paris, Delaye answered a similar question from Daniel Jacoby, then President of FIDH, by saying that it was better to talk to them than not to.[76] Challenged subsequently about the wisdom of meeting with representatives of a government engaged in genocide, Delaye stated that he had received 400 assassins and 2,000 drug traffickers in his office. "You cannot deal with Africa," he asserted, "without getting your hands dirty."[77]

---

[72]Réponse du Ministre des Affaires étrangères, M. Alain Juppé à une question orale à l'Assemblée nationale. 28 avril 1994.

[73]Human Rights Watch/FIDH interview, Paris, July 4, 1994.

[74]Alain Juppé, "Intervenir au Rwanda," *Libération*, June 16, 1994; Mitterrand also would use the plural "genocides" in a speech in November 1994. François Mitterand, "Discours de Monsieur François Mitterand," Biarritz, 8 November 1994, p.4

[75]Prunier, *The Rwanda Crisis,* p. 277; Alain Girma, French Embassy, Washington, D.C. to Holly Burkhalter, Human Rights Watch, April 28, 1994.

[76]Eric Gillet, "Le Génocide Devant La Justice," *Les Temps Modernes*, July-August, 1995, no. 583, p. 241, n. 33.

[77]Patrick de Saint-Exupèry, "France-Rwanda: un génocide sans importance...," *Le Figaro*, January 12, 1998.

During the 1998 inquiry at the National Assembly, Foreign Minister Hubert Védrine, who was secretary-general at the French Presidency in 1994, was asked why France had accorded legitimacy to the genocidal government. He responded that:

> It was not a question of legitimacy or illegitimacy, which is based in a democratic way of thinking not appropriate in the context of the period.... France does not select and does not judge some as more than legitimate than others. It saw that there was a terrible conflict which it watched with consternation since its purpose had been for years...to prevent that conflict. Hence its desire to negotiate a cease-fire, which required continuing a dialogue with all the parties.[78]

In fact, as shown above, other governments also continued discussions with the interim authorities but found more private ways to do so. If French officials chose such a highly visible way to maintain contact with the genocidal government, they did so fully aware of the political message being sent. It made genocide seem respectable in Paris, an encouragement to its supporters in Rwanda and a lever for the interim government to use in securing entry in other capitals abroad.

According to former minister of cooperation, Bernard Debré, Mitterrand at first remained "very attached to former President Habyarimana and his family, and to everything that was part of the old regime."[79] This attachment took the concrete form of a gift of some U.S.$40,000 to Madame Habyarimana at the time of her arrival in France, a sum that was designated as "urgent assistance for Rwandan refugees" and was taken from the budget of the Ministry of Cooperation.[80] This grant provoked such anger among staff of the ministry that information about it was leaked to the press. Ministry staff also formally and unanimously demanded that "money budgeted by the Ministry of Cooperation for Rwanda be used for humanitarian assistance for the people of the country" and deplored the French

---

[78]Assemblée Nationale, Mission d'information commune, *Enquête,* Tome III, Auditions, Volume I, p. 210.

[79]Quoted on Radio France Internationale, November 18, 1994.

[80]Alain Frilet and Sylvie Coma, "Paris, terre d'asile de luxe pour dignitaires hutus."

refusal to evacuate Rwandan employees, some of whom had worked with the French for many years.[81]

French authorities occasionally used their influence to protect people, as when they intervened at the Hotel Mille Collines. Just after the mid-May incident, an official at the foreign ministry remarked to a reporter that the success of the initiative "shows to what extent Paris can still influence events."[82] But when asked to use their power to produce a more general change in the policies of the interim government, French officials often professed having no means to do so. Two weeks after the first incident, Delaye told representatives of Médecins sans Frontières that he could not exert influence on Rwandan authorities because he could not get them on the telephone.[83] When asked to comment four years later on whether pressure from Paris had brought about change in the policies of the genocidal government, a high-ranking French official familiar with the Rwandan dossier replied, "What pressure? There was no pressure."[84]

Aid to the Rwandan Armed Forces

Official deliveries of arms by the French government to other governments are regulated by well-defined rules, but in the case of Rwanda—as in many others—the rules were rarely followed. According to the National Assembly investigative commission, thirty-one of thirty-six deliveries of weapons to Rwanda during the years 1990 to 1994 were made "without following the rules."[85] According to the commission, there were no legal and official deliveries of arms after April 8, 1994, a position reiterated by an official from the Ministry of Defense. But the commission left open the possibility of other kinds of deliveries linked to France, saying specifically that its report did not "exhaust the reality of the subject."[86]

---

[81]Guichaoua, *Les crises politiques*, pp. 718-19.

[82]Alain Frilet, "La France prise au piège de ses accords," *Liberation,* 18 mai 1994.

[83]Jean-Hervé Bradol and Anne Guibert, "Le temps des assassins et l'espace humanitaire, Rwanda, Kivu, 1994-1997," *Herodote*, Nos. 86-87, 1997, p.123

[84]Human Rights Watch/FIDH interview, Paris, November 12, 1998.

[85]Assemblée Nationale, Mission d'information commune, *Enquête,* Tome I, Rapport, p. 172.

[86]Ibid., p. 168; Human Rights Watch/FIDH interview, Paris, November 12, 1998.

Speaking privately, various military officers and officials in the ministries of cooperation and defense indicated that deliveries of weapons by French actors—perhaps unofficially, illegally, or transacted outside France—took place while the genocide was going on.[87] Bernard Debré reported his impression that France might have supplied arms for some time after the start of the genocide. He stated that he asked Mitterrand about this and the French president replied, "Do you think that the world woke up on April 7 saying today the genocide is beginning?"[88]

According to a U.N. military observer, one of the three French planes that delivered the troops of the evacuation mission also brought cases of ammunition for mortars. French officials had informed UNAMIR that the first planes bringing troops of the evacuation force would land at 6 a.m. on April 9 but they actually arrived more than two hours early. Rwandan soldiers, correctly informed of the arrival time, had removed the trucks blocking the runway to allow the plane to land. The ammunition was unloaded from the plane and taken away by Rwandan army vehicles.[89]

Research done by the Arms Division of Human Rights Watch established that the French government or French companies operating under government license delivered arms to the Rwandan forces five times in May and June through the town of Goma, just across the border from Gisenyi, in Zaire.[90] The first of these shipments may have taken place before May 17, when the Security Council imposed an embargo on the supply of arms to the interim government, but it was still done in disregard of its April 30 appeal "to refrain from providing arms or any military assistance" to the parties to the conflict. On one of the dates in question,

---

[87]Prunier, *The Rwanda Crisis,* p. 278; Callamard, "French Policy in Rwanda," p. 38, n. 7; Patrick Saint-Exupéry, "France-Rwanda: Des Silences d'Etat," *Le Figaro,* January 14, 1998.

[88]Assemblée Nationale, Mission d'information commune, *Enquête,* Tome III, Auditions, Volume 1, p. 414.

[89]Jean de la Guérivière, "Un Officier Belge Maintient Ses Déclarations sur l'Attitude de la France lors du Génocide Rwandais," *Le Monde,* July 23, 1995. The commander of the operation admitted that he had requisitioned Rwandan army vehicles but denied that his men had delivered ammunition for mortars. He did not mention the possibility that they might have delivered another kind of ammunition. Assemblée Nationale, Mission d'information commune, *Enquête,* Tome II, Annexes, pp 356-7.

[90]Human Rights Watch, "Rwanda/Zaire: Rearming with Impunity," pp. 6-8.

May 25, a plane from Malta landed at Goma with a single passenger, T. Bagosora, in addition to its cargo.[91]

Lt. Col. Cyprien Kayumba spent twenty-seven days in Paris in an effort to speed the supply of arms and ammunition to the Rwandan army. During that time, he was reportedly a regular visitor to the office of French military cooperation, where he frequently saw its head, General Huchon.[92] Just two days after the visit of Barayagwiza and Bicamumpaka to French officials, Kayumba submitted a large order for arms to SOFREMAS, Société Française d'Exploitation de Matériels et Systèmes d'Armement, an enterprise controlled by the French state that serves as intermediary between French arms manufacturers or dealers and countries seeking arms. According to correspondence later recovered from the archives of the Rwandan Ministry of Defense, SOFREMAS wrote Kayumba on May 5 at his Paris address, stating that they were prepared to ship U.S.$8 million worth of ammunition of South African manufacture as soon as they received a payment of 30 percent of the price and the necessary EUC/Zaire. EUC stands for End User Certificate, the formal attestation by a government that the arms purchased were for its own use and not for resale or transshipment elsewhere. This document was to be provided by Zaire in a clear attempt to hide the real purchaser of the arms, which would have been shipped to Goma, not to Kigali. Although the arms embargo had not yet been voted by the Security Council, SOFREMAS knew it would be embarassing to be discovered supplying arms to Rwanda during a period when a genocide was being executed.

On May 5, the day that SOFREMAS confirmed its deal with Kayumba, the French cabinet decided that all authorizations for the export of arms to Rwanda would be suspended and that no new authorisations would be accorded. This decision confirmed a provisional suspension that had been in effect since April 8.[93] The director of SOFREMAS, Germaine Guell, states that the U.S.$8 million order was cancelled by SOFREMAS once the arms embargo went into effect and that

---

[91]The government of Malta has been unable to provide clarification of this case. United Nations, Letter Dated 22 January 1998 from the Secretary-General Addressed to the President of the Security Council, S/1998/63, January 26,1998.

[92]Callamard, "French Policy in Rwanda," pp. 22, 36.

[93]Assemblée Nationale, Mission d'information commune, *Enquête,* Tome III, Annexes, volume I, p. 100.

company made no further shipments to Rwanda after May 17.[94] This carefully worded statement, like those of the government ministers, did not exclude deliveries to Zaire. In fact, Guell explicitly conceded that "it is possible and even probable that Mobutu's government agreed to have Goma serve as a conduit for material meant for Rwanda." He admitted that his company had been asked to deliver arms in this way—the mention of the End User Certificate in the document cited above proves that they had actually agreed to this arrangement—but he declares that they did not do so. He hastened to add that the practice of deliveries through Zaire must have ended quickly. He remarked, "It would take a pretty unscrupulous government to deliver materiel to Zaire that it knew would end up in Rwanda."[95]

Admiral Jacques Lanxade, chief of staff of the French army, discounted any impact of French-delivered arms on the genocide. In a radio interview on June 29, 1994 he said, "We cannot be reproached with having armed the killers. In any case, all those massacres were committed with sticks and machetes."[96] Lanxade was wrong about the importance of the use of firearms in the genocide, as data above shows. But even apart from any direct link between arms delivered by French actors and those used in massacring civilians, providing weapons desperately needed by the Rwandan armed forces in its war against the RPF strengthened a government engaged in genocide.

Lt. Col. Ephrem Rwabalinda of the Rwandan army came to Paris to press for more extensive aid than just arms. He reported on his four-day mission to the headquarters of French military assistance in a May 16 letter to the Rwandan minister of defense and chief of staff of the army.[97] On May 9, Rwabalinda had the first of a series of meetings with General Huchon. He requested French political support in the international community, French soldiers to be sent to Rwanda—at

---

[94]Patrick de Saint-Exupéry, "France-Rwanda: le temps de l'hypocrisie," *Le Figaro,* January 15, 1998.

[95]Bernard Duraud, "Rwanda: deux documents mettent la France en accusation," and Bruno Peuchamiel, "La réponse des sociétés mises en cause," *L'Humanité*, November 20, 1996.

[96]Prunier, *The Rwanda Crisis,* p. 278.

[97]Lt. Col. Ephrem Rwabalinda to Minister of Defense and Chief of Staff, Rwandan Army, May 16, 1994. Subsequent quotations about this meeting with Huchon are all from this document.

least some instructors who could "help out" under a military assistance program, and what he called the "indirect use of foreign soldiers, regular or irregular" (i.e., mercenaries). He also cited several "urgent needs": at least 2,000 rounds of 105mm ammunition and ammunition for individual arms, even if this had to be delivered indirectly through neighboring friendly countries.

By Rwabalinda's account, Huchon told him that a secure telephone to permit encoded conversations between himself and General Bizimungu had already been sent from Paris and was awaiting shipment from Ostend. The French had also sent seventeen small radio sets to facilitate communications between various units and Kigali. Huchon reportedly stressed that it was urgent to locate a usable airfield where landings could be made "in complete security." They agreed that Kamembe, in the southwestern town of Cyangugu, was the most likely site, provided that the runway was repaired and that "spies were driven away" from the airport.

When Rwabalinda pushed for more immediate aid, Huchon is said to have stated very clearly that "French soldiers had their hands and feet tied" and could not intervene to help the Rwandan army and interim government because of the bad press they had been getting. Unless something were done, Huchon reportedly stressed, Rwandan military and leaders will be "held responsible for the massacres committed in Rwanda." They must prove the legitimacy of their war "to turn international opinion back in favor of Rwanda in order to be able to resume bilateral aid." According to Rwabalinda, Huchon said that in the meantime the French military cooperation service "is preparing measures to save us."

Rwabalinda reported that Huchon returned several times to this point—that the "French government would not put up with accusations of helping a government condemned by international opinion if that government did not do what was necessary to defend itself. The media war is urgent and all subsequent operations depend on it." Huchon is said to have promised that the "urgent needs" Rwabalinda described would be evaluated in a "detailed and concrete" way once the secret telephone contact were established between him and Bizimungu.

Rwabalinda forwarded to his superiors the suggestion that a government spokesman who was up to the demands of the job be sent to Paris immediately. He reported that he had done his part to launch the media campaign by delivering some articles to one of his Rwandan colleagues there. Rwabalinda concluded his report with the suggestion that a visit "at high political" level would be a good idea to push for the desired assistance.

Assuming Rwabalinda reported the meeting accurately, Huchon and his aides were more concerned about the public perception of the killing than about the killing itself. The condition for important renewed French assistance was not to end the genocide but to make it more presentable in the international press.[98]

Some otherwise unidentified French generals did their part to improve the image of the interim goverment by depicting it as the victim of outside aggression. In early May—just about the same time when Rwabalinda was meeting with Huchon—they approached journalist Renaud Girard with private information about the presence of Ugandan batallions backing the RPF in its offensive on Kigali. Girard checked the "information" and found it to be false.[99]

The message about the need to improve the Rwandan image was also delivered in Rwanda. Two days after Rwabalinda wrote his report, RTLM told its listeners, "please, no more cadavers on the roads."

French Soldiers: A Private Initiative?

One of the needs mentioned by Rwabalinda was "foreign soldiers," whether regulars or mercenaries, to serve as "instructors." Captain Paul Barril, the former French policeman who had served as security consultant to Habyarimana, may have agreed to fill that need. Barril was reportedly linked to the French president directly as well as through Mitterrand's confidant De Grossouvre, who committed suicide at the presidency on April 7 (see above). According to one press report, a high-ranking military officer was so suspicious of Barril's activities in Rwanda in 1993 that he questioned Mitterrand directly about them, fearing that the president might be compromised by what Barril was doing. Mitterrand reportedly replied that Barril had received no orders from him.[100]

Barril claims to have been present in Rwanda from the beginning of the genocide through to its end. He maintains that he was one of the last to leave Kigali before the RPF victory, taken out by helicopter. In fact, he was in Europe for at least part of the period—he appeared on television at the end of June to describe

---

[98]Human Rights Watch/FIDH sought a meeting with General Huchon to discuss this letter, but were unable to arrange one. Rwabalinda's account is confirmed by a Rwandan military source and, in regard to the sending of the secure telephone, by a letter from Huchon to the Mission d'Information. Human Rights Watch/FIDH interview, Brussels, November 8, 1998; Assemblée Nationale, Mission d'information commune, *Enquête,* Tome II, Annexes, p 574. Although the commission apparently had a copy of the Rwabalinda letter, it did not publish it among the documents made public at the time of its report.

[99]Renaud Girard, "Rwanda: Les Faux Pas de la France," *Le Figaro,* May 19, 1994.

[100]Patrick de Saint-Exupéry, "France-Rwanda: des mensonges d'Etat."

his theory about how the RPF shot down Habyarimana's plane—but he seems to have been in Kigali on April 6 or soon after. He provides no specifics of his activities but relates that the Rwandans were so panic-stricken by Habyarimana's death that they "were running around like rabbits" and that senior officers of the Rwandan army, notably General Bizimungu, needed to turn to him for advice. The situation was "unimaginable," he says, explaining that this was "deepest Africa."[101] Barril declared that he acted on his own and "did not have to await for agreement from the ministry of foreign affairs to intervene," yet he also claims that he resided at the French embassy during the time after April 12 when he was in Kigali.[102] He says that he raised the flag over the embassy and that this pleased Rwandans who were waiting for the French to return.[103]

Rwandan military sources, assert that Barril was hired by the Rwandan Ministry of Defense to conduct a training program for 30 to 60 men, eventually to grow to 120, at Bigogwe military camp in the northwest. He was to provide training in marksmanship and infiltration tactics for an elite unit in preparation for attacks behind the RPF lines. The operation was code-named "Operation Insecticide," meaning an operation to exterminate the inyenzi or "cockroaches." In late April or early May, commanders of army and National Police units were ordered to recruit volunteers for the program. In June, Rwandan military officers decided to offer rewards to encourage participants in the training program to attack behind the RPF lines, which were vulnerable because stretched over a long distance. But the military situation changed too rapidly for them to put the decision into effect.[104]

According to Sébastien Ntahobari, then military attaché at the Rwandan embassy in Paris, Minister of Defense Bizimana transferred U.S.$1,200,000 from Nairobi to Paris in June 1994 and faxed Ntahobari to pay that sum to Barril for

[101]Human Rights Watch/FIDH interview, by telephone, Paris, September 22, 1998.

[102]Christian Chatillon, "Captain Barril," *Playboy* (French edition), March 1995, no. 29, p. 16.

[103]Human Rights Watch/FIDH interview, by telephone, Paris, September 22, 1998.

[104]Human Rights Watch/FIDH interviews, Brussels, May 26 and August 1, 1997, July 22, 1998.

otherwise unspecified "services and assistance." An assistant of Barril came to collect the money from the embassy.[105]

When asked about the training program in the course of an interview with a Human Rights Watch researcher, Barril denied knowledge of it and ended the conversation abruptly.[106]

UNAMIR, Rwandan army officers and RPF sources all reported seeing several white men in military uniform in Rwanda—and not part of UNAMIR—in early April and again after mid-May. Three or four French-speaking white men in military uniform ate at the Rwandan army officers' mess for several days in April and then left Kigali by helicopter for the northwest. Two or three, who spoke French and carried a considerable amount of gear, were transported to Bigogwe by Rwandan army helicopter in mid-May. They engaged in conversation with a Rwandan army officer and indicated by their questions that they were not familiar with Rwanda. According to one witness, the pilot of the helicopter was white and French-speaking.[107] At about this time, UNAMIR officers reported seeing whites in military uniform driving rapidly through Kigali on two occasions.[108] A Rwandan army officer and RPF sources both recall seeing one or more French-speaking soldiers at the Hotel Meridien in Gisenyi.[109] Other testimony reports French-speaking soldiers in the southern part of the country at about this same time.[110] When questioned about the reported presence of French-speaking soldiers in Rwanda at a time when regular troops were supposed to have left, one French

---

[105]Assemblée Nationale, Mission d'information commune, *Enquête,* Tome II, Annexes, p. 570.

[106]Human Rights Watch/FIDH interview, by telephone, Paris, September 22, 1998.

[107]Human Rights Watch/FIDH interviews, Brussels, August 1, 1997 and June 22, 1998; by telephone, July 22, 1998.

[108]Human Rights Watch/FIDH interview, Toronto, September 16, 1997.

[109]Human Rights Watch/FIDH interview, Brussels, October 19, 1997; Kamanzi, *Rwanda, Du Génocide à la Defaite,* p. 149, 152.

[110]Patrick Saint-Exupéry, "France-Rwanda: Des Mensonges d'Etat," *Le Figaro,* April 2, 1998.

officer replied that they were probably mercenaries.[111] If that were the case, it leaves unresolved the further question of whether Captain Barril or any other private agent had formal or informal support from French authorities in providing mercenaries to the Rwandan government.

Operation Turquoise

In mid-June, the French foreign minister announced that France would send troops to Rwanda "to stop the massacres and to protect the populations threatened with extermination."[112] At the time, French political leaders labored to convince press and public of the humanitarian nature of the operation and four years later they were still defending the reasons for undertaking it. Even those reportedly opposed to Operation Turquoise in 1994, such as then Prime Minister Edouard Balladur, responded angrily to criticism sparked by the National Assembly inquiry in 1998. Balladur insisted that France had sent its soldiers because it had a "duty to try to save lives." He found it "revolting" that others who had done nothing brought charges against France, "the only country in the world to have acted."[113]

Posturing and self-congratulation aside, Operation Turquoise did have another purpose besides saving lives: preventing a victory by the RPF. One observer reports that some military officers in Paris talked openly of "breaking the back of the RPF."[114] Others, like General Jean-Claude Lafourcade, commander of Operation Turquoise, spoke more discreetly of "putting the Arusha Accords back into operation," meaning implementing an agreement which required the RPF to share power with other parties.[115] The investigative commission of the National Assembly concluded that besides saving lives Operation Turquoise was meant to

---

[111]Patrick Saint-Exupéry, "France-Rwanda: Des Mensonges d'Etat."

[112]Juppé, "Intervenir au Rwanda."

[113]Assemblée Nationale, Mission d'information commune, *Enquête,* Tome III, Auditions, Volume I, pp. 88-90.

[114]Prunier, *The Rwanda Crisis,* p.285.

[115]Assemblée Nationale, Mission d'information commune, *Enquête,* Tome I, Rapport, p. 306.

preserve the necessary conditions for a cease-fire and subsequent political negotiations, that is, "territory and legitimacy" for the interim government.[116]

Mitterrand, who apparently continued to play the major role in determining policy towards Rwanda throughout the months of the genocide, reportedly disavowed Habyarimana's successors by mid-June, calling them "a bunch of killers."[117] According to former minister Bernard Debré, Mitterrand held that these Rwandan leaders could no longer be supported and must be punished "not only because there had been a genocide but also because his trust had been betrayed."[118] Mitterrand remained convinced, however, that "maintaining Hutu in power was the democratic thing to do." Whatever Mitterrand's personal repugnance towards the "bunch of killers," the French government had no immediate candidates to replace them. This, according to the commission, led France into the "untenable situation" of continuing to accept the legitimacy of the interim government, "either not taking account of the reality of the genocide, or not analyzing the responsibilities of the interim government for it."[119]

The French may have been planning a military intervention as early as the first part of May when, according to Rwabalinda, General Huchon said that the military cooperation service was preparing some way to help the Rwandan army. According to the Rwandan military attaché Ntahobari, the coded telephone discussed with Rwabalinda was meant to facilitate communications for Operation Turquoise "which was being prepared," even at that time.[120] Two or three weeks later—in late May or early June—the French "invited" the U.S. to join a military operation in Rwanda, hoping to obtain at least air transport for the undertaking. The U.S. refused—a decision "overshadowed by the ghost of Somalia," according to one

[116]Ibid., p. 307.

[117]Assemblée Nationale, Mission d'information commune, *Enquête,* Tome III, Auditions, Volume I, p. 395; Jean-Hervé Bradol and Anne Guibert, "Le temps des assassins et l'espace humanitaire, Rwanda, Kivu, 1994-1997," *Herodote,* Nos. 86-87, 1997, pp. 123-4.

[118]Assemblée Nationale, Mission d'information commune, *Enquête,* Tome III, Auditions, Volume I, p. 426.

[119]Assemblée Nationale, Mission d'information commune, *Enquête,* Tome I, Rapport, p. 344.

[120]Assemblée Nationale, Mission d'information commune, *Enquête,* Tome II, Annexes, p. 572.

Washington official. In addition to general concerns about becoming involved in an intractable conflict in Africa, the U.S. saw no interest in assisting the French to slow the advance of the RPF or to prop up the interim government. Policymakers in Washington, including those who did not favor the RPF, saw its victory as the most likely way to end the genocide.[121]

According to Gérard Prunier, who advised the Ministry of Defense on Operation Turquoise, Mitterrand was finally pushed into action in mid-June by the prospect that South Africa—another "Anglo-Saxon" country—might intervene in Rwanda. Humanitarian and human rights organizations had also been attacking French policy in Rwanda with increasing vigor throughout the end of May and early June and officials were anxious to quiet this criticism and, if possible, restore French honor.[122] While these considerations may have had their impact on thinking in Paris, the decision to act quickly in mid-June was more likely influenced by a serious deterioration in the position of Rwandan government forces. After a counter-offensive against the RPF failed in early June, the government army also lost the important town of Gitarama on June 13, leaving the way to the west largely free for further RPF advances. The government forces still held part of Kigali, but they were short on ammunition—apparently in part because officers in the northwestern town of Ruhengeri were hoarding their stock awaiting the French return in hopes of then launching an effective counterattack. General Bizimungu assessed the overall situation as hopeless and commented privately on June 17 that the government forces had lost the war.[123]

Mitterrand at first insisted that French troops must take control of all of Rwanda, a position he may have adopted under the influence of military officers like General Quesnot, who takes credit for persuading Mitterrand to intervene in the first place.[124] But Prime Minister Balladur firmly opposed such a large undertaking and the two compromised on a less ambitious objective, apparently that of establishing French authority over the part of Rwanda still controlled by the

---

[121]Human Rights Watch/FIDH interview, by telephone, November 14, 1998.

[122]Prunier, *The Rwanda Crisis,* p. 281; Bradol and Guibert, "Le temps des assassins et l'espace humanitaire," pp. 123-4.

[123]Human Rights Watch/FIDH interviews, Brussels, November 8, 1998.

[124]Assemblée Nationale, Mission d'information commune, *Enquête,* Tome III, Auditions, Volume I, p. 347.

Rwandan government forces.[125] At the U.N., French diplomats who were trying to rally support for Operation Turquoise at first showed a map with a proposed zone of French control that would have encompassed all territory west of a line running from Ruhengeri in the north, southeast to Kigali, then southwest down to Butare. This area would have encompassed Gisenyi, where the interim government had taken refuge, as well as the larger northwestern region that was the home of Habyarimana and many of the leading officers of the Rwandan army. This zone, where the government forces had concentrated substantial troops and supplies, would have served as the best location from which to launch a counteroffensive. Some important actors at the U.N.—including the U.S.—expressed hesitations about French plans to move into an area that was so large and so likely to provoke confrontations with the RPF. Prunier and others voiced the same reservations in Paris.[126]

Proponents of an aggressive strategy thought it essential for French troops to arrive in Kigali. By establishing a French presence there, they could enable the interim government to hang on to control of some parts of the city and thus more credibly claim to still govern Rwanda. Given that Operation Turquoise was supposedly a humanitarian operation, some French officials expected to find support for their position with humanitarian activists. The activist and politician Bernard Kouchner was one who had become known for his efforts to save lives. The RPF had solicited his aid in arranging for the evacuation of orphans and others besieged in Kigali and the U.N. secretary-general had given him an informal mandate to support his activities. Kouchner was ready to argue the case for sending French troops to the capital. On June 17, he and a French colleague visited General Dallaire in Kigali. According to one person present at the interview, the two French visitors brought with them a map marked with a line to delineate the zone that might come under French control. Like the map shown by French representatives at the U.N., it included most of western Rwanda and parts of the city of Kigali. Kouchner reportedly urged Dallaire to ask for French troops to rescue orphans and missionaries trapped behind "Interahamwe lines" in the capital. Such a plea by Dallaire might have persuaded sceptics at the U.N. or in Paris to agree to sending French forces to Kigali. Dallaire, suspicious of French intentions, responded, "Hell, no. I don't want to see any French around here. If you want to help, provide the

---

[125]Ibid., p. 417.

[126]Human Rights Watch/FIDH interview, by telephone, August 3, 1998; Prunier, *The Rwanda Crisis,* pp. 284-5.

troops waiting to join UNAMIR with the transport and equipment they need."[127] Kouchner confirms having made the visit and having brought along a map, which he remembers showing sites in Kigali where Tutsi or others were awaiting rescue. He recalls that he was given the map by officials in Paris, but not by whom.[128] With no appeal forthcoming from Dallaire, proponents of a relatively limited operation influenced the plan adopted. Prime Minister Balladur set a number of conditions for the undertaking, one of which was that it was to be based largely outside Rwanda—in effect in Zaire—with its troops making forays into Rwanda to assess the situation and to rescue people as needed.[129]

François Léotard, minister of defense in 1994, declared at the National Assembly hearings that orders for Operation Turquoise "prohibited French soldiers from making hostile military contact with the RPF."[130] At least one set of orders, those issued June 22, 1994, do not prohibit engaging in combat with the RPF. Leaving vague the actions to be undertaken, they focus on shaping how those actions might be interpreted:

> Adopt an attitude of strict neutrality to the different parties to the conflict. Insist on the idea that the French army has come to stop the massacres and not to fight the RPF or to support the FAR so that the actions undertaken not be interpreted as aiding the government troops.[131]

In explaining the context of the operation, the orders echoed the language of the interim government. They described "very serious ethnic clashes" and never mentioned the word "genocide" which had been used by Foreign Minister Juppé and other civilian officials more than a month before. They devote three paragraphs to recounting the RPF military advance and only then turn to the slaughter of Tutsi, which is laid to "groups of uncontrolled Hutu civilians and soldiers." The orders

---

[127]Human Rights Watch/FIDH interview, Toronto, September 16, 1997.

[128]Human Rights Watch/FIDH interview, by telephone, Paris, December 3, 1998.

[129]Prunier, *The Rwanda Crisis*, p. 287.

[130]Assemblée Nationale, Mission d'information commune, *Enquête,* Tome III, Auditions, Volume I, p. 109.

[131]Assemblée Nationale, Mission d'information commune, *Enquête,* Tome II, Annexes, p. 389.

state that the RPF seems to have also engaged in little known summary executions and "ethnic cleansing" and that "several hundred thousand persons of the Hutu and Tutsi ethnic groups" have been exterminated. By citing the Hutu first, they suggest that as many Hutu as Tutsi have been killed—or perhaps, even more.[132] Given that the mission of the troops was to stop the massacres, using force if necessary, the identification of Hutu as victims and the RPF as killers implied that soldiers could well be drawn into fighting the RPF.

When plans for the operation were discussed, Prunier had argued for sending troops into southwestern Rwanda at Cyangugu. From there, they could move quickly to rescue Tutsi at Nyarushishi, which would produce excellent publicity for the operation and firmly establish its humanitarian character. He had pointed out that sending troops into Rwanda at Gisenyi in the northwest might raise questions about the professed goal of saving lives since there were virtually no Tutsi left to save in that region. According to Prunier, Léotard was convinced by his logic and ordered the operation to proceed through Cyangugu. The military commanders also appeared to have accepted Prunier's reasoning: they ordered the troops to first assure protection for the Nyarushishi camp "to demonstrate the humanitarian character of the operation." Only after that were they to extend their area of control progressively over "Hutu country" and to move out from southwestern Rwanda towards Gisenyi in the northwest, towards Butare due east, and even "in the direction of Kigali."[133] As the French commanders must have known, their troops could not progress too far in those directions without encountering the RPF.

According to press accounts, the soldiers themselves believed that they were supposed to fight against the RPF. One officer stated, "At that time, the orders were very clear: it was planned to go as far as Kigali."[134] The soldiers were drawn from the elite of the reconnaissance and rapid reaction units. They included nearly 300 soldiers of the French special forces, more than had been deployed in any previous French operation.[135] Some, including several of the commanding officers, had

[132]Ibid., pp. 386-87.

[133]Prunier, *The Rwanda Crisis,* pp. 283-5; Assemblée Nationale, Mission d'information commune, *Enquête,* Tome II, Annexes, p. 387.

[134]Arnaud de la Grange, "Les ambiguités de 'Turquoise,'" *Le Figaro,* April 2, 1998.

[135]Agence France Presse, "Le ministre de la Défense constate la difficulté de l'opération Turquoise," BQA No. 14245, 30/6/94, p. 31.

previously served in Rwanda where their task had been to support the Rwandan troops in fighting the RPF, and for many of them the RPF had become their enemy as well. They had resented being withdrawn the year before in a move which had seemed to hand the RPF a victory and they were ready to "kick butt" according to one U.S. military officer who talked frequently with several of them.[136] The soldiers were well equipped to do just that with more than one hundred armored vehicles, a battery of 120mm. mortars, ten helicopters, four ground-attack jet planes and four reconnaissance jet planes. Amply supplied with heavy weaponry, the force lacked the ordinary vehicles, like trucks, needed to pick up civilians and ferry them to safety.[137]

The French authorities had initially hoped for some kind of international intervention, but in the end found only the Senegalese willing to send soldiers for the operation. They asked the Security Council for a Chapter VII mandate to cover Operation Turquoise, thus following the course suggested by the secretary-general on April 29. With the difficulties that the U.N. was experiencing in organizing UNAMIR II, it would have been difficult for the Security Council to refuse the request. When the French authorities decided to move, they wanted immediate action, probably because they feared the Rwandan government forces were so close to defeat. They were ready to send troops without a resolution and on the basis of "less formal cover," if the secretary-general agreed.[138] The French government did not even wait for the Security Council decision and landed its troops in Goma, which was to serve as the rear-base of the operation, hours before the council, with five abstentions, voted the mandate for Operation Turquoise.[139]

As planned, one detachment of troops entered Rwanda in the southwest and went directly to Nyarushishi. They were accompanied by the expected entourage of journalists who published the desired favorable reports about the rescue operation. Col. Didier Thibault was in command. According to Prunier, Thibault was a false name being used by Col. Didier Tauzin, who had previously served as

---

[136]Human Rights Watch/FIDH interview, by telephone, November 14, 1998; Assemblée Nationale, Mission d'information commune, *Enquête,* Tome I, Rapport, p. 305.

[137]Prunier, *The Rwanda Crisis,* p.291.

[138]Assemblée Nationale, Mission d'information commune, *Enquête,* Tome II, Annexes, p. 319.

[139]Ibid., p. 397; Human Rights Watch/FIDH interview, Plainsboro, New Jersey, June 14, 1996.

an adviser to the Rwandan army. The investigative commission identified Tauzin as head of the French operation that had helped the Rwandan forces "spectacularly save the situation" in turning back the RPF offensive in February 1993.[140] With much fanfare, Colonel Thibault and his men ordered militia to dismantle their barriers. One French officer confiscated a grenade from a militia member and gave him a reproving lecture before the journalists.[141]

At the very same time, and with virtually no attention from the foreign press, another detachment of 200 elite troops crossed into northwestern Rwanda at Gisenyi and began carrying out reconnaisance in the region.[142] Their arrival in Gisenyi was hailed gleefully by announcers on RTLM and Radio Rwanda.[143] Perhaps the only foreign reporter to cover the story wrote that French troops in the northwest were "discreet." Unlike their fellows to the south, they did not interfere with the militia at the barriers. Within the next day or two, they brought important quantities of equipment and supplies from Goma and set up camps in Gisenyi, ready to protect the town that housed the genocidal government.[144] The troops then moved east some fifteen miles to Mukamira, a military camp where the French had once trained Rwandan soldiers. There they were near Bigogwe, where Barril was supposedly carrying on a training program and well positioned to advance the twelve or so miles to the town of Ruhengeri, which was then besieged by the RPF. On June 24, Colonel Thibault said that the French were considering moving on to Ruhengeri.[145]

---

[140]Prunier, *The Rwanda Crisis*, p. 294, n. 27; Assemblée Nationale, Mission d'information commune, *Enquête,* Tome I, Rapport, p. 176.

[141]Robert Block, "French claim early success in Rwanda," *Independent,* June 29, 1994; Agence France Presse, "Les paras français aux miliciens: 'retournez chez vous travailler,'" BQA No. 14242, 27/06/94, p. 47.

[142]Agence France Presse, "L'arrivée des premiers soldats français au Rwanda," BQA No. 14241, 24/06/94, p. 33.

[143]UNAMIR, Notes, Radio Rwanda 19:00, June 25 and 26, 1994, RTLM, June 25, 1994.

[144]Agence France Presse, "Les troupes françaises consolident leurs positions à Gisenyi," BQA No. 14242, 27/06/94, p. 47.

[145]Mark Fritz, "First French commandos protect Tutsi refugees," *Independent,* June 25, 1994.

In a briefing in Paris on June 23 military spokesmen said that a small detachment had crossed the border to Gisenyi and that a larger force would arrive there subsequently. When questioned in Paris about the deployment two days later, however, Gen. Raymond Germanos, deputy chief of staff of the army, reportedly declared that a first contingent of thirty had crossed into northwestern Rwanda only at noon that day, June 25. It seems unlikely that General Germanos, identified as the officer in charge of the operation, did not know of the earlier deployment.[146] Perhaps he was simply distinguishing between information relating to humanitarian concerns and that dealing with "military secrets," a practice recommended in a confidential, official document about Operation Turquoise.[147] The inaccurate information delivered by General Germanos and the absence of discussion about the deployment in the northwest at the time and since—including in the report of the investigative commission—suggest that it was part of the "military secrets" of Operation Turquoise.[148]

The French commanders ordered their troops to encourage local civilian and military officials to "reestablish their authority," persisting in their view that the genocide resulted from governmental failure rather than governmental success.[149] The French soldiers followed orders. Even in regions where they dismantled barriers and chased away militia, they took no action against local authorities. They worked every day with Prefects Kayishema and Bagambiki and many of their subordinates, even though well aware of the evidence against them. Colonel Thibault described the Rwandan government and army as "legal organisations," meanwhile admitting that some of their officials "might have blood on their

---

[146]Agence France Presse, "Les miliciens hutus contrôlent l'entrée de Gisenyi," and "Des soldats français à Gisenyi," BQA No. 14242, 27/06/94, pp. 51, 53.

[147]De la Grange, "Les ambiguités de 'Turquoise.'"

[148]In an otherwise detailed description of the operation, Prunier never mentions the deployment in the northwest. The commission report mentions Gisenyi once in passing once but does not make clear that there was a substantial number of French troops in the area for more than a week.

[149]Assemblée Nationale, Mission d'information commune, *Enquête,* Tome II, Annexes, p. 387.

hands."[150] He declared that he had no mandate to replace these people and that "the legitimacy of this government is not my problem."[151] Thibault's opinions reflected those held at the highest levels of the French government. When questioned at the Presidency in early July, Bruno Delaye, the African adviser to Mitterrand, defended French collaboration with local authorities. He said that France had no choice but to continue relying on them because it lacked the personnel to replace them.[152]

Rwandan authorities at first believed that Operation Turquoise was the rescue mission promised by Huchon and they immediately became more assertive towards the RPF and towards UNAMIR.[153] Once French troops landed in Gisenyi and moved towards Ruhengeri, General Bizimungu—convinced a week before that the war was lost—declared that his forces would soon be launching an offensive against the RPF.[154] Ordinary people too anticipated French support and welcomed the troops with cheers, flowers, and banners. At one barrier a member of the Interahamwe "sporting a straw hat painted to resemble the tricolour, posed for the camera with his weapons—bows and arrows, a spear, and a machete—in front of a sign that read, "Vive La France."[155] The prefect of Gikongoro assured a warm welcome by having residents of the prefectural center gather to rehearse their "spontaneous" cheers and in Gisenyi authorities deployed entire schools of children to wave little French flags.[156]

As the dismantling of barriers in Cyangugu became known, some militia and government officials expressed anger and disappointment at the French. RTLM

---

[150]Chris McGreal, "French compromised by collaboration in Rwanda," *Guardian*, July 1, 1994.

[151]Block, "French claim early success"; Raymond Bonner, "Fear Is Still Pervasive in Rwanda Countryside," *New York Times*, June 29, 1994.

[152]Human Rights Watch/FIDH interview, Paris, July 4, 1994.

[153]ICTR-96-4-T, Testimony of Romeo Dallaire, February 25, 1998, p. 189.

[154]Agence France Presse, "Poursuite d'une guerre cruelle à Kigali," BQA No. 14242, 27/06/94, p. 58.

[155]Lindsey Hilsum, "Lindsey Hilsum in Butare," *Observer*, July 3, 1994.

[156]Agence France Presse, "Gikongoro se prépare à accueillir 'spontanement' les Français," BQA No. 14243, 28/06/94, p.25.

announcer Valerie Bemeriki sought to prevent any further erosion in relations between the interim government and the foreign troops. She urged listeners to make special efforts to seek out the French soldiers, to sing and dance for them, drink with them, invite them for dinner, and serve as guides when they went out in their cars. All these occasions should be used, she advised, to explain to them the "problem of Hutu and Tutsi" and the "wickedness of the Inyenzi and their supporters."[157] Announcer Gaspard Gahigi harangued the French about not interfering with roadblocks and directed officials to prepare people at the barriers with appropriate responses should the French ask what they were doing.[158]

   Several days after arriving in Cyangugu, Colonel Thibault and some of his troops moved further east to establish a base at the town of Gikongoro. There they took no action against militia and did not react to civilians carrying grenades. Asked why, Thibault reportedly answered that "the French army has no authority to disarm the militia or dismantle the road-blocks even though they are a threat to civilian lives."[159] French soldiers did confiscate a limited number of weapons from militia on an "empirical" basis according to a later statement by Colonel Thibaut. They reportedly collected about one hundred firearms Gikongoro and another one hundred in Kibuye. In some regions, the French soldiers permitted civilians to retain their arms if the local administrators indicated this was necessary "to assure usual police missions."[160] It is unclear why the French soldiers were ready to dismantle barriers and collect grenades in Cyangugu and not in Gisenyi or Gikongoro. Perhaps after having established the "humanitarian" nature of the operation in the first few days, they believed that it was no longer necessary to impress journalists. Perhaps as criticism by interim authorities grew, they wished to minimize any cause of conflict with them.[161] Or perhaps, as an official telegram reported in early July, they feared "provoking a general reaction" against their

---

[157]UNAMIR, Notes, RTLM, June 25, 1994.

[158]Ibid., and June 27, 1994.

[159]McGreal, "French compromised by collaboration in Rwanda"; Raymond Bonner, "Fear Is Still Pervasive in Rwanda Countryside," New York Times, June 29, 1994.

[160]Assemblée Nationale, Mission d'information commune, Enquête, Tome I, Rapport, pp. 328.

[161]Assemblée Nationale, Mission d'information commune, Enquête, Tome II, Annexes, p. 429.

troops by militia or government forces.[162] In Paris as well as in the region, high-ranking officers expressed this concern just as others in New York and elsewhere had previously voiced anxiety over the risk of injury to UNAMIR soldiers.[163]

The readiness of French soldiers to be swayed by local authorities accounts in part for their slowness in rescuing Tutsi at Bisesero, an incident that came to symbolize French indifference to the genocide. On June 26, journalist Sam Kiley informed French soldiers that Tutsi were being attacked nightly at Bisesero, the site of long-standing resistance described above. He showed them on a map exactly where the Tutsi were located, only a few miles distant from a French camp.[164] The commanding officer, Capt. Marin Gillier, sent a small patrol in that direction the next day. According to Tutsi survivors, they spoke with these soldiers who promised to return in three days. The Tutsi relate that the soldiers were accompanied by local authorities and that by having come out to speak with the French, they exposed themselves to an attack soon after that killed many of their number.[165] According to Gillier's account, the patrol found no Tutsi but were told by local authorities that RPF infiltrators had penetrated the region and were threatening them.[166] French soldiers had observed weapons fire on at least one occasion at Bisesero and Gillier knew, as he told reporters, that people were being killed every night. But he remarked that he did not want to "get involved in politics" and declined to say who were the victims and who the killers.[167]

---

[162]Ibid., p. 327.

[163]Agence France Presse, "Des soldats français à Gisenyi," and "'Tensions' dans certaines zones où interviennent les troupes françaises,"BQA No. 14242, 27/06/94, pp. 51, 56; Corine Lesnes, "M. Leotard craint de nouvelles difficultés pour le dispositif 'Turquoise,'"*Le Monde*, July 1, 1994.

[164]Gillier, perhaps seeking to preempt questions about why he did not act on information from the journalists, describes the encounter with misleading vagueness and says he took them for intelligence agents. Assemblée Nationale, Mission d'information commune, *Enquête,* Tome II, Annexes, p. 404.

[165]African Rights, *Resisting Genocide, Bisesero, April-June 1994*, Witness no. 8, pp. 61-64.

[166]Assemblée Nationale, Mission d'information commune, *Enquête*, Tome II, Annexes, p. 402.

[167]Robert Block, "French troops rescue starving Tutsi," *Independent*, July 1, 1994.

Gillier requested permission on June 27 and again on June 28 to investigate the situation in Bisesero. He received no response and hesitated to move on his own authority, he later explained, because his forces—according to the press nearly seventy elite French troops—might be put at risk.[168] The general staff of the operation, presumably referring to information Gillier had received from local authorities, told journalists that as many as one to two thousand well-armed RPF soldiers might have penetrated the government lines and infiltrated to the banks of Lake Kivu.[169] Remarkably enough, elite reconnaisance troops, equipped with such equipment as night-vision goggles, had found no evidence of infiltration and the commanding officers of the operation, with numerous sophisticated helicopters and airplanes at their disposition, apparently ordered no aerial reconnaissance to discover whether any RPF troops were actually in the area.

On June 29, Defense Minister François Léotard came to the French post near Bisesero on an inspection visit. Gillier briefed him on the situation, including the possibility that there were Tutsi needing rescue in the area. According to *New York Times* correspondent Raymond Bonner, who interviewed soldiers on the spot, Léotard "rejected any operation to evacuate or protect the embattled Tutsi at Bisesero," saying that the French did not have enough troops to protect everyone. A French journalist, however, reported that as Léotard was leaving, he turned back under the persistent questioning of the *New York Times* correspondent and ordered that troops be sent the next day. This account does not indicate where the soldiers were to be sent. Gillier later reported that their objective was to offer evacuation to a French priest at a church beyond Bisesero. He described locating the endangered Tutsi as an accident, the result of a chance sighting by some of his soldiers. Once he and most of his troops arrived at the church on June 30, he received a radio message from another part of the group who had turned back after having seen "some people different from those we had encountered since our arrival." They had discovered the Tutsi and called for urgent help.[170]

---

[168]Assemblée Nationale, Mission d'information commune, *Enquête,* Tome II, Annexes, p. 403.

[169]Agence France Presse, "Des forces du FPR seraient parvenus jusqu'au lac Kivu," BQA No. 14245, 30/06/94, p. 31.

[170]Raymond Bonner, "Grisly Discovery in Rwanda Leads French to Widen Role," *New York Times,* July 1, 1994; Corine Lesnes, "M. Léotard craint de nouvelles difficultés pour le dispositif 'Turquoise,'" *Le Monde,* July 1, 1994. Asked twice to comment on the accuracy of this account, Mr. Léotard replied that it would be inappropriate to resume

When Gillier and the rest of his force reached the site, they had no trouble seeing who were the killers and who the victims. A band of armed assailants had gathered on a nearby hill as the ragged, starving and wounded Tutsi survivors emerged from the bushes and caves. Confronted finally with the reality of the genocide, these French troops provided protection, food and medical help to the Tutsi survivors. Some 300 of the 800 who straggled out of the bush needed medical attention, about one hundred of them urgently so.[171]

The next morning, the soldiers walked through Bisesero valley, which had been inaccessible to their vehicles, and discovered hundreds of bodies, many of persons recently slain. It was, Gillier reported, "intolerable."[172] He urged a television cameraman to film the corpses, saying "People must see this."[173] The soldiers discovered no weapons or other evidence that the Tutsi were RPF infiltrators, leading Sgt. Maj. Thierry Prungnaud to complain, "We were manipulated. We thought the Hutu were the good guys and the victims."[174] Some of the soldiers who had been pleased at first by the warm welcome from militia now rejected their professions of friendship. As one said, "I've had enough of being cheered by murderers."[175] One French officer who had instructed soldiers of the Presidential Guard broke down and cried so moved was he at the crimes that might have been committed by men whom he had trained.[176] The commander of

---

debate on this "aid operation whose results have since enjoyed undisputed international recognition." François Léotard to Catherine Choquet, FIDH, September 25, 1996.

[171]Assemblée Nationale, Mission d'information commune, *Enquête,* Tome II, Annexes, p. 405.

[172]Ibid., p. 406.

[173]Raymond Bonner, "As French Aid the Tutsi, Backlash Grows" *New York Times,* July 2, 1994.

[174]Ibid.

[175]De la Grange, "Les ambiguités de 'Turquoise.'"

[176]Patrick de Saint-Exupéry, "France-Rwanda: le temps de l'hypocrisie." *Le Figaro,* January 15, 1998.

Operation Turquoise, General Lafourcade, declared that Rwandan officials had engaged in a deception to keep the French from intervening at Bisesero.[177]

Recognizing the crimes and deceptions of the genocidal authorities, however, did not make French military officers any more conciliatory towards the RPF. Seeing the government defense of Kigali crumbling before a persistent RPF attack, military experts in Paris predicted a "catastrophe" if the RPF were to win a "total victory."[178] On June 30, General Germanos ordered French soldiers in the north to maintain their forward position at Mukamira, some ten or twelve miles from the front at Ruhengeri, and directed those in the south to make forays as necessary to evacuate persons at risk in Butare.[179] A small French plane and a helicopter went to Butare on July 1 and returned the next day with some clergy, including the Bishop of Butare, and some faculty from the university.[180] During a second mission on July 3, described above, the French troops were fired on by the RPF. The next day, at noon, French troops at Gikongoro were ordered to hold the line against any RPF advance. They dug in, some of them at least seeming to anticipate combat with some relish. Colonel Thibault reportedly declared that if the RPF challenged the "line in the sand" drawn by the French, "we will open fire against them without any hesitation...and we have the means."[181]

Rwandan authorities at both local and national levels did their best to incite the French to open conflict with the RPF. Callixte Kalimanzira of the Interior Ministry asked the interim government to appeal urgently to the French to "protect the

---

[177]Corine Lesnes, "Le Chef de l'Opération "Turquoise" Prévoit que le FPR Va Progresser Jusqu'à la Limite de la Zone Humanitaire," *Le Monde,* July 3, 1994; Chris McGreal, "Hunted Rwandans Tell of Courage Amid Cruelty," *Guardian,* July 4, 1994.

[178]Agence France Presse, "Paris mise sur l'humanitaire et la diplomatie," BQA No. 14243, 30/06/94, p. 30.

[179]Assemblée Nationale, Mission d'information commune, *Enquête,* Tome I, Rapport, p. 311.

[180]Human Rights Watch/FIDH interview, by telephone, Antwerp, January 20, 1999.

[181]Raymond Bonner, "French Establish a Base in Rwanda to Block Rebels," *New York Times,* July 5, 1996.

innocent people threatened by the Inkotanyi" in Butare prefecture.[182] The prefect of Cyangugu insisted that the French must "go into the RPF area and free our civilian population taken as hostages by the rebels," a desire expressed also by the prefects of Butare and Ruhengeri.[183] Foreign Minister Bicamumpaka appealed to France to order its troops to stop the RPF advance and to intervene between the two sides.[184] The head of the Interahamwe, Robert Kajuga, assured a journalist that he was not concerned about the approaching RPF troops. "France is a great power, like America or England. They can stop the war."[185] Radio Rwanda and RTLM alternately pleaded with the French to come to Kigali and promised that they were sure to do so.[186]

On July 6, the French and the RPF decided not to make war.[187] Several days earlier, the French government announced that its forces would stay in Rwanda only if the Security Council authorized the creation of a "secure humanitarian zone" to "ensure that the people are safe from any threat from any side," according to Juppé.[188] The Security Council never authorized or approved the zone, but did acknowledge what amounted to a unilateral extension of the French mandate. The zone encompassed the southwestern quadrant of the country but did not include any of the northwest, nor did it reach to Kigali. French withdrawal from Gisenyi took place unheralded, presumably on or about July 5, and left the interim government and its troops without foreign protection in the northwest. French

---

[182]Telegram, Callixte Kalimanzira to Mininter-Minadef, no 94/066, June 28, 1994 (Butare prefecture).

[183]Prunier, *The Rwanda Crisis,* p. 293; Lindsey Hilsum, "Rwandan Rebels Advance as French Forces Hang Back," *Guardian*, July 2, 1994; Karin Davies, "Below the Volcanos, Hutus Wait for the Enemy," Associated Press, July 8, 1994.

[184]"Rwanda Asks France to Help Hold Off Rebels," *New York Times*, July 3, 1994.

[185]Lindsey Hilsum, "Lindsey Hilsum in Butare," *Observer*, July 3, 1994.

[186]UNAMIR, Notes, RTLM, June 26, June 27, June 30, July 3, 1994; Radio Rwanda, 19:00, June 26, 1994.

[187]Raymond Bonner, "France Backs Away from Battle in Rwanda," *New York Times*, July 6, 1994.

[188]SWB, AL/2039A/3, July 3 1994.

authorities thus signaled their readiness to stand aside for an RPF advance almost certain to result in the "total victory" that they had deplored just days before. In all likelihood, the withdrawal and the acceptance that it symbolized constituted part of an unpublicized agreement which ended the confrontation with the RPF.

Obviously distressed at the change in French policy, the interim authorities began to realize that the best they could hope for was passive protection rather than a more aggressive defense.[189] Ferdinand Nahimana, counselor at the Presidency, at first criticized the French bitterly for establishing an "Indian reservation," and then tried to persuade them to extend the zone at least to cover all the territory still more or less controlled by the Rwandan army.[190] Interim Prime Minister Kambanda and Interim President Sindikubwabo each made the same request formally to their French counterparts several days later, Sindikubwabo stressing the need to save nearly four million people threatened by massacres by the RPF.[191]

Once the French backed off from combat with the RPF, the French representative at Goma, Yannick Gérard, deputy director of African and Malagasay Affairs at the Ministry of Foreign Affairs, advocated severing links clearly and publicly with the interim government. He pointed out that Washington was preparing to do so and advised Paris:

> Their collective responsibility in calls to murder over Radio Mille Collines during these months seems to me well established. Members of this government cannot in any case, be considered valid interlocutors for a political settlement. Their usefulness lay in facilitating the good operation of Operation Turquoise. Now they will only try to complicate our task.[192]

---

[189]Patrick McDowell, "Tutsi rebels take over army HQ in Kigali push," *Daily Telegraph*, July 5, 1994.

[190]Agence France Presse, "Dix-sept partis s'engagent à favoriser un dialogue entre le FPR et le gouvernement déchu," July 4, 1994.

[191]Assemblée Nationale, Mission d'information commune, *Enquête,* Tome I, Rapport, pp. 323-24.

[192]Ibid., p. 321.

Gérard wrote the next day that further contact with the "discredited authorities" would be "useless and even harmful." He concluded, "We have nothing more to say to them, except to get lost as fast as possible."[193]

Administrative officials, members of militia and Rwandan army soldiers flooded into the secure zone along with ordinary civilians who feared the RPF advance. At this time, both officials and RTLM were ordering people to flee and warning that the RPF would surely kill them if they did not. The French joined in such warnings, telling people in Butare to flee west to Gikongoro and later warning people in Cyangugu to seek refuge across the border in Zaire.[194] On July 11, the commanding officer of Operation Turquoise reportedly stated that officials of the interim government could seek asylum in the zone if the RPF took Gisenyi.[195] Three days later, the Foreign Ministry in Paris countermanded the invitation and asked its local representative to inform Rwandan authorities that they were not welcome.[196] General Lafourcade informed Gérard on July 15, however, that several important figures of the interim government—they turned out to be the interim prime minister and interim president—were in Cyangugu and reconstituting their government. The ambassador immediately notified Paris:

> Since we consider their presence undesirable in the secure humanitarian zone and knowing as we do that the authorities bear a heavy responsibility for the genocide, we have no other choice, whatever the difficulties, but arresting them or putting them immediately under house arrest until a competent international judicial authority decides their case.[197]

The question of arrests involved also the numerous local authorities with whom the French had been collaborating, including the prefects of Kibuye and Cyangugu. As of July 10, French officers had compiled detailed information about their

[193]Ibid., p. 322.

[194]Human Rights Watch/FIDH interview, Butare, October 20, 1995; Chris McGreal, "French Accused of Protecting Killers, *Guardian Weekly,* September 4, 1994.

[195]Prunier, *The Rwanda Crisis,* p. 296.

[196]Assemblée Nationale, Mission d'information commune, *Enquête,* Tome I, Rapport, p. 325.

[197]Ibid., p. 325.

responsibilities in the genocide, which they had presumably communicated promptly to Paris.[198]

Gérard's insistence that the interim authorities be arrested seemed to accord with the position taken by Foreign Minister Juppé three weeks before when he wrote that "France will make no accomodation with the killers and their commanders...[and] demands that those responsible for these genocides be judged."[199] At the Presidency, however, Bruno Delaye insisted that arresting those accused of genocide did not fall within the French mandate. On July 16, the Foreign Ministry bowed to this view. In an uncanny echo of the pretexts used to explain U.N. failure to act, it declared that "our mandate does not authorize us to arrest them on our own authority. Such a task could undermine our neutrality, the best guarantee of our effectiveness."[200] The French government could have requested that the mandate be changed or could have unilaterally redefined the mandate, as it had in effect done by creating the secure humanitarian zone. Instead the French government, like the U.N., hid behind the cover of legal technicalities. After all the important authorities had left the zone, the French arrested a small number of persons who had not held government posts. In one case, they arrested nine persons accused of genocide, but failed to transfer them, as had been promised, to U.N. custody.[201]

When the French government declared that it would not arrest genocidal leaders, it was criticized at the U.N. and elsewhere for protecting persons guilty of genocide.[202] To end these criticisms and to avoid embarassment should the newly established Kigali government ask for these persons to be handed over to them, French authorities wanted them to leave the zone quickly. General Lafourcade maintains that once the Rwandan authorities understood that they were unwelcome,

---

[198] Assemblée Nationale, Mission d'information commune, *Enquête,* Tome II, Annexes, pp. 415, 494-500.

[199] Juppé, "Intervenir au Rwanda." Note the plural " genocides."

[200] Assemblée Nationale, Mission d'information commune, *Enquête,* Tome I, Rapport, p. 325.

[201] Chris McGreal, "French Accused of Protecting Killers."

[202] Assemblée Nationale, Mission d'information commune, *Enquête,* Tome II, Annexes, pp. 454, 457.

they left the zone on their own initiative and without French assistance.[203] A French military journal reported in October 1994, however, that the tactical general staff "initiated and organized" the evacuation of the transitional government to Zaire on July 17.[204] The report of the investigative commission confirms that French troops evacuated former prime minister Dismas Nsengiyaremye, who was to be part of the transitional government, from Cyangugu by air on July 17.[205] No charges had been made against Nsengiyaremye, but others who were supposed to serve in the transitional government were at the time serving as ministers in the interim government and were apparently implicated in the genocide: Minister of Defense Augustin Bizimana, Minister of Family and Women's Affairs Pauline Nyiramasuhuko, Minister of Planning André Ntagerura, and Minister of Commerce Justin Mugenzi. Ferdinand Nahimana, who was to serve as minister of higher education in the transitional government, had directed activities at RTLM and was an adviser to the presidency. Official French sources have not indicated if any of these five were part of the transitional government members who benefited from French assistance in leaving Rwanda on or about July 17.

After local officials most implicated in the genocide fled into exile, French soldiers kept the administration functioning through their own efforts and those of Rwandans whom they selected on the spot.[206] Presumably they could have achieved the same results several weeks before at a time when Delaye and others had asserted it was impossible for the French to replace local officials.

When French authorities decided to sever ties with the interim government, they continued to hope that some military officers could serve as valid representatives of the "Hutu" force that they wished to support. In a telegram of July 7, Gérard commented on the continuing authority of General Bizimungu. Expressing a wish that sounds almost like a directive, he wrote:

---

[203]Ibid., p. 535.

[204]Patrick de Saint-Exupéry, "Rwanda: les 'trous noirs' d'une enquête," *Le Figaro*, December 17, 1998.

[205]Assemblée Nationale, Mission d'information commune, *Enquête,* Tome I, Rapport, p. 326.

[206]Ibid., p. 315.

...it would be very desirable for the chief of staff of the FAR to dissociate himself very quickly politically from the Gisenyi authorities in order to strengthen his position as an interlocutor and negotiator.[207]

Bizimungu did not disavow the genocide, but other officers did, as discussed below. French soldiers evacuated at least some of those officers, perhaps hoping one of them would take the leadership role they had wanted Bizimungu to play.[208] Journalist Sam Kiley charged that French soldiers who arrived in Butare on July 1 also evacuated Colonel Bagosora, flying him out on July 2 along with a small number of other persons. Kiley's source was a high-ranking French officer who knew Bagosora well and who had reason to be well-informed about the details of the operation.[209] If the French did indeed provide this service for Bagosora, it was a mark of surprising consideration for a man who was characterized as "filth" by a French officer who dealt with him regularly.[210]

The French authorities permitted Rwandan soldiers to remain in and to transit through the secure zone without hindrance. In most circumstances they did not disarm them and in some cases, they assisted them on their way. One foreign soldier witnessed French soldiers refueling Rwandan army trucks before they departed for Zaire with their loads of goods looted from local homes and businesses. In Zaire, French soldiers drove their Rwandan colleagues around in official vehicles and, according to the report of the investigative commission, French soldiers delivered ten tons of food to Rwandan troops at Goma on July 21, 1994.[211]

---

[207]Assemblée Nationale, Mission d'information commune, *Enquête,* Tome II, Annexes, p. 412.

[208]Ibid., p. 451; Human Rights Watch/FIDH interview, by telephone, Brussels, September 22, 1998.

[209]Sam Kiley, "A French Hand in Genocide," *Times* (London), April 9, 1998; Human Rights Watch/FIDH interview, by telephone, September 22, 1998.

[210]Assemblée Nationale, Mission d'information commune, *Enquête,* Tome I, Rapport, p. 352.

[211]Ibid., pp. 327-29; Human Rights Watch/FIDH interview, by telephone, Montreal, September 26, 1996.

In the first days of the operation, the French authorities showed little interest in blocking RTLM or Radio Rwanda, but once those stations began propaganda hostile to the French forces, France announced at the U.N. that it would do everything possible to silence them. French officers made contact with the broadcasters of Radio Rwanda, who were operating in the secure humanitarian zone, and quickly obliged them to change the tone of their comments. When Bruno Delaye was asked to end broadcasts of RTLM, he said that the mandate did not cover such an operation and that, in any case, French forces had been unable to find its transmitters. But within days of beginning work on the problem, French agents were also able to locate some of the relay stations used by RTLM and to destroy them.[212]

Once the staunchest supporter of the interim government, France finally provided the resources that saved a substantial number of its intended victims. As the RPF advanced in June, killers hurried to finish their "work." The RPF managed to save thousands as it moved forward, but could not have reached the southwest and west quickly enough to save the groups of Tutsi already exhausted by months of attack, hunger and flight, who were hidden on mountain tops or in river valleys. The thousands who were confined at Nyarushishi were safe only because the local National Police commander, Lieutenant Colonel Bavugamenshi, insisted on protecting them. Had he been removed, they too would have faced attack and possible extermination before the RPF could have reached them.[213] To all those people, the French soldiers who came to their rescue were saviors, regardless of what had moved officials in Paris to send them to Rwanda.

According to French estimates, their 2,500 elite soldiers, equipped with the best equipment available, saved some 8,000 to 10,000 people at Nyarushishi, another 1,100 at Bisesero and another 6,000 in Gikongoro, a total of approximately 15,000 to 17,000 people.[214] UNAMIR, with its barely 500 men, poorly armed and equipped, protected at one time nearly twice that number. Like members of the U.N., the French could and did save lives when it suited their interests. And, when it did not, they too hid behind excuses of insufficient troops and concerns for their

---

[212]Human Rights Watch/FIDH interview, Paris, July 4, 1994; Assemblée Nationale, Mission d'information commune, *Enquête,* Tome I, Rapport, pp. 329-30.

[213]Human Rights Watch/FIDH interviews, Butare, February 25 and July 6, 1995.

[214]Assemblée Nationale, Mission d'information commune, *Enquête,* Tome I, Rapport, p. 310; Tome II, Annexes, pp. 397, 525.

safety or they used a supposed commitment to adhering to the mandate or to preserving neutrality as pretexts for inaction.

The Kigeme Declaration and the End to "Legitimacy"

Among those who profited from the security provided by the French were some of the military officers who had signed the original call for an end to violence on April 12. After that one effort, they had been disheartened and intimidated. They may have continued to dissent privately, but they took no further public position against the slaughter.

They came together once more within the secure zone under the leadership of Gatsinzi and Rusatira. At Kigeme on July 6—three months after the start of the slaughter—they signed a statement committing themselves to fighting the genocide which they "denounced and condemned" with all their strength. They deplored the elimination of Rwandans because of their political beliefs.They denounced a government that had reduced its people to silence by terror and the group of extremists who had ruled by intimidation. They urged a cease-fire and negotiations with the RPF.[215]

Had these high-ranking and respected officers issued such a statement in early April, they might have inspired others to join them in challenging the organizers of the killing campaign. They lacked the courage to take such a stand as well as the troops and equipment to back it up. Had the international community provided a counterweight to the Presidential Guard and its allies, had it taken a united and uncompromising stand—with the threat of the refusal of any future funding for the interim government—or had it silenced RTLM, these officers could have drawn on these sources of support to sustain their own efforts and to persuade others to join them.

At the time of the Kigeme Declaration and shortly after, foreigners—and not only the French—were still treating the Rwandan authorities as legitimate. But with the Rwandan army defeated and the interim government in flight, the international community finally recognized it for what it had always been—a band of killers. In Washington, the U.S. government ordered the Rwandan embassy closed and its assets frozen on July 15. Clinton said that the U.S. could not "allow representatives of a regime that supports genocidal massacres to remain on our soil," as if officials had just discovered that they were there or had just learned that the regime they

---

[215]Declaration de Kigeme, July 6, 1994.

represented was carrying out genocide.[216] The U.S. announced also that it would begin efforts to remove the Rwandan representative from the Security Council. Soon after, the Security Council, as if newly awakened to its power to control its own procedure, decided that Rwanda would not take its scheduled turn as president of the council. Decided on August 25, the measure came so late that it applied, ironically, to the government that ended the genocide rather than the one that perpetrated it.[217]

Had the international community denied the legitimacy of the interim government in the early stages of the genocide, some of the hesitant—like the officers at Kigeme—might have found the resolve to confront the organizers of the killing campaign. One former Rwandan army officer deplored his own lack of courage and that of other Rwandans who, in fear for their own lives, failed to oppose the interim authorities. He remarked, "We now must have the courage to pay the price of our cowardice." The same holds true for those international leaders who, secure in their distant offices, could have intervened—at no risk to their lives—and yet did not.

---

[216]The White House, Statement by the Press Secretary, July 15, 1994.

[217]United Nations, *The United Nations and Rwanda*, p. 334. Rwanda presided over the council in December.

THE RWANDAN PATRIOTIC FRONT

The Rwandan Patriotic Front ended the 1994 genocide by defeating the civilian and military authorities responsible for the killing campaign. Its troops encountered little opposition, except around Kigali, and they routed government forces in operations that began in early April and ended in July. As RPF soldiers advanced south down the eastern side of the country and then swept west, they even stopped the killers in the act of attacking or preparing to attack Tutsi at several churches or camps for the displaced. More often they rescued Tutsi with no dramatic confrontation. They drove military, militia, and other assailants from the region and so made it possible for Tutsi to return from the swamps and bush and to emerge from their hiding places. The RPF soldiers saved tens of thousands from annihilation and relentlessly pursued those whom they thought guilty of genocide.

In their drive for military victory and a halt to the genocide, the RPF killed thousands, including noncombatants as well as government troops and members of militia. As RPF soldiers sought to establish their control over the local population, they also killed civilians in numerous summary executions and in massacres. They may have slaughtered tens of thousands during the four months of combat from April to July. The killings diminished in August and were markedly reduced after mid-September when the international community exerted pressure for an end to the carnage. Carried out by soldiers who were part of a highly disciplined military organization, these killings by the RPF rarely involved civilian participation, except to identify the persons to be slain. In only a few cases, particularly in areas near the border with Burundi, civilian assailants reportedly joined soldiers in attacking other civilians.

Although the subject of substantial speculation, the RPF slaughter of civilians has been poorly documented. Even during the months when the RPF was just establishing its control, it was remarkably successful in restricting access by foreigners to certain parts of the country. Such limitations fed the speculation about RPF abuses but, at the same time, made it extremely difficult to prove wrongdoing.

Because this report focused on the genocide itself, we collected only limited data on crimes committed by the RPF. The information is sufficient, however, to demonstrate that certain kinds of RPF abuses occurred so often and in such similar ways that they must have been directed by officers at a high level of responsibility. It is likely that these patterns of abuse were known to and tolerated by the highest levels of command of the RPF forces.

RWANDA
The Advance of the RPF
April to July 1994

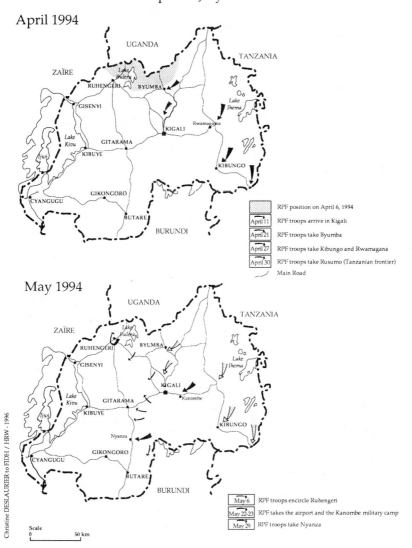

April 1994

UGANDA

ZAÏRE

TANZANIA

Lake
Bulera

RUHENGERI   BYUMBA

GISENYI

Lake
Ihema

KIGALI

Rwamagana

Lake
Kivu   GITARAMA

KIBUYE

Ijun

KIBUNGO

CYANGUGU

GIKONGORO

BUTARE

BURUNDI

RPF position on April 6, 1994

April 11	RPF troops arrive in Kigali
April 21	RPF troops take Byumba
April 27	RPF troops take Kibungo and Rwamagana
April 30	RPF troops take Rusumo (Tanzanian frontier)

Main Road

May 1994

UGANDA

ZAÏRE

TANZANIA

Lake
Bulera

RUHENGERI   BYUMBA

GISENYI

Lake
Ihema

KIGALI

Kanombe

Lake
Kivu   GITARAMA

KIBUYE

Ijun

KIBUNGO

Nyanza

CYANGUGU

GIKONGORO

BUTARE

BURUNDI

May 6	RPF troops encircle Ruhengeri
May 22-23	RPF takes the airport and the Kanombe military camp
May 29	RPF troops take Nyanza

Scale
0   50 km

Christine DESLAURIER to FIDH / HRW · 1996

June 1994

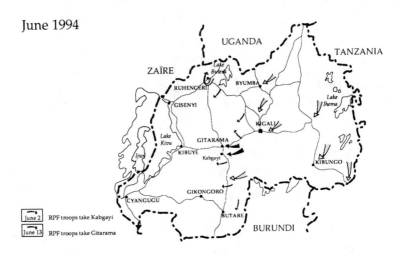

UGANDA

ZAÏRE

TANZANIA

Lake Bulera

RUHENGERI   BYUMBA

GISENYI

Lake Ihema

Lake Kivu

KIGALI

GITARAMA

Ijwi   KIBUYE

Kabgayi

KIBUNGO

GIKONGORO

CYANGUGU

BUTARE

BURUNDI

| June 2 | RPF troops take Kabgayi |
| June 13 | RPF troops take Gitarama |

July 1994

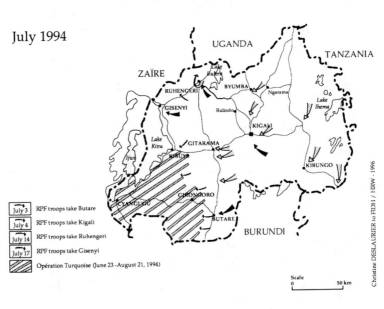

UGANDA

ZAÏRE

TANZANIA

Lake Bulera

RUHENGERI   BYUMBA   Ngarama

GISENYI   *Rulindo*

Lake Ihema

Lake Kivu

KIGALI

GITARAMA

Ijwi   KIBUYE

KIBUNGO

GIKONGORO

CYANGUGU

BUTARE

BURUNDI

July 3	RPF troops take Butare
July 4	RPF troops take Kigali
July 14	RPF troops take Ruhengeri
July 17	RPF troops take Gisenyi
▨	Opération Turquoise (June 23 -August 21, 1994)

Scale
0   50 km

Christine DESLAURIER to FIDH / HRW · 1996

"Not Hutu, Tutsi, nor Twa"
The Ideology of National Unity

Virtually all persons killed by RPF forces were Hutu, but the RPF explicitly disavowed any hostility based on ethnic distinctions and from its earliest days proclaimed a nationalist ideology. Whether or not born of conviction, the stress on national identity made sense politically for a group drawn mostly from the minority and aspiring to political power in a situation where ethnic differences had been exaggerated. The RPF called itself an *umuryango*, literally a lineage or kin group, suggesting that all who adhered to it were expected to feel strong bonds and perhaps even a common origin.[1]

The group taught that Rwandans had lived in harmony before the colonial regime introduced distinctions among ethnic groups. As one of the most famous RPF songs related:

It is the white man who has caused all that, children of Rwanda. He did it in order to find a secret way to pillage us. When they [the Europeans] arrived, we were living side by side in harmony. They were unhappy that they could not find a way to divide us. They invented different origins for us, children of Rwanda: some were supposed to have come from Chad, others from Ethiopia. We were a fine tree, its parts all in accord, children of Rwanda. Some of us were banished abroad, to never come back. We were separated by this division, children of Rwanda, but we have overcome the whiteman's trap....So, children of Rwanda, we are all called to unite our strength to build Rwanda....[2]

Once present in Rwanda and recruiting supporters, the RPF taught new members the same lesson. In training sessions during 1993 and early 1994, instructors presented extensive lessons on Rwandan history which stressed the destructive impact of colonialism on relations among Rwandans. They concluded by defining the RPF:

---

[1] Although the umuryango as usually defined included persons descended from a single ancestor and hence of only one ethnic group, the larger unit of *ubwoko* or clan traditionally could encompass Hutu, Tutsi, and Twa.

[2] Chrétien et al., *Rwanda, Les médias*, p. 359. See chapter one for a discussion of precolonial divisions and the impact of colonalism on them.

Inkotanyi are Rwandans who aim to lead Rwanda to development after too many years of poverty and darkness. Inkotanyi are not Hutu, Tutsi nor Twa...the Inkotanyi party accepts everyone who believes in its goals.[3]

After the genocide began, the RPF continued preaching the need for national identity to those who came under their control. At a just-established displaced persons camp at Rutare, north of Kigali, RPF organizer Athanasius Karisa explained the rules to new arrivals in mid-May 1994: they would be expected to elect their own leaders, to form work committees to build houses and gather food, to settle conflicts peacefully and to "forget who is Hutu and who is Tutsi." A resident of the Byumba camp recalled meetings to talk about "peace and living together."[4] A reporter who spoke to RPF soldiers found that many invoked the "code against ethnic bias, reciting it almost as if by rote."[5]

In their desire to emphasize bonds between Hutu and Tutsi, Kagame and other RPF leaders stressed the political rather than ethnic nature of the violence that began in April 1994.[6] Even when they used the term "genocide" to refer to Tutsi victims, they often hastened to add that moderate Hutu too were suffering from the killing campaign. Dr. Théogène Rudasingwa, then secretary general of the RPF, was quoted in *Der Spiegel* of May 30 as saying, "We are the only force that can put an end to the killing, and the Hutus, too, know that; they are just as much victims as the Tutsis."[7]

Recruiting Hutu Supporters

While still in exile, the RPF recruited well-known Hutu leaders, one of whom, Col. Alexis Kanyarengwe, was installed as chairman of the movement. Another,

---

[3]Notes of training session by Gasingwa Kamiri, December 23, 1993 in handwritten notebook of a recruit (Solidaire-Rwanda).

[4]Mark Fritz, "Rwanda-Life After Death," Associated Press, May 17, 1994; Human Rights Watch/FIDH interview, February 23, 1997.

[5]Mark Fritz, "Rwanda-Life After Death," Associated Press, May 17, 1994.

[6]"RPF radio says conflict is political not ethnic," SWB, AL/1980 A/3, April 25, 1994.

[7]"RPF Leader Views Reasons Behind Massacres," *Der Spiegel,* FBIS, AFR 94-104, 31 May 1994.

Seth Sendashonga, a bright young politician who had left the country because of dissatisfaction with Habyarimana's politics, served as liaison between the RPF and political parties opposed to Habyarimana within the country. As the RPF began more intensive organization within Rwanda in 1993, it continued to insist on the importance of attracting Hutu to its ranks. Its regulations supposedly specified that a new cell could be formally constituted only if the group included Hutu as well as Tutsi. This measure was meant to protect Tutsi from the risk of participating in easily identified monoethnic groups as well as to build a stronger, more broadly based party.

After the popularly acclaimed entrance of RPF troops to Kigali in late December 1993, numerous young Hutu found their way to training sessions at the CND or at RPF camps further north. Some prepared to be political organizers, others to be soldiers. At least one of the trainers was Hutu, as had been recommended by one RPF adviser.[8] In a document prepared for use within the party, the adviser stressed that party organizers must not be just Tutsi:

> These organizers should come from all social groups, with no discrimination whatsoever (Bahutu as well as Batutsi, Bakiga as well as Banyenduga [sic], educated people as well as those who are illiterate, officials from the central government as well as authorities from the private sector, etc...).[9]

Once the genocide began, RPF forces sought to locate and protect some Hutu leaders of political parties and civil society, arranging for their transport behind RPF lines as soon as it was possible. The most important of these leaders spent a brief period at Mulindi, the RPF headquarters in the north, while others were sent to the town of Byumba, or to camps like that at Rutare or to small centers like Kabuga. As RPF troops moved into communities, they quickly made contact with

---

[8]Human Rights Watch/FIDH interview, Kigali, February 14, 1997; handwritten notebook of a recruit.

[9]Anonymous, "L'Environment Actuel Et A Venir de l'Organisation," typescript, p. 11 (confidential source). "Bakiga," " the people of the hills," means northerners, while "Banyanduga" means people from the central and southern part of the country.

local leaders and educated persons and, initially anyway, sought the cooperation of those who were not clearly allied with the forces of genocide.[10]

Young Hutu at camps in RPF territory remember being heavily pressured in May, June, and July to join the RPF army or at the least to serve the party in other capacities. A medical student from the university was pressed by a lieutenant of military intelligence at Kacyiru in Kigali "to give us a hand, help us out." The student asked if he could not assist without becoming a soldier and was told no. When the lieutenant suggested that a continued refusal might raise suspicions about what he had done during the genocide, the student agreed to join the military medical service. One who declined military service ended by working in the civilian administration and another served as a liaison for the RPF with foreign humanitarian organizations.[11]

The RPF even went so far as to encourage members of the government army and of the militia to cross over and join their ranks. At the end of May, General Kagame said on Radio Muhabura: "Political party youthwingers who have been forced to join the Interahamwe to save their lives should denounce them" and come over to the RPF.[12] Kanyarengwe sent the same message, appealing to "members of the Interahamwe who are ready to put down their arms and stop their barbaric acts" to resume normal life behind RPF lines.[13] Not many Interahamwe responded to these calls, but some did.[14] According to one witness, one man who first terrorized the Marenga sector of Kayenzi commune as a member of the Interahamwe later joined the RPF troops, in which capacity he was able to intimidate people into

---

[10]Human Rights Watch/FIDH interviews, Butare, July 8, 1996; Nyabisindu, July 9, 1996; by telephone, Brussels, December 12, 1996; by telephone, Paris, February 19, 1998; by telephone, Washington, February 27, 1998.

[11]Human Rights Watch/FIDH interviews, Butare, September 2, 1996; February 27, 1997; Alter-Ciné interview, Nairobi, March 1996 (Alter-Ciné).

[12]"Government Soldiers Urged to Join RPF Army," Radio Muhabura, FBIS, AFR 94-100, 24 May 1994.

[13]"RPF Colonel Comments on Talking with Government," Radio Muhabura, FBIS, AFR 94-096, 18 May 1994.

[14]Human Rights Watch/FIDH interviews, Butare, February 12 and 23, 1995; Monique Mujyawamariya, "Rapport de Visite, Effectuée au Rwanda du 1/9/94 au 22/9/94," pp. 20-21.

keeping silent about his past abuses.[15] In another case, a councilor who had been involved in killing Tutsi women later identified victims for attack by the RPF in the commune of Rusatira.[16]

Stopping the Genocide

Before April 1994, RPF leaders were well aware of preparations for the killing campaign.[17] They sought to protect their adherents by calling on the international community to speed the implementation of the Arusha Accords. They also sought to strengthen bonds with various Hutu groups and even explored the possibility of joint training with militia of the MDR or the PSD, as mentioned above. When the genocidal forces began killing in Kigali and elsewhere, the RPF immediately warned that it would renew combat unless the slaughter halted. When the warning was ignored, RPF soldiers took to the field.

Military Action

According to two highly-placed RPF leaders, they anticipated that the international community would help defend civilians should killings be launched on a massive scale.[18] When neither the U.N. nor any foreign government showed any inclination to intervene, the RPF on April 9 proposed a joint operation with UNAMIR and the Rwandan army, with each to contribute 300 troops to end the slaughter. The RPF judged that number would suffice to stop the killings, most of which were being carried out by the Presidential Guard.[19] The Rwandan army rejected the bid the next day nor would UNAMIR participate.

After this initiative failed, the RPF undertook on its own to halt the genocide. In one of the most dramatic cases documented, RPF forces arrived in the vicinity as government soldiers and militia were in the midst of what would have been a final assault on Rukara church. An account based on witness testimony relates that as sounds of battle between the RPF and government troops grew closer, the

---

[15]Human Rights Watch interview, Kabgayi, August 28, 1994.

[16]Human Rights Watch/FIDH interview, Brussels, February 26, 1997.

[17]Alba Morasuti, "Seth Sendashonga dans 'L'Autre Afrique'" Rwandanet, February 4, 1998.

[18]Ibid; Human Rights Watch/FIDH interview, Kigali, February 14, 1997.

[19]Human Rights Watch/FIDH interview, by telephone, Nairobi, March 7, 1998.

soldiers fled and "the local militiamen threw their remaining stones and spears at the church, and then ran away, too."[20] In other locations, such as at Kabgayi diocese in central Rwanda, and at Rango south of Butare, militia waiting outside camps for the signal to attack Tutsi fled at the approach of RPF troops.[21]

The genocide took place in the context of war and the RPF wanted to win the war, not just to save theTutsi. In the first three days, the RPF 7th unit, commanded by Colonel Bagire and the 157th unit, commanded by Col. Fred Ibingira, defeated the Rwandan government forces in the northeast. The first mobile unit, under Col. Sam Kaka, pushed through to the capital, where they arrived on the afternoon of April 11, "in line, as if out for a stroll."[22] There they joined up with the 3rd battalion, headed by Lt. Col. Charles Kayonga, which had been stationed in the CND and had been engaged in action since the afternoon of April 7.

By April 12, these early successes caused RPF leaders to believe that they could win a total victory over the Rwandan army and they set out to do that.[23] The military strategy involved sending a substantial force down the eastern frontier while simultaneously engaging the Rwandan forces in the capital and further to the northwest in Ruhengeri. The RPF counted on the government being determined to defend the northwestern quadrant, the home region of Habyarimana and many of the military officers. By keeping alive a threat in that direction, they reduced the possibility that the government would shift an important part of its forces from the northwest to other regions. Rather than striking hard at this area of enemy strength, the RPF advanced rapidly through weaker regions in the east and south, then headed west and northwest again, building pressure on the capital and the northwest.[24] The RPF strategy, praised by other military experts, may have offered the best chance for military victory but did not present the best possible plan for rescuing Tutsi. The soldiers sent to Ruhengeri, where few Tutsi lived, had fewer

---

[20]U.S. Committee for Refugees, "Genocide in Rwanda," p. 16.

[21]Human Rights Watch/FIDH interviews, Kabgayi, August 28, 1994 and Butare, October 28, 1995.

[22]Morasuti, "Seth Sendashonga;" Kamanzi, *Rwanda, Du Genocide a la Defaite*, pp. 120-123.

[23]Human Rights Watch/FIDH interview, by telephone, Nairobi, March 7, 1998; Kamanzi, p. 123.

[24]Human Rights Watch/FIDH interview, by telephone, Brussels, May 2, 1998.

opportunities to save lives than they would have had in regions with a larger Tutsi population.

Rejection of UNAMIR II

When the Security Council discussed sending a larger peacekeeping force to Rwanda with a broader mandate to protect civilians, the RPF feared that the force might interfere with its goal of military victory. Its leaders may have been particularly concerned that the French might use the force to protect the interim government. Instead of welcoming the move and urging speedy implementation, the RPF spokesman in Brussels opposed it and asserted that there were no more Tutsi to be saved.[25] On April 30, Gerald Gahima and Claude Dusaidi of the RPF political bureau reiterated this position in a slightly less forceful statement which declared:

> The time for U.N. intervention is long past. The genocide is almost completed. Most of the potential victims of the regime have either been killed or have since fled.

The statement continued:

> Consequently, the Rwandese Patriotic Front hereby declares that it is categorically opposed to the proposed U.N. intervention force and will not under any circumstances cooperate in its setting up and operation. In view of the forgoing [sic] the Rwandese Patriotic Front:
>
>> a. Calls upon the U.N. Security Council not to authorize the deployment of the proposed force as U.N. intervention at this stage can no longer serve any useful purpose as far as stopping the massacres is concerned.[26]

The RPF was, of course, right in declaring that the U.N. had failed to respond at the appropriate time, but they were wrong to conclude that U.N. action, even if tardy, would "no longer serve any useful purpose." The tragic reality that hundreds

---

[25]Human Rights Watch interview by telephone, Brussels, April 30, 1994.

[26]Gerald Gahima and Claude Dusaidi, Statement by the Political Bureau of the Rwandese Patriotic Front on the Proposed Deployment of a U.N. Intervention Force in Rwanda, New York, April 30, 1994.

of thousands had already been slain in no way negated the need to rescue tens of thousands of others who were still alive. One member of the political bureau at the time claims that RPF leaders really believed that most Tutsi were dead and that only a few "pockets" remained.[27] But they certainly must have known, as did observers abroad, that some 30,000 people were gathered at various sites in Kigali and that more than 20,000 clung to life at Kabgayi with another 10,000 at Nyarushishi. They must have supposed that thousands more still remained in hiding in Butare prefecture, where the killing had become widespread only ten days before.

Representatives of Human Rights Watch and FIDH, who were then receiving frequent telephoned appeals for help from Tutsi hiding in Rwanda, were shocked by the RPF opposition to a force that could save Tutsi lives. They urged the RPF to reconsider its position. On May 2, Eric Gillet of the FIDH wrote Col. Kanyarengwe:

> We understand very well the reasons why the RPF would not want to accept an intervention force. But we cannot see any legitimate reason that the RPF might invoke to oppose a solution which would bring the necessary help to the civilian population without interfering with ongoing military operations.[28]

Diplomats at the Security Council also exerted pressure on the RPF, but without great success. On May 11, Radio Muhabura, the voice of the RPF, still maintained that "the genocide is already finished."[29] On May 18, the day after the Security Council authorized a second peacekeeping force, RPF vice-chairman Denis Polisi complained about the anticipated slowness in mounting the operation. He declared, "People are still suffering every day. People are still dying and we think a month or two is too long...."[30] But he was referring expressly to humanitarian assistance and "warned that if they did anything else then they would be considered an enemy force." Through late May the RPF continued to demand that the peacekeepers stick to purely humanitarian relief rather than engage in more

---

[27]Human Rights Watch/FIDH interview, by telephone, May 9, 1998.

[28]Eric Gillet, chargé de mission FIDH, to Col. Alexis Kanyarengwe, May 2, 1994.

[29]UNAMIR, Notes, Radio Muhabura, May 11, 1994.

[30]Buchizya Mseteka, "Rebels Blast U.N. Delays, Vow to Seize All Rwanda," Reuters, May 18, 1994.

active efforts to defend Tutsi from attack. It also insisted that the force be smaller than that the 5,500 troops set by the Security Council resolution of May 17.[31]

RPF opposition to UNAMIR II contributed to the reluctance of the U.S. and other powers to support such a force, a reluctance which in turn accounts at least in part for the slowness with which the operation was mounted.[32] It is impossible to judge how many lives would have been saved had the RPF welcomed the new force and had the U.S. and other U.N. member states been in turn galvanized to send military aid rapidly.

Human Rights Abuses by the RPF Before April 1994

According to investigations done by Human Rights Watch and the International Commission on Human Rights Abuse in Rwanda, mentioned above, the RPF was responsible for a number of serious human rights violations in the early years of the war in Rwanda. Between 1990 and 1993, RPF soldiers killed and abducted civilians and pillaged property in northeastern Rwanda. They attacked a hospital and displaced persons' camps. They forced the population of the border area to flee either to Uganda or to displaced persons camps further in the interior of the country. While professing a policy of openness and commitment to human rights, the RPF hindered the investigation of the International Commission and made it impossible for its members to speak freely and privately with potential witnesses in areas under RPF control. The commission gathered most of its information from victims of RPF abuses who had sought refuge at camps in the zone controlled by the government.[33]

According to Rwandan human rights organizations, RPF soldiers killed hundreds of civilians in the town and prefecture of Ruhengeri during the offensive of February 1993. In some cases, the soldiers reportedly asked the victims to produce their political party membership cards and then killed those who belonged

---

[31]Human Rights Watch interview, New York, May 23, 1994; Reuters, "U.N. Envoy Ends Talks with Rwanda Rebels," May 23, 1994.

[32]Human Rights Watch interview, New York, May 23, 1994; Human Rights Watch/FIDH interview, by telephone, May 7, 1998.

[33]Africa Watch, *Rwanda: Talking Peace and Waging War*; Report of the International Commission, pp. 37-39.

to the MRND or CDR.[34] The RPF was widely accused of killing civilians in two incidents in November 1993. Investigators from UNAMIR examined the cases, but never issued a public report.[35]

Killings and Other Abuses by the RPF, April to July 1994

The RPF killed thousands of civilians both during the course of combat, brief in most regions, and in the more lengthy process of establishing its control throughout the country. It had anticipated establishing a civilian administration in territory that it captured and, as mentioned above, had begun gathering information on local communities. This was particularly important because few of its leaders had ever known Rwanda as adults. It had also been training young civilians to serve as party organizers or cadres, "abakada." Once combat actually began, the RPF advanced further and faster than expected. Hundreds of thousands of civilians fled before its forces, reacting to stories of RPF abuses—many of them propaganda from the interim government—and following direct orders from local officials to leave. But hundreds of thousands of others remained and the RPF was apparently not fully prepared to begin administering such large numbers.

RPF leaders nonetheless quickly began moving civilians into camps, emptying the intervening zones of people. Kagame explained the policy on Radio Rwanda on July 27, saying that "harmful elements were hidden in bushes and banana plantations. Therefore a cleaning was necessary, especially to separate the innocent people with the killers...."[36]

Killings in the Course of Combat

In the course of combat, the RPF—as well as Rwandan government forces—killed and injured noncombatants, sometimes through attack by heavy weapons, sometimes in exchanges of small arms fire. A witness in Mukingi commune recalled the arrival of the RPF at Byimana. She reported, "There was shooting. We found the bodies afterwards, but we didn't know who had done the

---

[34]Association Rwandaise pour la Défense des Droits de la Personne et des Libertés Publiques, *Rapport sur les Droits de l'Homme au Rwanda, Octobre 1992-Octobre 1993*, Kigali: December 1993, pp. 171-73.

[35]Human Rights Watch/FIDH interview, Brussels, December 15, 1995; Embassy of Rwanda, Washington, Press Release, November 19, 1993.

[36]UNAMIR, Notes, Radio Rwanda, 19:00, July 27, 1994.

killing."[37] Outside of urban centers, the number of such casualties was relatively small, but certainly hundreds of unarmed civilians fell victim to weapons fire in the capital, in Byumba and in Gitarama.[38] Each party has been accused of shelling such sites as churches and the central hospital in Kigali. We lack the data to establish whether these attacks were deliberate or so negligent as to violate international humanitarian law.

As RPF troops advanced, militia fought against them in a number of locations. The CDR spokesman Stanislas Simbizi supposedly led a battalion of militia into battle, a feat that he boasted about in a broadcast on RTLM.[39] According to one account, the RPF advance guard striking south to Kigali in the opening days of the war met resistance from Interahamwe, as did troops at Kabarondo in Kibungo prefecture and at Gashora in the southern part of Kigali prefecture.[40] An officer of the former Rwandan government forces confirmed that militia from the capital fought in the battle over Rebero hill and in subsequent skirmishes in Kigali. According to him, ten regular soldiers ordinarily went into combat with one hundred or so Interahamwe, who were so unprepared that they became cannon fodder.[41] Members of the "civilian self-defense" force also were mustered against the RPF in battles in Gitarama and Butare, as discussed above, always with very heavy losses.

RPF leaders declared that members of the militia would be treated as combatants, a position in accord with international conventions. In late April, the RPF head of information, Maj. Wilson Rutayisire stated, "When we meet Interahamwe we kill them and we are going to keep killing them,"[42] a policy

---

[37]Human Rights Watch/FIDH interview, Mukingi, July 10, 1996.

[38]Joseph Matata, "Massacres de Civils Hutus en Commune Nyamabuye-Gitarama."

[39]Anonymous, "La Milice Interahamwe."

[40]Kamanzi, *Rwanda, Du Genocide a la Defaite*, p. 122. See also pp. 144-45.

[41]Human Rights Watch/FIDH interview, by telephone, Brussels, May 2, 1998.

[42]Cathy Watson, "Bloated Bodies Attest Carnage in Rwanda Church," Reuters, April 26, 1994.

reaffirmed in mid-May by Kagame who stressed that "armed militia at the frontline are a legitimate target."[43]

In a number of places where widespread genocidal killing had occurred or where RPF soldiers encountered or anticipated encountering active resistance from Interahamwe, RPF forces took no care to distinguish militia who were armed and potentially dangerous from civilians. Such a case happened on April 15 when Interahamwe who had killed many Tutsi in their home commune of Sake, in Kibungo prefecture, retreated towards the Tanzanian border. A large number of civilians left with them, either of their own volition or because forced to go along to shield the militia. According to witnesses, the RPF attacked the mixed group of hundreds of civilians and militia at the hill Kanazi and killed all except three persons.[44]

At Rutongo, north of Kigali, RPF soldiers reportedly went from house to house killing unarmed inhabitants[45] and at Murambi in Byumba prefecture, they killed seventy-eight persons, of whom forty-six were listed as children, between April 13 and 15.[46] In Gitwe, an RPF soldier shot an old man in the leg as he was hurrying towards his home.[47] When RPF troops took the church center of Kabgayi where thousands of Tutsi were confined in camps they killed Hutu civilians in the area and left some of their bodies, with the arms bound, in the woods on the church property.[48] Outside Butare, two teenagers and a woman and the baby on her back—all with identity cards showing they were Hutu—were found shot dead in a banana plantation immediately after RPF troops under Captain Théoneste

---

[43]"RPF General: Rebels Want 'Whole Country'" Radio Muhabura, FBIS, AFR 94-097, 19 May, 1994.

[44]Written communication to Human Rights Watch, February 9, 1996.

[45]Human Rights Watch/FIDH interview, by telephone, Atlanta, September 2, 1996.

[46]List prepared by families of victims of crimes attributed to the RPF.

[47]Human Rights Watch/FIDH interview, Gitwe, Murama commune, June 24, 1995.

[48]Human Rights Watch/FIDH interview, Kabgayi, August 28, 1994.

Rurangwa moved into the area.[49] According to several local and foreign witnesses, RPF soldiers killed civilians in the arboretum at the university and in the commune of Shyanda, at the home of Gatabazi, near Save.[50]

RPF forces also killed civilians in places where there had been little or no slaughter of Tutsi and where militia did not appear to threaten their advance. At Giti, for example, a commune known for its protection of Tutsi during the genocide, RPF soldiers "swept through like fire."[51]

In many battles RPF soldiers defeated enemy forces with ease, but they took few, if any, prisoners. Many of the defeated retreated rapidly, but others were shot by the RPF even after they had laid down their arms. In one incident filmed by a video journalist, RPF soldiers appeared with their weapons pointing at government soldiers who were wounded and on the ground. According to the journalist, the RPF shot the captured soldiers after he had shut off his camera.[52]

Kwitaba Imana and Kwitaba Inama: Massacres at Public Meetings

The RPF massacred groups of unarmed civilians at a number of locations in eastern, central, and southern Rwanda after combat was finished and the government forces were gone from the area. These deliberate slaughters of noncombatants were clear violations of international humanitarian law.

On or about April 20, the RPF drove government soldiers from the small town of Byumba and then transferred the headquarters of its general staff there from Mulindi. Many civilians followed the retreating government soldiers, but hundreds of others sought safety in the stadium. RPF soldiers reportedly massacred 300 or more of these people. Major John Birasa commanded the troops in Byumba, but most of the higher ranking officers of the general staff were also in the town at that

---

[49]Christopher McDougall, "A Few Hutu Hearts Prevail During Rwanda Massacres," Associated Press, July 13, 1994.

[50]Human Rights Watch/FIDH interview, by telephone, Montreal, November 23, 1996 and Brussels, October 19, 1997.

[51]Human Rights Watch/FIDH interview, by telephone, Nairobi, March 7, 1998.

[52]Human Rights Watch press release, June 6, 1994.

time. According to one observer, some of those shot may have been denounced by others as having participated in the genocide.[53]

In some places, RPF forces killed civilians at meetings organized soon after their arrival in the community, a practice which gave rise to the bitter joke that *kwitaba Imana*, meaning to die, had come to mean the same as *kwitaba inama*, to attend a meeting.[54] In Gishara on April 13, RPF soldiers invited the people to join a hunt to kill hippopotamus and enjoy a feast. After having questioned a few men about whether anyone in the crowd was a soldier or knew how to handle a gun, RPF troops launched grenades and shot into the crowd. Witnesses reported that they were attacked by RPF soldiers several days later in nearby Nyabwishongezi after having been called to a pacification meeting. Other residents of the same area related that family members or neighbors had been attacked by RPF soldiers who entered their houses and confiscated their identity papers before killing them.[55]

In several communities in Kibungo, people were promised food or salt if they would assemble as instructed. They were then attacked by soldiers. Twenty-two persons were reported killed near Rwamagana with others slain at Kayonza and Gahini.[56]

Witnesses declared that on June 5 in the Nteko sector, Mugina commune, Gitarama prefecture, RPF soldiers killed six men with old hoes and left their bodies in the woods at Cyumura. A week or so later, RPF forces surrounded and killed a group of civilians who had fled from the town of Gitarama to the hill of Muhanga at Gisoro. On June 20 and 23 and again on July 10, RPF soldiers reportedly attacked and each time killed some twenty people in Mugina sector of Mugina commune in Gitarama prefecture.[57]

---

[53]Human Rights Watch/FIDH interview, by telephone, Nairobi, May 9, 1998; Joseph Matata, "La Responsabilité du FPR dans le Génocide."

[54]Human Rights Watch/FIDH interview, by telephone, Nairobi, May 9, 1998.

[55]A witness from Rutongo commune also reported that RPF soldiers took identity cards before killing victims. Human Rights Watch, press release, June 6, 1994; Amnesty International, "Rwanda: Reports of killings and abductions by the Rwandese Patriotic Army, April-August 1994," October 20, 1994, pp. 5-6.

[56]Human Rights Watch/FIDH interviews, Brussels, July 16, 1995 and June 22, 1998.

[57]Matata, "Massacres des Civils Hutus."

In late July or early August, after thousands of people who had fled to the Zone Turquoise returned to Nyamabuye commune in Gitarama prefecture, the RPF was said to have summoned people living in or near the cell Kigarama to a meeting at Gatenzi. Witnesses declare that they were given salt and matches and were told that the meeting had been postponed until a larger number of people could gather. When the meeting was convoked again, dozens more people came. According to the witnesses, the men were tied up and taken to be killed with old hoes in the house of Rwamigabo. The women were slain in the house of Ntawugashira and the children were killed in the house of an old woman named Marguerite and then the house was burned.[58]

In Mututu, commune Muyira, Butare prefecture in early June, RPF soldiers asked children to go bring back the adults in their families who were hiding in the fields and bush. On June 10, after several hundred adults had returned, the soldiers directed them to assemble at the commercial center to be transported to a safer location to the east. The RPF reportedly killed a number of young men at the market place late in the afternoon and tied up some of the others. The crowd was directed to set out for the commune, about one hour away by foot. The soldiers reportedly killed some men on the way and threw their bodies in latrines or in a compost heap at a reservoir.[59] In another report from the same area, witnesses said that RPF soldiers and armed civilians gathered men and adolescent boys at the home of a man named Rutekereza and then killed them.[60]

In August, a group of Rwandans and foreigners who were in the region to investigate possible development projects encountered a badly frightened man who ran from them when they stopped their vehicle. When they had caught up with him, he begged for his life. He related that people from his community had come home from camps in the Zone Turquoise, believing that peace had been restored. RPF soldiers then assembled a large number of people, encircled them and shot them dead. He showed the visitors numerous bodies covered by leaves in banana plantations and fields of coffee plants.[61]

RPF soldiers reportedly killed dozens of people, probably Burundian refugees, at the Nzangwa mosque in the region known as Bugesera. Foreign humanitarian

---

[58]Ibid.

[59]Human Rights Watch/FIDH interview, by telephone, Paris, February 19, 1998.

[60]Amnesty International, "Rwanda: Killings and Abductions," p. 6.

[61]Human Rights Watch/FIDH interview, by telephone, February 27, 1998.

workers who tried to approach the site were prevented from doing so by RPF soldiers, but from a distance they could see that the building had been damaged, apparently by the blast of grenades.[62]

Witnesses from Nyaruhengeri commune reported that about a hundred people were killed by RPF soldiers at a meeting at Mumbeho. Others related similar incidents in the communes of Rusatira, Kigembe, and elsewhere in Butare prefecture.[63]

The only massacre by RPF forces that was documented in detail at the time was reported by Human Rights Watch/Africa in September 1994, as a result of an investigation carried out in late August. In that case, RPF soldiers arrived on June 19 from the direction of the hill Saruheshyi and assembled both local people and displaced persons from a neighboring camp in a field in the cell Nyagakombe, Rugogwe sector in the commune of Mukingi, Gitarama prefecture. They explained that they wanted to talk about transporting people to Rwabusoro in Bugesera. Without giving any reason, soldiers killed a woman named Sara and a man named Bihibindi. An hour and a half later, they opened fire on the crowd of hundreds of people. Some people fled down the road next to the field and were shot trying to escape by running through the woods on the adjacent hills. Others were caught and then killed with hammers, hoes, or other blunt instruments. The soldiers killed without regard to age, sex, or ethnic group. One of the victims was a Tutsi woman identified as the daughter-in-law of a man named Gahizi. Other victims of the attack included the wife, three children, and daughter-in-law of Karemangingo and ten people of the family of Rwabigwi.

Survivors hastily buried most of the bodies in three mass graves, one of which measured one meter by twenty meters and was said to hold about seventy bodies, mostly of women and children. Two other graves were considerably deeper and had originally been pits from which sand or clay had been excavated. The Human Rights Watch investigator photographed the graves and the remains of about twenty people scattered in the nearby woods. Approximately half of them were

---

[62]Human Rights Watch/Africa, "The Aftermath of Genocide in Rwanda," September 15, 1994, p. 5.

[63]Human Rights Watch/FIDH interview, Brussels, October 19, 1997; Monique Mujawamariya, "Rapport de Visite, Effectuée au Rwanda," p. 15; Jean Hélène, "Fuyant les exactions commises par le FPR," *Le Monde*, August 22, 1994.

women or children.[64] In addition, the body of a baby was visible floating in a nearby stream.[65]

Major Sam Bigabiro, who was reportedly implicated in the Mukingi killings, was later convicted by an RPA military court of having directed a similar slaughter in the nearby commune of Runda on July 2. After RPF soldiers offered local people the opportunity to move east to a zone fully controlled by the RPF, several dozen residents and displaced persons refused to leave. At Bigabiro's order, RPF soldiers killed thirty to forty of these people.[66]

Summary and Arbitrary Executions

Within a day or two of the renewal of conflict, RPF soldiers began assassinating persons associated with the Rwandan government, the army, or political groups thought to be hostile to the RPF. In many cases, the soldiers sought out the targeted persons at their homes and also killed family members or others, presumably to eliminate any witnesses. RPF troops reportedly killed Sylvestre Bariyanga, former prefect of Ruhengeri, and his family on April 9 in the Remera section of Kigali. They are also accused of slaying Col. Pontien Hakizimana, former officer of the National Police, his wife and children and Major Helene Bugenimana, National Police officer, and three of her children, who were at Hakizimana's house. On April 12, RPF soldiers dressed as government troops, supposedly killed Emile Nyungura, a leader of the PSD party. In the Gishushu section of Kigali, some RPF troops are said to have slain Felicien Mbanzarugamba, an administrator of the Bralirwa brewery and others are reported to have killed Emmanuel Hitayezu, former minister of planning as well as his Tutsi wife. Théoneste Mujyanama, former minister of justice, and his family, were executed on April 16 while in another incident, Phénéas Bwanakeye of Kibuye was slain with thirty-two others in the household of his son in the Remera section of Kigali. On April 13, Emmanuel Bahigiki, former secretary-general of the planning ministry, left his home with his family and some Tutsi whom he had been

---

[64]Because the investigation was interrupted, the numbers are approximate. See below.

[65]Human Rights Watch/Africa, "The Aftermath of Genocide in Rwanda," p. 6.

[66]Pronouncement of the judgement in trial RC/ 0025/ EMG/ KER/ RC0042/ CM/ KGL/ 97, Ministère Public v. Major Sam Bigabiro and Cpl. Denis Gato, January 30, 1998. For details, see below. As mentioned above, RPA refers to the Rwandan army after July 19, 1994.

protecting under the escort of RPF soldiers; the Tutsi were told to go on ahead but heard the shots that killed Bahigiki and his family. Claudien Habarushaka, former prefect of Kigali, was last seen being escorted by RPF soldiers.[67]

A number of people who had taken refuge under UNAMIR protection at Amahoro stadium were taken away by RPF soldiers and then "disappeared." Among them were Charles Ngendahimana, younger brother of the assassinated politician Emmanuel Gapyisi, and Doctor Prudence, a physician who had been treating the injured and wounded in the stadium.[68]

Outside of the capital, too, persons of some stature in the community were reportedly killed by RPF troops, sometimes after having been well-treated for a brief period. Josias Mwongereza, a prosperous merchant from Kigali, spent the months of April to June at Gasharu, in his home commune of Murama in Gitarama prefecture. Although known to be a member of the PSD, Mwongereza was not particularly active in politics. When the RPF first arrived at Gasharu, they found some fifty people at his residence, both family members and Tutsi to whom he had given shelter. After several days, the military authorities insisted that everyone be evacuated further behind the lines. They were moved to Ruhango for several days and then the group was divided. The Tutsi were sent to Kigali or Kabuga and on or about June 25 Mwongereza and his family were escorted away at night by RPF soldiers and were slain. Six of the seven vehicles in which the family had been traveling disappeared and one, a Mercedes 190, ended up at the Finance Ministry. RPF soldiers occupied Mwongereza's properties and declared that they would leave when the proprietor himself appeared to claim them back.[69]

When the RPF arrived in the commune of Muyira in Butare prefecture on June 7, they reportedly promised to protect a local leader named Faustin Sekamonyo and his Tutsi wife. The family took up residence in a house next to the commune and

[67]Human Rights Watch/FIDH interviews, Paris, April 22, 1996; by telephone, Montreal, November 23, 1996; Nairobi, February 8, 1997; Brussels, June 21, 1997 and October 19, 1997.

[68]Human Rights Watch/FIDH interviews, Paris, April 22, 1996; by telephone, Nairobi, May 9, 1998; Joseph Matata, "Les Massacres Planifiés de Civils Hutu dans la Prefécture de la Ville de Kigali," p.3.

[69]Anonymous, "Massacre Par le FPR en Juin 1994 d'Une Cinquantaine de Membres de la Famille du Commercant Mwongereza Josias en commune Murama-Prefecture de Gitarama au Rwanda," September 14, 1994; Human Rights Watch/FIDH interview, Paris, April 22, 1996.

children in the family worked for the RPF, including two sons who served as drivers for the soldiers. A family friend who came to visit them on June 10 found the house empty and said he was told by an RPF soldier that they had been killed by other soldiers.[70]

Eustache Kubwimana, a PSD leader and others of his party initially seemed to have established a good relationship with the RPF who arrived in their commune of Kigembe in Butare prefecture on July 7. But after they wrote the new authorities with suggestions on how to win public trust, five of those who had signed the letter were taken to the communal office by soldiers and never returned home. Kubwimana then fled to Burundi.[71]

A group of Americans and Rwandans working for Care International in Byumba prefecture sought to return to Kigali after hearing that Habyarimana's plane had been shot down. When they encountered a group of RPF soldiers, Daphrose Nyirangaruye, who was unarmed and posed no threat to military forces, was killed while others in the delegation were permitted to continue on their way.[72]

Also in Byumba, later in April, RPF soldiers killed a Spanish priest, Joaquin Valmajo, and three Rwandan priests: Abbés Joseph Hitimana, Faustin Mulindwa, and Fidèle Mulinda. On April 25 soldiers intercepted Father Valmajo and his Rwandan colleagues at Kageyo and prevented them from continuing on to Rwesero. They insulted them in front of UNAMIR soldiers, who did not intervene, and ordered them to go to the town of Byumba. Once there, Father Valmajo was in touch with Spanish authorities by radio for three days and then disappeared. After urgent inquiries from the Spanish government, an RPF official requested information from Col. Kayumba Nyamwasa, then deputy head of the general staff of the National Police and effectively the head of military intelligence. Colonel Kayumba reported that RPF soldiers had killed the priest and this conclusion was passed on to the Spanish government.[73]

RPF soldiers in some cases specially targeted the families of officers and soldiers of the Rwandan army. Several Rwandan army officers complained to Dallaire during April, May, and June about relatives who had been killed by the

---

[70]Human Rights Watch/FIDH interview, by telephone, Paris, February 19, 1998.

[71]Jean Hélène, "Fuyant les exactions commises par le FPR."

[72]Correspondence from family members, December 22, 1995.

[73]Human Rights Watch/FIDH interview, Paris, April 22, 1996; Société des Missionnaires d'Afrique, "Communique de Presse," June 24, 1994.

RPF. In one case, a Rwandan officer who signed the Kigeme declaration mentioned above found twenty-three of his family slain near the town of Gitarama.[74]

By April 25, the RPF had opened a corridor from Kigali to Byumba and had begun evacuating thousands of people to this position behind the lines. They took some from existing sites for the displaced in Kigali, like the Amahoro stadium or the Roi Faysal hospital, and collected others as they moved from house to house in those neighborhoods that they controlled in the city. Tens of thousands of other displaced persons gathered at Rutare, north of Kigali, where the RPF established a camp. Eventually some 35,000 persons would be housed in Byumba while another 150,000 would be at Rutare.[75]

At Byumba, the RPF executed some forty political leaders or persons of importance in civil society and at Rutare they killed another twenty or so. The RPF began executing these people even as they were escorting them to supposed places of safety. One human rights activist was taken to be killed on the road to Byumba but was saved by the screams of his wife. Because she was a Tutsi and the niece of a RPF officer, she was able to prevent the execution of her husband.[76]

The RPF Department of Military Intelligence (DMI) reportedly killed Celestin Seburikoko, an important Tutsi businessman originally from Butare, because he had supported the MRND. Like many in his position, he had contributed to Habyarimana's party as well as to the RPF and to the MDR, attempting to ensure his own security no matter which group ended up dominating the government. According to one witness, Kagame personally inquired about this case when the DMI seized Seburikoko at the end of April or beginning of May. Apparently convinced of Seburikoko's harmlessness, Kagame reportedly agreed to prevent his execution, but ultimately did not and the businessman was slain two or three days later.[77]

---

[74]Human Rights Watch/FIDH interviews, Brussels, June 21, 1997; Montreal, September 24, 1997; Jean Hélène, "Vengeances rwandaises," *Le Monde*, September 7, 1994.

[75]Human Rights Watch/FIDH interviews, Paris, April 22, 1996; by telephone, Nairobi, February 8, 1997; Faustin Kagame, "Je n'ai pas vu le même film d'horreur que vous," *L'Hebdo*, May 19, 1994, p. 15.

[76]Human Rights Watch/FIDH interviews, Brussels, June 21, 1997; New York, May 10, 1998.

[77]Human Rights Watch/FIDH interviews, Paris, April 22, 1996, Nairobi, by telephone, February 8, 1997.

A former sub-prefect and employee of the Ministry of Youth, Norbert Muhaturukundo, was also reportedly executed at Byumba as was Charles Mbabajende, one of the staff of the human rights organization LIPRODHOR, killed on May 8. In another case, a member of the human rights group ADL was detained for eight days and warned to give up his human rights activities when he was released.[78]

As tens of thousands of persons gathered at a huge RPF camp at Rutare, RPF authorities selected out community leaders and intellectuals whom they took away "to help organize the camp." They were not seen again. One of those was Come Kajemundimwe, a physics teacher at a secondary school in Kigali. Educated in the U.S.S.R. where he had founded an association to bring together Hutu and Tutsi students, he had often opposed the Habyarimana government. As punishment he had been relegated to teaching secondary school instead of being posted to the university. He was said to have protected more than fifty people, Tutsi and Hutu, at his home in Kacyiru during the genocide. He was preparing to move the entire group to his home region of Cyangugu when RPF soldiers arrived and sent them to Rutare camp. Several days later, Kajemundimwe disappeared in the company of other people of education and stature.[79]

Political leaders and leaders of civil society who had seen the RPF as their rescuers and who expected to collaborate with them were frightened and angered by the executions and "disappearances" of their colleagues. Some of them wanted to leave Byumba but the RPF, anxious to maintain the appearance of collaborating in a multi-ethnic, multi-party coalition, made it impossible for them to go. A number of them protested to Kagame and other RPF authorities, both orally and through written notes. Seth Sendashonga, responsible for liaisons between this group and the RPF, wrote six memoranda to Kagame about the "disappearances" and killings and the resulting disaffection among supposed collaborators. At one point, the protesters met with Sendashonga and RPF chairman Kanyarengwe to

---

[78]Human Rights Watch/FIDH interviews, Paris, April 22, 1996; by telephone, Nairobi, March 7, 1998; Mujawamariya, "Rapport de Visite, Effectuée au Rwanda," pp. 47-50.

[79]Human Rights Watch/FIDH interview, by telephone, Nairobi, March 7, 1998; written communication to Human Rights Watch/FIDH, Kigali, March 27, 1998.

voice their fear and anger. The RPF leaders promised to convey the concerns of the group to Kagame, but the effort brought no change.[80]

The most widely known and condemned of executions by RPF soldiers were the slayings of the Roman Catholic archbishop of Kigali, three other bishops, and ten priests at Byimana parish, near Kabgayi in early June. The one priest who survived the attack related that the group of clergy were arrested by the RPF at Kabgayi and moved to Byimana on June 2. Several days later soldiers who were guarding the clergy burst into the room where they were gathered and shot them dead. The priest who managed to flee was later captured by RPF soldiers who agreed to release him only after he accepted their version of events, that is, that the soldiers carried out the killings in reprisal for the slaughter of their own families. When the RPF officially admitted responsibility for the slayings several days later, it declared that one of the murderers had been killed in flight and that the others were being sought and would be tried. Apparently none was ever caught and RPF authorities have never made public any proof to substantiate their claim that the slayings were unauthorized reprisal killings. Archbishop Vincent Nsengiyumva was known for his closeness to Habyarimana, but not all in the group held such a position. Bishop Thaddée Nsengiyumva, who was also murdered, had favored political reform and had sought to distance the church from Habyarimana's government.[81]

Summary Execution of Persons Accused of Genocide

RPF authorities insisted that both personal acts of vengeance and more general killing of those thought to have committed genocide were prohibited. Even very young and just recruited soldiers understood and repeated this to foreign journalists.[82] On April 17, Kanyarengwe asserted that the RPF priority was to stop the killings and "to arrest the criminals and hand them over to courts, so that

---

[80]Ibid.; Human Rights Watch/FIDH interviews, by telephone, Nairobi, February 8, 1997; by telephone, Washington, February 27, 1998.

[81]Jef Vleugels and Guy Theunis, Société des Missionnaires d'Afrique, fax no. 17, June 9, 1994; Amnesty International, "Rwanda: Reports of killings," pp. 7-8; Prunier, *The Rwanda Crisis*, pp. 271-72.

[82]Mark Fritz, "Rwanda, Rebels with a Cause," Associated Press, May 16, 1994 and "Rwanda, Life After Death," Associated Press, May 17, 1994.

everyone could defend himself and be punished according to his crime."[83] RPF vice-chairman Denis Polisi reiterated the policy a month later. Speaking of some 2,000 prisoners captured by RPF troops, he declared:

They will be held until a time comes when we can try them in properly constituted legal institutions. We have no policy of killing any one of them and it is our intention that we bring them to justice.[84]

Four months later, RPF spokesman Major Wilson Rutayisire reportedly said that there were only "about 200" detained for genocide, raising the question of the fate of the others.[85] RPF soldiers apparently regularly executed persons whom they thought guilty of genocide and, in contrast to statements made to foreigners, some of them readily admitted this to other Rwandans. At Kabuga, a RPF post just outside Kigali, an officer named Gasore assured a person who inquired about the situation in the area south of Kigali, "Don't worry. We have taken vengence for you in Bugesera...." In that area, where thousands of Tutsi had been killed in and near Kanzenze, the RPF had killed 300 Hutu, he reportedly said.[86] Another survivor of the genocide who spent some time at an RPF post near Kizi, outside the town of Butare, declared:

I saw the the RPF soldiers bringing bodies in trucks at night and throwing them in toilets at Mwogo, near where they had dug their trenches. They brought men already wounded with their arms tied behind their backs. They brought no women. The soldiers were proud to show us that they were avenging us. We were ill at ease with this. We saw them dump bodies also in toilets of shops and houses at the little commercial center.[87]

---

[83]"RPF president interviewed on battle for Kigali, RPF objectives," Radio Muhabura, SWB, April 21, 1994.

[84]Buchizya Mseteka, "Rebels Blast U.N. Delays."

[85]Serge Arnold, "Government Considers Amnesty for Militiamen," AFP, September 23, 1994, FBIS-AFR-94-186, September 26, 1994.

[86]Human Rights Watch/FIDH interview, Brussels, December 12, 1996.

[87]Human Rights Watch/FIDH interview, by telephone, Washington, February 27, 1998.

Another witness related that persons leaving Zone Turquoise were held in the camp at Kizi, near the limit of the zone controlled by the French. There they were searched and interrogated. Survivors of the genocide who were temporarily lodged in shops at the commercial center joined in accusing those alleged to have participated in the genocide. In late August, the RPF supposedly put into effect a regulation requiring that an accused person had to be denounced by at least five persons before being executed. One accused person was reportedly hit on the head and thrown into a mass grave, but managed to escape and fled back to the Zone Turquoise.[88]

In some cases, RPF soldiers simply assumed that any people still alive in a community had killed Tutsi. When a survivor at Kabuga asked the RPF officer Gasore about the fate of people at Ndera, near Kigali, he is said to have replied that probably everyone in that region was dead, whether Hutu or Tutsi. "When we arrived," he said, "we supposed that those still alive were alive because they had collaborated and we killed them all."[89] According to another witness, RPF soldiers decided that the people they found alive in the Bugeramanga sector of Murama commune, Gitarama prefecture, had all participated in the genocide. They killed some thirty people by striking them with hoes and then throwing grenades into the house where they were gathered. Among those slain were some Tutsi as well as Hutu.[90] A witness from Butare prefecture related a similar event. Describing the arrival of RPF troops in early July, she said:

> The first day, they killed in turn. The militia killed those who came out of hiding to flee, and when the RPF arrived here and found the bodies, they killed the others who were still alive on the spot.[91]

After the first days of combat, the RPF made more of an effort to investigate the past behavior of people before condemning them to "disappearance" or execution. In some cases, they turned to survivors who were or appeared to be

---

[88]Jef Vleugels and Guy Theunis, Société des Missionnaires d'Afrique, fax no. 23, August 24, 1994.

[89]Human Rights Watch/FIDH interview, Brussels, December 12, 1996.

[90]Human Rights Watch/FIDH interview, by telephone, March 21, 1998.

[91]Alter-Ciné interview, Gikongoro, September, 1994.

Tutsi to judge others. One witness related his experience when the RPF arrived at his house in Kigali on April 20:

> They asked the women in the household, who looked Tutsi—but in fact were not—if the rest of us were "good." When the women answered, "yes," we were all taken away without trouble for evacuation.[92]

The soldiers consulted Tutsi first of all, but if they found Hutu whom they judged to be reliable, they also asked their opinion about others. In Muyira, the soldiers used survivors to guide them to the homes of supposed perpetrators and also asked a Hutu of importance in the community to name killers.[93] When RPF soldiers arrived in the commune of Rusatira in early July, they killed persons pointed out by a Hutu councilor. At most houses, they threw the dead into latrines, but at one house with a flush toilet, they burned the bodies.[94]

Soldiers sometimes arranged for survivors to denounce supposed killers among the crowds grouped at camps for displaced persons. In April, RPF soldiers separated the men from the women among the displaced who had taken refuge at the Amahoro stadium, then protected by UNAMIR. They brought in survivors to point out supposed killers among these people and then removed those identified from the stadium. Those persons were never seen again.[95]

On June 11, RPF soldiers directed some 1,500 people of Mukingi commune to gather in the sector of Mahembe, near the Nyagafunzo stream, where they stayed for about two weeks. During that time Corporal Mandevu and a soldier named André Pake (nicknamed Brown) were in charge. At one point, the soldiers separated the men from the women. They questioned survivors and others about

---

[92]Human Rights Watch/FIDH interview, February 23, 1997.

[93]Human Rights Watch/FIDH interview, Paris, February 19, 1998.

[94]Human Rights Watch/FIDH interview, Brussels, February 26, 1997.

[95]Human Rights Watch/FIDH interview, Paris, April 22, 1996; Nairobi, February 8, 1997; by telephone, Nairobi, May 9, 1998; Matata, "Les Massacres Planifiés de Civils Hutu," p.3.

who had participated in the genocide. On the basis of that information they took away some eighty people who were never seen again.[96]

In Rango, south of Butare, RPF soldiers summoned local people and displaced persons from neighboring communes to two meetings, one on July 8 and another on July 11. At the first meeting, they read a list of names of men, in most cases just their Christian names. They warned that any who did not come forward would be caught later. Those taken were locked up that night at the Rango Health Center and then "disappeared." When the wife of one man asked soldiers where he had gone, she was told that he had gone to be interrogated and would return. She never saw him again. At the second meeting, soldiers asked survivors to identify purported killers and they then took those named away in vehicles. Those taken away did not return.[97] On July 22, the hundreds of displaced persons who had been grouped at the parish of Save were called to a final meeting before being sent back to their homes. Soldiers asked the families of victims to point out the presumed killers. Some two hundred persons so indicated were taken away for interrogation. Most were never seen again but about a dozen were later released. Some of those freed, including a man named Mugiraneza, were taken away again by soldiers a few days later.[98]

In addition to gathering information from survivors and others in the community, RPF soldiers also conducted their own interrogations to discover supposed perpetrators of the genocide. During the last days of April or the first days of May, a foreigner reportedly witnessed the execution of persons in Gahini after they had been interrogated by soldiers.[99] In Byumba and Kigali it was mostly soldiers of the DMI who did the questioning. Soon after arrival in Byumba, displaced persons from Kigali were summoned one after another to be questioned. One witness observed that the number of persons lodging in the same large room of a secondary school with him dropped from some one hundred to about sixty in the course of several weeks. Those who left had all been taken away by RPF soldiers. If the person being summoned was with other family members, the whole group was generally taken at once. Sometimes they left under the impression that

[96]Human Rights Watch/FIDH interviews, Butare, July 8, 1996; Nyabisindu, July 9, 1996; Mukingi, July 10 and 13, 1996.

[97]Human Rights Watch interviews, Butare and Rango, August 27, 1994.

[98]Human Rights Watch/Africa, "The Aftermath of Genocide in Rwanda," p. 4.

[99]Human Rights Watch/FIDH interview, Brussels, June 22, 1998.

they were being moved to Mulindi where they would have better lodgings and where they could assist in formulating government programs. But they were never seen again. They were ordinarily transported in two vehicles, a Volkswagen Jetta and a minibus. One evening at about 7 p.m., the witness and another man were summoned by soldiers and transported to a house near the hospital. They were both questioned but were eventually permitted to return to their lodgings.[100] Another witness recalled his experience in Byumba:

> The first day, I was imprisoned with fourteen people. They then took them all out. The same thing happened the next day and the day after. They put people in the room with me, then took them out and they did not return. This went on for eight days when they released me.[101]

One woman recounted that she had seen many people "disappear" during the three months that she was at Byumba, including women, children and household workers. She declared,

> On June 2, two soldiers came to take my husband away. They came in civilian clothes, but I knew they were soldiers. Today they work for the DMI....After several weeks I went to the authorities to ask where my husband was. I went to Karera Denis, a captain who was the commander at Byumba. They said my husband was working for "the family," the "umuryango," as they called it. They said I should wait for him, that I might even have to wait four years before I heard from him. That was June 28, 1994.[102]

A foreign doctor working in Byumba reported two people killed and two wounded by RPF soldiers in mid-May and stated that others, including women, had come to the hospital for treatment for wounds they said had been inflicted by the RPF troops. He added that those recently wounded were "victims of witchhunts,

---

[100]Human Rights Watch/FIDH interview, Arusha, February 23, 1997.

[101]Human Rights Watch/FIDH interview, Kigali, May 14, 1996.

[102]Human Rights Watch/FIDH interview, Kigali, May 19, 1996.

suspected collaborators." He remarked that "There is a family-by-family screening" of new arrivals that amounts to "almost a paranoia."[103]

A witness from Rutare camp also declared that he saw groups of men being marched off behind a nearby school and that they did not return.[104]

When the RPF troops advanced through the commune of Ngenda, in the region known as Bugesera, south of Kigali, they reportedly directed the local people to a camp at Rutonde. After two days, the RPF soldiers took away the young men from the camp and, the day after, took away some older men. One who was taken but was able to return to the camp reported that others had been tied up, beaten on the head until dead and then thrown into the river. When the wife of one man who had supposedly been killed in that way tried to flee, she was caught by RPF soldiers who killed the child on her back and two other women by blows to the head. The woman herself was beaten on the head with a nail-studded club but survived. She showed a human rights investigator the scars of the beating.[105]

On July 13, RPF soldiers gathered several hundred displaced persons from Ntyazo, Ngenda, and Runyinya communes at a site near the town of Butare. They told them they were to be transported either to the stadium in town or back to their home communes. Instead they took them to buildings of the Groupe Scolaire and nearby veterinary school where they separated the men from women. The soldiers eventually released most of the women and a few of the men, but many of the men were held for interrogation and later "disappeared." Witnesses in the area declared that for two days they had heard the sounds of people being killed in the woods next to the school.[106]

RPF soldiers occupied the grounds of the Kivumu church, north of Gitarama, during the month of July and used the site as a camp for displaced persons. During that month, they killed several hundred men, apparently after having interrogated them. Those who helped bury the dead stated that most had their arms bound

---

[103] Aidan Hartley, "Western Doctors Toil to Save Survivors of Rwanda Killings," Reuters, May 18, 1994.

[104] Human Rights Watch/FIDH interviews, Kigali, May 14, 1996; February 23, 1997.

[105] Amnesty International, "Rwanda: Reports of killings," p. 7.

[106] Human Rights Watch/FIDH interviews, Butare and Rango, August 27, 1994.

behind their backs and that they had been beaten to death. A researcher from Human Rights Watch/Africa was shown three mass graves on the grounds.[107]

When the RPF took Kigali on July 4, they ordered the population to assemble in several locations around the city. One person who was directed towards the site in Kacyiru reported:

> And then they began to interrogate everyone there, especially the young men. To ask you what you were doing during this massacre. What you did. Especially since there were a lot of militia left when the city was taken by surprise. They didn't have time to get out of the city. They [the RPF] wanted to do a triage, the innocent and then the victims and those really guilty of genocide.[108]

The witness added that most of those interrogated had been men, that women were questioned less often. The questions asked concerned not just behavior during the genocide, but also political party membership and ethnic group. After questioning, those found suspect were put in a building apart which was called the house of the *ibipinga*, or the opponents. Those found probably trustworthy were pressed to join the RPF as soldiers and they were housed in a building belonging to the social security administration (*caisse sociale*). The new recruits were interrogated again concerning their activities and their ethnicity. The witness stated that relatively few Hutu passed the second interrogation. Those who did not were sent to the house of the ibipinga.[109]

After a few days, the new recruits were transferred to a RPF post at Masaka. According to the witness, some 120 of the new recruits were assigned to a detail called "manpower," which was carried out at the headquarters of the DMI at Masaka. There the recruits killed civilians, first tying their arms and legs and then striking them in the head with a hammer or other blunt instrument. According to the witness, the bodies were burned and what remained was buried. He declared that he could smell the burning flesh and see the smoke every day. Himself a medical assistant, he said he was never assigned to do this work, but he did give medical excuses to about ten recruits who were disgusted by the duty and wanted

---

[107]Human Rights Watch/Africa, "The Aftermath of Genocide in Rwanda," p. 3.

[108]Alter-Ciné interview with a former RPF soldier, Nairobi, March 1996.

[109]Ibid.

a way to avoid it. He said that from what he heard, he believed that thousands were slain in this way. The witness asserted that he was transferred about one month later to a military camp at Gabiro in the Akagera game park where the same kind of slaughter and burning of bodies took place in a detention camp adjacent to the military camp.[110]

The witness, described as credible by a former high-ranking RPF official, gave testimony that was convincing in its spontaneity and detail. Some of the practices he described, such as the screening by interrogation, the pressure on young men to join the RPF, and the use of the English term "manpower" among RPF soldiers, have been mentioned by other witnesses. We have no direct confirmation of his most serious charges, but there is some indirect corroboration. U.N. officials stumbled across a large number of bodies in a Kigali stadium several weeks after the RPF took power, to the great anger of RPF soldiers, and some U.N. officials had been told that there was a special RPF squad for disposing of bodies by burning them. (See below.) Journalists present in Kigali during July reported seeing a column of young men being marched under RPF guard to an unknown destination. When they questioned the authorities about them, they received different and not very credible explanations of who the young men were and where they were going.[111] Four months after the events described by the witness, several U.N. employees arrived unexpectedly by helicopter at the Gabiro camp and observed large numbers of civilians, including women and children, who rushed forward, apparently to try to make contact with them. Soldiers reportedly drove the people back, beating them with sticks. The RPF commander of the camp was extremely angry at the U.N. employees, interrogated them at length, and detained them for several hours. Agents of the DMI interrogated the U.N. employees several times in the days after the incident.[112]

---

[110]Ibid.

[111]Frédéric Fritscher, "Chasse à l'homme à Kigali," *Le Monde*, July 8, 1994; Agence France Presse, "Dans Kigali libére, une population encore parquée," July 6, 1994, BQA No., 14250, July 7, 1994.

[112]Lt. Col. Karenzi Karake to H.E. The Vice President and Minister of Defence, 21 December 1994, Re: Act of Threat to National Security; Human Rights Watch/FIDH interview, by telephone, Geneva, April 26, 1998.

Hindering Humanitarian Assistance

On several occasions, RPF soldiers violated the protection which is supposed to be accorded to medical facilities and other humanitarian assistance in general. At the end of June and the beginning of July, RPF authorities ordered the people in the central prefecture of Gitarama to move east to the region of Bugesera, in the southern part of Kigali prefecture. The forced removal of people from camps at Ruhango and Nyanza to Bugesera caused great misery to the 70,000 or so people who had to make the trek on foot. Soldiers reportedly obliged a group of orphans to wait at a river crossing for three days for no apparent reason and held up a truck full of sick and wounded patients for a day before it was allowed to proceed.[113]

RPF authorities also obliged humanitarian agencies to move east. The ICRC delegate in charge at Nyanza initially refused to close that hospital as directed by the RPF. According to witnesses not connected with the ICRC, the delegate was threatened several times by RPF soldiers, the last time by a Commander Bosco, accompanied by twelve heavily armed soldiers, one of whom pointed a rocket-propelled grenade launcher at his head. After the ICRC and MSF-Belgium opened a hospital at Rilima, in Bugesera, armed soldiers entered one night and abducted a woman and her child, who were never seen again.[114]

Control of Information

The RPF established close control over foreigners working or traveling in areas under its authority. Information and liaison officers worked hard at shaping the ideas of outsiders while persons employed by foreigners were ordered to report on their activities and conversations. Ordinarily journalists and aid workers were allowed to travel in RPF territory only in the company of officially designated "guides" who sought to ensure that they travel just to approved areas, usually via the main roads. The RPF closed whole regions to UNAMIR and other foreign observers for weeks at a time.[115]

Although professing commitment to the ideals of human rights and to the values of openness and honesty, the RPF sought to limit investigations that might produce evidence of abuses by their soldiers. When a researcher from Human

---

[113]Field notes, July 1994; Lindsey Hilsum, "Rwandan Rebels Advance as French Forces Hang Back," *Guardian*, July 2, 1994.

[114]Field notes, July 1994.

[115]Human Rights Watch interviews, Kigali, August 25, 1994.

Rights Watch, accompanied by a journalist, was investigating the June 19, 1994 massacre at Mukingi, she was interrupted by twenty-five soldiers armed with rocket-propelled grenade launchers and machine guns who arrived in two vehicles from one direction while a foot patrol of another ten soldiers came on the double from the other. The commanding officer, who would not give his name, directed the two women to get in his vehicle. He questioned them, including about the identities of persons whom they had talked with, and then escorted them from the area. When the researcher returned to her lodgings in the evening, an officer of the DMI was waiting to question her further about her work that day. RPF soldiers prohibited the head of the U.N. Human Rights Field Operation from entering such places as the area near the veterinary school in Butare where killings had reportedly taken place on a large scale (see below).[116]

Accusations of RPF Abuses

The first reports of misconduct by the RPF were vague and clouded by the blatantly exaggerated propaganda put out by the interim government. The U.N. High Commissioner for Refugees (UNHCR) began hearing accounts of RPF killings from refugees in early May and became sufficiently concerned to make public the allegations on May 17. At that time, a spokesman in Geneva reported that a field officer at the Tanzanian border had witnessed RPF soldiers shooting at refugees as they tried to flee across the Kagera River. He also stated that over the three previous days refugees coming from a dozen different locations in Rwanda had described RPF massacres. In some cases, refugees reported that people had been herded into a school and then attacked with machetes; in others, they declared that victims had been tied and thrown into the river alive.[117]

The RPF immediately denied the charges, which RPF vice-chairman Polisi characterized as "laughable."[118] On May 16, Radio Muhabura reported that "genocide victims" had been seen "tied with their hands behind their back and thrown into the River Nyabarongo" and stated that the bodies going down the river

---

[116]Human Rights Watch/Africa, "The Aftermath of Genocide in Rwanda," p. 8.

[117]Aidan Hartley, "U.N. Officials Accuse Rwanda Rebels of Atrocities," Reuters, May 17, 1994; Reuters, "U.N. Accuses Rwandan Rebels of Killings, Torture," May 17, 1994.

[118]Aidan Hartley, "U.N. Officials Accuse Rwanda Rebels of Atrocities."

were "said to be decomposing and not fresh corpses."[119] The broadcast appeared intended to explain away the presence of corpses in the river—surprising given that the RPF had driven away the militia and government troops—and the fact that many of the corpses were tied up, a practice usual for the RPF but rare for genocidal killers.

No further serious accusations followed these early charges by the UNHCR. In fact, journalists and aid workers present in RPF territory generally agreed that there was no evidence of large-scale killing by its troops. In making known these judgments, they rarely indicated how limited was the information from which they drew their conclusions.[120] According to the London-based organization African Rights, their researcher, unlike other foreigners, was permitted to travel "extensively in RPF-controlled areas of Rwanda, unescorted by RPF soldiers or civilian members" during the month of May. After visits to Byumba and Kibungo, she too reported that "there is absolutely no evidence that the RPF is responsible for large scale indiscriminate killing of civilians."[121]

The special rapporteur for Rwanda, named by the U.N. Commission on Human Rights at the end of May, René Degni-Ségui, visited Rwanda briefly in June. In a report issued on June 28, he stated that in areas controlled by the RPF, "the cases of massacres reported are rather rare, indeed virtually non-existent," but he added that this assessment might reflect lack of information rather than absence of killing.[122] The wise caution was pertinent: the massacre at Mukingi, for example, was being carried out on June 19, during the four day period when the special rapporteur was in Rwanda. He also declared that the RPF had been guilty of summary executions, such as of the clergy killed at Byimana, and had carried out

---

[119]"RPF Reports 2,000 'Rescued' in Southeast," Radio Muhabura, FBIS, AFR 94-096, 18 May 1994.

[120]"RPF Massacres Termed 'Government Propaganda," La Une Radio Network, FBIS, AFR 94-096, 18 May 1994; Mark Fritz, "Rwanda, Rebels With a Cause;" Aidan Hartley, "U.N. Officials Accuse Rwanda Rebels of Atrocities."

[121]African Rights, "Rwanda, Who is Killing; Who is Dying; What is to be done," May 1994, pp. 23-24.

[122]R. Degni-Ségui, Report on the situation of human rights in Rwanda submitted by Mr. R. Degni-Ségui, Special Rapporteur of the Commission on Human Rights, under paragraph 20 of Commission resolution E/CN.4/S-3/1 of 25 May 1994, E/CN.4/1995/7, 28 June 1994, p. 6.

murders "simply on the basis of a denunciation" which he characterized as "political assassinations."[123]

The U.N. Commission for Human Rights established a field operation in Rwanda in June. At the start, the "operation" consisted of a single person charged with the enormous tasks of gathering data on the genocide, monitoring the current situation, and establishing an office. She had no vehicle and virtually no resources. In addition, the mission was limited by the absence of a clear agreement between Rwandan authorities and the U.N., which meant that there were no official grounds for protest when the RPF excluded the investigator from certain areas. During this period, the operation issued no public reports of its findings, but submitted data to the high commissioner of human rights who was supposed to deliver them to the special rapporteur.[124]

The Gersony Mission

The first convincing evidence of wide-spread, systematic killings by the RPF was gathered by a UNHCR team dispatched for another purpose. When the team and the head of the UNHCR attempted responsibly to bring the information to the attention of the international community, the U.N. decided to suppress it, not just in the interests of the recently established Rwandan government but also to avoid further discredit to itself. The U.S., and perhaps other member states, concurred in this decision, largely to avoid weakening the new Rwandan government.

Scope and Conclusions

After the RPF victory, the UNHCR sent a three person mission headed by Robert Gersony to find ways to speed the repatriation of the nearly two million refugees who had fled the country since April. In a briefing for colleagues at the end of his mission, Gersony remarked that he had begun the work with high regard for the RPF, which he believed to be the most highly disciplined force he had encountered in years of fieldwork in Africa. Its communications system functioned very efficiently, more efficiently than that of UNAMIR itself, he was told by UNAMIR officers, and orders passed down the chain of command were well

---

[123]Ibid., p. 13.

[124]Human Rights Watch/FIDH interview, January 12, 1997; Human Rights Watch/Africa, "The Aftermath of Genocide in Rwanda," p.9. In fact, the special rapporteur reportedly did not receive the complete information submitted by the field operation to the high commissioner.

Document: Letter from the U.N. High Commissioner for Refugees stating that the Gersony Report "does not exist."

UNITED NATIONS
HIGH COMMISSIONER
FOR REFUGEES
Branch Office for Rwanda

NATIONS UNIES
HAUT COMMSSARIAT
POUR LES REFUGIES
Délégation pour le Rwanda

Telephone: (250) 85106
Telefax: (250) 85104

0 4 AVR. 1996

RWA/HCR/REP/96/0409

Monsieur:

Nous accusons réception de votre lettre datée du 29 Mars 1996 dans laquelle vous nous demandez de vous fournir une copie du "Rapport Gersony".

Nous vous informons que le "Rapport Gersony" n'existe pas. M. Gersony, à la fin de sa mission, en Septembre 1994 avait fait une présentation verbale de ses conclusions aux autorités locales et au Représentant Spécial du Secrétaire Général des Nations Unies.

Veuillez agréer, cher Monsieur, l'assurance de mes meilleures salutations.

W. R. Urasa
Délégué

Juge Edoukou Aka Kablan
Représentant du Rapporteur
Spécial pour le Rwanda
s/c HRFOR
Kigali, Rwanda

executed.[125] Although he and his team did not set out to gather information on RPF abuses, they became convinced in the course of the work that the RPF had engaged in "clearly systematic murders and persecution of the Hutu population in certain parts of the country."[126]

Although few in number and pressed for time, the team covered more of RPF territory and spoke to a wider number and variety of witnesses than any other foreigners working in Rwanda during this period. They were permitted to travel freely by the RPF, which may have expected the results of their work to support their efforts to bring the refugees home. From August 1 through September 5, the team visited ninety-one sites in forty-one of the 145 communes of Rwanda and gathered detailed information about ten others: In these places as well as in nine refugee camps in surrounding countries, they conducted more than two hundred individual interviews and another one hundred discussions with small groups. They found the information provided by witnesses detailed and convincing and they confirmed the most important parts of accounts by independent sources in other camps or inside Rwanda.[127]

In the northwest, they gathered data on an alleged RPF massacre on August 2 of some 150 persons who had been trying to return to Rwanda from Zaire and they noted systematic and arbitrary arrests and "disappearances" of adult men in the prefecture of Gisenyi. But their harshest criticism dealt with the prefectures of the south and southeast: Butare, part of Kigali, and Kibungo, particularly those communes adjacent to the border. They reported massacres following meetings convoked by the authorities, murders committed by assailants who went from house to house, and the hunting down and murder of people in hiding. They also reported ambushes and massacres of persons trying to flee across the border to Burundi. They stated that the victims were killed indiscriminately, with women, children, the elderly, and the handicapped being targeted as well as men. They concluded that "the great majority of these killings had apparently not been motivated by any suspicion whatsoever of personal participation by victims in the massacres of Tutsi in April 1994."[128] They added that in some cases, repatriated

---

[125]"Notes from briefing given by Bob Gersony" (confidential sources).

[126]Haut Commissariat des Nations Unies pour les réfugiés, "Note, La Situation au Rwanda," Confidentiel, September 23, 1994, p. 4.

[127]Ibid., pp. 1-2.

[128]Ibid., p. 3.

Tutsi refugees had joined the RPF in attacking local Hutu. They stated that during the last week of August and the first week of September, some five bodies a day on the average had been pulled from the Akagera River, many of them with their hands and feet bound.[129]

The team noted that field officers of the UNHCR, operating completely independent of themselves, had collected similar accounts from refugees fleeing Rwanda at various points along the border. In addition, UNHCR representatives had inadvertently discovered a large number of bodies when they made an unannounced visit to a stadium in Kigali which they were considering using for a transit center. They had also heard reports in Kigali that there was a special RPF squad designated for getting rid of the bodies of Hutu who had been killed and that it burned many of those bodies.[130]

A written note produced by the UNHCR estimated only that the RPF had killed "thousands of persons a month,"[131] but Gersony himself reportedly estimated that during the months from April to August the RPF had killed between 25,000 and 45,000 persons, between 5,000 and 10,000 persons each month from April through July and 5,000 for the month of August. In press accounts based on leaked information, the figure most often cited was 30,000.[132]

"The Gersony Report Does Not Exist"

Gersony reported the results of his mission to Madame Sadako Ogata, the U.N. High Commissioner for Refugees, who in turn informed the secretary-general. Boutros-Ghali and some of his subordinates were concerned not just about the extent of the abuses alleged and the eventual impact of the information on the still fragile Rwandan government, but also about the negative publicity for UNAMIR and other U.N. agencies operating in Rwanda with no apparent awareness of such atrocities. He directed Kofi Annan, who was traveling in northeastern Africa, to change his plans and go to Rwanda. There, on September 19, Annan, Gersony, and the secretary-general's special representative, Shaharyar Khan, briefed the Rwandan prime minister, the minister of foreign affairs and the interior minister on

---

[129]Ibid., p. 3.

[130]"Notes from briefing given by Bob Gersony."

[131]UNHCR "Note, La Situation au Rwanda," p. 4.

[132]Human Rights Watch/FIDH interview, by telephone, New York, March 22, 1998.

Gersony's findings.[133] The Rwandan government officials admitted that some soldiers had engaged in reprisal killings. But they rejected Gersony's allegations about the scale and the systematic nature of the killings and declared that it was impossible for thousands to have been killed without attracting attention.[134]

The news of Gersony's findings must have reached Washington soon after they arrived in New York. The U.S. Assistant Secretary of State for African Affairs George Moose contacted Deputy Assistant Secretary of State for African Affairs Prudence Bushnell in Bujumbura where she had just arrived from Kigali and directed her to return immediately to Rwanda to discuss the findings with officials there.

Annan and Khan went to visit one of the regions mentioned by Gersony and Bushnell, too, went down to the border region to attempt to check on Gersony's charges, but the time was too brief and their contacts too limited to allow them to learn anything new.[135]

Annan, apparently at Boutros-Ghali's direction, reportedly informed the Rwandan prime minister that the U.N. would do its best to minimize the attention given to Gersony's findings because the international community understood the difficult context in which the new government was operating. In the meantime, the information would be treated as awaiting confirmation—that is, it would be kept confidential. Without endorsing Gersony's findings, Annan nonetheless stressed that the killings must stop immediately. General Guy Tousignant, who had replaced General Dallaire as commander of UNAMIR, conveyed the same message even more bluntly to other ministers in the government, declaring that Gersony was probably right and that the slaughter must end.[136] In the meantime, the UNHCR suspended its organized repatriation of refugees and UNAMIR posted some one

---

[133]Ibid.; Human Rights Watch/FIDH interviews, by telephone, Nairobi, April 28, May 7 and May 9, 1998.

[134]Ibid. and UNHCR "Note, La Situation au Rwanda," p. 3.

[135]Human Rights Watch/FIDH interviews, by telephone, New York, March 22, 1998 and Nairobi, April 28, May 7 and May 9, 1998.

[136]Ibid.

hundred peacekeepers to the southeast, one of the regions where the most violence
had been reported.[137]

U.S. officials were aware of the U.N. decision not to make the report public
and agreed with it.[138]

Apparently in return for the understanding that the information would be kept
quiet, Rwandan authorities agreed to investigate the allegations. General
Tousignant and several other U.N. officials accompanied three Rwandan
government ministers and five uniformed RPF officers to the east where many
killings had supposedly taken place. The team reportedly worked for only one day,
the day after the departure of Gersony and Annan. They left Kigali late in the day
and spent some time in Kibungo, two hours distant by road. En route they visited
a grave site at Rwamagana which had been identified by Gersony. They found
grass already growing on the site and so decided that it was not recent enough to
confirm Gersony's data. They returned to Kigali and never made a proposed
second mission to the northwest because the presence of mines was supposed to
have made the area unsafe. One witness connected with the group dismisses the
investigation as a sham from the beginning, saying that no one wanted the truth
known.[139]

The substance of Gersony's findings was leaked to the press.[140] Rwandan
officials reacted with new denials and by unleashing renewed attacks on the U.N.
In New York, Boutros-Ghali ensured that there would never be a written document
to call into question the efficacy of the U.N. presence or the behavior of the
Rwandan forces. Gersony was told to write no report and he and his team were

---

[137]"U.N. Suspends Refugee Repatriation Program," AFP, September 28, 1994,
FBIS-AFR-94-190, September 30, 1994.

[138]Human Rights Watch/FIDH interviews, by telephone, Nairobi, April 28 and
May 9, 1998.

[139]Ibid.

[140]"Rwanda Asks U.N. to Probe New Atrocities," New York Times, September 24,
1994; Angus Shaw, "Much Trouble Remains for Returning Rwandans," Associated Press,
September 26, 1994; and Keith Richburg, "Leaders Struggling to Rebuild Their Nation,"
Washington Post, September 26, 1994.

directed to speak with no one about their findings.[141] The UNHCR produced a confidential note of some three and a half pages for internal use, but even this minimal statement was not shared with the special rapporteur on Rwanda of the Human Rights Commission. He received a shorter two and a half page statement.[142] When the representative of the special rapporteur tried in April 1996 to obtain more information about Gersony's findings from the UNHCR, he received a curt reply stating: "We wish to inform you that the 'Gersony Report *does not exist.*'"[143]

International Responsibility

Faced with full and horrifying information about a genocide where the moral and legal imperative to act was overwhelming, major actors at the U.N. and in various national governments had failed to intervene. Burdened with the guilt of this failure, they confronted a more complex situation when Gersony revealed the apparent extent of RPF killings.

Gersony's conclusions seemed solid, based as they were on a substantial body of data. Although the brief visits to the field by U.N. and U.S. representatives and the short-lived investigative commission did not confirm his findings, neither were they extensive enough to invalidate them. In addition, on September 15, Human Rights Watch/Africa published a report documenting the Mukingi massacre and other killings and reporting on the existence of mass graves at sites where RPF troops had organized a camp for the civilian population.

Leading authorities at the U.N. and in national governments were troubled by this information. They wanted the slaughter to end but they were reluctant to make any criticisms that might weaken the new Rwandan government. As one U.S. policymaker described the situation:

We have three choices. Support the former genocidal government. That is impossible. Support the RPF. That is possible. Support neither. That is

---

[141]Gersony continues to observe the order to say nothing about the mission and refused to talk with our researcher.

[142]Human Rights Watch/FIDH interview, by telephone, New York, March 22, 1998.

[143]W. R. Urasa, Délégué, UNHCR, Branch Office for Rwanda, to Juge Edoukou Aka Kablan, Représentant du Rapporteur Spécial pour le Rwanda, April 4, 1996 (underlined in the original).

unacceptable because it might result in the those responsible for the genocide coming back to win.[144]

Timothy Wirth, U.S. Undersecretary of State for Global Affairs, met Gersony in Kigali in late September and found the presentation of his work "compelling." Wirth discussed the killings of civilians described by Gersony and by the Human Rights Watch/Africa report with authorities in Kigali, but without getting any conclusive response from them. In a briefing in Washington several weeks later, both Wirth and Assistant Secretary of State Moose rejected the conclusion that RPF killings were "systematic" and Wirth suggested that Gersony had been misled by prejudiced informants. Moose remarked, however, that the U.S., like Belgium and Germany, was supporting the RPF "with its eyes open." He added that UNAMIR forces were going to be deployed more rapidly in Rwanda, presumably in hopes that their presence would reduce killings by the RPF.[145]

By refusing to deal openly and firmly with accusations of killings by the RPF, the U.N. and the international community shielded the RPF from reproach and from demands for increased international scrutiny of its policies and practices. The pressure brought by Annan, the U.S., and perhaps others behind the scenes, however, strengthened the position of moderates within the government who were seeking to end attacks on civilians. Partly in response to international pressure, partly in response to changes within Rwanda itself, RPF authorities ordered soldiers to stop killing civilians. The number of civilians slain diminished markedly after late September.[146]

Responsibility Within the RPF

When faced with accusations of killings and other abuses by their soldiers, RPF authorities sometimes denied the charges or they admitted the killings but tried to minimize the numbers involved, such as claiming that victims of killings documented by Gersony numbered only sixty to seventy. If it was clear that RPF soldiers had killed, as with the clergy at Byimana, they responded quickly with statements of regret, explanations, and promises of punishment for the offenders.

---

[144]Human Rights Watch interview, Washington, September, 1994.

[145]Human Rights Watch, notes from U.S. State Department briefings, September 22 and October 11, 1994.

[146]Human Rights Watch/FIDH interview, by telephone, Nairobi, April 28 and May 9, 1998.

RPF leaders occasionally sought to justify civilian deaths as the unavoidable consequence of combat but most often they portrayed the killings as spontaneous acts of vengeance by recently recruited young soldiers who were not yet fully trained. Certainly some soldiers killed out of personal grief and rage, but the RPF has not provided any evidence to establish that revenge was the motive in a substantial number of cases.

Vice-President Kagame and other Rwandan authorities have repeatedly declared their commitment to establishing accountability, including for soldiers who commit abuses against civilians. In September 1994, authorities said they had arrested soldiers who killed civilians and executed two of them.[147] When a Human Rights Watch researcher presented evidence of the Mukingi massacre to Kagame in September 1994, the vice-president expressed his appreciation for being given the details of an affair that, he said, he had known about only in general terms. He stated that Major Sam Bigabiro had been arrested for killing civilians and might have been in command at Mukingi.

The case of Major Bigabiro was brought to trial in Rwandan military court in January 1998, but he was charged with the slaying at Runda on July 2, mentioned above, not with killing civilians in Mukingi on June 19. Bigabiro admitted ordering his soldiers to shoot more than thirty civilians, but said there were Interahamwe among the group, from whom he had taken two weapons. Some witnesses suggested that Bigabiro had ordered the killings after a young woman spurned his sexual advances. While the details of motivation and execution remained unclear, all the military witnesses insisted that Bigabiro had acted on his own and several stated that he had directly contravened the orders of his superior, Col. Charles Muhire, to deliver the entire group to a safe zone and to leave punishing the Interahamwe to the appropriate services. Both Bigabiro and his subordinate, Cpl. Denis Gato, were found guilty and sentenced to prison, Bigabiro for life, Gato for forty-five months.[148] Twenty-one RPF soldiers had been charged with killing civilians in November 1994. Hundreds of others have since been arrested, but it is not known how many of this group are charged with serious human rights violations. Of the twenty-one arrested in 1994, six were tried by June 1998 and all found guilty. With the exception of Bigabiro, one lieutenant, and two sergeants, the others charged in 1994 were all either privates or corporals. Bigabiro received the

---

[147]Human Rights Watch/Africa, "The Aftermath of Genocide in Rwanda," p. 7.

[148]Pronouncement of the judgement in trial RC/ 0025/ EMG/ KER/ RC0042/ CM/ KGL/ 97, Ministère Géneral v. Major Sam Bigabiro and Cpl. Denis Gato, January 30, 1998.

harshest sentence of the six convicted by June 1998. Cpl. Innocent Niyonsenga, convicted of killing fifteen people—supposedly to avenge the deaths of family members—was sentenced to only three years in prison and Private Rurisa Kizityo, was sentenced to five years in prison after having been found guilty of killing five civilians. He, too, supposedly acted out a desire for revenge.[149]

Revenge killings by soldiers—or other crimes of passion—as well as the unintentional killing of civilians in combat situations could never account for the thousands of persons killed by the RPF between April and late July 1994. Much of the RPF slaughter is hard to document: many victims disappeared and have not been found, alive or dead. Because of this, determining the approximate number of victims slain by the RPF may be even more difficult than estimating the numbers of those killed in the genocide. Evidence gathered thus far suggests that the death toll was highest in certain communes of Kibungo, southern Kigali, Butare and Gitarama. These indications, partial and tentative, point to a minimum death toll of 25,000 to 30,000 people, a figure in the lower range of Gersony's estimates. Given the current state of our information, it is impossible to say how many of those were active participants in the genocide or were engaged in any military action against the RPF when they were killed.

RPF soldiers engaged in two kinds of deliberate killings of civilians outside of combat situations: the indiscriminate massacre of individuals and groups, bearing no arms, and posing no threat to them and the execution of individuals, selected according to their reputations, political party allegiance, denunciations by others in the community, or after interrogation by RPF soldiers. In the first situation, no pretence was made of selecting victims; all were judged to be the enemy by the fact of being alive, including, sometimes, people who were Tutsi and, often, people who had protected Tutsi. In the first kind of killing, massacres sometimes took place after people had been called to a meeting and after they had been reassured about the peaceable intentions of the RPF. In the second kind of killing, men were sometimes separated from women, and victims were often tied before being killed and were slain by blows of a heavy instrument or a machete.

These killings were wide-spread, systematic, and involved large numbers of participants and victims. They were too many and too much alike to have been unconnected crimes executed by individual soldiers or low-ranking officers. Given the disciplined nature of the RPF forces and the extent of communication up and down the hierarchy, commanders of this army must have known of and at least

---

[149]List entitled "Capital Offences" and list of soldiers convicted, June 3, 1998, received from the Auditorat Militaire, Ministry of Defense, June 3, 1998.

tolerated these practices. According to several informants, Kagame himself was told about the killings of civilians in Byumba and did not intervene to stop them. The RPF has declared that soldiers who kill civilians will be brought to justice, but thus far few have been tried and most of them have been ordinary soldiers or officers of low ranks. Col. Kayumba, recognized as the effective head of the DMI during the months when this agency was allegedly guilty of killing civilians, continues to enjoy the confidence of his high-ranking military colleagues. In early 1998, he was named chief of staff of the RPF.

When the U.S. and other powerful international actors insisted that the reported abuses be ended, killings diminished. Since RPA commanders had the capacity to reduce these abuses when subject to sufficient pressure, it appears that they had the capacity to halt the killings completely had they chosen to do so.

Despite talk of the need for accountability, the international community, like the RPA high command, has been satisfied with a mere pretense of justice for the 1994 abuses. It has not insisted on effective prosecutions of the most responsible officers, either within the Rwandan military system or from the international tribunal which is mandated to try crimes against humanity as well as genocide committed in Rwanda in 1994. Thus it has signaled that the killing of civilians, if perpetrated in the aftermath of a genocide, was understandable and would be tolerated, so opening the way to the further slaughter which took place in the months and years after.

CONCLUSION:
JUSTICE AND RESPONSIBILITY

There must be justice for the genocide, political murders, and other violations of human rights in Rwanda in 1994. The guilty must be punished and prevented from inflicting further harm. The innocent must be freed from unjust assumptions about their culpability and, if they are jailed, they must be released.

Demanding justice is morally and legally right and it is also politically sound. Without justice, there can be no peace in Rwanda, nor in the surrounding region. This truth, widely acknowledged in 1994, has become even clearer in the four years since: insurgents, including some responsible for the 1994 genocide, and RPA soldiers are killing and will keep on killing civilians until they become convinced that such a course is futile and costly.

Establishing the responsibility of *individual* Hutu is also the only way to diminish the ascription of *collective* guilt to all Hutu. The unexamined and incorrect assumption that all Hutu killed Tutsi, or at least actively participated in the genocide in some way, has become increasingly common both among Rwandans and outsiders. Fair trials, as well as other mechanisms for discovering the truth, such as missions of inquiry, can help establish a record of the events of 1994 that is credible to all Rwandans and thus useful in promoting reconciliation, distant though that prospect may be.

In addition, judicial decisions about responsibilities are necessary before the courts can decide on reparations, including allocating damages to the victims. Although such payments can never compensate for the suffering of victims, survivors must at least be able to recuperate lost property and see their destroyed homes rebuilt.

The international community, the Rwandan state, and other nations—all participants in some way in the genocide or witnesses to it—must share the burden of rendering justice for the crimes committed in Rwanda in 1994.[1] All recognize this responsibility but are slow to fulfill it. The international community took months to establish the international tribunal and then at first failed to fund it adequately or to oversee its proper administration. The new Rwandan government needed considerable foreign assistance to rebuild its devastated judicial system. Even after funds and technical assistance began to arrive, authorities required two

---

[1]For an examination of the complementary relationships between these systems, see Eric Gillet, "Le génocide devant la justice," *Les Temps Modernes,* 1994-1995, pp.228-71.

years more before beginning trials. Two years after that, fewer than 1,500 people had been tried while some 135,000 others were detained and awaiting trial.[2] Other national governments hesitate to prosecute alleged perpetrators because they expect the trials would be complex and expensive. Whatever the causes, the inadequate delivery of justice in all jurisdictions has aggravated the crisis in Rwanda and the larger region.

Rwandan government officials will be tried for their participation in the genocide, but foreign leaders whose inaction contributed to the scale and duration of the catastrophe will likely face the judgment only of history and public opinion. Some international authorities—including the U.N. secretary-general, the U.S. president, and leaders of the Belgian Senate—have rightly recognized their responsibility for failing to avert and halt the genocide. Some policymakers, however, have confused an appropriate recognition of the debt they owe to Rwandan genocide victims with a sense of obligation to current Rwandan authorities. This sense of obligation helps keep them silent before past and present abuses of the RPA, thus perpetuating the pattern of impunity for massive abuses. International efforts at justice will gain full credibility only if the victors in 1994 are held accountable for their alleged violations of international humanitarian law just as the losers are brought to justice for the genocide they executed.

The International Criminal Tribunal for Rwanda

On April 30, just over three weeks after the start of the genocide, the Security Council issued a presidential statement recalling the definition of genocide—still without using the term—and asking the secretary-general to make proposals for investigating such serious violations of international humanitarian law.[3] Following this first indication that the guilty would face international prosecution, other international actors began calling for justice for the genocide, adding to the demands of human rights and humanitarian organizations. Once the U.N. special rapporteur for Rwanda and a Commission of Experts named by the Security Council both concluded that Rwandan authorities had committed genocide and that

---

[2]Fondation Hirondelle, "Libérations de Suspects du Génocide: Controverses et Vengéances;" August 26, 1998, citing official sources. The U.N. Human Rights Field Operation estimated a total of 125,800 detainees at the end of March, 1998, 81,000 of them in central prisons, the rest in communal lockups. Arrests continued after that time, making 135,000 for the end of August a plausible figure. UNHRFOR *Report...January-March 1998,* p. 16.

[3]United Nations, *The United Nations and Rwanda,* pp. 55-56.

soldiers of the RPA were guilty of violations of international humanitarian law, the Security Council established the International Criminal Tribunal for Rwanda in November 1994.

Following the precedent of the International Tribunal for ex-Yugoslavia, the tribunal for Rwanda was established under Chapter VII of the U.N. charter, concerning threats to international peace. Acting under this authority, the council required member states of the U.N. to cooperate fully with the tribunal and to enact whatever domestic legislation was needed to do so. The tribunal is to judge persons accused of genocide, crimes against humanity, and violations of article 3 common to the Geneva Conventions and of Protocol II Additional to the Conventions. It is accorded jurisdiction over persons of whatever nationality accused of committing such crimes in Rwanda and over Rwandans charged with such crimes in neighboring states as well. The mandate of the tribunal extends to crimes committed from January 1, 1994 to December 31, 1994. In the limitation of the period covered by its mandate, the Rwandan tribunal differs from that for ex-Yugoslavia, for which no final date to its jurisdiction has been set.

The tribunal is competent to judge persons who "planned, instigated, ordered, committed or otherwise aided and abetted" in executing the crimes within its jurisdiction.[4] Since much of the planning took place before January 1, 1994, however, prosecuting planners of the genocide may be hampered by the time limits placed on the mandate. The Security Council intended the tribunal to try government authorities and specified that having held an official position at the time of the crime "shall not relieve such person of criminal responsibility nor mitigate punishment."[5] Officials are held responsible for the acts of subordinates, if they knew or had reason to know such acts were planned and failed to halt them.[6] Subordinates who committed crimes on the orders of their superiors cannot be

---

[4]Statute of the International Tribunal for Rwanda, Article 6,2. The resolution establishing the tribunal, S/RES/955, and the annexed statute is printed in United Nations, *The United Nations and Rwanda*, pp. 387-93. See also, E. David, "Le Tribunal pénal international des Nations Unies pour le Rwanda," *Dialogue,* no. 186, octobre-novembre 1995 and M.-A. Swartenbroeckx, "Le Tribunal pénal international des Nations Unies pour le Rwanda," in J.-F. Dupaquier, ed., *La justice internationale face au drame rwandais* (Paris: Karthala, 1996).

[5]Statute of the International Tribunal for Rwanda, Article 6,3.

[6]Ibid., Article 6,4.

exonerated for that reason, although the tribunal may take that into consideration in setting the punishment.[7]

The tribunal operates with a synthesis of common and civil law procedures, with heavier weight given to the common law system. In contrast to Rwandan courts where victims claiming damages as a result of the crime may speak at the trial, the international tribunal hears victims only if they are called to testify and then they speak as witnesses, not as injured parties. The tribunal operates with all the generally-recognized guarantees of due process, including the right to appeal the judgment. It may order punishment up to life imprisonment, but in accord with growing international practice, it does not impose the death penalty. It may order those found guilty to restore property taken from victims, but it has no procedure for ordering the payment of damages to the injured.

The tribunal was originally established with two chambers, each of three judges, and an appeals chamber of five judges. The Rwandan and the ex-Yugoslavia tribunals share the same appeals chamber in order to assure a single body of legal precedent for both. In response to the slow progress of trials and the large numbers of accused already in custody, the Security Council added a third chamber of three judges to the Rwandan tribunal on April 30, 1998.[8] One judge, Lennart Aspergen, announced in 1998 that he would not stand for re-election when his term expired in 1999. The U.N. has reportedly found it difficult to locate highly qualified candidates to stand for election to be judges.

The prosecutor for the tribunal for ex-Yugoslavia was charged also with investigating and presenting cases before the Rwandan tribunal, assisted by a deputy prosecutor. Although this arrangement has permitted some sharing of experience and resources between the prosecutorial staffs for the two courts, it initially hampered the work of the Rwandan tribunal. At the time of its establishment, the prosecutor, Judge Richard Goldstone, was already fully engaged in cases from the former Yugoslavia and found it difficult to take on the new responsibilities. A new prosecutor, Judge Louise Arbour, was named in 1996 and declared her intention to allocate more time to the work of the Rwandan tribunal. Although she has done so, she works primarily at the European headquarters of the tribunals in The Hague, leaving observers, particularly Rwandan observers, with the impression that the ex-Yugoslav tribunal remains the primary focus of her attention. In 1997 the Rwandan government attempted to secure the appointment

---

[7]Ibid., Article 6,5.

[8]United Nations, Security Council, S/RES/1165 (1998), 30 April 1998.

of a separate prosecutor for the Rwandan tribunal, arguing that the scale of the work demanded such a full-time post, but the effort failed.

When the Rwandan tribunal was first being discussed, Judge Goldstone hoped that the court would be established in Rwanda and that some of its sessions might even take place outside the capital, as near as possible to the site of the crimes. The Security Council, concerned about the safety of staff and trial participants as well as about logistical considerations, decided to place the trial chambers in Arusha, a small city in neighboring Tanzania. Although not much closer to major international airports than Kigali, Arusha offers a large conference center for the trial chambers. The office of the deputy prosecutor and his staff is located in Kigali. The division of personnel between the two African sites in addition to the distance of both from the general headquarters of the tribunals in The Hague complicates and slows communication among staff.

Relations Between the International Tribunal and National Jurisdictions

The tribunal takes precedence over the national courts of U.N. member states and can ask any national jurisdiction to defer to its competence. Persons tried by the tribunal cannot be charged for the same crime in national courts, nor vice versa, except if the national trial is deemed to have been only a charade. The statute of the tribunal sets terms for its cooperation with national jurisdictions. In addition, in a resolution passed in February 1995 (S/RES/978), the Security Council specifically asked member states to arrest those suspected of crimes that fell under the competence of the tribunal.

Belgium, Benin, Burkina Faso, Cameroon, Cote d'Ivoire, Kenya, Mali, Switzerland, Togo, and Zambia have arrested persons who were then transferred to the custody of the tribunal. One suspect, Elizaphan Ntakirutimana, was arrested in the United States, but a local court held unconstitutional the law providing for his delivery to the tribunal. The judge ruled that the law did not conform to the usual pattern of extradition treaties, which have to be negotiated with other nations and approved by the U.S. Senate. Ntakirutimana was released but was subsequently rearrested. A second judge found the law constitutional in August 1998 and ordered his release to the tribunal. Ntakirutimana's lawyer has announced that this decision will be appealed, to the U.S. Supreme Court, if necessary.[9]

---

[9]"Fighting Genocide Case," *Houston Chronicle*, August 22, 1998.

Administration of the International Tribunal

At the start, tribunal staff were obliged to spend a great deal of their time dealing with setting up and running offices. Drained by the search for paper clips, pens, and paper, they had little energy left for dealing with the complexities of understanding, investigating, and prosecuting the genocide of at least half a million people. Even the most basic supplies failed to arrive, sometimes because of lack of money, bureaucratic complications, or even corruption. Funded initially on a provisional basis, the tribunal offered contracts of three months to potential staff members and found it difficult to attract qualified personnel for employment of uncertain duration in a distant location lacking many of the amenities of city life. When competent people were hired, it could take U.N. headquarters up to a year to process their contracts and get them to central Africa.[10]

By late 1996, the problems of mismanagement were so obvious and constituted such an impediment to the work of the tribunal that they could not be ignored. After an investigation by a U.N. auditor, the registrar, responsible for daily functioning of the tribunal, and the deputy prosecutor were replaced. Subsequent audits have found considerable improvement but have noted the need for further changes in the administration.[11] Judge Aspergen cited incompetence and lack of committment in the administration of the tribunal as partly responsible for his decision, mentioned above, not to stand for election to another term.

By 1998, the tribunal was receiving regular funding on a yearly budget, which facilitated its operation. Although the sum available for 1998 was substantial, some U.S.$50 million, considerably more than half this amount was allocated to the registrar's office, about U.S.$34 million, while the office of the prosecutor, responsible for investigating and preparing the cases, was allocated only U.S.$14 million.[12] A substantial number of positions, including some for the senior prosecutorial staff, remained unfilled. The deputy prosecutor, Bernard Muna, remarked in February 1998 that the international tribunal was then functioning with

---

[10]Human Rights Watch/FIDH interviews, Kigali, January 24, 1995, July 13, 1996; Arusha, February 7, 1997.

[11]United Nations, General Assembly, Report of the Secretary-General on the activities of the Office of Internal Oversight Services, A/52/784, 6 February 1998.

[12]United Nations, International Criminal Tribunal for Rwanda, Press and Public Affairs Unit, ICTR Fact Sheet, May 14, 1998.

...stigators while 2,000 had been available to prepare cases for the Nuremburg tribunal after World War II.[13]

The tribunal has operated at a slow pace, in part because of administrative problems, such as assuring the attendance of witnesses and counsel for the defense, in part because of extended vacations taken by the judges. According to one study, the tribunal was in recess for four months during one twelve month period.[14]

Because of the slow progress of the tribunal, the right of the accused to be tried without undue delay may have been affected in certain cases. Joseph Kanyabashi, Elie Ndayambaje, and Gérard Ntakirutimana have been detained at Arusha since November 1996 and their trials had not yet begun two years later. Several of the accused have also experienced delays in being brought before a judge for confirmation of their detention or for having their motions heard.

The tribunal has recognized that delays present a serious problem, one that is likely to continue given the number of person already awaiting trial. The addition of another trial chamber is intended to help resolve this problem, as are several expedited procedures adopted by the tribunal in May 1998.

The tribunal has experienced great difficulty organizing its press and public relations office. Journalists from the independent news agencies Fondation Hirondelle and Ubutabera have kept the international community well informed about developments at the tribunal, but within Rwanda, the majority of the population knew little of what was happening at Arusha in the first years of the tribunal. It was only in 1998 that Radio Rwanda established a regular service to inform Rwandans about the trials.

Protection of Witnesses

The defense and, increasingly, the prosecution often find that potential witnesses fear reprisals if they testify and so refuse to do so.[15] The tribunal is charged with protecting all witnesses, but except for the time when witnesses are actually at Arusha, their safety is supposedly assured by local authorities in the country where they reside. In one case in September 1997, the tribunal sought the

---

[13]AFP, "UN war crimes court for Rwanda limited by funds: prosecutor," Kigali, February 24, 1998.

[14]Amnesty International, "International Criminal Tribunal for Rwanda, Trials and Tribulations," April 1998.

[15]Fondation Hirondelle, "Un Ancien Préfet en Mal de Témoins Directs pour sa Défense," June 17, 1998.

help of the Office of the U.N. High Commissioner for Refugees and of the Kenyan government to assure protection to defense witnesses in Kenya.[16] Most witnesses live in Rwanda and return there after testifying. In December 1996, a person scheduled to testify for the prosecution was killed in Rwanda; another was slain after testifying in March 1997. Seth Sendashonga, set to appear as a defense witness, was assassinated in Nairobi in May 1998. There is no proof that any of the three murders was directly related to the planned or past testimony of the victims, but the killings added to the sense of danger which discourages potential witnesses.

A number of the accused wish to call witnesses who currently live outside Rwanda. Some of these persons reside illegally in other African countries. Others have no valid passport because the Rwandan government has cancelled all passports issued by the previous government and these persons have been afraid to apply for new documents or have been unsuccessful in doing so. In order to assure the accused the right to call witnesses in their defense, the tribunal may have to make arrangements to permit witnesses to travel and to return to the countries where they now reside or to some other location which they deem secure.

The tribunal has occasionally failed to provide adequate safeguards for witnesses in its own hands, such as not shielding them adequately from public view. In one case, a prosecution lawyer inadvertently revealed the country of residence of a witness who wished to keep that information secret. In another, tribunal staff permitted unauthorized persons access to a list of possible witnesses whose identity was supposed to be kept confidential.[17]

The Prosecutions

When the tribunal was still getting organized, various national governments handed over suspects whom they had arrested but did not wish to try. Engaged in responding to the opportunities thus presented, prosecutors failed to develop a firm strategy for the cases they wished to pursue. Although the Security Council clearly intended the tribunal to focus on the highest officials and political leaders, the prosecutors found themselves putting together cases against officials of local importance who happened to have been surrendered to them.

---

[16]Fondation Hirondelle, "Cooperation du HCR et du Kenya pour la Protection de Témoins à Décharge," September 8, 1997.

[17]Fondation Hirondelle, "Imprudence du Parquet: Le Lieu de Réfuge d'Un Témoin Devoilé," June 17, 1998.

In 1997 prosecutors began to plan a more coherent strategy and to seek out the high-ranking officials who should be tried for the genocide. With the cooperation of Kenyan authorities, they arrested seven important suspects in July 1997 and they also took custody over several senior officials who had been arrested elsewhere in Africa. Prosecutors then envisaged joint trials to focus on the collaboration that existed among those responsible for the genocide. Their initial effort to join the indictments of several persons was rejected in 1998 both by the trial chamber and on appeal. But prosecutors planned to try again, developing trials focused either on one aspect of the genocide, such as the media used to incite killing, or on one region.

One of the most important Rwandan government officials now in the hands of the tribunal is the former interim prime minister, Jean Kambanda, who pleaded guilty to genocide in May 1998 and was sentenced to life imprisonment by the tribunal in early September 1998. On September 2, 1998, the tribunal found Jean-Paul Akayesu, former burgomaster of Taba, guilty of nine of fifteen charges, including genocide, inciting to genocide, and rape. He was the first person to be convicted of genocide after trial by an international court. The verdict was also the first to recognize rape as a form of genocide. In December 1998, Omar Serashago, a militia leader from Gisenyi pleaded guilty to four charges, including genocide and crimes against humanity. He was sentenced to fifteen years in prison. The tribunal heard final arguments in the case of Clément Kayishema, former prefect of Kibuye, and his co-defendant, businessman Obed Ruzindana, in late 1998 and was expected to issue a decision in early 1999. Among others awaiting trial at Arusha are Colonel Bagosora, CDR leader Barayagwiza, propagandist and RTLM head Ferdinand Nahimana, MRND president Mathieu Ngirumpatse, and former minister Pauline Nyiramasuhuko and her son Shalom Ntahobali.[18]

The initial indictments submitted by prosecutors made no mention of rape and other crimes of a sexual nature. After a coalition of nongovernmental organizations drew the attention of the tribunal staff to the importance of prosecuting these crimes as a category of genocide, the prosecutors amended the indictment against Akayesu and stated their intention to give greater attention to this matter in the future.

The resolution establishing the tribunal included crimes against humanity and violations of the Geneva Conventions within its mandate. As yet the prosecutors have taken no action against RPF soldiers who might be accused of such crimes,

---

[18]See the appendix for a list of those indicted and detained.

a circumstance which has provoked little commentary from major international actors but which risks undermining the credibility of the tribunal.

Rwandans and the International Tribunal

After having requested the establishment of the tribunal, the new government of Rwanda voted against the resolution creating the court because it was dissatisfied with some of the terms of its mandate. When the Office of the Prosecutor began its work in Rwanda, its staff encountered an atmosphere of general hostility to the U.N. Rwandans in general were disillusioned with its failure to intervene in the genocide and some authorities were dissatisfied with the ongoing operation of various of its agencies. In 1997 the Rwandan government sharply criticized the tribunal. It demanded that Judge Arbour be removed and that a separate prosecutor be designated exclusively to handle cases in Rwanda. Bernard Muna, appointed Deputy Prosecutor at this time, succeeded in improving relations with Rwandan authorities. The new good feeling between the tribunal and the Rwandan government was reflected in a statement made by Vice-President Kagame when the tribunal registrar, Agwu Ukiwe Okali, visited Kigali in July 1998. Kagame noted that his government and the tribunal were "partners," congratulated the tribunal on the significant progress made under difficult circumstances, and offered to provide any assistance needed in the future.[19] When the first verdict was announced in September 1998, however, Gerald Gahima, secretary-general of the Ministry of Justice, again expressed scepticism about the tribunal and declared that had Rwanda received one twentieth of the funds given to the tribunal, it "would have gone a long way towards solving our problems." He remarked, "I think there is something perverse about aspiring to provide good justice for genocide." And he continued, "People should aspire to prevent these crimes, not to punish them adequately after they have been committed."[20]

Beginning in 1996, the deteriorating security situation—the result of a growing insurgency—created new obstacles to investigations and the transport of witnesses needed for trials. Tribunal staff were unable to travel freely, particularly in the western part of the country. Were the tribunal to begin investigating charges

---

[19]United Nations, International Criminal Tribunal for Rwanda, Press Release, ICTR/INFO-9-2-133, July 24, 1998.

[20]Lara Santoro, "For Rwandans, Justice Done Only for Others," *The Christian Science Monitor*, September 11, 1998.

against RPF soldiers, assuring the safety of staff would presumably become even more difficult.

Perhaps more important than relations between the Rwandan government and the tribunal is the comprehension of the work of international justice by the Rwandan people. Conditioned by long experience of courts which operated only to serve the interests of the powerful, Rwandans could benefit from following the work of an independent tribunal which seeks to operate according to the highest standards of impartiality and respect for all parties.

Unfortunately, the tribunal is far from Judge Goldstone's original vision of delivering justice as near the site of the crime as possible. The court chambers at Arusha, even though in a neighboring country, are distant and hard to reach. Travel by car requires many hours over difficult roads. Travel by plane is far beyond the means not just of ordinary people but even of lawyers and other members of the elite. Although proposals to bring Rwandan magistrates, lawyers, victims, and ordinary people to witness the proceedings have been made to Rwandan authorities, tribunal staff, and various foreign aid officials, these suggestions have as yet produced little result. In 1998, some staff from the office of Rwandan prosecutors did finally attend court sessions and Rwandan representatives witnessed the announcement of the judgment against Akayesu, but the general public remains far removed from the proceedings. A plan to bring televised hearings to local communities has as yet to be realized, although, as mentioned above, Radio Rwanda now broadcasts news regularly from Arusha.

Distant in location, the tribunal is also alien in procedure. Rwandans are accustomed to presenting their own complaints to persons in authority, whether in a formal court or before the local burgomaster. Tribunal procedure obliges them to leave the process of accusation and presenting evidence in the hands of a professional legal staff with whom most of them have no contact. In the Rwandan capital, the office of the prosecution staff is well-guarded. Persons without prior appointment or acquaintance with tribunal personnel find it difficult to gain entrance. Reasonable though these precautions may be, they inhibit Rwandans from initiating contacts with staff whom they have never met. Should they be contacted by investigators, Rwandans can usually speak to them only through an interpreter and thus wonder if their real meaning is being communicated. As a result of these circumstances, many victims feel that the entire process has little to do with them and their suffering.

Rwandans are accustomed to a court case being heard in one or two days, with few or no witnesses, and being decided soon after. The lengthy presentation of evidence, complicated by the need to observe extensive safeguards for the rights of the accused, is foreign to them. Since neither the tribunal itself nor Rwandan authorities have successfully explained such aspects of tribunal procedure, most Rwandans see the slow pace of trials as simply one more proof of the inefficiency of the U.N., or worse still, of its indifference to Rwandan needs.

Rwandan law provides for the death penalty. In the years just before the genocide, there were no official executions of condemned criminals, but most Rwandans anticipated that the leaders of the genocide would be executed if found guilty. As with other aspects of court procedure, little has been said to Rwandans to explain why the international tribunal will not condemn those found guilty to death. With Rwandan courts prepared to execute some convicted of genocide even if they never exercised responsibility at high levels, the refusal of the tribunal to execute persons who directed the genocide at national level is doubly incomprehensible to some Rwandans.

According to the statute of the tribunal, the convicted are to serve their sentences in prisons in Rwanda or in other countries, as arranged by the tribunal. As of early 1999, several European and African governments had indicated a willingness to imprison convicted persons in national facilities, but only the government of Mali had signed an agreement with the tribunal.[21] Imprisoning the criminals in European or North American jails would anger those Rwandans who imagine foreign jails to be places of comfort, if not luxury.

The Rwandan Prosecution of Genocide

Justice, important in any orderly society, is arguably even more essential in a society that has suffered the trauma of a genocide. The guilty must be found guilty—and found guilty of crimes that they actually committed. Condemning a person for one crime even if he is in fact responsible for another allows a perpetrator to go unpunished and raises doubts among those who know that the judgment was wrong. To allow the innocent to be wrongly accused or, even worse, to find them guilty of crimes they did not commit makes the judicial process appear to be nothing more than politically-driven, organized reprisals. Without justice, there is no relief—psychological and material—for the victims and there is no hope of reconciliation for the society.

The proper prosecution of the genocide could permit the Rwandan state both to end impunity and to lay the foundation for the rule of law. These trials offer an opportunity to establish the independence of the judicial system from political

---

[21]Fondation Hirondelle, "Le Mali Accepte d'Acceuillir des Personnes Condamnees par le TPIR," February 16, 1999.

influence and to set the courts on the path of respect for the rights of all citizens, whether victims, accused, or neither.

Yet delivering justice after a genocide is extraordinarily difficult because of the enormous scale of the crime and because of the extent of suffering it has caused. Remarkably enough, some Rwandans who have suffered enormously recognize the need for fairness and honesty in judging alleged perpetrators. One woman who was raped during the genocide testified at the international tribunal:

> Not all the Hutu had wild hearts....I cannot say that all the Hutu have killed. There is a difference between Hutu and assassins.[22]

But other Rwandans, including some recently returned from decades in exile as well as some who survived the killing campaign, are not so careful about questions of guilt. In 1996 a professor at the national university published a magazine with a cover photograph of a person sitting in front of a pile of guns. The headline, as well as the article inside, implicated the subject of the photo in the genocide. The person had not been charged, far less convicted of genocide. When a researcher from Human Rights Watch/FIDH asked the professor if the photograph, which appeared to be a montage, was faked, he readily admitted that it was and explained that it had been created by combining an innocuous photograph of the subject with another unconnected photograph of a pile of arms. He added that it did not really matter, since the person in question was clearly guilty anyway. Having decided in his own mind that this person had committed genocide, he then apparently concluded that fairness and honesty were unnecessary in presenting "proofs" against him. The same reasoning seems to move witnesses at some genocide trials who recount events they could not possibly have seen and prosecutors and judges who accept their testimony without question.

Attempting to deliver justice for a genocide could overwhelm even the best organized judiciairy. In Rwanda, even before 1994, the judicial system was weak and subject to outside pressures, with relatively few attorneys, magistrates, and police professionally prepared by the study of the law. During the war, many of those persons were killed, themselves committed genocide, or fled the country. Court buildings, few and poorly equipped, were pillaged and in some cases partially or completely destroyed.

---

[22]Ubutabera, Arusha, No. 24, October 27, 1997, found at http://persoweb.francenet.fr/-intermed.

Beginning soon after the establishment of the new government, foreign donors offered considerable aid, both in funds and in training programs for judges, prosecutors, and other judicial staff. Although the National Assembly refused to accept the help of foreign judges in carrying out genocide trials, the government did accept other kinds of technical assistance provided by the U.N. Human Rights Field Operation, by foreign governments, and nongovernmental organizations, such as Réseau des Citoyens, the first to undertake training programs after the genocide. Courthouses were rebuilt and judges appointed at various levels of the system, including to the Supreme Court and to the supervisory Higher Council of Magistrates. A bar association was established in March 1997, permitting the setting of ethical standards for lawyers and the creation of a mechanism for legal assistance to the indigent.

Soon after the judicial system began to function, military officers, civilian officials, and other influential people began interfering with its operations. The essential issue of judicial independence has not been resolved with the passage of time, with the result that other gains in resources have not brought improvements to the extent anticipated in the functioning of the judicial system.

Legislation

Authorities in the new government sought legislative solutions to deal with the extraordinary number of arrests and projected prosecutions resulting from the genocide. In the first months after the end of the genocide, there were few civilian judicial authorities in place and neither courts nor prosecutors' offices were functioning. In the first efforts to bring the alleged perpetrators to justice, soldiers and others without legal authority to arrest detained thousands of persons without respecting their rights or legal formalities. The National Assembly first attempted to regularize these detentions by a law passed in June 1995, but the Supreme Court declared the statute unconstitutional on several grounds, including that it violated the right of the accused to be presumed innocent. A second law, passed on September 8, 1996, stipulated that such detentions must be regularized by December 31, 1997, and that pre-trial detentions must be limited to six months. As it became clear that the deadline would never be met, a law of December 26, 1997 set December 31, 1999 as the new deadline for regularizing detentions and set the length of pre-trial detention at a maximum of two years.

After long and bitter debate among advocates of different approaches to identifying and punishing those guilty of genocide, the Assembly passed a law on August 30, 1996 to regulate prosecutions for genocide, crimes against humanity, and other crimes committed in connection with them.[23] The law divided the accused into four categories according to the extent of their alleged participation in crimes committed after October 1, 1990 and before December 31, 1994.[24] Category one included the planners, organizers, inciters, supervisors, and leaders of genocide and crimes against humanity, including anyone who acted in a position of authority from the national level down to the level of the cell in political parties, the army, religious organizations, or the militia. It included all those who committed criminal acts or encouraged others to commit them. It also included notorious murderers, those known for the brutality of their crimes, and persons who committed acts of sexual torture.[25]

Category two included the authors of or accomplices in homicides or attacks that resulted in the death of the victim. Category three comprised those who caused serious injury to victims and category four included persons who committed crimes against property.

Those found guilty in category one were liable to punishment up to and including the death penalty. Legislators did not intend the death penalty to be mandatory, as was shown by their deleting the word *gusa* (only) from the kinyarwanda text of the law,[26] but many Rwandans expect that those condemned as category one criminals will be sentenced to death and in practice that has been

---

[23]"The Organic Law of 30 August 1996 on the Organization of the Prosecution of Offences Constituting the Crime of Genocide or Crimes Against Humanity," Government of Rwanda, *Official Journal*, September 1, 1996.

[24]"The Organic Law of 30 August 1996," article 7,2; Daniel de Beer, et al., *Rwanda, The Organic Law of 30 August 1996 on the Organization of the Prosecution of Offences Constituting the Crime of Genocide or Crimes Against Humanity, Commentary* (Alter Egaux Editions, 1997, no place of publication), pp. 41-45 (hereafter cited as *Commentary*).

[25]Although the legislators included crimes of sexual torture among those to be most severely sanctioned, judicial personnel have shown little interest in prosecuting such crimes. As of the end of March 1998, the United Nations Human Rights Field Operation in Rwanda had registered only eleven cases of persons charged with sexual crimes although such crimes were widely reported to have occurred during the genocide. United Nations Human Rights Field Operation in Rwanda, *Report on the Human Rights Situation in Rwanda and the Activities of HRFOR, January-March 1998*, HRFOR/RPF/16/January-March 1998/E, p. 12 (Hereafter cited as UNHRFOR, *Report...January-March 1998*).

[26]De Beer et al, *Commentary*, p. 46, n. 1.

the case. Persons found guilty of category two crimes were to be sentenced to punishment up to life imprisonment. Those convicted in category three were subject to imprisonment and the payment of damages as specified in the ordinary criminal code while those in category four were not to be imprisoned at all but were merely to deliver reparations to their victims in an amount settled by discussion between the parties and with the mediation of their fellow citizens in the community.[27]

Persons convicted in category one are "jointly and severally" liable for all damages caused anywhere in the country, regardless of where they personally committed a crime, while those convicted in other categories are liable for damages resulting from their own acts.[28] In addition, persons convicted in category one lose all civic rights for life, while those in category two may lose the right to vote, to stand for election, to serve as a witness (except for delivering simple factual information), to carry arms, and to serve as a member of the armed forces, as a policeman, or as a teacher. Persons convicted in category three may also lose civic rights for a period of up to twenty years, as provided for in the regular penal code.[29]

The definitions of category one are broad, including such terms as "notorious killers" and those who killed with "excessive malice" and "zeal." This vagueness leaves substantial latitude to prosecutors and judges and introduces the possibility that there may be significant variation from one jurisdiction to another in how the terms are applied. The consequences of assignment to a category are serious, since it is only criminals of category one who are liable to the death penalty.[30]

The chief prosecutor at the Supreme Court Procureur général près la Cour suprême was to publish a first list of persons placed in category one within three months and did so at the end of November 1996. The list of 1,946 names was hastily assembled, apparently by a foreign assistant in the justice ministry on the basis of information supplied by local administrative or judicial authorities. More than a dozen persons listed were dead at the time of publication, including one Tutsi killed in the early days of the genocide. One hundred and forty-three persons

---

[27]"The Organic Law of 30 August 1996," article 8.

[28]Ibid., article 30; De Beer et al, *Commentary*, p. 88.

[29]"The Organic Law of 30 August 1996," article 17; De Beer et al, *Commentary*, p. 47.

[30]De Beer et al, *Commentary*, p. 41; Stef Vandeginste, "Poursuite Des Présumés Responsables du Génocide et des Massacres Devant Les Juridictions Rwandaises," p. 2.

at the head of the list were mostly recognizable leaders of national importance. They were followed by names grouped according to commune. In some communes, local authorities apparently forwarded large numbers of names to the chief prosecutor for inclusion on the list. The commune of Kigoma was represented by 142 names and the commune of Mbogo by 234 names, considerably more than the number of national leaders and more than one tenth of those listed for the entire country. In other regions, authorities were less efficient in providing information to Kigali and some communes where major massacres took place were not mentioned at all or were represented by three or four names. Some persons were identified incompletely, without full name or other details, raising the possibility of future disputes over the identity of the person intended.[31]

In theory, being named on the list of category one does not infringe the presumption of innocence since those named must all be tried and convicted before being pronounced guilty. But many Rwandans assume otherwise, and except for those most scrupulous about legal procedure, consider those named on the list to be guilty. Those whose names are published lose the possibility of reducing their punishment by confessing in the plea-bargaining process established by the law and have no right to appeal having been placed on the list. Despite the importance of the list, it has not been revised in the two years since its publication.[32]

Persons convicted under the genocide law have the right to appeal the verdict, but only on the relatively narrow grounds of errors of law or flagrant errors of fact and only for the brief period of fifteen days after the verdict is handed down.[33]

The genocide law instituted a system of confession and reduced sentences modeled on the U.S. practice of plea-bargaining. If the accused made an apology and a full confession, including details concerning all others involved in the crime, he could benefit from lesser penalties. The extent of the reduction depended on whether or not the confession had been made before the trial had begun. Persons who might be assigned to category one and who confessed before trial could be placed in category two and hence avoid the death penalty, but only if their names had not already been published on the list of category one criminals.

---

[31]Government of Rwanda, *Journal Officiel*, numéro spécial, Novembre 30, 1996.

[32]Government of Rwanda, *Journal Officiel*, numéro spécial, Novembre 30, 1996.

[33]"The Organic Law of 30 August 1996," article 15,2; De Beer et al, *Commentary*, p. 98.

In some cases, the genocide law retained the penalties which were set in the ordinary penal code and in others reduced them. But in certain cases of crimes in category one, including sexual torture, serving as an accomplice to certain crimes, and committing genocide through the exercise of authority, the penalties—up to and including death—are greater than they were before the passage of the genocide law. In these cases, the genocide law seems to have violated the principle of non-retroactivity contained in Article 12 of the Rwandan constitution and in Article 15 of the International Convention on Civil and Political Rights.[34]

According to the law, trials for persons accused of genocide, crimes against humanity, and related crimes were to be held solely in specialized chambers to be created within ordinary civilian or military trial courts.

Detentions

In 1994, the RPF spokesman spoke of trying 2,000 persons for genocide, a figure later raised by judicial authorities to 10,000 and then increased by political leaders to 30,000.[35] In mid-1998, some 135,000 persons were incarcerated in prisons and communal lockups, most of them charged with genocide or related crimes.[36] Even four years after the defeat of the genocidal government and over a year after the end of the massive return of Rwandans who had fled to Zaire, Rwandan authorities were continuing to arrest persons for genocide.

An indeterminate number of those detained have been falsely accused by those who seek their posts or property or who wish retribution for some current or past

---

[34]Whether Article 15 of the ICCPR has been contravened is open to question since it provides that the prohibition of retroactivity must not be taken to inhibit the prosecution of crimes like genocide. It states:

1. No one shall be held guilty of any criminal offence on account of any act or omission which did not constitute a criminal offence, under national or international law, at the time when it was committed. Nor shall a heavier penalty be imposed than the one that was applicable at the time when the criminal offence was committed....

2. Nothing in this article shall prejudice the trial and punishment of any person for any act or omission which, at the time when it was committed, was criminal according to the general principles of law recognized by the community of nations.

[35]Human Rights Watch interview, Kigali, August 28, 1994; Serge Arnold, "Government Considers Amnesty for Militiamen," AFP, September 23, 1994, FBIS-AFR-94-186, September 26, 1994.

[36]Fondation Hirondelle, "Libérations de Suspects du Génocide: Controverses et Vengéances," August 26, 1998.

wrong, real or imagined. In some cases, authorities have wrongly charged political rivals with genocide and imprisoned them without good cause. In 1995, the prosecutor of Kigali estimated that 20 percent of detained persons were innocent;[37] in 1998, the prosecutor of Ruhengeri set the number as 15 percent.[38] Another person in the legal profession acquainted with prison conditions declared that some 60 percent of the persons held in Gitarama prison were either falsely accused or were at most guilty of category four crimes, which do not carry the punishment of a prison sentence.[39] Because the overburdened judicial system has failed to discover and punish false accusations, increasing numbers of people have brought false charges for their own interests. In some cases reported to our researchers, persons have been obliged to pay others in order to avoid being falsely accused and imprisoned or they have been asked to provide a substantial sum of money to officials in order to arrange for the release of a family member.[40] In 1997, two members of the prosecution staff in Ruhengeri and two judicial police inspectors were arrested for corruption and arbitrarily detaining innocent persons.[41]

In 1994, Minister of Justice Alphonse-Marie Nkubito and such subordinates as the prosecutor François-Xavier Nsanzuwera and Judge Gratien Ruhorahoza attempted to limit detentions to those persons for whom there were credible accusations of guilt. They also sought to insist that judicial files be promptly prepared to document charges against the accused. In late 1994, Judge Ruhorahoza "disappeared" after having ordered the release of some forty persons, whom he found had been detained without good cause. He was never seen again and the military promptly rearrested the persons who had been released.[42]

---

[37] Human Rights Watch/FIDH interview, by telephone, Brussels, October 9, 1998.

[38] Charles Sekabaraga, "Jugement Juste et Rapide des Présumés Coupables de Génocide," *Rwanda Liberation,* no. 33, April 18-May 18, 1998.

[39] Human Rights Watch/FIDH interview, June 22, 1998.

[40] Human Rights Watch/FIDH interviews, July 31 and August 10, 1998.

[41] United Nations Human Rights Field Operation in Rwanda, *Report on the Human Rights Situation in Rwanda and the Activities of HRFOR, January-December1997,* HRFOR/RPF/16-An/1/1777/E, p. 30 (hereafter cited as UNHRFOR, *Annual Report 1997*).

[42] Human Rights Watch/Africa, *Rwanda, A New Catastrophe,* vol. 6, no. 12, December 1994, p. 10.

Soon after, the minister of justice ordered the establishment of screening commissions, joint civilian and military committees, to examine cases of detainees who might be liberated. After sporadic activity in several prefectures, the screening commissions were disbanded in 1997 to be replaced by "mobile teams," which moved from one commune to another, supposedly to help prepare judicial files for detainees who had none and to speed the release of those who had been accused without sound basis. The teams, which received minimal training for two weeks, did facilitate the release of several hundred persons in some regions, but in others, such as Butare, Kibungo, and Kigali-rural prefectures they engaged in further large-scale arrests, sometimes together with harsh treatment or actual beatings of detainees.[43] In late 1997 the teams were generally superseded by Council Chambers, *Chambres du Conseil*, an institution that existed before the genocide in which presiding judges held hearings to determine whether detainees should be freed or kept in prison. Sitting in Kibungo, Kigali, Remera, Gikondo, Gitarama, Butare, Rilima, Gikongoro, Cyangugu, Byumba, and Nyanza these panels worked under pressure of the December 31, 1997 deadline described above and sought to dispose of the huge number of cases of persons detained without due process. They released hundreds of detainees, but once the 1997 deadline had been extended two years, their activity diminished to virtually nothing.[44] The panels began working more efficiently again in late 1998 in some areas but as of early 1999, none of the various efforts tried had yet reduced the prison population by any significant amount.

Trials

As the prison population swelled, trials progressed very slowly. The first began at the end of December 1996 and by the end of December 1997, 322 persons had been judged in 105 trials held in the specialized chambers created by the genocide law. Of this number, 111 of the accused were found guilty and sentenced to death while another 109 were condemned to life in prison and eighty-one to shorter terms. Nineteen persons were acquitted.[45]

---

[43]UNHRFOR, *Annual Report 1997*, p. 9.

[44]Fondation Hirondelle, "Liberation de Suspects du Génocide: Controverses et Vengeances," August 22, 1998; Avocats sans Frontières, Rapport Annuel 1997, pp. 17-18.

[45]UNHRFOR, *Annual Report 1997*, p. 26.

Acknowledging the extraordinarily slow rate of trials—a pace which would require literally hundreds of years before judging all those detained—Rwandan authorities set a goal of trying 5,000 persons during 1998. To this end, they began prosecuting larger groups of defendants together, the largest of which was fifty-one persons tried in the prefecture of Byumba. This practice offered some hope of disposing more rapidly of cases, but the confusion and logistical problems in dealing with such a large number of defendants at one time may prejudice the rights of some of them.[46] The Rwandan government stated that during 1998 courts had judged 864 persons, a considerable improvement over the previous year but still far short of their announced goal.

Prosecutorial staff often prepared cases extremely slowly, a circumstance which was only partly explained by the difficult conditions under which they often work. Many judicial police inspectors, those charged with doing on the spot investigation, lacked any means of transportation to get them quickly to the sites where they need to work. They sometimes did not appear at court or were not prepared and had to request a postponement.[47] Judges, too, were often absent from court, forcing postponements. According to one evaluation, some 60 percent of judicial hearings were postponed in the first half of 1998, about half of them for good reason, such as allowing the defendant to seek counsel or to prepare his defense, and the rest because of absenteeism, poor preparation of judicial personnel, or logistical problems.[48] Judicial staff are poorly paid, with judges earning only about U.S.$70 a month. In 1997, judicial salaries were subsidized by the U.N. Development Program, but this support finished at the end of 1997. To

---

[46]Human Rights Watch/FIDH, notes from trial observations, January to August, 1998; UNHRFOR *Report...January-March 1998,* p. 13; Ligue Rwandaise pour la Promotion et la Défense des Droits de l'Homme, Centre de Documentation et d'Information sur les Procès de Génocide, "Proces de Genocide: Un Nouvel Elan," July 1998, pp. 2-3 (Hereafter cited as CDIPG, "Procès"). The limited availability of lawyers will hinder efforts to speed up the trials. With only ten to fifteen lawyers available nationwide (see below), those involved at a large group trial will be unable to appear at other trials where they were scheduled to represent clients and those trials will have to be postponed.

[47]One small nongovernmental organization, Legal Aid Rwanda, assisted prosecutors in 1998 by meeting with more than 450 detainees at Kigali central prison, helping to clear up questions about their legal files. Higher officials at the ministry of justice, however, gave a negative evaluation to the project and its staff left Rwanda.

[48]The assessment apparently did not include the jurisdictions of Gisenyi, Ruhengeri and Kibuye. Avocats sans Frontières, *Rapport, 1 semestre 1998*, p. 15.

make the situation worse, judicial personnel did not receive even their regular salaries at least from December 24, 1997 through the end of March 1998, apparently because of the establishment of new procedures for payment.[49] Inadequate compensation, the overwhelming nature and scale of the work, and the risks involved in prosecuting the genocide help explain why judicial personnel fail to perform at maximum efficiency.

In the first trials for genocide, the accused were not represented by counsel, a situation which was strongly criticized by local and international human rights groups as well as by the U.N. Human Rights Field Operation. Soon after, the Belgian-based nongovernmental organization Avocats sans Frontières began providing foreign lawyers, many of whom were from other African countries. Of the forty-five who participated in 1997, most assisted defendants accused of genocide, but some also counseled victims who were seeking damages as civil claimants.[50] Between ten and twelve lawyers from Avocats sans Frontières were in Rwanda in early 1998, a figure that increased to between sixteen and twenty later in the year.[51] In 1998 several Rwandan lawyers also agreed to defend persons accused of genocide, a step that most had refused to take before, but even so, this meant that ordinarily there were fifteen or fewer lawyers available at any one time to assist persons charged with genocide. Some 56 percent of defendants in criminal trials during 1997 had no counsel, many of them in regions where local insecurity inhibited travel. None of the defendants in Kibuye was assisted by a lawyer and only about 20 percent of the accused in Ruhengeri and Gisenyi had representation at their trials. In contrast, 92 percent of those tried in the capital had legal advice.[52]

When trials began, many judges were completely inexperienced and had just completed a four month-long training program. Not surprisingly, many made errors, some of which violated the rights of the defendants. In some cases, for

---

[49]UNHRFOR *Report...January-March 1998,*p. 14.

[50]As in other countries using civil law, Rwanda permits civil complainants to make their case for damages as part of the criminal proceedings.

[51]Avocats sans Frontières, *Rapport, 1 semestre 1998*, p. 6. Persons other than lawyers are permitted to represent others in legal proceedings. The Danish Center for Human Rights provided the funds to train one hundred paralegal assistants who had completed training in early 1999.

[52]United Nations, High Commissioner for Human Rights Field Operation in Rwanda, Genocide Trials to 31 October 1997, HRFOR/STRPT/59/2, 19 December 1997/E.

example, they failed to inform the defendant of his right to have legal counsel or they refused to grant a postponement to permit the defendant to consult his file. In many of the early trials, neither the prosecution nor the defense presented witnesses and the judgment was based solely on the written file, including a summary of evidence by the prosecutor, and on any comments or responses made by the defendant. According to Rwandan law, prosecutors have the duty to seek out and present evidence that might establish the innocence of defendants, but they rarely did so.[53]

With experience, continued training, and criticism by attorneys who appeared before them, some judges have improved in the performance of their duties. They have shown greater willingness to grant postponements, such as to enable a defendant to seek counsel or to prepare his defense. Some conscientious judges have sought to resolve contradictions in witness testimony, even if doing so requires them to visit the site of the crime.[54] Other judges, however, still make no apparent effort to examine contradictions in testimony between witnesses—or even within the testimony of a single individual—and appear ready to accept without question any statement made by witnesses for the prosecution.[55]

Respect for the rights of the defendants and the victims, like the general decorum and efficiency of the proceedings, vary considerably from one courtroom to the next. The trials of the MDR leader Froduald Karamira and that of two soldiers and a civilian in a special chamber of a military court in Butare appear to have been conducted according to international standards of due process. In others, like that of Silas Munyagishali, there were apparently procedural errors as well as the intimidation of defense witnesses, and in the case of Dr. Geoffrey Gatera, judges failed to keep order and allowed the blatant harassment of the defense lawyer and of witnesses.[56]

Prosecutors have called witnesses to help establish proof of guilt with growing frequency. In 1997, witnesses testified for the prosecution in 63 percent of the trials. Defendants ordinarily made use of their right to examine these witnesses only if they had a lawyer present to assist them. In 1997, defendants presented

---

[53]Avocats sans Frontières, *Rapport, 1 semestre 1998*, p. 9.

[54]CDIPG, "Procès," p. 4.

[55]Human Rights Watch/FIDH interviews, May and June 1998 and notes from trial observations, 1998.

[56]Ibid.

witnesses on their behalf in about 18 percent of the cases.[57] In some cases, they were unaware that they had the right to do so. In other instances, they were unable to contact potential witnesses or to persuade them to appear. In one case documented by our researchers, a defense witness changed his testimony under pressure and falsely inculpated the defendant. The defendant was found guilty and condemned to death. The witness later went to beg the pardon of the defendant's wife and family.[58] In a case recorded by the U.N. Human Rights Field Operation, a witness who testified in defense of Jean-Baptiste Sebarame, a member of the assembly charged with genocide, was arrested by a judicial police inspector from the office of the Kigali prosecutor. He was detained from January 27 to February 15, 1998, without being charged with any crime. During this time, he was reportedly beaten severely and told to change his testimony to inculpate Sebarame.[59] *national courts*

Witnesses sometimes fail to appear at trials because they have not been informed in time or because they have found it too difficult to get there. In some cases, judges have moved proceedings to locations where witnesses will find it easier to come forward. In general this is an initiative worth encouraging if arrangements are made for the defendant to be present. In some cases, judges have held sessions away from the court chambers without the defendant and even without the prosecutor.[60]

Witnesses also refuse to testify for fear of reprisals. This may happen more often with those asked to present evidence for the defense, but it also happens with people asked to testify for the prosecution.[61] Judges, prosecutors and other members of the judiciary, as well as lawyers, also feel at risk because of their involvement in the genocide trials. Two Rwandan attorneys working with Avocats sans Frontières, Innocent Murengezi and André Ndikumana, were the victims of crimes that may have been linked to their willingness to defend persons accused of genocide. Murengezi disappeared in February 1997 and has never been found and Ndikumana was strangled, along with one of his household staff, in January 1998.

---

[57]UNHRFOR, *Annual Report 1997*, p. 27.

[58]Human Rights Watch/FIDH interview, August, 1998.

[59]UNHRFOR *Report...January-March 1998*, p. 11.

[60]Avocats sans Frontières, *Rapport, 1 semestre 1998*, p. 18.

[61]CDIPG, "Procès," pp. 3-4.

Another attorney working with Avocats sans Frontières received both written and oral threats in the course of his defense of Jean-Baptiste Sebarame, whose case is mentioned above.[62]

Material Compensation

The victims of genocide have the right to have their property returned and to be compensated, as far as is possible, for other losses, whether material or more abstract. Hundreds of thousands have been left destitute by the genocide, including many of the 300,000 children who now live without adult protection in households headed by minors and many of the women now solely responsible for the wellbeing of their households.[63] Some survivors, generally those based in urban centers, understand their right to damages from criminals who have harmed them or their families and have filed the necessary papers in court to receive compensation. Those who are in touch with organized groups formed to protect the interests of survivors understand best the procedures involved. In 1997, 27 percent of civil claimants were represented by lawyers in court.[64]

Often those most in need of compensation, such as elderly widows and children, are least informed or least able to act in their own interests and fail to claim damages at the appropriate time. In some cases, they live too far from court to appear or they are unaware that the case is being heard. In such cases, the court may set aside an amount of damages for claimants who have not yet made themselves known, but if it does not, those persons will never receive compensation.

In contrast, some survivors have learned how to exploit the system to their advantage and request damages from defendants who never harmed them. In one case that took place in Butare in 1998, a person filed for damages merely because the accused were charged with crimes that had taken place in her neighborhood the

---

[62]Ibid., p. 4; UNHRFOR *Report....January-March 1998*, p. 11.

[63]Doug Schwarz, "Rwanda's Orphans Find a Home—With One Another," *Christian Science Monitor,* May 12, 1998. Some 34 percent of Rwandan households are headed by women, but of course they are not all survivors of the genocide. United Nations, Commission on Human Rights, *Further Promotion and Encouragement of Human Rights and Fundamental Freedoms, Including the Work of the Commission: Report of the Special Rapporteur on violence against women, its causes and consequences, Addendum, Report of the Mission to Rwanda,* E/CN/4/1998/54/Add.1, February 4, 1998, p. 6.

[64]UNHRFOR, *Annual Report 1997*, p. 27; CDIPG, "Procès," p. 6.

same week her own residence had been attacked. She had no indication that the assailants involved had ever been at her residence. Some judges are extremely lenient in such cases and award damages without requiring a link to be established between the defendants and the supposed losses.[65] Persons convicted of category one crimes are liable for damages throughout Rwanda, as mentioned above, but no effort has yet been made to implement such compensation. The National Assembly has established an assistance fund for survivors, but its aid will be distributed according to need, not according to damages legally awarded.[66]

In 1995, administrators in some regions began encouraging the local settlement of claims by survivors against perpetrators of genocide through a customary process known as *gacaca*. Supposedly the result of negotiation between the injured party and the perpetrators, the process often took place before a community gathering. In case of subsequent conflict over the arrangement, the injured party could take the case to court to insist on its implementation.[67] Rwandan authorities reportedly began talking in late 1998 of using the procedure also to judge persons accused of causing injury or even death to others during the genocide, an extension of customary practice which would raise questions of due process for the accused.

The Executions of April 1998

In late April 1998, the Rwandan government carried out the executions of twenty-two people condemned to death for having led or participated in the genocide. The executions took place in public stadiums in several towns. Those in the capital attracted thousands of spectators, who watched the executions in a noisy, celebratory mood. Many expressed their satisfaction at the executions. Authorities had encouraged the public to attend, citing the "educational" effect of watching the condemned be executed.

Many international political and religious leaders as well as human rights organizations asked that the executions not be carried out and protested when they did take place. Human Rights Watch and FIDH oppose the death penalty because of its inherent cruelty and because no judicial system is free from the possibility of error. An error in a case resulting in capital punishment obviously can never be corrected. This logic is particularly compelling in the Rwandan situation where the

---

[65]Human Rights Watch/FIDH notes from trial observations, May-June, 1998.

[66]Avocats sans Frontières, *Rapport, 1 semestre 1998*, p. 20.

[67]Human Rights Watch/FIDH, notes from trial observations, May 10, 1998.

inexperience of the judges, the inadequate investigations by prosecutors, and the strongly emotional atmosphere of a post-genocide society increase the possibility that errors will occur. Many observers, Rwandan and foreign, believe, for example, that the guilt of former prosecutor Silas Munyagishali was not proven in the trial which resulted in his condemnation. He was one of those executed in April 1998. Several of the condemned had not had the benefit of counsel during their trials.

According to the Arusha Accords, the Rwandan government was bound to ratify all international human rights conventions, including the Second Optional Protocol to the International Convention on Civil and Political Rights, which abolishes the death penalty. Although the first minister of justice in the new government, Alphonse-Marie Nkubito, tried to persuade the government to fulfill its obligation to ratify the protocol, it refused to do so.

Among those condemned to death in 1998 but not yet executed is the husband of a Tutsi woman who lost all of her family except her husband and children during the genocide. She told our researchers that he was found guilty on the basis of testimony from witnesses who had been paid to lie against him, but she will not speak publicly about the perjury. Her husband insists that she remain silent to protect their children and she agrees with him that protecting their lives must take priority.

Confessions

In the first year after the genocide law was passed and the accused were offered the chance to confess in return for a reduction in punishment, fewer than sixty persons took advantage of the plea-bargaining opportunity. The number increased in 1998, particularly after the first executions. By the end of 1998, 8,615 people had begun the process of making confessions. Others refused to do so, citing mistrust of governmental authorities or fear of reprisals against themselves or members of their families. Some fear reprisals from fellow prisoners because in most prisons those who confess are not separated from the rest of the prison population.[68]

The confession procedure, even if it became widely used by detainees, would not quickly reduce the prison population. Each confession has to be examined by prosecutorial staff to determine its veracity and by judges to determine if the

---

[68]Neil Boisen, "Knowledge, Attitudes and Practices Among Inmates of Rwandan Detention Facilities Accused of Crimes of Genocide," The United States Institute of Peace, November 1997.

appropriate procedure has been followed. This process demands time and resources, although clearly somewhat less than a trial.

As authorities increase efforts to obtain confessions, even innocent persons may choose to "confess," particularly if they believe that doing so will bring them a faster release from prison. Such erroneous "confessions" of course will do nothing to advance the cause of justice: they will result in punishment of persons for crimes they did not commit and they may discourage efforts to find and prosecute the real perpetrators of the crimes.

Conditions in Prisons and Communal Lockups

In 1996 and 1997 Rwandan authorities expanded old prisons and opened new ones, temporarily relieving some of the overcrowding which had produced inhumane and in some cases life-threatening conditions in prior years. In the early months of 1998, however, thousands of prisoners previously housed in communal lockups were moved to central prisons, causing conditions there to deteriorate once more.[69] Conditions in the communal lockups are worse than those in the central prisons. The facilities are severely overcrowded and lack light, ventilation, and toilet facilities. In the first three months of 1998, 405 detainees died in central prisons and communal lockups. The International Committee of the Red Cross provides food at the central prisons but detainees at the communal lockups are supposed to be fed by their families. In households where the only adult male is detained, women often have great difficulty preparing and delivering food to communal jails, sometimes far removed from their homes, and at the same time cultivating the crops to feed children and others in the family. In the early months of 1998, U.N. monitors found that about two-thirds of the detainees were receiving no food from their families. The International Committee of the Red Cross provided high-protein biscuits in some communal lockups but in only three of eleven prefectures.[70]

Conditional Release

Rwandan authorities have expressed serious concern about the numbers of people detained. In August 1997, Vice-President Kagame declared that in addition to prisoners whose guilt is clear, there are others whose files have been lost or never even been opened. He continued:

[69]Avocats sans Frontières, *Rapport, 1 semestre 1998*, p. 15.

[70]UNHRFOR *Report. . . January-March 1998*, p. 16.

There is an incomprehensible situation, and this is the most essential: there are innocent people, arbitrarily detained. Justice must be done for these innocent people; no one should be unjustly detained.[71]

In addition to being wrong, keeping the innocent in prison is costly in terms of dollars and wasted human resources. The international community now supports the cost of feeding prisoners in the central prisons, a sum of more than U.S.$18 million per year, but presumably it will eventually require the Rwandan government to assume this expense. While the cost of maintaining the guilty in prison is a necessary expense in the interests of justice, it makes no sense to pay for detaining the innocent. Unjustified detentions are also politically costly, undermining the legitimacy of the government with those whose relatives and friends are the victims of injustice.

In July 1998, nearly a year after Kagame's statement and with the prison population still larger, authorities of the RPF talked about the possibility of releasing large numbers of detainees, perhaps as many as 80,000 people. They foresaw the provisional release of those accused in categories two, three, and four, including people who aided and abetted the genocide but did not actively participate in it.[72] Even were authorities to release only persons from category four, for whom punishment by imprisonment was never prescribed, this would reduce the prison population by a very significant number. The possibility of a massive release was not raised again until early October 1998, when the minister of justice once again told the press that ten thousand detainees might be provisionally released. He made clear that those persons would eventually be tried. In early December seventy-six persons were released, the first to be liberated under this plan.

The RPF authorities recognized that any large-scale release would first require substantial preparation of public opinion.[73] The return to their communities of released detainees or persons acquitted after trial—even discussion of plans for such release—has often resulted in demonstrations by survivors or those who purport to speak in the name of survivors. In a number of cases, those released or

---

[71]Fondation Hirondelle, "Liberation de Suspects du Génocide."

[72]Agence France Presse, "Release Considered for 80,000 Rwandans Held for Genocide," July 22, 1998.

[73]Ibid.

acquitted have been harassed by their neighbors. In one case investigated by Human Rights Watch and FIDH, an elderly man twice arrested and twice released chose to spend his days hidden at home rather than leave his house and risk insults or worse from others in the neighborhood.[74] In another case, researchers found that a child released from prison shortly before had been beaten by neighbors.[75] Persons provisionally released from detention were reportedly killed in Cyangugu and in December 1996 twenty-four persons who had been released were said to have been killed in several communes of Butare.[76] In August 1998 in the prefecture of Gitarama assailants killed thirteen persons in the household of a man who had recently been acquitted of genocide.[77] Many detainees continue, nonetheless, to have faith that their neighbors can discriminate between the innocent and the guilty and do not fear release.[78] To assure their safety, authorities must be prepared to act firmly and promptly to halt and punish any attacks on them.

Delivering justice for the genocide will continue to require extensive resources and a great deal of time. Large-scale provisional release of those against whom there is no credible evidence of guilt and those accused of category four offenses would at least signal the determination of Rwandan authorities to take decisive action. This in combination with improved efficiency in distributing resources throughout the system might encourage judicial personnel to work harder. Increased international technical assistance for judges, prosecutors, and other judicial personnel might also give renewed impetus to Rwandan authorities who are currently overwhelmed by the task.

Foreign Prosecutions and Other Proceedings

Rwandans implicated in the genocide began arriving in Europe and elsewhere in Africa even as the slaughter was going on, but judicial authorities in these areas have shown little determination to prosecute them. To do so means creating the necessary precedents and implementing hitherto untested criminal legislation. To invoke jurisdiction outside of Rwanda in common criminal cases would usually

---

[74]Human Rights Watch/FIDH interview, Gitarama, July 13, 1996.

[75]Human Rights Watch/FIDH interview, Kibungo, February 10, 1998.

[76]Fondation Hirondelle, "Liberation de Suspects du Génocide."

[77]Ibid.

[78]Boisen, "Knowledge, Attitudes and Practices Among Inmates."

require that either the perpetrator or the victim be of the same nationality as the prosecuting authority. But these criteria do not apply in many of these genocide cases where both accused and victim are Rwandan and where the crimes were committed on Rwandan soil. In most cases, prosecutions would involve reliance on the principle of universal jurisdiction, the right to prosecute certain crimes recognized by international law as so heinous as to require prosecution without regard to the site of the crime, when it took place, or the nationality of the accused or the victim.

The first legal action related to the genocide was undertaken in the U.S. in a civil rather than in a criminal court. An imaginative interpretation of a nineteenth-century law had established the precedent in the Filartiga case of suing human rights abusers for civil damages, even if neither abuser nor victim were U.S. citizens and even if the crime were not committed in the U.S. When Jean-Bosco Barayagwiza, the head of the CDR, came to New York in May 1994 to present the case of the Rwandan government to the U.N., Human Rights Watch used this precedent to sue him in the name of several Rwandans resident in the U.S. and related to persons killed in the genocide. Judge John Martin of the Second District Court in New York returned a strong verdict against Barayagwiza in April 1996. Declaring that he had never judged a case where monetary damages so inadequately compensated for the suffering inflicted, he ordered Barayagwiza to pay a total of U.S.$105 million to the Rwandan plaintiffs. Although the plaintiffs are unlikely ever to receive any of this money, the judgment was a strong symbolic statement, the clearest verdict that a U.S. court is likely to deliver on the Rwandan genocide.

In July 1994, several Rwandans and members of their families filed complaints with Belgian judicial authorities against four Rwandans, two burgomasters and two political leaders, then resident in Belgium. The four were arrested and two of them were later transferred to the International Tribunal which took over their prosecution. Belgian judicial authorities, initially slow to investigate the complaints, were stung to action by public protests by complainants and their attorneys. They assigned an examining magistrate who carried out extensive investigations in Belgium, Rwanda, and Arusha, but none of the prosecutions of those still in Belgium has been carried through to the stage of a trial. This delay, as well as an unexpected change in position by the Brussels prosecutor, who asked that the charges in one case be dropped, have raised questions about whether political influence has impeded the judicial process. In any case, in late 1998 the

Ministry of Justice suggested that the costs involved made any prosecutions for genocide unlikely.[79]

Also in Belgium, several Rwandan genocide victims, as well as the families of the Belgian peacekeepers killed in Rwanda, have taken the extraordinary step of filing complaints against Léo Delcroix and Willy Claes, respectively minister of national defense and minister of foreign affairs at the time of the genocide. They rely upon the strong language of a 1993 statute which specifically attributes to Belgian jurisdiction the right to prosecute serious violations of the 1949 Geneva Conventions regardless of the place of the crime or the nationality of the accused and the victim. The law defines as a crime not just the commission of such acts but also the failure to act by those who know such crimes are planned or have begun, who have the possibility to act to prevent or halt them, and who do not do so.

In France, charges have been brought against only one person, the priest Wenceslas Munyeshyaka. After his arrest, a French court held that it had no competence to try his case. This decision was later reversed by the Appeals Court of Nîmes. In January 1998, the Cour dc Cassation upheld the decision of the Appeals Court, ruling that the case could be tried on the basis of the 1984 Convention Against Torture and Other Cruel, Inhumane, or Degrading Treatment or Punishment, which has been incorporated into French criminal law. The case was returned to the trial court but has not been heard. Munyeshyaka is at liberty in France.

Swiss authorities arrested Alfred Musema, a politician and businessman, and later transferred his case to the International Tribunal. In 1998, authorities began proceeedings under Swiss law against a Rwandan burgomaster. Because violations of the genocide convention figure in military rather than civilian law in Switzerland, he will be tried by a military tribunal.

Canada has thus far undertaken no criminal proceedings, but, after a long hearing, an administrative arbiter decided that Léon Mugesera had incited to genocide by his notorious 1992 speech in northwestern Rwanda and ordered him expelled from Canada. The decision was appealed. In November 1998, an administrative tribunal heard new witnesses and confirmed the expulsion order with a decision of some one hundred pages. Mugesera has asked for the case to be further reviewed by federal court, but no action has yet been taken.

When an European Union (E.U.) delegation visited Rwanda in June 1998, British Minister of State Tony Lloyd said that E.U. countries were discussing how to ensure "that every suspected genocide perpetrator is arrested in every country

---

[79]Human Rights Watch/FIDH interview, by telephone, Brussels, October 9, 1998.

of the E.U."[80] Dozens of such suspects are now living in Europe and North America. Hundreds of others are in various African countries. Although many African governments have arrested suspects who were then transferred to the international tribunal, none has yet indicated a willingness to begin genocide trials in their own courts. Most cite lack of resources to undertake such prosecutions. Were other governments to offer either technical assistance or funds to support such trials, the judgment of alleged perpetrators in African courts could have considerable impact in the region.

Taking Responsibility

In May 1994, U.N. Secretary-General Boutros-Ghali admitted that the international community had failed the people of Rwanda in not halting the genocide. From that time through 1998, when U.S. President Bill Clinton apologized for not having responded to Rwandan cries for help and Secretary-General Kofi Annan expressed regret in vaguer terms, various world leaders have acknowledged responsibility for their failure to intervene in the slaughter. The archbishop of Canterbury has apologized on behalf of the Anglican church and the pope has called for clergy who are guilty to have the courage to face the consequences of their crimes.

Members of the Belgian Senate were the first to initiate an examination of the failures of their political leaders during the genocide. Spurred by a probing report by a preliminary ad hoc commission and by pressure from the families of the slain peacekeepers, the senators launched a broad inquiry into Belgian policy and actions during the genocide. After long hearings, they produced an extensive report in 1997 which lays out the successive errors in policy but does not treat the personal responsibility of the decision makers.

The next year, members of the French National Assembly investigated the policies of France, other foreign actors, and the U.N. in Rwanda, but unlike the Belgian senators, they did not take testimony under oath and they heard many important witnesses in closed session. In a report published at the end of 1998, they recognized that the French government had erred in supporting a government bent on genocide. They published less pertinent information on how decisions were made than did their Belgian counterparts and thus remained even further removed from establishing accountability for various political and military leaders.

---

[80]United Nations, Office for the Coordination of Humanitarian Affairs, Integrated Regional Information Network for Central and Eastern Africa, Update no. 429 for Central and Eastern Africa, June 3, 1998.

The Sub-Committee on International Operations and Human Rights of the International Relations Committee of the U.S. House of Representatives tried in May 1998 to investigate U.S. policy during the genocide in Rwanda, but only Richard McCall of U.S.A.I.D., the U.S. foreign assistance agency, gave testimony. Other senior officials from the State and Defense Departments declined to attend. No serious efforts have been made within the State Department to examine why decisions were made or what consequences they produced during the genocide.

The United Nations examined the conduct of its peacekeeping operation in Rwanda, but the inquiry focused more on the technical and logistical aspects of UNAMIR than on the larger issue of responsibilities of senior U.N. officials and of member states in failing to act vigorously to avert or halt the genocide. U.N. authorities permitted General Dallaire and Captain Lemaire to testify at the international tribunal but only on a limited range of questions. Otherwise, the U.N. has indicated that U.N. personnel will not be permitted to testify in such national investigations as that of the Belgian Senate.

These inquiries and others by the press and human rights organizations have revealed something of the roles played by individuals who were in positions of national or international authority during the genocide. Much of the truth remains hidden, however, by the laws, regulations and practices long used to protect political leaders from accountability. With the exception of the complaints against former ministers Delcroix and Claes in Belgium, no effort has been made to hold policymakers personally and legally responsible for refusing to halt the slaughter. Researchers must continue trying to go beyond the relatively painless, generalized confessions of political leaders to analyze the decisions taken by individuals, so that those persons can be obliged to acknowledge their responsibilities at least in the public domain, if not in a court of law. Only in this way can we hope to influence decision makers in the future to never again abandon a people to genocidal slaughter.

On several occasions, Rwandans and foreigners proposed some kind of truth commission to gather the accounts of survivors or to hear the confessions of the guilty. In June 1998, the Organization of African Unity created such a panel to inquire into the Rwandan genocide. It may provide an opportunity for at least some survivors to be heard who still believe their voices are ignored in the world community and even in their own country. By exposing the responsibilities of Rwandans and foreign leaders in the catastrophe, the commission may help deter other leaders in Africa and elsewhere in the world from following a similar disastrous course.

Conclusion

The Rwandan genocide stands alone for the way its organizers aimed to mobilize mass participation in murder. Far from hiding their objective, they advertised their goal of exterminating the Tutsi citizens of Rwanda in song and chant, through the press and over the radio. They exhorted Hutu to join the killing campaign, insisting that it "concerned everyone." They carried out the worst massacres in broad daylight and in many communities they left the dead in full view.

By focusing fear and hatred on the Tutsi, the organizers hoped to forge solidarity among Hutu. But beyond that, they also aimed at creating collective responsibility for the genocide. People were encouraged to kill together, just as soldiers in a firing squad are ordered to discharge their weapons simultaneously so that no one should bear individual or total responsibility for the execution. "No one person killed any one person," said one of the participants.

The leaders of the genocide, experienced at wielding power, knew how to use the state machinery and their network of personal contacts to mobilize large numbers of people. They expected to succeed and had planned carefully for the operation. With their quick, ruthless murders of political opponents that began on April 6, they intimidated the remaining dissidents. Then, strengthened by their apparent acceptance as a legitimate government by the international community, they pushed ahead with a speed and ease that may have exceeded their own expectations. By two weeks into the campaign, they had slain hundreds of thousands of Tutsi and squashed any significant open dissent.

But ultimately they failed in their goal of total mobilization for extermination. Hundreds of thousands of Hutu who lacked the courage or resources to openly oppose them resisted passively, most by withdrawing from political and community life, a few by working within the system to restrain its excesses.

Among those who did carry out genocide, actors participated in many ways: from the national leaders who aimed to extirpate the Tutsi down to the level of ordinary people who showed no taste for violence but wanted only to enrich themselves through pillage. As the roles varied, so did the motivations of the actors, some moved by virulent hatred, others by real fear, by ambition, by greed, by a desire to escape injury at the hands of those who demanded they participate, or by the wish to avoid fines for nonparticipation that they could not hope to pay. Whatever the role, whatever the motivation, participants must accept responsibility and be appropriately punished.

Outside Rwanda, most international leaders found mass slaughter of Tutsi tolerable provided it furthered or at least did not impinge on narrowly defined national interests. Many of their subordinates would not risk loss of favor and future advancement by arguing a moral position contrary to the course advocated by the powerful. A small number of foreigners did fight passionately to stop the slaughter, some in humanitarian and human rights organizations, some in governments and the U.N. An even smaller number struggled to save lives courageously within Rwanda.

Accurate accounts of the genocide must establish in all their complexity the roles of the leaders, the followers, and the dissidents within Rwanda as well as the parts played by various international actors. This is essential both for assessing fairly the behavior of individuals and for creating strategies for the future. We must find ways to increase the numbers and effectiveness of resisters against such crimes, whether within or outside the society at risk. We must understand how local and international protest can resonate back and forth to create the swell of outrage that will prevent or halt future genocides.

This work is one of the many that must come to establish the historical record, to lay the groundwork for justice for Rwandans and accountability for all others who failed to respond to the bonds of our common humanity. The story must be told.

INDEX

abakada, 702

Abakombozi, 55, 310

accomplices, see also ibyitso, 3, 5, 8, 31, 50, 59, 75, 76, 85, 89, 100, 103, 139, 142, 161, 190, 215, 228, 232, 250, 257, 270, 272, 278, 317, 322, 348, 365, 372, 411-2, 437, 441, 741

"accusation in a mirror", 66, 70, 80, 171, 227, 256, 649

ADL (Association Rwandaise pour la Défense des Droits de la Personne et des Libertés Publiques), 51, 92, 631, 713

African Rights, 725

AICF (Action Internationale Contre La Faim), 464

Akayesu, Jean-Paul 274-75, 744, 746

akazu, 44- 45, 62, 68, 103, 104, 196, 200, 223, 242, 260, 282, 305, 310, 317

Albania, 636, 649, 651

Albright, Madeleine, 631

Amahoro stadium, 167, 618, 630, 710, 712, 717

Amasasu, 103, 111, 129, 139, 231, 278

Amnesty International, 169

Angola, 167

Annan, Kofi, 152, 156, 601-02, 604-06, 650, 728-30, 732, 768

Anyidoho, Henry Kwami, 621

apostolic nuncio, 177

Arbour, Judge Louise, 739, 745

Archbishop of Kigali, see Nsengiyumva, Vincent

ARDHO (Association Rwandaise pour la Défense des Droits de

l'Homme), 51, 92, 145

Argentina, 19, 26, 175, 639, 643

Arms Division, Human Rights Watch, 28, 661

Arusha Accords, 61, 62, 84, 88, 96, 103, 105, 108, 120, 123-126, 130-32, 141, 148, 153, 157, 161-63, 169-70, 175, 178-81, 192, 194, 196, 619, 654, 655, 668, 697, 762

ASF (Avocats sans Frontières), 757, 759

Aspergen, Judge Lennard, 739, 741

AVP (Association des Volontaires de la Paix), 92, 143, 166

Bagambiki, 676

Bagaragaza, Michel, 200

Bagogwe, 32, 88, 90, 122

Bagosora, Théoneste, 5-7, 9, 11, 44, 103-8, 125-126, 128-29, 139, 172, 183, 185-87, 189-205, 208, 223-24, 228, 231, 261, 264, 267, 278-79, 281-82, 284, 286-87, 359, 425, 434, 595, 608-09, 633, 640, 652, 656, 662, 688, 744

Bahima, 32, 50, 79

Bakiga, 197, 303

Balladur, Edouard, 124, 670, 672

Bantu, 36, 72-3, 79-80

Baptist Church, 44, 355, 360, 364, 378, 396

bar association, 749

Baravuga, Laurent, 226, 437, 474-75

Barayagwiza, Jean-Bosco, 69, 126, 128, 158, 199, 222n., 285 and CDR militia, 199, 228-9; received by French 285, 658, 662, indicted by ICTR, 744; at U.N., 642; Human

Rights Watch sues, 191, n., 766
Baril, Maurice, 150, 173, 598
Barril, Captain Paul, 184-5, 665-68, 675
Batakanwa, Célestin, 360, 372, 410, 417, 420
Bavugamenshi, Lt. Col. Innocent, 187-88, 210, 267, 302, 689
Bazaramba, François, 360, 364, 366, 374, 383, 396-97, 401, 410, 417
Belgium, 2, 7, 17-19, 21-2, 28, 652, 732, 737, 740, 757, 769; Arusha Accords, 120, 124; threats and killings of Belgians, 184, 187, 189-91, 626, 200; colonial administration, 34-9; coordination of policy with U.S., 495-6, 622, 629-30; embargo, 286; evacuation, 603-8, 611-12; ETO, 615-8; interim government, 242, 245, 255, 543, 605, 635; mandate, 153, 161, 164-5, 169, 618; military aid, 50, 142, 267; public opinion, 619-20; response to warnings, 150-56, 176-7; UNAMIR troops and genocide, 598-600, 610-12, withdrawal, 618-23, 625
Bemeriki, Valérie, 70, 246, 253, 254-5, 373, 532, 542, 678
Benebikira, 492, 501, 504, 536, 545, 551
Benigna, Sister, 247
Bicamumpaka, Jérôme, 285, 450, 642, 658, 662, 683
Bigabiro, Maj. Sam, 709, 733
Bigogwe military camp, 88, 248, 266-67, 666-67, 675
Bikindi, Simon, 77, 83, 107, 315,

480
Biniga, Damien, 307-09, 311-12, 314-15, 332, 368, 370-71, 383, 392, 428, 532
Biramvu, Jean-Paul, 616
Birara, Jean, 163
Bisesero, 12, 16, 23, 216-21, 230, 295, 302, 549, 679, 680-82, 689
Bitare, 399, 401, 488, 495-96
Bivambagara, Maj. Protais, 281
Bizimana, Augustin, 128-29, 149, 162, 185, 224, 268, 666, 687
Bizimana, Lt. Pierre, 470
Bizimungu, Col. Augustin, 185, 223, 230-31, 264, 284, 286-87, 289-90, 292, 640-41, 664, 666, 670, 677, 687-88
Bizimungu, Maj. Christophe, 268, 311, 332
Bizimungu, Pasteur, 53n.
Booh-Booh, Jacques-Roger, 19, 152, 154, 156, 157, 160-62, 167, 172-73, 179, 186, 188, 622, 625-27
Boutros-Ghali, Boutros, 153, 154, 161, 164, 174, 176, 178-79, 604, 619, 621, 626, 635, 638, 642, 728-30, 768
Bucyana, Martin, 164, 366, 437-38, 456
Bucyibaruta, Laurent, 57, 307-11, 313, 319, 328, 345-347, 349, 350, 443
Bugesera, 12, 23, 39, 66, 68, 71, 87, 89-90, 92, 121, 146, 216, 221, 304, 542, 707-8, 715, 720, 723
Burundi, 4, 5, 7, 79-80, 106, 114, 124, 135, 137-8, 177, 181, 256, 329, 374, 376-81, 402, 406, 428-9, 463, 636; arms sales, 168, 365;

Chrétienne), 111
identity cards, 17, 37, 40, 42, 90,
92, 234, 238, 362, 404, 426, 474,
485, 487, 493, 501, 538, 572, 704
Imanishimwe, Lieut. Samuel, 266
Impuzamugambi, 56, 149, 230;
leadership, 228; military training,
118, 149
infiltrators and infiltration, 10, 23,
49, 88-89, 114, 181, 219, 229, 293,
305, 346, 349, 355, 362, 371, 427,
444, 469, 515, 519-20, 548; among
displaced, 240, 427, 445; at
Bisesero, 679-81; and military, 58,
61-63, 140; propaganda about, 74-
76, 89, 249, 254, 258; and civilian
self defense, 279, 282, 287
Inkotanyi, 73, 75, 84, 99, 145, 207,
208, 250-58, 271-74, 282, 292,
295, 302, 315, 319, 330, 333, 351,
362-3, 367, 373, 391, 404, 405,
407, 411, 413, 418, 420, 422, 425-
6, 430, 444, 493, 515, 522, 526,
538, 544, 546, 550, 555, 557, 574,
584-8, 585, 589-90, 648-9, 683,
694. See also RPF.
Inkuba, 55, 228, 310
intellectuals, 26, 47, 318, 337, 342-
3, 366, 371, 383, 432, 435; 553; at
barriers, 234; divisions in Butare,
435; interim government, 244, 258,
582; propaganda, 71, 81, 244, 713
Interafrican Union of Human and
Peoples' Rights, 28, 93, 169
Interahamwe, 4, 123, 159, 166,
191, 188, 230-53, 271-2, 274, 308,
348, 369-70, 383, 391, 406, 425,
463, 472, 484-5, 493, 539, 545,
556, 584, 590; and armed forces,

151, 160, 229, 231, 500; Bugesera
89;early violence, 148,-9, 157, 164;
French, 677, 683, 703-4; and
interim government, 222, 229, 275-
6; leaders 199, 210, 227, 474;
"pacification," 287, 289-91, 406,
429, 506, 509-10, 558 ; other
militia, 228; Setiba, 270; in Taba,
274; weapons, 143, 149,-50, 155;
Rwandex, 128; training, 5, 56, 118,
144; UNAMIR, 153, 155, 158
interim government, 11-13, 19, 22-
26, 88, 196-205, 402, 406, 441,
456, 522, 527, 542-4, 554, 577,
635-6; arms and arms embargo,
286, 290-2, 639, 649-50, 652-
3.Bisesero, 219; concern with
foreign image, 252-8; dissenters,
265-8; move to Gitarama, 271-2;
OAU summit, 643; pressure on
officials, 273-7, 278-80, 331, 393,
457-60, 515; and UNAMIR, 623,
638; UN Human Rights
Commission; and university, 244,
593. See also France.
International Criminal Tribunal for
Rwanda, 28, 238, 272, 274-5, 617,
620, 648-9, 735-6, 738-47, 766-67
International Committee of the Red
Cross (ICRC), 285, 287, 623, 634-
7, 723, 763
International Commission of
Inquiry on Human Rights Abuse in
Rwanda, 58, 93, 169, 304, 701
International Center for Human
Rights and Democratic
Development, 58, 93, 169
Inyenzi, 51, 73-4, 89, 110, 138,
167, 207, 249-51, 253, 258, 279,

498, 566
Mujawamariya, Monique, 92, 284
Mukamira, 675, 682
Mukarurangwa, Bernadette, 226,
550, 557
Mukingi, 14, 224, 275, 702, 708,
709, 717, 724-25, 331, 733
Muko, 209, 259, 312-13, 318, 325,
336-37, 338, 340, 345
Mulindi, 422, 462, 695, 705, 719
Muna, Bernard, 745
Mungwarareba, Modeste, 531-33
Munyemana, Sothene, 456, 478,
513, 535, 571, 578
Munyengango, Col. Francois, 571,
578
Munyeshyaka, Wenceslas, 247,
767
Murambi, site of interim
government, 198, 268, 271, 273
Murambi Technical School, 16,
309, 320
Murego, Donat, 112-13, 115, 157,
196, 199, 222, 269, 273, 361
Murengezi, Innocent, 759
Musabe, Pasteur, 69, 104
Musambira, 211, 215, 224, 272,
275, 277
Musebeya, 259, 263, 303, 306-07,
309-10, 313-14, 316-27, 329-30,
334-06, 338, 340, 343-44, 348,
350-52
Musema, Alfred, 218, 767
Museveni, Yoweri, 48,79, 105,
168, 182
Mutabaruka, Bernard, 513, 557
Mutabaruka, Celestin 317, 323,
329, 335
Mutwewingabo, Bernard 523, 544,

552-53
Muvunyi, Lt. Col. Tharcisse, 412-
13, 434, 440-42, 448, 492, 499-
500, 505, 519, 536, 551, 570-71

Nahimana, Ferdinand, 5, 37n, 68-9,
71, 110, 158, 170, 261, 684, 687,
744
National Assembly (France), 768
National Security Council, 624,
631, 642
National Resistance Army (NRA),
48, 63
Ndadaye, Melchior, 134-38, 305,
363
Ndagijimana, Callixte, 276-7
Ndagijimana, JMV, 242
Ndahimana, Mathiew, 235, 498,
581
Ndasingwa, Landoald, 191
Ndayambaje, Elie, 544, 581, 742
Ndikumana, André, 759
Ndindiliyimana, Gen. Augustin
149-50, 170, 187, 189, 190-95,
268-69, 284, 616, 650
Ndizihiwe, Jean-Chrysostome,
309-10, 316, 319, 321, 327, 329,
351-52
Ndora, 237-38, 442, 447, 454-55,
465-67, 488, 505, 522, 533, 535-
36, 548-50, 557, 567-68, 581, 583
Ndungutse, Francois 196, 448-49,
456
New Zealand, 19, 26, 175, 621,
629, 639, 643
Ngango, Félicien, 108, 191
Ngeze, Hassan, 70,89
Ngirabatware, Augustin, 69
Ngirumpatse, Mathieu, 69, 97, 111,